SO-DVF-143

Two ways to stay.
It's a great value either way.

1. Red Roof

Discover why **Red Roof is the perfect choice** for all
your travel plans – with **FREE Wi-Fi, flat-screen TVs**
in every room, and all the **conveniences** you'll need for
a clean, comfortable and affordable stay. We even welcome
your **family pet at no charge!**

2. Red Roof PLUS+®

Want to add a little **more WOW** to your Red Roof stay?
We're rolling out **Red Roof PLUS+®**. Discover an enhanced
experience with all new rooms, and our most requested
higher-end amenities. It's a completely remodeled and upgraded
stay! A little more pampering, all at an affordable rate you
expect from Red Roof.

Red Roof Mobile: Search, Book, Stay Connected

10% OFF* our already low rates for our AAA guests
Use VP+®/Promo Code 526810 to receive 10% off at
any of our locations. Simply visit redroof.com or call
800.RED.ROOF (800.733.7663) Español 877.733.7244

Restrictions may apply based on availability. Offer cannot be combined with any
other discount or offer. Not valid during special events.

*Discount off published rates

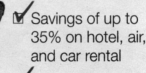

Pennsylvania

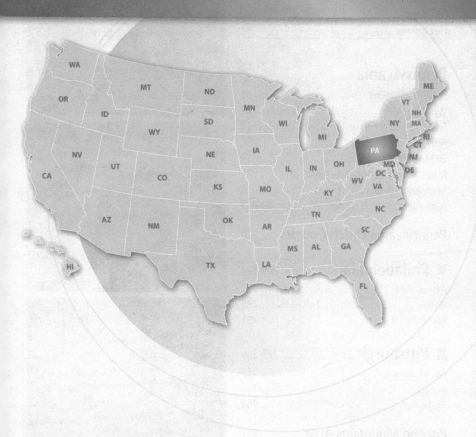

Published by AAA Publishing
1000 AAA Drive, Heathrow, FL 32746-5063
Copyright AAA 2015, All rights reserved

Advertising Rate and Circulation Information: (407) 444-8280

Printed in the USA by Quad/Graphics

This book is printed on paper certified by third-party standards for sustainably managed forestry and production.

Printed on recyclable paper.
Please recycle whenever possible.

Stock #4674

CONTENTS

Attractions, hotels, restaurants and other travel experience information are all grouped under the alphabetical listing of the city in which those experiences are physically located—or the nearest recognized city.

Pennsylvania

Pennsylvania Dutch Country 220

Pocono Mountains Area 371

Featured Information

Make the Most of Your Travels

Great vacations start long before you leave home, and they last long after you return. Savor every moment with TourBook resources that bring travel to life.

Dream
Picture the possibilities with visual references that inspire.

Plan
Navigate your way with vibrant maps you can trust.

Experience
Explore your destination with expert picks and itineraries.

Turn the page to begin your journey.

A to Z City Listings

Cities and places are listed alphabetically within each state or province. Attractions, hotels and restaurants are listed once — under the city in which they are physically located.

Cities that are considered part of a larger destination city or area have an expanded city header. The header identifies the larger region and cross-references pages that contain shared trip planning resources:

- Destination map – outline map of the cities that comprise a destination city or area
- Attraction spotting map – regional street map marked with attraction locations
- Hotel/restaurant spotting map and index – regional street map numbered with hotel and restaurant locations identified in an accompanying index

Cities that are not considered part of a larger destination city or area but have a significant number of listings may have these resources within the individual city section:

- Attraction spotting map
- Hotel/restaurant spotting map and index

Location Abbreviations

Directions are from the center of town unless otherwise specified, using these highway abbreviations:

Bus. Rte.=business route
CR=county road
FM=farm to market
FR=forest road
Hwy.=Canadian highway
I=interstate highway
LR=legislative route
R.R.=rural route
SR/PR=state or provincial route
US=federal highway

Maps

Use the navigable road maps and accompanying legend in the Atlas Section for route planning. Check the destination maps for general location reference. In select cities only, refer to the mass transit overview maps to cross-reference station names and numbers. For attraction and hotel/restaurant spotting maps, see the legend below to identify symbols and color coding.

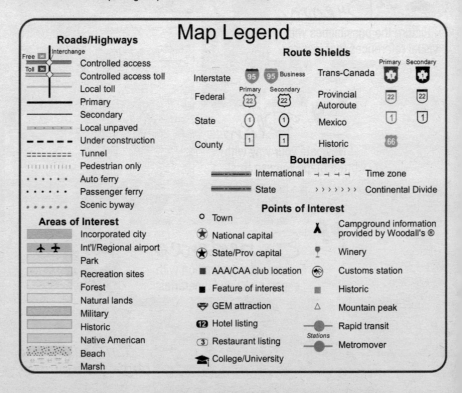

Map Legend

Roads/Highways

Free / Toll — Interchange	
Controlled access	
Controlled access toll	
Local toll	
Primary	
Secondary	
Local unpaved	
Under construction	
Tunnel	
Pedestrian only	
Auto ferry	
Passenger ferry	
Scenic byway	

Areas of Interest

- Incorporated city
- Int'l/Regional airport
- Park
- Recreation sites
- Forest
- Natural lands
- Military
- Historic
- Native American
- Beach
- Marsh

Route Shields

	Primary	Secondary
Interstate	95	95 Business
Federal	22 (Primary)	22 (Secondary)
State	1	1
County	1	1
Trans-Canada		
Provincial Autoroute	22	22
Mexico	1	1
Historic	66	

Boundaries

- International
- State
- Time zone
- Continental Divide

Points of Interest

- ○ Town
- ★ National capital
- ★ State/Prov capital
- ■ AAA/CAA club location
- ■ Feature of interest
- GEM attraction
- Hotel listing
- Restaurant listing
- College/University
- Campground information provided by Woodall's ®
- Winery
- Customs station
- Historic
- △ Mountain peak
- Rapid transit
- Stations Metromover

About Listed Establishments

AAA/CAA Approved attractions, hotels and restaurants are listed on the basis of merit alone after careful evaluation and approval by full-time, professionally trained AAA/CAA inspectors. An establishment's decision to advertise in the TourBook guide has no bearing on its evaluation or rating; nor does inclusion of advertising imply AAA endorsement of products and services.

Information in this guide was believed accurate at the time of publication. However, since changes inevitably occur between annual editions, please contact your AAA travel professional or visit AAA.com or download the AAA mobile app to confirm prices and schedules.

Attraction Listings

> **ATTRACTION NAME,** 3 mi. n. off SR 20A (Main Ave.), consists of 250 acres with Olmsted-designed gardens, a 205-foot marble and coquina bell tower and a Mediterranean-style mansion. One of the state's oldest attractions, the tower and gardens were dedicated to the American people in 1929 by President Calvin Coolidge on behalf of their founder, a Dutch immigrant.
>
> **Hours:** Gardens daily 8-6. Last admission 1 hour before closing. Visitor center daily 9-5. Estate tours are given at noon and 2. Carillon concerts are given at 1 and 3. Phone ahead to confirm schedule. **Cost:** $10; $3 (ages 5-12). Gardens and estate $16; $8 (ages 5-12). **Phone:** (555) 555-5555.
> Dupont Circle,13

AAA/CAA travel experts may designate an attraction of exceptional interest and quality as a AAA GEM — a *Great Experience for Members®. See GEM Attraction Index (listed on CONTENTS page) for a complete list of locations.*

Consult the online travel guides at AAA.com or visit AAA Mobile for additional things to do if you have time.

Cost

Prices are quoted without sales tax in the local currency (U.S. or Canadian dollars). Children under the lowest age specified are admitted free when accompanied by an adult. Most establishments accept credit cards, but a small number require cash, so please call ahead to verify.

Adventure Travel

Activities such as air tours, hiking, skiing and white-water rafting are listed to provide member information and do not imply AAA/CAA endorsement. For your safety, be aware of inherent risks and adhere to all safety instructions.

Icons

SAVE AAA Discounts & Rewards[SM] member discount

Electric vehicle charging station on premises. Domestic station information provided by the U.S. Department of Energy. Canadian station information provided by Plug'n Drive Ontario.

GT Guided Tours available

Camping facilities

Food on premises

Recreational activities

Pets on leash allowed

Picnicking allowed

In select cities only:

Mass transit station within 1 mile. Icon is followed by station name and AAA/CAA designated station number within listing.

Information-Only Attraction Listings

Bulleted listings, which include the following categories, are listed for informational purposes as a service to members:

- **Gambling establishments** (even if located in a AAA/CAA Approved hotel)
- **Guided food tours**
- **Participatory recreational activities** (those requiring physical exertion or special skills)
- **Wineries that offer tours and tastings**

Mobile Tags

 Scan QR codes throughout the TourBook guide to see online offers, menus, videos and more on your smartphone or tablet. If you need a QR scanner app, download one for free from your app store.

If you see a non-QR code in an ad, check the nearby text for details on which app you'll need to scan it.

Hotel and Restaurant Listings

1 Diamond Rating – AAA/CAA Approved hotels and restaurants are assigned a rating of one to five Diamonds. Red Diamonds distinguish establishments that participate in the AAA/CAA logo licensing program. For details, see p. 11 or AAA.com/Diamonds.

fyi indicates hotels and restaurants that are not AAA/CAA Approved and/or Diamond Rated but are listed to provide additional choices for members:

- **Hotels** may be unrated if they are too new to rate, under construction, under major renovation or not evaluated; or if they do not meet all AAA requirements. Hotels that do not meet all AAA requirements may be included if they offer member value or are the only option; details are noted in the listing.
- **Restaurants** may be unrated if they have not yet been evaluated by AAA.

2 Classification or Cuisine Type – Noted after the Diamond Rating.

- **Hotel Classifications** indicate the style of operation, overall concept and service level. Subclassifications may also be added. (See p. 12 list.)
- **Restaurant Cuisine Types** identify the food concept from more than 100 categories. If applicable, a classification may also be added. (See p. 13 list.)

3 Dollar Amounts – Quoted without sales tax in the local currency (U.S. or Canadian dollars), rounded up to the nearest dollar. Most establishments accept credit cards, but a small number require cash, so please call ahead to verify.

- **Hotel Rates** indicate the publicly available two-person rate or rate range for a standard room, applicable all year.
- **Restaurant Prices** represent the minimum and maximum entrée cost per person. Exceptions may include one-of-a-kind or special market priced items.

4 Spotting Symbol – Ovals containing numbers correspond with numbered location markings on hotel and restaurant spotting maps.

5 Parking – Unless otherwise noted, parking is free, on-site self parking.

6 Hotel Value Nationwide – Blue boxes highlight member benefits available at AAA/CAA Approved locations across a hotel chain. (See Just For Members section for details.)

7 Hotel Unit Limited Availability – Unit types, amenities and room features preceded by "some" are available on a limited basis, potentially as few as one.

8 Hotel Terms – Cancellation and minimum stay policies are listed. Unless otherwise noted, most properties offer a full deposit refund with cancellations received at least 48 hours before standard check-in. Properties that require advance payment may not refund the difference for early departures. "Resort fee" indicates a charge may apply above and beyond the quoted room rate.

9 Hotel Check-in/Check-out – Unless otherwise noted, check-in is after 3 p.m. and check-out is before 10 a.m.

10 Restaurant Dress Code – Unless otherwise noted, dress is casual or dressy casual.

11 Restaurant Menu – Where indicated, menus may be viewed in a secure online environment at AAA.com or, if a mobile tag is provided, via the restaurant's website.

12 Hotel Icons – May be preceded by CALL and/or SOME UNITS.

Member Information:

SAVE Rate guarantee: discounted standard room rate or lowest public rate available at time of booking for dates of stay.

ECO Eco-certified by government or private organization. Visit AAA.com/eco for details.

Electric vehicle charging station on premises. Domestic station information provided by the U.S. Department of Energy. Canadian station information provided by Plug'n Drive Ontario.

X Smoke-free premises

In select cities only:

Mass transit station within 1 mile. Icon is followed by station name and AAA/CAA designated station number within listing.

Services:

Airport transportation

Pets allowed (Call property for restrictions.)

Pets allowed (Call property for restrictions and fees.)

Restaurant on premises

Restaurant off premises

Room service for 2 or more meals

Full bar

HOTEL LISTING

HOTEL NAME (555)555-5555 **50**

♦♦♦ Hotel
$109-$199

LOGO **AAA Benefit:** Members save a minimum 5% off the best available rate.

Address: 300 Main St 55555 **Location:** I-275 exit 31 southbound; exit 30 northbound, 1.6 mi w on SR 688 (Oak Rd). ⊞ Dupont Circle, 13. **Facility:** 149 units, some efficiencies. 3 stories, interior corridors. **Parking:** on-site (fee). **Terms:** check-in 4 pm, cancellation fee imposed, resort fee. **Amenities:** video games. **Pool(s):** heated outdoor. **Activities:** hot tub, exercise room. **Guest Services:** valet and coin laundry. **Featured Amenity:**continental breakfast.

⟨SAVE⟩ ⟨ECO⟩ ⟨⎓⟩ ⟨¶¶⟩ CALL ⟨&M⟩ ⟨≈⟩ ⟨BIZ⟩ ⟨SHS⟩ ⟨≋⟩
⟨✕⟩ ⟨🎥⟩ ⟨▭⟩ /SOME UNITS ⟨🐾⟩ ⟨🗄⟩ ⟨▥⟩ ⟨🚇⟩

RESTAURANT LISTING

RESTAURANT NAME 555/555-5555

♦♦♦ Continental Fine Dining
$15-$35

AAA Inspector Notes: *Historic.* A romantic aura punctuates the modern and casual dining room, which is accented with floral arrangements and dramatic, freshly cut branches. The menu features seasonal ingredients. The pastry chef's decadent creations are popular. Semiformal attire. **Features:** full bar, patio dining, happy hour. **Address:** 26 N Main St 55555 **Location:** SR A1A southbound, 2.7 mi s of jct SR 520. ⊞ Dupont Circle, 13.

Menu on AAA.com ⟨ECO⟩ ⟨⎓⟩ ⟨L⟩ ⟨D⟩ ⟨🐾⟩ ⟨🚇⟩

⟨⛟⟩ Child care

⟨BIZ⟩ Business area

⟨&M⟩ Accessible features (Call property for available services and amenities.)

Activities:

⟨🎰⟩ Full-service casino

⟨≈⟩ Pool

⟨💪⟩ Health club on premises

In-Room Amenities:

⟨HS⟩ High-speed Internet service

⟨SHS⟩ High-speed Internet service (Call property for fees.)

⟨≋⟩ Wireless Internet service

⟨So⟩ Wireless Internet service (Call property for fees.)

⟨≋̸⟩ No wireless Internet service

⟨🎥⟩ Pay movies

⟨🗄⟩ Refrigerator

⟨▥⟩ Microwave

⟨▭⟩ Coffee maker

⟨AC̸⟩ No air conditioning

⟨TV̸⟩ No TV

⟨☎̸⟩ No telephones

13 **Restaurant Icons**

⟨SAVE⟩ AAA Discounts & Rewards℠ member discount

⟨ECO⟩ Eco-certified by government or private organization. Visit AAA.com/eco for details.

⟨⎓⟩ Electric vehicle charging station on premises. Domestic station information provided by the U.S. Department of Energy. Canadian station information provided by Plug'n Drive Ontario.

⟨AC̸⟩ No air conditioning

⟨&M⟩ Accessible features (Call property for available services and amenities.)

⟨🚬⟩ Designated smoking section

⟨B⟩ Breakfast

⟨L⟩ Lunch

⟨D⟩ Dinner

⟨24⟩ Open 24 hours

⟨LATE⟩ Open after 11 p.m.

⟨🐾⟩ Pet-friendly (Call property for restrictions.)

In select cities only:

⟨🚇⟩ Mass transit station within 1 mile. Icon is followed by station name and AAA/CAA designated station number within listing.

GET REAL
REAL INSPECTORS, REAL RATINGS

Just For Members

Understanding the Diamond Ratings

Hotel and restaurant evaluations are unscheduled to ensure our professionally trained inspectors encounter the same experience members do.

- When an establishment is Diamond Rated, it means members can expect a good fit with their needs. The inspector assigns a rating that indicates the type of experience to expect.
- While establishments at high levels must offer increasingly complex personalized services, establishments at every level are subject to the same basic requirements for cleanliness, comfort and hospitality. Learn more at AAA.com/Diamonds.

Hotels

Budget-oriented, offering basic comfort and hospitality.

Affordable, with modestly enhanced facilities, décor and amenities.

Distinguished, multifaceted with enhanced physical attributes, amenities and guest comforts.

Refined, stylish with upscale physical attributes, extensive amenities and high degree of hospitality, service and attention to detail.

Ultimate luxury, sophistication and comfort with extraordinary physical attributes, meticulous personalized service, extensive amenities and impeccable standards of excellence.

Restaurants

Simple, familiar specialty food at an economical price. Often self-service, basic surroundings.

Familiar, family-oriented experience. Home-style foods and family favorites, often cooked to order, modestly enhanced and reasonably priced. Relaxed service, casual surroundings.

Fine dining, often adult-oriented. Latest cooking trends and/or traditional cuisine, expanded beverage offerings. Professional service staff and comfortable, well-coordinated ambience.

Distinctive fine-dining, typically expensive. Highly creative chefs, imaginative presentations and fresh, top-quality ingredients. Proficient service staff, upscale surroundings. Wine steward may offer menu-specific knowledge.

Luxurious and consistently world-class. Highly acclaimed chefs, artistic and imaginative menu selections using the finest ingredients. Maitre d' and unobtrusive, expert service staff.

What's the difference?

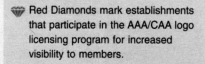

- Red Diamonds mark establishments that participate in the AAA/CAA logo licensing program for increased visibility to members.

- Black Diamonds identify all other AAA/CAA Approved and Diamond Rated establishments.

Hotel Classifications

Quality and comfort are usually consistent across each Diamond Rating level, but décor, facilities and service levels vary by classification.

Berry Manor Inn, Rockland, ME

Bed & Breakfast — Typically owner-operated with a high degree of personal touches. Guests are encouraged to interact during evening and breakfast hours. A continental or full, hot breakfast is included in the room rate.

Killarney Lodge, Algonquin Provincial Park, ON

Cabin — Often located in wooded, rural or waterfront locations. Freestanding units are typically rustic and of basic design. As a rule, essential cleaning supplies, kitchen utensils and complete bed and bath linens are supplied.

Hyatt Regency Clearwater Beach Resort & Spa, Clearwater Beach, FL

Condominium — Apartment-style accommodations of varying design or décor, units often contain one or more bedrooms, a living room, full kitchen and an eating area. As a rule, essential cleaning supplies, kitchen utensils and complete bed and bath linens are supplied.

Montpelier Plantation and Beach, St. Kitts and Nevis

Cottage — Often located in wooded, rural, or waterfront locations. Freestanding units are typically home-style in design and décor. As a rule, essential cleaning supplies, kitchen utensils and complete bed and bath linens are supplied.

Nottoway Plantation & Resort, White Castle, LA

Country Inn — Although similar in definition to a bed and breakfast, country inns are usually larger in scale with spacious public areas and offer a dining facility that serves breakfast and dinner.

The Shores Resort & Spa, Daytona Beach Shores, FL

Hotel — Typically a multistory property with interior room entrances and a variety of guest unit styles. The magnitude of the public areas is determined by the overall theme, location and service level, but may include a variety of facilities such as a restaurant, shops, a fitness center, a spa, a business center and meeting rooms.

Alexander Holiday Homes, Kissimmee, FL

House — Freestanding units of varying home-style design. Typically larger scale, often containing two or more bedrooms, a living room, a full kitchen, a dining room and multiple bathrooms. As a rule, essential cleaning supplies, kitchen utensils and complete bed and bath linens are supplied.

Bryce View Lodge, Bryce Canyon City, UT

Motel — A one- or two-story roadside property with exterior room entrances and drive up parking. Public areas and facilities are often limited in size and/or availability.

Vista Verde Guest Ranch, Clark, CO

Ranch — Typically a working ranch featuring an obvious rustic, Western theme, equestrian-related activities and a variety of guest unit styles.

Hotel Subclassifications

These additional descriptives may be added to the classification for more information:

- **Boutique** — Often thematic, typically informal yet highly personalized; may have a luxurious or quirky style that is fashionable or unique.
- **Casino** — Extensive gambling facilities are available, such as blackjack, craps, keno and slot machines.
- **Classic** — Renowned and landmark properties, older than 50 years, well known for their unique style and ambience.
- **Contemporary** — Overall theme reflects characteristics of present mainstream trends.
- **Extended Stay** — Offers a predominance of long-term accommodations with a designated full-service kitchen area within each unit.
- **Historic** — More than 75 years old with one of the following documented historical features: Maintains the integrity of the historical nature, listed on the National Register of Historic Places, designated a National Historic Landmark or located in a National Register Historic District.
- **Resort** — Extensive recreational facilities and programs may include golf, tennis, skiing, fishing, water sports, spa

treatments or professionally guided activities.

- **Retro** — Overall theme reflects a contemporary design that reinterprets styles from a past era.
- **Vacation Rental** — Typically houses, condos, cottages or cabins; these properties are "home away from home" self-catering accommodations.
- **Vintage** — Overall theme reflects upon and maintains the authentic traits and experience of a past era.

Restaurant Classifications

If applicable, in addition to the cuisine type noted under the Diamond Rating, restaurant listings may also include one or both classifications:

- **Classic** — Renowned and landmark operation in business for 25 plus years; unique style and ambience.
- **Historic** — Meets one of the following: Listed on National Register of Historic Places, designated a National Historic Landmark or located in a National Register Historic District.

Service Animals

Under the Americans with Disabilities Act (ADA), U.S. businesses that serve the public must allow people with disabilities to bring their service animals into all areas of the facility where customers are normally allowed to go.

Businesses may ask if an animal is a service animal and what tasks the animal has been trained to perform. Businesses may not ask about the person's disability, require special identification for the animal or request removal of the animal from the premises except in limited cases that require alternate assistance. Businesses may not charge extra fees for service animals, including standard pet fees, but may charge for damage caused by service animals if guests are normally charged for damage they cause.

Call the U.S. Department of Justice ADA Information Line: (800) 514-0301 or TTY (800) 514-0383, or visit ada.gov. Regulations may differ in Canada.

AAA/CAA Approved Hotels

For members, AAA/CAA Approved means quality assured.

- Only properties that meet basic requirements for cleanliness, comfort and hospitality pass inspection.
- Approved hotels receive a Diamond Rating that tells members the type of experience to expect.

Guest Safety

Inspectors view a sampling of rooms during evaluations and, therefore, AAA/CAA cannot guarantee the presence of working locks and operational fire safety equipment in every guest unit.

Member Rates

AAA/CAA members can generally expect to pay no more than the maximum TourBook listed rate for a standard room. Member discounts apply to rates quoted within the rate range and are applicable at the time of booking. Listed rates are usually based on last standard room availability. Within the range, rates may vary by season and room type. Obtain current AAA/CAA member rates and make reservations at AAA.com.

Exceptions

- Rates for properties operating as concessionaires for the U.S. National Park Service are not guaranteed due to governing regulations.
- Special advertised rates and short-term promotional rates below the rate range are not subject to additional member discounts.
- During special events, hotels may temporarily increase room rates, not recognize discounts or modify pricing policies. Special events may include Mardi Gras, the Kentucky Derby (including pre-Derby events), college football games, holidays, holiday periods and state fairs. Although some special events are listed in the TourBook guides and on AAA.com, it's always wise to check in advance with AAA travel professionals for specific dates.

If you are charged more than the maximum TourBook listed rate, question the additional charge. If an exception is not in effect and management refuses to adhere to the published rate, pay for the room and contact AAA/CAA. The amount paid above the stated maximum will be refunded if our investigation indicates an unjustified charge.

Reservations and Cancellations

When making your reservation, identify yourself as a AAA/CAA member and request written confirmation of your room type, rate, dates of stay, and cancellation and refund policies. At registration, show your membership card.

To cancel, contact the hotel, your AAA/CAA club office or AAA.com, depending on how you booked your reservation. Request a cancellation number or proof of cancellation.

If your room is not as specified and you have written confirmation of your reservation for a specific room type, you should be given the option of choosing a different room or receiving a refund. If management refuses to issue a refund, contact AAA/CAA.

Contacting AAA/CAA About Approved Properties

If your visit to a AAA/CAA Approved attraction, hotel or restaurant doesn't meet your expectations, please tell us about it — **during your visit or within 30 days**. Be sure to save your receipts and other documentation for reference.

Use the easy online form at AAA.com/TourBookComments to send us the details.

Alternatively, you can email your comments to: memberrelations@national.aaa.com or submit them via postal mail to: AAA Member Comments, 1000 AAA Dr., Box 61, Heathrow, FL 32746.

AAA/CAA Preferred Hotels

All AAA/CAA Approved hotels are committed to providing quality, value and member service. In addition, those designated as AAA/CAA Preferred Hotels also offer these extra values at Approved locations nationwide. Valid AAA/CAA membership required.

- **Best AAA/CAA member rates for your dates of stay.**
- **Seasonal promotions and special member offers.** Visit AAA.com to view current offers.
- **Member benefit.** See the blue boxes in hotel listings for the chains shown in the right-hand column below to find values offered at AAA/CAA Approved locations nationwide, subject to availability. Details valid at the time of publication and may change without notice.

- **Total satisfaction guarantee.** If you book your stay with AAA/CAA Travel and your stay fails to meet your expectations, you can apply for a full refund. Bring the complaint to the hotel's attention during the stay and request resolution; if the complaint is not resolved by the hotel, ask your AAA/CAA travel agent to request resolution through the AAA/CAA Assured Stay program.

Best Western, Best Western Plus and Best Western Premier

Hilton Hotels & Resorts, Waldorf Astoria Hotels & Resorts, Conrad Hotels & Resorts, Curio - A Collection by Hilton, DoubleTree, Embassy Suites Hotels, Hilton Garden Inn, Hampton Hotels, Homewood Suites, Home2 Suites and Hilton Grand Vacations

Park Hyatt, Andaz, Grand Hyatt, Hyatt Regency, Hyatt, Hyatt Place and Hyatt House

The Ritz-Carlton, Gaylord Hotels, JW Marriott Hotels, EDITION, Autograph Collection Hotels, Renaissance Hotels, AC Hotels, Marriott Hotels & Resorts, Courtyard, SpringHill Suites, Fairfield Inn & Suites, Residence Inn, and TownePlace Suites

starwood Hotels and Resorts

Aloft, Element, Four Points, Le Meridien, Sheraton, St. Regis, Westin, W Hotels and The Luxury Collection

DISCOUNTS »REWARDS™   Rewards

Member Discounts

Visit AAA.com/searchfordiscounts to find locations and available member discounts. Your AAA/CAA club may offer even greater discounts on theme park tickets. Amtrak and theme park discounts may be used for up to six tickets; restaurant savings may be used for up to six patrons. Other restrictions may apply. All offers subject to change. For complete restrictions, visit your AAA office or AAA.com/restrictions.

ATTRACTIONS

SeaWorld, Busch Gardens, Sesame Place

SEAWORLD PARKS & ENTERTAINMENT

- Save on admission at the gate, participating AAA/CAA offices or AAA.com/SeaWorld.
- Save 10% on up-close dining; visit Guest Relations for details.

Six Flags

- Save on admission at the gate, participating AAA/CAA offices or AAA.com/SixFlags.
- Save 10% on merchandise of $15 or more at in-park stores.

SixFlags

Universal Orlando Resort and Universal Studios Hollywood

BE EXTRAORDINARY

- Save on tickets at select AAA/CAA offices or AAA.com/Universal. In-park savings available in FL.

The Entertainment Capital of L.A.™

- Save on Blue Man Group tickets and at select food and merchandise venues at Universal CityWalk®.

BLUE MAN GROUP

DINING

Hard Rock Cafe

- Save 10% on food, nonalcoholic beverages and merchandise at all locations in the U.S. and Canada and select international locations.

Landry's Seafood House, The Crab House, Chart House, Oceanaire, Saltgrass Steak House, Muer Seafood Restaurants and Aquarium Restaurants

- Save 10% on food and nonalcoholic beverages at all of the above restaurants.
- Save 10% on merchandise at Aquarium, Downtown Aquarium and Rainforest Cafe restaurants.

SHOPPING

Banana Republic Factory Store

- Save 10% on all purchases, including sale merchandise.

BANANA REPUBLIC FACTORY STORE

Gap Outlet/Gap Factory Store

- Save 10% on all purchases, including sale merchandise.

Reebok/Rockport Outlet

- Save 20% on the entire purchase.

Reebok ®ROCKPORT OUTLET STORES

Tanger Outlet Centers

- Receive a free coupon book with discounts up to 20% at select merchants.

Tanger Outlets

TRANSPORTATION

Amtrak

- Save 10% on rail fare booked at least three days in advance of travel date at AAA.com/Amtrak.

AMTRAK

El Monte RV

- Save up to 10% on nightly rates booked at least 24 hours in advance of pickup at AAA.com/ElMonteRV or (800) 337-2156.

EL MONTE RV RENTALS • SALES

Hertz

- Save on daily, weekend, weekly and monthly rentals at AAA.com/Hertz or (800) 654-3080.

Hertz

RACK UP THE REWARDS

Make membership an even more rewarding experience.

Here at AAA, we believe that financial rewards and benefits are what our members have come to expect. The AAA Member Rewards Visa® credit card lets you earn reward points on all of your purchases. Open an account today and let the rewards start rolling in!

 Earn 1 point for every $1 in purchases with your AAA Member Rewards Visa® card!*

 Earn double points for gas, grocery and drug store purchases!

 Earn triple points on qualifying AAA and travel purchases!

 Redeem for a AAA Voucher that gives you up to 40% more value than cash back!**

 Exclusive rewards to make you smile!

VISIT AAA.com/creditcard   **STOP BY** any AAA branch

Pennsylvania has many beautiful covered bridges

Pennsylvania

Every state has its share of important "firsts," but if counting them were a game, Pennsylvania would be a tough player to beat.

Philadelphia was the first city in America to guarantee religious freedom. And if you've ever wondered about the first bank, stock exchange, hospital or zoo, each was established in Philly before anywhere else in the United States.

Some firsts heralded new hope: Pennsylvania was the first state to abolish slavery, and Dr. Jonas Salk developed a polio vaccine while at the University of Pittsburgh. Others have ushered in new ways of passing time. For instance, no one had ever eaten a banana split or played Bingo before each was first enjoyed in Pittsburgh.

You can see places associated with firsts. The Drake Well Museum in Titusville commemorates the spot where the world's first commercially successful oil well was drilled. Near Uniontown, Fort Necessity National

National Memorial Arch at Valley Forge National Historical Park

Battlefield preserves the site where the French and Indian War began, including the fort that Washington and his men built.

These Honored Dead

One of the most visited spots in Pennsylvania, Gettysburg National Military Park commemorates the July 1863 battle in which 51,000 Union and Confederate soldiers were wounded, captured or killed. Soldiers' National Monument, one of thousands in the park, stands near the spot where Lincoln made the famous speech.

Three other parks in Pennsylvania memorialize significant earlier war battles. Washington Crossing Historic Park, near Trenton, N.J., preserves the site where Gen. George Washington and 2,500 soldiers crossed the Delaware River to attack German mercenaries during the American Revolution.

The following year, in 1777, Washington and the Continental Army settled down for a 6-month encampment at Valley Forge, where a brutal winter contributed to nearly 2,000 deaths of his ill-equipped men. The National Memorial Arch at Valley Forge National Historical Park pays tribute to these soldiers.

More than 2 decades before he led the United States to victory in the American Revolution, Washington commanded troops at Fort Necessity, the first battle of the French and Indian War. Fort Necessity National Battlefield encompasses this site along with a reconstruction of the fort he built.

The Quaker State

The scene of such bloody conflict ironically began as an experiment in peaceful coexistence. In 1681 Quaker-convert William Penn established Pennsylvania as part of a "Holy Experiment" in applying Quaker principles to the practical business of governing a colony. Among those guiding beliefs was a commitment to religious tolerance.

If Penn were alive today in the state that bears his name, he would no doubt recognize his vision in the famed Pennsylvania Dutch Country. Here such religious groups as the Amish, Dunkers, Mennonites and others follow a simple, pastoral lifestyle that has changed little in the past 2 centuries.

More removed from the memories of epic battles won and lost on Pennsylvania soil is the natural tranquility of the Pocono Mountains. This highland wilderness of waterfalls, hiking trails and scenic overlooks has become a vacation playground for nature-hungry day-trippers from New York and Philadelphia and a favorite destination for honeymooners.

Even within the vast metropolis of Philadelphia you can forget conflict past and present at places like Fairmount Park, a lush oasis along the Schuylkill River's banks. Pittsburgh has its own enclaves of serenity—one such haven is a group of art, history and science museums collectively referred to as the Carnegie Museums of Pittsburgh.

Recreation

Practically any type of outdoor activity you can think of can be enjoyed in the Allegheny National Forest. Many recreation areas are near the 24-mile-long Allegheny Reservoir on the upper Allegheny River. Bradford and Warren are excellent starting points from which to explore this area. Among the forest's more than 200 miles of hiking trails is part of the constantly evolving North Country National Scenic Trail.

While the Allegheny Mountains are filled with challenging hiking terrain, other Pennsylvania paths offer easier walks, historic sites and bucolic scenery. The state's "rails to trails" program has converted unused railway lines into nearly 800 miles of wide, fairly smooth byways. The Ridley Creek, Wissahickon Gorge and Wilderness Trails make wonderful day trips and are all located within a 30-minute drive of Philadelphia.

The most famous of Pennsylvania's trails is the Appalachian National Scenic Trail, which runs for 220 miles from the south central to the northeastern part of the state on its span from Georgia to Maine. It is especially popular with leaf-peepers; fall colors are at their peak here mid- to late October.

The commonwealth touts some of the best trout fishing in the eastern United States. Good fishing holes can be found along the Delaware River and around Lake Erie. Limestone streams flowing throughout the state present a challenge to fly-fishers.

Some of Pennsylvania's best white-water rafting is in Ohiopyle State Park, which contains more than 14 miles of the Youghiogheny River Gorge. Several outfitters are based in nearby Ohiopyle.

The high mountain meadows, thick wooded forests and flat farmlands of the 2,400-square-mile Pocono Mountain region offer eight ski resorts as well as opportunities for cross-country skiing, snowshoeing, snowmobiling, ice fishing and ice-skating.

The Poconos are also a choice spot for mountain biking. Lehigh Gorge Trail, suitable for beginners and intermediate riders, travels along the Lehigh River for 26 miles and stretches from the outlet of the Francis E. Walter Dam to Jim Thorpe. Casual cruisers opt for the maple-lined streets of US 6 through Milford, Hawley and Honesdale, which pass historic buildings, wildlife sanctuaries and numerous waterfalls.

Gettysburg National Military Park

Historic Timeline

1681	Quaker William Penn receives title to Pennsylvania in a land grant from England's King Charles II.
1731	Benjamin Franklin establishes the first public library in Philadelphia.
1776	The newly adopted Declaration of Independence is read to 8,000 people in Independence Square.
1787	The United States Constitution is signed in Philadelphia's Independence Hall.
1856	James Buchanan, the only Pennsylvanian who has served as president of the United States, is elected.
1863	Union forces defeat the Confederate Army in the Battle of Gettysburg.
1887	Punxsutawney Phil sees his shadow at the first official ceremony at Gobbler's Knob.
1889	The Johnstown flood kills more than 2,000 people.
1940	The first section of the Pennsylvania Turnpike, America's first high-speed, multilane highway, opens.
2001	United Airlines Flight 93 is hijacked by terrorists and crashes into a Somerset County field.
2007	An archeology dig is performed at the Philadelphia site of the original presidential residence, home to Washington and Adams.

What To Pack

Temperature Averages Maximum/Minimum	JANUARY	FEBRUARY	MARCH	APRIL	MAY	JUNE	JULY	AUGUST	SEPTEMBER	OCTOBER	NOVEMBER	DECEMBER
Allentown	39 / 21	41 / 24	50 / 31	61 / 39	72 / 49	80 / 58	85 / 63	83 / 62	76 / 54	65 / 42	54 / 35	43 / 27
Erie	33 / 20	36 / 21	45 / 28	56 / 38	67 / 49	76 / 59	80 / 64	79 / 63	72 / 56	61 / 46	49 / 36	39 / 27
Harrisburg	38 / 23	41 / 25	51 / 33	63 / 42	73 / 51	81 / 61	86 / 66	84 / 64	76 / 57	64 / 45	53 / 36	42 / 28
Philadelphia	39 / 25	42 / 28	51 / 35	62 / 44	72 / 55	81 / 64	86 / 70	84 / 69	77 / 61	66 / 49	55 / 40	44 / 31
Pittsburgh	37 / 20	39 / 21	50 / 29	62 / 38	71 / 48	80 / 56	85 / 62	83 / 60	76 / 53	64 / 41	53 / 33	42 / 25
Scranton	34 / 18	37 / 20	47 / 28	59 / 38	71 / 48	78 / 57	83 / 61	81 / 60	72 / 53	61 / 42	49 / 34	39 / 24

From the records of The Weather Channel Interactive, Inc.

Good Facts To Know

ABOUT THE STATE

POPULATION: 12,773,801.

AREA: 46,054 square miles; ranks 33rd.

CAPITAL: Harrisburg.

HIGHEST POINT: 3,213 ft., Mount Davis.

LOWEST POINT: Sea level, Delaware River.

TIME ZONE(S): Eastern. DST.

GAMBLING

MINIMUM AGE FOR GAMBLING: 21.

REGULATIONS

TEEN DRIVING LAWS: Driving is not permitted 11 p.m.-5 a.m. During the first 6 months of driving, no more than one unrelated passenger under age 18, unless accompanied by a parent or guardian. After the first 6 months, no more than three unrelated passengers under 18, unless accompanied by a parent or guardian. Minimum age for unrestricted license is 17 years (with driver education). For more information about Pennsylvania's driver's license regulations phone (800) 932-4600 (within Pennsylvania) or (717) 412-5300 (outside Pennsylvania).

SEAT BELT/CHILD RESTRAINT LAWS: Seat belts or appropriate child safety restraints are required for driver and all passengers. Children 8 and younger must ride in a child safety seat or booster seat appropriate for their height and weight. Seat belts are required for passengers over 8 years old.

CELL PHONE RESTRICTIONS: Texting while driving is banned for all drivers.

HELMETS FOR MOTORCYCLISTS: Required for all drivers under age 21 and drivers over age 21 that have not completed a motorcycle safety course or have had a motorcycle license for less than 2 years. Required for passengers under age 21 and passengers of drivers required to wear helmets.

RADAR DETECTORS: Permitted. Prohibited for commercial vehicles.

MOVE OVER LAW: Driver is required to slow down and vacate the lane nearest stopped police, fire and rescue vehicles using audible or flashing signals. Law includes recovery vehicles, such as tow trucks.

FIREARMS LAWS: Vary by state or county. Contact Pennsylvania State Police Headquarters, 1800 Elmerton Ave., Harrisburg, PA 17110; phone (717) 783-5495.

SPECIAL REGULATIONS: Use of headlights is required in work zones in Pennsylvania.

HOLIDAYS

HOLIDAYS: Jan. 1 ▪ Martin Luther King Jr. Day, Jan. (3rd Mon.) ▪ Washington's Birthday/Presidents Day, Feb. (3rd Mon.) ▪ Memorial Day, May (last Mon.) ▪ July 4 ▪ Labor Day, Sept. (1st Mon.) ▪ Columbus Day, Oct. (2nd Mon.) ▪ Veterans Day, Nov. 11 ▪ Thanksgiving ▪ Christmas, Dec. 25.

MONEY

TAXES: Pennsylvania's statewide sales tax is 6 percent; individual counties can levy additional increments. Pittsburgh levies a 5 percent amusements tax. The statewide lodging tax is 6 percent, with local options to allow additional increments.

VISITOR INFORMATION

INFORMATION CENTERS: State welcome centers on the PA Turnpike : Zelienople at Milepost 21 ▪ and at North Neshaminy at Milepost 351. Others: I-90W .5 mi. w. of the New York line ▪ SR 15S 7 mi. s. of the New York line ▪ I-79N 5 mi. n. of the West Virginia line ▪ I-80E at the Ohio line w. of Farrell ▪ I-80W at the New Jersey line ▪ I-70W at the Maryland line near Warfordsburg ▪ I-70E near the West Virginia line ▪ I-83N at the Maryland line s. of Shrewsbury ▪ I-81N s. of Greencastle near the Maryland line ▪ I-84W just w. of Matamoras ▪ I-95N s. of Upland at the Delaware line ▪ I-78W e. of Glendon at the New Jersey line ▪ and I-81S s. of New York's Corbettsville. Open daily 7-7 but closed Jan. 1, Martin Luther King Jr. Day, Presidents Day, Easter, Thanksgiving and Christmas.

FURTHER INFORMATION FOR VISITORS:
Pennsylvania Tourism Office
Department of Community and Economic Development
400 North St.
4th Floor, Commonwealth Keystone Building
Harrisburg, PA 17120-0225
(866) 466-3972

NATIONAL FOREST INFORMATION:
Allegheny National Forest
4 Farm Colony Dr.
Warren, PA 16365
(814) 723-5150
(877) 444-6777 (reservations)

FISHING AND HUNTING REGULATIONS:
Pennsylvania Fish and Boat Commission
1601 Elmerton Ave.
Harrisburg, PA 17110
(717) 705-7800 (Headquarters)
(877) 707-4085 (Fishing Licenses)

Pennsylvania Game Commission
2001 Elmerton Ave.
Harrisburg, PA 17110-9797
(717) 787-4250

Pennsylvania Annual Events

Please call ahead to confirm event details.

JANUARY	FEBRUARY	MARCH
■ Orchid and Tropical Bonsai Show / Pittsburgh 412-622-6914 ■ Pennsylvania Farm Show Harrisburg 717-787-5373 ■ Mummers Parade Philadelphia 215-336-3050	■ Groundhog Day Punxsutawney 814-618-5591 ■ Mid-Winter Scottish-Irish Music Festival and Fair King of Prussia 610-825-7268 ■ Jim Thorpe Winterfest Jim Thorpe 888-546-8477	■ American Quilter's Society Quilt Show / Lancaster 270-898-7903, ext. 146 ■ Philadelphia St. Patrick's Day Parade / Philadelphia 215-983-7224 ■ PHS Philadelphia Flower Show / Philadelphia 215-988-8800

APRIL	MAY	JUNE
■ International Spring Festival Lansdale 215-855-3228 ■ Kaleidoscope Art Festival Slippery Rock 724-738-4586 ■ Spring Blooms Kennett Square 610-388-1000	■ Memorial Day Parade and Ceremonies / Gettysburg 717-334-6274 ■ Rhubarb Festival Intercourse 717-768-8261 ■ Philadelphia International Children's Festival Philadelphia 215-898-3900	■ Pennsylvania State Laurel Festival / Wellsboro 570-724-1926 ■ Gettysburg Fest Gettysburg 717-334-0853 ■ Delaware River Sojourn Bushkill 609-883-9500

JULY	AUGUST	SEPTEMBER
■ Pittsburgh Three Rivers Regatta / Pittsburgh 412-427-4893 ■ Iron Heritage Festival Danville 570-275-6700 ■ Kutztown Folk Festival Kutztown 888-674-6136	■ Riverfest / Towanda 570-265-2696 ■ Musikfest / Bethlehem 610-332-1300 ■ Pennsylvania Renaissance Faire / Manheim 717-665-7021, ext. 231	■ Lancaster Liederkranz German Oktoberfest Manheim 717-898-8451 ■ Whoopie Pie Festival Ronks 800-827-8635 ■ La Festa Italiana Scranton 570-348-4921

OCTOBER	NOVEMBER	DECEMBER
■ Autumn Timber Festival Shawnee On Delaware 570-421-7231 ■ Harvest Days / Lancaster 717-569-0401 ■ Woolly Worm Festival Lewisburg 570-594-4691	■ Victorian Christmas Williamsport 570-772-5671 ■ Christmas in Bethlehem Bethlehem 610-332-1300 ■ Philadelphia Thanksgiving Day Parade / Philadelphia 215-581-4502	■ Country Christmas Village Lancaster 717-569-0401 ■ Olde Time Christmas Jim Thorpe 570-325-5810 ■ Old Time Christmas Stroudsburg 870-992-6161

Longwood Gardens,
Kennett Square

The Pennsylvania State
University Nittany Lion statue,
State College

Codorus State Park,
Hanover (York County)

State Capitol, Harrisburg

Benjamin Franklin Bridge, Philadelphia

Index: Great Experience for Members

AAA editor's picks of exceptional note

Hersheypark

Devil's Den

Liberty Bell Center

Railroad Museum of Pennsylvania

See Orientation map on p. 36 for corresponding grid coordinates, if applicable.

Pittsburgh (G-2)

Carnegie Museum of Natural History *(See p. 339.)*

Carnegie Museums of Pittsburgh *(See p. 339.)*

Carnegie Science Center *(See p. 339.)*

Cathedral of Learning *(See p. 340.)*

Clayton *(See p. 341.)*

Fort Pitt Museum *(See p. 342.)*

Gateway Clipper Fleet *(See p. 344.)*

Hartwood *(See p. 341.)*

Phipps Conservatory and Botanical Gardens *(See p. 343.)*

The Pittsburgh Zoo & PPG Aquarium *(See p. 342.)*

Point State Park *(See p. 342.)*

Senator John Heinz History Center *(See p. 343.)*

Scranton (E-10)

Steamtown National Historic Site *(See p. 385.)*

Strasburg (I-10)

Railroad Museum of Pennsylvania *(See p. 399.)*

Stroudsburg (F-11)

Quiet Valley Living Historical Farm *(See p. 400.)*

Titusville (D-2)

Drake Well Museum *(See p. 403.)*

Valley Forge National Historical Park (A-8)

Valley Forge National Historical Park *(See p. 408.)*

Washington Crossing Historic Park (H-12)

Washington Crossing Historic Park *(See p. 412.)*

York (I-8)

Colonial Complex *(See p. 431.)*

York County Heritage Trust *(See p. 430.)*

Pennsylvania
Atlas Section

ROADS/HIGHWAYS
- INTERSTATE
- CONTROLLED ACCESS
- CONTROLLED ACCESS TOLL
- TOLL ROAD
- PRIMARY DIVIDED
- PRIMARY UNDIVIDED
- SECONDARY DIVIDED
- SECONDARY UNDIVIDED
- LOCAL DIVIDED
- LOCAL UNDIVIDED
- UNPAVED ROAD
- UNDER CONSTRUCTION
- TUNNEL
- PEDESTRIAN ONLY
- AUTO FERRY
- PASSENGER FERRY
- SCENIC BYWAY
- 10 DISTANCE BETWEEN MARKERS
- EXIT NUMBER-FREE/TOLL
- INTERCHANGE FULL/PARTIAL
- WELCOME CENTER
- REST AREA/ SERVICE CENTER

BOUNDARIES
- INTERNATIONAL
- STATE
- COUNTY
- TIME ZONE
- CONTINENTAL DIVIDE

ROAD SHIELDS
- INTERSTATE/BUSINESS
- U.S./STATE/COUNTY
- FOREST/INDIAN
- TRANS- CANADA
- PROVINCIAL AUTOROUTE
- MEXICO
- HISTORIC ROUTE 66
- VT 41 REFERENCE PAGE INDICATOR

AREAS OF INTEREST
- INDIAN
- MILITARY
- PARK
- FOREST
- GRASSLANDS
- HISTORIC
- INT'L/REGIONAL AIRPORT
- INCORPORATED CITY

POINTS OF INTEREST
- TOWN
- NATIONAL CAPITAL
- STATE/PROVINCIAL CAPITAL
- AAA/CAA CLUB LOCATION
- FEATURE OF INTEREST
- COLLEGE/UNIVERSITY
- CAMPGROUND INFORMATION PROVIDED BY WOODALL'S®
- CUSTOMS STATION
- HISTORIC
- LIGHTHOUSE
- MONUMENT/MEMORIAL
- STATE/PROVINCIAL PARK
- NATIONAL WILDLIFE REFUGE
- SKI AREA
- SPORTS COMPLEX
- DAM

CITIES/TOWNS are color-coded by size, showing where to find AAA Approved and Diamond rated lodgings or restaurants listed in the AAA TourBook guides and on AAA.com:

- Red - major destinations and capitals; many listings
- Black - destinations; some listings
- Grey - no listings

PENNSYLVANIA

Miles 15 0 15 30 Miles
Kilometers 15 0 15 30 Kilometers
ONE INCH EQUALS APPROXIMATELY 15 MILES OR 23.87 KILOMETERS 1:1,140,480

ER054-18

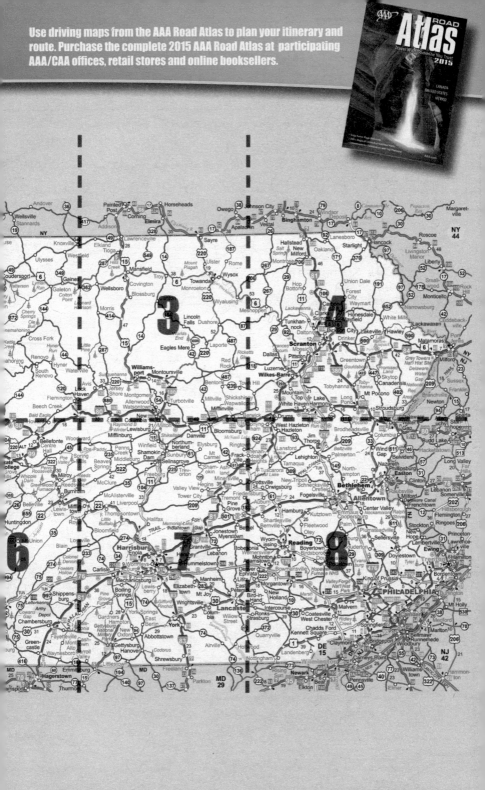

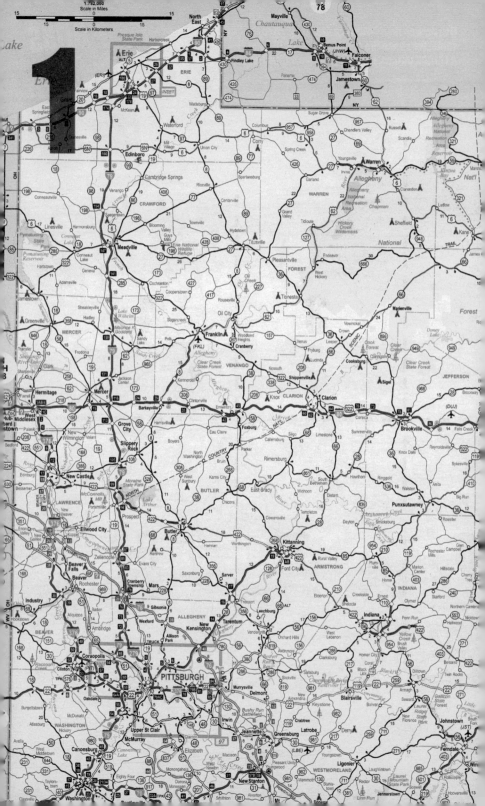

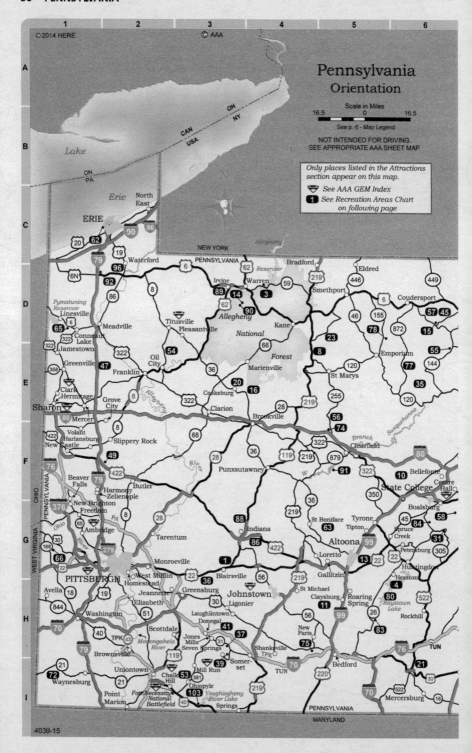

Pennsylvania
Orientation

Scale in Miles
16.5   0   16.5

See p. 6 - Map Legend

NOT INTENDED FOR DRIVING.
SEE APPROPRIATE AAA SHEET MAP.

Only places listed in the Attractions
section appear on this map.

See AAA GEM Index
See Recreation Areas Chart
on following page

©2014 HERE   © AAA

NEW YORK

PENNSYLVANIA

OHIO

WEST VIRGINIA

PENNSYLVANIA

MARYLAND

4039-15

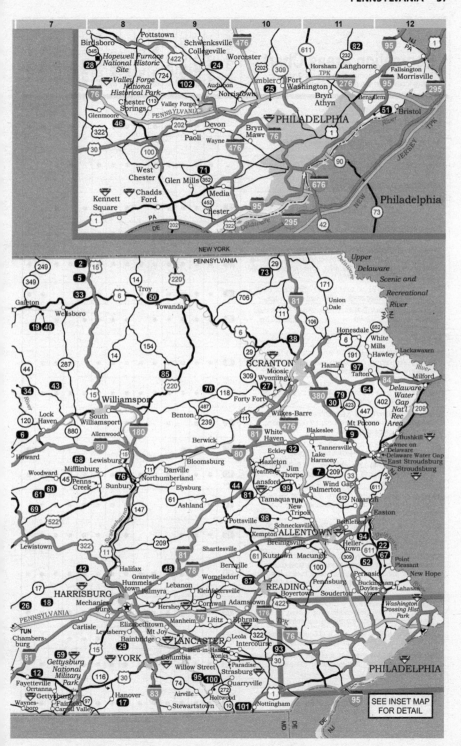

Recreation Areas Chart

The map location numerals in column 2 show an area's location on the preceding map.

	MAP LOCATION	CAMPING	PICNICKING	HIKING TRAILS	BOATING	BOAT RAMP	BOAT RENTAL	FISHING	SWIMMING	PETS ON LEASH	BICYCLE TRAILS	WINTER SPORTS	VISITOR CENTER	LODGE/CABINS	FOOD SERVICE
NATIONAL FORESTS *(See place listings.)*															
Allegheny (D-3) 516,000 acres. Northwestern Pennsylvania. Snowmobiling; all-terrain vehicle trails.		•	•	•	•	•	•	•	•	•	•	•	•		
NATIONAL RECREATION AREAS *(See place listings.)*															
Delaware Water Gap (E-12) 70,000 acres. Bird-watching, canoeing, cross-country skiing, hunting, kayaking, rafting, rock climbing, tubing.		•	•	•	•	•	•		•	•	•		•	•	
ARMY CORPS OF ENGINEERS															
Conemaugh River Lake (G-3) 7,609 acres 8 mi. n. of New Alexandria off SR 981. Ball field, canoe launch, dam tours, interpretive trail, playground.	**1**		•	•	•	•		•		•		•	•		
Cowanesque Lake (C-7) 3,200 acres 3 mi. w. of Lawrenceville off SR 15. Hunting, water skiing; amphitheater, playground.	**2**	•	•	•	•	•		•	•	•		•	•		
Kinzua Dam & Allegheny Reservoir (D-4) 26,541 acres 6 mi. e. of Warren via US 6 and SR 59. Cross-country skiing, ice fishing, playground, snowmobiling, water skiing. *(See Warren p. 409 and Allegheny National Forest p. 46.)*	**3**	•	•	•	•	•	•	•	•	•		•	•		
Raystown Lake (H-6) 29,300 acres s.w. of Huntingdon off SR 26. Water skiing; swimming beaches. *(See Huntingdon p. 159.)*	**4**	•	•	•	•	•	•	•	•	•		•	•	•	•
Tioga-Hammond Lakes (D-7) 6,700 acres 12 mi. n. of Mansfield on US 15. Hunting, water skiing; archery trail, horseshoe pits, swimming beach.	**5**	•	•	•	•	•		•	•	•		•	•		
STATE															
Bald Eagle (F-7) 5,900 acres off SR 150 to Main Park Rd. in Howard. Bird-watching, cross-country skiing, ice fishing, ice-skating, sledding, tobogganing; marina, swimming beach.	**6**	•	•	•	•	•		•	•	•		•	•		•
Beltzville (F-11) 3,002 acres 6 mi. e. of Lehighton off US 209. Bird-watching, cross-country skiing, hunting, ice boating, ice fishing, tobogganing, water skiing.	**7**		•	•	•	•		•	•	•		•			
Bendigo (E-5) 100 acres 3 mi. n.e. of Johnsonburg off US 219. Canoeing and kayaking only, cross-country skiing, sledding, snowshoeing; canoe launch.	**8**		•	•				•	•	•		•			•
Big Pocono (F-11) 1,306 acres off I-80 exit 299 at Tannersville. Historic. Downhill skiing, horseback riding, hunting.	**9**		•	•						•		•	•		
Black Moshannon (F-6) 3,394 acres 9 mi. e. of Philipsburg on SR 504. Cross-country skiing, hunting, ice boating, ice fishing, ice-skating, snowmobiling.	**10**	•	•	•	•	•	•	•	•	•		•		•	
Blue Knob (H-5) 6,128 acres .6 mi. n.w. of Pavia off SR 869. Cross-country and downhill skiing, horseback riding, hunting, snowmobiling.	**11**	•	•	•				•	•	•		•			•
Caledonia (I-7) 1,125 acres 4 mi. e. of Fayetteville on US 30. Historic. Cross-country skiing, golf (18 holes), hunting, theater. *(See Fayetteville p. 111.)*	**12**	•	•	•				•	•	•		•			•
Canoe Creek (G-5) 958 acres 7 mi. e. of Hollidaysburg off US 22. Bird-watching, boating (electric motors only), cross-country skiing, disc golf (9 holes), horseback riding, hunting, iceboating, ice fishing, ice-skating, sledding, tobogganing. *(See Altoona p. 54.)*	**13**	•	•	•	•	•		•	•	•		•			
Chapman (D-3) 805 acres 5 mi. w. of Clarendon off US 6. Boating (electric motors only), cross-country skiing, hunting, ice fishing, ice-skating, snowmobiling, tobogganing; warming hut.	**14**	•	•	•	•	•	•	•	•	•		•			
Cherry Springs (D-6) 48 acres 4 mi. e. of Coudersport on US 6, then 11 mi. s.e. on SR 44. Hunting, snowmobiling, star gazing.	**15**	•	•	•						•		•			
Clear Creek (E-4) 1,444 acres 4 mi. n. of Sigel off SR 949. Canoeing, cross-country skiing, hunting, sledding; canoe launch, playground.	**16**	•	•	•	•	•		•	•	•		•	•	•	
Codorus (I-8) 3,452 acres 2 mi. e. of Hanover off SR 216. Cross-country skiing, disc golf (54 holes), horseback riding, hunting, iceboating, ice fishing, ice skating, scuba diving, sledding, snowmobiling, tobogganing; horse trails, marina. *(See Hanover p. 133.)*	**17**	•	•	•	•	•	•	•	•	•		•	•	•	•

Recreation Areas Chart

The map location numerals in column 2 show an area's location on the preceding map.

Area	MAP LOCATION	CAMPING	PICNICKING	HIKING TRAILS	BOATING	BOAT RAMP	BOAT RENTAL	FISHING	SWIMMING	PETS ON LEASH	BICYCLE TRAILS	WINTER SPORTS	VISITOR CENTER	LODGE/CABINS	FOOD SERVICE
Colonel Denning (H-7) 273 acres 9 mi. n. of Newville off SR 233. Canoeing, cross-country skiing, hunting, ice-skating, tobogganing.	18	•	•	•	•	•		•	•	•		•	•		•
Colton Point (D-7) 368 acres 5 mi. s. of Ansonia off US 6. Cross-country skiing, hunting, interpretive center, snowmobiling. *(See Grand Canyon of Pennsylvania p. 416.)*	19	•	•	•	•			•				•	•		•
Cook Forest (E-3) 7,182 acres 1 mi. n. of Cooksburg off SR 36. Canoeing, cross-country skiing, horseback riding, hunting, ice-skating, sledding, snowmobiling, snowshoeing; craft center, horse rental, theater. *(See Cooksburg p. 88.)*	20	•	•	•	•			•		•	•	•	•	•	•
Cowans Gap (I-6) 1,085 acres n. of Fort Loudon off SR 75. Boating (electric motors only), cross-country skiing, hunting, ice fishing, ice-skating.	21	•	•	•	•	•	•	•	•			•			•
Delaware Canal (G-12) 60-mile area along SR 32; headquarters is in Upper Black Eddy. Bird-watching, canoeing, cross-country skiing, hunting, sledding.	22		•	•	•	•		•		•	•		•	•	
Elk (D-5) 3,192 acres 9 mi. e. of Wilcox. Hunting, iceboating, ice fishing.	23	•	•	•	•			•							
Evansburg (A-9) 3,349 acres 2 mi. e. of Collegeville on US 422. Cross-country skiing, golf (18 holes), horseback riding, hunting.	24	•	•	•				•		•	•	•			
Fort Washington (A-10) 493 acres at 500 Bethlehem Pike in Fort Washington. Bird-watching, cross-country skiing, disc golf (9 holes), sledding; observation deck, softball field.	25		•	•				•		•		•			
Fowlers Hollow (H-7) 104 acres 4 mi. s. of New Germantown off SR 274 on Upper Buck Ridge Rd. Cross-country skiing, horseback riding, hunting, mountain biking, snowmobiling.	26	•	•	•				•			•	•			
Frances Slocum (E-10) 1,035 acres 4 mi. e. of Dallas off SR 309. Boating (electric motors only), cross-country skiing, hunting, ice fishing, ice-skating, sledding. *(See Wilkes-Barre p. 422)*	27	•	•	•	•	•	•	•	•	•	•	•	•	•	•
French Creek (A-8) 7,339 acres about 5 mi. n.e. of Elverson off SR 345 (Hopewell Rd.). Bird-watching, boating (electric motors only), cross-country skiing, disc golf, horseback riding, hunting, ice fishing, ice-skating, sledding; mountain bicycle trails, softball field.	28	•	•	•	•	•	•	•	•	•	•	•	•	•	•
Gifford Pinchot (H-8) 2,338 acres 2 mi. e. of Rossville off SR 74. Boating (electric motors only), cross-country skiing, disc golf (18 holes), horseback riding, hunting, iceboating, ice fishing, ice-skating; swimming beach.	29	•	•	•	•	•	•	•	•	•	•	•	•		
Gouldsboro (E-11) 3,050 acres s. of Gouldsboro. Boating (electric motors only), cross-country skiing, hunting, ice fishing, ice-skating, snowmobiling; mountain bicycle trails.	30	•	•	•	•	•	•	•	•	•	•	•			
Greenwood Furnace (G-6) 423 acres 5 mi. n.w. of Belleville on SR 305. Canoeing and kayaking only, cross-country skiing, hunting, ice fishing, ice-skating, snowmobiling.	31	•	•	•				•	•	•		•	•		•
Hickory Run (F-10) 15,990 acres 5 mi. s.e. of White Haven on SR 534. Cross-country skiing, disc golf, hunting, ice fishing, ice-skating, snowmobiling; swimming beach. *(See White Haven p. 421.)*	32	•	•	•				•	•	•	•	•	•		•
Hills Creek (D-7) 407 acres 7 mi. n.e. of Wellsboro off SR 6. Boating (electric motors only), cross-country skiing, hunting, ice fishing, ice-skating, sledding, tobogganing.	33	•	•	•	•	•	•	•	•	•		•	•	•	•
Hyner Run (E-7) 180 acres 7 mi. e. of Renovo off SR 120. Hunting, hang-gliding, snowmobiling.	34	•	•	•				•	•	•		•	•		•
Kettle Creek (E-6) 1,793 acres 8 mi. n.w. of Westport off SR 120. Boating (electric motors only), cross-country skiing, horseback riding, hunting, ice fishing, sledding, snowmobiling; horse trail.	35	•	•	•	•	•	•	•		•		•			•
Keystone (H-3) 1,190 acres 3 mi. s.e. of New Alexandria on SR 981. Bird-watching, boating (electric motors only), cross-country skiing, hunting, ice fishing, ice-skating, sledding.	36	•	•	•	•	•	•	•	•	•		•	•	•	•
Kooser (H-3) 250 acres 10 mi. w. of Somerset on SR 31. Cross-country skiing, hunting.	37	•	•	•				•	•	•		•	•	•	

Recreation Areas Chart

The map location numerals in column 2 show an area's location on the preceding map.

	MAP LOCATION	CAMPING	PICNICKING	HIKING TRAILS	BOATING	BOAT RAMP	BOAT RENTAL	FISHING	SWIMMING	PETS ON LEASH	BICYCLE TRAILS	WINTER SPORTS	VISITOR CENTER	LODGE/CABINS	FOOD SERVICE
Lackawanna (D-10) 1,411 acres 3 mi. n. of Waverly on SR 407. Boating (electric motors only), cross-country skiing, horseback riding, hunting, ice fishing, ice-skating, mountain biking, sledding, tobogganing. *(See Scranton p. 384)*	38	•	•	•	•	•	•	•	•	•	•	•	•	•	•
Laurel Hill (I-3) 3,935 acres 10 mi. w. of Somerset off SR 31 near Trent. Boating (electric motors only), cross-country skiing, hunting, ice fishing, iceboating, mountain biking, snowmobiling, snowshoeing, tobogganing.	39	•	•	•	•	•	•	•	•	•	•	•		•	•
Leonard Harrison (D-7) 585 acres 10 mi. s.w. of Wellsboro off SR 660. *(See Grand Canyon of Pennsylvania p. 416.)*	40	•	•	•				•	•	•			•	•	•
Linn Run (H-3) 612 acres 10 mi. s.e. of Ligonier off SR 711. Horseback riding, hunting, snowmobiling.	41	•	•					•		•	•	•	•		
Little Buffalo (G-7) 830 acres 4 mi. s.w. of Newport off SR 34. Historic. Boating (electric motors only), cross-country skiing, hunting, ice fishing, ice-skating, sledding; playground.	42	•	•	•	•	•	•	•	•	•	•	•	•		
Little Pine (E-7) 2,158 acres 3 mi. n. of Waterville off SR 44. Boating (electric motors only), cross-country skiing, hunting, ice fishing, sledding, snowmobiling.	43	•	•	•	•	•	•	•	•	•	•	•			
Locust Lake (F-10) 1,089 acres 3 mi. s. of Mahanoy City off I 81 exit 131A. Hunting, ice fishing, ice-skating.	44	•			•	•	•	•	•	•		•			
Lyman Run (D-6) 595 acres 8 mi. s.w. of Galeton off US 6. Bird-watching, boating (electric motors only), hunting, ice fishing, ice-skating, snowmobiling; all-terrain vehicle trails, swimming beach.	45	•	•	•	•	•	•	•	•	•		•			•
Marsh Creek (B-8) 1,705 acres 5 mi. n.w. of Downingtown off SR 282. Bird-watching, boating (electric motors only), horseback riding, hunting, iceboating, ice fishing, ice-skating, sledding; horse rental.	46		•	•	•	•	•	•	•	•	•	•	•		• •
Maurice K. Goddard (E-2) 2,856 acres 14 mi. w. of Franklin on US 62. Bird-watching, cross-country skiing, hunting, iceboating, ice fishing, ice-skating, sledding, snowmobiling.	47		•	•	•	•	•	•	•	•		•	•	•	
Memorial Lake (G-9) 230 acres 5 mi. n.e. of Grantville off US 22 and I-81. Boating (electric motors only), cross-country skiing, ice fishing, ice-skating, sailing.	48		•	•	•	•	•	•		•		•		•	
Moraine (F-2) 16,725 acres 8 mi. n.w. of Butler off US 422. Cross-country skiing, disc golf (18 holes), horseback riding, hunting, iceboating, ice fishing, ice-skating, sledding, snowmobiling, windsurfing. *(See Butler p. 75)*	49	•	•	•	•	•	•	•	•	•	•	•	•	•	•
Mount Pisgah (D-8) 1,302 acres 10 mi. n.w. of Troy off US 6. Boating (electric motors only), cross-country skiing, hunting, ice fishing, ice-skating, snowmobiling.	50	•	•	•	•	•	•	•	•	•		•			
Neshaminy (B-12) 330 acres near Croydon off SR 132.	51		•	•				•	•	•			•		•
Nockamixon (G-11) 5,283 acres 5 mi. e. of Quakertown off CRs 513 and 563. Cross-country skiing, disc golf (18 holes), horseback riding, hunting, ice fishing, ice-skating, sledding, windsurfing; horse rental.	52		•	•	•	•	•	•	•	•	•	•	•	•	•
Ohiopyle (I-3) 20,499 acres 14 mi. e. of Uniontown on SR 381. Boating (white-water rafting only), cross-country skiing, horseback riding, hunting, rock climbing, mountain biking, sledding, snowmobiling, tobogganing, whitewater rafting; water slides. *(See Ohiopyle p. 216.)*	53	•	•	•	•	•	•	•		•	•	•	•	•	•
Oil Creek (E-2) 7,007 acres 4 mi. n. of Oil City on SR 8 via signs. Historic. Canoeing, cross-country skiing, hunting, kayaking; waterfalls. *(See Oil City p. 217)*	54	•	•	•				•		•	•	•	•		
Ole Bull (E-6) 132 acres 3 mi. s.w. of Oleona off SR 144. Cross-country skiing, hunting, mountain biking, snowmobiling.	55	•	•	•				•	•	•		•		•	•
Parker Dam (E-5) 968 acres 4 mi. e. of Penfield off SR 153. Boating (electric motors only), cross-country skiing, hunting, ice fishing, ice-skating, sledding, snowmobiling, sledding, snowshoeing.	56	•	•	•	•	•	•	•	•	•		•	•	•	•
Patterson (D-6) 10 acres off SR 44 between Cherry Springs and Sweden Valley. Hunting.	57	•	•	•				•		•	•				

Recreation Areas Chart

The map location numerals in column 2 show an area's location on the preceding map.

Recreation Area	MAP LOCATION	CAMPING	PICNICKING	HIKING TRAILS	BOATING	BOAT RAMP	BOAT RENTAL	FISHING	SWIMMING	PETS ON LEASH	BICYCLE TRAILS	WINTER SPORTS	VISITOR CENTER	LODGE/CABINS	FOOD SERVICE
Penn-Roosevelt (G-6) 41 acres 10 mi. w. of Milroy off US 322. Cross-country skiing, horseback riding, snowmobiling.	58	•	•	•				•	•	•		•			
Pine Grove Furnace (H-7) 696 acres at Pine Grove Furnace on SR 233. Boating (electric motors only), cross-country skiing, hunting, ice fishing, ice-skating, snowmobiling.	59	•	•	•	•	•	•	•	•	•	•	•	•	•	•
Poe Paddy (F-7) 23 acres n.e. of Milroy off US 322. Canoeing, snowmobiling; canoe launch.	60	•	•	•	•	•		•		•		•			
Poe Valley (F-7) 620 acres 10 mi. n.e. of Milroy off US 322. Boating (electric motors only), cross-country skiing, hunting, ice fishing, snowmobiling.	61	•	•	•	•	•	•	•	•	•		•			
Presque Isle (C-1) 3,200 acres 7 mi. n. of I-90 exit 18 on Peninsula Dr. (SR 832). Historic. Cross-country skiing, hunting, ice-boating, ice fishing, ice-skating, scuba diving, waterskiing; bike rentals, boat tours, marina. *(See Erie p. 106.)*	62		•	•	•	•	•	•	•	•	•	•	•	•	•
Prince Gallitzin (G-5) 7,335 acres 16 mi. n.w. of Altoona off SR 53. Cross-country skiing, disc golf (9 holes), horseback riding, hunting, iceboating, ice fishing, mountain biking, snowmobiling, tobogganing.	63	•	•	•	•	•	•	•	•	•	•	•	•		
Promised Land (E-11) 2,971 acres 10 mi. n. of Canadensis on SR 390. Boating (electric motors only), cross-country skiing, horseback riding, hunting, ice fishing, ice-skating, mountain biking, snowmobiling.	64	•	•	•	•	•	•	•	•	•		•	•	•	•
Pymatuning (D-1) 21,122 acres 4 mi. n. of Jamestown off US 322. Cross-country skiing, disc golf (18 holes), hunting, iceboating, ice fishing, ice-skating, sledding, snowmobiling. *(See Linesville p. 188.)*	65	•	•	•	•	•	•	•	•	•		•	•	•	•
Raccoon Creek (G-1) 7,572 acres 2 mi. n. of Frankfort Springs on SR 18. Boating (electric motors only), cross-country skiing, horseback riding, hunting, ice fishing, ice-skating, snowmobiling.	66	•	•	•	•	•	•	•	•	•		•	•		
Ralph Stover (G-12) 45 acres 9 mi. n.w. of New Hope on SR 32. Boating (white-water rafting only), rock climbing, tobogganing.	67		•	•				•		•		•			
Raymond B. Winter (F-7) 695 acres 20 mi. w. of Lewisburg on SR 192. Cross-country skiing, hunting, ice fishing, mountain biking, snowmobiling.	68	•	•	•	•	•		•	•	•		•	•		
Reeds Gap (G-7) 220 acres 13 mi. n.e. of Lewistown off US 322. Cross-country skiing, hunting.	69	•	•	•				•	•	•		•	•		
Ricketts Glen (E-9) 13,050 acres 4 mi. n. of Red Rock on SR 487. Boating (electric motors only), cross-country skiing, horseback riding, hunting, ice fishing, snowmobiling; beach, canoe rental. *(See Benton p. 61.)*	70	•	•	•	•	•	•	•	•					•	•
Ridley Creek (B-9) 2,606 acres 7 mi. e. of West Chester via SRs 3 or 352. Cross-country skiing, horseback riding, sledding; gardens.	71		•	•						•	•	•	•		
Ryerson Station (I-1) 1,164 acres 1 mi. s. of Wind Ridge off SR 21. Cross-country skiing, hunting, ice fishing, ice-skating, sledding, snowmobiling; swimming pool.	72	•	•	•				•	•	•		•	•		
Salt Springs (D-10) 405 acres 1 mi. w. of Franklin Forks off SR 29. Primitive. Cross-country skiing, hunting, sledding.	73	•	•	•					•	•		•		•	
S.B. Elliott (F-5) 318 acres 9 mi. w. of Clearfield on SR 153. Cross-country skiing, hunting, snowmobiling.	74	•	•	•					•	•		•	•	•	
Shawnee (H-4) 3,983 acres 9 mi. w. of Bedford off US 30. Boating (electric motors only), cross-country skiing, disc golf (9 holes), ice fishing, ice-skating, sledding, snowmobiling.	75	•	•	•	•	•	•	•	•	•		•	•	•	
Shikellamy (F-8) 132 acres 1 mi. n. of Shamokin Dam off SR 11; 3,000 acres off SR 147 between Sunbury and Northumberland. Marina, scenic overlook.	76		•	•	•	•	•	•	•	•		•		•	
Sinnemahoning (E-6) 1,910 acres 10 mi. n. of Sinnemahoning on SR 872. Boating (electric motors only), cross-country skiing, hunting, ice fishing, ice skating, snowmobiling.	77	•	•	•	•	•		•	•	•		•			
Sizerville (D-5) 386 acres at Sizerville off SR 155. Cross-country skiing, hunting, snowmobiling.	78	•	•	•				•	•	•		•	•	•	•

Recreation Areas Chart

The map location numerals in column 2 show an area's location on the preceding map.

	MAP LOCATION	CAMPING	PICNICKING	HIKING TRAILS	BOATING	BOAT RAMP	BOAT RENTAL	FISHING	SWIMMING	PETS ON LEASH	BICYCLE TRAILS	WINTER SPORTS	VISITOR CENTER	LODGE/CABINS	FOOD SERVICE
Tobyhanna (E-11) 5,440 acres 2 mi. e. of Tobyhanna on SR 423. Boating (electric motors only), hunting, ice fishing, ice-skating, mountain biking, snowmobiling.	79	•	•	•	•	•	•	•	•	•	•	•	•		
Trough Creek (H-5) 554 acres 3 mi. n. of Entriken off SR 994. Cross-country skiing, hunting, snowmobiling.	80	•	•	•				•				•	•	•	•
Tuscarora (F-10) 1,618 acres 5 mi. n.w. of Tamaqua off SR 309. Boating (electric motors only), hunting, ice fishing, ice-skating.	81	•	•	•	•	•	•	•	•	•		•	•	•	•
Tyler (A-11) 1,711 acres 1.5 mi. w. of Newtown off SR 413. Boating (electric motors only), canoeing, cross-country skiing, disc golf (27 holes), horseback riding, ice fishing, ice-skating, sledding; theater.	82		•	•	•	•		•	•		•	•	•	•	•
Warriors Path (H-5) 349 acres 1 mi. s. of Saxton on SR 26. Cross-country skiing, hunting.	83		•	•	•	•			•	•	•		•		
Whipple Dam (G-6) 256 acres 12 mi. s. of State College off SR 26. Boating (electric motors only), cross-country skiing, hunting, ice fishing, ice-skating, skiing, snowmobiling; volleyball court.	84		•	•	•	•	•	•	•	•	•	•			•
Worlds End (E-9) 780 acres 7 mi. n.w. of Laporte on SR 154. Boating (white-water rafting only), cross-country skiing, hunting, snowmobiling.	85	•	•	•	•			•	•	•		•	•	•	•
Yellow Creek (G-4) 2,981 acres 12 mi. e. of Indiana on US 422. Cross-country skiing, hunting, iceboating, ice fishing, ice-skating, mountain biking, sledding, snowmobiling. *(See Indiana p. 160)*	86	•	•	•	•	•		•	•	•	•	•	•	•	•
OTHER															
Blue Marsh Lake (H-10) 6,276 acres 8 mi. n. of Reading on SR 183. Historic. Horseback riding, hunting, iceboating, ice fishing, ice-skating, scuba diving, water skiing. Food service is available Memorial Day-Labor Day. *(See Reading p. 378)*	87		•	•	•	•		•	•	•	•	•	•		•
Blue Spruce Park (G-3) 650 acres 6 mi. n. of Indiana on SR 110. Bird-watching, cross-country skiing, hunting, sledding; playgrounds, sports field, volleyball court.	88	•	•	•				•		•		•			
Buckaloons Access Area (D-3) 5 mi. w. of Warren at jct. US 6 and US 62. Hunting.	89	•	•	•	•	•		•	•	•					
Chapman Lake (D-4) 68 acres near Montdale. Boating (electric motors only), cross-country skiing, ice fishing, ice-skating, sledding, snowmobiling.	90	•	•	•	•	•		•	•	•	•	•	•	•	•
Curwensville Lake (F-5) 362 acres 3 mi. s. of Curwensville on SR 453. Ice fishing; marina.	91	•	•	•	•	•	•	•	•	•	•	•			•
Edinboro Lake (D-2) 245 acres on SR 99 in Edinboro. Waterskiing; boat docks, fishing pier.	92	•			•	•	•	•						•	•
Hibernia Park (H-10) 900 acres 6 mi. n. of Coatesville on SR 82, then w. on Cedar Knoll Rd. Historic. Fishing pier, playground.	93	•	•	•				•		•		•	•		
Hugh Moore Park (G-11) 260 acres on SR 611 in Easton. Mule-drawn boat tour, museum. Boating is only permitted with rented canoes and kayaks. *(See Easton p. 99.)*	94		•	•	•					•			•	•	
Lake Aldred (I-9) 5,000 acres 25 mi. s.e. of York on SR 425. Hunting, waterskiing.	95	•	•	•	•	•		•		•					
Lake Leboeuf (D-2) 70 acres 2 blks. s. on Hazel St. in Waterford. *(See Waterford p. 414)*	96	•	•			•		•	•	•	•				
Lake Wallenpaupack (E-11) 5,700 acres 10 mi. e. of Hamlin off SR 590. Bird-watching, ice fishing, water skiing; horse rental. *(See Hawley p. 146.)*	97	•	•	•	•	•	•	•	•	•		•	•	•	•
Leaser Lake (G-10) 396 acres on SR 143 in Jacksonville. Boating (sailboats and boats with small electric motors only), horseback riding, ice fishing.	98	•	•	•	•	•		•		•			•		
Mauch Chunk Lake (F-10) 2,445 acres 4 mi. w. of Jim Thorpe. Boating (electric motors only), ice fishing, swimming beach. *(See Jim Thorpe p. 163)*	99	•	•	•	•	•	•	•	•	•			•	•	•	•
Muddy Run (I-9) 700 acres 4 mi. w. of Buck on SR 372. Boating (electric motors only). *(See Holtwood p. 156.)*	100	•	•	•	•	•	•	•	•		•	•		•		•

Recreation Areas Chart

The map location numerals in column 2 show an area's location on the preceding map.

	MAP LOCATION	CAMPING	PICNICKING	HIKING TRAILS	BOATING	BOAT RAMP	BOAT RENTAL	FISHING	SWIMMING	PETS ON LEASH	BICYCLE TRAILS	WINTER SPORTS	VISITOR CENTER	LODGE/CABINS	FOOD SERVICE
Nottingham (I-10) 651 acres .25 mi. s. of Nottingham at 150 Park Rd. Bird-watching, cross-country skiing. *(See Nottingham p. 215.)*	101		•	•				•		•	•	•	•		
Schuylkill Canal (A-9) 60 acres 3 mi. s. off US 422 on SR 29. Historic. Bird-watching, cross-country skiing, horseback riding.	102		•	•	•					•	•		•		
Youghiogheny Reservoir (I-3) 3,915 acres 20 mi. s.e. of Union-town on US 40. Hunting.	103	•	•		•	•	•	•	•	•	•	•		•	

Get There Better
with *TripTik® Travel Planner*

Much more than maps ... TripTik Travel Planner
is everything for a better journey.

- Itinerary builder for creating, saving and sharing trips
- Content-rich travel guides and custom drive trips
- Approved and Diamond Rated
  hotels and restaurants

Go with AAAmaps.com or the AAA or CAA Mobile app

ABBOTTSTOWN pop. 1,011

THE ALTLAND HOUSE INN AND SUITES   717/259-9535

▼▼▼ **Historic Country Inn.** Rates not provided. **Address:** 1 Center Square 17301 **Location:** Jct SR 194 and US 30; on circle. **Facility:** The building housing The Altland House has functioned continuously as an inn since 1790. 10 units, some kitchens. 3 stories (no elevator), interior corridors. **Dining:** The Altland House Grill & Pub, see separate listing.

🍴 🍸 📶 ⊠ ▣ / SOME UNITS 🛒 🔲 🖼️

WHERE TO EAT

THE ALTLAND HOUSE GRILL & PUB   717/259-9535

▼▼▼ American. Casual Dining. $8-$29 **AAA Inspector Notes:** *Historic.* Find the 1790 Altland House on the town square. The landmark property reflects a well-coordinated contemporary theme with neutral colors and modern furnishings. Peruse the menu for preparations of seafood, chicken, steak and pasta in addition to flavorful homemade soup, bread and dessert. **Features:** full bar, patio dining, early bird specials, Sunday brunch, happy hour. **Reservations:** suggested, weekends. **Address:** 20 W King St 17301 **Location:** Jct SR 194 and US 30; on circle; in The Altland House Inn and Suites. Ⓛ Ⓓ

ABINGTON

- **Hotels & Restaurants map & index p. 274**
- **Part of Philadelphia area — see map p. 230**

ALEXANDER'S KITCHEN BAR   215/576-9766 (79)

▼▼ American. Casual Dining. $9-$20 **AAA Inspector Notes:** Home-style American and Greek dishes are offered at this family-owned area favorite. Among the many specialties are dolmades, crabcakes and veal parmigiana. **Features:** full bar, happy hour. **Address:** 1482 Old York Rd 19001 **Location:** I-276 exit 343, 2.9 mi s on SR 611. 🏠 Crestmont, 295. Ⓑ Ⓛ Ⓓ 🚇

LEE'S HOAGIE HOUSE OF ABINGTON   215/659-3322 (78)

▼ Sandwiches. Quick Serve. $5-$17 **AAA Inspector Notes:** Fresh salads, wraps, cheesesteaks and of course, hoagies, fill the menu at this casual eatery. Sandwiches range from 6 to 18 inches, but larger groups may enjoy their party platters available upon request. **Address:** 1656 Old York Rd 19001 **Location:** I-276 exit 343, 2.2 mi s on SR 611. 🏠 Crestmont, 295. Ⓛ Ⓓ 🚇

ACME

POLYMATH PARK is at 187 Evergreen Ln.; tours begin at Tree Tops restaurant. The site is home to Frank Lloyd Wright's Duncan House which was originally constructed in Lisle, Ill. The house has been reconstructed in Polymath Park where it sits in close proximity to Balter House and Blum House, both designed by Peter Berndtson, apprentice to Wright. Shuttle service is provided during on a 1-hour tour. A 2-hour tour with the master builder is available on Sundays. **Hours:** House tours depart Mon.-Fri. 11:30, 12:30 and 1:30, Sun. 12:30 and 1:30, mid-March to mid-Oct. Master Builder tour Sun. at 11:30, mid-March to mid-Oct. **Cost:** House tour $22. Master Builder tour (includes lunch) $100. Reservations are required. **Phone:** (877) 833-7829. GT 🍴

BRADY'S RESTAURANT   724/423-4566

▼▼ American. Casual Dining. $4-$17 **AAA Inspector Notes:** The atmosphere is relaxed in the family-owned and -operated restaurant, a mainstay for home-cooked meals. **Features:** Sunday brunch. **Address:** 3242 State Rt 31 15610 **Location:** I-70/76 (Pennsylvania Tpke) exit 91, 1 mi w. Ⓑ Ⓛ Ⓓ

ADAMSTOWN (H-10) pop. 1,789, elev. 980'

- **Attractions map p. 221**
- **Hotels & Restaurants map & index p. 222**
- **Part of Pennsylvania Dutch Country area — see map p. 220**

Adamstown—called Antiques Capital, USA—and nearby Denver are considered gold mines by antiques lovers and collectors. Those shopping for furnishings or collectibles should not be disappointed.

Shopping areas: Between Adamstown and the nearby communities, there are nearly two dozen establishments selling antiques. Some of the shops are along SR 272 and can be accessed via the Pennsylvania Turnpike (I-76) exit 286. Some of the larger antique markets are Adamstown Antique Mall, Mad Hatter Antique Mall, Pine Hills Antique Mall, Renninger's Antique Market, Shupp's Grove, and Stoudt's Black Angus Antique Mall and Wonderful Good Market & Farmers Co-op. Stoudtburg Village, off SR 272 on Stoudtburg Road, is a Bavarian-inspired village with more than 40 shops.

ADAMSTOWN INNS & COTTAGES   (717)484-0800 ▣4

▼▼▼ **Historic Bed & Breakfast** $109-$270 **Address:** 144 W Main St 19501 **Location:** Center. **Facility:** This large Victorian inn features a magnificent intricately carved front door and a wraparound veranda. It's easy to feel at home since all of the oversize guest rooms include a fireplace and a hot tub. 9 units, some cottages. 3 stories (no elevator), interior/exterior corridors. **Terms:** 2-3 night minimum stay - weekends, 14 day cancellation notice-fee imposed.

🍴 📶 ⊠ 🚫 / SOME UNITS 🛒 🔲 🖼️ ▣

WHERE TO EAT

STOUDT'S BLACK ANGUS RESTAURANT   717/484-4386 ▣5

▼▼▼
American Casual Dining
$9-$39

AAA Inspector Notes: Victorian appointments decorate the casually upscale dining room, a favorite spot for special occasions. In addition to traditional German foods such as Wiener schnitzel, the menu delivers steaks, crab cakes and delicious homemade beer bread. The restaurant also is associated with the Stoudt Brewery and has a brewpub dispensing its products. **Features:** full bar, happy hour. **Reservations:** suggested. **Address:** 2800 N Reading Rd (SR 272) 19501 **Location:** I-76 (Pennsylvania Tpke) exit 286, 2.8 mi n on SR 272. Ⓓ

ZIA MARIA'S ITALIAN RESTAURANT   717/336-1333 ▣6

▼▼ Italian. Casual Dining. $7-$26 **AAA Inspector Notes:** Order a plate of the fresh, delicious bruschetta to share before perusing the daily specials at this casual eatery. Hearty portions of fresh food are a pleasant, albeit unexpected, staple at this gem in northern Lancaster County. You'll usually find the bar area packed with sports fans enjoying cold beers and heaping plates of wings or nachos. **Features:** full bar, patio dining. **Address:** 2350 N Reading Rd 17517 **Location:** I-76 (Pennsylvania Tpke) exit 286, 1 mi w to SR 272, then just n. Ⓛ Ⓓ

Choose real ratings you
can trust from professional
inspectors who've been there

THE BAHAMIAN RIVIERA AWAITS. Introducing a glamorous new playground with the world's most celebrated hotels, including the dazzling debut of the Baha Mar Casino & Hotel. Get ready for the rendezvous of the century in Nassau, The Bahamas. For an exclusive preview, visit BahaMar.com.

BAHA MAR CASINO & HOTEL | ROSEWOOD | SLS LUX | GRAND HYATT

AIRVILLE (I-9) elev. 679'

On the grounds of the Indian Steps Museum is a giant holly tree that is more than 375 years old. Each year a small branch of the tree is broken off and presented to the Pennsylvania Power and Light Co. as payment of rent for the land occupied by the museum.

INDIAN STEPS MUSEUM, 4.5 mi. n.e. on SR 425, then 1 mi. s.e. on Indian Steps Rd., houses Native American relics. More than 10,000 animal and Native American artifacts from 500-10,000 years old are imbedded in the walls, floors and exterior walkways of the century-old building. Also on display are locally found artifacts, including baskets, pottery shards and native clothing as well as dioramas. A nature trail winds through 26 acres of wooded hillsides.

Guided tours are available by appointment. **Time:** Allow 30 minutes minimum. **Hours:** Thurs.-Fri. 10-4, Sat.-Sun. and holidays 10-5, Apr. 15-Oct. 31. Phone ahead for special events schedule. **Cost:** Donations. $3. **Phone:** (717) 862-3948, or (717) 891-4828 in the off-season. 🏕

AKRON pop. 3,876

- **Hotels & Restaurants map & index p. 222**
- **Part of Pennsylvania Dutch Country area — see map p. 220**

BELLA VISTA BED & BREAKFAST   717/859-4227   **15**

▼▼▼ **Historic Bed & Breakfast.** Rates not provided. **Address:** 1216 E Main St 17501 **Location:** 1.2 mi e. Located in a residential area. **Facility:** At this historic B&B, the gardens, trees and a sprawling lawn enhance the acre-plus grounds. Built in 1912, the post-Victorian architecture is well preserved. 6 units. 3 stories (no elevator), interior corridors. **Terms:** check-in 4 pm, age restrictions may apply. 🛜 ✕ 🅿 / SOME UNITS 🎖

BOXWOOD INN   717/859-3466   **17**

▼▼▼ **Historic Bed & Breakfast.** Rates not provided. **Address:** 1320 Diamond St 17501 **Location:** SR 272, 0.4 mi se on Main St to Diamond St, 0.3 mi s. Located in a residential area. **Facility:** Each guest room in this restored 1768 stone farmhouse has a different décor theme. Set on three acres, this property includes a well-manicured backyard with a small stream, weeping willows and a stone deck. 5 units, some cottages. 2 stories (no elevator), interior/exterior corridors. 🛜 ✕ 🅿 / SOME UNITS 🐾 🖥 🖥 🖥

RODEWAY INN   (717)859-1654   **16**

▼ **Motel** $60-$100 **Address:** 116 S 7th St 17501 **Location:** Just s on SR 272. Located in a commercial area. **Facility:** 24 units. 1-2 stories (no elevator), exterior corridors. 🍴 🛜 ✕ 🖥 🖥

ALLEGHENY NATIONAL FOREST (D-4) elev. 1,867'

Elevations in the forest range from 1,071 ft. at Baker Island near Tionesta to 2,245 ft. at Tracy Ridge Recreation Area. Refer to AAA maps for additional elevation information.

Allegheny National Forest extends 40 miles south from the New York-Pennsylvania border through the counties of Warren, Forest, Elk and McKean. The only national forest in Pennsylvania, its 516,000 acres include 500 miles of fishing streams, 272 miles of hiking and cross-country ski trails, 366 miles of snowmobile trails and 108 miles of trail-bike and ATV routes. Several scenic drives traverse the area; contact the forest for recommended routes.

Six boat launches and a full-service marina provide access to the 12,000-acre Allegheny Reservoir *(see Warren p. 409 and Recreation Areas Chart)*, impounded by the Kinzua Dam *(see Warren p. 409 and Recreation Areas Chart)*. Water skiing is popular, and 10 of the forest's 20 campgrounds are on or near the shore. Five of these can be reached only by boat or on foot. Rimrock and Jake's Rocks overlooks offer picnicking and views of the dam and reservoir as well as spectacular displays of Pennsylvania's state flower, the mountain laurel, in June. Several other picnic areas are available throughout the forest—some with unsupervised swimming facilities.

Another recreational activity is hunting for deer, bears, grouse and small game. Canoeing is popular on the Allegheny Wild and Scenic River, the Clarion River and, in the early spring, Tionesta Creek. Heart's Content, a 120-acre primeval tract of 300- to 400-year-old hemlock and beech trees, is 15 miles south of Warren.

The 8,663-acre Hickory Creek Wilderness provides opportunities for primitive camping, hiking, hunting, fishing and wildlife watching. Allegheny Islands Wilderness, comprised of seven islands totaling 368 acres in the Allegheny River, holds the distinction of being the smallest federally designated wilderness in the United States.

For more information contact the Forest Supervisor, Allegheny National Forest, 4 Farm Colony Dr., Warren, PA 16365. Phone (814) 728-6100, (814) 723-5150, or TTY (814) 726-2710. *See Recreation Areas Chart.*

ALLENTOWN (G-11) pop. 118,032, elev. 304'

- **Hotels p. 52 • Restaurants p. 52**
- **Hotels & Restaurants map & index p. 49**

Allentown is nestled in the Lehigh Valley along with Bethlehem *(see place listing p. 62)* and Easton *(see place listing p. 99)*. Allentown was originally incorporated as Northamptontown; German settlers played a key role in its development. The city later adopted the name of its founder, Colonial Pennsylvania Supreme Court Chief Justice William Allen.

After the Battle of Brandywine in 1777 George Washington had no hope of saving Philadelphia from the British. The Liberty Bell and the bells of Christ Church were secretly removed to Allentown to be hidden in Zion's Church. The church now houses the Liberty Bell Museum *(see attraction listing p. 48)*.

Allentown has 2,000 acres of park grounds; recreational opportunities can be found on the city's bike paths, hiking trails and golf courses. Fishing is permitted in rivers and streams. The Old-Fashioned Garden and the Rose Garden, Parkway Boulevard and 27th Street, contain more than 100 varieties of

(See map & index p. 49.)

roses, water plants and many other flowers. Peak-bloom seasons are spring and fall. West Park features a fountain and war memorials surrounded by more than 200 types of trees; concerts are held in the summer at the band shell.

The city has three historic districts: Old Allentown; Old Fairgrounds; and West Park, which is centered around the city's first park and features Colonial Revival and Queen Anne architecture.

The 1,200-seat Miller Symphony Hall, 23 N. 6th St., is a renovated late 19th-century theater that is home to Allentown Symphony Orchestra. Musicals, theatrical events and symphony performances are given; phone (610) 432-6715 for the box office. Civic Theatre, 527 N. 19th St., offers live theater as well as independent and foreign films; phone (610) 433-8943.

Cedar Crest College and Muhlenberg College are institutions of higher education.

The Lehigh Valley IronPigs, Class AAA affiliate of the Philadelphia Phillies, play at Coca-Cola Park; phone (610) 841-7447.

🐝 Mayfair Festival of the Arts, one of the Northeast's largest visual and performing arts festivals, is held Memorial Day weekend at Cedar Beach Park. It includes art exhibits, concerts, dancers and storytellers; phone (610) 437-6900. Lehigh Valley SportsFest draws approximately 150,000 spectators and 10,000 amateur athletes, who compete in more than three dozen sporting events in parks across the city each July. In late August through early September the Great Allentown Fair, which supports the achievements of farmers, gardeners and homemakers, is held at the Allentown Fairgrounds. This annual event has been occurring since 1852 and features rides, games, shows and concerts; phone (610) 433-7541. Lights in the Parkway is a nearly 1.5-mile drive-through light display set to music along Lehigh Parkway, one of the city's parks, late November through late December; phone (610) 437-7530.

Lehigh County Historical Society operates the following nearby sites: Haines Mill Museum, 3600 Haines Mill Rd. in Cetronia; 1756 Troxell-Steckel Farmer Museum, 4229 Reliance St. in Egypt; and Lock Ridge Furnace Museum, 525 Franklin St. in Alburtis. For schedules phone (610) 435-1074.

Lehigh Valley Visitor Center: 840 Hamilton St., Suite 200, Allentown, PA 18101. **Phone:** (610) 882-9200 or (800) 747-0561.

Self-guiding tours: Brochures for the self-guiding Lehigh Valley Covered Bridges Tour, which leads past seven historic and picturesque bridges, are available at the convention and visitors bureau. Information about a local log cabin trail, the Lehigh Valley Wine Trail and bicycle trails also is available. Information about the Old Allentown historic district can be found at Lehigh Valley Visitor Center as well as at Old Allentown Preservation Association at 147 N. 10th St. and at City Hall.

Shopping areas: The Allentown Fairgrounds Farmers Market, 17th and Chew streets, features an Amish bakery, fresh produce, flowers, cheeses and specialty food items. It's open year-round Thursday through Saturday.

Lehigh Valley Mall, N. MacArthur Road and US 22, includes Boscov's, JCPenney and Macy's.

About 6.5 miles southeast of Allentown in Center Valley is The Promenade Shops at Saucon Valley, Center Valley Pkwy. and SR 309, which features more than 50 stores, including Banana Republic, Barnes & Noble, J. Jill and L.L. Bean.

ALLENTOWN ART MUSEUM is at 31 N. Fifth St. between Hamilton and Linden sts. Permanent exhibits include European Renaissance painting and sculpture; American painting and sculpture spanning three centuries; decorative arts; and Art Ways, an interactive gallery for families to explore together. Also featured are international textiles, works on paper, sculpture from southeast Asia and a library designed by Frank Lloyd Wright. Approximately 10 temporary exhibitions are presented throughout the year.

Time: Allow 1 hour minimum. **Hours:** Wed.-Sat. 11-4, Sun. noon-4. Closed Jan. 1, July 4, Thanksgiving and Christmas. **Cost:** $12; $10 (ages 6-12, ages 60+ and students with ID); free (active military with ID and to all on Sun. **Phone:** (610) 432-4333. 🎫

AMERICA ON WHEELS MUSEUM, 5 N. Front St. at jct. Hamilton St., presents creative exhibits portraying the many changes wheeled transportation has gone through over the years—from antique carriages to automobiles that run on alternative fuel sources. Cars, trucks, motorcycles and bicycles are displayed, and a gallery is dedicated to changing exhibits. Some of the interactive exhibits included let visitors test their knowledge about mechanics' tools, have their photo taken while sitting in the driver's seat of a miniature race car, and learn about the options for powering cars in the future.

Local history topics are tied into some of the exhibits. **Time:** Allow 1 hour, 30 minutes minimum. **Hours:** Tues.-Sat. 10-5, Sun. noon-5, Apr.-Dec. (10-3, Christmas Eve and Dec. 31); Wed.-Sun. 10-4, rest of year. Last ticket is sold 1 hour before closing. Closed Jan. 1 and Christmas. **Cost:** $8; $6 (ages 62+); $4 (ages 6-16); free (ages 0-12 on Sun.). **Phone:** (610) 432-4200. GT

🔺 **DA VINCI SCIENCE CENTER,** 3145 Hamilton Blvd. bypass, includes more than 100 interactive science exhibits designed to entertain and inspire. A 72-foot dark tunnel; an ocean touch tank; a fossil wall; bugs, butterflies and other critters; and Newton riding chairs are featured as well as GyroSphere, a gyroscope-style ride. The lobby memorializes Leonardo Da Vinci's design for a horse

(See map & index p. 49.)

sculpture, which was completed more than 500 years later with the help of Allentown native Charles C. Dent and others.

An area with activities designed for preschool children is available. Live and recorded programs also are offered throughout the year. **Time:** Allow 3 hours minimum. **Hours:** Mon.-Sat. 10-5, Sun. noon-5. **Cost:** $12.95; $11.95 (ages 62+ and military with ID); $9.95 (ages 4-12). GyroSphere tickets $4. **Phone:** (484) 664-1002.

DORNEY PARK AND WILDWATER KINGDOM is off I-78 exit 54, n.e. on Hamilton Blvd. (SR 222) and n. on Lincoln Ave. to jct. Dorney Park Rd. The site includes two parks spread across 200 acres and offers 100 attractions and thrill rides. With more than 125 years of experience, Dorney Park thrills guests with eight roller coasters, including Hydra: The Revenge, a floorless coaster; Talon: Grip of Fear, one of the Northeast's tallest inverted coasters; and Possessed, a U-shaped suspended impulse coaster. Planet Snoopy, inspired by the "Peanuts" comic strip, features 3.5 acres of rides and attractions that parents and children can enjoy together.

Wildwater Kingdom offers 28 waterslides, two tubing rivers, two giant wave pools, an aquatic fun house and three children's water-play areas. Kid-friendly afternoon and scarier evening Halloween programs are offered weekends in fall months.

Time: Allow a full day. **Hours:** Both parks open daily, Memorial Day-Labor Day. Dorney Park only, daily Sept. 18-Nov. 1 and Sat.-Sun. in May. Schedule may vary; phone to confirm. **Cost:** $54; $34.99 (under 48 inches tall and ages 62+); free (ages 0-2). Phone ahead to confirm all rates. **Parking:** $15. **Phone:** (610) 395-3724.

HISTORIC TROUT HALL, 414 W. Walnut St. at Fourth St., is a Georgian-style colonial stone mansion built as a summer retreat in 1770 for James Allen, son of community founder William Allen. The Allens, a Loyalist family, sought refuge here during

the Revolution. It was restored in 1918 by the Lehigh County Historical Society. The home is furnished in period. Entrance is by guided tour only. **Hours:** Sat.-Sun. 1-4, May-Sept. **Cost:** (includes Lehigh Valley Heritage Museum) $8; $3 (ages 5-12). **Phone:** (610) 435-1074.

LEHIGH VALLEY HERITAGE MUSEUM, 432 W. Walnut St., is the headquarters museum of the Lehigh County Historical Society. The museum collection includes thousands of artifacts and photographs, and the research library's collection contains nearly three million documents. The exhibit space comprises 13,000 square feet. Temporary exhibits also are given throughout the year.

Time: Allow 1 hour minimum. **Hours:** Museum Tues.-Sat. 10-4, Sun. noon-4. Library Tues.-Sat. 10-4. **Cost:** (includes admission to Historic Trout Hall, May-Sept.) $8; $3 (ages 5-12). **Phone:** (610) 435-1074. GT

LIBERTY BELL MUSEUM, in Zion's Reformed Church at 622 W. Hamilton St., is the site where the Liberty Bell was hidden during the American Revolution. Visitors can ring a replica of the bell. A mural, which features sound and light, describes the Liberty Bell's journey to Allentown in 1777.

A holiday puppet show is featured Thanksgiving through Jan. 3. **Hours:** Mon.-Sat. noon-4, Feb.-Dec. and second Sun. of each month. **Cost:** Free. $2; $1 (ages 5-17); free (ages 0-4). **Phone:** (610) 435-4232. GT

MUSEUM OF INDIAN CULTURE, 2825 Fish Hatchery Rd., is housed in an 18th-century stone farmhouse and features Native American artifacts and displays. The current exhibits spotlight Northeastern Woodland tribes, particularly the Lenape (Delaware) tribe and the Plains Indians. A nature trail is on the grounds.

Time: Allow 1 hour minimum. **Hours:** Thurs.-Sun. 10-4, June-Aug.; Fri.-Sun. 10-4, Sept.-Dec.; Sat.-Sun. 10-4, rest of year. Closed major holidays. **Cost:** $5; $4 (ages 63+ and 12-17); free (ages 0-11). Additional fees are charged for special events. **Phone:** (610) 797-2121. GT

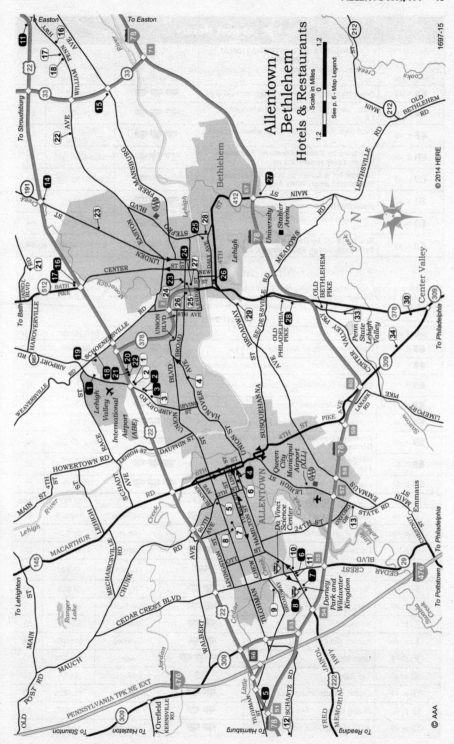

Allentown/
Bethlehem
Hotels & Restaurants

Scale in Miles

See p. 6 - Map Legend

© 2014 HERE

1697-15

✈ Airport Hotels

Map Page	LEHIGH VALLEY INTERNATIONAL AIRPORT (Maximum driving distance from airport: 2.0 mi)	Diamond Rated	Rate Range	Page
1 p. 49	Days Hotel Allentown Airport/Lehigh Valley, 1.0 mi	▽▽▽	$80-$159	52
2 p. 49	Hilton Garden Inn Allentown Bethlehem Airport, 1.8 mi	▽▽▽	$109-$219	52
3 p. 49	Staybridge Suites Allentown Bethlehem Airport, 1.8 mi	▽▽▽	Rates not provided	52
21 p. 49	**Courtyard by Marriott Allentown Bethlehem/ Lehigh Valley Airport, 2.0 mi**	▽▽▽	$125-$206 SAVE	63
22 p. 49	**Fairfield Inn & Suites by Marriott Allentown Bethlehem/Lehigh Valley Airport, 2.0 mi**	▽▽▽	$97-$160 SAVE	64
18 p. 49	Holiday Inn Express Hotel & Suites-Allentown area/Bethlehem Airport, 1.5 mi	▽▽▽	$89-$199	64
19 p. 49	Homewood Suites - Allentown/Bethlehem Airport, 1.3 mi	▽▽▽	$129-$199	64
20 p. 49	**Residence Inn by Marriott Allentown Bethlehem/Lehigh Valley Airport, 2.0 mi**	▽▽▽	$118-$194 SAVE	64

Allentown/Bethlehem

This index helps you "spot" where approved hotels and restaurants are located on the corresponding detailed maps. Hotel daily rate range is for comparison only. Restaurant price range is a combination of lunch and/or dinner. Turn to the listing page for more detailed rate and price information and consult display ads for special promotions.

ALLENTOWN

Map Page	Hotels	Diamond Rated	Rate Range	Page
1 p. 49	Days Hotel Allentown Airport/Lehigh Valley	▽▽▽	$80-$159	52
2 p. 49	Hilton Garden Inn Allentown Bethlehem Airport	▽▽▽	$109-$219	52
3 p. 49	Staybridge Suites Allentown Bethlehem Airport	▽▽▽	Rates not provided	52
4 p. 49	Holiday Inn-Allentown Center City	▽▽▽	$89-$149	52
5 p. 49	Holiday Inn Express & Suites Allentown West	▽▽▽	$75-$200	52
6 p. 49	**Allentown Howard Johnson Inn & Suites Dorney Park**	▽▽	$49-$159 SAVE	52
7 p. 49	Holiday Inn Express Hotel & Suites Allentown-Dorney	▽▽▽	Rates not provided	52
8 p. 49	Allentown Comfort Suites	▽▽▽	$99-$189	52

Map Page	Restaurants	Diamond Rated	Cuisine	Price Range	Page
① p. 49	Ichiban Japanese Steak House	▽▽	Japanese	$10-$28	53
② p. 49	Taste of Italy Ristorante	▽▽	Italian	$6-$27	53
③ p. 49	Copperhead Grille	▽▽	American	$9-$30	53
④ p. 49	Stahley's Family Restaurant & Sports Bar	▽	American	$5-$20	53
⑤ p. 49	Bellissimo Ristorante	▽▽	Italian	$8-$26	52
⑥ p. 49	Bay Leaf Restaurant	▽▽	Asian Fusion	$8-$31	52
⑦ p. 49	Wert's Cafe	▽▽	American	$7-$25	53
⑧ p. 49	Henry's Salt Of The Sea	▽▽	Seafood	$15-$40	53
⑨ p. 49	Grille 3501	▽▽▽	Asian	$10-$34	53
⑩ p. 49	Cali Burrito	▽	California	$4-$8	52
⑪ p. 49	Teppan Hibachi Steakhouse	▽▽	Japanese	$10-$25	53
⑫ p. 49	Sunset Grille	▽▽	Tex-Mex	$7-$17	53
⑬ p. 49	A1 Japanese Steak House	▽▽	Japanese	$8-$28	52

EASTON

Map Page	Hotel	Diamond Rated	Rate Range	Page
11 p. 49	Holiday Inn Express Hotel & Suites	◆◆◆	Rates not provided	100

Map Page	Restaurants	Diamond Rated	Cuisine	Price Range	Page
16 p. 49	Williams Family Restaurant	◆◆	American	$3-$16	101
17 p. 49	Nonna Lia Pizza Chef	◆◆	Italian	$6-$19	101
18 p. 49	Marblehead Grille and Chowder House	◆◆	Seafood	$13-$37	101

BETHLEHEM

Map Page	Hotels	Diamond Rated	Rate Range	Page
14 p. 49	The View Inn & Suites	◆◆	$69-$109	65
15 p. 49	**Courtyard by Marriott Bethlehem Lehigh Valley/I-78**	◆◆◆	$174-$286 SAVE	64
16 p. 49	**BEST WESTERN Lehigh Valley Hotel & Conference Center**	◆◆	$79-$119 SAVE	63
17 p. 49	Hampton Inn & Suites Bethlehem	◆◆	$119-$189	64
18 p. 49	Holiday Inn Express Hotel & Suites-Allentown area/Bethlehem Airport	◆◆◆	$89-$199	64
19 p. 49	Homewood Suites - Allentown/Bethlehem Airport	◆◆◆	$129-$199	64
20 p. 49	**Residence Inn by Marriott Allentown Bethlehem/Lehigh Valley Airport**	◆◆◆	$118-$194 SAVE	64
21 p. 49	**Courtyard by Marriott Allentown Bethlehem/Lehigh Valley Airport**	◆◆◆	$125-$206 SAVE	63
22 p. 49	**Fairfield Inn & Suites by Marriott Allentown Bethlehem/Lehigh Valley Airport**	◆◆◆	$97-$160 SAVE	64
23 p. 49	**Hyatt Place Bethlehem**	◆◆◆	$139-$249 SAVE	64
24 p. 49	Historic Hotel Bethlehem	◆◆◆	$165-$235	64
25 p. 49	**Sands Bethlehem** *(See ad p. 65.)*	◆◆◆◆	Rates not provided SAVE	65
26 p. 49	Comfort Suites University	◆◆	$95-$240	63
27 p. 49	Holiday Inn Express Hotel & Suites Bethlehem	◆◆◆	Rates not provided	64
28 p. 49	Wydnor Hall Inn	◆◆◆	Rates not provided	65

Map Page	Restaurants	Diamond Rated	Cuisine	Price Range	Page
21 p. 49	Hanoverville Roadhouse	◆◆	American	$7-$29	66
22 p. 49	Blue Grillhouse/Winebar	◆◆◆	Steak	$7-$47	66
23 p. 49	Stefano's Cafe	◆◆	Italian	$7-$26	66
24 p. 49	Edge Restaurant, Bar & Lounge	◆◆◆	French	$18-$38	66
25 p. 49	Bethlehem Brew Works Brewery & Restaurant	◆◆	American	$8-$22	66
26 p. 49	The Cafe	◆◆◆	Fusion	$5-$25	66
27 p. 49	**1741 on the Terrace**	◆◆◆	American	$24-$39	66
28 p. 49	Burgers and More by Emeril	◆◆	Burgers	$5-$14	66
29 p. 49	Benner Street Restaurant & Bar	◆◆	American	$5-$28	66
30 p. 49	Copperhead Grille	◆◆	American	$9-$23	66

CENTER VALLEY

Map Page	Restaurants	Diamond Rated	Cuisine	Price Range	Page
33 p. 49	Manor House Inn	◆◆◆	French	$9-$38	80
34 p. 49	Diana's Cafe & Catering	◆◆	American	$4-$11	80

(See map & index p. 49.)

ALLENTOWN COMFORT SUITES (610)437-9100 **8**

▼▼▼▼ Hotel $99-$189 Address: 3712 Hamilton Blvd 18103 Location: I-78 exit 54 (Hamilton Blvd), just n. Opposite Dorney Park and Wildwater Kingdom. Facility: 121 units. 4 stories, interior corridors. Amenities: safes. Activities: exercise room. Guest Services: valet laundry, area transportation.

⊞ ⑪ ⍥ BIZ 🤝 ✕ 🗄 🖥 🖳
/ SOME UNITS 🐾

ALLENTOWN HOWARD JOHNSON INN & SUITES DORNEY PARK (610)439-4000 **6**

▼▼ Hotel $49-$159

Address: 3220 Hamilton Rd 18103 Location: I-78 exit 54 (Hamilton Blvd), 0.8 mi n. Facility: 58 units. 2 stories. interior corridors. Amenities: safes. Pool(s): heated indoor. Activities: hot tub. Guest Services: coin laundry. Featured Amenity: continental breakfast.

SAVE ⑪ CALL ⓂM 🤝 🛜 🗄
🖥 🖳 / SOME UNITS 🐾

COMFORT INN LEHIGH VALLEY-WEST 610/391-0344

▼▼▼ Hotel. Rates not provided. Address: 7625 Imperial Way 18106 Location: I-78 exit 49B (SR 100), just n. Located in a business park. Facility: 123 units. 5 stories, interior corridors. Activities: exercise room. Guest Services: valet and coin laundry.

⍥ BIZ 🛜 🗄 🖳 / SOME UNITS 🐾 🖥

DAYS HOTEL ALLENTOWN AIRPORT/LEHIGH VALLEY (610)266-1000 **1**

▼▼▼ Hotel $80-$159 Address: 3400 Airport Rd 18109 Location: On SR 987 N (Airport Rd), 0.5 mi n of jct US 22. Located in a commercial area. Facility: 144 units. 2-3 stories (no elevator), interior corridors. Terms: cancellation fee imposed. Amenities: Some: safes. Dining: nightclub, entertainment. Pool(s): heated indoor. Activities: exercise room.

⊞ ⑪ ⍥ CALL ⓂM 🤝 BIZ 🛜 ✕ 🖳
/ SOME UNITS HS 🗄 🖥

HILTON GARDEN INN ALLENTOWN BETHLEHEM AIRPORT (610)443-1400 **2**

▼▼▼ Hotel $109-$219 Address: 1787-B Airport Rd 18109 Location: US 22 exit Airport Rd S, just s. Located in a commercial area. Facility: 106 units. 4 stories, interior corridors. Terms: 1-7 night minimum stay, cancellation fee imposed. Amenities: video games. Pool(s): heated indoor. Activities: hot tub, exercise room. Guest Services: valet and coin laundry, area transportation.

AAA Benefit: Members save 5% or more!

⊞ ⑪ ⍥ 🤝 BIZ HS 🛜 🎞 🗄 🖥 🖳

HOLIDAY INN-ALLENTOWN CENTER CITY (610)433-2221 **4**

▼▼▼▼ Hotel $89-$149 Address: 904 W Hamilton St 18101 Location: At 9th and Hamilton sts; downtown. Facility: 224 units. 9 stories, interior corridors. Parking: on-site (fee). Pool(s): heated indoor. Activities: game room, exercise room. Guest Services: valet and coin laundry.

⑪ ⍥ CALL ⓂM 🤝 BIZ 🛜 ✕ 🖳
/ SOME UNITS 🗄 🖥

Enjoy peace of mind with
AAA/CAA Insurance products

HOLIDAY INN EXPRESS & SUITES ALLENTOWN WEST (610)530-5545 **5**

▼▼▼▼ Hotel $75-$200 Address: 5630 Tilghman St 18104 Location: US 22 exit Kuhnsville westbound; I-78 exit 49 (SR 100 N), just n, then 2 mi e. Facility: 77 units, some two bedrooms and kitchens. 3 stories, interior corridors. Amenities: safes. Pool(s): heated indoor. Activities: exercise room. Guest Services: valet laundry.

⑪⊹ CALL ⓂM 🤝 BIZ HS 🛜 ✕ 🎞 🗄 🖥
🖳

HOLIDAY INN EXPRESS HOTEL & SUITES ALLENTOWN-DORNEY 610/437-9255 **7**

▼▼▼▼ Hotel. Rates not provided. Address: 3620 Hamilton Blvd 18103 Location: I-78 exit 54 (Hamilton Blvd), 0.5 mi n. Opposite Dorney Park and Wildwater Kingdom. Facility: 71 units. 3 stories, interior corridors. Activities: exercise room. Guest Services: valet laundry.

⑪⊹ CALL ⓂM BIZ 🛜 ✕ 🗄 🖥 🖳

STAYBRIDGE SUITES ALLENTOWN BETHLEHEM AIRPORT 610/443-5000 **3**

▼▼▼ Extended Stay Hotel. Rates not provided. Address: 1787-A Airport Rd 18109 Location: US 22 exit Airport Rd S, 0.3 mi s. Located in a commercial area. Facility: 108 efficiencies, some two bedrooms. 4 stories, interior corridors. Amenities: video games. Pool(s): heated outdoor. Activities: hot tub, exercise room. Guest Services: valet and coin laundry, area transportation.

⊞ ⑪⊹ CALL ⓂM 🤝 BIZ HS 🛜 ✕ 🎞 🗄
🖥 🖳 / SOME UNITS 🐾

WHERE TO EAT

A1 JAPANESE STEAK HOUSE 610/709-0998 **13**

▼▼▼ Japanese. Casual Dining. $8-$28 AAA Inspector Notes: Located within a small shopping mall storefront, this restaurant displays casual but attractive Japanese décor. There are four hibachi grill rooms, totaling 16 tables, for that popular method of preparation. In the 100-seat main dining room, guests may choose from the sushi bar or opt for sashimi, tempura or teriyaki dishes. Complementing the offerings is a full bar serving hot and cold sake and Japanese, American and international beers. Features: full bar. Reservations: suggested. Address: 3300 Lehigh St, Suite 320 18103 Location: I-78 exit 57 (Lehigh St), 0.6 mi s; in South Mall.

Ⓛ Ⓓ CALL ⓂM

BAY LEAF RESTAURANT 610/433-4211 **6**

▼▼▼ Asian Fusion. Casual Dining. $8-$31 AAA Inspector Notes: New American and Asian influences blend in delectable dishes along the lines of herb-crusted grouper fillet with sherry-vinegar reduction or fillet of sole with bananas, walnuts, crabmeat and maple-brandy sauce. Relax in the casually elegant dining room which displays Asian paintings and ceramics. Features: full bar. Reservations: suggested. Address: 935 Hamilton St 18101 Location: Jct 9th St, just s; downtown. Parking: on-site and street. Ⓛ Ⓓ

BELLISSIMO RISTORANTE 610/770-7717 **5**

▼▼ Italian. Casual Dining. $8-$26 AAA Inspector Notes: Featuring classic Sicilian cuisine, the dining room has a warm feel, with an attractive mosaic-inlaid tile floor, cultured marble-topped tables with fresh flowers and Italian background music. Imported marble statues of Roman gods and a fountain decorate the seasonal patio. On the menu are filet mignon, as well as preparations of veal, lobster, shrimp, crab and fresh ocean fish. Features: full bar, patio dining. Reservations: suggested, dinner. Address: 1243 Tilghman St 18102 Location: Jct Tilghman and 13th sts. Ⓛ Ⓓ

CALI BURRITO 610/351-1791 **10**

▼ California. Quick Serve. $4-$8 AAA Inspector Notes: A salsa bar features several varieties, all made in house at surfer-themed Cali Burrito. Large portions of fresh, Northern California-style tacos, quesadillas and burritos are offered. Smoked tofu is available in any of the dishes as a tasty filling alternative to meat. While service is curt, it is efficient. Address: 3104 Hamilton Blvd 18103 Location: I-78 exit 54 (Hamilton Blvd), 1.2 mi n. Ⓛ Ⓓ

(See map & index p. 49.)

COPPERHEAD GRILLE   610/403-4600   3
♥♥ ♥♥ American. Casual Dining. $9-$30 **AAA Inspector Notes:**
You can catch your favorite team playing on one of 11 flat screens or
three 130-inch high-definition projection screens. A bustling sports
lounge atmosphere prevails with a menu boasting nearly two dozen
appetizers along with sandwiches, steak, ribs, fajitas, pizza and pasta
dishes. Try the Copperhead's land and sea, a combination plate with
steak and a crab cake. If you're looking for a late-night snack, you
can order from the lounge menu until midnight. **Features:** full bar,
happy hour. **Reservations:** suggested, weekends. **Address:** 1731
Airport Rd 18109 **Location:** US 22 exit Airport Rd S, 0.5 mi s.
L D CALL ⼤M

GRILLE 3501   610/706-0100   9
♥♥ ♥♥ ♥♥ Asian. Fine Dining. $10-$34 **AAA Inspector Notes:** Fusion is the order of the day at this restaurant, which features an
eclectic martini bar, New-York-style Art Deco décor and early French
advertising posters. Artistically presented menu items, which merge
French and Asian cuisines, center on steak, seafood and homemade
pasta. Representative of the fare are wasabi-crusted tuna and veal
tenderloin wrapped in apple-wood-smoked bacon. **Features:** full bar,
happy hour. **Reservations:** suggested. **Address:** 3501 Broadway
18104 **Location:** I-78 exit 55 (Cedar Crest Blvd), 1.5 mi nw, then 0.3
mi w. L D

HENRY'S SALT OF THE SEA   610/434-2628   8
♥♥ ♥♥ Seafood. Casual Dining. $15-$40 **AAA Inspector Notes:**
A local favorite, this small seafood restaurant has a cozy atmosphere.
The menu offers a variety of fresh seafood and crab-stuffed entrées.
A full bar and salad bar also are offered. Be sure to make reserva-
tions, as this place fills up from the start with the early bird dinner
menu. **Features:** full bar. **Reservations:** suggested. **Address:** 1926
W Allen St 18104 **Location:** Just off 19th St; at Allen and Lafayette
sts. **Parking:** street only. D

ICHIBAN JAPANESE STEAK HOUSE   610/266-7781   1
♥♥ ♥♥ Japanese. Casual Dining. $10-$28 **AAA Inspector
Notes:** Ichiban lets you sample hibachi cooking, as well as sushi
and traditional Japanese favorites, with selections from its full-
service bar, which include fruity cocktails, wine and beer. **Fea-
tures:** full bar. **Address:** 1914 Catasauqua Rd 18109 **Location:**
US 22 exit Airport Rd S, just e; in Valley Plaza Shopping Center.
L D CALL ⼤M

STAHLEY'S FAMILY RESTAURANT & SPORTS BAR
                                     610/433-2468   4
♥♥ American. Casual Dining. $5-$20 **AAA Inspector Notes:**
Every neighborhood should have a pub like this one, where the TVs
are plentiful, the beer is cheap and the food is hearty. Sandwiches
and bar snacks, such as pierogies or corn nuggets, make up the majority of the menu, but old-school steak and pasta offerings also are
available. **Features:** full bar. **Address:** 1826 Hanover Ave 18109 **Location:** SR 378 exit 1, 2.2 mi e. L D LATE

SUNSET GRILLE   610/395-9622   12
♥♥ Tex-Mex. Casual Dining. $7-$17 **AAA Inspector Notes:**
This popular local spot offers a variety of Southwestern bar fare and
daily drink specials. Although the menu provides some south-of-the-
border options, we recommend trying one of their mouthwatering
burgers. **Features:** full bar, happy hour. **Reservations:** suggested,
weekends. **Address:** 6751 Ruppsville Rd 18106 **Location:** I-78 exit
49A, 0.9 mi e on Schantz Rd, then 0.5 mi ne on Industrial Blvd.
L D LATE

TASTE OF ITALY RISTORANTE   610/266-8011   2
♥♥ ♥♥ Italian. Casual Dining. $6-$27 **AAA Inspector Notes:** Dig
in to a hearty portion of pasta or maybe one of the fish or meat entrées at always-busy Taste of Italy. If you're in the mood for pizza,
you're still in luck. Although the wine list is limited, the choices are well
suited to the food. Pleasant service rounds out your experience. **Features:** full bar. **Address:** 1860 Catasauqua Rd 18109 **Location:** US
22 exit Airport Rd S, just s; in Valley Plaza Shopping Center.
L D CALL ⼤M

TEPPAN HIBACHI STEAKHOUSE   610/841-4799   11
♥♥ ♥♥ Japanese. Casual Dining. $10-$25 **AAA Inspector Notes:**
Dine among families, locals and business travelers, all of whom appreciate the bright and lively restaurant and its wide variety of Japanese dishes. Your kids will delight in the hibachi tables as the chefs
put on an entertaining show as they cook. Fresh and delicious sushi,
sashimi and maki are other options if you're feeling more adventurous. **Features:** full bar. **Address:** 3227 Hamilton Blvd 18103 **Location:** I-78 exit 54 (Hamilton Blvd), 1.1 mi n. L D

WERT'S CAFE   610/439-0951   7
♥♥ ♥♥ American. Casual Dining. $7-$25 **AAA Inspector Notes:**
This family owned- and operated-restaurant offers a cozy residential
feel inside along with friendly service. The menu consists of a variety
of homemade American cuisine at affordable prices. Be sure to try
the onion rings. **Features:** beer & wine. **Address:** 515 N 18th St
18104 **Location:** Between Allen and Liberty sts. L D

YOCCO'S-HOT DOG KING   610/264-1884
fyi Not evaluated. Stop by this well-known local favorite for a crisp,
juicy hot dog or plump pierogi. **Address:** 1930 Catasauqua Rd 18109
Location: US 22 exit Airport Rd S, just s; in Valley Plaza Shopping
Center.

ALLENWOOD (F-8) pop. 321, elev. 481'

CLYDE PEELING'S REPTILAND, 6 mi. n. of I-80
exit 210B on US 15, provides close-up views of
more than 40 species of alligators, tortoises, lizards
and frogs. Some of the snake species included are
cobras, mambas, pythons and vipers. Komodo
dragons and Aldabra tortoises are on display in a
naturalistic habitat. Visitors can watch a multimedia
presentation about reptiles as well as lectures and
feedings. Behind-the-Scenes tours provide a look at
the care facility, handling procedures and animal
husbandry. Seasonal butterfly and dinosaur exhibits
also are offered.

Time: Allow 1 hour, 30 minutes minimum. **Hours:**
Daily 9-6, Memorial Day-Labor Day; daily 10-5 (also
Sat.-Sun. 5-6), Apr. 1 the Friday before Memorial
Day and day after Labor Day-Oct. 31; daily 10-5,
rest of year. Multimedia presentations are shown at
10:30, noon, 1:30, 3 and 4:30. Phone for lecture,
tour and feeding schedules. Closed Jan. 1, Thanksgiving and Christmas. **Cost:** $16; $14 (ages 3-11),
Memorial Day-Labor Day. $14; $12 (ages 3-11), rest
of year. Behind-the-scenes tour $30; must be 12
and over for tour. **Phone:** (570) 538-1869 or (800)
737-8452. 🍴 🐾

ALLISON PARK pop. 21,552

• **Hotels & Restaurants map & index p. 348**
• **Part of Pittsburgh area — see map p. 326**

THE TUSCAN INN   412/486-7696   39
♥♥ ♥♥ Northern Italian. Casual Dining. $14-$29 **AAA Inspector
Notes:** An European feel prevails in the unpretentious dining room.
Aromatic Tuscan bread bakes in the wood-fired brick oven in one
section of the dining room. In addition to unusual pasta preparations,
the menu lists veal, chicken and seafood. The chef's great carrot
cake is worth a splurge. **Features:** full bar. **Address:** 2684 Wildwood
Rd 15101 **Location:** I-76 (Pennsylvania Tpke) exit 39, 2 mi s on SR
8, then 0.3 mi w. D

Get AAA/CAA travel information in the
digital and printed formats you prefer

ALTOONA (G-5) pop. 46,320, elev. 1,171'

Altoona was first settled in the mid-1700s. A series of stockades, including Fort Roberdeau, was built to protect the region against Native American raids. The region gained settlers and businesses with the completion of the Pennsylvania Canal in 1834, and within several years, the demand for lumber and coal gave rise to the railroad industry. The Allegheny Portage Railroad was founded in Altoona in 1849 during construction of the first railroad over the Alleghenies. For years the town's economy depended on railroad building and repair shops, but the area's economy has diversified and now includes manufacturing jobs.

Blair County Ballpark near Lakemont Park is home to Altoona's Class AA minor league baseball team, The Curve, which is affiliated with the Pittsburgh Pirates; phone (814) 943-5400 or (877) 992-8783 for ticket information.

The 958-acre Canoe Creek State Park, 12 miles east of Altoona, offers a wide assortment of summer and winter activities: fishing, swimming, horseback riding, boating, hiking, hunting, biking, cross-country skiing, iceboating, ice fishing, ice-skating and tobogganing. Environmental education and interpretive programs for families also are offered; phone (814) 695-6807. *See Recreation Areas Chart.*

Explore Altoona: 1216 11th Ave., Suite 216, Altoona, PA 16601. **Phone:** (814) 943-4183 or (800) 842-5866.

Shopping areas: The major shopping center is Logan Valley Mall, US 220 and Goods Lane. It features JCPenney, Macy's and Sears along with some 90 shops.

BAKER MANSION, 1 mi. w. of US 220 via Logan Blvd., was the home of ironmaster Elias Baker. The Greek Revival mansion, completed in 1849, is the headquarters of the Blair County Historical Society and the Blair County History Center. Items on display include carved oak furniture that Mr. Baker imported from Belgium and material about the Loyal War Governors Conference, a group that met in September 1862 in support of President Lincoln and the preservation of the Union. Railroad artifacts, memorabilia from the Civil War and World Wars I and II, and documents and other historical objects relating to the history and heritage of Blair County also are included.

A research library is available. Special events are held throughout the year. **Time:** Allow 1 hour minimum. **Hours:** Fri.-Sun. 1-4, Memorial Day-Labor Day. Last tour begins 1 hour before closing. Christmas tours are given the first 3 weekends in Dec.; phone for schedule. Library open Tues. and Fri. 9-noon. **Cost:** $7; $5 (ages 13-17 and 65+); $4 (ages 5-12). Library $3 (per day). **Phone:** (814) 942-3916. [GT]

FORT ROBERDEAU, in Sinking Valley, 9 mi. n.e. via I-99 Bellwood exit 41 to jct. Kettle and Fort Roberdeau rds., includes a reconstruction of a Revolutionary War fort with barracks, officers' quarters, a powder magazine, a miner's cabin, a storehouse and lead smelter. Gen. Daniel Roberdeau built the original fort to supply ammunition for American forces 1778-80 and to protect local settlers during British and Native American raids. The 230-acre county park also features exhibits, an education center and four nature trails.

Time: Allow 1 hour minimum. **Hours:** Grounds daily 8 a.m.-dusk. Guided tours of the historic area Tues.-Sat. 11-5, Sun.-Mon. 1-5, May-Oct. Phone ahead to confirm special event schedule. **Cost:** $4; $3 (ages 62+); $2 (ages 4-11). **Phone:** (814) 946-0048. [符]

HORSESHOE CURVE NATIONAL HISTORIC LANDMARK is at jct. 40th St. and Kittanning Point Rd. The site features the Horseshoe Curve, an 1854 engineering marvel that served as a vital link in early westward train travel. In allowing a more gradual ascent to the summit, locomotives were able to scale the Allegheny Mountains for the first time. It is still in use today as the Norfolk Southern main line. An incline plane ride takes visitors to an observation area where they can view the Curve and the Allegheny Mountains.

Hours: Mon.-Sat. 9-5, Sun. 11-5, Apr. 3-Nov. 1; Fri.-Sat. 9-5, Sun. noon-5, Nov. 6-Nov. 22 (weather permitting). Last admission 1 hour before closing. **Cost:** (includes Railroaders Memorial Museum) $10; $9 (ages 62+); $8 (ages 2-11). Horseshoe Curve only $7; free (ages 0-2). **Phone:** (814) 941-7743.

LAKEMONT PARK, 700 Park Ave., dates to 1894 when it opened as a trolley park. Today the amusement park offers more than 30 rides and attractions, including the Island Waterpark; go-carts; miniature golf; and two roller coasters, one of which was built in 1902. A Christmas themed holiday program is featured in winter.

Hours: Sat.-Sun. noon-8, Memorial Day weekend to early June and mid-Aug. to Labor Day weekend (also Memorial Day and Labor Day); Wed.-Sat. 11-9, Sun. 11-8, early June to mid-Aug. Holiday Lights on the Lake program daily 6-10 p.m., Fri. before Thanksgiving to Sun. after New Year's Day. Phone ahead to confirm schedule. **Cost:** Park free. Amusement park ride pass $5, Wed.-Fri.; $9.95, Sat.-Sun. before 5; $7.95, Sat.-Sun. after 5; free (ages 0-1). Holiday lights $12 per vehicle Fri.-Sun.; $10 per vehicle Mon.-Thurs. **Phone:** (814) 949-7275 or (800) 434-8006. [Ⅱ]

RAILROADERS MEMORIAL MUSEUM, 1300 9th Ave., traces the development of Pennsylvania Railroad (PRR) workers and the industry's effect on history. Interpretive exhibits and a historic film in the Norfolk Southern Theatre recall life in the small town where almost everyone was a PRR employee.

Time: Allow 2 hours minimum. **Hours:** Mon.-Sat. 9-5, Sun. noon-5, May-Oct.; Fri.-Sat. 9-5, Sun. noon-5, early Nov.-late Dec. and Apr. 3 to Apr. 26. **Cost:** (includes Horseshoe Curve National Historic Landmark) $10; $9 (ages 62+); $8 (ages 2-11); free (ages 0-2). **Phone:** (814) 946-0834 or (888) 425-8666.

WOPSONONOCK TABLELAND is on Juniata Gap Rd.; follow the sign at the top of the mountain. The site rises to an elevation of 2,580 feet and affords a panoramic view of the city and surrounding area. At the lookout, visitors can hike down into the valley. **Note:** Nighttime driving is not recommended. **Phone:** (814) 943-4183 (Explore Altoona).

COMFORT SUITES ALTOONA   (814)942-2600

Hotel
$109-$189

Address: 140 Stroehman Dr 16601 **Location:** I-99/US 220 exit 39, just n. **Facility:** 65 units. 3 stories, interior corridors. **Pool(s):** heated indoor. **Activities:** exercise room. **Guest Services:** valet and coin laundry. **Featured Amenity: full hot breakfast.**

COURTYARD BY MARRIOTT ALTOONA   (814)312-1800

Hotel $125-$206 **Address:** 2 Convention Center Dr 16602 **Location:** I-99/US 220 exit 31 (Plank Rd), just w, follow signs. Next to a convention center. **Facility:** 105 units. 4 stories, interior corridors. **Pool(s):** heated indoor. **Activities:** hot tub, exercise room. **Guest Services:** valet and coin laundry.

AAA Benefit: Members save 5% or more!

HAMPTON INN-ALTOONA   (814)941-3500

Hotel $109-$299 **Address:** 180 Charlotte Dr 16601 **Location:** I-99/US 220 exit 31 (Plank Rd), just w. Next to a shopping mall. **Facility:** 111 units. 5 stories, interior corridors. **Terms:** 1-7 night minimum stay, cancellation fee imposed. **Amenities:** video games. **Pool(s):** heated indoor. **Activities:** hot tub, exercise room. **Guest Services:** valet laundry.

AAA Benefit: Members save 5% or more!

HOLIDAY INN EXPRESS ALTOONA   (814)944-9661

Hotel $139-$299 **Address:** 3306 Pleasant Valley Blvd 16602 **Location:** I-99/US 220 exit 32, 0.5 mi w, then just n. **Facility:** 108 units. 2 stories, interior corridors. **Terms:** check-in 4 pm, 3 day cancellation notice-fee imposed. **Activities:** exercise room. **Guest Services:** valet and coin laundry.

MOTEL 6 #1415   814/946-7601

Motel. Rates not provided. **Address:** 1500 Sterling St 16602 **Location:** I-99/US 220 exit 31 (Plank Rd). **Facility:** 113 units. 1 story, exterior corridors. **Pool(s):** outdoor. **Guest Services:** coin laundry.

SUPER 8 ALTOONA   (814)942-5350

Motel $68-$91 **Address:** 3535 Fairway Dr 16602 **Location:** I-99/US 220 exit 32, just w. **Facility:** 62 units. 3 stories (no elevator), interior corridors. **Amenities:** Some: safes. **Activities:** limited exercise equipment. **Guest Services:** coin laundry.

ALLEGRO   814/946-5216

Italian
Casual Dining
$7-$31

AAA Inspector Notes: Veal, in such forms as osso buco, veal scaloppine, veal piccata and veal saltimbocca, is the specialty at this quiet restaurant. You'll also find seafood, Italian dishes and succulent filet mignon on the varied menu. Tiramisu and crème brûlée are the best bets among the homemade desserts. If your party includes four or more, you might consider ordering the traditional, family-style dinner. **Features:** full bar. **Reservations:** suggested, weekends. **Address:** 3926 Broad Ave 16601 **Location:** Jct Broad Ave and 40th St. _Menu on AAA.com_ D

FINELLI'S ITALIAN VILLA   814/943-8510

Northern Italian. Casual Dining. $10-$33 **AAA Inspector Notes:** Thoughtfully prepared traditional pasta dishes and tableside flambe are popular offerings at the relaxed neighborhood restaurant. An Old World atmosphere punctuates the dining room. Complimentary limousine service is offered to and from local lodgings. **Features:** full bar. **Reservations:** suggested. **Address:** 1808 4th Ave 16602 **Location:** I-99/US 220 exit 17th St, 0.9 mi w, then just w. D

KING'S FAMILY RESTAURANT   814/946-1136

American. Family Dining. $6-$17 **AAA Inspector Notes:** Fast and friendly service is offered here. The menu is large in size with descriptive menu items and pictures. The restaurant is also known for its ice cream and dessert menu. **Address:** 3001 6th Ave 16601 **Location:** I-99/US 220 exit 31 (Plank Rd).

AMBLER (A-10) pop. 6,417, elev. 217'
- Restaurants p. 56
- Hotels & Restaurants map & index p. 274
- Part of Philadelphia area — see map p. 230

THE AMBLER ARBORETUM OF TEMPLE UNIVERSITY, 580 Meetinghouse Rd., features about a dozen garden areas and a greenhouse. The site was once part of the Pennsylvania School of Horticulture for Women, which was founded in 1910. It merged with Temple University in 1958. Among the gardens are several buildings from the former school; most are from the early 1900s, but the first dormitory/classroom building dates to the 1700s. Gravel walkways meander through the gardens. Highlights include the formal perennial garden and the woodland gardens. The latter was planted in the 1920s by the school's students and staff; its focus is trees—beech, dogwood, sycamore and tulip—many of which are tall enough to provide shade, but there are flowers and shrubs as well.

Maps for self-guided tours are available in garden kiosks and in the welcome center. **Time:** Allow 1 hour, 30 minutes minimum. **Hours:** Gardens open daily dawn-dusk. Administration building open Mon.-Fri. 8:30-5. **Cost:** Donations. Guided tours $5. **Phone:** (267) 468-8000. GT

(See map & index p. 274.)

BRIDGET'S STEAKHOUSE   267/465-2000 (65)
ᵂᵂᵂᵂ Steak. Fine Dining. $11-$39 **AAA Inspector Notes:** This beautiful stone restaurant situated in downtown gives a warm and inviting atmosphere. Feel free to dine in the sunroom with its expansive windows and natural light or in the more formal dining room in the back. The menu provides a variety of mouthwatering steaks and fresh seafood options. **Features:** full bar, happy hour. **Reservations:** suggested. **Address:** 8 W Butler Ave 19002 **Location:** 0.6 mi w of jct Bethlehem Pike. ⓐ Ambler, 302. **Parking:** valet only.

ⓛ ⓓ 🅿

TRAX RESTAURANT AND CAFE   215/591-9777 (66)
ᵂᵂᵂᵂ American. Fine Dining. $24-$29 **AAA Inspector Notes:** Restored from the Old Ambler Train Station, this restaurant provides outstanding American dishes such as center-cut, bone-in pork chop over cranberry compote and oven-roasted Faroe Island salmon with cucumber dill sauce. Feel free to bring your favorite wine from home to pair with each course at this BYOB establishment. For the best value, look to dine between 4:30-6 pm Tuesday through Friday for the $30 prix fixe dinner. **Features:** patio dining. **Reservations:** suggested. **Address:** 27 W Butler Pike 19002 **Location:** 0.6 mi w of jct Bethlehem Pike. ⓐ Ambler, 302. ⓓ 🅿

AMBRIDGE (G-1) pop. 7,050, elev. 700'
• Part of Pittsburgh area — see map p. 326

🔻 **OLD ECONOMY VILLAGE,** at 270 16th St. at jct. Church St., derives its title from the town of Oekonomie, built 1824-30 by the Harmony Society *(see Harmony p. 134),* a German communal group. Comprising 6.5 acres, the village contains 17 historic structures available for touring; the restored buildings showcase collections from the society. Historic formal gardens also are featured. A visitor center offers an orientation film, permanent and changing exhibits and a Works Progress Administration (WPA) mural depicting the Harmony Society.

Time: Allow 2 hours minimum. **Hours:** Visitor center Tues.-Sat. 9-5, Sun. noon-5. Guided tours depart on the hour Tues.-Sat. 10-3, Sun. noon-3. Tour times vary; phone ahead to confirm. Closed major holidays except Memorial Day, July 4 and Labor Day. **Cost:** $10; $9 (ages 65+); $6 (ages 3-11); free (ages 0-3 and active military with ID). **Phone:** (724) 266-4500. (GT)

ARDMORE pop. 12,455
• Hotels & Restaurants map & index p. 274
• Part of Philadelphia area — see map p. 230

MIKADO THAI PEPPER   610/642-5951 (108)
ᵂᵂ Asian. Casual Dining. $8-$20 **AAA Inspector Notes:** Split into two distinct sections, the dining room at this spot reflects the atmosphere of a Thai steakhouse on one side while the other features tatami rooms and a full sushi bar. The design is a reflection of the menu, which hops back and forth between both types of cuisine. Duck kow chee is a tasty choice for those who prefer mildly spiced food. Tofu and curry dishes are established favorites. Maki options include such typical favorites as the California roll. **Features:** beer & wine. **Reservations:** suggested, weekends. **Address:** 64 E Lancaster Ave 19003 **Location:** On US 30; center. ⓐ Ardmore, 212. **Parking:** street only. ⓛ ⓓ 🅿

ASHLAND (F-9) pop. 2,817, elev. 885'

PIONEER TUNNEL COAL MINE AND STEAM TRAIN RIDE, 4 blks. s. off SR 61, following signs to jct. 20th and Oak sts., offers a tour through a coal mine in battery-powered mine cars. Another tour features a 1920s steam train pulling mine nearly a mile around a mountainside to an abandoned strip mine and bootleg coal hole. Smoke from a perpetual underground coal fire is visible. Note: Mine temperatures range from 48 to 52 degrees Fahrenheit. **Time:** Allow 1 hour, 30 minutes minimum. **Hours:** Mine tours and train rides daily 10:30-4:30, Memorial Day-Labor Day; hours vary Apr. 1-day before Memorial Day and day after Labor Day-Oct. 31. **Cost:** Mine tour $10; $7 (ages 2-11). Train ride $8; $6 (ages 2-11). Mine tour and train ride $16.20; $11.70 (ages 2-11). **Phone:** (570) 875-3850. (GT) (ℋ) (🅰)

AUDUBON (A-9) pop. 8,433, elev. 194'
• Part of Philadelphia area — see map p. 230

In the early 1900s some of the country's first feature-length motion pictures were produced a few miles east at a studio set up by Sigmund Lubin, a noted Philadelphia optician and movie producer. The lot, which accommodated 40 cowboys, 25 Native Americans and 100 horses, was used to film the "Battle of Shiloh," one of the first epic spectacles.

JOHN JAMES AUDUBON CENTER AT MILL GROVE is at Audubon and Pawlings rds. On the 175-acre nature preserve is Mill Grove, home in the early 1800s of John James Audubon, noted artist, author and naturalist. Now a museum, the house contains displays of Audubon's paintings, drawings and taxidermy specimens. Numerous trails wind through the grounds, which serve as a wildlife sanctuary.

Time: Allow 30 minutes minimum. **Hours:** Grounds daily dawn-dusk. Museum Tues.-Sat. 10-4, Sun. 1-4. Closed Jan. 1, Easter, July 4, Thanksgiving and Christmas. **Cost:** $5; $4 (ages 60+); $3 (ages 5-17). **Phone:** (610) 666-5593.

HOMEWOOD SUITES BY HILTON   (610)539-7300

ᵂᵂᵂ
Extended Stay Hotel
$109-$199

HOMEWOOD SUITES BY HILTON

AAA Benefit: Members save 5% or more!

Address: 681 Shannondell Blvd 19403 **Location:** US 422 exit S Trooper Rd, 1.2 mi n. **Facility:** 123 efficiencies, some two bedrooms. 5 stories, interior corridors. **Terms:** 1-7 night minimum stay, cancellation fee imposed. **Pool(s):** heated outdoor. **Guest Services:** valet and coin laundry, area transportation. **Featured Amenity:** full hot breakfast.

(SAVE) (🍴) CALL (&M) (🖥) (📶) (BIZ)
(HS) (📶) (✦) (🗄) (🖼) (🖥) / SOME UNITS (S🔚)

AVELLA (H-1) pop. 804, elev. 925'

MEADOWCROFT ROCKSHELTER AND HISTORIC VILLAGE is 3 mi. w. off SR 50, following signs. Meadowcroft Rockshelter is an excavated site featuring evidence of North American inhabitants dating back 16,000 years. A re-created 19th-century rural community with a one-room school, a working blacksmith, a covered bridge, a re-created 400-year-old Native American village and a 250-year-old frontier trading post are included.

Time: Allow 2 hours minimum. **Hours:** Wed.-Sat. noon-5, Sun. 1-5, Memorial Day-Labor Day; Sat. noon-5, Sun. 1-5, May 1-day before Memorial Day and day after Labor Day-Oct. 31. **Cost:** $12; $11 (ages 62+); $6 (ages 6-17). **Phone:** (724) 587-3412.

AVONDALE   pop. 1,265
• Part of Philadelphia area — see map p. 230

THE FARM HOUSE RESTAURANT   610/268-2235

♦♦♦♦ Continental. Fine Dining. $7-$40 **AAA Inspector Notes:** Candlelight, Oriental rugs, glowing fireplaces, country antiques and folk art lend a rustic ambience to the 18th-century farmhouse, a comfortable, casual place in which to unwind and enjoy well-prepared food. Menu favorites are crab cakes, lamb and veal. The seasonal patio overlooks a golf course. **Features:** full bar, Sunday brunch. **Reservations:** suggested, for dinner. **Address:** 514 McCue Rd 19311 **Location:** SR 41, 2 mi n on Church St, 0.5 mi w; US 1 exit Toughkenamon, 0.5 mi n on Newark Rd, 0.5 mi sw on Church St, then 0.5 mi w; on Loch Nairn Golf Course. L · D

BAINBRIDGE   (H-9) pop. 1,355, elev. 309'
• Part of Pennsylvania Dutch Country area — see map p. 220

WINERIES
• **Nissley Winery and Vineyards** is at 140 Vintage Dr. **Hours:** Guided tours (requiring a minimum of nine people) are available Fri. by appointment starting at 10. Self-guiding tours and tastings Mon.-Sat. 10-4:15, Sun. 1-3:15; last tour begins 45 minutes before closing. Closed Jan. 1, Easter, Thanksgiving and Christmas. **Phone:** (717) 426-3514, or (800) 522-2387 in state and surrounding states.

BALA-CYNWYD
• Hotels & Restaurants map & index p. 274
• Part of Philadelphia area — see map p. 230

AL DAR BISTRO   610/667-1245 (111)

♦♦ Mediterranean. Casual Dining. $7-$24 **AAA Inspector Notes:** Chefs grill over the gentle heat of glowing coals, employing a traditional Mediterranean style of cooking at this downtown restaurant. Settle in to the dining room, which evokes a casual European-style bistro atmosphere, to try the flavorful lamb shish kebab, marinated and grilled with peppers and onions and served with rice and fresh vegetables—it's a true standout. If you're seeking a lighter meal, consider the pizza, burgers, gyros and other convenience foods. **Features:** full bar. **Address:** 281 Montgomery Ave 19004 **Location:** Jct US 1 and SR 23, 1 mi w on SR 23 to Montgomery Ave. 🅿 Cynwyd, 219. L D 🍴

BARKEYVILLE   pop. 207

QUALITY INN-BARKEYVILLE   (814)786-7901

♦♦♦ **Address:** 137 Gibb Rd 16038 **Location:** I-80 exit 29, just n on SR 8. **Facility:** 73 units. 2 stories (no elevator), exterior corridors. **Activities:** limited exercise equipment. **Guest Services:** coin laundry. **Featured Amenity:** full hot breakfast.

Motel
$60-$130

WHERE TO EAT

KING'S FAMILY RESTAURANT   814/786-9494

♦♦ American. Family Dining. $6-$15 **AAA Inspector Notes:** Fast and friendly service is offered here. The menu is large in size with descriptive menu items and pictures. The restaurant is also known for its ice cream and dessert menu. **Address:** 5775 SR 8 16038 **Location:** I-80 exit 29, just n. B L D

BARNESVILLE

MAINSTAY SUITES BARNESVILLE/FRACKVILLE
                                          (570)773-5252

♦♦ Extended Stay Hotel $85-$135 **Address:** 1252 Morea Rd 18214 **Location:** I-81 exit 131A southbound; exit 131B northbound, just s. **Facility:** 70 efficiencies, some cottages. 3 stories, interior corridors. **Terms:** check-in 4 pm. **Activities:** limited exercise equipment. **Guest Services:** coin laundry.
CALL 🄼 HS 🛜   / SOME UNITS

BARTONSVILLE
• Hotels & Restaurants map & index p. 373
• Part of Pocono Mountains Area — see map p. 371

BAYMONT INN & SUITES   (570)476-1500 (35)

♦♦♦ **Address:** 116 Turtlewalk Ln 18321 **Location:** I-80 exit 302B, 0.4 mi n. Located in a commercial area. **Facility:** 114 units. 2 stories, interior corridors. **Amenities:** safes. **Pool(s):** heated indoor. **Activities:** hot tub, playground, game room, limited exercise equipment. **Guest Services:** coin laundry. **Featured Amenity:** breakfast buffet.

Hotel
$90-$150

SAVE 🍴 🚗 BIZ 🛜
 / SOME UNITS 🔌 🖨

BEAVER   pop. 4,531
• Hotels & Restaurants map & index p. 348
• Part of Pittsburgh area — see map p. 326

BERT'S WOODEN INDIAN   724/774-7992 (29)

♦♦ American. Casual Dining. $4-$15 **AAA Inspector Notes:** *Classic.* This is a family-run operation that has been in business for more than 40 years. This old-fashioned neighborhood restaurant is where the service and atmosphere is casual and the food is tasty and filling. The staff makes diners feel welcomed and sees to their needs. The restaurant is suitable for most occasions such as a family, social or business meal. **Reservations:** suggested. **Address:** 308 Leopard Ln at Sharon Rd 15009 **Location:** 0.5 mi n on SR 51; in Bridgewater/Beaver. L D CALL 🄼

THE WOODEN ANGEL   724/774-7880 (30)

♦♦ American. Fine Dining. $12-$40 **AAA Inspector Notes:** For a truly memorable dining experience, try the pappardelle noodles with sautéed lamb; this is the signature dish at this romantic, candlelit restaurant. Rack of lamb also is featured, and specials change seasonally. The owner's love of wine is evident in articles and awards that decorate the walls, as well as on the extensive wine list of American vintages. **Features:** full bar. **Reservations:** suggested. **Address:** 308 Leopard Ln at Sharon Rd 15009 **Location:** 0.5 mi n on SR 51; in Bridgewater/Beaver. L D CALL 🄼

BEAVER FALLS   (F-1) pop. 8,987, elev. 787'
• Hotels p. 58 • Restaurants p. 58
• Part of Pittsburgh area — see map p. 326

Beaver Falls, home to Geneva College, is along the banks of the Beaver River. When the Harmony Society purchased the site in 1859, an industrial boom began, which resulted in the area being referred to as a miniature Pittsburgh.

Beaver County Recreation and Tourism Department: 121 Bradys Run Rd., Beaver Falls, PA 15010. **Phone:** (724) 770-2062 or (800) 342-8192.

AIR HERITAGE MUSEUM, at the Beaver County Airport, 2 mi. n. on SR 51, houses memorabilia from World Wars I and II and the Vietnam War. Uniforms; flight suits; and airplane models, including an F-15 Eagle, are on display. Visitors can observe vintage aircraft being restored. **Time:** Allow 30 minutes minimum. **Hours:** Mon.-Sat. 10-5, Sun. by appointment. Closed major holidays. **Cost:** Donations. **Phone:** (724) 843-2820.

BEAVER FALLS HISTORICAL SOCIETY AND MUSEUM is at 1301 Seventh Ave. (SR 18), in the basement of the Carnegie Free Library. Historical items displayed include vintage fire department equipment, china, photo albums, clothing and 1800s Chinese cutlery. **Time:** Allow 1 hour minimum. **Hours:** Mon.-Thurs. 10-2. Closed federal holidays. Closed major holidays. Phone ahead to confirm schedule. **Cost:** Donations. **Phone:** (724) 846-4340 for the library.

PARK INN BY RADISSON BEAVER FALLS　　724/846-3700
▼▼▼▼ **Hotel.** Rates not provided. **Address:** 7195 Eastwood Rd 15010 **Location:** I-76 (Pennsylvania Tpke) exit 13, just n. **Facility:** 156 units. 3 stories, interior corridors. **Amenities:** video games. **Pool(s):** heated indoor. **Activities:** hot tub, playground, exercise room. **Guest Services:** valet and coin laundry.

WHERE TO EAT

GIUSEPPE'S TUSCANY GRILL　　724/843-5656
▼▼▼ Italian. Casual Dining. $6-$27 **AAA Inspector Notes:** Choices abound at this laid-back restaurant, which delivers plentiful portions of all kinds of pasta as well as veal, steak and seafood. Homemade bread, soup and sauces are aromatic and flavorful. Diners can expect friendly and prompt service. **Features:** full bar. **Reservations:** suggested. **Address:** 7072 Big Beaver Blvd 15010 **Location:** I-76 (Pennsylvania Tpke) exit 13, just s.

BEDFORD　(H-5) pop. 2,841, elev. 1,060'

The Allegheny mountain area of Bedford was first settled in 1751 by Robert Ray, after whom Fort Raystown was named when it was built in 1758. Eventually the community was renamed in honor of the Duke of Bedford.

Several historic buildings have been preserved in Bedford, including the Espy House, which served as President Washington's headquarters in 1794 when he led Federal troops into western Pennsylvania to quell the Whiskey Rebellion. Also, the Anderson House, 137 E. Pitt St., was built 1814-15 and housed what is believed to be the first bank west of the Allegheny Mountains. The original bank vault still can be seen.

During the French and Indian War historic Forbes Road (US 30) was used by Gen. John Forbes on his

way to capture Fort Duquesne, now known as Pittsburgh. The road winds through the farmlands and valleys of Bedford County and over more than 14 covered bridges. Schellsburg Old Log Church, built in 1806, also is along Forbes Road.

In the early 1900s, Forbes Road became a vital link in nation's first transcontinental artery, the Lincoln Highway. Unusual tourist attractions and landmarks dotted the route, including an 18-foot-high coffee pot that lured travelers to a local luncheonette. Restored to its former glory, the architectural oddity can be seen on US 30, in the Bedford County Fairgrounds. This is one of many such sites commemorated by the Lincoln Highway Roadside Museum, a 200-mile, statewide heritage corridor that features historic buildings, road makers, exhibits and nostalgic murals. A brochure and driving tour map are available from the visitors bureau.

Free guided tours of the downtown historic district are offered Fri. at 3:30, May-Oct.; phone (800) 765-3331.

Bedford County Conference and Visitors Bureau: 131 S. Juliana St., Bedford, PA 15522. **Phone:** (814) 623-1771 or (800) 765-3331.

Self-guiding tours: Brochures for walking, driving and bicycling tours are available at the visitors bureau.

FORT BEDFORD MUSEUM, 110 Fort Bedford Dr., is housed in a reproduction of an early blockhouse. The museum displays a scale model of the original fort. **Hours:** Wed.-Sun. 11-5, early May-Oct. 31. **Cost:** $5; $4.50 (ages 65+); $3.50 (ages 6-18); free (active military with ID). **Phone:** (814) 623-8891.

OLD BEDFORD VILLAGE is w. off US 220 Bus. Rte. at 220 Sawblade Rd. The Claycomb covered bridge leads to this depiction of Pennsylvania village life 1750-1850. Thirty-five buildings, including log cabins, two one-room schoolhouses and other structures, were brought from their original locations and reassembled. Various crafts of the era are demonstrated by interpreters dressed in period clothing.

Time: Allow 1 hour, 30 minutes minimum. **Hours:** Thurs.-Tues. 9-5, Memorial Day weekend-Labor Day; Thurs.-Sun. 9-5, day after Labor Day-Oct. 31. **Cost:** $10; $9 (ages 62+ and military with ID); $5 (ages 6-18). **Phone:** (814) 623-1156 or (800) 238-4347.

FAIRFIELD INN & SUITES BY MARRIOTT BEDFORD
(814)623-3444
▼▼▼ **Hotel** $111-$183 **Address:** 4436 Business Rt 220 15522 **Location:** I-70/76 (Pennsylvania Tpke) exit 146, just n. **Facility:** 84 units. 5 stories, interior corridors. **Pool(s):** heated indoor. **Activities:** hot tub, exercise room. **Guest Services:** valet and coin laundry.

| AAA Benefit: |
| Members save 5% |
| or more! |

HAMPTON INN OF BEDFORD   (814)624-0101

Hotel
$129-$169

AAA Benefit: Members save 5% or more!

Address: 4235 Business Rt 220 15522 **Location:** I-70/76 (Pennsylvania Tpke) exit 146, 0.5 mi s. **Facility:** 71 units. 4 stories, interior corridors. **Terms:** check-in 3:30 pm, 1-7 night minimum stay, cancellation fee imposed. **Pool(s):** heated indoor. **Activities:** hot tub, exercise room. **Guest Services:** valet laundry. **Featured Amenity: breakfast buffet.**

JUDY'S MOTEL-PA DUTCH HERITAGE   814/623-9118

Motel. Rates not provided. **Address:** 3521 Business Rt 220 15522 **Location:** I-70/76 (Pennsylvania Tpke) exit 146, 1.7 mi s. **Facility:** 12 units. 1 story, exterior corridors.

OMNI BEDFORD SPRINGS RESORT & SPA
814/623-8100

Historic Resort Hotel
Rates not provided

Address: 2138 Business Rt 220 15522 **Location:** I-70/76 (Pennsylvania Tpke) exit 146, 3.9 mi s. **Facility:** The resort, nestled in the Allegheny Mountains of southwest Pennsylvania, has been restored to its original grandeur to match its rich history. 216 units, some two bedrooms. 4 stories, interior corridors. **Parking:** valet only. **Terms:** check-in 4 pm. **Amenities:** safes. **Dining:** 5 restaurants, also, The Crystal Room, The Frontier Tavern, see separate listings. **Pool(s):** heated outdoor, heated indoor. **Activities:** hot tub, fishing, regulation golf, tennis, recreation programs, bicycles, playground, exercise room, spa. **Guest Services:** valet laundry, area transportation.

QUALITY INN BEDFORD   (814)623-5188

Hotel
$79-$165

Address: 4407 Business Rt 220 N 15522 **Location:** I-70/76 (Pennsylvania Tpke) exit 146, just n. **Facility:** 65 units. 1-2 stories (no elevator), interior/exterior corridors. **Pool(s):** outdoor. **Guest Services:** valet laundry. **Featured Amenity: breakfast buffet.**

TRAVELODGE BEDFORD   (814)623-9006

Hotel $50-$82 **Address:** 4517 Business Rt 220 15522 **Location:** I-70/76 (Pennsylvania Tpke) exit 146, 0.3 mi n. **Facility:** 104 units. 1-2 stories (no elevator), interior/exterior corridors. **Pool(s):** outdoor. **Activities:** sauna, hot tub, game room, exercise room. **Guest Services:** valet and coin laundry.

Take your imagination to new destinations with the online AAA/CAA Travel Guides

---

WHERE TO EAT

THE CRYSTAL ROOM   814/623-8100

American. Fine Dining. $20-$38 **AAA Inspector Notes:** *Historic.* The main dining room at this elegant resort is one of the oldest restaurants in America and features an upscale, traditional ambience. The menu features many fine regional specialties, including Pennsylvania cheeses and charcuterie. Do not miss the bread pudding at the end of your meal. **Features:** beer & wine. **Reservations:** suggested. **Address:** 2138 Business Rt 200 15522 **Location:** I-70/76 (Pennsylvania Tpke) exit 146, 3.9 mi s; in Omni Bedford Springs Resort & Spa. **Parking:** valet only. B L D

ED'S STEAK HOUSE   814/623-8894

Steak. Casual Dining. $6-$24 **AAA Inspector Notes:** As the name suggests, this local favorite is known for traditional steakhouse fare-beef and seafood-as well as tasty breakfasts. Daily specials are reasonably priced and well planned. **Features:** full bar. **Reservations:** suggested. **Address:** 4476 Business Rt 220 N 15522 **Location:** I-70/76 (Pennsylvania Tpke) exit 146, 0.3 mi n. B L D

THE FRONTIER TAVERN   814/623-8100

American. Casual Dining. $9-$23 **AAA Inspector Notes:** *Historic.* Set in the restored 1806 Stone Inn building, this restaurant offers all-American cuisine, large comfy chairs, a full bar, root beer on tap and local artisanal brews. After savoring a great homemade dessert, relax in one of the custom-built, ergonomic rocking chairs. **Features:** full bar. **Address:** 2138 Business Rt 220 15522 **Location:** I-70/76 (Pennsylvania Tpke) exit 146, 3.9 mi s; in Omni Bedford Springs Resort & Spa. L D CALL

THE GREEN HARVEST CO. CAFE   814/623-3465

Natural/Organic. Casual Dining. $4-$12 **AAA Inspector Notes:** *Historic.* Located in the downtown historic area, this café with a vegan owner offers a completely organic menu. A lot of distinctive local art hangs throughout the building and is for sale. Half specialty market, half restaurant there is a complete section dedicated to organic dry mixes and spreads—very cool and very good. Service is great and the food is very good. **Address:** 110 E Pitt St 15522 **Location:** Between Penn and Richard sts; downtown. **Parking:** street only. B L

HOSS'S FAMILY STEAK & SEA   814/623-2793

Steak. Casual Dining. $7-$28 **AAA Inspector Notes:** Folks can bring the whole family to enjoy this restaurant's 100-item salad bar, homemade soups and bread, steaks, fresh seafood and chicken entrées. **Address:** 4308 Business Rt 220 15522 **Location:** I-70/76 (Pennsylvania Tpke) exit 146, just n. L D

JEAN BONNET TAVERN   814/623-2250

American. Casual Dining. $8-$28 **AAA Inspector Notes:** *Historic.* Once owned by friends of William Penn and George Washington, the tavern came under the ownership of Jean Bonnet in 1780. The dining room sports stone walls, exposed beams, twig and slat seating as well as some bench seats. Light to hearty choices of chicken, beef or fish are accompanied by a medley of vegetables. It is rumored that a friendly ghost has called the restaurant home since the 18th century. **Features:** full bar. **Reservations:** suggested, weekends. **Address:** 6048 Lincoln Hwy 15522 **Location:** Jct US 30 and SR 31. L D

BELLEFONTE (F-6) pop. 6,187, elev. 747'
• Hotels p. 60 • Restaurants p. 60

Bellefonte is built on several hills at the base of Bald Eagle Mountain. Many of the town's homes are fine examples of early Victorian architecture. Known as the Home of Governors, seven of the town's residents have become governors of Pennsylvania and other states. Several times per year, the Bellefonte Historical Railroad carries passengers through some of central Pennsylvania's most scenic landscapes; phone (814) 355-1053 or (814) 355-2917.

If you're interested in catch and release fly-fishing for trout, head to Fisherman's Paradise on Spring Creek Road, which parallels much of Spring Creek. A state fishing license is required; fishing is permitted daily dawn to dusk. For more information and location details phone (610) 369-0464, for Fishermans Paradise, and (814) 359-5250 or (877) 707-4085 for the Pennsylvania Fish and Boat Commission.

Bellefonte Area Chamber of Commerce: Train Station, 320 W. High St., Bellefonte, PA 16823. **Phone:** (814) 355-2917.

Self-guiding tours: A walking-tour brochure can be obtained from the chamber of commerce.

ECONO LODGE   (814)355-5561

Motel $59-$199 **Address:** 3482 Benner Pike 16823 **Location:** I-99 exit 78B, 1.3 mi. **Facility:** 47 units. 1 story, exterior corridors.

REYNOLDS MANSION BED AND BREAKFAST   814/353-8407

Historic Bed & Breakfast $129-$325 **Address:** 101 W Linn St 16823 **Location:** Corner of Allegheny and Linn sts; downtown. **Facility:** Located 10 miles from Penn State, this 1800s Victorian mansion offers 10,000 square feet of luxurious comfort. Spacious rooms each have fireplaces and modern amenities. Most rooms also have a hot tub. 8 units. 3 stories (no elevator), interior corridors. **Parking:** on-site and street. **Terms:** check-in 4 pm, 14 day cancellation notice-fee imposed. **Guest Services:** complimentary and valet laundry.

WHERE TO EAT

BONFATTO'S   814/353-3330

Italian. Casual Dining. $8-$22 **AAA Inspector Notes:** Friendly service in a relaxed atmosphere offers panini, sandwiches, burgers, pizza, homemade soups and pasta dishes for dinner. Carry out is offered in a drive up window. Owner, Mr. Letterman gives his top 10 favorites among offerings of mostly chicken, steak and pasta. **Features:** full bar. **Address:** 205 Park Pl, Suite 1 16823 **Location:** 1.5 mi w on SR 550 (Zion Rd).

THE GAMBLE MILL   814/355-7764

Continental. Casual Dining. $9-$24 **AAA Inspector Notes:** Historic. Once a mill, this 1786 landmark has evolved into a popular restaurant. Its distinctive antique timbers and brick provide a backdrop for local artwork displays. Revel in the feel of history in their tavern with one of the in-house craft beers. **Features:** full bar. **Address:** 160 Dunlap St 16823 **Location:** At Lamb St Bridge; downtown.

BELLE VERNON pop. 1,093
• Part of Pittsburgh area — see map p. 326

COMFORT INN   (724)929-3177

Hotel
$119-$169

Address: 4300 SR 51 S 15012 **Location:** I-70 exit 46B, just n. **Facility:** 52 units. 2 stories (no elevator), interior corridors. **Amenities:** safes. **Pool(s):** outdoor. **Activities:** exercise room. **Guest Services:** coin laundry. **Featured Amenity: full hot breakfast.**

HAMPTON INN-BELLE VERNON   (724)929-8100

Hotel $109-$200 **Address:** 1525 Broad Ave Ext 15012 **Location:** I-70 exit 43A westbound; exit 43 eastbound. **Facility:** 70 units. 3 stories, interior corridors. **Terms:** 1-7 night minimum stay, cancellation fee imposed. **Pool(s):** heated indoor. **Activities:** exercise room. **Guest Services:** valet laundry.

AAA Benefit: Members save 5% or more!

HOLIDAY INN EXPRESS & SUITES   724/930-0100

Hotel. Rates not provided. **Address:** 181 Finley Rd 15012 **Location:** I-70 exit 43A westbound; exit 43 eastbound. **Facility:** 70 units. 3 stories, interior corridors. **Pool(s):** heated indoor. **Activities:** hot tub, exercise room. **Guest Services:** valet and coin laundry.

BENSALEM (A-11) elev. 70'
• Hotels & Restaurants map & index p. 274
• Part of Philadelphia area — see map p. 230

Visit Bucks County: 3207 Street Rd., Bensalem, PA 19020. **Phone:** (215) 639-0300 or (800) 836-2825.

NATIONAL SHRINE OF SAINT KATHARINE DREXEL, 1663 Bristol Pike, is the tomb of the founder of the Sisters of the Blessed Sacrament. Born into the wealthy Philadelphia Drexel family in 1858, Katharine Drexel devoted her life to the church and donated her $20 million inheritance to benefit African-Americans and Native Americans. **Note:** The schedule of the shrine may change in September 2015 during the World Meeting of Families. Phone ahead for schedule updates. **Hours:** Daily 10-5. Closed major holidays. **Cost:** Free. **Phone:** (215) 244-9900.

Cornwells Heights, 254

GAMBLING ESTABLISHMENTS
• **Parx Casino and Racing** is at 2999 Street Rd. **Hours:** Daily 24 hours. **Phone:** (215) 639-9000 or (888) 588-7279.

BEST WESTERN PLUS PHILADELPHIA BENSALEM
(215)638-1500

Hotel
$99-$139

AAA Benefit: Members save up to 20%!

Address: 3499 Street Rd 19020 **Location:** I-276 (Pennsylvania Tpke) exit 351, just s on US 1, then 0.3 mi e on SR 132. Located in a commercial area. **Facility:** 121 units. 2 stories, interior/exterior corridors. **Pool(s):** outdoor. **Activities:** exercise room. **Guest Services:** valet and coin laundry. **Featured Amenity: full hot breakfast.**

(See map & index p. 274.)

EXTENDED STAY AMERICA-PHILADELPHIA/BENSALEM
215/633-6900 **45**

◆◆ ◆◆ **Extended Stay Hotel.** Rates not provided. **Address:** 3216 Tillman Dr 19020 **Location:** I-95 exit 37 (SR 132), 2.5 mi w, then just s; I-276 (Pennsylvania Tpke) exit 351, 0.9 mi on US 1, 1.4 mi e, then just s. **Facility:** 99 efficiencies. 3 stories, interior corridors. **Activities:** exercise room. **Guest Services:** coin laundry.

HAMPTON INN AND SUITES PHILADELPHIA BENSALEM
(267)332-2200 **47**

◆◆◆ **Hotel** $99-$149 **Address:** 3660 Street Rd 19020 **Location:** I-276 exit 351, just s on US 1, then just e on SR 132. **Facility:** 101 units. 4 stories, interior corridors. **Terms:** 1-7 night minimum stay, cancellation fee imposed. **Amenities:** safes. **Pool(s):** heated indoor. **Activities:** exercise room. **Guest Services:** valet laundry.

> **AAA Benefit:** Members save 5% or more!

HOLIDAY INN BENSALEM-PHILADELPHIA AREA
(215)639-9100 **44**

◆◆◆◆ **Hotel** $89-$299 **Address:** 3327 Street Rd 19020 **Location:** I-276 (Pennsylvania Tpke) exit 351, just s on US 1, then just e on SR 132. Located in a commercial area. **Facility:** 167 units. 6 stories, interior corridors. **Amenities:** safes. **Pool(s):** outdoor. **Activities:** exercise room. **Guest Services:** valet and coin laundry.

HOLIDAY INN EXPRESS PHILADELPHIA NORTHEAST/BENSALEM
(215)245-5222 **46**

◆◆◆◆ **Hotel** $89-$159 **Address:** 1329 Bristol Pike 19020 **Location:** I-95 exit 35 (Woodhaven Rd), just s via US 13/Bristol Pike. Located in a commercial area. Ⓡ Cornwells Heights, 254. **Facility:** 141 units. 3 stories, interior corridors. **Terms:** cancellation fee imposed. **Pool(s):** outdoor. **Activities:** exercise room. **Guest Services:** valet laundry. **Featured Amenity:** full hot breakfast.

QUALITY INN & SUITES
(215)245-0111 **41**

◆◆◆ **Hotel** $79-$179 **Address:** 3671 Street Rd 19020 **Location:** I-276 (Pennsylvania Tpke) exit 351, just s on US 1, then just e on SR 132. Located in a commercial area. **Facility:** 95 units. 5 stories, interior corridors. **Activities:** exercise room. **Guest Services:** coin laundry. **Featured Amenity:** breakfast buffet.

SLEEP INN & SUITES-BENSALEM
(215)244-2300 **43**

◆◆ ◆◆ **Hotel** $90-$120 **Address:** 3427 Street Rd 19020 **Location:** I-276 (Pennsylvania Tpke) exit 351, just s on US 1, then 0.3 mi e on SR 132. Located in a commercial area. **Facility:** 64 units. 3 stories, interior corridors. **Activities:** exercise room. **Guest Services:** valet laundry.

WHERE TO EAT

FISHER'S TUDOR HOUSE
215/244-9777 **72**

◆◆ ◆◆ ◆◆ Seafood. Casual Dining. $10-$22 **AAA Inspector Notes:** Mouthwatering baked goods and nicely prepared dishes of chicken, seafood, beef and veal are what this popular restaurant offers. Angus beef and panini are features on the menu. Wine by the glass and a changing menu of bottle or draft beers also are featured. The restaurant provides a lovely and relaxed setting. Murder mystery dinner theater shows are conducted on Saturday evenings. **Features:** full bar. **Reservations:** suggested, for dinner. **Address:** 1858 Street Rd 19020 **Location:** I-95 exit 37 (SR 132), 1 mi w. L D

TIJUANA FLATS
215/639-5418

◆◆ Tex-Mex. Quick Serve. $6-$9 **AAA Inspector Notes:** The first one of these restaurants opened in Central Florida way back in 1995 and has since spawned over sixty more locations! The menu specializes in Tex-Mex with some all-time favorites such as burritos, chimichangas, quesadillas, tacos, enchiladas and nachos. Well known for their hot sauce bar, this eatery has a slew of them from which to choose. Careful, some are really hot! Although the restaurant is considered quick serve, the food is cooked to order. **Address:** 2814 Street Rd 19020 **Location:** I-276 (Pennsylvania Tpke) exit 351, just s on US 1, then 0.5 mi e on SR 132. L D

BENTLEYVILLE pop. 2,581
• Part of Pittsburgh area — see map p. 326

BEST WESTERN GARDEN INN
(724)239-4321

◆◆ **Hotel** $130

> **AAA Benefit:** Members save up to 20%!

Address: 101 Gosai Dr 15314 **Location:** I-70 exit 32B, just s. **Facility:** 83 units. 3 stories, interior corridors. **Pool(s):** heated indoor. **Activities:** exercise room. **Guest Services:** valet and coin laundry.

HOLIDAY INN EXPRESS BENTLEYVILLE
(724)239-7700

◆◆◆◆ **Hotel** $129-$160 **Address:** 25 Smita Ln 15314 **Location:** I-70 exit 32B, 0.5 mi s on Main St. **Facility:** 61 units. 3 stories, interior corridors. **Terms:** cancellation fee imposed. **Pool(s):** heated outdoor. **Activities:** exercise room. **Guest Services:** valet and coin laundry.

WHERE TO EAT

KING'S FAMILY RESTAURANT
724/239-6202

◆◆ ◆◆ American. Family Dining. $6-$14 **AAA Inspector Notes:** Fast and friendly service is offered here. The menu is large in size with descriptive menu items and pictures. The restaurant is also known for its ice cream and dessert menu. **Address:** 206 Wilson Rd 15314 **Location:** I-70 exit 32B, 0.5 mi s. B L D

BENTON (COLUMBIA COUNTY) (E-9)
pop. 824, elev. 800'

RICKETTS GLEN STATE PARK is 11.3 mi. n. on SR 487. In the Glens Natural Area, 22 waterfalls are formed as Kitchen Creek winds through two deep gorges; Ganoga Falls is the tallest at 94 feet. There are 26 miles of hiking trails in the park. A full loop on the longest trail is 7 miles, and a 3-mile hike passes most of the falls. Other activities include snowmobiling, boating, fishing and swimming. *See Recreation Areas Chart.*

Hiking boots are recommended. **Hours:** Daily dawn-dusk. **Cost:** Free. Fee for camping, cabins and boat rental. **Phone:** (570) 477-5675, or (888) 727-2757 for reservations. 🅰 ⊠ 🏕

BERNVILLE (G-10) pop. 955, elev. 317'

KOZIAR'S CHRISTMAS VILLAGE is 1.5 mi. s.w. via SR 183, following signs to Christmas Village Rd. This is one of the largest displays in the country of various Christmas theme exhibits. The village, a converted farm with more than a dozen decorated buildings, features more than a half-million colored lights, holiday music and walk-through displays arranged in themed sections. There also is an indoor/outdoor miniature train display. Children can visit with Santa Claus.

Time: Allow 1 hour minimum. **Hours:** Mon.-Fri. 6-9 p.m., Sat. 5-9:30, Sun. 5-9, Thanksgiving-Jan. 1; Fri. 6-9 p.m., Sat. 5:30-9:30, Sun. 5:30-9, early Nov.-day before Thanksgiving. Phone ahead to confirm schedule. **Cost:** $9; $8 (ages 65+); $7 (ages 4-10). **Phone:** (610) 488-1110. 🍴

BERWICK (F-9) pop. 10,477, elev. 505'

Berwick was founded as a religious refuge in 1786 by the Quaker Evan Owen, who named his community after Berwick-upon-Tweed, an English town on the Scottish border. Berwick is an industrial community that produces clothing, boxes, decorative ribbons, containers, snack foods, manufactured housing and metal parts.

The Columbia Montour Chamber of Commerce: 107 S. Market St., Suite 6, Berwick, PA 18603. **Phone:** (570) 752-3612 or (570) 784-2522.

SUSQUEHANNA ENERGY INFORMATION CENTER AND RIVERLANDS, 5 mi. n. on US 11, has displays about nuclear energy as well as a nature center exhibit. Next to the center is Riverlands, a 1,200-acre recreation and nature area that offers picnicking, fishing, canoeing, boating (electric motors only), cross-country skiing and nature trails.

Hours: Energy information center open Mon.-Fri. 8:30-4:30. Riverlands open daily 8 a.m.-dusk. Closed Jan. 1, Easter, Thanksgiving, Christmas Eve and Christmas. Phone ahead to confirm holiday schedule. **Cost:** Free. **Phone:** (866) 832-3312.

BERWYN pop. 3,631
• Part of Philadelphia area — see map p. 230

RESIDENCE INN BY MARRIOTT PHILADELPHIA-VALLEY FORGE   (610)640-9494
♦♦♦ **Extended Stay Hotel** $146-$240 **Address:** 600 W Swedesford Rd 19312 **Location:** US 202 exit Paoli/SR 252, 1 mi n. Located in a commercial area. **Facility:** 88 kitchen units, some two bedrooms. 2 stories (no elevator), exterior corridors. **Pool(s):** heated outdoor. **Activities:** exercise room. **Guest Services:** valet and coin laundry. **AAA Benefit: Members save 5% or more!**
🌱 🛗 CALL 📶 🚐 BIZ 🛜 ✕ 🛢 🖨 🖥
/ SOME UNITS 🛏

WHERE TO EAT

LOTUS INN CHINESE & JAPANESE RESTAURANT   610/725-8888
♦♦ Asian. Casual Dining. $7-$26 **AAA Inspector Notes:** In a shopping plaza storefront, this restaurant presents extensive dine-in and takeout menus with offerings from both the Chinese and Japanese traditions. A small sushi bar is a prevalent element of the dining room. Pan-seared diver scallops with mango salsa, honey spicy walnut chicken and crispy cod fillet with Szechuan black bean sauce are among the delicious menu options. **Features:** full bar. **Address:** 402 W Swedesford Rd 19312 **Location:** US 202 exit Valley Forge Rd, 0.5 mi s; in Swedesford Plaza. Ⓛ Ⓓ

NECTAR   610/725-9000
♦♦♦ Asian. Fine Dining. $10-$37 **AAA Inspector Notes:** Warm earth tones, big open windows and candle-filled walls lend to the intimate feel at this spot amid the suburban sprawl of the Main Line. Seafood, Chinese vegetables and tasty sauces come together in satisfying wok dishes. Many entrées mingle elements of Indian, Japanese and Chinese cuisines. The edamame dumplings and seared tuna roll come highly recommended. **Features:** full bar, patio dining. **Reservations:** suggested, dinner. **Address:** 1091 Lancaster Ave 19312 **Location:** 7 mi e of jct US 202. Ⓟ Berwyn, 202.
Ⓛ Ⓓ CALL 📶 🚃

BETHEL (BERKS COUNTY)

COMFORT INN-BETHEL/MIDWAY   (717)933-8888

♦♦ Hotel $85-$129
Address: 41 Diner Dr 19507 **Location:** I-78 exit 16, just w. **Facility:** 71 units. 3 stories, interior corridors. **Pool(s):** heated indoor. **Activities:** game room, limited exercise equipment. **Featured Amenity: continental breakfast.**

SAVE 🛗 CALL 📶 🚐 🛜 🖥
/ SOME UNITS 🛏 🛢 🖨

BETHEL PARK pop. 32,313
• Hotels & Restaurants map & index p. 348
• Part of Pittsburgh area — see map p. 326

CROWNE PLAZA PITTSBURGH SOUTH (412)833-5300 📶
♦♦♦ Hotel $119-$219 **Address:** 164 Ft Couch Rd 15241 **Location:** 1 mi n on US 19. Opposite South Hills Village Mall. Ⓟ Bethel Village, 13. **Facility:** 179 units, some kitchens. 2-8 stories, interior corridors. **Amenities:** video games. **Pool(s):** heated outdoor. **Activities:** exercise room. **Guest Services:** valet and coin laundry, area transportation.
🛗 🍴 🍽 CALL 📶 🚐 BIZ HS 🛜 ✕ 📹
🖨 / SOME UNITS 🛏 🛢 🖨 🖥

BETHLEHEM (G-11) pop. 74,982, elev. 236'
• Restaurants p. 66
• Hotels & Restaurants map & index p. 49

Bethlehem is nestled in the Lehigh Valley along with Allentown *(see place listing p. 46)* and Easton *(see place listing p. 99).*

In 1741 a group of Moravian missionaries from Europe arrived in what is now Bethlehem and established a community. They christened their settlement during the traditional vigils on Christmas Eve with their patron, Count von Zinzendorf, who was visiting from Europe. Many of the large stone buildings constructed by the Moravians are still in use;

(See map & index p. 49.)

the structures are considered among the finest examples of pre-Revolutionary German architecture in the country. The visitor center offers guided tours of the historic district.

Burnside Plantation, an 18th-century farm at 1461 Schoenersville Rd., was the first privately owned Moravian residence in Bethlehem. Guided tours of the grounds are offered throughout the year by appointment only; phone (610) 691-6055. Colonial Industrial Quarter, along Monocacy Creek at 459 Old York Rd., is a restored 1700s industrial site that features a tannery, mill, blacksmith shop, waterworks and a children's museum; phone (610) 691-6055. The 1810 Goundie House, at 501 Main St., is a Federalist-style brick home built by the town's brewer. A kitchen, dining room and parlor have been furnished in period, and changing exhibitions depict the story of 1800s Bethlehem; phone (610) 691-6055.

Bethlehem is the home of three institutions of higher education: Lehigh University, Moravian College and Northampton Community College. Moravian, established in 1742, is one of America's oldest colleges, and Lehigh is a major research university.

🦅 Musikfest is a celebration of music, theater, and arts and crafts held in the historic downtown early- to mid-August. Celebrate the holiday season at 🦅 Christkindlmarkt, which takes place on Main and Spring streets mid-November to late December.

Historic Bethlehem Museums & Sites: 74 W. Broad Street, Suite 260, Bethlehem, PA 18018. **Phone:** (610) 691-6055 or (800) 360-8687.

Self-guiding tours: Brochures of the Old Bethlehem historic district and tickets for guided walks of the area are available at the visitor center.

THE KEMERER MUSEUM OF DECORATIVE ARTS, 427 N. New St., offers period rooms, galleries and changing exhibits that present more than 250 years of folk art, furnishings, paintings and decorative arts. Collections of cast-iron toys, maps, prints and textiles provide insight into the past.

Time: Allow 1 hour minimum. **Hours:** Fri.-Sat. 11-4, Sun. noon-4. Some extended hours during winter holidays. Closed major holidays. Phone ahead to confirm schedule. **Cost:** (includes Moravian Museum of Bethlehem) $12; $6 (ages 4-12). Phone ahead to verify rates. **Phone:** (610) 691-6055 or (610) 868-6868.

MORAVIAN MUSEUM OF BETHLEHEM, downtown at 66 W. Church St., is housed in the 1741 Gemeinhaus (community house), the oldest building in Bethlehem. The site shares stories about the art, culture and dreams of the early Moravian settlers. The structure has served as a home, school, church and a work space. See the 1752 Apothecary, the 18th century Nain-Schober House and the Moravian Single Sisters' House.

Hours: Fri.-Sat. noon-4. Some extended hours Nov. 29-Dec. 30. Closed major holidays. Phone ahead

to confirm schedule. **Cost:** (includes The Kemerer Museum of Decorative Arts) $12; $6 (ages 4-12). **Phone:** (610) 691-6055 or (610) 868-6868. GT

SUN INN, 564 Main St., was established in 1758 by the Moravians. Guests included George Washington, the Marquis de Lafayette and John Adams. It is restored and furnished in period. A self-guiding tour is available. **Time:** Allow 30 minutes minimum. **Hours:** Self-guiding tours Sat.-Sun. Phone ahead to confirm schedule. **Cost:** Self-guiding tour free. Guided tour $7; $3 (ages 6-12). **Phone:** (610) 866-1758.

GAMBLING ESTABLISHMENTS

- **Sands Bethlehem** is at 77 Sands Blvd. **Hours:** Daily 24 hours. **Phone:** (877) 726-3777. *(See ad p. 65.)*

BEST WESTERN LEHIGH VALLEY HOTEL & CONFERENCE CENTER   (610)866-5800 **16**

 Hotel $79-$119   **AAA Benefit:** Members save up to 20%!

Address: 300 Gateway Dr 18017 **Location:** US 22 exit Center St and SR 512. Located in a commercial area. **Facility:** 192 units. 2 stories (no elevator), interior/exterior corridors. **Terms:** check-in 4 pm, 3 day cancellation notice. **Dining:** nightclub. **Pool(s):** outdoor. **Activities:** exercise room. **Guest Services:** valet laundry.

COMFORT SUITES UNIVERSITY   (610)882-9700 **26**

Hotel $95-$240 **Address:** 120 W 3rd St 18015 **Location:** SR 378 exit 3rd St; jct W 3rd and Brodhead sts; center. Located in a commercial area. **Facility:** 124 units. 4 stories, interior corridors. **Dining:** entertainment. **Activities:** exercise room. **Guest Services:** valet laundry, area transportation.

COURTYARD BY MARRIOTT ALLENTOWN BETHLEHEM/LEHIGH VALLEY AIRPORT
          (610)317-6200 **21**

 Hotel $125-$206   COURTYARD Marriott **AAA Benefit:** Members save 5% or more!

Address: 2160 Motel Dr 18018 **Location:** US 22 exit Airport Rd S, 0.8 mi se on Catasauqua Rd. Located in a commercial area. **Facility:** 114 units. 3 stories, interior corridors. **Pool(s):** heated indoor. **Activities:** exercise room. **Guest Services:** valet and coin laundry, boarding pass kiosk, area transportation.

Visit AAA.com/searchfordiscounts to save on dining, attractions, hotels and more

64 BETHLEHEM, PA

(See map & index p. 49.)

COURTYARD BY MARRIOTT BETHLEHEM LEHIGH VALLEY/I-78
(610)625-9500 **15**

Hotel
$174-$286

AAA Benefit: Members save 5% or more!

Address: 2220 Emrick Blvd 18020 **Location:** SR 33 exit Freemansburg Ave, just w. **Facility:** 138 units. 4 stories, interior corridors. **Pool(s):** heated indoor. **Activities:** hot tub, exercise room. **Guest Services:** valet and coin laundry, rental car service, area transportation.

FAIRFIELD INN & SUITES BY MARRIOTT ALLENTOWN BETHLEHEM/LEHIGH VALLEY AIRPORT
(610)867-8681 **22**

Hotel
$97-$160

AAA Benefit: Members save 5% or more!

Address: 2140 Motel Dr 18018 **Location:** US 22 exit Airport Rd S, 0.8 mi se on Catasauqua Rd. Located in a commercial area. **Facility:** 103 units. 3 stories, interior corridors. **Pool(s):** outdoor. **Activities:** hot tub. **Guest Services:** valet and coin laundry, area transportation. **Featured Amenity:** breakfast buffet.

HAMPTON INN & SUITES BETHLEHEM
(610)868-2442 **17**

Hotel $119-$189 **Address:** 200 Gateway Dr 18017 **Location:** US 22 exit Center St and SR 512. Located in a commercial area. **Facility:** 110 units, some efficiencies. 3 stories, interior corridors. **Terms:** 1-7 night minimum stay, cancellation fee imposed. **Pool(s):** heated indoor. **Activities:** exercise room. **Guest Services:** valet and coin laundry.

AAA Benefit: Members save 5% or more!

HISTORIC HOTEL BETHLEHEM
(610)625-5000 **24**

Historic Hotel $165-$235 **Address:** 437 Main St 18018 **Location:** SR 378 S exit 3 (City Center), just n on 3rd Ave, 0.3 mi e on Union, then 0.3 mi s. **Facility:** Downtown, adjacent to the Moravian historic district, this nine-story brick hotel retains architectural features from its 1922 construction, including a brass mail chute that can be seen on each floor. 128 units. 9 stories, interior corridors. **Parking:** on-site (fee). **Terms:** check-in 4 pm, 2 night minimum stay - seasonal and/or weekends, 7 day cancellation notice-fee imposed. **Dining:** 2 restaurants, also, 1741 on the Terrace, see separate listing. **Activities:** exercise room. **Guest Services:** valet laundry, area transportation.

Enjoy great member rates and benefits at AAA/CAA Preferred Hotels

HOLIDAY INN EXPRESS HOTEL & SUITES-ALLENTOWN AREA/BETHLEHEM AIRPORT
(610)882-2255 **18**

Hotel $89-$199 **Address:** 3375 High Point Blvd 18017 **Location:** US 22 exit SR 378/Schoenersville Rd, follow signs for Schoenersville Rd, then 0.6 mi n. **Facility:** 100 units, some efficiencies. 3 stories, interior corridors. **Terms:** cancellation fee imposed. **Pool(s):** heated outdoor. **Activities:** exercise room. **Guest Services:** valet laundry, area transportation.

HOLIDAY INN EXPRESS HOTEL & SUITES BETHLEHEM
610/838-6110 **27**

Hotel. Rates not provided. **Address:** 2201 Cherry Ln 18015 **Location:** I-78 exit 67, just s on SR 412, then just e. **Facility:** 80 units. 4 stories, interior corridors. **Amenities:** safes. **Pool(s):** heated indoor. **Activities:** hot tub, exercise room. **Guest Services:** valet and coin laundry, area transportation.

HOMEWOOD SUITES - ALLENTOWN/BETHLEHEM AIRPORT
(610)264-7500 **19**

Extended Stay Hotel $129-$199 **Address:** 2031 Avenue C 18017 **Location:** US 22 exit SR 378/Schoenersville Rd, follow signs for Schoenersville Rd, then 0.7 mi n. **Facility:** 113 efficiencies, some two bedrooms. 3 stories, interior corridors. **Terms:** 1-7 night minimum stay, cancellation fee imposed. **Pool(s):** heated indoor. **Activities:** hot tub. **Guest Services:** valet and coin laundry, area transportation.

AAA Benefit: Members save 5% or more!

HYATT PLACE BETHLEHEM
(610)625-0500 **23**

Hotel
$139-$249

AAA Benefit: Members save 10%!

Address: 45 W North St 18018 **Location:** SR 378 exit 2 (Eighth Ave), just s, 0.7 mi w on Broad St, just n on Main St, then just w. **Facility:** 124 units. 6 stories, interior corridors. **Terms:** cancellation fee imposed. **Amenities:** video games. **Pool(s):** heated indoor. **Activities:** exercise room. **Guest Services:** valet laundry, rental car service, area transportation. **Featured Amenity:** breakfast buffet.

RESIDENCE INN BY MARRIOTT ALLENTOWN BETHLEHEM/LEHIGH VALLEY AIRPORT
(610)317-2662 **20**

Extended Stay Hotel
$118-$194

AAA Benefit: Members save 5% or more!

Address: 2180 Motel Dr 18018 **Location:** US 22 exit Airport Rd S, 0.8 mi se on Catasauqua Rd. Located in a commercial area. **Facility:** 120 units, some two bedrooms, efficiencies and kitchens. 3 stories, interior corridors. **Pool(s):** heated outdoor. **Activities:** tennis, exercise room. **Guest Services:** valet and coin laundry, area transportation. **Featured Amenity:** breakfast buffet.

(See map & index p. 49.)

SANDS BETHLEHEM
484/777-7690 **25**

Contemporary Resort Hotel
Rates not provided

Address: 77 Sands Blvd 18015 **Location:** I-78 exit 67, just off SR 412. **Facility:** This modern-style resort offers spacious guest rooms with 42-inch flat-screen LCD HDTVs, pillowtop beds and upscale glass-enclosed showers. Several Emeril Lagasse restaurants are on the premises. 302 units. 10 stories, interior corridors. **Parking:** valet and street only. **Amenities:** safes. **Dining:** 3 restaurants, also, Burgers and More by Emeril, see separate listing. **Pool(s):** heated indoor. **Activities:** exercise room, spa. **Guest Services:** valet laundry. **Featured Amenity:** continental breakfast. *(See ad this page.)*

Play Your Way at Sands Bethlehem!

THE VIEW INN & SUITES
(610)865-6300 **14**

Hotel $69-$109 **Address:** 3191 Highfield Dr 18020 **Location:** US 22 exit SR 191, just s. Located in a commercial area. **Facility:** 113 units. 2 stories (no elevator), interior/exterior corridors. **Activities:** exercise room.

WYDNOR HALL INN
610/867-6851 **28**

Bed & Breakfast. Rates not provided. **Address:** 3612 Old Philadelphia Pike 18015 **Location:** I-78 exit 60, 0.3 mi s to Center Valley Pkwy, 2.3 mi e to SR 378, 1.5 mi n to Black River Rd, just w to Old Philadelphia Pike, then 0.3 mi s. **Facility:** In a scenic and peaceful setting, this charming B&B offers five spacious rooms with large personal bathrooms. For a more private stay or if you're traveling with the family, ask about the bi-level cottage. 6 units, some cottages. 3 stories (no elevator), interior corridors.

Use travel time to share driving tips and rules of the road with your teens

▼ See AAA listing this page ▼

AAA.com/ TourBook Comments

Let Your Voice Be Heard

If your visit to a TourBook-listed property doesn't meet your expectations, tell us about it.

AAA.com/TourBookComments

(See map & index p. 49.)

WHERE TO EAT

1741 ON THE TERRACE   610/625-5000   ②⑦

▼▼▼

American
Fine Dining
$24-$39

AAA Inspector Notes: *Historic.* Order off a seasonal menu listing contemporary cuisine to enjoy dishes prepared using just-plucked fresh ingredients, many of which are locally grown. If you're looking to sample a few items, the three-course tasting menu is a smart option. Relax in the dining room boasting soaring Palladian windows, which open onto views of the surrounding valley and quaint downtown shops. **Features:** full bar, Sunday brunch. **Reservations:** suggested. **Address:** SR 378 S exit 3 (City Center), just n on 3rd Ave, 0.3 mi e on Union, then 0.3 mi s; in Historic Hotel Bethlehem. *Menu on AAA.com* D CALL &M

BENNER STREET RESTAURANT & BAR   610/861-8181   ②⑨

▼▼ American. Casual Dining. $5-$28 **AAA Inspector Notes:** *Historic.* Functioning as a small hotel through much of its history, this historic 1886 structure is now a restaurant. You'll find a comfortable gathering place for enjoying American/classical country French cuisine with affordable pricing. The menu features such delectable entrées as crab cakes, rack of lamb, filet mignon and even burgers. **Features:** full bar, happy hour. **Reservations:** suggested, for dinner. **Address:** 1028 Broadway 18015 **Location:** 0.6 mi s on SR 378, 0.5 mi sw. L D

BETHLEHEM BREW WORKS BREWERY & RESTAURANT
                                    610/882-1300   ②⑤

▼▼ American. Gastropub. $8-$22 **AAA Inspector Notes:** At any one time, this microbrewery offers six hand-crafted beers, ales and lagers in addition to cigars and a good selection of single malts and bourbons. More than 90 Belgian beers are available in the on-site Belgian beer lounge. Three large murals depict the city's once-famed steel industry. Examples of preparations served in the casual dining rooms are diamond-plate pork marinated in beer and spices and Bethlehem pasta, a spicy Cajun dish with mushrooms. **Features:** full bar, happy hour. **Address:** 569 Main St 18018 **Location:** Jct Broad St; downtown. L D LATE

BLUE GRILLHOUSE/WINEBAR   610/691-8400   ②②

▼▼▼ Steak. Fine Dining. $7-$47 **AAA Inspector Notes:** Employing mahogany walls and ceilings, plush carpeting and modern decorative lighting, the dining room exudes a sophisticated yet relaxed ambience. A seasonal dining patio is another option. Signature martinis, cognacs and cocktails are served in the upscale wine bar. An extensive wine list, including 60 by-the-glass choices, complements a menu that features prime steaks, chops and seafood. **Features:** full bar, Sunday brunch. **Reservations:** suggested. **Address:** 4431 Easton Ave 18020 **Location:** SR 33 exit William Penn Hwy, 1 mi w. L D

BURGERS AND MORE BY EMERIL   484/777-7777   ②⑧

▼▼ Burgers. Casual Dining. $5-$14 **AAA Inspector Notes:** The bright Burgers and More by Emeril is a great place to get some tasty malts and shakes, crispy fries and onion rings and large burgers, prime chuck and short rib brisket blend, all made from grass-fed beef. **Features:** full bar. **Address:** 77 Sands Blvd 18015 **Location:** I-78 exit 67, just off SR 412; in Sands Bethlehem. **Parking:** valet and street only. L D CALL &M

THE CAFE   610/866-1686   ②⑥

▼▼▼ Fusion. Fine Dining. $5-$25 **AAA Inspector Notes:** Ponder an interesting blend of Thai and Continental cuisines in addition to French pastries at this café. Fresh seafood and vegetarian dishes are always available, and you'll savor the taste of items such as rack of lamb prepared with either Thai curry sauce or mustard sauce. You can request seating in one of the eight intimate dining rooms, which are decorated in the Victorian style, or on the seasonal patio. **Features:** full bar, patio dining. **Reservations:** suggested, for dinner. **Address:** 221 W Broad St 18018 **Location:** Just w of downtown. **Parking:** on-site and street. L D

COPPERHEAD GRILLE   610/282-4600   ③⓪

▼▼ ▼▼ American. Casual Dining. $9-$23 **AAA Inspector Notes:** Lending to the bustling sports lounge atmosphere are 10 flat screens and a 130-inch high-definition projection screen for sports viewing; a cigar lounge; and karaoke, DJs or live bands from varying genres Tuesday through Saturday evenings. In addition to nearly two dozen appetizers, the menu lists sandwiches, steaks, ribs, fajitas, pizza and Italian specialties. A good choice is the land and sea combination plate with steak and a crab cake. Patrons can order from the lounge menu until midnight. **Features:** full bar, happy hour. **Address:** 5737 Rt 378 N 18015 **Location:** On SR 378, 5 mi s. L D

EDGE RESTAURANT, BAR & LOUNGE   610/814-0100   ②④

▼▼▼ French. Fine Dining. $18-$38 **AAA Inspector Notes:** Near the downtown historic district, this modern, upscale dining room nurtures a casual but still sophisticated New York-style atmosphere and incorporates marble and elegant hardwood elements into the décor. Asian-influenced French cuisine choices on the quarterly changing menu might include grilled filet mignon, porcini-crusted pork tenderloin, oven-roasted rack of lamb and sesame seed- and pepper-crusted ahi tuna. **Features:** full bar, happy hour. **Reservations:** suggested. **Address:** 74 W Broad St 18018 **Location:** SR 378 S exit 3 (Center City); at W Broad and Main sts; in Liberty Center Building. **Parking:** street only. D CALL

HANOVERVILLE ROADHOUSE   610/837-1122   ②①

▼▼ American. Casual Dining. $7-$29 **AAA Inspector Notes:** A wood-burning brick fireplace and antique furnishings are featured elements of the dining rooms in the circa 1825 Colonial-style farmhouse. The menu centers on steaks, prime rib and fresh seafood, particularly the noteworthy crab cakes. **Features:** full bar. **Reservations:** suggested. **Address:** 5001 Hanoverville Rd 18017 **Location:** US 22 exit Center St and SR 512, 0.8 mi n on SR 512, 0.8 mi e on Brodhead Rd, then 0.4 mi n on Township Line Rd. L D

STEFANO'S CAFE   610/867-7775   ②③

▼▼ Italian. Casual Dining. $7-$26 **AAA Inspector Notes:** This popular spot gives you the option of casual family-style dining or more formal, café-oriented dining in a Mediterranean atmosphere. Featuring both Northern and Southern Italian cuisines, the menu includes steak, veal, seafood and even wild game. The delicious tilapia Patrizia is a lightly sauteed fillet finished with white-wine butter sauce and topped with fresh tomato, herbs and jumbo lump crabmeat—we highly recommend it. **Features:** full bar. **Address:** 2970 Linden St 18017 **Location:** US 22 exit SR 191, 1.7 mi s. L D CALL &M

BIRD-IN-HAND (H-9) pop. 402, elev. 360'

• **Attractions map p. 221**
• **Hotels & Restaurants map & index p. 225**
• **Part of Pennsylvania Dutch Country area — see map p. 220**

   Bird-in-Hand took its name from a tavern sign that pictured a bird resting in a hand. Taverns of the period chose pictures over words because it was immediately recognizable to travelers, many of whom could not read. Four hotels have since stood on the site of the original Bird-in-Hand, which was built to serve travelers on the Philadelphia Turnpike.

Shopping areas: The Bird-in-Hand Farmers Market, 2710 Old Philadelphia Pike, is a great place to sample the area's specialty foods and crafts. The market is open Wed.-Sat. 8:30-5:30, July-Oct. Hours vary rest of year; phone (719) 393-9674.

   The Old Village Store and Bird-in-Hand Village Antique Market, on SR 340, features an operating hardware store and an antique market with about 40 dealers. It is said to be one of the oldest hardware stores in the country. Bike and scooter rentals also are available; phone 717-278-1991.

(See map & index p. 225.)

ABE'S BUGGY RIDES, 2596 Old Philadelphia Pike, offers tours through Amish country in a horse-drawn Amish family carriage. The 7-mile tour stops at an Amish home or a Mennonite craft and bake shop. A petting zoo also is offered. **Hours:** Mon.-Sat. 9-5 (also Sat. 5-6), Apr.-Dec. (weather permitting). Hours vary; phone ahead. **Cost:** $10-$60; $5-$15 (ages 3-12). Cash only. **Phone:** (717) 392-1794. ⊞

PLAIN AND FANCY FARM, 1.5 mi. e. on SR 340 to 3121 Old Philadelphia Pike, is an interpretive cultural center where visitors can enjoy buggy rides and tours, explore crafts and gift shops and dine on fresh, farm-to-table Amish cuisine. **Hours:** Open daily 9-7:30, June-Oct.; 10-7, mid-Mar. through May 31 and Nov.-Dec. **Cost:** Varies per activity. **Phone:** (717) 768-4400. ⑪

Amish Country Homestead, 3121 Old Philadelphia Pike at Plain and Fancy Farm, is furnished to reflect the Amish way of life. Guided tours lasting 45 minutes take visitors through nine rooms on two stories and an adjoining one-room Amish school. Background information is provided on such topics as plain clothes, education and living without electricity.

Hours: Daily 10-4, mid-Mar. through Nov. 30; Sat. (also Dec. 26-Dec. 31) 10-4, in Dec. Last tour begins at closing. Closed Thanksgiving and Christmas. Phone ahead to confirm schedule. **Cost:** $11.95; $8.50 (ages 4-12). Combination ticket with The Amish Experience Theater $21.95; $15.95 (ages 4-12). **Phone:** (717) 768-8400, ext. 210.

Amish Country Tours at Plain & Fancy Farm depart 1.5 mi. e. on SR 340 from 3121 Old Philadelphia Pike. Narrated bus tours lasting 1.5 hours include views of scenic Amish farmlands in eastern Lancaster County and Amish-related stops. Tours include a 3-hour Amish VIP (Visit In Person) tour where visitors can observe and talk with the Amish at three different properties. Tours are limited to 14 passengers.

The VIP tour is limited to 14 passengers and is not recommended for young children. **Hours:** Farmland tour departs daily at 10, noon, 2 and 4, Mar.-Nov. VIP tour departs Mon.-Sat. at 5, Apr.-Nov. 30. **Cost:** Farmland tour $28.95; $15.95 (ages 0-12). VIP tour $55.95. Reservations are recommended. **Phone:** (717) 768-8400, ext. 210.

The Amish Experience Theater, 3121 Old Philadelphia Pike at Plain and Fancy Farm, features a 30-minute multimedia presentation about a teenager who must choose between remaining in the modern, outside world or joining the Amish church and adopting the Amish lifestyle. Events from Amish history are re-created using special effects.

Hours: Presentations are given daily 10-5, mid-Mar. through Nov. 30; Sat. (also Dec. 26-31) 10-5, in Dec. Closed Thanksgiving and Christmas. **Cost:** $11.95; $8.50 (ages 4-12). Combination ticket with

Amish Country Homestead $21.95; $15.95 (ages 4-12). **Phone:** (717) 768-8400, ext. 210.

AMISH COUNTRY MOTEL (717)768-8396 **42**

◆◆ Motel $84-$120 **Address:** 3013 Old Philadelphia Pike (Rt 340) 17505 **Location:** On SR 340, 1 mi e. Located in a quiet rural area. **Facility:** 25 units. 1-2 stories (no elevator), exterior corridors. **Terms:** closed 11/30-3/12, cancellation fee imposed. **Pool(s):** outdoor.

🏊 🛜 ✕ 🍴 💻 / SOME UNITS 🐾 📶

AMISH VIEW INN & SUITES 717/768-1162 **41**

◆◆◆ Hotel
Rates not provided

Address: 3125 Old Philadelphia Pike (Rt 340) 17505 **Location:** On SR 340, 2 mi e. Located in a semi-rural area. **Facility:** 86 units, some two bedrooms and efficiencies. 3 stories, interior corridors. **Pool(s):** heated indoor. **Activities:** hot tub, game room, exercise room. **Guest Services:** coin laundry. **Featured Amenity: full hot breakfast.** (See ad p. 175.)

SAVE ⑪ 🛜 🔲 BIZ HS 🛜 ✕ 🍴 💻 📶

BIRD-IN-HAND FAMILY INN (717)768-8271 **44**

◆◆ Hotel $69-$189 **Address:** 2740 Old Philadelphia Pike (Rt 340) 17505 **Location:** On SR 340, 0.3 mi e. **Facility:** 125 units. 1-3 stories, interior/exterior corridors. **Terms:** cancellation fee imposed. **Pool(s):** heated outdoor, heated indoor. **Activities:** hot tub, miniature golf, tennis, playground, game room, exercise room. **Guest Services:** coin laundry.

⑪ 🛜 BIZ 🛜 ✕ 🍴 💻 / SOME UNITS 📶

BIRD-IN-HAND VILLAGE INN & SUITES 717/768-1535 **43**

◆◆◆ Historic Country Inn. Rates not provided. **Address:** 2695 Old Philadelphia Pike (Rt 340) 17505 **Location:** Center. **Facility:** This restored 1852 inn offers rooms distinctively appointed with period furnishings. The newer units across the street have the ambience of a modern boutique hotel. 24 units, some two bedrooms and efficiencies. 2-3 stories (no elevator), interior/exterior corridors. **Terms:** age restrictions may apply.

⑪ BIZ 🛜 ✕ 🍴 / SOME UNITS 📶 💻

LEAMAN'S LANCASTER COUNTRY LODGING 717/656-7483 **40**

◆◆◆ Bed & Breakfast $69-$89 **Address:** 155 Glenbrook Rd 17505 **Location:** Jct SR 23 and 772 W, 1 mi w on SR 772 (Glenbrook Rd). Located in a rural area. **Facility:** This cozy home with relaxed country-style furnishings is beautifully landscaped and you're free to wander through the 40 acres of farmland just across the street. 5 units. 1 story, interior corridors. **Terms:** cancellation fee imposed.

🛜 ✕ ⓩ / SOME UNITS 🐾

WHERE TO EAT

PLAIN & FANCY FARM RESTAURANT
717/768-4400 **23**

◆◆ Regional American Family Dining $7-$19

AAA Inspector Notes: Stop and treat yourself and your family to a traditional Pennsylvania Dutch dinner. Sit down to a family-style offering of fried chicken, roast beef, chicken pie, real mashed potatoes, dried corn, apple dumplings and the like. Wood accents add to the rustic charm of the barn-like dining room. Before you leave, check out the homemade wares in the large gift shop near the entry. **Address:** 3121 Old Philadelphia Pike (Rt 340) 17505 **Location:** On SR 340, 2 mi e; at Plain & Fancy Farm. Ⓛ Ⓓ CALL ⑤Ⓜ

BIRDSBORO (A-8) pop. 5,163, elev. 163'

DANIEL BOONE HOMESTEAD, 1 mi. n. off US 422 on Daniel Boone Rd., was the 1734 birthplace of the famous frontiersman. The 579-acre site incorporates the restored 10-room stone house built 1730-1800 by the Boones and other subsequent families. The house is furnished with mid-18th-century Pennsylvania furniture.

Included on the site are a restored blacksmith shop, sawmill and barn, the 1737 Bertolet log house, hiking trails and a visitor center. A 15-minute orientation video also is available at the visitor center. **Time:** Allow 1 hour minimum. **Hours:** Grounds Tues.-Fri. 9-5, Sat. 10-5, Sun. 11-5. Visitor center and historic area Tues.-Sat. 10-4, Sun. noon-4, mid-June to Aug.; Fri.-Sat. 10-4, Sun. noon-4, Mar. to mid-June and Sept.-Dec.; Sat. 10-4, Sun. noon-4, rest of year. Phone to confirm tour times. Closed major holidays. **Cost:** Self-guiding historic grounds $3; free (ages 0-2). Historic grounds and guided house tour $6; $5.50 (ages 65+ and inactive military); $4 (ages 5-11); free (active military with ID). **Phone:** (610) 582-4900. 🛅

BLAIRSVILLE (G-3) pop. 3,412, elev. 1,017'

BLAIRSVILLE HISTORICAL SOCIETY, 116 E. Campbell St., is housed in a 1909 home that now showcases local history with its large collection of antiques, which includes books, decorative items, dolls, furniture, kitchen items, maps, photographs and wedding dresses. **Time:** Allow 20 minutes minimum. **Hours:** Tues.-Sat. 10-2 and by appointment. Closed major holidays. **Cost:** Donations. **Phone:** (724) 459-0580. 🔘

HAMPTON INN & SUITES BLAIRSVILLE   (724)459-5920

♦♦♦ **Hotel** $129-$199 **Address:** 1762 Old William Penn Hwy 15717 **Location:** Jct US 119 and 22, just s. Adjacent to a golf course. **Facility:** 93 units. 5 stories, interior corridors. **Terms:** 1-7 night minimum stay, cancellation fee imposed. **Pool(s):** heated indoor. **Activities:** hot tub, exercise room. **Guest Services:** valet and coin laundry.

AAA Benefit: Members save 5% or more!

🔢 CALL 🅖 🈁 BIZ HS 🛜 🅱 🖼 💻

WHERE TO EAT

PIE CUCINA RISTORANTE   724/459-7145

♦♦ Italian. Casual Dining. $15-$27 **AAA Inspector Notes:** The décor is simple yet you'll take one step inside and know this is the perfect spot to dine with someone special. The family-run establishment takes special care in preparing meals with distinctive sauces. The menu features traditional favorites such as hand-tossed pizzas, calzones and pasta dishes. The dinner menu offers items like bruschetta, calamari, fresh salads, Alfredo or tomato basil pastas, veal mozzarella and chicken Parmesan. **Features:** full bar. **Address:** 181 Brown St 15717 **Location:** 1 mi e on W Market, 0.3 mi e on S East Ln, just e. L D CALL 🅖

Visit the AAA and CAA senior driving websites for valuable resources

BLAKESLEE (F-11) elev. 1,677'

• Part of Pocono Mountains Area — see map p. 371

RECREATIONAL ACTIVITIES

Skiing and Snowboarding

• **Jack Frost Mountain** is off I-80 exit 284, 6 mi. s. on CR 115 to SR 940 at 1 Jack Frost Mountain Rd., following signs. Snow tubing also is available. **Hours:** Ski resort Mon.-Fri. 9-4, Sat.-Sun. 8-4, mid-Dec. to mid-Mar. Snow tubing park (weather permitting) Fri.-Sun. 10-4, mid-Jan. to late Feb.; Sat.-Sun. 10-4, late Dec. to mid-Jan. Closed Christmas. Phone ahead to confirm schedule. **Phone:** (570) 443-8425.

BEST WESTERN INN AT BLAKESLEE-POCONO
(570)646-6000

Hotel $77-$250

AAA Benefit: Members save up to 20%!

Address: 107 Parkside Ave 18610 **Location:** I-80 exit 284, just n. **Facility:** 85 units. 3 stories, interior corridors. **Pool(s):** heated indoor. **Activities:** sauna. **Guest Services:** coin laundry. **Featured Amenity:** full hot breakfast.

SAVE CALL 🅖 🈁 🛜 🖂 💻 / SOME UNITS 🐾 🅱

BLAWNOX pop. 1,432

• Hotels & Restaurants map & index p. 348
• Part of Pittsburgh area — see map p. 326

COMFORT INN & SUITES   (412)963-0600 62

♦♦♦ **Hotel** $99-$249

Address: 180 Gamma Dr 15238 **Location:** I-76 (Pennsylvania Tpke) exit 48, 3.3 mi s; SR 28 (RIDC) exit 10. **Facility:** 223 units, some efficiencies. 2 stories, interior corridors. **Pool(s):** heated indoor. **Activities:** exercise room. **Guest Services:** valet and coin laundry, area transportation. **Featured Amenity:** breakfast buffet. (See ad p. 365.)

SAVE 🈁 BIZ HS 🛜 🖂 💻 / SOME UNITS 🅱 🖼

BLOOMSBURG (F-9) pop. 14,855, elev. 530'

Its location on the Susquehanna River helped Bloomsburg emerge as an important player in the region's flourishing 19th-century iron industry. Today's downtown historic district features some 650 buildings that represent a variety of architectural styles from earlier eras.

CHILDREN'S MUSEUM is at 2 W. 7th St. A variety of changing interactive exhibits about science, the arts and humanities encourages hands-on learning for school-age children. Exhibits include an interactive coal mine, an Egyptian tomb and a giant bird'snest. A seasonal outdoor butterfly garden is featured. Special programs and workshops are held throughout the year. **Time:** Allow 2 hours minimum.

Hours: Tues.-Sat. 10-4. Closed major holidays. Phone ahead to confirm schedule. **Cost:** $6; free (ages 0-2). **Phone:** (570) 389-9206.

BUDGET HOST PATRIOT INN (570)387-1776

Motel
$67-$110

Address: 6305 Columbia Blvd 17815 **Location:** I-80 exit 241A eastbound; exit 241 westbound, 0.5 mi s on US 11. Located in a commercial area. **Facility:** 59 units. 1 story, interior corridors. **Guest Services:** valet laundry.

COMFORT SUITES BLOOMSBURG (570)387-9100

Hotel
$139-$159

Address: 120 Plaza Dr 17815 **Location:** I-80 exit 232 (SR 42), just e; in Buckhorn Plaza. **Facility:** 82 units, some efficiencies. 3 stories, interior corridors. **Pool(s):** heated indoor. **Activities:** game room, exercise room. **Guest Services:** valet and coin laundry. **Featured Amenity:** breakfast buffet.

ECONO LODGE (570)387-0490

Hotel
$55-$150

Address: 189 Columbia Mall Dr 17815 **Location:** I-80 exit 232 (SR 42), just n. Adjacent to Columbia Mall. **Facility:** 80 units. 2 stories (no elevator), interior corridors. **Activities:** limited exercise equipment. **Guest Services:** coin laundry. **Featured Amenity:** continental breakfast.

HAMPTON INN BLOOMSBURG (570)380-1020

Hotel
$119-$209

AAA Benefit: Members save 5% or more!

Address: 255 Paper Mill Rd 17815 **Location:** I-80 exit 236 eastbound; exit 236A westbound, just sw. **Facility:** 70 units. 3 stories, interior corridors. **Terms:** 1-7 night minimum stay, cancellation fee imposed. **Pool(s):** heated indoor. **Activities:** hot tub, exercise room. **Guest Services:** valet and coin laundry.

THE INN AT TURKEY HILL (570)387-1500

Country Inn $140-$250 **Address:** 991 Central Rd 17815 **Location:** I-80 exit 236 eastbound; exit 236A westbound, just s. Located in a quiet area. **Facility:** This is the place to stay as this charming property is convenient to the highway but feels miles away with shady trees and a duck pond. A fine dining restaurant and casual brew pub also are on site. 23 units. 1-2 stories (no elevator), interior/exterior corridors. **Terms:** check-in 4 pm. **Dining:** The Farmhouse at Turkey Hill, Turkey Hill Brewing Company Pub & Grille, see separate listings. **Guest Services:** valet laundry.

WHERE TO EAT

THE FARMHOUSE AT TURKEY HILL 570/387-1500

Regional American. Fine Dining. $18-$38 **AAA Inspector Notes:** This is a great stop for a relaxing meal with an interesting menu combining fresh and organic produce from area farms and some specialty and exotic game meats. Menus change regularly and dessert is a highlight of the meal. Sit on the enclosed porch and enjoy the serene view of the duck pond and gardens. **Features:** full bar. **Reservations:** suggested. **Address:** 991 Central Rd 17815 **Location:** I-80 exit 236 eastbound; exit 236A westbound, just s; in The Inn at Turkey Hill.

LA FONTANA RISTORANTE & PIZZERIA 570/245-0057

Italian. Casual Dining. $8-$23 **AAA Inspector Notes:** Located in the historic downtown area, you can find this casual Italian spot offering up all types of pizzas, pastas, strombolis, calzones and homemade soups. Feel free to dine inside or outdoors on the patio when weather permits. For those on the go, feel free to call ahead for take-out and delivery. **Features:** full bar. **Address:** 105 W Main St 17815 **Location:** Between Market St and Murray Ave; downtown. **Parking:** street only.

MARLEY'S BREWERY & GRILLE 570/784-9600

Comfort Food Pizza. Casual Dining. $8-$21 **AAA Inspector Notes:** This family-friendly restaurant offers more than just great beer; the menu offers a good range of familiar salads, sandwiches, burgers, steaks and pastas as well as brick-oven pizzas. **Features:** full bar, patio dining, happy hour. **Address:** 1323 Columbia Blvd 17815 **Location:** 1 mi w of SR 487.

TURKEY HILL BREWING COMPANY PUB & GRILLE 570/387-8422

American. Casual Dining. $10-$19 **AAA Inspector Notes:** Whether you're a family, couple or just someone looking for a meal, you won't be disappointed at this casual eatery set in a renovated farmhouse. The hand-crafted beers on tap are a specialty of the area. The menu focuses on American fare, and I highly recommend the Buffalo chicken dip as a hearty starter. **Features:** beer & wine. **Address:** 991 Central Rd 17815 **Location:** I-80 exit 236 eastbound; exit 236A westbound, just s; in The Inn at Turkey Hill.

BLUE BELL pop. 6,067

- Hotels & Restaurants map & index p. 274
- Part of Philadelphia area — see map p. 230

BLUE BELL INN 215/646-2010 (82)

Steak Seafood. Fine Dining. $11-$40 **AAA Inspector Notes:** *Historic.* The charming inn, which was marked on George Washington's military maps of 1777, has been steadfast with its hospitality. Today guests enjoy well-prepared food, such as prime rib with asparagus, served in a traditional American atmosphere. **Features:** full bar, happy hour. **Reservations:** suggested. **Address:** 601 Skippack Pike 19422 **Location:** SR 73, 1.5 mi e of jct US 202.

BLUE MOUNTAIN

KENMAR MOTEL   (717)423-5915

🔻🔻 🔻
Motel
$65-$90

Address: 17788 Cumberland Hwy 17240 **Location:** I-76 (Pennsylvania Tpke) exit 201, just e on SR 997 N. Located in a quiet area. **Facility:** 15 units. 1 story, exterior corridors. **Terms:** 3 day cancellation notice. **Featured Amenity: continental breakfast.**

 / SOME UNITS

BOALSBURG (G-6) pop. 3,722, elev. 1,096'

An early stagecoach stop founded in 1808, Boalsburg has retained much of its original architecture and street layout.

Boalsburg lays claim as the site of the original Memorial Day, after a group of women honored those who died during the Civil War during a ceremony in 1864. Warrenton, Va., Charleston, S.C. and Savannah, Ga. also claim that they were the first to begin the holiday to honor soldiers who died in battle.

Shopping areas: The Village of Boalsburg offers taverns and quaint shops filled with antiques, art, flowers, crafts, gifts and collectibles. Many of the shops are in historic houses.

COLUMBUS CHAPEL AND BOAL MANSION MUSEUM is at 163 Boal Estate Dr. The Columbus Chapel was imported from Spain—where it was part of the Columbus Castle in Asturias—in 1909 by Col. Theodore Davis Boal, the husband of a descendant of Christopher Columbus. It features an admiral's desk said to have belonged to Columbus, 15th- and 16th-century artwork by European masters and two pieces of the cross on which Jesus Christ died. The mansion displays an array of Boal family items, including furnishings, papers, portraits, tools and weapons.

Time: Allow 1 hour, 30 minutes minimum. **Hours:** Tues.-Sat. 10-5, Sun. noon-5, mid-June through Labor Day; Tues.-Sun. 1:30-5, early May to mid-June and day after Labor Day-Oct. 31. Phone ahead to confirm schedule. **Cost:** $10; $6 (ages 7-11). **Phone:** (814) 466-6210.

PENNSYLVANIA MILITARY MUSEUM, on S. Atherton St. (US 322 Bus. Rte.), showcases the state's 20th-century military history. The 28th Infantry Division Shrine honors the Pennsylvania National Guard's service in World Wars I and II. A walking path, large-scale artifacts, vehicles and memorials also are displayed.

Time: Allow 1 hour, 30 minutes minimum. **Hours:** Wed.-Sat. 10-4, Sun. noon-4, Mar. 12-Nov. 30. Closed major holidays except Memorial Day, July 4th and Labor Day. Closed Thanksgiving. Phone ahead to confirm schedule. **Cost:** $6; $5.50 (ages

65+); $4 (ages 3-11); free (military with ID). **Phone:** (814) 466-6263.

DUFFY'S TAVERN   814/466-6241

🔻🔻 American. Casual Dining. $6-$29 **AAA Inspector Notes:** *Historic.* Opened in 1819, this tavern used to be a stopping point for weary travelers and local patrons. Still open today in the historic section of town, the eatery has the remnants of the early days. The large menu will satisfy any appetite. **Features:** full bar. **Reservations:** suggested. **Address:** 113 E Main St 16827 **Location:** Between N Church and Academy sts; in historic area. ⬜L⬜ ⬜D⬜

BOILING SPRINGS pop. 3,225

BOILING SPRINGS TAVERN   717/258-3614

🔻🔻🔻 American. Fine Dining. $10-$24 **AAA Inspector Notes:** *Historic.* Enjoy fresh fish and aged Western beef in this 1832 Federal-style inn constructed of native limestone. The quaint, historic spot is a nice place for a relaxed meal. Be sure to try the wildberry tart, one of the refreshing, wonderful desserts. **Features:** full bar. **Reservations:** suggested. **Address:** First & Front sts 17007 **Location:** On the square; downtown. ⬜L⬜ ⬜D⬜

BOYERTOWN (H-11) pop. 4,055, elev. 386'

Known to the Pennsylvania Dutch who settled here as Boyer's Eck or Boyer's Corner, this community prospered because of its foundries and the craftsmen who manufactured caskets and vehicles. Today its orchards attract visitors.

Shopping areas: Several antique shops can be found in various areas throughout the town.

BOYERTOWN MUSEUM OF HISTORIC VEHICLES, 85 S. Walnut St., displays southeastern Pennsylvania vehicles from the 18th-, 19th- and 20th centuries. Sleighs, carriages, wagons, motorcycles and bicycles are exhibited as well as electric-, steam- and gas-powered vehicles and the tools used to assemble them. A collection of early and contemporary electric vehicles, examples of roadside architecture and a 19th century carriage factory also are displayed. **Time:** Allow 1 hour minimum. **Hours:** Tues.-Sun. 9:30-4. Closed major holidays. **Cost:** $6; $5 (ages 60+); $4 (ages 6-18). **Phone:** (610) 367-2090.

TWIN TURRETS INN   610/367-4513

🔻🔻🔻🔻 Historic Bed & Breakfast $124-$154 **Address:** 11 E Philadelphia Ave 19512 **Location:** SR 100 exit Boyertown, 1 mi w on SR 73; downtown. **Facility:** A Victorian home built in 1865, this inn is furnished with beautiful antiques but also offers modern amenities. 10 units. 3 stories (no elevator), interior corridors.
⬜↑+⬜ ⬜BIZ⬜ 🛜 ⬜✕⬜

BRADFORD (C-4) pop. 8,770, elev. 1,437'
• Restaurants p. 72

Bradford was settled on the Tunungwant Creek in 1823 in the region known as the Tuna Valley but wasn't charted as a city until 1879. In 1871 oil was discovered and the price of land soared from 6.25 cents to $1,000 an acre. In less than 25 years the city boomed; residents sank wells everywhere. As the oil industry expanded in the area, the town became the world's first billion-dollar oil field. Bradford also has become a leader in manufacturing: Timber products, wooden toys, electronic parts, case knives and Zippo lighters are produced.

Of particular interest in the Downtown Bradford National Historic District are the Hooker-Fulton Building, a prime example of Art Deco architecture, and the still-operating Cline Oil Well on Main Street. Students at the University of Pittsburgh at Bradford campus can choose from more than 40 majors; phone (814) 362-7500. Bromeley Family Theater, 300 Campus Dr., presents a series of touring productions; phone (814) 362-5113 for ticket information.

One mile north of Bolivar Drive on the Seaward Avenue extension is Crook Farm, a collection of restored 19th-century buildings that includes a farmhouse, barn, carpenter shop, one-room schoolhouse, train depot and nature trails. Guided tours are given on Monday, Wednesday and Friday; phone (814) 362-3906 for information.

The Marilla Trail System is an interconnecting system of five trails: Marilla Bridges, Marilla Springs, Indian Pipe, White Pine and Hidden Valley. These trails offer raised boardwalks, covered bridges, wildlife viewing, fishing, canoeing and scenic hiking along Marilla Reservoir. Bradford is a launching site for hiking excursions within the Allegheny National Forest *(see place listing p. 46 and Recreation Areas Chart)* and New York's Allegany State Park, where there are more than 600 miles of trails available year-round.

Allegheny National Forest Visitors Bureau: 80 E. Corydon St., Bradford, PA 16701. **Phone:** (814) 368-9370 or (800) 473-9370.

PENN-BRAD OIL MUSEUM, 901 South Ave., features a 72-foot-tall wooden standard drilling rig used in developing the first billion-dollar oil field. A museum displays items from the town's oil-producing days in the 1890s, including a vintage player piano. **Time:** Allow 1 hour minimum. **Hours:** Tours are given Mon.-Fri. 9-4, Sat. 9-2. **Cost:** $5; $4.50 (ages 65+); free (ages 0-11 with adult). **Phone:** (814) 362-1955.

ZIPPO/CASE MUSEUM, 1932 Zippo Dr., displays hundreds of rare production Zippo models and prototypes; interactive displays; and ZAC (Zippo and Case), an audio/kinetic ball machine with sound and motion. Visitors can watch technicians repair lighters at the Zippo Repair Clinic. **Hours:** Mon.-Sat. 9-5, Sun. 11-4. Closed Jan. 1, Easter, Thanksgiving and Christmas. **Cost:** Free. **Phone:** (814) 368-1932.

BEST WESTERN PLUS BRADFORD INN
(814)362-4501

Hotel
$105-$145

AAA Benefit: Members save up to 20%!

Address: 100 Davis St S 16701 **Location:** US 219 exit Forman St southbound, just w to Davis St, then 0.3 mi s; exit Elm St northbound, just w. **Facility:** 112 units. 3 stories, interior/exterior corridors. **Pool(s):** heated outdoor. **Activities:** exercise room. **Featured Amenity:** breakfast buffet.

COMFORT INN-BRADFORD   (814)368-6772

▼▼▼ Hotel $79-$150 **Address:** 76 Elm St 16701 **Location:** US 219 exit Forman St southbound, just w to Davis St, then 0.3 mi s; exit Elm St northbound, just w. **Facility:** 48 units. 2 stories, interior corridors. **Amenities:** safes. **Pool(s):** heated indoor. **Activities:** hot tub.

GLENDORN   (814)362-6511

▼▼▼
Historic Country Inn
$450-$2275

Address: 1000 Glendorn Dr 16701 **Location:** US 219 exit Forman St, just s on Mechanic St, then 4.3 mi w on W Corydon St. Located in a quiet secluded area. **Facility:** Set on a forested 1,280-acre family estate, this lodge offers heated sidewalks, expansive grounds and guest rooms and private cottages with a rustic yet luxurious ambience. 14 units, some cabins and cottages. 1-2 stories (no elevator), interior/exterior corridors. **Terms:** 2 night minimum stay - seasonal and/or weekends, 30 day cancellation notice-fee imposed, resort fee. **Pool(s):** heated outdoor. **Activities:** steamroom, fishing, tennis, cross country skiing, snowmobiling, sledding, ice skating, recreation programs, bicycles, game room, lawn sports, picnic facilities, trails, spa. **Guest Services:** valet laundry. **Featured Amenity:** full hot breakfast.

HOLIDAY INN EXPRESS BRADFORD   814/362-7090

▼▼▼ Hotel. Rates not provided. **Address:** 30 Tarport Dr Ext 16701 **Location:** US 219 exit Forman St, just w. **Facility:** 75 units, some two bedrooms. 3 stories, interior corridors. **Pool(s):** heated indoor. **Activities:** limited exercise equipment. **Guest Services:** coin laundry.

THE MOUNTAIN LAUREL INN   (814)362-8006

▼▼▼ Historic Bed & Breakfast $105-$135 **Address:** 136 Jackson Ave 16701 **Location:** US 219 exit Forman St southbound, just w to Davis St, then 0.3 mi n; exit Elm St northbound, just w to Davis St, then 0.7 mi n. **Facility:** This meticulously maintained 1894 home features Greek and Colonial Revival architecture. 7 units. 3 stories (no elevator), interior corridors. *Bath:* shower only. **Parking:** on-site and street. **Terms:** check-in 4 pm, age restrictions may apply, 5 day cancellation notice-fee imposed.

Ask about on-the-go vehicle battery testing and replacement

WHERE TO EAT

BEEFEATERS   814/362-9717

♦♦ American. Casual Dining. $7-$24 **AAA Inspector Notes:** Composed of three busy dining rooms in a restored library building, this restaurant is in the city's historic district. The roast beef dinner, a specialty, swims in au jus and comes with a creamy baked potato. Beef on a wick also is flavorful. **Features:** full bar. **Address:** 27 Congress St 16701 **Location:** Just s of Main St; corner of E Corydon St; center. **Parking:** street only. D

BREEZEWOOD

BEST WESTERN PLAZA INN   (814)735-4352

Motel
$80-$100

AAA Benefit: Members save up to 20%!

Address: 16407 Lincoln Hwy 15533 **Location:** I-76 (Pennsylvania Tpke) exit 161, just w on US 30; I-70 exit 147. **Facility:** 82 units. 2 stories (no elevator), exterior corridors. **Pool(s):** outdoor.

SAVE 🍴 🏊 BIZ 🛜 ✕ 💻 / SOME UNITS 🍴 HS 🚫 🖨

HOLIDAY INN EXPRESS BREEZEWOOD   (814)735-7666

♦♦♦ Hotel $126-$155 **Address:** 16503 Lincoln Hwy 15533 **Location:** I-76 (Pennsylvania Tpke) exit 161, just w; I-70 exit 147, just e on US 30. **Facility:** 79 units. 4 stories, interior corridors. **Pool(s):** heated outdoor. **Activities:** exercise room.

🍴 CALL 🅼 🏊 BIZ HS 🛜 ✕ 💻 / SOME UNITS 🚫 🖨

QUALITY INN-BREEZE MANOR   (814)735-4311

♦♦ Motel $84-$150 **Address:** 16621 Lincoln Hwy 15533 **Location:** I-76 (Pennsylvania Tpke) exit 161, just e on US 30. **Facility:** 50 units. 1-2 stories (no elevator), exterior corridors. **Pool(s):** outdoor. **Guest Services:** coin laundry.

🍴 CALL 🅼 🏊 💻 / SOME UNITS 🚫 🖨

WILTSHIRE MOTEL   814/735-4361

♦ Motel. Rates not provided. **Address:** 140 S Breezewood Rd 15533 **Location:** I-76 (Pennsylvania Tpke) exit 161, just w on US 30; I-70 exit 147. **Facility:** 12 units. 1 story, exterior corridors.

🍴 🛜 💻 / SOME UNITS 🐕

BREINIGSVILLE (G-11) pop. 4,138, elev. 407'

WINERIES

• **Clover Hill Vineyards & Winery** is 2.7 mi. w. of SR 100 via Schantz Rd., then e. on Newtown Rd. **Hours:** Free tastings Mon.-Sat. 10-5:30, Sun. noon-5. Closed major holidays. Phone ahead to confirm schedule. **Cost:** Tastings free. Tour by appointment, $10. **Phone:** (610) 395-2468.

• **Vynecrest Winery** is at 172 Arrowhead Ln. **Hours:** Daily 11-5. Tours are available some weekends, May-Aug.; phone ahead. **Phone:** (610) 398-7525 or (800) 361-0725. GT

BRIDGEVILLE pop. 5,148

• **Hotels & Restaurants map & index p. 348**
• **Part of Pittsburgh area — see map p. 326**

HAMPTON INN   (412)319-7706 101

♦♦♦ Hotel $139-$189 **Address:** 150 Old Pond Rd 15017 **Location:** I-79 exit 54 (SR 50), just w. **Facility:** 84 units. 5 stories, interior corridors. **Terms:** 1-7 night minimum stay, cancellation fee imposed. **Pool(s):** heated indoor. **Activities:** limited exercise equipment. **Guest Services:** valet and coin laundry.

AAA Benefit: Members save 5% or more!

🏊 BIZ 🛜 ✕ 🚫 🖨 💻

HOLIDAY INN EXPRESS   412/914-2000 102

♦♦♦ Hotel
Rates not provided

Address: 3053 Washington Pike 15017 **Location:** I-79 exit 54 (SR 50), just e. **Facility:** 70 units. 3 stories, interior corridors. **Terms:** check-in 4 pm. **Pool(s):** heated indoor. **Activities:** exercise room. **Guest Services:** valet laundry. **Featured Amenity:** breakfast buffet. *(See ad p. 366.)*

SAVE 🍴 CALL 🅼 🏊 BIZ HS 🛜 ✕ 🚫 🖨 💻

WHERE TO EAT

KING'S FAMILY RESTAURANT   412/221-1119

♦♦ American. Family Dining. $6-$15 **AAA Inspector Notes:** Fast and friendly service is offered here. The menu is large in size with descriptive menu items and pictures. The restaurant is also known for its ice cream and dessert menu. **Address:** 3049 Washington Pike 15017 **Location:** I-79 exit 54 (SR 50), just s. B L D

LABELLA BEAN COFFEE HOUSE & EATERY   412/257-2202 89

♦ American. Casual Dining. $3-$10 **AAA Inspector Notes:** Located in the downtown area, the restaurant offers great sandwiches and salads, not to mention an over abundance of flavored coffee drinks and teas. It's very busy—make sure you get there early for any meal so you can grab a seat. It's guaranteed to make you smile. Plenty of regulars like this place, too. **Address:** 609 Washington Ave 15017 **Location:** I-79 exit 54 (SR 50), just off exit. **Parking:** on-site (fee) and street. B L

PETERS PLACE   412/221-5000 87

♦♦ American. Casual Dining. $8-$42 **AAA Inspector Notes:** This simply decorated dining room corresponds with the relaxed style of service. Among menu favorites are chicken, steak and seafood dishes. The toasted coconut ice cream ball is a tasty treat. **Features:** full bar. **Reservations:** suggested. **Address:** 1199 Washington Pike 15017 **Location:** I-79 exit 55 (Kirwin Heights), 0.5 mi w on SR 50. L D

TAMBELLINI BRIDGEVILLE RESTAURANT   412/221-5202 88

♦♦ Italian. Casual Dining. $6-$25 **AAA Inspector Notes:** Located one street back from Main Street, this family-run restaurant offers good Italian fare. On the menu are a selection of pasta dishes, as well as meats and fish. Pastas and desserts are made fresh on the premises. **Features:** full bar. **Reservations:** suggested. **Address:** 413 Railroad St 15017 **Location:** I-79 exit 54 (SR 50), 0.3 mi e on Washington Pike, just s on Station St, then just e. **Parking:** street only. L D CALL 🅼

BRISTOL (A-12) pop. 9,726, elev. 21'
• Part of Philadelphia area — see map p. 230

MARGARET R. GRUNDY MEMORIAL MUSEUM, 610 Radcliffe St., was built in the early 19th century. In later years when it served as the family home of Sen. Joseph R. Grundy, it was remodeled and furnished in the Victorian style. Named for the senator's sister, the house overlooks the Delaware River and features an abundance of antiques. **Time:** Allow 30 minutes minimum. **Hours:** Tours depart Tues.-Thurs. and Sat. at 1:15, 2:15 and 3:15, Apr.-Dec.; by appointment rest of year. **Cost:** Free. **Phone:** (215) 788-7891. GT 🔲 Bristol, 257

BROOKVILLE (F-4) pop. 3,924, elev. 1,230'
Brookville was settled about 1800 when Moses Knapp built a mill at the confluence of the North Fork and the Sandy Lick. Growth was slow, but in 1830 the town was named the county seat and settlement began in earnest. Between 1865 and 1874 Brookville had a thriving lumber industry and supplied all the lumber markets in Pittsburgh and along the Ohio. The arrival of the railroad in 1874 augmented industrial and commercial development.

Many of the town's 19th-century buildings have been preserved. Two such buildings are the 1867 three-story Greek Revival and Victorian Jefferson County Courthouse, Main and Pickering streets, and the Marlin Opera House, a 900-seat Italianate hall, which was in use 1884-1902.

PA Great Outdoors Visitors Bureau: 2801 Maplevale Rd., Brookville, PA 15825. **Phone:** (814) 849-5197.

Self-guiding tours: Maps detailing a walking tour of the historic district are available at the local AAA office at 288 Main St.

JEFFERSON COUNTY HISTORY CENTER, 172-176 Main St., features 12 exhibit areas of changing displays and a large Bowdish-style model railroad layout. Living on the Land showcases how the people of Jefferson County have lived, worked and traveled since the days when Native Americans inhabited the area; the exhibit is permanent but the contents will occasionally change. A research room offers genealogical materials, books, maps, newspapers and periodicals. **Time:** Allow 1 hour minimum. **Hours:** Wed.-Sat. noon-5. Bowdish trains run first Sat. of the month 1-3, Mar.-Dec. Closed major holidays. Phone ahead to confirm schedule. **Cost:** $5; $1 (ages 0-12); $7 (family). Fees are charged for some programs and for research. **Phone:** (814) 849-0077.

THE COURTHOUSE GRILLE & PUB   814/849-2557
🟡🟡 American. Casual Dining. $6-$15 **AAA Inspector Notes:** *Historic.* Built in 1871 across from the historic Jefferson County Court House and Jail, the casual restaurant has a fresh look and a new menu. An enticing breakfast menu has been added, along with Italian and Greek specialties, pizza, stromboli, subs, Pittsburgh-style sandwiches and other hometown favorites. **Features:** full bar. **Address:** 209 Main St 15825 **Location:** Center. **Parking:** street only.
B L D

BROWNSVILLE (H-2) pop. 2,331, elev. 380'
Brownsville is part of the Laurel Highlands *(see place listing p. 183).* Dunlap Creek Bridge, built in 1839, was the first cast-iron bridge built in America; it crosses Dunlap Creek, carrying US 40 through downtown Brownsville and connecting High and Market streets. A metal truss bridge known as the Intercounty Bridge was built in 1917; it separates Fayette County from Washington County.

FLATIRON BUILDING HERITAGE CENTER, at 69 Market St., features exhibits about Westward Expansion (National Road era) and the Industrial Era. Regional industrial history is explored with displays about steamboats; the river; the railroad; coal; and the National Road, the first federally funded road. The Frank L. Melega Art Museum features multimedia art representing local industries. The 1830s Flatiron Building, so named for its curved front facade and peaked roof resembling an old-fashioned clothing iron, is of architectural interest.

Time: Allow 1 hour minimum. **Hours:** Mon.-Sun. 10:30-3:30, Sat. 1-4; otherwise by appointment. Phone ahead to confirm schedule. **Cost:** Donations. Reservations are recommended. **Phone:** (724) 785-9331.

NEMACOLIN CASTLE, Brashear and Front sts., was built in 1789. The stately brick mansion features 22 rooms furnished in various periods from Colonial times through the late Victorian era. Ghost tours and Christmas tours are offered seasonally.

Time: Allow 1 hour minimum. **Hours:** Fri.-Sun. noon-5, June-Aug.; Sat.-Sun. noon-5, Easter-May 31 and Sept.-Oct. Ghost tours offered Sat.-Sun. 6-10 p.m., in Oct.; phone for departure times. Christmas tours Fri.-Sun. 9-5, day after Thanksgiving-Christmas; phone for departure times. **Cost:** History tour $8; $4 (ages 0-12). Ghost tour $9; $4 (ages 0-12). Fees may vary. **Phone:** (724) 785-6882.

BRYN ATHYN (A-11) pop. 1,375, elev. 200'
• Part of Philadelphia area — see map p. 230

BRYN ATHYN CATHEDRAL, SR 232 and Cathedral Rd., was constructed 1914-30 by craft guilds for the Swedenborgian faith. The building exemplifies Gothic Revival and English Arts and Crafts architecture and features stained-glass windows. The structure was built to have a bowing effect to represent the course of human growth; the walls have no straight or right angles.

Hours: Mon.- Sat. 9-4, Sun. 1-4. Sun. services at 9:30 and 11. Guided tours are offered 1-4; reservations are recommended. Phone ahead to confirm schedule. **Cost:** Free. **Phone:** (267) 502-4600.

Keep a current AAA/CAA

Road Atlas in every vehicle

BRYN MAWR (B-10) pop. 3,779, elev. 412'
- **Hotels & Restaurants map & index p. 274**
- **Part of Philadelphia area — see map p. 230**

HARRITON HOUSE is 1.2 mi. n. of US 30 on Morris Ave., .5 mi. w. on Old Gulph Rd., then n. on Harriton Rd. to the entrance. Built in 1704, the three-story stone house was the home of Charles Thomson, first secretary of the Continental Congress and designer of the Great Seal of the United States. The house has been restored to its original appearance and has some of the first owner's furnishings. The grounds cover 23 acres.

Guided tours are available by appointment. **Hours:** Wed.-Sat. 10-4. Closed major holidays. Phone ahead to confirm schedule. **Cost:** $5; free (students with ID). **Phone:** (610) 525-0201.

⛩ 🏢 Rosemont, 209

TANGO   610/526-9500 (114)

▼▼▼ American. Casual Dining. $7-$29 **AAA Inspector Notes:** The cozy, intimate restaurant occupies a former baggage depot for the Main Line Railroad, which was constructed in the early 1900s. Representative of contemporary American cuisine are such tasty items as grilled ahi tuna, sashimi and grilled thyme porterhouse steak with Gorgonzola and onions. Seating in the al fresco deck and bar area can be requested seasonally. **Features:** full bar, patio dining, Sunday brunch, happy hour. **Reservations:** suggested, weekends. **Address:** 39 Morris Ave 19010 **Location:** Just n of US 30; center. 🏢 Bryn Mawr, 210. [L] [D] 🏢

BUCKINGHAM (H-12) elev. 234'
- **Part of Philadelphia area — see map p. 230**

WINERIES

- **Buckingham Valley Vineyards and Winery** is at 1521 SR 413. **Hours:** Tours and tastings Tues.-Sat. 11-6, Sun. noon-5. **Phone:** (215) 794-7188. [GT]

BUCKS COUNTY
- **Part of Philadelphia area — see map p. 230**

One of the commonwealth's largest and most historic counties, Bucks County stretches into the countryside surrounding northern Philadelphia. This quiet, wooded region bordering the Delaware River is replete with rolling hills, old stone houses and covered bridges. William Penn named the county for its resemblance to Buckinghamshire in England. An interesting driving tour covering much of Bucks County follows the Delaware River along SR 32.

The narrow, winding streets of Doylestown, once an overnight stagecoach stop between Philadelphia and Easton, capture Bucks County's historic charm, as do Fallsington and Washington Crossing Historic Park.

The Delaware Canal, on which construction was begun in 1817, flows through New Hope, an artists' and writers' colony settled along the river. New Hope is known for its natural settings, book and antiques shops, art galleries and cafes on the banks of both the river and the canal. The town also is home to one of the nation's oldest and most famous

summer theaters, the Bucks County Playhouse; phone (215) 862-2121.

Places and towns in Bucks County listed individually are Bensalem, Bristol, Buckingham, Doylestown, Fallsington, Lahaska, Langhorne, Morrisville, New Hope, Perkasie, Point Pleasant, Quakertown, Southampton and Washington Crossing Historic Park.

Visit Bucks County: 3207 Street Rd., Bensalem, PA 19020. **Phone:** (215) 639-0300 or (800) 836-2825.

BURNHAM pop. 2,054

QUALITY INN & SUITES OF LEWISTOWN
(717)248-4961

Motel
$89-$269

Address: 13015 Ferguson Valley Rd 17009 **Location:** US 322 exit Burnham, just w. **Facility:** 111 units. 2 stories (no elevator), exterior corridors. **Pool(s):** outdoor. **Guest Services:** valet and coin laundry.

[SAVE] 🍽 🍸 🏊 [BIZ] 📶 💻
/SOME UNITS 🛑 🔲 🖨

SUPER 8 BURNHAM-LEWISTOWN
(717)242-8888

Hotel
$60-$129

Address: 12886 Ferguson Valley Rd 17009 **Location:** US 322 exit Burnham, just w; 3.1 mi n of jct US 22 and 522. **Facility:** 57 units. 2 stories, interior corridors. **Terms:** 2 night minimum stay - seasonal and/or weekends, cancellation fee imposed. **Amenities:** safes.

[SAVE] 🍽 📶 ✕ 💻
/SOME UNITS 🛑 🖨

BUSHKILL (F-12) elev. 371'
- **Part of Pocono Mountains Area — see map p. 371**

Bushkill is best known for its scenic waterfalls nestled deep within the wooded mountains.

◆GEM **BUSHKILL FALLS**, 2 mi. n.w. off US 209 on Bushkill Falls Rd., is not just one but eight waterfalls that can be seen via a series of rustic trails and wooden stairs and bridges over a 2-mile area. The falls' source is Bushkill Creek, which descends through the Pocono Mountains to the Delaware River, passing rocky walls, rushing through gorges and over boulders and tumbling over misty precipices along the way. Lush foliage, ferns, mosses, verdant forested areas and wildflowers line the pathways.

A choice of four color-coded trails of varying difficulties provides access to the falls for all levels of hikers. The simplest and shortest, the Green Trail, is a brief 10- to 15-minute trek to a scenic overlook of the Main Falls, which cascades in a 100-foot drop.

Follow the yellow markers for views of the Main Falls, the Lower Gorge Falls, Laurel Glen and the Upper Canyon; plan on spending about 45 minutes. Approximately 75 minutes on the Blue Trail takes hikers to Pennell Falls, while about 2.5 hours (and 2 miles) of hiking on the Red Trail covers all eight cataracts, including Bridal Veil Falls. Benches along the trails provide spots to rest for a bit.

The entrance to the trails is through an indoor wildlife exhibit featuring native animals in dioramas. Families with children will appreciate the 18-hole miniature golf course; paddleboat rides; fishing; and an exhibit showcasing the Native American lifestyle and featuring a life-size replica of a Lenni Lenape longhouse.

Comfortable, non-slip walking shoes and bottles of water are recommended. Pets must remain on a leash and not be left unattended. **Time:** Allow 2 hours minimum. **Hours:** Open daily at 9, Apr.-Oct. (also Nov., weather permitting). Phone for closing times, which vary by season. Last admission 1 hour before closing. Closed Thanksgiving. Phone ahead to confirm schedule. **Cost:** $12.50; $11.50 (ages 62+); $7 (ages 4-10). Fees for activities are additional. **Phone:** (570) 588-6682.

POCONO INDIAN MUSEUM, off I-80 exit 309 then 8 mi. n. on US 209, depicts the lifestyle of the Delaware Indians and displays examples of their bark houses, pottery, food and weapons. Many of the items displayed were unearthed in the Delaware Water Gap area. A 30-minute self-guiding audio tour is available. **Time:** Allow 30 minutes minimum. **Hours:** Daily 10-6. Closed Easter, Thanksgiving and Christmas. Phone ahead to confirm schedule. **Cost:** $6; $3 (ages 6-16). **Phone:** (570) 588-9338.

BUTLER (F-2) pop. 13,757, elev. 1,040'
• Part of Pittsburgh area — see map p. 326

Butler County was named for Revolutionary War hero Gen. Richard Butler, who served with Gen. George Washington.

The county has more than 1,200 farms. Moraine State Park (see Recreation Areas Chart), 8 miles northwest on US 422, offers year-round recreation, including boating, swimming, hiking, biking and cross-country skiing.

Butler County Chamber of Commerce: 101 E. Diamond St., Lower Level Suite 116, P.O. Box 1082, Butler, PA 16003-1082. **Phone:** (724) 283-2222.

ASSOCIATED ARTISTS OF BUTLER COUNTY: THE ART CENTER is downtown at 344 S. Main St. Changing exhibits feature pieces by regional artists who work in various media. Lectures, classes, workshops and annual holiday events also are offered. **Time:** Allow 30 minutes minimum. **Hours:** Wed.-Fri. noon-6, Sat. noon-4. **Cost:** Donations. **Phone:** (724) 283-6922.

THE MARIDON MUSEUM is downtown at 322 N. McKean St. An extensive collection of Chinese and Japanese art includes jade and ivory sculptures, landscape paintings, tapestries, silk prints and ink-on-paper scrolls. An impressive display of Meissen porcelain, with some items dating to the early 18th century, also is featured. The entire collection, which totals more than 1,000 pieces, was acquired and donated by Mary Phillips, a lifelong Butler resident.

Time: Allow 1 hour minimum. **Hours:** Wed.-Sat. 11-4; other times by appointment. Closed major holidays. **Cost:** $4; $3 (ages 60+ and students with ID); free (ages 0-8 with an adult). Reservations are recommended 1 week in advance for guided tours. **Phone:** (724) 282-0123.

BUTLER DAYS INN CONFERENCE CENTER   (724)287-6761
Hotel $89-$399 **Address:** 139 Pittsburgh Rd 16001 **Location:** 2 mi s. **Facility:** 143 units, some efficiencies. 2 stories (no elevator), interior corridors. **Terms:** cancellation fee imposed. **Amenities:** safes. **Pool(s):** heated indoor. **Activities:** exercise room. **Guest Services:** coin laundry.

FAIRFIELD INN & SUITES BY MARRIOTT BUTLER
                                                          (724)283-0009
Hotel $97-$160 **Address:** 200 Fairfield Ln 16001 **Location:** Just sw of jct US 422 and SR 8. **Facility:** 75 units. 3 stories, interior corridors. **Pool(s):** heated indoor. **Activities:** hot tub, exercise room. **Guest Services:** valet and coin laundry.

AAA Benefit: Members save 5% or more!

LOCUST BROOK LODGE   (724)283-8453
Bed & Breakfast $90 **Address:** 179 Eagle Mill Rd 16001 **Location:** 5 mi w on US 422 to jct Eagle Mill Rd, 0.8 mi s; I-79 exit 99, 10 mi e on US 422 to jct Eagle Mill Rd, then 0.8 mi s. Located in a rural setting. **Facility:** 6 units, some two bedrooms. 3 stories (no elevator), interior/exterior corridors. **Terms:** 3 day cancellation notice-fee imposed.

SUPER 8   (724)287-8888
Motel $51-$72 **Address:** 138 Pittsburgh Rd 16001 **Location:** 2 mi s. **Facility:** 66 units. 3 stories (no elevator), interior corridors.

WHERE TO EAT

THE BRICK HOUSE RESTAURANT   724/284-1159
American. Casual Dining. $7-$23 **AAA Inspector Notes:** The distinctive, modern restaurant presents a menu of delicious food. The chef prides himself on the final course: dessert. Public parking is available. **Features:** full bar, happy hour. **Address:** 118 N Main St 16001 **Location:** Center of downtown. **Parking:** street only.

KING'S FAMILY RESTAURANT   724/282-1216
American. Family Dining. $6-$13 **AAA Inspector Notes:** Fast and friendly service is offered here. The menu is large in size with descriptive menu items and pictures. The restaurant is also known for its ice cream and dessert menu. **Address:** 191 New Castle Rd 16001 **Location:** On SR 356. B L D

CAMP HILL pop. 7,888
• Hotels & Restaurants map & index p. 138

RADISSON HOTEL HARRISBURG   (717)763-7117 🟠35

▼▼▼▼ **Hotel** $95-$189 **Address:** 1150 Camp Hill Bypass 17011 **Location:** Jct US 11, 15 and Erford Rd. Located in a quiet area. **Facility:** 250 units. 1-3 stories (no elevator), interior/exterior corridors. **Terms:** cancellation fee imposed. **Amenities:** *Some:* safes. **Pool(s):** outdoor. **Activities:** game room, exercise room. **Guest Services:** valet laundry, area transportation.

[icons]

WHERE TO EAT

FLINCHY'S   717/761-9000 26

▼▼ ▼▼ American. Casual Dining. $7-$32 **AAA Inspector Notes:** This casual spot offers a small, comfortable dining room that includes a long wooden bar and TVs for popular sporting events. The friendly staff provides a neighborhood-like feel and is helpful with making menu recommendations. However, we strongly advise you go with their signature Hot Rock entrées, which are prepared over a 500-degree volcano rock right at your table. **Features:** full bar, patio dining, happy hour. **Address:** 1833 Hummel Ave 17011 **Location:** I-83 exit 42, 0.3 mi n on S 3rd St, then 1.2 mi s. [L] [D]

MASALA BISTRO   717/975-9091 27

▼▼ ▼▼ Indian. Casual Dining. $9-$18 **AAA Inspector Notes:** You always can order from the menu at this casual spot, but if you want to sample a variety of flavors come for the lunchtime buffet. In a heavy commercial area near hotels, this bistro prepares authentic cuisine such as lamb vindaloo and rasmalai. You can surf the Web with free Wi-Fi as you relax in the India-themed setting. **Address:** 3401 Hartzdale Dr, Suite 120 17011 **Location:** I-76 (Pennsylvania Tpke) exit 236 (US 15), 3.5 mi n, then 0.6 mi on Yale Ave. [L] [D]

CANADENSIS

• Hotels & Restaurants map & index p. 373
• Part of Pocono Mountains Area — see map p. 371

BROOKVIEW MANOR INN   (570)595-2451 12

▼▼▼▼ Bed & Breakfast $155-$250 **Address:** 4534 Rt 447 18325 **Location:** Jct SR 390, 1 mi s. **Facility:** Set on a hill in a rural area, this 1911 frame house features a glassed-in sun porch where you can enjoy the beauty of the grounds year-round. 10 units, some two bedrooms. 3 stories (no elevator), interior corridors. **Terms:** 2 night minimum stay - weekends, age restrictions may apply, 14 day cancellation notice. [icons]

CANONSBURG pop. 8,992
• Part of Pittsburgh area — see map p. 326

Washington County Tourism Promotion Agency: 375 Southpointe Blvd., Suite 240, Canonsburg, PA, 15317. **Phone:** (724) 228-5520 or (866) 927-4969.

HILTON GARDEN INN PITTSBURGH/SOUTHPOINTE   (724)743-5000

▼▼▼▼ Hotel $139-$229

🅷 Hilton Garden Inn **AAA Benefit:** Members save 5% or more!

Address: 1000 Corporate Dr 15317 **Location:** I-79 exit 48, 0.3 mi w, then w on Southpointe Blvd. **Facility:** 175 units. 4 stories, interior corridors. **Terms:** 1-7 night minimum stay, cancellation fee imposed. **Amenities:** video games. **Dining:** Jacksons-Restaurant-Rotisserie-Bar, see separate listing. **Pool(s):** heated indoor. **Activities:** exercise room. **Guest Services:** valet and coin laundry.

[icons]

HOLIDAY INN EXPRESS - SOUTHPOINTE   724/743- 4300

▼▼▼ Hotel. Rates not provided. **Address:** 4000 Horizon Vue Dr 15317 **Location:** I-79 exit 48, 1.7 mi w, then w on Consol Dr. **Facility:** 90 units. 3 stories, interior corridors. **Amenities:** *Some:* video games. **Pool(s):** heated indoor. **Activities:** limited exercise equipment. **Guest Services:** valet and coin laundry.

[icons]

HOMEWOOD SUITES PITTSBURGH-SOUTHPOINTE   (724)745-4663

▼▼▼ Extended Stay Hotel $149-$229 **Address:** 3000 Horizon Vue Dr 15317 **Location:** I-79 exit 48, 1.7 mi w, then w on Consol Dr. **Facility:** 113 efficiencies, some two bedrooms. 5 stories, interior corridors. **Terms:** check-in 4 pm, 1-7 night minimum stay, cancellation fee imposed. **Pool(s):** heated indoor. **Activities:** hot tub, exercise room. **Guest Services:** valet and coin laundry, area transportation.

AAA Benefit: Members save 5% or more!

[icons]

WHERE TO EAT

BIG FELLA'S PIZZA, DELI & WING CO   724/873-9222

▼▼ Pizza. Casual Dining. $4-$18 **AAA Inspector Notes:** Featuring a family atmosphere with a friendly staff, the restaurant has a large menu board that specializes in pizzas, hoagies and wings. This is a great place where diners can eat in or take out; delivery is also available. **Features:** beer only. **Address:** 47 E Pike St 15317 **Location:** Center. **Parking:** on-site (fee). [L] [D]

JACKSONS-RESTAURANT-ROTISSERIE-BAR   724/743-5005

▼▼ ▼▼ American. Casual Dining. $9-$55 **AAA Inspector Notes:** Patrons can watch the chefs prepare food through large windows peering into the open kitchen. The establishment's rotisserie-cooked chicken and pork and wood-fired chicken dishes are highly recommended. **Features:** full bar. **Reservations:** suggested. **Address:** 1000 Corporate Dr 15317 **Location:** I-79 exit 48, 0.3 mi w, then w on Southpointe Blvd; in Hilton Garden Inn Pittsburgh/Southpointe. [L] [D]

KING'S FAMILY RESTAURANT   724/745-2552

▼▼ ▼▼ American. Casual Dining. $6-$18 **AAA Inspector Notes:** Fast and friendly service is offered here. The menu is large in size with descriptive menu items and pictures. The restaurant is also known for its ice cream and dessert menu. **Address:** 580 McClelland Rd 15317 **Location:** Just n off US 19. [B] [L] [D]

CARBONDALE pop. 8,891

BEST WESTERN PIONEER PLAZA   (570)536-6020

Hotel
$109-$169

AAA Benefit:
Members save up to 20%!

Address: 25 S Main St 18407 **Location:** Center of downtown. **Facility:** 61 units. 4 stories, interior corridors. **Amenities:** safes. **Activities:** exercise room.

🆂🆅 🍽 📶 📺 CALL 🄶M BIZ
HS 📶 ✉ 🔌 💻
/SOME UNITS 📠

WHERE TO EAT

BEN-MAR RESTAURANT   570/282-5970
♥♥ Italian. Casual Dining. $6-$24 **AAA Inspector Notes:** Expect reasonably priced food served in ample portions at this friendly neighborhood restaurant. Gracious servers contribute to the warm, inviting atmosphere. The varied menu includes American and Italian preparations of seafood, beef, veal and poultry. **Features:** full bar. **Address:** 89 N Main St 18407 **Location:** On US 6; center.

B L D

CARLISLE (H-7) pop. 18,682, elev. 469'
• Hotels p. 78 • Restaurants p. 79

Founded in 1751, Carlisle was the home of James Smith, James Wilson and George Ross, three signers of the Declaration of Independence. The First Presbyterian Church, facing the town's main square, was built 1757-72. In this church the citizens of Carlisle chose Smith, Wilson and Ross to represent them at the Continental Congress. Mary Hays McCauley, the famous Molly Pitcher of the Battle of Monmouth, also lived in Carlisle. A life-size memorial in a cemetery on E. South Street marks her grave.

On Walnut Bottom Road, once a busy thoroughfare, is Two Mile House. This 1820 residence was built in the Federal style and served as a tavern 1826-1857. The house, which was named for its distance from the town square, features twelve rooms, ten of which have a fireplace. Tours may be arranged with the Cumberland County Historical Society (see attraction listing this page); phone (717) 243-3437 or (717) 249-7610.

During the Confederate invasion in 1863 Gen. Richard S. Ewell's infantry corps, some of whom camped on the grounds of Dickinson College, occupied Carlisle for nearly 3 days. After their departure Union troops arrived but soon encountered additional Confederate cavalry under the command of Gen. Jeb Stuart, who ordered their surrender. The Union troops refused and the Confederates shelled the town until an urgent message from Gen. Robert E. Lee arrived directing all Confederate troops to converge on Gettysburg.

Originally founded as a British frontier outpost in 1757 to curb Native American attacks during the French and Indian war, Carlisle Barracks still serves as one of the oldest posts in the Army. The Carlisle Indian School, one of the first non-reservation

schools for Native Americans, was established in 1879 at Carlisle Barracks, which is now the site of the U.S. Army War College. During its 39 years of existence the school attained an enrollment of more than 10,000 students representing all tribes in the United States. Jim Thorpe, winner of the pentathlon and the decathlon in the 1912 Olympic Games, attended the school. Monuments at the courthouse square, High and Hanover streets, honor Thorpe and Cumberland County's Civil War dead.

Activities at the 1,454-acre Kings Gap State Park, off Kings Gap Rd., include hiking (16 miles of trails), hunting and bird-watching. Woodpeckers, great horned owls, white-tailed deer, snakes, turtles and wild turkeys are some of the park's inhabitants. Recreational and environmental education programs are offered throughout the year; the grounds are open daily dawn to dusk; offices are open weekdays 8-4; phone (717) 486-5031.

In nearby Boiling Springs, 🆂🆅 Allenberry Resort Inn and Playhouse is a 57-acre country estate that offers professional Broadway shows. Murder mystery weekends also are offered; phone (717) 254-0766.

Cumberland Valley Visitors Center: 33 W. High St., Carlisle, PA 17013. **Phone:** (888) 513-5130.

CARLISLE BARRACKS is 1 mi. n. on US 11 at 122 Forbes Ave. This was the site of a Revolutionary War forge and is one of the oldest Army posts in the United States. The Hessian Powder Magazine Museum is in the 1777 structure built by Hessian prisoners who had been captured at the Battle of Trenton the previous December. The army post is home to the U.S. Army War College.

Note: All vehicles and individuals must pass through security before entering the barracks gates. **Hours:** Mon.-Fri., 8-4. Closed major holidays except Memorial Day, Independence Day, Labor Day and Veterans Day. Phone ahead to confirm schedule. **Cost:** Free. **Phone:** (717) 245-4101.

CUMBERLAND COUNTY HISTORICAL SOCIETY MUSEUM AND LIBRARY is at 21 N. Pitt St. More than a dozen galleries feature exhibits about Schimmel woodcarvings, the Carlisle Indian School and other topics that change throughout the year. The library contains genealogy resources and archival materials about local history. Docents are available to answer questions during museum hours. **Hours:** Tues.-Fri. 10-4, Mon. 4-8, Sat. 10-2. Closed major holidays. Phone ahead to confirm schedule. **Cost:** Museum free. Library $5. **Phone:** (717) 249-7610.

THE TROUT GALLERY is at 240 W. High St. in the Emil R. Weiss Center for the Arts on the Dickinson College campus. The gallery houses the college's collections of art, which span from ancient Greek through contemporary periods. It also presents a changing schedule of thematic exhibitions. **Time:** Allow 30 minutes minimum. **Hours:** Tues.-Sat. 10-4.

Closed Thanksgiving and during Christmas and other school holidays. Phone ahead to confirm schedule. **Cost:** Free. **Phone:** (717) 245-8159 or (717) 245-1344.

U.S. ARMY HERITAGE AND EDUCATION CENTER, 950 Soldiers Dr., features archives, a museum a library and a research facility with a focus on U.S. soldier history. Visitors can tour the interactive Soldiers Experience Gallery and other indoor exhibits. On the grounds is the Heritage Trail, a 1-mile trail with two large outdoor exhibits, including tanks, helicopters and displays from all eras of U.S. Army history. **Hours:** Mon.-Sat. 10-5, Sun. 12-5. Closed federal holidays except Memorial Day, July 4, Labor Day and Veterans Day. Research facility closed Sun. **Cost:** Free. **Phone:** (717) 245-3972.

BEST WESTERN CARLISLE   (717)243-6200

Hotel
$79-$199

AAA Benefit: Members save up to 20%!

Address: 1155 Harrisburg Pike 17013 **Location:** I-76 (Pennsylvania Tpke) exit 226, just s. **Facility:** 72 units. 1 story, interior corridors. **Pool(s):** outdoor. **Activities:** exercise room. **Guest Services:** coin laundry.

COMFORT SUITES HOTEL   (717)960-1000
Hotel $89-$169 **Address:** 10 S Hanover St 17013 **Location:** I-81 exit 47, 0.8 mi n on SR 34, just s of square; downtown. Located in a commercial area. **Facility:** 105 units. 5 stories, interior corridors. **Parking:** on-site (fee). **Activities:** exercise room. **Guest Services:** valet laundry.

COUNTRY INN & SUITES BY CARLSON - CARLISLE, PA   (717)241-4900

Hotel
$99-$249

Address: 1529 Commerce Ave 17015 **Location:** I-81 exit 44 (Plainfield Rd), s on SR 465 (Allen Rd), then left. **Facility:** 70 units. 3 stories, interior corridors. **Terms:** cancellation fee imposed. **Pool(s):** heated indoor. **Activities:** hot tub, exercise room. **Guest Services:** valet and coin laundry, area transportation. **Featured Amenity:** full hot breakfast.

DAYS INN CARLISLE-SOUTH   (717)258-4147

Hotel
$79-$175

Address: 101 Alexander Spring Rd 17015 **Location:** I-81 exit 45, just sw. **Facility:** 136 units. 2-3 stories, interior corridors. **Amenities:** Some: safes. **Pool(s):** outdoor. **Activities:** game room, exercise room. **Guest Services:** valet and coin laundry.

FAIRFIELD INN & SUITES BY MARRIOTT CARLISLE   (717)243-2080
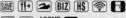
Hotel $94-$154 **Address:** 1528 E Commerce Ave 17015 **Location:** I-81 exit 44 (Plainfield Rd), just s, then just e. **Facility:** 84 units. 5 stories, interior corridors. **Pool(s):** heated indoor. **Activities:** hot tub, exercise room. **Guest Services:** valet and coin laundry.

AAA Benefit: Members save 5% or more!

HAMPTON INN CARLISLE   (717)240-0200

Hotel
$129-$209

AAA Benefit: Members save 5% or more!

Address: 1164 Harrisburg Pike 17013 **Location:** I-76 (Pennsylvania Tpke) exit 226, just n; I-81 exit 52 (US 11) southbound; exit 52B northbound, 0.8 mi s. **Facility:** 97 units. 3 stories, interior corridors. **Terms:** 1-7 night minimum stay, cancellation fee imposed. **Pool(s):** heated indoor. **Activities:** hot tub, exercise room. **Guest Services:** valet and coin laundry. **Featured Amenity:** breakfast buffet.

PHEASANT FIELD BED & BREAKFAST   717/258-0717

Historic Bed & Breakfast
$135-$255

Address: 150 Hickorytown Rd 17015 **Location:** I-76 (Pennsylvania Tpke) exit 226, 0.4 mi n on US 11, 2.3 mi right on S Middlesex Rd, 0.4 mi left on Ridge Dr, then right. Located in a quiet rural area. **Facility:** Once a stop on the Underground Railroad, this 200-year-old Federal-style brick farmhouse offers a serene location near the Appalachian Trail. 8 units. 2 stories (no elevator), interior/exterior corridors. **Terms:** check-in 4 pm, 7 day cancellation notice-fee imposed. **Guest Services:** complimentary laundry.

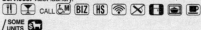

Show you care with AAA/CAA

Gift Membership, perfect for any occasion

RESIDENCE INN BY MARRIOTT HARRISBURG CARLISLE

(717)610-9050

Extended Stay Hotel
$111-$183

Residence Inn *Marriott*

AAA Benefit: Members save 5% or more!

Address: 1 Hampton Ct 17013 **Location:** I-76 (Pennsylvania Tpke) exit 226, just n; I-81 exit 52 (US 11) southbound; exit 52B northbound, 0.8 mi s. **Facility:** 78 units, some two bedrooms, efficiencies and kitchens. 3 stories, interior corridors. **Pool(s):** heated indoor. **Activities:** hot tub, exercise room. **Guest Services:** valet and coin laundry. **Featured Amenity: breakfast buffet.**

 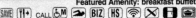

SLEEP INN CARLISLE

(717)249-8863

 Hotel $90-$189 **Address:** 5 E Garland Dr 17013 **Location:** I-81 exit 47 northbound; exit 47A southbound, just ne. **Facility:** 99 units. 3 stories, interior corridors. **Bath:** shower only. **Pool(s):** heated indoor. **Activities:** exercise room. **Guest Services:** valet and coin laundry.

SUPER 8/CARLISLE SOUTH

(717)245-9898

Motel
$49-$160

Address: 100 Alexander Spring Rd 17015 **Location:** I-81 exit 45, just se. **Facility:** 60 units. 3 stories, interior corridors. **Terms:** cancellation fee imposed. **Amenities:** safes. **Featured Amenity: continental breakfast.**

WHERE TO EAT

HOSS'S FAMILY STEAK & SEA

717/258-4468

Steak. Casual Dining. $7-$28 **AAA Inspector Notes:** Folks can bring the whole family to enjoy this restaurant's 100-item salad bar, homemade soups and bread, steaks, fresh seafood and chicken entrees. A children's menu is available. **Address:** 1151 Harrisburg Pike 17013 **Location:** I-76 (Pennsylvania Tpke) exit 226, just s; I-81 exit 52 (US 11) southbound; exit 52B northbound, 1 mi s.

MARKET CROSS PUB AND BREWERY

717/258-1234

American. Casual Dining. $7-$25 **AAA Inspector Notes:** Come to this English-style pub located in the heart of downtown. It offers a variety of American dishes as well as some traditional favorites like shepherd's pie, beef 'n' Guinness and bangers and mash. Wash it all down with one of the hand-crafted beers on tap, which change seasonally. **Features:** full bar, Sunday brunch. **Address:** 113 N Hanover St 17013 **Location:** I-81 exit 47, 1 mi n on SR 34. **Parking:** street only.

NORTH HANOVER GRILLE

717/241-5517

American. Casual Dining. $6-$17 **AAA Inspector Notes:** Buffalo wings are a specialty at this casual bar and restaurant, but its selection of sandwiches and entrées will leave you more than satisfied. Try to get one of the few outdoor tables when weather permits. **Features:** full bar. **Address:** 37 N Hanover St 17013 **Location:** I-81 exit 47, 1 mi n on SR 34. **Parking:** on-site (fee) and street.

PIATTO REGIONAL ITALIAN CUISINE

717/249-9580

Italian. Fine Dining. $16-$34 **AAA Inspector Notes:** Find the quaint restaurant tucked in Carlisle's historic residential section. It's the perfect place for a quiet dinner. Daily specials feature seasonal and local organic produce, and all of the desserts, including the refreshing gelati, are made in house by a pastry chef. **Features:** full bar, patio dining, happy hour. **Address:** 22 W Pomfret St 17013 **Location:** Jct US 11, just w. **Parking:** street only.

RILLO'S

717/243-6141

Italian. Casual Dining. $13-$36 **AAA Inspector Notes:** Rillo's satisfies your craving for Italian food in a comfortable, friendly atmosphere. Start with one or more of the creative appetizers, then move on to a delicious pasta, veal, chicken, seafood or hearty steak dish for your main course. Be sure to save room for a sumptuous dessert. **Features:** full bar. **Reservations:** suggested. **Address:** 60 Pine St 17013 **Location:** I-81 exit 48, 0.4 mi w, then just s on Spruce St.

CARNEGIE pop. 7,972
• Part of Pittsburgh area — see map p. 326

KING'S FAMILY RESTAURANT

412/276-4544

American. Family Dining. $6-$15 **AAA Inspector Notes:** Fast and friendly service is offered here. The menu is large in size with descriptive menu items and pictures. The restaurant is also known for its ice cream and dessert menu. **Address:** 2100 Washington Pike 15106 **Location:** I-376 W exit 64B, 2.3 mi s on SR 50.

CARROLL VALLEY (I-7) pop. 3,876, elev. 607'

RECREATIONAL ACTIVITIES

Skiing and Snowboarding

• **Liberty Mountain Resort** is at 78 Country Club Tr. Snow tubing and summer activities also are offered. **Hours:** Skiing and snowboarding Mon.-Fri. 9 a.m.-10 p.m., Sat.-Sun. 8 a.m.-10 p.m., mid-Dec. to mid-Mar. (8-5, Christmas Eve; noon-10, Christmas), weather permitting. Snow tubing Mon.-Fri. 4-10 (also Fri. 9-4), Sat.-Sun. 8 a.m.-10 p.m. (8-5, Christmas Eve; noon-10, Christmas), weather permitting. Hours are extended day after Christmas-early Jan., Martin Luther King Jr. weekend and Presidents' Day weekend. Phone ahead to confirm schedule. **Phone:** (717) 642-8282 for general information, or (717) 642-9000 for the snow report.

CASTLE SHANNON pop. 8,316
• Hotels & Restaurants map & index p. 348
• Part of Pittsburgh area — see map p. 326

CALABRIA'S

412/885-1030 (92)

Italian. Casual Dining. $7-$27 **AAA Inspector Notes:** Serving the area since 1992, this family-owned restaurant offers ample portions of Italian and American dishes from recipes passed down for generations. **Features:** full bar. **Address:** 3107 Library Rd 15234 **Location:** On SR 88, 1 mi s of SR 51. Killarney, 50.

CENTER VALLEY
• Hotels & Restaurants map & index p. 49

DIANA'S CAFE & CATERING   610/797-2525 (34)
▼▼ American. Casual Dining. $4-$11 **AAA Inspector Notes:**
This restaurant has a homey, casual, relaxed atmosphere, with a
large wall mural of a garden. The menu features crab bisque, steaks,
seafood, chicken, pasta and homemade desserts. Sea scallops with
herb crust and salmon Dijonnaise are examples from the menu.
Family friendly, the restaurant offers a five-item children's menu. **Address:** 4907 Rt 309 18034 **Location:** I-78 exit 60, 1.5 mi e to Camp
Meeting Rd, just e to SR 309 N, U-turn, then 0.5 mi n.

(B) (L)

MANOR HOUSE INN   610/865-8166 (33)
▼▼▼ French. Fine Dining. $9-$38 **AAA Inspector Notes:** This
place exudes country charm. Set in a circa 1740 fieldstone manor,
the restaurant's dining room nurtures a French Colonial atmosphere
while its menu is comprised of country French cuisine. A delectable
example is clove-studded rack of lamb with lingonberry sauce. **Features:** full bar. **Reservations:** suggested. **Address:** 4508 Old Bethlehem Pike 18034 **Location:** I-78 exit 60, 0.3 mi s to Center Valley
Pkwy, 2.1 mi e to Old Bethlehem Pike, then 0.5 mi s.

(L) (D)

CENTRE HALL (F-6) pop. 1,265, elev. 1,187'

PENN'S CAVE & WILDLIFE PARK, 5 mi. e.
on SR 192 at 222 Penn's Cave Rd., is America's only all-water cavern and wildlife park. A 45-
minute guided motorboat tour through the cavern
features limestone formations and Lake Nitanee.
The site is still a working farm.

Also offered is a guided 90-minute tour of some of
the 1,600 acres of the Wildlife Park's fields, farmland, grazing pastures and mountain trails. Highlights include bison, bobcats, white-tailed deer, elk,
black bears, Texas longhorn cattle, timber wolves,
bighorn sheep, a butterfly garden and a mountain
lion den. A 4,800-square-foot Miner's Maze and
gemstone panning also are offered. A 2-hour off-
road jeep tour is available by reservation.

Note: The cave's temperature is a constant 52 F.
Hours: Cave tours depart daily 9-7, June-Aug.; daily
9-5, Apr.-May and Sept.-Oct.; daily 10-5 in Mar. and
Nov.; Sat.-Sun. 11-4, in Feb. and Dec. Departure
time for last cave tour varies; phone ahead. Wildlife
Park tours available daily, Apr.-Oct., Sat.-Sun., in
Nov.; phone ahead to confirm schedule. Closed
Thanksgiving and Christmas.

Cost: Cave tour $16.95; $15.95 (ages 65+);
$14.25 (military with ID); $8.95 (ages 2-12); $7.50
(military child ages 2-12). Wildlife Park tour $19.95;
$18.95 (ages 65+); $14.25 (military with ID); $11.95
(ages 2-12); $7.50 (military child ages 2-12). Com-
bined cave and wildlife tour $30.95; $29.95 (ages
65+); $28.50 (military with ID); $16.95 (ages 2-12);
$15 (military child ages 2-12). Gemstone panning
$10.50 (large bag); $5.95 (small bag). **Phone:** (814)
364-1664. (GT)

Pick up vibrant, top-quality
travel guides and atlases
at AAA/CAA offices

CHADDS FORD (C-8) elev. 129'
• Part of Philadelphia area — see map p. 230

Chadds Ford is in the Brandywine Valley where
the Revolutionary War engagement, the Battle of
Brandywine, occurred. Chadds Ford also is home to
the Wyeth family of artists. A river walk connects the
Brandywine River Museum of Art *(see attraction
listing)* with the circa 1725 John Chads House. The
1714 Barns-Brinton Tavern & House is nearby. Tours
of the homes are given on weekends 1-5, Memorial
Day weekend through Labor Day weekend, and by
appointment. Contact the Chadds Ford Historical
Society Barn Visitors Center, 1736 N. Creek Rd., for
more information; phone (610) 388-7376. The visitor
center, which was built to resemble the types of historic barns found in the area, has a small museum
with a combination of permanent and temporary exhibits pertaining to local history. The site is open
weekdays 9-2 year-round, with additional weekend
hours Memorial Day through Labor Day.

BRANDYWINE BATTLEFIELD PARK embraces 50
acres along the n. side of US 1, 1 mi. e. of Creek
Rd. The Battle of Brandywine was fought nearby
Sept. 11, 1777. This defeat of the American forces
under George Washington left Philadelphia open to
advancing British troops. The visitor center contains
exhibits about the battle. A reproduction of the farmhouse used by Washington as a headquarters is on
the grounds can only be seen on guided tours. An
18-minute video presentation features a re-
enactment of the battle.

Time: Allow 1 hour minimum. **Hours:** Visitor
center Wed.-Sat. 9-4, Sun. noon-4, May to mid-June
and Sept. to mid-Dec.; Tues.-Sat. 9-4, Sun. noon-4,
mid-June to Aug. 31. Hours vary rest of year. Tours
are given at 10, 11, 1, 2 and 3 during visitor center
hours. Closed major holidays. Phone ahead to confirm schedule. **Cost:** Battlefield free. Visitor center
(includes house tour and film) $8; $7 (ages 60+); $5
(ages 6-17). Museum and film only $3. Phone
ahead to confirm rates. **Phone:** (610) 459-3342.

BRANDYWINE RIVER MUSEUM OF ART,
on US 1 at 1 Hoffman's Mill Rd., is a 19th-
century gristmill converted into a museum housing a
collection of American art and illustration. Works by
three generations of the Wyeth family are featured,
with individual galleries devoted to N.C., Andrew
and Jamie Wyeth. The galleries in the restored mill
have original beams, pine floors and white plaster
walls. The museum grounds are landscaped with
native plants and wildflowers.

Via a shuttle bus connection, visitors may take a
1-hour guided tour of the nearby Andrew Wyeth
Studio, where the artist worked 1940-2008; the N.C.
Wyeth house and studio, restored to their 1945 appearance, or Kuerner Farm, the inspiration for more
than 1,000 paintings completed during Andrew Wyeth's 70-year friendship with the Kuerner family.

Time: Allow 1 hour, 30 minutes minimum. **Hours:**
Museum open daily 9:30-4:30. House and studio

tours or Kuerner Farm tours are given early Apr. to mid-Nov.; phone for schedule. Food is available daily 10-3. Closed Christmas. Phone ahead to confirm schedule. **Cost:** $12; $8 (ages 65+); $6 (ages 6-12 and students with ID). Off-site tours additional $8. Ages 0-5 are not permitted on off-site tours. **Phone:** (610) 388-2700, or (610) 388-8326 for off-site tour information.

WINERIES
- **Chaddsford Winery** is 1.8 mi. e. of jct. Kennett Pike (SR 52) at 632 Baltimore Pike (US 1). **Hours:** Tues.-Sun. 11-7. Tastings noon-6:45. Guided tours Sat.-Sun. 1-4, Apr.-Sept. Closed Jan. 1, Easter, Thanksgiving and Christmas. **Cost:** Tasting fee $5. Guided tour $15. **Phone:** (610) 388-6221. GT

BRANDYWINE RIVER HOTEL   (610)388-1200

W W **Hotel** $129-$159 **Address:** 1609 Baltimore Pike, Bldg 300 19317 **Location:** Jct US 1 (Baltimore Pike) and SR 100, 2 mi w of US 202 (Wilmington Pike). Located amidst a collection of upscale gift shops. **Facility:** 39 units. 2 stories, interior corridors. **Terms:** cancellation fee imposed. **Activities:** exercise room.

WHERE TO EAT

THE GABLES AT CHADDS FORD   610/388-7700

W W W American. Fine Dining. $10-$32 **AAA Inspector Notes:** Located in a restored 19th-century barn, this dining room offers a casually elegant atmosphere with rustic touches. Another option is a seasonal dining patio within an old barn foundation. The menu offers contemporary American dishes with Asian and French influences. Their specialty is fresh fish, but the wild game courses are just as delicious. A prix-fixe menu is available Tuesday and Wednesday nights. **Features:** full bar, Sunday brunch, happy hour. **Reservations:** suggested, dinner. **Address:** 423 Baltimore Pike 19317 **Location:** Jct SR 100, 1.5 mi s on US 1 (Baltimore Pike). L D

MING VILLAGE   610/459-3900

W W Chinese. Casual Dining. $7-$20 **AAA Inspector Notes:** Guests will be pleasantly surprised at the simple yet charming Asian décor and attentive service at this restaurant located inside Painters Crossing Shopping Center. Locals flock here for the bargain prices and quick lunch service. The sushi menu is a tad limited; we recommend sticking with some of the traditional Chinese and Thai entrées. **Address:** 136 Painters Crossing 19317 **Location:** 0.3 mi s; jct Wilmington Pike (US 202). L D

CHALFONT pop. 4,009
• Part of Philadelphia area — see map p. 230

LOS SARAPES AUTHENTIC MEXICAN RESTAURANT & VILLA TEQUILA BAR   215/822-8858

W W W
Mexican
Casual Dining
$8-$25

AAA Inspector Notes: Traditionally prepared family recipes, including an extensive selection of beef, chicken and seafood dishes, are made from authentic ingredients. A buffet is set up for Sunday lunches. An extensive selection of Mexican dishes is available. **Features:** full bar, Sunday brunch, happy hour. **Address:** 17 Moyer Rd 18914 **Location:** Just s of US 202. Chalfont, 311.

L D

Check DrivingLaws.AAA.com
for local motor vehicle laws
when traveling

CHALK HILL (I-2) pop. 141, elev. 2,000'

Chalk Hill is part of the Laurel Highlands *(see place listing p. 183).*

FRANK LLOYD WRIGHT'S HOUSE ON KENTUCK KNOB, 6 mi. n. of US 40 at 723 Kentuck Rd. (Chalk Hill-Ohiopyle Rd.), was designed for Bernardine and I.N. Hagan in 1953 by renowned American architect Frank Lloyd Wright. The couple had admired Fallingwater, a house Wright had designed for the Kaufmann family, and asked him to design a house for them as well.

The house is one of Wright's Usonian designs and is constructed of tidewater red cypress and 800 tons of native sandstone; it appears to be part of the mountainous western Pennsylvania terrain. The design is based on a hexagonal grid with an open floor plan and expanses of glass, blurring the distinction between the indoor and outdoor spaces. The grounds include a meadow with contemporary sculptures and woodland trails. A former greenhouse now serves as a visitor center.

Time: Allow 1 hour, 30 minutes minimum. **Hours:** Guided tours are given Thurs.-Tues. 9-5, Wed. noon-5, Mar.-Oct.; Thurs.-Tues. 10-4, Wed. noon-4, in Nov.; Fri.-Sun. 10-4, in Dec. In-depth tours are also offered on selected days. Closed Jan. 1, Thanksgiving, Christmas Eve and Christmas. Phone ahead to confirm schedule. **Cost:** $22; $15.50 (ages 6-12). In-depth tour $60.50. Ages 0-5 are not permitted. Reservations are recommended for guided tours and are required for in-depth tours. **Phone:** (724) 329-1901.

THE LODGE AT CHALK HILL   (724)438-8880

W W W
Motel
$70-$150

Address: 2920 National Pike Rd 15421 **Location:** I-40 exit 14B, just w. **Facility:** 61 units, some kitchens. 1 story, exterior corridors. **Terms:** closed 12/15-1/15, check-in 4 pm. **Activities:** fishing, playground. **Featured Amenity: continental breakfast.**

CHAMBERSBURG (I-6) pop. 20,268, elev. 613'
• Hotels p. 82 • Restaurants p. 83

Nestled in the historic Cumberland Valley, Chambersburg experienced three raids by Confederate troops during the Civil War. The last incursion culminated in 1864 with the burning of the city after its refusal to pay an indemnity. In Memorial Square in the historic district is the five-tiered Memorial Fountain and its statue of a Union soldier; the memorial was dedicated in 1878 to honor Civil War soldiers. Facing south, the statue symbolizes protection against future invasions. Also in Memorial Square are Central Presbyterian Church, with its Tiffany glass windows, and the Franklin County Courthouse, which was rebuilt after the fire of 1864.

In the summer of 1859 Chambersburg served as a base of operations for abolitionist John Brown. His headquarters were at a local boarding house. Now known as the John Brown House, the building is at 225 E. King St.; phone (717) 264-1667 for schedule information.

Founding Fathers Park, on the historic site of Chambers Fort, has walkways and benches.

Chambersburg Heritage Center/Chamber of Commerce: 100 Lincoln Way E., Chambersburg, PA 17201. **Phone:** (717) 264-7101.

Self-guiding tours: Brochures of walking and driving tours highlighting local historical sites are available at the chamber of commerce. Driving tour brochures are $1; walking tour brochures are free.

CHAMBERSBURG HERITAGE CENTER, 100 Lincoln Way E. on the town square, is housed in the restored white marble Valley National Bank Building. A 15-minute film and exhibits about Native American tribes, the Revolutionary War, transportation and the Civil War showcase the town's history. **Time:** Allow 1 hour minimum. **Hours:** Mon.-Fri. 8-5 (also Sat. 10-3, May-Oct.). Closed major holidays. **Cost:** Donations. Guided tour $5. **Phone:** (717) 264-7101. [GT]

THE OLD JAIL, 175 E. King St., was built in 1818 and was one of the few buildings that survived the burning of Chambersburg by Confederate forces in 1864. The building, featuring an early drugstore, pioneer kitchen, changing exhibits and genealogical library, houses the Franklin County Historical Society.

Hours: Museum Tues.-Sat. 10-4, May-Oct.; Thurs.-Sat. 10-4, rest of year. Library Tues.-Sat. 10-4 (also Tues. 4-8), May-Oct.; Thurs.-Sat. 10-4, Tues. 5-8, rest of year. Closed major holidays. **Cost:** Museum $5; $4 (ages 6-17); $10 (family). Library $5. **Phone:** (717) 264-1667.

BEST WESTERN CHAMBERSBURG   (717)262-4994

 Hotel $70-$300

 AAA Benefit: Members save up to 20%!

Address: 211 Walker Rd 17201 **Location:** I-81 exit 16, just w on US 30, then just n. **Facility:** 46 units. 1 story, interior corridors. **Pool(s):** outdoor. **Activities:** exercise room. **Guest Services:** coin laundry.

CANDLEWOOD SUITES   717/263-2800

 Extended Stay Hotel. Rates not provided. **Address:** 231 Walker Rd 17201 **Location:** I-81 exit 16, just w on US 30, then just n. **Facility:** 70 efficiencies. 3 stories, interior corridors. **Pool(s):** heated indoor. **Activities:** hot tub, exercise room. **Guest Services:** complimentary and valet laundry.

CLARION INN CHAMBERSBURG   (717)263-9191

Hotel $65-$200 **Address:** 1123 Lincoln Way E 17201 **Location:** I-81 exit 16, just w on US 30. **Facility:** 126 units. 3 stories, interior corridors. **Pool(s):** heated indoor. **Activities:** exercise room. **Guest Services:** valet and coin laundry.

COUNTRY INN & SUITES BY CARLSON   717/261-0900

Hotel. Rates not provided. **Address:** 399 Bedington Blvd 17201 **Location:** I-81 exit 17 (Walker Rd), 0.6 mi s, then just w. **Facility:** 70 units. 3 stories, interior corridors. **Pool(s):** heated indoor. **Activities:** hot tub, exercise room. **Guest Services:** complimentary and valet laundry.

HAMPTON INN   (717)261-9185

Hotel $103-$160

 AAA Benefit: Members save 5% or more!

Address: 955 Lesher Rd 17202 **Location:** I-81 exit 14, just e on SR 316. **Facility:** 121 units. 3 stories, interior corridors. **Terms:** 1-7 night minimum stay, cancellation fee imposed. **Pool(s):** heated outdoor. **Activities:** exercise room. **Guest Services:** valet laundry.

HOLIDAY INN EXPRESS HOTEL & SUITES   717/709-9009

Hotel. Rates not provided. **Address:** 1097 Wayne Ave 17201 **Location:** I-81 exit 14, just w on SR 316. **Facility:** 77 units. 3 stories, interior corridors. **Pool(s):** heated indoor. **Activities:** hot tub, exercise room. **Guest Services:** complimentary and valet laundry.

LA QUINTA INN & SUITES CHAMBERSBURG   (717)446-0770

Hotel $89-$254 **Address:** 199 Walker Rd 17201 **Location:** I-81 exit 16, just w on US 30, then just n. **Facility:** 49 units. 3 stories, interior corridors. **Pool(s):** heated indoor. **Activities:** exercise room. **Guest Services:** valet and coin laundry.

QUALITY INN & SUITES   (717)263-3400

Hotel $69-$130 **Address:** 1095 Wayne Ave 17201 **Location:** I-81 exit 14, just w on SR 316. **Facility:** 124 units. 2 stories (no elevator), interior corridors. **Amenities:** safes. **Pool(s):** heated outdoor. **Activities:** exercise room. **Guest Services:** valet and coin laundry.

SLEEP INN & SUITES (717)263-0596

▼▼▼ **Hotel** $74-$130 **Address:** 1435 Doron Dr 17202 **Location:** I-81 exit 20, just w. **Facility:** 69 units. 2 stories, interior corridors. **Amenities:** safes. **Pool(s):** heated indoor. **Activities:** exercise room. **Guest Services:** coin laundry.

CALL ⌖M 🚐 BIZ HS 🛜 📶 🖨 💻 / SOME UNITS 🆂

WHERE TO EAT

BISTRO 71 RESTAURANT & BAR 717/261-0007

▼▼▼ American. Casual Dining. $16-$29 **AAA Inspector Notes:** In the heart of downtown, the bistro is a wonderful spot to enjoy a pleasant dinner. The staff will make you feel welcome and relaxed and will be happy to assist with menu and beverage choices. The setting is comfortable and intimate with a rustic, upscale ambience. The kitchen will please your palate with creative American dishes. The menu is changed seasonally and is driven by the availability of fresh, quality ingredients. **Features:** full bar, patio dining. **Reservations:** suggested. **Address:** 71 N Main St 17201 **Location:** I-81 exit 16, 1.5 mi w on US 30 (Lincoln Way); downtown. **Parking:** street only. D CALL ⌖M 🐾

COPPER KETTLE RESTAURANT 717/264-3109

▼▼▼ American. Fine Dining. $10-$45 **AAA Inspector Notes:** Don't look for a conventional building when looking for this restaurant; the Kettle is housed in a converted home. Prime rib may be the specialty, but the menu offers a variety of other steak, chicken and seafood entrées. The interior is kept simple, with few decorations, but the candlelight and background music are indications of the experience they strive to provide. **Features:** full bar. **Reservations:** suggested. **Address:** 1049 Lincoln Way E 17201 **Location:** I-81 exit 16, 0.3 mi w on US 30. L D

MARIO'S ITALIAN RESTAURANT 717/263-9397

▼▼ Italian. Casual Dining. $9-$27 **AAA Inspector Notes:** This family-owned and -operated restaurant provides a variety of piping-hot homemade pasta dishes, chicken and veal entrées, gourmet pizzas and seafood classics. The casual setting makes it a great spot for any lunch or dinner. **Features:** full bar, patio dining. **Address:** 831 Wayne Ave 17201 **Location:** I-81 exit 14, 0.6 mi nw on SR 316. L D

MONTEZUMA 717/709-1003

▼▼ Mexican. Casual Dining. $6-$16 **AAA Inspector Notes:** This eatery has become the locals' choice; chefs prepare consistently good Mexican food. Choose from tacos, burritos and enchiladas as well as specialty dishes from the kitchen. The restaurant lacks a full bar, but you can enjoy a margarita or daiquiri. The atmosphere is casual, comfortable and colorful, suitable for most any occasion. **Features:** beer & wine, patio dining, happy hour. **Address:** 820 Wayne Ave 17201 **Location:** I-81 exit 14, 0.6 mi nw on SR 316. L D

THE ORCHARDS 717/264-4711

▼▼▼ American. Fine Dining. $8-$37 **AAA Inspector Notes:** Let your cares slip away in the sophisticated dining room of The Orchards, where you can start your meal with delicious saganaki, which is pan-fried beside your table, before lingering over tasty bites of your choice of pasta, seafood or steak. **Features:** full bar, patio dining, happy hour. **Reservations:** suggested. **Address:** 1580 Orchard Dr 17201 **Location:** I-81 exit 14, 0.4 mi e on SR 316, then 0.6 mi s. L D CALL ⌖M

ROSALIE'S FAB GRILL & WOOD-FIRED OVEN 717/262-4981

▼▼ Italian Pizza Sandwiches. Family Dining. $6-$20 **AAA Inspector Notes:** When the locals are looking for a good Italian restaurant, they come here. The eatery has been in business for more than 17 years. It's casual, small and comfortable—great for families. The kitchen prepares everything from subs and pizzas to pasta, veal and seafood dishes. Alcohol is not served, but you can bring your own bottle, with no corkage fee. The restaurant is a short drive off the interstate along rural roads. If you're hungry, it's worth the drive. **Address:** 1901 Scotland Ave 17201 **Location:** I-81 exit 20, just w to Scotland Ave, then 3.6 mi sw. L D

CHESTER (C-10) pop. 33,972, elev. 23'
• Hotels & Restaurants map & index p. 274
• Part of Philadelphia area — see map p. 230

Settled by Swedes and Finns in 1644, Chester is one of the oldest settlements in Pennsylvania. Until its power waned in 1683, it was the most important town in the colony and the seat of its courts. The first meeting of the Pennsylvania Assembly was held in Chester in 1682, the year William Penn arrived.

The Caleb Pusey House, 2 miles west at 15 Race St. on Landingford Plantation in Upland, is a restored cottage built in 1683 of handmade bricks.

GAMBLING ESTABLISHMENTS

• **Harrah's Chester Casino & Racetrack** is at 777 Harrah's Blvd. **Hours:** Daily 24 hours. **Phone:** (484) 490-1800 or (800) 480-8020.

BEST WESTERN PLUS PHILADELPHIA AIRPORT SOUTH AT WIDENER UNIVERSITY (610)872-8100 **142**

▼▼▼ Hotel $120-$150

Best Western PLUS

AAA Benefit: Members save up to 20%!

Address: 1450 Providence Ave (SR 320) 19013 **Location:** I-95 exit 6, just e to SR 320, follow signs. Across from Widener University. 🅿 Chester T.C., 172. **Facility:** 60 units. 4 stories, interior corridors. **Amenities:** safes. **Activities:** exercise room. **Guest Services:** boarding pass kiosk, area transportation.

SAVE ➔ 🍴 BIZ HS 🛜 ✕
📶 🖨 💻 / SOME UNITS 🆂 🚉

CHESTER SPRINGS (B-8) elev. 275'
• Part of Philadelphia area — see map p. 230

HISTORIC YELLOW SPRINGS, 1685 Art School Rd., was built around three mineral-rich springs and consists of several early American buildings, including a circa 1840 home, 1722 health spa, an inn, military hospital ruins, a school for Civil War orphans, a cultural center, a theater, an arts school and a library.

Brochures are available for self-guiding tours. An annual art show in early May showcases more than 170 artists. **Time:** Allow 1 hour, 30 minutes minimum. **Hours:** Grounds daily dawn-dusk. Buildings Mon.-Fri. 9-4. Closed major holidays. **Cost:** Free. **Phone:** (610) 827-7414.

CLARION (E-3) pop. 5,276, elev. 1,500'
• Hotels p. 84 • Restaurants p. 84

SUTTON-DITZ HOUSE MUSEUM & FULTON LIBRARY is at 18 Grant St.; the library is at 17 S. 5th Ave., across the street from the museum. The three-story brick house was built in 1850 by attorney Thomas Sutton and remodeled in 1908 in the Greek Revival style by merchant John Ditz. Furniture, home accessories, children's toys and clothing from the mid-1800s through 1940 are displayed. Changing exhibits are presented in the Industrial

Room and Military Room. Fulton Library houses Clarion County history and genealogy library and archives.

Time: Allow 30 minutes minimum. **Hours:** Mon.-Fri. 10-5 and by appointment. Guided tours are available by appointment. Closed major holidays. Phone ahead to confirm schedule. **Cost:** Donations. **Phone:** (814) 226-4450.

RECREATIONAL ACTIVITIES
Horseback Riding

• **Cook Forest Area Scenic Trailride** is 7 mi. e. on Scott Dr. Self-guiding trails and 1- to 5-hour guided trail rides are offered. Other activities also are available. **Hours:** Trail rides daily 9-5, May 15-Oct. 15. **Phone:** (814) 226-5985.

COMFORT INN-CLARION (814)226-5230

▼▼ ▼▼ Hotel $70-$135 **Address:** 129 Dolby St 16214 **Location:** I-80 exit 62, 0.6 mi n on SR 68. **Facility:** 76 units, some efficiencies. 2 stories (no elevator), interior corridors. **Pool(s):** heated indoor. **Activities:** hot tub, limited exercise equipment. **Guest Services:** coin laundry.

HAMPTON INN-CLARION (814)226-4444

▼▼▼▼
Hotel
$139-$209

AAA Benefit: Members save 5% or more!

Address: 4 Hospital Dr 16214 **Location:** I-80 exit 62, just n. **Facility:** 72 units. 3 stories, interior corridors. **Terms:** 1-7 night minimum stay, cancellation fee imposed. **Pool(s):** heated indoor. **Activities:** exercise room. **Guest Services:** coin laundry. **Featured Amenity:** breakfast buffet.

PARK INN BY RADISSON CLARION (814)226-8850

▼▼ ▼▼ Hotel $109-$149 **Address:** 45 Holiday Inn Rd 16214 **Location:** I-80 exit 62, 0.5 mi n on SR 68. **Facility:** 121 units. 2 stories (no elevator), interior corridors. **Pool(s):** heated indoor. **Activities:** exercise room. **Guest Services:** coin laundry.

WHERE TO EAT

FAIRWAY CASUAL DINING RESTAURANT 814/226-8850

▼▼ ▼▼ American. Casual Dining. $8-$19 **AAA Inspector Notes:** Offering a golfing theme, this contemporary facility offers an excellent variety of sandwiches, burgers, steaks, seafood, chops and ribs, which are served in hearty portions. **Features:** full bar. **Address:** 45 Holiday Inn Rd 16214 **Location:** I-80 exit 62, 0.5 mi n on SR 68.

B L D

RRR ROADHOUSE 814/227-2000

▼▼ ▼▼ Steak. Casual Dining. $10-$40 **AAA Inspector Notes:** Located in the Clarion Mall, this local favorite has a bustling yet casual atmosphere with rustic décor. The dining room is paneled in knotty pine. Portions are generous and USDA Prime steak, ribs and chops are aged and hand cut. Some seafood, chicken and pasta are among other choices. The staff is energetic and attentive. **Features:** full bar. **Address:** 22631 State Hwy 68 16214 **Location:** I-80 exit 62, 0.5 mi n; in Clarion Mall. L D CALL&M

CLARK (E-1) pop. 640, elev. 774'

◀▬ **TARA,** just e. on SR 258 at 2844 Lake Rd., recalls the antebellum era of "Gone With the Wind." Spacious lawns, seasonal blossoms and a long veranda with white wicker furniture enhance the Southern atmosphere of this 1854 Greek Revival mansion, now an inn. Each room, named after a character from the Margaret Mitchell epic, is decorated with period furnishings and original works of art. Opulent chandeliers, Oriental rugs and a large collection of art and antiques create an atmosphere of Southern elegance. Tours are conducted by guides in Civil War-era costumes. **Time:** Allow 1 hour minimum. **Hours:** Tours depart Sat.-Sun. on the hour 10-3. Phone ahead to confirm schedule. **Cost:** $5. **Phone:** (724) 962-3535 or (800) 782-2803. 🍴

TARA-A-COUNTRY INN 724/962-3535

fyi Not evaluated. **Address:** 2844 Lake Rd 16113 **Location:** I-80 exit 4B, 8 mi n on SR 18. Facilities, services, and décor characterize a mid-scale property. Themed after the fictional Southern mansion of the same name from the epic film "Gone With the Wind," the inn offers individually decorated guest rooms featuring antiques and original art.

CLARKS SUMMIT pop. 5,116

COMFORT INN (570)586-9100

▼▼▼▼
Hotel
$100-$150

Address: 811 Northern Blvd 18411 **Location:** I-81 exit 194, on US 6 and 11; I-476 (Pennsylvania Tpke) exit 131. **Facility:** 65 units. 4 stories, interior corridors. **Guest Services:** valet laundry, boarding pass kiosk. **Featured Amenity:** continental breakfast.

HAMPTON INN-CLARKS SUMMIT (570)586-1515

▼▼▼▼
Hotel
$129-$179

AAA Benefit: Members save 5% or more!

Address: 890 Northern Blvd 18411 **Location:** I-81 exit 194; I-476 (Pennsylvania Tpke) exit 131, 0.5 mi nw on US 6 and 11. Located in a commercial area. **Facility:** 68 units. 4 stories, interior corridors. **Terms:** 1-7 night minimum stay, cancellation fee imposed. **Pool(s):** heated indoor. **Activities:** hot tub, exercise room. **Guest Services:** valet and coin laundry. **Featured Amenity:** full hot breakfast.

NICHOLS VILLAGE HOTEL & SPA 570/587-1135

▼▼▼▼ Boutique Hotel. Rates not provided. **Address:** 1101 Northern Blvd 18411 **Location:** I-81 exit 194, just w; I-476 (Pennsylvania Tpke) exit 131, 0.7 mi w on US 6 and 11. **Facility:** A woodsy setting with patios, courtyards and gardens accent the grounds of this hotel, which staffs a professional, friendly and welcoming staff. Some rooms have a balcony. 116 units, some kitchens. 2-4 stories, interior corridors. **Pool(s):** heated indoor. **Activities:** exercise room, spa. **Guest Services:** valet and coin laundry.

CLAYSBURG (H-5) pop. 1,625, elev. 1,148'

RECREATIONAL ACTIVITIES
Skiing and Snowboarding
• **Blue Knob All Seasons Resort** is at 1424 Overland Pass. Cross-country and downhill skiing, snowboarding, tubing and other activities are offered. **Hours:** Mon.-Thurs. 10-9, Fri. 10-10, Sat. 9 a.m.-10 p.m., Sun. 9-9, mid-Dec. to mid-Mar. (weather permitting). **Phone:** (814) 239-5111 or (800) 458-3403.

CLEARFIELD (F-5) pop. 6,215, elev. 1,100'

Visit Clearfield: 511 Spruce St. Suite 8, Clearfield, PA 16830. **Phone:** (814) 765-5734 or (866) 469-4537.

GRICE CLEARFIELD COMMUNITY MUSEUM is at 119 N. Fourth St. The 25,000-square-foot building houses collections of approximately 75 classic cars and about 400 wild game and fish mounts. Rotating exhibits also are on display. **Time:** Allow 30 minutes minimum. **Hours:** Mon.-Sat. 10-4, Sun. noon-4, Memorial Day weekend-Sept. 30; Sat.-Sun. 10-4, in Oct. **Cost:** $5; free (ages 0-11 with adult). **Phone:** (814) 768-7892.

BEST WESTERN PLUS CLEARFIELD   (814)768-1049

Hotel
$87-$135

AAA Benefit:
Members save up to 20%!

Address: 14424 Clearfield Shawville Hwy (Rt 879) 16830 **Location:** I-80 exit 120, just s. **Facility:** 69 units. 3 stories, interior corridors. **Pool(s):** heated indoor. **Activities:** hot tub, exercise room. **Guest Services:** valet and coin laundry. **Featured Amenity:** continental breakfast.

CLEARFIELD RODEWAY INN   814/765-7587

Motel
Rates not provided

Address: 6259 Clearfield Woodland Hwy (US 322 E) 16830 **Location:** I-80 exit 120, 1.5 mi sw on SR 879, then 1.3 mi e. **Facility:** 34 units. 2 stories (no elevator), exterior corridors.

COMFORT INN CLEARFIELD   (814)768-6400
🦅🦅🦅 Hotel $99-$185 **Address:** 1821 Industrial Park Rd 16830 **Location:** I-80 exit 120, just s. **Facility:** 70 units. 3 stories, interior corridors. **Terms:** check-in 4 pm. **Pool(s):** heated indoor. **Activities:** limited exercise equipment. **Guest Services:** valet laundry.

HAMPTON INN   (814)765-8300
🦅🦅🦅 Hotel $104-$189 **Address:** 1777 Industrial Park Rd 16830 **Location:** I-80 exit 120, just s. **Facility:** 69 units. 3 stories, interior corridors. **Terms:** 1-7 night minimum stay, cancellation fee imposed. **Pool(s):** heated indoor. **Activities:** exercise room. **Guest Services:** valet laundry.

AAA Benefit:
Members save 5% or more!

HOLIDAY INN EXPRESS HOTEL & SUITES CLEARFIELD   (814)768-7500
🦅🦅🦅 Hotel $100-$160 **Address:** 1625 Industrial Park Rd 16830 **Location:** I-80 exit 120, just s. **Facility:** 80 units. 3 stories, interior corridors. **Terms:** cancellation fee imposed. **Pool(s):** heated indoor. **Activities:** exercise room. **Guest Services:** valet laundry.

SUPER 8-CLEARFIELD   (814)768-7580
🦅🦅 Motel $68-$103 **Address:** 14597 Clearfield Shawville Hwy (Rt 879) 16830 **Location:** I-80 exit 120, just s. **Facility:** 80 units. 2 stories (no elevator), interior corridors. **Guest Services:** coin laundry.

WHERE TO EAT

DUTCH PANTRY FAMILY RESTAURANT   814/765-2137
🦅🦅 American. Family Dining. $7-$15 **AAA Inspector Notes:** This restaurant is distinguished by its red and white exterior, visible from the interstate. You'll find family-style dining with comfort foods for every taste and beverages served in Mason jars. **Address:** 14680 Clearfield Shawville Hwy 16830 **Location:** I-80 exit 120, just s.
[B] [L] [D]

HEDGE'S FINE FOOD & SPIRITS   814/765-7441
🦅 American. Casual Dining. $8-$22 **AAA Inspector Notes:** Located downtown, this informal tavern-style restaurant presents a four-page menu of Italian dishes, steaks, seafood, burgers and sandwiches. This is a good place for comfort foods such as liver and onions or spaghetti and meatballs. Dominated by an open bar, there is nothing fancy here, just good food. Open at 4 pm on Saturday. **Features:** full bar. **Address:** 315 E Market St 16830 **Location:** Downtown; just e. **Parking:** on-site and street. [L] [D]

MOENA   814/765-1564
🦅🦅 Italian. Casual Dining. $7-$25 **AAA Inspector Notes:** This restaurant offers a generous variety of contemporary Italian fare, including pasta, steak and pizza. All desserts are created on the premises, with varied selections prepared daily. The décor, from the charming red brick facade to the newly varnished hardwood floors, is evocative of the turn-of-the-century era when this small town flourished. **Features:** full bar. **Reservations:** suggested. **Address:** 215 E Market St 16803 **Location:** Downtown. **Parking:** street only.
[L] [D]

CLINTON pop. 434
• Part of Pittsburgh area — see map p. 326

JANOSKI FARMS COUNTRY RESTAURANT   724/899-2344
🦅 American. Family Dining. $3-$14 **AAA Inspector Notes:** This cozy country restaurant is one aspect of the working farm, which also incorporates a farmer's market, gift shop, garden center and bakery. **Address:** 1714 US 30 15026 **Location:** On US 30, 2.1 mi nw. [B] [L] [D] CALL🅖Ⓜ

Remember, car seats, booster seats and seat belts save lives

COATESVILLE pop. 13,100
• Part of Philadelphia area — see map p. 230

COURTYARD BY MARRIOTT PHILADELPHIA COATESVILLE/
EXTON   (610)380-8700

▼▼▼ Hotel $104-$171 Address:
600 Manor Rd 19320 Location: On US   **AAA Benefit:**
30 (Lincoln Hwy), just s. Facility: 125   Members save 5%
units. 4 stories, interior corridors.   or more!
Pool(s): heated indoor. Activities: hot
tub, exercise room. Guest Services: valet and coin laundry, boarding
pass kiosk.

[Y] CALL [&M] [➡] [BIZ] [HS] [📶] [✕] [🛗] [🏢] [🖥]

COLLEGEVILLE (A-9) pop. 5,089, elev. 155'
• Part of Philadelphia area — see map p. 230

BERMAN MUSEUM OF ART, 601 E. Main St. on
the Ursinus College campus, features more than
4,000 paintings, sculpture, prints, drawings and historical artifacts. Works by contemporary regional artists and turn-of-the-20th-century Pennsylvanians
are highlighted. Large-scale outdoor sculptures are
featured throughout the campus. Time: Allow 1 hour
minimum. Hours: Tues.-Fri. 10-4. Closed Thanksgiving, day after Thanksgiving, Christmas Eve-Jan.
2 and college holidays. Cost: Free. Phone: (610)
409-3079.

COURTYARD BY MARRIOTT PHILADELPHIA VALLEY FORGE/
COLLEGEVILLE   (484)974-2600

▼▼▼ Hotel $153-$252 Address:
600 Campus Dr 19426 Location: Just w   **AAA Benefit:**
of US 422. Facility: 132 units. 5 stories, Members save 5%
interior corridors. Pool(s): heated indoor.   or more!
Activities: exercise room. Guest Ser-
vices: valet and coin laundry, boarding pass kiosk, area
transportation.

[Y] CALL [&M] [➡] [BIZ] [HS] [📶] [✕] [🛗] [🖥]
/ SOME [🖼]
  UNITS

COLUMBIA (H-9) pop. 10,400, elev. 252'
• Attractions map p. 221
• Hotels & Restaurants map & index p. 222
• Part of Pennsylvania Dutch Country area — see
map p. 220

Founded in the early 1700s, Columbia is in the
Susquehanna River Valley, a location that encouraged the development of the town's livelihood as a
transportation and commercial center.

The Susquehanna Chamber of Commerce and
Visitors Center: 445 Linden St., P.O. Box 510, Columbia, PA 17512. Phone: (717) 684-5249.

THE NATIONAL WATCH AND CLOCK MU-
SEUM is off US 30 and SR 441 at 514
Poplar St. at jct. Fifth St. The museum, in a stately
columned building, has what is said to be the largest
collection of timepieces in North America as well as
interactive exhibits that introduce visitors to ho-
rology, the study of time and timekeeping. After
viewing a 10-minute introductory film explaining how
clocks work, visitors enter the galleries through the
Time Tunnel and begin a chronological examination
of timekeeping and timepieces.

The history of timepieces is traced from Stone-
henge to early water clocks to mechanisms used in
early monasteries to clockmaking in the United
States. Clockmaking in this country did not develop
until after 1775, when tall case (grandfather) clocks
were first made. During this time period, cabinets
were made by a cabinetmaker and the clock mecha-
nism by a clockmaker. One of the museum's finest
collections is the large group of 18th- and 19th-
century tall case clocks.

Other interesting displays include collections of
European clocks, including German cuckoo clocks;
vintage pocket watches; and old and new wrist-
watches. Sound effects accompany many exhibits,
and murals and graphics provide background information about the timepieces displayed.

In addition, visitors can see timekeeping items
from around the world including movements, tools
and machinery; a cabinetmaker's workshop; a watch
factory; a replica train master's office; a turn-of-the-
20th-century watch and clock shop; and examples
of various technological developments, from the earliest mechanical timepieces to the futuristic atomic
clock. Temporary exhibits also are featured. A reference library and a computer-catalogued index are
available.

Time: Allow 1 hour minimum. Hours: Tues.-Sat.
10-5, Sun. noon-4, Apr.-Nov. (also Mon. 10-5, Memorial Day-Labor Day); Tues.-Sat. 10-4, rest of year.
Closed Jan. 1, Easter, July 4, Thanksgiving and
Christmas. Cost: $8; $7.50 (military with ID); $7
(ages 65+); $4 (ages 5-16); $20 (family, two adults
and children under 18 in same household). Phone:
(717) 684-8261.

TURKEY HILL EXPERIENCE, 301 Linden St. at jct.
Third St., offers nine interactive exhibit areas showcasing the history and the inner workings of the
Turkey Hill Dairy in Lancaster County. Though not a
factory tour, visitors will learn how the company's ice
cream and iced tea are made. They can milk a mechanical cow, make their own Turkey Hill commercial and enjoy free samples of ice cream and iced
tea. In the Taste Lab, ice cream lovers can make
their own "virtual" flavor. Time: Allow 1 hour, 30 minutes minimum. Hours: Daily 9:30-5:30, June 15-
Sept. 1; Tues.-Fri. 10-4, Sat.-Sun. 10-5, Sept. 2 to
late Dec. (also Sat.-Sun. 5-6, Oct. 11-26). Schedule
varies rest of year. Closed Thanksgiving and
Christmas. Phone ahead to confirm schedule. Cost:
Turkey Hill Experience $9.95; $8.95 (62+); $7.95
(ages 5-17); Free (ages 0-4); Combo tickets including Taste Lab: $14.50; $13.50 (62+); $12.50
(ages 5-17); $4.55 (ages 0-4). Reservations re-
quired for Taste Lab. Phone: (844) 847-4884. [🍴]

WRIGHT'S FERRY MANSION, Second and Cherry
sts., was the Colonial home of Susanna Wright, a lit-
erary Quaker. The restored 1738 English stone
house contains a collection of early 18th-
centuryPhiladelphia furniture and reflects life in a

(See map & index p. 222.)

Pennsylvania Quaker household prior to 1750. **Time:** Allow 1 hour minimum. **Hours:** Guided tours are offered Tues.-Wed. and Fri.-Sat. 10-3, May-Oct. Last tour begins at closing. Closed July 4. **Cost:** $5; $2.50 (ages 6-18). **Phone:** (717) 684-4325.

COMFORT INN   (717)285-9100   **34**

 Hotel $90-$170 **Address:** 3903 Abel Dr 17512 **Location:** US 30 exit Prospect Rd, just s to Columbia Ave, 0.4 mi e to Sylvan Retreat Rd, then just n. **Facility:** 60 units, some kitchens. 3 stories, interior corridors. **Pool(s):** heated indoor. **Activities:** hot tub, exercise room. **Guest Services:** valet and coin laundry.

CONCORDVILLE
• Part of Philadelphia area — see map p. 230

BEST WESTERN PLUS CONCORDVILLE HOTEL
             (610)358-9400

Hotel
$119-$179

AAA Benefit: Members save up to 20%!

Address: 780 Baltimore Pike 19331 **Location:** Jct US 322 W and 1. Located in a commercial area. **Facility:** 115 units. 5 stories, interior corridors. **Amenities:** safes. **Dining:** Concordville Inn, see separate listing. **Pool(s):** heated indoor. **Activities:** sauna, game room, exercise room. **Guest Services:** valet and coin laundry, area transportation. **Featured Amenity:** full hot breakfast.

HAMPTON INN & SUITES CHADDS FORD
             (610)358-9540

Hotel
$129-$169

AAA Benefit: Members save 5% or more!

Address: 40 State Farm Dr 19342 **Location:** Jct US 202, just n on US 1, just w. **Facility:** 124 units. 4 stories, interior corridors. **Terms:** check-in 4 pm, 1-7 night minimum stay, cancellation fee imposed. **Pool(s):** heated indoor. **Activities:** hot tub, exercise room. **Guest Services:** valet and coin laundry. **Featured Amenity:** breakfast buffet.

WYNDHAM GARDEN GLEN MILLS
             (610)358-1700

Hotel
$99-$344

Address: 1110 Baltimore Pike 19331 **Location:** Jct US 1 and 202. Located in a commercial area. **Facility:** 136 units, some two bedrooms and efficiencies. 5 stories, interior corridors. **Amenities:** safes. **Pool(s):** outdoor. **Activities:** game room, exercise room. **Guest Services:** valet and coin laundry, area transportation. **Featured Amenity:** full hot breakfast.

 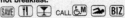

CONCORDVILLE INN   610/459-2230

 American. Casual Dining. $7-$40 **AAA Inspector Notes:** *Historic.* Baked crab-imperial-stuffed mushrooms are a favorite appetizer at this casual restaurant in a historic inn. The menu lists soups, pasta, salads and such entrées as prime rib, filet mignon and Atlantic salmon. Guests looking for a more relaxed environment may enjoy the bar and lounge area. **Features:** full bar, patio dining, Sunday brunch, happy hour. **Reservations:** suggested. **Address:** 780 Baltimore Pike 19331 **Location:** Jct US 322 W and 1; in BEST WESTERN PLUS Concordville Hotel. [L] [D]

CONNEAUT LAKE (D-1) pop. 653, elev. 1,083'

Conneaut Lake is Pennsylvania's largest natural lake and offers fishing, swimming, boating, water-skiing and sailing.

WINERIES
• **Conneaut Cellars Winery** is on US 322 at 12005 Conneaut Lake Rd. **Hours:** Daily 10-6. Guided tours are given at 11 and on the hour 1-5. Closed Jan. 1, Easter, Thanksgiving and Christmas. **Phone:** (814) 382-3999 or (877) 229-9463. [GT]

CONSHOHOCKEN pop. 7,833
• Hotels & Restaurants map & index p. 274
• Part of Philadelphia area — see map p. 230

RESIDENCE INN BY MARRIOTT PHILADELPHIA/CONSHOHOCKEN
             (610)828-8800   **75**

 Extended Stay Hotel $174-$286 **Address:** 191 Washington St 19428 **Location:** I-76 (Schuylkill Expwy) exit 332 (SR 23), 0.3 mi over Fayette Bridge to Elm St, then just se along river. Located in a commercial area. Conshohocken, 235. **Facility:** 137 units, some two bedrooms, efficiencies and kitchens. 6 stories, interior corridors. **Pool(s):** heated indoor. **Activities:** hot tub, exercise room. **Guest Services:** valet and coin laundry, area transportation.

AAA Benefit: Members save 5% or more!

BLACKFISH   610/397-0888   **99**

Continental. Fine Dining. $10-$34 **AAA Inspector Notes:** Chef Chip Roman has won countless awards and recognition for this outstanding fine dining establishment. Whether ordering a la carte or off the chef's tasting menu, guests will experience unbelievable flavor profiles in this sophisticated daily changing menu that may feature Washington Canyon swordfish in a ham and savory broth or pastrami spiced flat iron steak topped with lobster mushrooms and Chinese eggplant. Also, this restaurant allows guests to bring their favorite wine from home. **Address:** 119 Fayette St 19428 **Location:** Between 1st and 2nd aves. Conshohocken, 235. **Parking:** street only. [L] [D]

(See map & index p. 274.)

COYOTE CROSSING   610/825-3000 (98)
▽▽▽▽ Mexican. Casual Dining. $8-$28 **AAA Inspector Notes:**
Lending to the colorful décor are faux cacti, a fireplace, track lighting
and modern-art wall hangings. The dining patio is open seasonally.
An excellent choice is sea bass and shrimp with Mexican herbs and
white wine served with cilantro cream sauce. **Features:** full bar, patio
dining, happy hour. **Reservations:** suggested, for dinner. **Address:**
800 Spring Mill Ave 19428 **Location:** I-76 (Schuylkill Expwy) exit 331
westbound; exit 332 (SR 23) eastbound, 1.1 mi ne over Fayette
Bridge, then 0.4 mi s on 8th Ave. 🚇 Spring Mill, 234.

L D 🚇

SPRING MILL CAFE   610/828-2550 (97)
▽▽▽▽ French. Casual Dining. $10-$37 **AAA Inspector Notes:**
The intimate Spring Mill Cafe, housed in a rustic building that was
once a post office, concentrates on upscale French cuisine. The seasonally changing menu choices can vary from Moroccan spiced
game hen to seared scallops over Japanese rice. Servers are knowledgeable and prompt. You can bring your own bottle of wine and they
will serve it to you. **Features:** Sunday brunch. **Reservations:** suggested. **Address:** 164 Barren Hill Rd 19428 **Location:** I-76
(Schuylkill Expwy) exit 332 (SR 23), 0.3 mi n over Fayette Bridge, 0.6
mi e on Elm St to Hector St, 0.8 mi e to Barren Hill Rd, then just s.
🚇 Spring Mill, 234. L D 🚇

COOKSBURG (E-3) elev. 1,197'

Cook Forest State Park is 1 mile north off SR 36.
The park comprises some 7,182 acres of scenic
drives and hiking trails set against the backdrop of
the winding Clarion River. Once known as the
"Black Forest," the area is famous for its stands of
old growth forest and its abundance of deer. Canoeing and tubing are popular, as are camping,
horseback riding, waterslides and winter sports.
Mountain streams and reservoirs in the vicinity offer
good trout fishing. *See Recreation Areas Chart.*

GATEWAY LODGE   814/744-8017
▽▽▽ **Country Inn** $179-$250 **Address:** 14870 Rt 36 16217
Location: I-80 exit 78 westbound, 15 mi n; exit 60 eastbound, 15 mi
n to SR 36, then 7.5 mi se. Located in a wooded area. **Facility:** Adjacent to Allegheny National Forest, the rustic inn offers many spacious, luxurious guest rooms and a few modest ones; public areas
are cozy and quaint. 31 units. 2 stories (no elevator), interior corridors. **Terms:** check-in 4 pm, age restrictions may apply. **Dining:** restaurant, see separate listing. **Activities:** game room, picnic facilities,
trails, limited exercise equipment, spa.

🍴 🍸 📶 ✕ / SOME UNITS 📺 🐄 🍴 🖫

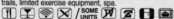

WHERE TO EAT

GATEWAY LODGE   814/744-8017
▽▽ American. Casual Dining. $14-$36 **AAA Inspector Notes:**
Adjacent to the Allegheny National Forest, this rustic dining room has
antiques, log walls and hardwood floors. Selections from a good wine
list pair with well-prepared and moderately creative American cuisine,
including preparations of beef tenderloin, sea bass, chicken and
pasta. Dishes are a little pricey, but the quality is good. Service is casual but attentive in the relaxed setting. **Features:** full bar. **Reservations:** suggested. **Address:** 14870 Rt 36 16217 **Location:** I-80 exit
78 westbound, 15 mi n; exit 60 eastbound, 15 mi n to SR 36, then 7.5
mi se. B D

CORAOPOLIS pop. 5,677
• **Hotels & Restaurants map & index p. 348**
• **Part of Pittsburgh area — see map p. 326**

COURTYARD BY MARRIOTT PITTSBURGH AIRPORT
(412)264-5000 (70)
▽▽▽ Hotel $146-$240 **Address:**   **AAA Benefit:**
450 Cherrington Pkwy 15108 **Location:**   Members save 5%
Business I-376 Loop exit Thorn Run Rd.   or more!
Facility: 148 units. 2-3 stories, interior
corridors. **Pool(s):** heated indoor. **Activ-**
ities: exercise room. **Guest Services:** valet and coin laundry,
boarding pass kiosk, area transportation.

ECO 🛗 🍴 🍸 CALL 🅼 🔁 BIZ 📶 ✕ 🖫
/ SOME UNITS 🍴 🖵

DOUBLETREE BY HILTON PITTSBURGH AIRPORT
(412)329-1400 (65)
▽▽▽ Hotel $159-$299

DOUBLETREE BY HILTON

AAA Benefit:
Members save 5% or
more!

Address: 8402 University Blvd 15108
Location: Jct Business I-376 Loop, 0.8
mi e. **Facility:** 135 units, some two bedrooms. 7 stories, interior corridors.
Terms: 1-7 night minimum stay, cancellation fee imposed. **Amenities:** video
games, safes. **Dining:** Jacksons
Restaurant-Rotisserie-Bar, see separate
listing. **Pool(s):** heated indoor. **Activ-**
ities: hot tub, exercise room. **Guest**
Services: valet laundry, area transportation.

SAVE 🛗 🍴 🍸 CALL 🅼 🔁 BIZ HS 📶 ✕
📺 🖵 / SOME UNITS 🍴 🖫

EMBASSY SUITES-PITTSBURGH INTERNATIONAL
AIRPORT   (412)269-9070 (71)
▽▽▽ Hotel $139-$279

EMBASSY SUITES
HOTELS®

AAA Benefit:
Members save 5%
or more!

Address: 550 Cherrington Pkwy 15108
Location: Business I-376 Loop exit
Thorn Run Rd. **Facility:** 223 units. 5 stories, interior corridors. **Terms:** check-in 4
pm, 1-7 night minimum stay, cancellation
fee imposed. **Pool(s):** heated indoor.
Activities: hot tub, game room, exercise
room. **Guest Services:** valet and coin
laundry, area transportation. **Featured**
Amenity: full hot breakfast.

SAVE 🛗 🍴 🍸 CALL 🅼 🔁 BIZ 📶 🍴 🖫
🖵 / SOME UNITS 🐄

HAMPTON INN PITTSBURGH AIRPORT
(412)264-0020 (66)
▽▽▽ Hotel $149-$179 **Address:**   **AAA Benefit:**
8514 University Blvd 15108 **Location:**   Members save 5%
Jct Business I-376 Loop, 0.5 mi n. **Fa-** or more!
cility: 127 units. 5 stories, interior corridors. **Terms:** 1-7 night minimum stay,
cancellation fee imposed. **Guest Services:** valet laundry, area
transportation.

🛗 🕇 CALL 🅼 🔁 BIZ 📶 🍴 🖫 🖵
/ SOME UNITS 🐄

**Use travel time to share driving tips
and rules of the road with your teens**

(See map & index p. 348.)

HYATT REGENCY PITTSBURGH INTERNATIONAL AIRPORT
(724)899-1234 **72**

Hotel
$99-$359

AAA Benefit: Members save 10%!

Address: 1111 Airport Blvd 15231 **Location:** I-376 exit 53 (Airport Blvd). Adjacent to airport. **Facility:** 336 units. 11 stories, interior corridors. **Parking:** on-site (fee). **Terms:** cancellation fee imposed. **Amenities:** video games, safes. **Dining:** Olive Press, see separate listing. **Pool(s):** heated indoor. **Activities:** sauna, hot tub, exercise room. **Guest Services:** valet laundry, area transportation.

LA QUINTA INN PITTSBURGH AIRPORT
(412)269-0400 **67**

Hotel $92-$194 **Address:** 8507 University Blvd 15108 **Location:** Jct Business I-376 Loop, 1 mi n. **Facility:** 129 units. 3 stories, interior corridors. **Parking:** on-site (fee). **Activities:** limited exercise equipment. **Guest Services:** coin laundry.

PITTSBURGH AIRPORT SUPER 8
(412)264-7888 **68**

Motel $60-$70 **Address:** 8991 University Blvd 15108 **Location:** Jct Business I-376 Loop, 1 mi n. **Facility:** 50 units. 3 stories, interior corridors. **Terms:** cancellation fee imposed.

Access trusted AAA/CAA services on the go with the AAA and CAA Mobile apps

SHERATON PITTSBURGH AIRPORT HOTEL
(412)262-2400 **69**

Hotel
$99-$289

AAA Benefit: Members save up to 15%, plus Starwood Preferred Guest® benefits!

Address: 1160 Thorn Run Rd 15108 **Location:** Business I-376 Loop exit Thorn Run Rd. **Facility:** 200 units. 9 stories, interior corridors. **Pool(s):** outdoor. **Activities:** exercise room. **Guest Services:** valet and coin laundry, area transportation. *(See ad this page.)*

WHERE TO EAT

ARMSTRONG'S RESTAURANT
412/262-9355 **51**

American. Family Dining. $6-$20 **AAA Inspector Notes:** In a small shopping center storefront, the comfortable, casual restaurant encourages family visits. Homemade pastas and desserts, fresh calzones and fresh seafood are prepared in an open kitchen. Large portions are standard. **Address:** 1136 Thorn Run Rd 15108 **Location:** Business I-376 Loop exit Thorn Run Rd, just n; jct Thorn Run and Beaver Grade rds; in Thorn Run Crossing Shopping Center.

HYEHOLDE RESTAURANT
412/264-3116 **50**

Continental. Fine Dining. $25-$42 **AAA Inspector Notes:** Rack of lamb, elk and seafood are specialties on this menu, which is well complemented by an extensive wine list. The French country setting—a re-creation of an old English castle—is quaint and refined. Enjoy the chef's table in the new kitchen and "HyeTea" weekdays between 4 and 6 pm. **Features:** full bar. **Reservations:** suggested. **Address:** 1516 Coraopolis Heights Rd 15108 **Location:** Jct Coraopolis Heights and Beaver Grade rds. **Parking:** valet only.

▼ See AAA listing this page ▼

(See map & index p. 348.)

JACKSONS RESTAURANT-ROTISSERIE-BAR
412/329-1405 ⑷

🔻🔻🔻 American. Casual Dining. $10-$40 **AAA Inspector Notes:** The newer restaurant nurtures a trendy atmosphere suitable for business meetings and relaxing in the lounge. The chef's great menu—which comprises soups, salads and Jackson's power lunch box at midday, as well as a larger selection of grilled entrées, rotisserie chicken and beef items for dinner—lists some special features. **Features:** full bar. **Address:** 8402 University Blvd 15108 **Location:** Jct Business I-376 Loop, 0.8 mi e; in DoubleTree by Hilton Pittsburgh Airport. (B) (L) (D) CALL (&)(M)

OLIVE PRESS
724/899-6050 ⑸

🔻🔻🔻 Mediterranean. Fine Dining. $8-$35 **AAA Inspector Notes:** This restaurant, sitting off from the hotel lobby, is decorated in retro style with modern-day artwork. A Mediterranean-inspired menu is offered, in addition to steaks, surf and turf and stay fit cuisine choices. **Features:** full bar. **Reservations:** suggested. **Address:** 1111 Airport Blvd 15231 **Location:** I-376 exit 53 (Airport Blvd) in Hyatt Regency Pittsburgh International Airport.

(B) (L) (D) CALL (&)(M)

WINGS, SUDS & SPUDS
412/264-1866 ⑸

🔻 American. Casual Dining. $5-$12 **AAA Inspector Notes:** The atmosphere is casual but bustling at this restaurant, which is noted for its chicken wings, salads, sandwiches and other finger foods. All can be ordered for takeout. The small full-service bar carries 20 varieties of American and imported beers. **Features:** full bar. **Address:** 8806 University Blvd 15108 **Location:** 0.5 mi n of jct Business I-376 Loop. (L) (D) (LATE)

CORNWALL (H-9) pop. 4,112, elev. 620'

The Cornwall Ore Banks, on the knobs of South Mountain, Grassy Hill, Middle Hill and Big Hill, contain one of the most valuable deposits of iron ore in the East. The mines operated 1735-1972.

[SAVE] **CORNWALL IRON FURNACE** is off US 322, following markers on SR 419 to 94 Rexmont Rd. The furnace, built by Peter Grubb in 1742, operated until 1883. Structures on the grounds include the original furnace stack; the blast machinery; blowing tubs; wagon and blacksmith shops; the open-pit mine; and the ironmaster's mansion. Exhibits in the Charcoal House, now a visitor center, depict mining operations, charcoal making and iron making.

Time: Allow 1 hour, 15 minutes minimum. **Hours:** Thurs.-Sat. 9-5, Sun. noon-5. Last tour begins 1 hour, 15 minutes before closing. Closed major holidays except Memorial Day, July 4 and Labor Day. Phone ahead to confirm schedule. **Cost:** $8; $7 (ages 65+); $4 (ages 3-11). **Phone:** (717) 272-9711. (GT) (🎫)

COUDERSPORT (D-6) pop. 2,546, elev. 1,650'

Coudersport is a manufacturing community on the banks of the Allegheny River. It was founded by John Keating, an Irish mercenary who managed the Ceres Land Co., which owned most of the county. Keating gave 50 acres to each of the first 50 settlers and named the community after Jean Samuel Couderc, a Dutch banker. A monument to David Zeisberger, a Moravian missionary who camped nearby in October 1767, is in the county courthouse square at Second and Main streets.

Potter County Visitors Association: P.O. Box 245, 188 N. Main St., Coudersport, PA 16915. **Phone:** (814) 274-3365.

WESTGATE INN
814/274-0400

🔻🔻 Hotel $82-$99 **Address:** 307 Rt 6 W 16915 **Location:** On US 6, 1 mi w. **Facility:** 58 units. 1-3 stories, interior corridors. **Terms:** cancellation fee imposed.

(📶) (🍴) (▤) / SOME UNITS (🔌) (💻)

CRABTREE pop. 277

CARBONE'S
724/834-3430

🔻🔻 Italian. Casual Dining. $9-$27 **AAA Inspector Notes:** *Classic.* In business since 1938, the restaurant delivers steak, chops and seafood as well as specialty pizza and Italian dishes with home-made sauces. Mediterranean accents such as wrought iron, brick and red walls decorate the comfortable dining room. Located in a small town off a highway through a residential area. They are known for their Italian sauces, which are offered for sale in cans. House-made onion rings also are highly popular. **Features:** full bar. **Address:** 2582 Rt 119 15624 **Location:** 3 mi s of US 22; center. (D)

CRAFTON pop. 5,951

• Hotels & Restaurants map & index p. 348
• Part of Pittsburgh area — see map p. 326

SAPPORO JAPANESE STEAKHOUSE 412/920-2988 ⑹

🔻🔻 Japanese. Casual Dining. $7-$38 **AAA Inspector Notes:** Chefs prepare meals tableside with fresh seafood, meats and veggies. Tropical drinks accompany any dish. **Features:** full bar. **Reservations:** suggested. **Address:** 4260 Steubenville Pike 15205 **Location:** I-79 exit 60A, 1.5 mi e on SR 60. (L) (D)

CRANBERRY

HOLIDAY INN EXPRESS HOTEL & SUITES

(814)677-2640

Hotel
$123-$149

Address: 225 Singh Dr 16319 **Location:** Jct US 322, just n on SR 257. Next to Cranberry Mall. **Facility:** 65 units. 3 stories, interior corridors. **Parking:** winter plug-ins. **Terms:** cancellation fee imposed. **Pool(s):** heated indoor. **Activities:** exercise room. **Guest Services:** valet and coin laundry. **Featured Amenity:** breakfast buffet.

(SAVE) (🍴) CALL (&)(M) (🛏) (BIZ) (📶)
(✕) (▤) (💻)

CRANBERRY TOWNSHIP

• Restaurants p. 92
• Hotels & Restaurants map & index p. 348
• Part of Pittsburgh area — see map p. 326

CANDLEWOOD SUITES (724)591-8666 ㉛

🔻🔻🔻 Extended Stay Hotel $149-$189 **Address:** 20036 Rt 19 16066 **Location:** I-76 (Pennsylvania Tpke) exit 28; I-79 exit 76 northbound; exit 78 southbound. **Facility:** 75 kitchen units. 4 stories, interior corridors. **Parking:** winter plug-ins. **Pool(s):** heated indoor. **Activities:** hot tub, exercise room. **Guest Services:** complimentary laundry.

(🍴) CALL (&)(M) (🛏) (BIZ) (📶) (✕) (▤) (💻)
/ SOME UNITS (🔌) (HS)

Plan complete trip routings with the
online and mobile TripTik® Travel Planner

(See map & index p. 348.)

COURTYARD BY MARRIOTT PITTSBURGH NORTH/CRANBERRY WOODS   (724)776-1900 27

▼▼▼▼ **Hotel** $146-$240 **Address:** 150 Cranberry Woods Dr 16066 **Location:** I-79 exit 78 to Cranberry Woods Dr. Located in a quiet area. **Facility:** 125 units. 5 stories, interior corridors. **Amenities:** *Some:* safes. **Pool(s):** heated indoor. **Activities:** exercise room. **Guest Services:** valet and coin laundry.

 / SOME UNITS

FAIRFIELD INN BY MARRIOTT PITTSBURGH CRANBERRY TOWNSHIP   (724)772-0600 29

▼▼▼ Hotel $118-$194

FAIRFIELD INN & SUITES® Marriott

Address: 30 St. Francis Way 16066 **Location:** I-76 (Pennsylvania Tpke) exit 28, 0.3 mi n on US 19; I-79 exit 76 northbound; exit 78 southbound, 0.5 mi n on US 19. Located in a quiet area. **Facility:** 102 units. 3 stories, interior/exterior corridors. **Pool(s):** heated outdoor. **Activities:** limited exercise equipment. **Guest Services:** valet laundry. **Featured Amenity:** full hot breakfast.

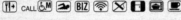

HAMPTON INN CRANBERRY   (724)776-1000 26

▼▼▼▼ **Hotel** $99-$189 **Address:** 210 Executive Dr 16066 **Location:** I-79 (Pennsylvania Tpke) exit 76, 0.5 mi n on US 19, then 0.3 mi w on Freedom Rd; exit 78 southbound, 0.5 mi w on Freedom Rd. Located in a commercial area. **Facility:** 116 units. 4 stories, interior corridors. **Terms:** 1-7 night minimum stay, cancellation fee imposed. **Pool(s):** heated indoor. **Activities:** hot tub. **Guest Services:** valet laundry.

 / SOME UNITS

HILTON GARDEN INN PITTSBURGH/ CRANBERRY   (724)779-9999 24

▼▼▼▼ **Hotel** $149-$199 **Address:** 2000 Garden View Ln 16066 **Location:** I-79 exit 78 to Cranberry Woods Dr. Located in a quiet area. **Facility:** 136 units. 5 stories, interior corridors. *Bath:* shower only. **Terms:** 1-7 night minimum stay, cancellation fee imposed. **Pool(s):** heated indoor. **Activities:** hot tub, picnic facilities, exercise room.

HOLIDAY INN EXPRESS CRANBERRY TOWNSHIP   (724)772-1000 33

▼▼▼▼ **Hotel.** Rates not provided. **Address:** 20003 Rt 19 16066 **Location:** I-76 (Pennsylvania Tpke) exit 28; I-79 exit 76 northbound; exit 78 southbound, just s. **Facility:** 101 units. 2 stories, interior corridors. **Activities:** recreation programs, exercise room. **Guest Services:** valet laundry.

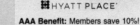

HYATT PLACE PITTSBURGH/CRANBERRY   (724)779-7900 30

▼▼▼ Hotel $84-$199

⋈ HYATT PLACE®

Address: 136 Emeryville Dr 16066 **Location:** I-76 (Pennsylvania Tpke) exit 28; I-79 exit 76 northbound; exit 78 southbound, 0.3 mi s on US 19. **Facility:** 127 units. 6 stories, interior corridors. **Terms:** cancellation fee imposed. **Amenities:** safes. **Pool(s):** heated indoor. **Activities:** exercise room. **Guest Services:** valet laundry. **Featured Amenity:** breakfast buffet. *(See ad this page.)*

▼ See AAA listing this page ▼

(See map & index p. 348.)

PITTSBURGH MARRIOTT NORTH   (724)772-3700  25

▼▼▼▼ **Hotel** $154-$253 **Address:** | **AAA Benefit:**
100 Cranberry Woods Dr 16066 **Loca-** | Members save 5%
tion: I-79 exit 78 to Cranberry Woods Dr. | or more!
Located in a quiet area. **Facility:** 295
units. 8 stories, interior corridors.
Pool(s): heated indoor. **Activities:** exercise room. **Guest Services:**
valet and coin laundry.

🍴 🍸 CALL 🔊M 🏊 BIZ HS 📶 ✕ 🎥 📠
/ SOME UNITS 🛗 🖥

RED ROOF INN PITTSBURGH NORTH CRANBERRY TOWNSHIP   724/776-5670 32

Motel
Rates not provided

Address: 20009 Rt 19 16066 **Location:**
I-76 (Pennsylvania Tpke) exit 28; I-79
exit 76 northbound; exit 78 southbound.
Facility: 108 units. 2 stories (no elevator), exterior corridors. **Amenities:**
safes. **Guest Services:** coin laundry.

SAVE 🍴 📶 ✕
/ SOME UNITS 🐾 🛗 🖥 ☕

RESIDENCE INN BY MARRIOTT PITTSBURGH CRANBERRY
TOWNSHIP   (724)779-1000 28

▼▼▼▼ **Extended Stay Hotel** | **AAA Benefit:**
$167-$275 **Address:** 1308 Freedom Rd | Members save 5%
16066 **Location:** I-76 (Pennsylvania | or more!
Tpke) exit 76, 0.5 mi n on US 19, then
0.3 mi w; I-79 exit 78 southbound, 0.5 mi
w. Located in a commercial area. **Facility:** 96 units, some two bedrooms, efficiencies and kitchens. 4 stories, interior corridors. **Pool(s):**
heated indoor. **Activities:** sauna, hot tub, exercise room. **Guest Services:** valet and coin laundry.

🍽 📶 CALL 🔊M 🏊 BIZ 📶 ✕ 🛗 🖥 📠
/ SOME UNITS 🍳 HS

FLAVOR OF INDIA   724/772-9191 26
▼▼ Indian. Casual Dining. $11-$15 **AAA Inspector Notes:** Located in a strip mall, this restaurant offers authentic Indian cuisine
presented in a modern décor dining room with Indian art. Rasmalai
and tandoori chicken are fantastic. Good service is offered, especially
during the very busy lunch hour when a buffet is available. Free Wi-Fi
is offered. **Features:** happy hour. **Address:** 10 St. Francis Way, Suite
6 16066 **Location:** I-76 (Pennsylvania Tpke) exit 28, just n on US
19. L D

MONTE CELLO'S CRANBERRY   724/772-3133 25
▼▼ American. Casual Dining. $5-$18 **AAA Inspector Notes:**
Tucked in a shopping plaza, guests can sample a variety of pizzas
while relaxing in front of a big-screen TV. The kitchen is consistent
and has pleased locals for more than 10 years. Enjoy a well-prepared
menu of standard Italian favorites such as fettuccine Alfredo, homemade lasagna, stromboli, pasta and more. **Features:** full bar. **Address:** 20325 Rt 19 Perry Hwy 16066 **Location:** I-76 (Pennsylvania
Tpke) exit 28, 1 mi n. L D LATE

PRIMANTI BROTHERS RESTAURANT   724/772-5757
▼▼ American. Casual Dining. $6-$14 **AAA Inspector Notes:**
Looking for a sandwich that offers piled-high fries and coleslaw on top
of each sandwich, then this is the place to be. The bar restaurant
theme is every Pittsburgh's dream with memorabilia for each sports
fan. **Features:** full bar. **Address:** 200 Executive Dr 16066 **Location:**
I-76 (Pennsylvania Tpke) exit 28, 0.5 mi n on US 19, then 0.3 mi w
on Freedom Rd; I-79 exit 78 southbound, 0.5 mi w on Freedom Rd.
L D CALL 🔊M

CRESCO
• **Hotels & Restaurants map & index p. 373**
• **Part of Pocono Mountains Area — see map
p. 371**

CRESCENT LODGE   570/595-7486 15
▼▼▼▼ **Country Inn.** Rates not provided. **Address:** 5854 Paradise Valley Rd 18326 **Location:** 3 mi s on SR 191 at SR 940. Located in a quiet rural area. **Facility:** Manicured grounds enhance this
charming property. You can choose to stay in the main inn or in an
outlying cottage that offers homelike amenities, including a full
kitchen, living room and outdoor patio. 30 units, some kitchens and
cottages. 1-3 stories (no elevator), interior/exterior corridors. **Dining:**
restaurant, see separate listing. **Pool(s):** heated outdoor. **Activities:**
tennis, trails. 🍴 🏊 📶 ✕ / SOME UNITS 🛗 📠

CRESCENT LODGE   570/595-7486 13
▼▼▼▼ Continental. Casual Dining. $16-$29 **AAA Inspector
Notes:** Warm, upscale country décor is featured throughout the
charming dining room, which is subtly illuminated with candlelight.
The menu features Châteaubriand for two, filet mignon, duck, lamb,
chicken and seafood. A pianist performs on weekends. **Features:** full
bar. **Reservations:** suggested. **Address:** 5854 Paradise Valley Rd
18326 **Location:** 3 mi s on SR 191 at SR 940. D

DALLAS pop. 2,804

CONNOR'S GRILLROOM   570/674-5100
▼▼ New Continental Small Plates. Fine Dining. $12-$36
AAA Inspector Notes: A cheerful, contemporary, bistro-style atmosphere punctuates the restaurant, which presents a weekly changing
menu that takes advantage of market-fresh availability and kitchen
creativity from a new chef. Exciting traditional and trendy items such
as Vermont cheddar mac 'n cheese with almonds, roasted mushrooms and truffled crumbs, Californian duck breast with raspberry-
vanilla glaze, butternut squash gnocchi, baby spinach duck confit and
toasted pistachios offer a break toward the unusual. **Features:** full
bar. **Reservations:** suggested. **Address:** 55 Memorial Hwy 18612
Location: Jct SR 118, 0.8 mi e on Memorial Hwy (SR 309).
D

DANVILLE (F-9) pop. 4,699, elev. 456'

Columbia Montour Visitors Bureau: 316 Mill St.,
Danville, PA 17821-2058. **Phone:** (570) 284-4455.

MONTOUR PRESERVE, 5 mi. w. of I-80 exit 224 on
SR 54, then 4.5 mi. n.e., following signs, is a nature
preserve and recreation area centering on 165-acre
Lake Chillisquaque. Visitors enjoy boating, hiking
and fishing in summer and cross-country skiing and
ice fishing in winter. There are marked trails and a
visitor center displaying nature, wildlife and history
exhibits.

Pets are not permitted on the grounds. **Time:**
Allow 1 hour minimum. **Hours:** Visitor center daily
8-4, Memorial Day-Labor Day; hours vary rest of
year. Trails daily dawn-dusk. Phone ahead to confirm schedule. **Cost:** Free. **Phone:** (570) 437-3131.
✕ 🍴

BEST WESTERN PLUS DANVILLE INN   (570)275-5750

Hotel
$119-$139

AAA Benefit:
Members save up to 20%!

Best
Western
PLUS

Address: 79 Old Valley School Rd 17821 **Location:** I-80 exit 224, just s. **Facility:** 58 units. 3 stories, interior corridors. **Pool(s):** heated indoor. **Activities:** exercise room. **Guest Services:** valet laundry.

DANVILLE SUPER 8   (570)275-4640

Motel
$130-$230

Address: 35 Sheraton Rd 17821 **Location:** I-80 exit 224, just sw on SR 54. **Facility:** 120 units. 2 stories (no elevator), exterior corridors. **Terms:** 3 day cancellation notice-fee imposed. **Activities:** game room, exercise room. **Guest Services:** coin laundry. **Featured Amenity: continental breakfast.**

HAMPTON INN DANVILLE   (570)271-2500

Hotel
$123-$170

AAA Benefit:
Members save 5% or more!

Hampton

Address: 97 Old Valley School Rd 17821 **Location:** I-80 exit 224, just s on SR 54. Located in a commercial area. **Facility:** 71 units. 3 stories, interior corridors. **Terms:** 1-7 night minimum stay, cancellation fee imposed. **Pool(s):** heated indoor. **Activities:** hot tub, exercise room. **Guest Services:** valet and coin laundry. **Featured Amenity:** breakfast buffet.

DELAWARE WATER GAP (F-12) pop. 746, elev. 509'
• Hotels & Restaurants map & index p. 373
• Part of Pocono Mountains Area — see map p. 371

Tucked within the Delaware Water Gap National Recreation Area, the small town caters to those exploring the great outdoors. Businesses lining Main Street offer river trips, biking, kayaking and other recreational pursuits. One of the access points to the Appalachian Trail is near Main Street off Mountain Road; from the trailhead, hikers can venture to the top of Mount Minsi for a panorama of the Delaware Water Gap.

The Antoine Dutot Museum, open 1-5 on weekends from Memorial Day weekend through Columbus Day, presents local history displays and art exhibits in a mid-19th-century brick schoolhouse; phone (570) 476-4240 for information. In early September, the Celebration of the Arts presents a weekend of jazz performances in a hillside amphitheater and at various venues throughout town; phone (570) 424-2210.

The Delaware River Scenic Drive, just outside town heading south on SR 611, affords views of the river cutting through an Appalachian Mountain ridge, known as a water gap. Drivers can pull off at Resort Point Overlook, Point of Gap Overlook and Arrow Island Overlook to enjoy the verdant scenery.

Water Gap Trolley offers tours lasting a little more than an hour that will mostly appeal to those who have an interest in the area.

. Sites along the route include the historic Shawnee Church, Cold Air Cave, Indian Head and Shawnee Playhouse. Two short stops are made at roadside parking areas in the Delaware Water Gap National Recreation Area. Phone (570) 476-9766.

A Pennsylvania State Welcome Center providing local information is situated on Broad Street near its intersection with River Road.

WATER GAP COUNTRY CLUB   570/476-4653 **32**
Historic Hotel. Rates not provided. **Address:** 288 Mountain Rd 18327 **Location:** I-80 exit 310, 0.8 mi s on SR 611, then 0.7 mi sw. **Facility:** This appealing small hotel is perched in the hills and surrounded by its own historic 18-hole golf course. Rooms are a bit modest in décor and amenities but are large and comfortable. 24 units. 3 stories (no elevator), interior corridors. *Bath:* shower only. **Pool(s):** outdoor. **Activities:** regulation golf.

WHERE TO EAT

SYCAMORE GRILLE   570/426-1200 **29**
American. Casual Dining. $8-$30 **AAA Inspector Notes:** Dine minutes away from the Delaware River at this cozy restaurant. The lunch menu lists an array of sandwiches, wraps and panini, while dinner offers more sophisticated entrées, including veal T-bone vino bianco, filet mignon au poivre and seafood St. Jacques. **Features:** full bar. **Address:** 92 Main St 18327 **Location:** I-80 exit 310, follow signs to SR 611 S; downtown. L D

DELAWARE WATER GAP NATIONAL RECREATION AREA (E-12) elev. 361'
• Part of Pocono Mountains Area — see map p. 371

Stretching for 40 miles along the Delaware River in New Jersey and Pennsylvania, Delaware Water Gap National Recreation Area encompasses nearly 70,000 acres. Popular with artists and wealthy vacationers during the late 1800s, the gap is a picturesque break in the Kittatinny Ridge of the Appalachian Mountains. The park is threaded by the Delaware River. Wooded Mount Tammany and Mount Minsi rise abruptly 1,200 feet above the river at the Water Gap.

More than 200 miles of scenic roads meander through the valleys and ridges of the park. Trails, wildlife, historic structures and waterfalls can be viewed along the way. A 27-mile portion of the Appalachian Trail winds its way along Kittatinny Ridge in New Jersey and Pennsylvania.

A variety of trails offer hiking, horseback riding and cross-country skiing opportunities. Camping is permitted in the many area campgrounds. Backcountry camping is permitted only along the Appalachian Trail, where regulations are in effect. Open fires are prohibited. In the summer lifeguards are on duty at Smithfield Beach and Milford Beach; these facilities charge a fee. Canoeing, kayaking, boating and fishing (with state license) are permitted on the Delaware River. There are multiple access points; developed access points charge fees.

New Jersey's Millbrook Village, 12 miles north of Kittatinny Point Visitor Center along Old Mine Road, is a re-created rural community featuring residences and other buildings of the late 19th century. On weekends in summer interpreters in period dress demonstrate rural lifestyles; phone (908) 841-9531 on weekends Memorial Day weekend through Labor Day. During Millbrook Days on the first full weekend in October, a hundred interpreters bring the village to life.

Raymondskill Falls, off US 209 at Milepost 18 on Raymondskill Road, is Pennsylvania's tallest waterfall. The upper falls are reached via a hike through a hemlock ravine, and the middle falls are reached via a hike with steep, uneven stairs. The upper falls hike is a quarter-mile round-trip, and the middle falls hike is a half-mile round-trip.

Dingmans Falls, Pennsylvania's second highest waterfall, is off Johnny Bee Road between Mileposts 12 and 13 on US 209 in Dingmans Ferry. A level, quarter-mile boardwalk leads to the bottom of the falls; for those who want to venture to the top, a steep, 240-step staircase awaits. The trail is open daily dawn-dusk (weather permitting); the road closes in winter due to snow and ice. Dingmans Falls Visitor Center offers information daily 9-5, Memorial Day weekend through Labor Day and Thursday through Monday, day after Labor Day to late October. Phone (570) 828-6125.

Kittatinny Point Visitor Center, just off the I-80 toll bridge that crosses into New Jersey, has exhibits and free literature. The center is open daily 9-5, Memorial Day weekend through Labor Day and on weekends in the fall; phone (908) 496-4458.

Park headquarters is in Bushkill, Pa., 1 mile east of US 209 on River Road. It is open Mon.-Fri. 8-4:30; closed federal holidays. Phone (570) 426-2452.

Peters Valley Craft Center, at the junction of CR 615 and Old Mine Road near Layton, N.J., has several historic buildings that have been converted into studios for artisans, a gallery and a craft store; phone (973) 948-5202.

Pennsylvania's Pocono Environmental Education Center is off US 209 on Brisco Mountain Road, 7 miles north of Bushkill. The center offers guided treks, weekend ecology camps and naturalist-led activities; phone (570) 828-2319.

DELMONT   pop. 2,686
• Part of Pittsburgh area — see map p. 326

HOLIDAY INN EXPRESS MURRYSVILLE/DELMONT
724/468-1050

WWWW **Motel.** Rates not provided. **Address:** 6552 Rt 22 15626 **Location:** 0.3 mi w of jct SR 66. Located in a quiet area. **Facility:** 71 units. 3 stories, interior corridors. **Activities:** limited exercise equipment. **Guest Services:** valet laundry.

SUPER 8
(724)468-4888

WW **Hotel** $70-$110 **Address:** 180 Sheffield Dr 15626 **Location:** SR 66, just s of US 22. **Facility:** 46 units. 2 stories (no elevator), interior corridors.

WHERE TO EAT

KING'S FAMILY RESTAURANT
724/468-6020

WW **American. Family Dining.** $6-$15 **AAA Inspector Notes:** Fast and friendly service is offered here. The menu is large in size with descriptive menu items and pictures. The restaurant is also known for its ice cream and dessert menu. **Address:** 200 Sheffield Dr 15626 **Location:** SR 66, just s of US 22.

B L D LATE

LAMPLIGHTER RESTAURANT
724/468-4545

WW
American
Casual Dining
$5-$35

AAA Inspector Notes: Breakfast is served all day at this family restaurant. The dining room offers the very freshest of seafood and prime rib is served daily. Soup, bread and dessert are all homemade. The delicious Boston cream pie is moist and flavorful. A lunch buffet is available Monday through Friday. On Sunday a dinner buffet is offered. Evil Knievel has eaten here. **Features:** full bar, Sunday brunch. **Reservations:** suggested. **Address:** 6566 Rt 22 15626 **Location:** Just w of jct SR 66.

B L D CALL

DENVER   pop. 3,861
• Hotels & Restaurants map & index p. 222
• Part of Pennsylvania Dutch Country area — see map p. 220

COMFORT INN LANCASTER COUNTY NORTH
(717)336-7541   37

WWWW **Hotel** $95-$135 **Address:** 1 Denver Rd 17517 **Location:** I-76 (Pennsylvania Tpke) exit 286, 1 mi w to SR 272, then just s. Located in a commercial area. **Facility:** 110 units. 2 stories, interior corridors. **Pool(s):** outdoor. **Activities:** exercise room. **Guest Services:** coin laundry.

RED ROOF INN DENVER
717/336-4649   38

WW **Hotel.** Rates not provided. **Address:** 2017 N Reading Rd 17517 **Location:** I-76 (Pennsylvania Tpke) exit 286, 1 mi w to SR 272, then just s. Located in a commercial area. **Facility:** 45 units. 2 stories (no elevator), interior corridors. **Activities:** exercise room.

AAA Vacations® packages ...
unforgettable experiences and unrivaled value

(See map & index p. 222.)

WHERE TO EAT

THE BLACK HORSE RESTAURANT & TAVERN
717/336-6555 ③0

♦♦ American. Casual Dining. $14-$34 **AAA Inspector Notes:** Jumbo lump Maryland crab cakes, barbecued smoked baby back ribs, pork tenderloin and artfully presented fresh vegetables are specialties at this casually upscale restaurant. Beef dishes are prepared from aged certified Angus beef. House-prepared soups, desserts and ice creams offer excellent flavor. Six juried regional microbrews, 500 distilled spirits and 100 international bottled beers are served in the comfortable European-style tavern. Servers are pleasant and knowledgeable. **Features:** full bar. **Reservations:** suggested. **Address:** 2170 N Reading Rd 17517 **Location:** I-76 (Pennsylvania Tpke) exit 286, 1 mi w to SR 272, then 0.3 mi n; in Black Horse Lodge and Suites. Ⓓ

DEVON (B-9) pop. 1,515, elev. 499'
• Part of Philadelphia area — see map p. 230

JENKINS ARBORETUM & GARDENS is off US 202 Devon/Valley Forge Rd. exit, .6 mi. s. on N. Valley Forge Rd. (which becomes Devon State Rd.), then .3 mi. w. to 631 Berwyn Baptist Rd. Azaleas, rhododendrons and wildflowers dominate the grounds of this 46-acre botanical garden, which include 1 mile of paved pathways lined with signs and labels informing visitors about the plants and ongoing ecological projects.

Animal residents include flying squirrels, foxes, green herons, kingfishers, owls, red-tailed hawks, turtles and more than 100 other bird species. A self-guiding map of the grounds is available in the John J. Willaman Education & Visitors Center. Educational activities are held and special exhibitions are on display throughout the year. Garden paths are not wheelchair accessible. Pets are not permitted. **Time:** Allow 1 hour, 30 minutes minimum. **Hours:** Gardens open daily 8 a.m.-dusk. Education center open daily 9-4. **Cost:** Free. **Phone:** (610) 647-8870. ⊞ Berwyn, 202

SHANGRILA
610/687-8838

♦♦♦ Asian. Fine Dining. $8-$29 **AAA Inspector Notes:** A must-try at this upscale and contemporary restaurant is the apple-whiskey-glazed duck Margaret served with pearl onions, baby carrots and wasabi mashed potatoes. The menu offers sashimi and tempura but also dishes that are a fusion of various Asian cuisines. A subtle impression of Japanese architecture can be found in the casual décor of light-colored woodwork in both the main dining room, the private areas and the sushi bar. **Features:** full bar, early bird specials, happy hour. **Reservations:** suggested. **Address:** 120 W Swedesford Rd 19333 **Location:** US 202 exit Valley Forge Rd, just s on SR 252 (Swedesford Rd). Ⓛ Ⓓ CALL &M

DICKSON CITY pop. 6,070

FAIRFIELD INN BY MARRIOTT-SCRANTON   (570)346-3222

♦♦ ♦♦ Hotel $104-$194 **Address:** 949 Viewmont Dr 18519 **Location:** I-81 exit 190, just e, follow signs to Viewmont Dr. Near Viewmont Mall. **Facility:** 81 units. 3 stories, interior corridors. Pool(s): heated indoor. **Guest Services:** valet laundry.

AAA Benefit: Members save 5% or more!

 ⦅ǁ⦆ CALL &M ⊠ 🛜 ⊠ 💻 / SOME UNITS 🛏 🖨

HOLIDAY INN EXPRESS & SUITES   (570)307-4437

♦♦♦ Hotel $99-$179 **Address:** 1265 Commerce Blvd 18519 **Location:** I-81 exit 190 northbound, 2 mi n on Viewmont Dr, then just s: exit 191B (US 6 E) southbound, 2.3 mi ne, then just s on Viewmont Dr. **Facility:** 102 units. 4 stories, interior corridors. Pool(s): heated indoor. **Activities:** hot tub, game room, exercise room. **Guest Services:** valet and coin laundry, area transportation.

➡ ⦅ǁ⦆ CALL &M ⊠ BIZ HS 🛜 ⊠ 🛏 🖨 💻

MICROTEL INN & SUITES BY WYNDHAM DICKSON CITY/SCRANTON   (570)307-1200

♦♦♦♦
Hotel
$79-$130

Address: 232 Main St 18519 **Location:** I-81 exit 190, just n. **Facility:** 62 units. 3 stories, interior corridors. **Activities:** exercise room. **Guest Services:** valet and coin laundry. **Featured Amenity:** continental breakfast.

SAVE CALL &M HS 🛜 ⊠ 💻 / SOME UNITS 🛏 🖨

RESIDENCE INN BY MARRIOTT-SCRANTON   (570)343-5121

♦♦♦ Extended Stay Hotel $111-$206 **Address:** 947 Viewmont Dr 18519 **Location:** I-81 exit 190, just e, follow signs to Viewmont Dr. Located near Viewmont Mall. **Facility:** 78 units,

AAA Benefit: Members save 5% or more!

some two bedrooms, efficiencies and kitchens. 3 stories, interior corridors. Pool(s): heated indoor. **Activities:** exercise room. **Guest Services:** valet and coin laundry.

⦅ǁ⦆ ⊠ 🛜 ⊠ 🛏 🖨 💻 / SOME UNITS ⬛ HS

WHERE TO EAT

COLARUSSO'S COAL-FIRED PIZZA   570/489-2627

♦ Pizza. Casual Dining. $9-$14 **AAA Inspector Notes:** Local food? This place takes it further by using local coal to heat the oven that turns out great thin-crust pizzas as well as roasted chicken wings, hearty meatballs and toasty baked sandwiches. They also have a large bar with TVs. The easy location is convenient for nearby hotels or those traveling on I-81. **Features:** full bar. **Address:** 1126 Commerce Blvd 18519 **Location:** I-81 exit 190 northbound, 2 mi n on Viewmont Dr, then just s; exit 191B (US 6 E) southbound, 2.3 mi ne, then just s on Viewmont Dr; in Target shopping plaza.

Ⓛ Ⓓ CALL &M

DONEGAL (H-3) pop. 120, elev. 1,811'

Just off I-76, the small community of Donegal is part of the Laurel Highlands *(see place listing p. 183)* and is surrounded by the Laurel Mountains. It is convenient for hiking on the 70-mile Laurel Highlands Trail, which runs from Ohiopyle State Park to just northwest of Johnstown.

DAYS INN AT DONEGAL (724)593-7536

▼▼▼ **Hotel** $84-$94 **Address:** 3620 Rt 31 15628 **Location:** I-70/76 (Pennsylvania Tpke) exit 91, just e. **Facility:** 51 units. 2 stories (no elevator), interior/exterior corridors. **Amenities:** safes. **Pool(s):** heated outdoor. **Activities:** game room, exercise room. **Guest Services:** coin laundry.

HOLIDAY INN EXPRESS & SUITES (724)593-1881

▼▼▼
Hotel
$83-$129

Address: 3695 SR 31 15628 **Location:** I-70/76 (Pennsylvania Tpke) exit 91, just e. **Facility:** 73 units. 3 stories, interior corridors. **Terms:** cancellation fee imposed. **Pool(s):** heated indoor. **Activities:** hot tub, exercise room. **Featured Amenity:** full hot breakfast.

WHERE TO EAT

OUT OF THE FIRE CAFE 724/259-8887

▼▼ American. Casual Dining. $9-$38 **AAA Inspector Notes:** Nestled into a quiet residential neighborhood next to a stream, this restaurant offers great smoked salmon. Other menu items include appetizers, salads and entrées such as sesame-crusted ahi tuna, fennel-and-orange-dusted duck breast, hand-cut steaks, tasty grilled veal tenderloin and pan-seared Alaskan scallops. A nice selection of wine is available by the glass. A popular outdoor patio is available in season. **Reservations:** suggested. **Address:** 3784 SR 31 15628 **Location:** I-70/76 (Pennsylvania Tpke) exit 91, 1.4 mi e.

DOWNINGTOWN pop. 7,891

• **Part of Philadelphia area — see map p. 230**

THE OLIVE TREE MEDITERRANEAN GRILL 610/873-7911

▼▼ Mediterranean. Casual Dining. $9-$28 **AAA Inspector Notes:** This BYOB spot offers outstanding Greek-focused cuisine, including such options as branzino, char-grilled salmon, lamb souvlaki, moussaka and gyros. Perfect for families or couples, the colorful interior décor features large wall murals and ample seating. You won't be disappointed. **Address:** 379 W Uwchlan Ave 19335 **Location:** Jct US 30 and SR 113, 1.2 mi n.

DOYLESTOWN (H-12) pop. 8,380, elev. 351'

• **Part of Philadelphia area — see map p. 230**

Settled in 1735, Doylestown is in Bucks County *(see place listing p. 74)*, one of Pennsylvania's finest farming areas.

On the campus of Delaware Valley College at 700 E. Butler Ave. is the 60-acre Henry Schmieder Arboretum. The site, which is a nice place for picnics, is open daily dawn to dusk except for major holidays; phone (215) 489-2283. The best time to visit is late afternoons and weekends because there is less student activity.

Central Bucks Chamber of Commerce: Bailiwick Office Campus, Suite 23, 252 W. Swamp Rd., Doylestown, PA 18901. **Phone:** (215) 348-3913.

FONTHILL CASTLE, E. Court St. at SR 313 (Swamp Rd.), is the castle-like dream house of Dr. Henry Chapman Mercer. Built 1908-12, this concrete mansion was designed by the owner from the inside out; he designed the interiors of the rooms and then planned the exteriors to accommodate them. The multilevel dwelling has more than 44 rooms, 32 stairways and more than 200 windows. Works in tile, prints, engravings and memorabilia of Mercer's life are featured.

Time: Allow 1 hour minimum. **Hours:** Guided tours are offered Mon.-Sat. 10-5, Sun. noon-5. Last tour begins 1 hour before closing. Closed Jan. 1, Thanksgiving and Christmas. **Cost:** $14; $12 (ages 65+); $8 (ages 6-17). Reservations are strongly recommended. **Phone:** (215) 348-9461.

JAMES A. MICHENER ART MUSEUM, 138 S. Pine St., is in the renovated 1884 Bucks County prison. The permanent collection features Daniel Garber's 22-foot-mural, "A Wooded Watershed," as well as 19th- and 20th-century regional American art, including many fine pieces by Pennsylvania Impressionists. A permanent exhibit about author James A. Michener re-creates the Bucks County office where he wrote "Tales of the South Pacific." The Patricia D. Pfundt Sculpture Garden features items that pay homage to the area landscape. Nationally touring special exhibitions and regional artists also are showcased.

Time: Allow 1 hour, 30 minutes minimum. **Hours:** Tues.-Fri. 10-4:30, Sat. 10-5. Closed major holidays. **Cost:** $18; $17 (ages 65+); $16 (students with ID); $8 (ages 6-18). Phone ahead to confirm rates. **Phone:** (215) 340-9800. Doylestown, 314

MERCER MUSEUM, 84 S. Pine St. at jct. Ashland St., traces the pre-industrial history of the nation from colonization to the Civil War. Artifacts and implements from the 18th- and 19th centuries represent more than 60 crafts and trades. There also are folk art displays and changing exhibits. Changing exhibits are featured in the gallery.

Time: Allow 2 hours minimum. **Hours:** Museum Mon.-Sat. 10-5, Sun. noon-5. Library Tues.-Thurs.

1-5, Fri.-Sat. 10-5. Closed Jan. 1, Thanksgiving and Christmas. **Cost:** $14; $12 (ages 62+); $8 (ages 6-17); free (first Fri. of the month 6-9 p.m.). Combination ticket with Fonthill Castle $20; $12 (ages 6-17). **Phone:** (215) 345-0210.

 Doylestown, 314

MORAVIAN POTTERY AND TILE WORKS, 130 Swamp Rd., is the restored building used by Dr. Henry Chapman Mercer (1856-1930) for the production of decorative tile and mosaics for public and private buildings throughout the country. A video presentation features Mercer and his production techniques, and a self-guiding tour illustrates the tile making process. **Hours:** Daily 10-4:45. Last tour begins 45 minutes before closing. Closed major holidays. **Cost:** $5; $4 (ages 60+); $3 (ages 7-17). **Phone:** (215) 348-6098.

NATIONAL SHRINE OF OUR LADY OF CZESTO-CHOWA (chen-sto-HO-va) is 1.5 mi. n. on SR 611, 1.5 mi. n.w. on SR 313, then 2 mi. w. on Ferry Rd. On a picturesque tract of 250 acres, the shrine includes a monastery, a visitor center, a rosary garden and a cemetery. The upper church's striking stained-glass windows depict 1,000 years of Polish Christianity. "The Holy Trinity" sculpture is above the altar area; below the sculpture is a copy of the icon "Our Lady of Czestochowa." A small exhibition hall in the visitor center displays religious relics and artwork. **Hours:** Church daily 7:30-5. Visitor center daily 9-4:30. Food is available on Sun. **Cost:** Free. **Phone:** (215) 345-0600. ⊤⊥

HONEY   215/489-4200
▼▼▼ New American. Fine Dining. $14-$36 **AAA Inspector Notes:** This restaurant artfully blends traditional American dishes with ingredients and methods borrowed from other cultures. The Chinese 5 spice sweet potato fries and the foie gras slickers with duck bacon and red wine fig ketchup will awaken every inch of diners' taste buds. The mood is intimate and romantic in this sweet suburban foodie paradise. With a frequently changing seasonal menu, it is worthwhile to visit several times a year. **Features:** full bar. **Reservations:** suggested. **Address:** 42 Shewell Ave 18901 **Location:** Jct SR 611, 1 mi ne on US 202, continue to W Court St, left to N Main St, then just w. Doylestown, 314. **Parking:** street only. ⅅ ⊞

DRUMS

HOLIDAY INN EXPRESS HOTEL & SUITES   570/788-8081
▼▼▼ Hotel. Rates not provided. **Address:** 1 Corporate Dr 18222 **Location:** I-80 exit 262, just s on SR 309. **Facility:** 80 units. 3 stories, interior corridors. **Activities:** exercise room. **Guest Services:** valet laundry.
CALL 🅼 BIZ HS 🛜 💻 /SOME UNITS 🍽 🖨

DUBLIN pop. 2,158
• **Part of Philadelphia area — see map p. 230**

LUBERTO'S TRATTORIA   215/249-0688
▼▼ Italian. Casual Dining. $4-$14 **AAA Inspector Notes:** The Luberto family serves pizza, pasta and entrées topped with home-made sauces at this casual, comfortable spot. An order of garlic bread is more than ample to accompany the meal of a large group. Be prepared to take some food home. **Address:** 169 N Main St 18917 **Location:** Jct SR 413, 3.6 mi n on SR 313.
Ⓛ ⅅ CALL 🅼

DU BOIS pop. 7,794

BEST WESTERN PLUS INN & CONFERENCE CENTER
(814)371-6200

▼▼▼▼
Hotel
$109-$149

AAA Benefit:
Members save up to 20%!

Address: 82 N Park Pl 15801 **Location:** I-80 exit 97 eastbound, 2.5 mi e on DuBois Ave (US 219/SR 255), then just s; exit 101 westbound, 2.7 mi w on DuBois Ave (US 219/SR 255), then just s on US 219. Opposite DuBois Campus, Penn State. **Facility:** 55 units. 2-3 stories (no elevator), interior corridors. **Activities:** playground, picnic facilities, exercise room. **Guest Services:** valet and coin laundry.
SAVE 🍴 BIZ 🛜 🔲 💻 /SOME UNITS 🍽 🖨

FAIRFIELD INN & SUITES BY MARRIOTT DU BOIS
(814)371-2260
▼▼▼ Hotel $101-$166 **Address:** 2219 Bee Line Hwy 15801 **Location:** I-80 exit 101, 1 mi s on SR 255. **Facility:** 91 units. 3 stories (no elevator), interior corridors. **Pool(s):** heated indoor. **Activities:** exercise room. **Guest Services:** coin laundry.

AAA Benefit:
Members save 5% or more!

🍴 🏊 BIZ 🛜 ✕ 🔲 🖨 💻

HAMPTON INN - DU BOIS   (814)375-1000
▼▼▼ Hotel $135-$175 **Address:** 1582 Bee Line Hwy 15801 **Location:** I-80 exit 101, 1 mi s on SR 255. **Facility:** 96 units. 3 stories, interior corridors. **Terms:** 1-7 night minimum stay, cancellation fee imposed. **Pool(s):** heated indoor. **Activities:** hot tub, limited exercise equipment. **Guest Services:** valet and coin laundry.

AAA Benefit:
Members save 5% or more!

🍴 CALL 🅼 🏊 BIZ 🛜 🔲 🖨 💻

HOLIDAY INN EXPRESS & SUITES   814/371-8900
▼▼▼ Hotel. Rates not provided. **Address:** 1690 Rich Hwy 15801 **Location:** I-80 exit 97 eastbound, just s; exit 101 westbound, just s on US 219. **Facility:** 79 units. 3 stories, interior corridors. **Parking:** winter plug-ins. **Pool(s):** heated indoor. **Activities:** hot tub, exercise room. **Guest Services:** coin laundry.
🍴 CALL 🅼 🏊 BIZ HS 🛜 ✕ 🔲 🖨 💻

WHERE TO EAT

THE FORT WORTH RESTAURANT   814/371-7570
▼▼ Steak. Casual Dining. $8-$24 **AAA Inspector Notes:** This Western-themed steakhouse has a small inn and nightclub attached to it. The restaurant is owned by local butcher company Palumbo Market, so the steaks are amazingly tender and fresh. Service is very good, and a large bar is available. **Features:** full bar. **Address:** 229 W Long Ave 15801 **Location:** In downtown historic area.
Ⓛ ⅅ

ITALIAN OVEN   814/371-6836
▼▼ Italian. Casual Dining. $8-$15 **AAA Inspector Notes:** The full-service, family-friendly restaurant serves large portions of tasty favorites. All pasta dishes and entrees come with the signature "bottomless salad" and fresh oven-baked herb bread. Brick oven pizza, strombolis and calzones are among choices that can be eaten in the dining room or carried out. Service is casual but efficient and friendly. Those who don't arrive early can expect a wait. **Features:** full bar. **Address:** 5548 Shaffer Rd 15801 **Location:** I-80 exit 101, 1.2 mi w on SR 255; in DuBois Mall. Ⓛ ⅅ CALL 🅼

Get AAA/CAA travel information in the digital and printed formats you prefer

LUIGIS RISTORANTE   814/375-9113

▼▼ ▼▼ Italian. Casual Dining. $6-$22 **AAA Inspector Notes:** In the business district, the family-owned-and-operated restaurant stays busy for both lunch and dinner. Italian food is at the heart of the menu. **Features:** full bar. **Address:** 32 N Brady St 15801 **Location:** Center of business district. **Parking:** on-site (fee).

L D CALL ♿M

THUNDERBIRD RESTAURANT & LOUNGE   814/371-0799

▼▼ ▼▼ American. Casual Dining. $10-$26 **AAA Inspector Notes:** Traditional surf and turf fare, including well-prepared fresh seafood, steak and chops, is what to expect at this relaxed restaurant. A fireplace and accents of stone and wood contribute to the rustic atmosphere. Homemade apple dumplings are a light, sweet treat. **Features:** full bar. **Reservations:** suggested, weekends. **Address:** 1 Thunderbird Rd 15851 **Location:** SR 255, 2.6 mi s on US 219, 1 mi s on US 119, then 1 mi w. D

DUNCANSVILLE pop. 1,233

COMFORT INN ALTOONA   (814)693-1800

Hotel
$99-$179

Address: 130 Patchway Rd 16635 **Location:** I-99 exit 31 (Plank Rd), 2 mi s on Business Rt US 220. **Facility:** 78 units. 3 stories, interior corridors. **Pool(s):** heated indoor. **Activities:** hot tub, exercise room. **Guest Services:** valet and coin laundry. **Featured Amenity:** full hot breakfast.

SAVE ▮⬤ CALL ♿M ⇌ BIZ 🛜
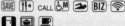
🛏 🖥 💻

WYE MOTOR LODGE   814/695-4407

Motel
$59-$89

Address: 200 Plank Rd 16635 **Location:** I-99 exit 31 (Plank Rd), 2.5 mi s. **Facility:** 36 units. 1 story, exterior corridors. **Parking:** winter plug-ins. **Terms:** 7 day cancellation notice-fee imposed.

SAVE ▮⬤ 🛜 🛏 🖥

WHERE TO EAT

HOSS'S FAMILY STEAK & SEA   814/695-8543

▼▼ Steak. Casual Dining. $7-$29 **AAA Inspector Notes:** Folks can bring the whole family to enjoy the restaurant's 100-item salad bar, homemade soups and bread, steaks, fresh seafood and chicken entrees. A children's menu is available. **Address:** 110 Patchway Rd 16635 **Location:** I-99 exit 31 (Plank Rd), 2 mi e on Business Rt US 220. L D

DUNMORE pop. 14,057

BEST WESTERN PLUS SCRANTON EAST HOTEL & CONVENTION CENTER   570/343-4771

▼▼ ▼▼
Hotel
Rates not provided

Best Western
PLUS

AAA Benefit:
Members save up to 20%!

Address: 200 Tigue St 18512 **Location:** I-84/380 exit 1 (Tigue St), 0.3 mi e of jct I-81. **Facility:** 139 units. 3 stories, interior corridors. **Pool(s):** heated indoor. **Activities:** hot tub, game room, exercise room. **Guest Services:** valet and coin laundry.

SAVE ▮⬤ ▼ ⇌ BIZ 🛜 🎦
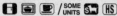
🛏 🖥 💻 / SOME UNITS 🆂⬤ HS

QUALITY INN SCRANTON   (570)348-6101

▼▼ ▼▼
Hotel
$79-$299

Address: 1226 Oneill Hwy 18512 **Location:** I-81 exit 188 (Throop), just e at SR 347 N (Oneill Hwy). Located in a commercial area. **Facility:** 77 units. 4 stories, interior corridors. **Amenities:** safes. **Activities:** limited exercise equipment. **Guest Services:** coin laundry. **Featured Amenity:** continental breakfast.

SAVE ▮⬤ 🛜 🛏 🖥 💻 / SOME UNITS 🆂⬤

SLEEP INN & SUITES   (570)961-1116

▼▼ ▼▼ Hotel $80-$107 **Address:** 102 Monahan Ave 18512 **Location:** I-81 exit 188 (Throop), just e at SR 347 N (Oneill Hwy), then just s. **Facility:** 78 units. 3 stories, interior corridors. **Amenities:** safes. **Pool(s):** heated indoor. **Activities:** hot tub, limited exercise equipment. **Guest Services:** valet and coin laundry, area transportation.

➕ ▮⬤ CALL ♿M ⇌ HS 🛜 🛏 🖥 💻 / SOME UNITS 🆂⬤

WHERE TO EAT

SIBIO'S RESTAURANT   570/961-9274

▼▼ ▼▼ Italian. Casual Dining. $8-$28 **AAA Inspector Notes:** Simple elegance and casual style make this Italian restaurant a local favorite. Salads can be plain or dressed up with apples, almonds, dried cranberries and the house balsamic vinaigrette. Experts in the pasta arena, they also have delicious seafood offerings such as panroasted filet of salmon served on a bed of sautéed spinach, white beans, sun-dried tomatoes and roasted garlic. A nice selection of wines is available for every taste. For dessert, try the popular rum cake. **Features:** full bar. **Address:** 1240 Quincy Ave 18509 **Location:** I-81 exit 188 (Throop), s on Blakely St, then just ne. L D

DUPONT pop. 2,711

HOLIDAY INN EXPRESS   (570)654-3300

 Hotel $90-$159 **Address:** 30 Concorde Dr 18641 **Location:** I-81 exit 178A, just e. Adjacent to Wilkes-Barre/Scranton International Airport. **Facility:** 99 units. 5 stories, interior corridors. **Pool(s):** heated outdoor. **Activities:** exercise room. **Guest Services:** valet and coin laundry, area transportation.

EAGLES MERE pop. 120

CRESTMONT INN   (570)525-3519

 Historic Country Inn $120-$250 **Address:** 180 Crestmont Dr 17731 **Location:** Just n on SR 42 (Eagles Mere Ave), just w on Lakewood Ave. Located in a quiet area. **Facility:** Surrounded by the Endless Mountains in a picturesque Victorian village, the inn offers gracious hospitality. A couple of economy rooms are offered. 15 units, some two bedrooms. 3 stories (no elevator), interior corridors. **Terms:** 7 day cancellation notice-fee imposed. **Activities:** tennis, cross country skiing.

EAST EARL pop. 1,144
• Hotels & Restaurants map & index p. 222

SHADY MAPLE SMORGASBORD   717/354-8222 16

American Family Dining
$10-$24

AAA Inspector Notes: This excellent buffet, fresh and filling, offers such Pennsylvania Dutch cuisine as ham balls, stewed tomatoes, dried corn and noodle-based chicken pot pie. An ample dessert bar is filled with fresh-baked pies, cakes and cookies along with a wide variety of toppings. Specials change throughout the week and include prime rib Wednesday. **Address:** 129 Toddy Dr 17519 **Location:** Jct SR 23, 0.9 mi e on US 322, just n.

B L D

EAST GREENVILLE pop. 2,951
• Part of Philadelphia area — see map p. 230

SCHULTHEIS CARRIAGE HOUSE   215/679-7700

Continental. Casual Dining. $9-$39 **AAA Inspector Notes:** This renovated 18th-century farmhouse offers a cozy, warm atmosphere and an excellent selection of steak, seafood, poultry and pasta entrées. Weekly specials include prime rib on Thursday nights and a lobster special on Friday nights. When weather permits, the beautiful patio area is a great place to enjoy a meal. **Features:** full bar, patio dining, happy hour. **Address:** 745 Gravel Pike 18041 **Location:** I-476 exit 44, 4.8 mi w on SR 663, then 2.3 mi n.

L D

EAST NORRITON pop. 13,590
• Hotels & Restaurants map & index p. 274
• Part of Philadelphia area — see map p. 230

HYATT HOUSE PHILADELPHIA/PLYMOUTH MEETING
(610)313-9990 58

Extended Stay Hotel
$94-$299

HYATT house™
AAA Benefit: Members save 10%!

Address: 501 E Germantown Pike 19401 **Location:** I-476 exit 20, 2.5 mi w. Located in a commercial area. **Facility:** 131 efficiencies, some two bedrooms. 4 stories, interior corridors. **Terms:** cancellation fee imposed. **Pool(s):** heated outdoor. **Activities:** hot tub, exercise room. **Guest Services:** valet and coin laundry, area transportation. **Featured Amenity:** breakfast buffet. (See ad p. 306.)

SAVE BIZ / SOME UNITS

EASTON (G-11) pop. 26,800, elev. 211'
• Hotels p. 100 • Restaurants p. 101
• Hotels & Restaurants map & index p. 49

Easton is nestled in the Lehigh Valley along with Allentown (see place listing p. 46) and Bethlehem (see place listing p. 62).

Easton served as a focal point of the Revolutionary War. The first public reading of the Declaration of Independence in the Colonies occurred on the steps of Northampton County Courthouse when it was in Centre Square. Easton also was the home of George Taylor, a signer of the Declaration of Independence. The Parson-Taylor House, a stone house built in 1757, still stands on S. 4th Street.

During the 19th century Easton became one of America's earliest industrial centers due to its strategic location at the confluence of the Delaware and Lehigh rivers, the Morris Canal and five major railroads. It was during the height of the canal era that many of Easton's fine examples of American architecture were built.

Easton's industrial prosperity was reflected in the founding of Lafayette College in 1832. Daniel Chester French's bronze statue of the Marquis de Lafayette, the French aristocrat who fought with the American Colonists against the British, stands above the city on the Lafayette College campus.

Lehigh Valley Visitor Center—Easton at Sigal Museum: 342 Northampton St., Easton, PA 18042. **Phone:** (610) 253-1222.

Shopping areas: The downtown area surrounding the Crayola Experience features coffee houses, art galleries, antiques shops, restaurants, stores and historic architecture. Since 1752, the Easton Farmers Market has taken place downtown at Centre Square Sat. 9-1 May through November.

SAVE **CRAYOLA EXPERIENCE,** 30 Centre Sq., houses more than 20 interactive experiences on four floors. Guests can see how crayons are made in

(See map & index p. 49.)

a live demonstration as well as learn the history and fun facts about crayons. The attraction offers a personalized crayon label station, customized coloring pages, interactive digital art stations, drip art stations where you can paint with melted wax, a two-story crayon-themed playground and a live theater show. Themes for craft projects are tied to the seasons, and changing exhibits also are presented.

Note: Backpacks are not permitted in the building. **Time:** Allow 3 hours minimum. **Hours:** Daily 10-6, Memorial Day-Labor Day; 9:30-4 rest of year. Closed Easter, Thanksgiving and Christmas. Phone ahead to confirm schedule. **Cost:** $17.99; $13.99 (ages 65+); free (ages 0-1). Ages 0-15 must be with an adult. Additional fees for some craft activities. **Phone:** (610) 515-8000 or (800) 272-9652. 🔟

NATIONAL CANAL MUSEUM, in Hugh Moore Park at 2750 Hugh Moore Park Rd., contains interactive exhibits about the history and technology of Pennsylvania's 19th-century canals. Artifacts, photos and documents housed in the Emrick Center museum building reveal how the canals and the coal transported on them contributed to the Industrial Revolution.

The mule-drawn canal boat *Josiah White II* operates a 45-minute trip on a restored section of the Lehigh Canal. The canal's towpath allows foot and bicycle access to the park's working locks and 19th-century industrial ruins. During summer weekends an 1890s lock tender's house is staffed by a costumed interpreter.

The park offers picnic tables, a children's playground, and paddleboat and canoe rentals. **Hours:** Wed.-Sun. 11:30-4:30, June 7-Aug. 31 (also Memorial Day weekend); Sat.-Sun. noon-5, early Sept.-Sept. 30. Canal boat rides depart on the hour 1-3. Closed Jan. 1, Easter, Thanksgiving, Christmas Eve and Christmas. Phone ahead to confirm schedule. **Cost:** $12; $11 (senior citizens); $9 (ages 3-15). **Phone:** (610) 923-3548. 🅰️

SIGAL MUSEUM, 342 Northampton St., has permanent and changing exhibits about pre- and post-European settlement in the Easton/Bethlehem area. Exhibits illustrate the history of the area from 10,000 years ago to the present. Objects on display include documents, decorative arts, clothing, textiles, military memorabilia and farming implements. The Jane S. Moyer Genealogical Research Library is on-site as well. Docent-led tours are a self-guiding cell phone audio tour are available.

Time: Allow 1 hour minimum. **Hours:** Museum Tues.-Sun. 10-4, June-Labor Day; Wed.-Sat. 10-4, Sun. noon-4, rest of year. Library Wed.-Fri. 9:30-2. Closed Jan. 1, Easter, Memorial Day, July 4, Labor Day, Thanksgiving and Christmas. **Cost:** $7; $5 (ages 3-12). **Phone:** (610) 253-1222. 🄶🅃

SOLDIERS AND SAILORS MONUMENT is on the square in the business district. On this site stood

Northampton County's first courthouse, built in 1765 on a tract presented by the Penn family at an annual rent of one red rose. **Hours:** Daily 24 hours. **Cost:** Free. **Phone:** (610) 250-6711.

COMFORT INN   (610)253-0546

▼▼ **Hotel** $70-$140 **Address:** 2415 Nazareth Rd 18042 **Location:** US 22 exit 25th St, just e on N Service Rd. Adjacent to a shopping plaza. **Facility:** 79 units. 4 stories, interior corridors. **Activities:** exercise room. **Guest Services:** valet laundry.

🔟➕ BIZ 🛜 🟦 🖥️ 🖥️

GRAND EASTONIAN SUITES HOTEL   (610)258-6350

▼▼▼ **Hotel** $109-$239 **Address:** 140 N Northampton St 18042 **Location:** US 22 exit 4th St (SR 611), just e to 3rd St, just s to downtown square, then e towards river. **Facility:** 37 units, some two bedrooms, three bedrooms and kitchens. 10 stories, interior corridors. **Terms:** check-in 4 pm. **Amenities:** safes. **Pool(s):** heated indoor. **Activities:** exercise room. **Guest Services:** coin laundry.

🔟 CALL 🆘Ⓜ 🔄 BIZ HS 🛜 ✖️ 🖥️
/SOME UNITS 🆘 🖥️ 🖥️

HAMPTON INN EASTON   (610)250-6500

▼▼▼ **Hotel** $119-$169 **Address:** 3723 Easton-Nazareth Hwy 18045 **Location:** SR 33 exit SR 248 (Easton-Nazareth Hwy), 0.4 mi e. Located in a commercial area. **Facility:** 97 units. 5 stories, interior corridors. **Terms:** 1-7 night minimum stay, cancellation fee imposed. **Pool(s):** heated indoor. **Activities:** exercise room. **Guest Services:** valet laundry.

> **AAA Benefit:** Members save 5% or more!

🔟➕ 🍽️ CALL 🆘Ⓜ 🔄 BIZ HS 🛜 ✖️ 📹 🖥️ 🖥️ 🖥️

HOLIDAY INN EXPRESS HOTEL & SUITES   610/923-9495 🔟

▼▼▼ **Hotel.** Rates not provided. **Address:** 90 Kunkle Dr 18045 **Location:** US 22 exit 25th St, 0.5 mi w, follow signs. **Facility:** 68 units. 3 stories, interior corridors. **Pool(s):** heated indoor. **Activities:** exercise room. **Guest Services:** valet and coin laundry.

🔟➕ CALL 🆘Ⓜ 🔄 BIZ HS 🛜 ✖️ 🖥️ 🖥️ 🖥️

THE LAFAYETTE INN   610/253-4500

▼▼▼ **Historic Bed & Breakfast.** Rates not provided. **Address:** 525 W Monroe St 18042 **Location:** US 22 exit 4th St (SR 611), just n on 3rd St, 0.3 mi ne on College Ave, then 0.3 mi n on Cattell St to jct Monroe St. Located in a residential area. **Facility:** Elaborately carved headboards are among the elegant period antiques furnishing the three floors of guest rooms at this 1895 grand mansion. 18 units, some kitchens. 4 stories (no elevator), interior/exterior corridors. **Guest Services:** valet laundry.

🔟➕ 🛜 ✖️ /SOME UNITS 🆘 🖥️ 🖥️ 🖥️

TOWNEPLACE SUITES BY MARRIOTT - BETHLEHEM/EASTON   (610)829-2000

▼▼▼
Extended Stay Hotel
$118-$194

TownePlace SUITES Marriott

> **AAA Benefit:** Members save 5% or more!

Address: 3800 Easton-Nazareth Hwy 18045 **Location:** SR 33 exit SR 248 (Easton-Nazareth Hwy), 0.6 mi w. **Facility:** 86 units, some two bedrooms, efficiencies and kitchens. 4 stories, interior corridors. **Terms:** check-in 4 pm. **Pool(s):** heated indoor. **Activities:** hot tub, exercise room. **Guest Services:** valet and coin laundry. **Featured Amenity:** continental breakfast.

🆂🅰️🆅🅴 🔟➕ 🔄 BIZ HS 🛜 ✖️ 🖥️ 🖥️ 🖥️
/SOME UNITS 🆘

(See map & index p. 49.)

WHERE TO EAT

GARDEN BUFFET   610/258-6668

Asian. Casual Dining. $5-$12 **AAA Inspector Notes:** Enjoy this restaurant's extensive buffet, which offers such Asian favorites as teriyaki chicken, steamed dumplings, wonton soup, snow crab legs and sesame beef. **Address:** 3758 Nazareth Rd 18045 **Location:** SR 33 exit SR 248 (Nazareth Rd), just e. [L] [D]

MARBLEHEAD GRILLE AND CHOWDER HOUSE
                                                            610/258-4301   [18]

Seafood. Casual Dining. $13-$37 **AAA Inspector Notes:** Nautically themed, this casual restaurant is notable for its fresh seafood. What happens next is up to you. Get your favorite items grilled, baked, poached, blackened or prepared Cajun style. If you're a landlubber, perhaps you'd prefer prime rib or filet mignon. The 2-plus-pound lobster and the salmon, which is marinated and rubbed with spices, then grilled and served over colorful Southwestern corn relish, are particularly recommended. **Features:** full bar. **Reservations:** suggested. **Address:** 4101 William Penn Hwy 18045 **Location:** Jct US 22 and SR 33, 0.5 mi s on SR 33 exit William Penn Hwy, 1 mi e. [L] [D]

MORICI'S RESTAURANT   610/253-6257

Italian. Casual Dining. $5-$19 **AAA Inspector Notes:** Mostly known by the local Lafayette College students for its take-out counter, this restaurant also offers a sizable menu of Italian specialties including broccoli rabe and Italian sausage, chicken parmigiana and tomato pie. Beer and a small selection of wines also are available. **Features:** beer & wine. **Address:** 218 Cattell St 18045 **Location:** US 22 exit 4th St (SR 611), just n on 3rd St, 0.5 mi ne on College Ave, then just s of jct High St. **Parking:** street only. [L] [D]

NONNA LIA PIZZA CHEF   610/258-5800   [17]

Italian. Family Dining. $6-$19 **AAA Inspector Notes:** Bring the family to this locally popular, cozy spot. Here you can sample fresh pizza, pasta and sandwiches. **Address:** 4011 William Penn Hwy 18045 **Location:** SR 33 exit William Penn Hwy, 1.2 mi e. [L] [D]

PEARLY BAKER'S ALE HOUSE   610/253-9949

American. Casual Dining. $6-$30 **AAA Inspector Notes:** *Historic.* Pearly Baker's Ale House has a lot more style than you might expect for a building that got its start as a YMCA. It was built in 1863 and was converted in 1935, and the present dining room still reflects that 1930s style. A beautiful chandelier and historic memorabilia decorate the walls, and the lounge area features a 50-foot marble bar and a skylight with open-tram windows. The affordable menu changes with the seasons and focuses on steak, seafood and pub classics. **Features:** full bar. **Reservations:** suggested, weekends. **Address:** 11 Centre Square 18042 **Location:** US 22 exit 4th St (SR 611), just e to 3rd St, then just s to southeast quadrant of downtown square. **Parking:** street only. [L] [D]

RIVER GRILLE   610/923-5110

American. Fine Dining. $7-$33 **AAA Inspector Notes:** Just off the downtown square, this hip restaurant is known for delivering contemporary cuisine reflecting Latin American, Asian and Italian influences at very reasonable prices. Of special interest is a delectable variety of gourmet pizzas and fresh seafood dishes. The upscale décor is casual but sophisticated. **Features:** full bar. **Reservations:** suggested. **Address:** 243 Northampton St 18042 **Location:** US 22 exit 4th St (SR 611), just e to 3rd St, just s to downtown square, then just e. [L] [D] CALL [M]

WILLIAMS FAMILY RESTAURANT   610/253-8281   [16]

American. Family Dining. $3-$16 **AAA Inspector Notes:** It is hard to tell if the loyal patrons come for the hefty portions of affordable, yummy classics (such as chicken Parmigiana, stuffed shells, Philly cheesesteak or corn fritters) or if they are here to catch up with the friendly, attentive staff. Either way, the experience offers a comforting taste of home amid a sea of mediocre diners. **Address:** 3630 William Penn Hwy 18045 **Location:** SR 33 exit William Penn Hwy, 1.6 mi e. [B] [L] [D] CALL [M]

EAST STROUDSBURG (F-11) pop. 9,840, elev. 427'
• Hotels & Restaurants map & index p. 373
• Part of Pocono Mountains Area — see map p. 371

RECREATIONAL ACTIVITIES
Tubing
• **Fernwood Resort,** 5785 Milford Rd., offers year-round tubing. Other activities also are offered. **Hours:** Schedule varies by season; phone for details. **Phone:** (888) 337-6966 or TTY (888) 316-3844.

BUDGET INN & SUITES   (570)424-5451   [40]

Hotel
$70-$116

Address: 320 Greentree Dr 18301 **Location:** I-80 exit 308, just se. **Facility:** 112 units. 2-3 stories (no elevator), interior/exterior corridors. **Dining:** The Roasted Tomato, see separate listing. **Activities:** limited exercise equipment. **Guest Services:** valet and coin laundry.

DAYS INN EAST STROUDSBURG   (570)424-1951   [38]

Hotel
$60-$120

Address: 838 Seven Bridges Rd 18301 **Location:** I-80 exit 309, just se. **Facility:** 106 units. 2 stories (no elevator), exterior corridors. **Terms:** cancellation fee imposed. **Pool(s):** heated indoor. **Activities:** game room, exercise room. **Guest Services:** coin laundry. **Featured Amenity:** continental breakfast.

SUPER 8 EAST STROUDSBURG   (570)424-7411   [39]

Motel $55-$149 **Address:** 340 Greentree Dr 18301 **Location:** I-80 exit 308, just se. **Facility:** 57 units. 3 stories (no elevator), interior corridors. **Terms:** cancellation fee imposed. **Amenities:** safes. **Guest Services:** coin laundry.

WHERE TO EAT

HOLY GUACAMOLE   570/420-1909   [33]

Mexican. Quick Serve. $3-$7 **AAA Inspector Notes:** This bright, spacious spot may feature a short menu, but the fresh salsa, meats, cheeses and veggies can be combined into dozens of combinations. The staff is extremely friendly and a filling meal can be had on the cheap. **Address:** 107 Brown St 18301 **Location:** I-80 exit 308, 0.4 mi n on Prospect St, just w on Ridgeway St, then just sw; in Pocono Plaza Shopping Center. [L] [D] CALL [M]

Keep your focus safely

on the road when driving

(See map & index p. 373.)

PEPPE'S BISTRO 570/421-4460 [32]

Northern
Italian
Casual Dining
$9-$33

AAA Inspector Notes: This updated modern, casual bistro is popular with locals, and it's easy to see why. The menu offers some familiar Italian favorites, pizzas and pastas as well as a few chef specialty entrées such as the veal chop stuffed with prosciutto and mozzarella or the sea bass with a crispy panko crust and lemon caper sauce. The staff is very friendly, and the atmosphere is relaxed and comfortable both in the dining room and the inviting lounge. **Features:** full bar, early bird specials, happy hour. **Reservations:** suggested, weekends. **Address:** 100 Eagle Valley Mall 18301 **Location:** Jct SR 447 N and Business Rt US 209; at Eagle Valley Mall. [D]

THE ROASTED TOMATO 570/424-5451 [34]

American
Casual Dining
$9-$22

AAA Inspector Notes: Nestled in the Pocono Mountains, this restaurant is known for its weekend breakfast buffet and 42-item super fresh salad bar. On the dinner menu are such items as grilled marinated salmon, zesty crunchy cod, Mediterranean chicken, New York strip steak and baby back ribs. The lunch menu is a bit more casual with sandwiches and burgers offered. Service is laid back yet thorough. **Features:** full bar. **Address:** 320 Greentree Dr 18301 **Location:** I-80 exit 308, just se; in Budget Inn & Suites. *Menu on AAA.com* [B] [L] [D]

EBENSBURG pop. 3,351

COMFORT INN 814/472-6100

Hotel. Rates not provided. **Address:** 111 Cook Rd 15931 **Location:** Jct US 219, just e on US 22. **Facility:** 77 units. 3 stories, interior corridors. **Amenities:** safes. **Pool(s):** heated indoor. **Activities:** hot tub, limited exercise equipment. **Guest Services:** valet and coin laundry.

THE NOON-COLLINS INN 814/472-4311

Historic Bed
& Breakfast
$90

Address: 114 E High St 15931 **Location:** Just e of jct High and Center sts; downtown. **Facility:** This 1834 restored historic Federal-style property resides in the heart of Ebensburg. Every room is thoughtfully arranged and decorated to reflect a cozy country style. 6 units. 2 stories (no elevator), interior corridors. *Bath:* shower only. **Terms:** 7 day cancellation notice-fee imposed. **Featured Amenity:** full hot breakfast.

ECKLEY (F-10) elev. 1,654'

ECKLEY MINERS' VILLAGE is off SR 940, following signs. This living-history museum is a 19th-century anthracite mining village with approximately 50 buildings. Exhibits, pictures and a 17-minute video presentation shown in the visitor center depict the lives of miners and their families. Some houses not open to the public are occupied by descendants of miners.

Time: Allow 2 hours minimum. **Hours:** Museum center Mon.-Sat. 9-5, Sun. noon-5. Guided walking tours are offered at Mon.-Sat. at 11 and 2 and Sun. at 2, Memorial Day weekend-Labor Day. Closed holidays except Memorial Day, July 4 and Labor

Day. **Cost:** (includes guided tour) $10; $9 (ages 65+); $8 (ages 3-11). Museum only $8; $7 (ages 65+); $6 (ages 3-11). Walking tour only, $2. **Phone:** (570) 636-2070.

EDINBORO pop. 6,438

COMFORT SUITES (814)969-7000

Hotel $89-$189 **Address:** 1007 Market Place Dr 16412 **Location:** I-79 exit 166, just e. **Facility:** 82 units. 3 stories, interior corridors. **Pool(s):** heated indoor. **Activities:** hot tub, exercise room. **Guest Services:** coin laundry.

ELDRED (C-5) pop. 825, elev. 1,500'

ELDRED WWII MUSEUM is at 201 Main St. The war's history and its effect on the region is depicted with electronic exhibits, sound and light effects, dioramas, photographs, a dateline, documents and audiovisual history narrations. A sculpture exhibit re-creates a local defense plant and honors the women who worked on its production line. A research library is included. **Time:** Allow 1 hour minimum. **Hours:** Tues.-Sat. 10-4, Sun. 1-4. **Cost:** $5; free (ages 0-18). **Phone:** (814) 225-2220 or (866) 686-9944.

ELIZABETH (H-2) pop. 1,493, elev. 752'
• Part of Pittsburgh area — see map p. 326

ROUND HILL PARK AND EXHIBIT FARM, .5 mi. e. of SR 51 on SR 48, then s. on Round Hill Rd., is a complete small-scale working exhibit farm built in 1790. Highlights include a brick farmhouse built in 1838 and livestock, including dairy and beef cattle, sheep, pigs, chickens and horses. There also are an adjoining park, a picnic area and duck pond. Walking and bridle trails, an exhibit garden and children's splash park are available. **Time:** Allow 30 minutes minimum. **Hours:** Farm daily 8-dusk. Dairy cows are milked at 4. Office Mon.-Fri. 8-4. **Cost:** Free. **Phone:** (412) 384-4701.

ELIZABETHTOWN (H-9) pop. 11,545, elev. 462'
• Hotels & Restaurants map & index p. 222
• Part of Pennsylvania Dutch Country area — see map p. 220

THE MASONIC VILLAGE of the Grand Lodge of Free and Accepted Masons of Pennsylvania is on the s.w. edge of town on SR 241 at One Masonic Dr. The 1,400-acre scenic campus, which includes a retirement community and children's home, features many Gothic-style granite buildings dating to the early 1900s. Exhibits displayed in the cultural center depict the village's history.

An extensive model train layout, a farm market and 7 miles of walking paths are other highlights. Unusual trees and plants are found in a 6.5-acre formal garden. An eternal flame monument to veterans also is on site. Pets are not permitted on the grounds. **Hours:** Grounds daily dawn-dusk. Cultural

(See map & index p. 222.)

center Mon.-Sat. 9-noon and 1-4, Sun. 1-4. **Cost:** Free. **Phone:** (717) 367-1121. **GT**

HOLIDAY INN EXPRESS ELIZABETHTOWN (HERSHEY AREA) (717)367-4000 **24**

◆◆◆ Hotel $131-$175

Address: 147 Merts Dr 17022 **Location:** SR 283 exit Elizabethtown/ Rheems. **Facility:** 82 units. 2 stories, interior corridors. **Activities:** exercise room. **Guest Services:** valet laundry. **Featured Amenity:** continental breakfast. *(See ad p. 154.)*

SAVE CALL M BIZ HS 🛜
✕ 🖊 🍽 💻 / SOME UNITS 🔒

WHERE TO EAT

FLOWERS IN THE KITCHEN 717/361-9158 **22**
◆◆ American. Casual Dining. $5-$15 **AAA Inspector Notes:** In an 1840 former men's clothing store, this converted restaurant has displays of handmade crafts. Menu items, which are fittingly named for flowers, are of the light gourmet variety. Attention is focused on presenting health-conscious selections. An early dinner menu is available Friday and Saturday only. No credit cards are accepted, but an ATM machine is nearby. **Address:** 8 S Market St 17022 **Location:** Jct SR 743 and 230, just w; downtown. **Parking:** on-site (fee) and street. B L

ELLWOOD CITY pop. 7,921
• Part of Pittsburgh area — see map p. 326

CHAPEL VALLEY ESTATE BED AND BREAKFAST 724/201-0811
◆◆◆ Bed & Breakfast. Rates not provided. **Address:** 297 Chapel Dr 16117 **Location:** I-79 exit 88 (US 19/Perry Hwy), left on SR 588, then 7 mi w. **Facility:** This property was built with recycled materials from an existing original farmhouse dating back to the 1800s. 5 units, some kitchens. 2 stories (no elevator), interior/exterior corridors. **Guest Services:** valet laundry.
BIZ 🛜 ☎ / SOME UNITS 🖊 🍽

WHERE TO EAT

SHAKESPEARE'S RESTAURANT & PUB AT OLDE STONEWALL GOLF COURSE 724/752-4653
◆◆◆ American. Casual Dining. $8-$28 **AAA Inspector Notes:** You will feel like a king or queen dining at this large, beautiful castle that sits on several acres of lush green golf course. The dining room incorporates design elements from Old World England with a knight who greets you upon entrance, dark wooden paneling, a painted tin ceiling and a coat of arms adorning the walls. The dining room also is large in size and height; this matches the menu, which offers an array of chicken, pork, steaks and seafood dishes. **Features:** full bar, Sunday brunch, happy hour. **Address:** 1495 Mercer Rd 16117 **Location:** Jct SR 65 and Chapel Dr.
L D CALL M

Ask about on-the-go
vehicle battery testing
and replacement

ELYSBURG (F-9) pop. 2,194, elev. 587'

KNOEBELS AMUSEMENT RESORT, 2 mi. n. on SR 487 at 391 Knoebels Blvd., features more than 60 rides, 26 games, miniature golf, an 18-hole golf course, a swimming pool and waterslides. A bald eagle habitat, a mining museum and a carousel museum also are on the premises. The Scenic Skyride takes visitors up and down a mountainside for views of the valley and park.

Time: Allow 6 hours minimum. **Hours:** Mon.-Sat. 11-10, Memorial Day weekend-Labor Day; hours vary rest of year. Phone ahead to confirm schedule. **Cost:** Park free. Rides 75c-$3 each. All-day ride pass available Mon.-Fri., mid-June to late-Aug.; Sat.-Sun. in May and Sept. Swimming pool and waterslides are additional; phone ahead to confirm rates. **Phone:** (570) 672-2572 or (800) 487-4386.
🔺 🎴

EMPORIUM (E-5) pop. 2,073, elev. 1,040'

BUCKTAIL STATE PARK NATURAL AREA is on SR 120 between Emporium and Lock Haven. The 16,433-acre park was named for the Civil War soldiers from the local Bucktail Regiment who built rafts in order to travel from Driftwood to the endangered State Capitol as quickly as possible.

A scenic drive follows Sinnemahoning Creek and the West Branch of the Susquehanna River through a narrow valley called the Bucktail Trail, also known as the Sinnemahoning Trail, which Native Americans used for traveling between the Susquehanna and Allegheny rivers. **Hours:** Daily dawn-dusk. **Cost:** Free. **Phone:** (814) 486-3365.

ENOLA pop. 6,111
• Hotels & Restaurants map & index p. 138

QUALITY INN ENOLA (717)732-0785 **32**

◆◆◆ Motel $69-$299

Address: 501 N Enola Rd 17025 **Location:** I-81 exit 65, 1.7 mi s on US 11. **Facility:** 71 units. 2 stories (no elevator), interior corridors. **Amenities:** safes. **Activities:** exercise room. **Guest Services:** coin laundry. **Featured Amenity:** continental breakfast.

SAVE 🍴 BIZ HS 🛜 🖊 💻
/ SOME UNITS 🍽

WHERE TO EAT

TAVERN ON THE HILL 717/732-2077 **23**
◆◆◆ Steak Seafood. Fine Dining. $20-$35 **AAA Inspector Notes:** You may rub elbows with dignitaries from the state's capital at Tavern on the Hill, an appropriately named spot that sits hillside. The relaxed setting and helpful staff help you unwind after a busy day. **Features:** full bar, happy hour. **Reservations:** suggested. **Address:** 109 Howard St 17025 **Location:** Jct US 11 and 15, follow signs.
D CALL M

(See map & index p. 138.)

VISAGGIO'S RISTORANTE 717/697-8082

Italian. Fine Dining. $22-$35 **AAA Inspector Notes:** *Classic.* Sample flavorful cuisine from the Abruzzi region of Italy in this 200-year-old converted barn. Boasting original chestnut beams and stone pillars, the dining space is decorated with antiques. **Features:** full bar. **Reservations:** suggested. **Address:** 6990 Wertzville Rd 17025 **Location:** I-81 exit 57, 1.1 mi w. D

EPHRATA (H-10) pop. 13,394, elev. 381'
• Attractions map p. 221
• Hotels & Restaurants map & index p. 222
• Part of Pennsylvania Dutch Country area — see map p. 220

Ephrata Chamber of Commerce: 16 E. Main St., Suite 1, Ephrata, PA 17522. **Phone:** (717) 738-9010.

Shopping areas: The Green Dragon Farmers Market, 955 N. State St., offers a wide variety of goods at its indoor and outdoor stands Fri. 9-9, Mar.-Dec. (9-8, Jan.-Feb.).

  EPHRATA CLOISTER, 632 W. Main St., was one of America's earliest communal societies. The cloister was established in 1732 by Conrad Beissel, a German immigrant who came to Pennsylvania to be able to worship freely under William Penn's policy of religious tolerance. The charismatic Beissel espoused a life of solitude and self-denial that included celibacy and Saturday as the main day of worship.

A small group of followers joined him, and at its height in the mid-18th century the community consisted of 80 celibate Brothers and Sisters and a group of approximately 200 known as the Householders, married family groups who supported Beissel with funds and assistance but were unwilling to live the austere life of the Brothers and Sisters.

The community of religious celibates practiced a Spartan, regimented lifestyle, emphasizing spiritual goals rather than material ones. They wore long white robes, ate only one meal a day, were allowed only 6 hours of sleep each night and built and occupied a distinctive group of European-style wooden buildings.

The cloister was an early center for publishing and printing, and the residents were known for their detailed hand-illuminated books and German-style calligraphy known as *Frakturschriften.* The self-reliant Brothers made their own ink and paper and had their own bindery. They also composed their own a cappella music and hymns. After Beissel's death in 1768, the community began to decline; the last celibate member died in 1813.

Nine of the original buildings on the 28-acre site have been restored and furnished to re-create the atmosphere of the 18th-century communal village. Following a 15-minute introductory film in the visitor center, 45-minute tours are conducted by knowledgeable costumed guides. The five-story, half-timbered meetinghouse and the four-story dormitory known as the Sisters' House can only be seen on the guided tour. Self-guided and cell phone tours also are available. Special events are offered throughout the year.

Time: Allow 1 hour, 30 minutes minimum. **Hours:** Mon.-Sat. 9-5, Sun. noon-5, Apr.-Oct.; Tues.-Sat. 9-5, Sun. noon-5, Mar.-Dec.; Wed.-Sat. 9-5, Sun. noon-5, rest of year. Tour times vary; phone ahead to confirm schedule. Closed Jan. 1, Easter, Veterans Day, Columbus Day, Thanksgiving, day after Thanksgiving and Christmas. **Cost:** $10; $9 (ages 65+); $6 (ages 3-11). Phone ahead to confirm rates. **Phone:** (717) 733-6600.

HAMPTON INN & SUITES EPHRATA-MOUNTAIN SPRINGS (717)733-0661 **7**

 Hotel $129-$165

 AAA Benefit: Members save 5% or more!

Address: 380 E Main St 17522 **Location:** US 322, 1.3 mi w, just n on Spring Garden St, then just w on Hill St. **Facility:** 72 units. 4 stories, interior corridors. **Terms:** 1-7 night minimum stay, cancellation fee imposed. **Pool(s):** heated indoor. **Activities:** exercise room. **Guest Services:** valet laundry. **Featured Amenity:** full hot breakfast.

WHERE TO EAT

AROMAS DEL SUR 717/738-0101 **10**

Colombian. Casual Dining. $9-$22 **AAA Inspector Notes:** While the dining room features a simple décor with blue tablecloths and metal chairs, the food is what keeps guests coming back. Flavorful dishes of flank steak, empanadas, tamales, grilled pork and plantains fill the Spanish-inspired menu. Remember to bring your favorite wine from home to this BYOB establishment. **Features:** patio dining. **Address:** 548 S State St 17522 **Location:** 0.6 mi w of jct US 322 and State St. L D

ISAAC'S FAMOUS GRILLED SANDWICHES 717/733-7777

Deli Sandwiches. Quick Serve. $8-$12 **AAA Inspector Notes:** The modern, New York-style delicatessen specializes in overstuffed grilled sandwiches named after birds, plants and flowers. Salads and homemade soups also are popular. A tropical feel is prevalent in the colorful, casual dining room. **Address:** 120 N Reading Rd 17522 **Location:** SR 272, just n of jct US 322; in Cloister Shopping Center. L D

LILY'S ON MAIN 717/738-2711 **9**

American. Fine Dining. $9-$33 **AAA Inspector Notes:** Lending to the upscale Art Deco style in the dining area of this restaurant are a cascading lobby waterfall, lush woodwork and decorative brass window treatments. Try a variety of classic American favorites prepared with an artistic flair, including horseradish salmon and raspberry chicken. Be sure to call ahead for brunch reservations. **Features:** full bar, Sunday brunch. **Reservations:** suggested, weekends. **Address:** 124 E Main St 17522 **Location:** Jct US 322 and Lake St; on 2nd Floor of Brossman Business Complex. L D

ERIE (C-2) pop. 101,786, elev. 710'
• Hotels p. 107 • Restaurants p. 108

Pennsylvania's only port on the Great Lakes was founded in 1795 after the purchase of the Erie Triangle. The region's first inhabitants were the Eriez Indians, for whom the lake and city were named. In 1753 a French military expedition built Fort Presque Isle on the site of Erie and Fort LeBoeuf on the site of Waterford *(see place listing p. 414).* The French abandoned their forts in 1759; the next year the English took possession and rebuilt them.

Three years later the English were driven out by Native Americans led by Chief Pontiac, who destroyed both forts. The region remained free of Europeans until the spring of 1795, when 200 men from Gen. Anthony Wayne's army built a building on the bluff overlooking the bay. During the War of 1812 ships built at Erie under the command of Commodore Oliver Hazard Perry were instrumental in eliminating British naval control of the Great Lakes.

As the state's fourth largest city, modern Erie is a center of diversified industry and commerce that also offers a variety of entertainment and recreational opportunities. The Bayfront District, off the Bayfront Parkway via I-79 and I-90, is set against the backdrop of Presque Isle Bay. The cornerstone of the district is the Raymond M. Blasco M.D. Memorial Library, the Erie Maritime Museum and US Brig *Niagara (see attraction listing)* and the Bayfront Convention Center. Water-taxi service connects the Bayfront to Presque Isle State Park *(see attraction listing)* as well as Dobbins Landing and Liberty Park where outdoor concerts, festivals and performances are held seasonally; phone (814) 881-2502 for water taxi and (814) 455-7557 for Liberty Park amphitheater.

Erie's miles of inland waterways can be explored via private boats or sightseeing cruises. Boat rentals are available at many local marinas. Weekend sightseeing boat trips depart from the Perry Monument in Presque Isle State Park from mid-May to mid-June and from the second week in September to September 30; phone (814) 836-0201 or (800) 988-5780 for reservations. Charter fishing services are generally available May through October.

A portion of the Seaway Trail, a scenic byway, includes SR 5, the Bayfront Parkway Loop and Peninsula Drive from West Sixth Street to Presque Isle State Park. It continues on into New York for some 450 miles paralleling Lake Erie, Niagara River and part of the St. Lawrence Seaway.

The city is home to the Class AA Erie SeaWolves, an affiliate of the Detroit Tigers. Baseball season runs April through October with games played at the 6,000-seat Jerry Uht Park; phone (814) 456-1300. The Erie Otters, part of the Ontario Hockey League, play at the Erie Insurance Arena late September through mid-March; phone (814) 452-4857 or (814) 456-7070. The arena also is home to the Erie BayHawks, November through April; the team is part of the NBA Development League and affiliated with the

Cleveland Cavaliers and Toronto Raptors; phone (814) 790-5600.

VisitErie: 208 E. Bayfront Pkwy., Suite 103, Erie, PA 16507. **Phone:** (814) 454-1000 or (800) 524-3743.

Shopping areas: The major shopping center in Erie is Millcreek Mall, US 19 and Interchange Road, featuring some 175 stores, including The Bon-Ton, JCPenney, Macy's and Sears. The mall complex also includes adjacent plazas. The Bayfront District offers gift shops.

ASBURY WOODS NATURE CENTER is off I-90 exit 18, 4.7 mi. n. on SR 832, 1.8 mi. w. on 38th St., then just s. to 4105 Asbury Rd. This 200-acre site includes an education center, Children's Discovery Room, a restored barn, live animal exhibits, and nature trails through 4.5 miles of trails through a variety of natural habitats. Hiking, fishing, cross-country skiing, snowshoeing and mountain biking are permitted. Fishing is available at nearby Walnut Creek.

Time: Allow 1 hour minimum. **Hours:** Mon.-Sat. 10-5, Sun. noon-5, June-Aug.; Tues.-Sat. 10-4, Sun. noon-4, rest of year. Trails daily dawn-dusk. Closed major holidays. **Cost:** Free. **Phone:** (814) 835-5356.

BICENTENNIAL TOWER, 7 State St., was built at Dobbins Landing in 1995 to celebrate Erie's 200th birthday. The 187-foot tower overlooks the historic bay-front district and Presque Isle Bay. Visitors may take the elevator to the observation decks, which feature open-air and enclosed viewing areas; the highest one is at 138 feet.

Time: Allow 30 minutes minimum. **Hours:** Daily 9:30 a.m.-10 p.m., day after Memorial Day-Labor Day; daily 10-8, May 1 to day before Memorial Day; daily 10-6, mid-Apr. to late Apr. and day after Labor Day to Sept. 30; daily 10-5, early Apr. 1 to mid-Apr.; Sat.-Sun. noon-4, rest of year. Phone ahead to confirm schedule. **Cost:** $3; $2 (ages 7-12); free (first Sun. of the month). **Phone:** (814) 455-7577.

ERIE ART MUSEUM is at 411 State St.; visitors can enter the museum at 20 E. 5th St. The galleries in this 1839 Greek Revival brick and marble building house historical and contemporary works of art, including community-based work, contemporary craft, folk art, multi-disciplinary installations and traditional media. Temporary exhibits, performances, classes, workshops and lectures also are offered.

Time: Allow 1 hour minimum. **Hours:** Tues.-Sat. 11-5, Sun. 1-5. Closed major holidays. **Cost:** $7; $5 (senior citizens and students with ID); free (ages 0-5, each Wed. and second Sun. of each month). **Phone:** (814) 459-5477.

ERIE MARITIME MUSEUM AND US BRIG *NIAGARA* is at 150 E. Front St. just off Bayfront Pkwy. Regional maritime heritage with emphasis on the War of 1812 and the history of the USS

Michigan/Wolverine is interpreted through interactive exhibits and multimedia presentations. In the Live Fire exhibit a section of a re-created wooden warship illustrates the rigors of fighting at sea. The *Niagara*, a re-creation of Oliver Hazard Perry's relief flagship, sails frequently and operates as a sailing school vessel in summer months. Guided tours are available when it is in port.

Time: Allow 2 hours minimum. **Hours:** Mon.-Sat. 9-5, Sun. noon-5, Apr.-Sept.; Thurs.-Sat. 9-5, Nov.-Mar.; Mon.-Sat. 9-5 in Oct. Open Mon. holidays. Closed Jan. 1, Thanksgiving and Christmas. **Cost:** $10 (includes museum and ship when in port); $8 (ages 65+); $5 (ages 3-11); free (active military with ID and immediate family). **Phone:** (814) 452-2744. 🍴

ERIE ZOO is 3 mi. n. of I-90 exit 27 at 423 W. 38th St. The main zoo contains more than 400 animals on 15 acres. The Wild Asia exhibit features exotic mammals, reptiles and primates, including a family of Bornean orangutans. Several botanical gardens and a children's zoo also are offered. A train ride and carousel are offered seasonally (weather permitting).

Time: Allow 1 hour minimum. **Hours:** Daily 10-5, Mar.-Nov. **Cost:** $8.50; $6 (ages 62+); $5 (ages 2-12). Train ride and carousel $2. **Phone:** (814) 864-4091. 🍴

EXPERIENCE CHILDREN'S MUSEUM is at 420 French St. The museum's three floors offer hands-on art, science, reading and imaginative play exhibits for kids from toddlers to 10 years old. Exhibits include an interactive water table, a bedrock cave and a creativity center as well as Old Town, which features a doctor's office, a bank, a delicatessen and a kids market.

Time: Allow 1 hour, 30 minutes minimum. **Hours:** Tues.-Sat. 10-4, Sun. 1-4. Closed major holidays. Phone ahead to confirm schedule. **Cost:** $6; free (ages 0-1). Phone ahead to confirm rates. **Phone:** (814) 453-3743.

HAGEN HISTORY CENTER, 356 W. Sixth St. in the West Sixth Street Historic District, is a three-building campus that includes the Watson-Curtze Mansion, a 24-room mansion built in 1891. It features stained-glass windows, friezes and decorative stone and woodwork. Exhibits by the Erie County Historical Society will vary throughout the year and may be geared to different age levels.

The carriage house will be renovated with a reading room and gift shop. A new 10,000-square-foot archive building is also a part of the site.

At press time, the Hagen History Center was still undergoing renovations. A grand reopening is scheduled for 2015. Phone ahead for updates. **Time:** Allow 1 hour minimum. **Hours:** Tues.-Sat. 11-4. Closed major holidays. Phone ahead to confirm schedule. **Cost:** $9; $7 (ages 4-12). **Phone:** (814) 454-1813.

PRESQUE ISLE STATE PARK is 7 mi. n. of I-90 exit 18 at 301 Peninsula Dr. (SR 832). This 3,200-acre peninsula on Lake Erie offers bicycling, boating, fishing, hiking, in-line skating and swimming. In winter, ice fishing, ice-skating and cross-country skiing are available (weather permitting). *See Recreation Areas Chart.* **Hours:** Park daily dawn-dusk. Phone ahead to confirm schedule. **Cost:** Free. **Phone:** (814) 833-7424.
🍴 🎿 🚤 ⛺

Tom Ridge Environmental Center is at 301 Peninsula Dr. at the entrance of Presque Isle State Park. The state-of-the-art facility was designed to be a green building with environment-friendly features and includes 7,000 square feet of exhibit space. Two floors of exhibits and hands-on displays chronicle the natural history of the area. A 15-minute orientation film is shown in a 60-seat theater every 20 minutes. A 75-foot observation tower provides panoramic views of Lake Erie. The Big Green Screen, a 4-story, 45-foot-wide giant screen theater, offers science and entertainment films.

Time: Allow 2 hours minimum. **Hours:** Daily 10-6. Phone ahead to confirm movies and for movie times. Closed Jan. 1, Thanksgiving and Christmas. **Cost:** Center free. Movie $5-$7.50; phone to confirm. **Phone:** (814) 833-7424. 🍴

SPLASH LAGOON INDOOR WATER PARK RESORT is off I-90 exit 24, then s. to 8091 Peach St. The indoor water park features waterslides, a wave pool, a lazy river, family whirlpools, a 1,000-gallon tipping bucket and a five-story interactive Tiki Tree House. The Tree Tops Ropes Course above the water park includes a tightrope, rickety bridges and balance beams. There also is an arcade and laser tag space.

Time: Allow 2 hours minimum. **Hours:** Hours vary; phone for schedule. **Cost:** Peak Day Pass $44.95; $34.95 (under 42 inches tall); $19.95 (spectator); free (ages 0-2). Peak Day Pass after 4 p.m. $34.95; $26.95 (under 42 inches tall); $17.95 (spectator); free (ages 0-2). Non-Peak Day Pass $39.95; $29.95 (under 42 inches tall and ages 65+); $14.95 (spectator); free (ages 0-2). Non-Peak Day Pass after 4 p.m. $29.95; $21.95 (under 42 inches tall and ages 65+); $12.95 (spectator); free (ages 0-2). Peak days vary per month; phone to confirm rates. Ropes course (one climb) $7; $10 (all-day access). Aqua Tumbler $7. **Phone:** (814) 217-1111 or (866) 377-5274. 🍴

WALDAMEER PARK & WATER WORLD, 7 mi. n. of I-90 exit 18 on Peninsula Dr. (SR 832) at the entrance to Presque Isle State Park, is an amusement and water park complex. The amusement park offers 32 rides, a live music stage show, midway entertainment and a video-game arcade. The water park features 16 slides, an "endless" river ride and a large wave pool.

Hours: Waldameer Park Tues.-Sun. and Mon. holidays noon-10 (weather permitting), late June-Labor Day. Water World Tues.-Sun. and Mon. holidays 11-7 (weather permitting), late June-Labor Day. Phone ahead to confirm schedule.

Cost: Waldameer Park entry free. Unlimited ride pass $26.99; $17.99 (under 48 inches tall). Individual ride tickets are available. Water World $23.99; $17.99 (under 48 inches tall). Combination unlimited rides and Water World pass $34.99; $24.99 (under 48 inches tall and ages 65+). **Phone:** (814) 838-3591 or (877) 817-1009.

GAMBLING ESTABLISHMENTS

- **Presque Isle Downs & Casino** is off I-90 exit 27 to 8199 Perry Hwy. **Hours:** Casino daily 24 hours. Racetrack Sun.-Thurs. 5:25-9, mid-May through Sept. 30. Racetrack schedule may vary; phone ahead to verify. **Phone:** (814) 860-8999 or (866) 374-3386.

BAYMONT INN ERIE PA　(814)866-8808
Hotel $72-$189 **Address:** 8170 Perry Hwy 16509 **Location:** I-90 exit 27, just s. **Facility:** 110 units, some two bedrooms. 4 stories, interior corridors. **Activities:** exercise room. **Guest Services:** valet and coin laundry.

CLARION LAKE ERIE & BEL AIR CONFERENCE CENTER　(814)833-1116
Hotel $70-$190 **Address:** 2800 W 8th St 16505 **Location:** I-79 exit 183B, 1.5 mi w on SR 5, then just n. Located in a commercial area. **Facility:** 131 units. 3 stories, interior corridors. **Terms:** check-in 4 pm. **Pool(s):** heated indoor. **Activities:** sauna, hot tub, exercise room. **Guest Services:** valet and coin laundry, area transportation.

COMFORT INN PRESQUE ISLE　(814)835-4200
Hotel $62-$180 **Address:** 3041 W 12th St 16505 **Location:** I-79 exit 183B, 1.5 mi w on SR 5. **Facility:** 100 units. 3 stories, interior corridors. **Terms:** check-in 4 pm. **Pool(s):** heated outdoor. **Guest Services:** valet and coin laundry, area transportation.

COUNTRY INN & SUITES BY CARLSON SOUTH　(814)864-5810
Hotel $69-$199 **Address:** 8040 Oliver Rd 16509 **Location:** I-90 exit 24, just s, then 0.5 mi w. Located in a commercial area. **Facility:** 75 units. 3 stories, interior corridors. **Terms:** cancellation fee imposed. **Pool(s):** heated indoor. **Activities:** hot tub, exercise room. **Guest Services:** valet and coin laundry.

COURTYARD BY MARRIOTT/ERIE　(814)860-8300
Hotel $83-$194 **Address:** 7792 Peach St 16509 **Location:** I-90 exit 24, just n. Located in a commercial area. **Facility:** 110 units. 6 stories, interior corridors. **Activities:** sauna, hot tub, exercise room. **Guest Services:** valet and coin laundry.
AAA Benefit: Members save 5% or more!

FAIRFIELD INN BY MARRIOTT ERIE　(814)868-0985
Hotel $69-$148 **Address:** 2082 Interchange Rd 16565 **Location:** I-79 exit 180, just e; in Pavilion Marketplace. **Facility:** 79 units. 4 stories, interior corridors. **Pool(s):** heated indoor. **Activities:** hot tub. **Guest Services:** valet laundry.
AAA Benefit: Members save 5% or more!

GLASS HOUSE INN　(814)833-7751
Motel $75-$137 **Address:** 3202 W 26th St 16506 **Location:** I-79 exit 182, 1.4 mi w on US 20. **Facility:** 30 units. 1 story, exterior corridors. **Terms:** 2 night minimum stay - seasonal and/or weekends, cancellation fee imposed. **Pool(s):** heated outdoor.

HAMPTON INN ERIE SOUTH　(814)866-6800
Hotel $99-$199 **Address:** 8050 Old Oliver Rd 16509 **Location:** I-90 exit 24, just s, then 0.5 mi w. **Facility:** 101 units. 4 stories, interior corridors. **Terms:** check-in 4 pm, 1-7 night minimum stay, cancellation fee imposed. **Pool(s):** heated indoor. **Activities:** exercise room. **Guest Services:** valet and coin laundry.
AAA Benefit: Members save 5% or more!

HILTON GARDEN INN　(814)866-1390
Hotel $109-$329 **Address:** 2225 Downs Dr 16509 **Location:** I-90 exit 24, just n on Peach St, then just w. **Facility:** 104 units. 5 stories, interior corridors. **Terms:** 1-7 night minimum stay, cancellation fee imposed. **Pool(s):** heated indoor. **Activities:** hot tub, exercise room. **Guest Services:** valet and coin laundry.
AAA Benefit: Members save 5% or more!

HOLIDAY INN EXPRESS HOTEL & SUITES　814/217-1100

Hotel Rates not provided **Address:** 8101 Peach St 16509 **Location:** I-90 exit 24, just s. Adjacent to indoor water park. **Facility:** 112 units. 5 stories, interior corridors. **Terms:** check-in 4 pm. **Amenities:** Some: video games. **Activities:** exercise room. **Guest Services:** valet and coin laundry. **Featured Amenity:** breakfast buffet.

HOMEWOOD SUITES BY HILTON　814/866-8292
Extended Stay Hotel. Rates not provided. **Address:** 2084 Interchange Rd 16565 **Location:** I-79 exit 180, just e; in Pavilion Marketplace. **Facility:** 89 units, some two bedrooms, efficiencies and kitchens. 4 stories, interior corridors. **Pool(s):** heated indoor. **Activities:** exercise room. **Guest Services:** valet and coin laundry.
AAA Benefit: Members save 5% or more!

LA QUINTA INN & SUITES　(814)864-1812
Hotel $65-$244 **Address:** 7820 Perry Hwy 16509 **Location:** I-90 exit 27, just n. **Facility:** 71 units. 3 stories, interior corridors. **Bath:** shower only. **Amenities:** safes. **Pool(s):** heated indoor. **Activities:** exercise room. **Guest Services:** valet laundry.

MICROTEL INN BY WYNDHAM ERIE　　(814)864-1010

Motel
$59-$119

Address: 8100 Peach St 16509 **Location:** I-90 exit 24, just s. Across from indoor water park. **Facility:** 97 units. 3 stories, interior corridors. **Terms:** cancellation fee imposed. **Amenities:** safes. **Activities:** exercise room. **Guest Services:** valet and coin laundry. **Featured Amenity:** breakfast buffet.

RED ROOF INN ERIE　　814/868-5246

Motel
Rates not provided

Address: 7865 Perry Hwy 16509 **Location:** I-90 exit 27, just s. **Facility:** 110 units. 2 stories (no elevator), interior/exterior corridors. **Amenities:** safes.

SHERATON ERIE BAYFRONT HOTEL　　(814)454-2005

Hotel
$109-$399

Sheraton
HOTELS & RESORTS

AAA Benefit: Members save up to 15%, plus Starwood Preferred Guest® benefits!

Address: 55 West Bay Dr 16507 **Location:** Waterfront. I-90 exit 22B to Bayfront Connector; I-79 to Bayfront Pkwy. Next to convention center. **Facility:** 200 units. 8 stories, interior corridors. **Parking:** on-site (fee). **Terms:** 2 night minimum stay - seasonal and/or weekends. **Dining:** Bayfront Grille, see separate listing. **Pool(s):** heated indoor. **Activities:** hot tub, fishing, exercise room. **Guest Services:** valet and coin laundry.

SPRINGHILL SUITES BY MARRIOTT ERIE　　(814)864-5000

Hotel $83-$171 **Address:** 2087 Interchange Rd 16509 **Location:** I-79 exit 180, just e; in Millcreek Marketplace. **Facility:** 117 units. 4 stories, interior corridors. **Pool(s):** heated indoor. **Activities:** exercise room. **Guest Services:** valet and coin laundry.

AAA Benefit: Members save 5% or more!

TOWNEPLACE SUITES BY MARRIOTT ERIE　　(814)866-7100

Extended Stay Hotel $83-$171 **Address:** 2090 Interchange Rd 16565 **Location:** I-79 exit 180, just e; in Pavilion Marketplace. **Facility:** 99 units, some two bedrooms and kitchens. 4 stories, interior corridors. **Terms:** check-in 4 pm. **Pool(s):** heated indoor. **Activities:** hot tub, exercise room. **Guest Services:** valet and coin laundry.

AAA Benefit: Members save 5% or more!

Add AAA or CAA Associate Members

to bring home the benefits of membership

WINGATE BY WYNDHAM　　(814)860-3050

Hotel $109-$179 **Address:** 8060 Old Oliver Rd 16509 **Location:** I-90 exit 24, just s on Peach St, just w, just n, then just e. **Facility:** 100 units. 4 stories, interior corridors. **Amenities:** safes. **Pool(s):** heated indoor. **Activities:** hot tub, exercise room. **Guest Services:** valet laundry.

WHERE TO EAT

BAYFRONT GRILLE　　814/454-2005

American. Casual Dining. $9-$29 **AAA Inspector Notes:** Located on the Erie bayfront with a beautiful view of the water and incoming/outgoing boats. The all-American menu features trendy choices. Although the ambiance is upscale, you will be comfortable in casual dress. Seasonal patio dining facing the waterfront is offered. **Features:** full bar, Sunday brunch. **Reservations:** suggested, for dinner. **Address:** 55 West Bay Dr 16507 **Location:** I-90 exit 22B to Bayfront Connector; I-79 to Bayfront Pkwy; in Sheraton Erie Bayfront Hotel. B L D CALL

BERTRAND'S BISTRO　　814/871-6477

French. Fine Dining. $18-$34 **AAA Inspector Notes:** Owned by Certified Master Chef Bertrand Artiques, this little eatery is great for festive occasions or a very special meal. It's located in the business district across from Perry Square. The authentic French cuisine is noted for its rich, buttery goodness, so make sure you sample one of the seven homemade crêpes. Not surprisingly, they are also well known for an excellent wine selection. **Features:** full bar, Sunday brunch. **Reservations:** suggested. **Address:** 18 N Park Row 16501 **Location:** I-79 exit 183A, just e on W 12th St, left on State St, then just n off State St; downtown. **Parking:** street only. D

LATINO'S RESTAURANT & BAR　　814/452-1966

Mexican
Casual Dining
$14-$22

AAA Inspector Notes: Authentic Mexican cuisine without preservatives is the cornerstone of this restaurant's success. Delicious family recipes sometimes take all day to prepare, but the result is downright delicious. The very casual atmosphere and family-friendly staff put guests at ease. **Features:** full bar. **Address:** 1315 Parade St 16503 **Location:** I-90 exit 27 (State St), 3.3 mi n on SR 97 (Old French Rd), then 0.9 mi n; between 13th and 14th sts. **Parking:** on-site and street. *Menu on AAA.com* D

PUFFERBELLY ON FRENCH STREET　　814/454-1557

American. Casual Dining. $8-$25 **AAA Inspector Notes:** Recalling the nickname given to steam pumpers and engines of the late 1800s, this eatery is decorated with artifacts of the Erie Fire Department. Constructed in 1907, the historic fire station closed in 1979. The menu centers on creative, seasonal dishes. **Features:** full bar, Sunday brunch. **Reservations:** suggested, for dinner. **Address:** 414 French St 16507 **Location:** Just se of public dock. **Parking:** street only. L D

SENSORY 3 AT PRESQUE ISLE DOWNS & CASINO

814/866-8359

Steak Seafood. Fine Dining. $25-$55 **AAA Inspector Notes:** Located in the Presque Isle Downs Casino, this upscale American steakhouse offers high-quality cuts of beef, pork, seafood, shellfish and homemade desserts. Their creative tapas menu offers intriguing choices such as shark tacos and pick-up sticks. Its new bistro atmosphere is great for any special occasion or a great meal for the foodies out there. They offer an extensive wine list. After 10 pm the lounge crowd may enjoy music and cocktails. No one under 21 may be admitted. **Features:** full bar. **Reservations:** suggested. **Address:** 8199 Perry Hwy 16509 **Location:** I-90 exit 27, just n on Perry Hwy, follow signs for Presque Isle Downs & Casino. **Parking:** on-site and valet. D CALL

SYD'S PLACE　　814/838-3089

American. Casual Dining. $6-$20 **AAA Inspector Notes:** This is a great spot for seafood at a reasonable price. Clam chowder, hearty Lake Erie perch, stuffed grouper, coconut shrimp, homemade deserts and crabcakes are some of the specialties served by this husband-and-wife team. Although the focus is on ocean favorites, landlubber fare also shares menu space. **Features:** full bar. **Address:** 2992 W Lake Rd 16505 **Location:** I-79 exit 183B, 1.5 mi w on SR 5, then just s. D

ERWINNA
• Part of Philadelphia area — see map p. 230

GOLDEN PHEASANT INN   610/294-9595
 Historic Country Inn. Rates not provided. **Address:** 763 River Rd 18920 **Location:** SR 32, 0.5 mi n of jct Dark Hollow Rd. **Facility:** Just off the Delaware River, this historic inn provides elegantly appointed rooms with luxurious plush bedding, upscale furnishings, marble bathrooms and gas fireplaces. 4 units. 3 stories (no elevator), interior corridors. *Bath:* shower only. **Terms:** check-in 4 pm. **Amenities:** safes. **Dining:** restaurant, see separate listing. ⓘ 📶 ✕ ☎

WHERE TO EAT

GOLDEN PHEASANT INN   610/294-9595
French
Fine Dining
$22-$45
AAA Inspector Notes: Between the Delaware River and canal, this restored 1857 mule-barge stop now is a favorite spot in which to enjoy distinctive cuisine. Maine day boat scallops, wild Alaskan halibut and Lancaster County lamb shank are among the well-prepared specialties. Two original dining rooms with fireplaces, beamed ceilings, exposed stone walls and an attractive plate and ceramics collection offer a romantic setting. **Features:** full bar, patio dining, Sunday brunch. **Reservations:** suggested. **Address:** 763 River Rd 18920 **Location:** SR 32, 0.5 mi n of jct Dark Hollow Rd.
D

ESSINGTON
• Hotels & Restaurants map & index p. 274
• Part of Philadelphia area — see map p. 230

THE CLARION HOTEL CONFERENCE CENTER
(610)521-9600 135
Hotel $109-$229 **Address:** 76 Industrial Hwy 19029 **Location:** I-95 exit 9A, 0.4 mi sw on SR 291. Located in a commercial area. **Facility:** 297 units. 7 stories, interior corridors. **Pool(s):** outdoor. **Activities:** exercise room. **Guest Services:** valet and coin laundry.
✕ ⓘ 🐾 Y 🏊 BIZ 📶 ✕ 🎥 ▯
/ SOME UNITS 🛗 🍽

HOLIDAY INN EXPRESS PHILADELPHIA AIRPORT
(610)521-1200 136
Hotel $129-$159 **Address:** 101 Taylor Ave 19029 **Location:** I-95 exit 9A, 0.9 mi s on US 420, then just w. **Facility:** 72 units. 4 stories, interior corridors. **Activities:** exercise room. **Guest Services:** valet and coin laundry.
✕ CALL 🔊M BIZ HS 📶 ✕ 🍽 ▯

RED ROOF INN PHILADELPHIA AIRPORT
610/521-5090 133

Motel
Rates not provided
Address: 49 Industrial Hwy 19029 **Location:** I-95 exit 9A, 0.3 mi sw on SR 291. Located in a commercial area. **Facility:** 135 units. 2-3 stories, exterior corridors. **Amenities:** safes. **Guest Services:** coin laundry.

WYNDHAM GARDEN HOTEL PHILADELPHIA AIRPORT
(610)521-2400 134
Hotel
$89-$239
Address: 45 Industrial Hwy 19029 **Location:** I-95 exit 9A, 0.3 mi sw on SR 291. Located in a commercial area. **Facility:** 308 units. 6 stories, interior corridors. **Terms:** check-in 4 pm. **Amenities:** safes. **Pool(s):** heated outdoor. **Activities:** exercise room. **Guest Services:** valet laundry, area transportation.
SAVE ✕ ⓘ Y CALL 🔊M
🏊 BIZ 📶 ✕ 🍽 ▯

WYNDHAM
🟦 GARDEN

Great airport location. Park and fly packages. Close to Harrah's Casino, easy access from I-95.

EXTON pop. 4,842
• Restaurants p. 110
• Part of Philadelphia area — see map p. 230

DULING-KURTZ HOUSE & COUNTRY INN   610/524-1830
Historic Country Inn. Rates not provided. **Address:** 146 S Whitford Rd 19341 **Location:** Jct SR 100, 1 mi w on Business Rt US 30, 0.3 mi s. Located in a commercial area. Whitford, 197. **Facility:** This inn offers 15 guest rooms, each named and themed for a famous historical figure and appointed with reproduction furniture. Several upscale shopping centers are within a short drive. 13 units. 3 stories (no elevator), interior corridors. **Terms:** age restrictions may apply. **Dining:** restaurant, see separate listing.
ⓘ Y 📶 ✕ 🐾

HILTON GARDEN INN EXTON/WEST CHESTER
(610)458-8822

Hotel
$119-$199
Hilton Garden Inn
AAA Benefit: Members save 5% or more!

Address: 720 Eagleview Blvd E 19341 **Location:** I-76 exit 312, 0.4 mi s, then just w. **Facility:** 135 units. 5 stories, interior corridors. *Bath:* shower only. **Terms:** 1-7 night minimum stay, cancellation fee imposed. **Pool(s):** heated indoor. **Activities:** hot tub, exercise room. **Guest Services:** valet and coin laundry, area transportation.
SAVE Y CALL 🔊M 🏊 BIZ HS
📶 ✕ 🍽 ▯

HOLIDAY INN EXPRESS   (610)524-9000
Hotel $139-$169 **Address:** 120 N Pottstown Pike 19341 **Location:** I-76 (Pennsylvania Tpke) exit 312, 3 mi s at Business Rt US 30 and SR 100. Located in Whiteland Towne Center. Exton, 198. **Facility:** 124 units. 4 stories, interior corridors. **Pool(s):** outdoor. **Activities:** exercise room. **Guest Services:** valet laundry.
ⓘ CALL 🔊M 🏊 BIZ 📶 ✕ ▯
/ SOME UNITS 🍽 🐾

Keep a current AAA/CAA Road Atlas in every vehicle

WHERE TO EAT

DULING-KURTZ HOUSE & COUNTRY INN   610/524-1830

♦♦♦♦ Continental. Fine Dining. $18-$42 **AAA Inspector Notes:** *Historic.* Friendly servers in formal attire go to great lengths to satisfy you at this 1830s country inn, which has seven intimate dining rooms appointed with lovely antiques. From the enclosed porch dining room you can see the small fountain and gazebo in the lovely gardens. As you browse the menu of veal, lamb and farm-raised game, take an extra minute to ponder hickory-smoked buffalo fillet with a pearl onion and pine nut sauce. **Features:** full bar, happy hour. **Reservations:** suggested. **Address:** 146 S Whitford Rd 19341 **Location:** Jct SR 100, 1 mi w on Business Rt US 30, 0.3 mi s. ♨ Whitford, 197. ⓛ ⓓ 🍴

THE POUR HOUSE   610/280-7900

♦♦ American. Casual Dining. $8-$15 **AAA Inspector Notes:** While many will come to this local favorite to be "poured" one of the 100-plus beers offered, the menu is nothing to ignore with out-standing bar snacks, hearty salads, savory appetizers, delicious sandwiches and award-winning burgers. The spacious dining room features a wraparound bar at the center, a fresh shucked oyster bar and multiple TVs for ample viewing. **Features:** full bar, happy hour. **Address:** 116 N Pottstown Pike 19341 **Location:** I-76 (Pennsylvania Tpke) exit 312, 3 mi s at Business Rt US 30 and SR 100. ♨ Exton, 198. ⓛ ⓓ CALL 🍴

RIVER STONE CAFE   610/594-2233

♦♦♦♦ American. Casual Dining. $5-$15 **AAA Inspector Notes:** This restaurant presents an upscale contemporary appear-ance. A water wall, river pebbles in the clear glass door handles and ceiling disks that suggest millstones all evoke the restaurant's name. Crab cakes are a specialty on a menu of innovative American cuisine. The raw bar features oysters from around the world. **Features:** full bar, Sunday brunch, happy hour. **Reservations:** suggested, week-ends. **Address:** 143 W Lincoln Hwy 19341 **Location:** I-76 (Pennsyl-vania Tpke) exit 312, 3 mi s on SR 100; in Whiteland Towne Center. ♨ Exton, 198. ⓛ ⓓ 🍴

SHIP INN   610/363-7200

♦♦♦♦ Seafood Steak. Fine Dining. $10-$39 **AAA Inspector Notes:** *Historic.* Choose from two dining experiences in this historic fieldstone building, a former stagecoach tavern that's been serving its guests continuously since 1796. Head to the rear Grill Room, a lounge offering more contemporary décor, or dine in one of the front rooms for a more formal meal. If you choose the latter, you'll dine by candlelight amid fireplaces, soft padded damask-print walls and ship paintings. The surf and turf, crab imperial and Roquefort steak come highly recommended. **Features:** full bar, patio dining. **Reservations:** suggested, for dinner. **Address:** 693 E Lincoln Hwy 19341 **Location:** Jct SR 100, 1 mi e on Business Rt US 30. ♨ Exton, 198.

ⓛ ⓓ CALL 🍴

WINNER'S CIRCLE SPORTS GRILLE   610/524-2424

♦♦ American. Casual Dining. $5-$20 **AAA Inspector Notes:** This casual restaurant carries out a sports-nostalgia theme. Satellite broadcasts of major automobile races and other sporting events can be viewed on 35 TVs with individual table speakers. Theme nights in-clude karaoke on Wednesdays and Quizzo trivia on Thursdays. The menu of traditional American cuisine lists steaks, seafood, ribs, wings, nachos and potato skins. **Features:** full bar, happy hour. **Ad-dress:** 143 W Lincoln Hwy 19341 **Location:** I-76 (Pennsylvania Tpke) exit 312, 3 mi s on SR 100; in Whiteland Towne Center. ♨ Exton, 198. ⓛ ⓓ ⓛⒶⓉⒺ 🍴

FAIRFIELD (I-7) pop. 507, elev. 531'

STRAWBERRY HILL NATURE PRESERVE is off SR 116, then 3.5 mi. n.w. on Bullfrog Rd. to 1537 Mt. Hope Rd. This 609-acre preserve offers 10 miles of walking trails through woodlands with mountain streams and ponds as well as a restored mineral quarry. **Hours:** Nature center Mon.-Fri. 10-5; Sat. 10-2. Additional hours are offered some Saturdays; phone ahead. Trails daily dawn-dusk. Closed major holidays. **Cost:** Free. **Phone:** (717) 642-5840. 🐾

HISTORIC FAIRFIELD INN   717/642-5410

♦♦ Classic Bed & Breakfast. Rates not provided. **Address:** 15 W Main St 17320 **Location:** On SR 116; center. **Facility:** This B&B has hosted many famous people, from Patrick Henry and Thad-deus Stevens to generals Robert E. Lee and J.E.B. Stuart and the Eisenhowers. Parts of the inn date back to 1757. 6 units. 3 stories (no elevator), interior corridors. **Terms:** age restrictions may apply. **Dining:** The Historic Fairfield Inn 1757, see separate listing.

🍽 📶 ✖ 🚭 💻 / SOME UNITS 🛁

WHERE TO EAT

THE HISTORIC FAIRFIELD INN 1757   717/642-5410

♦♦ American. Casual Dining. $18-$33 **AAA Inspector Notes:** *Historic.* Built 19 years before the Declaration of Independence was signed, the inn is steeped in history and remains one of America's oldest inns that once was a Civil War hospital. The inn's two chefs offer an imaginative menu of grilled and roasted game, pasta, sea-food and mouthwatering steaks. Four centuries of fine service and culinary expertise make dining here a unique experience. There's a live Civil War dinner theater each night at 7 pm. **Features:** full bar, Sunday brunch. **Address:** 15 W Main St 17320 **Location:** On SR 116; center; in Historic Fairfield Inn. ⓓ

FALLSINGTON (A-12) elev. 82'
• **Part of Philadelphia area — see map p. 230**

HISTORIC FALLSINGTON is just off Tyburn Rd. be-tween US 1 and US 13 at 4 Yardley Ave. This well-preserved Quaker village has pre-Revolutionary, Federal and Victorian buildings, including three Friends meetinghouses set around a picturesque square. The restored buildings contain period furnishings.

    Time: Allow 1 hour minimum. **Hours:** Tues.-Sat. 10:30-3:30, mid-May to mid-Oct.; Tues.-Fri. by ap-pointment, rest of year. Tours are given every 30 minutes. Closed major holidays. **Cost:** $7; $6 (ages 65+); $3 (ages 0-12). Reservations are required for guided tours during winter months. **Phone:** (215) 295-6567. ⒼⓉ

FARMINGTON pop. 767

HISTORIC SUMMIT INN   724/438-8594

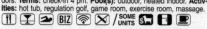 **Historic Hotel. Rates not provided. Address:** 101 Skyline Dr 15437 **Location:** On US 40; center. Near many attractions. **Facility:** Built in 1907, the historic hotel is atop a densely wooded mountain and offers a front porch with sweeping views. Original stained-glass windows, a rustic fireplace and a carved oak staircase adorn the public area. 94 units. 4 stories (no elevator), interior corridors. **Terms:** check-in 4 pm. **Pool(s):** outdoor, heated indoor. **Activities:** hot tub, regulation golf, game room, exercise room, massage.

NEMACOLIN WOODLANDS RESORT   (724)329-8555

Resort Hotel
$209-$969

Address: 1001 Lafayette Dr 15437 **Location:** 1 mi e on US 40. **Facility:** Serenely set in a wooded area on a hillside, this hidden gem and multifaceted resort encompasses 2,000 acres and offers limitless recreational opportunities and adventures. 280 units, some two bedrooms, kitchens, houses and condominiums. 4-5 stories, interior/exterior corridors. **Parking:** on-site and valet. **Terms:** check-in 4 pm, 2-3 night minimum stay - weekends, 14 day cancellation notice-fee imposed, resort fee. **Amenities:** *Some:* safes. **Dining:** 10 restaurants, also, Lautrec, see separate listing, available. **Pool(s):** heated outdoor. **Activities:** sauna, hot tub, steamroom, fishing, regulation golf, miniature golf, tennis, downhill & cross country skiing, snowmobiling, bicycles, playground, game room, spa. **Guest Services:** valet laundry.

NEMACOLIN
WOODLANDS RESORT

**Expect the unexpected at this
2,000 acre resort nestled in the
PA Laurel Highlands!**

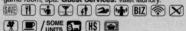 **WHERE TO EAT**

AQUEOUS   724/329-6417

American
Fine Dining
$28-$72

AAA Inspector Notes: This chic dining room of stone and wood overlooks the 18th green of the resort's championship golf course and offers a wildly creative menu. The artful chef specializes in cutting-edge techniques that transforms luxury ingredients into distinctive displays—a traditional steak might be accented by a foie gras powder or a rich bisque served with a Parmesan powder. **Features:** full bar. **Reservations:** suggested. **Address:** 150 Falling Rock Blvd 15437 **Location:** 1 mi e on US 40; in Falling Rock at Nemacolin Woodlands Resort. **Parking:** valet only.

LAUTREC   724/329-8555

French
Fine Dining
$110-$270

AAA Inspector Notes: This elegant and upscale restaurant gives diners a night to remember. Stepping into the lobby is like setting foot in elegant Paris. Rich fabrics drape the dining room, and the walls display reproductions of the works of famed artist Henri de Toulouse-Lautrec. Professional servers cater to the diner's every whim. Selections start with a four-course prix-fixe dinner and range all the way to a 12-course grand tasting menu. **Features:** full bar. **Reservations:** suggested, weekends. Semiformal attire. **Address:** 1001 Lafayette Dr 15437 **Location:** 1 mi e on US 40; in Nemacolin Woodlands Resort. **Parking:** on-site and valet.

FAYETTEVILLE (I-7) pop. 3,128, elev. 792'

In Caledonia State Park *(see Recreation Areas Chart)*, Totem Pole Playhouse is a 450-seat theater that presents summer stock productions featuring nationally known actors, directors and designers. Performances are held June through August. The box office opens March 1; phone (717) 352-2164 or (888) 805-7056.

Also of interest in the park are artifacts and displays in the reconstructed Thaddeus Stevens' Blacksmith Shop and the Caledonia Iron Furnace. Recreational facilities include an Olympic-size swimming pool, an 18-hole golf course, nature trails and cross-country ski trails.

FERNDALE   pop. 1,636

• Part of Philadelphia area — see map p. 230

FERNDALE INN   610/847-2662

 American. Fine Dining. $12-$32 **AAA Inspector Notes:** *Historic.* Traditional cuisine is served in this Pennsylvania fieldstone former stagecoach stop. It has been in operation since 1862. Candles and fresh flowers contribute to the intimate mood of the dining rooms. **Features:** full bar. **Reservations:** suggested. **Address:** 551 Church Hill Rd 18921 **Location:** Jct SR 611.

FLOURTOWN   pop. 4,538

• Hotels & Restaurants map & index p. 274
• Part of Philadelphia area — see map p. 230

SCOOGI'S   215/233-1063

 Italian. Casual Dining. $10-$30 **AAA Inspector Notes:** You'll find classic dishes being served in this friendly, casual and comfortable place. Chicken Française, veal parmigiana and rigatoni with broccoli and sun-dried tomatoes are just a few of the tasty choices. Those looking for a cocktail and something quick may prefer the bar and lounge area. **Features:** full bar. **Reservations:** suggested. **Address:** 738 Bethlehem Pike 19031 **Location:** I-276 (Pennsylvania Tpke) exit 339, 0.5 mi s on US 30, 0.4 mi w on Valley Green Rd, then just s.

FOGELSVILLE

• Restaurants p. 112

GLASBERN   610/285-4723

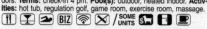 Historic Country Inn. Rates not provided. **Address:** 2141 Packhouse Rd 18051 **Location:** I-78 exit 49B (SR 100), 0.3 mi n to 1st traffic light, 0.3 mi w on Main St, 0.6 mi n on Church St, then 0.8 mi ne. **Facility:** This is a beautiful country inn that provides true rustic elegance and a variety of large guest suite options. It's a great couples getaway and offers multiple packages, including visits to nearby vineyards. 34 units, some cottages. 2 stories (no elevator), interior/exterior corridors. **Terms:** check-in 4 pm. **Amenities:** safes. **Dining:** restaurant, see separate listing. **Pool(s):** heated outdoor. **Activities:** exercise room. **Guest Services:** valet laundry.

HAMPTON INN-ALLENTOWN   (610)391-1500

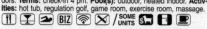 Hotel $89-$149 **Address:** 7471 Keebler Way 18106 **Location:** I-78 exit 49A, 0.3 mi s on SR 100. Located in Wm Penn Business Center. **Facility:** 124 units. 5 stories, interior corridors. **Terms:** 1-7 night minimum stay, cancellation fee imposed. **Activities:** exercise room. **Guest Services:** valet and coin laundry.

AAA Benefit:
Members save 5% or more!

HAWTHORN SUITES BY WYNDHAM HOTELS   (610)366-9422

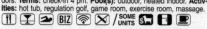 Hotel $79-$170 **Address:** 7720 Main St (I-78) 18051 **Location:** I-78 exit 49B (SR 100), just n. Located in a shopping plaza. **Facility:** 64 units. 3 stories, interior corridors. **Activities:** exercise room. **Guest Services:** valet and coin laundry.

HILTON GARDEN INN ALLENTOWN WEST   (610)398-6686

▼▼▼ **Hotel** $99-$209 **Address:** 230 Sycamore Rd 18031 **Location:** I-78 exit 49A, just s. Located in a commercial area. **Facility:** 111 units. 3 stories, interior corridors. **Terms:** 1-7 night minimum stay, cancellation fee imposed. **Amenities:** video games. **Pool(s):** heated indoor. **Activities:** hot tub, exercise room. **Guest Services:** valet and coin laundry.

AAA Benefit:
Members save 5% or more!

⬦ ☂ CALL ⬦ᴹ ➳ BIZ HS 🛜 ✕ 🐾 🔌
🖥 ▣

HOLIDAY INN CONFERENCE CENTER   610/391-1000

▼▼▼
Hotel
Rates not provided

Address: 7736 Adrienne Dr 18031 **Location:** I-78 exit 49A, 0.3 mi s on SR 100. **Facility:** 175 units. 3 stories, interior corridors. **Pool(s):** outdoor. **Activities:** exercise room. **Guest Services:** valet and coin laundry, area transportation.

SAVE ⬦ 🍴 🖐 ☂ CALL ⬦ᴹ
➳ BIZ HS 🛜 ✕ 🔌 ▣
/SOME UNITS 🅂 🖥

SLEEP INN   (610)395-6603

▼▼ **Hotel** $69-$129 **Address:** 327 Star Rd 18106 **Location:** I-78 exit 49A, 0.3 mi s on SR 100, e at traffic light, then n on service road. Located in a commercial area. **Facility:** 62 units. 3 stories, interior corridors. **Bath:** shower only. **Guest Services:** valet and coin laundry.

🍴 CALL ⬦ᴹ BIZ HS 🛜 🔌 🖥 ▣ /SOME UNITS 🅂

STAYBRIDGE SUITES-ALLENTOWN WEST   610/841-5100

▼▼▼ **Extended Stay Hotel.** Rates not provided. **Address:** 327 Star Rd 18106 **Location:** I-78 exit 49A, 0.3 mi s on SR 100, e at traffic light, then n on service road. Located in commercial area. **Facility:** 83 efficiencies, some two bedrooms. 3 stories, interior corridors. **Pool(s):** heated indoor. **Activities:** hot tub, exercise room. **Guest Services:** valet and coin laundry.

🍴 ➳ BIZ HS 🛜 🔌 🖥 ▣ /SOME UNITS 🅂

WHERE TO EAT

GLASBERN   610/285-4723

▼▼▼ American. Fine Dining. $18-$36 **AAA Inspector Notes:** In the great hall of a country inn, a converted 19th-century barn, this charming dining room is an inviting spot in which to enjoy attentive, prompt service as you dine on seasonally changing American preparations of beef, seafood, chicken and game. The farm-to-table concept incorporates many ingredients from their own Pennsylvania garden. **Features:** full bar. **Reservations:** suggested, for dinner. **Address:** 2141 Packhouse Rd 18051 **Location:** I-78 exit 49B (SR 100), 0.3 mi n to 1st traffic light, 0.3 mi w on Main St, 0.6 mi w on Church St, then 0.8 mi ne. D

STARLITE DINER   610/395-4031

▼▼ American. Casual Dining. $5-$18 **AAA Inspector Notes:** With gleaming stainless steel, neon lights and granite, this restaurant evokes a retro-diner feel. Added attractions are two large pillar-style aquariums stocked with tropical fish. The menu lists many regional and Pennsylvania Dutch foods, as well as seafood and steaks. All are complemented by a 30-item soup and salad bar. A cabinet displaying many mouthwatering desserts captures the eye at the restaurant's entrance. **Features:** full bar. **Address:** 233 N Rt 100 18051 **Location:** I-78 exit 49A, 0.3 mi s, left at 1st traffic light, then immediate left on service road. B L 24

Discover a wealth of savings and offers

on the AAA/CAA travel websites

FOREST HILLS pop. 6,518
• **Hotels & Restaurants map & index p. 348**
• **Part of Pittsburgh area — see map p. 326**

DREWS FAMILY RESTAURANT   412/271-1556   56

▼▼ American. Family Dining. $4-$16 **AAA Inspector Notes:** In addition to a standard menu, the family restaurant prepares daily specials and homemade desserts. **Address:** 2060 Ardmore Blvd 15221 **Location:** I-376 exit 78A, 0.5 mi e on US 30. B L D

FORT NECESSITY NATIONAL BATTLEFIELD (I-2) elev. 1,952'

Eleven miles east of Uniontown on US 40, Fort Necessity National Battlefield surrounds a reconstruction of the fort built by George Washington in 1754. The Battle of Fort Necessity, in which Washington led the Colonial Virginia Regiment alongside the British regulars from South Carolina against a strong force of French and Native Americans, occurred at the site on July 3, 1754. This was Washington's first major event in his military career and it marked the beginning of the French and Indian War.

Reconstructions of the fort, entrenchments and earthworks have been erected on their original sites. Picnic facilities are available. A visitor center features exhibits and a 20-minute video presentation. Mount Washington Tavern, on US 40 near the fort, is a restored 19th-century stagecoach inn. Visitor programs are available (weather permitting).

A mile west on US 40 is a monument marking the grave site of Gen. Edward Braddock. During the Battle of the Monongahela, Braddock was fatally wounded; his troops carried his body back as far as the site of the Old Orchard Camp, where he died. He was buried in the road that his men had built, and then the soldiers marched over the area to prevent the Native Americans from finding the body and defiling it. George Washington, who had joined the campaign as a volunteer aide, officiated at Braddock's burial ceremony. In 1804 remains said to be those of Braddock were moved to the present grave site, marked by a monument.

Jumonville Glen, 7.5 miles from Fort Necessity, is reached via Jumonville Road (LR 26115), 2.5 miles north of US 40 at Mount Summit. It was the site of a 15-minute skirmish between French and British forces that led to the battle of Fort Necessity.

Park open daily dawn-dusk. Visitor center open daily 9-5. Mount Washington Tavern open Apr. 15-Oct. 31; phone ahead to verify hours. Closed federal holidays except Memorial Day, July 4, Labor Day and Columbus Day. Admission (valid for 7 days) $5; free (ages 0-15). The general entrance fee covers the fort, tavern, visitor center, Jumonville Glen, Braddock's grave and the park grounds, and is payable at the visitor center. Phone (724) 329-5512.

FORT WASHINGTON (A-10) pop. 5,446, elev. 174'
• **Restaurants p. 114**
• **Hotels & Restaurants map & index p. 274**
• **Part of Philadelphia area — see map p. 230**

THE HIGHLANDS MANSION AND GARDENS is off Pennsylvania Tpke./I-276 exit 339, .5 mi. n.w. on

(See map & index p. 274.)

W. Pennsylvania Ave., 1 mi. s. on S. Bethlehem Pike, 1 mi. w. on Skippack Pike, then n.e. to 7001 Sheaff Ln. Quaker Anthony Morris' Georgian manor house was completed in 1796. Comprising 44 acres, the estate includes a two-story octagonal springhouse, an icehouse and a three-level bank barn. A 2-acre walled garden with statuary, a fountain and a Gothic Revival cottage exemplifies 19th- and 20th-century landscape architecture.

Guides conduct 45-minute tours of the house and grounds. **Time:** Allow 1 hour minimum. **Hours:** Grounds daily dawn-dusk. Manor house and garden tours are offered Mon.-Fri. at 1:30 and by appointment. Closed major holidays. **Cost:** Grounds free. House and garden tour $5; $4 (seniors); $3 (students with ID). Reservations are recommended for tours. **Phone:** (215) 641-2687. Fort Washington, 301

HOPE LODGE is off Pennsylvania Tpke./I-276 exit 339, .8 mi. n.w. on Pennsylvania Ave., then s. on Bethlehem Pike, following signs. Built 1743-48 for prosperous Quaker gristmill operator Samuel Morris, the Georgian mansion now is filled with antique art and furnishings from the 18th- through 20th centuries representing both the Colonial and Colonial Revival styles. Beautiful Colonial Revival gardens surround the home.

Note: Due to lack of funding, Hope Lodge tours are currently not available. Phone for further updates. Visitors may still walk the grounds, and special public events are held occasionally. **Time:** Allow 1 hour minimum. **Hours:** Fri.-Sat. 10-5, Sun. noon-5. Closed Jan. 1, Columbus Day, Nov. 11, day after Thanksgiving and Christmas. Guided tours third Sun. of every month at 1, 2 and 3, June-Oct. Phone ahead to confirm schedule. **Cost:** $5; $4 (ages 65+); free (ages 0-5). **Phone:** (215) 646-1595. Fort Washington, 301

BEST WESTERN FORT WASHINGTON INN
(215)542-7930

Hotel
$95-$141

AAA Benefit: Members save up to 20%!

Address: 285 Commerce Dr 19034 **Location:** I-276 (Pennsylvania Tpke) exit 339 (SR 309 S), just w on Pennsylvania Ave, just n to Commerce Dr, then 0.3 mi e. Located in a commercial area. Fort Washington, 301. **Facility:** 106 units, some efficiencies. 4 stories, interior corridors. **Amenities:** safes. **Pool(s):** outdoor. **Activities:** exercise room. **Guest Services:** coin laundry.

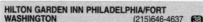

HILTON GARDEN INN PHILADELPHIA/FORT WASHINGTON (215)646-4637

Hotel
$119-$229

AAA Benefit: Members save 5% or more!

Address: 530 W Pennsylvania Ave 19034 **Location:** I-276 (Pennsylvania Tpke) exit 339 (SR 309 S), just w. Fort Washington, 301. **Facility:** 146 units. 6 stories, interior corridors. **Terms:** 1-7 night minimum stay, cancellation fee imposed. **Amenities:** video games. **Pool(s):** heated indoor. **Activities:** hot tub, exercise room. **Guest Services:** valet and coin laundry. *(See ad this page.)*

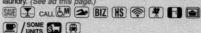

Ask about on-the-go vehicle battery testing and replacement

▼ See AAA listing this page ▼

(See map & index p. 274.)

WHERE TO EAT

CANTINA FELIZ   215/646-1320 (69)

▼▼◆▼▼ Mexican. Casual Dining. $11-$24 **AAA Inspector Notes:** After working under Food Network's Iron Chef Jose Garces, executive chef Tim Spinner has been able to provide authentic Mexican cuisine here in Fort Washington. Inside you will find vibrant colors, decorative art pieces and architectural enhancements that provide a feeling of being south of the border. The menu is filled with all traditional favorites including carnitas, huarache and enchiladas. At lunch time, try their $13.95 two-course menu with drink. **Features:** full bar, happy hour. **Reservations:** suggested. **Address:** 424 S Bethlehem Pike 19034 **Location:** I-276 (Pennsylvania Tpke) exit 339, just w on S Bethlehem Pike, just nw on Lafayette Ave, then just s on Morris Rd. 🐾 Fort Washington, 301. Ⓛ Ⓓ 🏧

FORTY FORT (E-10) pop. 4,214, elev. 554'

Built in 1790, the Nathan Denison House is 1 mile north via Wyoming Avenue at 35 Denison St. The house was built by Nathan Denison, a Revolutionary War colonel and later a Luzerne County judge. His 1717 ancestral homestead is in Mystic, Conn.

Col. Denison was among the first 40 settlers, for whom the Forty Fort settlement was named. Denison's property is considered to be the oldest frame dwelling in the Wyoming Valley. The restored house is mostly furnished with authentic 18th-century pieces. Events and programs of historical interest are presented throughout the year, concluding with an afternoon of Colonial hospitality in December. The house is open Sundays 1-4, late May through September. Guided tours are available. Phone (570) 288-5531 for appointments or events information.

The 1807 Forty Fort Meeting House, 20 River St., was built by New England settlers from the Congregationalist, Presbyterian and Methodist congregations and was in use until the late 1840s. A cemetery dating to the late 18th century also is on the grounds; Col. Nathan Denison is among those interred here. The site is open Sundays and holidays 1-3 from Memorial Day weekend through late September; phone (570) 287-5214 to confirm schedule or to set up a tour by appointment.

FOXBURG pop. 183

THE FOXBURG INN HOTEL   724/659-3116

▼▼◆▼▼
Hotel
$129-$199

Address: 20 Main St 16036 **Location:** I-80 exit 42; in town square. **Facility:** 24 units. 3 stories, exterior corridors. **Terms:** cancellation fee imposed. **Amenities:** safes. **Dining:** 2 restaurants. **Activities:** regulation golf, bicycles.

SAVE 🍴 Ⓗ🅢 🛜 ✕ 🛗

Find thousands of pet-friendly places to stay, play and dine with *The AAA PetBook*

FOX CHAPEL pop. 5,388
• Part of Pittsburgh area — see map p. 326

ATRIA'S RESTAURANT & TAVERN   412/963-1514

▼▼ ▼▼ American. Casual Dining. $10-$28 **AAA Inspector Notes:** Guests feel right at home in this dining room decorated in bright shades of yellow, green and red and with rich wood tables and chairs. Tasty and well-seasoned entrees, including the local favorite, bourbon-glazed pot roast nachos, make up the menu. This place is great for a fast sit-down lunch or relaxed dinner. **Features:** full bar. **Address:** 1374 Freeport Rd 15238 **Location:** SR 28 exit 9 northbound, just w; exit 8 southbound, just s, then 0.8 mi e. Ⓛ Ⓓ

FRACKVILLE pop. 3,805

COUNTRY INN & SUITES BY CARLSON - FRACKVILLE
    570/544-5201

▼▼◆▼▼ Hotel. Rates not provided. **Address:** 100 Keystone Blvd E 17901 **Location:** I-81 exit 119 (Highridge Park Rd), follow signs. **Facility:** 79 units. 3 stories, interior corridors. **Pool(s):** heated indoor. **Activities:** hot tub, exercise room. **Guest Services:** coin laundry.
🏊 🄱🄸🅉 Ⓗ🅢 🛜 ✕ 🛗 📠 🖥

HOLIDAY INN EXPRESS & SUITES FRACKVILLE
    570/874-1700

▼▼◆▼▼ Hotel. Rates not provided. **Address:** 958 Schuylkill Mall Rd 17931 **Location:** I-81 exit 124A (SR 61), just s. Located at Schuylkill Mall. **Facility:** 65 units. 3 stories, interior corridors. **Activities:** exercise room. **Guest Services:** complimentary laundry.
📶 CALL🄼 🄱🄸🅉 Ⓗ🅢 🛜 ✕ 🛗 📠 🖥

FRANKLIN (VENANGO COUNTY) (E-2)
pop. 6,545, elev. 1,017'

Franklin is believed to be the only city in Pennsylvania to have had four different forts within its boundaries. The town's history dates back to the French Fort Machault, built in 1753 near the confluence of French Creek and the Allegheny River. In 1760 the British built Fort Venango, which fell to the Native Americans during Pontiac's Conspiracy. American soldiers built Fort Franklin in 1787; it served as a defense against Native Americans. The fourth fort within the city, the Old Garrison, stationed federal troops 1796-99 and later served as the first jail of Venango County until 1819.

The county of Venango was established in 1800 with Franklin as the county seat. The town retained its rural atmosphere until the start of the oil boom in 1859. Drilling began in Franklin shortly after Edwin Drake's successful well came in near Titusville *(see place listing p. 403)*. Refineries were started, and Franklin's population more than tripled in the 1860s; three railroads came into the community, new businesses flourished, hotels were built and Franklin became a city in 1868.

Displays about local history can be seen at the Venango County Historical Society at 301 S. Park St. in the Hoge-Osmer House, a circa 1865 building; phone (814) 437-2275. Thirty Tiffany stained-glass windows adorn St. John's Episcopal Church on Buffalo Street; phone (814) 432-5161. The Barrow-Civic Theatre, a restored 1913 vaudeville house, features performing arts; phone (814) 437-3440 or (800) 537-7769.

Walking and bicycling can be enjoyed on the Allegheny River Trail and the Samuel Justis Trail.

Applefest, held Friday through Sunday the first full weekend in October, is an arts and crafts festival with live entertainment, a 5K race, an apple pie baking contest and an antique and classic car show. Apple orchards can be found in the surrounding area, but the main connection Franklin has with the fruit has to do with folk hero Johnny Appleseed's ties to the area. The festival draws nearly 100,000 to the Victorian downtown.

Franklin Area Chamber of Commerce: 1327 Liberty St., Franklin, PA 16323. **Phone:** (814) 432-5823.

Self-guiding tours: Booklets outlining a walking tour can be obtained at the chamber of commerce for $1.

Shopping areas: A farmers market is held on 12th Street on Saturdays 8-1, May-Oct.

DEBENCE ANTIQUE MUSIC WORLD is at 1261 Liberty St. A collection of more than 100 automated music machines ranges from small music boxes to large carousel organs including a nickelodeon, a calliope and an orchestrion. Historical facts and demonstrations of machines are provided. Phonographs and other antiques are displayed.

Time: Allow 1 hour minimum. **Hours:** Tues.-Sat. 11-4, Sun. 12:30-4, Apr.-Oct.; by appointment rest of year. Last tour begins 30 minutes before closing. Phone ahead to confirm schedule. **Cost:** $8; $7 (ages 60+); $5 (high school and college students with ID); $3 (grade school students). **Phone:** (814) 432-8350.

FRANKLIN SUPER 8   (814)432-2101

▼▼ **Hotel** $64-$125 **Address:** 847 Allegheny Blvd 16323 **Location:** 2 mi n on SR 8. **Facility:** 40 units. 2 stories (no elevator), interior corridors. **Guest Services:** coin laundry.

QUALITY INN & CONFERENCE CENTER   (814)437-3031

▼▼▼▼
Hotel
$89-$120

Address: 1411 Liberty St 16323 **Location:** On US 62 and SR 8; center. **Facility:** 85 units. 5 stories, interior corridors. **Activities:** exercise room. **Guest Services:** valet and coin laundry.

WHERE TO EAT

KING'S FAMILY RESTAURANT   814/437-6997

▼▼ American. Family Dining. $6-$11 **AAA Inspector Notes:** Fast and friendly service is offered here. The menu is large in size with descriptive menu items and pictures. The restaurant is also known for its ice cream and dessert menu. **Address:** 821 Allegheny Blvd 16323 **Location:** On US 62 and SR 8. B L D

FREEDOM (G-1) pop. 1,569, elev. 781'
• Part of Pittsburgh area — see map p. 326

• Part of Pittsburgh area — see map p. 326

THE CAPTAIN WILLIAM VICARY MANSION, 1235 Third Ave., is a three-story sandstone house built by Vicary 1826-29. One of the 20 rooms is furnished in period, but the highlight of the structure is the Federal architecture itself. Throughout the home, specially created viewing windows allow visitors to see what lies underneath the plaster and flooring. An archival room contains local history items and a library. Interactive living history and craft classes as well as five special events are held throughout the year.

Time: Allow 45 minutes minimum. **Hours:** Mon.-Fri. 10-2 and other times by appointment. Closed major holidays. Phone ahead to confirm schedule. **Cost:** Donations. **Phone:** (724) 775-1848. GT

GAINES

LOG CABIN INN   814/435-8808

▼▼ ▼▼ Steak. Casual Dining. $7-$29 **AAA Inspector Notes:** Set in the mountains, the cozy log cabin has evergreen landscaping and a dining room appointed in rustic decor, including a recently acquired 400-pound stuffed Pennsylvania black bear and other hunting trophies. The focus of the menu is on simple preparations of steak and seafood, including the specialty camper's trout. **Features:** full bar, Sunday brunch. **Reservations:** suggested, Fri & Sat. **Address:** 3501 Rt 6 16921 **Location:** 5 mi e. D

GALETON (D-6) pop. 1,149, elev. 1,319'

PENNSYLVANIA LUMBER MUSEUM, 11.2 mi. w. on US 6 to 5660 US 6W, interprets the history of the state's lumber industry—from the days when pine and hemlock were the wealth of the nation to the present. More than 3,000 objects can be seen—ranging from axes to logging locomotives. Visitors can tour a recreated logging camp and expanded visitors center with new exhibits. The Sustainable Forestry Trail highlights timber management practices.

Time: Allow 1 hour minimum. **Hours:** Starting April 2015: Wed.-Sun. 9-5. Closed some holidays. Phone ahead to confirm schedule. **Cost:** $8; $7 (ages 65+); $4 (ages 3-11). **Phone:** (814) 435-2652.

GALLITZIN (G-5) pop. 1,668, elev. 2,182'

ALLEGHENY PORTAGE RAILROAD NATIONAL HISTORIC SITE is off US 22 Gallitzin exit, following signs. Considered to be a 19th-century technological wonder, this site employed a series of inclined planes for transporting trains and canal boats over the Allegheny Mountains. Models, exhibits and artifacts depict its significance as a critical link in westward travel and trade.

An 1830s tavern, the Skew Arch Bridge, Incline Plane No. 6 and stone railroad ties can still be seen. Interpretive programs are offered in summer. **Time:** Allow 1 hour, 30 minutes minimum. **Hours:** Daily 9-5. Closed major holidays. **Cost:** Admission, valid for seven days, $4; free (ages 0-15). **Phone:** (814) 886-6150.

GETTYSBURG (I-7) pop. 7,620, elev. 520'
- Hotels p. 121 • Restaurants p. 125
- Attractions map p. 127
- Hotels & Restaurants map & index p. 119

Marsh Creek Settlement was founded between two low ridges just north of the Mason-Dixon Line in the 1780s. Renamed Gettysburg in honor of Gen. James Gettys, the town grew quickly after being incorporated in 1806. Its square, at the crossroads of four major highways and several secondary roads, was a stopping point for travelers. This strategic location led to the town's involvement in one of the bloodiest battles of the Civil War *(see Gettysburg National Military Park p. 126).*

Though the battlefield is the main draw for visitors, there are several reasons to venture downtown. On Lincoln Square, formed from Baltimore, Chambersburg, Carlisle and York streets, you'll find buildings from the Civil War era, including the David Wills House *(see attraction listing p. 126),* where President Lincoln was a guest the evening before he delivered his Gettysburg Address on Nov. 19, 1863. Outside the building is a statue entitled " Return Visit" depicting Lincoln pointing toward the house and standing with a man dressed in late 20th-century attire who is reading a copy of the Gettysburg Address.

Not far from the Wills House is the restored Historic Gettysburg Railroad Station at 35 Carlisle St., which also serves as the **Destination Gettysburg** visitors center. Original construction on the Italianate-style building was completed in 1859. During the battle of Gettysburg, it served as a hospital, and a few months later it was where Lincoln arrived in and departed from Gettysburg, but there is no proof that he ever actually went inside the station. There is proof, however, that he visited Gettysburg Presbyterian Church. The present building was built in 1963, but it contains the original pew, now marked with a plaque, in which Lincoln sat when he attended a patriotic service after the cemetery dedication. President and Mrs. Eisenhower were later members of the church and a plaque marks their pew as well.

Next to the railroad station is the Majestic Theater, built in 1925 in the Colonial Revival style and used for vaudeville shows and presentations of silent films. The interior boasts exquisite detail, from its custom-woven wool carpet to its pressed tin ceiling. Today films are shown and live performances are given. Two additional cinemas were added, and each was designed to have a 1950s look. For schedule information phone (717) 337-8200.

The small town is also home to the 200-acre campus of Gettysburg College, a liberal arts school with nearly 2,600 students. It is affiliated with the Lutheran faith and has its roots in abolitionist principles. Antislavery theologian Samuel Simon Schmucker founded the school—originally called Pennsylvania College—in 1832, and the institution eventually moved into Pennsylvania Hall, which was on land provided by abolitionist Thaddeus Stevens,

who assisted in the Underground Railroad and began to establish American civil rights as a member of Congress. Pennsylvania Hall was used as a hospital during and after the battle. Another noteworthy building on campus is the admissions office, named Eisenhower House for the former president who served on the college's board of trustees and wrote his memoirs in the building.

In early July, ♋ Gettysburg Civil War Heritage Days features living-history encampments, reenactments, a book and paper show, a collectors' show, band concerts and a Civil War lecture series throughout Gettysburg and the Adams County area.

Destination Gettysburg: 35 Carlisle St., Gettysburg, PA 17325. **Phone:** (717) 334-6274 or (800) 337-5015.

Self-guiding tours: Sightseeing excursions include a 14-block walking tour past 90 restored buildings. Driving tours include a 36-mile tour of the surrounding valley, and a 40-mile driving tour that explores East Cavalry Field, Victorian New Oxford and Early American East Berlin. Free brochures describing these tours are available from the Destination Gettysburg Visitors Center.

Shopping areas: Gettysburg shops lining Steinwehr Avenue and Baltimore, Chambersburg, Carlisle and York streets feature an assortment of antiques, books, collectibles, souvenirs and other specialty items. There also are more than a dozen art galleries.

A farmers market is held on Lincoln Square Saturdays 7 a.m.-noon from late April through late September (October schedule varies).

The Outlet Shoppes at Gettysburg, US 15 and SR 97, features more than 70 outlets, including Eddie Bauer, The Gap, Jones New York, Tommy Hilfiger and Van Heusen, in a village setting.

DAVID WILLS HOUSE—see Gettysburg National Military Park p. 126.

▼ **EISENHOWER NATIONAL HISTORIC SITE** is accessible by a shuttle bus that departs from the Museum and Visitor Center at Gettysburg National Military Park on SR 97 at 1195 Baltimore Pike. The 231-acre Eisenhower farm was the only home ever owned by President Dwight D. Eisenhower and his wife Mamie. The house, grounds and buildings are preserved. Visitors can see the Eisenhower's formal living room, sun porch, original furniture and photographs as well as many of the president's paintings, gifts and other items. An 11-minute video presentation and exhibits about the president's life also are featured.

Among the dignitaries who visited the estate were Winston Churchill, Charles DeGaulle and Nikita Khrushchev. Self-guiding walking tours (with or without a cell phone audio tour) of the cattle barns, skeet shooting range and grounds are available. Summer programs include Ike and the Men of

(See map & index p. 119.)

D-Day, a 30-minute interactive presentation featuring the weapons and equipment used for the invasion, and Exploring Eisenhower, a ranger-led walking tour focusing on various topics relating to Eisenhower's life. Children ages 7-12 can participate in the Junior Secret Service Agent Program.

Hours: Twenty-minute tours of the grounds are conducted daily (weather permitting). A shuttle departs at regular intervals daily 9-4. Tickets are sold at the Museum and Visitor Center at Gettysburg National Military Park daily 8-6, Apr.-Oct.; 8-5, rest of year. Closed Jan. 1, Thanksgiving and Christmas. Phone ahead to confirm schedule. **Cost:** $7.50; $5 (ages 6-12). **Phone:** (717) 338-9114, or (717) 253-9256 for audio tour.

EXPLORE & MORE CHILDREN'S MUSEUM is .2 mi. s. on Baltimore Pike, then .1 mi. e. on High St. The museum offers a great variety of hands-on activities that focus on learning. The 1860s house features seven rooms, including an art room, an exploration room, a construction room and re-creations of a period house and general store. **Hours:** Mon.-Sat. 10-5, Apr.-Sept.; Mon.-Tues. and Thurs.-Sat., 10-5, Sun. noon-5, rest of year. Closed major holidays. **Cost:** $7 (ages 2-14); $5 (adults). **Phone:** (717) 337-9151.

FARNSWORTH HOUSE MUSEUM AND TOURS is at 401 Baltimore St. The 1810 house, which includes a brick portion that was added in 1833, has been restored to its 1863 appearance when it held Confederate sharpshooters during the 3-day siege in the Civil War. A south wall still holds more than 100 bullet holes. Weapons, bullets and artifacts from the house and battlefield are displayed in the attic area. The home was used by Union veterans during the 75th anniversary of the battle in 1938. Uniforms and props used by actors Sam Elliott and Tom Berenger from the 1993 film "Gettysburg" are also displayed.

Nightly ghost tours of Farnsworth House given by guides in period clothing include walks by other Gettysburg sites. A seated presentation in the cellar featuring ghost tales and stories about Victorian mourning is also offered nightly. Other offerings are A Day in the Life of a Soldier tour and a dinner theater, which is available December 1 through Easter. The museum can only be seen on a guided tour.

Time: Allow 1 hour minimum. **Hours:** Tours depart Fri.-Sat. at 2. Ghost tour and seated presentation daily 7-11 p.m., Apr.-Oct.; Sat.-Sun. 7-11 p.m., rest of year. A Day in the Life of a Soldier tour offered Mar.-Nov.; phone for schedule. Closed Jan. 1, Thanksgiving and Christmas. Phone ahead to confirm schedule. **Cost:** House tour $7.25; $5 (ages 6-12). Ghost presentation $9-$20. **Phone:** (717) 334-8838. ⊞

GENERAL LEE'S HEADQUARTERS MUSEUM is on historic Seminary Ridge, 401 Buford Ave. at US 30W. On July 1, 1863, Gen. Robert E. Lee established his personal headquarters in this old stone house, which dates from the early 1800s. Displays include Union and Confederate military equipment from the Battle of Gettysburg and other Civil War artifacts. **Time:** Allow 1 hour minimum. **Hours:** Daily 9-5, mid-Mar. through Nov. 30. Hours are extended in summer. Phone ahead to confirm schedule. **Cost:** Donations. $3; $1 (ages 0-15). **Phone:** (717) 334-3141.

GETTYSBURG BATTLEFIELD BUS TOURS departs from 778 Baltimore St. Two-hour tours of the Gettysburg Battlefield are offered; choose from an audio tour with dramatized narration aboard an air-conditioned coach or a double-decker bus.

Hours: Daily 8-7, early June to mid-Aug.; daily 8-5, Mar. 1-early June and Sept.-Dec.; Fri.-Mon. 9-4, rest of year. Closed Jan. 1, Thanksgiving and Christmas. Phone ahead to confirm schedule. **Cost:** Audio tour $26; $15 (ages 6-12). Guided tour $30; $19 (ages 6-12). Phone ahead to confirm rates. **Phone:** (717) 334-6296 or (877) 680-8687.

GETTYSBURG BATTLE THEATRE, 571 Steinwehr Ave., offers an orientation program about the Battle of Gettysburg with a diorama, an electronic map and a film that features multimedia battle re-enactments. **Time:** Allow 1 hour minimum. **Hours:** Open daily at 9, Mar.-Oct.; phone for closing times and for schedule rest of year. **Cost:** $6.95; $6.25 (ages 60+); $3.50 (ages 6-12). **Phone:** (717) 334-6100. ⊞

GETTYSBURG HERITAGE CENTER is 1 mi. s. on US 15 Bus. Rte. at 297 Steinwehr Ave. The space formerly housed the American Civil War Wax Museum, but new owners began a multi-year renovation project in 2014 that continues. The new interactive gallery will feature artifacts, historical documents, interactive displays and replica weapons from the Battle of Gettysburg. A film about the Battle of Gettysburg is also available. Note: Admission may be waived if construction on the new gallery space is still continuing. **Time:** Allow 1 hour minimum. **Hours:** Daily 9-5, Mar.-Dec.; Sat.-Sun. and holidays 9-5, rest of year. Hours are extended May-Aug.; phone for details. Last admission 45 minutes before closing. Closed Jan. 1, Thanksgiving and Christmas. **Cost:** $7.95; $4.95 (ages 6-17). **Phone:** (717) 334-6245.

GETTYSBURG SEMINARY RIDGE MUSEUM, 111 Seminary Ridge, is housed in the four-story 1832 Schmucker Hall on the Lutheran Theological Seminary campus. The building served as a hospital during the Gettysburg battle. Voices of Duty and Devotion details the first day of the Battle of Gettysburg along Seminary Ridge. It showcases the nurses and doctors who treated the wounded, and it tells stories about the fugitive slaves and African-Americans who served in the United States Colored Troops. The exhibit also focuses on the civic and spiritual debates related to faith and freedom that waged during the Civil War era. Murals, video screens, audio recordings and artifacts (including uniforms and weapons) are used throughout.

(See map & index p. 119.)

There is a 1-mile outdoor trail with exhibits on the campus, and cupola tours also are offered. **Time:** Allow 1 hour minimum for the museum; 1 hour, 30 minutes minimum for the museum and cupola. **Note:** Cupola tours require visitors to climb stairs. **Hours:** Daily 10-5, Mar.-Nov.; Thurs.-Sun. 10-5, rest of year. Closed Jan. 1, Easter and Christmas. Phone ahead to confirm schedule. **Cost:** $9; $7 (ages 6-12 and 65+). Museum and cupola tour $29; $27 (ages 65+). Reservations are required for cupola tour; ages 0-12 are not permitted. **Phone:** (717) 339-1300.

[SAVE] **HALL OF PRESIDENTS,** 789 Baltimore St., displays life-size wax representations of the United States presidents. Audio presentations begin every 20 minutes. **Time:** Allow 1 hour minimum. **Hours:** Daily 9-5 in May and Sept.-Oct.; Sun.-Thurs. 9-6, Fri.-Sat. 9-7, early June to mid-Aug.; 10-4, Sun.-Thurs., 10-5, Fri.-Sat. Nov. 1 through Sun. after Thanksgiving. Closed Thanksgiving. Phone ahead to confirm schedule. **Cost:** $7.50; $3.50 (ages 6-12). Phone ahead to confirm rates. **Phone:** (717) 334-5717.

HISTORIC TOUR CO. tours depart from 55 Steinwehr Ave. Premier Gettysburg Battlefield Tours and Battlefield Tours for Kids—2 and 2.5 hours long—are conducted in vintage Yellowstone Park buses. A 4.5-hour tour of two local wineries is offered in a modern motor coach. Other tours also are available.

Hours: Premier Gettysburg Battlefield Tour departs daily at 10, noon and 2. Wineries Tour departs Mon., Wed. and Sat. at 1. Battlefield Tour for Kids departs daily at 10:30 and 2:30. Phone ahead to confirm schedule. **Cost:** Premier Battlefield Tour $24.95. Battlefield Tour for Kids $18. Winery tour $25. Family discounts available. Reservations are recommended for battlefield tour and are required for wineries tour. **Phone:** (717) 334-8000.

[SAVE] **JENNIE WADE HOUSE,** 548 Baltimore St., is the house in which the only civilian killed in the Battle of Gettysburg died. Guides in period attire lead visitors throughout the home, which is furnished as it might have been at the time of the historic battle.

Time: Allow 1 hour minimum. **Hours:** Daily 9-7, early June to mid-Aug. and in Oct.; Mon.-Thurs. 10-4, Fri. 10-6, Sat. 9-6, Sun. 9-5 in Mar.; Sun.-Thurs. 9-5, Fri.-Sat. 9-6, in Apr. and Sept.; Mon.-Thurs. 10-4, Fri.-Sun. 9-5 in Nov. Closed Thanksgiving and Christmas. Phone ahead to confirm rates. **Cost:** $8; $5 (ages 6-12). Phone ahead to confirm rates. **Phone:** (717) 334-4100. [GT]

[SAVE] **LAND OF LITTLE HORSES FARM PARK,** 5 mi. w. off US 30 at 125 Glenwood Dr., features educational displays, events and performing animals. Petting and feeding areas are offered. **Hours:** Mon.-Sat. 10-5, Sun noon-5, in May and Sept.-Oct.;

Mon.-Sat 10-5, Sun. noon-5, June-Aug. 23. Show times vary; phone ahead. **Cost:** $15.95; $13.95 (ages 6-11); $11.95 (ages 2-5). **Phone:** (717) 334-7259. [¶]

THE LINCOLN TRAIN MUSEUM, 425 Steinwehr Ave., features items from early American history and interactive train layouts. Visitors take a simulated trip aboard the recreated Funeral Car United States as it follows the funeral route of President Abraham Lincoln through the post-Civil War countryside. **Time:** Allow 1 hour minimum. **Hours:** Daily 9-9, Apr. to the day before Labor Day; Sun.-Thurs. 9-6, Fri.-Sat. 9-8, Labor Day to Nov. 30; Thurs.-Mon. 10-6, rest of year. Closed Thanksgiving. Phone ahead to confirm schedule. **Cost:** $7; $6 (military, police, fire and EMT personnel with ID); $5 (ages 65+); $4 (ages 6-12); free (ages 0-5). Phone ahead to confirm rates. **Phone:** (717) 334-5678.

RUPP HOUSE HISTORY CENTER, 451 Baltimore St., is the former home of the Rupp family, who hid in their cellar during the battle at Gettysburg. Due to damage caused by Union and Confederate soldiers during the battle, the house was rebuilt in 1868. Exhibits focus on civilian life during the Civil War and the life of soldiers who fought in the Gettysburg area. Exhibits feature interactive elements, and the museum hosts several living history events April through October. **Hours:** Fri. noon-8, Sat. 10-8, and Sun. noon-5, Apr. 4-Nov. 2. Phone ahead to confirm schedule. **Cost:** Free. **Phone:** (717) 339-2157.

SHRIVER HOUSE MUSEUM, 309 Baltimore St., restored and furnished to its 1860s appearance. Guides in period costumes conduct tours and interpret the Shriver family's experience of living deep within Civil War battle lines. During the Battle of Gettysburg, Confederate sharpshooters took aim from positions in the attic; the house also served as a hospital for wounded soldiers. Candlelight tours are offered by reservation during the holiday season.

Time: Allow 45 minutes minimum. **Hours:** Sun.-Thurs. 10-5, Fri.-Sat. 10-6, Apr.-Thanksgiving; Sat. noon-9, in Dec.; hours vary rest of year. Phone ahead to confirm schedule. **Cost:** $8.95; $6.95 (ages 7-12). **Phone:** (717) 337-2800.

STARS AND STRIPES TOURS meets passengers at area hotels. The Washington, D.C. tour is a 12-hour narrated motor coach trip and includes visits to the World War II, Lincoln, Iwo Jima, Vietnam Veterans and Korean War Veterans memorials. Around noon, passengers are dropped off at the Smithsonian Institution for 3 hours of independent sightseeing. The return trip includes a dinner stop in Thurmont, Md. Other tours are available.

Hours: Tours Tues. and Thurs., May-Oct. (also Wed., July-Aug.). Departure times and length of trips may vary. Phone ahead to confirm schedule. **Cost:** $85; $80 (ages 4-12). **Phone:** (717) 528-1660 or (877) 723-1863.

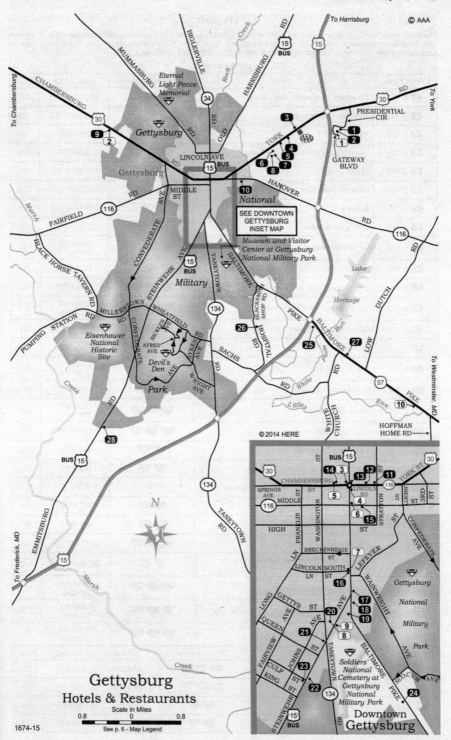

To Harrisburg

© AAA

To Chambersburg

CHAMBERSBURG

MUMMASBURG RD

BIGLERVILLE RD

Rock Creek

HARRISBURG RD

15 BUS

15

Eternal Light Peace Memorial

34

To York

RD

30

PRESIDENTIAL CIR

3

1 2

1

GATEWAY BLVD

9 2

30

Gettysburg

YORK

LINCOLN AVE

15 BUS

4

5

6 8 7

Gettysburg

RD

MIDDLE ST

10

HANOVER

National

FAIRFIELD

116

SEE DOWNTOWN GETTYSBURG INSET MAP

RD

116 RD

Museum and Visitor Center at Gettysburg National Military Park

Marsh

RD

CONFEDERATE AVE

STEINWEHR AVE

15 BUS

TANEYTOWN RD

BALTIMORE

Military

Lake

Heritage

BLACK HORSE TAVERN RD

MILLERSTOWN RD

WHEATFIELD RD

134

BLACKSMITH SHOP RD

PIKE

DUTCH

Run

PUMPING STATION RD

Eisenhower National Historic Site

CONFEDERATE

SICKLES AVE

AYRES AVE

SYKES AVE

RD

SACHS RD

26

HOSPITAL RD

25

BALTIMORE

27

LOW

To Westminster, MD

Devil's Den

WRIGHT AVE

RD

White Run

97

PIKE

10

Creek

Park

Littles Run

CHURCH

HOFFMAN HOME RD →

28

© 2014 HERE

BUS 15

134

N

TANEYTOWN RD

15

To Emmitsburg

To Frederick, MD

Marsh

Creek

Gettysburg
Hotels & Restaurants

Scale in Miles

0.8   0.8

See p. 6 - Map Legend

1674-15

Downtown Gettysburg inset

30

BUS 15

14 3

13 12

11

30

CHAMBERSBURG

SPRINGS AVE

MIDDLE

116

LINCOLN SQ

5

4

116

YORK ST

JS

3RD ST

FRANKLIN LN

WASHINGTON ST

6

15

ST

STRATTON ST

CONFEDERATE AVE

HIGH

BRECKENRIDGE ST

7

LEFEVER ST

WAINWRIGHT AVE

Gettysburg

LINCOLN LN

SOUTH ST

16

National

LONG LN

GETTYS ST

17

18

19

Military

QUEEN AVE

ST

20

9

8

AVE

TANEYTOWN ST

BALTIMORE

Park

FAIRVIEW AVE

21

CULP ST

JOHNS ST

23

Soldiers' National Cemetery at Gettysburg National Military Park

SLOCUM AVE

24

KING ST

22

134

STEINWEHR AVE

15 BUS

Downtown Gettysburg

Gettysburg

This index helps you "spot" where approved hotels and restaurants are located on the corresponding detailed maps. Hotel daily rate range is for comparison only. Restaurant price range is a combination of lunch and/or dinner. Turn to the listing page for more detailed rate and price information and consult display ads for special promotions.

GETTYSBURG

Map Page	Hotels	Diamond Rated	Rate Range	Page
❶ p. 119	**Courtyard by Marriott Gettysburg**	◆◆◆	$69-$194 SAVE	122
❷ p. 119	**Wyndham Gettysburg**	◆◆◆	$119-$349 SAVE	125
❸ p. 119	Hampton Inn	◆◆◆	$89-$269	124
❹ p. 119	Hilton Garden Inn-Gettysburg *(See ad p. 124.)*	◆◆◆	$89-$259	124
❺ p. 119	**Econo Lodge**	◆◆	$69-$119 SAVE	122
❻ p. 119	**Days Inn Gettysburg**	◆◆	$42-$249 SAVE	122
❼ p. 119	**Super 8**	◆◆	$49-$210 SAVE	125
❽ p. 119	Quality Inn & Suites	◆◆	$45-$119	124
❾ p. 119	**Inn at Herr Ridge**	◆◆◆	Rates not provided SAVE	124
❿ p. 119	Keystone Inn	◆◆◆	$119-$179	124
⓫ p. 119	The Swope Manor Bed & Breakfast	◆◆◆	$145-$205	125
⓬ p. 119	The Brafferton Inn Bed & Breakfast	◆◆◆	Rates not provided	121
⓭ p. 119	**Gettysburg Hotel** *(See ad p. 123.)*	◆◆◆	$109-$199 SAVE	123
⓮ p. 119	James Gettys Hotel	◆◆◆	$150-$275	124
⓯ p. 119	The Gaslight Inn	◆◆◆	Rates not provided	123
⓰ p. 119	Farnsworth House Inn	◆◆	$145-$175	123
⓱ p. 119	The Brickhouse Inn	◆◆◆	Rates not provided	121
⓲ p. 119	1863 Inn of Gettysburg	◆◆◆	$105-$345	121
⓳ p. 119	Gettysburg Travelodge	◆◆	$76-$130	123
⓴ p. 119	Gettystown Inn Bed & Breakfast	◆◆	$69-$195	123
㉑ p. 119	**Budget Host Three Crowns Motor Lodge**	◆	$40-$99 SAVE	121
㉒ p. 119	Quality Inn Gettysburg Motor Lodge	◆◆	$67-$192	124
㉓ p. 119	Americas Best Value Inn	◆◆	$57-$156	121
㉔ p. 119	**Comfort Suites Gettysburg**	◆◆◆	$80-$190 SAVE	121
㉕ p. 119	**Country Inn & Suites By Carlson** *(See ad p. 122.)*	◆◆	$89-$189 SAVE	122
㉖ p. 119	Baladerry Inn at Gettysburg	◆◆◆	Rates not provided	121
㉗ p. 119	The Lightner Farmhouse Bed & Breakfast	◆◆◆	Rates not provided	124
㉘ p. 119	Battlefield Bed & Breakfast Inn	◆◆◆	Rates not provided	121

Map Page	Restaurants	Diamond Rated	Cuisine	Price Range	Page
① p. 119	1863 Restaurant	◆◆◆	American	$9-$38	125
② p. 119	**Inn at Herr Ridge**	◆◆◆	American	$10-$34	125
③ p. 119	The Pub and Restaurant	◆◆	American	$11-$29	126
④ p. 119	Blue and Gray Bar and Grill	◆◆	American	$8-$23	125

Map Page	Restaurants (cont'd)	Diamond Rated	Cuisine	Price Range	Page
⑤ p. 119	The Blue Parrot Bistro	▼▼	American	$10-$33	125
⑥ p. 119	Cafe Saint-Amand	▼▼	French	$7-$25	125
⑦ p. 119	**Farnsworth House**	▼▼	American	$17-$25	125
⑧ p. 119	Alexander Dobbin Dining Rooms in the Dobbin House	▼▼▼	American	$25-$36	125
⑨ p. 119	Springhouse Tavern at the Dobbin House	▼▼	American	$9-$29	126
⑩ p. 119	Olivia's Restaurant	▼▼	Mediterranean	$9-$26	126

1863 INN OF GETTYSBURG   (717)334-6211 18
▼▼▼▼ **Hotel** $105-$345 **Address:** 516 Baltimore St 17325 **Location:** Jct US 15 business route and SR 97. **Facility:** 110 units. 2-5 stories, interior/exterior corridors. **Terms:** 7 day cancellation notice-fee imposed. **Pool(s):** outdoor. **Activities:** exercise room. **Guest Services:** coin laundry.

AMERICAS BEST VALUE INN   (717)334-1188 23
▼▼▼ **Motel** $57-$156 **Address:** 301 Steinwehr Ave 17325 **Location:** 1 mi s on US 15 business route, just s of jct SR 134. **Facility:** 76 units. 2 stories, interior/exterior corridors. **Pool(s):** outdoor. **Activities:** hot tub.

BALADERRY INN AT GETTYSBURG   717/337-1342 26
▼▼▼ **Historic Bed & Breakfast.** Rates not provided. **Address:** 40 Hospital Rd 17325 **Location:** US 15 exit SR 134, 1 mi on Blacksmith Shop Rd. **Facility:** Within minutes of the battlefield and downtown Gettysburg, the inn sits on four acres and offers a peaceful retreat. Rooms are charming, and some have a patio or gas fireplace. 10 units, some two bedrooms. 2 stories (no elevator), interior corridors. **Terms:** age restrictions may apply. **Activities:** hot tub.

BATTLEFIELD BED & BREAKFAST INN   717/334-8804 28
▼▼▼ **Historic Bed & Breakfast.** Rates not provided. **Address:** 2264 Emmitsburg Rd 17325 **Location:** 3.8 mi s on Steinwehr Ave/Emmitsburg Rd from jct Baltimore St. **Facility:** This handsome stone house was built in 1809, with a second section added later. Public areas feature portraits by Dale Gallon, a local artist. 10 units, some two bedrooms and cottages. 2 stories (no elevator), interior corridors.

THE BRAFFERTON INN BED & BREAKFAST
717/337-3423 12
▼▼▼ **Historic Bed & Breakfast.** Rates not provided. **Address:** 44 York St 17325 **Location:** US 30, just e of traffic circle. **Facility:** This B&B—a restored 1786 fieldstone house and a 19th-century brick carriage house—invokes a bit of history with Colonial and Antebellum furnishings and décor. Four designated units offer free parking. 17 units, some two bedrooms and kitchens. 1-3 stories (no elevator), interior/exterior corridors. **Parking:** on-site (fee). **Terms:** age restrictions may apply.

THE BRICKHOUSE INN   717/338-9337 17
▼▼▼ **Historic Bed & Breakfast.** Rates not provided. **Address:** 452 Baltimore St 17325 **Location:** From traffic circle, 0.5 mi s on US 15 business route. **Facility:** The landscaped garden and spacious common areas invite you to relax at this charming B&B built in the 1800s. Rooms are decorated with needlepoints and period antiques and vary in size. 15 units. 2-3 stories (no elevator), interior/exterior corridors. **Terms:** age restrictions may apply.

BUDGET HOST THREE CROWNS MOTOR LODGE
(717)334-3168 21

▼ **Motel** $40-$99
Address: 205 Steinwehr Ave 17325 **Location:** 0.5 mi s on US 15 business route; jct SR 134. **Facility:** 29 units. 1 story, exterior corridors. **Terms:** 3 day cancellation notice-fee imposed. **Pool(s):** outdoor.

COMFORT SUITES GETTYSBURG   (717)334-6715 24

▼▼▼ **Hotel** $80-$190
Address: 945 Baltimore Pike 17325 **Location:** US 15 business route, 0.5 mi s on SR 97. **Facility:** 70 units, some two bedrooms. 4 stories, interior corridors. **Terms:** resort fee. **Amenities:** safes. **Pool(s):** heated indoor. **Activities:** exercise room.

(See map & index p. 119.)

COUNTRY INN & SUITES BY CARLSON

(717)337-9518 **25**

Hotel
$89-$189

Address: 1857 Gettysburg Village Dr 17325 **Location:** US 15 exit SR 97, just e. Next to factory outlet stores. **Facility:** 83 units. 3 stories, interior corridors. **Pool(s):** heated indoor. **Activities:** hot tub, exercise room. **Guest Services:** coin laundry. **Featured Amenity: breakfast buffet.** (See ad this page.)

COURTYARD BY MARRIOTT GETTYSBURG

(717)334-5600 **1**

Hotel
$69-$194

 AAA Benefit: Members save 5% or more!

Address: 115 Presidential Cir 17325 **Location:** US 15 exit York St, just e on US 30. **Facility:** 152 units. 5 stories, interior corridors. **Pool(s):** heated indoor. **Activities:** hot tub, exercise room. **Guest Services:** complimentary laundry.

DAYS INN GETTYSBURG

(717)334-0030 **6**

Hotel
$42-$249

Address: 865 York Rd 17325 **Location:** 1 mi e on US 30. **Facility:** 112 units. 5 stories, interior corridors. **Terms:** check-in 4 pm, cancellation fee imposed. **Pool(s):** outdoor. **Activities:** exercise room. **Guest Services:** coin laundry. **Featured Amenity: continental breakfast.**

ECONO LODGE

(717)334-4208 **5**

Motel
$69-$119

Address: 983 York Rd 17325 **Location:** 1.2 mi e on US 30. **Facility:** 30 units. 2 stories (no elevator), exterior corridors. **Featured Amenity: continental breakfast.**

▼ *See AAA listing this page* ▼

(See map & index p. 119.)

FARNSWORTH HOUSE INN   717/334-8838   **16**

 Historic Bed & Breakfast $145-$175 **Address:** 401 Baltimore St 17325 **Location:** Just s on US 15 business route. **Facility:** You'll take a step back in time at this inn, one of the original homes remaining from the Civil War period. Used by Confederate snipers during the battle, many soldiers died in the house. 10 units. 1-2 stories (no elevator), interior corridors. **Terms:** age restrictions may apply, 14 day cancellation notice-fee imposed. **Dining:** Farnsworth House, see separate listing.

THE GASLIGHT INN   717/337-9100 **15**

Historic Bed & Breakfast. Rates not provided. **Address:** 33 E Middle St 17325 **Location:** Just s on US 15 business route from traffic circle, just e. **Facility:** A charming 1872 Victorian with contemporary furnishings and modern conveniences, this cheerful inn offers some rooms with gas fireplaces and some with steam showers. 9 units. 3 stories (no elevator), interior corridors. **Terms:** age restrictions may apply.

GETTYSBURG HOTEL   (717)337-2000 **13**

Historic Hotel
$109-$199

Address: One Lincoln Square 17325 **Location:** On US 30; center of downtown. **Facility:** Established in 1797, this restored hotel has a ballroom that was once a bank. The restaurant offers upscale American comfort food. All guest rooms have a king or two queen beds. 119 units, some two bedrooms. 6 stories, interior corridors. **Parking:** on-site (fee). **Terms:** check-in 4 pm, 3 day cancellation notice. **Pool(s):** outdoor. **Activities:** exercise room. *(See ad this page.)*

Walking distance to the battlefield, attractions, shops & restaurants. Located in Historic Downtown.

GETTYSBURG TRAVELODGE   (717)334-9281 **19**

 **Motel** $76-$130 **Address:** 613 Baltimore St 17325 **Location:** On SR 97; at US 15 business route. **Facility:** 47 units. 1-2 stories, interior/exterior corridors. **Amenities:** safes. **Guest Services:** coin laundry.

GETTYSTOWN INN BED & BREAKFAST   (717)334-2100 **20**

 **Historic Country Inn** $69-$195 **Address:** 89 Steinwehr Ave 17325 **Location:** US 15 business route, just n of jct SR 134 S. **Facility:** Period furnishings adorn the Civil War-era home, which is within walking distance of museums, antique shops and some battlefields. The on-site restaurant and tavern provide great dining options. 10 units, some efficiencies, kitchens and houses. 1-2 stories (no elevator), interior/exterior corridors. **Terms:** 2 night minimum stay - seasonal and/or weekends. **Dining:** Springhouse Tavern at the Dobbin House, see separate listing.

Get There Better

TripTik® Travel Planner

Plan your trips with better maps and better travel information.
AAAmaps.com

▼ See AAA listing this page ▼

(See map & index p. 119.)

HAMPTON INN   (717)338-9121 **3**

▼▼▼ **Hotel** $89-$269 **Address:**
1280 York Rd 17325 **Location:** US 15
exit US 30, just w. **Facility:** 79 units. 4
stories, interior corridors. **Terms:** 1-7
night minimum stay, cancellation fee im-
posed. **Pool(s):** heated indoor. **Activities:** hot tub, exercise room.
Guest Services: coin laundry.

AAA Benefit:
Members save 5%
or more!

[icons]

HILTON GARDEN INN-GETTYSBURG   (717)334-2040 **4**

AAA Benefit:
Members save 5% or more!

▼▼▼ **Hotel** $89-$259 **Address:**
1061 York Rd 17325 **Location:** 0.9 mi e
on US 30. **Facility:** 88 units. 4 stories, interior corridors. **Terms:** 1-7 night
minimum stay, cancellation fee imposed.
Pool(s): heated indoor. **Activities:** hot
tub, exercise room. **Guest Services:** valet and coin laundry. **(See
ad this page.)**

[icons] CALL

INN AT HERR RIDGE   717/334-4332 **9**

▼▼▼
Historic
Country Inn
Rates not provided

Address: 900 Chambersburg Rd 17325
Location: 1.7 mi w on US 30. **Facility:**
All the rooms (some of which are very
spacious) at this hilltop property have
gas fireplaces, and many have balconies and hot tubs. 17 units. 3 stories (no
elevator), interior/exterior corridors.
Terms: check-in 4 pm, age restrictions
may apply. **Amenities:** safes. **Dining:**
restaurant, see separate listing. **Activities:** massage. **Featured Amenity: full
hot breakfast.**

[SAVE icons]

JAMES GETTYS HOTEL   (717)337-1334 **14**

▼▼▼ **Historic Bed & Breakfast** $150-$275 **Address:** 27
Chambersburg St 17325 **Location:** From traffic circle, just w on US
30. **Facility:** The small inn, with more than 200 years of rich Gettysburg history, is on the National Register of Historic Places. Dating
from 1804, the comfortable guest rooms are suited for long-term
stays. 12 units, some efficiencies. 4 stories, interior corridors. **Terms:**
2 night minimum stay - weekends, 5 day cancellation notice-fee
imposed. [icons]

KEYSTONE INN   (717)337-3888 **10**

▼▼▼ **Historic Bed & Breakfast** $119-$179 **Address:** 231
Hanover St 17325 **Location:** US 30, just e on SR 116. **Facility:** This
1913 home offers a front porch overlooking seasonal gardens in a
quiet, cozy residential area of town. DVD players are in all rooms.
They offer a guest library with board games and DVDs. 8 units. 3 stories (no elevator), interior corridors. **Terms:** 2 night minimum stay -
seasonal and/or weekends, 14 day cancellation notice-fee imposed.
[icons] / SOME UNITS

THE LIGHTNER FARMHOUSE BED & BREAKFAST
                                              717/337-9508 **27**

▼▼▼ **Historic Bed & Breakfast.** Rates not provided. **Address:** 2350 Baltimore Pike 17325 **Location:** US 15 Bypass exit SR
97, 0.7 mi s. **Facility:** Set on 23 acres, this 1862 Federal-style brick
manor was Sheriff Lightner's house during the Civil War and also
served as a Union field hospital. 7 units, some cottages. 3 stories (no
elevator), interior corridors. **Terms:** age restrictions may apply.
[icons] / SOME UNITS

QUALITY INN & SUITES   (717)337-2400 **8**

▼▼ **Hotel** $45-$119 **Address:** 871 York Rd 17325 **Location:** 1
mi e on US 30. **Facility:** 77 units. 2 stories, interior corridors. **Amenities:** safes. **Pool(s):** heated indoor. **Activities:** hot tub, limited exercise equipment. **Guest Services:** coin laundry.
[icons] / SOME UNITS

QUALITY INN GETTYSBURG MOTOR LODGE
                                              (717)334-1103 **22**

▼▼ **Motel** $67-$192 **Address:** 380 Steinwehr Ave 17325 **Location:** 1 mi s on US 15 business route; just s of jct SR 134. **Facility:**
109 units, some efficiencies. 2 stories (no elevator), interior/exterior
corridors. **Pool(s):** outdoor, heated indoor. **Activities:** hot tub, exercise room. **Guest Services:** coin laundry.
[icons] / SOME UNITS

▼ See AAA listing this page ▼

(See map & index p. 119.)

SUPER 8   (717)337-1400 **7**

Motel
$49-$210

Address: 869 York Rd 17325 **Location:** 1 mi e on US 30. **Facility:** 50 units. 2 stories (no elevator), interior corridors. **Terms:** cancellation fee imposed. **Amenities:** safes. **Pool(s):** heated indoor. **Activities:** hot tub. **Guest Services:** complimentary laundry.

SAVE ¶†↑ CALL &M ≥ BIZ
🛰 🛗 🍽 💻 / SOME UNITS 🛏

1 mile from heart of town. Near Gettysburg National Military Park, historic sites & area attractions.

THE SWOPE MANOR BED & BREAKFAST
     (717)398-2655 **11**

▼▼▼ **Historic Bed & Breakfast** $145-$205 **Address:** 58-60 York St 17325 **Location:** US 30, just e of traffic circle, jct Stratton St. **Facility:** This historic brick residence, built in 1836, is an easy walk to shops and a restaurant. The B&B offers well-appointed common areas and guest rooms. Each room is individually decorated and furnished. 13 units. 3 stories (no elevator), interior corridors. **Parking:** on-site (fee). **Terms:** 2-4 night minimum stay - seasonal and/or weekends, 15 day cancellation notice-fee imposed.

¶†↑ CALL &M 🛰 ✕ ✆

WYNDHAM GETTYSBURG   (717)339-0020 **2**

Hotel
$119-$349

Address: 95 Presidential Cir 17325 **Location:** US 15 exit York St, just e on US 30. **Facility:** 248 units. 6 stories, interior corridors. **Terms:** cancellation fee imposed. **Amenities:** safes. **Dining:** 1863 Restaurant, see separate listing. **Pool(s):** heated indoor. **Activities:** hot tub, exercise room. **Guest Services:** complimentary laundry, rental car service.

SAVE ¶† 🛗 ▯ 📶 CALL &M ≥
BIZ HS 🛰 ✕ 💻
/ SOME UNITS 🛏

WHERE TO EAT

1863 RESTAURANT   717/339-0020 **1**

▼▼▼ American. Fine Dining. $9-$38 **AAA Inspector Notes:** This restaurant is great both for a meal with your family or for discussing business with associates. The acclaimed chef who operates this place focuses on American cuisine, including daily homemade desserts and soups served in nice plate presentations. A wonderful lounge is also available just off the formal dining room, featuring oversized leather chairs, dark wood accents and a fully-stocked bar. **Features:** full bar, happy hour. **Reservations:** suggested. **Address:** 95 Presidential Cir 17325 **Location:** US 15 exit York St, just e on US 30; in Wyndham Gettysburg.

B L D CALL &M

ALEXANDER DOBBIN DINING ROOMS IN THE DOBBIN HOUSE   717/334-2100 **8**

▼▼▼ American. Casual Dining. $25-$36 **AAA Inspector Notes:** *Historic.* Staff members dressed in period garb act as though they are from another era as they circulate through this relaxed dining room, which is decorated with antiques and historic furnishings. Fresh homemade breads accompany every meal. House specialties include seafood Isabella (crabmeat and scallops on pasta), pork tenderloin with raspberry sauce and lamb chops. Children must be at least 10 years old to enter. Additional dining is available in the tavern, which serves meals from 11:30 am to 9 pm. **Features:** full bar. **Reservations:** suggested. **Address:** 89 Steinwehr Ave 17325 **Location:** US 15 business route, just n of jct SR 134 S; adjacent to Gettystown Inn Bed & Breakfast. D

BLUE AND GRAY BAR AND GRILL   717/334-1999 **4**

▼▼ American. Casual Dining. $8-$23 **AAA Inspector Notes:** Conveniently located in the center of the square, this sports bar offers 12 flat-panel TVs and a lively atmosphere. The menu focuses on casual pub fare and includes a large option of buffalo wings and a variety of burgers named after Union and Confederate generals. **Features:** full bar. **Address:** 2 Baltimore St 17325 **Location:** On US 30; center of downtown. **Parking:** street only.

L D LATE

THE BLUE PARROT BISTRO   717/337-3739 **5**

▼▼ American. Casual Dining. $10-$33 **AAA Inspector Notes:** Situated downtown, this charming bistro offers an eclectic menu, including Cajun catfish, lamb loin chops, chicken souvlaki salad and smoked trout pâté. The casual atmosphere makes it a great spot for a drink at the bar or for a full dining experience. **Features:** full bar, patio dining. **Address:** 35 Chambersburg St 17325 **Location:** From traffic circle, just w on US 30. **Parking:** street only. L D

CAFE SAINT-AMAND   717/334-2700 **6**

▼▼ French. Casual Dining. $7-$25 **AAA Inspector Notes:** This cozy bistro is in the heart of downtown. The menu lists a nice selection of French and American classic dishes, as well as light fare with a selection of sandwiches and crepes. In addition to the menu, the chef prepares daily specials. Desserts are made in house. They do not offer beer or wine, but you are able to BYOB for no corkage fee. **Address:** 48 Baltimore St 17325 **Location:** Jct Middle St; downtown. **Parking:** street only. B L D

FARNSWORTH HOUSE   717/334-8838 **7**

◆◆
American
Casual Dining
$17-$25

AAA Inspector Notes: *Historic.* This place triumphs in recreating the dining experience that one would have enjoyed in the Civil War era. Everything from the menu, which features items such as spoon bread and game pie, to the complementing service ware makes this a real treat that should not be passed up. Look for the more than 100 bullet holes that attest to the place in history the Farnsworth will forever claim. The tavern offers lunch and dinner service. **Features:** full bar, patio dining. **Reservations:** suggested. **Address:** 401 Baltimore St 17325 **Location:** Just s on US 15 business route; in Farnsworth House Inn. *Menu on AAA.com*

D

INN AT HERR RIDGE   717/334-4332 **2**

◆◆◆
American
Fine Dining
$10-$34

AAA Inspector Notes: *Historic.* Fireplaces lend to the appeal of this 1816 public house's four dining rooms, which are decorated with antiques and lanterns. Gourmet cuisine is prepared and served in a refined atmosphere. Small plates include baked baby Brie with local raspberry and rosemary gastrique and crab and corn chowder. Satisfying main entrées include a char-crusted pork tenderloin and seared sea scallops with preserved lemon and pancetta risotto. Friday and Saturday nights feature prime rib. **Features:** full bar, patio dining, happy hour. **Reservations:** suggested, weekends. **Address:** 900 Chambersburg Rd 17325 **Location:** 1.7 mi w on US 30. L D

(See map & index p. 119.)

OLIVIA'S RESTAURANT   717/359-9357   [10]

WWW WWW   Mediterranean. Casual Dining. $9-$26 **AAA Inspector Notes:** This casual and relaxed restaurant offers a large menu of seafood, burgers and sandwiches along with hickory chargrilled entrées of beef, lamb and chicken. Weekends usher in live entertainment. Parrot Island is the open deck around back. Enjoy a drink or a meal in the festive atmosphere. DJ night is on Thursday. **Features:** full bar, patio dining, happy hour. **Address:** 3015 Baltimore Pike 17325 **Location:** US 15 Bypass exit SR 97, 1.2 mi e.

[L] [D]

THE PUB AND RESTAURANT   717/334-7100   [3]

WWW WWW   American. Casual Dining. $11-$29 **AAA Inspector Notes:** Located in the center of the square and within walking distance of shops and lodging, this busy pub is the perfect place to have a bite to eat and relax before going off and touring the Gettysburg sites. This place is closed on Sunday during December and January. They do not serve breakfast on Tuesday and Wednesday. **Features:** full bar. **Address:** 20 Lincoln Square 17325 **Location:** On US 30; center of downtown. **Parking:** street only. [B] [L] [D]

SPRINGHOUSE TAVERN AT THE DOBBIN HOUSE
                                   717/334-2100   [9]

WWW WWW   American. Casual Dining. $9-$29 **AAA Inspector Notes:** *Historic.* Part of a circa 1776 Underground Railroad stop and Civil War hospital now serves as Springhouse Tavern, a quaint ale house where you'll be treated to sandwiches, salads, ribs, steak, homemade soups and tasty "pecan pye." Expect efficient, thoughtful service. **Features:** full bar. **Address:** 89 Steinwehr Ave 17325 **Location:** US 15 business route, just n of jct SR 134 S; in Gettystown Inn Bed & Breakfast. [L] [D]

GETTYSBURG NATIONAL MILITARY PARK (I-7) elev. 495'

• Attractions map p. 127

Gettysburg National Military Park virtually surrounds the town of Gettysburg; the main entrance is at the Museum and Visitor Center at 1195 Baltimore Pike. The park comprises the Gettysburg battlefield, where one of the most important and hotly contested battles of the Civil War was fought July 1-3, 1863. It also was the bloodiest battle of the war, resulting in 51,000 wounded, captured or killed.

The Federal Army of the Potomac, under Major Gen. George Meade, met the Confederate Army of Northern Virginia, under Gen. Robert E. Lee. Some 168,000 soldiers were at Gettysburg. The battlefield covers 25 square miles.

After his victory at Chancellorsville, Va., Lee invaded Pennsylvania, hoping to draw the Union Army away from Richmond. On the morning of July 1 two Confederate brigades attacked Gen. John Buford's cavalry division. Fierce fighting followed, and the Union forces were driven back to the heights south of town, known as Cemetery Hill, Cemetery Ridge and Culp's Hill. That night the armies moved into battle position. Confederate assaults on both Union flanks gained some ground late the next day in some of the heaviest fighting of the battle.

On the third day, after a heavy 2-hour artillery barrage, a Confederate force advanced on the center of the Union line in the face of deadly fire that shattered their ranks. They retreated on the evening of July 4, ending the last major offensive of Lee's army and presaging the war's outcome 22 months later.

On Nov. 19, 1863, President Lincoln dedicated Soldiers' National Cemetery on the battlefield, delivering his most famous speech, the Gettysburg Address.

There are now 1,328 monuments and memorials, three observation towers and 31 miles of marked avenues.

On Cemetery Ridge, Meade, commander of the Union forces, is depicted on his horse. His headquarters on Taneytown Road is preserved. In the spring, summer and fall there are interpretive walks to the High Water Mark, where there is a monument to the bravery of both armies, and to the National Cemetery as well as to such other sites as the Peach Orchard and McPherson's Ridge.

Many states have erected monuments in the park. The Virginia memorial is surmounted by a statue of Lee, and the North Carolina memorial was designed and carved by Gutzon Borglum, sculptor of Mount Rushmore.

The park roads are open daily 6 a.m.-10 p.m., Apr.-Oct.; 6 a.m.-7 p.m., rest of year. Phone (717) 334-1124, or (877) 874-2478 for advance ticket purchases.

DAVID WILLS HOUSE is at 8 Lincoln Sq. on the downtown square, within Gettysburg National Military Park. The site reveals what Gettysburg was like during the weeks after the Civil War battle through displays, two interactive exhibits and two films. Much of the recovery phase was centered around the three-story brick house of David Wills, a prominent lawyer. From here local women cared for wounded soldiers, and state leaders convened to discuss burial options for the Union casualties. Pennsylvania's governor, Andrew Curtin, placed Wills in charge of organizing a national cemetery.

On Nov. 2, 1863, Wills wrote to President Lincoln, inviting him to deliver "a few appropriate remarks" at the cemetery's dedication on Nov. 19. To many people's amazement, the president accepted and arrived the evening before the event. Mr. and Mrs. Wills welcomed him into their home, where they were hosting a dinner for nearly three dozen guests. That night from his bedroom (Mrs. Wills had prepared her own for the president), he completed the Gettysburg Address he would give the next day.

The museum collection features original furnishings, including the bed Lincoln slept in, and the saddle he used on his trip to the cemetery. A model with 260 buildings is a powerful visual representation of the 1863 town. Photography is permitted. **Time:** Allow 45 minutes minimum. **Hours:** Daily 10-5, May-Aug.; Wed.-Mon. 10-4, in Apr. and Sept.-Oct.; Thurs.-Mon. 10-4, in Mar.; Sat.-Sun. 10-4, Nov.-Dec.; Sat. 10-4, Sun. 10-3, rest of year. Closed Jan. 1, Thanksgiving and Christmas. Phone ahead to confirm schedule. **Cost:** $6.50; $4 (ages 6-12). **Phone:** (717) 334-2499 or (866) 486-5735.

DEVIL'S DEN, off Warren Ave. and just w. of Little Round Top within Gettysburg National Military Park, is a group of huge boulders from which

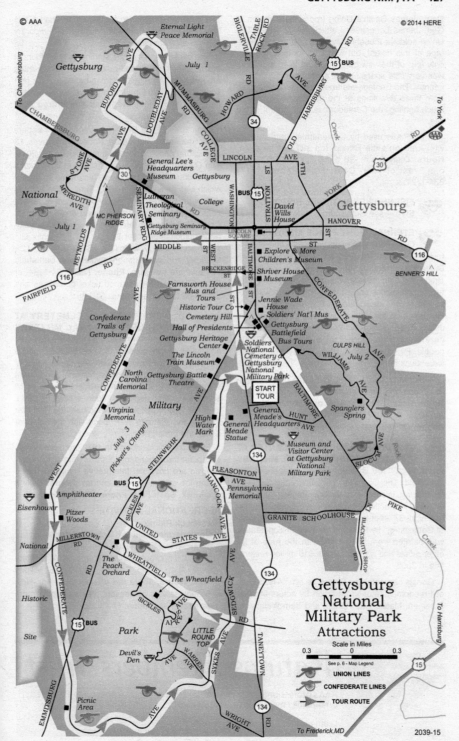

© AAA

© 2014 HERE

Eternal Light
Peace Memorial

Gettysburg

July 1

BIGLERVILLE RD

TABLE ROCK RD

15 BUS

To Chambersburg

CHAMBERSBURG

BUFORD AVE

DOUBLEDAY AVE

MUMMASBURG RD

HOWARD AVE

COLLEGE AVE

34

OLD HARRISBURG AVE

Rock Creek

RD

To York

AAA

STONE AVE

MEREDITH AVE

National

July 1

REYNOLDS AVE

30

SEMINARY RDG

MC PHERSON RIDGE

General Lee's
Headquarters
Museum

Lutheran
Theological
Seminary

Gettysburg
Seminary
Ridge Museum

LINCOLN AVE

Gettysburg
College

WASHINGTON ST

STRATTON ST

BUS 15

David
Wills
House

4TH ST

YORK ST

30

Gettysburg

HANOVER RD

MIDDLE

WEST ST

LINCOLN SQUARE

BALTIMORE ST

116

FAIRFIELD

116

RD

BRECKENRIDGE ST

Explore & More
Children's Museum

Shriver House
Museum

CONFEDERATE AVE

BENNER'S HILL

Confederate
Trails of
Gettysburg

CONFEDERATE AVE

North
Carolina
Memorial

Virginia
Memorial

Military

Farnsworth House
Mus and
Tours

Historic Tour Co

Hall of Presidents

Gettysburg Heritage
Center

The Lincoln
Train Museum

Gettysburg Battle
Theatre

Jennie Wade
House

Cemetery Hill

Soldiers' Nat'l Mus

Gettysburg
Battlefield
Bus Tours

Soldiers
National
Cemetery a
Gettysburg
National
Military Park

CULPS HILL

July 2

WILLIAMS AVE

Spanglers
Spring

SLOCUM AVE

Rock Creek

July 3
(Pickett's Charge)

STEINWEHR AVE

High
Water
Mark

General
Meade
Statue

START
TOUR

General
Meade's
Headquarters

BALTIMORE

HUNT AVE

Museum and
Visitor Center
at Gettysburg
National
Military Park

WEST

BUS 15

Amphitheater

Eisenhower

Pitzer
Woods

National

MILLERSTOWN RD

CONFEDERATE RD

The Peach
Orchard

Historic

15 BUS

Site

Park

Devil's
Den

SICKLES AVE

UNITED STATES AVE

WHEATFIELD RD

SICKLES AVE

AYRES AVE

LITTLE
ROUND
TOP

WARREN AVE

AVE

The Wheatfield

HANCOCK AVE

PLEASONTON AVE

Pennsylvania
Memorial

134

SEDGWICK AVE

SYKES AVE

134

GRANITE SCHOOLHOUSE

BLACKSMITH SHOP RD

PIKE

Blacksmith Creek

To Harrisburg

15

Gettysburg
National
Military Park
Attractions

Scale in Miles

0.3   0   0.3

See p. 6 - Map Legend

UNION LINES

CONFEDERATE LINES

TOUR ROUTE

EMMITSBURG

Picnic
Area

AVE

TANEYTOWN RD

WRIGHT AVE

134

To Frederick, MD

To Frederick, MD

2039-15

Capt. James Smith's Union troops were driven in Gen. James Longstreet's attack July 2, 1863. The Union soldiers thought they would be at an advantage at this height, but with little room at the top, only four of their six guns could be used and there was very little space left for ammunition supplies or infantry. The Confederate troops eventually attacked from three directions at the same time, and after much fighting, the Confederates took control of the site.

A barricade used by Confederate sharpshooters who fired on Little Round Top still can be seen. **Hours:** Daily 6 a.m.-10 p.m., Apr.-Oct.; 6 a.m.-7 p.m., rest of year. **Cost:** Free. **Phone:** (717) 334-1124.

 EISENHOWER NATIONAL HISTORIC SITE—see Gettysburg p. 116.

 ETERNAL LIGHT PEACE MEMORIAL, on Oak Ridge in the northwest section of Gettysburg National Military Park, commemorates the Battle of Gettysburg. The project was suggested by Union and Confederate veterans in 1913, and after funding difficulties and construction delays were resolved, it was dedicated by President Franklin D. Roosevelt on the 75th anniversary of the battle on July 3, 1938. Some Civil War veterans attended the ceremony, which drew an estimated 250,000 people. Perhaps another 100,000 would-be visitors were stuck in nearby traffic.

A perpetual flame burns at the top of the monument, and an inscription reads, "Peace Eternal in a Nation United." **Hours:** Park daily 6 a.m.-10 p.m., Apr.-Oct.; 6 a.m.-7 p.m., rest of year. **Cost:** Free. **Phone:** (717) 334-1124.

MUSEUM AND VISITOR CENTER AT GETTYSBURG NATIONAL MILITARY PARK is at 1195 Baltimore Pike, adjacent to the battlefield. The Civil War, particularly the Battle of Gettysburg, is chronicled through archival materials, artifacts, interactive exhibits and a cyclorama: a 42-foot high, 377-foot-long canvas painting. "The Battle of Gettysburg," by French artist Paul Philippoteaux was painted from 1883-1884 with the help of 20 other artists and went through a $15 million restoration in 2008.

Guests can watch the 22-minute film "A New Birth of Freedom," featuring narration by actors Morgan Freeman, Marcia Gay Harden and Sam Waterston.

The museum's collection includes more than 1 million items, though not all are displayed. Temporary exhibits also are offered.

The center serves as the starting point for tours of the battlefield. Both self-guiding and guided tours are available. Arrangements can be made for a personally conducted 2-hour tour with a licensed battlefield guide. Ranger programs are offered April through December.

Treasures of the Civil War: Legendary Leaders Who Shaped a War and a Nation showcases 13 noteworthy people and runs through June 16, 2016. The Cyclorama painting is displayed in the Visitor's Center building, not in the Cyclorama building, which was demolished in 2013. **Time:** Allow 2 hours minimum. **Hours:** Daily 8-6, Apr.-Oct.; 8-5, rest of year. Closed Jan. 1, Thanksgiving and Christmas. **Cost:** Visitor center free. Museum, film and cyclorama combination ticket $12.50; $11.50 (senior citizens and military with ID); $8.50 (ages 6-12). Multiday and combination passes with battlefield bus tour are available. **Phone:** (717) 334-1124, or (877) 874-2478 for advance ticket purchases and battlefield tour reservations. GT ⑪

SOLDIERS' NATIONAL CEMETERY AT GETTYSBURG NATIONAL MILITARY PARK, at 97 Taneytown Rd., just n. of the museum and visitor center, consists of 17 acres and contains the graves of 3,555 Union Civil War dead, 1,600 of them unknown. The Soldiers' National Monument stands near the spot where President Lincoln delivered his immortal dedication address Nov. 19, 1863, to some 15,000 people. Veterans from the Civil War through the Vietnam War, along with their dependents, are buried here.

Since the official closing in 1972, no more burials except for the dependents of those veterans already interred are possible. Interpretive walks are given during the spring, summer and fall. **Hours:** Daily 8 a.m.-dusk. **Cost:** Free. **Phone:** (717) 334-1124.

RECREATIONAL ACTIVITIES
Horseback Riding
- **Confederate Trails of Gettysburg** 1 to 2-hour horseback tours depart from McMillan Woods Youth Campground's parking area on W. Confederate Ave., within Gettysburg National Military Park. **Hours:** Tours are offered daily Apr.-Nov. Schedules vary by season; phone to confirm departure times. **Phone:** (717) 315-7433.

GIBSONIA pop. 2,733
- **Hotels & Restaurants map & index p. 348**
- **Part of Pittsburgh area — see map p. 326**

QUALITY INN & SUITES PITTSBURGH-GIBSONIA
(724)444-8700   **41**

🎗🎗 **Motel** $90-$200 **Address:** 5137 William Flynn Hwy 15044 **Location:** I-76 (Pennsylvania Tpke) exit 39, just n. **Facility:** 59 units, some efficiencies. 3 stories, exterior corridors. **Activities:** limited exercise equipment. **Guest Services:** coin laundry.

WHERE TO EAT

KING'S FAMILY RESTAURANT   724/443-4280

🎗🎗 American. Family Dining. $6-$13 **AAA Inspector Notes:** Fast and friendly service is offered here. The menu is large in size with descriptive menu items and pictures. The restaurant is also known for its ice cream and dessert menu. **Address:** 112 Northtowne Square 15044 **Location:** I-76 (Pennsylvania Tpke) exit 39, 2 mi n on SR 8, then just e. B L D

THE PINES TAVERN   724/625-3252   **33**

🎗🎗🎗 Traditional American. Casual Dining. $10-$36 **AAA Inspector Notes:** A local landmark since 1914, this warm country inn is appointed with antiques, flowers and candles. Lamb, crab cakes and pasta are preparations on an ever-evolving menu. Diners enjoy a fine selection of desserts and coffees. **Features:** full bar, patio dining. **Reservations:** suggested. **Address:** 5018 Bakerstown Rd 15044 **Location:** West from jct SR 8 and 910. L D

GLEN MILLS (B-9) elev. 230'
- **Part of Philadelphia area — see map p. 230**

NEWLIN GRIST MILL consists of 150 acres on Baltimore Pike/US 1 at Cheyney Rd. The restored gristmill, with a 16-foot water-powered wheel, dates from 1704. The miller's stone house, built in 1739, is furnished in period. A blacksmith shop, bank barn, springhouse and log cabin are in the park, as is the Markham Train Station, which serves as a visitor center. There are 8 miles of nature trails along the millrace and the stream.

Time: Allow 1 hour minimum. **Hours:** Grounds daily dawn-dusk. Guided tours Mon.-Fri. at 11 and 2, Sat.-Sun. at 10, 11, 1 and 2. **Cost:** Grounds free. Tour $5. **Phone:** (610) 459-2359. GT ⛲

SWEETWATER FARM BED & BREAKFAST   610/459-4711

🎗🎗🎗 **Historic Bed & Breakfast** $150-$435 **Address:** 50 Sweetwater Rd 19342 **Location:** US 1, 2 mi w on Valley Rd, 0.6 mi s. **Facility:** Set on 50 acres, this beautifully appointed B&B and winery features suites located in spacious cottages as well as comfortable guest rooms in an 18th-century manor house. 15 units, some two bedrooms, kitchens and cottages. 1-2 stories (no elevator), interior/exterior corridors. **Terms:** 2 night minimum stay - seasonal and/or weekends, 14 day cancellation notice-fee imposed. **Pool(s):** outdoor. **Activities:** hot tub, exercise room.

GLENMOORE (B-8) elev. 560'
- **Part of Philadelphia area — see map p. 230**

SPRINGTON MANOR FARM, 5 mi. w. off US 322 on Springton Rd., is a 300-acre demonstration farm. Features include the giant Great Barn, a sheep barn, poultry house and a petting area. A nature trail and wildlife pond are on the grounds. Educational programs also are offered in spring and fall at the agricultural museum on the grounds. Catch-and-release fishing is offered to visitors with a valid state fishing license. **Time:** Allow 1 hour minimum. **Hours:** Grounds daily 8-dusk. Barn and agricultural museum daily 10-2:30. **Cost:** Free. **Phone:** (610) 942-2450. ⛲

GORDONVILLE pop. 508
- **Hotels & Restaurants map & index p. 225**
- **Part of Pennsylvania Dutch Country area — see map p. 220**

AFTER EIGHT B&B   (717)687-3664   **52**

🎗🎗🎗 **Historic Bed & Breakfast** $118-$188 **Address:** 2942 Lincoln Hwy E 17529 **Location:** On US 30 (Lincoln Hwy), 1 mi w. Located in a rural area. **Facility:** Located in an 1818 Colonial brick home and surrounded by Amish farmland, this B&B offers individually decorated rooms with antiques. Those looking for more room should inquire about the available cottages. 10 units, some two bedrooms, kitchens and cottages. 2 stories (no elevator), interior/exterior corridors. **Terms:** 2 night minimum stay - seasonal and/or weekends, 14 day cancellation notice-fee imposed.

MOTEL 6-LANCASTER #4174   717/687-3880   **51**

🎗🎗 **Motel** **Rates not provided**   **Address:** 2959 Lincoln Hwy E 17529 **Location:** On US 30 (Lincoln Hwy); center. Located in a commercial area. **Facility:** 40 units. 2 stories, interior corridors.

GRANTVILLE (H-9) elev. 531'
- **Restaurants p. 130**

GAMBLING ESTABLISHMENTS
- **Hollywood Casino at Penn National Race Course** is at 777 Hollywood Blvd. **Hours:** Daily 24 hours. **Phone:** (717) 469-2211.

DAYS INN GRANTVILLE-HERSHEY   (717)469-0631

🎗🎗 **Motel** $90-$110 **Address:** 252 Bow Creek Rd 17028 **Location:** I-81 exit 80, 0.3 mi s. **Facility:** 100 units. 2-3 stories (no elevator), exterior corridors. **Activities:** exercise room.

HAMPTON INN-GRANTVILLE/HARRISBURG/HERSHEY
(717)469-7689

🎗🎗🎗 **Hotel** $119-$239 **Address:** 255 Bow Creek Rd 17028 **Location:** I-81 exit 80, 0.3 mi s. **Facility:** 79 units. 4 stories, interior corridors. **Terms:** 1-7 night minimum stay, cancellation fee imposed. **Pool(s):** heated indoor. **Activities:** hot tub, exercise room. **Guest Services:** coin laundry.

AAA Benefit: Members save 5% or more!

HOLIDAY INN HARRISBURG-HERSHEY AREA, I-81
(717)469-0661

Hotel
$99-$229

Address: 604 Station Rd 17028 **Location:** I-81 exit 80. **Facility:** 200 units. 4 stories, interior corridors. **Terms:** check-in 4 pm, cancellation fee imposed. **Dining:** 2 restaurants, entertainment. **Pool(s):** outdoor, heated indoor. **Activities:** hot tub, exercise room. **Guest Services:** valet and coin laundry, area transportation. (See ad p. 154.)

Located just minutes to Hersheypark and attractions!

FINAL CUT STEAKHOUSE   717/469-2211
[fyi] Not evaluated. The wood-fire grilled steaks, seafood and pork chops are a few of the offerings that are available at this elegant restaurant. **Address:** 777 Hollywood Blvd 17028 **Location:** I-81 exit 80, 0.5 mi n; in Hollywood Casino at Penn National Race Course.

GREENCASTLE pop. 3,996

COMFORT INN   (717)597-8164

Hotel
$70-$120

Address: 50 Pine Dr 17225 **Location:** I-81 exit 3, just s on US 11. **Facility:** 71 units. 3 stories, interior corridors. **Amenities:** Some: safes. **Guest Services:** valet laundry. **Featured Amenity:** full hot breakfast.

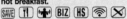

GREENSBURG (H-3) pop. 14,892, elev. 1,114'

Greensburg is part of the Laurel Highlands (see place listing p. 183). Incorporated in 1799, Greensburg was named in honor of Revolutionary War Gen. Nathanael Greene. A monument and marker for Gen. Arthur St. Clair, who served as president of the Continental Congress and was the first governor of the Northwest Territory, is in St. Clair Park.

In the early 1900s, Greensburg joined dozens of other small towns linked across the nation by the newly created Lincoln Highway. Known today as US 30, its heritage sites across the state are commemorated by the Lincoln Highway Roadside Museum. This 200-mile corridor features historic buildings, architectural oddities, exhibits and nostalgic murals. A brochure and driving tour map are available from the Lincoln Highway Heritage Corridor office at 3435 US 30E in Latrobe; phone (724) 879-4241.

The Five Star Trail, which is along the Southwestern Pennsylvania Railroad corridor and accommodates walkers, bikers and cross-country skiers,

begins at Lynch Field and continues 6 miles south to Hillis Street in Youngwood. Just before the southern terminus, the trail branches east at Depot Street and continues about 1.5 miles to connect with Westmoreland County Community College and then to Armburst. For brochures or more information contact Westmoreland County Parks and Recreation, 194 Donohoe Rd., Greensburg, PA 15601; phone (724) 830-3950.

Westmoreland Chamber of Commerce: 241 Tollgate Hill Rd., Greensburg, PA 15601. **Phone:** (724) 834-2900.

Shopping areas: Westmoreland Mall, US 30 and Donohoe Rd., features The Bon-Ton, JCPenney, Macy's and Sears.

HISTORIC HANNA'S TOWN is 3 mi. n. via US 119, following signs to 809 Forbes Trail Rd. The town marks the site of a 1773 settlement that included the first English court west of the Allegheny Mountains. The town was attacked and burned in 1782. The reconstructed village includes the tavern/courthouse, jail, three early 19th-century log houses, a reconstructed Revolutionary War fort and a Conestoga wagon.

Time: Allow 1 hour minimum. **Hours:** Wed.-Sat. 10-4, Sun. 1-4, Memorial Day-Labor Day; Sat. 10-4, Sun. 1-4, May 1-day before Memorial Day and day after Labor Day-Oct. 31. **Cost:** Guided tour $5; $4 (senior citizens and students through high school); free (ages 0-5). **Phone:** (724) 532-1935.

WESTMORELAND MUSEUM OF AMERICAN ART, 221 N. Main St., features American and southwestern Pennsylvania paintings, sculpture, drawings, prints and decorative arts. The collection includes works by Mary Cassatt, George Hetzel, Louis Comfort Tiffany and Benjamin West. Several changing exhibits are presented each year. Visitors can also experience KidSpace, an interactive gallery for families and children.

Note: The museum has temporarily relocated to 4764 SR 30 while its permanent location at 221 N. Main St. is being renovated. Admission prices and schedule for the temporary museum (being called Westmoreland @RT30) are subject to change. **Time:** Allow 1 hour minimum. **Hours:** Tues.-Sun. 11-5 (also some Fri. 5-8). Closed major holidays. Phone ahead to confirm schedule. **Cost:** Free. Phone for admission price updates. **Phone:** (724) 837-1500.

COURTYARD BY MARRIOTT PITTSBURGH GREENSBURG
(724)834-3555

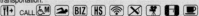

Hotel $132-$217 **Address:** 700 Powerline Dr 15601 **Location:** Jct US 30 and SR 66, 0.6 mi e. **Facility:** 102 units. 4 stories, interior corridors. **Pool(s):** heated indoor. **Activities:** hot tub, exercise room. **Guest Services:** valet and coin laundry, area transportation.

AAA Benefit: Members save 5% or more!

HAMPTON INN GREENSBURG
(724)838-8800

▼▼▼▼ **Hotel** $129-$189 **Address:** 1000 Towne Square Dr 15601 **Location:** I-76 (Pennsylvania Tpke) exit 75, 5.6 mi on US 119 N, 1.1 mi on US 30 E exit Mt Pleasant, just n, then just e. **Facility:** 69 units. 3 stories, interior corridors. **Terms:** 1-7 night minimum stay, cancellation fee imposed. **Pool(s):** heated indoor. **Activities:** exercise room. **Guest Services:** valet and coin laundry.

AAA Benefit:
Members save 5%
or more!

[icons]

RAMADA HOTEL AND CONFERENCE GREENSBURG
(724)836-6060

▼▼▼▼ **Hotel** $85-$140 **Address:** 100 Ramada Inn Dr 15601 **Location:** I-76 (Pennsylvania Tpke) exit 75, 5.6 mi on US 119 N, 3 mi e on US 30, then just n. **Facility:** 146 units. 2 stories (no elevator), interior corridors. **Terms:** cancellation fee imposed. **Dining:** Vista Plateau Restaurant, see separate listing, entertainment. **Pool(s):** heated indoor. **Activities:** exercise room. **Guest Services:** valet laundry, area transportation.

[icons] / SOME UNITS

RODEWAY INN GREENSBURG
(724)836-1648

▼▼ **Hotel** $60-$130 **Address:** 5351 E State Rt 30 15601 **Location:** I-70 E to New Station; SR 66/US 119 N to US 30, 4 mi e. **Facility:** 50 units. 2 stories (no elevator), exterior corridors. **Guest Services:** coin laundry.

[icons] / SOME UNITS

WHERE TO EAT

KING'S FAMILY RESTAURANT
724/523-5371

▼▼ American. Family Dining. $6-$13 **AAA Inspector Notes:** Fast and friendly service is offered here. The menu is large in size with descriptive menu items and pictures. The restaurant is also known for its ice cream and dessert menu. **Address:** Hempfield Plaza Pointe (US 30) 15601 **Location:** I-76 (Pennsylvania Tpke) exit 75, 5.6 mi on US 119, then 4.5 mi w on US 30.

[B] [L] [D] [LATE] CALL [icons]

PEPPERWOOD GRILLE
724/853-8121

▼▼ ▼▼ American. Casual Dining. $8-$32 **AAA Inspector Notes:** This modern restaurant sits in front of Westmoreland Mall. The restaurant offers a wide range of salads, beef and veal, lamb, seafood and poultry dishes. Choose from a variety of brick-oven pizzas or wood-grilled burgers; the pizza dough and semi-hard rolls are baked fresh in the kitchen daily. **Features:** full bar. **Address:** 5290 E Pittsburgh St, Rt 30 15601 **Location:** I-76 (Pennsylvania Tpke) exit 75, 5.6 mi on US 119 N, then 3 mi e. [L] [D]

PRIMANTI BROTHERS RESTAURANT
724/689-1300

▼ American. Casual Dining. $6-$18 **AAA Inspector Notes:** Looking for a sandwich that offers piled-high fries and coleslaw on top of each sandwich, then this is the place to be. The bar restaurant theme is every Pittsburgher's dream with memorabilia for each sports fan. **Features:** full bar. **Address:** 830 E Pittsburgh St 15601 **Location:** On Business Rt US 30. [L] [D]

ROBOKYO JAPANESE STEAKHOUSE AND SUSHI
724/834-7423

▼▼▼▼ Japanese. Casual Dining. $10-$50 **AAA Inspector Notes:** The upscale, casual steakhouse reflects a contemporary décor, with deep reds, grays and black accents throughout. Guests will appreciate the restaurant's unique setting, which is located in a renovated historic home. Try the Robokyo roll—it's incredible. **Features:** full bar, patio dining. **Reservations:** suggested. **Address:** 910 E Pittsburgh St 15601 **Location:** Just s on SR 819 and US 119, 1.2 mi e on SR 130 (E Pittsburgh St), just se on Toll House Rd, then just e on St. Clair Cemetery Rd. [L] [D]

VALLOZZI'S RESTAURANT
724/836-7663

▼▼▼▼ Italian. Casual Dining. $15-$43 **AAA Inspector Notes:** This popular family-owned-and-operated dining spot is the place to be on any given night. The chef offers variety in the menu, which lists steaks, poultry and pasta dishes, along with daily specials. **Features:** full bar. **Reservations:** suggested. **Address:** 855 Georges Station Rd E 15601 **Location:** I-76 (Pennsylvania Tpke) exit 75, 5.6 mi on US 119 N, then 4 mi e. [L] [D]

VISTA PLATEAU RESTAURANT
724/836-6060

▼▼ American. Casual Dining. $6-$25 **AAA Inspector Notes:** It's nice to get a table by the window to enjoy lovely views of Greensburg county in the daylight hours. This cozy spot offers a comfortable vibe with its spacious dining room, small lounge and personable staff. The chef tries to cater to all cravings by offering such traditional staples as burgers, pastas and steaks but always throws in some innovative daily specials. Lighter eaters will enjoy a variety of large salads, which can be topped with any of the menu proteins. **Features:** full bar. **Address:** 100 Sheraton Dr 15601 **Location:** I-76 (Pennsylvania Tpke) exit 75, 5.6 mi on US 119 N, 3 mi e on US 30, then just n; in Ramada Hotel and Conference Greensburg. [B] [L] [D] CALL [icons]

GREEN TREE pop. 4,432

DOUBLETREE BY HILTON PITTSBURGH-GREEN TREE
(412)922-8400 **95**

▼▼▼▼ Hotel $189-$289

AAA Benefit:
Members save 5% or more!

Address: 500 Mansfield Ave 15205 **Location:** I-376 exit 67, 1.1 mi nw to Mansfield Ave. **Facility:** 460 units. 7 stories, interior corridors. **Terms:** 1-7 night minimum stay, cancellation fee imposed. **Amenities:** safes. **Dining:** 2 restaurants. **Pool(s):** heated outdoor, heated indoor. **Activities:** hot tub, exercise room. **Guest Services:** valet laundry, area transportation.

[SAVE] [icons] / SOME UNITS

HAMPTON INN PITTSBURGH GREEN TREE
(412)922-0100 **94**

▼▼▼▼ Hotel $109-$199 **Address:** 555 Trumbull Dr 15205 **Location:** I-376 exit 67; jct US 22 and 30, 1 mi nw via Mansfield Ave. **Facility:** 132 units. 6 stories, interior corridors. **Terms:** 1-7 night minimum stay, cancellation fee imposed. **Pool(s):** heated outdoor. **Activities:** exercise room. **Guest Services:** valet laundry, area transportation.

AAA Benefit:
Members save 5%
or more!

[icons] / SOME UNITS

HOLIDAY INN EXPRESS HOTEL & SUITES PITTSBURGH WEST-GREENTREE
(412)922-7070 **93**

▼▼▼ Hotel $109-$399 **Address:** 875 Green Tree Rd 15220 **Location:** I-376 exit 67, 0.4 mi e. **Facility:** 150 units. 8 stories, interior corridors. **Terms:** cancellation fee imposed. **Pool(s):** heated indoor. **Activities:** exercise room. **Guest Services:** valet and coin laundry, area transportation.

[icons]

(See map & index p. 348.)

(See map & index p. 348.)

WHERE TO EAT

TAMARIND SAVORING INDIA 412/278-4848 ⑦⑦
♥♥ ♥♥ Indian. Casual Dining. $7-$15 **AAA Inspector Notes:** The small eatery prepares such dishes as vegetarian thali: an assortment of curries, sambar, rasam, chapathi and rice. The buffet is the only option for lunch. **Features:** full bar. **Address:** 2101 Green Tree Rd 15220 **Location:** I-376 exit 67, 2.6 mi sw at Scott Town Centre (Yellow Belt). Ⓛ Ⓓ

VINCENT'S OF GREEN TREE 412/921-8811 ⑦⑥
♥♥ ♥♥ Italian. Casual Dining. $7-$19 **AAA Inspector Notes:** This old-fashioned neighborhood restaurant is noted for its specialty pizzas, which you can enjoy inside or for takeout. The restaurant resembles a tree house, with a rustic wraparound deck with great views. The menu provides a large amount of tasty Italian entrées along with American cuisine. Private dining rooms are available for large groups. **Features:** full bar. **Address:** 333 Mansfield Ave 15220 **Location:** Just se of Poplar St. Ⓛ Ⓓ ⓁⒶⓉⒺ

GREENVILLE (E-1) pop. 5,919, elev. 945'

GREENVILLE RAILROAD PARK AND MUSEUM, 314 Main St., features Steam Engine #604—one of the largest switch engines in the world used by the steel industry. Built in 1936, the engine hauled iron ore on the Duluth, Missabe and Iron Range Railroad. Also displayed are a coal tender, hopper car, a 1913 Empire touring car, a 1952 caboose and a display related to the parachute designed by Greenville citizen Stefan Banic in 1921.

Time: Allow 30 minutes minimum. **Hours:** Tues.-Sun. 1-5, second weekend in June-Labor Day; Sat.-Sun. 1-5 in May and weekend after Labor Day-Oct. 31. **Cost:** Free. **Phone:** (724) 588-4009. ⒼⓉ

GROVE CITY (E-2) pop. 8,322, elev. 1,245'

Eastern Mercer County's first gristmill, built in 1799 by Valentine Cunningham, drew settlers to the village then known as Pine Grove. Several historical markers downtown on Broad Street describe noteworthy buildings, events and people related to Grove City. Two murals depict scenes related to the town's history; one is at 118 S. Broad St. and the other is at 232 S. Broad St. Today's Grove City is a prosperous community best known as the home of Grove City College.

Grove City Area Chamber of Commerce: 119 S. Broad St., Grove City, PA 16127. **Phone:** (724) 458-6410.

Shopping areas: Downtown offers more than a dozen small shops, but the big draw is Grove City Premium Outlets, I-79 and SR 208, where retailers include Banana Republic, Calvin Klein, Gap, J. Crew, Jones New York, Nike and Polo Ralph Lauren. One mile east of the mall on SR 208 is Slovak Folk Crafts, which features animated wood-carving displays, handmade crafts and decorative items imported from Eastern Europe.

BEST WESTERN GROVE CITY INN 724/748-5836

Hotel
Rates not provided

AAA Benefit:
Members save up to 20%!

Address: 1924 Leesburg Grove City Rd 16127 **Location:** I-79 exit 113, just w. Across from outlet mall. **Facility:** 60 units. 2 stories (no elevator), interior corridors. **Amenities:** safes. **Pool(s):** heated indoor. **Activities:** sauna, hot tub, limited exercise equipment. **Guest Services:** coin laundry.

ⓈⒶⓋⒺ ⓎⒾ→ CALL Ⓔ𝖬 ⏩ ⒷⒾⓏ ⒽⓈ 📶 📠 🖥 🖨

COMFORT INN (724)748-1005
♥♥ ♥ Hotel $85-$160 **Address:** 118 Garrett Dr 16127 **Location:** I-79 exit 113, just w. **Facility:** 70 units. 3 stories, interior corridors. **Terms:** check-in 4 pm. **Pool(s):** heated indoor. **Activities:** limited exercise equipment. **Guest Services:** coin laundry.
ⓎⒾ→ CALL Ⓔ𝖬 ⏩ ⒷⒾⓏ 📶 ✕ 📠 🖥 🖨

HAMPTON INN & SUITES OF GROVE CITY (724)748-5744
♥♥♥ ♥ Hotel $109-$159 **Address:** 4 Holiday Blvd 16127 **Location:** I-79 exit 113, just w. **Facility:** 90 units. 4 stories, interior corridors. **Terms:** 1-7 night minimum stay, cancellation fee imposed. **Amenities:** video games. **Pool(s):** heated indoor. **Activities:** hot tub, exercise room. **Guest Services:** valet and coin laundry.

AAA Benefit:
Members save 5% or more!

ⓎⒾ→ CALL Ⓔ𝖬 ⏩ ⒷⒾⓏ ⒽⓈ 📶 🎞 📠 🖥 🖨

HOLIDAY INN EXPRESS 724/748-5514
♥♥♥ ♥ Hotel. Rates not provided. **Address:** 21 Holiday Blvd 16127 **Location:** I-79 exit 113, just w on SR 208. **Facility:** 74 units. 3 stories, interior corridors. **Pool(s):** heated indoor. **Activities:** hot tub, limited exercise equipment. **Guest Services:** coin laundry.
ⓎⒾ→ CALL Ⓔ𝖬 ⏩ ⒷⒾⓏ ⒽⓈ 📶 ✕ 🎞 📠 🖥 🖨

TERRA NOVA HOUSE B&B (724)450-0712
♥♥♥ ♥ Historic Bed & Breakfast $120-$150 **Address:** 322 W Poplar St 16127 **Location:** I-80 exit 24, 3.4 mi s on SR 173, then just w; I-79 exit 113, 3 mi e on SR 208, 0.4 mi n on Stewart Ave, then just e. **Facility:** Nestled in a quiet residential neighborhood, this beautifully restored Victorian home was built in the early 1900s. Each room is individually themed, offering personal touches and upgraded bedding. 6 units. 2 stories (no elevator), interior corridors. **Terms:** 10 day cancellation notice-fee imposed.
ⓎⒾ→ Ⓣ 🖥 📶 ✕ 🎞 Ⓩ✉

WHERE TO EAT

KING'S FAMILY RESTAURANT 724/748-1015
♥♥ ♥ American. Family Dining. $6-$15 **AAA Inspector Notes:** Fast and friendly service is offered here. The menu is large in size with descriptive menu items and pictures. The restaurant is also known for its ice cream and dessert menu. **Address:** 1920 Leesburg Grove City Rd 16127 **Location:** I-79 exit 113, just w; across from outlet mall. Ⓑ Ⓛ Ⓓ

GWYNEDD
• Part of Philadelphia area — see map p. 230

WILLIAM PENN INN   215/699-9272

▼▼▼ Continental. Fine Dining. $13-$45 **AAA Inspector Notes:** Pore over a vast menu of international fare such as delicious pan-seared jumbo sea scallops and roasted Hudson Valley duck over an autumn fruit chutney. You can count on the incredible staff to deliver prompt, attentive service. **Features:** full bar, Sunday brunch. **Reservations:** suggested. **Address:** 1017 Dekalb Pike 19436 **Location:** Jct US 202 and Sumneytown Pike. [L] [D]

HALIFAX (G-8) pop. 841, elev. 407'

LAKE TOBIAS WILDLIFE PARK, 760 Tobias Rd., offers safari tours in a 150-acre wildlife park. Hundreds of animals are featured, including alligators, bears, buffalo, emus, ostriches, lions, llamas, monkeys, tigers and zebras. Also offered are animal and reptile shows and a petting zoo.

Time: Allow 3 hours minimum. **Hours:** Mon.-Fri. 10-6, Sat.-Sun. 10-7, June-Labor Day; Mon.-Fri. noon-6, Sat.-Sun. 10-7, in May; Sat.-Sun. 10-7, in Sept.; Sat.-Sun. 10-6, in Oct. Last safari tour departs 1 hour before closing. Phone ahead to confirm schedule. **Cost:** Zoo or safari tour $6; free (ages 0-2). Discounts available for active military with ID. Phone to verify rates. **Phone:** (717) 362-9126. [¶] [⊞]

HALLSTEAD pop. 1,303

COLONIAL BRICK INN & SUITES   570/879-2162

▼▼ Motel $95-$130

Address: 25161 SR 11 18822 **Location:** I-81 exit 230 (Great Bend-Hallstead), just w. Located in a light-commercial area. **Facility:** 52 units, some kitchens. 2 stories (no elevator), interior/exterior corridors.

[SAVE] [¶+] [🛜] [🛏] [🖥] [▭]

Easy On, Easy Off Great Bend Exit 230, I-81, golf & ski packages, in plaza with many restaurants.

HAMBURG pop. 4,289

MICROTEL INN & SUITES BY WYNDHAM HAMBURG
                                           (610)562-4234

▼▼ Hotel $77-$118 **Address:** 50 Industrial Dr 19526 **Location:** I-78 exit 29B, 0.3 mi n on SR 61, then just e. Located in a commercial area. **Facility:** 69 units. 3 stories, interior corridors. **Activities:** game room. **Guest Services:** valet and coin laundry.
[¶] [⊤] CALL [&M] [🛜] / SOME UNITS [🖥] [🐕] [🛏] [🖥] [▭]

Take your imagination to new destinations

with the online AAA/CAA Travel Guides

HAMLIN (E-11) elev. 555'
• Part of Pocono Mountains Area — see map p. 371

COMFORT INN-POCONO LAKES REGION   (570)689-4148

▼▼ Hotel $80-$160 **Address:** 117 Twin Rocks Rd 18427 **Location:** I-84 exit 17, just n on SR 191. **Facility:** 124 units. 2 stories (no elevator), interior corridors. **Terms:** check-in 4 pm. **Activities:** game room, exercise room. **Guest Services:** coin laundry.
[¶+] CALL [&M] [🛜] [🛏] [🖥] [▭] / SOME UNITS [🐕] [⊞]

WHERE TO EAT

MY BROTHERS PLACE   570/689-4410

▼▼▼ American. Casual Dining. $18-$26 **AAA Inspector Notes:** Slow-cooked prime rib and surf and turf are popular menu items. A warm, Old World atmosphere prevails in the romantic, candlelit, dining room. **Features:** full bar. **Address:** 4446 Hamlin Hwy 18427 **Location:** 0.8 mi w on SR 590; 5 mi e of jct SR 590 and 435; at Elmhurst. [D]

HANOVER (YORK COUNTY) (I-8)
pop. 15,289, elev. 599'
• Hotels p. 134

In its early days, Hanover was called Digg's Choice or Rogue's Roost, names that originated from the many outlaws who migrated to the area due to the lack of law enforcement that ensued after the Pennsylvania-Maryland boundary dispute. In 1763 Col. Richard McAllister founded the town by drawing up a formal plan; hence it was called McAllister's Town. In order to gain favor with Germans who occupied the land, McAllister named it Hanover, meaning "on the high banks." The town was incorporated as a borough in 1815.

On June 30, 1863, the first Civil War battle north of the Mason-Dixon Line was fought in Hanover when Union generals Hugh Kilpatrick and George Custer defeated Confederate general J.E.B. Stuart and prevented him from reaching Gettysburg until the day after that major battle.

Hanover is the base for several industries that produce furniture, machine tools and such foods as potato chips and pretzels. The city's most famous product, however, is the horse. Just south on SR 194, Hanover Shoe Farms, is one of the largest Standardbred horse breeders in the world. The 4,000-acre farm, founded in 1926, is home to some 1,800 horses, many of which are record-breaking trotters and pacers. The grounds and buildings are open daily dawn-dusk for self-guiding tours; phone (717) 637-8931.

A variety of concerts and theater events are presented at the Eichelberger Performing Arts Center, 195 Stock St. Tours of the restored 1896 building also are offered; phone (717) 637-7086. Two miles east of town is Codorus State Park *(see Recreation Areas Chart)*, which offers a 1,275-acre lake with 26 miles of shoreline. Swimming, boating, fishing, camping and picnicking are popular activities. Also in the area are nature trails and snowmobiling and sledding facilities.

Hanover Area Chamber of Commerce: 146 Carlisle St., Hanover, PA 17331. **Phone:** (717) 637-6130.

BASILICA OF THE SACRED HEART OF JESUS is 2 mi. n. on Second St. from SR 116. The original 1741 log chapel was replaced in 1787 by the present stone structure. Designated a minor basilica in 1962, it contains frescoes, statues and paintings. **Time:** Allow 30 minutes minimum. **Hours:** Daily dawn-dusk. Mass Sat. at 5:30 p.m., Sun. at 7:30 a.m. and 10 a.m. **Cost:** Free. **Phone:** (717) 637-2721.

UTZ QUALITY FOODS INC., 900 High St., allows visitors to observe the potato chip production process from an elevated, glass-enclosed observation gallery in its 535,000-square-foot plant. **Time:** Allow 1 hour minimum. **Hours:** Mon.-Thurs. 8-4. Closed Jan. 1, Easter, Memorial Day, July 4, Labor Day, Thanksgiving and Christmas. **Cost:** Free. **Phone:** (717) 637-6644 or (800) 367-7629.

HAMPTON INN   (717)633-1117

▼▼▼▼ **Hotel** $134-$234 **Address:** 309 Wilson Ave 17331 **Location:** 1.4 mi n on SR 94, 0.5 mi e on Eisenhower Dr. **Facility:** 83 units. 3 stories, interior corridors. **Terms:** 1-7 night minimum stay, cancellation fee imposed. **Pool(s):** heated indoor. **Activities:** hot tub, exercise room. **Guest Services:** coin laundry.

AAA Benefit:
Members save 5%
or more!

🛏️ CALL Ⓜ️ 🛗 BIZ 📶 🛗 🖥️ 💻

HANOVER SUPER 8   (717)630-8888

▼▼ ▼▼ **Hotel** $59-$281 **Address:** 40 Wetzel Dr 17331 **Location:** 1.5 mi n on SR 94, just w. **Facility:** 46 units. 2 stories (no elevator), interior corridors. **Amenities:** safes. 🛏️ 📶 🛗 💻

HOLIDAY INN EXPRESS   717/637-1228

▼▼▼▼ **Hotel.** Rates not provided. **Address:** 305 Wilson Ave 17331 **Location:** 1.4 mi n on SR 94, 0.5 mi e on Eisenhower Dr. **Facility:** 63 units. 3 stories, interior corridors. **Activities:** exercise room. **Guest Services:** valet and coin laundry.
🛏️ CALL Ⓜ️ (HS) 📶 🛗 🖥️ 💻

HARLANSBURG (F-1) elev. 1,125'

HARLANSBURG STATION MUSEUM OF TRANSPORTATION, jct. US 19 and SR 108, showcases transportation history from railroading and seafaring days to the era of air travel. A replica of a train station was built to house four 80-foot-long train cars, which have been set up with an array of artifacts, including rail memorabilia, photographs and railroad lanterns as well as a model train display. A baggage wagon, postal buggy and a collection of train tracks and gauges are on the grounds.

The maritime history area includes vintage river tow boats and model boats, automotive history is presented through memorabilia like signs and collectible toy cars and trucks, and aviation exhibits cover commercial and military aircraft history as well as the air mail program. **Time:** Allow 45 minutes minimum. **Hours:** Tues.-Sat. 10-5, Sun. noon-5, June-Aug.; Sat. 10-5, Sun. noon-5, Mar.-May and Sept.-Dec. Closed major holidays. **Cost:** $5; $4 (ages 0-12). **Phone:** (724) 652-9002. (GT)

HARMARVILLE

- **Hotels & Restaurants map & index p. 348**
- **Part of Pittsburgh area — see map p. 326**

HOLIDAY INN EXPRESS   412/828-9300 54

▼▼ ▼▼
Hotel
Rates not provided

Address: 10 Landings Dr 15238 **Location:** I-76 (Pennsylvania Tpke) exit 48, just s on Freeport Rd. **Facility:** 63 units. 3 stories, interior corridors. **Pool(s):** heated indoor. **Activities:** exercise room. **Guest Services:** valet and coin laundry. **Featured Amenity:** breakfast buffet. *(See ad p. 367.)*

(SAVE) 🛏️ CALL Ⓜ️ 🎁 BIZ
(HS) 📶 ❌ 🖼️
/ SOME UNITS 🛗 🖥️

SUPER 8   (412)828-8900 55

▼▼ ▼▼ **Motel** $70-$110 **Address:** 8 Landings Dr 15238 **Location:** I-76 (Pennsylvania Tpke) exit 48, just s on Freeport Rd. **Facility:** 60 units. 3 stories, interior corridors. **Guest Services:** valet and coin laundry. 🛏️ BIZ 📶 💻 / SOME UNITS 🛗 🖥️

VALLEY MOTEL   412/828-7100 56

▼▼ **Motel.** Rates not provided. **Address:** 2571 Freeport Rd 15238 **Location:** I-76 (Pennsylvania Tpke) exit 48, 1 mi s; SR 28 exit 11. **Facility:** 28 units. 1 story, exterior corridors. 🛏️ 📶 🛗

WHERE TO EAT

KING'S FAMILY RESTAURANT   412/826-9170

▼▼ ▼▼ American. Casual Dining. $6-$18 **AAA Inspector Notes:** Fast and friendly service is offered here. The menu is large in size with descriptive menu items and pictures. The restaurant is also known for its ice cream and dessert menu. **Address:** 5 Alpha Dr E 15238 **Location:** I-76 (Pennsylvania Tpke) exit 48, just s on Freeport Rd, then just n. (B) (L) (D) (LATE)

PRIMANTI BROTHERS RESTAURANT   412/826-9680

▼▼ American. Casual Dining. $6-$9 **AAA Inspector Notes:** If you are looking for a sandwich that offers piled-high fries and coleslaw on top of each sandwich, then this is the place to be. The bar restaurant theme is every Pittsburghers dream with memorabilia for each sports fan. **Features:** full bar. **Address:** 6 Anchor Dr 15238 **Location:** I-76 (Pennsylvania Tpke) exit 48, 1.1 mi w on Freeport Rd, then just n on SR 910. (L) (D)

HARMONY (F-1) pop. 890, elev. 913'
- **Part of Pittsburgh area — see map p. 326**

George Rapp and his Harmony Society set up their first communal settlement on Connoquenessing Creek in 1804. During the following 10 years about 100 members died and were buried in a little graveyard. The graves, according to custom, were not marked. This cemetery and a number of substantial brick buildings remain from the original settlement.

In 1814 the society migrated to Indiana and founded New Harmony; 10 years later they returned to Pennsylvania and established the community of Old Economy, later renamed Ambridge *(see place listing p. 56).*

HARMONY MUSEUM, on the Diamond in the town center, offers guided tours of an 1809 warehouse, an 1811 Harmony Society building and an 1830s Mennonite family log house. The Harmony Society was founded in 1804 by German Lutheran Separatists. Exhibits showcase the 1815 Mennonite resettlement, Delaware Native American history and Maj. George Washington's 1753 military mission to the area. Target and hunting rifles made by 19th-century gunsmith Charles Flowers also are displayed.

Visitors can add guided tours of other nearby historic sites (two cemeteries; a barn; a meetinghouse; and Rapp's Seat, a seat carved into a rock used for meditation) onto the guided museum tour with advance notice and for an additional fee. **Time:** Allow 1 hour minimum. **Hours:** Tues.-Sun. 1-4. Closed major holidays. **Cost:** $7; $6 (ages 60+); $3 (ages 6-17). **Phone:** (724) 452-7341.

LOG CABIN INN   724/452-4155

♦♦ ♦♦ American. Casual Dining. $6-$26 **AAA Inspector Notes:** A rustic 160-year-old log cabin is surrounded by this restaurant building, which retains its rural atmosphere. Diners enjoy a meal in the casual and relaxing spot. Friendly servers can assist in deciding among aged Certified Angus beef, steaks, pork chops, fresh seafood and salads. **Features:** full bar. **Address:** 430 Perry Hwy (US 19) 16037 **Location:** I-79 exit 88, 0.5 mi w to US 19, then 1.7 mi n.

[L] [D] CALL ⑤M

HARRISBURG (H-8) pop. 49,528, elev. 358'

• **Hotels p. 141** • **Restaurants p. 145**
• **Attractions map p. 135**
• **Hotels & Restaurants map & index p. 138**

Around 1710 John Harris established a trading post in the area that is now Harrisburg; in 1733 he obtained a grant of 800 acres of land. His son, John Harris Jr., the founder of Harrisburg, and William Maclay, Pennsylvania's first U.S. senator, laid out the town in 1785, including four acres in what now is Capitol Park with hopes of it becoming the commonwealth's capital.

Incorporated as a borough in 1791, Harrisburg officially replaced Lancaster as the state capital in 1812. Today's Capitol Complex includes the ornate Capitol Building, The State Museum of Pennsylvania, plazas and fountains, and landscaped areas open to the public. An early residence, the 1766 John Harris/Simon Cameron Mansion, was built by the city's founder and later expanded in 1863 by Simon Cameron, a former U.S. senator and President Lincoln's first secretary of war. Mansion tours are available Mon.-Thurs. at 1, 2 and 3 and the second Sun. of each month. The house also includes a library with documents relating to local history and genealogical information; phone (717) 233-3462.

Paxton Presbyterian Church, at Paxtang Boulevard and Sharon Street, is one of the oldest Presbyterian churches still in use in the United States. The present structure dates from 1740. In the sanctuary are the baptismal font and pulpit light holder that have been in use for more than 200 years. The archives contain a pewter communion set that was used as early as 1734.

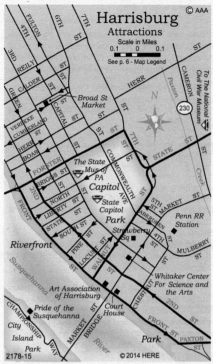

The adjacent cemetery, which dates from the early 1700s, contains the graves of John Harris Jr.; Rev. John Elder, the fighting parson of the Revolution; and William Maclay. A brochure describing a self-guiding tour of the graveyard is available.

City Island is in the middle of the Susquehanna River across from downtown. Owned by the city and operated by its Parks and Recreation Department, this setting offers nature trails, a swimming beach and a playground. Also in the park are commercial amusement and recreational facilities. The Harrisburg Senators, a AA league baseball team affiliated with the Washington Nationals, play here at Metro Bank Park; phone (717) 231-4444. Events also take place on the island.

The Capital Area Greenbelt, a 20-mile parkway used for bicycling, jogging, walking and nature studies, loops around the city and passes through many scenic parks. Reservoir Park, 22nd and Market streets, has art galleries, gardens, plazas, fountains, playgrounds, basketball courts and other facilities. Riverfront Park (see attraction listing p. 136), along a 5-mile stretch of scenic waterfront, features sunken gardens, public art and various memorials. Other recreational facilities are in Italian Lake Park, 3rd and Division streets. Phone (717) 255-3020 for more information.

The Pennsylvania Farm Show Complex & Expo Center covers 14 acres at N. Cameron and Maclay

(See map & index p. 138.)

streets; phone (717) 787–5373. Among the many events held here are the Pennsylvania Farm Show and Pennsylvania Auto Show in January, the Great American Outdoor Show in February, and the Pennsylvania National Horse Show in October.

Center City, City Island and City-Wide Sites brochures are available free by contacting the Mayor's Office, 10 N. 2nd St., Harrisburg, PA 17101; phone (717) 255-3040.

Hershey Harrisburg Regional Visitors Bureau: 3211 North Front St., Harrisburg, PA 17101. **Phone:** (717) 231-7788 or (877) 727-8573.

Shopping areas: Two major malls are Colonial Park, US 22 and Colonial Road, and Harrisburg at I-83 and Paxton Street. The former has more than 70 stores, including The Bon-Ton, Boscov's and Sears; the latter offers more than 90 stores, including Macy's. Nearby Camp Hill has Capital City at the Highland Park exit off US 15, featuring JCPenney, Macy's and Sears.

The historic Broad Street Market is open Thurs.-Fri. 7-5 and Sat. 7-4. This farmers market, which sells fresh produce, meat, poultry, confections and food, has been operating since 1860 and is housed in two buildings dating from 1863 and 1874. The market is one-half mile north of the Capitol Complex, at 1233 N. 3rd St.; phone (717) 236-7923.

ART ASSOCIATION OF HARRISBURG, 21 N. Front St. across from Riverfront Park, is housed in the Italianate Gov. Findlay Mansion. Five galleries present works by regional and national artists in various styles and media. **Hours:** Mon.-Thurs. 9:30-9, Fri. 9:30-4, Sat. 10-4, Sun. 2-5. Closed major holidays. **Cost:** Free. **Phone:** (717) 236-1432.

FORT HUNTER MANSION AND PARK is 6 mi. n. at 5300 N. Front St. overlooking the Susquehanna River Valley. Built in 1787 on the site of old Fort Hunter and enlarged in 1814, the stone house is decorated with 19th-century items including pewter, pitchers, furniture, costumes and toys. The dwelling retains the original fireplace. A 35-acre park surrounds the mansion and includes an 1881 covered bridge, other historic buildings, playgrounds and nature trails.

Time: Allow 1 hour minimum. **Hours:** Park 8 a.m.-dusk. Mansion Tues.-Sat. 10-4:30, Sun. noon-4:30, May to late Dec. Closed major holidays. **Cost:** $5; $4 (ages 61+); $3 (ages 6-17). **Phone:** (717) 599-5751. 🛤

THE NATIONAL CIVIL WAR MUSEUM, at 1 Lincoln Cir. at Reservoir Park, is reportedly the only museum in the nation to cover the entire American Civil War from beginning to end. In bringing history to life, the museum includes collections of Union and Confederate artifacts, life-size dioramas and audiovisual presentations.

Seventeen galleries focus on the multitude of human experiences that made up the war. From slavery, to camp life, to the turmoil of 19th-century politics, the museum immerses visitors in the Civil War, with an equal emphasis given to both sides of the conflict.

Time: Allow 1 hour, 30 minutes minimum. **Hours:** Mon.-Sat. 10-5 (also Wed. 5-8), Sun. noon-5. Closed Jan. 1, Easter, Thanksgiving and Christmas. **Cost:** $11; $10 (ages 60+); $9 (students with ID); free (ages 0-5); $40 (family, two adults and three children). **Phone:** (717) 260-1861.

THE PENNSYLVANIA NATIONAL FIRE MUSEUM, 1820 N. 4th St., is in a restored 1899 firehouse. The collection, which includes items spanning the 18th-through 21st centuries, features an 1867 carriage, interactive displays, a stovepipe hat collection and firefighters' apparatus and uniforms. A DVD presentation is shown. **Time:** Allow 30 minutes minimum. **Hours:** Tues.-Sat. 10-4, Sun. 1-4. Closed major holidays. **Cost:** $6; $5 (ages 60+ and students with ID); free (ages 0-4); $20 (family, two adults and children). **Phone:** (717) 232-8915.

PRIDE OF THE SUSQUEHANNA, at City Island via the Market Street Bridge, offers a cruise of the Susquehanna River on an authentic paddle wheeler. A history of the city and island is given on the 40-minute narrated cruise. Dinner and murder mystery cruises, live music cruises and other themed trips are available.

Hours: Sightseeing tours depart daily (weather permitting) at noon-3, June-Aug. Some weekend cruises available Sept.-Nov. Phone ahead to confirm schedule. **Cost:** $10; $8 (ages 59+); $5 (ages 3-12). Reservations are required for dinner and event cruises. **Phone:** (717) 234-6500.

RIVERFRONT PARK, on the Capital Area Greenbelt, extends 5 mi. along the e. bank of the Susquehanna River, bordering Front St. The area contains war memorials, the Sunken Garden and Peace Garden. At the foot of a bank on the riverside is a promenade where Harrisburg's 13 front steps descend to the water's edge, representing the original colonies. **Hours:** Daily dawn-dusk. **Cost:** Free. **Phone:** (717) 255-3020.

STATE CAPITOL is on Capitol Hill. A magnificent building in a 13-acre park, the Capitol covers 2 acres and contains more than 600 rooms. The 272-foot dome, bronze doors, statuary, mural paintings and stained-glass windows are notable features. The marble grand staircase is designed after the one in the Paris Grand Opera House. Flanking the central entrance are two groups of statuary by the Pennsylvania-born sculptor George Grey Barnard. The welcome center, in the East Wing of the Capitol, offers 18 exhibits.

Note: All visitors must pass through metal detectors; all bags and packages will be X-rayed and are

(See map & index p. 138.)

subject to hand inspection. The security screening may require a whole body pat-down. **Hours:** Thirty-minute guided tours are offered Mon.-Fri. every half-hour 8:30-4, Sat.-Sun. and some holidays at 9, 11, 1 and 3. Welcome center open Mon.-Fri. 8:30-4:30. Closed Jan. 1, Easter, Thanksgiving and Christmas. Phone ahead to confirm schedule. **Cost:** Free. **Phone:** (717) 787-6810 or (800) 868-7672.

THE STATE MUSEUM OF PENNSYL-VANIA, 300 North St., presents Pennsylvania's heritage from the Earth's beginning to the present. Archeological artifacts, decorative arts, fine art galleries and industrial and technological innovations can be seen. A Civil War exhibit includes Peter F. Rothermel's 1870 "The Battle of Gettysburg: Pickett's Charge" painting. Curiosity Connection is a hands-on learning environment for children ages 5 and younger. Additional features are Nature Lab, Mammal Hall, a restored mastodon skeleton and a planetarium.

Time: Allow 2 hours minimum. **Hours:** Wed.-Sat. 9-5, Sun. noon-5. Planetarium shows are offered Wed.-Fri. at 11 and noon; Sat. on the hour 11-2, Sun. at 1 and 2. Curiosity Connection Wed.-Sat. 10-4. Closed state holidays. **Cost:** Museum $7; $6 (ages 65+); $5 (ages 1-11); free (active military with ID). Planetarium additional $3. **Phone:** (717) 787-4980.

SAVE **WHITAKER CENTER FOR SCIENCE AND THE ARTS,** downtown at 225 Market St., serves as a regional center for science, art and culture. The complex presents more than 100 hands-on exhibits and displays on three floors. The Backstage Studio exhibit gallery features interactive exhibits that focus on the technology used to make movies, TV, music and theater like sound and special effects. Educational documentaries and Hollywood movies are shown on a six-story-high IMAX screen. A 664-seat performance theater hosts plays, concerts and dance events throughout the year. Art on the Curved Wall, an exhibit in the lobby, features artwork by local artists.

Hours: Tues.-Sat. 9:30-5, Sun. 11:30-5. IMAX documentary films $9.50; $8 (ages 3-17). IMAX feature films $13.75; $11.75 (ages 3-17). Combination tickets $19.75; $16.75 (ages 3-17). Closed Thanksgiving, part of Christmas Eve and Christmas. Holiday hours vary. Phone ahead to confirm schedule. **Cost:** Science center $16; $12.50 (ages 3-17, ages 55+ and students with ID). Phone for IMAX theater rates. Combination tickets are available. Phone to confirm all prices. **Parking:** $5. **Phone:** (717) 214-2787.

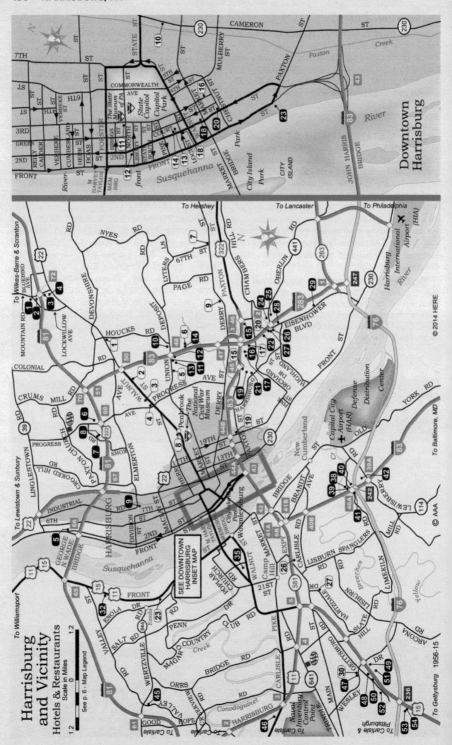

Downtown Harrisburg

Harrisburg
and Vicinity
Hotels & Restaurants

Scale in Miles

See p. 6 - Map Legend

© 2014 HERE

© AAA

To Gettysburg   1956-15

✈ Airport Hotels				
Map Page	**HARRISBURG INTERNATIONAL AIRPORT** (Maximum driving distance from airport: 6.3 mi)	Diamond Rated	Rate Range	Page
25 p. 138	Holiday Inn Harrisburg East-Airport, 6.3 mi	◈◈◈	$99-$179 (SAVE)	143
28 p. 138	Red Roof Inn Harrisburg - Hershey, 6.3 mi	◈◈	Rates not provided (SAVE)	144
24 p. 138	Sheraton Harrisburg Hershey, 6.2 mi	◈◈◈	$161-$329 (SAVE)	144
29 p. 138	Wingate by Wyndham Harrisburg East, 5.3 mi	◈◈◈	$89-$149	145

Harrisburg and Vicinity

This index helps you "spot" where approved hotels and restaurants are located on the corresponding detailed maps. Hotel daily rate range is for comparison only. Restaurant price range is a combination of lunch and/or dinner. Turn to the listing page for more detailed rate and price information and consult display ads for special promotions.

HARRISBURG

Map Page	Hotels	Diamond Rated	Rate Range	Page
1 p. 138	Candlewood Suites Harrisburg	◈◈◈	$110-$200	141
2 p. 138	Ramada Harrisburg	◈◈	$75-$165 (SAVE)	144
3 p. 138	Quality Inn	◈◈	$80-$160 (SAVE)	144
4 p. 138	Comfort Inn Harrisburg/Hershey	◈◈	$75-$175 (SAVE)	141
5 p. 138	Days Inn Harrisburg North	◈◈	$80-$130 (SAVE)	142
6 p. 138	Red Roof Inn Harrisburg North	◈◈	Rates not provided (SAVE)	144
7 p. 138	Hampton Inn & Suites Harrisburg North	◈◈◈	$89-$199	142
8 p. 138	SpringHill Suites by Marriott Harrisburg/Hershey	◈◈◈	$111-$217	144
9 p. 138	Staybridge Suites Harrisburg	◈◈◈	Rates not provided (SAVE)	144
10 p. 138	Hampton Inn Harrisburg East (Hershey Area)	◈◈◈	$109-$225	142
11 p. 138	Holiday Inn Express East	◈◈◈	$99-$199	143
12 p. 138	Country Inn & Suites By Carlson, Harrisburg at Union Deposit Rd	◈◈◈	$89-$199 (SAVE)	142
13 p. 138	Fairfield Inn & Suites by Marriott-Harrisburg/Hershey	◈◈◈	$104-$206	142
14 p. 138	BEST WESTERN PREMIER The Central Hotel & Conference Center	◈◈◈	$100-$200 (SAVE)	141
15 p. 138	Residence Inn by Marriott Harrisburg-Hershey	◈◈◈	$118-$217	144
16 p. 138	Homewood Suites by Hilton-Harrisburg East (Hershey Area)	◈◈◈	$129-$219 (SAVE)	143
17 p. 138	Hilton Garden Inn Harrisburg East	◈◈◈	$119-$209 (SAVE)	142
18 p. 138	Hilton Harrisburg	◈◈◈	$159-$219 (SAVE)	143
19 p. 138	TownePlace Suites by Marriott Harrisburg Hershey	◈◈◈	$139-$229 (SAVE)	145
20 p. 138	Crowne Plaza Harrisburg-Hershey	◈◈◈	$129-$199 (SAVE)	142
21 p. 138	Candlewood Suites Harrisburg-Hershey	◈◈◈	$80-$240	141
22 p. 138	Sleep Inn & Suites Harrisburg/Hershey	◈◈◈	$74-$169	144
23 p. 138	Comfort Inn Riverfront	◈◈◈	$79-$189	141
24 p. 138	Sheraton Harrisburg Hershey	◈◈◈	$161-$329 (SAVE)	144
25 p. 138	Holiday Inn Harrisburg East-Airport *(See ad p. 143.)*	◈◈◈	$99-$179 (SAVE)	143
26 p. 138	Wyndham Garden Hotel-Harrisburg/Hershey	◈◈◈	$147-$349	145
27 p. 138	Courtyard by Marriott-Harrisburg/Hershey	◈◈◈	$132-$229	142

HARRISBURG (cont'd)

Map Page	Hotels (cont'd)	Diamond Rated	Rate Range	Page
28 p. 138	**Red Roof Inn Harrisburg - Hershey**	◇◇	Rates not provided SAVE	144
29 p. 138	Wingate by Wyndham Harrisburg East	◇◇◇	$89-$149	145

Map Page	Restaurants	Diamond Rated	Cuisine	Price Range	Page
1 p. 138	El Rodeo	◇◇	Mexican	$7-$17	145
2 p. 138	Gabriella Italian Restaurant	◇◇	Italian	$11-$25	145
3 p. 138	Progress Grill	◇◇	American	$14-$38	146
4 p. 138	M Sushi House and Restaurant	◇◇	Japanese	$9-$23	146
5 p. 138	Empire Asian Bistro	◇◇	Asian	$7-$14	145
6 p. 138	T. Brendan O'Reilly's Irish Pub	◇◇	American	$9-$24	146
7 p. 138	The Wharf	◇◇	American	$6-$25	146
8 p. 138	Meiji	◇◇	Vietnamese	$7-$11	146
9 p. 138	Pho Kim's	◇◇	Vietnamese	$7-$12	146
10 p. 138	Appalachian Brewing Co	◇◇	American	$8-$16	145
11 p. 138	Mangia Qui	◇◇	Italian	$9-$32	146
12 p. 138	The Fire House Restaurant	◇◇	American	$8-$38	145
13 p. 138	Stock's on 2nd	◇◇	American	$9-$34	146
14 p. 138	Cafe Fresco	◇◇	American	$9-$30	145
15 p. 138	Hibachi Buffet Grill	◇	Asian	$8-$13	145
16 p. 138	Bricco	◇◇◇	International	$11-$40	145
17 p. 138	Lancaster Brewing Company	◇◇	American	$7-$26	145
18 p. 138	Zia's Trattoria At Red Door	◇◇◇	Italian	$8-$29	146
19 p. 138	Bangkok 56 Thai Cuisine	◇◇	Thai	$10-$16	145
20 p. 138	Leeds Restaurant and Lounge	◇◇	American	$8-$40	146

ENOLA

Map Page	Hotel	Diamond Rated	Rate Range	Page
32 p. 138	**Quality Inn Enola**	◇◇	$69-$299 SAVE	103

Map Page	Restaurant	Diamond Rated	Cuisine	Price Range	Page
23 p. 138	Tavern on the Hill	◇◇◇	Steak Seafood	$20-$35	103

CAMP HILL

Map Page	Hotel	Diamond Rated	Rate Range	Page
35 p. 138	Radisson Hotel Harrisburg	◇◇◇	$95-$189	76

Map Page	Restaurants	Diamond Rated	Cuisine	Price Range	Page
26 p. 138	Flinchy's	◇◇	American	$7-$32	76
27 p. 138	Masala Bistro	◇◇	Indian	$9-$18	76

NEW CUMBERLAND

Map Page	Hotels	Diamond Rated	Rate Range	Page
38 p. 138	Fairfield Inn & Suites by Marriott Harrisburg West	◇◇◇	$97-$194	211
39 p. 138	Comfort Inn New Cumberland	◇◇◇	$60-$170	211
40 p. 138	**Clarion Hotel & Conference Center Harrisburg**	◇◇◇	Rates not provided SAVE	211
41 p. 138	**BEST WESTERN PLUS New Cumberland Inn & Suites**	◇◇◇	$95-$170 SAVE	210

NEW CUMBERLAND (cont'd)

Map Page	Hotels (cont'd)	Diamond Rated	Rate Range	Page
42 p. 138	Days Inn Harrisburg South	▽▽	$65-$110	211

MECHANICSBURG

Map Page	Hotels	Diamond Rated	Rate Range	Page
45 p. 138	Holiday Inn Express & Suites Harrisburg West/ Mechanicsburg	▽▽▽	$108-$162	196
46 p. 138	Park Inn by Radisson Harrisburg West	▽▽▽	$99-$179	197
47 p. 138	Comfort Inn Capital City	▽▽	$79-$189 SAVE	196
48 p. 138	Courtyard by Marriott Harrisburg West/Mechanicsburg	▽▽▽	$118-$194 SAVE	196
49 p. 138	Hampton Inn-Harrisburg West	▽▽▽	$109-$189	196
50 p. 138	Country Inn & Suites By Carlson, Harrisburg West	▽▽▽	$99-$179 SAVE	196
51 p. 138	Homewood Suites by Hilton-Harrisburg West	▽▽▽	$119-$199	196
52 p. 138	Econo Lodge	▽▽	$55-$75	196
53 p. 138	Motel 6	▽▽	$60-$120	196
54 p. 138	Wingate by Wyndham Mechanicsburg/Harrisburg West	▽▽▽	$109-$269	197

Map Page	Restaurant	Diamond Rated	Cuisine	Price Range	Page
30 p. 138	Peppermill Family Restaurant	▽▽	American	$4-$15	197

BEST WESTERN HARRISBURG HERSHEY HOTEL
(717)652-0101

▽▽▽
Motel
$59-$109

AAA Benefit:
Members save up to 20%!

Address: 7500 Allentown Blvd 17112 **Location:** I-81 exit 77, 1 mi s on SR 39, then 1.2 mi w on US 22. **Facility:** 56 units. 3 stories, interior corridors. **Pool(s):** heated indoor. **Activities:** limited exercise equipment. **Guest Services:** coin laundry. **Featured Amenity:** continental breakfast.

BEST WESTERN PREMIER THE CENTRAL HOTEL & CONFERENCE CENTER
(717)561-2800 14

▽▽▽▽
Hotel
$100-$200

AAA Benefit:
Members save up to 20%!

Address: 800 E Park Dr 17111 **Location:** I-83 exit 48, just e on Union Deposit Rd, then 0.5 mi s. **Facility:** 174 units. 3 stories, interior corridors. **Amenities:** safes. **Dining:** T. Brendan O'Reilly's Irish Pub, see separate listing. **Pool(s):** heated indoor. **Activities:** game room, exercise room. **Guest Services:** valet and coin laundry, area transportation.

CANDLEWOOD SUITES HARRISBURG
(717)652-7800 1

▽▽▽ Extended Stay Hotel $110-$200 **Address:** 504 N Mountain Rd 17112 **Location:** I-81 exit 72B, 0.4 mi n. **Facility:** 93 efficiencies. 3 stories, interior corridors. **Pool(s):** heated indoor. **Activities:** hot tub, exercise room. **Guest Services:** valet and coin laundry.

CANDLEWOOD SUITES HARRISBURG-HERSHEY
(717)561-9400 21

▽▽▽ Extended Stay Hotel $80-$240 **Address:** 413 Portview Dr 17111 **Location:** I-83 exit 45, 0.7 mi n on Paxton St, then 0.4 mi s. **Facility:** 71 efficiencies. 4 stories, interior corridors. **Terms:** 3 day cancellation notice. **Pool(s):** heated indoor. **Activities:** hot tub, exercise room. **Guest Services:** valet and coin laundry.

COMFORT INN HARRISBURG/HERSHEY
(717)657-2200 4

▽▽
Hotel
$75-$175

Address: 5680 Allentown Blvd 17112 **Location:** I-81 exit 72, just s on N Mountain Rd, then just w on US 22. **Facility:** 76 units. 2 stories, interior corridors. **Pool(s):** outdoor. **Guest Services:** coin laundry.

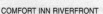

COMFORT INN RIVERFRONT
(717)233-1611 23

▽▽▽ Hotel $79-$189 **Address:** 525 S Front St 17104 **Location:** I-83 exit 43, 0.5 mi n. **Facility:** 115 units. 2 stories (no elevator), interior corridors. **Amenities:** safes. **Pool(s):** outdoor. **Activities:** exercise room. **Guest Services:** valet and coin laundry.

(See map & index p. 138.)

COMFORT SUITES HERSHEY/HARRISBURG
(717)566-3000

Hotel
$104-$244

Address: 320 Milroy Rd 17036 **Location:** I-283 exit 3C, 3.4 mi e on US 322. **Facility:** 80 units. 4 stories, interior corridors. **Terms:** check-in 4 pm. **Amenities:** safes. **Pool(s):** heated indoor. **Activities:** exercise room. **Guest Services:** coin laundry. **Featured Amenity:** continental breakfast.

SAVE CALL 🔊M ➰ BIZ HS 📶
✕ 🛅 🖼

COUNTRY INN & SUITES BY CARLSON, HARRISBURG AT UNION DEPOSIT RD
(717)558-9200 12

Hotel
$89-$199

Address: 1025 Peiffers Ln 17109 **Location:** I-83 exit 48, just w. **Facility:** 78 units. 5 stories, interior corridors. **Terms:** 3 day cancellation notice. **Pool(s):** heated indoor. **Activities:** hot tub, exercise room. **Guest Services:** valet and coin laundry.

SAVE ➠ CALL 🔊M ➰ BIZ HS
📶 ✕ 🛅 🖼 🖥

COUNTRY INN & SUITES BY CARLSON HARRISBURG NORTHEAST
717/651-5100

Hotel. Rates not provided. **Address:** 8000 Jonestown Rd 17112 **Location:** I-81 exit 77, just s. **Facility:** 79 units. 3 stories, interior corridors. **Pool(s):** heated indoor. **Activities:** hot tub, exercise room. **Guest Services:** coin laundry.

CALL 🔊M ➰ BIZ HS 📶 ✕ 🛅 🖼 🖥

COURTYARD BY MARRIOTT-HARRISBURG/HERSHEY
(717)558-8544 27

Hotel $132-$229 **Address:** 725 Eisenhower Blvd 17111 **Location:** I-283 exit 2, just n. **Facility:** 128 units. 4 stories, interior corridors. **Terms:** check-in 4 pm. **Pool(s):** indoor. **Activities:** exercise room. **Guest Services:** valet and coin laundry, boarding pass kiosk.

AAA Benefit: Members save 5% or more!

🍽 ➰ BIZ HS 📶 ✕ 🎣 🛅 🖥
/ SOME UNITS 🖼

CROWNE PLAZA HARRISBURG-HERSHEY
(717)234-5021 20

Hotel
$129-$199

Address: 23 S 2nd St 17101 **Location:** Jct Chestnut St; downtown. **Facility:** 261 units. 10 stories, interior corridors. **Parking:** on-site (fee) and valet. **Terms:** check-in 4 pm, cancellation fee imposed. **Pool(s):** heated indoor. **Activities:** exercise room. **Guest Services:** valet and coin laundry.

SAVE 🍽 🎣 🍸 CALL 🔊M ➰
BIZ 📶 ✕ 🖥 / SOME UNITS 🛅

DAYS INN HARRISBURG NORTH
(717)233-3100 5

Hotel
$80-$130

Address: 3919 N Front St 17110 **Location:** I-81 exit 66, just n. **Facility:** 115 units, some efficiencies. 3 stories, exterior corridors. **Pool(s):** outdoor. **Activities:** playground, exercise room. **Guest Services:** coin laundry. **Featured Amenity:** continental breakfast.

SAVE 🔊+ ➰ BIZ 📶 🖥
/ SOME UNITS 🛅 🖼

FAIRFIELD INN & SUITES BY MARRIOTT-HARRISBURG/HERSHEY
(717)412-4326 13

Hotel $104-$206 **Address:** 1018 Briarsdale Rd 17109 **Location:** I-83 exit 48, just w. **Facility:** 94 units. 3 stories, interior corridors. **Pool(s):** heated indoor. **Activities:** hot tub, exercise room. **Guest Services:** valet and coin laundry.

AAA Benefit: Members save 5% or more!

🍽 ➰ BIZ HS 📶 ✕ 🛅 🖥 / SOME UNITS 🖼

HAMPTON INN & SUITES HARRISBURG NORTH
(717)540-0900 7

Hotel $89-$199 **Address:** 30 Capital Dr 17110 **Location:** I-81 exit 69, just w on Kohn Rd, then just e. **Facility:** 106 units. 4 stories, interior corridors. **Terms:** check-in 4 pm, 1-7 night minimum stay, cancellation fee imposed. **Pool(s):** heated indoor. **Activities:** exercise room. **Guest Services:** valet and coin laundry.

AAA Benefit: Members save 5% or more!

🍽 CALL 🔊M ➰ BIZ 📶 ✕ 🖥
/ SOME UNITS HS 🛅 🖼

HAMPTON INN HARRISBURG EAST (HERSHEY AREA)
(717)545-9595 10

Hotel $109-$225 **Address:** 4230 Union Deposit Rd 17111 **Location:** I-83 exit 48, just e. **Facility:** 145 units. 5 stories, interior corridors. **Terms:** 1-7 night minimum stay, cancellation fee imposed. **Pool(s):** heated outdoor. **Activities:** exercise room. **Guest Services:** valet and coin laundry.

AAA Benefit: Members save 5% or more!

🍽 CALL 🔊M ➰ BIZ 📶 🛅 🖼 🖥 / SOME UNITS HS

HILTON GARDEN INN HARRISBURG EAST
(717)635-7299 17

Hotel
$119-$209

Hilton **Garden Inn** **AAA Benefit:** Members save 5% or more!

Address: 3943 TecPort Dr 17111 **Location:** I-83 exit 45, 0.5 mi se on Paxton St. **Facility:** 126 units. 5 stories, interior corridors. **Terms:** check-in 4 pm, 1-7 night minimum stay, cancellation fee imposed. **Pool(s):** heated outdoor, heated indoor. **Activities:** hot tub, exercise room. **Guest Services:** valet and coin laundry. **Featured Amenity:** full hot breakfast.

SAVE 🔁 🍸 CALL 🔊M ➰ BIZ HS 📶 ✕ 🛅
🖼 🖥

Recommend places you'd like us to inspect
at AAA.com/TourBookComments

(See map & index p. 138.)

HILTON HARRISBURG
(717)233-6000

Hotel
$159-$219

AAA Benefit: Members save 5% or more!

Address: One N 2nd St 17101 **Location:** Jct Market St; downtown. **Facility:** 341 units, some two bedrooms. 15 stories, interior corridors. **Parking:** on-site (fee) and valet. **Terms:** 1-7 night minimum stay, cancellation fee imposed. **Amenities:** safes. **Dining:** 2 restaurants, entertainment. **Pool(s):** heated indoor. **Activities:** exercise room, massage. **Guest Services:** valet and coin laundry, area transportation.

HOLIDAY INN EXPRESS EAST
(717)561-8100

Hotel $99-$199 **Address:** 4021 Union Deposit Rd 17109 **Location:** I-83 exit 48, just w. **Facility:** 114 units. 5 stories, interior corridors. **Pool(s):** heated outdoor. **Activities:** exercise room. **Guest Services:** valet and coin laundry.

HOLIDAY INN EXPRESS HARRISBURG NE - HERSHEY
(717)540-8400

Hotel
$69-$229

Address: 7744 Linglestown Rd 17112 **Location:** I-81 exit 77, 0.5 mi w. **Facility:** 80 units. 3 stories, interior corridors. **Terms:** check-in 4 pm. **Pool(s):** heated indoor. **Activities:** hot tub, exercise room. **Guest Services:** coin laundry. **Featured Amenity:** continental breakfast.

HOLIDAY INN HARRISBURG EAST-AIRPORT
(717)939-7841

Hotel
$99-$179

Address: 4751 Lindle Rd 17111 **Location:** I-283 exit 2, just e. **Facility:** 274 units. 2-4 stories, interior corridors. **Terms:** check-in 4 pm, cancellation fee imposed. **Amenities:** Some: safes. **Pool(s):** outdoor, heated indoor. **Activities:** hot tub, tennis, playground, game room, exercise room. **Guest Services:** valet and coin laundry, area transportation. *(See ad this page.)*

 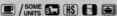

Located just minutes from downtown Harrisburg and Hershey. Close to various downtown attractions.

HOMEWOOD SUITES BY HILTON-HARRISBURG EAST (HERSHEY AREA)
(717)909-4663

Extended Stay Hotel
$129-$219

AAA Benefit: Members save 5% or more!

Address: 3990 TecPort Dr 17111 **Location:** I-83 exit 45, 0.5 mi se on Paxton St. **Facility:** 105 efficiencies, some two bedrooms. 3 stories, interior corridors. **Terms:** check-in 4 pm, 1-7 night minimum stay, cancellation fee imposed. **Pool(s):** heated indoor. **Activities:** hot tub, exercise room. **Guest Services:** valet and coin laundry. **Featured Amenity:** breakfast buffet.

▼ *See AAA listing this page* ▼

(See map & index p. 138.)

LA QUINTA INN & SUITES HARRISBURG HERSHEY
(717)566-7666

WWW Hotel $79-$274 Address: 265 N Hershey Rd 17112 Location: I-81 exit 77, just s. Facility: 81 units. 3 stories, interior corridors. Pool(s): heated indoor. Activities: hot tub, exercise room.

QUALITY INN
(717)540-9339 **3**

Hotel
$80-$160

Address: 200 N Mountain Rd 17112 Location: I-81 exit 72A northbound; exit 72 southbound. Facility: 65 units. 3 stories, interior corridors. Activities: exercise room. Guest Services: valet and coin laundry.

RAMADA HARRISBURG
(717)652-7180 **2**

Hotel
$75-$165

Address: 300 N Mountain Rd 17112 Location: I-81 exit 72 southbound; exit 72B northbound, just s. Facility: 101 units. 2-3 stories, interior corridors. Pool(s): heated indoor. Activities: hot tub, exercise room. Guest Services: coin laundry. Featured Amenity: continental breakfast.

RED ROOF INN HARRISBURG - HERSHEY
717/939-1331 **28**

Motel
Rates not provided

Address: 950 Eisenhower Blvd 17111 Location: I-283 exit 2, just e. Facility: 110 units. 2 stories (no elevator), interior/exterior corridors. Amenities: safes.

RED ROOF INN HARRISBURG NORTH
717/657-1445 **6**

Motel
Rates not provided

Address: 400 Corporate Cir 17110 Location: I-81 exit 69 (Progress Ave), just n. Located in a quiet area. Facility: 110 units. 2 stories (no elevator), interior/exterior corridors. Amenities: video games, safes.

RESIDENCE INN BY MARRIOTT HARRISBURG-HERSHEY
(717)561-1900 **15**

WWW Extended Stay Hotel $118-$217 Address: 4480 Lewis Rd 17111 Location: US 322 exit Penhar Dr, just e. Facility: 122 units, some two bedrooms, efficiencies and kitchens. 2-3 stories (no elevator), interior/exterior corridors. Terms: check-in 4 pm. Pool(s): outdoor, heated indoor. Activities: exercise room. Guest Services: valet and coin laundry.

AAA Benefit:
Members save 5%
or more!

SCOTTISH INN & SUITES
(717)901-8383

WWW Motel $59-$119 Address: 7975 Jonestown Rd 17112 Location: I-81 exit 77, just s. Facility: 32 units. 2 stories, interior corridors. Terms: cancellation fee imposed.

SHERATON HARRISBURG HERSHEY
(717)564-5511 **24**

WWW
Hotel
$161-$329

Sheraton

AAA Benefit: Members save up to 15%, plus Starwood Preferred Guest® benefits!

Address: 4650 Lindle Rd 17111 Location: I-283 exit 2, just e. Facility: 347 units. 10 stories, interior corridors. Terms: 3 day cancellation notice-fee imposed. Amenities: video games, safes. Pool(s): heated outdoor, heated indoor. Activities: hot tub, massage. Guest Services: valet and coin laundry, area transportation.

SLEEP INN & SUITES HARRISBURG/HERSHEY
(717)564-8888 **22**

WWW Hotel $74-$169 Address: 631-A Eisenhower Blvd 17111 Location: I-283 exit 2, just n. Facility: 74 units. 4 stories, interior corridors. Amenities: safes. Pool(s): heated indoor. Activities: exercise room. Guest Services: valet and coin laundry.

SPRINGHILL SUITES BY MARRIOTT HARRISBURG/HERSHEY
(717)540-5100 **8**

WWW Hotel $111-$217 Address: 15 Capital Dr 17110 Location: I-81 exit 69 (Progress Ave), just w on Kohn Rd, then just e. Facility: 118 units. 4 stories, interior corridors. Pool(s): heated indoor. Activities: exercise room. Guest Services: valet and coin laundry, area transportation.

AAA Benefit:
Members save 5%
or more!

STAYBRIDGE SUITES HARRISBURG
717/233-3304 **9**

Extended Stay
Hotel
Rates not provided

Address: 920 Wildwood Park Dr 17110 Location: I-81 exit 67A/B, just w. Facility: 127 efficiencies, some two bedrooms. 5 stories, interior corridors. Pool(s): heated indoor. Activities: exercise room. Guest Services: valet and coin laundry, area transportation.

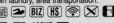
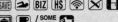

(See map & index p. 138.)

TOWNEPLACE SUITES BY MARRIOTT HARRISBURG HERSHEY
(717)558-0200 **19**

Extended Stay Hotel
$139-$229

AAA Benefit: Members save 5% or more!

Address: 450 Friendship Rd 17111 **Location:** I-83 exit 45, 0.7 mi on Paxton St, then 0.3 mi s. Near a shopping mall and restaurants. **Facility:** 107 units, some two bedrooms, efficiencies and kitchens. 4 stories, interior corridors. **Terms:** check-in 4 pm. **Pool(s):** heated indoor. **Activities:** hot tub, exercise room. **Guest Services:** valet and coin laundry. **Featured Amenity: continental breakfast.**

WINGATE BY WYNDHAM HARRISBURG EAST
(717)985-1600 **29**

Hotel $89-$149 **Address:** 1344 Eisenhower Blvd 17111 **Location:** I-76 (Pennsylvania Tpke) exit 247, just n. **Facility:** 85 units. 4 stories, interior corridors. **Terms:** check-in 4 pm, cancellation fee imposed. **Amenities:** safes. **Activities:** hot tub, exercise room. **Guest Services:** coin laundry.

WYNDHAM GARDEN HOTEL-HARRISBURG/HERSHEY
(717)558-9500 **26**

Hotel $147-$349 **Address:** 765 Eisenhower Blvd 17111 **Location:** I-283 exit 2, just w. **Facility:** 167 units. 6 stories, interior corridors. **Terms:** cancellation fee imposed. **Pool(s):** heated outdoor. **Activities:** exercise room. **Guest Services:** valet and coin laundry, area transportation.

WHERE TO EAT

APPALACHIAN BREWING CO
717/221-1080 **10**

American. Casual Dining. $8-$16 **AAA Inspector Notes:** On any given day you can sample several types of beer at this microbrewery, where brews are named after locations in the state of Pennsylvania. Burgers, sandwiches and pub fare are offered as are traditional favorites like chicken Kiev and homemade meatloaf. Parking is tight in the two small parking lots, but you might find a spot on the street. **Features:** full bar. **Address:** 50 N Cameron St 17101 **Location:** I-81 exit 67A, 2 mi s; 0.5 mi past Farm Show Complex.

BANGKOK 56 THAI CUISINE
717/236-2931 **19**

Thai. Casual Dining. $10-$16 **AAA Inspector Notes:** This casual, relaxed spot keeps the locals coming back for its savory traditional Thai dishes and affordable pricing. While the menu provides a lot, we recommend sticking with the curry or noodle entrée dishes. Remember to also bring your favorite beer or wine from home at this B.Y.O. establishment. **Address:** 1917 Paxton St 17104 **Location:** I-83 exit 44B, just s.

THE BLUE MOOSE BAR AND GRILLE
717/651-9493

American. Casual Dining. $8-$20 **AAA Inspector Notes:** A bit out of the way, this casual restaurant and bar has a ski-lodge feel and offers a great spot for a quick bite or a just a draft beer at the bar. Make sure to call ahead and ask about their weekly live music and karaoke events. **Features:** full bar, Sunday brunch. **Address:** 6791 Linglestown Rd 17112 **Location:** I-81 exit 72B, 1.2 mi n.

BRICCO
717/724-0222 **16**

International. Casual Dining. $11-$40 **AAA Inspector Notes:** Breeze into a Mediterranean setting marked by vibrant colors and a pleasant staff busily moving from table to table to help you and other guests choose sure-to-satisfy dishes. The chef's innovative preparations of fresh seafood, steak and stone-oven pizza, which change with the seasons, often incorporate imported and local cheeses. **Features:** full bar, happy hour. **Reservations:** suggested. **Address:** 31 S 3rd St 17101 **Location:** I-83 exit 43, 0.4 mi n, just e on Market St, then just s. **Parking:** street only.

CAFE FRESCO
717/236-2599 **14**

American. Casual Dining. $9-$30 **AAA Inspector Notes:** Relax during lunchtime in this modern-style café and order a cup of coffee and pizza or a sandwich and dessert. During dinner, the atmosphere becomes more intimate and the entrées a bit more gourmet. Regardless of when you come, this is a great place to enjoy a specialty cocktail. **Features:** full bar. **Reservations:** suggested, for dinner. **Address:** 215 N 2nd St 17101 **Location:** I-83 exit 43; City Center. **Parking:** street only.

EL RODEO
717/652-5340 **1**

Mexican. Casual Dining. $7-$17 **AAA Inspector Notes:** Nibble on tortilla chips with homemade salsa before digging in to your favorite off El Rodeo's menu of yummy options. Prompt, pleasant servers lend to a relaxed dining experience. **Features:** full bar. **Address:** 4659 Jonestown Rd 17109 **Location:** Just e of Colonial Park Mall on US 22.

EMPIRE ASIAN BISTRO
717/558-9258 **5**

Asian. Casual Dining. $7-$14 **AAA Inspector Notes:** Whether you want sushi, General Tso's chicken or pad thai, you can find your favorite Asian dish here. It has become popular among locals due to its great prices, large portions, and most importantly, delicious food. **Features:** full bar. **Reservations:** suggested. **Address:** 3819 Union Deposit Rd 17109 **Location:** I-83 exit 48, 0.4 mi w.

THE FIRE HOUSE RESTAURANT
717/234-6064 **12**

American. Casual Dining. $8-$38 **AAA Inspector Notes:** Classic. Originally built in 1871 as the historic Hope Station, this restaurant has kept most of its original architecture and features a beautiful brick exterior. Inside, red and black firehouse memorabilia decorate the walls and inside the dining room. The menu continues to impress offering hearty, flavorful courses such as garlic-studded filet mignon, blackened chicken cheese steak, cedar plank salmon and Hungarian stuffed peppers. **Features:** full bar, happy hour. **Address:** 606 N 2nd St 17101 **Location:** Jct 2nd and Liberty sts; downtown. **Parking:** street only.

GABRIELLA ITALIAN RESTAURANT
717/540-0040 **2**

Italian. Casual Dining. $11-$25 **AAA Inspector Notes:** This classic restaurant offers all the traditional favorites, but we highly recommend their specialty chicken and veal entrées. The staff is energetic and the dishes are hearty. **Features:** beer & wine. **Reservations:** suggested. **Address:** 3907 Jonestown Rd 17109 **Location:** I-83 exit 50A, just e on US 22.

HIBACHI BUFFET GRILL
717/889-7008 **15**

Asian. Casual Dining. $8-$13 **AAA Inspector Notes:** Expect great value at this buffet-style restaurant that offers an array of food, including crawfish, snow crab legs, sushi, sirloin, crispy duck and bourbon chicken. After you're finished with dinner, make sure you've saved some room for their variety of desserts. **Features:** patio dining. **Address:** 421 Friendship Rd 17111 **Location:** I-83 exit 45, 0.7 mi w on Paxton St, then just s.

LANCASTER BREWING COMPANY
717/564-4448 **17**

American. Casual Dining. $7-$26 **AAA Inspector Notes:** You'll be greeted with friendly and prompt service at the Lancaster Brewing Company, an outlet of a local microbrewery. Expect hearty portions of flavorful American fare, which are just as tempting as the beer selections. Food samples are available at the bar during happy hour. **Features:** full bar. **Reservations:** suggested, weekends. **Address:** 469 Eisenhower Blvd 17111 **Location:** I-283 exit 2, just w on SR 441, then 0.6 mi n.

(See map & index p. 138.)

LEEDS RESTAURANT AND LOUNGE   717/564-4654   (20)
▼▼ American. Casual Dining. $8-$40 **AAA Inspector Notes:**
You can peruse a vast menu of pasta, chicken, steak and seafood
dishes as you relax in the inviting dining room, or outside on the patio,
when the weather allows. **Features:** full bar. **Reservations:** suggested. **Address:** 750 Eisenhower Blvd 17111 **Location:** I-283 exit 2,
just n. [L] [D]

MANGIA QUI   717/233-7358   (11)
▼▼ Italian. Casual Dining. $9-$32 **AAA Inspector Notes:**
Upon entering the restaurant, guests will have the option to dine
downstairs at Mangia Qui or walk upstairs to their separated tapas-
style restaurant. Once inside, you will be surrounded by a variety of
vibrant colors and original artwork along the walls. The diverse menu
puts forth tasty dishes ranging from rib-eye rollitini to blackened mahi
mahi with tzatziki sauce. Lunchtime provides the best value for your
dollar. **Features:** full bar, Sunday brunch. **Reservations:** suggested.
Address: 272 North St 17101 **Location:** Jct 3rd and North sts;
downtown. **Parking:** street only. [L] [D]

MEIJI   717/213-9300   (8)
▼▼ Vietnamese. Casual Dining. $7-$11 **AAA Inspector
Notes:** This modest storefront offers flavorful, healthy and authentic
cuisine that will not come anywhere close to breaking the bank. Service is prompt and helpful. Guests are welcome to bring the wine or
beer of their choice to accompany their meal. **Address:** 2306 Walnut
St 17103 **Location:** I-83 exit 50B (US 22 W/Progress Ave), 2 mi w;
in Penbrook Plaza Shopping Center. [L] [D]

M SUSHI HOUSE AND RESTAURANT   717/545-8885   (4)
▼▼ Japanese. Casual Dining. $9-$23 **AAA Inspector Notes:**
You'll enjoy casual Japanese cuisine and a large variety of specialty
sushi rolls at this casual spot. Lunch specials are as low as $8 and
offer curry, noddle, chicken and sushi options. The staff is extremely
attentive and courteous. **Address:** 3402 Walnut St 17109 **Location:**
I-83 exit 50B, 1.1 mi w. [L] [D]

PHO KIM'S   717/836-7562   (9)
▼▼ Vietnamese. Casual Dining. $7-$12 **AAA Inspector
Notes:** Reasonably priced Vietnamese favorites such as pho, vermicelli noodle bowls, rice plates, stir-fry dishes and spring rolls keep the
locals frequenting this establishment. If there is anything that tastes
particularly fantastic, the owners also have a conveniently located
Asian grocery store next door. **Address:** 5490 Derry St 17111 **Location:** I-83 exit 47, 1.1 mi e. [L] [D]

PROGRESS GRILL   717/652-7348   (3)
▼▼ American. Casual Dining. $14-$38 **AAA Inspector Notes:**
Only fresh ingredients are used in grilled and broiled preparations of
delicious seafood, particularly the specialty crabcakes. Subdued
lighting and dark plaid wallpaper give the feeling of a cozy club. Service is professional and prompt. **Features:** full bar. **Reservations:**
suggested. **Address:** 3526 Walnut St 17109 **Location:** I-83 exit 50B
(US 22 W/Progress Ave), 0.9 mi w. [D]

STOCK'S ON 2ND   717/233-6699   (13)
▼▼ American. Casual Dining. $9-$34 **AAA Inspector Notes:**
Take stock of your wonderful options at Stock's on 2nd, an inviting
spot on downtown's restaurant row. The seasonally changing menu
creatively and deftly describes the creative dishes that the chef prepares in the display kitchen in the dining room's back corner. Keep it
simple with the fabulous peanut butter pie for dessert. **Features:** full
bar, happy hour. **Reservations:** suggested. **Address:** 211 N 2nd St
17101 **Location:** I-83 exit 43, 0.5 mi n. [L] [D]

T. BRENDAN O'REILLY'S IRISH PUB   717/564-2700   (6)
▼▼ American. Casual Dining. $9-$24 **AAA Inspector Notes:**
A broad drink selection, including 24 frequently changing beers on
tap, can be found here. Order up some of the typical Irish pub fare
and listen to the live music or partake in karaoke offered weekly. **Features:** full bar, happy hour. **Address:** 800 E Park Dr 17111 **Location:**
I-83 exit 48, just e on Union Deposit Rd, then 0.5 mi s; in BEST
WESTERN PREMIER The Central Hotel & Conference Center.
[L] [D] CALL 🖐M

THE WHARF   717/564-9920   (7)
▼▼ American. Casual Dining. $6-$25 **AAA Inspector Notes:**
Known for its signature kickin' clam and corn chowder soup, this
eatery provides a classic charm with green leather booths and light
wood furnishings. Nine flat-panel televisions fill the walls and current
music plays through the surround-sound speakers. While a variety of
entrées are available, we recommend sticking with the seafood specialties such as jumbo lump crab cakes and fish and chips. **Features:**
full bar, patio dining, happy hour. **Address:** 6852 Derry St 17111 **Location:** I-83 exit 47, 2.8 mi e. [L] [D]

ZIA'S TRATTORIA AT RED DOOR   717/920-0330   (18)
▼▼▼ Italian. Fine Dining. $8-$29 **AAA Inspector Notes:** Patrons are sure to enjoy a fresh classic Italian meal in a relaxed,
modern atmosphere. House specialties include dishes such as veal
Oscar, Tuscan-style New York strip and seafood scarpiello. Save
room for dessert; try homemade panna cotta. **Features:** full bar, patio
dining, happy hour. **Reservations:** suggested. **Address:** 110 N 2nd
St 17101 **Location:** Between Locust and Walnut sts; downtown.
Parking: street only. [L] [D] [🛒]

HAVERTOWN
• **Hotels & Restaurants map & index p. 274**
• **Part of Philadelphia area — see map p. 230**

NAIS CUISINE   610/789-5983   (127)
▼▼ French. Casual Dining. $15-$27 **AAA Inspector Notes:**
An Oriental flair punctuates such French-style dishes as leg of lamb,
filet mignon, roast duck and fresh salmon. Classical music plays in
the background of the warm, cozy dining room. For dessert, savor the
excellent crème brûlée or French chocolate pie. **Reservations:** suggested. **Address:** 13-17 W Benedict Ave 19083 **Location:** I-476 exit
9 (SR 3), 2.3 mi e, 1.2 mi nw on Darby Rd, then just w. [🚇] Wynnewood Rd, 89. **Parking:** street only. [D] [🚇]

HAWLEY (E-11) pop. 1,211, elev. 906'
• **Part of Pocono Mountains Area — see map
p. 371**

**Hawley-Lake Wallenpaupack Chamber of Com-
merce:** 2512 US 6, Suite 2, Hawley, PA 18428.
Phone: (570) 226-3191.

**LAKE WALLENPAUPACK ENVIRONMENTAL PRE-
SERVE** is just w. of US 6 and has multiple access
points in Hawley and nearby towns; the learning
center is at 126 PPL Dr. The highlight is 5,700-acre,
13-mile Lake Wallenpaupack, the state's third
largest man-made lake. Recreational opportunities,
including boating, fishing, hiking, waterskiing and ice
fishing, are abundant. Lake Wallenpaupack Overlook, on SR 590, and Tafton Dike Observation Area,
junction US 6 and SR 507, provide scenic views.

A good place to start exploring the area is the
PPL Wallenpaupack Environmental Learning
Center, which features displays about the lake, a cut
glass display from a local collector, a Native
American dugout canoe and a library. *See Recre-
ation Areas Chart.* **Hours:** Learning center Mon.-
Sat. 10-4, Memorial Day weekend-Labor Day; Mon.-
Fri. 10-4, rest of year. Phone ahead to confirm
schedule. **Cost:** Free. **Phone:** (570) 253-7001.
🅰 ⊠ 🏕

WALLENPAUPACK SCENIC BOAT TOUR, 3.6 mi.
s. to 2487 US 6 at the Wallenpaupack Observation-
Dike, is given aboard either a 28-foot or 32-foot pon-
toon boat. The 1-hour tour on the 5,700-acre man-
made Lake Wallenpaupack offers splendid views of

the lake region as well as a bit of area history and facts about how the lake was created.

Hours: Departures require a minimum of four passengers. Trips depart daily on the hour 11-7 (last tour sometimes departs at 7), Sat.-Sun. 11-6, mid-June through Labor Day; Sat.-Sun. on the hour noon-4, early May to mid-June and early Sept.-early Oct. Phone ahead to confirm schedule. **Cost:** $15; $14 (ages 60+); $11 (ages 2-12). **Phone:** (570) 226-3293 or (877) 226-8226.

EHRHARDT'S WATERFRONT RESORT & CONFERENCE CENTER 570/226-4388

▼▼ **Resort Hotel** $63-$275 **Address:** 205 Rt 507 18428 **Location:** I-84 exit 26, 5.2 mi n on SR 390, then 0.5 mi n. **Facility:** Located on the shores of Lake Wallenpaupack, this family resort offers year-round activities. A variety of rooms and housekeeping units feature private porches and some have a fireplace and hot tub. 30 units, some two bedrooms and cottages. 1-3 stories (no elevator), interior/exterior corridors. **Terms:** 2 night minimum stay - seasonal and/or weekends, 21 day cancellation notice-fee imposed. **Dining:** Ehrhardt's Waterfront Restaurant, see separate listing. **Pool(s):** heated outdoor. **Activities:** self-propelled boats, boat dock, fishing, playground.

THE LODGE AT WOODLOCH (570)685-8500

▼▼▼▼ **Resort Hotel** $618-$1458 **Address:** 109 River Birch Ln 18428 **Location:** Waterfront. Jct US 6, 6.3 mi e on SR 590 E. **Facility:** This four-seasons destination sits on 150 private, woodland acres and offers luxurious rooms and baths. Extensive public areas and grounds all overlook a private lake. 57 units. 3 stories, interior corridors. **Parking:** valet only. **Terms:** check-in 4 pm, 2 night minimum stay - seasonal and/or weekends, cancellation fee imposed, resort fee. **Amenities:** safes. **Dining:** entertainment. **Pool(s):** heated indoor. **Activities:** sauna, hot tub, self-propelled boats, fishing, regulation golf, recreation programs, bicycles, trails, spa. **Guest Services:** complimentary laundry, area transportation.

THE SETTLERS INN AT BINGHAM PARK 570/226-2993

▼▼▼ **Historic Country Inn.** Rates not provided. **Address:** 4 Main Ave 18428 **Location:** On Main Ave (US 6), 0.3 mi w. Across from Bingham Park. **Facility:** This 1927 English Arts and Crafts inn features extensive herb and flower gardens. The guest rooms vary in size and are furnished with an eclectic blend of antiques and luxury bedding. 22 units, some two bedrooms. 3 stories (no elevator), interior corridors. **Dining:** restaurant, see separate listing. **Activities:** bicycles.

TANGLWOOD RESORTS (570)226-6161

▼▼▼ **Resort Condominium** $90-$165 **Address:** 9 Crest Dr 18428 **Location:** Waterfront. I-84 exit 26, 5.1 mi n on SR 390, then 1.3 mi n on SR 507 to jct US 6. **Facility:** This condo-style resort offers activities both in and around the immediate area. Located across from Lake Wallenpaupack. 75 condominiums. 1-2 stories (no elevator), exterior corridors. **Terms:** check-in 4 pm, 2 night minimum stay - seasonal and/or weekends, cancellation fee imposed, resort fee. **Pool(s):** outdoor. **Activities:** fishing, tennis, recreation programs, game room. **Guest Services:** coin laundry.

WHERE TO EAT

EHRHARDT'S WATERFRONT RESTAURANT
570/226-2124

▼▼ **American Casual Dining** $8-$28 **AAA Inspector Notes:** Offering nice views of Lake Wallenpaupack, this multi-tiered restaurant has been family-owned since 1943. A background of mountains encompass the idyllic setting, and friendly service is well-suited to the relaxing atmosphere. **Features:** full bar. **Address:** 205 Rt 507 18428 **Location:** I-84 exit 26, 5.2 mi n on SR 390, then 0.5 mi n; in Ehrhardt's Waterfront Resort & Conference Center. *Menu on AAA.com* [L] [D]

THE SETTLERS INN AT BINGHAM PARK 570/226-2993

▼▼▼ **Regional American Fine Dining** $9-$38 **AAA Inspector Notes:** Local organic ingredients and products, including fresh herbs from the owner's garden, are used in such menu preparations as the grilled pork tenderloin with rhubarb ginger chutney or pasture-raised chicken roulade with fresh mozzarella, local tomatoes and basil aïoli. All is served in the pale warm glow of the amber lamps in the Arts and Crafts-style dining room or on the covered porch overlooking the gardens. **Features:** full bar, patio dining, Sunday brunch. **Reservations:** suggested. **Address:** 4 Main Ave 18428 **Location:** On Main Ave (US 6), 0.3 mi w. [B] [L] [D]

HAZLETON (F-10) pop. 25,340, elev. 1,624'
• Restaurants p. 148

The first seven miles of the Greater Hazleton Rails to Trails follows old rail bed—the 1842 Delaware Susquehanna and Schuylkill line—on SR 93 (E. Broad St.) and includes picnic areas, benches, flowers and plants.

Just northeast of town on SR 940 is the Sacred Heart Shrine. Its landscaped grounds contain depictions of the life of Christ. Picnicking is permitted. The Greater Hazleton Historical Society Museum, 55 N. Wyoming St., is open by appointment and contains exhibits relating to Native Americans, the mining and railroad industries, music, sports, the military and the life of native son, actor Jack Palance. Reservations must be made one week in advance; phone (570) 455-8576.

Greater Hazleton Chamber of Commerce: 20 W. Broad St., Hazleton, PA 18201. **Phone:** (570) 455-1509.

BEST WESTERN GENETTI INN & SUITES
(570)454-2494

▼▼ **Hotel** $91-$101 **AAA Benefit:** Members save up to 20%!

Address: 1341 N Church St 18202 **Location:** I-80 exit 262, 6 mi s on SR 309. Located in a commercial area. **Facility:** 77 units, some kitchens. 1-3 stories (no elevator), interior/exterior corridors. **Terms:** 3 day cancellation notice-fee imposed. **Pool(s):** heated outdoor. **Activities:** playground. **Guest Services:** valet and coin laundry. **Featured Amenity:** continental breakfast.

RAMADA INN HAZLETON   (570)455-2061

▼▼ **Hotel** $70-$140 **Address:** 1221 N Church St 18202 **Location:** I-80 exit 262, 6 mi s on SR 309. Located in a commercial area. **Facility:** 106 units. 2 stories (no elevator), interior/exterior corridors. **Pool(s):** outdoor. **Activities:** limited exercise equipment. **Guest Services:** valet and coin laundry.

⊤ ⤳ 📶 🛏 🖥 🖵 / SOME UNITS 🛎

RESIDENCE INN BY MARRIOTT-HAZLETON   (570)455-9555

▼▼▼ **Extended Stay Hotel** $90-$148 **Address:** 1 Station Circle Dr 18202 **Location:** I-81 exit 143, just s on SR 924 S; at Humboldt Station, just e on Commerce Dr. **Facility:** 92 units, some two bedrooms, efficiencies and kitchens. 3 stories, interior corridors. **Pool(s):** heated indoor. **Activities:** hot tub, exercise room. **Guest Services:** valet and coin laundry.

AAA Benefit:
Members save 5% or more!

CALL 🄻🄼 ⤳ 🄱🄸🅉 🄷🅂 📶 ✖ 🛏 🖥 🖵 / SOME UNITS 🛎

WHERE TO EAT

OVALON BAR & GRILL   570/454-0853

▼▼ Italian. Casual Dining. $14-$39 **AAA Inspector Notes:** *Classic.* This restaurant, in continuous operation downtown for more than 50 years, offers both a tavern section and a more formal dining area. But no matter where you sit, you'll be presented with a menu of Italian-American cuisine that includes steaks, seafood, veal, chicken and homemade pasta. You can choose a lighter meal or an upscale dinner. With its friendly hometown feel, the restaurant has a loyal local following. **Features:** full bar. **Reservations:** suggested, weekends. **Address:** 254 N Wyoming St 18201 **Location:** Jct SR 309 and 93, 1.3 mi n on SR 309, just e on Diamond Ave to Wyoming St. **Parking:** street only. Ⓓ

HELLERTOWN (G-11) pop. 5,898, elev. 278'

LOST RIVER CAVERNS AND THE GILMAN MUSEUM are .5 mi. e. of SR 412 at 726 Durham St. The limestone cavern contains five chambers of crystal formations. One chamber, the Crystal Chapel, was used for weddings and baptisms. The formations include stalagmites, stalactites, flowstone and dripstone. Displays include a tropical garden, museum of natural history, rocks, minerals, gems and antique weapons. A nature trail, a picnic grove and gem panning also are available.

Time: Allow 1 hour minimum. **Hours:** Guided walking tours daily 9-6, Memorial Day weekend-Labor Day; 9-5, rest of year. Closed Jan. 1, Easter morning, Thanksgiving and Christmas. **Cost:** $12.50; $7.75 (ages 3-12). Gem panning $4. **Phone:** (610) 838-8767. 🏕

HERMITAGE (E-1) pop. 16,220, elev. 1,076'

THE AVENUE OF 444 FLAGS is in Hillcrest Memorial Park at 2619 E. State St. A paved avenue is lined with 444 American flags, one for each day that 53 American hostages were held captive in Iran under the reign of the Ayatollah Khomeini. The flags fly 24 hours a day as a symbol of hope and freedom. A monument and eternal flame are dedicated to the eight U.S. servicemen who died trying to rescue the hostages in April 1980. Veterans of other wars also are honored. **Hours:** Daily 24 hours. **Cost:** Free. **Phone:** (724) 346-3818.

KRAYNAK'S SANTA'S CHRISTMASLAND AND EASTER BUNNY LANE is off I-80 exit 4B, 3.1 mi. n. on SR 18N, then .7 mi. w. to 2525 E. State St. Santa's Christmasland has more than 100 decorated trees with animated figures depicting religious themes, traditional Christmas scenes and favorite childhood characters. Easter Bunny Lane features flowering trees and lights. Animated figures, bunnies and chicks accent the Easter scenes.

Time: Allow 30 minutes minimum. **Hours:** Santa's Christmasland Mon.-Sat. 9-9, Sun. (and Christmas Eve) 10-5, Sept. 10-Christmas Eve. Easter Bunny Lane Mon.-Sat. 9-9, Sun. 10-5, Feb. 15-Mon. after Easter. Closed Easter, Thanksgiving and Christmas. **Cost:** Free. **Phone:** (724) 347-4511.

COMBINE BROTHERS BAR & GRILLE   724/983-1057

▼▼ Italian. Casual Dining. $11-$27 **AAA Inspector Notes:** An industrial theme prevails in this casual restaurant, where diners can enjoy hearty portions of food prepared by the owner-chef. Expect to wait at least a half-hour for the popular homemade bread, pastry, sausage and meatballs during peak hours. They open daily at 3:30 pm. **Features:** full bar. **Address:** 2376 S Hermitage Rd (SR 18) 16148 **Location:** I-80 exit 4B (SR 60), just w to SR 18, then 1 mi n. Ⓓ

HERSHEY (H-9) pop. 14,257, elev. 423'
• Hotels p. 152 • Restaurants p. 156
• Attractions map p. 149

The aroma of chocolate pervades Hershey, a name synonymous with the confection. In the rich Lebanon Valley, the town was founded in 1903 by Milton S. Hershey, who planned and built an attractive industrial community. The Hershey Foods Corp. factory is one of the largest chocolate and cocoa plants in the world.

The 550-acre campus of Penn State Milton S. Hershey Medical Center, on US 322 at 500 University Dr., includes Penn State College of Medicine, Penn State Hershey Children's Hospital, Penn State Hershey Cancer Institute and other health facilities; phone (717) 531-8521.

Giant Center, a 12,500-seat arena, is home to the Hershey Bears AHL hockey club. Hersheypark Stadium presents outdoor sports events and concerts; it seats 30,000. Next to the stadium is Star Pavilion, an 8,000-seat amphitheater that features musical events in summer. Phone (717) 534-3911 or (877) 598-6504 for additional information.

One-hour tours of Hershey Theatre, built by Milton S. Hershey in 1933, are given Friday mornings (also Sunday afternoons, Memorial Day through Labor Day). The performing arts center features Broadway shows and other entertainers; phone (717) 534-3405 for ticket information or (717) 533-6299 for tour information.

Shopping areas: 🅂🄰🅅🄴 Tanger Outlet Center, 46 Outlet Sq., offers nearly 60 stores, including Anne Taylor, Calvin Klein, Coach, J. Crew, Reebok and Tommy Hilfiger.

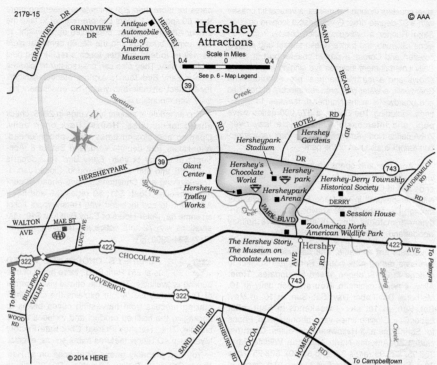

2179-15

GRANDVIEW DR

GRANDVIEW DR

Antique Automobile Club of America Museum

Hershey
Attractions

Scale in Miles

0.4   0   0.4

See p. 6 - Map Legend

© AAA

© 2014 HERE

ANTIQUE AUTOMOBILE CLUB OF AMERICA MUSEUM is 1 mi. n. of Hersheypark Dr. on US 39W. Eight decades of antique cars, motorcycles and memorabilia are presented in themed exhibits. The Museum of Bus Transportation depicts the evolution of public transit and how it influenced the development of modern society; nearly a dozen buses are displayed. A large collection of Tucker Automobiles and related artifacts are also on display. **Time:** Allow 1 hour minimum. **Hours:** Daily 9-5 (also first Thurs. of every month). Closed Jan. 1, Thanksgiving, Christmas Eve and Christmas. **Cost:** $12; $11 (ages 61+); $9 (ages 4-12). **Phone:** (717) 566-7100.

FOUNDERS HALL, 1.2 mi. e. of jct. SR 743 and US 322, is a tribute to Milton Hershey and his wife, Catherine, founders of the Milton Hershey School for children from families of low income and in social need. Founders Hall, the centerpiece of the school, features a grand marble rotunda, a student dining room, a 2,600-seat chapel/auditorium, special exhibits and a visitor center. A 12-minute video presentation about the school is shown upon request in the visitor center. **Hours:** Daily 10-3. Closed school holidays. **Cost:** Free. **Phone:** (717) 520-2000.

HERSHEY-DERRY TOWNSHIP HISTORICAL SOCIETY is off SR 39 (Hersheypark Dr.), then just s. to 40 Northeast Dr. Hershey's history before and after the arrival of the chocolate factory and park is showcased through artifacts and a research library. Exhibits include a collection of World War II memorabilia about Maj. Dick Winters and an exhibit about the Hershey Bears hockey team franchise. During the Christmas holiday, an extensive collection of model trains is on display. Guided tours are available by appointment. **Time:** Allow 30 minutes minimum. **Hours:** Mon., Wed. and Fri. 9-4:30, Sat. 9-1. **Cost:** Donations. **Phone:** (717) 520-0748.

HERSHEY GARDENS, 170 Hotel Rd. across from The Hotel Hershey, is a 23-acre botanical garden. Visitors stroll among seasonal displays, rare trees, numerous theme gardens, a seasonal butterfly house and thousands of rose bushes. The Children's Garden features 23 themed areas designed for hands-on learning and entertainment.

Time: Allow 1 hour minimum. **Hours:** Gardens daily 9-7, May 23-Sept. 1; 9-5, Apr. 5-May 22 and Sept. 2-Nov. 2; Fri.-Sun. 10-4, Nov. 3-Dec. 31. Butterfly house daily 9-5, May 23 to mid-Sept. Closed Thanksgiving. **Cost:** $10.50; $9.50 (ages 62+); $7.50 (ages 3-12). **Phone:** (717) 534-3492.

HERSHEYPARK, just off SR 743 and US 422, dates to 1907 when the park was founded by Milton S. Hershey as a recreational gathering place for employees of his chocolate company. The park's appearance has changed over the past century but has retained its original charm.

There are now more than 70 rides and attractions, including 13 roller coasters. Laff Trakk, an indoor, spinning "glow coaster," debuts in 2015. Other wood and steel coasters include Fahrenheit, a vertical lift coaster with a 97-degree drop; Great Bear, a looping coaster; Storm Runner, a hydraulic launch coaster with inversions; Skyrush, the park's tallest, fastest and longest coaster; and Comet, a classic coaster built in 1946. Daily entertainment includes live singing and dancing shows and a marine mammal presentation. The Boardwalk, a water play area reminiscent of beaches and boardwalks in the Northeast, features 14 attractions, including The Shore, a 378,000-gallon wave pool, and Intercoastal Waterway, a lazy river. ZooAmerica North American Wildlife Park *(see attraction listing)* is also part of the park.

In April the park opens up for a 2-weekend preview called Springtime in the Park, and on weekends in mid-October the park celebrates Halloween with Hersheypark in the Dark. From mid-November through December 31 Hersheypark Christmas Candylane transforms the park into a festive holiday wonderland.

Lockers are available, and day-use kennels are available during park hours. Prices are subject to change in 2015; phone ahead for updates. **Time:** Allow 4 hours minimum. **Hours:** Open daily at 10, Memorial Day-Labor Day; Sat.-Sun. at 10, in May; Sat.-Sun. at 10, select weekends in Sept. after Labor Day. Closing times vary; phone ahead. Phone for Springtime and Halloween schedules. **Cost:** (includes ZooAmerica North American Wildlife Park) $56.95; $35.95 (ages 3-8 and 55-69); $22.95 (ages 70+). Sunset admission (after 3 when park closes at 6, after 4 when park closes at 8, after 5 when park closes at 10 and 11) $28.95; $24.95 (ages 3-8 and 55-69); $17.95 (ages 70+). Other admission packages, including multiday options, are available. **Phone:** (800) 437-7439. 🍴

Falconry Experience departs from The Hotel Hershey at 100 Hotel Rd. Guests are then shuttled to a nearby field for the 1.5-hour Falconry Experience where they can watch simulated hunt demonstrations and see the birds in flight. Falconry, now a field sport, is a 4,000-year-old technique where hunters used trained birds of prey to hunt game for food. Falconers provide background on falconry and willing participants can hold a bird of prey. Participants can visit ZooAmerica the same day. **Hours:** 11-12:30 Wed.-Mon, late May-early Sept. and Sat.-Sun. in Sept.-Oct. Offered on select dates in March, April and May. Winter and holiday schedule varies based on availability. **Cost:** $75. $65 for hotel guests; $25 (hotel guests ages 0-15). Fee includes admission to ZooAmerica. Reservations are recommended. **Phone:** (800) 437-7439.

ZooAmerica North American Wildlife Park is at 201 Park Ave., opposite Hersheypark; during Hersheypark's season, visitors can also enter via a walking bridge from the Kissing Tower area of the park. This 11-acre zoo depicts native plants and animals from five North American regions: Big Sky Country, The Great Southwest, Eastern Woodlands, Southern Swamps, and Northlands. ZooAmerica

cares for more than 200 animals representing more than 60 species. Visitors can pre-register to take the 2-hour After-Hours Tour, conducted by flashlight, to see animal buildings and the health center at night as well as to feed an otter, touch a reptile and hold a bird of prey. They also can pre-register to take the 2-hour Early Bird Tour to explore outdoor exhibits, feed select animals and watch an enrichment activity with mountain lions.

Zoo schedule is subject to change in 2015; check ahead for updates. **Hours:** Park open daily. Opening and closing times vary; phone ahead. After-Hours Tour departs Wed. and Sat. at 8, Apr.-Sept.; at 6, rest of year. Early Bird Tour departs Tues., Fri. and Sun. at 8, year-round. Closed Jan. 1, Thanksgiving and Christmas. Phone ahead to confirm schedule. **Cost:** $11; $9 (ages 3-8 and 55+). Admission to zoo included with Hersheypark ticket on same day. After-Hours or Early Bird tour $49; reservations with 72-hour notice are required. **Phone:** (717) 534-3900. 🎢

🔻 GEM SAVE **HERSHEY'S CHOCOLATE WORLD** is at 251 Park Blvd.; three hours of free parking is available. This is the official visitor center of The Hershey Co. A tour explains the chocolate-making process from harvesting cocoa beans to packaging the finished product and includes a free sample. The "Hershey's Great Chocolate Factory Mystery in 4D" show features many special effects.

You can probably guess what goes on at Hershey's Chocolate Tasting Adventure. This 20-minute session combines chocolate lore with the opportunity to taste a variety of chocolate types. Desserts, including Hershey's S'mores, can be created at Hershey's Dessert Creation Studio. For a more involved experience, visitors can head to the Create Your Own Candy Bar area to experience a real factory environment and create and make their own candy bar, including the packaging design.

Time: Allow 30 minutes minimum. **Hours:** Open daily at 9; phone ahead to verify closing times. Closed Christmas. **Cost:** Tour free. "Hershey's Great Chocolate Factory Mystery in 4D" $7.95; $7.45 (ages 62+); $6.95 (ages 3-12). Hershey's Create Your Own Candy Bar $14.95. Fees for candy and dessert creations vary. Phone ahead to confirm rates. **Phone:** (717) 534-4900. 💳 🍴

Hershey Trolley Works tours depart from the main lobby inside Hershey's Chocolate World at 251 Park Blvd. The 1-hour History and Chocolate Tour takes visitors through the town while sharing information about Milton Hershey. It includes a stop at Founders Hall at the Milton Hershey School. The 45-minute Trolley Adventure also takes visitors around town, but there is entertainment provided by two actors who reveal aspects of the time when Mr. Hershey lived; sing-alongs and mini chocolates are in abundance. During the holiday season, the Trolley Adventure becomes The Christmas Adventure.

Hours: Trolley Adventure runs daily, Memorial Day-Labor Day. History and Chocolate Tour runs daily, late Mar.-day before Memorial Day and day after Labor Day-Oct. 31; Mon.-Fri., Jan. 2-late Mar. Tour times vary; phone ahead for schedule. Christmas Adventure Tour is offered select days Nov.-Dec. (weather permitting). Closed Christmas. Phone ahead to confirm schedule. **Cost:** $14.95; $10.95 (ages 3-12). **Phone:** (717) 533-3000.

THE HERSHEY STORY, THE MUSEUM ON CHOCOLATE AVENUE is downtown at 63 W. Chocolate Ave. (US 422). This museum features exhibits about Milton S. Hershey's life, including his chocolate factory, the town he created and his philanthropic legacy. Visitors can sample various flavors of single-origin warm drinking chocolate in Cafe Zooka. Chocolate Lab classes related to making and working with chocolate—including techniques like tempering, dipping and molding—also are offered.

Time: Allow 1 hour, 30 minutes minimum. **Hours:** Open daily at 9. Closing times vary; phone ahead. Closed Thanksgiving and Christmas. **Cost:** Museum or Chocolate Lab $10; $9 (ages 62+); $7.50 (ages 3-12). Museum and Chocolate Lab $17.50; $16.50 (ages 62+); $14 (ages 4-12). Children under 4 not permitted in lab. **Phone:** (717) 534-8939.

INDIAN ECHO CAVERNS—see Hummelstown p. 159.

SESSION HOUSE, 248 E. Derry Rd. at Derry Presbyterian Church, is one of Hershey's most historic buildings. The 1732 cabin was built of hand-hewn logs and originally served as a school. Later functions included church meetings, Sunday School classes and a post office. A letter drop slot can still be seen on one of the doors. Since 1929 the cabin has been enclosed in glass thanks to funding from Milton S. Hershey. In order to preserve it for years to come, visitors can now only view it from the outside.

The cemetery on the church grounds dates to 1735. The grave of the area's first pastor, Rev. William Bertram (who began in 1732), is buried in the southwest corner of the cemetery. Revolutionary War soldiers are interred here as well. **Hours:** Daily dawn-dusk. **Cost:** Free. **Phone:** (717) 533-9667.

BEST WESTERN INN HERSHEY   (717)533-5665

Motel
$79-$329

AAA Benefit:
Members save up to 20%!

Address: US 422 & Sipe Ave 17033 **Location:** Jct US 322, just e. **Facility:** 123 units, some efficiencies. 3 stories (no elevator), interior/exterior corridors. **Terms:** check-in 4 pm, 3 day cancellation notice. **Pool(s):** heated outdoor. **Activities:** hot tub, game room, exercise room. **Guest Services:** valet and coin laundry. *(See ad this page.)*

Located 2 miles from Hersheypark attractions!

BLUEGREEN VACATIONS SUITES AT HERSHEY, AN ASCEND RESORT COLLECTION MEMBER
(717)534-2003

Extended Stay Hotel
$229-$509

Address: 176 E Hersheypark Dr 17033 **Location:** Jct Northeast Dr. Across from Outlets at Hershey. **Facility:** 74 two-bedroom kitchen units. 4 stories, interior corridors. **Terms:** check-in 4 pm. **Pool(s):** heated outdoor, heated indoor. **Activities:** hot tub, recreation programs, playground, game room, exercise room, massage. **Guest Services:** complimentary laundry.

Choose real ratings you can trust from professional inspectors who've been there

COMFORT INN AT THE PARK   (717)566-2050

Hotel
$89-$399

Address: 1200 Mae St 17036 **Location:** Jct US 322, 422 and SR 39 (Hersheypark Dr); just off Hersheypark Dr. **Facility:** 125 units, some two bedrooms. 7 stories, interior corridors. **Terms:** check-in 4 pm. **Amenities:** safes. **Pool(s):** heated indoor. **Guest Services:** coin laundry. **Featured Amenity: breakfast buffet.**

Recently renovated, 2 mi from Hersheypark, free hot breakfast, Wi-Fi, indoor pool, smoke free hotel.

DAYS INN HERSHEY   (717)534-2162

Hotel
$110-$300

Address: 350 W Chocolate Ave 17033 **Location:** On US 422; center. **Facility:** 89 units. 4 stories, interior corridors. **Terms:** check-in 4 pm. **Amenities:** safes. **Pool(s):** heated indoor. **Activities:** hot tub, game room, exercise room. **Guest Services:** valet and coin laundry, area transportation. **Featured Amenity: continental breakfast.**

FAIRFIELD INN & SUITES BY MARRIOTT-HERSHEY
(717)520-5240

Hotel $92-$309 **Address:** 651 Areba Ave 17033 **Location:** US 322 exit 46B. **Facility:** 108 units. 5 stories, interior corridors. **Pool(s):** heated indoor. **Activities:** exercise room. **Guest Services:** coin laundry, boarding pass kiosk.

AAA Benefit:
Members save 5% or more!

▼ *See AAA listing this page* ▼

HAMPTON INN & SUITES HERSHEY (717)533-8400

Hotel
$99-$239

AAA Benefit:
Members save 5% or more!

Address: 749 E Chocolate Ave 17033 **Location:** 0.9 mi e on US 422. **Facility:** 110 units, some efficiencies. 3 stories, interior corridors. **Terms:** 1-7 night minimum stay, cancellation fee imposed. **Pool(s):** heated indoor. **Activities:** hot tub, game room, exercise room. **Guest Services:** valet and coin laundry. **Featured Amenity:** full hot breakfast.

HAMPTON INN & SUITES HERSHEY NEAR THE PARK (717)566-3369

Hotel $99-$299 **Address:** 195 Hershey Rd 17036 **Location:** I-81 exit 77 (SR 39 W), 3.5 mi sw. **Facility:** 86 units. 3 stories, interior corridors. **Terms:** 1-7 night minimum stay, cancellation fee imposed. **Pool(s):** heated indoor. **Activities:** exercise room. **Guest Services:** coin laundry.

AAA Benefit:
Members save 5% or more!

  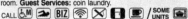

HERSHEY LODGE 717/533-3311

Hotel
Rates not provided

Address: 325 University Dr 17033 **Location:** Jct US 322, 2.5 mi w on US 422. **Facility:** 665 units. 2-5 stories, interior/exterior corridors. **Parking:** onsite and valet. **Terms:** check-in 4 pm. **Amenities:** safes. **Dining:** 5 restaurants. **Pool(s):** outdoor, heated indoor. **Activities:** sauna, hot tub, miniature golf, tennis, recreation programs, playground, game room, exercise room. **Guest Services:** valet laundry, area transportation.

HILTON GARDEN INN HERSHEY (717)566-9292

AAA Benefit:
Members save 5% or more!

Hotel $89-$399 **Address:** 550 E Main St 17036 **Location:** Just nw of jct US 322, 422 and SR 39 (Hersheypark Dr). **Facility:** 99 units. 3 stories, interior corridors. **Terms:** check-in 4 pm, 1-7 night minimum stay, cancellation fee imposed. **Pool(s):** heated indoor. **Activities:** hot tub, exercise room. **Guest Services:** valet and coin laundry, area transportation. *(See ad this page.)*

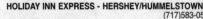

HOLIDAY INN EXPRESS - HERSHEY/HUMMELSTOWN (717)583-0500

Hotel
$99-$259

Address: 610 Walton Ave 17036 **Location:** Just nw of jct US 322, 422 and SR 39 (Hersheypark Dr); just off Hersheypark Dr. **Facility:** 78 units. 3 stories, interior corridors. **Pool(s):** heated indoor. **Activities:** hot tub, exercise room. **Guest Services:** valet and coin laundry. **Featured Amenity:** full hot breakfast.

▼ See AAA listing this page ▼

Keep Your Hands, Eyes
and *Mind* on the Road

**Even voice-activated features can cause
driver distraction.**

AAA.com/distraction

THE HOTEL HERSHEY
717/533-2171

Classic Historic Hotel
Rates not provided

Address: 100 Hotel Rd 17033 **Location:** Jct US 322, 2.3 mi n on SR 39 (Hersheypark Dr). **Facility:** Set on a hill overlooking 300 acres of lush manicured grounds, this hotel is styled after a 19th-century Mediterranean palace. Luxury cottages also are available. 276 units, some cottages. 1-5 stories, interior corridors. **Parking:** on-site and valet. **Terms:** check-in 4 pm. **Amenities:** safes. **Dining:** 3 restaurants, also, The Circular, Trevi 5, see separate listings. **Pool(s):** heated outdoor, heated indoor. **Activities:** sauna, hot tub, miniature golf, tennis, recreation programs, bicycles, playground, game room, spa. **Guest Services:** valet laundry, area transportation.

HOWARD JOHNSON INN
(717)533-9157

Hotel
$67-$200

Address: 845 E Chocolate Ave 17033 **Location:** 1 mi e on US 422. **Facility:** 52 units. 1-2 stories (no elevator), interior/exterior corridors. **Terms:** cancellation fee imposed. **Dining:** What If...of Hershey, see separate listing. **Pool(s):** heated outdoor. **Activities:** limited exercise equipment. **Guest Services:** coin laundry. **Featured Amenity:** continental breakfast.

  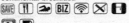

Savings for Your Inner Child

AAA.com/searchfordiscounts

RODEWAY INN & SUITES
(717)533-7054

Motel
$40-$300

Address: 43 W Areba Ave 17033 **Location:** Just s of US 422 on SR 743, just w. Located in a residential area. **Facility:** 22 units, some two bedrooms and kitchens. 2 stories (no elevator), exterior corridors. **Pool(s):** heated indoor. **Featured Amenity:** continental breakfast. *(See ad this page.)*

LOCATED IN THE HEART OF HERSHEY, WITHIN HALF A MILE FROM HERSHEYPARK.

SPRINGHILL SUITES BY MARRIOTT HERSHEY
(717)583-2222

Hotel $90-$332 **Address:** 115 Museum Dr 17033 **Location:** Jct US 322, 3.4 mi nw on SR 39 (Hersheypark Dr). **Facility:** 80 units. 3 stories, interior corridors. **Pool(s):** heated indoor. **Activities:** hot tub, exercise room. **Guest Services:** valet and coin laundry, area transportation.

AAA Benefit:
Members save 5% or more!

WHITE ROSE MOTEL
717/533-9876

Motel $59-$155 **Address:** 1060 E Chocolate Ave 17033 **Location:** Jct SR 743, 1.3 mi e on US 422. **Facility:** 25 units, some cottages. 2 stories (no elevator), exterior corridors. **Terms:** 4 day cancellation notice-fee imposed. **Pool(s):** heated outdoor. **Guest Services:** coin laundry.

▼ See AAA listing this page ▼

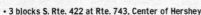

WHERE TO EAT

THE CHOCOLATE AVENUE GRILL   717/835-0888
▼▼ American. Casual Dining. $9-$28 **AAA Inspector Notes:** Located near Hersheypark, this is a great place for the family to grab dinner or lunch. The menu includes both vegetarian and vegan options and ranges from lobster risotto to homemade lasagna. The warm, friendly staff is more than happy to assist with any requests and provide recommendations for the area. **Features:** full bar, patio dining. **Address:** 114 W Chocolate Ave 17033 **Location:** On US 422; center. Ⓛ Ⓓ CALL ⓂⓂ

THE CIRCULAR   717/534-8800
▼▼▼ ▼▼▼ ▼▼▼
Continental
Fine Dining
$23-$49

AAA Inspector Notes: This dining room has an elegant, contemporary Mediterranean character, with breathtaking views of the gardens and reflecting pools. Staff provide an iPad for guests to search the expansive wine list to help assist with the perfect pairing. The kitchen expertly prepares sophisticated American and Continental specialties, enhanced by the sinfully delicious chocolate desserts. Schedule may vary seasonally. **Features:** full bar, Sunday brunch, happy hour. **Reservations:** suggested. **Address:** 100 Hotel Rd 17033 **Location:** Jct US 322, 2.3 mi n on SR 39 (Hersheypark Dr); in The Hotel Hershey. **Parking:** on-site and valet. Ⓑ Ⓛ Ⓓ

DAFNOS ITALIAN GRILLE   717/533-8999
▼ Italian. Casual Dining. $6-$18 **AAA Inspector Notes:** Just minutes from Hersheypark and in the midst of several lodgings, this Italian restaurant employs friendly staffers who serve traditional favorites including lasagna, veal parmigiana and minestrone soup. **Features:** beer & wine. **Address:** 1190 W Chocolate Ave 17036 **Location:** Jct US 322 and 422. Ⓛ Ⓓ CALL ⓂⓂ

DEVON SEAFOOD GRILL   717/508-5460
▼▼▼ Seafood. Fine Dining. $11-$55 **AAA Inspector Notes:** A newer addition to the city's dining scene, this place offers fresh seafood and dry-aged steaks with a great wine selection. Knowledgeable servers make a meal here a memorable one. **Features:** full bar, Sunday brunch, happy hour. **Reservations:** suggested, for dinner & Sunday brunch. **Address:** 27 W Chocolate Ave 17033 **Location:** Corner of Park and W Chocolate aves; downtown.
Ⓛ Ⓓ CALL ⓂⓂ

FENICCI'S OF HERSHEY   717/533-7159
▼▼ ▼▼
Italian
Casual Dining
$9-$30

AAA Inspector Notes: The menu lines up a large selection of dishes served in large portions. Guests who can finish the lasagna earn a certificate of accomplishment. **Features:** full bar, happy hour. **Address:** 102 W Chocolate Ave 17033 **Location:** Center. **Parking:** street only.

Menu on AAA.com Ⓛ Ⓓ Ⓛ̲ᴬᵀᴱ

THE HERSHEY PANTRY   717/533-7505
▼▼ American. Casual Dining. $11-$23 **AAA Inspector Notes:** Convenient to Hersheypark, this busy restaurant serves breakfast, lunch and dinner in a casual atmosphere. Breads and desserts are homemade and hearty specials are featured daily. **Features:** Sunday brunch. **Address:** 801 E Chocolate Ave 17033 **Location:** 0.9 mi e on US 422. Ⓑ Ⓛ Ⓓ

SODA JERK DINER & DAIRY BAR   717/566-7707
▼ American. Casual Dining. $5-$17 **AAA Inspector Notes:** The 1950s and '60s come alive at this diner. Sit back and enjoy the oldies but goodies playing in the background. The menu offers hamburgers, hot dogs, milk shakes and ice cream sundaes. However, they also branch out with some of their specialty Greek dishes. **Address:** 403 E Main St 17036 **Location:** 1.2 mi nw of jct US 322, 422 and SR 39 (Hersheypark Dr). Ⓑ Ⓛ Ⓓ

TREVI 5   717/534-8800
▼▼▼▼ Italian. Casual Dining. $18-$35 **AAA Inspector Notes:** This stylish café provides a casual, comfortable atmosphere. You can dine inside or out on the terrace, shaded by umbrellas and offering sweeping views of the countryside. The menu offers a good variety of pasta dishes, gourmet pizza, veal and fresh fish. Save room for one of the distinctive chocolate desserts. **Features:** full bar, patio dining. **Reservations:** suggested, 9/6-6/30. **Address:** 100 Hotel Rd 17033 **Location:** Jct US 322, 2.3 mi n on SR 39 (Hersheypark Dr); in The Hotel Hershey. **Parking:** on-site and valet. Ⓛ Ⓓ

WHAT IF...OF HERSHEY   717/533-5858
▼▼▼▼ International. Casual Dining. $10-$33 **AAA Inspector Notes:** After an exciting day at Hersheypark, visitors often stop in at this restaurant located just underneath the Howard Johnson hotel. Patrons should not walk away hungry after sampling any of a wide range of steaks, pasta dishes, specialty entrées and freshly made desserts. **Features:** full bar. **Reservations:** suggested, for dinner. **Address:** 845 E Chocolate Ave 17033 **Location:** 1 mi e on US 422; in Howard Johnson Inn. Ⓛ Ⓓ

HESSTON (G-6) elev. 744'

SEVEN POINTS MARINA, *PRINCESS* **LAKE CRUISES,** departing from 5922 Seven Points Marina Dr., offers narrated 2-hour sightseeing cruises on Raystown Lake featuring wildlife sightings and historical points of interest. Specialty and dinner cruises with some narration also are offered.

Hours: Sightseeing cruise departs daily at 1:30 mid-June to mid-Aug.; Sat.-Sun. early May to early Oct. Phone ahead to confirm schedule. **Cost:** Sightseeing fare $15; $14 (ages 65+); $7.50 (ages 4-12); $7 (ages 65+ Thurs., late June-late Aug.). A buy-one, get-one ticket (equal or lesser value) free program is offered Tues., mid-June to mid-Aug. **Phone:** (814) 658-3074.

HOLLIDAYSBURG pop. 5,791

THE DREAM FAMILY RESTAURANT   814/696-3384
▼▼ American. Casual Dining. $7-$20 **AAA Inspector Notes:** Bring the whole clan to this restaurant for a tasty, like-home meal. The family-style spot is a great place to enjoy daily specials of roasted turkey, beef and pork, as well as Italian pasta dishes, while you have some good conversation. Tempting aromas from the on-site bakery remind you to save room for the freshly baked breads, pies, cookies and apple dumplings. **Address:** 1500 Allegheny St 16648 **Location:** SR 36, 0.6 mi e on US 22. Ⓑ Ⓛ Ⓓ

HOLTWOOD (I-9) elev. 387'

• **Part of Pennsylvania Dutch Country area — see map p. 220**

MUDDY RUN INFORMATION CENTER, 172 W. Bethesda Church Rd., offers exhibits that highlight resource conservation and information about wildlife, nuclear waste management and power generation. Audiovisual and nature programs also are presented. The center is part of a 700-acre Muddy Run recreation area; nature programs are offered through the park. *See Recreation Areas Chart.* **Time:** Allow 1 hour minimum. **Hours:** Fri.-Sat. 8-3, Apr.-Sept. Boating is permitted mid-Mar. to mid-Oct. **Cost:** Free. **Phone:** (717) 284-5850. 🅰 ❌ 🎒 ⛺

HOMESTEAD (G-2) pop. 3,165, elev. 787'
• Hotels & Restaurants map & index p. 348
• Part of Pittsburgh area — see map p. 326

Homestead, which lies in the Rivers of Steel National Heritage Area in southwestern Pennsylvania, was the setting for a labor strike that held national interest in 1892. The Amalgamated Association of Iron and Steel Workers held out against Carnegie Steel Co. from June 29-Nov. 21 despite the arrival of 300 Pinkerton guards by barge on July 6; 12 men lost their lives in the confrontation between the guards and the laborers, families and supporters. In the end the strikers lost. Visitors can still see remnants of the steel era like the pump house and smokestacks, but the main draw now is the Monongahela River waterfront's shopping and entertainment.

Self-guiding tours: The "History to Go: Homestead Walking Tour" utilizes portable DVD players to guide visitors through the community and mill site. Archival footage is used throughout. Part of the route overlaps with the Steel Valley Trail, which runs along the Monongahela River and contains interpretive signs. Portable DVD players may be rented or purchased from the Rivers of Steel Visitor Center in the Bost Building, 623 E. Eighth Ave., Mon.-Sat. 10-3; phone (412) 464-4020. Steel Valley Trail brochures are usually available as well.

Shopping areas: The Waterfront is a shopping and entertainment locale that has taken over the land once occupied by the Homestead steel mill.

BOST BUILDING, 623 E. Eighth Ave., serves as the visitor center for the Rivers of Steel National Heritage Area. The 1892 building was used as the Amalgamated Association of Iron and Steel Workers Union headquarters during the lockout and strike that same year at the Homestead steel plant. Rooms that were used by union leaders during the strike have been restored and there are changing exhibits related to the region's cultural and industrial heritage. **Time:** Allow 1 hour minimum. **Hours:** Mon.-Fri. 10-4. Closed major holidays. **Cost:** $3; $1 (ages 0-14). **Phone:** (412) 464-4020.

COURTYARD BY MARRIOTT PITTSBURGH-WATERFRONT
(412)462-7301 **90**

WWWW **Hotel** $146-$240 **Address:** 401 W Waterfront Dr 15120 **Location:** Just off Hi-Level Bridge. Located in Waterfront Town Square. **Facility:** 94 units. 4 stories, interior corridors. **Pool(s):** heated indoor. **Activities:** hot tub, exercise room. **Guest Services:** valet and coin laundry.

AAA Benefit:
Members save 5% or more!

Add AAA or CAA Associate Members to bring home the benefits of membership

---

HAMPTON INN & SUITES PITTSBURGH WATERFRONT
(412)462-4226 **89**

Hotel
$149-$219

AAA Benefit:
Members save 5% or more!

Address: 301 W Waterfront Dr 15120 **Location:** Waterfront. Just off Hi-Level Bridge. Located in Waterfront Town Square. **Facility:** 113 units. 5 stories, interior corridors. **Terms:** 1-7 night minimum stay, cancellation fee imposed. **Amenities:** _Some:_ video games. **Pool(s):** heated indoor. **Activities:** exercise room. **Guest Services:** valet and coin laundry. **Featured Amenity:** breakfast buffet.

WHERE TO EAT

MITCHELL'S FISH MARKET   412/476-8844 **66**

WWWW Seafood. Casual Dining. $17-$30 **AAA Inspector Notes:** A variety of fresh, never-frozen fish is flown in daily, and market availability determines the daily specials. Diners may order fish grilled, broiled, blackened or steamed in the Shanghai-style with ginger, spinach and sticky rice. Among other choices are steak, pasta and chicken selections. **Features:** full bar. **Reservations:** suggested. **Address:** 185 W Waterfront Dr 15120 **Location:** Just off Hi-Level Bridge; in Waterfront Town Square.

P.F. CHANG'S CHINA BISTRO   412/464-0640 **67**

WWW Chinese. Fine Dining. $10-$25 **AAA Inspector Notes:** Trendy, upscale decor provides a pleasant backdrop for New Age Chinese dining. Appetizers, soups and salads are a meal by themselves. Vegetarian plates and sides, noodles, chow meins, chicken and meat dishes are created from exotic, fresh ingredients. **Features:** full bar. **Reservations:** suggested, for dinner. **Address:** 148 W Bridge St 15120 **Location:** Just off Hi-Level Bridge; in Waterfront Town Square.

HONESDALE (D-11) pop. 4,480, elev. 982'
• Restaurants p. 158
• Part of Pocono Mountains Area — see map p. 371

Established in 1828 as a terminal for canal barges carrying coal to New York markets, Honesdale was the site of the first use of a commercial steam locomotive in the United States. Imported from England, the locomotive Stourbridge Lion made its trial run on Aug. 8, 1829. Too heavy for the rails, it was withdrawn from service. A full-size replica can be seen in the Wayne County Historical Society Museum (see attraction listing).

Stourbridge Line Rail Excursions are offered by the chamber of commerce during holiday seasons, beginning in spring for the Easter holiday. Departure times vary; phone (570) 253-1960 or (800) 433-9008 for schedule updates.

Chamber of the Northern Poconos: 32 Commercial St., Suite 200, Honesdale, PA 18431. **Phone:** (570) 253-1960.

WAYNE COUNTY HISTORICAL SOCIETY MUSEUM, 810 Main St., is housed in the 1860 former office of the D&H Canal Co. Exhibits include a life-size replica of the first commercial steam engine, the Stourbridge Lion; a Native American archeology collection; and changing displays about the history of Wayne County. Also on-site is a research library. **Hours:** Wed.-Sat. 10-4, (also Sun. Memorial Day-Columbus Day) late Apr.-Dec. 31. Closed Thanksgiving and Christmas. Phone ahead to confirm schedule. **Cost:** $5; free (children and students with ID). **Phone:** (570) 253-3240.

BISTRO 1202   570/253-3290

American Casual Dining $7-$25

AAA Inspector Notes: In a renovated old hotel, this bistro-style restaurant offers a wide selection including wings, baby back barbecue ribs, pasta, steaks, calamari and caprese salad. **Features:** full bar. **Address:** 1202 Main St 18431 **Location:** Center; in Hotel Wayne. **Parking:** on-site and street. L D

HOPEWELL FURNACE NATIONAL HISTORIC SITE (A-8) elev. 472'

Hopewell Furnace National Historic Site is about 5 miles south of Birdsboro on SR 345 and also is accessible via the Morgantown exit off the Pennsylvania Turnpike, using SRs 23 and 345. The 848-acre site is one of the finest examples of an early American 18th- and 19th-century iron-making community.

Englishman William Bird was prominent in the early iron industry in Pennsylvania. His son Mark built Hopewell Furnace on French Creek in 1771. Around the furnace developed a small industrial settlement where many of the employees lived in tenant houses. A resident manager lived on the site in the ironmaster's mansion.

The furnace cast pig iron, hollowware, stoves and many other items; during the Revolutionary War it produced cannon and shot. The furnace operated until 1883, when more advanced technology made it unprofitable.

Many of the structures have been restored and refurnished. The waterwheel, blast machinery, bridge house, cooling shed, barn, store, ironmaster's mansion and tenant houses can be seen. The ruin of an 1853 anthracite furnace has been uncovered and stabilized.

A visitor center features an audiovisual program and an exhibit area with original iron castings produced at Hopewell Furnace and tools associated with the operation of 18th- and 19th-century cold-blast charcoal furnaces. Allow 2 hours minimum. Daily 9-5, mid-June to late Aug.; Wed.-Sun. and some holidays 9-5, rest of year. Closed Jan. 1, Martin Luther King Jr. Day, Presidents Day, Thanksgiving and Christmas. Admission free. Phone (610) 582-8773.

Keep a current AAA/CAA
Road Atlas in every vehicle

HOPWOOD pop. 2,090

HOPWOOD MOTEL OF UNIONTOWN   724/437-7591

Motel. Rates not provided. **Address:** 1151 National Pike (US 40 E) 15401 **Location:** On US 40 business route, 1 mi e of Uniontown: US 40/119 (George C Marshall Pkwy) exit Hopwood, 0.7 mi w. **Facility:** 15 units. 1 story, exterior corridors.

WHERE TO EAT

THE SUN PORCH   724/439-5734

American. Family Dining. $6-$16 **AAA Inspector Notes:** The bright, cheerful restaurant is known for its evening buffet, which lays out a good array of traditional, home-style foods. Many types of pies and cakes, as well as ice cream sundaes, are sure to satisfy a sweet tooth. **Features:** Sunday brunch. **Address:** 1141 National Pike 15445 **Location:** US 40/119 (George C Marshall Pkwy) exit Hopwood, 0.5 mi e. L D

HORSHAM (A-11) pop. 14,842, elev. 249'
• Hotels & Restaurants map & index p. 274
• Part of Philadelphia area — see map p. 230

SAVE **GRAEME PARK**, .5 mi. w. off US 611 at 859 County Line Rd., was the home of Sir William Keith, the provincial governor of Pennsylvania 1717-26. Built during his years as governor, the well-preserved stone house is a fine example of 18th-century architecture. The home is furnished with period pieces and contains original paneling and flooring. Writer Elizabeth Graeme Fergusson also lived in the house 1739-93.

Time: Allow 1 hour minimum. **Hours:** Fri.-Sat. 10-4, Sun. noon-4. Last tour begins 1 hour before closing. Closed Jan. 1, Easter, day after Thanksgiving and Christmas. **Cost:** Grounds free. House tour $6; $5 (ages 65+); $3 (ages 3-11). **Phone:** (215) 343-0965.

DAYS INN-HORSHAM/PHILADELPHIA
(215)674-2500   25

Hotel $59-$130

Address: 245 Easton Rd 19044 **Location:** I-276 (Pennsylvania Tpke) exit 343 (SR 611), 1 mi n. Located in a commercial area. **Facility:** 171 units. 4 stories, interior corridors. **Amenities:** safes. **Activities:** exercise room. **Guest Services:** valet and coin laundry. **Featured Amenity:** continental breakfast.

10% off for AAA Members. Free continental breakfast. Walk to restaurants. Kids stay free.

EXTENDED STAY AMERICA-PHILADELPHIA/HORSHAM
215/784-9045   27

Extended Stay Hotel. Rates not provided. **Address:** 114 Welsh Rd 19044 **Location:** I-276 (Pennsylvania Tpke) exit 343 (SR 611), s toward Jenkintown, 0.6 mi w on Maryland Rd, 0.5 mi sw on Computer Ave, then just n. **Facility:** 116 efficiencies. 3 stories, interior corridors. **Guest Services:** coin laundry.

(See map & index p. 274.)

RESIDENCE INN BY MARRIOTT-WILLOW GROVE
(215)443-7330 **26**

◆◆◆◆◆ **Extended Stay Hotel**
$139-$229 **Address:** 3 Walnut Grove Dr
19044 **Location:** I-276 (Pennsylvania
Tpke) exit 343, 1 mi n on Easton Rd,
then 1.3 mi w on Dresher Rd. Located in
Pennsylvania Business Campus. **Facility:** 118 units, some two bedrooms, efficiencies and kitchens. 2 stories (no elevator), exterior corridors. **Terms:** check-in 4 pm. **Pool(s):** heated outdoor. **Activities:**
exercise room. **Guest Services:** valet and coin laundry.

AAA Benefit:
Members save 5% or more!

CALL ⬛M 🏊 BIZ 🛜 ✕ 🍴 📶 📺 / SOME UNITS 💲🔔

LEE'S HOAGIE HOUSE OF HORSHAM   215/674-8000

◆ Sandwiches. Quick Serve. $6-$17 **AAA Inspector Notes:**
Nosh on your favorite wraps, hoagies and cheesesteaks at this quick-
bite spot that has multiple locations in the Pennsylvania area. Those
on the go will have the ability to call their orders in ahead of time or
even order online. Once inside, enjoy such tasty options such as
Lee's Italian hoagie with Genoa salami, pepper ham and capocollo or
the ultimate chicken wrap with bacon, honey mustard and American
cheese. **Address:** 870 Easton Rd 19044 **Location:** I-276 (Pennsylvania Tpke) exit 343, 2.8 mi n. L D

OTTO'S BRAUHAUS   215/675-1864 **62**

◆◆◆ German. Casual Dining. $6-$25 **AAA Inspector Notes:**
This restaurant focuses on steaks, seafood and a variety of German
favorites such as schnitzel, spaetzle and sauerbraten. Inside you will
find a large dining room with decoratively dressed servers. **Features:**
full bar. **Reservations:** suggested, weekends. **Address:** 233 Easton
Rd 19044 **Location:** I-276 (Pennsylvania Tpke) exit 343, 1 mi n.

B L D LATE

HOWARD (F-6) pop. 720, elev. 669'

CURTIN VILLAGE is at 251 Curtin Village Rd. The
1830 Federal-style mansion was the home of Ro-
land Curtin, owner of the Eagle Iron Works. Curtin's
30,000 acres provided products for making iron as
well as food for the entire community, and the village
was self-sufficient until the Eagle Iron Works burned
and closed down in 1921, ending 111 years of production. Guided 40-minute and 1-hour tours are
available. **Hours:** Sat. 10-4, Sun. 11-4, Memorial
Day-Oct. 31. **Cost:** $4; $1 (ages 1-11). Phone
ahead to confirm rates. **Phone:** (814) 355-1982 or
(814) 357-6981.

HUMMELSTOWN (H-8) pop. 4,538, elev. 384'

SAVE **INDIAN ECHO CAVERNS,** off US 322, then 3
mi. w., offers a 45-minute guided, narrated
tour amid the natural beauty of stalagmites, stalactites, columns, flowstone and lakes. The caverns are
electronically lighted, contain level pathways and
maintain a constant temperature of 52 degrees
Fahrenheit. Visitors may pan for gemstones at Gem
Mill Junction or interact with goats in the petting zoo.
Hayrides also are offered in the fall.

Guests who cannot walk through the caverns can
enjoy a non-walking video tour. **Note:** Backpacks
and large bags are prohibited inside the caverns.
Two covered picnic pavilions are available. **Hours:**
Daily 9-6, Memorial Day-Labor Day; 10-4, rest of
year. Closed Jan. 1, Thanksgiving and Christmas.

Cost: $14; $12 (ages 62+); $8 (ages 3-11). Phone
ahead to confirm rates. **Phone:** (717) 566-8131.
🅰

HUNTINGDON (G-6) pop. 7,093, elev. 630'
• Hotels p. 160 • Restaurants p. 160

Near Huntingdon is Raystown Lake *(see Recreation Areas Chart),* the largest man-made lake
wholly within Pennsylvania. Recreation available at
the lake includes hunting, boating, camping, swimming and fishing, especially for smallmouth and lar-
gemouth bass, striped bass and lake trout. Wildlife
inhabiting the area includes deer, turkeys, grouse
and squirrels.

ISETT ACRES MUSEUM, 2.1 mi. W on SR 22, 2.5
mi. N on Stone Creek Ridge Rd., showcases three
buildings brimming with an array of historical items
related to 19th- and 20th-century life in Huntingdon
and the vicinity. Items include farm equipment and
clothing, toys and musical instruments. **Time:** Allow
1 hour minimum. **Hours:** Mon.-Sat. 8-5, Sun.
noon-5, Apr.-Nov.; Mon.-Fri. 8-5, rest of year. Closed
major holidays. **Cost:** $6; $4 (students with ID).
Cash only. **Phone:** (814) 643-9600. GT 🅰

JUNIATA COLLEGE, n. edge of town, was founded
in 1876. The L.A. Beeghly Library has an extensive
collection of Pennsylvania-German printed materials. The Juniata College Museum of Art, at 17th
and Moore sts. in Carnegie Hall, presents regular
exhibits of paintings, prints and photographs. The
Cloister dormitory, built in 1928, exemplifies the
Pennsylvania-German style of architecture.

Hours: Library Mon.-Thurs. 8 a.m.-1 a.m., Fri.
8-8, Sat. 10-9:45, Sun. noon-1 a.m. Museum Mon.-
Fri. 10-4, Sat. noon-4, Sept.-Apr.; Wed.-Fri. noon-4,
rest of year. Closed school holidays and breaks.
Cost: Free. **Phone:** (814) 641-3000, or (814)
641-3505 for the museum.

SAVE **LINCOLN CAVERNS,** 3 mi. w. on US 22 at
7703 William Penn Hwy., offers 1-hour interpretive tours through two crystal caverns that display a variety of formations. Children may pan for
gemstones in a sluice. Nature trails also are
available.

Cavern temperature is 52 degrees Fahrenheit. A
light jacket is recommended. **Hours:** Guided tours
are offered daily 9-6, July 1-Labor Day; daily 9-5,
Memorial Day weekend-June 30; daily 9-4, Apr.
1-late May and early Sept.-Oct. 31 (also some extended weekends in Oct.); Thurs.-Mon. 9-4, in Mar.
and Nov.; Sat.-Sun. 11-3, in Dec.; by appointment
rest of year. **Cost:** Tour $13.98; $12.98 (ages 65+);
$7.98 (ages 4-12). Tour and gem panning $13.48
(ages 4-12, mid-Mar. to mid-Nov. only). Phone
ahead to verify rates. **Phone:** (814) 643-0268.
🅰 🅰

SWIGART MUSEUM, 4 mi. e. on US 22 at 12031
William Penn Hwy., contains a rotating collection of

nearly 150 antique and rare automobiles with 30 to 35 vehicles on display at any given time. The collection includes two Tuckers, a 1920 Carroll, a 1916 Scripps-Booth and a 1936 Duesenberg as well as Herbie the Love Bug, a 1960s Volkswagen Beetle that appeared in the Walt Disney movie.

Domestic and foreign license plates, name plates, antique toys, horns, lights and other accessories also are displayed. **Time:** Allow 1 hour minimum. **Hours:** Daily 10-5 (also Fri. 5-6), Memorial Day-Oct. 31. **Cost:** $7; $6.50 (ages 65+); $3 (ages 6-12). **Phone:** (814) 643-0885.

COMFORT INN   (814)643-1600

Hotel
$63-$159

Address: 100 S 4th St 16652 **Location:** I-99 exit 48, 8.8 mi on SR 453, then 9.8 mi on US 22 and S 4th St; just off US 22. **Facility:** 69 units. 3 stories, interior corridors. **Pool(s):** heated indoor. **Activities:** limited exercise equipment. **Guest Services:** coin laundry.

[SAVE] [↑↑] CALL [&M] [≈] [BIZ] [≈]
[⊟] [⊡] [⊡] / SOME UNITS [S⊞]

HUNTINGDON MOTOR INN   814/643-1133

▼▼ **Motel.** Rates not provided. **Address:** 6920 Motor Inn Dr 16652 **Location:** On US 22 (William Penn Hwy) at SR 26. Located in a quiet area. **Facility:** 48 units. 1-2 stories (no elevator), exterior corridors. [↑↑] [≈] [⊟] [⊡] / SOME UNITS [S⊞] [⊡]

THE INN AT SOLVANG   814/643-3035

▼▼▼ **Bed & Breakfast.** Rates not provided. **Address:** 10611 Standing Stone Rd 16652 **Location:** On SR 26, 3.4 mi n. **Facility:** The southern Colonial home, situated in the privacy of a country estate, features classical furnishings like Persian rugs, murals and period artwork. 5 units. 3 stories (no elevator), interior/exterior corridors. **Terms:** age restrictions may apply. **Activities:** massage. **Guest Services:** valet and coin laundry. [≈] [X]

THE MILL STONE MANOR   (814)643-0108

▼▼ ▼▼ **Motel** $49-$100 **Address:** 11979 William Penn Hwy 16652 **Location:** On US 22 (William Penn Hwy); 3 mi n of downtown. **Facility:** 27 units, some two bedrooms. 2 stories (no elevator), interior/exterior corridors. *Bath:* shower only. **Parking:** winter plug-ins. **Terms:** 3 day cancellation notice-fee imposed. **Activities:** limited exercise equipment. **Guest Services:** coin laundry.

[≈] [X] [⊡] / SOME UNITS [S⊞] [⊟] [⊡]

WHERE TO EAT

HOSS'S FAMILY STEAK & SEA   814/643-6939

▼▼ Steak. Casual Dining. $7-$28 **AAA Inspector Notes:** Folks can bring the whole family to enjoy the restaurant's 100-item salad bar, homemade soups and bread, steaks, fresh seafood and chicken entrees. A children's menu is available. **Address:** 9016 William Penn Hwy 16652 **Location:** On US 22 (William Penn Hwy), just e of jct SR 26. [L] [D]

HUNTINGDON VALLEY
• **Hotels & Restaurants map & index p. 274**
• **Part of Philadelphia area — see map p. 230**

WHITE ELEPHANT RESTAURANT   215/663-1495 [85]

▼▼ ▼ Thai. Casual Dining. $9-$25 **AAA Inspector Notes:** Elephant paintings and sculptures and many plants turn the storefront restaurant into an inviting little getaway. Fresh herbs and spices such as lemongrass, basil, mint, galangal, cilantro and kaffir lime leaves are employed in innovative, flavorful, exotic dishes that range from mild to hot. A good choice is heavenly fish: pan-seared Chilean sea bass filled with spinach, crabmeat and onion and served with Thai classic tamarind sauce. Bring-your-own-bottle wine service is available. **Reservations:** suggested, weekends. **Address:** 759 Huntingdon Pike 19006 **Location:** Jct SR 232 and 63, 2.7 mi s on SR 232; in Huntingdon Valley Shopping Center. [🚗] Fox Chase, 274.

[L] [D] [🚲]

INDIANA (INDIANA COUNTY) (G-3)
pop. 13,975, elev. 1,310'

Indiana was founded in 1805 when George Clymer of Philadelphia, a signer of the Declaration of Independence, donated 250 acres of land for county buildings. Later, before the Civil War, Indiana became an important station on the Underground Railroad. In more recent history, the town was the birthplace and childhood home of actor Jimmy Stewart. A bronze statue of the actor, unveiled for his 75th birthday, stands on the lawn of the Indiana County Courthouse on Philadelphia Street. Crosswalk audio clips at 7th and 9th streets and Philadelphia and 9th streets feature safety tips and personal tidbits from Jimmy Stewart (thanks to a voice impersonator).

Northern Indiana County is Amish country. Horse-drawn buggies are common sights, as are Christmas trees—more than one million trees per year are marketed by local growers in the area.

Historic buildings can be seen on the campus of Indiana University of Pennsylvania. John Sutton Hall, built in 1875, houses University Museum's changing art exhibits and displays; phone (724) 357-2397.

Year-round recreational opportunities include hunting, fishing and boating. For information about game areas phone the Pennsylvania Game Commission Southwest Regional office at (724)

238-9523. For fishing information and boating regulations phone the Pennsylvania Fish and Boat Commission regional office at (814) 443-9841. Yellow Creek State Park *(see Recreation Areas Chart)* is about 12 miles east of town. The Ghost Town, Hoodlebug and West Penn trails offer nearly 65 miles of rails-to-trails that give hikers and bikers the opportunity to pass through scenic areas, historic sites and other natural attractions. Maps are available at the Indiana County Tourist Bureau; phone (724) 463-7505. The Indiana County Parks & Trails office, 1128 Blue Spruce Rd. in Blue Spruce Park, has brochures about the Ghost Town and Hoodlebug trails; phone (724) 463-8636.

Indiana County Tourist Bureau: 2334 Oakland Ave., Suite 68, Indiana, PA 15701. **Phone:** (724) 463-7505.

The office is in Indiana Mall.

Shopping areas: Yarnick Farmers Market, in business for nearly 30 years, is open daily 9-6 at 155 Thomas Covered Bridge Rd. Indiana County Farmers Market, downtown at 8th and Church streets, Sat. 9-noon and at Wayne Avenue across from the Kovalchick Complex Wed. 3:30-5:30. The town also features antique and specialty shops.

THE JIMMY STEWART MUSEUM, 835 Philadelphia St. at jct. 9th St., on the third floor of the Indiana Free Library, is dedicated to the life and career of film icon Jimmy Stewart. Displays include original movie posters and photo stills; family photographs; and items reflecting his personal, public and military life. A film is shown in a 50-seat theater.

Time: Allow 2 hours minimum. **Hours:** Mon.-Sat. 10-4, Sun. noon-4. Closed federal holidays. **Cost:** $7; $6 (ages 62+, military with ID and students with ID); $5 (ages 7-17). **Phone:** (724) 349-6112 or (800) 835-4669.

BEST WESTERN INDIANA INN   724/349-4600

 Hotel
Rates not provided

AAA Benefit: Members save up to 20%!

Address: 111 Plaza Rd 15701 **Location:** US 422 exit SR 286, just n. **Facility:** 67 units. 3 stories, interior corridors. **Activities:** exercise room. **Guest Services:** valet laundry.

COMFORT INN INDIANA   (724)465-7000

Hotel $110-$150 **Address:** 1350 Indian Springs Rd 15701 **Location:** US 422 exit Oakland Ave, 0.7 mi e. **Facility:** 72 units. 4 stories, interior corridors. **Amenities:** safes. **Pool(s):** heated indoor. **Activities:** limited exercise equipment. **Guest Services:** valet laundry.

Discover a wealth of savings and offers
on the AAA/CAA travel websites

HAMPTON INN INDIANA   (724)349-7700

Contemporary Hotel $149-$159 **Address:** 1275 Indian Springs Rd 15701 **Location:** US 422 exit Oakland Ave, 1.1 mi e. **Facility:** 72 units. 3 stories, interior corridors. **Terms:** 1-7 night minimum stay, cancellation fee imposed. **Pool(s):** heated indoor. **Activities:** hot tub, exercise room. **Guest Services:** valet and coin laundry.

AAA Benefit: Members save 5% or more!

PARK INN BY RADISSON   (724)463-3561

Hotel $109-$159 **Address:** 1395 Wayne Ave 15701 **Location:** US 422 exit Wayne Ave, 1 mi n. **Facility:** 158 units. 2 stories (no elevator), interior/exterior corridors. **Terms:** cancellation fee imposed. **Pool(s):** heated indoor. **Activities:** game room, exercise room. **Guest Services:** valet and coin laundry.

WHERE TO EAT

BENJAMIN'S   724/465-4446

Mediterranean. Casual Dining. $7-$29 **AAA Inspector Notes:** The rooms of this Victorian house have been turned into quaint, cozy dining rooms in which locals are served flavorful seafood, chicken, beef and pasta, as well as gourmet pizza. Other options include chicken piccata, artichoke tilapia, grilled flat-iron steak and crab Alfredo linguine. Lunch selections include burgers, wraps, sandwiches, salads and pizza. **Features:** full bar. **Reservations:** suggested. **Address:** 458 Philadelphia St 15701 **Location:** Center.

INDUSTRY pop. 1,835
• Part of Pittsburgh area — see map p. 326

WILLOWS INN   724/643-4500

Motel. Rates not provided. **Address:** 1830 Beaver Midland Rd 15052 **Location:** I-376 exit 38 (State St), 4 mi w on SR 68. **Facility:** 30 units. 1 story, exterior corridors. **Dining:** Willows Inn Family Smorgasbord, see separate listing. **Guest Services:** valet laundry.

WHERE TO EAT

WILLOWS INN FAMILY SMORGASBORD   724/643-4500

American. Family Dining. $6-$10 **AAA Inspector Notes:** Enjoy casual family dining featuring a large buffet which includes a salad bar, dessert bar and good selection of meats and vegetables. Certain days feature dinner themes such as Italian or seafood. This restaurant offers a great value for large families. **Features:** full bar, Sunday brunch. **Address:** 1830 Beaver Midland Rd 15052 **Location:** I-376 exit 38 (State St), 4 mi w on SR 68; in Willows Inn.

INTERCOURSE (H-10) pop. 1,274, elev. 436'
• **Hotels p. 162** • **Restaurants p. 162**
• **Attractions map p. 221**
• **Hotels & Restaurants map & index p. 225**
• **Part of Pennsylvania Dutch Country area — see map p. 220**

In the heart of Pennsylvania Dutch Country, Intercourse was founded in 1754. First called Cross Keys after a local tavern, the town was renamed in 1814. Its name is believed to have evolved from either the entrance to the old racecourse (the Entercourse) just outside of town or from the joining, or intercourse, of the Old Kings Highway and the Wilmington-Erie Road.

162   INTERCOURSE, PA

(See map & index p. 225.)

Shopping areas: Amish and Mennonite crafts, including such items as quilts, toys and tablecloths, can be found at the Old Country Store on Old Philadelphia Pike. Across the street Kitchen Kettle Village contains more than 40 stores offering Amish and other handmade items as well as antiques, food and furniture.

INTERCOURSE CANNING CO. is e. on SR 772 to 13 Center St. Newport Rd. Jams, pickled vegetables, peanut butter and sauces are produced at this factory. Visitors may watch canning operations through a small observation window. **Time:** Allow 30 minutes minimum. **Hours:** Wed.-Sat. 11-3. **Cost:** Free. **Phone:** (717) 768-0156.

THE INN & SPA AT INTERCOURSE VILLAGE   717/768-2626 **37**

Historic Bed & Breakfast. Rates not provided. **Address:** 3542 Old Philadelphia Pike 17534 **Location:** Just s of SR 772; in Intercourse Village. **Facility:** Guest rooms at this restored 1909 home have fireplaces and Victorian furnishings, and suites offer a modern twist on traditional Amish Country style. 12 units. 1-3 stories (no elevator), interior/exterior corridors. **Terms:** age restrictions may apply. **Activities:** spa.

THE INN AT KITCHEN KETTLE VILLAGE   (717)768-8261 **35**

Country Inn $99-$270 **Address:** 3529 Old Philadelphia Pike 17534 **Location:** Jct SR 772 and 340. Located in a complex of tourist-related shops. **Facility:** Set in the quaint Kettle Village, where you can pick up traditional Pennsylvania Dutch wares, this inn's spacious guest rooms offer comfortable, modern furnishings. 17 units, some two bedrooms and kitchens. 1-2 stories, interior/exterior corridors. **Terms:** cancellation fee imposed. **Dining:** The Kling House Restaurant, see separate listing.

TRAVELERS REST MOTEL   (717)768-8731 **34**

Motel $76-$126 **Address:** 3701 Old Philadelphia Pike (Rt 340) 17534 **Location:** 0.5 mi e on SR 340. **Facility:** 40 units. 1 story, exterior corridors. **Terms:** closed 12/13-2/11, cancellation fee imposed. **Activities:** playground.

WHERE TO EAT

THE KLING HOUSE RESTAURANT   717/768-2746 **20**

Regional American. Family Dining. $6-$13 **AAA Inspector Notes:** Originally a stagecoach stop, this restaurant is now located on the grounds of a Pennsylvania Dutch tourist retail village. Intimate dining rooms with country motifs and an enclosed porch overlook the village activity. The menu offers Pennsylvania Dutch cuisine, frequently employing the sauces and relishes of Kitchen Kettle Foods Corporation, which owns the facility. Italian sausage, clam soup and baked chicken pie are favorites. **Address:** 3529 Old Philadelphia Pike 17534 **Location:** Jct SR 772 and 340; in The Inn at Kitchen Kettle Village.

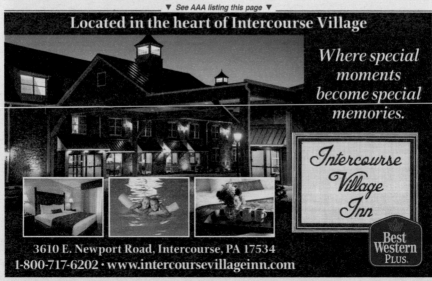

IRVINE (D-3) elev. 1,168'

WILDER MUSEUM: WARREN COUNTY'S HISTORY CENTER is at 51 Erie Ave. Local area history is portrayed through artifacts and antiques. Some featured topics are fashion, furniture, transportation and the oil and lumber industries. Native American artifacts 8,000 years old are included. **Time:** Allow 30 minutes minimum. **Hours:** Tues. and Fri.-Sat. 1-5, mid-May to early Oct. Closed major holidays. **Cost:** Self-guiding tour $1. Guided tour $2. **Phone:** (814) 563-7773 or (814) 723-1795. GT

IRWIN pop. 3,973
• Part of Pittsburgh area — see map p. 326

HOLIDAY INN EXPRESS   (724)861-9000

WWWW Hotel $123-$139 **Address:** 8400 US 30 15642 **Location:** I-76 (Pennsylvania Tpke) exit 67, use access road immediately after toll booth. **Facility:** 62 units. 3 stories, interior corridors. **Activities:** limited exercise equipment. **Guest Services:** valet laundry.

[I+] CALL [&M] [BIZ] [HS] 🛜 🖥 🖭 🖵

WHERE TO EAT

PASQUALINO'S ITALIAN EATERY   724/864-9600

W Italian. Casual Dining. $7-$18 **AAA Inspector Notes:** This casual little spot has been serving diners since 1971. It is highly popular, prides itself on offering the highest-quality fresh ingredients and makes everything from scratch. The restaurant specializes in homemade pizza, classic simple Italian dishes and sandwiches. **Features:** full bar. **Address:** 8711 Rt 30 15642 **Location:** I-76 (Pennsylvania Tpke) exit 67, 0.4 mi w. [L] [D] CALL [&M]

TEDDY'S RESTAURANT   724/863-8180

WW American. Casual Dining. $6-$25 **AAA Inspector Notes:** Family-owned and -operated for more than 20 years, the restaurant employs friendly staffers who serve hot, fresh entrees in a casual, family-focused atmosphere. Those who try french-fried shrimp or stuffed mushroom caps will be asking for more. Homemade desserts are placed on a dessert cart that travels around the dining area. Save room for a sweet surprise. **Features:** full bar. **Reservations:** suggested. **Address:** 8695 Rt 30 15642 **Location:** I-76 (Pennsylvania Tpke) exit 67, 0.4 mi w. [L] [D] CALL [&M]

JAMESTOWN (E-1) pop. 617, elev. 990'

PYMATUNING DEER PARK, .5 mi. e. of US 322 on SR 58E, is a family-owned animal park containing more than 250 exotic and domestic animals, including bears, camels, cougars, llamas, lions, monkeys, panthers, tigers, various birds, wolves, zebras and several species of deer. A highlight is the petting zoo. Visitors can purchase food and feed the animals. Pony and train rides also are available.

Hours: Mon.-Fri. 10-5, Sat.-Sun. and holidays 10-6, Memorial Day weekend-Labor Day; Sat.-Sun. 10-5, day after Labor Day-Sept. 30. **Cost:** $8.95; $7.95 (ages 65+); $6.95 (ages 2-12). Pony or train ride $2; free (ages 0-1). **Phone:** (724) 932-3200.

Say YES to ERS text updates
to stay posted when your
tow truck is on the way

JEANNETTE (H-2) pop. 9,654, elev. 1,033'
• Part of Pittsburgh area — see map p. 326

BUSHY RUN BATTLEFIELD, SR 66N to SR 993W (Bushy Run Rd.), is the site of a military encounter in 1763 between the British and the Native Americans. The British victory at Bushy Run marked the turning point in Pontiac's War. A visitor center displays artifacts and reproductions from the period, and an exhibit describes the battle.

Time: Allow 30 minutes minimum. **Hours:** Battlefield daily 9-5. Visitor center Wed.-Sat. 9-5, Sun. noon-5, May-Oct. Both closed major holidays except Memorial Day, July 4 and Labor Day. **Cost:** $5; $4.50 (ages 65+); $3 (ages 3-11). **Phone:** (724) 527-5584. GT 🏛

MAURO'S RISTORANTE & LOUNGE   724/523-3391

WW Italian. Casual Dining. $8-$20 **AAA Inspector Notes:** When dining at the restaurant, patrons should come with an appetite. Overflowing entrées mean folks won't walk out hungry. The specialty here is pasta, of course, in a variety of shapes and with sauces that range from marinara to Alfredo. You'll also find such main dishes as chicken Marsala and veal Parmesan, plus daily specials. There is a full bar and the menu selections are reasonably priced. **Features:** full bar. **Address:** 202 Baughman Ave 15644 **Location:** Just w of jct Lowry and Baughman aves. [L] [D] CALL [&M]

JENNERSTOWN pop. 695

GREEN GABLES RESTAURANT   814/629-9201

WW American. Casual Dining. $9-$35 **AAA Inspector Notes:** A stream winds behind this quiet restaurant, which resides in a picturesque setting. A companion facility to a popular summer-stock theater, this place can be crowded on matinee days. Beef tenderloin with garlic mashed potatoes, pan-roasted antelope loin with wild-rice risotto and Amish chicken breast are among specialty dishes. **Features:** full bar, Sunday brunch. **Reservations:** suggested. **Address:** 7712 Somerset Pike 15547 **Location:** 0.5 mi n on SR 985. [L] [D] [AX]

JERMYN pop. 2,169

WINDSOR INN   570/876-4600

W
American
Casual Dining
$9-$15

AAA Inspector Notes: The relaxed family restaurant is known locally for its flavorful hot wings and delicious, homemade cheesecake. Mirrors, Tiffany-style lamps and assorted memorabilia contribute to the rustic ambience of the dining room. Servers are prompt and friendly. **Features:** full bar. **Address:** 669 Washington Ave 18433 **Location:** SR 107, 0.3 mi s of jct US 6; downtown. Menu on AAA.com [L] [D]

JIM THORPE (F-10) pop. 4,781, elev. 531'
• Hotels p. 164 • Restaurants p. 164
• Part of Pocono Mountains Area — see map p. 371

In the foothills of the Pocono Mountains, the town of Jim Thorpe was named after the famous Olympic athlete who won each pentathlon event but the javelin throw in the 1912 Olympic Games in Stockholm. He was later stripped of his honors because of previous professional sports activities.

In response to Thorpe's widow's search for a memorial for him, two Pennsylvania communities—

Mauch Chunk and East Mauch Chunk—joined by incorporating as Jim Thorpe in the mid-1950s. The new community gave the man a final and fitting memorial, while also gaining economic stability for itself. Jim Thorpe was reinstated in the Olympic records in 1982, and the medals he won in the 1912 games were presented to his family. The Jim Thorpe Memorial is a half-mile east on SR 903.

St. Mark's & St. John's Episcopal Church, on Race Street, contains Italian marble altars, brass gas standards flanking the baptismal font and Tiffany stained-glass windows. Guided tours are available Wednesday-Sunday noon-4, May 30 through August; tour times vary rest of year. Phone (570) 325-2241.

Mauch Chunk Lake Park *(see Recreation Areas Chart)* offers recreational opportunities, including picnicking, hiking, boating, fishing, swimming and cross-country skiing.

Concerts are often held at Penn's Peak at 325 Maury Rd.; phone (610) 836-9000 or (866) 605-7325.

ASA PACKER MANSION, off US 209 on Packer Hill, was the 1860 Victorian home of the well-known 19th-century industrialist and philanthropist Asa Packer. While the exterior has changed somewhat from its original appearance, the interior remains nearly the same, containing original furnishings, woodcarvings and paintings.

Parking is not available at the mansion; for a fee, visitors may park in the train station lot at the Pocono Mountain Visitors Bureau on US 209. **Time:** Allow 1 hour minimum. **Hours:** Daily 11-4, Memorial Day weekend-Oct. 31; Sat.-Sun. 11-4, Apr. 1-day before Memorial Day and Nov. 1 to mid-Dec. Last tour begins at closing. **Cost:** $8; $7 (ages 55+); $5 (ages 6-18); $3 (ages 0-5). **Phone:** (570) 325-3229.

LEHIGH GORGE SCENIC RAILWAY tours depart from 1 Susquehanna St. One-hour round-trip rides are offered, except in October when rides are 45 minutes. Passengers will travel in a 1920s coach along the Lehigh River into the Lehigh Gorge State Park to Old Penn Haven. See beautiful views of the mountains, river and trees on your journey while listening to narration about the area. Themed excursions that vary in length are offered throughout the year including a bike train in which riders can opt to cycle a 25-mile path back into town.

The side of train facing away from the station offers better views. **Hours:** Trips depart Sat.-Sun. and select weekdays at 11, 1, 3, May-Sept. and Nov.-Dec; Fri.-Sun. on the hour 10-4, in Oct. Phone to confirm schedule and for themed tour schedules. **Cost:** Open-air car fare $18; $10 (ages 3-12). Coach fare $13; $9 (ages 3-12). **Phone:** (570) 325-8485.

RECREATIONAL ACTIVITIES
White-water Rafting
* **Jim Thorpe River Adventures** is 1 mi. n. of the Lehigh River Bridge on SR 903, following signs. Other activities are available. Minimum age requirements may apply. **Hours:** Trips are offered

mid-Mar. to late Oct. **Phone:** (570) 325-2570 or (800) 424-7238.

* **Pocono Whitewater Rafting** trips depart 8 mi. n.e. of the Lehigh River Bridge on SR 903. Other activities are available. Ages 0-3 are not permitted on raft trips. **Hours:** Trips are offered daily Apr.-Oct. Phone ahead to confirm schedule. Reservations are required. **Phone:** (570) 325-3655 or (800) 944-8392.

THE INN AT JIM THORPE   (570)325-2599

Historic
Country Inn
$105-$189

Address: 24 Broadway 18229 **Location:** Just w of jct SR 209. **Facility:** In historic downtown, this 1840s inn features wrought iron banisters and guest room décor that mixes Victorian features with modern amenities. 45 units, some two bedrooms. 4 stories, interior corridors. **Terms:** 2 night minimum stay - seasonal and/or weekends, 5 day cancellation notice-fee imposed. **Dining:** Broadway Grille and Pub, see separate listing. **Activities:** game room, exercise room, massage.

WHERE TO EAT

BROADWAY GRILLE AND PUB   570/732-4343

 American. Casual Dining. $11-$29 **AAA Inspector Notes:** Come to this cozy spot that pairs the building style, including exposed brick walls, with a colorful, newly-designed contemporary decor. The menu touches on a variety of different cuisines including a one pound bone-in porterhouse and a pan seared wild salmon over creamy polenta. Certain weekdays highlight specialty items such as "Tapas Tuesday" and "Sushi Night Thursday." **Features:** full bar, happy hour. **Reservations:** suggested, weekends. **Address:** 24 Broadway 18229 **Location:** Just w of jct SR 209; in The Inn at Jim Thorpe. **Parking:** street only. B L D

JOHNSTOWN (H-4) pop. 20,978, elev. 1,178'
* Hotels p. 166 • Restaurants p. 166

Four times disastrous floods have claimed Johnstown, which is in a deep, irregular valley formed by Stony Creek and the Little Conemaugh and Conemaugh rivers. The first two floods, in 1862 and 1889, were a result of the collapse of the South Fork Dam, about 12 miles east on the Conemaugh. Some of the older buildings still show high water marks of the 1889 disaster, one of the country's worst peacetime catastrophes. Debris held behind a stone bridge area caught fire and added to the losses, which included some 2,200 lives. The Path of the Flood Trail is a hiking/biking trail following the roughly 14-mile path of the 1889 flood. The trail begins in Ehrenfeld and then joins the National Park Service's Staple Bend Tunnel Site for a short distance. There is about a .75-mile gap until it picks up again just past the Franklin Ballfield area to Pershing Avenue/Clapboard Run Road; the route then continues into Johnstown and ends at the Johnstown Flood Museum. Kiosks and interpretive panels along the way detail the devastating event. For more information about the route contact the Cambria County Conservation & Recreation Authority; phone (814) 472-2110.

In 1936 a third flood caused a great deal of damage to the city and its environs. A fourth flood occurred in July 1977, when heavy rains caused rivers and streams to overflow throughout the Conemaugh Valley. Once again damage was severe.

Conemaugh Gap, a gorge cut by the Conemaugh River as it passes through Laurel Hill Ridge Mountain, extends 7 miles and is about 1,700 feet deep.

Pasquerilla Performing Arts Center at the University of Pittsburgh at Johnstown stages plays, dance performances and concerts as well as productions for children; phone (814) 269-7200 or (800) 846-2787. The Johnstown Symphony Orchestra also provides musical entertainment; its 1,000-seat theater is at the performing arts center; phone (814) 535-6738.

Greater Johnstown/Cambria Convention and Visitors Bureau: 111 Roosevelt Blvd., Suite A, Johnstown, PA 15906. **Phone:** (814) 536-7993 or (800) 237-8590.

Shopping areas: The Johnstown Galleria, SR 219, has more than 100 specialty stores, including The Bon-Ton, Boscov's, JCPenney and Sears. In addition, numerous shops line Scalp Avenue.

FRANK & SYLVIA PASQUERILLA HERITAGE DISCOVERY CENTER is at 201 6th Ave.; the parking lot entrance is at jct. Broad St. and 7th Ave. The center presents the experiences of Southern and Eastern European immigrants whose arrival at the turn of the 20th century shaped the region's culture, economy and industry. Daily experiences, difficulties and accomplishments are depicted through several fictional immigrants who give personal accounts of events in their lives. Some of the scenes depicted are an Italian funeral, a Ukrainian wedding, a bar mitzvah, an ethnic social club and a butcher shop.

Interactive exhibits about coal mines and steel mills also are featured. The Iron & Steel Gallery presents additional exhibits about the steel industry. It also shows the film "Mystery of Steel," which chronicles Johnstown's 19th-century history as a technological innovator in steelmaking. The Johnstown Children's Museum is housed here as well.

Time: Allow 1 hour, 30 minutes minimum. **Hours:** Tues.-Sun. 10-5, May-Oct.; Wed.-Sat., Sun. noon-5, rest of year. Closed Jan. 1, Easter, Thanksgiving and Christmas. **Cost:** (includes Johnstown Children's Museum, Johnstown Flood Museum and Wagner-Ritter House & Garden up to 5 days after ticket is purchased) $9; $7 (ages 62+); $6 (ages 3-18 and 62+). **Phone:** (814) 539-1889. [T]

Johnstown Children's Museum is at 201 6th Ave. at jct. Broad St. and 7th Ave., on one floor of the Frank & Sylvia Pasquerilla Heritage Discovery Center. Many of the interactive exhibits introduce children to local history topics, including mining and steel mills. There is a water room where youngsters can learn about dams, rain, fish and municipal plumbing; a rooftop garden with native Pennsylvania plants; an area to learn about maps and city planning; role play and dress-up activities; and a coal mine-theme climbing structure.

Time: Allow 1 hour minimum. **Hours:** Daily 10-5, Apr.-Sept.; Wed.-Sun. 10-5, rest of year. **Cost:** (includes Frank & Sylvia Pasquerilla Heritage Discovery Center, Johnstown Flood Museum and Wagner-Ritter House & Garden up to 5 days after ticket is purchased) $9; $7 (ages 3-18 and 62+). **Phone:** (814) 539-1889. [T]

Wagner-Ritter House & Garden is at 418 Broad St., 1 blk. e. of the Frank & Sylvia Pasquerilla Heritage Discovery Center. This two-story house depicts three generations of working-class German immigrants 1860-1990. Guided tours take visitors through the kitchen, living area and bedrooms, all of which have been furnished with original items as well as reproductions. A small garden also is on the property.

Time: Allow 45 minutes minimum. **Hours:** Sat. noon-5, Apr.-Sept. Closed major holidays. Phone ahead to confirm schedule. **Cost:** $3; free (ages 0-2). **Phone:** (814) 539-1889.

GRANDVIEW CEMETERY, 2.5 mi. s. on SR 271 to Millcreek Rd., contains the Unknown Plot, where 777 unidentified victims of the 1889 flood are buried. **Hours:** Daily 7:30 a.m.-dusk, May-Oct.; 7:30-5, rest of year. **Cost:** Free. **Phone:** (814) 535-2652.

INCLINED PLANE, SR 56 and Johns St., is 996 feet long with a grade of 71 percent, making it one of the steepest passenger inclined planes in the world. It connects the central part of Johnstown with a residential suburb on a plateau 502 feet above the city. Both cars and pedestrians are carried. An observation platform at the top overlooks the city.

Time: Allow 30 minutes minimum. **Hours:** Mon.-Thurs. 8 a.m.-10 p.m., Fri. 8 a.m.-11 p.m., Sat. 9 a.m.-11 p.m., Sun. 9 a.m.-10 p.m., Apr.-Sept.; Sun.-Thurs. 11-9, Fri.-Sat. 10-10, Oct.-Dec.; Fri. 4-10, Sat. noon-10, Sun. noon-9, rest of year. Closed Jan. 1 and Christmas. Phone ahead to confirm schedule. **Cost:** Round-trip fare $4; $2.50 (ages 2-12); free (ages 65+). One-way fare $2.25; $1.50 (ages 2-12). Cars, vans and trucks one-way fare $6; motorcycles $4; bicycles free. **Phone:** (814) 536-1816. [T]

JOHNSTOWN FLOOD MUSEUM is at 304 Washington St. at Walnut St. This 1891 building was one of the first Carnegie libraries, built with a donation from philanthropist Andrew Carnegie. The museum chronicles the cause and course of events prior to, during and after the devastating flood of May 31, 1889, and features the 26-minute 1989 Academy Award-winning documentary film "The Johnstown Flood." Oklahoma houses, prefabricated structures designed for Oklahoma Territory homesteaders, were used for emergency housing after the flood; an original is displayed.

A 24-foot, 3-D relief map with sound effects and animation illustrates the devastation wrought by the 40-foot-high wall of water. Some 2,200 people were killed as it swept through the Conemaugh Valley, destroying everything in its path. Another exhibit is dedicated to the relief provided by the American Red Cross, including the efforts of the group's founder, Clara Barton. Recovered artifacts also are displayed.

Time: Allow 1 hour, 30 minutes minimum. **Hours:** Daily 10-5, Apr.-Sept.; Wed.-Sat. 10-5, rest of year. Film is shown every hour. Closed Jan. 1, Easter, Thanksgiving and Christmas. **Cost:** (includes Frank & Sylvia Pasquerilla Heritage Discovery Center, Johnstown Children's Museum and Wagner-Ritter House & Garden up to 5 days after ticket is purchased) $9; $7 (ages 3-18 and 62+). **Phone:** (814) 539-1889.

JOHNSTOWN FLOOD NATIONAL MEMORIAL— see St. Michael p. 383.

COMFORT INN & SUITES   (814)266-3678
◆◆◆ **Hotel** $99-$112 **Address:** 455 Theatre Dr 15904 **Location:** US 219 exit Elton (SR 756), just e. Across from Walmart Supercenter. **Facility:** 115 units. 5 stories, interior corridors. **Amenities:** safes. **Pool(s):** heated indoor. **Activities:** hot tub, exercise room. **Guest Services:** valet and coin laundry, area transportation.

ECONO LODGE   (814)536-1114
◆◆ **Motel** $80-$190 **Address:** 430 Napoleon Pl 15901 **Location:** Jct SR 271 and 403; downtown. **Facility:** 49 units. 3 stories, interior corridors. **Guest Services:** coin laundry.

HAMPTON INN   (814)262-7700
◆◆◆ **Hotel** $129-$179 **Address:** 129 Commerce Ct 15904 **Location:** US 219 exit Elton (SR 756), just e, just n on Donald Ln, then just w. Located in a quiet secluded area. **Facility:** 70 units. 3 stories, interior corridors. **Terms:** 1-7 night minimum stay, cancellation fee imposed. **Pool(s):** heated outdoor. **Activities:** exercise room. **Guest Services:** valet laundry.

> **AAA Benefit:** Members save 5% or more!

HOLIDAY INN DOWNTOWN   814/535-7777
◆◆◆ **Hotel.** Rates not provided. **Address:** 250 Market St 15901 **Location:** Corner of Market and Vine sts; downtown. **Facility:** 159 units. 5 stories, interior corridors. **Pool(s):** heated indoor. **Activities:** sauna, hot tub, exercise room. **Guest Services:** valet and coin laundry, area transportation.

HOLIDAY INN EXPRESS JOHNSTOWN   814/266-8789
◆◆ **Motel.** Rates not provided. **Address:** 1440 Scalp Ave 15904 **Location:** US 219 exit Windber (SR 56 E), just e. **Facility:** 95 units. 3 stories, interior corridors. **Activities:** exercise room. **Guest Services:** valet and coin laundry, area transportation.

SLEEP INN   (814)262-9292
◆◆ ◆◆ **Hotel** $81-$89 **Address:** 453 Theatre Dr 15904 **Location:** US 219 exit Elton (SR 756), just e. Across from a shopping mall. **Facility:** 62 units. 3 stories, interior corridors. **Guest Services:** valet laundry.

SUPER 8 JOHNSTOWN   (814)535-5600
◆◆
Hotel
$60-$150
Address: 627 Solomon Run Rd 15904 **Location:** US 219 exit Galleria Dr, just w. **Facility:** 65 units. 3 stories, interior corridors. **Guest Services:** coin laundry. **Featured Amenity: continental breakfast.**

WHERE TO EAT

HARRIGAN'S CAFE & WINE DECK   814/361-2620
◆◆ ◆◆ American. Casual Dining. $8-$24 **AAA Inspector Notes:** Peruse a menu with a wide variety of American classic favorites at this restaurant with a contemporary, lively atmosphere. **Features:** full bar, happy hour. **Address:** 250 Market St 15901 **Location:** Corner of Market and Vine sts; downtown. [L] [D]

JONES MILLS (H-3) elev. 1,560'

Jones Mills is part of the Laurel Highlands *(see place listing p. 183).*

LIVING TREASURES ANIMAL PARK, 288 SR 711, has hundreds of animals from around the world, and visitors can feed some of them. The park also offers a petting zoo with a variety of animals, including goats, llamas, sheep and baby camels. **Hours:** Daily 10-dusk, Apr. 1-Oct. 31. Extended hours Sat.-Sun. in Oct.; phone ahead. **Cost:** $12.99; $10.99 (ages 62+); $9.99 (ages 3-11). Pony rides $3. Shire rides $4. **Phone:** (724) 593-8300.

RECREATIONAL ACTIVITIES
Skiing and Snowboarding
* **Hidden Valley Resort** is e. on SR 31, then s. to 1 Craighead Dr. Skiing, snowboarding and snow tubing are offered. **Hours:** Mon.-Tues. 10-4:30, Wed.-Thurs. 10-9, Fri.-Sat. 9 a.m.-9:30 p.m., Sun. 9-7. Tubing Fri. 6-9 p.m., Sat. 10-9, Sun. 10-4. Phone for holiday schedules and to verify other schedules. **Phone:** (814) 443-8000.

LOG CABIN LODGE & SUITES   724/593-8200
◆◆ **Motel.** Rates not provided. **Address:** 288 Rt 711 15646 **Location:** I-76 (Pennsylvania Tpke) exit 91, 2 mi on SR 31 E, then just s. Adjacent to Living Treasures Animal Park. **Facility:** 34 units, some two bedrooms, three bedrooms and efficiencies. 2 stories (no elevator), exterior corridors. **Terms:** check-in 4 pm.

JONESTOWN pop. 1,905

BEST WESTERN LEBANON VALLEY INN & SUITES
(717)865-4234

Hotel
$79-$119

AAA Benefit: Members save up to 20%!

Address: 4 Fisher Ave 17038 **Location:** I-81 exit 90, just e. **Facility:** 60 units. 3 stories, interior corridors. **Amenities:** safes. **Pool(s):** heated indoor. **Activities:** exercise room. **Guest Services:** coin laundry.

COMFORT INN LEBANON VALLEY-FT. INDIANTOWN GAP
(717)865-8080

Motel
$79-$169

Address: 16 Marsanna Ln 17038 **Location:** I-81 exit 90, just w. **Facility:** 50 units. 3 stories, interior corridors. **Pool(s):** outdoor. **Activities:** exercise room. **Guest Services:** coin laundry. **Featured Amenity:** continental breakfast.

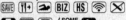

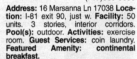

DAYS INN LEBANON/FORT INDIANTOWN GAP   (717)865-4064

Hotel $89-$219 **Address:** 3 Everest Ln 17038 **Location:** I-81 exit 90. **Facility:** 80 units, some efficiencies and kitchens. 4 stories, interior corridors. **Terms:** cancellation fee imposed. **Activities:** hot tub, exercise room. **Guest Services:** coin laundry.

KANE (D-4) pop. 3,730, elev. 2,020'

Located in northwestern Pennsylvania, Kane was founded in 1863 by Gen. Thomas L. Kane, who recruited the renowned Bucktail Regiment for Civil War combat. With an average snowfall of 107 inches per year, the area draws winter sports enthusiasts. Ice fishing, snowmobiling and cross-country skiing are popular. The Allegheny National Forest *(see place listing p. 46 and Recreation Areas Chart)* surrounds the city and offers year-round recreation.

KEMPTON (G-10) pop. 169, elev. 430'

HAWK MOUNTAIN SANCTUARY, at 1700 Hawk Mountain Rd. on Blue Mountain, offers birdwatching opportunities during the fall raptor migrations. Designated as a national natural landmark, the 2,600-acre site features scenic views of the forested Appalachian mountaintops, bold rock promontories and 8 miles of hiking trails. The visitor center contains birds of prey exhibits and a museum. Hawk and eagle migrations take place late August through late November.

Pets are not permitted. **Time:** Allow 2 hours minimum. **Hours:** Trails daily dawn-dusk. Visitor center daily 9-5, Dec.-Aug., 8-5, rest of year. Visitor center closed Jan. 1, Thanksgiving and Christmas. **Cost:** Holidays and Sept.-Nov. Sat.-Sun. $8; $4 (ages 6-12). Rest of year $6; $5 (senior citizens); $3 (ages 6-12). **Phone:** (610) 756-6961.

KENNETT SQUARE (C-8) pop. 6,072, elev. 260'
• Part of Philadelphia area — see map p. 230

The Chester County Visitors Center, just outside the gates of Longwood Gardens, is housed in a 19th-century Quaker meetinghouse and offers exhibits, video presentations and a wide range of visitor information. Across the street is a Quaker cemetery begun in the mid-1800s.

Chester County Conference and Visitors Bureau: 300 Greenwood Rd., Kennett Square, PA 19348. **Phone:** (484) 770-8550.

LONGWOOD GARDENS is 3 mi. n.e. at jct. US 1 and SR 52. Once the country estate of industrialist Pierre S. du Pont, Longwood is famous for its superb grounds that include elaborate fountains, two lakes, meadows, woodlands, 20 outdoor formal and informal gardens and a conservatory. The Peirce-du Pont House, occupied by du Pont until 1954, contains an exhibit tracing the 300-year historical and horticultural evolution of Longwood Gardens through photographs, artifacts, videotapes and family home movies.

Fountains, a water lily display and more than 11,000 types of plants are the main summer outdoor attractions. Masses of flowering plants adorn the 4-acre heated conservatory, which is particularly colorful November through April.

Time: Allow 2 hours minimum. **Hours:** Grounds daily 9-6. Closing times may vary; phone ahead to confirm schedule. **Cost:** $20; $17 (ages 62+); $10 (ages 5-18). **Phone:** (610) 388-1000, or (800) 737-5500 in state and surrounding states.

FAIRFIELD INN & SUITES BY MARRIOTT KENNETT SQUARE BRANDYWINE VALLEY   (610)444-8995

Hotel $97-$171 **Address:** 719 E Baltimore Pike 19348 **Location:** Jct Kennett Pike, 1.8 mi e, follow signs. **Facility:** 109 units. 4 stories, interior corridors. **Pool(s):** heated indoor. **Activities:** hot tub, exercise room. **Guest Services:** valet and coin laundry.

AAA Benefit: Members save 5% or more!

HILTON GARDEN INN KENNETT SQUARE
(610)444-9100

Hotel
$130-$180

AAA Benefit: Members save 5% or more!

Address: 815 E Baltimore Pike 19348 **Location:** 1.5 mi e on US 1. Located in a commercial area. **Facility:** 92 units. 3 stories, interior corridors. **Terms:** check-in 4 pm, 1-7 night minimum stay, cancellation fee imposed. **Pool(s):** heated indoor. **Activities:** hot tub. **Guest Services:** valet and coin laundry.

KENNETT HOUSE BED & BREAKFAST
610/444-9592

Bed & Breakfast. Rates not provided. **Address:** 503 W State St 19348 **Location:** Just off US 1. **Facility:** Whether you're lounging on the wraparound stone porch or relaxing in the beautifully landscaped grounds you will feel at ease at this fabulous B&B. 4 units. 3 stories (no elevator), interior corridors. **Parking:** street only. **Terms:** check-in 4 pm.

KING OF PRUSSIA pop. 19,936
• Part of Philadelphia area — see map p. 230

BEST WESTERN PLUS THE INN AT KING OF PRUSSIA
(610)265-4500

Hotel
$99-$219

AAA Benefit: Members save up to 20%!

Address: 127 S Gulph Rd 19406 **Location:** I-76 (Pennsylvania Tpke) exit 326 (Valley Forge Rd), 1.3 mi e to jct US 202 N and S Gulph Rd; Schuylkill Expwy exit 328A (Mall Blvd), just e. Opposite King of Prussia Mall. **Facility:** 168 units. 2-3 stories, interior corridors. **Pool(s):** heated outdoor. **Activities:** hot tub, exercise room. **Guest Services:** valet and coin laundry. **Featured Amenity:** full hot breakfast.

Directly across from the King of Prussia Mall

CASINO HOTEL TOWER-VALLEY FORGE RESORT
610/265-1500

Hotel. Rates not provided. **Address:** 1210 1st Ave 19406 **Location:** I-76 (Pennsylvania Tpke) exit 326 (Valley Forge Rd), 1.3 mi n on N Gulph Rd; Schuylkill Expwy exit 328A (Mall Blvd). Located at Valley Forge Convention Plaza. **Facility:** Guest rooms here are incredibly spacious and offer lovely triple-sheeted bedding. Gaming and dining options abound, and sometimes headline entertainment is featured. 160 units. 6 stories, interior corridors. **Amenities:** video games, safes. **Dining:** 2 restaurants, nightclub. **Pool(s):** heated outdoor. **Activities:** exercise room, spa. **Guest Services:** valet laundry, area transportation.

COMFORT INN VALLEY FORGE
(610)962-0700

Hotel
$99-$139

Address: 550 W Dekalb Pike 19406 **Location:** I-76 (Pennsylvania Tpke) exit 326 (Valley Forge Rd), 1 mi ne on US 202 N; exit 328B (US 202 N), 2 mi ne. Near King of Prussia Mall. **Facility:** 121 units. 5 stories, interior corridors. **Activities:** exercise room. **Guest Services:** valet and coin laundry.

CROWNE PLAZA PHILADELPHIA/VALLEY FORGE
(610)265-7500

Hotel
$109-$349

Address: 260 Mall Blvd 19406 **Location:** I-76 (Pennsylvania Tpke) exit 326 (Valley Forge Rd), 1 mi e; Schuylkill Expwy exit 328A (Mall Blvd), just n; just w off US 202 N. Next to a shopping mall. **Facility:** 226 units. 5 stories, interior corridors. **Terms:** cancellation fee imposed. **Amenities:** video games. **Guest Services:** valet laundry, area transportation.

DOUBLETREE BY HILTON PHILADELPHIA VALLEY FORGE
(610)337-1200

Hotel
$104-$199

AAA Benefit: Members save 5% or more!

Address: 301 W Dekalb Pike 19406 **Location:** I-76 (Pennsylvania Tpke) exit 326 (Valley Forge Rd), 1.4 mi ne on US 202 N. **Facility:** 327 units. 9 stories, interior corridors. **Terms:** 1-7 night minimum stay, cancellation fee imposed. **Amenities:** video games, safes. **Dining:** 2 restaurants. **Pool(s):** heated outdoor. **Activities:** exercise room. **Guest Services:** valet laundry, area transportation.

FAIRFIELD INN VALLEY FORGE/KING OF PRUSSIA
(610)337-0700

Hotel
$153-$252

AAA Benefit: Members save 5% or more!

Address: 258 Mall Blvd 19406 **Location:** I-76 (Pennsylvania Tpke) exit 326 (Valley Forge Rd); Schuylkill Expwy exit 328A (Mall Blvd), just off US 202 N. Next to a shopping mall. **Facility:** 80 units. 5 stories, interior corridors. **Guest Services:** valet laundry, area transportation. **Featured Amenity:** continental breakfast.

Get your vehicle vacation ready at a

AAA/CAA Approved Auto Repair facility

HAMPTON INN PHILADELPHIA/KING OF PRUSSIA
(610)962-8111

 Hotel $149-$179 **Address:** 530 W Dekalb Pike 19406 **Location:** I-76 (Pennsylvania Tpke) exit 326 (Valley Forge Rd), 2 mi ne on US 202 N. Located in a commercial area. **Facility:** 147 units. 7 stories, interior corridors. **Terms:** 1-7 night minimum stay, cancellation fee imposed. **Activities:** exercise room. **Guest Services:** valet laundry.

AAA Benefit: Members save 5% or more!

HOLIDAY INN EXPRESS HOTEL & SUITES- KING OF PRUSSIA
(610)768-9500

Hotel $99-$299

Address: 260 N Gulph Rd 19406 **Location:** I-76 (Pennsylvania Tpke) exit 326 (Valley Forge Rd), 0.5 mi n. Next to King of Prussia Mall. **Facility:** 155 units. 7 stories, interior corridors. **Terms:** cancellation fee imposed. **Activities:** hot tub, exercise room. **Guest Services:** valet laundry. **Featured Amenity:** breakfast buffet.

HYATT HOUSE PHILADELPHIA/KING OF PRUSSIA
(610)265-0300

Hotel $109-$349

HYATT house™

AAA Benefit: Members save 10%!

Address: 240 Mall Blvd 19406 **Location:** I-76 (Pennsylvania Tpke) exit 326 (Valley Forge Rd), 1 mi n of jct US 202 on Gulph Rd. **Facility:** 147 units, some efficiencies. 4 stories, interior corridors. **Terms:** cancellation fee imposed. **Pool(s):** heated indoor. **Activities:** hot tub, exercise room. **Guest Services:** valet and coin laundry, area transportation. **Featured Amenity:** breakfast buffet.

HYATT PLACE PHILADELPHIA/KING OF PRUSSIA
(484)690-3000

Hotel $99-$249

HHYATT PLACE™

AAA Benefit: Members save 10%!

Address: 440 American Ave 19406 **Location:** I-76 (Pennsylvania Tpke) exit 326 (Valley Forge Rd); Schuylkill Expwy exit 328A (Mall Blvd), 1.3 mi n on N Gulph Rd, 1 mi ne on 1st Ave, then just e. Located in a commercial area. **Facility:** 129 units. 6 stories, interior corridors. **Terms:** cancellation fee imposed. **Pool(s):** heated indoor. **Activities:** hot tub, exercise room. **Guest Services:** valet and coin laundry, area transportation. **Featured Amenity:** breakfast buffet.

Pick up vibrant, top-quality travel guides and atlases at AAA/CAA offices

RADISSON VALLEY FORGE HOTEL
(610)337-2000

  Hotel $119-$499 **Address:** 1160 1st Ave 19406 **Location:** I-76 (Pennsylvania Tpke) exit 326 (Valley Forge Rd), 1.3 mi n on N Gulph Rd; Schuylkill Expwy exit 328A (Mall Blvd). Located at Valley Forge Convention Plaza. **Facility:** 327 units. 15 stories, interior corridors. **Terms:** cancellation fee imposed. **Amenities:** video games, safes. **Dining:** 2 restaurants, nightclub. **Pool(s):** heated outdoor. **Activities:** exercise room, spa. **Guest Services:** valet laundry, area transportation.

SHERATON VALLEY FORGE
(484)238-1800

Hotel $99-$349

Sheraton HOTELS & RESORTS

AAA Benefit: Members save up to 15%, plus Starwood Preferred Guest® benefits!

Address: 480 N Gulph Rd 19406 **Location:** I-76 (Pennsylvania Tpke) exit 326 (Valley Forge Rd), 0.5 mi w. Located in commercial area. **Facility:** 180 units. 6 stories, interior corridors. **Terms:** cancellation fee imposed. **Amenities:** safes. **Pool(s):** heated indoor. **Activities:** hot tub, exercise room. **Guest Services:** valet laundry, area transportation.

SPRINGHILL SUITES BY MARRIOTT PHILADELPHIA/ VALLEY FORGE/KING OF PRUSSIA
(610)783-1400

Hotel $139-$229 **Address:** 875 Mancill Mill Rd 19406 **Location:** I-76 (Pennsylvania Tpke) exit 328A (Mall Blvd), 2.8 mi n on US 422, 0.3 mi e on SR 23 (Valley Forge Rd), then just n. **Facility:** 131 units. 5 stories, interior corridors. **Pool(s):** heated outdoor. **Activities:** exercise room. **Guest Services:** valet and coin laundry.

AAA Benefit: Members save 5% or more!

WHERE TO EAT

THE CAPITAL GRILLE
610/265-1415

Steak. Fine Dining. $13-$48 **AAA Inspector Notes:** Cherry wood and red leather assist in making this clubby dining room a beautiful spot to dine on excellent cuts of dry-aged beef. The staff is highly attentive and knowledgeable. **Features:** patio dining. **Reservations:** suggested, for dinner. **Address:** 236 Mall Blvd 19406 **Location:** I-76 (Pennsylvania Tpke) exit 326 (Valley Forge Rd), 1 mi n of jct US 202 on Gulph Rd.

CREED'S SEAFOOD & STEAKS
610/265-2550

Continental. Fine Dining. $12-$39 **AAA Inspector Notes:** If visiting Valley Forge or shopping at King of Prussia Mall, this restaurant is a hop, skip and a jump away. Once a roadside stone inn during the late 19th-century, the eatery now employs attentive servers who deliver tasty seafood dishes and selections off a superb wine list. A piano bar is a nice place to unwind. **Features:** full bar, happy hour. **Reservations:** suggested. **Address:** 499 N Gulph Rd 19406 **Location:** I-76 (Pennsylvania Tpke) exit 326 (Valley Forge Rd), 0.3 mi w.

MAGGIANO'S LITTLE ITALY
610/992-3333

Italian. Fine Dining. $11-$47 **AAA Inspector Notes:** Diners savor scrumptious, traditional favorites served in a bustling atmosphere reminiscent of Little Italy. The dining area projects an early-20th-century feel; loud conversations bouncing off high ceilings evoke a sense of the Roaring 20's. **Features:** full bar. **Reservations:** suggested. **Address:** 205 Mall Blvd 19406 **Location:** I-76 (Pennsylvania Tpke) exit 326 (Valley Forge Rd), 0.5 mi n of jct US 202 on Gulph Rd. **Parking:** on-site and valet.

MICHAEL'S DELICATESSEN & RESTAURANT   610/265-3265

▽ American. Casual Dining. $7-$15 AAA Inspector Notes: Operating in the same location for more than 20 years, this establishment offers a blend of restaurant, delicatessen and convenience store, making it convenient for both dining in or taking out. The menu features an all-day breakfast, salads, a huge selection of sandwiches, including Italian hoagies, and such dinner entrées as steak, chicken, seafood, pork, veal and brisket of beef. Features: beer only. Address: 130 Town Center Rd 19406 Location: I-76 (Pennsylvania Tpke) exit 326 (Valley Forge Rd), 1.5 mi ne on US 202 N; in Valley Forge Shopping Center. ⬙ Dekalb St, 103.

(B) (L) (D) (🍽)

PEACE A PIZZA   610/962-9900

▽ Pizza. Quick Serve. $11-$18 AAA Inspector Notes: A delicious variety of traditional and exotic pizza slices, including vegetarian options, can be savored at this casual pizzeria. The staff prepares fresh salads from ingredients of the diner's choosing or from a menu of scrumptious combinations. Address: 143-149 S Gulph Rd 19406 Location: I-76 (Pennsylvania Tpke) exit 326 (Valley Forge Rd), 1.3 mi e to jct US 202 N and S Gulph Rd, then just s; Schuylkill Expwy exit 328A (Mall Blvd), just e, then just s. (L) (D)

PEPPERS ITALIAN RESTAURANT AND BAR   610/265-2416

▽ Italian. Casual Dining. $6-$18 AAA Inspector Notes: Large portions and reasonable prices are the orders of the day at this casual restaurant. Representative of the cuisine are such dishes as seafood pescatora, chicken amaretto and Peppers penne. The children's menu lists 10 items. Features: full bar, happy hour. Address: 239 Town Center Rd 19406 Location: I-76 (Pennsylvania Tpke) exit 326 (Valley Forge Rd), 1.5 mi ne on US 202 N; in Valley Forge Shopping Center. ⬙ Dekalb St, 103. (L) (D) (🍽)

SULLIVAN'S STEAKHOUSE   610/878-9025

▽▽▽ Steak. Fine Dining. $12-$59 AAA Inspector Notes: Named for John L. Sullivan, heavyweight champion of the world in the 1880s, the upscale steakhouse prepares a wide selection of steaks, chops and seafood. The décor features black-and-white photographs of Sullivan, Jack Dempsey and other boxing legends. Features: full bar. Reservations: suggested. Address: 700 W Dekalb Pike 19406 Location: I-76 (Pennsylvania Tpke) exit 326 (Valley Forge Rd), 1.5 mi ne on US 202 N; next to King of Prussia Mall. Parking: valet only. (L) (D)

KITTANNING pop. 4,044

HOLIDAY INN EXPRESS & SUITES   724/543-5200

▽▽▽ Hotel. Rates not provided. Address: 13 Hilltop Plaza 16201 Location: SR 28 exit 19A; on SR 268. Located in a shopping plaza. Facility: 66 units. 3 stories, interior corridors. Pool(s): heated indoor. Activities: exercise room. Guest Services: valet and coin laundry.

(🍴) CALL (🔐M) (🚲) (BIZ) (📶) (✕) (🔒) (🖥) (💻)

QUALITY INN ROYLE   (724)543-1159

▽▽▽ Hotel. $85-$140 Address: 405 Butler Rd 16201 Location: SR 28 exit US 422 W. Facility: 59 units, some efficiencies and kitchens. 2 stories (no elevator), interior/exterior corridors. Activities: exercise room. Guest Services: valet laundry.

(🍴) (BIZ) (📶) (✕) (🔒) (🖥) (💻) /SOME UNITS (🔐)

▮ WHERE TO EAT ▮

KING'S FAMILY RESTAURANT   724/545-3340

▽▽ American. Family Dining. $6-$14 AAA Inspector Notes: Fast and friendly service is offered here. The menu is large in size with descriptive menu items and pictures. The restaurant is also known for its ice cream and dessert menu. Address: 16 Hilltop Plaza 16201 Location: SR 28 exit 19A. (B) (L) (D)

Check DrivingLaws.AAA.com for local motor vehicle laws when traveling

KLEINFELTERSVILLE (H-9) elev. 581'

MIDDLE CREEK WILDLIFE MANAGEMENT AREA, 2 mi. s. on Hopeland Rd., is administered by the Pennsylvania Game Commission. The 6,254-acre area, which includes a visitor center, provides a habitat for waterfowl and wildlife. Nature trails, educational programs and a self-guiding driving tour also are available. Hours: Visitor center Tues.-Sat. 8-4, Sun. noon-5, Feb. 1-day before Thanksgiving. Self-guiding driving tour Mar. 1-Sept. 15. Limited winter hours are offered; phone ahead to confirm schedule. Cost: Free. Phone: (717) 733-1512.

KULPSVILLE pop. 8,194

• Part of Philadelphia area — see map p. 230

HOLIDAY INN LANSDALE   215/368-3800

▽▽▽▽ Hotel. Rates not provided. Address: 1750 Sumneytown Pike 19443 Location: I-476 (Pennsylvania Tpke NE Ext) exit 31, just e. Facility: 182 units. 4 stories, interior corridors. Pool(s): outdoor. Activities: exercise room. Guest Services: valet and coin laundry.

(🍴) (🍸) CALL (🔐M) (🚲) (BIZ) (HS) (📶) (🔒) (🖥) (💻) /SOME UNITS (🔐)

KUTZTOWN (G-10) pop. 5,012, elev. 423'

Kutztown was settled in 1771 by Pennsylvania Germans and named for founder George Kutz. An 1892 schoolhouse at White Oak and Normal avenues portrays a classroom and library of the era. On display are Keith Haring sketches, antique toys and a 1799 newspaper announcing George Washington's death. It is open by appointment; phone (610) 683-7697. Also in town is Kutztown State University.

The ▽ Kutztown Folk Festival celebrates the town's heritage with traditional food, crafts and family entertainment. The celebration begins at the Kutztown Fairgrounds the Saturday before July 4 and continues through the following Sunday; phone (888) 674-6136.

Northeast Berks Chamber of Commerce: 110 W. Main St., Kutztown, PA 19530. Phone: (610) 683-8860.

Shopping areas: Renninger's Antique & Farmers Market, 740 Noble St., is open Fri.-Sat. (antique market Sat. only).

CRYSTAL CAVE, 2 mi. n. off US 222, following signs, is named for the crystalline formations found in the cavern. Also on the grounds are a miniature golf course, theater, museum and nature trail. Panning for gemstones is offered.

The underground temperature is a constant 54 F. A jacket and comfortable walking shoes are recommended. Time: Allow 1 hour, 30 minutes minimum. Hours: Daily 9-6 (also Sat.-Sun. and holidays 6-7 p.m.), Memorial Day weekend-Labor Day; 9-5, Mar. 1-day before Memorial Day weekend and day after Labor Day-Nov. 30. Cost: $13.50; $9.50 (ages 4-11). Gem panning $6-$11. Miniature golf $4.50. Phone: (610) 683-6765. (🍴) (⛲)

PENNSYLVANIA GERMAN CULTURAL HERITAGE CENTER, .5 mi. s. off US 222 at 22 Luckenbill Rd., is a museum that highlights the history of early German immigrants. On its 30 acres is an 1830 one-room schoolhouse, an 1810 stone farmhouse, a 19th-century barn and washhouse and two reconstructed 18th-century log houses. Also on the premises is a genealogy and cultural library. **Time:** Allow 1 hour minimum. **Hours:** Mon.-Fri. 10-noon and 1-4. Closed major holidays; phone ahead. **Cost:** Library $5; $3 (ages 0-11 and 65+). Grounds only free. Reservations are required. **Phone:** (610) 683-1589. GT

LACKAWAXEN (E-12) elev. 687'
• **Part of Pocono Mountains Area — see map p. 371**

ZANE GREY MUSEUM, at 135 Scenic Dr., is situated along the Delaware River in the house where Zane Grey began his writing career. Exhibits include photographs, books and personal belongings of the Western author and his wife, Dolly. **Time:** Allow 30 minutes minimum. **Hours:** Daily 10-5, Memorial Day-Sept; Sat.-Sun. 10-5, Oct. 1-19. **Cost:** Free. **Phone:** (570) 685-4871.

RECREATIONAL ACTIVITIES
Skiing and Snowboarding

• **Ski Big Bear at Masthope Mountain** is at the end of Karl Hope Blvd. Other activities also are available. **Hours:** Fri.-Sat. 9-9, Wed.-Thurs. noon-9, Sun.-Mon. 9-4:30, Jan. 1 to mid-Mar. Hours are extended during holiday season; phone ahead. **Phone:** (570) 685-1400.

ROEBLING INN ON THE DELAWARE   570/685-7900
WWW **Historic Bed & Breakfast.** Rates not provided. **Address:** 155 Scenic Dr 18435 **Location:** Waterfront. Just off SR 590; center. Located on Delaware River. **Facility:** The stately 1870 Greek Revival home overlooks the Delaware River and the Roebling Bridge, North America's oldest suspension bridge. Near Zane Grey and Minisink Battleground, the hotel is surrounded by history. 6 units, some kitchens and cottages. 1-2 stories (no elevator), interior/exterior corridors. **Activities:** fishing.

WHERE TO EAT
SUMMIT RESTAURANT AT MASTHOPE MOUNTAIN   570/685-1173
WW **American. Casual Dining.** $8-$23 **AAA Inspector Notes:** In the modern lodge perched atop the Big Bear ski area, this casual and friendly restaurant offers sweeping views and high-quality food. The menu covers a lot of ground with something for everyone. There is an interesting selection of sandwiches and salads as well as entrées ranging from ribs to grilled steaks, ahi tuna, roasted rainbow trout, mango chicken and even some Italian pasta dishes. Note that hours can vary a bit between the ski and summer seasons. **Features:** full bar. **Address:** 192 Karl Hope Blvd 18435 **Location:** 2.8 mi n on Masthope Plank Rd, 0.8 mi w on Westcolang Rd; at summit of Ski Big Bear.

LAHASKA (H-12) elev. 315'
• **Part of Philadelphia area — see map p. 230**

PEDDLER'S VILLAGE is at US 202 and SR 263. This 18th-century-style village is a shopping, dining and entertainment complex with 65 specialty shops;

an inn; five restaurants; and Giggleberry Fair, an indoor family entertainment center that features an antique operating carousel and the region's largest obstacle course. The site presents 12 annual festivals and seasonal events set on 42 acres of landscaped gardens and brick pathways.

Time: Allow 2 hours minimum. **Hours:** Mon.-Sat. 10-9, Sun. 11-7, late Nov.-Dec. 30; Mon.-Thurs. 10-6, Fri.-Sat. 10-9 p.m., Sun. 11-6, rest of year. Shops close at 4 Christmas Eve and Dec. 31. Shops closed Thanksgiving Day and Christmas Day. Restaurants closed Christmas Day. Phone ahead to confirm schedule. **Cost:** Free. **Phone:** (215) 794-4000.

GOLDEN PLOUGH INN   (215)794-4004

Country Inn
$190-$490

Address: Rt 202 & Street Rd 18931 **Location:** In Peddler's Village. **Facility:** Located in a retail complex with multiple shops and restaurants, the property boasts a country theme throughout its spacious guest rooms. 71 units. 2-3 stories, interior corridors. **Terms:** cancellation fee imposed. **Dining:** Buttonwood Grill, see separate listing. **Activities:** exercise room. **Guest Services:** valet laundry. **Featured Amenity:** continental breakfast.

WHERE TO EAT
BUTTONWOOD GRILL   215/794-4040
WW **American. Casual Dining.** $6-$28 **AAA Inspector Notes:** This casual eatery is the perfect stop for a quick bite when visiting Peddler's Village. The large outdoor patio is equipped with a full bar and is a common place for visitors to grab cocktails. The vast menu provides a variety of delicious choices, but we recommend the famous mouthwatering burgers, prepared fresh daily. **Features:** full bar, patio dining, happy hour. **Address:** Rt 202 & Street Rd 18931 **Location:** In Peddler's Village; in Golden Plough Inn.

COCK 'N BULL RESTAURANT   215/794-4000
WW **American Casual Dining $7-$34 AAA Inspector Notes:** The atmosphere bustles at this cozy restaurant, a family favorite for traditional food. The Thursday King Henry's feast buffet lays out a sumptuous collection. An eclectic collection of folk art contributes to the bright appeal of the dining room. **Features:** full bar, Sunday brunch. **Reservations:** suggested, for dinner. **Address:** SR 263 & Street Rd 18931 **Location:** In Peddler's Village.

EARL'S BUCKS COUNTY   215/794-4020
WWW **American Casual Dining $9-$44 AAA Inspector Notes:** This sophisticated steak and seafood house is quite upscale. A granite-topped bar with a brushed-aluminum front contributes to the cosmopolitan, urban atmosphere, and a high-energy lounge hops with live entertainment on select days. The menu features the finest Black Angus steaks from Omaha, fresh seafood flown in daily, selections from a raw bar and an extensive wine collection. A two- or three-course lunch option is served 11-4, Monday through Saturday. **Features:** full bar, happy hour. **Reservations:** suggested, for dinner. **Address:** 2400 Street Rd 18931 **Location:** In Peddler's Village.

LAKE ARIEL E-11 elev. 1,434'

• Part of Pocono Mountains Area — see map p. 371

CLAWS 'N' PAWS WILD ANIMAL PARK is at 1475 Ledgedale Rd. The park includes 120 species of exotic animals in a wooded setting. Featured are birds of prey, bears, leopards, monkeys, otters, reptiles, tropical birds, rare white tigers and wolves. A petting zoo with tame deer and farm animals and a walk-in tortoise area also are presented. The Dinosaur Outpost features fossil hunts and gemstone panning. Animal shows as well as hand-feedings of lories and the giraffe are scheduled throughout the day.

Pets are not permitted. **Time:** Allow 2 hours minimum. **Hours:** Daily 10-6, May 1 to mid-Oct. Last admission 45 minutes before closing. **Cost:** $17; $16 (ages 65+); $12 (ages 2-11). **Phone:** (570) 698-6154.

TWIN ROCKS DINER 570/689-9112

American Family Dining $7-$15

AAA Inspector Notes: Popular with locals and tourists alike, the informal restaurant—family-owned and -operated since 1976—is welcoming to families. The menu centers on home-cooked food, which is simply prepared and flavorful. Service is friendly and attentive. **Address:** 117 Twin Rocks Rd 18436 **Location:** I-84 exit 17, just n on SR 191. [B] [L] [D]

LAKE HARMONY (F-11) elev. 1,870'

• Part of Pocono Mountains Area — see map p. 371

RECREATIONAL ACTIVITIES

Skiing and Snowboarding

• **Big Boulder Ski Area** is off I-80 exit 284 to SR 115 at 1 S. Lake Dr., following signs. Snow tubing also is available. **Hours:** Skiing and snowboarding Mon.-Thurs. 3-9, Fri. 3-10, Sat. 8 a.m.-10 p.m., Sun. 8-8, mid-Dec. to mid-Mar. (also Christmas 4-10). Tubing Mon.-Thurs. 3-9, Fri. 3-10, Sat. 10-10, Sun. 10-8, mid-Dec. to mid-Mar. (also Christmas 4-10). Holiday hours vary. Closed Christmas Eve. Phone ahead to confirm schedule. **Phone:** (570) 443-8425.

NICK'S LAKE HOUSE 570/722-2500

American. Casual Dining. $9-$27 **AAA Inspector Notes:** Whether approaching by car, foot or boat, guests receive a warm welcome—and a dock when needed—at Lake Harmony Resort's oldest hotel, originally built in 1923 as an icehouse and now a lakefront restaurant. A seasonal deck overlooks the scenic lake and plays host to weekend entertainment. The casual American menu features steaks, seafood and sautéed dishes. **Features:** full bar, happy hour. **Reservations:** suggested, weekends. **Address:** 110 S Lake Dr 18624 **Location:** I-80 exit 284, 1.8 mi se on SR 115, 1.9 mi sw on SR 903, then 1.4 mi nw on Lake Harmony Rd. [L] [D]

Gear up with

head-to-toe savings at

AAA.com/searchfordiscounts

LAKEVILLE

• Part of Pocono Mountains Area — see map p. 371

COVE HAVEN RESORT 570/226-4506

Resort Hotel
Rates not provided

Address: 194 Lakeview Dr 18438 **Location:** Waterfront. Just off SR 590, 7 mi w of jct US 6; on Lake Wallenpaupack. **Facility:** This spacious couples-only resort has many accommodations with in-room pools, steam baths and fireplaces. Heart-shaped and hot tubs also are offered in many of the king units. 256 units. 1-2 stories (no elevator), interior/exterior corridors. **Terms:** check-in 3:30 pm, age restrictions may apply. **Dining:** 2 restaurants, nightclub, entertainment. **Pool(s):** heated outdoor, heated indoor. **Activities:** sauna, hot tub, steamroom, self-propelled boats, fishing, miniature golf, tennis, sledding, ice skating, bicycles, game room, lawn sports, trails, massage.

LAMAR pop. 562

COMFORT INN OF LAMAR (570)726-4901

Hotel $85-$210 **Address:** 31 Hospitality Ln 17751 **Location:** I-80 exit 173, just n on SR 64. **Facility:** 131 units. 3 stories, interior corridors. **Terms:** check-in 4 pm. **Amenities:** safes. **Pool(s):** outdoor. **Activities:** exercise room. **Guest Services:** coin laundry.

HAMPTON INN & SUITES OF LAMAR (570)726-3939

Hotel $89-$99 **Address:** 24 Hospitality Ln 16848 **Location:** I-80 exit 173, just n on SR 64. **Facility:** 75 units. 3 stories, interior corridors. **Terms:** 1-7 night minimum stay, cancellation fee imposed. **Pool(s):** heated indoor. **Activities:** hot tub, exercise room. **Guest Services:** coin laundry.

LANCASTER (H-9) pop. 59,322, elev. 377'

• Hotels p. 175 • Restaurants p. 180
• Attractions map p. 221
• Hotels & Restaurants map & index p. 222, 225
• Part of Pennsylvania Dutch Country area — see map p. 220

During the Revolutionary War Lancaster was the largest inland city in the Colonies. It was capital of the nation for 1 day on Sept. 27, 1777, when Congress stopped in Lancaster as it fled Philadelphia after the Battle of Brandywine *(see Chadds Ford p. 80)*. Lancaster was the state capital 1799-1812.

The city is in the heart of Lancaster County and is known for its Amish and Mennonite population, its picturesque and productive farms and its heaping platters of Pennsylvania Dutch food. The Pennsylvania Dutch Convention and Visitors Bureau, on US 30 at the Greenfield Road exit, presents a brief orientation to the area through exhibits, a multi-image program, brochures and maps.

Pennsylvania Dutch Convention and Visitors Bureau: 501 Greenfield Rd., Lancaster, PA 17601. **Phone:** (717) 299-8901 or (800) 723-8824.

(See maps & indexes p. 222, 225.)

Shopping areas: Farmers markets at various locations around town offer such delicacies as souse, schmiercase, cup cheese, schnitz, old-fashioned Bavarian pretzels and shoofly pie. **Central Market**, Penn Sq., is one of the oldest enclosed markets in the country. Visitors can shop for fresh fruits, vegetables, flowers, meats and baked goods. The site is open Tues. and Fri. 6-4 and Sat. 6-2.

Lancaster has a large number of factory outlets, including the [SAVE] Tanger Outlet Center at 311 Stanley K. Tanger Blvd. and **Totes Factory Store**, offering umbrellas and rainwear off Lincoln Highway E. at 35 S. Willowdale Dr. **Rockvale Square Factory Outlet Village**, at SR 30E and SR 896, is another large center; it contains more than 120 factory outlets. Several specialty shops are located on Lincoln Highway E.

AMERICAN MUSIC THEATRE is at 2425 Lincoln Hwy. E. A variety of original shows, national Broadway tours and concerts are featured year-round. An original Christmas production is presented each holiday season.

Hours: Christmas show, Nov. 4-Dec. 30. Phone for show times and to confirm schedule and for schedules of other shows. Closed Thanksgiving, Christmas Eve and Christmas. **Cost:** Christmas show $42; $21 (children). Phone for other show ticket prices. **Phone:** (717) 397-7700 or (800) 648-4102.

THE AMISH FARM AND HOUSE is 5 mi. e. on US 30 (Lincoln Highway). Tours of this 1805 farmhouse and of the furnished one-room schoolhouse explain the past and present Amish lifestyle. Farm equipment, barns, animals and an original Conestoga wagon and an 1855 covered bridge can be seen on the 15-acre farm. Whittling demonstrations are available April through October. A 90-minute minibus tour of the nearby countryside is offered as well; phone for details. Sunset, covered bridges and historic Lancaster city tours also are available.

Time: Allow 1 hour, 30 minutes minimum. **Hours:** Farm and house daily 9-6, June-Aug.; 9-5 Apr.-May and Sept.-Nov.; 10-4, rest of year. Phone for countryside bus tour schedule. Closed Jan. 1, Thanksgiving and Christmas. **Cost:** $9.25; $8.25 (ages 60+); $6.25 (ages 5-11). Countryside tour $20.95; $13.95 (ages 5-11); $4.95 (ages 0-4). Combination ticket (includes bus tour and house tour) $27.95; $17.95 (ages 5-11); $4.95 (ages 0-4). Countryside tour reservations are recommended on Sun. **Phone:** (717) 394-6185.

DUTCH WONDERLAND FAMILY AMUSEMENT PARK is 4 mi. e. on US 30 to 2249 E. Lincoln Hwy. More than 30 family-friendly rides, shows and attractions are highlights of this park. Duke's Lagoon features child-friendly water activities and slides. **Time:** Allow 4 hours minimum. **Hours:** Open daily at 10 (weather permitting), Memorial Day-Labor Day; Sat.-Sun. at 10, Apr. 27-day before Memorial Day and

day after Labor Day-Oct. 13. Closing times vary. Events are held select weekends in the fall and winter. Phone ahead to confirm schedule.

Cost: $37.99; $32.99 (ages 60-69); $24.99 (ages 70+); free (ages 0-2). Other admission packages and combination tickets are available. Phone ahead to confirm all rates. **Phone:** (717) 291-1888 or (866) 386-2839. [🍴]

HANDS-ON HOUSE, CHILDREN'S MUSEUM is at 721 Landis Valley Rd. The museum encourages learning through imaginative play. Interactive exhibits include a child-size grocery store, a machine shop and assembly line as well as an indoor farm exhibit with a tractor and cow. Face painting and a play garden also are offered.

Picnic facilities are limited; phone ahead for availability. **Time:** Allow 2 hours minimum. **Hours:** Mon.-Sat. 10-5 (also Fri. 5-8), Sun. noon-5, Memorial Day-Labor Day; Tues.-Fri. 11-4 (also Fri. 4-8), Sat. 10-5, Sun. noon-5, rest of year. Closed major holidays. **Cost:** $8.50. Children under 16 must be with an adult. **Phone:** (717) 569-5437. [🎨]

HISTORIC LANCASTER WALKING TOUR, departing from 5 W. King St., is a 90-minute tour of the city led by a costumed guide who explains the cultural, economic, religious and architectural development of Lancaster. An audiovisual presentation is included. **Hours:** Tours are offered daily at 1 (also Tues. and Fri.-Sat. at 10), Apr.-Oct. Phone ahead to confirm schedule. **Cost:** $7; $6 (ages 62+); $1 (ages 16 and college students with ID). **Phone:** (717) 392-1776.

HISTORIC ROCK FORD PLANTATION, in Lancaster County Park at 881 Rockford Rd., is the preserved 18th-century brick Georgian plantation (built circa 1794) of Edward Hand, Adjutant General to George Washington during the Revolutionary War. Each of the four floors is laid out with four corner rooms branching off of a center hall. The house still includes original flooring, doors, rails, paneling, cupboards, shutters and windowpanes. **Hours:** Wed.-Sun. 11-3, Apr.-Oct. Last tour begins at closing. **Cost:** $8; $7 (ages 65+); $6 (ages 6-12). **Phone:** (717) 392-7223.

HOLY TRINITY LUTHERAN CHURCH, 31 S. Duke St., was originally constructed in 1730 and rebuilt 1761-66. The spire, with statues of apostles Matthew, Mark, Luke and John, dates from 1794. **Hours:** Tours are available by prior arrangement Mon.-Fri. 8:30-4:30. Guide service is available Sun. at 9:45 and noon (after services). **Cost:** Free. **Phone:** (717) 397-2734.

LANCASTERHISTORY.ORG, 230 N. President Ave. at jct. Marietta Ave., houses a 15,000-item artifact collection featuring more than 200 paintings and prints, textiles, glass, ceramics and furniture. The family history research center and library contain more than 1 million historic manuscripts, 50,000

(See maps & indexes p. 222, 225.)
Lancaster County photographs and an Amish quilt collection.

The 10-acre grounds include the Tanger Arboretum with more than 100 species of trees from around the world, and President James Buchanan's Wheatland *(see attraction listing)*. **Hours:** Mon.-Sat. 9:30-5 (also Tues. and Thurs. 5-8). Closed major holidays. **Cost:** Museum, exhibitions and library $7; $5 (ages 65+); free (ages 0-10). **Phone:** (717) 392-4633.

LANCASTER MUSEUM OF ART, 135 N. Lime St., is housed in the 1845 Greek Revival mansion of Clement Grubb, a wealthy citizen who was a patron of 19th-century regional artists. The museum fosters the visual arts through permanent and changing exhibits of works in a variety of media. **Time:** Allow 30 minutes minimum. **Hours:** Tues.-Sat. 10-4, Sun. noon-4. Closed major holidays. Phone ahead to confirm schedule. **Cost:** Donations. **Phone:** (717) 394-3497.

LANCASTER NEWSPAPERS NEWSEUM is 1 blk. s. of the center square at 28 S. Queen St. A window display depicts the history of Lancaster newspapers and includes exhibits of historical newspaper printing equipment, major front pages dating to 1795, a video presentation about the importance of newspapers and a map showing countries with a free and restricted press. **Hours:** Daily 8 a.m.-10 p.m. **Cost:** Free. **Phone:** (717) 291-8600.

LANCASTER SCIENCE FACTORY, 454 New Holland Ave., encourages children to learn about science and engineering with interactive exhibits. The hands-on stations demonstrate concepts such as light, electricity, magnetism, mechanics, motion, sound and vision. . **Hours:** Tues.-Sat. 10-5 (also Mon. 10-5, Memorial Day-Labor Day), Sun. noon-5. Closed Jan. 1, Easter, Thanksgiving and Christmas. **Cost:** $8.50; free (ages 0-2). **Phone:** (717) 509-6363.

LANDIS VALLEY VILLAGE & FARM MUSEUM is 2.5 mi. n. on Oregon Pike (SR 272), following signs to 2451 Kissel Hill Rd. This living-history complex interprets 1740-1940 Pennsylvania German rural life with a mixture of modern and historic buildings on more than 100 acres. An orientation film program and exhibits are offered at the visitor center.

Brothers Henry and George Landis, both devoted collectors of historic memorabilia, founded the museum in 1925 in the barn of their Landis Valley homestead in order to preserve the heritage and culture of the Pennsylvania German region and their family; their collection eventually grew to more than 100,000 items.

From arrowheads gathered in their childhood, the brothers' collections expanded to include decorative arts and examples of early implements and tools used by their farming ancestors that were rapidly being replaced by more modern, mass-produced

items. The museum continued to expand and eventually historic buildings (and some new ones) were acquired and moved to the site.

At the 1870s Landis Brothers House visitors can see the brothers' Victorian home interpreted as it might have appeared around the turn of the 20th century. The house originally belonged to the brothers' parents. The Erisman House, which dates to the 1800s, was moved from Lancaster to the village. In its current setting it is interpreted as the modest home of a seamstress.

Though built in 1941, the stone Tavern, with its huge kitchen and nearby barroom, was constructed to resemble one of the inns prevalent in this area in the early 19th century. An exhibit of Pennsylvania rifles, powder horns, handguns and gunsmithing tools can be seen at the Gun Shop, another of the "newer" buildings. The Country Store is stocked with items typical of a rural store of the early 1900s. Other buildings include a blacksmith shop, a schoolhouse and a barn.

Interpreters dressed in period clothing are stationed at many of the buildings and provide insights into everyday life. Traditional craft and skills demonstrations also are given. Special events are held throughout the year.

Time: Allow 2 hours minimum. **Hours:** Mon.-Sat. 9-5, Sun. noon-5, mid-Mar. to Dec. 31; Wed.-Sat. 9-5, Sun. noon-5, rest of year. Phone ahead to verify craft demonstrations and holiday schedules. Closed Jan. 1, Martin Luther King Jr. Day, Presidents Day, Easter, Columbus Day, Veterans Day, Thanksgiving, day after Thanksgiving and Christmas. **Cost:** $12; $10 (ages 65+); $8 (ages 3-11). Additional fees may be charged during special events. **Phone:** (717) 569-0401.

MENNONITE INFORMATION CENTER AND BIBLICAL TABERNACLE REPRODUCTION is 4.5 mi. e. at 2209 Millstream Rd., just off US 30. The information center features exhibits and a three-screen film presentation that explain the faith and culture of the Amish and Mennonites. Mennonite guides are available to ride with visitors in their own vehicles for a personal, 2-hour tour of the Amish farmlands. Next door is a reproduction of the Biblical Tabernacle. Lecture tours about the tabernacle's history, construction, function and significance are available.

Time: Allow 30 minutes minimum. **Hours:** Center Mon.-Sat. 8-5, Apr.-Oct.; Mon.-Sat. 8:30-4:30, rest of year. Film shown Mon.-Sat. on the hour 9-4. Tabernacle tours depart Mon.-Sat. on the hour 9-4, Apr.-Oct.; Mon.-Sat. on the hour 10-3, in Mar. and Nov.; Mon.-Sat. at 10, noon and 2, rest of year. Closed Jan. 1, Thanksgiving and Christmas. **Cost:** Center free. Film $8; $5.50 (ages 6-16). Tabernacle tours $7.50; $5 (ages 6-16). Personal 2-hour tour (maximum seven people per vehicle) $49; $16 each additional hour. **Phone:** (717) 299-0954, or (800) 858-8320 for tour reservations.

(See maps & indexes p. 222, 225.)

[SAVE] **NORTH MUSEUM OF NATURE & SCIENCE,** at 400 College Ave., contains exhibits about regional geology, Native Americans and dinosaurs. Mounted animals, an 80-seat planetarium, a live animal room, the Hall of the Cosmos and a children's hands-on discovery room also are featured.

Note: The museum is at a temporary location at the corner of Water and Chestnut sts. while the original building undergoes a renovation. The museum is expected to reopen at the 400 College Ave. location in 2015. Hours at the temporary location are Tues.-Fri. 9-5, Sat. 9-4. **Hours:** Tues.-Sat. 10-5, Sun. noon-5 (also Mon. 10-5, June 24-Aug. 19, on Martin Luther King Jr. Day, Presidents Day and Columbus Day). Planetarium shows on the hour Sat. 11-3 and Sun. 1-3. Closed Jan. 1, Easter, July 4, Labor Day, Thanksgiving and Christmas. Phone ahead to confirm schedule. **Cost:** Museum $7.50; $6.50 (ages 3-17 and 65+). Museum and planetarium $10; $9 (ages 3-17 and 65+). Prices may vary during renovations. **Phone:** (717) 291-3941.

[GEM] [SAVE] **PRESIDENT JAMES BUCHANAN'S WHEATLAND** is at 1120 Marietta Ave. (SR 23). Wheatland, home of the 15th U.S. president James Buchanan from 1848-68, highlights the life of America's only bachelor president and the only Pennsylvanian to hold the office. During Buchanan's presidential years the home served as his personal retreat and offered respite from public life. He conducted his 1856 campaign from here, and it also served as Democratic Party headquarters. From the front porch he accepted his party's nomination and the general election results.

Tours of the 1828 Federal-style mansion include public and private rooms furnished in period. Interpreters in period dress help illustrate Buchanan's life and times. The grounds include gardens, a carriage house, ice house and privy. Living history and Yuletide tours also are offered.

Time: Allow 1 hour minimum. **Hours:** House tours are offered Mon.-Sat. on the hour 10-4, Presidents Day to mid-Nov.; by appointment (with at least 24-hour notice), Jan.-Feb. Last tour begins one hour before closing. Living history tours are offered the first Sat. of the month, Mar.-Oct.; phone for tour times. Yuletide tours begin the Fri. after Thanksgiving; phone for tour times. Closed major holidays except Presidents Day. **Cost:** $10; $8 (ages 14-18 and 65+). **Phone:** (717) 392-4633.

AUSTRALIAN WALKABOUT INN B&B   717/464-0707 [23]

[WWW] **Historic Bed & Breakfast.** Rates not provided. **Address:** 837 Village Rd 17602 **Location:** Just w on SR 741. Located in a quiet, small town area. **Facility:** Set in a rural village, this Australian-style B&B features attractive guest rooms with many antique furnishings. 5 units, some cottages. 3 stories (no elevator), interior/exterior corridors. **Terms:** age restrictions may apply.

BEST WESTERN PREMIER EDEN RESORT & SUITES
(717)569-6444 [4]

Hotel
$105-$180

AAA Benefit: Members save up to 20%!

Address: 222 Eden Rd 17601 **Location:** Jct US 30 (Lincoln Hwy) and SR 272 (Oregon Pike). Located in a commercial area. **Facility:** 301 units, some two bedrooms and kitchens. 3 stories, interior/exterior corridors. **Amenities:** video games, safes. **Dining:** Arthur's Terrace Restaurant, see separate listing. **Pool(s):** heated outdoor, heated indoor. **Activities:** sauna, hot tub, playground, game room, exercise room. **Guest Services:** valet and coin laundry, area transportation.

▼ See AAA listing p. 67 ▼

(See maps & indexes p. 222, 225.)

CLASSIC INN   (717)291-4576 18
◆◆ Motel $39-$89 Address: 2302 Lincoln Hwy E 17602 Location: On US 30 (Lincoln Hwy), 5 mi e. Located in a commercial area. Facility: 18 units, some kitchens. 2 stories (no elevator), interior/exterior corridors. Terms: cancellation fee imposed.

COMFORT SUITES AMISH COUNTRY   (717)299-7000 16
◆◆◆ Hotel $129-$299 Address: 2343 Lincoln Hwy E (US 30 E) 17602 Location: On US 30 E (Lincoln Hwy), 4.8 mi e. Facility: 76 units. 3 stories, interior corridors. Terms: check-in 4 pm. Amenities: safes. Pool(s): heated indoor. Activities: exercise room. Guest Services: coin laundry.

CONTINENTAL INN   (717)299-0421 17
◆◆◆ Hotel $75-$145
Address: 2285 Lincoln Hwy E 17602 Location: On US 30 (Lincoln Hwy), 5 mi e. Adjacent to an amusement park. Facility: 165 units. 2 stories (no elevator), interior/exterior corridors. Terms: 3 day cancellation notice-fee imposed. Pool(s): outdoor, heated indoor. Activities: sauna, hot tub, tennis, playground, game room. Guest Services: coin laundry. (See ad this page.)

CORK FACTORY HOTEL   717/735-2075 8
◆◆◆ Historic Hotel. Rates not provided. Address: 480 New Holland Ave, Suite 3000 17602 Location: US 30 (Lincoln Hwy) exit New Holland Ave, 1.4 mi sw. Facility: Located in what once was a cork manufacturing plant, the buildings have been completely reconditioned to residential-style guest rooms that still have kept the original warehouse character. 77 units. 3-4 stories, interior corridors. Amenities: safes. Activities: exercise room, spa.

COUNTRY INN & SUITES BY CARLSON
                               (717)299-4460 19
◆◆◆ Hotel $89-$299
Address: 2260 Lincoln Hwy E 17602 Location: On US 30 (Lincoln Hwy), 5 mi e. Located in a commercial area. Facility: 78 units, some two bedrooms. 4 stories, interior corridors. Terms: check-in 4 pm. Amenities: safes. Pool(s): heated indoor. Activities: hot tub, exercise room. Guest Services: coin laundry. Featured Amenity: continental breakfast.

COUNTRY INN OF LANCASTER   (717)393-3413 13
◆◆◆ Hotel $129-$279
Address: 2133 Lincoln Hwy E 17602 Location: On US 30 (Lincoln Hwy), 4.5 mi e. Located in a commercial area. Facility: 125 units. 2 stories, interior corridors. Terms: cancellation fee imposed. Pool(s): heated indoor. Activities: hot tub. Guest Services: valet laundry. Featured Amenity: continental breakfast. (See ad p. 177.)

COUNTRY LIVING INN   717/295-7295 7
◆◆ Country Inn. Rates not provided. Address: 2406 Old Philadelphia Pike 17602 Location: SR 340, 2 mi e of jct US 30 (Lincoln Hwy). Located in a semi-rural area. Facility: 34 units. 2 stories (no elevator), interior corridors. Guest Services: area transportation.

COURTYARD BY MARRIOTT-LANCASTER
                               (717)393-3600 6
◆◆◆ Hotel $115-$206 Address: 1931 Hospitality Dr 17601 Location: US 30 (Lincoln Hwy) exit Greenfield Rd, just n, then just e on Hempstead Rd. Facility: 133 units. 5 stories, interior corridors. Pool(s): heated indoor. Activities: hot tub, exercise room. Guest Services: valet and coin laundry, boarding pass kiosk, area transportation.

AAA Benefit:
Members save 5% or more!

(See maps & indexes p. 222, 225.)

DOUBLETREE RESORT BY HILTON HOTEL LANCASTER

(717)464-2711 **24**

Hotel
$99-$279

AAA Benefit:
Members save 5% or more!

Address: 2400 Willow Street Pike 17602 **Location:** On US 222, 3.8 mi s. **Facility:** 185 units, some two bedrooms. 5 stories, interior corridors. **Terms:** check-in 4 pm, 1-7 night minimum stay, cancellation fee imposed. **Pool(s):** heated indoor. **Activities:** hot tub, regulation golf, recreation programs, game room, exercise room. **Guest Services:** valet and coin laundry, area transportation.

SAVE ✈ 〒| 🛎 〒 🛎 CALL 🖐M 🏊 BIZ 📶 ⊠ 🖥 🛏 💻

DOUBLETREE RESORT
BY HILTON
LANCASTER

Enjoy Hilton hospitality, in the heart of the Pennsylvania Dutch Country.

Remember, car seats, booster seats and seat belts save lives

FAIRFIELD INN & SUITES BY MARRIOTT LANCASTER

(717)581-1800 **2**

Hotel $104-$229 **Address:** 150 Granite Run Dr 17601 **Location:** Jct SR 72 and 283. Located in a commercial area. **Facility:** 130 units. 3 stories, interior corridors. **Pool(s):** heated outdoor. **Activities:** hot tub, exercise room. **Guest Services:** valet and coin laundry, area transportation.

AAA Benefit:
Members save 5% or more!

〒|➔ CALL 🖐M 🏊 BIZ HS 📶 ⊠ 🛏 💻 / SOME UNITS 🖥

FULTON STEAMBOAT INN

717/299-9999 **20**

Hotel. Rates not provided. **Address:** 2510 Lincoln Hwy E 17602 **Location:** Jct US 30 (Lincoln Hwy) and SR 896. Located in a commercial area. **Facility:** 97 units. 3 stories, interior corridors. **Pool(s):** heated indoor. **Activities:** hot tub, playground, game room, exercise room. **Guest Services:** valet and coin laundry.

〒| 〒 🏊 BIZ 📶 ⊠ 🛏 🖥 💻

HAMPTON INN-LANCASTER

(717)299-1200 **5**

Hotel $164-$214 **Address:** 545 Greenfield Rd 17601 **Location:** 3.3 mi e on US 30 (Lincoln Hwy) exit Greenfield Rd, 0.4 mi n. Located in a commercial area. **Facility:** 129 units. 4 stories, interior corridors. **Terms:** 1-7 night minimum stay, cancellation fee imposed. **Pool(s):** heated outdoor. **Activities:** limited exercise equipment. **Guest Services:** valet and coin laundry.

AAA Benefit:
Members save 5% or more!

🔌 〒|➔ 🏊 BIZ 📶 🛏 🖥 💻

▼ See AAA listing p. 176 ▼

(See maps & indexes p. 222, 225.)

HAWTHORN SUITES BY WYNDHAM
(717)290-7100 **12**

Hotel
$89-$170

Address: 2045 Lincoln Hwy 17602 **Location:** Jct US 30 (Lincoln Hwy). Located in a commercial area. **Facility:** 73 units. 3 stories, interior corridors. **Terms:** check-in 4 pm, cancellation fee imposed. **Activities:** exercise room. **Guest Services:** valet and coin laundry. **Featured Amenity:** full hot breakfast.

HERITAGE HOTEL LANCASTER
(717)898-2431 **1**

Hotel
$109-$149

Address: 500 Centerville Rd 17601 **Location:** 5 mi w on US 30 (Lincoln Hwy) exit Centerville Rd, just nw. Located in a commercial area next to dinner theater. **Facility:** 166 units. 3 stories, interior corridors. **Pool(s):** outdoor. **Activities:** exercise room. **Guest Services:** valet laundry.

Save on brand-name luggage and travel accessories at AAA/CAA Travel Stores

HILTON GARDEN INN LANCASTER
(717)560-0880 **3**

Hotel $135-$259 **Address:** 101 Granite Run Dr 17601 **Location:** Jct SR 72 (Manheim Pike) and 283. Located in a commercial area. **Facility:** 156 units. 2 stories, interior corridors. **Terms:** 1-7 night minimum stay, cancellation fee imposed. **Pool(s):** heated indoor. **Activities:** hot tub, exercise room. **Guest Services:** valet and coin laundry.

AAA Benefit:
Members save 5% or more!

HOLIDAY INN EXPRESS - LANCASTER - ROCKVALE OUTLETS
(717)293-9500 **21**

Hotel
$99-$259

Address: 24 S Willowdale Dr 17602 **Location:** On US 30 (Lincoln Hwy), 6.5 mi e. Located in Rockvale Square Outlets. **Facility:** 111 units. 2 stories, interior corridors. **Terms:** check-in 4 pm, 2 night minimum stay - seasonal and/or weekends, 3 day cancellation notice-fee imposed. **Pool(s):** heated outdoor. **Activities:** exercise room. **Guest Services:** coin laundry. **Featured Amenity:** full hot breakfast.

HOMEWOOD SUITES BY HILTON LANCASTER
(717)381-4400 **1**

Extended Stay Hotel $175-$329 **Address:** 200 Granite Run Dr 17601 **Location:** Jct SR 72 (Manheim Pike) and 283, just ne. **Facility:** 98 efficiencies, some two bedrooms. 3 stories, interior corridors. **Terms:** check-in 4 pm, 1-7 night minimum stay, cancellation fee imposed. **Pool(s):** heated indoor. **Activities:** exercise room. **Guest Services:** valet and coin laundry, area transportation.

AAA Benefit:
Members save 5% or more!

KING'S COTTAGE BED AND BREAKFAST
717/397-1017 **11**

Historic Bed & Breakfast $175-$289 **Address:** 1049 E King St 17602 **Location:** 1.5 mi e on SR 462. Located in a residential neighborhood. **Facility:** This is an elegantly restored Spanish-style mansion, which features a grand wooden staircase, original stained-glass windows and antique furnishings. 8 units. 3 stories (no elevator), interior/exterior corridors. **Terms:** check-in 4 pm, 2 night minimum stay - weekends, 15 day cancellation notice-fee imposed.

LANCASTER ARTS HOTEL
(717)299-3000 **9**

Contemporary Hotel
$189-$359

Address: 300 Harrisburg Ave 17603 **Location:** US 30 (Lincoln Hwy) exit Harrisburg Pike, 1.5 mi s; just n of jct Mulberry St. **Facility:** 63 units. 5 stories, interior corridors. **Terms:** cancellation fee imposed. **Activities:** exercise room. **Guest Services:** valet laundry. **Featured Amenity:** continental breakfast.

THE LANCASTER BED AND BREAKFAST
717/293-1723 **10**

Historic Bed & Breakfast. Rates not provided. **Address:** 1105 East King St 17602 **Location:** 1.5 mi e on SR 462. Located in a residential area. **Facility:** This 1910 Dutch Colonial-style B&B was built for the Armstrong family, famous as flooring manufacturers. The large bright rooms are individually decorated with antiques and quality reproductions. 6 units, some two bedrooms. 3 stories (no elevator), interior corridors. **Terms:** check-in 4 pm, age restrictions may apply.

(See maps & indexes p. 222, 225.)

LANCASTER MARRIOTT AT PENN SQUARE

(717)239-1600   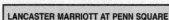 **22**

Hotel
$125-$235

AAA Benefit:
Members save 5% or more!

Address: 25 S Queen St 17603 **Location:** US 222 S to US 30 (Lincoln Hwy) exit Walnut St, left on Prince St, then left on King St. **Facility:** 299 units. 19 stories, interior corridors. **Parking:** on-site (fee) and valet. **Terms:** check-in 4 pm. **Amenities:** safes. **Pool(s):** heated indoor. **Activities:** hot tub, massage. **Guest Services:** valet laundry. (See ad this page.)

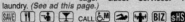

MARRIOTT

Remarkable presence in historic Lancaster near Central Mkt, Fulton Theatre & unique shopping/dining.

RED ROOF INN LANCASTER

717/299-9700   **15**

Motel
Rates not provided

Address: 2307 Lincoln Hwy E 17602 **Location:** On US 30 (Lincoln Hwy), 5 mi e. Located in a commercial area. **Facility:** 92 units. 3 stories, interior/exterior corridors. **Amenities:** safes. **Pool(s):** heated outdoor. **Activities:** limited exercise equipment. **Guest Services:** coin laundry. **Featured Amenity:** continental breakfast.

 / SOME UNITS

WINGATE BY WYNDHAM LANCASTER

(717)299-6604   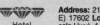 **14**

Hotel
$109-$239

Address: 2110 Lincoln Hwy E (Rt 30 E) 17602 **Location:** On US 30 (Lincoln Hwy), 4.3 mi e. **Facility:** 70 units. 3 stories, interior corridors. **Amenities:** safes. **Activities:** hot tub, exercise room. **Featured Amenity:** continental breakfast.

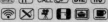

WINGATE
BY WYNDHAM

Located in the heart of PA Dutch country; premium outlet shopping & the famous Dutch Wonderland Pk.

▼ See AAA listing this page ▼

(See maps & indexes p. 222, 225.)

WHERE TO EAT

ARTHUR'S TERRACE RESTAURANT   717/569-6444   1

◆◆◆ American. Casual Dining. $10-$30 **AAA Inspector Notes:** Known locally for an extensive brunch and dinner buffet, this restaurant also features a number of a la carte options, including charbroiled New York strip steak, lump crabcakes and pan-seared sea scallops. **Features:** full bar, Sunday brunch. **Reservations:** required, for Sunday brunch. **Address:** 222 Eden Rd 17601 **Location:** Jct US 30 (Lincoln Hwy) and SR 272 (Oregon Pike); in BEST WESTERN PREMIER Eden Resort & Suites.

B   L   D

THE BELVEDERE INN   717/394-2422   9

◆◆◆ Continental. Fine Dining. $7-$32 **AAA Inspector Notes:** The city-chic ambience at this spot likely is unexpected due to its location in the midst of Amish country. Food is fresh and modern, and the bar offers an extensive variety of liquors, wines and cigars. From Wednesday through Sunday, nightly entertainment is offered upstairs at Crazy Shirley's. **Features:** full bar, patio dining. **Reservations:** suggested, weekends. **Address:** 402 N Queen St 17603 **Location:** Jct Lemon St. L   D

THE BRASSERIE RESTAURANT & BAR
717/299-1694   10

◆◆
American
Casual Dining
$10-$28

AAA Inspector Notes: *Historic.* Tomato bisque and tenderloin tips with mushrooms over fettuccine are specialties at this cozy restaurant. The converted 1925 home contains five small dining rooms and a bar that once was the judge's bench from the old city courthouse. **Features:** full bar. **Reservations:** suggested, weekends. **Address:** 1679 Lincoln Hwy E 17602 **Location:** 2 mi e on SR 462. L   D

EL SERRANO RESTAURANTE   717/397-6191   13

◆◆ Mexican. Casual Dining. $7-$20 **AAA Inspector Notes:** Employing mahogany, bronze, terra cotta and ceramic elements, this restaurant offers a Spanish décor feel. On the menu is a mix of Mexican and Peruvian dishes, including fajitas and pollo fundido — grilled marinated chicken breast folded in a flour tortilla, topped with homemade cheese sauce and served with rice and beans. **Features:** full bar. **Address:** 2151 Columbia Ave 17603 **Location:** 3 mi w on SR 462. L   D

GIBRALTAR   717/397-2790   5

◆◆◆ Seafood. Fine Dining. $15-$33 **AAA Inspector Notes:** Unwind in the contemporary setting of the elegant, open and airy dining room or at the Aquabar Lounge, a martini lounge in which tapas and raw bar items are served. The weekly changing main menu centers on Mediterranean cuisine, 75 percent of which is seafood. Varied whole fishes are prepared and deboned tableside. Breads are prepared on site in an Old World style. **Features:** full bar. **Reservations:** suggested. **Address:** 931 Harrisburg Pike 17603 **Location:** Jct US 30 (Lincoln Hwy) and Harrisburg Pike, 1.4 mi se; in College Square Building; opposite Franklin & Marshall College.

L   D   CALL🅼

THE GREENFIELD RESTAURANT   717/393-0668   2

◆◆◆
American
Fine Dining
$7-$32

AAA Inspector Notes: Capable, attentive servers take care of you at this moderately upscale restaurant, which occupies a 1780 Pennsylvania stone farmhouse. You can feel comfortable bringing your children along for a meal of fresh seafood or steak (or both). Order the well-prepared and nicely garnished seafood crêpes. **Features:** full bar, Sunday brunch. **Reservations:** suggested. **Address:** 595 Greenfield Rd 17601 **Location:** 3.3 mi e on US 30 (Lincoln Hwy) exit Greenfield Rd, then 0.5 mi n.

L   D

HORSE INN RESTAURANT   717/392-5528   8

◆◆◆
American
Casual Dining
$18-$40

AAA Inspector Notes: This casual spot offers a smaller menu focusing on ingredients from the local area. The dining room features dark wood furnishings and exposed brick walls with chalkboards displaying the day's menu options. Hand-crafted cocktails pair well with any dish. **Features:** full bar. **Reservations:** suggested, weekends. **Address:** 540 E Fulton St 17602 **Location:** Access via 200 blk of N Marshall St; in alley, just n of Chestnut St. *Menu on AAA.com* D

ISAAC'S FAMOUS GRILLED SANDWICHES

◆ Deli Sandwiches. Quick Serve. $8-$12 **AAA Inspector Notes:** The modern, New York-style delicatessen specializes in overstuffed grilled sandwiches named after birds, plants and flowers. Salads and homemade soups also are popular. A tropical feel is prevalent in the colorful, casual dining room. L   D

For additional information, visit AAA.com

LOCATIONS:

Address: 1559 Manheim Pike 17601 **Location:** Jct SR 72 and 283, just n on SR 72; in Granite Run Square. **Phone:** 717/560-7774

Address: 25 N Queen St, Suite 101 17603 **Location:** Just n of town square; in Central Market Mall. **Phone:** 717/394-5544

Address: 245 Centerville Rd 17603 **Location:** US 30 (Lincoln Hwy) exit Centerville Rd, just s; in Sycamore Court Plaza. **Phone:** 717/393-1199

Address: 565 Greenfield Rd 17601 **Location:** 3.3 mi e on US 30 (Lincoln Hwy) exit Greenfield Rd, 0.3 mi n. **Phone:** 717/393-6067

JIMMEE'S DELUXE GRILLE   717/509-1919   3

◆ Burgers. Quick Serve. $3-$12 **AAA Inspector Notes:** Order up freshly made burgers, cheesesteaks and fries at this casual grill where all is served with a smile. **Features:** beer & wine. **Address:** 1153 Lititz Pike 17601 **Location:** US 222 S, 0.5 mi s of US 30 (Lincoln Hwy). L   D   CALL🅼

LEMON GRASS THAI RESTAURANT   717/295-1621   6

◆◆ Thai. Casual Dining. $9-$18 **AAA Inspector Notes:** Thai wall tapestries, parasols with bamboo poles and many plants turn the storefront restaurant into an inviting little getaway. Fresh herbs and spices such as lemongrass, basil, mint, galangal, cilantro and Kaffir lime leaves are used in innovative, flavorful, exotic dishes that range from mild to hot. A delicious menu example is angel breast: spinach- and shrimp-stuffed chicken in a delicate orange sauce. Vegetarian choices are extensive. **Address:** 603 Prince St 17603 **Location:** Jct N Prince and W Frederick sts.

L   D

THE PRESSROOM   717/399-5400   12

◆◆ American. Casual Dining. $10-$30 **AAA Inspector Notes:** A renovated hardware building is the scene for bistro-type cuisine. Green lights and cherry-wood accents detail the open, airy dining room in which you can sample delicious crab cakes, lamb chops, pizza and burgers. Live jazz trios perform each Wednesday and Saturday evening. **Features:** full bar, happy hour. **Address:** 26-28 W King St 17603 **Location:** Jct Market and King sts.

L   D

STOCKYARD INN   717/394-7975   4

◆◆◆
Steak
Seafood
Fine Dining
$8-$45

AAA Inspector Notes: The former home of President James Buchanan, this converted restaurant carries out a Colonial theme with the help of large murals, candlelight, background music and freshly cut flowers. Expect traditional cuisine such as chicken croquettes and baked flounder. **Features:** full bar, patio dining. **Reservations:** suggested. **Address:** 1147 Lititz Pike 17601 **Location:** 0.5 mi s of US 30 (Lincoln Hwy) on US 222 S. *Menu on AAA.com* L   D

(See maps & indexes p. 222, 225.)

SYMPOSIUM MEDITERRANEAN RESTAURANT
717/391-7656 ⬛2

▼▼▼▼ Mediterranean. Casual Dining. $9-$28 **AAA Inspector Notes:** Stop in several nights each week to be treated to live music while you indulge in Mediterranean and American specialty dishes. If the weather's nice you can request a seat on the patio. Unwind with an appropriate wine from an exceptional list that complements menu offerings such as coconut-curry shrimp and lamb tenderloin. **Features:** full bar, happy hour. **Address:** 125 S Centerville Rd 17603 **Location:** 5 mi w on US 30 (Lincoln Hwy) exit Centerville Rd, 0.8 mi s.
Ⓛ Ⓓ ⓁⒶⓉⒺ CALL 📞Ⓜ

TOBIAS S FROGG 717/394-8366 ⬛14

▼▼ ▼▼ American. Casual Dining. $7-$27 **AAA Inspector Notes:** The menu mainstays at this local favorite are fine steak and seafood. Try one of Tobias S Frogg's several house specialties or the don't-miss Caribbean shrimp. Everything is served amid a relaxed, tree-lined setting. Peruse the good wine list for an appropriate pairing. **Features:** full bar, patio dining. **Address:** 1766 Columbia Ave 17603 **Location:** 2.5 mi w on SR 462. Ⓛ Ⓓ ⓁⒶⓉⒺ

TONY WANG'S CHINESE RESTAURANT
717/399-1915 ⬛11

▼▼ ▼▼
**Chinese
Casual Dining
$6-$24**

AAA Inspector Notes: The quaint storefront-type dining room serves Cantonese and Szechuan cuisines; an extensive takeout menu is offered. Among tasty examples are sliced chicken with broccoli in garlic sauce and General Tso's chicken, in which large chunks of marinated spring chicken are deep fried and sauteed with scorched red peppers in a tangy sauce. Bring-your-own-bottle wine service is offered. **Reservations:** suggested, weekends. **Address:** 2217 Lincoln Hwy E (Rt 30) 17602 **Location:** On US 30 (Lincoln Hwy), 4.7 mi e. *Menu on AAA.com*
Ⓛ Ⓓ

VENICE PIZZA & PASTA 717/396-1100 ⬛1

▼ Italian. Quick Serve. $6-$23 **AAA Inspector Notes:** From such typical toppings as pepperoni and sausage to the exotic—potato, cheddar and bacon, and shrimp fettuccine—pizza lovers will indulge in hefty slices on freshly prepared crust served at this eatery. Locals swear by the juicy chicken cheesesteaks and cold hoagies, also available all day. **Features:** beer & wine. **Address:** 3079 Columbia Ave 17603 **Location:** US 30 (Lincoln Hwy) exit Centerville Rd, 0.9 mi e, just s; in Western Corners Shopping Plaza. Ⓛ Ⓓ

WALNUT STREET GRILLE AT LANCASTER BREWING COMPANY 717/391-6258 ⬛7

▼▼ ▼▼ Regional American. Casual Dining. $9-$28 **AAA Inspector Notes:** Converted from a turn-of-the-20th-century tobacco warehouse, the casual eatery's industrial-like dining room overlooks the brass kettles of the microbrewery. You always have eight to 10 beers to choose from, and four varieties are sold in bottles and kegs. Beer also factors into the regional American cuisine. The menu features seafood, steaks, prime rib, pork and sauerkraut, varied sandwiches and appetizers and Chicago-style deep-dish pizza. **Features:** full bar, patio dining, happy hour. **Address:** 302 N Plum St 17603 **Location:** Jct Walnut and Plum sts; downtown. Ⓛ Ⓓ

LANGHORNE (A-12) pop. 1,622, elev. 103'
- **Restaurants p. 182**
- **Hotels & Restaurants map & index p. 274**
- **Part of Philadelphia area — see map p. 230**

ⓈⒶⓋⒺ **SESAME PLACE** is at 100 Sesame Rd. This family theme park based on the show "Sesame Street" offers a variety of interactive attractions for all ages. The fun includes the Neighborhood Street Party parade, water play activities in The Count's Splash Castle, live stage shows, the Vapor Trail roller coaster, character meet-and-greets, and exciting rides in Elmo's World.

Swimwear is required for water attractions. Stroller, wheelchair and locker rentals are available. Pets are not permitted. **Time:** Allow 5 hours minimum. **Hours:** Opens daily at 10, May 1-early Sept.; Sat.-Sun. at 10, early Sept.-late Oct.; select days at 1, mid-Nov. through Dec. 31. Closing times vary. **Cost:** $60.99; $55.99 (ages 55+); free (ages 0-1). Prices may vary. Character dining is available for an additional fee. **Parking:** $17-$30. **Phone:** (866) 464-3566. 🍽

COURTYARD BY MARRIOTT PHILADELPHIA-LANGHORNE
(215)945-7980

▼▼ ▼▼ Hotel $167-$332 **Address:** 5 E Cabot Blvd 19047 **Location:** I-95 exit 46A (Oxford Valley Rd), just e off US 1 N; 0.5 mi n of Sesame Place. Located in a business/retail complex. **Facility:** 118 units. 5 stories, interior corridors. **Terms:** check-in 4 pm. **Pool(s):** heated indoor. **Activities:** hot tub, exercise room. **Guest Services:** valet and coin laundry, boarding pass kiosk, area transportation.

AAA Benefit:
Members save 5% or more!

📺 CALL 📞Ⓜ 🚪 BIZ HS 📶 ✕ 🛄 🖨 🖥 / SOME UNITS 🖨

HOLIDAY INN EXPRESS-LANGHORNE OXFORD VALLEY
215/757-4500

▼▼ ▼▼ Hotel. Rates not provided. **Address:** 3101 Cabot Blvd W 19047 **Location:** I-95 exit 46A (Oxford Valley Rd), just e off US 1 N; 0.5 mi n of Sesame Place. Located in a commercial area. **Facility:** 87 units. 4 stories, interior corridors. **Terms:** check-in 4 pm. **Pool(s):** outdoor. **Activities:** exercise room. **Guest Services:** valet laundry.

🍽➕ CALL 📞Ⓜ 🚪 BIZ 📶 ✕ 🛄 🖨 🖥

RED ROOF INN PHILADELPHIA OXFORD VALLEY
215/750-6200

▼▼ ▼▼
Motel
Rates not provided

Address: 3100 Cabot Blvd W 19047 **Location:** I-95 exit 46A (Oxford Valley Rd), just n of Sesame Place. **Facility:** 91 units. 3 stories, exterior corridors. **Amenities:** video games, safes.

ⓈⒶⓋⒺ 📶 ✕ 📷 🎥 🖥 / SOME UNITS 🐾 🛄 🖨

RESIDENCE INN BY MARRIOTT PHILADELPHIA LANGHORNE
(215)946-6500

▼▼ ▼▼ Extended Stay Hotel $153-$367 **Address:** 15 E Cabot Blvd 19047 **Location:** I-95 exit 46A (Oxford Valley Rd), just e off US 1 N; 0.5 mi n of Sesame Place. **Facility:** 100 efficiencies, some two bedrooms. 4 stories, interior corridors. **Pool(s):** heated indoor. **Activities:** hot tub, exercise room. **Guest Services:** valet and coin laundry, area transportation.

AAA Benefit:
Members save 5% or more!

🍽➕ CALL 📞Ⓜ 🚪 BIZ HS 📶 ✕ 🛄 🖨 🖥 / SOME UNITS 🍽

**Choose real ratings you can trust
from professional inspectors
who've been there**

(See map & index p. 274.)

SHERATON BUCKS COUNTY HOTEL   (215)547-4100

Hotel
$89-$289

Sheraton
HOTELS & RESORTS

AAA Benefit: Members save up to 15%, plus Starwood Preferred Guest® benefits!

Address: 400 Oxford Valley Rd 19047 **Location:** I-95 exit 46A (Oxford Valley Rd), 0.8 mi e to exit off US 1 N. Opposite Sesame Place. **Facility:** 186 units. 15 stories, interior corridors. **Terms:** cancellation fee imposed. **Pool(s):** heated indoor. **Activities:** hot tub, game room, exercise room. **Guest Services:** valet laundry, area transportation.

SPRINGHILL SUITES BY MARRIOTT   (215)891-5501

Hotel $98-$275 **Address:** 200 N Buckstown Dr 19047 **Location:** I-95 exit 46A (Oxford Valley Rd), 0.8 mi e to exit off US 1 N. **Facility:** 91 units. 4 stories, interior corridors. **Pool(s):** heated indoor. **Activities:** hot tub, exercise room. **Guest Services:** valet and coin laundry.

AAA Benefit: Members save 5% or more!

WHERE TO EAT

J. B. DAWSON'S   215/702-8119   (58)

American. Casual Dining. $9-$28 **AAA Inspector Notes:** You can watch as breads, sauces and desserts come together in the open kitchen. Servers bring out entrées centered on steak, chops, seafood and pasta. Locals know this area chain for its ample portions, which probably means you'll have to clear space in your refrigerator for the takeout containers you'll be bringing home. The slow-roasted prime rib comes highly recommended but is only available after 4 pm. **Features:** full bar, happy hour. **Address:** 92 N Flowers Mill Rd 19047 **Location:** US 1 exit Maple Ave, just n; in Flowers Mill Shopping Center.

PICCOLO TRATTORIA   215/750-3639   (59)

Italian. Casual Dining. $6-$23 **AAA Inspector Notes:** This casual eatery provides attentive service and features a variety of traditional pasta dishes, panini sandwiches, steak entrées and seafood items. Guests also are able to bring their favorite wine from home to be served. Be sure to save room for their dessert tray. **Address:** 144 N Flowers Mill Rd 19047 **Location:** US 1 exit Maple Ave, just n.

LANSDALE pop. 16,269
• Part of Philadelphia area — see map p. 230

COURTYARD BY MARRIOTT PHILADELPHIA LANSDALE
(215)412-8686

Hotel $179-$230 **Address:** 1737 Sumneytown Pike 19446 **Location:** I-476 exit 31, just e. **Facility:** 135 units. 6 stories, interior corridors. **Pool(s):** heated indoor. **Activities:** exercise room. **Guest Services:** valet and coin laundry, boarding pass kiosk.

AAA Benefit: Members save 5% or more!

AAA Vacations® packages ... unforgettable
experiences and unrivaled value

HOMEWOOD SUITES BY HILTON-LANSDALE   (215)362-6400

Extended Stay Hotel $129-$209 **Address:** 1200 Pennbrook Pkwy 19446 **Location:** I-476 (Pennsylvania Tpke NE Ext) exit 31, 3.9 mi e on Sumneytown Pike, then 1.5 mi n on Church Rd. Pennbrook, 306. **Facility:** 170 efficiencies, some two bedrooms. 6 stories, interior corridors. **Terms:** 1-7 night minimum stay, cancellation fee imposed. **Pool(s):** outdoor. **Activities:** hot tub, exercise room. **Guest Services:** valet and coin laundry.

AAA Benefit: Members save 5% or more!

WHERE TO EAT

UMAI JAPANESE RESTAURANT   215/855-5544

Japanese. Casual Dining. $10-$24 **AAA Inspector Notes:** This cozy Japanese restaurant offers a warm yet intimate atmosphere to go along with a variety of high-grade maki, sushi and specialty rolls. Traditional entrées such as Teriyaki Chicken and Bento boxes are also available. Those with a sweet tooth will enjoy a complimentary fried banana at the end of the meal. Also, guests are able to bring their favorite wine from home during weekdays. **Address:** 220 Penbrook Pkwy 19446 **Location:** I-476 exit 31, 3.9 mi e on Sumneytown Pike, then 1.5 mi n on Church Rd. Pennbrook, 306.

LANSFORD (F-10) pop. 3,941, elev. 1,134'
• Part of Pocono Mountains Area — see map p. 371

NO. 9 MINE & MUSEUM is off SR 209, following signs to 9 Dock St. A battery-operated mine car transports visitors 1,600 feet horizontally into the mountainside where anthracite coal was mined 1855-1972. No. 9, owned by Lehigh Coal & Navigation Co., was said to be the world's oldest continuously operated anthracite coal mine.

You'll need to duck and bend over as you climb into the bright yellow metal mine car, which noisily clanks and rumbles its way into the dark, dank, chilly world of the coal miners and their search for black gold.

A guided walking tour leads down a maze of narrow, dimly lit passageways, as the dangers and hard work required to bring the coal to the surface are related. This is a no-frills tour. Illumination is often only by the light on the guide's hard hat. Deposits of rust can be seen above and on the sides of the walls, and water drips, forming puddles of water on the floor.

You'll see the muleway (the path taken by the mules that were lowered into the mine to haul the heavy carloads of coal out before electric motors came into use); a "hospital" cut into the stone of the mine (more like a room with a cot, some chairs, bandages, crutches and blankets); the 900-foot-deep elevator shaft used to transfer the loaded coal cars to the surface; and an assortment of mining equipment.

Above ground, the museum is housed in the former 1923 wash shanty; it features miners' clothes hanging from the ceiling, a kitchen typical of a miner's home, photographs, tools and mining memorabilia.

Note: A jacket or sweater and comfortable closed-toe walking shoes are recommended; the mine temperature averages 52 to 54 degrees Fahrenheit. **Time:** Allow 2 hours minimum. **Hours:** Museum open Wed.-Sun. 11-4, May-Nov. Mine tours depart Wed.-Sun. on the hour 11-3. Phone ahead to confirm schedule. **Cost:** (includes mine and museum) $10; $6.50 (ages 5-10); free (ages 0-4). Museum only, $3. Cash only. **Phone:** (570) 645-7074.

LATROBE pop. 8,338

WINGATE BY WYNDHAM   (724)539-0400
▼▼▼▼ **Hotel** $99-$135 **Address:** 3970 US Rt 30 15650 **Location:** Jct US 30 and SR 981. **Facility:** 80 units. 3 stories; interior corridors. **Terms:** check-in 4 pm. **Amenities:** video games, safes. **Activities:** hot tub, exercise room. **Guest Services:** valet laundry, area transportation.

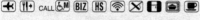

WHERE TO EAT

DENUNZIO'S ITALIAN CHOPHOUSE AND SINATRA BAR
                                      724/539-3980
▼▼▼ Italian. Fine Dining. $7-$30 **AAA Inspector Notes:** On the top floor of Arnold Palmer Regional Airport, this place affords great views of planes taking off and landing. Rat Pack artwork hangs throughout. In addition to a good wine list, this place offers a large bar. Professional, knowledgeable servers can explain excellent Italian dishes such as mushroom ravioli and mussel bisque. **Features:** full bar, patio dining, Sunday brunch, happy hour. **Reservations:** suggested, weekends. **Address:** 148 Aviation Ln 15650 **Location:** 12 mi n on SR 66, 1.7 mi e, 0.3 mi se. Ⓛ Ⓓ

DISALVO'S STATION RESTAURANT   724/539-0500
▼▼ Italian. Casual Dining. $8-$33 **AAA Inspector Notes:** Historic. Built in 1903, this renovated Pennsylvania railroad station is a dining and socializing complex with five distinct dining areas and a downstairs cigar bar. The fact that Mrs. DiSalvo still does the baking makes it worthwhile to save room for dessert. **Features:** full bar, Sunday brunch. **Reservations:** suggested. **Address:** 325 McKinley Ave 15650 **Location:** On Depot St; downtown. **Parking:** on-site (fee). Ⓛ Ⓓ

LAUGHLINTOWN (H-3) elev. 1,289'

Laughlintown is part of the Laurel Highlands *(see place listing this page)*.

THE COMPASS INN MUSEUM, on US 30, is a restored 1799 stagecoach inn. A barn displays a Conestoga wagon, stagecoach and tools. A blacksmith and carpenter shop as well as an outdoor cookhouse contain implements of the time. Costumed docents conduct tours of the complex.

Time: Allow 1 hour, 30 minutes minimum. **Hours:** Tues.-Sat. and Mon. holidays 11-4, Sun. 1-5, May-last Sun. in Oct. Candlelight tours are offered Sat.-Sun. 3-7, Nov. 1 to mid-Dec. **Cost:** $9; $8 (ages 65+); $6 (students through high school); free (ages 0-5). **Phone:** (724) 238-4983.

LAUREL HIGHLANDS

In Southwestern Pennsylvania, the Laurel Highlands cover a 100-square-mile region in the Allegheny Mountain foothills, which includes Fayette, Somerset and Westmoreland counties. Once the exclusive country retreat of Pittsburgh's wealthy industrialists, it is now a popular four-season resort area. Its mountain vistas, rolling countryside and recreational rivers yield a wide range of activities and experiences.

Inspired by the surrounding natural beauty, renowned architect Frank Lloyd Wright left his touch on the area with two landmark homes, Fallingwater *(see attraction listing p. 200)* and House on Kentuck Knob *(see attraction listing p. 81)*. Nearby is Fort Necessity National Battlefield, built by George Washington in 1754 *(see place listing p. 112)*.

Excellent white-water rafting is possible on the Youghiogheny River, which runs southeastward from McKeesport to the Maryland border *(see Ohiopyle p. 216)*. Boating on Conemaugh Lake and Youghiogheny Reservoir also is popular. The Laurel and Chestnut ridges of the Allegheny Mountains provide for excellent stream fishing in season as well as downhill and cross-country skiing in winter. The region also offers more than 25 hiking, bicycling and horse trails and some 30 golf courses. Cyclists can travel 132 continuous miles on the Great Allegheny Passage *(see Insider Info p. 216)*, which runs through the heart of the Laurel Highlands, connecting Cumberland, Md., to McKeesport, outside of Pittsburgh.

In warmer months photographers appreciate the profusion of wildflowers; mountain laurel blooms at higher elevations for about 3 weeks in June. The fall foliage is at its peak mid- to late October. Views are dramatic along the Laurel Highlands Scenic Byway—begin at Farmington, follow SR 381 north through Ohiopyle State Park onto SR 711, continue north at Normalville, then end the trip with a stop for ice cream in historic Ligonier. Forbes State Forest in the central highlands and Mount Davis, the state's highest point, also provide great vistas.

Another scenic route, the Pennsylvania Turnpike/I-76, traverses the region. Exits 67, 75, 91 and 110 off I-76, and exit 27 off I-70 provide direct access to Laurel Highlands.

LEBANON (LEBANON COUNTY) (H-9)
pop. 25,477, elev. 466'
• Hotels p. 184 • Restaurants p. 184
• Attractions map p. 221

A community of German agricultural and English industrial origins, Lebanon was founded in 1750 and named after the White Mountain of Biblical times.

Lebanon's historic churches include the 1760 Tabor United Church of Christ at 10th and Walnut streets and the 1760 Salem Lutheran Church at Eighth and Willow streets. Both churches are open for tours by appointment.

North of Lebanon off SR 72 at Tunnel Hill Road is Union Canal Tunnel, one of the oldest tunnels in the

United States. When it was completed in 1827, the tunneling through 729 feet of rock was considered an engineering marvel. The feat completed the canal between Harrisburg and Reading.

Lebanon County Tourism Promotion Agency: 80 Rocherty Rd., Lebanon, PA 17042. **Phone:** (717) 228-4427.

LEBANON COUNTY HISTORICAL SOCIETY, 924 Cumberland St., contains such reconstructed rooms as a drugstore, one-room schoolhouse, Victorian parlor and general store as well as exhibits about early industries and regional crafts. The front part of the building, constructed in 1780's as a residence, was used from 1813-1818 as the county courthouse, where James Buchanan, the 15th U.S. president, practiced law as a young attorney.

Time: Allow 1 hour, 30 minutes minimum. **Hours:** Museum and library Mon. 1-8, Thurs. 9-4:30, Sat. 9-3 and Sun. 1-4:30. Last tour begins 1 hour, 30 minutes before closing. Closed major holidays. **Cost:** $5; $4 (ages 65+); $2 (ages 9-18). **Phone:** (717) 272-1473. GT

BERRY PATCH BED AND BREAKFAST   (717)865-7219
▼▼▼ **Bed & Breakfast** $135-$239 **Address:** 115 Moore Rd 17046 **Location:** I-81 exit 90, 2.8 mi s on SR 72, 1 mi e on New Bunker Hill St, 0.8 mi s on S Lancaster St, then just e, follow signs. **Facility:** On a hilltop amid 10 acres of scenic countryside, this spacious log home is reminiscent of a Swiss chalet; murder-mystery weekends are offered. 6 units. 2 stories (no elevator); interior/exterior corridors. **Terms:** check-in 4 pm, 2 night minimum stay - seasonal and/or weekends, age restrictions may apply, 14 day cancellation notice-fee imposed. **Activities:** game room, massage. **Guest Services:** coin laundry, area transportation.

WHERE TO EAT

GIN MILL   717/273-2729
▼▼ American. Casual Dining. $7-$25 **AAA Inspector Notes:** You have great options here when it comes to steak. Order it drunken, with brandy cream demi-glace; black and blue, blackened and topped with bleu cheese; or scampi style. Not in the mood for beef? The chef also turns out good seafood, ribs, chicken and pasta. Keep occupied while you wait for your entrée with freshly baked crab-stuffed pretzels or a more traditional appetizer such as fried mozzarella sticks. This place exudes fun, and the friendly staffers further the mood. **Features:** full bar, patio dining, happy hour. **Address:** 324 E Cumberland St 17042 **Location:** US 422, just w of jct 4th St.
L D

LEECHBURG pop. 2,156

KING'S FAMILY RESTAURANT   724/842-0361
▼▼ American. Family Dining. $6-$13 **AAA Inspector Notes:** Fast and friendly service is offered here. The menu is large in size with descriptive menu items and pictures. The restaurant is also known for its ice cream and dessert menu. **Address:** 315 Hyde Park Rd 15656 **Location:** Just s of SR 56; just n of SR 356.
B L D

Enjoy peace of mind with

AAA/CAA Insurance products

LEHIGHTON pop. 5,500
• **Part of Pocono Mountains Area — see map p. 371**

COUNTRY INN & SUITES BY CARLSON   (610)379-5066

▼▼▼ **Hotel** $92-$300 **Address:** 1619 Interchange Rd 18235 **Location:** I-476 (Pennsylvania Tpke NE Ext) exit 74 (US 209), just w. **Facility:** 64 units. 3 stories, interior corridors. **Terms:** cancellation fee imposed. **Pool(s):** heated indoor. **Activities:** hot tub, exercise room. **Guest Services:** coin laundry. **Featured Amenity:** continental breakfast.
SAVE T+ CALL &M ⊠ BIZ HS
🛜 🖥 🖨 🖵 / SOME UNITS 🐾

HAMPTON INN LEHIGHTON (JIM THORPE AREA)
                                        (610)377-3400
▼▼▼ Hotel $99-$169 **Address:** 877 Interchange Rd 18235 **Location:** I-476 (Pennsylvania Tpke NE Ext) exit 74 (US 209), 0.8 mi w. **Facility:** 78 units. 3 stories, interior corridors. **Terms:** 1-7 night minimum stay, cancellation fee imposed. **Pool(s):** heated indoor. **Activities:** hot tub, limited exercise equipment. **Guest Services:** valet laundry.

AAA Benefit: Members save 5% or more!

T+ CALL &M ⊠ BIZ 🛜 ⊠ 🖥 🖨 🖵

SWEET REFLECTIONS B&B   570/386-5406
▼▼ Bed & Breakfast. Rates not provided. **Address:** 574 Oak Grove Dr 18235 **Location:** I-476 (Pennsylvania Tpke NE Ext) exit 74 (US 209), 2.8 mi sw to US 209 (which becomes SR 443/Blakeslee Blvd), 2.9 mi sw to Gilberts Hill Rd, just s to Oak Grove Dr, then 0.5 mi sw. Located in a rural residential area. **Facility:** 3 units. 2 stories (no elevator), interior corridors. **Terms:** age restrictions may apply.
🖥 ⊠ 🆔

WHERE TO EAT

PJ WHELIHAN'S PUB & RESTAURANT   610/377-1819
▼▼ American. Casual Dining. $5-$20 **AAA Inspector Notes:** This immensely popular pub offers a welcoming atmosphere and delicious salads, sandwiches, wings, burgers, steaks and seafood. Notable menu favorites are the clam chowder, prime rib, baked ziti and Buffalo wings. The early-bird menu is an excellent value and well worth stopping by for before 6 pm. The ambience is reminiscent of a British or Irish pub with dark woods, stained-glass light fixtures and dim lighting adding to the atmosphere. **Features:** full bar, patio dining, early bird specials, happy hour. **Reservations:** suggested, weekends. **Address:** 101 Harrity Rd 18235 **Location:** I-476 (Pennsylvania Tpke NE Ext) exit 74 (US 209), just e. L D

LEOLA (H-10) elev. 430'
• **Attractions map p. 221**
• **Hotels & Restaurants map & index p. 222, 225**
• **Part of Pennsylvania Dutch Country area — see map p. 220**

MASCOT ROLLER MILLS AND RESSLER FAMILY HOME is 3.4 mi. s.e. off SR 23 to jct. Stumptown and Newport rds. A mill has been on this site since the mid-1730s, and it was owned and operated by three generations of the Ressler family 1865-1977. The mill also acted as the town's post office 1890-1934.

Guided tours of the operational mill offer information about early rural life as well as the milling process; old equipment can be seen. The 1855 house features period antiques. **Time:** Allow 1 hour, 30 minutes minimum. **Hours:** Mon.-Sat. 10-4, mid-May

(See maps & indexes p. 222, 225.)

to mid-Oct. Closed major holidays. **Cost:** Free. **Phone:** (717) 656-7616.

THE INN AT LEOLA VILLAGE   (717)656-7002 ③

Boutique Hotel
$159-$349

Address: 38 Deborah Dr 17540 **Location:** On SR 23; center. Located in a commercial area. **Facility:** An upscale country-inn ambiance characterizes this property, which features an outstanding, upscale restaurant and full-service spa. Each room is individually decorated with elegant furnishings. 62 units, some two bedrooms and kitchens. 1-3 stories, interior/exterior corridors. **Terms:** cancellation fee imposed. **Amenities:** Some: safes. **Dining:** TE, see separate listing. **Pool(s):** outdoor. **Activities:** sauna, exercise room, spa. **Guest Services:** valet and coin laundry, area transportation. **Featured Amenity:** continental breakfast.

WHERE TO EAT

TÈ   717/556-8715 ⑰

Italian
Fine Dining
$89-$159

AAA Inspector Notes: Experience an absolutely unbelievable dining experience at this one-of-a-kind upscale Italian restaurant. A team of six staff members, including a certified sommelier, will assist with your every need and provide extensive information on either the five- or nine-course prix fixe menu options. Unique flavors like white chocolate lobster risotto and seared scallops with pork bell are among a few of the options. With only five tables available, make sure to call ahead for a reservation. **Features:** full bar. **Reservations:** required. Semiformal attire. **Address:** 38 Deborah Dr 17540 **Location:** On SR 23; center; in The Inn at Leola Village.

LEVITTOWN   pop. 52,983

• Hotels & Restaurants map & index p. 274
• Part of Philadelphia area — see map p. 230

COMFORT INN LEVITTOWN/BENSALEM   (215)547-5000 ㊴

Hotel
$65-$159

Address: 6401 Bristol Pike 19057 **Location:** I-276 (Pennsylvania Tpke) exit 358, 0.4 mi n. **Facility:** 71 units, some kitchens. 2 stories (no elevator), interior corridors. **Amenities:** safes. **Pool(s):** outdoor. **Activities:** exercise room. **Guest Services:** coin laundry. **Featured Amenity:** continental breakfast.

RAMADA INN   (215)946-1100 ㊵

Hotel
$90-$170

Address: 6201 Bristol Pike 19057 **Location:** I-276 (Pennsylvania Tpke) exit 358, just n. Located in a commercial area. **Facility:** 120 units. 2 stories (no elevator), interior corridors. **Amenities:** video games, safes. **Pool(s):** outdoor. **Activities:** playground, exercise room. **Guest Services:** valet and coin laundry.

LEWISBERRY   (H-8) pop. 362, elev. 436'

RECREATIONAL ACTIVITIES

Skiing and Snowboarding

• **Roundtop Mountain Resort** is at 925 Roundtop Rd. Snow tubing and summer activities also are offered. **Hours:** Skiing and snowboarding Mon.-Fri. 9 a.m.-10 p.m.; Sat.-Sun. 8 a.m.-10 p.m., early Dec. to mid-Mar., weather permitting. Snow tubing Mon.-Thurs. 4-10, Fri. noon-10, Sat.-Sun. 9 a.m.-10 p.m., early Dec. to mid-Mar., weather permitting. Holiday hours vary. Phone for summer activity schedules. **Phone:** (717) 432-9631.

LEWISBURG   (F-8) pop. 5,792, elev. 460'
• Hotels p. 186 • Restaurants p. 186

Lewisburg, on the West Branch of the Susquehanna River, is noted for its late Federal and Victorian architecture. It also is a college town: Bucknell University is a private liberal arts college.

Susquehanna River Valley Visitors Bureau: 81 Hafer Rd., Lewisburg, PA 17837. **Phone:** (570) 524-7234 or (800) 525-7320.

Shopping areas: An interesting shopping center is Country Cupboard, 3 miles north on SR 15. It offers crafts, gifts, Christmas items and specialty foods. Another unusual collection of shops is Brookpark Farm, 1 mile west of SR 15 on SR 45, offering rugs, gourmet foods, crafts, antiques, collectibles and Christmas items. Roller Mills Marketplace, 517 St. Mary St., features more than 400 antiques dealers. The Street of Shops, in a restored woolen mill at 100 N. Water St., is home to 125 unique boutique-style shops offering artwork, handcrafted items, collectibles and vintage furniture.

PACKWOOD HOUSE MUSEUM, 15 N. Water St., features an extensive decorative arts collection that spans the 18th- through 20th centuries. More than 10,000 pieces are featured in the 27-room house built in the 1790's. The museum specializes in central Pennsylvania decorative arts, including furniture and more than 240 quilts. Exhibits of works by local artists are offered in the Kelly Gallery. Visitors will see three stories and 18 rooms of the house.

Time: Allow 1 hour minimum. **Hours:** Tues.-Sat. 10-5. Guided tours are offered Thurs.-Sat. at 11 and 1. Closed major holidays. **Cost:** $10; free (ages 0-12). **Phone:** (570) 524-0323. ㏿

SAMEK ART MUSEUM is at jct. Moore Ave. and 7th St. on the third floor of the Elaine Langone Center on the Bucknell University campus (there also is a satellite gallery downtown at 416 Market St.). The permanent collection comprises more than 5,500 works in a variety of media by American and international artists from various time periods as well as objects from different cultures and countries. Highlights include the Kress collection of Renaissance paintings and the Sordoni collection of Japanese art.

A student art show is held annually, and temporary exhibits accompanied by lectures are held throughout the year. **Time:** Allow 30 minutes minimum. **Hours:** Tues.-Sun. noon-5 (both locations). **Cost:** Free. **Phone:** (570) 577-3792.

SLIFER HOUSE MUSEUM, 1 mi. n. on US 15, was built 1860-62 and is an excellent example of Victorian architecture. Designed by architect Samuel Sloan, the mansion was once the home of Eli Slifer, Secretary of the Commonwealth of Pennsylvania during the Civil War. Period furnishings and decorative arts from the Victorian and Civil War eras are displayed. **Time:** Allow 1 hour minimum. **Hours:** Guided tours are offered Tues.-Sat. 1-4, mid-April to mid-Dec.; by appointment rest of year. Last tour begins 1 hour before closing. **Cost:** $7; $6 (ages 60+); $5 (students with ID); $3 (ages 5-17). **Phone:** (570) 524-2245.

BEST WESTERN PLUS COUNTRY CUPBOARD INN
(570)524-5500

Hotel
$120-$180

AAA Benefit: Members save up to 20%!

Address: 7701 Westbranch Hwy (US 15) 17837 **Location:** I-80 exit 210A (US 15/New Columbia), 4.8 mi s on US 15. Located in a commercial area. **Facility:** 136 units. 3 stories, interior corridors. **Dining:** Country Cupboard Restaurant, see separate listing. **Pool(s):** heated outdoor, heated indoor. **Activities:** sauna, hot tub, exercise room. **Guest Services:** valet and coin laundry. **Featured Amenity: full hot breakfast.**

COMFORT SUITES
(570)524-8000

Hotel
$104-$199

Address: 4775 Westbranch Hwy 17837 **Location:** I-80 exit 210A (US 15/New Columbia), 7 mi s on US 15. Near Bucknell University. **Facility:** 60 units. 3 stories, interior corridors. **Pool(s):** heated indoor. **Activities:** exercise room. **Guest Services:** valet and coin laundry. **Featured Amenity: full hot breakfast.**

COUNTRY INN & SUITES BY CARLSON
(570)524-6600

Hotel
$115-$225

Address: 134 Walter Dr 17837 **Location:** I-80 exit 210A (US 15/New Columbia), 4.8 mi s on US 15. **Facility:** 84 units. 3 stories, interior corridors. **Terms:** 3 day cancellation notice-fee imposed. **Pool(s):** heated indoor. **Activities:** hot tub, exercise room. **Guest Services:** valet and coin laundry. **Featured Amenity: full hot breakfast.**

Get AAA/CAA travel information in the digital and printed formats you prefer

---

HAMPTON INN
(570)522-8500

Hotel
$129-$249

AAA Benefit: Members save 5% or more!

Address: 140 International Dr 17837 **Location:** I-80 exit 210A (US 15/New Columbia), 5 mi s, then just w. **Facility:** 70 units. 4 stories, interior corridors. **Terms:** 1-7 night minimum stay, cancellation fee imposed. **Pool(s):** heated indoor. **Activities:** hot tub, exercise room. **Guest Services:** valet and coin laundry.

WHERE TO EAT

COUNTRY CUPBOARD RESTAURANT   570/523-3211

American. Family Dining. $7-$16 **AAA Inspector Notes:** The comfortable, country-casual family restaurant delivers wholesome, familiar fare: ham, chicken, steak, seafood, sandwiches and homemade soup, all of which is so popular that they're sold at the attached one-acre gift shop. Daily specials offer good value. Buffets are served at lunch and dinner, and the menu service is fast and friendly. Treats from the in-house bakery are delicious. **Address:** 101 Hafer Rd 17837 **Location:** I-80 exit 210A (US 15/New Columbia), 4.8 mi s on US 15; adjacent to BEST WESTERN PLUS Country Cupboard Inn.

ELIZABETH'S AN AMERICAN BISTRO   570/523-8088

American. Casual Dining. $8-$32 **AAA Inspector Notes:** Located in historic downtown, this bistro offers a distinctive flair of Asian, French and Italian cuisines. The breads and desserts are all made in-house each morning. Feast on pasta, frittatas, five-spice grilled hen or shrimp, brick-fired pizza, adobe porterhouse pork chops or a balsamic-grilled salmon over roasted corn with thyme-truffle risotto. All fresh produce is seasonal, local or organic while more than 100 wines complement the meal. **Features:** full bar. **Reservations:** suggested. **Address:** 412 Market St 17837 **Location:** Center of downtown. **Parking:** on-site (fee).

LEWISBURG HOTEL   570/523-7800

American. Casual Dining. $7-$31 **AAA Inspector Notes:** Step inside the beautifully restored Lewisburg Hotel to find rich oak woodwork and an antique-style, tin-type ceiling. Expect an air of subtle sophistication while you dine on traditional fare. Order from a menu listing several Italian and vegetarian selections, and the unfussy servers will happily take care of you. **Features:** full bar. **Reservations:** suggested. **Address:** 136 Market St 17837 **Location:** Between 2nd and Front sts; downtown. **Parking:** street only.

REBA & PANCHO'S A MODERN AMERICAN RESTAURANT
570/522-7006

New American. Casual Dining. $10-$28 **AAA Inspector Notes:** New American fusion unites Mediterranean and Mexican for an innovative and distinctive menu. Freshness and creativity in dishes such as the main plates with two fish choices, both spicy or not, veal loin chop with lentils, vegetarian ravioli with goat cheese and spinach or great starters—gorditas, tostadas, skinny pizza or spring roll. Menu choices are virtually all over the map. Reba, the chef and owner, is a Culinary Institute of America graduate. Bring your own bottle. **Address:** 2006 W Market St 17837 **Location:** Jct US 15 and SR 45, 0.5 mi w on SR 45.

TEMPERANCE HOUSE   570/524-2558

American. Casual Dining. $9-$29 **AAA Inspector Notes:** Subtle lighting and local artwork add to the relaxed ambience to your choice of comfortable dining rooms. The menu centers on such tried-and-true dishes as steak, chicken, seafood, sandwiches and salad. The friendly, attentive staff deliver timely follow-up in a casual atmosphere. **Features:** full bar. **Reservations:** suggested. **Address:** 50 N 2nd St 17837 **Location:** Jct US 15, just n, 0.5 mi e on SR 45.

LEWISTOWN (G-7) pop. 8,338, elev. 495'

Lewistown, named in honor of Quaker legislator William Lewis, was a thriving Native American community prior to its incorporation in 1795. European immigrants later settled in the region; their traces are still visible at many local historical sites. The borough lies within a scenic region: To the east is Lewistown Narrows, a 6-mile section of land through which the Juniata River flows; the river meets the Susquehanna River some 35 miles downstream. The river offers year-round fishing, recreation and natural beauty.

The Stone Arch Bridge, curiously constructed without a keystone, was once part of the early turnpike that connected Harrisburg and Pittsburgh. The arch is off US 22/322W Lewistown exit on Jacks Creek Road. North of Lewistown is the Seven Mountain District, known for good hunting and fishing. Kishacoquillas Valley, also called the Big Valley, is 8 miles north of Lewistown on SR 655W and is home to a large Amish population. Amish and Mennonites sell produce, plants, flowers, antiques and handcrafted items in this 25-mile-long valley. Farmers markets, flea markets and livestock auctions are held on Wednesdays, March through November.

The Pennsylvania State Fire Academy is in Lewistown. Firefighters from Pennsylvania and other states attend classes throughout the year.

The original county courthouse, built in 1843, is on Monument Square and is home to the chamber of commerce and visitors bureau and the Mifflin County Historical Society. Nearby is McCoy House, the 1874 birthplace and home of soldier-statesman Maj. Gen. Frank Ross McCoy. It now houses a museum. Tours are offered Sun. 1:30-4, mid-May through mid-Oct.; phone (717) 242-1022.

Juniata River Valley Chamber of Commerce & Visitors Bureau: One W. Market St., Lewistown, PA 17044. **Phone:** (717) 248-6713.

LIGONIER (H-3) pop. 1,573, elev. 1,201'
• Hotels p. 188

Part of the Laurel Highlands *(see place listing p. 183)*, Ligonier is sheltered by Laurel Mountain to the east and Chestnut Ridge to the west. It is a quiet, picturesque village with a turn-of-the-20th-century atmosphere. Steeped in history, the town was a key British defense post during the French and Indian War. In the early 1800s it served as a stagecoach stop along the new Philadelphia-Pittsburgh Turnpike, which a century later became part of the Lincoln Highway.

Quaint shops and eateries border the town square, where a Victorian bandstand on a grassy lawn is surrounded by benches and pretty flora. Metered parking is available for those eager to explore the downtown area on foot. Boutiques, taverns and antique dealers also are dotted along Main Street, branching off the town square. You'll encounter the occasional coffee shop or ice cream parlor tucked in between novelty shops and art galleries displaying hand-crafted works. The commercial area eventually gives way to tidy historic homes with well-manicured lawns and flower gardens.

Live stage productions, children's theater shows, concerts, movies and cabaret nights are offered at The Ligonier Theater, 208 W. Main St.; phone (724) 238-6514. The musically inclined can witness some fancy guitar picking at the Laurel Highlands Bluegrass Festival, held in mid-June just northeast of town at the Ligonier Township Fire Department's fairgrounds. Exhibits relating to Eastern Orthodox Christianity as well as Middle Eastern and Eastern European culture are featured at the Antiochian Heritage Museum, 6 miles north of US 30 on SR 711; phone (724) 238-3677.

Ligonier is one of many places included along a statewide heritage corridor known as the Lincoln Highway Roadside Museum. Though not a museum in the traditional sense, this 200-mile stretch of US 30 features some 250 landmarks, both historical and whimsical, commemorating the colorful history of the nation's first coast-to-coast highway. A brochure and driving tour map are available at the visitors bureau as well as from the Lincoln Highway Heritage Corridor office at 3435 US 30E in Latrobe; phone (724) 879-4241. Another pleasant drive, the Laurel Highlands Scenic Byway, extends from SR 711 in Ligonier to Donegal; travelers can view hilly, bucolic countryside dotted by farms along this stretch.

Laurel Highlands Visitors Bureau: 120 E. Main St., Ligonier, PA 15658. **Phone:** (724) 238-5661 or (800) 333-5661.

FORT LIGONIER, US 30 and SR 711 at 200 S. Market St., is a full-scale, on-site reconstruction and restoration of a British fort built in 1758. The fort, a stronghold during the French and Indian War, contains a fascine cannon battery with reproduced British artillery pieces. A museum includes The French and Indian War Art Gallery of Original Art and an in-depth exhibit entitled The World Ablaze: An Introduction to the Seven Years' War, which features more than 200 original items that were acquired from a variety of countries.

Time: Allow 1 hour minimum. **Hours:** Mon.-Sat. 10-4:30, Sun. noon-4:30, mid-Apr. to early Nov.; by appointment rest of year. **Cost:** $10; $8 (seniors and students with ID); $6 (ages 6-16); free (active military with ID). Phone ahead to verify rates. **Phone:** (724) 238-9701.

IDLEWILD PARK, 2.5 mi. w. on US 30, features several theme areas. Jumpin' Jungle offers interactive play features, including a 3-story net climb/tree house and a ball pit and slides. Nursery rhyme characters roam through Story Book Forest. Olde Idlewild features 11 main rides, an antique carousel and two roller coasters. Among the SoakZone offerings are the

Family Wavepool, the Lazy River, the three-level Aqua-Play structure, more than a dozen waterslides, giant tipping buckets and an interactive children's pool. Hootin' Holler, resembling an old mining town, offers live entertainment and rides. Raccoon Lagoon has 14 rides for children. A trolley runs through Daniel Tiger's Neighborhood of Make Believe.

Hours: Gates open daily at 10:30, late May-Labor Day. Rides and attractions open by 11:30; closing times vary. Phone ahead to confirm schedule. **Cost:** $41.99; $32.99 (ages 60+); free (ages 0-2). Phone ahead to confirm rates. **Phone:** (724) 238-3666.

CAMPBELL HOUSE B&B   (724)238-9812
Historic Bed & Breakfast $90-$175 **Address:** 305 E Main St 15658 **Location:** Just e of Ligonier Diamond. **Facility:** The décor at this B&B set in a restored turn-of-the-century 1868 city cottage is vintage chic with bits of historic touches. 6 units. 2 stories (no elevator), interior/exterior corridors. **Terms:** 3 day cancellation notice-fee imposed. **Guest Services:** valet laundry, area transportation.

CHAMPION LAKES B&B AND GOLF CLUB   724/238-5440
Bed & Breakfast. Rates not provided. **Address:** 4743 Rt 711 15923 **Location:** On SR 711, 7 mi n. **Facility:** 17 units, some kitchens. 2 stories (no elevator), interior corridors. **Activities:** regulation golf.

LINCOLN FALLS

MORGAN CENTURY FARM   570/924-4909
Bed & Breakfast. Rates not provided. **Address:** 7043 Rt 154 18616 **Location:** Just w on SR 87, 0.6 mi s; in village. Next to Elk Creek. **Facility:** The restored family farmhouse offers gracious rooms meticulously decorated with family antiques. Enjoy a book in the apple tree swing or in the screened-in gazebo by Elk Creek. Credit cards not accepted. 5 units, some cottages. 2 stories (no elevator), interior/exterior corridors. *Bath:* shower only. **Terms:** age restrictions may apply. **Activities:** fishing, cross country skiing.

LINESVILLE (D-1) pop. 1,040, elev. 1,034'

Pymatuning Reservoir arcs through Crawford County for 16 miles, its south end near Jamestown on US 322 and its northern apex near Linesville on US 6. Its western shore curves into Ohio. Pymatuning State Park *(see Recreation Areas Chart)* surrounds the Pennsylvania shoreline. At the spillway in the park visitors can buy bread to feed the fish; the site is known as the place where the fish are reputedly so numerous that ducks walk on the fishes' backs. The lake is home to bass, bluegill, crappie, muskellunge, perch and walleye. Recreational activities include hunting and fishing.

The upper part of the reservoir is a state waterfowl sanctuary. A number of islands mark this part of the reservoir. Cabins, campgrounds and boat rentals are available at Pymatuning State Park; phone (724) 932-3142 for information and (888) 932-3141 for cabin and campground reservations.

Pymatuning Holeshot Raceway, 15729 Maple Rd., offers dirt bike, ATV and quad racing competitions April through October; phone (814) 683-5655.

PENNSYLVANIA GAME COMMISSION PYMATUNING WILDLIFE LEARNING CENTER is 2 mi. s. at 12590 Hartstown Rd. It features more than 250 mounted birds and animals as well as stamp and patch collections. Wildlife educational activities and materials are available. The center overlooks Pymatuning Lake and several bald eagle nests. A paved .75-mile nature trail is on the grounds. **Note:** The attraction and grounds are closed while a new building is being built to replace the old one. The new center is expected to be completed in 2016.

LIONVILLE
• Part of Philadelphia area — see map p. 230

COMFORT SUITES EXTON   (610)594-4770
Hotel $119-$200 **Address:** 700 W Uwchlan Ave 19341 **Location:** I-76 (Pennsylvania Tpke) exit 312, 1 mi s on SR 100. **Facility:** 91 units, some efficiencies. 4 stories, interior corridors. **Amenities:** safes. **Pool(s):** heated indoor. **Activities:** hot tub, exercise room. **Guest Services:** valet and coin laundry.

EXTENDED STAY AMERICA-PHILADELPHIA/EXTON
                                         610/524-7185
Extended Stay Hotel. Rates not provided. **Address:** 877 N Pottstown Pike (Rt 100) 19353 **Location:** I-76 (Pennsylvania Tpke) exit 312, 1.8 mi s. Located in a commercial area. **Facility:** 101 efficiencies. 3 stories, interior corridors. **Guest Services:** coin laundry.

FAIRFIELD INN BY MARRIOTT PHILADELPHIA GREAT VALLEY/EXTON   (610)524-8811
Hotel $90-$148 **Address:** 5 N Pottstown Pike 19341 **Location:** I-76 (Pennsylvania Tpke) exit 312, 0.5 mi s; jct SR 113 and 100. Located in a commercial area. **Facility:** 104 units. 4 stories, interior corridors. **Pool(s):** heated indoor. **Activities:** exercise room. **Guest Services:** valet and coin laundry.

AAA Benefit: Members save 5% or more!

HAMPTON INN EXTON/DOWNINGTOWN   (610)363-5555
Hotel $119-$159 **Address:** 4 N Pottstown Pike 19341 **Location:** I-76 (Pennsylvania Tpke) exit 312, 0.5 mi s; jct SR 113 and 100. Located in a commercial area. **Facility:** 122 units. 4 stories, interior corridors. **Terms:** 1-7 night minimum stay, cancellation fee imposed. **Pool(s):** heated outdoor. **Guest Services:** valet and coin laundry.

AAA Benefit: Members save 5% or more!

RESIDENCE INN BY MARRIOTT PHILADELPHIA GREAT VALLEY/EXTON   (610)594-9705
Extended Stay Hotel $132-$217 **Address:** 10 N Pottstown Pike 19341 **Location:** I-76 (Pennsylvania Tpke) exit 312, 1 mi s on SR 100. Located in a commercial area. **Facility:** 96 units, some two bedrooms, efficiencies and kitchens. 4 stories, interior corridors. **Pool(s):** heated indoor. **Activities:** exercise room. **Guest Services:** valet and coin laundry.

AAA Benefit: Members save 5% or more!

WYNDHAM GARDEN EXTON VALLEY FORGE (610)363-1100

▼▼▼ **Hotel** $100-$180 **Address:** 815 N Pottstown Pike 19341 **Location:** I-76 (Pennsylvania Tpke) exit 312, 2 mi s on SR 100. Located in a commercial area. **Facility:** 217 units. 4 stories, interior corridors. **Dining:** Arthur's Steakhouse Restaurant, see separate listing. **Pool(s):** outdoor. **Activities:** exercise room. **Guest Services:** valet and coin laundry.

[icons]

WHERE TO EAT

ARTHUR'S STEAKHOUSE RESTAURANT 610/363-1100

▼▼ American. Casual Dining. $5-$20 **AAA Inspector Notes:** This restaurant offers comfortable, casual library décor with large windows overlooking the hotel's swimming pool area. The menu features bistro fare and focuses on fresh seafood and quality steaks. Try the signature dish, the sirloin steak au poivre. **Features:** full bar, Sunday brunch. **Address:** 815 N Pottstown Pike 19341 **Location:** I-76 (Pennsylvania Tpke) exit 312, 2 mi s on SR 100; in Wyndham Garden Exton Valley Forge. [D]

ISAAC'S FAMOUS GRILLED SANDWICHES 484/875-5825

▼ Deli Sandwiches. Quick Serve. $8-$12 **AAA Inspector Notes:** The modern, New York-style delicatessen specializes in overstuffed grilled sandwiches named after birds, plants and flowers. Salads and homemade soups also are popular. A tropical feel is prevalent in the colorful, casual dining room. **Address:** 630 W Uwchlan Ave 19341 **Location:** I-76 (Pennsylvania Tpke) exit 312, 0.6 mi s; in Crossroads Square Shopping Center. [L] [D] CALL [icons]

LITITZ (H-9) pop. 9,369, elev. 360'

- **Restaurants p. 190**
- **Attractions map p. 221**
- **Hotels & Restaurants map & index p. 222**
- **Part of Pennsylvania Dutch Country area — see map p. 220**

Dedicated in 1756 as a Moravian community, Lititz was named for the place in Bohemia where the Moravian Church was founded in 1456. Until 1855 the entire community was owned by the church. Linden Hall, one of the oldest girls' residence schools in the United States, was founded by Moravians in 1746. Originally a day school, it began boarding students in 1794. The Lititz Moravian Archives Museum, at Church Square and Main Street, provides guided tours of the church buildings by appointment May to October; phone (717) 626-8515.

Lititz Springs Park, on SR 501 just north of jct. SR 772, is illuminated by thousands of candles on July 4. The celebration dates from the early days of the town's settlement.

Self-guiding tours: A brochure outlining a walking tour of historic buildings and houses on E. Main Street is available from the Lititz Historical Foundation at the Johannes Mueller House *(see attraction listing)*.

GRAVE OF GEN. JOHN A. SUTTER is in the Moravian Cemetery behind the church on E. Main St. It was the discovery of gold on Gen. Sutter's property near Sacramento, Calif., that started the rush of 1849. From 1871, Sutter lived in Lititz while petitioning Congress to receive compensation for damages to his California property caused by gold seekers. Sutter died in 1880 without Congress having decided the matter. **Hours:** Daily 24 hours. **Cost:** Free. **Phone:** (717) 626-8515.

JOHANNES MUELLER HOUSE, 137-145 E. Main St., was built in 1792 and consists of a stone house and an adjoining log structure. The log portion contains Mueller's workshop. The stone house is furnished in period. A museum next to the house features a collection of early Lititz artifacts, paintings and special exhibits. Heritage and water gardens are on the premises.

45-minute tours are conducted by costumed guides. **Time:** Allow 30 minutes minimum. **Hours:** House and museum open Mon.-Sat. 10-4, Memorial Day-last Sat. in Oct. (museum also open Fri.-Sat. 10-4, Nov. 1-Sat. before Christmas). **Cost:** Museum by donation. House $5; $4 (ages 62+); $3 (ages 10-18). **Phone:** (717) 627-4636.

JULIUS STURGIS PRETZEL BAKERY is at 219 E. Main St. In 1861 Julius Sturgis established what is said to be the first pretzel bakery in the United States. Handmade soft pretzels are baked on the premises. Visitors are taught how to twist pretzel dough and about baking in the 1860s.

Time: Allow 15 minutes minimum. **Hours:** Guided tours are given Mon.-Sat. every half-hour 9:30-4:30, mid-Mar. through Dec. 31; 10:30-3:30, mid-Jan. to mid-Mar. Closed Jan. 1, Thanksgiving and Christmas. **Cost:** $3.50; $2.50 (children). **Phone:** (717) 626-4354.

WILBUR CHOCOLATE CANDY AMERICANA MUSEUM AND STORE is in the Wilbur Chocolate Co. building at 48 N. Broad St. The museum displays antique confectionery equipment, including molds, tins, trays, wooden boxes and a collection of more than 150 antique chocolate pots. A video presentation details the history of the cocoa bean to present-day chocolate products.

Visitors can watch hand-dipped candies being made. The museum has a strong aroma of chocolate from the adjoining factory. The candy outlet resembles an old country store. **Hours:** Mon.-Sat. 10-5. Closed Jan. 1, Thanksgiving and Christmas. **Cost:** Free. **Phone:** (717) 626-3249 or (888) 294-5287.

ALDEN HOUSE BED & BREAKFAST 717/627-3363 ⑪

▼▼▼ **Historic Bed & Breakfast.** Rates not provided. **Address:** 62 E Main St 17543 **Location:** SR 501 (Lititz Pike), just e on SR 772; downtown. Located in a historic district. **Facility:** An attractive garden and patio enhance this restored 1850s Colonial-style building located in the heart of the shopping and tourism area. 7 units. 3 stories (no elevator), interior corridors. *Bath:* shower only. **Terms:** age restrictions may apply.

[icons]

HOLIDAY INN EXPRESS & SUITES (717)625-2366 ⑫

▼▼▼ **Hotel** $121-$308 **Address:** 101 Crosswinds Dr 17543 **Location:** 1.4 mi s on SR 501 (Lititz Pike), just w on Trolley Run Rd. **Facility:** 90 units. 3 stories, interior corridors. **Terms:** check-in 4 pm. **Pool(s):** heated indoor. **Activities:** hot tub, exercise room. **Guest Services:** valet and coin laundry. **Featured Amenity:** continental breakfast.

[icons] SAVE [icons] CALL [icons] BIZ HS

[icons] / SOME UNITS

(See map & index p. 222.)

SWISS WOODS BED & BREAKFAST   717/627-3358 **10**

WWWW **Bed & Breakfast.** Rates not provided. **Address:** 500 Blantz Rd 17543 **Location:** 4 mi n on SR 501 (Lititz Pike), 1 mi w on Brubaker Valley Rd, just n. Located in a rural area. **Facility:** Find Swiss-style décor at this inn that's tucked away in the woods. A beautifully landscaped garden and outdoor patios are sure to tempt you to spend a lot of time outdoors. 7 units. 2 stories (no elevator), interior corridors. **Terms:** age restrictions may apply.

BIZ 🛜 ✕ 🚭 / SOME UNITS 🛗 📶

WHERE TO EAT

ISAAC'S FAMOUS GRILLED SANDWICHES   717/625-1181

W **Deli Sandwiches.** Quick Serve. $8-$12 **AAA Inspector Notes:** The modern, New York-style delicatessen specializes in overstuffed grilled sandwiches named after birds, plants and flowers. Salads and homemade soups also are popular. A tropical feel is prevalent in the colorful, casual dining room. **Address:** 4 Trolley Run Rd 17543 **Location:** 1.4 mi s on SR 501 (Lititz Pike), just w.

L   D   LATE

MOJO ASIAN CUISINE & SUSHI BAR   717/509-3888 **13**

WW **Asian.** Casual Dining. $7-$20 **AAA Inspector Notes:** You'll be thankful for the abundant comfortable booths here, as it may take you awhile to narrow choices from a widely diverse menu that incorporates sushi, Chinese, Japanese and Thai cuisines. Although that diversity doesn't carry over to the limited dessert menu, a dish of green tea ice cream is more than enough after a filling meal. **Reservations:** suggested. **Address:** 245 Bloomfield Dr 17543 **Location:** Jct SR 772, 2.9 mi s on SR 501 (Lititz Pike); in Shoppes at Bloomfield.   L   D

LOCK HAVEN (F-7) pop. 9,772, elev. 563'

Lock Haven was laid out at the site of Fort Reed, which had once protected frontier settlers from the Native Americans. The 1778 evacuation of the fort during a fierce Native American raid became known as the great runaway. During the 19th century Lock Haven was a major lumber center and an important port on the Pennsylvania Canal.

Clinton County Economic Partnership: 212 N. Jay St., Lock Haven, PA 17745. **Phone:** (570) 748-5782 or (888) 388-6991.

Self-guiding tours: Guided walking tours are offered by appointment at the Ross Library at 232 W. Main St. Tour schedules and themes vary; phone (570) 748-3321.

SAVE **HEISEY MUSEUM,** 362 E. Water St., is in a restored two-story 1831 Victorian house. Tours lasting about 90 minutes reveal the period rooms and furnishings as well as local memorabilia. **Hours:** Wed.-Thurs. 10-3, mid-Jan. to mid-Dec. (also second Sun. of the month 2-4, Feb.-Nov.); other times by appointment. Phone ahead to confirm schedule. **Cost:** Donations. **Phone:** (570) 748-7254.

SAVE **PIPER AVIATION MUSEUM,** 1 Piper Way, chronicles the life of William T. Piper Sr., founder of Piper Aircraft, and his contribution to the airline industry's demand for light personal aircraft.

His company once boasted three manufacturing facilities in Pennsylvania and two in Florida. The museum includes aircraft, artifacts, models, advertising, historic photographs and archives.

Guided tours are available by appointment. **Time:** Allow 1 hour minimum. **Hours:** Mon.-Fri. 9-4, Sat. 10-4, Sun. noon-4. **Cost:** $6; $5 (ages 55+); $3 (ages 7-15). **Phone:** (570) 748-8283.

BEST WESTERN LOCK HAVEN   (570)748-3297

Hotel
$99-$199

 AAA Benefit: Members save up to 20%!

Address: 101 E Walnut St 17745 **Location:** US 220 exit 111 (SR 120 W), just w. **Facility:** 67 units. 4 stories, interior corridors. **Terms:** 30 day cancellation notice-fee imposed, resort fee. **Activities:** exercise room. **Guest Services:** valet and coin laundry. **Featured Amenity: continental breakfast.**

SAVE 🍴➜ 🛜 🛗 💻 / SOME UNITS 🐾 📶

FAIRFIELD INN & SUITES BY MARRIOTT   (570)748-1580

Hotel
$101-$166

FAIRFIELD INN & SUITES **Marriott**   **AAA Benefit:** Members save 5% or more!

Address: 50 Spring St 17745 **Location:** US 220 exit 109 (Mill Hall), 2 mi n on SR 150 (Bellefonte Ave), just w. **Facility:** 65 units. 3 stories, interior corridors. **Pool(s):** heated indoor. **Activities:** hot tub, exercise room. **Guest Services:** valet and coin laundry. **Featured Amenity: breakfast buffet.**

SAVE 🍴➜ CALL 📞M 🚐 BIZ HS
🛜 ✕ 💻 / SOME UNITS 🛗 📶

WHERE TO EAT

DUTCH HAVEN RESTAURANT   570/748-7444

WW **American.** Casual Dining. $6-$22 **AAA Inspector Notes:** Classic American fare is prepared from fresh ingredients. The friendly staff provides attentive service in a relaxing atmosphere. **Features:** full bar, Sunday brunch. **Address:** 201 E Bald Eagle St 17745 **Location:** US 220 exit Walnut St, just w, then just n; corner of Grove St.

L   D

LORETTO (G-4) pop. 1,302, elev. 1,942'

SOUTHERN ALLEGHENIES MUSEUM OF ART, on the campus of St. Francis College, displays a fine collection of American art with emphasis on 19th- and 20th-century paintings and graphics. Regional and national artists are represented in the permanent collection and changing exhibits. **Time:** Allow 30 minutes minimum. **Hours:** Tues.-Fri. 10-5, Sat. 1-5. Closed major holidays. **Cost:** Free. **Phone:** (814) 472-3920.

LUDWIGS CORNER

• Part of Philadelphia area — see map p. 230

LUDWIG'S GRILLE AND OYSTER BAR   610/458-5336

♦♦ ♦♦ Seafood. Casual Dining. $8-$32 **AAA Inspector Notes:** The casual, country restaurant, set in a charming shopping plaza organized in village fashion, employs a nautical theme in several dining rooms. You can choose from seafood, including crab cakes, lobster and crab bisque. The extensive oyster bar offers 10 to 20 varieties at any given time. **Features:** full bar, patio dining. **Reservations:** suggested, weekends. **Address:** 2904 Conestoga Rd 19343 **Location:** Jct SR 100 and 401; in The Shoppes At Ludwig's Village.

[L] [D] CALL[&M]

LUZERNE pop. 2,845

ANDY PERUGINO'S RESTAURANT   570/288-5337

♦♦ Italian. Casual Dining. $6-$30 **AAA Inspector Notes:** Pictures of food and maps of Italy decorate the walls of this comfortable restaurant. Its popularity stems from its great tasting sauces of the Italian dishes, such as lasagna, ravioli and other pasta. American selections offer diversity. Portion sizes are generous. **Features:** full bar. **Reservations:** suggested. **Address:** 258 Charles St 18709 **Location:** Cross Valley Expwy exit 6 northbound; exit 5 southbound, right on Bennett St, then right on Ryman St to Charles St.

[L] [D]

MACUNGIE (G-11) pop. 3,074, elev. 390'

RECREATIONAL ACTIVITIES

Skiing and Snowboarding

• **Bear Creek Mountain Resort & Conference Center** is at 101 Doe Mountain Ln. Snow tubing and warm-weather activities also are offered. **Hours:** Mon.-Fri. 9 a.m.-10 p.m., Sat.-Sun. (also Jan. and Feb. long holiday weekends and Christmas-Dec. 30) 8:30 a.m.-10 p.m. (Dec. 31, 8:30 a.m.-1 a.m.; Jan. 1, 10-10), Dec.-Mar. (weather permitting). Phone for schedule rest of year. **Phone:** (610) 682-7100 or (866) 754-2822.

BEAR CREEK MOUNTAIN RESORT & CONFERENCE CENTER   (610)682-7100

♦♦♦♦♦♦
Hotel
$159-$450

Address: 101 Doe Mountain Ln 18062 **Location:** 0.5 mi w of State St. **Facility:** 117 units, some two bedrooms, three bedrooms and efficiencies. 5-8 stories, interior corridors. **Terms:** check-in 4 pm, 2-3 night minimum stay - seasonal and/or weekends, 7 day cancellation notice. **Amenities:** safes. **Dining:** 2 restaurants. **Pool(s):** heated outdoor, heated indoor. **Activities:** hot tub, tennis, playground, game room, exercise room, spa. **Guest Services:** coin laundry, area transportation. **Featured Amenity: full hot breakfast.**

[SAVE] [+] [¶] [Y] CALL[&M] [⊛]
[BIZ] [📶] [X] [🔌] [▭] [▱] /[SOME UNITS] [HS]

WHERE TO EAT

THE GRILLE AT BEAR CREEK   610/641-7149

♦♦ ♦♦ American. Casual Dining. $12-$35 **AAA Inspector Notes:** After a day on the slopes, come to this casual spot that resembles a beautiful ski lodge with dark wood furnishings and stone accents. The menu touches on a variety of different cuisines and includes such options as the Saigon sandwich with lemon grass or the Montreal pork loin with apple smoked bacon. Other items include Buffalo wings, shrimp cocktail, the Bear Creek cheeseburger and steak Cobb salad. **Features:** full bar, happy hour. **Address:** 101 Doe Mountain Ln 18062 **Location:** 0.5 mi w of State St. [D] CALL[&M]

MALVERN pop. 2,998

• Restaurants p. 192
• Part of Philadelphia area — see map p. 230

COURTYARD BY MARRIOTT - PHILADELPHIA GREAT VALLEY/MALVERN   (610)993-2600

♦♦♦♦♦♦ Hotel $160-$263 **Address:** 280 Old Morehall Rd 19355 **Location:** I-76 (Pennsylvania Tpke) exit 324, jct US 202 exit SR 29 N. **Facility:** 127 units. 5 stories, interior corridors. **Pool(s):** heated indoor. **Activities:** exercise room. **Guest Services:** valet and coin laundry, area transportation.

| **AAA Benefit:** Members save 5% or more! |

[Y] CALL[&M] [⊛] [BIZ] [HS] [📶] [X] [🎥] [🔌] [▭] /[SOME UNITS] [▤]

THE DESMOND HOTEL AND CONFERENCE CENTER MALVERN   (610)296-9800

♦♦♦♦♦♦ Hotel $169-$299 **Address:** 1 Liberty Blvd 19355 **Location:** US 202 exit SR 29 N, 0.5 mi w. Located in Great Valley Corporate Center. **Facility:** 194 units. 4 stories, interior corridors. **Terms:** cancellation fee imposed. **Dining:** 2 restaurants, also, The Hunt Room, see separate listing. **Pool(s):** heated indoor. **Activities:** hot tub, trails, exercise room. **Guest Services:** valet laundry, area transportation.

[¶] [+] [Y] [⊛] [BIZ] [📶] [X] [▱]
/[SOME UNITS] [🐾] [HS] [🔌]

EXTENDED STAY AMERICA MALVERN   610/695-9200

♦♦ ♦♦ Extended Stay Hotel. Rates not provided. **Address:** 8 E Swedesford Rd 19355 **Location:** Just w of US 202 and SR 29 N. Opposite Great Valley Corporate Center. **Facility:** 78 efficiencies. 3 stories, interior corridors. **Pool(s):** heated indoor. **Activities:** exercise room. **Guest Services:** coin laundry.

[+] [⊛] [📶] [X] [🔌] [▭] [▱] /[SOME UNITS] [🐾]

EXTENDED STAY AMERICA-PHILADELPHIA GREAT VALLEY   610/240-0455

♦♦ ♦♦ Extended Stay Hotel. Rates not provided. **Address:** 300 Morehall Rd (SR 29) 19355 **Location:** US 202 exit SR 29 N. **Facility:** 104 efficiencies. 3 stories, interior corridors. **Guest Services:** coin laundry.

[+] CALL[&M] [📶] [🔌] [▭] [▱] /[SOME UNITS] [🐾]

HAMPTON INN GREAT VALLEY/MALVERN   (610)699-1300

♦♦♦♦♦♦ Hotel $129-$179 **Address:** 635 Lancaster Ave 19355 **Location:** On US 30, just e of jct US 202. Located in a commercial area. **Facility:** 125 units. 5 stories, interior corridors. **Terms:** 1-7

| **AAA Benefit:** Members save 5% or more! |

night minimum stay, cancellation fee imposed. **Pool(s):** outdoor. **Activities:** exercise room. **Guest Services:** valet and coin laundry, area transportation.

[+] CALL[&M] [⊛] [BIZ] [📶] [X] [🔌] [▭] [▱]

HOLIDAY INN EXPRESS MALVERN FRAZER   610/651-0400

♦♦♦♦♦♦
Hotel
Rates not provided

Address: 1 Morehall Rd 19355 **Location:** Jct US 30 at SR 29. [🍴] Malvern, 199. **Facility:** 88 units. 4 stories, interior corridors. **Activities:** exercise room. **Guest Services:** valet laundry. **Featured Amenity: full hot breakfast.**

[SAVE] [+] CALL[&M] [BIZ] [📶] [X]
[🔌] [▭] [▱] [🚌]

HOMEWOOD SUITES BY HILTON   (610)296-3500

  Extended Stay Hotel
$129-$249 **Address:** 12 E Swedesford
Rd 19355 **Location:** US 202 exit SR 29,
follow signs. Opposite Great Valley Corporate Center. **Facility:** 123 efficiencies,
some two bedrooms. 4 stories, interior corridors. **Terms:** 1-7 night
minimum stay, cancellation fee imposed. **Pool(s):** heated indoor. **Activities:** hot tub, exercise room. **Guest Services:** valet and coin
laundry, area transportation.

AAA Benefit:
Members save 5%
or more!

SHERATON GREAT VALLEY HOTEL   (610)524-5500

Hotel
$109-$229

Sheraton

AAA Benefit: Members
save up to 15%, plus
Starwood Preferred
Guest® benefits!

Address: 707 Lancaster Pike 19355
Location: Jct US 202 and 30 E. Located in a commercial area. **Facility:**
193 units. 5 stories, interior corridors.
Terms: cancellation fee imposed. **Amenities:** safes. **Pool(s):** heated indoor.
Activities: hot tub, exercise room.
Guest Services: valet and coin laundry,
area transportation.

SONESTA ES SUITES MALVERN   610/296-4343

**Extended Stay
Hotel**
Rates not provided

Address: 20 Morehall Rd 19355 **Location:** Jct US 30 and SR 29, just nw. Located in a commercial area. Malvern,
199. **Facility:** 120 kitchen units, some
two bedrooms. 2 stories (no elevator),
interior/exterior corridors. **Terms:**
check-in 4 pm. **Amenities:** safes.
Pool(s): outdoor. **Activities:** exercise
room. **Guest Services:** valet and coin
laundry, area transportation.

WHERE TO EAT

ANTHONY'S PIZZA AND ITALIAN RESTAURANT 610/647-7400

 Italian. Casual Dining. $7-$23 **AAA Inspector Notes:** This
family-owned and -operated restaurant offers Italian-themed décor
and a warm atmosphere. The menu consists of traditional favorites
served in large portions. A large variety of Neopolitan and Sicilian
pizzas are available. This spot offers great value and is a local favorite. **Address:** 127 W King St 19355 **Location:** US 30, 0.5 mi se
on Old Lincoln Hwy, just s on Bridge St, then just w on E King St.
 Malvern, 199.

DIXIE PICNIC   484/320-8024

 Southern American. Quick Serve. $6-$14 **AAA Inspector
Notes:** Whether choosing baby back ribs, French toast, shrimp and
grits or a box lunch, taste buds, belly and budget will all be satisfied.
The upcake alone (a cupcake frosted on all sides but one and served
upside down) is reason enough to venture away from nearby King of
Prussia Mall. Once meal choices are made, ring the bell at the counter
to summon a cheerful staff member from the kitchen to take your order.
Address: 215 Lancaster Ave 19355 **Location:** Jct SR 29, 0.8 mi w on
US 30; in Lincoln Court Shopping Plaza.

HISTORIC GENERAL WARREN INNE   610/296-3637

 Continental. Fine Dining. $10-$37 **AAA Inspector
Notes:** *Historic.* This charming 18th-century country inn features
candlelit dining rooms with original working fireplaces, some with
hand-carved mantelpieces. Diners also might choose seating on the
heated, year-round, canopied deck or the seasonal brick patio. The
menu mixes American and Continental cuisines, including such
classic dishes as snapper soup, Wiener schnitzel and crabcakes.
Tableside service is expert. **Features:** full bar. **Reservations:** suggested, for dinner. **Address:** 9 Old Lancaster Rd 19355 **Location:**
Jct US 30 and SR 29, just e on US 30, just s on Old Lincoln Hwy,
then just w. Malvern, 199.

THE HUNT ROOM   610/296-9800

 Regional American. Fine Dining. $11-$32 **AAA Inspector Notes:** This modestly elegant restaurant with beautiful
blond-wood paneling and decorative brass chandeliers overlooks a
pond with a fountain set amid nicely landscaped grounds. Representative of the well-prepared entrées on the seasonally revised menu is
rack of lamb. **Features:** full bar, Sunday brunch. **Reservations:** suggested. **Address:** 1 Liberty Blvd 19355 **Location:** US 202 exit SR 29
N, 0.5 mi w; in The Desmond Hotel and Conference Center
Malvern.

MARGARET KUO'S MANDARIN   610/647-5488

 Chinese. Casual Dining. $9-$38 **AAA Inspector Notes:**
Asian décor elements such as a Chinese drum, elegant paintings of
costumed Mandarins and beautiful black-lacquered chairs with patterned silk seats provide a striking contrast to the dining room's stark
white walls. Guests can bring wine to enjoy with delicious, nicely presented entrées of classic Mandarin and Szechuan cuisine. Dishes
center on duck, fish, pork, chicken, seafood and steak. Also offered is
a Japanese sushi bar. The weekday lunch buffet and weekend dim
sum are popular. **Reservations:** suggested, weekends. **Address:**
190 Lancaster Ave 19355 **Location:** US 30, 0.5 mi w of jct SR 29.

MANHEIM (H-9) pop. 4,858, elev. 400'
- **Attractions map p. 221**
- **Hotels & Restaurants map & index p. 222**
- **Part of Pennsylvania Dutch Country area — see map p. 220**

Baron Henry William Stiegel, along with Charles
and Alexander Stedman, founded Manheim in 1762.
The trio bought the land from Mary Norris, granddaughter of James Logan. Logan was William
Penn's secretary and was given the 720 acres from
Penn's widow and sons in 1734. Stiegel also was
the originator of Stiegel glass, which is blown and
colored. Its three types include enameled, pattern-molded, and cut and engraved.

The Pennsylvania Renaissance Faire is held
on the grounds of the 35-acre 19th-century Mount
Hope Estate and Winery, .5 mi. s. of the Pennsylvania Tpke. exit 266 on SR 72, weekends August
through October (also Labor Day). The grand traditions of the 16th century, including arts, literature
and music, are re-created with artisans, jousters,
merchants, more than 90 stage performances and
hundreds of people in Elizabethan costumes. Each
weekend offers its own theme. Food—including contemporary and ethnic fare as well as fare that would
have been served during the era—is available.

Visit AAA.com/searchfordiscounts to save
on dining, attractions, hotels and more

(See map & index p. 222.)

Manheim Area Chamber of Commerce: 13 E. High St., Manheim, PA 17545. **Phone:** (717) 665-6330.

HAMPTON INN-MANHEIM (717)665-6600 [20]

WWW **Hotel** $99-$229 **Address:** 2764 Lebanon Rd 17545 **Location:** I-76 (Pennsylvania Tpke) exit 266, 0.3 mi s on SR 72. **Facility:** 95 units. 4 stories, interior corridors. **Terms:** 1-7 night minimum stay, cancellation fee imposed. **Pool(s):** heated outdoor. **Activities:** exercise room. **Guest Services:** coin laundry.

AAA Benefit: Members save 5% or more!

LANCASTER INN & SUITES (717)665-5440 [21]

WWW **Hotel** $101-$199 **Address:** 1475 Lancaster Rd 17545 **Location:** 2.5 mi s on SR 72. Located in a commercial area. **Facility:** 60 units. 3 stories, interior corridors. **Terms:** cancellation fee imposed. **Pool(s):** heated outdoor. **Activities:** exercise room. **Guest Services:** valet and coin laundry, area transportation.

WHERE TO EAT

THE CAT'S MEOW 717/664-3370 [19]

WW American. Casual Dining. $8-$24 **AAA Inspector Notes:** Small-town Manheim was once an important railroad crossroads, and you'll find this eatery nestled in the center of town in a historic 1869 brick hotel that serviced the railroad industry. Its name, which comes from a phrase that became popular during the Roaring '20s, has décor reminiscent of that era, including mannequins dressed as famed Public Enemy Number One, John Dillinger and his "Lady in Red." You'll even find a bathtub gin tap system at the bar. **Features:** full bar. **Reservations:** suggested. **Address:** 215 S Charlotte St 17545 **Location:** SR 72, just w on W Stiegel St, just s.

MANSFIELD pop. 3,625

COMFORT INN (570)662-3000

WWWW **Hotel** $109-$179

Address: 300 Gateway Dr 16933 **Location:** Jct US 6 and 15. Located in a quiet secluded area. **Facility:** 100 units. 2 stories, interior corridors. **Parking:** winter plug-ins. **Activities:** exercise room. **Featured Amenity:** full hot breakfast.

HAMPTON INN & SUITES (570)662-7500

WWW **Hotel** $149-$209 **Address:** 98 Dorsett Heights 16933 **Location:** US 15 exit US 6/Mansfield, just e, then just s. **Facility:** 83 units. 4 stories, interior corridors. **Terms:** 1-7 night minimum stay, cancellation fee imposed. **Pool(s):** heated indoor. **Activities:** hot tub, exercise room. **Guest Services:** coin laundry.

AAA Benefit: Members save 5% or more!

MICROTEL INN & SUITES BY WYNDHAM MANSFIELD (570)662-9300

WWW **Hotel** $99-$190 **Address:** 90 Dorsett Heights 16933 **Location:** US 15 exit US 6/Mansfield, just n. **Facility:** 85 units. 3 stories, interior corridors. **Pool(s):** heated indoor. **Activities:** hot tub, exercise room. **Guest Services:** valet and coin laundry.

WHERE TO EAT

LAMB'S CREEK 570/662-3222

WWW American. Casual Dining. $7-$28 **AAA Inspector Notes:** Dark woods accented by stained-glass lamps enhance the lounge and dining rooms at this casual restaurant. The chef creates delicious comfort food and creative choices such as the Texas grilled meatloaf, grilled Atlantic salmon, chicken Parmesan, prime rib every night and their specialty, the Lamb's Creek salad with apples and candied walnuts. The house-made desserts should not be missed. The Italian lemon cream cake is memorable. Seasonal patio dining available. **Features:** full bar, Sunday brunch. **Address:** 200 Gateway Dr 16933 **Location:** US 15 exit US 6/Mansfield, just e, just n on Lamb's Creek Rd, then just w.

MARIENVILLE (E-4) pop. 3,137, elev. 1,732'

Marienville, cradled between the half-million-acre Allegheny National Forest *(see place listing p. 46 and Recreation Areas Chart)* and the 7,182-acre virgin timber Cook Forest State Park *(see Recreation Areas Chart)*, is attractive to outdoor enthusiasts year-round.

THE FOREST LODGE & CAMPGROUND 814/927-8790

W **Motel.** Rates not provided. **Address:** 44078 Rt 66 16239 **Location:** 6 mi n of town. Direct access to Allegheny National Forest. **Facility:** 12 units, some cabins. 1 story, interior/exterior corridors. **Terms:** check-in 4 pm. **Activities:** snowmobiling, playground, picnic facilities, trails.

MARIETTA pop. 2,588, elev. 259'

• **Hotels & Restaurants map & index p. 222**
• **Part of Pennsylvania Dutch Country area — see map p. 220**

RAILROAD HOUSE RESTAURANT BED & BREAKFAST 717/426-4141 [33]

WWW American. Casual Dining. $8-$25 **AAA Inspector Notes:** A Victorian flair punctuates the dining room, which is decorated with antiques, stenciling and Oriental appointments. The menu focuses on preparations of beef, poultry, seafood and pasta, all of which are complemented by a nice wine list. **Features:** full bar. **Address:** 280 W Front St 17547 **Location:** Jct US 30 (Lincoln Hwy), 2.2 mi n on SR 441, 1.3 mi w on Market St, then just s on Perry St.

MARS pop. 1,699

• **Hotels & Restaurants map & index p. 348**
• **Part of Pittsburgh area — see map p. 326**

COMFORT INN CRANBERRY TOWNSHIP (724)772-2700 [37]

WWW **Hotel** $99-$159 **Address:** 924 Sheraton Dr 16046 **Location:** I-76 (Pennsylvania Tpke) exit 28; I-79 exit 76 (US 19) northbound; exit 78 southbound, 0.5 mi s on US 19. **Facility:** 103 units. 5 stories, interior corridors. **Activities:** exercise room. **Guest Services:** valet and coin laundry.

Recommend places

you'd like us to inspect at

AAA.com/TourBookComments

(See map & index p. 348.)

DOUBLETREE BY HILTON PITTSBURGH CRANBERRY
724/776-6900

 Hotel
Rates not provided

AAA Benefit: Members save 5% or more!

Address: 910 Sheraton Dr 16046 **Location:** I-76 (Pennsylvania Tpke) exit 28, 0.5 mi s on US 19; I-79 exit 76 (US 19) northbound; exit 78 southbound. **Facility:** 189 units. 5 stories, interior corridors. **Amenities:** video games, safes. **Dining:** 2 restaurants. **Pool(s):** heated outdoor, heated indoor. **Activities:** sauna, hot tub, exercise room. **Guest Services:** valet laundry.

SUPER 8-CRANBERRY   (724)776-9700
Hotel $90-$175 **Address:** 929 Sheraton Dr 16046 **Location:** I-76 (Pennsylvania Tpke) exit 28; I-79 exit 76 (US 19 N) northbound; exit 78 southbound, 0.5 mi s on US 19. **Facility:** 65 units. 3 stories, interior corridors. **Guest Services:** valet laundry.

MARSHALLS CREEK
• Hotels & Restaurants map & index p. 373
• Part of Pocono Mountains Area — see map p. 371

POCONO PALACE RESORT   570/588-6692

Resort Hotel
Rates not provided

Address: 5241 Milford Rd (Rt 209) 18335 **Location:** I-80 exit 309, 7.4 mi n on SR 209. Located in a rural area. **Facility:** Snuggle up to your guest-room fireplace at this classic couples-only, all-inclusive resort. A variety of room types are available, including lakeside chalets and huge multi-level suites. 188 units. 1-4 stories, interior/exterior corridors. **Terms:** check-in 3:30 pm, age restrictions may apply. **Dining:** 2 restaurants, nightclub, entertainment. **Pool(s):** heated outdoor, heated indoor. **Activities:** sauna, hot tub, steamroom, motor boats, fishing, regulation golf, miniature golf, tennis, cross country skiing, snowmobiling, recreation programs, bicycles, game room, trails, exercise room, massage.

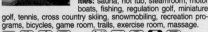

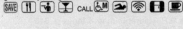 WHERE TO EAT

BIG "A" GRILLEHOUSE   570/223-1700
American. Casual Dining. $8-$32 **AAA Inspector Notes:** This comfortable place welcomes you with a friendly staff and a familiar menu of steaks, seafood and pastas. Although the original buildings are gone, the restaurant traces its roots in the Poconos to the 1920s. **Features:** full bar, Sunday brunch. **Address:** One Fox Run Ln 18302 **Location:** I-80 exit 309, 7.3 mi n on SR 209.
L   D

Enjoy great member rates and benefits at AAA/CAA Preferred Hotels

MATAMORAS pop. 2,469
• Part of Pocono Mountains Area — see map p. 371

BEST WESTERN INN AT HUNT'S LANDING
(570)491-2400

 Hotel
$109-$199

 AAA Benefit: Members save up to 20%!

Address: 120 Rt 6 & 209 18336 **Location:** I-84 exit 53, just s. **Facility:** 109 units. 4 stories, interior corridors. **Terms:** resort fee. **Pool(s):** heated indoor. **Activities:** limited exercise equipment. **Guest Services:** coin laundry. **Featured Amenity:** full hot breakfast.

HAMPTON INN   (570)491-5280
Hotel $129-$189 **Address:** 122 Westfall Town Dr 18336 **Location:** I-84 exit 53, just s. **Facility:** 98 units. 4 stories, interior corridors. **Terms:** check-in 4 pm, 1-7 night minimum stay, cancellation fee imposed. **Pool(s):** heated indoor. **Activities:** exercise room. **Guest Services:** coin laundry.

AAA Benefit: Members save 5% or more!

MAYFIELD pop. 1,807

ALEXANDER'S FAMILY RESTAURANT   570/876-9993
American. Family Dining. $7-$20 **AAA Inspector Notes:** The pleasant, diner-style restaurant delivers ample portions of reasonably priced, home-style food. The menu is extensive, with many sandwiches, salads and entrees ranging from the simple to the more elaborate. Mouthwatering treats are made in the bakery. **Features:** full bar. **Address:** 604 Rt 6 18433 **Location:** Jct SR 107, 0.6 mi ne.
B   L   D

McELHATTAN pop. 598

RESTLESS OAKS   570/769-7385
American. Family Dining. $5-$12 **AAA Inspector Notes:** Pass under a covered bridge-like roof lined with stones and carved with sage sayings and be greeted by a life sized carved wooden bear at this log cabin restaurant. The decor also features a stone fireplace, buffalo hide, antique tools hanging from the ceiling and a soaring eagle. Casual American fare is offered. **Address:** 119 Pine Mountain Rd 17748 **Location:** US 220 exit McElhattan-Woolrich, just n.
B   L   D

MEADVILLE (D-1) pop. 13,388, elev. 1,078'

The invention of the hookless fastener by Whitcomb L. Judson in Chicago came to the attention of Meadville's Col. Lewis Walker in 1893. Impressed by the new idea, Walker persuaded Judson to build a machine to produce the fastener. After several years of failure, Walker moved the enterprise to Meadville, where Gideon Sundback invented the fastener as it is currently known. The fastener did not become a commercial success, however, until 1923, when the B.F. Goodrich Co. decided to put it on a new line of galoshes. The popular new galoshes were called Zippers, a name that has evolved to mean the fastener itself.

The first direct primary took place here in 1842, and use of this system eventually spread across the country.

Of architectural interest is the Unitarian Church in Diamond Park. Built in 1835, it is a fine example of Greek Revival architecture. The Meadville Market House on Market Street has been used as an open-air marketplace since its founding about 1870 and is said to be the state's oldest continuously operating such marketplace; it is the cultural hub of the community. The Meadville Council on the Arts occupies the second floor.

If you head 13 miles northeast on SR 77 then just south to 17620 John Brown Rd. in Guys Mills, you'll reach the site of the John Brown Tannery, which was operated by the abolitionist 1825-35. All that remains of the tannery are its 8-foot stone walls. Interpretive markers at the site guide visitors to different points of interest, including the graves of Brown's first wife and two of their sons.

Crawford County Convention and Visitors Bureau: 16709 Conneaut Lake Rd., Meadville, PA 16335. **Phone:** (814) 333-1258 or (800) 332-2338.

ALLEGHENY COLLEGE, 520 N. Main St., was founded in 1815 and is a liberal arts college with 2,100 students. The college's 562-acre campus has a number of buildings constructed in the early 19th century, including Bentley Hall, a fine example of Federal architecture. **Phone:** (814) 332-3100.

BALDWIN-REYNOLDS HOUSE MUSEUM, 639 Terrace St., was built 1841-43 for U.S. Supreme Court Justice Henry Baldwin. The home is furnished in period with displays that change monthly. Also on the grounds are Dr. Mosier's 19th-century doctor's office, which was relocated here in 1982, and an 1875 icehouse.

Photography is not permitted. **Hours:** One-hour tours depart Wed.-Sun. on the hour noon-3, mid-May to late Aug. Last tour begins at closing. Phone ahead to confirm schedule. **Cost:** $5; $3 (ages 6-18). **Phone:** (814) 333-9882, or (814) 724-6080 in the off-season.

JOHNSON-SHAW STEREOSCOPIC MUSEUM is downtown at 423 Chestnut St. Housed in an 1856 building, the museum features a collection of items showcasing Meadville company Keystone View, which was the country's largest manufacturer of stereoscopic views and was in operation 1892-1976. The collection includes equipment and stereoscopic photos, and the exhibits explain the technology's uses in leisure, education, military and optometric applications. Meadville history is featured with stereoscopic views from the turn of the 20th century-1940s as well as with ledger books from the Holland Land Co. that originally occupied the building.

Time: Allow 30 minutes minimum. **Hours:** Wed.-Fri. 10-4, second Sat. of the month 10-5, Apr.-Dec.; by appointment rest of year. **Cost:** $5; $3 (children, students and senior citizens). **Phone:** (814) 720-4306 or (814) 333-4326. GT

ECONO LODGE   (814)724-6366

Motel $70-$80 **Address:** 11237 Shaw Ave 16335 **Location:** I-79 exit 147A, just e on US 322. **Facility:** 63 units. 3 stories, interior corridors. **Guest Services:** coin laundry.

HAMPTON INN   (814)807-1446

Hotel $119-$169 **Address:** 11446 Dawn Dr 16335 **Location:** I-79 exit 147B, just w on US 322. **Facility:** 73 units. 3 stories, interior corridors. **Terms:** 1-7 night minimum stay, cancellation fee imposed. **Pool(s):** heated indoor. **Activities:** hot tub, exercise room. **Guest Services:** valet and coin laundry.

AAA Benefit:
Members save 5% or more!

HOLIDAY INN EXPRESS   (814)724-6012

Hotel $109-$149 **Address:** 18240 Conneaut Lake Rd 16335 **Location:** I-79 exit 147A, just e on US 322. **Facility:** 68 units. 3 stories, interior corridors. **Terms:** cancellation fee imposed. **Pool(s):** heated indoor. **Activities:** hot tub, exercise room. **Guest Services:** valet laundry.

QUALITY INN MEADVILLE   814/333-8883

Motel. Rates not provided. **Address:** 17259 Conneaut Lake Rd 16335 **Location:** I-79 exit 147B, just w on US 322. **Facility:** 61 units. 3 stories, interior/exterior corridors. **Activities:** exercise room. **Guest Services:** valet and coin laundry.

WHERE TO EAT

CHOVY'S ITALIAN CASUAL   814/724-1286

Italian. Casual Dining. $5-$25 **AAA Inspector Notes:** Light and open, the dining room has the aura of a cozy bistro with subdued warm tones accentuated with murals and art. While the focus is on pastas, they are well known for their chops, prime rib, fresh fish and poultry accentuated with fresh herbs and tantalizing sauces. Neatly attired servers have extensive first-hand knowledge of the menu and extensive wine list. A heart-healthy menu is available. **Features:** full bar. **Address:** 18228 Conneaut Lake Rd 16335 **Location:** I-79 exit 147A, 0.3 mi e on US 322. L D

COMPADRES MEXICAN RESTAURANT   814/336-6633

Mexican. Casual Dining. $6-$20 **AAA Inspector Notes:** In a commercial area near a shopping mall, the restaurant sports the vibrant decor typical of south-of-the-border heritage. Representative of Mexican cuisine are burritos, taquitos, tamales, tacos, quesadillas and homemade desserts, which diners can enjoy with great margaritas. Service is casual in the small dining room, which has limited seating and gets busy during dinner. **Features:** full bar. **Address:** 16704 Conneaut Lake Rd 16335 **Location:** I-79 exit 147B, 4.2 mi w on US 322. L D

KING'S FAMILY RESTAURANT   814/333-8938

American. Family Dining. $6-$15 **AAA Inspector Notes:** Fast and friendly service is offered here. The menu is large in size with descriptive menu items and pictures. The restaurant is also known for its ice cream and dessert menu. **Address:** 16494 Conneaut Lake Rd 16335 **Location:** I-79 exit 147B, 1.5 mi w on US 322. B L D

MECHANICSBURG (H-8) pop. 8,981, elev. 433'
• Hotels & Restaurants map & index p. 138

AMERICA'S MUSEUM & RESEARCH FACILITY FOR ROLLS-ROYCE AND BENTLEY MOTOR-CARS, 189 Hempt Rd., provides guided tours of its collection of Rolls-Royce and Bentley automobiles (about 12 are usually displayed) and related historical items. Tour guides explain the cultural role these vehicles have played for more than a century. A noncirculating library features books, technical manuals, handbooks, sales literature, periodicals and other historic documents.

Time: Allow 1 hour minimum. **Hours:** Mon.-Fri. 10-4; last tour begins 1 hour before closing. Parties with more than six people must schedule an appointment. Schedule may vary; phone ahead to confirm. **Cost:** Donations. **Phone:** (717) 795-9400.

BAYMONT INN & SUITES MECHANICSBURG HARRISBURG WEST   (717)790-1520
♦♦ Hotel $75-$149 Address: 350 Bentcreek Blvd 17050 Location: I-81 exit 57, 1 mi e on SR 114. Located in a quiet area. Facility: 69 units. 3 stories, interior corridors. Amenities: safes. Pool(s): heated indoor. Activities: hot tub, limited exercise equipment. Guest Services: valet and coin laundry.

COMFORT INN CAPITAL CITY   (717)766-3700   **47**
♦♦♦ Hotel $79-$189

Address: 1012 Wesley Dr 17055 Location: I-76 (Pennsylvania Tpke) exit 236, 1 mi n to Wesley Dr exit, then just w. Adjacent to Wesley Drive Plaza. Facility: 64 units. 4 stories, interior corridors. Pool(s): outdoor. Activities: exercise room. Guest Services: valet and coin laundry. Featured Amenity: full hot breakfast.

COUNTRY INN & SUITES BY CARLSON, HARRISBURG WEST   (717)796-0300   **50**
♦♦♦ Hotel $99-$179

Address: 4943 Gettysburg Rd 17055 Location: US 15 exit Rossmoyne Rd/Wesley Dr. Facility: 66 units. 3 stories, interior corridors. Terms: 7 day cancellation notice-fee imposed. Pool(s): heated indoor. Activities: hot tub, exercise room. Guest Services: coin laundry. Featured Amenity: continental breakfast.

Keep your focus safely

on the road when driving

COURTYARD BY MARRIOTT HARRISBURG WEST/
MECHANICSBURG   (717)766-9006   **48**
♦♦♦ Hotel $118-$194

COURTYARD Marriott

AAA Benefit: Members save 5% or more!

Address: 4921 Gettysburg Rd 17055 Location: I-76 (Pennsylvania Tpke) exit 236, 1 mi n to Wesley Dr, just w, then 0.5 mi s. Facility: 91 units. 3 stories, interior corridors. Pool(s): heated indoor. Activities: hot tub, exercise room. Guest Services: valet and coin laundry, boarding pass kiosk.

ECONO LODGE   (717)766-4728   **52**
♦♦ Motel $55-$75 Address: 650 Gettysburg Rd 17055 Location: I-76 (Pennsylvania Tpke) exit 236, 1 mi n to Wesley Dr exit, just w, then 0.8 mi s. Located in a commercial area. Facility: 41 units. 1 story, exterior corridors. Pool(s): outdoor.

HAMPTON INN-HARRISBURG WEST   (717)691-1300   **49**
♦♦♦ Hotel $109-$189 Address: 4950 Ritter Rd 17055 Location: I-76 (Pennsylvania Tpke) exit 236, 1 mi n to Rossmoyne Rd exit. Located in a quiet commercial area. Facility: 129 units. 4 stories, interior corridors. Terms: 1-7 night minimum stay, cancellation fee imposed. Pool(s): heated outdoor. Activities: exercise room. Guest Services: valet and coin laundry.

AAA Benefit: Members save 5% or more!

HOLIDAY INN EXPRESS & SUITES HARRISBURG WEST/
MECHANICSBURG   (717)732-8800   **45**
♦♦♦ Hotel $108-$162 Address: 2055 Technology Pkwy 17050 Location: I-81 exit 61, 1 mi s on Wertzville Rd. Facility: 103 units. 5 stories, interior corridors. Pool(s): heated indoor. Activities: exercise room. Guest Services: valet and coin laundry.

HOLIDAY INN EXPRESS HARRISBURG SW-MECHANICSBURG   (717)790-0924
♦♦♦ Hotel $119-$209 Address: 6325 Carlisle Pike 17050 Location: Jct Carlisle Pike and US 11, 1 mi w on US 11. Located in light-commercial area. Facility: 109 units. 4 stories, interior corridors. Pool(s): outdoor. Activities: exercise room. Guest Services: valet and coin laundry.

HOMEWOOD SUITES BY HILTON-HARRISBURG WEST   (717)697-4900   **51**
♦♦♦ Extended Stay Hotel $119-$199 Address: 5001 Ritter Rd 17055 Location: I-76 (Pennsylvania Tpke) exit 236, 1 mi n to Rossmoyne Rd exit. Located in a quiet commercial area.

AAA Benefit: Members save 5% or more!

Facility: 116 efficiencies, some two bedrooms. 2 stories, interior corridors. Terms: check-in 4 pm, 1-7 night minimum stay, cancellation fee imposed. Pool(s): heated outdoor. Activities: exercise room. Guest Services: valet and coin laundry, area transportation.

MOTEL 6   (717)766-0238   **53**
♦♦ Motel $60-$120 Address: 381 Cumberland Pkwy 17055 Location: I-76 (Pennsylvania Tpke) exit 236, just s, then exit Cumberland Pkwy. Located in a commercial area. Facility: 35 units. 2 stories (no elevator), exterior corridors. Pool(s): outdoor.

(See map & index p. 138.)

PARK INN BY RADISSON HARRISBURG WEST
(717)697-0321 **46**

▼▼▼▼ **Hotel** $99-$179 **Address:** 5401 Carlisle Pike 17050 **Location:** Jct Carlisle Pike and US 11, just w. Located in a commercial area. **Facility:** 219 units. 2 stories (no elevator), interior/exterior corridors. **Terms:** check-in 4 pm, cancellation fee imposed. **Dining:** nightclub, entertainment. **Pool(s):** outdoor, heated indoor. **Activities:** miniature golf, playground, picnic facilities, exercise room. **Guest Services:** valet and coin laundry, rental car service, area transportation.

[icons]

WINGATE BY WYNDHAM MECHANICSBURG/HARRISBURG WEST
(717)766-2710 **54**

▼▼▼ **Hotel** $109-$269 **Address:** 385 Cumberland Pkwy 17055. **Location:** I-76 (Pennsylvania Tpke) exit 236, just s. **Facility:** 93 units. 4 stories, interior corridors. **Amenities:** safes. **Pool(s):** heated indoor. **Activities:** hot tub, exercise room. **Guest Services:** valet and coin laundry.

[icons]

WHERE TO EAT

DROSOS SILVER SPRING DINER   717/691-7070

▼ American. Casual Dining. $5-$14 **AAA Inspector Notes:** Fast and friendly service is standard at this diner, where the menu lists salads, burgers and specialty homemade entrées. **Address:** 6520 Carlisle Pike 17050 **Location:** Jct SR 114 and US 11; in Silver Spring Shopping Plaza. [B] [L] [D] [24]

ISAAC'S FAMOUS GRILLED SANDWICHES

▼ Deli Sandwiches. Quick Serve. $8-$12 **AAA Inspector Notes:** The modern, New York-style delicatessen specializes in overstuffed grilled sandwiches named after birds, plants and flowers. Salads and homemade soups also are popular. A tropical feel is prevalent in the colorful, casual dining room. [L] [D] CALL [icon]

For additional information, visit AAA.com

LOCATIONS:

Address: 4940 Ritter Rd 17055 **Location:** I-76 (Pennsylvania Tpke) exit 236 (US 15), 1 mi n to Rossmoyne Rd exit. **Phone:** 717/766-1111
Address: 6520 Carlisle Pike 17050 **Location:** Jct SR 114 and US 11; in Silver Spring Commons. **Phone:** 717/795-1925

PEPPERMILL FAMILY RESTAURANT   717/697-3111 **30**

▼▼ American. Casual Dining. $4-$15 **AAA Inspector Notes:** Join the locals who frequent this family-owned and -operated restaurant. Peppermill attracts a casual family crowd that comes for the homemade American fare served by an efficient and friendly staff. **Features:** Sunday brunch. **Address:** 1010 Wesley Dr, Suite 100 17055 **Location:** I-76 (Pennsylvania Tpke) exit 236, 1 mi n to Wesley Dr exit, then just w; in Wesley Drive Plaza. [B] [L] [D]

MEDIA (C-9) pop. 5,327, elev. 210'
• Part of Philadelphia area — see map p. 230

Media, named for its central location in Delaware County, was laid out in 1848 after being designated county seat. Midway between Philadelphia and Wilmington, Del., it has remained a thriving business and government center.

Just south on Rose Valley Road in an 1840 gristmill is the 1923 Hedgerow Theatre, one of the oldest repertory theaters in the country; phone (610) 565-4211. Another sign of the past still rumbles along State Street—an early 20th-century trolley that takes passengers to shops, restaurants and the

Delaware County Courthouse. On Wednesday evenings from May to September, a portion of State Street is closed to traffic for Dining Under the Stars, an event sponsored by local restaurants. Several music festivals occur throughout the year, including the Americana Roots Ramble in April, the State Street Blues Stroll in June and the Jazz by Night Celebration in November.

Delaware County's Brandywine Conference and Visitor's Bureau: 1501 N. Providence Rd., Media, PA 19063. **Phone:** (800) 343-3983.

TYLER ARBORETUM, 515 Painter Rd., is one of the nation's oldest and largest arboretums. The 650-acre property contains renowned horticultural collections, including the Wister Rhododendron Garden, meadows, wetlands and forest. There are 17 miles of marked hiking trails, historic buildings dating to 1738 and many natural areas. Nature walks, educational programs for children and adults, special events and nature camps are offered year-round. Maps are available for self-guiding tours.

Hours: Mon.-Fri. 9-5, Sat.-Sun. 9-6, Mar.-Oct.; Mon.-Fri. 9-4, Sat.-Sun., 9-6, rest of year. Closed Thanksgiving, Christmas Eve and Christmas. Phone ahead to confirm schedule. **Cost:** $11; $9 (ages 65+); $7 (ages 3-15). **Phone:** (610) 566-9134. [icon]

QUALITY INN   (610)565-5800

▼▼ **Motel** $90-$165 **Address:** 4 S New Middletown Rd 19063 **Location:** US 1, just s on SR 352. Located in a commercial area. [icon] Elwyn, 194. **Facility:** 83 units. 2-3 stories, exterior corridors. **Amenities:** safes. **Activities:** exercise room. **Guest Services:** valet and coin laundry.

[icons]

MENDENHALL
• Part of Philadelphia area — see map p. 230

INN AT MENDENHALL, AN ASCEND HOTEL COLLECTION MEMBER
(610)388-2100

▼▼▼ **Hotel** $98-$164 **Address:** 323 Kennett Pike (Rt 52) 19357 **Location:** Jct US 1, 1 mi s. **Facility:** 70 units. 3 stories, interior corridors. **Amenities:** safes. **Dining:** Mendenhall Inn, see separate listing. **Activities:** exercise room. **Guest Services:** valet laundry.

[icons]

WHERE TO EAT

MENDENHALL INN   610/388-1181

▼▼▼ Continental. Fine Dining. $16-$38 **AAA Inspector Notes:** Rustic appointments and antiques decorate the old country inn, which has six dining rooms that range from upscale casual to more formal. The restaurant is known for fine Continental cuisine, an example of which is the 12-ounce center-cut veal chop enriched with Mediterranean seasonings and topped with sautéed domestic mushrooms and sherry wine. Remnants of farm buildings constructed by the Mendenhalls' son are incorporated into the present structure. **Features:** full bar, patio dining, Sunday brunch, happy hour. **Reservations:** suggested, for brunch & dinner. **Address:** 323 Kennett Pike (Rt 52) 19357 **Location:** Jct US 1, 1 mi s; in Inn at Mendenhall, an Ascend Hotel Collection Member. [D]

Ask about on-the-go vehicle
battery testing and replacement

MERCER (E-1) pop. 2,002, elev. 1,006'

Founded near the banks of the Neshannock Creek in 1803, Mercer was named for Brig. Gen. Hugh Mercer, a Scottish physician who moved to America and fought in the Revolutionary War. The city is a light industrial center in a farming region.

Mercer Chamber of Commerce: 143 N. Diamond St., Mercer, PA 16137. **Phone:** (724) 662-4185.

MERCER COUNTY HISTORICAL SOCIETY MUSEUM, 119 S. Pitt St., chronicles the history and development of Mercer County. Exhibits include clothing, dolls, furniture, photographs and toys. A genealogical reference library is available. **Time:** Allow 30 minutes minimum. **Hours:** Tues.-Fri. 10-4:30, Sat. 10-3. Closed major holidays. **Cost:** Free. **Phone:** (724) 662-3490.

WENDELL AUGUST FORGE, 2074 Leesburg-Grove City Rd., is one of the few remaining forges in the country that produces handcrafted metal giftware forged from aluminum, bronze, pewter and sterling silver. Visitors can watch items being created on a self-guiding workshop tour or can tour the forge's history center. **Hours:** Mon.-Sat. 9-5, Sun. noon-5; phone ahead for extended hours. **Cost:** Free. **Phone:** (724) 748-9501 or (800) 923-4438.

COMFORT INN MERCER   (724)748-3030

▼▼ **Hotel** $90-$120 **Address:** 835 Perry Hwy 16137 **Location:** I-80 exit 15, just n on US 19. Located in a quiet area. **Facility:** 100 units. 2 stories (no elevator), interior corridors. **Pool(s):** heated indoor. **Activities:** hot tub. **Guest Services:** valet and coin laundry.

CALL 🔊ᴹ ➡️ BIZ 🛜 🚪 🖥️ 🖥️ /SOME UNITS 🅂🄻 (HS)

WHERE TO EAT

IRON BRIDGE INN   724/748-3626

▼▼ American. Casual Dining. $8-$30 **AAA Inspector Notes:** Just 5 minutes away from the bustle of downtown, this charming eatery is nestled along a river and next to an old iron bridge. The restaurant resembles that of an old fish camp with a rustic wooden facade and tin roof. Stuffed animals and a storied time line of pictures decorate the dining rooms. The menu items include burgers, lamb, filet mignon, prime rib, shrimp, chicken and a strip steak. Entrées are hearty and typically come with two sides, so bring your appetite. **Features:** full bar, Sunday brunch. **Address:** 1438 Perry Hwy 16137 **Location:** I-80 exit 15, 2 mi s on US 19. (L) (D)

MY BROTHER'S PLACE   724/748-3840

▼▼ American. Casual Dining. $10-$25 **AAA Inspector Notes:** This eatery, owned by former Steeler Ray Mathews and run by his family, offers good food at reasonable prices. **Features:** full bar. **Address:** 2058 Leesburg Grove City Rd 16137 **Location:** I-79 exit 113, 1 mi w. (L) (D)

RACHEL'S ROADHOUSE   724/748-3193

▼▼▼ American. Casual Dining. $6-$20 **AAA Inspector Notes:** The exterior resembles a large, country Victorian home, but don't be fooled as this restaurant sports a high-energy, fun-loving atmosphere. Start with the homemade chips or Rachel's wings appetizer. The standard menu offers American bar and grill favorites such as burgers, Reuben sandwiches, pizzas, pasta dishes such as the Linguine Alfredo, steaks and seafood. If you're really hungry try the Frankenstein burger with everything but the kitchen sink. They have very reasonable prices, daily specials and a helpful waitstaff. **Features:** full bar. **Address:** 1553 Perry Hwy 16137 **Location:** I-80 exit 15, 2.5 mi s on US 19. (L) (D)

SPRINGFIELD GRILLE   724/748-3589

▼▼▼▼ American. Casual Dining. $8-$31 **AAA Inspector Notes:** This restaurant's rustic and cozy atmosphere is a nice spot in which to enjoy aged Angus beef, pasta, salads and delicious homemade desserts. The food is very tasty and served in huge portions. **Features:** full bar. **Address:** 1226 Perry Hwy 16137 **Location:** I-80 exit 15, 2 mi s on US 19. (D)

MERCERSBURG (I-6) pop. 1,561, elev. 581'

BUCHANAN'S BIRTHPLACE STATE PARK is 1 mi. n.w. off SR 16. The 18.5-acre birthplace site is run by Cowans Gap State Park (see Recreation Areas Chart). Activities include fishing; picnic table also are available. A stone monument marks the birthplace of James Buchanan, the only Pennsylvanian to become a U.S. president. **Hours:** Daily dawn-dusk. **Cost:** Free. **Phone:** (717) 485-3948. 🎣 🏕️

MERCERSBURG ACADEMY, 10 mi. w. on SR 16, is an independent coeducational secondary school (boarding school) and the site of President James Buchanan's 1791 log cabin birthplace, which was moved from its original location. The interior is not open to the public, but visitors can look through a window to see inside the mostly unfurnished cabin. A plaque contains information about the structure.

Also on campus is the McFadden Railroad Museum, containing Lionel trains and accessories, including 148 engines and more than 500 cars. Concerts and performances are offered at the Burgin Center for the Arts. The academy chapel houses a 50-bell carillon.

Time: Allow 1 hour minimum. **Hours:** Cabin site open daily dawn-dusk. Carillon recitals are performed Sun. at 3 during the academic year. Phone for art center schedule. Museum open by appointment. **Cost:** Free. **Phone:** (717) 328-2151.

RECREATIONAL ACTIVITIES
Skiing and Snowboarding
• **Whitetail Resort** is at 13805 Blairs Valley Rd. Other activities also are offered. **Hours:** Daily 8:30 a.m.-10 p.m., Thanksgiving to mid-Mar. (8:30-5 on Christmas Eve, noon-10 on Christmas, 8:30 a.m.-1 a.m. on Dec. 31). **Phone:** (717) 328-9400.

MIDDLETOWN (DAUPHIN COUNTY)

ALFRED'S VICTORIAN RESTAURANT   717/944-5373

▼▼ Continental. Fine Dining. $14-$44 **AAA Inspector Notes:** Historic. Set in an 1888 Victorian home, Alfred's intimate dining rooms are interestingly decorated with antiques, carved wood and gingerbread accents. If you're seeking a romantic spot, this is it. Screens separate some tables to provide extra privacy. The kitchen, which emphasizes fresh ingredients, is known for its Tuscan cooking, but the menu also offers American and European selections. An herb garden blossoms in the backyard. **Features:** full bar. **Reservations:** suggested. **Address:** 38 N Union St 17057 **Location:** SR 441, 3.3 mi s of SR 283. **Parking:** street only. (D)

MIFFLINBURG (F-8) pop. 3,540, elev. 583'

Established in 1792 and renamed in honor of Governor Thomas Mifflin in 1827, Mifflinburg was a buggy-making town. Between 1841 and 1924, 75 independent buggy makers called this borough home. Because of the quality of its product, the town produced more buggies per capita than any other Pennsylvania town, as many as 6,000 vehicles annually. In fact, in 1880 the town came to be known by the nickname "Buggy Town."

MIFFLINBURG BUGGY MUSEUM, s. on 5th St. then w. to 598 Green St., offers exhibits about buggy making and Mifflinburg as well as guided tours of four historic buildings that include a 19th-century carriage factory, a furnished coach maker's house and a carriage showroom. Exhibits include thousands of tools, a 1910 New Holland engine, a hands-on work bench and 25 horse-drawn vehicles. An introductory video also is shown.

Time: Allow 1 hour minimum. **Hours:** Visitor center and historic buildings Thurs.-Sat. 10-5, Sun. 1-5, Apr.-Oct. **Cost:** Visitor center and historic buildings $10; $5 (children). Visitor center only $3; $1.50 (children). **Phone:** (570) 966-1355.

CARRIAGE CORNER RESTAURANT   570/966-3866
♦♦ American. Family Dining. $5-$16 **AAA Inspector Notes:** Friendly service is a hallmark of this family-style restaurant, which occupies a country Victorian setting. The kitchen prepares old-fashioned, tried-and-true recipes. Weekly specials focus on buffet service. A piece of homemade shoofly pie or lemon sponge pie makes a tasty dessert. **Address:** 257 E Chestnut St 17844 **Location:** 0.5 mi e on SR 45; center. [L] [D]

MIFFLINTOWN pop. 936

ECONO LODGE   (717)436-5981
♦♦
Motel
$70-$160

Address: 29 Stop Plaza Dr 17059 **Location:** Jct US 322/22 and SR 35. **Facility:** 47 units, some kitchens. 2 stories (no elevator), interior/exterior corridors.

[SAVE] [tt+] [BIZ] [HS] [📶] [🛏] [🍽]
/ SOME UNITS [🖨]

MIFFLINVILLE pop. 1,253

SUPER 8 - MIFFLINVILLE   (570)759-6778
♦♦ Motel $65-$110 **Address:** 450 W 3rd St 18631 **Location:** I-80 exit 242 (SR 339), just n. **Facility:** 54 units. 2 stories (no elevator), exterior corridors.
[tt+] [📶] [🛏] [🍽] [🖨] / SOME UNITS [Sn]

MILFORD (E-12) pop. 1,021, elev. 492'
• Restaurants p. 200
• Part of Pocono Mountains Area — see map p. 371

Situated along the early Milford-Owego Turnpike, the village became an important transportation stop during the nation's 19th-century westward expansion. Today numerous historic buildings, tree-lined streets and country inns make it a pleasant vacation stop. The Columns is a Victorian mansion housing

the museum of the Pike County Historical Society. The artifact collection includes the flag that supposedly was used to cradle President Lincoln's head after he was shot at Ford's Theatre; several tests have confirmed its authenticity. Native Americans and Underground Railroad are other local history topics that are showcased. The museum is downtown at 608 Broad St. and is usually open Wednesdays and weekends 1-4; phone (570) 296-8126.

Pike County Chamber of Commerce: 209 E. Harford St., Milford, PA 18337. **Phone:** (570) 296-8700.

Self-guiding tours: A brochure developed by the Pike County Historical Society features information about 40 historical sites in Milford and is available from the chamber of commerce for $1. The chamber also offers brochures for driving tours of the area.

Shopping areas: Milford has a large variety of antique and specialty shops.

GREY TOWERS NATIONAL HISTORIC SITE is .5 mi. w. on US 6, then .3 mi s.w. on Old Owego Tpke. This 1886 estate was the summer home of conservationist Gifford Pinchot, a former Pennsylvania governor and first chief of the USDA Forest Service. Designed to resemble a French château, the stone mansion is built of native materials and furnished in 1920s style. Guided 1-hour tours of the first floor are given. Visitors may wander through the restored gardens and walking trails on their own.

Pets are not permitted in the mansion. **Time:** Allow 1 hour, 30 minutes minimum. **Hours:** Grounds daily dawn-dusk, all year. Guided tours of the mansion and gardens are offered Memorial Day weekend-Oct. 31. Tour times vary; phone ahead for schedule. **Cost:** $8; $7 (ages 62+); $5 (ages 12-17). **Phone:** (570) 296-9630. [🎫]

THE UPPER MILL, on Sawkill Creek at 150 Water St., is a restored gristmill built in the early 1800s. A three-story waterwheel powers the mill. Specialty shops, a bakery and eateries on the grounds are open year-round. **Time:** Allow 30 minutes minimum. **Hours:** The waterwheel operates daily 10-5, May-Oct. **Cost:** Free. **Phone:** (570) 409-4646. [tt]

HOTEL FAUCHÈRE   (570)409-1212
♦♦♦ Historic Hotel $189-$594 **Address:** 401 Broad St 18337 **Location:** In historic downtown. **Facility:** In the charming downtown, this landmark historic hotel has meticulously restored public areas and rooms with a more modern aesthetic. The baths are decked out in marble and have heated floors. 16 units. 3 stories, interior corridors. **Terms:** check-in 4 pm, 2 night minimum stay - seasonal and/or weekends, 14 day cancellation notice-fee imposed. **Dining:** 2 restaurants, also, Bar Louis, see separate listing. **Activities:** spa. **Guest Services:** valet laundry.
[tt] [🛋] [Y] [📶] [✕] [🖨] / SOME UNITS [Sn] [🛏]

MYER COUNTRY MOTEL   570/296-7223
♦♦ Cottage. Rates not provided. **Address:** 600 Rt 6 & 209 18337 **Location:** US 6 and 209, 0.5 mi ne. Located in a semi-rural area. **Facility:** 19 cottages, some efficiencies. 1 story, exterior corridors. [tt+] [📶] [🛏] [🍽]

SCOTTISH INNS (570)491-4414

◆◆◆◆ ◆◆◆◆
Motel
$50-$110

Address: 274 Rt 6 & 209 18337 **Location:** I-84 exit 53, 1 mi s. Located in a semi-rural area. **Facility:** 18 units, some kitchens. 1 story, exterior corridors. **Terms:** 3 day cancellation notice-fee imposed.

⊞ ⁑ HS 🛜 🖥 🖼 ▭ / SOME UNITS 🅂🔓

WHERE TO EAT

APPLE VALLEY FAMILY RESTAURANT 570/296-6831

◆◆◆ American. Casual Dining. $7-$25 **AAA Inspector Notes:** On eight scenic acres, the tourist village restaurant is surrounded by seven specialty shops, an 1800 schoolhouse and fish and duck ponds. The casual dining room's rustic walls are constructed from wood paneling taken from a 19th-century barn. A seasonal deck offers another seating option. Live entertainment is provided two nights weekly. Many microbrewed beers are available from the lounge. The menu focuses on prime rib, steaks and burgers. **Features:** full bar. **Address:** 104 Rt 6 18337 **Location:** I-84 exit 46, 1.1 mi s.

Ⓛ Ⓓ

BAR LOUIS 570/409-1212

◆◆◆◆ New American. Casual Dining. $10-$38 **AAA Inspector Notes:** Whether you are staying at its historic hotel or just sightseeing in this quaint small town, this a great stop for lunch or dinner. Here you will find excellent creative cuisine crafted from fresh seasonal ingredients and the bounty of local farms. The menu changes regularly but includes great charcuterie plates, salads with fresh produce and artisan cheeses, grilled fish entrées, roasted chicken and Prime steak. **Reservations:** suggested. **Address:** 401 Broad St 18337 **Location:** In historic downtown; in Hotel Fauchère. **Parking:** on-site and street. Ⓛ Ⓓ CALL🔓Ⓜ

MILFORD DINER 570/296-8611

◆◆◆ American. Casual Dining. $5-$15 **AAA Inspector Notes:** The friendly staff quickly serves large portions of comfort food, Greek specialties and fresh-baked desserts. This is a great place to stop for breakfast when touring historic downtown Milford. **Features:** Sunday brunch. **Address:** 301 Broad St 18337 **Location:** Just n of jct US 6 and 209; downtown. Ⓑ Ⓛ Ⓓ

VILLAGE DINER 570/491-2819

◆◆◆ Comfort Food. Casual Dining. $5-$18 **AAA Inspector Notes:** At first you'll notice the look of this classic 1956 steel diner complete with counter and booths, but what you'll remember is the great food and friendly service. It's all here: full breakfasts, salads, sandwiches, a huge burger selection, meatloaf, pastas and, of course, homemade pies and cakes for dessert. **Address:** 268 Rt 6 & 209 18337 **Location:** I-84 exit 53, 1 mi s. Ⓑ Ⓛ Ⓓ

WATER WHEEL CAFE 570/296-2383

◆◆◆ Comfort Food. Casual Dining. $6-$28 **AAA Inspector Notes:** Here you will enjoy a casual lunch of homemade soups, fresh salads and sandwiches ranging from the familiar roast turkey to Vietnamese-style banh mi. Dinner offers more of a fine dining experience with a menu of entrées like roasted red snapper with garlic aioli, crispy hazelnut pork chops and a few Vietnamese dishes. The café is within the historic Upper Mill, and you can see and tour the working waterwheel and grist mill with its gears, shafts and belt-driven machinery. **Features:** full bar, patio dining. **Address:** 150 Water St 18337 **Location:** Just w of W Harford St (US 6) on Mill St; in Upper Mill. Ⓑ Ⓛ Ⓓ

Add AAA or CAA Associate Members to bring home the benefits of membership

---

MILL RUN (I-3) elev. 1,383'

Mill Run is part of the Laurel Highlands *(see place listing p. 183)*.

BEAR RUN NATURE RESERVE, on SR 381, includes more than 5,000 acres of forest, 20 miles of trails, more than eight miles of streams and is the Western Pennsylvania Conservancy's largest property. The organization's goal is to preserve the diversity of local ecosystems by protecting, conserving and restoring land, water and foliage. Hiking, primitive camping, bird-watching, hunting, fishing, snowshoeing and cross-country skiing are permitted. **Hours:** Daily dawn-dusk. **Cost:** Free. **Phone:** (724) 329-8501. 🅰 ❎

💎 **FALLINGWATER,** on SR 381 at 1491 Mill Run Rd., was a weekend home designed by Frank Lloyd Wright in 1935 and was entrusted to Western Pennsylvania Conservancy in 1963. Constructed of reinforced concrete and native stone, the house is dramatically cantilevered over a waterfall. The famous house blends so well with the mountainous terrain that it seems to grow out of its site. It has been acclaimed by the American Institute of Architects. Self-guiding grounds tours, 1-hour guided house tours, 2-hour in-depth tours and other special tours are offered. A visitor center is on-site.

Hours: Thurs.-Tues. 10-4, mid-Mar. through Thanksgiving weekend; Sat.-Sun. 11:30-3 in Dec. (also day after Christmas-Dec. 31) and first two weekends in Mar. (weather permitting). Phone for other special tour schedules. Closed Jan. 1, Thanksgiving, Christmas Eve and Christmas. **Cost:** $25; $17 (ages 6-12). In-depth tour $72. Grounds only $8. Advanced ticket purchase is required to guarantee tour availability; discounts are applied to advance ticket purchases. Ages 0-5 are not permitted on regular tour. Ages 0-6 are not permitted on in-depth and other special tours. **Phone:** (724) 329-8501. ⁑

COUNTRY SEASONS BED AND BREAKFAST INN
724/455-6825

◆◆◆ Bed & Breakfast. Rates not provided. **Address:** 100 Stewarton Rd 15464 **Location:** I-70/76 (Pennsylvania Tpke) exit 91 (SR 31), 2 mi s, w on SR 381, then 13.5 mi s; corner of SR 381 and Stewarton Rd. **Facility:** Situated in the Laurel Highlands, this B&B offers casual accommodations and friendly ownership. There is a large, well-manicured yard and a large front porch to enjoy a glass of iced tea on. 4 units. 2 stories (no elevator), interior corridors. **Terms:** age restrictions may apply. 🛜 ❎ 🈂

MILROY pop. 1,498

BEST WESTERN NITTANY INN MILROY (717)667-9595

◆◆◆ ◆◆◆
Hotel
$80-$100

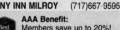

Best Western

AAA Benefit: Members save up to 20%!

Address: 5 Commerce Dr 17063 **Location:** US 322 exit Milroy, just e. **Facility:** 41 units. 2 stories, interior corridors. **Pool(s):** heated outdoor. **Activities:** exercise room. **Guest Services:** valet and coin laundry.

⊞ ⁑ Ⓨ 🛒 BIZ 🛜 ❎

🖥 🖼 ▭ / SOME UNITS 🅂🔓

MOHNTON pop. 3,043

EMILY'S   610/856-7887

▼▼ ▼▼ American. Casual Dining. $7-$30 **AAA Inspector Notes:** *Historic.* This restaurant is named for the ghost that some claim resides in this 200-year-old building, which has previously functioned as a hotel and post office. The dining rooms feature Victorian décor; another seating option is on a seasonal awning-covered dining deck. The menu offers casual contemporary cuisine, including Cajun pasta, fried calamari, mixed grills, Chesapeake chicken and rack of lamb. **Features:** full bar, patio dining. **Reservations:** suggested. **Address:** 3790 Morgantown Rd 19540 **Location:** I-176 (Morgantown Expwy) exit 7, 1.3 mi s on SR 10. L D

MONACA pop. 5,737

- Hotels & Restaurants map & index p. 348
- Part of Pittsburgh area — see map p. 326

COMFORT SUITES   (724)728-9480 **48**

▼▼ ▼▼ Hotel $109-$155 **Address:** 1523 Old Brodhead Rd 15061 **Location:** I-376 exit 39, 1 mi e. **Facility:** 40 units. 3 stories, interior corridors. **Activities:** exercise room. **Guest Services:** valet and coin laundry.

FAIRFIELD INN & SUITES BY MARRIOTT   (724)888-2696 **47**

▼▼ ▼▼ Hotel $132-$169 **Address:** 1438 Brodhead Rd 15061 **Location:** I-376 exit 39, 0.9 mi e. **Facility:** 82 units. 4 stories, interior corridors. **Amenities:** *Some:* safes. **Pool(s):** heated indoor. **Activities:** exercise room. **Guest Services:** valet and coin laundry.

AAA Benefit: Members save 5% or more!

HAMPTON INN BEAVER VALLEY/PITTSBURGH   (724)774-5580 **51**

▼▼ ▼▼ Hotel $134-$164 **Address:** 202 Fairview Dr 15061 **Location:** I-376 exit 39, just n. **Facility:** 57 units. 4 stories, interior corridors. **Terms:** 1-7 night minimum stay, cancellation fee imposed. **Pool(s):** heated indoor. **Activities:** exercise room. **Guest Services:** valet parking.

AAA Benefit: Members save 5% or more!

HOLIDAY INN EXPRESS HOTEL & SUITES-CENTER TOWNSHIP   724/728-5121 **50**

▼▼ ▼▼ Hotel. Rates not provided. **Address:** 105 Stone Quarry Rd 15061 **Location:** I-376 exit 39 (SR 18 N/Frankfort Rd), just n. **Facility:** 66 units. 4 stories, interior corridors. **Pool(s):** heated indoor. **Activities:** hot tub, exercise room. **Guest Services:** valet and coin laundry.

THE INN   724/728-9270 **49**

▼▼ ▼▼ Hotel. Rates not provided. **Address:** 1525 Old Brodhead Rd 15061 **Location:** I-376 exit 39, 1 mi e. **Facility:** 20 units, some kitchens. 2 stories (no elevator), interior corridors.

WHERE TO EAT

KING'S FAMILY RESTAURANT   724/774-7760

▼▼ ▼▼ American. Family Dining. $6-$11 **AAA Inspector Notes:** Fast and friendly service is offered here. The menu is large in size with descriptive menu items and pictures. The restaurant is also known for its ice cream and dessert menu. **Address:** 1451 N Brodhead Rd 15061 **Location:** Just w of jct N Branch Rd. B L D

MONROEVILLE (G-2) pop. 28,386, elev. 1,204'

- Hotels p. 202 • Restaurants p. 203
- Hotels & Restaurants map & index p. 348
- Part of Pittsburgh area — see map p. 326

SRI VENKATESWARA TEMPLE, off Thompson Run Rd. on S. McCully Dr., is one of the earliest Hindu temples established in North America. It is modeled after a temple in southern India. The ornate white towers contain representations of Hindu deities. Guided tours are available by appointment. **Hours:** Daily 9-8:30 (also Fri. 8:30-9:30 p.m.), mid-Mar. to late Oct.; Mon.-Fri. 9-7:30 (also Fri. 7:30-8:30 p.m.), Sat.-Sun. 9-7:30, rest of year. **Cost:** Free. **Phone:** (412) 373-3380.

(See map & index p. 348.)

COMFORT SUITES MONROEVILLE   (412)373-0911
  Contemporary Hotel $100-$144 Address: 2731 Mosside Blvd 15146 Location: I-76 (Pennsylvania Tpke) exit 57, 0.8 mi w. Facility: 40 units. 4 stories, interior corridors. Bath: shower only. Activities: limited exercise equipment. Guest Services: valet and coin laundry.

▼ See AAA listing this page ▼

Courtyard Pittsburgh Monroeville

3962 William Penn Highway
Monroeville, PA 15146
412-856-8680 • marriott.com

Our hotel features a new lobby with inviting, flexible spaces to work or relax, free Wi-Fi throughout and easy access to the latest news, weather and airport conditions via our GoBoard.

The highlight of our new lobby experience is 'The Bistro - Eat. Drink. Connect.' – providing guests with healthy food and beverage offerings in the morning as well as evening dinner service with cocktails.

Discover a wealth of savings and offers
on the AAA/CAA travel websites

COURTYARD BY MARRIOTT PITTSBURGH MONROEVILLE   (412)856-8680

Hotel $104-$171

COURTYARD Marriott

AAA Benefit: Members save 5% or more!

Address: 3962 William Penn Hwy 15146 Location: I-76 (Pennsylvania Tpke) exit 57, 1 mi w on US 22. Facility: 98 units. 4 stories, interior corridors. Pool(s): heated indoor. Activities: hot tub, exercise room. Guest Services: valet and coin laundry. (See ad this page.)

DOUBLETREE BY HILTON HOTEL PITTSBURGH - MONROEVILLE CONVENTION CENTER   (412)373-7300

Hotel $99-$169

DOUBLETREE BY HILTON

AAA Benefit: Members save 5% or more!

Address: 101 Mall Blvd 15146 Location: I-76 (Pennsylvania Tpke) exit 57, 2 mi w on US 22. Adjacent to Monroeville Mall. Facility: 191 units. 14-15 stories, interior corridors. Terms: 1-7 night minimum stay, cancellation fee imposed. Amenities: video games. Pool(s): heated indoor. Activities: hot tub, exercise room. Guest Services: valet laundry.

EXTENDED STAY AMERICA-PITTSBURGH-MONROEVILLE   412/856-8400
  Extended Stay Hotel. Rates not provided. Address: 3851 Northern Pike 15146 Location: I-76 (Pennsylvania Tpke) exit 57, 1.2 mi w on Business Rt US 22. Facility: 104 efficiencies. 3 stories, interior corridors. Guest Services: coin laundry.

HAMPTON INN MONROEVILLE/PITTSBURGH   (412)380-4000
Hotel $109-$159 Address: 3000 Mosside Blvd 15146 Location: I-76 (Pennsylvania Tpke) exit 57; I-376 exit 84A, 0.3 mi s on SR 48. Facility: 140 units. 9 stories, interior corridors.

AAA Benefit: Members save 5% or more!

Terms: 1-7 night minimum stay, cancellation fee imposed. Pool(s): heated indoor. Activities: exercise room.

HOLIDAY INN PITTSBURGH-MONROEVILLE   (412)372-1022
Hotel $95-$159

Address: 2750 Mosside Blvd 15146 Location: I-76 (Pennsylvania Tpke) exit 57, 0.4 mi s on SR 48; I-376 exit 84A, 0.4 mi s on SR 48. Facility: 187 units. 4 stories, interior corridors. Pool(s): outdoor. Activities: exercise room. Guest Services: valet and coin laundry.

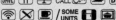

(See map & index p. 348.)

RED ROOF INN PITTSBURGH EAST - MONROEVILLE

412/856-4738 **20**

Motel

Rates not provided

Address: 2729 Mosside Blvd 15146 **Location:** I-76 (Pennsylvania Tpke) exit 57; I-376 exit 84A, 0.8 mi s on SR 48. **Facility:** 116 units. 3 stories, exterior corridors. **Amenities:** safes. **Guest Services:** coin laundry.

SPRINGHILL SUITES BY MARRIOTT PITTSBURGH MONROEVILLE

(412)380-9100 **17**

Hotel
$97-$160

AAA Benefit: Members save 5% or more!

Address: 122 Daugherty Dr 15146 **Location:** I-76 (Pennsylvania Tpke) exit 57; I-376 exit 84A, 0.5 mi s on SR 48. **Facility:** 86 units. 4 stories, interior corridors. **Pool(s):** heated indoor. **Activities:** exercise room. **Guest Services:** valet and coin laundry. **Featured Amenity:** breakfast buffet. *(See ad this page.)*

SUPER 8 PITTSBURGH/MONROEVILLE   (724)733-8008 **13**

Motel $80-$175 **Address:** 1807 Golden Mile Hwy (Rt 286) 15239 **Location:** I-76 (Pennsylvania Tpke) exit 57; I-376 exit 84A, 2 mi e on US 22 E, then 2 mi e. **Facility:** 49 units. 2 stories (no elevator), interior corridors. **Terms:** cancellation fee imposed.

WHERE TO EAT

GATEWAY GRILL   412/372-2977 **19**

American. Casual Dining. $5-$20 **AAA Inspector Notes:** Enjoy the city's only restaurant that offers wood-fire-grilled dinners and pizzas while you watch a variety of sporting events on several TVs. The décor is simple and you can expect good and straightforward food with entrées such as pizza, salads, wings, pastas, subs, sandwiches and even gyros. **Features:** full bar, Sunday brunch. **Address:** 4251 Northern Pike 15146 **Location:** Just w of jct SR 48.

B L D

KING'S FAMILY RESTAURANT   412/373-3110

American. Family Dining. $6-$15 **AAA Inspector Notes:** Fast and friendly service is offered here. The menu is large in size with descriptive menu items and pictures. The restaurant is also known for its ice cream and dessert menu. **Address:** 4310 Northern Pike 15146 **Location:** I-76 (Pennsylvania Tpke) exit 57; I-376 exit 84A, 1.2 mi s on SR 48, then just e. B L D CALL

LUCCIA SHEA'S   412/372-5859 **17**

American. Casual Dining. $7-$36 **AAA Inspector Notes:** The large picture window in the front of the building brightens the dining room. This restaurant has been pleasing locals for more than 12 years with homemade pastas, fresh seafood and succulent marinated prime rib, which is the house specialty. Tasty soups and sauces are prepared daily by the chef. **Features:** full bar. **Address:** 4733 William Penn Hwy 15146 **Location:** I-76 (Pennsylvania Tpke) exit 57, 1.2 mi e on US 22 E. L D CALL

Say YES to ERS text updates to stay posted when your tow truck is on the way

(See map & index p. 348.)

MONTEREY BAY FISH GROTTO
412/374-8530 ㉒

▼▼▼ Seafood. Fine Dining. $8-$39 **AAA Inspector Notes:** This restaurant sits above the business district in the Jonnett Building. It features a cozy wine bar and offers a wide array of tempting seafood and steak dishes such as steamed clams, pan-fried shrimp, a popular lobster Caesar salad, Caribbean-style wild salmon and filet mignon. Daily fresh catches come from the west, the east and the Florida coast. The menu consists of mostly seafood with some steak and pasta entrées. **Features:** full bar. **Reservations:** suggested. **Address:** 705 Mall Circle Dr 15146 **Location:** Business Rt US 22; in Monroeville Mall. ⬜Ⓛ ⬜Ⓓ CALL ⬜Ⓜ ⬜

RUDY'S SUBMARINES
412/372-9738 ⑱

▼ American. Quick Serve. $4-$10 **AAA Inspector Notes:** Guests step up to the counter to order one of the many submarine sandwiches listed on the menu board and then head off to the small eat-in area. Service is speedy. **Features:** beer only. **Address:** 3942 William Penn Hwy (US 22) 15146 **Location:** I-76 (Pennsylvania Tpke) exit 57, 1 mi w on US 22. ⬜Ⓑ ⬜Ⓛ ⬜Ⓓ

SHOGUN
412/372-0700 ㉑

▼▼ Japanese. Casual Dining. $8-$40 **AAA Inspector Notes:** Guests sit around the hibachi grill while the chef prepares their meals right before their eyes. Shrimp and filet mignon are among the chef's specialties. The menu includes sushi rolls, tempura, katsu, and stir-fry and teriyaki dishes. An extensive selection of sushi, including octopus, yellow tail, eel and calamari, is most popular. **Features:** full bar. **Reservations:** suggested, weekends. **Address:** 8 Tech One Dr 15146 **Location:** 0.5 mi s of Monroeville Mall's back entrance. ⬜Ⓛ ⬜Ⓓ

TAIPEI-TOKYO
412/373-5464 ⑳

▼▼ Chinese. Casual Dining. $5-$22 **AAA Inspector Notes:** Among offerings of Chinese and Japanese fare are sushi bar preparations. The menu also offers tempura, teriyaki and noodle dishes. Friendly atmosphere and service lend to an enjoyable meal. **Features:** full bar. **Reservations:** suggested, weekends. **Address:** 304 Mall Blvd 15146 **Location:** Just s of jct US 22 and Mall Blvd; adjacent to Monroeville Mall. ⬜Ⓛ ⬜Ⓓ CALL ⬜Ⓜ

MONTGOMERYVILLE pop. 12,624
• Part of Philadelphia area — see map p. 230

COMFORT INN
(215)361-3600

▼▼▼ Hotel $89-$179 **Address:** 678 Bethlehem Pike 18936 **Location:** Jct SR 463 and US 202, 0.3 mi n on SR 309. **Facility:** 84 units. 3 stories, interior corridors. **Amenities:** safes. **Guest Services:** valet and coin laundry.

COURTYARD BY MARRIOTT PHILADELPHIA-MONTGOMERYVILLE
(215)699-7247

▼▼▼ Hotel $132-$217 **Address:** 544 Dekalb Pike 19454 **Location:** Jct SR 309, just s. Across from Montgomery Mall. **Facility:** 102 units. 4 stories, interior corridors. **Pool(s):** heated indoor. **Activities:** hot tub, exercise room. **Guest Services:** valet and coin laundry.

AAA Benefit: Members save 5% or more!

RESIDENCE INN BY MARRIOTT PHILADELPHIA/MONTGOMERYVILLE
(267)468-0111

▼▼▼ Extended Stay Hotel $132-$217 **Address:** 1110 Bethlehem Pike 19454 **Location:** I-276 (Pennsylvania Tpke) exit 339, 6.5 mi n on SR 309. **Facility:** 96 units, some two bedrooms, efficiencies and kitchens. 3 stories, interior corridors. **Pool(s):** heated indoor. **Activities:** exercise room. **Guest Services:** valet and coin laundry.

AAA Benefit: Members save 5% or more!

BACCO
215/699-3361

▼▼ Southern Italian. Casual Dining. $8-$22 **AAA Inspector Notes:** Tasty preparations of Southern Italian fare come to the table in family-style servings large enough to feed two or more people in your party. You'll kick back in Bacco's inviting setting over offerings of pasta, pizza, soup and entrées. **Features:** full bar, happy hour. **Reservations:** suggested. **Address:** 587 Dekalb Pike 19454 **Location:** I-276 (Pennsylvania Tpke) exit 339, 9.2 mi n on SR 309, then just w. ⬜Ⓛ ⬜Ⓓ CALL ⬜Ⓜ

IRON HILL BREWERY & RESTAURANT
267/708-2000

▼▼ American. Casual Dining. $8-$27 **AAA Inspector Notes:** The signature microbrews taste great with the steaks, fish and wood-oven pizzas prepared in the open kitchen. Don't pass on dessert, especially the sublime banana Bundt cake. A gluten-free menu also is available. **Features:** full bar, happy hour. **Address:** 1460 Bethlehem Pike 19454 **Location:** I-276 (Pennsylvania Tpke) exit 339, 5.5 mi s on SR 309; in English Village Shoppes. ⬜Ⓛ ⬜Ⓓ CALL ⬜Ⓜ

MONTOURSVILLE pop. 4,615

JOHNSON'S CAFÉ
570/368-8351

▼▼ American. Casual Dining. $7-$20 **AAA Inspector Notes:** This casual restaurant has its roots as a former farmhouse and stagecoach stop. Transformed into a restaurant nearly 60 years ago and handed down from family members, it now serves American fare with Mexican on Thursday and Italian night on Saturday. The versatile menu succeeds because of the passion for good food and fine service. Awesome salads combine interesting ingredients such as cranberries, grilled yellowfin tuna, caramelized pear and Buffalo chicken. The patio opens seasonally. **Features:** full bar. **Address:** 334 Broad St 17754 **Location:** Center. ⬜Ⓛ ⬜Ⓓ

MOON RUN
• Hotels & Restaurants map & index p. 348
• Part of Pittsburgh area — see map p. 326

COMFORT SUITES
(412)494-5750 ㉙

▼▼▼ Hotel $109-$199 **Address:** 750 Aten Rd 15108 **Location:** I-376 exit 58 (Montour Run Rd). **Facility:** 74 units. 3 stories (no elevator), interior corridors. **Pool(s):** heated indoor. **Activities:** limited exercise equipment. **Guest Services:** valet and coin laundry.

EXTENDED STAY AMERICA PITTSBURGH AIRPORT
412/490-0979 ㉘

▼▼ Extended Stay Hotel. Rates not provided. **Address:** 200 Chauvet Dr 15275 **Location:** I-376 exit 59 (Robinson Town Center Blvd), left on Summit Park Dr, then just s. **Facility:** 85 kitchen units. 3 stories, interior corridors. **Activities:** limited exercise equipment. **Guest Services:** coin laundry.

 CALL

HOLIDAY INN EXPRESS & SUITES PITTSBURGH AIRPORT
(412)788-8400 ㉘

▼▼▼
Hotel
$109-$229

Address: 5311 Campbells Run Rd 15205 **Location:** I-376 exit 60B (Crafton/SR 60 S), just w. **Facility:** 148 units. 3 stories, interior corridors. **Pool(s):** heated outdoor. **Activities:** hot tub, exercise room. **Guest Services:** valet laundry, area transportation.

(See map & index p. 348.)

HOMEWOOD SUITES
(412)490-0440 **76**

Extended Stay Hotel $129-$219 **Address:** 2000 GSK Dr 15108 **Location:** I-376 exit 59 (Montour Run Rd), 0.9 mi w, then just w to Fedex Dr; jct Montour Run Rd and Fedex Dr. **Facility:** 117 efficiencies. 4 stories, interior corridors. **Terms:** 1-7 night minimum stay, cancellation fee imposed. **Pool(s):** heated indoor. **Activities:** exercise room. **Guest Services:** valet and coin laundry, area transportation.

| AAA Benefit: Members save 5% or more! |

HYATT PLACE PITTSBURGH AIRPORT
(412)494-0202 **83**

Hotel $89-$209

HYATT PLACE®

AAA Benefit: Members save 10%!

Address: 6011 Campbells Run Rd 15205 **Location:** I-376 exit 60B (Crafton/SR 60 S), just w. **Facility:** 127 units. 6 stories, interior corridors. **Parking:** winter plug-ins. **Terms:** cancellation fee imposed. **Amenities:** safes. **Pool(s):** heated indoor. **Activities:** exercise room. **Guest Services:** valet laundry, area transportation. **Featured Amenity:** breakfast buffet. *(See ad p. 364.)*

MAINSTAY SUITES PITTSBURGH AIRPORT
(412)490-7343 **81**

Extended Stay Hotel $90-$120 **Address:** 1000 Park Lane Dr 15275 **Location:** I-376 exit 58 (Montour Run Rd), just w on Cliff Mine Rd, then just s. **Facility:** 101 efficiencies. 3 stories, interior corridors. **Activities:** exercise room. **Guest Services:** valet and coin laundry, area transportation.

PITTSBURGH AIRPORT MARRIOTT
(412)788-8800 **78**

Hotel $188-$309 **Address:** 777 Aten Rd 15108 **Location:** I-376 exit 58 (Montour Run Rd). **Facility:** 318 units. 15 stories, interior corridors. **Amenities:** video games. **Pool(s):** heated indoor. **Activities:** hot tub, exercise room. **Guest Services:** valet and coin laundry, area transportation.

| AAA Benefit: Members save 5% or more! |

PITTSBURGH COMFORT INN
(412)922-7555 **77**

Hotel $109-$299 **Address:** 4770 Steubenville Pike 15205 **Location:** I-79 exit 60A, just s on SR 60 (Steubenville Pike). **Facility:** 47 units. 3 stories, interior corridors. **Activities:** limited exercise equipment. **Guest Services:** valet and coin laundry.

RED ROOF INN PLUS PITTSBURGH SOUTH - AIRPORT
412/787-7870 **82**

Motel
Rates not provided

Address: 6404 Steubenville Pike 15205 **Location:** I-79 exit 60A, 3.2 mi w on SR 60 (Steubenville Pike). **Facility:** 120 units. 2 stories (no elevator), interior/exterior corridors. **Amenities:** safes.

RESIDENCE INN BY MARRIOTT PITTSBURGH AIRPORT CORAOPOLIS
(412)787-3300 **80**

Extended Stay Hotel $133-$219 **Address:** 1500 Park Lane Dr 15275 **Location:** I-376 exit 58 (Montour Run Rd), just w on Cliff Mine Dr to Summit Park Dr, just s to Park Lane Dr, then just e. **Facility:** 156 units, some two bedrooms, efficiencies and kitchens. 3 stories, interior corridors. **Pool(s):** heated outdoor. **Activities:** hot tub, recreation programs in season, exercise room. **Guest Services:** valet and coin laundry, area transportation.

| AAA Benefit: Members save 5% or more! |

SPRINGHILL SUITES BY MARRIOTT-PITTSBURGH AIRPORT
(412)494-9446 **85**

Hotel $132-$217 **Address:** 239 Summit Park Dr 15275 **Location:** I-376 exit 59 (Robinson Town Center Blvd), just s. Located in a shopping complex. **Facility:** 102 units. 4 stories, interior corridors. **Pool(s):** heated indoor. **Activities:** hot tub, exercise room. **Guest Services:** valet and coin laundry, area transportation.

| AAA Benefit: Members save 5% or more! |

 WHERE TO EAT

DITKA'S RESTAURANT
412/722-1555 **60**

Steak. Fine Dining. $10-$60 **AAA Inspector Notes:** The comfortable dining room carries out an upscale, contemporary look with bright colors of yellow, green and red along with rich wood tables and chairs. The menu is large with tasty entrées. This restaurant is great for a fast sit-down lunch or a relaxed and casual dinner. **Features:** full bar. **Address:** 1 Robinson Plaza 15205 **Location:** US 22 W exit 59B, just s on SR 60 (Steubenville Pike); in Robinson Manor Plaza. [L] [D]

KING'S FAMILY RESTAURANT
412/937-0300

American. Family Dining. $6-$13 **AAA Inspector Notes:** Fast and friendly service is offered here. The menu is large in size with descriptive menu items and pictures. The restaurant is also known for its ice cream and dessert menu. **Address:** 4900 Steubenville Pike 15205 **Location:** I-79 exit 60A, just e on SR 60 (Steubenville Pike). [B] [L] [D] [LATE]

(See map & index p. 348.)

MAD MEX   412/494-5656

▼▼ Mexican. Casual Dining. $7-$17 **AAA Inspector Notes:** The colorful décor and lively music will make for a fun experience. The kitchen prepares unique steak, seafood and chicken dishes using authentic Mexican ingredients, as well as tacos, enchiladas, quesadillas, sizzling fajitas and "Mad Mex" burritos. At the restaurant's large bar area, guests can order from a wide range of beers in bottles or on draft, as well as specialty drinks. **Features:** full bar. **Address:** 2 Robinson Plaza 15205 **Location:** Jct US 22 and 30 exit Moon Run Rd, 1 mi w; in Robinson Manor Plaza. Ⓛ Ⓓ

PRIMANTI BROTHERS RESTAURANT   412/921-6677

▼ American. Casual Dining. $6-$10 **AAA Inspector Notes:** Looking for a sandwich that offers piled-high fries and coleslaw on top of each sandwich, then this is the place to be. The bar restaurant theme is every Pittsburgher's dream with memorabilia for each sports fan. **Address:** 4501 Steubenville Pike 15205 **Location:** I-79 exit 60A, 1.1 mi e on SR 60 (Steubenville Pike).

Ⓛ Ⓓ ⓛⒶⓉⒺ CALL ⒼⓂ

YA FEI   412/788-9388 ㊉

▼ Chinese. Casual Dining. $7-$19 **AAA Inspector Notes:** A favorite among local businesses in the shopping area, this restaurant employs a warm, welcoming staff. Offerings include fresh seafood, poultry and beef preparations. **Features:** full bar. **Reservations:** suggested. **Address:** 1980 Park Manor Blvd 15205 **Location:** Just w; in Robinson Town Centre. Ⓛ Ⓓ

MOOSIC (E-10) pop. 5,719, elev. 636'

ⓈⒶⓋⒺ **MONTAGE MOUNTAIN WATERPARK,** 1000 Montage Mountain Rd., offers a wave pool, lazy river, children's pool, waterslides and bumper boats. The facility also has batting cages and a miniature golf course. **Time:** Allow 4 hours minimum. **Hours:** Daily 11-6, Memorial Day-Labor Day weekend. Phone ahead to confirm schedule. **Cost:** $24.99; $20.99 (children under 48 inches tall); free (ages 0-2). Phone ahead to confirm rates. **Phone:** (570) 969-7669 or (888) 754-7946. ┚ 🏞

RECREATIONAL ACTIVITIES

Skiing and Snowboarding

• **Montage Mountain Resort** is at 1000 Montage Mountain Rd. Snow tubing, air boarding and 26 cross-country trails also are offered. **Hours:** Mon.-Fri. 9-9 (also Fri. 9-10 p.m.), Sat.-Sun. 8:30 a.m.-10 p.m., Dec.-Mar. **Phone:** (570) 969-7669, or (800) 468-7669 Dec.-Mar.

MORGANTOWN pop. 826

HOLIDAY INN   610/286-3000

▼▼▼ Hotel. Rates not provided. **Address:** 6170 Morgantown Rd 19543 **Location:** I-76 (Pennsylvania Tpke) exit 298, just s on SR 10. Adjacent to a furniture mall. **Facility:** 187 units. 4 stories, interior corridors. **Pool(s):** heated indoor. **Activities:** exercise room. **Guest Services:** valet and coin laundry.

┚ 🍸 🏊 ⒷⒾⓏ ⒽⓈ 🛜 ✕ ▣
/ SOME UNITS 🅂🄷 📶 🖥

**Show you care with
AAA/CAA Gift Membership,
perfect for any occasion**

THE WINDMILL RESTAURANT   610/286-5980

▼▼ American. Family Dining. $5-$19 **AAA Inspector Notes:** Located on the eastern edge of Pennsylvania Dutch Country, this family-oriented restaurant is a favorite for wholesome food prepared the Pennsylvania Dutch way—and in hearty portions. Chicken-corn soup is a tasty specialty, as are homemade pies and breads. An ice cream stand and gift shop also occupy prominent positions here. **Address:** 2838 Main St 19543 **Location:** I-76 (Pennsylvania Tpke) exit 298, 0.5 mi w of jct SR 10 and 23. Ⓑ Ⓛ Ⓓ

MORRISVILLE (A-12) pop. 8,728, elev. 21'

• Part of Philadelphia area — see map p. 230

PENNSBURY MANOR, 5 mi. s. on the Delaware River at 400 Pennsbury Memorial Rd., was the country estate of William Penn. The 43-acre historic site contains reconstructed versions of a worker's cottage, a smokehouse, a bake-and-brew house, an icehouse, a blacksmith shop, stables and the 1683 manor house. Costumed guides conduct tours of the manor; the buildings display 17th- and 18th-century artifacts. William Penn: The Seed of a Nation includes artifacts, dioramas and activities. Farm animals and formal and kitchen gardens also can be seen.

Picnicking is permitted in the pavilion. **Time:** Allow 1 hour, 30 minutes minimum. **Hours:** Tues.-Sat. 9-5, Sun. noon-5. Tours depart Tues.-Sat. at 11:30, 1:30 and 3:30, Sun. at 12:30, 1:30, 2:30 and 3:30, Mar.-Oct.; Tues.-Sat. at 11:30 and 1:30, Sun. at 12:30 and 2:30, Nov.-Dec. Rest of year by appointment. Phone ahead to confirm schedule. **Cost:** Grounds $3. Tours $9; $7 (ages 65+); $5 (ages 3-11). **Phone:** (215) 946-0400. 🏞

COMFORT INN NJ STATE CAPITAL AREA
                         (215)428-2600

▼▼▼ Hotel $89-$190

Address: 7 S Pennsylvania Ave 19067 **Location:** US 1 exit Pennsylvania Ave, just n. Located in a commercial area. **Facility:** 59 units. 2 stories, interior corridors. **Amenities:** safes. **Pool(s):** heated outdoor. **Activities:** limited exercise equipment. **Guest Services:** coin laundry. **Featured Amenity:** breakfast buffet.

ⓈⒶⓋⒺ ┚ CALL ⒼⓂ 🏊 🛜 ✕
🛜 🖥 ▣ / SOME UNITS 🅂🄷

MOUNTAIN TOP pop. 10,982

DAMENTI'S RESTAURANT   570/788-2004

▼▼▼ Continental. Casual Dining. $26-$46 **AAA Inspector Notes:** In business for more than 60 years, this restaurant is set in a restored home and bears the last name of the original owner. The ambience is set for romance as the dining room features rustic woods, low ceilings, dim lighting and soft music playing in the background. The menu features Continental cuisine with such selections as jumbo lump crab meat, cherry stone clams, a New York strip steak, veal, rack of lamb, liver, duck and Florida grouper. The seasoned staff are well dressed. **Features:** full bar. **Reservations:** suggested. **Address:** 870 N Hunter Hwy 18707 **Location:** I-80 exit 262, 1.3 mi n on SR 309. Ⓓ

MOUNT JOY (H-9) pop. 7,410, elev. 360'
- **Attractions map p. 221**
- **Hotels & Restaurants map & index p. 222**
- **Part of Pennsylvania Dutch Country area — see map p. 220**

BUBE'S BREWERY, 102 N. Market St., is a mid-19th-century brewery that operated until Prohibition. Built by Alois Bube, a German immigrant, the brewery is 43 feet below street level beneath a Victorian hotel that also houses three restaurants, a brewery museum and an art gallery. Guided tours include a history tour and a brewer-led tour. **Hours:** Tours are offered to dining and non-dining guests daily. History tour Sat. at 9. Brewer's tour Sat. at 2 when brewing is in progress. **Cost:** Free. **Phone:** (717) 653-2056.

HILLSIDE FARM B&B   717/653-6697 27
 Bed & Breakfast. Rates not provided. **Address:** 607 Eby Chiques Rd 17552 **Location:** SR 283 exit Salunga, 1.2 mi sw on Spooky Nook Rd, then 0.3 mi nw. Located in a rural farm area. **Facility:** 4 units, some cottages. 3 stories (no elevator), interior corridors. **Terms:** check-in 4:30 pm, age restrictions may apply.

WHERE TO EAT

THE CATACOMBS   717/653-2056 26
 American. Casual Dining. $22-$39 **AAA Inspector Notes:** *Historic.* Several stories underground in the stone-lined cellars of a 19th-century brewery, the restaurant attracts a broad crowd for its unusual setting and tasty food. Baked tomato soup and chicken Costello stand out on a menu of well-prepared dishes. **Features:** full bar. **Reservations:** suggested. **Address:** 102 N Market St 17552 **Location:** Just n of SR 230; in Bube's Brewery. D

COUNTRY TABLE RESTAURANT   717/653-4745 27
 Regional American. Family Dining. $4-$13 **AAA Inspector Notes:** Wholesome, home-style cooking is what you'll get at the casual, family-oriented Country Table, which features such Pennsylvania Dutch favorites as ham loaf, turkey and filling and honey-broiled chicken. The homemade desserts are sure to satisfy your sweet tooth. **Address:** 740 E Main St 17552 **Location:** 1 mi e on SR 230. B L D

THE WATERING TROUGH   717/653-6181 25
 American. Casual Dining. $6-$20 **AAA Inspector Notes:** Old-time photographs hang on the walls of the small, intimate dining room. The menu centers on charbroiled steak and seafood, including a full seafood bar called "Shucks." Carrot cake and peanut butter pie are among the tempting desserts. **Features:** full bar, happy hour. **Address:** 905 W Main St (SR 230) 17552 **Location:** 0.9 mi w of jct SR 772. L D

MOUNT LEBANON pop. 33,137
- **Hotels & Restaurants map & index p. 348**
- **Part of Pittsburgh area — see map p. 326**

SPRINGHILL SUITES BY MARRIOTT PITTSBURGH MT. LEBANON   (412)563-6300
 [fyi] Hotel $119-$159 Too new to rate, opening scheduled for January 2015. **Address:** 611 Washington Rd 15228 **Location:** Jct SR 19. Mt Lebanon, 42. **Amenities:** 194 units.

AAA Benefit: Members save 5% or more!

WHERE TO EAT

DEBLASIO'S   412/531-3040 80
 Italian. Casual Dining. $6-$30 **AAA Inspector Notes:** In a busy shopping plaza, this family-owned restaurant is a popular dining spot with locals. Friendly servers bring out piping-hot food. **Features:** full bar. **Address:** 1717 Cochran Rd 15220 **Location:** Jct Greentree and Cochran rds; in Virginia Manor Shoppes. L D

MOUNT PLEASANT pop. 4,454
- **Part of Pittsburgh area — see map p. 326**

HOLIDAY INN EXPRESS   724/547-2095
 Hotel. Rates not provided. **Address:** 250 Bessemer Rd 15666 **Location:** Jct US 119 and SR 819. **Facility:** 68 units. 3 stories, interior corridors. **Activities:** exercise room. **Guest Services:** valet laundry.

WHERE TO EAT

MARGARITA'S   724/547-5478
 Mexican. Casual Dining. $5-$22 **AAA Inspector Notes:** Stucco walls, arches and traditional Mexican decor accent this restaurant, where patrons sit down to large portions of traditional south-of-the-border favorites. Flan or sopaipilla make for a yummy dessert. **Features:** full bar. **Address:** 318 Countryside Plaza 15666 **Location:** SR 819; in Countryside Plaza. L D

VILLAGE RESTAURANT   724/547-3529
 Italian. Casual Dining. $8-$18 **AAA Inspector Notes:** Just east of the center of town sits the real deal in Italian food. It's worth a trip for the satisfying pastas, fines sauces, value-priced specials and eager-to-please service. Generous portions and outstanding pizza shine at this restaurant. Pasta favorites include spaghetti in freshly made red sauce, penne with fresh tomatoes and basil and gnocchi. You'll find traditional Italian versions of veal, chicken and seafood. **Address:** 236 W Main St 15666 **Location:** On SR 31; center. D

MOUNT POCONO (F-11) pop. 3,170, elev. 1,658'
- **Hotels p. 208 • Restaurants p. 208**
- **Hotels & Restaurants map & index p. 373**
- **Part of Pocono Mountains Area — see map p. 371**

From a hundred viewpoints at and near Mount Pocono, the colossal notch of the Delaware Water Gap is plainly visible, even though it is 25 miles away. Southwest of town is Pocono Raceway, where two annual NASCAR 500 automobile races and other motorsports races are held.

POCONO KNOB, s. on US 611, then e. on Knob Rd. to scenic overlook, is one of the well-known viewpoints of the region. The panorama extends across the Pocono Mountains into New Jersey and New York.

GAMBLING ESTABLISHMENTS
- SAVE **Mount Airy Casino Resort** is at 312 Woodland Rd. **Hours:** Daily 24 hours. **Phone:** (877) 682-4791.

Get your vehicle vacation ready at a
AAA/CAA Approved Auto Repair facility

(See map & index p. 373.)

MOUNT AIRY CASINO RESORT   570/243-4800   19

Contemporary Resort Hotel
Rates not provided

Address: 312 Woodland Rd 18344 **Location:** I-380 exit 3, 1.8 mi e on SR 940, 2 mi s on SR 611, then just e. **Facility:** Setting the bar high for lodgings in the Poconos area, this casino resort offers upscale accommodations and exciting amenities, including an impressive indoor/outdoor pool complex and luxury spa. 188 units. 6 stories, interior corridors. **Parking:** on-site and valet. **Terms:** check-in 4 pm. **Amenities:** safes. **Dining:** 5 restaurants, also, Guy Fieri's Mt. Pocono Kitchen, see separate listing, nightclub, entertainment. **Pool(s):** heated outdoor, heated indoor. **Activities:** sauna, hot tub, steamroom, cabanas, regulation golf, snowmobiling, trails, spa. **Guest Services:** valet laundry, area transportation.

PARADISE STREAM RESORT   570/839-8881   18

Resort Hotel
Rates not provided

Address: Rt 940 & Carlton Rd 18344 **Location:** Waterfront. I-380 exit 3 (SR 940), 5 mi e, then just w of SR 390. Located in a semi-rural area. **Facility:** This couples-focused, all-inclusive resort offers a variety of accommodations from lakeside villas to champagne-tower suites. 143 units. 1 story, exterior corridors. **Terms:** check-in 3:30 pm, age restrictions may apply. **Dining:** 2 restaurants, nightclub, entertainment. **Pool(s):** heated outdoor, heated indoor. **Activities:** hot tub, self-propelled boats, fishing, miniature golf, tennis, recreation programs, bicycles, game room, trails, exercise room, spa. **Guest Services:** coin laundry, area transportation.

WHERE TO EAT

BAILEYS GRILLE & STEAKHOUSE   570/839-9678   16

Steak. Casual Dining. $16-$36 **AAA Inspector Notes:** Visit this relaxed steakhouse for super steaks, prime rib, seafood, hickory-smoked baby back ribs, London broil, crab cakes, chicken, fajitas and the ultimate onion. The giant rack of smoked beef ribs known as dinosaur bones is a popular item. A salad bar also is available, and the family-friendly spot lists eight dishes on its children's menu. **Features:** full bar, patio dining. **Reservations:** suggested, weekends. **Address:** 604 Pocono Blvd 18344 **Location:** SR 611, 0.6 mi n of jct SR 611, 940 and 196. L D

GUY FIERI'S MT. POCONO KITCHEN   570/580-9990   17

New Comfort Food. Casual Dining. $13-$28 **AAA Inspector Notes:** The popular TV personality brings his brand of brash and bold food to an energetic spot just off the casino floor. Giant burgers, sweet and spicy motley 'cue barbecue sandwiches and meatloaf with a mac 'n' cheese crust are some of the staples at lunch and dinner. Desserts here are massive. Breakfast includes more twists, including chunky monkey pancakes and a pulled pork omelet. **Features:** full bar. **Address:** 312 Woodland Rd 18344 **Location:** I-380 exit 3, 1.8 mi e on SR 940, 2 mi s on SR 611, then just e. **Parking:** on-site and valet. B L D LATE CALL &M

MOUNTVILLE   pop. 2,802
• Hotels & Restaurants map & index p. 222
• Part of Pennsylvania Dutch Country area — see map p. 220

MAINSTAY SUITES   (717)285-2500   31

Extended Stay Hotel
$90-$160

Address: 314 Primrose Ln 17554 **Location:** US 30 (Lincoln Hwy) exit Mountville, just n on Stoney Battery Rd, just w on Highland Dr, then just s. Located in a light-commercial area. **Facility:** 71 efficiencies, some two bedrooms. 3 stories, interior corridors. **Activities:** exercise room. **Guest Services:** coin laundry. **Featured Amenity: continental breakfast.** (See ad p. 178.)

SLEEP INN & SUITES LANCASTER COUNTY   (717)285-0444   30

Hotel
$90-$170

Address: 310 Primrose Ln 17554 **Location:** US 30 (Lincoln Hwy) exit Mountville, just n on Stoney Battery Rd, just w on Highland Dr, then just s. Located in a light-commercial area. **Facility:** 80 units. 3 stories, interior corridors. **Pool(s):** heated indoor. **Activities:** hot tub, exercise room. **Guest Services:** valet laundry. **Featured Amenity: breakfast buffet.** (See ad p. 178.)

MURRYSVILLE   pop. 20,079
• Part of Pittsburgh area — see map p. 326

ATRIA'S RESTAURANT & TAVERN   724/733-4453

American. Casual Dining. $10-$28 **AAA Inspector Notes:** With bright shades of yellow, green and red and rich wood tables and chairs, guests feel right at home in this dining room. Tasty and well-seasoned entrees fill the large menu. This place is great for a fast sit-down lunch or relaxed dinner. **Features:** full bar. **Address:** 4869 William Penn Hwy 15668 **Location:** I-76 (Pennsylvania Tpke) exit 57, 4.1 mi e. L D

MYERSTOWN   pop. 3,062

MOTEL SKANDIA   717/866-6447

Motel. Rates not provided. **Address:** 922 E Lincoln Ave 17067 **Location:** 2 mi e on US 422. Located in a country setting. **Facility:** 15 units. 1-2 stories (no elevator), exterior corridors.

WHERE TO EAT

COUNTRY FARE RESTAURANT BAKERY & DELI   717/866-9043

American. Casual Dining. $5-$18 **AAA Inspector Notes:** A favorite among locals, this restaurant focuses on Pennsylvania Dutch food, including a large selection of such items as the top-selling henny penny chicken, potpie and chow chow. The bakery cranks out homemade desserts such as yummy shoofly pie. **Address:** 498 E Lincoln Ave 17067 **Location:** 1.5 mi of jct US 422 and SR 501. B L D CALL &M

NAZARETH (G-11) pop. 5,746, elev. 530'

The area was originally part of a 5,000-acre tract of land owned as a feudal estate by the William Penn family. In 1740 evangelist George Whitefield purchased the land. He employed Peter Boehler and a small band of Moravians, a group of Protestants from Germany, to oversee the construction of what is now called the Whitefield House, at 214 E. Center St. The house now contains the Moravian Historical Society's Museum and Research Library; phone (610) 759-5070. The following year the Moravians bought the property and Nazareth remained exclusively a Moravian settlement for more than a century. Nazareth Hall, built in 1755, was a boys' military academy 1759-1929.

Nazareth Area Chamber of Commerce and Visitor Center: 201 N. Main St., P.O. Box 173, Nazareth, PA 18064. **Phone:** (610) 759-9188.

MARTIN GUITAR CO., 510 Sycamore St., offers a 1-hour guided tour through the factory. Visitors view each step in the production process, from shaping the wood to testing the instrument's sound. A museum displays unusual and vintage Martin guitars and memorabilia dating to the company's founding in 1833. **Time:** Allow 1 hour, 30 minutes minimum. **Hours:** Museum Mon.-Fri. 8-5. Guided tours are given at regular intervals 11-2:30. Closed major holidays. **Cost:** Free. **Phone:** (610) 759-2837.

CLASSIC VICTORIAN ESTATE INN   610/759-8276

▼▼▼ **Historic Bed & Breakfast.** Rates not provided. **Address:** 35 N New St 18064 **Location:** US 22 exit SR 191, 5 mi n; SR 33 exit SR 191, 2.5 mi s. **Facility:** This inviting home, which dates from 1908, is decorated in a Victorian style and boasts a charming historic atmosphere. 3 units. 2 stories, interior corridors.

WHERE TO EAT

HANA SUSHI   610/759-2810

▼▼ Japanese Sushi. Casual Dining. $9-$15 **AAA Inspector Notes:** Quick service and tasty food are the hallmarks here. Try a traditional miso soup and chicken teriyaki or explore the various specialty rolls featuring spicy tuna, salmon, yellow tail and eel. Come hungry to this small downtown spot where the sushi rolls are huge. **Reservations:** suggested. **Address:** 6 Belvidere St 18064 **Location:** US 22 exit SR 191, 4.1 mi n, follow signs to SR 191 N for 0.7 mi, then just w. **Parking:** street only. L D

NEWBURG INN   610/759-8528

▼▼ American. Casual Dining. $7-$33 **AAA Inspector Notes:** Head to the charming Newburg Inn, established in the mid-18th century as an Indian trading post and stagecoach stop, for specialties of prime rib and fresh seafood. Although it now bears little resemblance to its pioneer-day appearance, the cozy dining room is decorated with raisin racks and old photographs. For dessert, you can't go wrong with the wonderful chocolate peanut butter pie. **Features:** full bar, happy hour. **Reservations:** suggested. **Address:** 4357 Newburg Rd 18064 **Location:** On SR 191, 2 mi n of US 22. L D

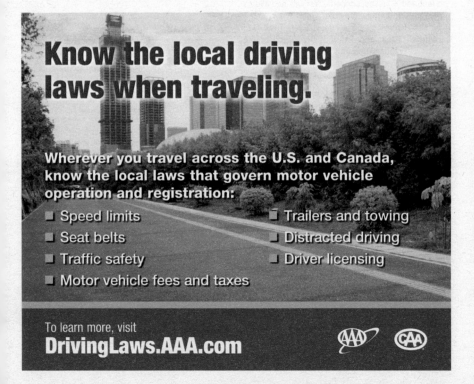

NEW BRIGHTON (G-1) pop. 6,025, elev. 738'
• Part of Pittsburgh area — see map p. 326

MERRICK ART GALLERY, 1100 Fifth Ave., was founded with the collection of local industrialist Edward Dempster Merrick. The majority of works features American and European paintings from the 18th- and 19th centuries, and the highlight is a collection of Hudson River School paintings. The museum also includes contemporary art, a music room and a library as well as rock, mineral and zoological collections.

Time: Allow 45 minutes minimum. **Hours:** Tues.-Sat. 10-4:30, Sun. 1-4, day after Labor Day-day before Memorial Day; Wed.-Sat. 10-4, every other Sun. 1-4, rest of year. Closed major holidays and during special events; phone ahead to confirm schedule. **Cost:** Donations. **Phone:** (724) 846-1130.

NEW CASTLE (F-1) pop. 23,273, elev. 806'

Lawrence County Tourist Promotion Agency: Cilli Central Station, 229 S. Jefferson St., New Castle, PA 16101. **Phone:** (724) 654-8408 or (888) 284-7599.

HOYT CENTER FOR THE ARTS, 124 E. Leasure Ave., includes an art center and museum housed in two 1917 mansions within the North Hill historic district. Art collections, exhibitions and period rooms are featured. Classes, concerts, festivals and events are offered throughout the year. **Time:** Allow 1 hour minimum. **Hours:** Galleries (Hoyt East) Tues.-Sat. 11-4 (also Tues. and Thurs. 4-8). Period house (Hoyt West) tours Tues.-Sat. 11-4. **Cost:** Galleries by donation. Period house guided tour $5. Reservations are required. **Phone:** (724) 652-2882. GT

LIVING TREASURES ANIMAL PARK, off I-79 exit 99, then 4 mi. w. on US 422 to 268 Fox Rd., is in a wooded environment and features more than 300 animals from around the world. Included are parrots and exotic birds, giraffes, grizzly bears, Asian small-clawed river otters, reptiles, big cats, a white tiger, several species of primates and a Barbary white lion, which is extinct in the wild. Horse-drawn safari tours and camel and pony rides are offered, and visitors can get their picture taken with animals at a park photo center.

Time: Allow 1 hour minimum. **Hours:** Daily 10-8, June-Aug..; 10-6, Apr.-May before Memorial Day and early Sept. to mid-Nov. **Cost:** $12.99; $10.99 (ages 62+); $9.99 (ages 3-11). Camel ride $5. Pony ride $3. **Phone:** (724) 924-9571. [11]

COMFORT INN-NEW CASTLE   (724)658-7700
🏨🏨 Hotel $79-$139 **Address:** 1740 New Butler Rd (US Business 422) 16101 **Location:** Jct SR 65, 1 mi e on US 422, 1 mi w on US 422 business route. **Facility:** 79 units. 2 stories (no elevator), interior corridors. **Amenities:** safes. **Activities:** sauna, exercise room.
[BIZ] [HS] 🛜 🍴 🖨 🖵 / SOME UNITS 🛏

HAMPTON INN & SUITES NEW CASTLE   (724)656-0000
🏨🏨🏨 **Contemporary Hotel** $109-$299 **Address:** 2608 W State St 16101 **Location:** I-376 exit 13, just w. Near a shopping area. **Facility:** 74 units, some efficiencies. 3 stories, interior corridors. **Parking:** winter plug-ins. **Terms:** 1-7 night minimum stay, cancellation fee imposed. **Pool(s):** heated indoor. **Activities:** hot tub, exercise room. **Guest Services:** valet and coin laundry.

AAA Benefit: Members save 5% or more!

[11] CALL [M] 🚗 [BIZ] [HS] 🛜 ✖ 🍴 🖨 🖵

SUPER 8   (724)658-8849
🏨🏨 Hotel $86-$126 **Address:** 1699 New Butler Rd (US Business 422) 16101 **Location:** Jct SR 65, 1.1 mi e on US 422, 1 mi w on US 422 business route. **Facility:** 57 units. 3 stories (no elevator), interior corridors. [BIZ] 🛜 🍴 🖨 🖵

WHERE TO EAT

ELHAM RESTAURANT   724/652-6611
🍷 Mediterranean. Casual Dining. $6-$16 **AAA Inspector Notes:** In a strip mall, the restaurant puts forth a menu of Middle Eastern cuisine, including kebabs and grape leaf wraps, in addition to varied desserts. The decor is basic, but the food is very good. **Address:** 2650 Ellwood Rd 16101 **Location:** US 422 W, just off Ellwood Rd; in Kmart Shopping Center. [L] [D]

KING'S FAMILY RESTAURANT   724/656-0699
🍷🍷 American. Family Dining. $6-$16 **AAA Inspector Notes:** Fast and friendly service is offered here. The menu is large in size with descriptive menu items and pictures. The restaurant is also known for its ice cream and dessert menu. **Address:** 2541 W State St 16101 **Location:** On US 224, just e of jct SR 60. [B] [L] [D] [LATE]

NEW COLUMBIA pop. 1,013

HOLIDAY INN EXPRESS   (570)568-1100
🏨🏨🏨
Hotel
$99-$229

Address: 160 Commerce Park Dr 17856 **Location:** I-80 exit 210A (US 15/New Columbia), just s. Located in a quiet area. **Facility:** 101 units. 3 stories, interior corridors. **Pool(s):** heated indoor. **Activities:** hot tub, exercise room. **Guest Services:** valet and coin laundry. **Featured Amenity:** full hot breakfast.

[SAVE] [11] CALL [M] 🚗 [BIZ] 🛜 ✖ 🖵 / SOME UNITS 🛏 🍴 🖨 🖵

NEW CUMBERLAND pop. 7,277
• Hotels & Restaurants map & index p. 138

BEST WESTERN PLUS NEW CUMBERLAND INN & SUITES   (717)774-4440 [41]
🏨🏨🏨
Hotel
$95-$170

[Best Western PLUS logo]

AAA Benefit: Members save up to 20%!

Address: 702 Limekiln Rd 17070 **Location:** I-83 exit 40A, just w. **Facility:** 64 units. 3 stories, interior corridors. **Pool(s):** heated indoor. **Activities:** hot tub, exercise room. **Guest Services:** valet and coin laundry.

[SAVE] [11] 🚗 [BIZ] [HS] 🛜 🍴 🖵 / SOME UNITS 🛏

(See map & index p. 138.)

CLARION HOTEL & CONFERENCE CENTER
HARRISBURG   717/774-2721 **40**

Hotel
Rates not provided

Address: 148 Sheraton Dr 17070 **Location:** I-83 exit 40A, just se. Located in a commercial area. **Facility:** 195 units. 2 stories, interior corridors. **Terms:** check-in 4 pm. **Pool(s):** heated indoor. **Activities:** exercise room. **Guest Services:** valet and coin laundry, area transportation. **Featured Amenity:** breakfast buffet.

COMFORT INN NEW CUMBERLAND   (717)774-8888 **39**
Hotel $60-$170 **Address:** 130 Limekiln Rd 17070 **Location:** I-83 exit 40A, just ne. **Facility:** 88 units. 3 stories, interior corridors. **Pool(s):** heated outdoor. **Activities:** exercise room. **Guest Services:** valet and coin laundry.

DAYS INN HARRISBURG SOUTH   (717)774-4156 **42**
Hotel $65-$110 **Address:** 353 Lewisberry Rd 17070 **Location:** I-83 exit 39A, just ne. Located in a quiet area. **Facility:** 61 units. 2 stories (no elevator), interior corridors. **Pool(s):** outdoor. **Activities:** exercise room. **Guest Services:** coin laundry.

FAIRFIELD INN & SUITES BY MARRIOTT HARRISBURG
WEST   (717)774-0100 **38**
Hotel $97-$194 **Address:** 185 Beacon Hill Blvd 17070 **Location:** I-83 exit 40A, just ne. **Facility:** 83 units. 3 stories, interior corridors. **Pool(s):** heated indoor. **Activities:** hot tub, exercise room. **Guest Services:** valet and coin laundry.

AAA Benefit:
Members save 5% or more!

NEW HOLLAND pop. 5,378
- **Hotels & Restaurants map & index p. 222, 225**
- **Part of Pennsylvania Dutch Country area — see map p. 220**

COMFORT INN AMISH COUNTRY   (717)355-9900 **28**
Hotel $110-$180 **Address:** 626 W Main St 17557 **Location:** 0.5 mi w on SR 23. Located in a commercial area. **Facility:** 69 units. 2 stories, interior corridors. **Activities:** exercise room. **Guest Services:** valet laundry.

COUNTRY SQUIRE MOTOR INN   (717)354-4166 **27**
Motel $60-$90 **Address:** 504 E Main St 17557 **Location:** 0.8 mi e on SR 23. Located in a commercial area. **Facility:** 31 units. 1-2 stories (no elevator), interior/exterior corridors. **Terms:** 3 day cancellation notice-fee imposed.

NEW HOPE (G-12) pop. 2,528, elev. 86'
- **Restaurants p. 212**
- **Part of Philadelphia area — see map p. 230**

The picturesque town of New Hope, an artists' and writers' colony, is a favorite spot for antiques hunting. The village along the banks of the Delaware River across the river from the antique-rich Lambertville, N.J. features lovely guest homes and charming restaurants; make reservations early for these popular eateries.

Bucks County Playhouse stages its performances on the site of a former mill dating from the 1780s. Broadway productions are staged April through December; phone (215) 862-2121.

New Hope Visitors Center: 1 W. Mechanic St., New Hope, PA 18938. **Phone:** (215) 862-5030.

NEW HOPE & IVYLAND RAILROAD, jct. Bridge and Stockton sts., offers a 9-mile, round-trip ride through the Pennsylvania countryside. The 1925 vintage steam train crosses over Pauline's Trestle, upon which actress Pearl White was bound in the 1914 silent film serial "The Perils of Pauline." Dinner and children's excursions also are offered.

Time: Allow 1 hour minimum. **Hours:** Train departs Mon.-Fri. on the hour 11-4, Sat.-Sun. and holidays 11-5, day after Memorial Day-Labor Day and in Oct.; Mon.-Thurs. noon-3, Fri. 11-4, Sat.-Sun. 11-5, day after Labor Day-Sept. 30; Fri. noon-3, Sat.-Sun. 11-4, day after Easter-Memorial Day and Nov. 1 through weekend before Thanksgiving; Sat.-Sun. noon-3, Jan. 2-Easter. Departures vary day after Thanksgiving-day after Christmas; phone ahead. Closed Jan. 1, Thanksgiving, Christmas Eve and Christmas. Phone ahead to confirm schedule. **Cost:** Coach fare $19.95; $17.95 (ages 2-11); $3.95 (ages 0-1). First-class fare $27.90; $25.90 (ages 2-11); $3.95 (ages 0-2). Phone ahead to confirm rates. **Phone:** (215) 862-2332.

1870 WEDGWOOD INN OF NEW HOPE   215/862-2570
Historic Bed & Breakfast. Rates not provided. **Address:** 111 W Bridge St (SR 179) 18938 **Location:** 0.5 mi w of SR 32; downtown. **Facility:** Just off Main Street, this cute B&B features an elaborate outdoor area that includes two gazebos, brick walkways and a dining area. Bike and canoe rentals are available for the nature-oriented guest. 8 units, some two bedrooms. 2 stories (no elevator), interior corridors. **Activities:** bicycles.

AARON BURR HOUSE INN & CONFERENCE CENTER
                                     215/862-3937
Historic Bed & Breakfast. Rates not provided. **Address:** 80 W Bridge St (SR 179) 18938 **Location:** 0.5 mi w of SR 32; at W Bridge and Chestnut sts. **Facility:** Cozy up in front of the gas fireplace found in each guest room while enjoying the complimentary breakfast-in-bed that's served to those who so desire. 7 units. 2 stories (no elevator), interior corridors. **Activities:** bicycles.

FOX & HOUND BED & BREAKFAST OF NEW HOPE
                                     215/862-5082
Bed & Breakfast. Rates not provided. **Address:** 246 W Bridge St 18938 **Location:** 0.5 mi s on SR 179; downtown. **Facility:** A little off Main Street, this B&B is a beautiful three-story house with pleasing landscaping, exposed stone accents and bay windows. 8 units. 3 stories (no elevator), interior corridors. **Guest Services:** coin laundry.

THE INN AT BOWMAN'S HILL 215/862-8090

Bed & Breakfast
Rates not provided

Address: 518 Lurgan Rd 18938 **Location:** 2.9 mi s on S Main St/River Rd, 0.5 mi w. **Facility:** This is an absolutely breathtaking B&B with precise attention to detail. The backyard offers beautiful landscaping, an outdoor sitting/dining area, an expansive koi pond and a stunning outdoor pool. 8 units, some two bedrooms. 2 stories (no elevator), interior corridors. **Terms:** age restrictions may apply. **Amenities:** safes. **Pool(s):** heated outdoor. **Activities:** hot tub, bicycles, massage. **Featured Amenity:** full hot breakfast.

SAVE [!+] CALL [M] [≈] [HS] [≈]
[⊠] [■] [▣]

PINEAPPLE HILL INN B&B 215/862-1790

Historic Bed & Breakfast. Rates not provided. **Address:** 1324 River Rd 18938 **Location:** 4.6 mi s on SR 32. Located in a rural area. **Facility:** Rooms at this stone-and-frame 18th-century Colonial manor house are traditionally furnished and each has a private balcony or gas fireplace. 9 units, some two bedrooms and kitchens. 3 stories (no elevator), interior/exterior corridors. **Terms:** age restrictions may apply. **Pool(s):** outdoor.

[≈] [≈] [⊠] [☎] / SOME UNITS [■]

WHERE TO EAT

BOWMAN'S TAVERN 215/862-2972

American. Casual Dining. $9-$24 **AAA Inspector Notes:** This casual American eatery focuses on fresh and local ingredients in a fun, relaxing environment. Live music is performed often in the lounge area each week. The menu offers a large variety of options, all with exceptional flavor. Try the wood-roasted lamb sandwich or the butternut squash risotto. **Features:** full bar, happy hour. **Address:** 1600 River Rd 18938 **Location:** Jct River and Lurgan rds.

[L] [D]

CENTRE BRIDGE INN 215/862-2048

Continental. Fine Dining. $24-$36 **AAA Inspector Notes:** Historic. Dishes on the seasonally changing menu rely on the availability of fresh ingredients, and you can follow them up with homemade desserts. Friendly, efficient servers tend the rustic and quaint Colonial-style inn, which was originally constructed in 1705 and rebuilt in the 1800s after it burned to the ground. Diners can dine in front of the blazing fireplace in the main dining room or in the glass-enclosed terrace room overlooking the Delaware River. **Features:** full bar, patio dining, Sunday brunch. **Reservations:** suggested. Semiformal attire. **Address:** 2998 N River Rd 18938 **Location:** 4 mi n at jct SR 32 and 263. **Parking:** on-site and valet. [D]

FRAN'S PUB 215/862-5539

Pizza. Casual Dining. $8-$25 **AAA Inspector Notes:** Even though pizza is the star at the pub, where patrons fill the seats year-round, the filling daily specials (often Italian entrées) and sandwiches shouldn't be ignored. Although guests can't get dessert here, ice cream and dessert shops are within walking distance. **Features:** full bar, patio dining, happy hour. **Address:** 116 S Main St 18938 **Location:** On SR 32; center. **Parking:** street only.

[L] [D] [LATE]

HAVANA BAR 215/862-9897

Cuban. Casual Dining. $13-$39 **AAA Inspector Notes:** This Caribbean-based restaurant provides its own flair on such traditional favorites as ahi tuna tartare tostadas, Jamaican jerk chicken wings and the always-popular Cuban panini. The eatery also offers an incredible outdoor dining terrace that overlooks Main Street, a perfect people-watching spot. Be sure to check the calendar for nightly entertainment performances. **Features:** full bar, patio dining, happy hour. **Address:** 105 Main St 18938 **Location:** On SR 32; center. **Parking:** street only. [L] [D] [LATE]

THE LANDING RESTAURANT 215/862-5711

Regional American. Casual Dining. $7-$29 **AAA Inspector Notes:** On the banks of the scenic Delaware River, this casually upscale restaurant features an intimate dining room with fireplaces as well as a seasonal brick patio with colorful flowers. Fresh ingredients enhance the flavor of well-prepared regional cuisine. **Features:** full bar, patio dining, happy hour. **Address:** 22 N Main St 18938 **Location:** On SR 32, just n of jct W SR 179. **Parking:** street only. [L] [D]

MARSHA BROWN CREOLE KITCHEN 215/862-7044

Creole. Fine Dining. $14-$48 **AAA Inspector Notes:** Reared in Louisiana, Marsha Brown goes back to her roots in her eponymous restaurant, which tempts you with such sophisticated fare as gumbo, crayfish and sublime baked macaroni and cheese. The Main Street restaurant occupies a former church and incorporates many of the original pews, stained glass and paintings into the décor. **Features:** full bar, happy hour. **Reservations:** suggested. **Address:** 15 S Main St 18938 **Location:** On SR 32; downtown. **Parking:** valet and street only. [L] [D] CALL [M]

MARTINE'S RIVER HOUSE 215/862-2966

Continental. Casual Dining. $10-$35 **AAA Inspector Notes:** Historic. Martine's serves well-prepared Continental dishes in a 1752 canal tollhouse with a rustic, cozy pub atmosphere. The menu changes seasonally, but you're likely to find seafood, beef, pasta and vegetarian options. A seasonal outdoor terrace is sometimes available. **Features:** full bar. **Reservations:** suggested. **Address:** 14 E Ferry St 18938 **Location:** On SR 32; center. **Parking:** street only. [L] [D]

TRIUMPH BREWING COMPANY 215/862-8300

American. Casual Dining. $12-$24 **AAA Inspector Notes:** Head on downtown and indulge in some finely crafted beers and a variety of tasty American dishes made with ingredients from local and nearby organic farms. Whether you want to dine in the extremely spacious indoor dining room or outside at the lovely patio, you won't be disappointed. Call ahead to check on live music performances and other weekly events. **Features:** full bar. **Address:** 400 Union Square Dr 18938 **Location:** Just w of SR 32, just n. **Parking:** on-site (fee). [L] [D]

C'EST LA VIE 215/862-1956

[fyi] Not evaluated. This spot tucked away off the main road offers a delicious selection of fresh pastries and baked goods. **Address:** 20 N Main St 18938 **Location:** On SR 32; downtown.

NEW KENSINGTON pop. 13,116

• Part of Pittsburgh area — see map p. 326

KING'S FAMILY RESTAURANT 724/339-2234

American. Family Dining. $6-$15 **AAA Inspector Notes:** Fast and friendly service is offered here. The menu is large in size with descriptive menu items and photos. The restaurant is also known for its ice cream and dessert menu. **Address:** 2400 Leechburg Rd, Suite 1000 15068 **Location:** 1.6 mi s of SR 28 exit 14; south end of Tarentum Bridge Rd. [B] [L] [D]

NEW MILFORD pop. 868

HOLIDAY INN EXPRESS GIBSON (570)465-5544

Hotel $129-$169 **Address:** 1561 Oliver Rd 18834 **Location:** I-81 exit 219, just w. **Facility:** 92 units. 3 stories, interior corridors. **Parking:** winter plug-ins. **Terms:** cancellation fee imposed. **Pool(s):** heated indoor. **Activities:** exercise room. **Guest Services:** coin laundry.

[!+] CALL [M] [≈] [BIZ] [HS] [≈] [■] [▣] [▣]

WHERE TO EAT

ARMETTA'S PIZZERIA & PUB   570/465-5492

Italian. Casual Dining. $6-$12 **AAA Inspector Notes:** Located in a former State Police barracks, the restaurant serves ample dishes of classic Italian food with a large selection of appetizers, pizza specialties, salads, subs, wings and grilled-to-order Angus burgers. If you're in a hurry, meals can be prepared for on-the-go consumption. **Features:** full bar, patio dining. **Address:** RR 1, Box 222 E 18834 **Location:** I-81 exit 219, just e; on east side of interstate. D

NEW PARIS (H-4) pop. 186, elev. 1,280'

REYNOLDSDALE FISH CULTURAL STATION, SR 56 to Fish Hatchery Rd., is a modern plant operated by the Pennsylvania Fish and Boat Commission for the propagation of trout for public fishing. A visitor center offers displays and a two-story-high aquarium. **Hours:** Daily 8-3:30. **Cost:** Free. **Phone:** (814) 839-2211.

NEW SMITHVILLE

DE MARCO'S ITALIAN RESTAURANT, PIZZERIA & BAR
610/285-2278

Italian. Casual Dining. $4-$12 **AAA Inspector Notes:** De Marco's prepares modestly priced specialties of Old Italy in a historic structure with a warm and casual family feel. Peruse the seemingly endless menu for poultry, veal and seafood favorites made with homemade pasta and sauces. Don't skip the freshly baked Italian bread. A fine selection of domestic and imported wines complements the superb cuisine. **Features:** full bar. **Address:** 10240 Old Rt 22 19530 **Location:** I-78 exit 45, just s on SR 863. L D

NEW STANTON pop. 2,173

• Restaurants p. 214

COMFORT INN NEW STANTON   (724)755-2400

Hotel $120-$150 **Address:** 106 Bair Blvd 15672 **Location:** I-76 (Pennsylvania Tpke) exit 75, 0.7 mi sw; I-70 exit 57B westbound; exit 57 eastbound. **Facility:** 70 units. 3 stories, interior corridors. **Pool(s):** heated indoor. **Activities:** limited exercise equipment. **Guest Services:** valet laundry.

**FAIRFIELD INN & SUITES BY MARRIOTT
PITTSBURGH/NEW STANTON**   (724)755-0800

Hotel
$97-$160

FAIRFIELD
INN & SUITES
Marriott

AAA Benefit: Members save 5% or more!

Address: 107 Bair Blvd 15672 **Location:** I-76 (Pennsylvania Tpke) exit 75, 0.7 mi sw; I-70 exit 57B westbound; exit 57 eastbound. **Facility:** 63 units. 3 stories, interior corridors. **Pool(s):** heated indoor. **Activities:** hot tub, limited exercise equipment. **Guest Services:** valet and coin laundry. **Featured Amenity:** breakfast buffet. *(See ad this page.)*

SUPER 8-NEW STANTON   (724)925-8915

Motel $69-$84 **Address:** 103 Bair Blvd 15672 **Location:** I-76 (Pennsylvania Tpke) exit 75, 0.5 mi se; I-70 exit 57B westbound; exit 57 eastbound. **Facility:** 60 units. 3 stories (no elevator), interior corridors. **Amenities:** safes. **Activities:** limited exercise equipment. **Guest Services:** coin laundry.

   / SOME UNITS

LA TAVOLA RISTORANTE   724/925-9440

▼▼▼ Northern Italian. Casual Dining. $14-$35 **AAA Inspector Notes:** Cheese ravioli with tomato-basil cream and such chicken entrées as chicken Contadina are among specialties on a menu of Northern Italian fare. A Continental influence is evident in many dishes. Servers in professional attire—black pants and white tuxedo shirts—are attentive. The lounge sits off of the dining room. **Features:** full bar. **Reservations:** suggested. **Address:** 400 S Center Ave 15672 **Location:** I-76 (Pennsylvania Tpke) exit 75, 0.6 mi n; I-70 exit 57B westbound; exit 57 eastbound, just s.

L D CALL 👁M

NEWTOWN (BUCKS COUNTY)
• Part of Philadelphia area — see map p. 230

HOMEWOOD SUITES-NEWTOWN   (215)860-5080

▼▼▼ **Extended Stay Hotel**
$119-$239 **Address:** 110 Pheasant Run 18940 **Location:** I-95 exit 49, 1.8 mi w on SR 332, just n on Penn's Tr, then just w. **Facility:** 104 efficiencies, some two bedrooms. 5 stories, interior corridors. **Terms:** 1-7 night minimum stay, cancellation fee imposed. **Pool(s):** heated indoor. **Activities:** exercise room. **Guest Services:** valet and coin laundry.

AAA Benefit:
Members save 5% or more!

🍴➕ 🏊 BIZ HS 📶 🔒 🖨 ☕

MARCO'S PIZZERIA   215/497-4992

▼ Italian. Casual Dining. $9-$19 **AAA Inspector Notes:** This local favorite draws much of its attention with its variety of pizzas sold by the slice, but its hearty pasta dishes and sandwiches prove to be delicious options as well. Great for a quick bite in a casual setting. **Address:** 2102 S Eagle Rd 18940 **Location:** I-95 exit 49, 1.5 mi w on SR 322, 2 mi n on Newton-Yardley Rd, then just e; in Village at Newtown South Shopping Center. L D

NEW TRIPOLI (G-10) pop. 898, elev. 578'

WINERIES
• **Blue Mountain Vineyards** is off SR 143 to Madison St., then 1 mi. e. to 7627 Grape Vine Dr. **Hours:** Tastings daily 11-6. Tours are available; phone ahead for schedule. Closed Jan. 1, Easter, Thanksgiving and Christmas. **Cost:** $5 tasting fee (redeemable with wine purchase). **Phone:** (610) 298-3068. GT

NORRISTOWN (A-10) pop. 34,324, elev. 83'
• Part of Philadelphia area — see map p. 230

ELMWOOD PARK ZOO, on Harding Blvd., following signs, is home to bison, jaguars, bald eagles and other animals. Visitors learn about and may observe animals found in North, South and Central America. Seasonal features include a petting barn, pony rides, face painting, a playground and an exhibit where visitors can hand-feed giraffes.

Time: Allow 1 hour minimum. **Hours:** Daily 10-5, Apr.-Oct.; 10-4, rest of year. Last admission 30 minutes before closing. Closed Jan. 1, Sept. 14, Thanksgiving and Christmas Eve-Dec. 31. **Cost:** $14; $12 (students with ID); $10 (ages 3-12 and 65+). **Phone:** (610) 277-3825.

🌲 🚃 Elm St-Norristown, 238

NORTH EAST (C-2) pop. 4,294, elev. 803'

North East and the vicinity grow an abundance of fruit and vegetables—especially grapes. With the help of Lake Erie's moderating effect on the climate and proper soil conditions, grape production is thriving. The first vines were planted in 1850 and today there are thousands of acres of vineyards, several wineries and a large Welch's processing plant. Locals take pride in their agricultural region: More than two dozen banners sporting an image of a large grape bunch are displayed around downtown and public school students are known as the Grapepickers. Local produce can be bought at markets, farms (including pick-your-own fruit and vegetable farms) and roadside stands. A farmers market is held Thursdays 11-7 from June through September in Gibson Park. Bicyclists and motorists on SR 5, which parallels Lake Erie and is part of the Great Lakes Seaway Trail (a national scenic byway), get great views of the sprawling vineyards and lake.

Recreational opportunities are certainly not lacking. Lake Erie offers boating, fishing and swimming. North East Marina, 11950 E. Lake Rd., provides various marine services, including fishing charters and free access to four boat ramps. The season runs mid-April to mid-October; phone (814) 725-8244. Freeport Beach is about 2 miles west of the marina at the end of SR 89. Lifeguards are on duty 10 a.m. until dusk early June through Labor Day. The adjacent Halli Reid Park, named for the first woman to swim across Lake Erie from Canada, has a playground, covered picnic areas and grills. There are several other small parks in the area, and North East has places to camp, golf, hike, hunt and cross-country ski as well. Tributary streams 16-Mile Creek and 20-Mile Creek can be used for steelhead trout fishing.

North East is home to a branch of Erie's Mercyhurst College. The 84-acre Catholic-affiliated Mercyhurst North East campus, which opened in 1991, was home to St. Mary's Seminary until the mid-1980s. Some of the historic buildings date between 1868 and 1920.

Lake Erie Speedway, 10700 Delmas Dr., hosts auto racing in six divisions Saturday evenings on its 3/8-mile asphalt track; the stands can seat up to 8,000. Pop into the post office lobby at 38 S. Lake St. to see a sculpture of a town crier, created during the Great Depression as part of President Roosevelt's WPA program; it resides above the drop-off area.

The extensive calendar of events in North East includes two festivals celebrating local agriculture. The North East Cherry Festival takes place in mid-July and the Wine Country Harvest Festival is held the last full weekend in September.

North East Area Chamber of Commerce: 17 E. Main St., North East, PA 16428. **Phone:** (814) 725-4262.

Self-guiding tours: Pick up a brochure, which includes a detailed map of the area, at the chamber of commerce and enjoy the exteriors of downtown's many historic buildings, including the library, Masonic Temple and several churches and residences.

Shopping areas: In addition to all the edible goodies you can find in North East, there are boutiques and antique shops in some of the downtown historic buildings. More antiques can be found at Interstate Antique Mall, 5446 Station Rd. (SR 89), just off I-90.

LAKE SHORE RAILWAY MUSEUM, 31 Wall St. at jct. Robinson St., is in an 1889 passenger train station containing railroading relics. There are 26 pieces of rolling stock on the grounds, and more than 60 trains traverse the nearby tracks daily. **Time:** Allow 45 minutes minimum. **Hours:** Wed.-Sun. noon-4, June 1-Labor Day; Sat.-Sun. noon-4, mid-Apr. to day before Memorial Day. Closed major holidays. **Cost:** Donations. **Phone:** (814) 725-1911 or (814) 673-0679.

RECREATIONAL ACTIVITIES
Horseback Riding
- **Eden Run Farms,** 11610 Cole Rd., offers guided trail rides. **Hours:** Daily 8-5, Apr.-Oct. **Phone:** (814) 725-2996.

HOLIDAY INN EXPRESS & SUITES (814)725-4400

Hotel
$100-$300

Address: 6310 Old Station Rd NE 16428 **Location:** I-90 exit 41, just n on SR 89. **Facility:** 61 units. 4 stories, interior corridors. **Amenities:** safes. **Pool(s):** heated indoor. **Activities:** sauna, hot tub, exercise room. **Guest Services:** valet and coin laundry.

NORTHERN CAMBRIA pop. 3,835

CITY HOTEL BAR & GRILL 814/951-0303
Hotel. Rates not provided. **Address:** 1014 Maple Ave 15714 **Location:** SR 219 S, just e on Cottonwood St, just s. **Facility:** 18 units, some kitchens. 3 stories (no elevator), interior corridors. **Parking:** winter plug-ins. **Guest Services:** valet laundry, area transportation.

NORTHUMBERLAND (F-8) pop. 3,804, elev. 452'

JOSEPH PRIESTLEY HOUSE, 472 Priestley Ave., contains the laboratory and scientific apparatus of Dr. Joseph Priestley, the Unitarian theologian who discovered oxygen. The house contains period furnishings. An introductory exhibit and an orientation video at the visitor center depict the life of Dr. Priestley, who emigrated from England in 1794.

Time: Allow 1 hour minimum. **Hours:** Visitor center open Sat.-Sun. 1-4, Mar. 8-Nov. 29. Guided tours depart on the hour 1-3; other times by appointment. Phone ahead to confirm schedule. **Cost:** $6;

$5.50 (ages 60+); $4 (ages 3-11); free (active military with ID and family). **Phone:** (570) 473-9474.

FRONT STREET STATION 570/473-3626
American. Casual Dining. $8-$28 **AAA Inspector Notes:** *Historic.* Some tables at this 1910 railway station-turned-restaurant overlook tracks where trains still shunt back and forth. Friendly, efficient servers bring tasty pastas, seafood entrées, salads, burgers and sandwiches while you enjoy the old railroad atmosphere. **Features:** full bar, happy hour. **Reservations:** suggested, weekends. **Address:** 2 Front St 17857 **Location:** Jct US 11 and SR 147, just n.

NORTH VERSAILLES pop. 10,229
• Part of Pittsburgh area — see map p. 326

KING'S FAMILY RESTAURANT 412/823-0324
American. Family Dining. $6-$15 **AAA Inspector Notes:** Fast and friendly service is offered here. The menu is large in size with descriptive menu items and pictures. The restaurant is also known for its ice cream and dessert menu. **Address:** 1820 Lincoln Hwy 15137 **Location:** 1 mi e of center; just w of jct Mosside Blvd and Jacks Run Rd.

PRIMANTI BROTHERS RESTAURANT 412/829-4700
American. Casual Dining. $6-$18 **AAA Inspector Notes:** *Classic.* Looking for a sandwich that offers piled-high fries and coleslaw on top of each sandwich, then this is the place to be. The bar restaurant theme is every Pittsburgher's dream with memorabilia for each sports fan. **Features:** full bar. **Address:** 921 E Pittsburgh McKeesport Blvd 15137 **Location:** Just s from US 30 (Lincoln Hwy).

NORTH WALES pop. 3,229
• Part of Philadelphia area — see map p. 230

JOSEPH AMBLER INN 215/362-7500
Historic Bed & Breakfast. Rates not provided. **Address:** 1005 Horsham Rd 19454 **Location:** On SR 463; between Upper State and Stump rds. **Facility:** Situated on 12 acres, the B&B features a variety of renovated historic buildings with exposed stone and brick features. Special amenities include a complimentary pass to facilities at a nearby country club. 52 units. 2-3 stories (no elevator), exterior corridors. **Activities:** exercise room. **Guest Services:** valet laundry.

NOTTINGHAM (I-10) elev. 551'
• Part of Philadelphia area — see map p. 230

Nottingham County Park *(see Recreation Areas Chart)* offers opportunities for bicycling, camping, cross-country skiing, fishing, hiking and horseback riding, and it is also home to Nottingham Serpentine Barrens. The 630-acre site is rare because its desert-like landscape looks nothing like the typical surroundings of Southeastern Pennsylvania. The plants you'll find here have become highly adaptive to their environment because the soil is low in nutrients and high in metals; prairie grasses and pitch pines are common. The park, 150 Park Rd., is open daily 8 a.m.-dusk.

HERR'S SNACK FACTORY TOUR, US 1 and SR 272 at 271 Old Baltimore Pike, offers tours of the snack food production from preparation to packaging. Each tour begins with a short presentation in Chipper's Theatre. Visitors sample freshly made potato chips right off the assembly line. **Time:** Allow 1 hour minimum. **Hours:** Mon.-Thurs. 9-11 and 1-3, Fri. 9-11. Hours may be extended in summer and during the Christmas season; phone ahead. Closed major holidays. **Cost:** Free. Reservations are required. **Phone:** (800) 284-7488. [🍽]

OAKDALE pop. 1,459
• **Hotels & Restaurants map & index p. 348**
• **Part of Pittsburgh area — see map p. 326**

QUALITY INN PITTSBURGH AIRPORT (412)787-2600 [98]
[▼▼] **Hotel** $95-$199 **Address:** 7011 Old Steubenville Pike 15071 **Location:** I-376 exit 60A; jct US 22 and 30. **Facility:** 66 units. 2 stories (no elevator), interior/exterior corridors. **Amenities:** safes. **Activities:** exercise room. **Guest Services:** valet and coin laundry.
[🍽][CALL][&M][BIZ][🛜][🅿][📷][📺]/[SOME UNITS][S⊾]

WHERE TO EAT

KING'S FAMILY RESTAURANT 724/695-3922
[▼▼] American. Family Dining. $6-$13 **AAA Inspector Notes:** Fast and friendly service is offered here. The menu is large in size with descriptive menu items and pictures. The restaurant is also known for its ice cream and dessert menu. **Address:** 500 Marketplace Dr 15071 **Location:** US 22 exit US 30, just n, just w on W Steuben St, then just s. [B] [L] [D]

OAKMONT pop. 6,303
• **Hotels & Restaurants map & index p. 348**
• **Part of Pittsburgh area — see map p. 326**

DOONE'S INN AT OAKMONT 412/828-0410 [59]
[▼▼▼] Bed & Breakfast. Rates not provided. **Address:** 300 Rt 909 15147 **Location:** From Hulton Bridge, 1.7 mi e on Hulton Rd (SR 909). Across from Oakmont East Golf Course. **Facility:** In a serene location, this service-oriented B&B is located across the street from a world-class golf course. Its very spacious guest rooms are all decorated in a golf theme. 8 units. 2 stories (no elevator), interior corridors. **Activities:** exercise room, massage. **Guest Services:** valet laundry.
[🍽][🛜][📷][☎]

WHERE TO EAT

CHELSEA GRILLE 412/828-0570 [43]
[▼▼] American. Casual Dining. $7-$30 **AAA Inspector Notes:** This is an old-fashioned neighborhood restaurant where the service and atmosphere are casual and the food is tasty and filling. Lasagna, spaghetti and chicken Parmesan are specialties. The menu also lists a handful of American choices. **Features:** full bar. **Reservations:** suggested. **Address:** 515 Allegheny Ave 15139 **Location:** Center. **Parking:** on-site and street. [L] [D]

SOMMA PIZZA & SPORTS BAR 412/826-1500 [42]
[▼] American. Casual Dining. $5-$18 **AAA Inspector Notes:** Across from the famous Oakmont East Golf Course, home of the U.S. Open, the eatery pays tribute to Pittsburgh sports teams in a dining room that bleeds Steelers gold and black and displays memorabilia everywhere. Drinks from the full bar complement items such as pizza and subs. Outdoor seating is available. **Features:** full bar. **Address:** 380 Rt 909 15147 **Location:** I-76 (Pennsylvania Tpke) exit 48 (SR 28), left over Hulton Bridge, then 2.1 mi e. [L] [D]

Use travel time to share

driving tips and rules of the

road with your teens

OAKS
• **Part of Philadelphia area — see map p. 230**

HAMPTON INN & SUITES-VALLEY FORGE/OAKS
(610)676-0900

[▼▼▼]
Hotel
$99-$159

AAA Benefit: Members save 5% or more!

Address: 100 Cresson Blvd 19456 **Location:** US 422 exit Oaks. Located in a commercial area. **Facility:** 107 units, some efficiencies. 5 stories, interior corridors. **Terms:** 1-7 night minimum stay, cancellation fee imposed. **Pool(s):** outdoor. **Activities:** exercise room. **Guest Services:** valet and coin laundry, area transportation. **Featured Amenity: full hot breakfast.**
[SAVE] [🍽] [CALL][&M] [🔑] [BIZ] [HS] [🛜] [✕] [📺]
/[SOME UNITS] [🅿] [📷]

HILTON GARDEN INN VALLEY FORGE/OAKS
(610)650-0880

[▼▼▼]
Hotel
$109-$229

Hilton Garden Inn **AAA Benefit:** Members save 5% or more!

Address: 500 Cresson Blvd 19456 **Location:** US 422 exit Oaks. **Facility:** 135 units. 5 stories, interior corridors. **Terms:** 1-7 night minimum stay, cancellation fee imposed. **Pool(s):** heated indoor. **Activities:** hot tub, exercise room. **Guest Services:** valet and coin laundry, area transportation.
[SAVE] [☎] CALL[&M] [🔑] [BIZ] [HS]
[🛜] [🅿] [📷] [📺]

OHIOPYLE (I-3) pop. 59, elev. 1,221'

Ohiopyle is part of the Laurel Highlands *(see place listing p. 183)*. Once a hunting area of the Delaware, Shawnee and Iroquois, the area was named Ohiopehhle by the Native Americans for the white frothy water of the Youghiogheny River. Ohiopyle State Park *(see Recreation Areas Chart)* provides overlook platforms to the falls. It also is a trailhead for the Great Allegheny Passage and the Laurel Highlands Hiking Trail.

Ohiopyle is best known as a popular starting point for white-water rafting. Trips can be arranged through several outfitters in town.

Laurel Highlands Information Center: 7 Sheridan St., Ohiopyle, PA 15470. **Phone:** (724) 329-1127 (May-Oct.).

The information center is in Ohiopyle State Park; it is not staffed during the off-season but brochures are available.

INSIDER INFO:
Great Allegheny Passage
The Great Allegheny Passage is one of the longest multipurpose recreational trails in the eastern United States, spanning 141 continuous miles between Homestead, just east of Pittsburgh, and Cumberland, Md. The last 9 miles from Homestead to

Pittsburgh are not yet complete; phone for updates. Bicyclists, cross-country skiers, walkers and, in some places, equestrians travel through the Laurel Highlands along the scenic Youghiogheny and Casselman rivers. The 3,200-foot Big Savage Tunnel near the Mason-Dixon Line is usually closed Dec. 1-April 10 (phone ahead to verify dates); there is no alternate route.

The passage connects with the C&O Canal Towpath, providing a 325-mile motor-free route to Washington, D.C. Restrooms and facilities are available at several towns along the trail, which include (running west to east) Cedar Creek Park, Whitsett; Connellsville; Ohiopyle; Confluence; Rockwood; Meyersdale; Frostburg, Md.; and Cumberland, Md. The trail passes through Ohiopyle State Park (see Recreation Areas Chart), which offers white-water rafting and cottages for camping. Fallingwater, one of Frank Lloyd Wright's architectural landmarks, also is nearby.

For more information contact the Allegheny Trail Alliance at P.O. Box 501, Latrobe, PA 15650; phone (888) 282-2453.

RECREATIONAL ACTIVITIES
White-water Rafting
- **Laurel Highlands River Tours** is on SR 381. Other activities are offered. **Hours:** Trips depart daily, Apr.-Oct. **Phone:** (724) 329-8531 or (800) 472-3846.
- **White Water Adventurers Inc.** is at 6 Negley St. Other activities are offered. **Hours:** Trips are offered Apr.-Oct. **Phone:** (800) 992-7238 for reservations.
- **Wilderness Voyageurs** is at 103 Garrett St. **Hours:** Trips depart daily, Apr. 1 to mid-Oct. **Phone:** (724) 329-5517 or (800) 272-4141.

OIL CITY (E-2) pop. 10,557, elev. 1,028'

The discovery of oil in 1860 precipitated the almost overnight settlement of Oil City. The narrow ravine of Oil Creek became the busiest valley on the continent and in a short time was covered with derricks from Oil City to Titusville. From 1860 to 1870, 17 million barrels of oil were shipped from this region to Pittsburgh. McClintock Well No. 1, drilled in 1861, is still producing. Phone (814) 817-2797 for information.

The Oil Creek and Titusville Railroad offers 27-mile round-trips in restored 1930s passenger cars between Titusville and Rynd Farm in Oil City. Along the way there are stops at Drake Well Park and Petroleum Centre Station in Oil Creek State Park. (see Titusville p. 403).

Hasson Park Arboretum on E. Bissell Avenue bursts into color in the spring when more than 500 rhododendron bloom. Summer and winter recreational activities are offered at Oil Creek State Park (see Recreation Areas Chart) off SR 8 between Oil City and Titusville; phone (814) 676-1733.

Oil Region Alliance of Business, Industry and Tourism: 217 Elm St., Oil City, PA 16301-1412. **Phone:** (814) 677-3152 or (800) 483-6264.

VENANGO MUSEUM OF ART, SCIENCE AND INDUSTRY, 270 Seneca St., has exhibits dedicated to ten thematic areas regarding the discovery of oil. The Black Gold or Black Magic exhibit showcases the role oil still plays in our lives. "Fuel-less," a 16-minute video explaining the importance of recycling, shows how very different life would be if there were no longer any products made from petroleum. The museum features a restored 1928 Wurlitzer organ, which is demonstrated for visitors. A 1937 Cord Phaeton automobile also is on display.

Time: Allow 30 minutes minimum. **Hours:** Tues.-Fri. 10-4, Sat.-Sun. 11-4, early Apr.-Dec. 31. **Cost:** $7; $5 (students with ID and senior citizens); $3 (ages 5-11). **Phone:** (814) 676-2007.

OLD FORGE pop. 8,313

ARCARO & GENELL 570/457-5555
▼▼ ▼▼ Italian. Casual Dining. $6-$20 **AAA Inspector Notes:** This old-style tavern offers authentic Italian favorites such as generous portions of delicious marinara, pastas, steaks and chops, all served by friendly staff. **Features:** full bar. **Address:** 443 S Main St 18518 **Location:** Center. [L] [D]

ORRTANNA (I-7) pop. 173, elev. 670'

WINERIES
- **Adams County Winery** is at 251 Peach Tree Rd. **Hours:** Self-guiding tours and tastings daily 10-6. Guided tours are offered by appointment. Closed Jan. 1, Thanksgiving and Christmas. **Phone:** (717) 334-4631. [GT]

HICKORY BRIDGE FARM BED & BREAKFAST 717/642-5261
▼▼▼ Historic Country Inn. Rates not provided. **Address:** 96 Hickory Bridge Rd 17353 **Location:** Southwest end of town, follow signs. Located in a quiet rural area. **Facility:** A functioning farm is the setting for this picturesque B&B, which offers a variety of unit types, including cottages and rooms with a hot tub. A farm museum and country store are on the property. 7 units, some three bedrooms and cottages. 1-2 stories (no elevator), interior/exterior corridors. **Dining:** Hickory Bridge Farm Restaurant, see separate listing.

WHERE TO EAT

HICKORY BRIDGE FARM RESTAURANT 717/642-5261
▼▼ ▼▼ American. Casual Dining. $26 **AAA Inspector Notes:** Historic. Soak up the ambience of the 150-year-old barn while passing around dishes with salad, home-cooked entrées, sides and desserts, all of which are served family-style. Liken the hearty food to what the first German settlers who came to Pennsylvania would have favored. If you're exploring south central Pennsylvania (or just passing through), don't miss this memorable spot. **Reservations:** suggested. **Address:** 96 Hickory Bridge Rd 17353 **Location:** Southwest end of town, follow signs; in Hickory Bridge Farm Bed & Breakfast. [D]

Save on brand-name luggage and travel accessories at AAA/CAA Travel Stores

ORWIGSBURG pop. 3,099

OAK HILL INN 570/366-3881
▼▼▼ American. Casual Dining. $8-$27 **AAA Inspector Notes:** The hillside inn, established in 1993, offers innovative American cuisine served in a country-style dining room or on the seasonal dining deck. The deck is a great place because if you spot a deer then you get a beer. The menu includes a variety of dishes such as lamb, veal, New York strip steak, Atlantic haddock, ahi tuna and scallops. The featured selections are the Black Forest filet mignon and Maryland jumbo lump crab cakes. I suggest the delightful raspberry Brie-stuffed chicken. **Features:** full bar. **Reservations:** suggested. **Address:** 655 Rt 61 S 17961 **Location:** SR 61, 1 mi s of jct SR 443. ⒹD

OSTERBURG

SLICK'S IVY STONE RESTAURANT 814/276-3131
▼▼ American. Casual Dining. $5-$20 **AAA Inspector Notes:** Antiques and servers in Colonial attire lend to the homey charm of the warm, cozy restaurant. The menu centers on family-style meals of such dishes as fried chicken, roast turkey and waffles. Also delicious are the homemade soup, bread and desserts. **Address:** 8785 William Penn Rd 16667 **Location:** Jct I-99/US 220 exit 7 (Osterburg/St. Clairsville), 2 mi n on unmarked Old US 220.
Ⓛ Ⓓ

PALMERTON (F-11) pop. 5,414, elev. 400'
• Part of Pocono Mountains Area — see map p. 371

RECREATIONAL ACTIVITIES
Skiing and Snowboarding
• **Blue Mountain Ski Area** is at 1660 Blue Mountain Dr. Snow tubing also is available. **Hours:** Sat.-Sun. and holidays 8 a.m.-10 p.m., Mon.-Fri. 8:30 a.m.-10 p.m., early Dec.-late Mar. (weather permitting). Tubing Mon.-Thurs. 4-10, Fri. 10-10, Sat.-Sun. 8 a.m.-10 p.m. Closed Christmas. **Phone:** (610) 826-7700, or (877) 754-2583 for conditions.

PALMYRA (LEBANON COUNTY) (H-9)
pop. 7,320, elev. 450'

Founded by John Palm in the late 1700s, Palmyra bases its economy on food manufacturing and farming. Of interest 3 miles north of Main and Railroad streets is the 1803 Bindnagles Evangelical Lutheran Church, a two-story brick structure with round arch windows and doors. The grave of John Palm is in the churchyard.

AMERICAS BEST VALUE INN (717)838-4761
▼▼ Motel $55-$275 **Address:** 2951 Horseshoe Pike 17078 **Location:** Jct SR 743, 3 mi e on US 322. Located in a rural area. **Facility:** 32 units. 1-2 stories (no elevator), exterior corridors. **Terms:** cancellation fee imposed. **Pool(s):** outdoor. **Activities:** tennis.

KNIGHTS INN (717)838-1324
▼▼ Motel $60-$139 **Address:** 1071 E Main St 17078 **Location:** On US 422. **Facility:** 35 units. 1-2 stories (no elevator), exterior corridors. **Terms:** 3 day cancellation notice-fee imposed. **Pool(s):** outdoor.

WHERE TO EAT

HOMETOWN FAMILY RESTAURANT 717/838-0877
▼▼ American. Casual Dining. $8-$18 **AAA Inspector Notes:** You'll rub elbows with plenty of locals who frequent this restaurant for hearty Pennsylvania Dutch food, including the top-selling henny penny chicken, potpie and chow chow. Sinfully good shoofly pie and other homemade desserts churn out of the bakery. **Address:** 1 N Londonderry Square 17078 **Location:** On US 422; in Cinema Center of Palmyra. Ⓑ Ⓛ Ⓓ CALLⒼⓂ

PAOLI (B-9) pop. 5,575, elev. 541'
• Part of Philadelphia area — see map p. 230

A short distance from Valley Forge National Historical Park near the junction of US 76 and 276 is the rustic Wharton Esherick Studio. Esherick, known as the "dean of American craftsmen" worked here until his death in 1970. Displayed are more than 200 of his pieces, including paintings, woodcuts, ceramics, sculpture, furniture and utensils. Guided studio tours are available. Reservations are required; phone (610) 644-5822 for more information.

Just west of Paoli in Malvern at the junction of Monument and Wayne avenues is Paoli Battlefield Historic Site, the scene of the Battle of Paoli during the American Revolution. The grounds contain plaques describing the massacre. The oldest monument on the grounds dates to 1817. The site is open daily dawn to dusk; phone (484) 320-7173.

WAYNESBOROUGH, 1 mi. s. of US 30 via SR 252 at 2049 Waynesborough Rd., is the birthplace and former home of Revolutionary War hero Maj. Gen. "Mad" Anthony Wayne. The restored two-and-a-half-story Georgian house was built of native stone quarried on the property. It is furnished in period and includes objects that belonged to Wayne and his family. A DVD presentation tells the history of the family and the house.

Time: Allow 30 minutes minimum. **Hours:** Tours Thurs.-Sun. 1-3, late Mar. to mid-Dec. Last tour begins 30 minutes before closing. Closed holidays and some Sat. **Cost:** $10; $7 (senior citizens and students with ID); free (ages 0-5); $20 (family). **Phone:** (610) 647-1779. Paoli, 200

LE SAIGON 610/889-4870
▼▼ Vietnamese. Casual Dining. $6-$21 **AAA Inspector Notes:** Although it's located in the storefront of a large shopping center, Le Saigon sustains a cozy and romantic atmosphere. Vietnamese cuisine such as crispy boneless tangerine duck and jumbo coconut shrimp is prepared with a French flair. You are welcome to bring your own bottle of wine. **Address:** 82 E Lancaster Ave 19301 **Location:** Jct US 30 and SR 252; in Paoli Shopping Center. Paoli, 200. Ⓛ Ⓓ

PARADISE (LANCASTER COUNTY)
(H-10) pop. 1,129, elev. 457'
• Attractions map p. 221
• Hotels & Restaurants map & index p. 225

SAVE **NATIONAL CHRISTMAS CENTER** is 2 mi. e. on US 30 at 3427 E. Lincoln Hwy. Christmas history, traditions and memories are celebrated with

(See map & index p. 225.)

an array of antiques, decorations, toys, trains and life-size scenes displayed in 15 main galleries and numerous smaller exhibits. Visitors can walk through re-created toy and Christmas departments from an F.W. Woolworth Co. 5 & 10 Cent Store where counters and displays are filled with vintage items. In the animated storybook village of Tudor-Towne, more than 125 animal characters in Old World costumes celebrate Christmas.

Time: Allow 1 hour, 30 minutes minimum. **Hours:** Daily 10-6, May 1-Jan. 4 (also Fri.-Sat. 6-8 p.m., day after Thanksgiving-Christmas Eve); Sat.-Sun. 10-6, Mar.-Apr. Closed Jan. 1, Easter, Thanksgiving and Christmas. **Cost:** $12; $5 (ages 3-12). **Phone:** (717) 442-7950.

BEST WESTERN PLUS REVERE INN & SUITES
(717)687-7683 **55**

Hotel
$89-$149

AAA Benefit: Members save up to 20%!

Address: 3063 Lincoln Hwy E (Rt 30) 17562 **Location:** On US 30 (Lincoln Hwy), 0.3 mi w. Located in a commercial area. **Facility:** 95 units, some two bedrooms. 2-3 stories, interior/exterior corridors. **Dining:** Revere Tavern, see separate listing. **Pool(s):** heated outdoor, heated indoor. **Activities:** hot tub, game room, exercise room. **Guest Services:** coin laundry.

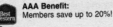

WHERE TO EAT

REVERE TAVERN 717/687-8601 **29**

American Casual Dining $7-$33

AAA Inspector Notes: *Historic.* This restaurant is found within a stone building built in 1740 as a stagecoach inn. Prior to his presidency, James Buchanan owned the building. His sister-in-law's brother, Stephen Foster, wrote some of his songs here. The menu features steaks, veal, pork, seafood and chicken. Try the veal Capri, tender medallions of veal, jumbo gulf shrimp and diced tomatoes sautéed in a tarragon cream sauce. **Features:** full bar. **Address:** 3063 Lincoln Hwy E (Rt 30) 17562 **Location:** On US 30 (Lincoln Hwy), 0.3 mi w; in BEST WESTERN PLUS Revere Inn & Suites.
L D

TWO COUSINS PIZZA 717/687-8606 **30**

Italian. Quick Serve. $5-$12 **AAA Inspector Notes:** On your way into Lancaster, stop by this casual spot for some gourmet pizzas, hot subs, calzones, salads or traditional Italian entrées. The dining area provides pleasant décor and ample seating. **Address:** 3099 Lincoln Hwy E 17562 **Location:** On US 30 (Lincoln Hwy), 0.3 mi w.
L D

PENNSBURG (G-11) pop. 3,843, elev. 380'
• **Part of Philadelphia area — see map p. 230**

SCHWENKFELDER LIBRARY AND HERITAGE CENTER is w. on 2nd St. from jct. Main St. (SR 29), then n. to 105 Seminary St. This center interprets

local Perkiomen Valley history and the history of the Schwenkfelders, a religious group that emigrated to the area in the 1700s to escape persecution in their native Germany. The center's collections include fraktur, handwritten and hand-colored documents; textiles; and objects relating to daily rural life from the 18th- to early 20th centuries.

Time: Allow 1 hour minimum. **Hours:** Tues.-Fri. 9-4 (also Thurs. 4-8), Sat. 10-3, Sun. 1-4. Closed federal holidays, Christmas Eve, day after Christmas and Dec. 31. Phone ahead to confirm schedule. **Cost:** Donations. **Phone:** (215) 679-3103.

PENNS CREEK (F-8) pop. 715, elev. 568'

Named for the stream that flows nearby, Penns Creek is surrounded by rich, rolling farmland. Just east at US 11 and US 15 is the site where the Penns Creek Massacre occurred Oct. 16, 1755, when Native Americans killed or captured 26 settlers.

PENNSYLVANIA DUTCH COUNTRY

The simple lifestyle of the Pennsylvania Dutch defines this bucolic area in southeastern Pennsylvania. Well-kept white farmhouses with expansive porches and black roofs dot the gently rolling hills. Tall silos stand like sentinels next to barns and neat vegetable gardens border houses, sharing space with clotheslines filled with dark trousers and prim dresses drying in the breeze.

Meandering two-lane roads wind past fields where bearded men in broad-brimmed hats guide plows pulled by teams of hard-working horses or mules. Horse-drawn carriages hospitably share roads with cars and trucks, the noisy clatter of the buggy's wheels against the pavement practically drowning out the rhythmic clip-clop of the horse's hooves.

The Amish settled this rich farmland in the early 18th century, coming here mainly from Germany in response to William Penn's promise of religious tolerance. Actually, the Amish were one of three similar spiritual groups who left Germany in search of freedom of worship in this new land. All three faiths-the Amish, the Mennonites and the Brethren-share the same beliefs concerning baptism, the importance of family and community, and the authority of the Bible.

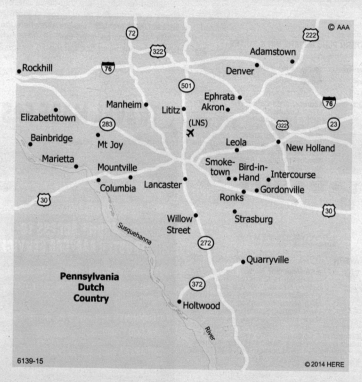

This map shows cities in the Pennsylvania Dutch Country where you will find attractions, hotels and restaurants. Cities are listed alphabetically in this book on the following pages.

Where the groups differ is in how much they allow the "outside world" to touch their everyday lives. The devout Amish are the most conservative of the groups. While most Mennonites and Brethren wear clothing much like their "English" (i.e., non-Amish) counterparts, Amish men are easily recognizable by their distinctive plain dark suits, solid-color shirts, suspenders and wide-brimmed hats. Amish women favor modest attire, generally consisting of long-sleeved dresses with full skirts (no prints), a cape and an apron, their hair hidden by demure prayer coverings.

Many Mennonites and Brethren allow contemporary conveniences such as electricity, phones and cars, but the Amish restrict such technology to reinforce their separation from the rest of the world. You won't see any power lines running to Amish homes, but the "Plain People" (as they are sometimes called) do manage to enjoy modern household appliances by using propane instead of electricity.

The Amish view of education also differs from that of the "English." The Amish build and operate their own one-room schools, which are placed every mile or two apart so that children can walk to them; teachers are generally young, single Amish women. Students (about 30 per school) attend classes only through the eighth grade; any further education, it is believed, would threaten their value system, loosen tight family ties and cause the children to become more secular.

And speaking of children, the Amish tend to have large families-seven or eight kids are average. Families are paramount to the group, and it's common for several generations to live in the same household. Although English is spoken away from home, Pennsylvania Dutch (a dialect of German) is the language of choice when conversing with family members.

Approximately 25 families comprise each Amish church district. Services, conducted every other Sunday, are held in church members' homes. Hymns are sung (in German), but there is no musical accompaniment. Visiting is the order of the day on the Sundays when there is no church service, and the children take advantage of this time by playing softball, volleyball or, in winter, hockey.

You certainly can't come to this part of the country without sampling the justly famous Pennsylvania Dutch cuisine. Numerous restaurants feature traditional Amish cooking served family style. Diners, seated at long tables, share heaping platters of all-you-can-eat down-home cooking, beginning with local delicacies such as chow chow, a mix of pickled vegetables, and homemade bread and apple butter. Dishes overflowing with fried chicken, sausages, mashed potatoes, bread stuffing, noodles with browned butter and fresh, seasonal veggies follow, not to mention shoofly pie for dessert. Other regional specialties to try include pretzels (the first pretzel bakery was established in Lititz in 1861),

whoopie pies (the cream-filled confections were first made in Lancaster County) and schnitz, dried apples typically made into pies.

Pennsylvania's Lancaster County is home to the nation's largest concentration of Amish. Many of the sect still hold to their farming heritage, but the majority now are spread out among the community and work in such diverse industries as manufacturing, construction, retail and crafts.

One of the crafts most associated with Pennsylvania Dutch Country is quilting, an art form perfected by the Amish. Beautiful quilts and other handmade items such as "quillows" (a small quilt that folds up to become a pillow) can be found in shops throughout the region. Other quality handcrafted items made locally include furniture and pottery.

If you like to rummage about in search of treasures from the past, be sure to visit some of the antique malls that Lancaster County is known for. Adamstown has more than its share of these emporiums. Other fun ways to shop are at the area's outlet malls and, if you're in the area in spring, at "mud sales." Named after the condition of the ground as it thaws out from the cold winter, these sales are typically held to benefit local volunteer fire departments. You'll find a mixture of Amish and English checking out everything from buggies to quilts to baked goods.

A ride through the rolling farmland of Pennsylvania Dutch Country, whether in a car or as part of a horse-drawn buggy tour, often reveals some of Lancaster County's hidden treasures-more than two dozen historic covered bridges. The Pennsylvania Dutch Convention and Visitors Bureau in Lancaster has several self-guiding driving tours available.

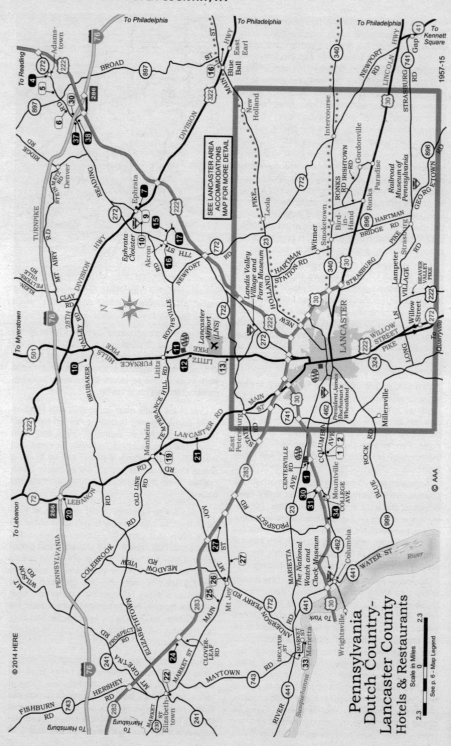

Pennsylvania
Dutch Country-
Lancaster County
Hotels & Restaurants

Scale in Miles

See p. 6 - Map Legend

© 2014 HERE

© AAA

1957-15

Pennsylvania Dutch Country-Lancaster County

This index helps you "spot" where approved hotels and restaurants are located on the corresponding detailed maps. Hotel daily rate range is for comparison only. Restaurant price range is a combination of lunch and/or dinner. Turn to the listing page for more detailed rate and price information and consult display ads for special promotions.

LANCASTER

Map Page	Hotel	Diamond Rated	Rate Range	Page
1 p. 222	**Heritage Hotel Lancaster**	🔹🔹	$109-$149 SAVE	178

Map Page	Restaurants	Diamond Rated	Cuisine	Price Range	Page
① p. 222	Venice Pizza & Pasta	🔹	Italian	$6-$23	181
② p. 222	Symposium Mediterranean Restaurant	🔹🔹🔹	Mediterranean	$9-$28	181

ADAMSTOWN

Map Page	Hotel	Diamond Rated	Rate Range	Page
4 p. 222	Adamstown Inns & Cottages	🔹🔹🔹	$109-$270	44

Map Page	Restaurants	Diamond Rated	Cuisine	Price Range	Page
⑤ p. 222	**Stoudt's Black Angus Restaurant**	🔹🔹	American	$9-$39	44
⑥ p. 222	Zia Maria's Italian Restaurant	🔹🔹	Italian	$7-$26	44

EPHRATA

Map Page	Hotel	Diamond Rated	Rate Range	Page
7 p. 222	**Hampton Inn & Suites Ephrata-Mountain Springs**	🔹🔹🔹	$129-$165 SAVE	104

Map Page	Restaurants	Diamond Rated	Cuisine	Price Range	Page
⑨ p. 222	Lily's On Main	🔹🔹🔹	American	$9-$33	104
⑩ p. 222	Aromas del Sur	🔹🔹	Colombian	$9-$22	104

LITITZ

Map Page	Hotels	Diamond Rated	Rate Range	Page
10 p. 222	Swiss Woods Bed & Breakfast	🔹🔹🔹	Rates not provided	190
11 p. 222	Alden House Bed & Breakfast	🔹🔹🔹	Rates not provided	189
12 p. 222	**Holiday Inn Express & Suites**	🔹🔹🔹	$121-$308 SAVE	189

Map Page	Restaurant	Diamond Rated	Cuisine	Price Range	Page
⑬ p. 222	Mojo Asian Cuisine & Sushi Bar	🔹🔹	Asian	$7-$20	190

AKRON

Map Page	Hotels	Diamond Rated	Rate Range	Page
15 p. 222	Bella Vista Bed & Breakfast	🔹🔹🔹	Rates not provided	46
16 p. 222	Rodeway Inn	🔹	$60-$100	46
17 p. 222	Boxwood Inn	🔹🔹🔹	Rates not provided	46

MANHEIM

Map Page	Hotels	Diamond Rated	Rate Range	Page
20 p. 222	Hampton Inn-Manheim	🔹🔹🔹	$99-$229	193
21 p. 222	Lancaster Inn & Suites	🔹🔹	$101-$199	193

Map Page	Restaurant	Diamond Rated	Cuisine	Price Range	Page
⑲ p. 222	The Cat's Meow	🔹🔹	American	$8-$24	193

ELIZABETHTOWN

Map Page	Hotel	Diamond Rated	Rate Range	Page
24 p. 222	Holiday Inn Express Elizabethtown (Hershey Area) (See ad p. 154.)	◆◆	$131-$175 SAVE	103

Map Page	Restaurant	Diamond Rated	Cuisine	Price Range	Page
22 p. 222	Flowers in the Kitchen	◆◆	American	$5-$15	103

MOUNT JOY

Map Page	Hotel	Diamond Rated	Rate Range	Page
27 p. 222	Hillside Farm B&B	◆◆	Rates not provided	207

Map Page	Restaurants	Diamond Rated	Cuisine	Price Range	Page
25 p. 222	The Watering Trough	◆◆	American	$6-$20	207
26 p. 222	The Catacombs	◆◆	American	$22-$39	207
27 p. 222	Country Table Restaurant	◆◆	Regional American	$4-$13	207

MOUNTVILLE

Map Page	Hotels	Diamond Rated	Rate Range	Page
30 p. 222	Sleep Inn & Suites Lancaster County (See ad p. 178.)	◆◆	$90-$170 SAVE	208
31 p. 222	MainStay Suites (See ad p. 178.)	◆◆	$90-$160 SAVE	208

COLUMBIA

Map Page	Hotel	Diamond Rated	Rate Range	Page
34 p. 222	Comfort Inn	◆◆	$90-$170	87

DENVER

Map Page	Hotels	Diamond Rated	Rate Range	Page
37 p. 222	Comfort Inn Lancaster County North	◆◆◆	$95-$135	94
38 p. 222	Red Roof Inn Denver	◆◆	Rates not provided	94

Map Page	Restaurant	Diamond Rated	Cuisine	Price Range	Page
30 p. 222	The Black Horse Restaurant & Tavern	◆◆	American	$14-$34	95

EAST EARL

Map Page	Restaurant	Diamond Rated	Cuisine	Price Range	Page
16 p. 222	Shady Maple Smorgasbord	◆◆	American	$10-$24	99

MARIETTA

Map Page	Restaurant	Diamond Rated	Cuisine	Price Range	Page
33 p. 222	Railroad House Restaurant Bed & Breakfast	◆◆	American	$8-$25	193

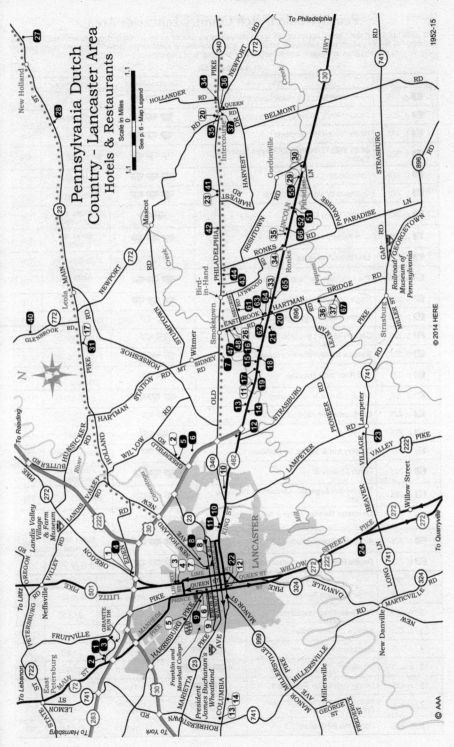

Pennsylvania Dutch
Country - Lancaster Area
Hotels & Restaurants

Scale in Miles
See p. 6 - Map Legend

1952-15

© 2014 HERE

© AAA

Pennsylvania Dutch Country-Lancaster Area

This index helps you "spot" where approved hotels and restaurants are located on the corresponding detailed maps. Hotel daily rate range is for comparison only. Restaurant price range is a combination of lunch and/or dinner. Turn to the listing page for more detailed rate and price information and consult display ads for special promotions.

LANCASTER

Map Page	Hotels	Diamond Rated	Rate Range	Page
1 p. 225	Homewood Suites by Hilton Lancaster	◆◆◆	$175-$329	178
2 p. 225	Fairfield Inn & Suites by Marriott Lancaster	◆◆◆	$104-$229	177
3 p. 225	Hilton Garden Inn Lancaster	◆◆◆	$135-$259	178
4 p. 225	**BEST WESTERN PREMIER Eden Resort & Suites**	◆◆◆	$105-$180 SAVE	175
5 p. 225	Hampton Inn-Lancaster	◆◆◆	$164-$214	177
6 p. 225	Courtyard by Marriott-Lancaster	◆◆◆	$115-$206	176
7 p. 225	Country Living Inn	◆◆	Rates not provided	176
8 p. 225	Cork Factory Hotel	◆◆◆	Rates not provided	176
9 p. 225	**Lancaster Arts Hotel**	◆◆◆	$189-$359 SAVE	178
10 p. 225	The Lancaster Bed and Breakfast	◆◆◆	Rates not provided	178
11 p. 225	King's Cottage Bed and Breakfast	◆◆◆	$175-$289	178
12 p. 225	**Hawthorn Suites by Wyndham**	◆◆	$89-$170 SAVE	178
13 p. 225	**Country Inn of Lancaster** (See ad p. 177.)	◆◆	$129-$279 SAVE	176
14 p. 225	**Wingate by Wyndham Lancaster**	◆◆◆	$109-$239 SAVE	179
15 p. 225	**Red Roof Inn Lancaster**	◆◆	Rates not provided SAVE	179
16 p. 225	Comfort Suites Amish Country	◆◆◆	$129-$299	176
17 p. 225	**Continental Inn** (See ad p. 176.)	◆◆	$75-$145 SAVE	176
18 p. 225	Classic Inn	◆◆	$39-$89	176
19 p. 225	**Country Inn & Suites By Carlson**	◆◆	$89-$299 SAVE	176
20 p. 225	Fulton Steamboat Inn	◆◆◆	Rates not provided	177
21 p. 225	**Holiday Inn Express - Lancaster - Rockvale Outlets**	◆◆◆	$99-$259 SAVE	178
22 p. 225	**Lancaster Marriott at Penn Square** (See ad p. 179.)	◆◆◆	$125-$235 SAVE	179
23 p. 225	Australian Walkabout Inn B&B	◆◆◆	Rates not provided	175
24 p. 225	**DoubleTree Resort by Hilton Hotel Lancaster**	◆◆◆	$99-$279 SAVE	177

Map Page	Restaurants	Diamond Rated	Cuisine	Price Range	Page
① p. 225	Arthur's Terrace Restaurant	◆◆	American	$10-$30	180
② p. 225	**The Greenfield Restaurant**	◆◆◆	American	$7-$32	180
③ p. 225	Jimmee's Deluxe Grille	◆	Burgers	$3-$12	180
④ p. 225	**Stockyard Inn**	◆◆◆	Steak Seafood	$8-$45	180
⑤ p. 225	Gibraltar	◆◆◆	Seafood	$15-$33	180
⑥ p. 225	Lemon Grass Thai Restaurant	◆◆	Thai	$9-$18	180
⑦ p. 225	Walnut Street Grille at Lancaster Brewing Company	◆◆	Regional American	$9-$28	181
⑧ p. 225	**Horse Inn Restaurant**	◆◆	American	$18-$40	180

Map Page	Restaurants (cont'd)	Diamond Rated	Cuisine	Price Range	Page
⑨ p. 225	The Belvedere Inn	◆◆◆	Continental	$7-$32	180
⑩ p. 225	**The Brasserie Restaurant & Bar**	◆◆	American	$10-$28	180
⑪ p. 225	**Tony Wang's Chinese Restaurant**	◆◆	Chinese	$6-$24	181
⑫ p. 225	The Pressroom	◆◆	American	$10-$30	180
⑬ p. 225	El Serrano Restaurante	◆◆	Mexican	$7-$20	180
⑭ p. 225	Tobias S Frogg	◆◆	American	$7-$27	181

NEW HOLLAND

Map Page	Hotels	Diamond Rated	Rate Range	Page
㉗ p. 225	Country Squire Motor Inn	◆	$60-$90	211
㉘ p. 225	Comfort Inn Amish Country	◆◆◆	$110-$180	211

LEOLA

Map Page	Hotel	Diamond Rated	Rate Range	Page
㉛ p. 225	**The Inn at Leola Village**	◆◆◆◆	$159-$349 [SAVE]	185

Map Page	Restaurant	Diamond Rated	Cuisine	Price Range	Page
⑰ p. 225	**TÈ**	◆◆◆◆	Italian	$89-$159	185

INTERCOURSE

Map Page	Hotels	Diamond Rated	Rate Range	Page
㉞ p. 225	Travelers Rest Motel	◆◆	$76-$126	162
㉟ p. 225	The Inn at Kitchen Kettle Village	◆◆◆	$99-$270	162
㊱ p. 225	**BEST WESTERN PLUS Intercourse Village Inn & Restaurant** *(See ad p. 162.)*	◆◆◆	$95-$145 [SAVE]	162
㊲ p. 225	The Inn & Spa at Intercourse Village	◆◆◆	Rates not provided	162

Map Page	Restaurant	Diamond Rated	Cuisine	Price Range	Page
⑳ p. 225	The Kling House Restaurant	◆◆	Regional American	$6-$13	162

BIRD-IN-HAND

Map Page	Hotels	Diamond Rated	Rate Range	Page
㊵ p. 225	Leaman's Lancaster Country Lodging	◆◆◆	$69-$89	67
㊶ p. 225	**Amish View Inn & Suites** *(See ad p. 175.)*	◆◆◆	Rates not provided [SAVE]	67
㊷ p. 225	Amish Country Motel	◆◆	$84-$120	67
㊸ p. 225	Bird-In-Hand Village Inn & Suites	◆◆◆	Rates not provided	67
㊹ p. 225	Bird-In-Hand Family Inn	◆◆	$69-$189	67

Map Page	Restaurant	Diamond Rated	Cuisine	Price Range	Page
㉓ p. 225	**Plain & Fancy Farm Restaurant**	◆◆	Regional American	$7-$19	67

SMOKETOWN

Map Page	Hotels	Diamond Rated	Rate Range	Page
㊼ p. 225	**Smoketown Inn (of Lancaster County)**	◆◆	$59-$89 [SAVE]	391
㊽ p. 225	Mill Stream Country Inn	◆◆	Rates not provided	391

Map Page	Restaurant	Diamond Rated	Cuisine	Price Range	Page
㉖ p. 225	**Good 'N Plenty Restaurant**	◆◆	Regional American	$8-$21	391

GORDONVILLE

Map Page	Hotels	Diamond Rated	Rate Range	Page
51 p. 225	**Motel 6-Lancaster #4174**	◆◆	Rates not provided [SAVE]	129
52 p. 225	After Eight B&B	◆◆◆	$118-$188	129

PARADISE (LANCASTER COUNTY)

Map Page	Hotel	Diamond Rated	Rate Range	Page
55 p. 225	**BEST WESTERN PLUS Revere Inn & Suites**	◆◆◆	$89-$149 [SAVE]	219

Map Page	Restaurants	Diamond Rated	Cuisine	Price Range	Page
29 p. 225	**Revere Tavern**	◆◆	American	$7-$33	219
30 p. 225	Two Cousins Pizza	◆	Italian	$5-$12	219

RONKS

Map Page	Hotels	Diamond Rated	Rate Range	Page
61 p. 225	Quiet Haven Motel	◆	$52-$96	382
62 p. 225	**Days Inn Lancaster PA Dutch Country**	◆◆	$59-$169 [SAVE]	381
63 p. 225	**La Quinta Inn & Suites**	◆◆◆	$82-$189 [SAVE]	381
64 p. 225	**Eastbrook Inn**	◆◆	$65-$109 [SAVE]	381
65 p. 225	Candlelight Inn Bed & Breakfast	◆◆◆	Rates not provided	381
66 p. 225	**Sleep Inn & Suites**	◆◆	$110-$185 [SAVE]	382
67 p. 225	**Hershey Farm Inn**	◆◆	$50-$170 [SAVE]	381

Map Page	Restaurants	Diamond Rated	Cuisine	Price Range	Page
33 p. 225	Jennie's Diner	◆	American	$6-$17	382
34 p. 225	**Miller's Smorgasbord & Bakery**	◆◆	Regional American	$8-$24	382
35 p. 225	Dienner's Country Restaurant	◆◆	American	$3-$12	382
36 p. 225	Katie's Kitchen	◆◆	American	$7-$13	382
37 p. 225	**Hershey Farm Restaurant**	◆◆	Regional American	$6-$26	382

PERKASIE (G-11) pop. 8,511, elev. 414'
• Part of Philadelphia area — see map p. 230

[SAVE] THE PEARL S. BUCK HOUSE, 1 mi. s.w. of SR 313 at 520 Dublin Rd., was the home of author and humanitarian Pearl S. Buck. The 1825 stone farmhouse displays her Nobel and Pulitzer prizes and many personal mementos collected in China, including decorative screens, rare Asian artwork and porcelain. The desk and typewriter on which she wrote "The Good Earth" are displayed, and her personal collection of Pennsylvania country furniture also is featured. During the Festival of Trees display in November and December, the house is decorated for the holidays and includes more than a dozen trees. A welcome center features exhibits.

Hours: Guided tours are offered Mon.-Sat. at 11, 1 and 2, Sun. at 1 and 2. Hours may vary during special events; phone ahead. Closed major holidays. **Cost:** $15; $12 (ages 62+); $7 (students with ID); free (ages 0-5). **Phone:** (215) 249-0100.

PERRYOPOLIS pop. 1,784

LENORA'S   724/736-2509
◆◆ American. Fine Dining. $20-$50 **AAA Inspector Notes:** Located about an hour from Pittsburgh, this quaint restaurant is in a beautiful Victorian home. The menu includes items such as French onion soup, chicken and lobster in cognac cream, and bananas Foster. The dress code is business casual. **Features:** full bar. **Reservations:** required. **Address:** 301 Liberty St 15473 **Location:** I-70 (Pennsylvania Tpke) exit 46A/B, 5 mi s on SR 51 to light, 0.5 mi e to traffic circle, then just s. [D]

PETERSBURG (G-6) pop. 480, elev. 680'

SHAVER'S CREEK ENVIRONMENTAL CENTER is off SR 26, then 1.7 mi. w. on SR 1029 to Stone Valley Recreation Area east entrance. Walking trails wind through woodlands, hillsides and marshes. A raptor center houses injured birds of prey. Bird feeding stations, a beehive, bat boxes and interactive exhibits are offered. Seasonal walks and events also are featured throughout the year. **Hours:** Daily 10-5, mid-Feb. to mid-Dec. Closed Thanksgiving. **Cost:** Free. **Phone:** (814) 863-2000 or (814) 667-3424.

Philadelphia

Then & Now

So, why is the Liberty Bell cracked?

There are many tales concerning the circumstances of the bell's first crack, but consensus has it that the fracture dangerously expanded and ultimately rendered the bell unusable after it rang in 1846 to commemorate George Washington's birthday. It was probably a fitting occasion for its final performance.

Philadelphia teems with icons like this hallowed bell that inspire an undeniable sense of history and awe. These vestiges of the past send shivers down the spines of visitors and residents alike as it hits home that this is indeed America's birthplace. Have lunch at City Tavern like Washington did, or tour Christ Church, where he worshipped along with Benjamin Franklin and members of Congress. Or wander inside the Betsy Ross House to learn about the woman who reputedly sewed the first stars and stripes on Old Glory.

To experience Philadelphia to the fullest, a good place to start is where it all began:

Independence National Historical Park. You can easily spend the entire day here, exploring landmarks that represent the nation's founding. There's Congress Hall, the site that hosted the inauguration of John Adams and the second inauguration of Washington, and of course, that famous bell.

Outside of this historic square mile, there are other nooks and crannies of the Old City ripe for exploration.

Stroll down narrow Elfreth's Alley, said to be America's oldest continuously inhabited residential street. Take the self-guiding tour at the U.S. Mint to see the birth of currency, or learn about Quaker life at the brick Historic Arch Street Meeting House, built as a gathering spot in 1804.

Now that you have a sense of the old, you can appreciate the new. Skyscrapers like Comcast Center, One Liberty Place and Bell Atlantic-Verizon Tower soar over Center City, and statues of historical figures meld with those of modern day heroes. Gaze at the commanding statue of city founder William Penn presiding over his "City of Brotherly Love" from a perch atop City Hall's clock tower.

Penn's brotherly love and the strong sense of family and tradition instilled by the Quakers are still values held near and dear to Philadelphians. Philly's neighborhoods have histories of their own. To the south, there's Bella Vista,

(Continued on p. 232.)

Independence Hall

Destination Philadelphia

This map shows cities in the Philadelphia vicinity where you will find attractions, hotels and restaurants. Cities are listed alphabetically in this book on the following pages.

© AAA

Fast Facts

ABOUT THE CITY

POP: 1,526,006 ▪ **ELEV:** 39 ft.

MONEY

SALES TAX: Pennsylvania's statewide sales tax is 6 percent. An additional 2 percent is collected by Philadelphia County, as is an 8.2 percent hotel tax.

WHOM TO CALL

EMERGENCY: 911

POLICE (non-emergency): 911 (Calls are transferred to appropriate department.)

HOSPITALS: Aria Health (Torresdale Campus), (215) 612-4000 ▪ Hospital of the University of Pennsylvania, (215) 662-4000 ▪ Methodist Hospital, (215) 952-9000 ▪ Pennsylvania Hospital, (215) 829-3000 ▪ Roxborough Memorial Hospital, (215) 483-9900 ▪ Temple University Hospital, (215) 836-7536.

WHERE TO LOOK AND LISTEN

NEWSPAPERS: Philadelphia has two daily papers: the Philadelphia *Inquirer (online at www.philly.com)* and the *Daily News (online at www.philly.com/dailynews).*

RADIO: Philadelphia radio station KYW (1060 AM) is an all-news/weather station ▪ WHYY (90.9 FM) is a member of National Public Radio.

VISITOR INFORMATION

Independence Visitor Center: One N. Independence Mall W., Philadelphia, PA 19106. **Phone:** (215) 965-7676.

Tours of area attractions, including Independence National Historical Park, may be booked here. It's open daily 8:30-7, Memorial Day-Labor Day; 8:30-6, Apr. 1-day before Memorial Day and day after Labor Day-Sept. 30; 8:30-5, rest of year.

Visit Philadelphia also provides information at the center about the city's attractions, neighborhoods, hotels, restaurants and events and neighboring Bucks, Chester, Delaware and Montgomery Counties.

TRANSPORTATION

AIR TRAVEL: Philadelphia International Airport (PHL) is 6.5 miles south of the business district via I-76 (Schuylkill Expressway) and SR 291 (Penrose Avenue). SEPTA's airport rail line runs daily on the half-hour 5 a.m.-midnight between the airport and Market Street East Station, Suburban Station and 30th Street Station. Advance fare $6.50; onboard fare $8. Discounted fares are available for children, senior citizens and disabled guests.

RENTAL CARS: Hertz, at the Philadelphia International Airport, (215) 492-7205 or (800) 654-3131, offers discounts to AAA members.

RAIL SERVICE: Amtrak trains pull into both the main 30th Street Station terminal at 30th and Market streets and the North Philadelphia Station at N. Broad Street and W. Glenwood Avenue. If your destination is midcity, disembark at 30th Street Station. Phone (800) 872-7245, or TTY (800) 872-7245.

BUSES: The major bus terminal is Greyhound Lines Inc., (215) 931-4075, at 10th and Filbert streets. Peter Pan Trailways, (800) 343-9999, also serves the city. New Jersey Transit buses, (973) 275-5555, depart for southern New Jersey and shore points.

TAXIS: Yellow Cab Co., (215) 333-3333, charges a $2.70 base rate plus $2.50 per mile. A fuel surcharge also may be added. One-way fares between the airport and central Philadelphia locations are a flat $28.50 fee.

PUBLIC TRANSPORTATION: A system of buses, trolleys, subways and regional rails serves Philadelphia. Operated by the Southeastern Pennsylvania Transportation Authority (SEPTA), all vehicles charge $2.25, plus $1 for a transfer; exact change is required. Senior citizens ride free. RiverLink Ferry offers ferry service from Penn's Landing to the Adventure Aquarium in Camden, N.J. *See Public Transportation.*

(Continued from p. 229.)

characterized by the colorful, aromatic Italian Market. In Chinatown, diners can indulge culinary cravings at all hours. Handsome 18th-century Colonials flanked by quaint courtyards grace the fashionably preserved Society Hill area, while Rittenhouse Square exudes luxury and wealth.

Although many head to Philadelphia to explore attractions focusing on history and patriotism, a healthy cultural and sports scene also are part of the mix. The Philadelphia Museum of Art houses great works of art, and immortalizes fictional boxer Rocky Balboa with his larger-than-life likeness at the base of its steps. The Philadelphia Orchestra offers a popular summer concert series, and the Philadelphia Ballet's annual "Nutcracker" performances enchant holiday audiences. The Franklin Institute and Philadelphia Zoo stimulate the imaginations of all ages.

And Philadelphians turn out in droves to show their love for the Phillies (baseball), Eagles (football), Flyers (hockey) and 76ers (basketball).

Must Do: AAA Editor's Picks

- Book your tickets in advance to see one of the world's most celebrated collections of post-impressionist and early modern art at ⬥ **The Barnes Foundation.** You'll be mesmerized by a diverse ensemble of works that spans multiple cultures and time periods.

- Stroll down **South Street** between Front and 9th, the "hippest street in town." After checking out the funky boutiques and tattoo parlors, pull up a chair at one of the outdoor cafés or bars. In the City of Brotherly Love, this is where you go for people watching, and you'll see it all—preppies, punk rockers, old hippies, pierced skateboarders and lawyers in business suits.

- For romance, hail a **horse-drawn cab** at 5th and Chestnut streets. As the horse trots down Society Hill's 18th-century cobblestone streets, enjoy the sights: Colonial and Federal architecture, row houses and intimate courtyards. Other routes include a trip through Independence National Historical Park's tree-lined lanes and a peek at the bustling Old City area, featuring such sites as the **Betsy Ross House** and **Elfreth's Alley.**

- Think about it—or go to the **Rodin Museum** and leave the pondering to Auguste Rodin's best-known sculpture, "The Thinker." While you're here, tour the museum and discover other sculptures to consider, contemplate and regard.

- Cheer for one of Philly's **sports teams.** If there's a nip in the air, you can head to **Lincoln Financial Field** and take your chances on tickets for an Eagles game. And if football's not your thing, applaud at **Wells Fargo Center** as a 76er dunks the ball or a Flyer hooks the puck. In spring and summer, go to a Phillies game at **Citizen's Bank Park** and catch a foul ball on the third base line. The latest addition for area sports fans is the region's first Major League Soccer club, the Philadelphia Union, that plays at **PPL Park.** Warning: Philadelphia sports fans are *very* loyal to their teams.

- Jog to the top of the steps at the ⬥ **Philadelphia Museum of Art** and—like Rocky Balboa in the movie—pump your arms in the air! Once you catch your breath, enter the museum to enjoy one of the world's premier art collections. With some 225,000 objects onsite, it's a challenge to see everything, so consider joining one of the daily tours.

- Enjoy music the old-fashioned way at Macy's twice daily **Wanamaker Organ** recitals Monday through Saturday. One of the largest musical instruments in the world, this grand organ fills the store atrium with classical and contemporary tunes from seven floors above the cosmetic counters, downtown at 13th and Market streets. During the holidays, there's a light show to go along with the musical numbers.

- There's no better way to experience the founding of our nation than to visit ⬥ **Independence National Historical Park.** It's packed full of history, Colonial architecture and iconic sights like the Liberty Bell.

- Chow down on a **Philly cheesesteak**, the famous hoagie made with thinly sliced rib eye, melted cheese and grilled onions. Most South Philly sandwich shops are open 24-7-365 (and most claim *they* cooked up the original idea). Two of the best are **Pat's King of Steaks** and **Geno's Steaks.** Want more culinary options? Stop by Reading Terminal Market for a wonderful selection of tried-and-true Philly favorites as well as ethnic offerings and delectable baked goods.

- Gawk at the strange, spine-tingling exhibits at the **Mütter Museum of The College of Physicians of Philadelphia.** Exhibits at this College of Physicians of Philadelphia museum include the Soap Lady, celebrity body parts and casts of patients who suffered from gigantism, eye diseases and other deformities.

The Wanamaker Organ at Macy's

Philadelphia 1- day Itinerary

AAA editors suggest these activities for a great short vacation experience. Those staying in the area for a longer visit can access a 3-day itinerary at AAA.com/TravelGuide.

Morning

- Begin your first day in the City of Brotherly Love at **Independence Visitor Center** in ✈ **Independence National Historical Park** located at the corner of 6th and Market streets in Center City. If you arrive early, you'll be ahead of the crowds. Get free tickets and sign up for a National Park Service walking tour; for a historical overview, catch one of the two films that run throughout the day.

- Head to ✈ **Independence Hall.** Many landmark events in American history occurred within these halls: On July 4, 1776, the Declaration of Independence was adopted in the Assembly Room of this Georgian structure; the Articles of Confederation and the U.S. Constitution sprang to life in the same room.

- Your next stop should be ✈ **Liberty Bell Center.** In the late 1800s, the 2,000-pound bell made a pilgrimage from its perch in the Pennsylvania State House to various states in the union, holding court at various events to heal the nation after the Civil War. In 1915, Philadelphia became the revered symbol of liberty's final resting place.

- Continue touring Independence National Historical Park and see the following: ✈ **National Constitution Center,** where hands-on activities and a self-guiding audio tour provide a unique historical perspective; ✈ **Congress Hall,** where you can participate in a ranger-led program; and the ✈ **Second Bank of the United States Portrait Gallery,** now featuring a cell phone audio tour and the "People of Independence" display, an assortment of paintings highlighting early leaders who influenced the nation.

Afternoon

- Walk north on 5th Street. Stop at Christ Church's modest burial ground, where Benjamin Franklin and other signers of the Declaration of Independence are interred.

- For lunch, dine in an Old City restaurant—take your pick of places, from upscale establishments to casual diners and sandwich joints. Try **Fork** (306 Market); **Sonny's Famous Steaks** (2nd and Market); or **Amada** (2nd and Chestnut), offering a delectable selection of Spanish tapas. For a Philly cheesesteak, why not visit the most popular place in the neighborhood? Hoof it to **Jim's Steaks** at 4th and South streets. You'll also discover lunch trucks serving the famous sandwich on just about every corner.

- After lunch, walk (or bus it) back to ✈ **Christ Church.** This time go inside to see where the American Episcopal Church got its start and where some of the Founding Fathers

Elfreth's Alley, America's oldest residential street

worshipped. Then head to 239 Arch St. to tour the **Betsy Ross House;** you'll experience 18th-century life and encounter Betsy and other period-costumed Colonials plying their trades. Afterward, stroll down **Elfreth's Alley,** America's oldest continually inhabited street.

- In the late afternoon, walk southeast to Head House Square (Lombard and S. 3rd streets). Take a romantic horse-drawn carriage ride. Meander through Society Hill's 18th-century cobblestone streets and take in the architecture, row houses and intimate courtyards.

Evening

- For dinner, try one of Old City's restaurants or head back toward Independence National Historical Park. If you're in the mood for some hip Asian cuisine, try the fusion **Buddakan** at 3rd and Chestnut. If meatloaf or macaroni and cheese are more your speed, head to **Jones,** a colorfully funky eatery known for its innovative comfort food.

- After dinner, head to Penn's Landing on the waterfront, scene of Friday night concerts all summer and Thursday film screenings under the stars in July and August. In the winter, you can practice your turns on the outdoor ice-skating rink. Afterward, nab a cocktail on "The Hippest Street in Town." The popular song's lyrics don't lie: as you amble down South Street between Front and 9th, you'll find plenty of bistros and bars where you can swill that nightcap.

Top Picks for Kids

Under 13

- Thrill wee ones by taking a trip to **Sesame Place** in nearby **Langhorne**. Rides and waterslides entertain tots, as do huggable Sesame Street friends like Big Bird, Abby Cadabby, Elmo and Cookie Monster. For an educational experience that's also tons of fun, attend the Neighborhood Street Party parade.

- Ages 5-12 will have a blast at ⧖ **The Franklin Institute.** The Train Factory mesmerizes young conductors as they learn about operating a 350-ton locomotive, while aspiring astronauts can command a mission and examine space expedition equipment. Kids can also walk through a two-story-high giant heart with sound and lighting effects or peer through a telescope in the fourth-floor observatory. A special exhibit of 70 massive Lego® sculptures and art masterpieces including a 20-foot-long T. Rex and Vincent Van Gogh's Starry Night will be featured through Sept. 6.

- The **Please Touch Museum** in Fairmont Park amuses young children with interactive exhibits that stimulate learning through touching and playing. Adventures include exploring a neighborhood in City Capers, experimenting with balance at Flight Fantasy or winding through Wonderland's maze.

Teens

- Teens love intrigue, and they'll find it at **Ghost Tours of Philadelphia.** And what's more, they'll be exposed to a little history in addition to pondering such dilemmas as whether Edgar

Allan Poe's spirit lingers in the Old City. Guides conduct a candlelit stroll past Philly's spooky nooks and crannies, telling tales of haunted houses and ghostly encounters. And, of course, there's the requisite cemetery stop.

- Philadelphia is known for its iconic treats, and **Reading Terminal Market** is the perfect venue in which to sample the city's delectable tidbits. In this enclosed historic farmers market built underneath the Reading Railroad's train shed in 1892, you'll find everything from cheesesteaks to soft pretzels to whoopie pies.

- Guided tours aboard the cruiser *Olympia* and the World War II submarine *Becuna* at the **Independence Seaport Museum** spark the imaginations of students as they investigate these historic vessels. The "What Floats Your Boat?" display inside the museum features hands-on activities that illustrate the concepts of speed and gravity.

- For a buggy endeavor, head to **The Insectarium,** a museum devoted entirely to creepy-crawlies. You can handle some of the live creatures if you choose, but if you'd rather admire them from afar there are plenty of exhibits, including mounted specimens.

All Ages

- ⧖ **Independence National Historical Park** awes history buffs with the revered Liberty Bell and sites like ⧖ **Independence Hall** that played a pivotal role in the nation's development.

- The 42-foot-long T. rex welcoming visitors into **The Academy of Natural Sciences of Drexel University** certainly makes a lasting impression, as do the other residents in Dinosaur Hall. Or, maybe it's the Egyptian mummy in the Africa Hall that will fascinate your family. A live animal center housing critters that have been injured or born in captivity provides an inside look into their care and feeding, and a tropical butterfly garden presents a palette of vibrant color.

- At the **Philadelphia Zoo,** rides like the carousel, train and swan boats excite tots, while older kids are eager to saddle up on a pony or camel. Habitats are plentiful, and include Monkey Junction, Bear Country, African Plains and First Niagara Big Cat Falls, where you'll come face to face with the endangered inhabitants.

- Several Philly events bring joy to the entire crew. The **Mummers Parade** on New Year's Day is a merry extravaganza with colorful costumes, elaborate floats and entertainment. **Odunde,** which is celebrating its 40th anniversary in 2015, is one of the country's largest African-American festivals. **Wawa Welcome America** in early July has a number of fun activities leading up to its Independence Day festivities. For the culturally inclined, the Philadelphia Orchestra Family Concert Series on occasional Saturdays from October through April makes for a nice outing.

Philadelphia Zoo

Arriving

By Car

I-95 is the major route from the northeast and south, connecting the city with Philadelphia International Airport. From New Jersey on the east, I-676 joins US 30 and traverses the north side of downtown as the Vine Street Expressway (I-676). From the northwest, I-76 leaves the Pennsylvania Turnpike at Valley Forge and enters Philadelphia at the Schuylkill Expressway. Follow either I-95 or I-76 to I-676 to the city center; enter the business district at 15th Street.

US 1 (Roosevelt Boulevard) traverses northeast Philadelphia, but both the north and south entrances into town are heavily commercialized and rather slow. From the east both the New Jersey Turnpike and I-295, which run north-south in New Jersey, provide ready access to either US 30, which enters the city center via the Benjamin Franklin Bridge and I-676, or to New Jersey SR 42 (North-South Freeway or Atlantic City Expressway), which approaches the Walt Whitman Bridge and south Philadelphia. When crossing either bridge from New Jersey, there is a $5 toll.

Getting Around

Street System

It would be wise to leave your automobile behind when going downtown because the old streets, though arrow straight, are very narrow. Unless you *must* have your car, allow a bus or cab driver to negotiate the congested, often two-lane, streets.

Most north-south streets, beginning with Front Street west of the Delaware River, are numbered;

Ride a SEPTA trolley around the city

east-west streets are named. Broad Street, the major north-south artery, is the equivalent of 14th Street. All downtown north-south streets are alternate one-way with the exception of Broad, which has two lanes in each direction. Market Street is one-way eastbound between 20th and 15th streets. Westbound motorists should use JFK Boulevard at this point. Chestnut Street is closed to all traffic except buses between 8th and 18th streets from 6 a.m. to 7 p.m.

Since Market Street is the principal east-west artery, north and south numbering begins at this street. Westward numbering begins at Front Street.

Right turns on red are permitted after a full stop, unless otherwise posted. Rush hours in general are 7-9:30 a.m. and 4-6:30 p.m. The speed limit on most streets is 25 mph, or as posted.

Parking

Though chances of getting on-street parking on the clogged streets are virtually zero, some metered parking is permitted on side streets and less traveled avenues: Parking meter rates in Center City are $2.50 per hour. Rates in the numerous lots and garages range from about $3-$8 for 30 minutes; $7-$24 for 2 hours; $16-$20 for 12 hours and $22-$43 for 24 hours.

Public Transportation

A SEPTA day pass provides up to eight rides on all SEPTA buses, trolleys and subways; the pass is $8. For information about schedules, routes and locations where day pass and tokens may be purchased, phone (215) 580-7800, or TTY (215) 580-7853.

The Speedline, operated by Port Authority Transit Corporation (PATCO), connects with SEPTA's subway with three stops on Locust St. between 9th and 16th sts. and one at 8th and Market sts. One-way fare between any Philadelphia station $1.40; free (ages 0-5). Fare from Philadelphia into New Jersey $1.60-$3. Phone (215) 922-4600 or (856) 772-6900.

PHLASH, the downtown visitor shuttle, services 20 key locations, including attractions, hotels, shopping, cultural sites and historic districts. Passengers may board at any stop. Buses run daily 10-6, Memorial Day-Labor Day; Fri.-Sun. 10-6, in May and September-October. Fare (single-trip) $2; free (ages 0-6 and 65+). All-day pass $5; phone (215) 389-8687 to confirm information.

RiverLink Ferry offers ferry service from Penn's Landing to the Adventure Aquarium in Camden, N.J. *(see attraction listing p. 315).* The ferry departs Penn's Landing Mon.-Fri. on the hour 10-6 (weather permitting) and departs Camden Mon.-Fri. on the half-hour 9:30-5:30 (weather permitting), Memorial Day through Labor Day; Saturday and Sunday, May 1-day before Memorial Day and day after Labor Day-Sept. 30. Hours may vary during special events; phone ahead. Tickets may be purchased at either terminal or at the Independence Visitor

Center. Fare $7; $6 (ages 3-12 and 65+). Phone (215) 925-5465.

Shopping

Sure, big name department stores like Bloomingdale's and Nordstrom are available at the area malls.

But those on the hunt for fabulous finds know that the heart and soul of Philly shopping lies in its unique neighborhoods and its nearby suburbs.

Oh, and did we mention that there's no sales tax on clothing or shoes in Pennsylvania?

Even if you're not in the market, Center City's quaint **Antique Row,** bordered by Locust and Lombard streets from 9th to Broad streets, delights with its engaging window displays. Here, anything goes, from kitschy bargains to refined elegance: You can pick up an unusual $4 china plate or a $40,000 Chippendale highboy, barter for a mustache cup or negotiate for a priceless silver service. Historic samplers and needlework are the specialty at M. Finkel & Daughter (936 Pine), while stained glass and porcelain entice at Kohn & Kohn (1112 Pine).

The section of **Chestnut Street** from 8th to 18th streets is a busy corridor where Philadelphians find a mixed bag of stores convenient for generic, everyday shopping. Athletes and sports fans sprint to Mitchell & Ness (1318 Chestnut) to ogle the amazing collection of reproduction pro jerseys and jackets. At 17th and Chestnut, you'll find the Shops at Liberty Place, an urban mall with the typical retail potpourri enhanced by a stunning glass atrium. The **Market & Shops at Comcast Center,** a block north at John F. Kennedy Boulevard and N. 17 Street, has a handful of shops and eateries catering to downtown office workers. A cluster of stores on 13th Street between Walnut and Chestnut is worthy of investigation.

Jewelers' Row, on Sansom between 7th and 8th streets (between Chestnut and Walnut streets), is Center City's diamond district, second in size only to New York's and reputedly the nation's oldest. You'll surely find a trinket that tickles your fancy in this treasure trove of shops, many operated by the same Philadelphia families for generations. Don't buy on first impulse—checking out the competition generally pays off, since many of the jewelers do offer discounts.

Those inclined toward high-end tidbits land in the **Rittenhouse Square** area, in a class all its own. As you browse along Walnut Street from Broad to 20th, you'll come across fashion-forward designs at Coach, Diesel, Kenneth Cole, Urban Outfitters (originally launched in Pennsylvania) and a multitude of other chic retailers. For some great deals, peruse the sale racks in the lower level of Anthropologie, another sophisticated chain born in the Keystone State. Pricey designs with an edgy flair are all the rage at Joan Shepp, while Boyd's on nearby Chestnut Street is the arbiter of classic elegance amid upper crust digs complete with chandeliers—it even has a sushi lounge. Savor

Antique Row offers a unique shopping experience

some lunch or the luxury goods of Tiffany, Polo Ralph Lauren and other upscale merchants at Shops at the Bellevue, Broad and Walnut streets. At 16th and Walnut, the Apple Store draws the technically savvy masses into its packed quarters.

Foodies must stop by the happily bustling [SAVE] **Reading Terminal Market,** 12th and Arch streets, a cornucopia of palate-pleasing sensations. Indulge in a steaming cheese steak, freshly baked soft pretzels, succulent pastry and other culinary treats. (Hint: It's also an affordable breakfast stop.) The [SAVE] **Hard Rock Cafe Philadelphia,** is located nearby at 12th and Market streets. Urbanites looking for a mall-type experience with moderate prices dash into the glass-roofed **Gallery at Market East,** on Market Street between 8th and 11th, and **Market Place East,** in a historically handsome building right across the street. Shoppers in redecorating mode may be interested in venturing to **Marketplace Design Center** (2400 Market St.), with some 50 showrooms exhibiting the latest and greatest in decor.

For a slice of history with your purchases, duck into **Macy's Center City** in the Wanamaker Building (1300 Market St.), where you are serenaded by the music of the Wanamaker Grand Organ as you shop. Out-of-state visitors get extra discounts.

Young hipsters love to pop into the trendy emporiums clustered about **Old City** to search for modish clothes, new age home designs and vintage furniture. This neighborhood just north of Independence National Historical Park also is dotted with some of the most happening galleries in Philly's art scene. If you're around, you can sample wine and hors d'oeuvres during the "First Friday" evening of the month, when galleries host an open house that turns into a wandering street party. **The Bourse,** a renovated 1895 grain and stock exchange just across from the Liberty Bell at 21 S. 5th St., is a good place for tourists to pick up some souvenirs. Weary shoppers seek refuge in the food court, a comfortable oasis within a stylish multilevel atrium.

Those in the know who also want to feel good about themselves when they shop stop into **The Wardrobe Boutique** (1822 Spring Garden St.), near the Philadelphia Museum of Art. Proceeds from sales of the gently-used clothing and accessories goes to help local women - and these designer duds can perk up any closet.

South Street, just south of Society Hill, has an eclectic assortment of funky shops with unique baubles. If you're into vintage and have a hankering for the exotic, this is your turf—the scene heats up at night. You can't help but notice Magic Gardens, a folk art gallery and sculpture garden housed within a whimsical building adorned with mosaics. Antique hounds should note that a few dealers branch off the main drag. Head a little farther south and you'll come across the Bella Vista neighborhood, home of the **9th Street Italian Market.** Running along 9th from Wharton to Fitzwater streets, the market tantalizes your senses with the aromas of garlic and freshly baked bread along with the colorful displays of fresh vegetables, pastas, spices and cheeses. For culinary delights sure to tease your taste buds, stop by Di Bruno Bros., a foodie haven brimming with cheeses and other gourmet specialties. The market's a great lunch spot—roasted garlic pizza is

a hit at Sarcone's, while locals swear by both Pat's King of Steaks and Geno's Steaks for mouthwatering cheese steaks, a short jaunt south down 9th Street. **Fabric Row,** at S. 4th Street and Fitzwater, is a hub of textile-related concerns featuring custom draperies, tailors, designer fabrics and sewing supplies.

In Philadelphia's Northern Liberties neighborhood, a few blocks north of the Old City, the **Piazza at Schmidts** (2nd Street and Germantown Avenue) is a landscaped open-air plaza surrounded by art studios and boutiques; it's also the site of concerts, festivals and other events. **Liberties Walk,** 1040 N. American St., is a pedestrian walkway that travels past boutiques and restaurants.

On the fringes of Philly, wander the charming cobblestone streets of pretty **Chestnut Hill** and relish the assortment of some 125 shops. An easy trip from downtown, this northwest enclave with a moneyed vibe attracts those on the prowl for art and antiques, suburbanites out for a spin, and those just happy to park in a quaint café and do a little people watching. Individually owned boutiques touting specialized merchandise co-exist with established chains. About 7 miles northwest of Center City, **Main Street Manayunk** offers an assortment of galleries and shops interspersed with restaurants. You can browse for home furnishings, jewelry, boutique-style fashions, and vintage and consignment finds.

If you only visit one suburban shopping mall, make it the **King of Prussia** (US 202 at Schuylkill Expressway), a monstrous labyrinth of stores that makes fighting traffic almost worthwhile. Reputedly the East Coast's largest, the megamall features more than 350 shops and seven major anchors, including Bloomingdale's, Lord & Taylor and Neiman Marcus. You can replenish your energy in one of the numerous eateries, including upscale steakhouse Morton's of Chicago.

Nightlife

Philly is a drinking town, as evidenced by the number of handsome brewpubs and classy lounges. But the city which gave birth to television sensation "American Bandstand" also continues to party hearty with a decent selection of trendy dance clubs and good ol' rock 'n' roll.

Clubs providing entertainment may include cover charges, and usually require drink or food minimums. To avoid surprises, phone ahead and confirm prices, opening hours, scheduled acts and dress codes.

Nowadays, you never know where you'll find great late-night places to eat or drink as pop-up restaurants and food trucks and beer gardens have been sprouting up everywhere.

Case in point: **The Independence Beer Garden** (Independence Mall West/(215) 922-7100) offers 20,000 square feet of space to relax and unwind with 40 beers on tap. The new space also offers food and other cocktails for those who aren't into hops.

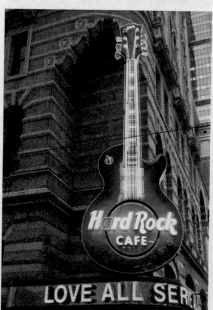
Stop for a bite at the Hard Rock Cafe Philadelphia

In fact, every neighborhood has its favorite brewpub, but there are definitely standouts. Homey touches like an antique wooden bar, brick accents and an inviting fireplace make young movers and shakers want to snuggle up with a cold one and some first-rate munchies at **The Black Sheep** (Rittenhouse Square/(215) 545-9473). **Fergie's** (Center City/(215) 928-8118), a rip-roaring Irish pub, throws quite a party on St. Pat's Day—the jovial spot attracts a multifarious gang, including those eager for some good music or fresh mussels along with their brew. Savor one of Philly's best burgers with your brewski at **Good Dog** (Center City/(215) 985-9600), where youngish patrons like to shoot pool and select tunes from an Internet jukebox amid canine-inspired decor. The packed taproom at **Monk's** (Center City/(215) 545-7005) specializes in beer from Belgium, with one of their ales actually custom brewed in that country—you might be able to escape the throngs of kids by nabbing a seat at the back bar. An edgy, 20-to-30 something set hangs out at **Standard Tap** (Northern Liberties/(215) 238-0630), home of well-crafted drafts and a cranking jukebox—the pub grub is heavenly, from the roast pork sandwich to the duck confit salad.

If your idea of fun is similar to a contact sport—more specifically, a sea of bodies gyrating to a thumping beat—then you'll find bliss partying in Philadelphia's dance clubs. Philly's most coveted DJs spin funk, punk, rock 'n' roll, trance, progressive and what not in this sleek, high-tech danceteria serving up potent drinks. The party begins behind the retro façade of **Silk City** (Northern Liberties/(215) 592-8838). Grab a nosh at the diner and then migrate to the club, where you can burn the calories on a dance floor accented by disco balls, neon lighting and a mob pumped-up by '80s and '90s hits.

Jazz aficionados head to **Chris' Jazz Café** (Center City/(215) 568-3131), a locally touted joint featuring top hometown acts and the occasional touring show in cozy digs. It's not the tasty soul food that has them singing the blues at **Warmdaddy's** (South Philly/(215) 462-2000)—it's the top-notch sound system. Tuesday jam sessions showcase local cool cats at this down-home find with a laid-back vibe. **The Raven Lounge** (Rittenhouse Square/(215) 840-3577), which draws a disparate bunch in search of tunes in an unpretentious atmosphere, has been known to put up a live jazz or blues ensemble on its music stage upstairs.

For those who like to sit and sip, Philly offers plenty of swank lounges and happening bars. In summer, the rooftop deck at **Continental Mid-town** (Center City/(215) 567-1800) is a major hangout—inside, a trendy crowd sips apple martinis and soaks up the ambience of the chicly decorated space. VIPs hobnob in a stylish, sophisticated setting at **Whisper** (Rittenhouse Square/(215) 735-6700), where the pricey bottle service lures beautiful

Plumbing-themed front door at the Standard Tap

people who like to make an entrance. Mellow-minded hipsters who would rather skip the scene, settle in a comfy chair and peruse a decent wine list choose **L'Etage** (South Street/(215) 592-0656) for a low-key evening with a French flair. For drinkable assets, brave the line at **Franklin Mortgage & Investment Co.** (Rittenhouse Square/(267) 467-3277), a snug and dimly lit subterranean speakeasy that captivates patrons with designer cocktails.

If you're not averse to spending some serious coin, turn left after entering **The Farmers' Cabinet** (Center City/(215) 923-1113) and you'll discover beer nirvana with 26 brews on tap and nearly 150 bottles of European crafts. Or, take a right for enticing cocktail creations, enriched by seasonally inspired ingredients. Either way, you'll relish your costly libation amid Victorian décor reminiscent of the Prohibition era. **Vango Lounge & Skybar** (Rittenhouse Square/(215) 568-1020) boasts an outdoor lounge on the top level, where you can sink into plush couches and appreciate a skyline panorama—get there early if you want to avoid the crowd and gaze at the twinkling lights of Center City in peace.

The Old World style wine bar at **Ristorante Panorama** (Old City/(215) 922-7800) in the Penn's View Hotel impresses oenophiles with its state-of-the-art dispensing system—if you are new to the wine game, this is a great place to order a "flight," a sampling of five different vintages to taste. Eclectic touches like a wine bottle chandelier, stamped-tin ceiling and exposed brick walls entice connoisseurs at the **Vintage Wine Bar** (Center City/(215) 922-3095), where Old City character melds with a new Philadelphia vibe. Reasonable prices along with open-air seating, yummy nibbles and a popular happy hour draw a youngish clientele to **Jet Wine Bar** (South Street/(215) 735-1116), a friendly and funky neighborhood nook just right for quiet conversation. **Tria Cafe** (Center City/(215) 972-8742) delights foodies who like to select from the tempting assortment of cheeses and appetizers to pair with their wine (or beer).

Rock 'n' roll is alive and kicking in the City of Brotherly Love. A mostly under-thirty set likes to check out the up and comers at **North Star** (Art Museum Area/(215) 787-0488), a neighborhood hangout small enough to call "intimate" with bar food that's cheap and good. For a refined experience in a café-style venue enhanced by candlelight, try **Tin Angel** (Old City/(215) 928-0978), home to soft rock, bluegrass, folk, country, rockabilly and other acoustic gigs. Twenty-something punkers and rockers infiltrate **Trocadero** (Chinatown/(215) 922-6888) in hopes of discovering hard-hitting, edgy talent—the roomy Chinatown club's ornate accents hint at its past stint as a burlesque house. The focus isn't on mainstream music at **World Cafe Live** (University City/(215) 222-1400), a modernistic live-music venue hosting a diverse global line-up, from indie bands to hip-hop to acoustical performances. Happy hours are a hot bargain. **Johnny Brenda's** (Northern Liberties/(215) 739-9684) is a gastro-pub that also happens to have a concert hall upstairs—the small Fishtown space has a welcoming, relaxed feel and showcases indie rock acts and the latest in Philly's rock scene at a value.

Philly's sports fans are fanatical, and there are lots of watering holes where they like to go get their

Enjoy Old City character at the Vintage Wine Bar

game on. **XFINITY Live!** (South Philadelphia/(267) 443-6416), a dining and entertainment complex with a sports theme, presents a range of options for your viewing pleasure—wherever you land, you can rest assured you'll receive a healthy dose of team spirit. In the same part of town, hungry fans ease their jitters by cracking crabs at **Chickie's and Pete's** (South Philadelphia/(215) 218-0500), probably the next best place to catch an Eagles game if home field tickets aren't available. Downtown at **Locust Rendezvous** (Center City/(215) 985-1163), revved-up spectators are lured by the dive-bar ambience, ample big screens, cheap beverages and decent vittles. And **McGillin's Olde Ale House** (Center City/(215) 735-5562), a tried-and-true pick that's been serving drafts since the 1860s, always throws open a welcoming door for Philly's "phanatics."

Big Events

Philadelphia's calendar is packed throughout the year with events including the huge Mummers and Thanksgiving Day parades, flower and antiques shows, and folk festivals.

The brightly-colored ⚜ **Mummers Parade** starts off the new year and attracts some 15,000 costumed Mummers String Bands, fancies and comics. Philadelphia then settles down for the **Philadelphia Home Show** in late January. The **Philadelphia International Auto Show** is held in early February at the **Pennsylvania Convention Center.**

February is **Black History Month,** observed in Philadelphia with exhibitions, lectures and music at **The African American Museum in Philadelphia** (*see attraction listing p. 242*).

The **PHS Philadelphia Flower Show,** held in early March at the convention center, is one of the world's largest indoor flower exhibitions.

The wearing of the green is toasted during the **Philadelphia St. Patrick's Day Parade.** The **Easter Promenade** offers music, entertainment, pony rides and a petting zoo on **Head House Square** on Easter Sunday.

The **Penn Relays** at **Franklin Field** in April is one of the world's oldest and largest track meets. In late April, the **Philadelphia Antiques Show** is conducted at the **Pennsylvania Convention Center,** 1101 Arch St. Also in late April **Valborgsmassoafton,** the traditional Swedish welcoming of spring, is observed at the **American Swedish Historical Museum.**

In May, the city's historic homes open their doors during the **Society Hill Open House and Garden Tour.**

The **Dad Vail Regatta,** held in early May, is one of the largest college regattas in the country. High school rowers get their turn in the spotlight shortly thereafter when the ⚜ **Stotesbury Cup Regatta** takes place on the **Schuylkill River** in mid-May. This event has been taking place annually since 1927.

Additional events in May include the **Rittenhouse Square Flower Market for Children's Charities,** 18th and Walnut streets at **Rittenhouse Square** and the **Philadelphia International Children's Festival** at the **Annenberg Center,** 3680 Walnut St.

Summer kicks off in June with the **Rittenhouse Square Fine Arts Show** (also held in September) and **Elfreth's Alley Fête Days.** The latter celebrates patriotism and Colonial history; events include tours of private homes.

The **Odunde Festival,** held the second Sunday in June, is a 12-block African street festival filled with music, dance, food, crafts and culture. The day kicks off with a procession to celebrate the Yoruba New Year.

A special treat for those in the Delaware River region in the summer of 2015 will be the arrival of the **Tall Ships Philadelphia Camden 2015.** Twelve ships will be docked at Penn's Landing and the Camden Waterfront from June 24-28 and visitors will be able to tour the giant vessels with massive sails.

Wawa Welcome America! explodes the first week in July to celebrate the country's birth in its hometown. Parades, concerts and fireworks displays are among the more than 40 scheduled events. Mid-August brings the **Philadelphia Folk Festival,** which features folk music concerts and workshops at suburban **Old Poole Farm** in Schwenksville.

The **German-American Steuben Parade** takes place in September as do the **Philadelphia Live Arts Festival and Philly Fringe** and the **Puerto Rican Day Parade.**

For 2015, the City of Brotherly Love will welcome tens of thousands of people and Pope Francis for the **World Meeting of Families** at the Pennsylvania Convention Center from Sept. 22-27.

The **Pulaski Day Parade** and **Columbus Day Parade** are in October.

The Convention Center stages the **Philadelphia Museum of Art Crafts Show** in early November, a major exhibition of crafts by the nation's top artisans. Later in November the holidays begin in grand and traditional fashion with the **Philadelphia Thanksgiving Day Parade,** complete with celebrities, enormous balloons and national TV coverage.

The Philadelphia holiday season begins at Thanksgiving and includes various events, including a tree lighting ceremony at **Macy's Center City** (also Macy's Christmas Light Show and the Dickens Village inside the store), concerts, a parade and New Year's Eve fireworks.

The city was proud to be awarded title of host city of the **Army-Navy Football Classic** for five games over eight years, including in December of 2015, when the game will again be played at Lincoln Financial Field.

Take in a show at Merriam Theater

Sports & Rec

Philadelphia, with a representative in every major sports league—**baseball, football, hockey, basketball** and **soccer**—is a paradise for spirited spectator sports fans. The NFL's **Eagles** play at Philadelphia's **Lincoln Financial Field** at S. Broad and Pattison streets; and the **Phillies** of baseball's National League suit up at **Citizens Bank Park,** 10th Street and Pattison Avenue. The **Wells Fargo Center,** also at S. Broad and Pattison streets, plays host to the NHL's **Flyers** and the NBA's **76ers.** For ticket information, phone (215) 463-1000 for the Phillies; (215) 463-5500 for the Eagles; (215) 339-7676 for the 76ers; and (215) 218-7825 for the Flyers. Philly's newest team, the **Philadelphia Union,** plays soccer at **PPL Park** in nearby Chester; (877) 218-6466.

Minor league baseball is just across the river in New Jersey at **Campbell's Field,** with the **Camden Riversharks.**

The Philadelphia **Kixx,** affiliated with the National Soccer League, play at the **Liacouras Center** on the campus of Temple University; phone (888) 888-5499.

Rowing is popular on the **Schuylkill River;** sculls are often seen skimming the water. Periodic races and spectacular annual rowing regattas can be seen from Fairmount Park.

Polo is played by the suburban **Brandywine Polo Club,** which has games on Sunday afternoons May through September; phone (610) 268-8692. **Cricket** matches are held in **Fairmount Park** on weekends in the summer.

Fairmount Park caters to nearly everyone's recreational appetite, with **archery, bicycling, canoeing,** fishing, golf, hiking, horseback riding, lawn bowling and tennis. The Robert P. Levy Tennis Pavilion, located on the campus of University of Pennsylvania, offers indoor tennis courts; phone (215) 898-4741.

From the Schuylkill River Trail (a small portion of which runs through Philadelphia) to the Delaware Canal National Heritage Trail, there are plenty of hiking, jogging and biking opportunities. Maps showing good routes for running and walking are available at downtown hotels. Runners enjoy the Philadelphia Rock 'n' Roll Half-Marathon in September and the full Philadelphia Marathon through the historic city each November. Note: The Bartram Trail section of the Schuylkill River Trail is near, or crosses, state game lands, so wearing blaze orange is recommended during hunting seasons; contact the Pennsylvania Game Commission, (717) 787-4250, for details.

If you want to play the ponies, Parx Casino and Racing (see attraction listing p. 60) in Bensalem offers Thoroughbred racing all year; phone (215) 639-9000. Delaware Park, near Wilmington, Del., offers Thoroughbred races spring through fall; phone (302) 994-2521.

Note: Policies concerning admittance of children to pari-mutuel betting facilities vary. Phone for information.

Performing Arts

The Philadelphia Orchestra, one of the country's finest symphonies, presents its winter series in The Kimmel Center for the Performing Arts (see attraction listing p. 257). The Philly Pops Christmas Spectacular is popular for families. The Kimmel Center also hosts Broadway musicals, speakers and special concerts; phone (215) 731-3333 for tickets. Opera Philadelphia and the Pennsylvania Ballet perform at the Academy of Music, one block north at Broad and Locust streets; phone (215) 893-1999 for orchestra, opera and ballet tickets. The Opera celebrates its 40th anniversary in 2015 with several special performances.

In summer, the orchestra's rich tones ring through Fairmount Park's Mann Center for the Performing Arts (see attraction listing p. 249). Tickets are sold at the box office, 52nd street and Parkside Avenue. Summer concerts are also held at Penn's Landing. Check at the visitor center for times.

Philadelphia theater is popular. The Forrest Theatre presents pre-Broadway and hit shows with name stars; national touring companies appear at the Annenberg Center and the Merriam Theater.

There also are numerous regional and community theater companies, including the Arden Theatre Company, the Bristol Riverside Theatre, the Freedom Theatre, the Hedgerow Theatre, the People's Light and Theatre Company, the Philadelphia Theatre Company, the Prince Music Theater, the Society Hill Playhouse, the Walnut Street Theatre and the Wilma Theater. College theater can be enjoyed at Temple University or Villanova University.

Painted Bride Art Center presents an array of performing arts and music performances as well as art exhibits.

A special public art project in 2015 sponsored by the city's Mural Arts Program called "Open Source: Engaging Audiences in Public Space" will bring art throughout Philadelphia. The public art project ends during Mural Arts Month in October.

INSIDER INFO:
CityPASS

Philadelphia CityPASS offers savings to those who plan to visit many Philadelphia attractions. The pass includes tickets to: Adventure Aquarium (in nearby Camden, N.J.); The Franklin Institute; Philadelphia Trolley Works and Big Bus Co., an option for either the Philadelphia Zoo or National Constitution Center; and an option for either Eastern State Penitentiary or Please Touch Museum.

A pass, valid for 9 consecutive days from first date of use, will save travelers 46 percent off the combined cost of purchasing individual tickets to all of the included attractions. Philadelphia CityPASS can be purchased online or from the participating attractions; phone (208) 787-4300 or (888) 330-5008.

ATTRACTIONS

THE ACADEMY OF NATURAL SCIENCES OF DREXEL UNIVERSITY is at 19th St. and Benjamin Franklin Pkwy. Founded in 1812, it is the oldest continually operating institution of its kind in America. Outstanding among the natural science exhibits are the children's nature center, Outside-In; and Dinosaur Hall, where fossils of prehistoric giants are displayed. The Butterflies! exhibit is a walk-through tropical garden with live butterflies from around the world and a display of live pupae. The Art of Science gallery features changing exhibits of contemporary and historic artworks that explore the beauty of science. Live animal shows, historical dioramas, films and special programs also are offered.

Time: Allow 1 hour, 30 minutes minimum. Hours: Mon.-Fri. 10-4:30, Sat.-Sun. and holidays 10-5. Closed Jan. 1, Thanksgiving and Christmas. Cost: $15.95; $13.95 (ages 3-12, ages 65+ and students and military with ID). Phone: (215) 299-1000. 19th, 69

THE AFRICAN AMERICAN MUSEUM IN PHILADELPHIA, n.w. corner of 7th and Arch sts., traces the history of African-American culture in the Americas and throughout the world. The special achievements of people of African descent are documented through documents, drawings and multimedia presentations. Temporary exhibits feature artifacts, clothing, diaries, furniture, photographs

© 2014 HERE

© AAA

Philadelphia SEPTA System Map

Market-Frankford Line
Broad Street Line & Broad-Ridge Spur
Norristown High Speed Line
Trolley Lines
PATCO Line
Regional Rail Lines

① Station ① Transfer Station

SEE PHILADELPHIA AREA
MAPS FOR METRO STATION
LOCATIONS WITH AAA
DESIGNATED NUMBERS

Amtrak to:
Harrisburg
Pittsburgh
Chicago

Schuylkill River

Amtrak to:
New York
Boston
Montreal
NJ Transit to:
New York
New Jersey Points

River Line
to Camden

291 West Trenton

259 Trenton

290 Yardley
289 Woodbourne
288 Langhorne
287 Neshaminy Falls
286 Trevose
285 Somerton
284 Forest Hills
283 Philmont
282 Meadowbrook
281 Rydal
280 Noble
279 Fern Rock Trans Center

258 Levittown
257 Bristol
256 Croydon
255 Eddington
254 Cornwells Heights
253 Torresdale
252 Holmesburg Junction
251 Tacony
250 Bridesburg

Doylestown
314 Delaware Valley College
313 New Britain
312 Chalfont
311 Link Belt
310 Colmar
309 Fortuna
308 Lansdale
307 Pennbrook
306 North Wales
305 Gwynedd Valley
304 Penllyn
303 Ambler
302 Fort Washington
301 Oreland
300 North Hills
299 Glenside

298 Warminster
297 Hatboro
296 Willow Grove
295 Crestmont
294 Roslyn
293 Ardsley
292 Bethayres

51 Frankford Term
(Bridge-Pratt)
52 Margaret-Orthodox
53 Church
54 Torresdale
55 Toga
56 Allegheny
57 Somerset
58 Huntingdon
59 York-Dauphin
60 Berks
61 Girard
225 Girard

Fox Chase
274 Ryers
273 Olney
272 Lawndale
271 Olney
270 Wyoming
134 Logan
133 Wister
132 Wyoming
131 Hunting Park
130 Erie
129 Allegheny
128 North Philadelphia
127 Susquehanna-Dauphin
126 Cecil B. Moore
223 Girard

Cheltenham
277 Fern Rock Trans Center
276 Elkins Park
275 Melrose Park

Jenkintown Wyncote

224 40th

227 Temple University
228 North Broad
249 North Philadelphia
123 Fairmount
121 Fairmount

Chestnut Hill East
260 Gravers
261 Mt Airy
262 Sedgwick
263 Stenton
264 Washington Lane
265 Carpenter
266 Upsal
267 Tulpehocken
268 Germantown
269 Wayne Junction

Chestnut Hill West
240 Highland
241 St Martins
242 Allen Lane
243 Carpenter
244 Upsal
245 Tulpehocken
246 Chelten Avenue
247 Queen Lane
248 Allegheny

Norristown Transportation Center
236 Norristown Transp Ctr
237 Main Street
238 Norristown/Elm Street

105 Norristown Transportation Center
104 Bridgeport
103 DeKalb
102 Hughes Park
101 Gulph Mills
100 Matsonford
99 County Line
208 Villanova
209 Rosemont
210 Bryn Mawr
211 Haverford
212 Ardmore
213 Wynnewood
214 Narberth
215 Merion

235 Spring Mill
234 Miquon
233 Ivy Ridge
232 Manayunk
231 Wissahickon
230 East Falls
229 Allegheny

219 Bala
218 Cynwyd
217 Wynnefield Avenue

195 Thorndale
196 Downingtown
197 Whitford
198 Exton
199 Malvern
200 Paoli
201 Daylesford
202 Berwyn
203 Devon
204 Strafford
205 Wayne
206 St Davids
207 Radnor
98 Radnor
97 Villanova
96 Stadium
95 Garrett Hill
94 Roberts
93 Bryn Mawr
92 Haverford
91 Ardmore Avenue
90 Ardmore Junction
89 Wynnewood Road

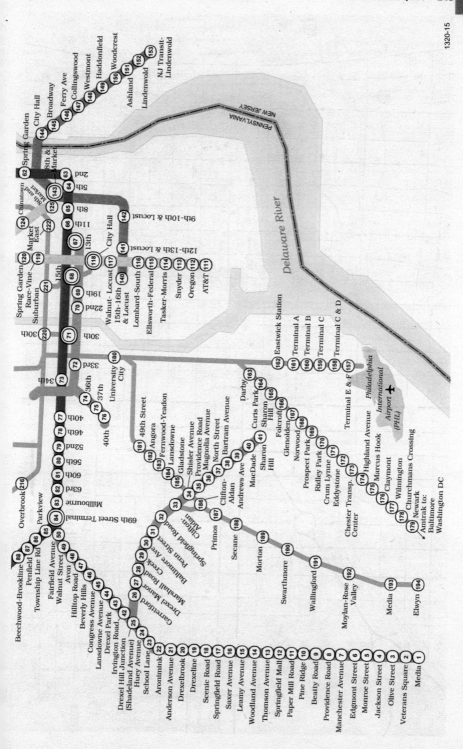

1320-15

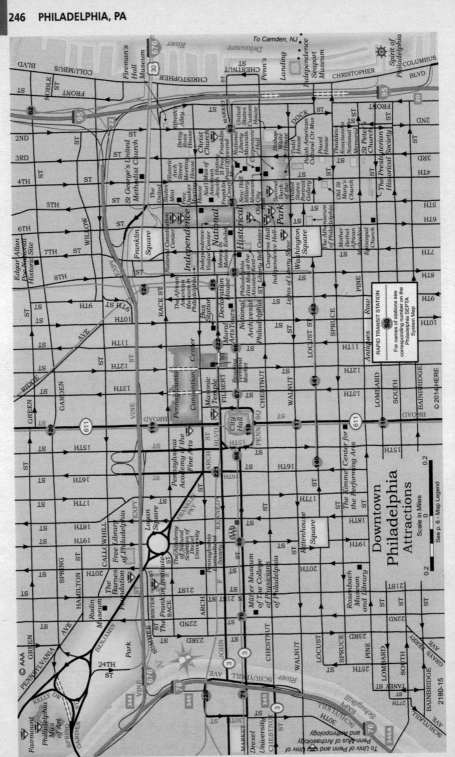

Downtown
Philadelphia
Attractions

Scale in Miles

See p. 6 · Map Legend

0.2   0   0.2

2180-15

© 2014 HERE

RAPID TRANSIT STATION

50   For names of stations see
corresponding number on the
Philadelphia SEPTA
System Map

and works of art. The exhibit Audacious Freedom: African Americans in Philadelphia 1776-1876 recounts how people of African descent contributed to the cause of civil rights in Philadelphia.

Time: Allow 2 hours minimum. **Hours:** Thurs.-Sat. 10-5 (also Martin Luther King Jr. Day), Sun. noon-5. Closed Jan. 1, Easter, Thanksgiving and Christmas. **Cost:** $14; $10 (ages 4-12, ages 60+, physically impaired visitors, and students with ID). **Phone:** (215) 574-0380. 🖨 8th and Market, 125

AMERICAN PHILOSOPHICAL SOCIETY (APS) MUSEUM—see Independence National Historical Park p. 253.

AMERICAN SWEDISH HISTORICAL MUSEUM,
1900 Pattison Ave. in Franklin Delano Roosevelt Park, features 12 permanent galleries as well as changing exhibits. A research library focuses on the history of Swedes in America from the establishment of the New Sweden Colony in 1638 to modern accomplishments in technology, architecture, and the fine and decorative arts. Original drawings of the USS *Monitor* and other works by John Ericsson also are presented.

Traditional Swedish holidays are celebrated year-round. **Hours:** Tues.-Fri. 10-4, Sat.-Sun. noon-4. Closed major holidays. **Cost:** $8; $6 (ages 61+ and students with ID); $4 (ages 5-11). **Phone:** (215) 389-1776. 🖨 AT&T, 111

HISTORIC ARCH STREET MEETING HOUSE, 320
Arch St., was built on burial ground originally granted by William Penn. The meetinghouse has been in continual use since 1804, when it was constructed to serve as a meeting space and place of worship for the Society of Friends (Quakers). Exhibits explore the history and role of Quakers in the United States. **Time:** Allow 30 minutes minimum. **Hours:** Tues.-Sat. 10-4. Closed holidays except Memorial Day, July 4 and Labor Day. **Cost:** Donations. **Phone:** (215) 413-1804. GT 🖨 5th, 64

THE ATHENAEUM OF PHILADELPHIA, 219 S. 6th
St., is named for Athena, the Greek goddess of wisdom. Built in 1847, this three-story Italianate Revival building houses American fine and decorative arts from the first half of the 19th century and a research library and reading room. Changing exhibits can be seen in the first-floor gallery. Guided tours are offered by appointment.

Time: Allow 30 minutes minimum. **Hours:** Mon.-Fri. 9-5 (also first three Sat. of the month 11-3, Sept.-June). Closed major holidays, Good Friday, day after Thanksgiving, Christmas Eve and Dec. 31. Research by appointment only. **Cost:** Free. **Phone:** (215) 925-2688. 🖨 9th-10th & Locust, 142

AWBURY ARBORETUM, 1 Awbury Rd., is a 55-
acre public garden with several trails among indigenous trees, flowers and plants. There also is a secret garden, bird sanctuary and ponds. The 19th-century Francis Cope House is on the grounds and visitors can get information about the Cope family as well as trail maps. Pets on leashes are permitted. **Time:** Allow 2 hours minimum. **Hours:** Grounds daily dawn-dusk. Cope house Mon.-Fri. 9-5. Closed major holidays. **Cost:** Donations. **Phone:** (215) 849-2855. 🐕 🎍 🖨 Washington Lane, 266

BARTRAM'S GARDEN is entered from Lindbergh
Blvd. w. of 54th St. Formerly the 18th-century farm of Colonial botanist John Bartram, the estate is now a 45-acre public park on the banks of the Schuylkill River. The grounds feature the furnished Bartram family home, the botanical garden, a wildflower meadow, wetlands and a historic cider press. **Note:** The Bartram house will be closed in 2015 due to conservation work on the building. Phone ahead for updates. **Time:** Allow 1 hour minimum. **Hours:** Grounds daily 9-5. Phone for tour times. Closed major holidays. **Cost:** Grounds free. Guided tour $15; $10 (ages 3-16 and 62+ and students with ID). **Phone:** (215) 729-5281. GT 🖨 49th St, 181

BETSY ROSS HOUSE, 239 Arch St., was the Colo-
nial home and business of upholsterer Betsy Ross. Although historians debate whether or not she actually stitched the first American flag in 1777, she is popularly credited with having done so. The restored house is furnished to simulate an 18th-century Philadelphia dwelling. Self-guiding tours and audio guides are offered. A Betsy Ross re-enactor greets visitors in her 18th century upholstery shop. Other interactive programming and changing exhibits also are available. Special events such as Betsy Ross' birthday are celebrated throughout the year.

Concessions are available daily May-Oct. and Thurs.-Sun., Mar.-Apr. **Hours:** Daily 10-5, Mar.-Nov.; Tues.-Sun., Dec.-Feb. Phone for special programs schedule. Closed Jan. 1, Thanksgiving and Christmas. **Cost:** $5; $4 (children, students, military with ID and ages 55+). House with audio guide $7; $6 (children, students, military with ID and ages 55+). **Phone:** (215) 629-4026. 🍴 🖨 2nd, 63

CHEMICAL HERITAGE FOUNDATION, 315
Chestnut St. between 3rd and 4th sts. in the renovated 1865 First National Bank building, offers a collection of exhibits to highlight the important role chemistry, chemical engineering and other related sciences has played in advancing everyday life. Historical items in the collection include scientific instruments, rare books, the personal papers of scientists and artwork. Temporary exhibits are included. Guest speakers discuss various topics the first Friday evening of each month from March through December.

Time: Allow 45 minutes minimum. **Hours:** Mon.-Fri. 10-5 (also first Fri. of the month 5-8). Closed Jan. 1, Martin Luther King Jr. Day, Memorial Day, Labor Day, Thanksgiving, day after Thanksgiving and Christmas. **Cost:** Donations. **Phone:** (215) 925-2222. 🖨 2nd, 63

CITY HALL is at Penn Sq., Broad and Market sts.; tours depart from the visitor center, room 121. This was planned to be the tallest structure in the world when construction began in 1871. However, it was surpassed in height by the Washington Monument and the Eiffel Tower before its completion in 1901. A 37-foot-high bronze statue of William Penn tops the City Hall tower. The document in Penn's left hand represents the state's charter.

The elevator for the tower observation deck tour holds four adults at one time. **Hours:** Two-hour guided history and architecture tours of City Hall and the tower are offered Mon.-Fri. at 12:30. Fifteen-minute tower tours are offered Mon.-Fri. every 15 minutes 9:30-4:15. Phone ahead to confirm availability. Closed major holidays. **Cost:** Two-hour tour $12; $8 (ages 65+, students and military with ID). Fifteen-minute tour $6; $4 (ages 65+, students and military with ID). Reservations are recommended. **Phone:** (215) 686-2840. 🚇 City Hall, 118

CLIVEDEN, 6401 Germantown Ave., was built 1763-67 for Pennsylvania Chief Justice Benjamin Chew. The house was damaged during the 1777 Battle of Germantown; scars from the battle remain in the walls. The mid-Georgian home is furnished with 18th- and 19th-century pieces, original Chippendale furnishings, Chinese porcelain, paintings and other decorative arts. A short film and interactive displays also are available. The grounds consist of 5.5 acres.

Time: Allow 1 hour, 30 minutes minimum. **Hours:** Thurs.-Sun. noon-4, Apr.-Dec. Last tour begins 30 minutes before closing. Closed Easter, Thanksgiving

and Christmas. **Cost:** $10; $8 (ages 65+ and students with ID). **Phone:** (215) 848-1777.
GT 🚇 Upsal, 245

SAVE **EASTERN STATE PENITENTIARY,** 2027 Fairmount Ave., opened in 1829 with a revolutionary design in prison facilities: private cells with skylights, individual recreation areas and cellblocks radiating from a central rotunda. Also new was the reform concept that replaced brutality with isolation and productive work. Multimedia displays and art exhibitions portray life on the inside. Original cell blocks, center surveillance hub, a baseball diamond, Al Capone's cell and Death Row can be seen. An audio tour, a 1-hour guided tour and interactive exhibits are available. One-hour Winter Adventure Tours also are given.

Note: The building is unheated, and access to tour sites may change due to weather.

Time: Allow 1 hour, 30 minutes minimum. **Hours:** Daily 10-5. Theme guided tours depart at various times; phone ahead to confirm schedule. Last admission is 1 hour before closing. Winter Adventure Tours are given Dec.-Mar.; phone for schedule. Closed Jan. 1, Thanksgiving, Christmas Eve and Christmas. **Cost:** (includes audio tour, guided tour and exhibits) $14; $12 (ages 65+); $10 (ages 7-12 and students with ID). Tour is not recommended for children under 7. **Phone:** (215) 236-3300.
GT 🚇 Fairmount, 121

EDGAR ALLAN POE NATIONAL HISTORIC SITE, 532 N. 7th St. at jct. Spring Garden St., contains a visitor center that has exhibits, an audiovisual program and a reading room as well as the house where Poe lived 1843-44 with his wife, Virginia; mother-in-law, Maria Clemm; and their cat, Catterina. Poe lived in Philadelphia, a thriving publishing center, for six years. During these years he wrote some of his most famous works, including "Murders in the Rue Morgue," "The Black Cat," "The Gold-Bug" and "The Tell-Tale Heart." Poe rented several residences during his years here, but this is the only one that remains.

Hours: Fri.-Sun. 9-noon and 1-5. Guided tour times vary; phone for schedule. Closed Jan. 1, Veterans Day, Thanksgiving and Christmas. **Cost:** Free. **Phone:** (215) 597-8780 (voice or TTY), or (267) 519-4295, ext. 31 for audio tour.
🚇 Chinatown, 124

ELFRETH'S ALLEY, off 2nd St. between Arch and Race sts., is one of many narrow streets lined with houses that have stood since the days of Penn's Greene Countrie Towne. It is said to be the country's oldest continually inhabited residential street. House tours and information are available at the Elfreth's Alley Museum, 124 Elfreth's Alley. **Hours:** Fri.-Sun. noon-5, Apr.-Sept. Closed major holidays. **Cost:** Museum $5. **Phone:** (215) 627-8680. 🚇 2nd, 63

FAIRMOUNT PARK is reached by Benjamin Franklin Pkwy. This beautiful park system covers 9,200 acres throughout the city. It is threaded

City Hall

by miles of scenic drives, walks, a bicycle route and horse trails. Visitors can see sculls racing on the Schuylkill, hear band concerts in Pastorious Park or symphony orchestras at Mann Center for the Performing Arts, or visit numerous museums and historic houses.

The park system, founded in 1876, was the site of the Centennial Exposition. Of almost 200 buildings erected for the fair, only Memorial Hall and the Ohio House remain. Glendenning Rock Garden and Horticultural Hall Gardens are noteworthy. Within the park boundaries are several Colonial estates *(see Fairmount Park Historic Houses)* and public squares, including Franklin Square, which features a carousel and playgrounds, and Logan Square, with the beautiful Swann Memorial Fountain that is lit at night.

Historic RittenhouseTown, on Wissahickon Avenue, was the site of America's first paper mill. Today seven buildings remain and can be viewed from the outside via a guided walking tour. The boat houses along the Schuylkill River are lit at night with strings of white lights that reflect in the water; they are best seen from the Schuylkill Expressway across the river. **Phone:** (215) 438-5711 for Historic RittenhouseTown. ⊠ 𝄔

The Barnes Foundation, 2025 Benjamin Franklin Pkwy. within Fairmount Park, displays a collection of early French Modern and Post-Impressionist paintings that include works by Paul Cézanne, Edgar Degas, Henri Matisse, Amedeo Modigliani, Claude Monet, Pablo Picasso, Pierre Auguste Renoir, Georges Seurat and Vincent Van Gogh. Native American pottery, Pennsylvania German decorative furniture, sculpture, ceramics and metalwork are displayed. Other noted collections include art from Africa, Central America, China, Greece and Rome.

What differentiates this art collection from most others is the way the pieces are displayed; each room displays American and European furniture and metalwork in ways that enhance and accentuate characteristics of the artworks. Therefore, don't be surprised to see painting masterpieces next to an antique tool or an Amish chest. The presentation is unconventional, exactly how founder Albert Barnes wanted it to be.

Time: Allow 1 hour, 30 minutes minimum. **Hours:** Wed.-Mon. 10-6 (also some Fri. 6-8 p.m.). **Cost:** $22; $20 (ages 65+); $10 (ages 6-18 and students with ID). Guided tour additional $5. Reservations are required. **Parking:** $12. **Phone:** (215) 278-7000. 🔵 GT ⊞ 🚆 19th, 69

Fairmount Water Works Interpretive Center is within Fairmount Park behind the Philadelphia Museum of Art at 640 Waterworks Dr. Serving as a model for more than 30 other American water delivery systems, the Fairmont Water Works was a 19th-century engineering wonder providing clean water to the growing Philadelphia vicinity.

Operating 1815-1909, it now houses historical and interactive environmental exhibits, galleries, a theater and displays that invite visitors to discover the wonders of water. **Time:** Allow 2 hours minimum. **Hours:** Tues.-Sat. 10-5, Sun. 1-5. Closed major holidays. **Cost:** Free. **Phone:** (215) 685-0723. 🚆 30th, 220

Horticulture Center, 100 N. Horticultural Dr. at jct. Belmont Ave. and Montgomery Dr. within Fairmount Park, includes a landscaped arboretum with a large reflecting pool, seasonal greenhouse displays and outdoor gardens. **Time:** Allow 30 minutes minimum. **Hours:** Grounds daily 8-6, Apr.-Oct.; 8-5, rest of year. Display house daily 9-3. Closed major holidays. **Cost:** Donations. **Phone:** (215) 685-0096.

Japanese House and Garden is off Montgomery Dr. at Belmont Mansion Dr. next to the Horticulture Center within Fairmount Park. The house was built in Japan in 1953 in a style that would have been intended for an educated upper-class person living in the 16th- or 17th-century; the house displays a combination of elements from both centuries. The America-Japan Society of Tokyo gave it to New York's Museum of Modern Art for an exhibition, and afterward it was moved to Philadelphia.

A tea house adjoins the main house. A pond and ornamental garden also are on the grounds. A tea ceremony is held on occasional Sunday afternoons by reservation. **Time:** Allow 1 hour minimum. **Hours:** Wed.-Fri. 10-4, Sat.-Sun. 11-5, Apr. and Oct. Closed major holidays. Phone ahead to confirm schedule. **Cost:** $7; $5 (ages 3-17, ages 65+ and students with ID). **Phone:** (215) 878-5097. GT

Laurel Hill Cemetery, 3822 Ridge Ave. within Fairmount Park, incorporates striking architecture and landscape design elements into its 78 acres. The cemetery represents one of the nation's earliest examples of landscape architecture. It is shaded by large trees and contains interesting statuary. Many notable historical figures are buried here, including 40 Civil War-era generals, Philadelphia industrialists and six passengers aboard the RMS *Titanic.*

A cemetery map and cell phone audio tour brochure are available at the office. Monthly guided tours are available (schedule varies). **Hours:** Grounds Mon.-Fri. 8-4:30, Sat.-Sun. 9:30-4:30. Closed major holidays. Phone ahead to confirm schedule. **Cost:** Grounds, cell phone tour and map free. Monthly tour fees vary; phone ahead to confirm. **Phone:** (215) 228-8200, or (215) 525-1548 for audio tour. 🚆 East Falls, 229

Mann Center for the Performing Arts, 52nd St. and Parkside Ave. within Fairmount Park, is an outdoor cultural arts center that presents summer concerts, opera, dance and visiting performers. Picnicking is permitted at orchestra concerts only. **Hours:** The season runs May-Sept.; phone for schedules. **Cost:**

Please Touch Museum

Ticket prices $10-$125. **Phone:** (215) 893-0400 for general information, or (800) 745-3000 for box office. Wynnefield Ave, 217

Philadelphia Museum of Art, end of Benjamin Franklin Pkwy. at 26th St., in Fairmount Park, ranks among the largest art museums in the United States. Founded in 1876, the museum's collections offer a full range of both fine and decorative arts from Asia, Europe and the United States. Spanning more than 2,000 years, the museum is home to more than 227,000 objects, including masterpieces of painting, sculpture, works on paper, arms and armor, costumes and textiles.

Included are works by Paul Cézanne, Claude Monet, Pierre Auguste Renoir, Pablo Picasso, Marcel Duchamp, Henri Matisse and Joan Miró as well as those by modern artists. The American collections survey three centuries of paintings, furniture and decorative arts with an emphasis on Philadelphia's traditions. Special programs for children and families, lectures, concerts and films also are presented.

Special exhibits for 2015 include "Discovering the Impressionists," featuring Paul Durand-Ruel, running from June 24-Sept. 13 and "Audubon to Warhol: The Art of American Still Life" from Oct. 27-Jan. 10. **Note:** Sign-language interpreted tours can be arranged with advanced notice. **Hours:** Tues.-Sun. and some Mon. holidays 10-5 (also Wed. and Fri. 5-8:45). Closed July 4, Thanksgiving and Christmas. **Cost:** (includes Mount Pleasant, Rodin Museum, and the Ruth and Raymond G. Perelman Building), valid for 2 consecutive days, $20; $18 (ages 65+); $14 (ages 13-18 and students with ID);

donations (first Sun. of the month). Additional fees may be charged for special exhibitions. **Phone:** (215) 763-8100 or TTY (215) 763-7600. GT 30th, 220

Philadelphia Zoo, 3400 Girard Ave. W. within Fairmount Park, first opened on July 1, 1874. Today the 42-acre Victorian garden is home to more than 1,300, including many rare and endangered species. Zoo360 is an animal trail system that enables primates and big cats to roam above the zoo, creating interesting viewing opportunities for visitors. First Niagara Big Cat Falls offers guests an up close look at endangered cats from around the globe. PECO Primate Reserve offers an encounter with primates and the McNeil Avian Center provides lush walk-through habitats where visitors discover more than 100 birds, many of them rare and endangered. KidZooU features hands-on experiences for children, wildlife displays and rare breeds.

Time: Allow 2 hours minimum. **Hours:** Daily 9:30-5, Mar.-Oct.; 9:30-4, rest of year. Phone for special activity schedules. Closed Jan. 1, Thanksgiving, Christmas Eve, Christmas and Dec. 31. **Cost:** Mar.-Oct. $20; $18 (ages 2-11, 65+ and active military with ID). Rest of year $16. Phone for special activity additional fees. **Parking:** $15. **Phone:** (215) 243-1100. 40th, 224

Please Touch Museum, 4231 Avenue of the Republic (formerly N. Concourse Dr.) at Memorial Hall in Fairmount Park, occupies a building used as an art gallery during the 1876 Centennial Exhibition. Abundant hands-on educational activities encourage children under age 8 and their families to use their senses as they play. Children can run a supermarket, medical practice or construction site. Flight Fantasy teaches experimentation through flight simulations. Older children and adults will enjoy Centennial Exploration, which showcases the historical World's Fair building.

Events and daily theater performances also are offered. **Time:** Allow 3 hours minimum. **Hours:** Mon.-Sat. 9-5, Sun. 11-5. Closed Thanksgiving and Christmas. **Cost:** $17; free (under 1). Carousel $3 (per ride). Every five children must be accompanied by one adult. **Parking:** $8. **Phone:** (215) 581-3181.

Rodin Museum, jct. Benjamin Franklin Pkwy. and 22nd St. in Fairmount Park, is a Beaux Arts-style building displaying a priceless collection of Auguste Rodin originals and casts, the largest collection outside Paris. Many sculptures are housed in the garden, including casts of "The Burghers of Calais" and "The Thinker."

Rodin worked on "The Gates of Hell," a pair of doors intended for a Paris museum, for 37 years, but it was only cast in bronze after his death. The piece measures nearly 21 feet tall and 13 feet wide and contains more than 200 sculptures of human figures. A tour introduces visitors to the history of the work that consumed so much of Rodin's career.

Photography is permitted. A free shuttle departs the Philadelphia Museum of Art's west entrance Wed.-Sun. 10-5 every 45 minutes after the hour and the Rodin Museum 50 minutes after the hour. **Time:** Allow 30 minutes minimum. **Hours:** Wed.-Mon. 10-5. The Rediscovering Rodin tour departs at 1:30. Closed July 4, Thanksgiving and Christmas.

Cost: Museum and Gardens, donations. Combination ticket with Mount Pleasant, Philadelphia Museum of Art, and the Ruth and Raymond G. Perelman Building, valid for 2 consecutive days, $20. **Phone:** (215) 568-6026 or TTY (215) 763-7600. 🚇 30th, 220

Ruth and Raymond G. Perelman Building is at 2525 Pennsylvania Ave. at jct. Fairmount Ave., across from the Philadelphia Museum of Art. This 1927 Art Deco building (formerly the Fidelity Mutual Life Insurance Co.) is an extension of the art museum and features frequently changed exhibitions of contemporary art, including costumes, photography, sculpture and textiles. An art library contains about 200,000 auction catalogs, books and periodicals published since the 16th century as well as electronic resources.

A free shuttle provides transportation between the Perelman Building and the Philadelphia Museum of Art Tues.-Sun. every 10 to 15 minutes. **Time:** Allow 1 hour, 30 minutes minimum. **Hours:** Museum Tues.-Sun. 10-5; closed July 4, Thanksgiving and Christmas. Library Tues.-Fri. 10-4 (also Sat. 10-4, mid-Sept. to mid-May); closed Nov. 24-28, Christmas Eve, Christmas and day after Christmas.

Cost: $10; $8 (ages 65+); $6 (ages 13-18 and students with ID); donations (first Sun. of the month). Combination ticket with Mount Pleasant, Philadelphia Museum of Art and Rodin Museum, valid for 2 consecutive days, $20; $18 (ages 65+); $14 (ages 13-18 and students with ID); donations (first Sun. of the month). Additional fees may be charged for special exhibitions. **Phone:** (215) 763-8100. GT 🍴 🚇 30th, 220

FAIRMOUNT PARK HISTORIC HOUSES, along the banks of the Schuylkill River within Fairmount Park, are the former homes of wealthy 18th- and 19th-century Philadelphians. They include Cedar Grove, Laurel Hill, Lemon Hill, Mount Pleasant, Strawberry Mansion, Sweetbriar Mansion and Woodford Mansion. **Hours:** Hours vary per house. **Cost:** Per house $5; $3 (ages 65+); $2 (ages 6-12). **Phone:** (215) 684-7926, or (215) 222-1333 for Sweetbriar Mansion.

Cedar Grove, at 1 Cedar Grove Dr. within Fairmount Park, is an 18th-century summer home that served five generations of the same Quaker family. It features many original family furnishings, household articles and decorative arts. **Hours:** Thurs.-Sun. tour given at 11, Apr.-Dec. **Cost:** $5; $3 (ages 65+); free (ages 0-12); donations (first Sun. of the month). Combination ticket with Philadelphia Museum of Art, Rodin Museum and Ruth and Raymond

G. Perelman building, valid for two consecutive days, $20; $18 (ages 65+); $14 (ages 13-18 and students with ID). **Phone:** (215) 763-8100. GT

Laurel Hill, Kelly Dr. to Fountain Green Dr., following signs to jct. E. Edgeley and Reservoir drs. within Fairmount Park, offers views of the Schuylkill River and features paneling, an 1818 Broadwood fortepiano, a 1783 Philadelphia tall chest and an octagonal drawing room with Federal architectural details. Costumed guides conduct tours of the home. **Hours:** Thurs.-Sun. 10-4, Apr.-Dec. **Cost:** $5; $3 (ages 65+); $2 (ages 6-12). **Phone:** (215) 235-1776 or (215) 684-7926.

Lemon Hill, jct. Kelly and Sedgley drs. within Fairmount Park, is a masterpiece of 19th-century architecture with three oval-shaped rooms crafted with curved fireplaces, windows and doors. Staffordshire dishware with scenes of old Philadelphia and a 200-piece set of Chinese dinnerware also are on display. Tours are offered by docents. **Hours:** Thurs.-Sun. 10-4, early Apr. to mid-Dec.; by appointment rest of year. **Cost:** $5; $3 (ages 65+ and students with ID). **Phone:** (215) 232-4337 or (215) 684-7926. 🚇 40th, 224

Mount Pleasant, off Kelly Dr. to 3800 Mt. Pleasant Dr. within Fairmount Park, was built 1762-65 by Scottish sea captain John Macpherson. The Middle Georgian mansion features classical architecture and craftsmanship of Colonial Philadelphia. **Hours:** Tours Thurs.-Sun. at 1 and 2:30, Apr.-Dec. **Cost:** $5; $3 (ages 65+); free (ages 0-12); donations (first Sun. of the month). Combination ticket with Philadelphia Museum of Art, Rodin Museum and Ruth and Raymond G. Perelman Building, valid for 2 consecutive days, $20; $18 (ages 65+); $14 (ages 13-18 and students with ID); donations (first Sun. of the month). **Phone:** (215) 763-8100 or (215) 684-7926. GT

Strawberry Mansion, at 2450 Strawberry Mansion Dr. within Fairmount Park, is the largest of the Fairmount Park historic mansions and is furnished in Empire style. The house features period furnishings, a doll collection, antique toys and other early American artifacts. **Hours:** Tues.-Sun. 10-4, early Apr. to mid-Dec.; by reservation rest of year. **Cost:** $5. **Phone:** (215) 228-8364. GT

Woodford Mansion, jct. 33rd St. and W. Dauphin Dr. within Fairmount Park, is a fine example of Colonial architecture and is decorated with a collection of 18th-century American crafted furniture, 17th- and 18th-century Delftware, and Colonial pewter and clocks. **Hours:** Tues.-Sun. 10-4. Closed major holidays. **Cost:** $5; $3 (ages 65+); $2 (ages 6-12). **Phone:** (215) 229-6115. GT

FIREMAN'S HALL MUSEUM, 147 N. 2nd St. above Arch St., is housed in a firehouse built in 1902. The history of fire fighting is depicted using memorabilia, graphics, films and early fire-fighting equipment. An interactive exhibit illustrates fire prevention techniques. Also featured is a photographic tribute to firefighters killed during the attacks of Sept. 11, 2001. **Time:** Allow 1 hour minimum. **Hours:** Tues.-Sat. 10-4:30 (also first Fri. of the month 4:30-9). Closed major holidays. **Cost:** Donations. **Phone:** (215) 923-1438. 🖐 2nd, 63

FORT MIFFLIN, jct. Fort Mifflin and Hog Island rds., was built in 1771 by the British to protect the Colonies. Ironically, during the Revolutionary War, Americans used the fort to prevent the occupying British army from receiving supplies, a delay that allowed General Washington to establish winter quarters in Valley Forge. The fort also was garrisoned for the war of 1912, was a federal prison during the Civil War and was used as a munitions depot until it was decommissioned in 1812. The 14 structures on-site date to 1778-1875. Interpretive guides in Revolutionary or Civil War attire are available some weekends. Living history events are held throughout the year.

Time: Allow 1 hour minimum. **Hours:** Wed.-Sun. 10-4, Mar. 1 to mid-Dec.; by appointment rest of year. Closed Easter, Thanksgiving and Christmas. **Cost:** $8; $6 (ages 65+); $4 (ages 5-12 and veterans with ID). **Phone:** (215) 685-4167. 🖐

THE FRANKLIN INSTITUTE is at N. 20th St. and Benjamin Franklin Pkwy. Three floors of interactive exhibits are offered. The Sports Challenge offers a climbing wall, pitching cage and other interactive displays; KidScience: The Island of the Elements teaches children basic science concepts;

Your Brain explores developments in neuroscience; The Train Factory features a 350-ton moving locomotive; The Franklin Air Show includes an aircraft hangar, a midway, and a pilot training area where visitors can try various maneuvers in a flight simulator; and SkyBike, a two-wheel bicycle that balances riders on a 28-foot-high cable. Franklin 3D Theater, the Joel N. Bloom Observatory, Sir Isaac's Loft and a giant walk-through heart also are featured.

Other exhibits relate to astronomy, aviation, electricity, math and physics. The Benjamin Franklin National Memorial, in the museum's rotunda, features a 20-foot-tall statue of Franklin. Fels Planetarium and Tuttleman IMAX Theater are other highlights.

Note: An exhibit of 70 Lego® sculptures and art masterpieces including a 20-foot-long T. Rex dinosaur and Vincent Van Gogh's Starry Night will be featured through Sept. 6. **Time:** Allow 4 hours minimum. **Hours:** Museum daily 9:30-5. Holiday hours vary; phone ahead. IMAX theater daily 10-6 (also Fri.-Sat. 6-9 p.m.). Closed Thanksgiving and Christmas. **Cost:** (includes Fels Planetarium) $18.50; $17.50 (military with ID); $14.50 (ages 3-11). IMAX theater $9; price varies for feature films. Combination ticket with Fels Planetarium and IMAX theater and other combination tickets are available. SkyBike additional $3 (riders must be at least 56 inches tall). Flight simulator additional $5. **Phone:** (215) 448-1200. 🔲 🖐 19th, 69

Fels Planetarium, 222 N. 20th St. at The Franklin Institute, presents multimedia shows about astronomy and the night skies. The Space Command Exhibit simulates life on an Earth-orbiting research station. **Hours:** Show times vary; phone ahead. Closed Thanksgiving and Christmas.

Cost: (includes The Franklin Institute) $18.50; $17.50 (military with ID); $14.50 (ages 3-11). Combination ticket with The Franklin Institute and Tuttleman IMAX Theater and other combination tickets are available; phone for prices. **Phone:** (215) 448-1200. 🖐 19th, 69

Tuttleman IMAX Theater, 222 N. 20th St. at The Franklin Institute, projects films about science and adventure onto a four-story, 79-foot-wide dome screen with 56 audio speakers. Diverse topics include space exploration, nature and the human body.

Hours: Daily 10-6 (also Fri.-Sat. 6-9 p.m.). Phone ahead to confirm schedule. **Cost:** $9. Price varies for major motion films. Combination ticket with The Franklin Institute and Fels Planetarium is available; phone for prices. **Phone:** (215) 448-1200 for show information. 🔲 🖐 19th, 69

FREE LIBRARY OF PHILADELPHIA, Logan Sq. at 1901 Vine St., has a variety of exhibits about art, architecture, photography, books and local history. Free concerts, films and lecture programs are presented some Sundays; phone for times. **Hours:** Mon.-Thurs. 9-9, Fri. 9-6, Sat. 9-5, Sun. 1-5. Tours

The Franklin Institute

of the library are given Tues. and Thurs. at 10, Sat.-Sun. at 10 and 2. Tours of the rare book room are conducted Mon.-Fri. at 11. **Cost:** Free. **Phone:** (215) 686-5322. 19th, 69

GERMANTOWN HISTORICAL SOCIETY AND HISTORIC GERMANTOWN, 5501 Germantown Ave. on Market Sq., features a research library/archives and a small exhibit area with a decorative arts collection depicting Germantown history through the centuries. Germantown was America's first German settlement, the scene of the Revolutionary Battle of Germantown, the birthplace of writer Louisa May Alcott and an Underground Railroad site.

Settled mainly by Germans and the Dutch, many of Germantown's old houses are distinguished by Dutch doors and arched cellar windows. It is home to 16 historic sites. **Hours:** Museum, library and archives Tues. 9-1, Thurs. and first Sun. of each month, 1-5. **Cost:** Museum and library $5; free (ages 0-12). **Phone:** (215) 844-1683. Germantown, 267

GERMANTOWN WHITE HOUSE (formerly Deshler-Morris House) is at 5442 Germantown Ave. Affiliated with Independence National Historical Park, this is where George Washington spent the fall of 1793 to escape Philadelphia's yellow fever epidemic. Though he was away from the capital, he continued his duties as president, including holding four cabinet meetings in the residence. In the summer of 1794 he returned with his family. The restored 1752 house is furnished in period.

Hours: Sat.-Sun. 10-4, Memorial Day-Labor Day. Closed major holidays. Phone ahead to confirm schedule. **Cost:** Free. **Phone:** (215) 965-2305 or (215) 597-7130. Germantown, 267

GLORIA DEI (OLD SWEDES') CHURCH, Columbus Blvd. at Christian St., is believed to be Pennsylvania's oldest church and the first in Colonial America to use an organ during services. The church was built in 1700, but its congregation was founded in 1643. The oversized Hook and Hastings organ, with approximately 1,300 pipes, has been in continual use since 1902.

Of special interest is a chandelier modeled after two ships that brought the first colonists to the area; an exact replica of the original 11th-century angel Gabriel found in Gothenburg, Sweden; and a plaque featuring two cherub faces and a bible brought here from Sweden prior to 1646. **Hours:** Grounds daily 9-4. Church open Tues.-Sun. 9-4. Sun. services at 10. **Phone:** (215) 389-1513.

INDEPENDENCE NATIONAL HISTORICAL PARK, with its main area extending from 2nd to 6th sts. between Walnut and Arch sts., includes some 20 buildings that are closely associated with the Colonial period, the founding of the nation and Philadelphia's early role as the U.S. capital. It features the nation's best-known symbol of freedom—the Liberty Bell—as well as Independence Hall, where the Declaration of Independence and the U.S. Constitution were created. Within the 54-acre park is a site where Benjamin Franklin's home once stood; exhibits here depict his life and teachings.

The centerpiece in Washington Square is the memorial to George Washington and the unknown soldiers of the American Revolution. Walkways under mature trees lead to the memorial, where a statue of Washington stands guard over the tomb of one unknown soldier.

Free, timed tickets are required for tours of Independence Hall from March through December. Tickets are available at the Independence Visitor Center (see attraction listing), at 6th and Market streets, or may be ordered in advance for a small fee through the National Park Reservation Service. The visitor center, open daily, presents exhibits and continuous showings of a 30-minute John Huston film, "Independence." Inquire at the center for a walking tour map and the latest information about events, attractions and activities in the Philadelphia region.

Note: Access to Congress Hall, Independence Hall and the Liberty Bell Center requires visitors to pass through security screening. The security entrance for Independence Square is at 5th and Chestnut streets. For the Liberty Bell Center, the security entrance is at 6th and Market streets.

Time: Allow 5 hours minimum. **Hours:** Many buildings are open daily 9-5. Hours may be extended in summer and reduced other times of year. Closed Christmas. Phone ahead to confirm schedule. **Cost:** All attractions are free except the National Constitution Center and the Benjamin Franklin Museum in Franklin Court. **Phone:** (215) 965-2305, or (877) 444-6777 for National Park Reservation Service. 5th, 64

American Philosophical Society (APS) Museum is at 104 S. 5th St. at jct. Chestnut St., adjacent to Independence Hall; the museum falls within the boundaries of Independence National Historical Park but is not part of the park. This scholarly society, founded in 1743 by Benjamin Franklin, included John Adams, Thomas Jefferson and many other prominent early Americans. Rotating exhibits are created from the society's collection, which includes artworks, 300,000 books, important documents, 11 million manuscripts, maps, scientific specimens and instruments, and other items tracing American history from the Founding Fathers to the computer age. Exhibitions showcase the connections between history, science and art. Three exhibitions about Thomas Jefferson are scheduled to run from April 2014 through December 2016.

Time: Allow 1 hour minimum. **Hours:** Thurs.-Sun. 10-4, mid-Apr. to late Dec. Guided tours Mon.-Wed., 10-4. Closed holidays and when exhibitions are being changed. Phone ahead to confirm schedule.

Bishop White House

Cost: Donations. Guided tours $5; $2 (students with ID). **Phone:** (215) 440-3442. 5th, 64

B. Free Franklin Post Office and Museum, 316 Market St. within Independence National Historical Park, commemorates Franklin's 1775 appointment as first postmaster general. The only post office operated by the U.S. Postal Service that does not fly the American flag, it is named after Franklin's unique signature. It is assumed that his use of Free as part of his signature referred to America's struggle for freedom. Philatelists prize the hand-canceled letters from this post office.

Hours: Mon.-Sat. 9-5. Closed major holidays. Phone ahead to confirm schedule. **Cost:** Free. **Phone:** (215) 592-1292. 5th, 64

Bishop White House, 309 Walnut St. within Independence National Historical Park, was built by Pennsylvania's first Protestant Episcopal bishop in 1787; he was also the rector of Christ Church and St. Peter's Church. The restored house contains many original articles.

Time: Allow 1 hour minimum. **Hours:** Hours vary. Phone ahead to confirm schedule. **Cost:** Free. **Phone:** (215) 965-2305 for visitor information. 2nd, 63

Carpenters' Hall, 320 Chestnut St. within Independence National Historical Park, was lent by the Carpenters' Co. of Philadelphia for the First Continental Congress in 1774. A collection of early carpentry tools as well as chairs used by the Congress are inside. An 11-minute video presentation chronicles the history of the Carpenters' Co., which still owns and operates the hall.

Hours: Tues.-Sun. 10-4, Mar.-Dec.; Wed.-Sun. 10-4, rest of year. Closed Jan. 1, Easter, Thanksgiving, Christmas Eve and Christmas. **Cost:** Free. **Phone:** (215) 925-0167. 5th, 64

Christ Church (Episcopal), on 2nd St. between Market and Arch sts. within Independence National Historical Park, was the house of worship of 15 signers of the Declaration of Independence. Brass plaques mark the pews once occupied by Benjamin Franklin, Betsy Ross and George Washington. The 1727 structure typifies early Georgian architecture. It has one of the oldest Palladian windows in North America. It also contains the font from which William Penn was baptized in 1644 in London.

Christ Church Burial Ground, 5th and Arch streets, contains the graves of Benjamin Franklin and four other signers of the Declaration of Independence.

Time: Allow 30 minutes minimum. **Hours:** Church Mon.-Sat. 9-5, Sun. 1-5, Mar.-Dec.; Wed.-Sat. 9-5, Sun. 1-5, rest of year. Services Sun. at 9 and 11 a.m., Wed. at noon. Burial ground (weather permitting) Mon.-Sat. 10-4, Sun. noon-4, Mar.-Nov.; Fri.-Sat. noon-4, in Dec. Burial ground guided tours depart every 15 minutes; last tour departs at 3:30. Closed Jan. 1, Easter, Thanksgiving and Christmas. **Cost:** Church by donation. Burial ground admission $2; $1 (ages 5-16). Guided tour (includes Burial Ground) $5; $2 (ages 5-16). **Phone:** (215) 922-1695. GT 2nd, 63

Congress Hall, 6th and Chestnut sts. within Independence National Historical Park, was built 1787-89 as the Philadelphia County Court House but was occupied by the U.S. Congress 1790-1800 until Congress was moved to Washington, D.C. On the first floor is the chamber of the House of Representatives; the second floor contains the elaborate chamber of the Senate and various committee rooms. The hall was the setting for the inaugurations of George Washington (his second) and John Adams.

Note: Access requires visitors to pass through security screening. **Hours:** Daily 9-5. Tours depart every 20 minutes. Closed Christmas. Phone ahead to confirm schedule. **Cost:** Free. **Phone:** (215) 965-2305. 5th, 64

Declaration House, s.w. corner of 7th and Market sts. within Independence National Historical Park, is a reconstruction of the dwelling in which Thomas Jefferson drafted the Declaration of Independence in June 1776. **Hours:** Hours vary; phone ahead for schedule. **Cost:** Free. **Phone:** (215) 965-2305. 8th, 65

Franklin Court, between 3rd, 4th, Chestnut and Market sts. within Independence National Historical

Park, was once owned by Benjamin Franklin. This was his home when he was part of the Continental Congress and Constitutional Convention until his death in 1790. The brick house was demolished in 1812 and there are no records describing the architectural appearance, but the foundation can be seen and a 54-foot-tall steel skeletal structure provides an outline to give visitors a feel for the space it once occupied.

The complex includes the Benjamin Franklin Museum as well as five Market Street houses, the exteriors of which have been restored to period. The buildings contain the refinished *Aurora* newspaper office historically operated by Franklin's grandson, a working reproduction of an 18th-century printing press and bindery operation and a post office.

Hours: Daily 9-5. A Ben Franklin reenactor is available in summer only. Phone ahead to confirm schedule. **Cost:** Franklin Court (including Market Street buildings) free. Benjamin Franklin Museum $5; $2 (ages 4-16). **Phone:** (215) 965-2305, or (267) 519-4295, ext. 22, 23 and 221 for audio tour. 🚇 5th, 64

Free Quaker Meeting House is at 500 Arch St. at jct. 5th St. within Independence National Historical Park. Built in 1783, the building served as a meeting and worship house for the 30 to 50 men and women, including Betsy Ross, that had been disowned by the Quakers for going against their principle of pacifism and supporting the Colonial militia. Displays detail Quaker history, including their role in the American Revolution.

A guide dressed in 18th-century Quaker attire is available to answer questions and share information about Quaker religious beliefs and the revolution. **Hours:** Hours vary. Phone ahead to confirm schedule. **Cost:** Free. **Phone:** (215) 965-2305. GT 🚇 5th, 64

Independence Archeology Lab, 313 Walnut St. within Independence National Historical Park, is a laboratory where you can watch archeologists at work and learn how the small artifacts they study help piece together what life was like in 18th- and 19th-century Philadelphia. The items being studied were excavated 2000-03 before and during the National Constitution Center construction. Visitors may see archeologists at work in the park (weather permitting).

Time: Allow 30 minutes minimum. **Hours:** Entrance is by appointment only. Tours are offered on a space-available basis to visitors ages 16 and older in groups up to 4 persons. **Cost:** Free. **Phone:** (215) 861-4956 for tour reservations. 🚇 2nd, 63

Independence Hall is between 5th and 6th sts. on Chestnut St. on Independence Square within Independence National Historical Park. Within this graceful 1732 brick building, built as the Pennsylvania State House, the Second Continental Congress voted to break with England, the

Declaration of Independence and Constitution were signed, and George Washington accepted the role of commander in chief of the Colonial armies. The Assembly Room has been restored to look as it did when used by the founding fathers 1775-87. It contains the original Rising Sun chair that Washington occupied during the drafting of the Constitution.

Across the hallway is the restored Pennsylvania Supreme Court Chamber. Upstairs, the Governor's Council Chamber, Long Room and Committee Room have been restored and furnished in period. The west wing's Great Essentials Exhibit features original rare, printed copies of the Declaration of Independence, the Articles of Confederation and the Constitution as well as the silver inkstand that is believed to have been used by the signers of the Declaration of Independence and the Constitution.

Note: Access requires visitors to pass through security screening. Admission is by guided tour only (except for the west wing). Tickets are issued for specific times and are available at the Independence Visitor Center at 6th and Market streets. For a small handling fee, the National Park Reservation Service will arrange advance tickets (tickets are not necessary Jan.-Feb.). **Hours:** Daily 9-5. Closed Christmas. **Cost:** Free. **Phone:** (215) 965-2305, or (877) 444-6777 for National Park Reservation Service. 🚇 5th, 64

Independence Visitor Center, jct. 6th and Market sts. at 1 N. Independence Mall W. within Independence National Historical Park, is a 50,000-square-foot facility that provides a range of tourism services for Independence National Historic Park and the Philadelphia region. These include orientation films, hotel and dining reservations, tour and attraction information and ticket sales. The visitor center is the only location to obtain free timed tickets for Independence Hall on the day of your visit.

Time: Allow 30 minutes minimum. **Hours:** Daily 8:30-7, Memorial Day-Labor Day; 8:30-6, rest of year. Closed Thanksgiving and Christmas. **Cost:** Free. **Phone:** (215) 965-2305 or (800) 537-7676. 🍴 🚇 5th, 64

Liberty Bell Center, on 6th St. between Chestnut and Market sts. within Independence National Historical Park, houses the renowned bell that announced America's birth as a new nation in 1776 and was used as a symbol in the 19th-century abolition movement. Today the 2,080-pound bell is encased in a glass chamber, and admirers will see Independence Hall in the background. The bell's yoke, made of American elm, is believed to be the original.

The center includes exhibits about the bell's significance as a worldwide symbol of freedom. An 11-minute video presentation, available in a dozen languages, tells the story of its origins. **Note:** Access requires visitors to pass through security screening. **Time:** Allow 30 minutes minimum. **Hours:** Daily 9-5. Closed Christmas. **Cost:** Free. **Phone:** (215) 965-2305. 🚇 5th, 64

National Constitution Center occupies a city block between 5th and 6th sts. at 525 Arch St. within Independence National Historical Park. Devoted to preserving the legacy of the U.S. Constitution and inspiring active citizenship, this museum features hundreds of interactive exhibits, rare artifacts and films. Signers' Hall is sure to amaze with its 42 life-size bronze sculptures of the nation's founding fathers. Don't miss the 17-minute presentation of "Freedom Rising," a 360-degree theatrical production illustrating important milestones in American history.

Note: One of the 12 original copies of the Bill of Rights is on display in a special exhibition through 2017. **Time:** Allow 2 hours, 30 minutes minimum. **Hours:** Mon.-Sat. 9:30-5 (also Sat. 5-6), Sun. noon-5. Closed Jan. 1, Thanksgiving and Christmas. **Cost:** $14.50; $13 (ages 65+); $8 (ages 4-12); free (active military with ID). **Parking:** $8-$18. **Phone:** (215) 409-6700 for ticket information. 🍴 🅿 🚇 5th, 64

New Hall Military Museum, on Chestnut St. between 3rd and 4th sts. within Independence National Historical Park, is a reconstruction of a 1791 building. The museum commemorates the history of the U.S. Army, Navy and Marine Corps 1775-1805. **Note:** At press time, the attraction was closed due to sequestration. Phone for further details. **Hours:**

National Constitution Center

Hours vary. Phone ahead to confirm schedule. **Cost:** Free. **Phone:** (215) 965-2305, or (267) 519-4295, ext. 24, for audio tour. 🚇 5th, 64

Old City Hall, s.w. corner of 5th and Chestnut sts. within Independence National Historical Park, was the home of the U.S. Supreme Court 1791-1800. The exterior and the room used by the Supreme Court have been restored. **Hours:** Daily 9-5, July-Aug.; hours vary rest of year. Phone ahead to confirm schedule. **Cost:** Free. **Phone:** (215) 965-2305 or TTY (215) 597-1785. 🚇 5th, 64

President's House Site, 600 Market St. at jct. 6th St. within Independence National Historical Park, is the site of the former residence of Presidents George Washington and John Adams 1790-1800. Although the structure no longer exists, the exhibit "Freedom and Slavery in the Making of a New Nation," which features video installations, panels and illustrated glass, tells the story of their time here. Archeological fragments unearthed from the site in 2007 can be viewed in a glass enclosure.

The contradiction of Washington's belief in freedom with his use of slaves is pointed out, profiling nearly a dozen of the Africans who worked here. A memorial honors all the enslaved who lived on the grounds. A cell phone audio tour is available. Note: the attraction is outdoors and offers no shelter from inclement weather. **Time:** Allow 45 minutes minimum. **Hours:** Daily 24 hours. **Cost:** Free. **Phone:** (215) 965-2305. 🚇 5th, 64

Second Bank of the United States Portrait Gallery is at 420 Chestnut St. within Independence National Historical Park. The 1824 structure, modeled after the Parthenon, now houses the People of Independence Portrait Gallery. Some 185 late 18th- and early 19th-century portraits, many by Charles Willson Peale, illustrate Philadelphia's role as the capital city 1790-1800. Many of the portraits represent members of the military and signers of the Declaration of Independence and Constitution. Works by artists James Sharples and Thomas Sully also are included.

Hours: Wed.-Sun. 11-5. Hours vary; phone ahead to confirm schedule. **Cost:** Free. **Phone:** (215) 965-2305. 🚇 5th, 64

Todd House, 4th and Walnut sts. within Independence National Historical Park, was the home of Dolley Payne Todd before her marriage to James Madison, fourth president of the United States. The restored 1775 home reflects life in the 18th century. Admission is by tour only and includes the Bishop White House.

Time: Allow 1 hour minimum. **Hours:** Hours vary. Phone ahead to confirm schedule. **Cost:** Free. **Phone:** (215) 956-2305 for visitor information. 🚇 5th, 64

INDEPENDENCE SEAPORT MUSEUM, on Penn's Landing at 211 S. Columbus Blvd. at jct. Walnut St., depicts the maritime heritage of the

Delaware River, Delaware Bay and its tributaries. Visitors can climb aboard the World War II submarine *Becuna*, a Guppy-1A type submarine that went on missions in the Pacific before being refitted for missions during the Korean and Vietnam Wars, and *Olympia*, Adm. George Dewey's flagship during the Spanish-American War. Guided engine room tours are available. Exhibits include "Disasters on the Delaware: Rescues on the River, Homeport Philadelphia." In the Workshop on the Water, boatbuilders can be seen practicing their craft; models, blueprints and replicas of a variety of small watercraft pay tribute to generations of boat builders and enthusiasts.

Time: Allow 1 hour minimum. **Hours:** Sun.-Wed., 10-5, Thurs.-Sat. 10-7, Memorial Day-Labor Day. Closed Jan. 1, Thanksgiving and Christmas. **Cost:** $13.50; $10 (ages 3-12 and 65+, college students and military with ID); donations (Sun. 10-noon). **Phone:** (215) 413-8655. 🚇 2nd, 63

THE INSECTARIUM is off I-95 exit 30; take Cottman Ave. 1.2 mi. w., then .8 mi. n. to 8046 Frankford Ave. Spiders, scorpions and other arthropods—live and mounted—can be seen in exhibits and hands-on activities. Two live insect displays are a working beehive and a glass-enclosed kitchen pervaded by cockroaches. At the petting corner, visitors also can touch some of the resident creatures. **Time:** Allow 1 hour minimum. **Hours:** Mon.-Sat. 10-4. Closed Jan. 1, Thanksgiving and Christmas. **Cost:** $9; free (ages 0-2). **Phone:** (215) 335-9500.
🚇 Holmesburg Jct, 252

JOHN HEINZ NATIONAL WILDLIFE REFUGE AT TINICUM is off I-95S exit 14, 1.5 mi. n.e. on Bartram Ave., then 1 mi. n. on 84th St., following signs to 86th St. & Lindbergh Blvd. The refuge contains 1,000 acres of what was once tidal wetlands. More than 300 bird species have been recorded at the site, and approximately 80 of those species nest here. Opossums, raccoons, deer, foxes, muskrats and state-endangered turtles and frogs also can be seen.

The Cusano Environmental Education Center presents nature exhibits. Boardwalks and trails offer opportunities for wildlife observation, hiking, fishing and bicycling. Naturalists conduct nature walks and education programs. **Time:** Allow 2 hours minimum. **Hours:** Refuge daily dawn-dusk. Education center daily 8:30-4; closed major holidays. **Cost:** Free. **Phone:** (215) 365-3118. 🚇 Eastwick, 161

JOHNSON HOUSE HISTORIC SITE is at 6306 Germantown Ave. The house was built in 1768 by a Quaker family and was used in the 1850s by slaves escaping the South. The tour provides insights into the Johnson family, the Underground Railroad and the abolitionist movement. **Time:** Allow 1 hour, 30 minutes minimum. **Hours:** Guided tours are offered Thurs.-Fri. 10-4, Sat. 1-4. Phone ahead to confirm schedule. **Cost:** $8; $6 (senior citizens); $4 (ages 0-12 and students with ID). Cash only. Reservations are recommended. **Phone:** (215) 438-1768.
🚇 Upsal, 245

THE KIMMEL CENTER FOR THE PERFORMING ARTS, on Avenue of the Arts between S. Broad and Spruce sts., is home to the Philadelphia Orchestra, the Pennsylvania Ballet, Opera Philadelphia and several music and theater companies. Comprised of the 2,500-seat Verizon Hall and the 650-seat Perelman Theater, the center is enclosed within an arched-glass atrium.

The Building and Theater tour gives an overview of the history of the Kimmel theaters, and once a month begins with a 15-minute demonstration of the Fred J. Cooper Memorial Organ. Access to performance halls varies with event scheduling. The Art and Architecture tour focuses on the art displayed within the Kimmel and aspects of the building itself. **Time:** Allow 1 hour minimum. **Hours:** Daily 10-6. Building & Theater Tour departs Tues.-Sun. at 1. Art & Architecture Tour departs Sat. at 10:30. Organ demonstrations first Sat. of each month. Closed major holidays. Phone ahead to confirm schedule. **Cost:** Free. **Phone:** (215) 790-5800 for general information, or (215) 790-5886 for tour information. GT 🍴 🚇 Lombard-South, 116

LIBERTY 360 3D SHOW, is at 600 Chestnut St. at jct. 6th St., in the Historic Philadelphia Center's PECO Theater. Visitors stand in the theater to watch the 20-minute 360-degree 3-D film, hosted by a Benjamin Franklin interpreter, about the importance of liberty in America. It includes visual effects and original music. A brief history of our country is told along with the meanings of American symbols of freedom like the Great Seal of the United States and the Statue of Liberty.

Hours: Mon.-Sat. 10-8, Sun. 10-6, June 24-Aug. 10; Mon.-Sat. 10-6, Sun. 11-5, Sept. 3-May 27 (10-3 on Christmas Eve); daily 10-6 (also Thurs. and Labor Day weekend 6-8 p.m.), Aug. 11-Labor Day weekend; daily 10-6, rest of year. Closed Thanksgiving and Christmas. Phone ahead to confirm schedule. **Cost:** $6; $5 (ages 0-12, students with ID, senior citizens and military with ID); $20 (family of four). **Phone:** (215) 629-4026. 🚇 5th, 64

MARIAN ANDERSON HISTORICAL SOCIETY MUSEUM, 762 S. Martin St., is located in the former residence of the renowned contralto singer. Anderson purchased the home in 1924 and resided there for much of her life. The museum offers tours where guests can view memorabilia and exhibits and also learn about her life and career touring Europe and America. **Hours:** Mon.-Sat. 10-4. **Cost:** $10. Reservations are recommended. **Phone:** (215) 732-9505. GT 🚇 Lombard-South, 116

MARIO LANZA INSTITUTE AND MUSEUM, 712 Montrose St. in the Columbus House, displays treasures from the life of the singer and actor, including many portraits, photographs and personal items.

Masonic Temple

counterfeit detection, electronic banking and monetary policy represent the more recent changes in the nation's financial situation. Various types of currency are displayed; a highlight is currency that was used in the original 13 colonies.

Time: Allow 1 hour minimum. **Hours:** Mon.-Fri. 9:30-4:30, Mar.-Dec. (also Sat. 9-3, Sun. 11-3, June-Aug.); Mon.-Fri. 10-2, rest of year. Last admission 30 minutes before closing. Closed major holidays. **Cost:** Free. **Phone:** (215) 574-6257 or (866) 574-3727. 🚇 5th, 64

MORRIS ARBORETUM OF THE UNIVERSITY OF PENNSYLVANIA is at 100 E. Northwestern Ave., between Germantown and Stenton aves. in Chestnut Hill. Within its 92 acres of ever-changing landscape are 13,000 labeled trees and shrubs and colorful gardens. Highlights include a formal rose garden; a glasshouse fernery; and Out on a Limb, a 450-foot canopy walk exhibit (wheelchair accessible) that takes visitors 50 feet into the treetops.

Time: Allow 1 hour, 30 minutes minimum. **Hours:** Daily 10-4 (also Sat.-Sun. 10-5, Apr.-Oct.) Guided tours are available Sat.-Sun. at 2. Closed Jan. 1, Thanksgiving, Christmas Eve and Christmas. **Cost:** $16; $14 (ages 65+); $8 (ages 3-17, students and active military with ID). **Phone:** (215) 247-5777. GT

MOTHER BETHEL AFRICAN METHODIST EPISCOPAL CHURCH is at 419 Richard Allen Ave. at S. 6th between Pine and Lombard sts. The 1890 church is the fourth structure on the site; the original 1794 building is said to have been the nation's first AME Church. It was a stop on the Underground Railroad. Of note are the symbolic stained-glass windows, which have been restored.

The church also houses the Richard Allen Museum, containing items belonging to the church's founder, including original pews and Allen's pulpit and Bible. Allen and his wife, Sarah, are interred here. **Hours:** Museum hours Tues.-Sat. 10-3 (also Sun. after services); other times by appointment. Sun. services at 8 and 11. Phone ahead to confirm schedule. **Cost:** Donations. **Phone:** (215) 925-0616. 🚇 9th-10th & Locust, 142

MUMMERS MUSEUM, 1100 S. 2nd St. at Washington Ave., features interactive displays, video presentations, costumes and musical instruments that depict the history of the Mummers and their New Year's Day parade. Guided tours are available by reservation.

Time: Allow 1 hour minimum. **Hours:** Wed.-Sat. 9:30-4:30, May-Oct. String band concerts are given (weather permitting) May-Sept. Phone ahead for concert schedule. Closed major holidays. **Cost:** $3.50; $2.50 (ages 0-11, ages 65+ and students with ID). **Phone:** (215) 336-3050.

MÜTTER MUSEUM OF THE COLLEGE OF PHYSICIANS OF PHILADELPHIA is just s. of Market St. at 19 S. 22nd St. Thomas Dent Mütter, a professor of surgery at Jefferson Medical College, donated his

Among the highlights is a bust of Lanza made behind the Iron Curtain by a Hungarian sculptor. **Time:** Allow 30 minutes minimum. **Hours:** Mon.-Tues. and Fri.-Sat. 11:30-3:30. Closed major holidays. Phone ahead to confirm schedule. **Cost:** Donations. **Phone:** (215) 238-9691. 🚇 Ellsworth-Federal, 115

🔷 **MASONIC TEMPLE,** 1 N. Broad St., was built 1868-73 and is one of the city's striking architectural landmarks. Each of the temple's seven lodge halls exemplifies a different architectural style—Corinthian, Ionic, Italian Renaissance, Norman, Gothic, Oriental and Egyptian. The hallways and stairways are enhanced by chandeliers, paintings, statuary and artwork. A large stained-glass window overlooks the marble grand staircase.

Tours of the building include the Grand Lodge Museum, which is a Byzantine room housing Masonic treasures. Included in the collection are jewels, George Washington's Masonic apron, furniture, Liverpool and Lowestoft ware, cut glass and statues by William Rush. Visitors must be accompanied by guides. **Hours:** Tours are offered Tues.-Fri. at 10, 11, 1, 2 and 3, Sat. on the hour 10-noon. Closed major holidays and special events. Phone ahead to confirm schedule. **Cost:** $10; $6 (students with ID); $5 (ages 62+ and children); $25 (family, 4 or more individuals). **Phone:** (215) 988-1810. 🚇 13th, 67

MONEY IN MOTION EXHIBIT is in the Federal Reserve Bank at jct. 6th and Arch sts. America's financial history is presented through interactive exhibits. Topics include the role of the Federal Reserve Bank and the history of America's currency. Exhibits about

collection of unique medical materials to The College of Physicians of Philadelphia in 1858. The collection now has more than 20,000 items, including medical instruments as well as anatomical and pathological specimens and models. Displays about diseases, viruses and treatment throughout history also can be seen. The building, designed by Cope & Stewardson, dates to 1908.

Time: Allow 1 hour, 30 minutes minimum. **Hours:** Daily 10-5. Closed Jan. 1, Thanksgiving, Christmas Eve and Christmas. **Cost:** $15; $13 (ages 65+ and military with ID); $10 (ages 6-17 and students with ID). Combination ticket with the University of Pennsylvania Museum of Archaeology and Anthropology $26; $22 (ages 65+); $16 (ages 6-17, students and military with ID). **Phone:** (215) 563-3737.
🚇 22nd, 70

NATIONAL LIBERTY MUSEUM is downtown at 321 Chestnut St. between 2nd and 3rd sts. Glass art, exhibits, films and interactive centers portray American democracy throughout the nation's history. The museum explores such topics as the relationship between character, leadership and heroism, and the potential for people of all ages and backgrounds to be heroes. The Welcome to Liberty Gallery features an immersive theater. A collection of contemporary glass art is on display, including a 20-foot glass sculpture by artist Dale Chihuly. The Heroes of Character and Heroes of 9/11 exhibits and an original collection of presidential White House china also are featured.

Time: Allow 2 hours minimum. **Hours:** Daily 10-5. Phone for holiday hours. **Cost:** $7; $6 (ages 56+); $5 (students with ID); $2 (ages 5-17 with adult); $15 (family, two adults and their children). **Phone:** (215) 925-2800 or (888) 542-7678. 🚇 5th, 64

NATIONAL MUSEUM OF AMERICAN JEWISH HISTORY, 101 S. Independence Mall E. at jct. 5th and Market sts., is a Smithsonian affiliate and the only major museum dedicated to chronicling the American Jewish experience. The museum's three floors contain documents, artifacts, photographs, films and interactive exhibits preserving the history of Jewish life from the arrival of the first Jewish community in New York in 1654 to the present. Some of the topics covered include early Jewish lifestyles, the evolution of religious practices, and immigration obstacles and discrimination.

Time: Allow 1 hour, 30 minutes minimum. **Hours:** Tues.-Fri. 10-5, Sat.-Sun. 10-5:30. Highlight tours are given at 11:30 and 2:30. Closed Jan. 1, first two days of Passover, Rosh Hashanah, Yom Kippur and Thanksgiving. **Cost:** $12; $11 (ages 13-21 and 65+); free (ages 0-12 and active military with ID). **Parking:** Validation provided for a discount at The Bourse garage at 400 Ranstead St. **Phone:** (215) 923-3811. GT ⑪ 🚇 5th, 64

NATIONAL SHRINE OF ST. JOHN NEUMANN, 1019 N. 5th St. at jct. Girard Ave., is dedicated to the life and canonization of Philadelphia's fourth

Catholic bishop. Featured are stained-glass windows depicting his life and a glass altar containing his remains. A museum includes portraits, relics and personal items. **Time:** Allow 1 hour, 30 minutes minimum. **Hours:** Shrine and museum Mon.-Fri. 7 a.m.-6 p.m., Sun. 7 a.m.-4:30 p.m. Guided tours are given by appointment. Closed major holidays and during services. **Cost:** Donations. **Phone:** (215) 627-3080. 🚇 Girard, 61

OLD ST. MARY'S CHURCH is on 4th St. between Locust and Spruce sts. Built in 1763 and enlarged in 1810, this was the second Roman Catholic church in Philadelphia. George Washington and John Adams are two of the many early American leaders who attended services here.

On July 4, 1779, the Continental Congress commemorated the Declaration of Independence, which marked the first public religious commemoration of the document. Another first came in 1810 when it was made the city's first cathedral. The cemetery dates to 1759. **Hours:** Daily 9-5. Closed during religious services. **Cost:** Free. **Phone:** (215) 923-7930. 🚇 5th, 64

ONCE UPON A NATION is at 600 Chestnut St., in the Historic Philadelphia Center in the Public Ledger building. The variety of living history tours include Storytelling Benches in and around Independence National Historic Park. The ten benches are marked with "Once Upon a Nation." Independence After Hours is a guided tour of Independence Hall with some of the founding fathers and dinner at City Tavern. A colonial pub crawl is also offered seasonally. **Hours:** Tues.-Sat. 5:30, mid-June to mid-August; Fri.-Sat. 5:30 mid-Aug. to late Oct. **Cost:** Storytelling Benches: Free. Independence After Hours: $85; $80 (senior citizens, students and military); $55 (ages 0-11). Reservations are recommended. **Phone:** (215) 629-4026. 🚇 5th, 64

PENN'S LANDING, between Washington Ave. and Spring Garden St. along the Delaware River waterfront, marks the site where William Penn landed in 1682. The 37-acre site offers scenic views of the Ben Franklin Bridge and the Delaware River. RiverStage at the Great Plaza at Columbus Blvd. and Chestnut St. and Festival Pier at Columbus Blvd. and Spring Garden St. host more than 50 festivals, concerts and events in summer.

Other highlights include Independence Seaport Museum, the historic ship and restaurant *Moshulu* and Blue Cross RiverRink Winterfest (open seasonally). **Phone:** (215) 629-3200 for program information, or (215) 925-7465 for the ice-skating rink. 🚇 2nd, 63

PENNSYLVANIA ACADEMY OF THE FINE ARTS, 118-128 N. Broad St., was founded in 1805 and is the nation's first museum and school of fine arts. The majority of major American artists has studied, taught or exhibited here. The building, a

Victorian Gothic beauty with all its exterior embellishments, dates to 1876 and houses art from the 18th century to the present. Changing exhibits of multimedia works by students, faculty and alumni can be viewed at the Samuel M.V. Hamilton Building.

The collection showcases American art since the 1760s. Among the PAFA founders was painter/scientist Charles Willson Peale; his self-portrait, "The Artist in His Museum," portrays him lifting a curtain to reveal scientific specimens. Other artists represented throughout the collection include Mary Cassatt, Thomas Eakins, Childe Hassam, Robert Henri, Edward Hopper, Georgia O'Keefe, William Rush, Henry Ossawa Tanner, Benjamin West and Andrew Wyeth. Scheduled for 2015 are an exhibition on American Impressionism and the Garden Movement and a retrospective of the works of 20th century artist Norman Lewis. **Time:** Allow 1 hour minimum. **Hours:** Tues. and Thurs.-Fri. 10-4; Wed. 10-9, Sat.-Sun. 11-5. Guided tours are offered Tues.-Sun. at 1 and 2. Phone ahead to confirm tour schedule. Closed federal holidays. **Cost:** $15; $12 (ages 60+ and students with ID); $8 (ages 12-18); free (military with ID). **Phone:** (215) 972-7600. Race-Vine, 119

Samuel M.V. Hamilton Building, 128 N. Broad St., is part of the Pennsylvania Academy of the Fine Arts and features two floors of galleries with changing exhibits of multimedia works by American artists, including students, faculty and alumni. The early 20th-century building is a former automobile showroom and storage facility.

Powel House

Time: Allow 1 hour minimum. **Hours:** Tues.-Fri. 10-4, Wed. 10-9, Sat.-Sun. 11-5. Closed major holidays. Phone ahead to confirm schedule. **Cost:** $15; $12 (ages 60+ and students with ID); $8 (ages 13-18); free (military with ID). **Phone:** (215) 972-7600. Race-Vine, 119

PENNSYLVANIA HORTICULTURAL SOCIETY, 100 N. 20th St. on the fifth floor, houses gardening literature; a library is on the first floor. **Time:** Allow 30 minutes minimum. **Hours:** Mon.-Fri. 9:30-5. Closed major holidays. **Cost:** Free. **Phone:** (215) 988-8800. 19th, 69

SAVE **PHILADELPHIA HISTORY MUSEUM AT THE ATWATER KENT,** 15 S. 7th St., includes over 100,000 objects hundreds of items covering 330 years of Philadelphia history. Portraiture, sports and political memorabilia are on display. Objects from the city's founders and residents include President George Washington's writing desk from the 1790s and Joe Fraziers boxing gloves from the 1970s. Themed galleries fitted with interactive elements tell stories about such topics as culture and local manufacturing. **Hours:** Tues.-Sat. 10:30-4:30. **Cost:** $10; $8 (ages 64+); $6 (ages 13-18 and students with ID). **Phone:** (215) 685-4830. 8th, 65

 PHILADELPHIA MUSEUM OF ART—see Fairmount Park p. 250.

PHILADELPHIA ZOO—see Fairmount Park p. 250.

POLISH AMERICAN CULTURAL CENTER MUSEUM, opposite Independence National Historical Park at 308 Walnut St., maintains a portrait collection celebrating well-known Polish figures. Among the scientists, artists and leaders portrayed are Revolutionary War hero Gen. Casimir Pulaski and late 20th-century freedom fighter Lech Walesa. **Time:** Allow 30 minutes minimum. **Hours:** Mon.-Sat. 10-4, May-Dec.; Mon.-Fri. 10-4, rest of year. Closed major holidays. **Cost:** Free. **Phone:** (215) 922-1700. 2nd, 63

POWEL HOUSE is at 244 S. 3rd St. Built in 1765, this mansion has elegant furnishings and lovely gardens. **Time:** Allow 30 minutes minimum. **Hours:** Thurs.-Sat. noon-5, Sun. 1-5, Mar.-Dec. 31; by appointment rest of year. Last tour begins 1 hour before closing. Closed for events and holidays. **Cost:** $8; $6 (ages 62+ and students with ID); free (ages 0-6); $20 (family). **Phone:** (215) 627-0364. 2nd, 63

THE PRESBYTERIAN HISTORICAL SOCIETY, at 425 Lombard St., is the national archives and historical research center of the Presbyterian Church (U.S.A.). It was founded in 1852 to preserve the church's history. Changing exhibits also are presented. **Time:** Allow 30 minutes minimum. **Hours:** Mon.-Fri. 8:30-4:30. Reading room closes 15 minutes before closing. Closed major holidays. **Cost:** Donations. **Phone:** (215) 627-1852. 9th-10th & Locust, 142

RODIN MUSEUM—see Fairmount Park p. 250.

ROSENBACH MUSEUM AND LIBRARY, 2008-2010 Delancey Pl., exhibits books, manuscripts and fine and decorative art collected by the Rosenbach brothers. Though not always on view at the same time, collection highlights include manuscripts by Geoffrey Chaucer, Charles Dickens and James Joyce as well as books once owned by Abraham Lincoln and Herman Melville. Other authors and political figures represented include William Blake, Lewis Carroll, Miguel de Cervantes, Bram Stoker, Phyllis Wheatley, Thomas Jefferson and George Washington. Illustrations and manuscripts by author Maurice Sendak also are featured.

Note: The library will celebrate the 150th anniversary of Alice's Adventures in Wonderland with special exhibits and events about Lewis Carroll, his characters and the creation of Alice's fascinating world that brought us favorites like The Cheshire Cat, The Mad Hatter and The Queen of Hearts. It starts Oct. 14, 2015 and runs through Spring 2016. **Time:** Allow 1 hour minimum. **Hours:** Wed.-Thurs. noon-8, Tues. and Fri. noon-5, Sat.-Sun. noon-6. Last hour begins 1 hour before closing. Library open by appointment. Closed major holidays. **Cost:** $10; $8 (ages 65+); $5 (ages 5-18 and students with ID). **Phone:** (215) 732-1600.
GT 15th-16th & Locust, 140

RYERSS MUSEUM AND LIBRARY is at 7370 Central Ave. in Burholme Park. This Victorian house is on a hilltop and was built by the Ryerss family in 1859 to be used as a summer home. Since they loved animals, much of the interior is adorned with pieces related to animals including numerous portraits, and there is a pet cemetery on the grounds. Furnishings include Colonial and Victorian antiques as well as art and artifacts from Asia, the Americas and Europe. The house also includes a lending library.

Time: Allow 2 hours minimum. **Hours:** Fri.-Sun. 10-4. Self-guiding tours 10-3. Guided tours depart at 11 and 2. Closed major holidays. **Cost:** Free. **Phone:** (215) 685-0599 or (215) 685-0544.
GT Ryers, 273

ST. GEORGE'S UNITED METHODIST CHURCH, 235 N. 4th St. at the Benjamin Franklin Bridge, was dedicated in 1769 and is said to be one of the oldest Methodist churches continuously used for worship. In 1784 St. George's licensed the first African-American Methodist preacher in the United States. The adjoining Methodist Historical Center contains historic artifacts.

For guide service ring the bell at the side entrance on New Street. **Time:** Allow 30 minutes minimum. **Hours:** Mon.-Fri. 10-3. Access to historical library and archives by appointment only. Closed Jan. 1, Thanksgiving and Christmas. Phone

ahead to confirm schedule. **Cost:** Donations. **Phone:** (215) 925-7788. 5th, 64

ST. PETER'S CHURCH is at 313 Pine St. The Episcopal church was erected in 1761. Four signers of the Declaration of Independence worshiped at St. Peter's. Docents are available to answer questions on weekends. An audio tour of the church and churchyard also is available by cell phone. **Hours:** Daily 8-4. Sun. services at 9 and 11. Docents are available Sat. 11-3 and Sun. 1-3. **Cost:** Free. **Phone:** (215) 925-5968, or (215) 554-6161 for audio tour. 2nd, 63

THE SCHUYLKILL CENTER FOR ENVIRONMENTAL EDUCATION is off the Schuylkill Expwy. (I-76) exit 338, .9 mi. e. on Green Ln., 2.3 mi. n. on Ridge Ave., .2 mi. w. on Port Royal Ave., then just n. to 8480 Hagy's Mill Rd., following signs. Covering 340 acres of fields and forests, the site features 3.5 miles of hiking trails, ponds, streams, wetlands, outdoor art installations and a 2-acre organic farm. Hickory, buttonwood, tulip, poplar and sumac trees are abundant, as are mica schist and quartzite rocks.

Previously an agricultural area, the center now houses a children's discovery center, an environmental art gallery, interactive exhibits and meeting space. Pets are not permitted. **Time:** Allow 1 hour, 30 minutes minimum. **Hours:** Trails daily dawn to dusk. Center Mon.-Sat. 9-5. Trail maps are available outside main building on Sun. Closed major holidays. **Cost:** Free. **Phone:** (215) 482-7300.

THADDEUS KOSCIUSZKO NATIONAL MEMORIAL, 3rd and Pine sts., presents exhibits and audiovisual displays in English and Polish describing military engineer Thaddeus Kosciuszko's career in Poland as well as his contributions to the American Revolution. He rented a room in this boarding house 1797-98 after his exile from his native Poland. He was recovering from battle wounds and received many visitors, including Vice President Thomas Jefferson and Chief Little Turtle of the Miami tribe.

The exterior of the house has been restored and the interior is furnished in period. Military artifacts, books and paintings are on display; some are on loan from museums in Poland. **Time:** Allow 30 minutes minimum. **Hours:** Hours vary. Closed Jan. 1, Thanksgiving and Christmas. Phone ahead to confirm schedule. **Cost:** Free. **Phone:** (215) 597-9618, or (267) 519-4295, ext. 30, for audio tour. 2nd, 63

THE UNITED STATES MINT is at 151 N. Independence Mall East between Arch and Race sts.; the entrance is at the corner of Fifth and Arch sts. Utilizing video, audio, photographs, historic documents and samples of currency, the U.S. Mint gives visitors a thorough description of American coin production from the late 1700s to today. Visitors can watch coining operations from a vantage point 40 feet above the factory floor.

Note: Photo ID is required. Visitors must pass through a metal detector and are subject to search. Photography, food, purses, bags and packages are not permitted. **Time:** Allow 1 hour minimum. **Hours:** Mon.-Fri. 9-4:30 (also Sat. 9-4:30, early Sept.-late May). Closed major holidays, except Memorial Day, Labor Day and July 4. Phone ahead to confirm schedule. **Cost:** Free. **Phone:** (215) 408-0112.

🚇 5th, 64

UNIVERSITY OF PENNSYLVANIA, bounded by Chestnut, Pine, 32nd and 40th sts., was founded in 1740 and is considered to be one of the nation's leading educational centers. In 1765 the country's first medical school was established here. The 269-acre main campus in west Philadelphia is comprised of 151 buildings including the University of Pennsylvania Hospital. Tours of the campus are available through the Office of Undergraduate Admissions at 1 College Hall. **Hours:** Phone ahead for tour schedule. **Cost:** Free. **Phone:** (215) 898-7507.

🚇 36th, 74

Institute of Contemporary Art, 36th and Sansom sts. at the University of Pennsylvania, presents changing exhibitions of contemporary art. **Time:** Allow 1 hour minimum. **Hours:** Wed.-Fri. 11-6, Sat.-Sun. 11-5. Guided tours are available by appointment. Closed Jan. 1, Thanksgiving, Christmas and when exhibitions are being changed. Phone ahead to confirm schedule. **Cost:** Free. **Phone:** (215) 898-7108. 🚇 36th, 74

Penn Museum, 3260 South St. on the University of Pennsylvania urban campus, displays outstanding archeological and anthropological collections from around the world. Exhibits include artifacts from ancient Egypt, the Near East, Asia, Central America, North America, Mesopotamia and the Mediterranean. Visitors can see conservators at work on Egyptian mummies in an artifact lab. Special events are held throughout the year.

Time: Allow 1 hour minimum. **Hours:** Tues.-Sun. 10-5 (also first Wed. of the month 5-8). Closed major holidays. **Cost:** $15; $13 (ages 65+); $10 (ages 6-17 and students with ID); free (military with ID). Combination ticket with Mütter Museum of the College of Physicians of Philadelphia $26; $22 (ages 65+); $16 (ages 6-17, students and military with ID). **Phone:** (215) 898-4000.

🍴 🚇 University City, 180

WAGNER FREE INSTITUTE OF SCIENCE is at 1700 W. Montgomery Ave. Incorporated in 1855, the institute contains more than 100,000 mineral, fossil and zoological specimens. Displayed in cherry wood cases built in the 1880s, the exhibits include mounted animal skeletons and shells from around the world. As a continuing resource for scholarly research, it houses the Library and Archives, which

also showcases items highlighting the history of the institution.

Evening and weekend events are held throughout the year. **Time:** Allow 1 hour, 30 minutes minimum. **Hours:** Museum and library Tues.-Fri. 9-4. Guided tours and library use are available by appointment; library appointments should be made at least 1 week in advance. Closed major holidays. **Cost:** Donations. Guided tour $15; $10 (ages 65+); $5 (ages 0-17 with adult). **Phone:** (215) 763-6529.

🚇 Cecil B. Moore, 126

THE WOODLANDS, 4000 Woodland Ave., is the former 600-acre estate of William Hamilton. Originally built in the 1740s, Hamilton embarked some 40 years later on a major renovation that more than doubled size of the house and re-created it in the neoclassical style of architects Robert and James Adam. .

Today the property spans 54 acres and is still home to Hamilton's house and a cemetery that dates back to 1840. Artists Thomas Eakins and Rembrandt Peale are among the more than 30,000 interred. Hamilton's influence remains as many of the trees and plant varieties once thrived in his English-style garden. The grounds are commonly used as a park and to hold events such as special cemetery tours and craft fairs. House tours are offered. Rubbings of gravestones are not permitted. **Hours:** Grounds open daily dawn-dusk. Hamilton Mansion tours depart Wed. on the hour 10-2, Apr.-Oct. Visitors should arrive 10-15 minutes prior to tour departure. Walk-in tours are offered at other times based on staff availability. . Closed major holidays. **Cost:** Grounds free. Hamilton Mansion tour $10; $8 (senior citizens). **Phone:** (215) 386-2181. 🄶🅃

WOODMERE ART MUSEUM, 4 mi. s. of Pennsylvania Tpke./I-276 exit 333 at 9201 Germantown Ave., has paintings and decorative art spanning the 18th- through 20th centuries. The Victorian home and art collection of Charles Knox Smith form the nucleus of the museum. Of particular interest is the collection of 19th-century American paintings, which includes works by Thomas Anshutz, Frederic Church, Jasper Cropsey, Edward Moran and Benjamin West.

Changing exhibits often focus on local artists. **Time:** Allow 30 minutes minimum. **Hours:** Tues.-Fri. 10-5 (also Fri. 5-8:45), Sat. 10-6, Sun. 10-5. Closed major holidays. **Cost:** Donations. A fee is charged for special exhibitions. **Phone:** (215) 247-0476.

🚇 Chestnut Hill East, 260

WYCK HOUSE, GARDEN, AND FARM, 6026 Germantown Ave., is the 2.5-acre estate that served as the home to nine generations of a prominent Quaker family who lived here 1689-1973. Tour guides show visitors through the house, which is filled with mementos and furniture offering a glimpse into American history. The grounds include a well-groomed rose garden widely recognized as the oldest rose garden growing in its original plan; a sprawling farm and woodlot; and several outbuildings, including a coach house, icehouse and smokehouse.

Time: Allow 2 hours minimum. **Hours:** House and garden guided tours are offered Thurs.-Sat. 1-4, Apr.-Nov. Self-guiding tours are available Fri. 1-4, June-Nov. (during the weekly farmers market). Closed major holidays. **Cost:** Guided tour $8. Self-guiding tour free. **Phone:** (215) 848-1690.
⛩ 🚇 Germantown, 267

Sightseeing
Boat Tours
The *Spirit of Philadelphia* offers narrated 2-hour lunch and dinner sightseeing cruises on the Delaware River. Cruises depart from Columbus Boulevard and Lombard Circle at Penn's Landing; phone (866) 455-3866.

RIDE THE DUCKS tours depart from jct. 6th and Chestnut sts. 80-minute tours are given aboard an amphibious vehicle, taking visitors through historic Philadelphia on land and on a cruise on the Delaware River. Four of the sightseeing highlights are Betsy Ross House, Independence Hall, the Philadelphia Museum of Art and City Hall. The captain provides humorous commentary while giving historical information about the sites along the way.

Time: Allow 1 hour, 30 minutes minimum. **Hours:** Tours daily, Apr.-Oct. Departure times vary; phone ahead to confirm schedule. **Cost:** $29; $26 (ages 62+ and military with ID); $19 (ages 4-12); $5 (ages 0-3). **Phone:** (215) 227-3825, or (877) 887-8225 for tickets. 🚇 5th, 64

Bus and Trolley Tours

MURAL ARTS TOURS depart from Mural Arts at The Gallery kiosk, on the second level of The Gallery at Market East, at the 9th and Market sts. entrance (most tours). Guided trolley and walking tours highlight community history and the stories behind the creation of the murals. The neighborhoods and themes of the 2-hour trolley tours vary each week, but most tours showcase about 35 murals. The Center City and Broad Street neighborhood tours showcase most of the murals. Other tours include two Mural Mile Walking Tours highlighting a wide variety of iconic Center City murals, and the Love Letter train tour featuring 50 rooftop murals in West Philadelphia. Other trolley tours, walking tours and bike tours also are available.

Hours: Trolley tours depart Fri. at 11, Sat. at 10, June-Aug. Mural Mile tours depart Wed. and Sat.-Sun. at 11, June-Aug. Love Letter tours depart Sat. at 10:30 and Sun. at 1; phone for departure times. Phone ahead to confirm schedule. **Cost:** $20-$30 depending on tour. Reservations are recommended. **Phone:** (215) 925-3633 or (800) 537-7676.
🚇 8th and Market, 125

PHILADELPHIA TROLLEY WORKS, THE BIG BUS CO. AND 76 CARRIAGE CO. tours depart from jct. 5th and Market sts. with 21 stops along the

Mural Arts Tours

loop. The 90-minute tour aboard a double-decker bus or a Victorian-style trolley passes and stops at most of Philadelphia's major attractions, from Independence Visitor Center to Philadelphia Zoo, and includes the Please Touch Museum, Philadelphia Museum of Art, The Franklin Institute, and Penn's Landing. Horse-drawn carriage and walking tours also are available.

Tickets can be purchased at the Independence Visitor Center. Free unlimited, interchangeable reboarding is permitted on the bus or trolley for the timeframe specified on the ticket. **Hours:** Daily 9:30-5, Apr.-Nov. (also Sat.-Sun. 5-6, July-Aug.); daily 10-4, rest of year. Hours vary frequently; phone ahead to confirm schedule. Closed Jan. 1 and Christmas. **Cost:** Fare, valid for 24 hours, $27; $10 (ages 4-12). Fare, valid for 48 hours, $32; $30 (senior citizens) $10 (ages 4-12). Phone ahead to confirm rates. **Phone:** (215) 923-8516 for horse drawn carriage. 🚇 40th, 76

Food Tours
The following bulleted tour is presented for informational purposes as a service to members and has not been inspected by AAA.

- **TASTE OF PHILLY FOOD TOUR** departs from the Reading Terminal Market information desk at jct. 12th and Filbert sts. The 75-minute walking tour, which provides a historical overview of the market includes stops at several of the market's vendors, including longtime merchants. Participants receive several small food bites so they can experience some of Philly's iconic treats. **Hours:** Wed. and Sat. at 10; additional tours are offered in summer. Phone ahead to confirm schedule.

Cost: $15.95; $8.95 (ages 7-11). Reservations are required. **Phone:** (215) 545-8007.

Guided Walking Tours

Joining Chef Joe Poon's narrated Wok 'n Walk Tour is a good way to see Philadelphia's Chinatown. Tours, which depart daily from 1002 Arch St. in Chinatown, include a five-course meal. Reservations are required; phone (215) 928-9333.

THE CONSTITUTIONAL WALKING TOUR departs from the main entrance of the National Constitution Center (near the stone benches) at 525 Arch St., and includes 21 stops on a 1.25-mile route. Knowledgeable and friendly guides provide historical context for some of the city's most prominent sites, including the Betsy Ross House, Christ Church and its nearby burial ground, Congress Hall, Declaration House, Franklin Court, Independence Hall, Liberty Bell Center, National Constitution Center and Old City Hall.

The tour does not include the interiors of any of the buildings. **Time:** Allow 1 hour, 15 minutes minimum. **Hours:** Tours depart Mon.-Sat. at 10, noon and 2, Sun. at 11, 1 and 3, Apr.-Nov. **Cost:** $17.50; $12.50 (ages 3-12); $55 (family, two adults and two children ages 3-12). Reservations are required. **Phone:** (215) 525-1776. 🈲 5th, 64

FRANKLIN'S FOOTSTEPS WALKING TOUR departs from the Independence Visitor Center at jct. 6th and Market sts.; tickets can be purchased inside the visitor center. The route includes more than 30 sites and offers visitors a thorough history of Revolutionary Philadelphia from the perspective of Benjamin Franklin, whose many titles include diplomat, inventor and philosopher. Detailed insights into Independence National Historical Park are shared at such stops as Carpenters' Hall, Christ Church, Independence Hall and Liberty Bell Center.

The tour does not include the interiors of any of the buildings. **Time:** Allow 1 hour, 30 minutes minimum. **Hours:** Tours depart Mon.-Fri. 11-3, Sat.-Sun. 11-4, May-Oct. **Cost:** $19; $17 (ages 65+); $12 (ages 4-12). Combination ticket with Big Bus and Walking Tour $42; $40 (seniors). Phone ahead to confirm rates. **Phone:** (215) 389-8687. 🈲 5th, 64

SAVE **GHOST TOURS OF PHILADELPHIA** departs from Signers Garden at jct. 5th and Chestnut sts.; tickets can be purchased at Ben and Betsy's Gift Shop at 401 Chestnut St. and from the Independence Visitor Center at jct. 6th and Market sts. This 90-minute candlelight walking tour through Society Hill, Old City and Independence National Historical Park takes visitors past places that are said to be haunted and includes a number of ghost stories. Stops on the route include Independence Hall, Washington Square and the cemetery at St. Peter's Church. Along the way you'll hear about early American history, folklore, and maybe even about Edgar Allan Poe's time in Philadelphia. Other tours also are offered on a more limited basis; phone for details.

The tour does not include the interiors of any of the buildings. **Hours:** Tours depart daily at 7:30 (also Thurs.-Sat. at 9:30), July-Aug.; daily at 7:30 (also Fri.-Sat. at 9:30), in June and Oct.; daily at &:30 (also Sat. at 9:30) in Sept.; daily at 7:30, Apr.-May; Fri.-Sat. at 7:30, in Mar. and Nov. Visitors should arrive 15 minutes prior to departure. **Cost:** $17; $10 (ages 4-12). With advance reservations $10; $8 (ages 4-12). Reservations are recommended. **Phone:** (215) 413-1997 for information or to purchase tickets. 🈲 5th, 64

SPIRITS OF '76 GHOST TOUR departs from Mrs. K's Koffee Shop at 325 Chestnut St. at jct. 4th St. Guides share haunted Philadelphia facts and folklore, including tales about Edgar Allan Poe and the only prisoner to escape the city's Eastern State Penitentiary without being captured, on this tour through Old City. The route features more than 20 sites, some of which are said to be haunted.

The tour does not include the interiors of any of the buildings. **Time:** Allow 1 hour, 15 minutes minimum. **Hours:** Tours depart Mon.-Wed. at 7:30, Thurs.-Fri. at 7:30 and 9:30, Sat. at 6, 7:30 and 9:30, Sun. at 6 and 7:30, in Oct.; daily at 7:30 (also Thurs.-Sat. at 9:30), July-Aug.; Wed.-Sun. at 7:30, in June and Sept.; Thurs.-Sat. at 7:30, in May; Thurs.-Sat. at 7:30, in Apr. and Nov. Phone ahead to confirm schedule. **Cost:** $17.50; $12.50 (ages 3-12); $55 (family, two adults and two children ages 3-12). Reservations are recommended. **Phone:** (215) 525-1776. 🈲 5th, 64

Self-guiding Tours

The heart of historic Philadelphia lends itself to a walking tour. A stroll through the narrow cobblestone streets among restored Georgian and Colonial buildings is the best way to discover the essence of the city and to assimilate its 18th-century atmosphere. A good way to see historic Philadelphia is to combine the walking tour with stops at the attractions along the way. The names of sites listed in detail in the Attractions section are printed in bold type. Even if you do not tour a listed site, reading the attraction listing when you reach that point will make the tour more interesting. This tour takes approximately 5 hours, which allows for a leisurely pace.

Start at **City Hall** at Centre Square. Walking east on Market Street, you pass Macy's department store on the right. If you're in this area on a weekday afternoon, stop in for the 1-hour 3:30 tour of the historic Wanamaker building ($10, cash only); phone (215) 241-9000 (press 1, then ext. 2408). A few blocks farther on Market Street at 9th Street is a major shopping mall, the Gallery at Market East, which includes Burlington Coat Factory.

Continue east on Market Street to 7th Street, where you will find the shops and restaurants of Market Place East and the **Declaration House.**

Cross 7th Street to the **Philadelphia History Museum at the Atwater Kent.** Upon leaving the museum, take the walkway to the right to 6th Street for a stop at the **Liberty Bell Center,** which houses the famous symbol of American freedom. From there, walk across Chestnut Street to **Independence Hall.**

Within the next 3 blocks of Chestnut are numerous historical buildings that are part of the **Independence National Historical Park.** They include **Congress Hall** and **Old City Hall,** which flank Independence Hall; **Second Bank of the United States Portrait Gallery;** the **New Hall Military Museum; Carpenters' Hall; Todd House;** and the **Bishop White House.**

Facing Independence Hall is the renovated Philadelphia Bourse. The historic merchants' exchange now houses shops, restaurants and an information center on the first floor.

Just east on Chestnut Street is a path leading to **Franklin Court,** where a steel frame suggests the shape of Franklin's home, destroyed in 1812. Traces of the original foundation are visible.

From Franklin Court, exit onto Market Street and walk east to 2nd Street. Take 2nd Street north to **Christ Church,** on the left. Continue north 1.5 blocks, then stroll through **Elfreth's Alley** on the right. The 6-foot-wide alley is lined with a number of quaint, modest houses from the early 1700s. Farther north on 2nd Street is **Fireman's Hall Museum,** a museum depicting the history of fire fighting in America with memorabilia, graphics, films and antique equipment.

From this point turn around and return to Arch Street. Turn right on Arch Street and walk a half-block to the **Betsy Ross House,** on your right. After a visit, proceed west and cross 3rd Street toward the **Historic Arch Street Meeting House,** a Quaker gathering place since the early 1800s, which is on the left. The next block is occupied by the **United States Mint,** where pocket change and commemorative coins are made.

To end the tour, walk south to Market Street on 5th Street. You will pass the **Free Quaker Meeting House** on the right. Once on Market Street you can walk back to the Gallery at Market East to do some shopping or perhaps rest your feet, relax and refresh at one of the many restaurants in the area. At City Tavern, tucked away at 2nd and Walnut, diners experience a taste of the Colonial past. The 1792 building was once an unofficial meeting place for the First Continental Congress.

Another excellent area for the visitor on foot is **Penn's Landing,** which hosts concerts and events during summer. Catch a glimpse of Philadelphia's nautical past at the **Independence Seaport Museum,** home to the World War II submarine *Becuna.* The Philadelphia Vietnam Veterans Memorial, Columbus Boulevard and Spruce Street, and A World Sculpture Garden, with sculpture given to the city during the Bicentennial, also are at Penn's Landing.

Pennsylvania Quest for Freedom: Philadelphia, features stops showcasing African-American history, including the Underground Railroad. Brochures can be picked up at the Independence Visitor Center and at many of the tour's sites.

The Historic Philadelphia Center offers brochures about the Once Upon A Nation storytelling program. Between Memorial Day and Labor Day, there are 13 benches scattered throughout historic Philadelphia where passersby can stop to listen to stories about historic sites and influential people from the past.

Philadelphia boasts more than 3,000 murals, so check some out while you're in the city. Seventeen murals in Center City make up Mural Mile; a plaque at each stop contains the mural hotline number, (215) 525-1577, so you can call to hear audio commentary on your cell phone.

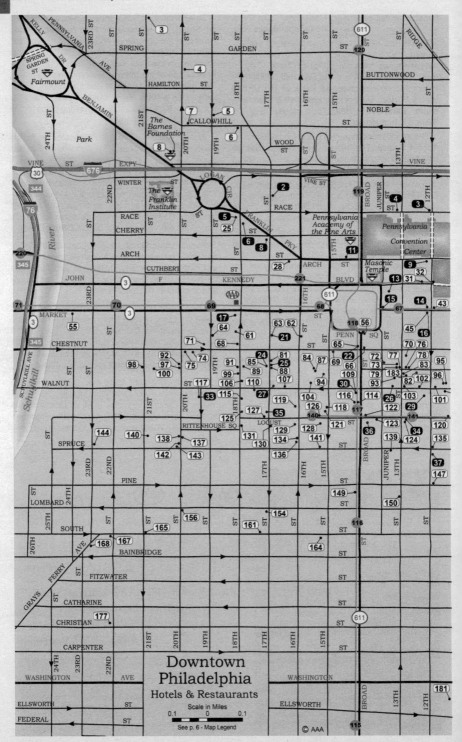

Downtown
Philadelphia
Hotels & Restaurants

Scale in Miles
0.1   0   0.1

See p. 6 - Map Legend

© AAA

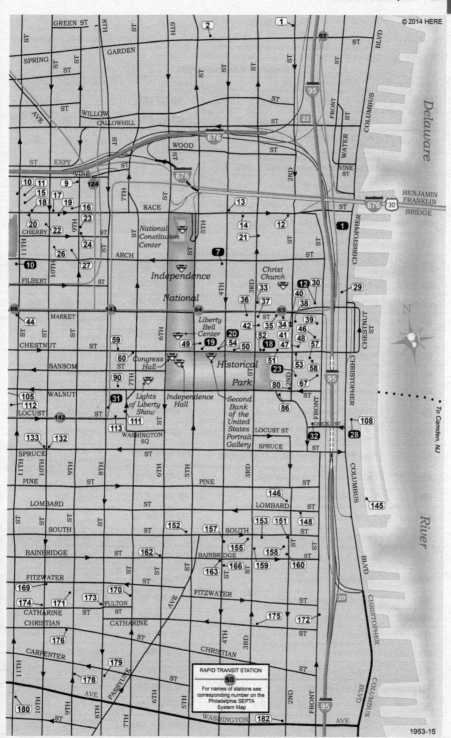

© 2014 HERE

1953-15

Downtown Philadelphia

This index helps you "spot" where approved hotels and restaurants are located on the corresponding detailed maps. Hotel daily rate range is for comparison only. Restaurant price range is a combination of lunch and/or dinner. Turn to the listing page for more detailed rate and price information and consult display ads for special promotions.

DOWNTOWN PHILADELPHIA

Map Page	Hotels	Diamond Rated	Rate Range	Page
1 p. 266	Holiday Inn Express Philadelphia/Penn's Landing	◆◆◆	Rates not provided	288
2 p. 266	**Sheraton Philadelphia Downtown**	◆◆◆	$129-$499 (SAVE)	290
3 p. 266	**Four Points by Sheraton - Philadelphia City Center**	◆◆◆	$109-$459 (SAVE)	286
4 p. 266	**Hampton Inn Philadelphia Center City/Convention Center** *(See ad p. 286.)*	◆◆◆	$139-$309 (SAVE)	287
5 p. 266	Four Seasons Hotel Philadelphia	◆◆◆◆	Rates not provided	286
6 p. 266	Embassy Suites Hotel Philadelphia - Center City	◆◆◆	$159-$579	286
7 p. 266	**Wyndham Philadelphia Historic District**	◆◆◆	$129-$409 (SAVE)	291
8 p. 266	**The Windsor Suites**	◆◆◆	Rates not provided (SAVE)	291
9 p. 266	Home2 Suites by Hilton Philadelphia Convention Center	◆◆◆	$149-$399	288
10 p. 266	Hilton Garden Inn Philadelphia Center City	◆◆◆	$139-$309	287
11 p. 266	**Le Meridien Philadelphia**	◆◆◆◆	$139-$999 (SAVE)	288
12 p. 266	**Penn's View Hotel**	◆◆◆	$159-$349 (SAVE)	289
13 p. 266	Courtyard by Marriott Philadelphia Downtown	◆◆◆	$167-$275	285
14 p. 266	**Philadelphia Downtown Marriott Hotel**	◆◆◆	$216-$355 (SAVE)	289
15 p. 266	Residence Inn by Marriott Center City Philadelphia	◆◆◆	$174-$286	289
16 p. 266	**Loews Philadelphia Hotel**	◆◆◆	$149-$489 (SAVE)	289
17 p. 266	**Sonesta Philadelphia**	◆◆◆	Rates not provided (SAVE)	290
18 p. 266	**BEST WESTERN PLUS Independence Park Hotel**	◆◆◆	$99-$320 (SAVE)	285
19 p. 266	**Hotel Monaco Philadelphia, A Kimpton Hotel**	◆◆◆◆	Rates not provided (SAVE)	288
20 p. 266	**Omni Hotel at Independence Park**	◆◆◆◆	Rates not provided (SAVE)	289
21 p. 266	**The Westin Philadelphia**	◆◆◆◆	$109-$1999 (SAVE)	290
22 p. 266	The Ritz-Carlton Philadelphia	◆◆◆◆	Rates not provided	290
23 p. 266	**The Thomas Bond House B & B**	◆◆	$125-$205 (SAVE)	290
24 p. 266	**Sofitel Philadelphia**	◆◆◆◆	Rates not provided (SAVE)	290
25 p. 266	**Hotel Palomar-Philadelphia**	◆◆◆◆	Rates not provided (SAVE)	288
26 p. 266	**Holiday Inn Express Midtown**	◆◆◆	$169-$349 (SAVE)	287
27 p. 266	**The Latham Hotel**	◆◆◆	$129-$549 (SAVE)	288
28 p. 266	**Hilton Philadelphia at Penn's Landing**	◆◆◆	$99-$499 (SAVE)	287
29 p. 266	Rodeway Inn	◆◆	$79-$700	290
30 p. 266	**Hyatt at The Bellevue**	◆◆◆◆	$119-$449 (SAVE)	288
31 p. 266	**Morris House Hotel**	◆◆◆	$199-$499 (SAVE)	289
32 p. 266	**Sheraton Philadelphia Society Hill**	◆◆◆	$159 (SAVE)	290
33 p. 266	**The Rittenhouse**	◆◆◆◆◆	Rates not provided (SAVE)	289

DOWNTOWN PHILADELPHIA (cont'd)

Map Page	Hotels (cont'd)	Diamond Rated	Rate Range	Page
34 p. 266	**The Independent Hotel Philadelphia**	◆◆◆	$129-$296 [SAVE]	288
35 p. 266	**Radisson Blu Warwick Hotel, Philadelphia**	◆◆◆	$229-$599 [SAVE]	289
36 p. 266	**DoubleTree by Hilton Philadelphia Center City**	◆◆◆	$89-$309 [SAVE]	286
37 p. 266	**Alexander Inn** *(See ad p. 285.)*	◆◆◆	$119-$159 [SAVE]	285

Map Page	Restaurants	Diamond Rated	Cuisine	Price Range	Page
1 p. 266	Seiko Japanese Restaurant	◆◆	Japanese	$7-$24	302
2 p. 266	Silk City Diner, Bar & Lounge	◆◆	American	$8-$18	302
3 p. 266	The Belgian Cafe	◆◆	Belgian	$9-$20	292
4 p. 266	McCrossen's Tavern	◆◆	American	$9-$19	298
5 p. 266	Rose Tattoo Cafe	◆◆	Continental	$11-$30	301
6 p. 266	Sabrina's Cafe & Spencer's Too	◆◆	American	$6-$18	302
7 p. 266	Pizzeria Vetri	◆◆	Pizza	$8-$18	300
8 p. 266	The Garden Restaurant	◆◆◆	American	$14-$19	296
9 p. 266	Sang Kee Peking Duck House	◆◆	Chinese	$7-$16	302
10 p. 266	Vietnam Palace Restaurant	◆◆	Vietnamese	$8-$16	304
11 p. 266	Vietnam Restaurant	◆◆	Vietnamese	$8-$15	304
12 p. 266	Race Street Cafe	◆◆	American	$8-$19	301
13 p. 266	Kisso Sushi Bar	◆◆	Japanese	$7-$23	297
14 p. 266	DiNardo's Famous Seafood	◆◆	Seafood	$11-$48	294
15 p. 266	Yakitori Boy	◆◆	Japanese	$5-$18	304
16 p. 266	Pho Xe Lua Viet Thai Restaurant	◆◆	Vietnamese	$5-$12	300
17 p. 266	Rising Tide	◆◆	Chinese	$6-$15	301
18 p. 266	Ocean Harbor	◆◆	Chinese	$5-$15	299
19 p. 266	Shiao Lan Kung	◆◆	Chinese	$8-$18	302
20 p. 266	Joy Tsin Lau Chinese Restaurant	◆◆	Chinese	$7-$28	296
21 p. 266	La Locanda Del Ghiottone	◆◆	Italian	$16-$31	297
22 p. 266	Imperial Inn	◆◆	Chinese	$6-$20	296
23 p. 266	Ray's Cafe	◆◆	Regional Chinese	$8-$19	301
24 p. 266	Harmony Vegetarian Restaurant	◆◆	Vegetarian	$6-$13	296
25 p. 266	Fountain Restaurant	◆◆◆◆	Continental	$21-$44	295
26 p. 266	Penang	◆◆	Asian	$6-$20	299
27 p. 266	Rangoon Burmese Restaurant	◆◆	Burmese	$7-$17	301
28 p. 266	Tir na Nog, Bar & Grill	◆◆	Irish	$9-$27	303
29 p. 266	La Veranda	◆◆◆	Italian	$10-$40	297
30 p. 266	Ristorante Panorama	◆◆◆	Regional Italian	$22-$30	301
31 p. 266	Maggiano's Little Italy	◆◆◆	Italian	$10-$47	298
32 p. 266	Di Nic's Roast Beef & Pork	◆	Sandwiches	$5-$8	294
33 p. 266	Bistro 7	◆◆◆	French	$24-$32	292
34 p. 266	Campo's Deli	◆	Sandwiches	$7-$10	293
35 p. 266	Marmont Steakhouse & Bar	◆◆	American	$8-$45	298

Map Page	Restaurants (cont'd)	Diamond Rated	Cuisine	Price Range	Page
36 p. 266	Fork	◆◆◆	American	$16-$40	295
37 p. 266	Pizzicato	◆◆	Italian	$7-$26	300
38 p. 266	The Continental Restaurant & Martini Bar	◆◆◆	American	$8-$32	294
39 p. 266	La Famiglia	◆◆◆	Italian	$7-$43	297
40 p. 266	Cuba Libre Restaurant & Rum Bar	◆◆◆	Cuban	$8-$33	294
41 p. 266	Serrano	◆◆	International	$14-$25	302
42 p. 266	Farmicia	◆◆◆	Continental	$8-$29	295
43 p. 266	Hard Rock Cafe	◆◆	American	$15-$23 [SAVE]	296
44 p. 266	Down Home Diner	◆◆	American	$5-$13	295
45 p. 266	Bank and Bourbon	◆◆◆	American	$12-$34	292
46 p. 266	Spasso Italian Grill	◆◆	Italian	$11-$25	303
47 p. 266	The Plough and The Stars Irish Restaurant & Bar	◆◆◆	Continental	$8-$24	300
48 p. 266	Han Dynasty	◆◆	Chinese	$12-$23	296
49 p. 266	Red Owl Tavern	◆◆	American	$14-$26	301
50 p. 266	Buddakan	◆◆◆	Asian	$15-$48	293
51 p. 266	Amada	◆◆◆	Spanish Small Plates	$15-$45	291
52 p. 266	Barra Restaurant	◆◆◆	Italian	$9-$26	292
53 p. 266	Ariana Restaurant	◆◆	Afghan	$8-$16	291
54 p. 266	Azalea	◆◆◆	American	$11-$30	291
55 p. 266	Bistro St. Tropez	◆◆◆	Regional French	$8-$29	293
56 p. 266	McCormick & Schmick's	◆◆◆	Seafood	$12-$46	298
57 p. 266	Karma Restaurant & Bar	◆◆	Indian	$11-$22	297
58 p. 266	Kabul, Cuisine of Afghanistan	◆◆	Afghan	$15-$20	296
59 p. 266	Morimoto	◆◆◆◆	Japanese	$26-$45	299
60 p. 266	Jones	◆◆	Continental	$10-$26	296
61 p. 266	Pastrami & Things	◆	Deli	$4-$10	299
62 p. 266	R2L	◆◆◆	New American	$26-$42	301
63 p. 266	Winthorpe & Valentine Bar and Grill	◆◆◆	American	$10-$34	304
64 p. 266	Matyson	◆◆◆	American	$10-$27	298
65 p. 266	10 Arts Bistro & Lounge by Eric Ripert	◆◆◆	American	$12-$35	291
66 p. 266	The Capital Grille	◆◆◆	Steak	$13-$48	293
67 p. 266	Pagoda Noodle Cafe	◆◆	Chinese	$6-$28	299
68 p. 266	The Continental Midtown	◆◆	American	$6-$32	293
69 p. 266	Del Frisco's Double Eagle Steak House	◆◆◆	Steak	$14-$59	294
70 p. 266	Spice 28	◆◆	Asian Fusion	$8-$26	303
71 p. 266	Devil's Alley Bar and Grill	◆◆	American	$10-$19	294
72 p. 266	McGillin's Olde Ale House	◆◆	American	$6-$13	298
73 p. 266	Lolita	◆◆◆	Mexican	$18-$24	297
74 p. 266	Le Castagne	◆◆◆	Northern Italian	$16-$45	297

Map Page	Restaurants (cont'd)	Diamond Rated	Cuisine	Price Range	Page
75 p. 266	Jane G's	◆◆	Chinese	$10-$29	296
76 p. 266	El Vez	◆◆◆	Mexican	$8-$28	295
77 p. 266	Barbuzzo	◆◆◆	Mediterranean	$10-$17	292
78 p. 266	Raw Sushi & Sake Lounge	◆◆◆	Sushi	$10-$29	301
79 p. 266	Zavino	◆◆◆	Italian	$13-$18	304
80 p. 266	**City Tavern**	◆◆◆	American	$9-$27	293
81 p. 266	Davio's Northern Italian Steakhouse	◆◆◆	Northern Italian	$12-$55	294
82 p. 266	Fergie's Pub	◆◆	Irish	$6-$14	295
83 p. 266	Vintage Wine Bar & Bistro	◆◆	French	$11-$22	304
84 p. 266	Nodding Head Brewery & Restaurant	◆◆	American	$5-$20	299
85 p. 266	Liberté	◆◆◆	French	$14-$32	297
86 p. 266	Positano Coast by Aldo Lamberti	◆◆◆	Southern Italian Small Plates	$7-$30	300
87 p. 266	Oyster House	◆◆	Seafood	$14-$28	299
88 p. 266	Square 1682	◆◆	New American	$11-$32	303
89 p. 266	Tria	◆◆◆	Continental	$4-$10	303
90 p. 266	El Fuego	◆	Mexican	$4-$10	295
91 p. 266	The Dandelion	◆◆◆	American	$13-$28	294
92 p. 266	Tinto	◆◆◆	Spanish	$10-$55	303
93 p. 266	Sampan	◆◆◆	Asian	$10-$25	302
94 p. 266	Ocean Prime	◆◆◆	American	$27-$49	299
95 p. 266	Irish Pub	◆◆	Irish	$4-$9	296
96 p. 266	Maoz Vegetarian	◆	Vegetarian	$5-$8	298
97 p. 266	Village Whiskey	◆◆◆	American	$10-$26	304
98 p. 266	Day by Day	◆◆	American	$7-$15	294
99 p. 266	Serafina Rittenhouse	◆◆◆	Italian	$9-$29	302
100 p. 266	Porcini Restaurant	◆◆	Italian	$18-$26	300
101 p. 266	Caribou Café	◆◆	French	$10-$23	293
102 p. 266	Aki Japanese Fusion Restaurant & Sake Bar	◆◆	Japanese	$9-$26	291
103 p. 266	Walnut Street Supper Club	◆◆◆	Italian	$17-$35	304
104 p. 266	Tiramisu	◆◆◆	Italian	$12-$35	303
105 p. 266	Moriarty's Restaurant & Irish Pub	◆◆	American	$8-$24	298
106 p. 266	a.kitchen	◆◆	American	$8-$26	291
107 p. 266	Alma de Cuba	◆◆◆	Cuban	$5-$32	291
108 p. 266	Keating's River Grill	◆◆◆	American	$12-$32	297
109 p. 266	**XIX (Nineteen) Restaurant**	◆◆◆◆	American	$11-$40	304
110 p. 266	Pietro's Coal Oven Pizzeria	◆◆	Italian	$9-$18	300
111 p. 266	Talula's Garden	◆◆◆	American	$30-$50	303
112 p. 266	Strangelove's	◆◆	American	$10-$19	303
113 p. 266	Ristorante La Buca	◆◆	Italian	$11-$30	301
114 p. 266	Bliss	◆◆◆	New American	$12-$36	293

Map Page	Restaurants (cont'd)	Diamond Rated	Cuisine	Price Range	Page
115 p. 266	Rouge	▼▼▼	American	$12-$28	301
116 p. 266	The Palm Restaurant	▼▼▼	American	$31-$57	299
117 p. 266	**Lacroix At The Rittenhouse**	▼▼▼▼	American	$18-$75	297
118 p. 266	Shiroi Hana Japanese Restaurant	▼▼	Japanese	$11-$35	302
119 p. 266	Bellini Grill	▼▼	Italian	$12-$32	292
120 p. 266	Garces Trading Company	▼▼	Continental	$8-$29	295
121 p. 266	Good Dog Bar & Restaurant	▼▼	American	$9-$21	296
122 p. 266	Varalli Restaurant	▼▼▼	Northern Italian	$18-$24	304
123 p. 266	Perch Pub	▼▼	American	$8-$19	300
124 p. 266	Little Nonna's	▼▼▼	Italian	$11-$26	297
125 p. 266	Devon Seafood Grill	▼▼▼	Seafood	$13-$66	294
126 p. 266	Misconduct Tavern	▼▼	American	$8-$15	298
127 p. 266	The Prime Rib	▼▼▼	Steak	$20-$50	300
128 p. 266	Fado Irish Pub	▼▼	Irish	$10-$17	295
129 p. 266	Los Catrines Tequila's	▼▼▼	Mexican	$10-$28	297
130 p. 266	The Black Sheep Pub & Restaurant	▼▼	American	$8-$23	293
131 p. 266	Barclay Prime	▼▼▼▼	Steak	$20-$100	292
132 p. 266	Varga Bar	▼▼	American	$8-$21	304
133 p. 266	Kanela	▼▼	Mediterranean	$9-$32	297
134 p. 266	Bistro La Viola	▼▼	Italian	$14-$18	292
135 p. 266	Tria	▼▼▼	Continental	$9-$11	303
136 p. 266	Monk's Cafe	▼▼	Belgian	$7-$24	298
137 p. 266	Twenty Manning Grill	▼▼▼	American	$13-$27	304
138 p. 266	D'Angelo's Ristorante Italiano	▼▼	Italian	$10-$40	294
139 p. 266	Vetri	▼▼▼▼	Italian	$155	304
140 p. 266	Friday Saturday Sunday	▼▼	American	$21-$29	295
141 p. 266	Fox and Hound	▼▼	American	$8-$16	295
142 p. 266	Seafood Unlimited	▼▼	Seafood	$11-$18	302
143 p. 266	Audrey Claire	▼▼▼	Mediterranean	$17-$26	291
144 p. 266	Mama Palma's	▼▼	Italian	$8-$25	298
145 p. 266	**Moshulu**	▼▼▼▼	International	$15-$35	299
146 p. 266	Pizzeria Stella	▼▼	Pizza	$9-$19	300
147 p. 266	Mixto	▼▼	Latin American	$8-$24	298
148 p. 266	**Bistro Romano**	▼▼▼	Regional Italian	$17-$29	292
149 p. 266	Sbraga	▼▼▼	American	$55-$95	302
150 p. 266	Amis	▼▼▼	Italian	$10-$26	291
151 p. 266	Bridget Foy's	▼▼	American	$11-$22	293
152 p. 266	South Street Souvlaki	▼▼	Greek	$5-$25	303
153 p. 266	Lovash Indian Cuisine	▼▼	Northern Indian	$9-$25	298
154 p. 266	Bistro La Baia	▼▼	Italian	$11-$16	292

Map Page	Restaurants (cont'd)	Diamond Rated	Cuisine	Price Range	Page
(155) p. 266	Jon's Bar & Grille	♦♦	American	$7-$29	296
(156) p. 266	Pub and Kitchen	♦♦♦	American	$9-$26	300
(157) p. 266	Alyan's	♦	Middle Eastern	$5-$14	291
(158) p. 266	Fez Moroccan Cuisine	♦♦	Moroccan	$13-$25	295
(159) p. 266	Hosteria Da Elio	♦♦	Italian	$12-$27	296
(160) p. 266	Mustard Greens	♦♦	Chinese	$7-$24	299
(161) p. 266	Pumpkin	♦♦♦	Mediterranean	$30-$50	300
(162) p. 266	Beau Monde	♦♦	Northern French	$10-$29	292
(163) p. 266	Famous 4th Street Delicatessen	♦♦	Deli	$9-$27	295
(164) p. 266	The Cambridge	♦♦	American	$10-$20	293
(165) p. 266	Ten Stone	♦♦	American	$8-$12	303
(166) p. 266	Southwark	♦♦♦	Continental	$19-$26	303
(167) p. 266	My Thai	♦♦	Thai	$10-$18	299
(168) p. 266	Grace's Tavern	♦♦	American	$5-$14	296
(169) p. 266	Morning Glory	♦♦	American	$4-$15	299
(170) p. 266	Saloon	♦♦♦	Italian	$10-$42	302
(171) p. 266	Ralph's Italian Restaurant	♦♦	Southern Italian	$9-$34	301
(172) p. 266	Catahoula	♦♦	Cajun	$10-$19	293
(173) p. 266	Cucina Forte	♦♦	Italian	$13-$32	294
(174) p. 266	Dante & Luigi's	♦♦	Italian	$7-$30	294
(175) p. 266	Dmitri's	♦♦	Mediterranean	$8-$20	294
(176) p. 266	Sabrina's Cafe	♦♦	American	$9-$23	302
(177) p. 266	The Sidecar Bar and Grille	♦♦	American	$10-$18	302
(178) p. 266	Paesano's	♦	Sandwiches	$7-$9	299
(179) p. 266	Bibou	♦♦♦	French	$26-$32	292
(180) p. 266	Ratchada Thai & Laos Cuisine	♦♦	Asian	$9-$25	301
(181) p. 266	Pho & Cafe Viet Huong	♦♦	Vietnamese	$4-$14	300
(182) p. 266	Snockey's Oyster and Crab House	♦	Seafood	$7-$51	303
(183) p. 266	Charlie was a Sinner	♦♦	Vegan Small Plates	$7-$12	293

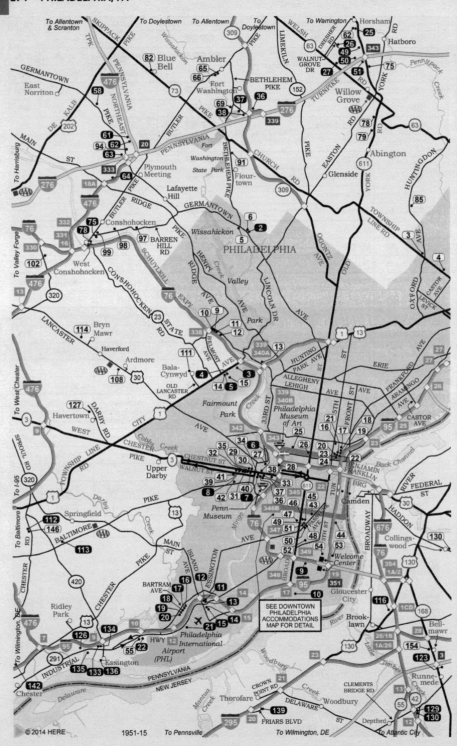

© 2014 HERE 1951-15

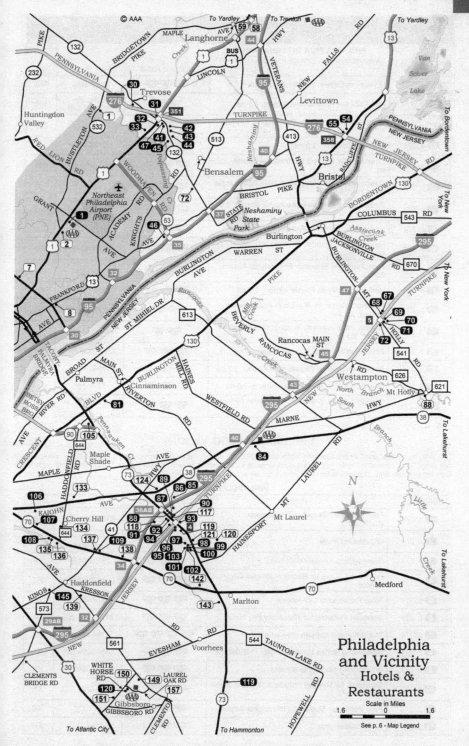

Philadelphia
and Vicinity
Hotels &
Restaurants

Scale in Miles

See p. 6 - Map Legend

✈ Airport Hotels

Map Page	PHILADELPHIA INTERNATIONAL (Maximum driving distance from airport: 5.9 mi)	Diamond Rated	Rate Range	Page
136 p. 274	Holiday Inn Express Philadelphia Airport, 5.0 mi	◇◇◇	$129-$159	109
133 p. 274	Red Roof Inn Philadelphia Airport, 4.8 mi	◇◇	Rates not provided (SAVE)	109
134 p. 274	Wyndham Garden Hotel Philadelphia Airport, 4.7 mi	◇◇◇	$89-$239 (SAVE)	109
12 p. 274	Aloft Philadelphia, 2.0 mi	◇◇◇	$129 (SAVE)	305
19 p. 274	Courtyard by Marriott Philadelphia Airport, 3.6 mi	◇◇◇	$160-$263 (SAVE)	305
10 p. 274	Courtyard by Marriott Philadelphia South at the Navy Yard, 5.9 mi	◇◇◇	$181-$298 (SAVE)	305
14 p. 274	DoubleTree by Hilton Philadelphia Airport, 2.0 mi	◇◇◇	$109-$329 (SAVE)	305
20 p. 274	Embassy Suites-Philadelphia Airport, 3.4 mi	◇◇◇	$139-$329	305
18 p. 274	Fairfield Inn by Marriott - Philadelphia Airport, 3.0 mi	◇◇◇	$118-$217	305
11 p. 274	Four Points by Sheraton Philadelphia Airport, 2.2 mi	◇◇◇	$99 (SAVE)	306
17 p. 274	Hampton Inn-Philadelphia Airport, 2.9 mi	◇◇◇	$129-$189 (SAVE)	306
15 p. 274	Hawthorn Suites by Wyndham Philadelphia Airport, 2.2 mi	◇◇	$111-$179 (SAVE)	306
16 p. 274	Microtel Inn & Suites by Wyndham Philadelphia Airport, 3.0 mi	◇◇	$70-$110	307
21 p. 274	Philadelphia Airport Marriott Hotel, 2.6 mi	◇◇◇	$202-$332 (SAVE)	307
22 p. 274	Renaissance Hotel Philadelphia Airport, 3.3 mi	◇◇◇	$140-$230 (SAVE)	307
13 p. 274	Sheraton Suites Philadelphia Airport, 2.0 mi	◇◇◇	$129 (SAVE)	308
126 p. 274	SpringHill Suites by Marriott Philadelphia Airport/ Ridley Park, 5.4 mi	◇◇◇	$118-$206	380

Philadelphia and Vicinity

This index helps you "spot" where approved hotels and restaurants are located on the corresponding detailed maps. Hotel daily rate range is for comparison only. Restaurant price range is a combination of lunch and/or dinner. Turn to the listing page for more detailed rate and price information and consult display ads for special promotions.

PHILADELPHIA

Map Page	Hotels	Diamond Rated	Rate Range	Page
1 p. 274	Four Points by Sheraton Philadelphia Northeast	◇◇◇	$125-$235 (SAVE)	306
2 p. 274	Chestnut Hill Hotel	◇◇◇	Rates not provided	305
3 p. 274	Crowne Plaza - Philadelphia West	◇◇◇	$159-$499	305
4 p. 274	Homewood Suites by Hilton/Philadelphia City Avenue	◇◇◇	$139-$249	307
5 p. 274	Hilton Philadelphia City Avenue	◇◇◇	$139-$249	307
6 p. 274	Sheraton Philadelphia University City Hotel	◇◇◇	$119-$399 (SAVE)	308
7 p. 274	The Hilton Inn at Penn (See ad p. 287.)	◇◇◇◇	$119-$359 (SAVE)	307
8 p. 274	Homewood Suites University City Philadelphia	◇◇◇	$169-$399	307
9 p. 274	Holiday Inn Philadelphia Stadium	◇◇◇	$129-$999	307
10 p. 274	Courtyard by Marriott Philadelphia South at the Navy Yard	◇◇◇	$181-$298 (SAVE)	305
11 p. 274	Four Points by Sheraton Philadelphia Airport	◇◇◇	$99 (SAVE)	306
12 p. 274	Aloft Philadelphia	◇◇◇	$129 (SAVE)	305

PHILADELPHIA (cont'd)

Map Page	Hotels (cont'd)	Diamond Rated	Rate Range	Page
13 p. 274	**Sheraton Suites Philadelphia Airport**	▽▽▽	$129 SAVE	308
14 p. 274	**DoubleTree by Hilton Philadelphia Airport**	▽▽▽	$109-$329 SAVE	305
15 p. 274	**Hawthorn Suites by Wyndham Philadelphia Airport**	▽▽	$111-$179 SAVE	306
16 p. 274	Microtel Inn & Suites by Wyndham Philadelphia Airport	▽▽	$70-$110	307
17 p. 274	**Hampton Inn-Philadelphia Airport**	▽▽▽	$129-$189 SAVE	306
18 p. 274	Fairfield Inn by Marriott - Philadelphia Airport	▽▽▽	$118-$217	305
19 p. 274	**Courtyard by Marriott Philadelphia Airport**	▽▽▽	$160-$263 SAVE	305
20 p. 274	Embassy Suites-Philadelphia Airport	▽▽▽	$139-$329	305
21 p. 274	**Philadelphia Airport Marriott Hotel**	▽▽▽	$202-$332 SAVE	307
22 p. 274	**Renaissance Hotel Philadelphia Airport**	▽▽▽	$140-$230 SAVE	307

Map Page	Restaurants	Diamond Rated	Cuisine	Price Range	Page
1 p. 274	Pho Palace	▽▽	Vietnamese	$7-$20	311
2 p. 274	Las Margaritas	▽▽	Mexican	$5-$17	310
3 p. 274	Makiman Sushi	▽▽	Sushi	$10-$27	310
4 p. 274	Country Club Restaurant	▽▽	American	$5-$14	309
5 p. 274	McNally's Tavern	▽▽	Sandwiches	$4-$12	310
6 p. 274	Chestnut Grill and Sidewalk Cafe	▽▽	American	$8-$20	308
7 p. 274	Jannie	▽▽	Asian	$5-$18	309
8 p. 274	Mayfair Diner	▽	American	$7-$15	310
9 p. 274	Zesty's	▽▽▽	Mediterranean	$10-$50	312
10 p. 274	Derek's	▽▽▽	American	$11-$34	309
11 p. 274	Jake's & Cooper's Wine Bar	▽▽▽	American	$13-$32	309
12 p. 274	Winnie's Le Bus	▽▽	American	$6-$18	312
13 p. 274	Johnny Mañana's	▽▽	Tex-Mex	$7-$20	310
14 p. 274	Delmonico's Steak House	▽▽▽	Steak	$15-$35	309
15 p. 274	Chun Hing	▽▽	Chinese	$5-$15	308
16 p. 274	Las Cazuelas Restaurant	▽▽	Mexican	$7-$19	310
17 p. 274	Bar Ferdinand	▽▽▽	Spanish	$10-$30	308
18 p. 274	Standard Tap	▽▽	American	$8-$26	311
19 p. 274	Circles Contemporary Asian	▽▽	Asian Fusion	$8-$19	309
20 p. 274	Honey's Sit 'n Eat	▽▽	Comfort Food	$6-$16	309
21 p. 274	North 3rd	▽▽	American	$10-$19	311
22 p. 274	Green Eggs Cafe	▽▽	American	$9-$13	309
23 p. 274	Il Cantuccio	▽▽	Italian	$8-$23	309
24 p. 274	The Abbaye	▽▽	American	$5-$20	308
25 p. 274	Jack's Firehouse Restaurant	▽▽▽	American	$8-$32	309
26 p. 274	Osteria	▽▽▽	Italian	$12-$30	311
27 p. 274	Sabrina's Cafe @ Powelton	▽▽	American	$7-$20	311
28 p. 274	JG Domestic	▽▽	American	$12-$22	310

Map Page	Restaurants (cont'd)	Diamond Rated	Cuisine	Price Range	Page
29 p. 274	Distrito	▽▽▽	New Mexican	$8-$32	309
30 p. 274	Thai Singha House	▽▽	Thai	$4-$18	312
31 p. 274	New Delhi	▽	Indian	$10-$15	311
32 p. 274	Pattaya Thai Cuisine	▽▽	Thai	$8-$17	311
33 p. 274	New Deck Tavern	▽▽	American	$8-$17	311
34 p. 274	Pod	▽▽▽	Japanese	$9-$30	311
35 p. 274	Tandoor India	▽▽	Indian	$9-$16	312
36 p. 274	Penne Restaurant & Wine Bar	▽▽▽	Italian	$10-$28	311
37 p. 274	White Dog Cafe	▽▽	American	$12-$32	312
38 p. 274	The Fat Ham	▽▽▽	American	$6-$15	309
39 p. 274	The Restaurant School At Walnut Hill College	▽▽▽	Continental	$13-$21	311
40 p. 274	Bobby's Burger Palace	▽	Burgers	$6-$9	308
41 p. 274	Abyssinia Ethiopian Restaurant	▽▽	Ethiopian	$6-$15	308
42 p. 274	Marigold Kitchen	▽▽▽	American	$24-$45	310
43 p. 274	Bitar's	▽	Eastern Mediterranean	$4-$9	308
44 p. 274	Warmdaddy's	▽▽	American	$8-$23	312
45 p. 274	The VictorCafe	▽▽▽	Italian	$16-$36	312
46 p. 274	Green Eggs Cafe	▽▽	American	$9-$13	309
47 p. 274	Circles	▽▽	Asian	$8-$19	308
48 p. 274	Mamma Maria	▽▽	Italian	$25-$55	310
49 p. 274	Mr. Martino's Trattoria	▽▽	Italian	$11-$20	310
50 p. 274	Los Caballitos Cantina	▽▽	Mexican	$7-$23	310
51 p. 274	Marra's Cucina Italiana	▽▽	Italian	$8-$21	310
52 p. 274	Bomb Bomb Bar-be-que Grill	▽▽	Italian Barbecue	$8-$26	308
53 p. 274	Tony Luke's Beef and Beer Sports Bar	▽▽	Sandwiches	$6-$9	312
54 p. 274	Oregon Diner	▽▽	American	$5-$18	311
55 p. 274	The Sanctuary	▽▽▽	American	$6-$36	311

HORSHAM

Map Page	Hotels	Diamond Rated	Rate Range	Page
25 p. 274	Days Inn-Horsham/Philadelphia	▽▽	$59-$130 SAVE	158
26 p. 274	Residence Inn by Marriott-Willow Grove	▽▽▽	$139-$229	159
27 p. 274	Extended Stay America-Philadelphia/Horsham	▽▽	Rates not provided	158

Map Page	Restaurant	Diamond Rated	Cuisine	Price Range	Page
62 p. 274	Otto's Brauhaus	▽▽	German	$6-$25	159

TREVOSE

Map Page	Hotels	Diamond Rated	Rate Range	Page
30 p. 274	Crowne Plaza Philadelphia-Bucks County Hotel	▽▽▽	Rates not provided SAVE	405
31 p. 274	Red Roof Inn Philadelphia Trevose	▽▽	Rates not provided SAVE	405
32 p. 274	Comfort Inn Trevose	▽▽▽	$85-$105	405
33 p. 274	Radisson Hotel Philadelphia Northeast	▽▽▽	$119-$199	405

FORT WASHINGTON

Map Page	Hotels	Diamond Rated	Rate Range	Page
36 p. 274	**BEST WESTERN Fort Washington Inn**	◆◆◆	$95-$141 SAVE	113
38 p. 274	**Hilton Garden Inn Philadelphia/Fort Washington** *(See ad p. 113.)*	◆◆◆	$119-$229 SAVE	113

Map Page	Restaurant	Diamond Rated	Cuisine	Price Range	Page
69 p. 274	Cantina Feliz	◆◆◆	Mexican	$11-$24	114

BENSALEM

Map Page	Hotels	Diamond Rated	Rate Range	Page
41 p. 274	**Quality Inn & Suites**	◆◆	$79-$179 SAVE	61
42 p. 274	**BEST WESTERN PLUS Philadelphia Bensalem**	◆◆◆	$99-$139 SAVE	60
43 p. 274	Sleep Inn & Suites-Bensalem	◆◆	$90-$120	61
44 p. 274	Holiday Inn Bensalem-Philadelphia Area	◆◆◆	$89-$299	61
45 p. 274	Extended Stay America-Philadelphia/Bensalem	◆◆	Rates not provided	61
46 p. 274	**Holiday Inn Express Philadelphia Northeast/Bensalem**	◆◆◆	$89-$159 SAVE	61
47 p. 274	Hampton Inn and Suites Philadelphia Bensalem	◆◆◆	$99-$149	61

Map Page	Restaurant	Diamond Rated	Cuisine	Price Range	Page
72 p. 274	Fisher's Tudor House	◆◆	Seafood	$10-$22	61

WILLOW GROVE

Map Page	Hotels	Diamond Rated	Rate Range	Page
49 p. 274	**Courtyard by Marriott Philadelphia Willow Grove**	◆◆◆	$160-$263 SAVE	426
50 p. 274	**SpringHill Suites by Marriott Philadelphia Willow Grove**	◆◆◆	$132-$217 SAVE	427
51 p. 274	Hampton Inn-Willow Grove	◆◆◆	$99-$199	427

Map Page	Restaurant	Diamond Rated	Cuisine	Price Range	Page
75 p. 274	Ooka Japanese Sushi & Hibachi Steak House	◆◆	Japanese	$13-$29	427

LEVITTOWN

Map Page	Hotels	Diamond Rated	Rate Range	Page
54 p. 274	**Comfort Inn Levittown/Bensalem**	◆◆◆	$65-$159 SAVE	185
55 p. 274	**Ramada Inn**	◆◆	$90-$170 SAVE	185

EAST NORRITON

Map Page	Hotel	Diamond Rated	Rate Range	Page
58 p. 274	**HYATT house Philadelphia/Plymouth Meeting** *(See ad p. 306.)*	◆◆◆	$94-$299 SAVE	99

PLYMOUTH MEETING

Map Page	Hotels	Diamond Rated	Rate Range	Page
61 p. 274	**Courtyard by Marriott-Philadelphia Plymouth Meeting**	◆◆◆	$146-$240 SAVE	370
62 p. 274	DoubleTree Suites by Hilton Philadelphia West	◆◆◆	$109-$209	370
63 p. 274	**SpringHill Suites by Marriott Philadelphia/Plymouth Meeting**	◆◆◆	$146-$240 SAVE	370
64 p. 274	Hampton Inn Plymouth Meeting	◆◆◆	$129-$179	370

Map Page	Restaurant	Diamond Rated	Cuisine	Price Range	Page
94 p. 274	Redstone American Grill	◆◆	American	$13-$39	370

WESTAMPTON, NJ

Map Page	Hotels	Diamond Rated	Rate Range	Page
67 p. 274	Courtyard by Marriott Burlington Mt. Holly/Westampton	◆◆◆	$130-$213	324

WESTAMPTON, NJ (cont'd)

Map Page	Hotels (cont'd)	Diamond Rated	Rate Range	Page
68 p. 274	Holiday Inn Express Hotel & Suites	▽▽▽	$99-$149	324
70 p. 274	Hilton Garden Inn Mt. Holly/Westampton	▽▽▽	Rates not provided	324
71 p. 274	**BEST WESTERN Burlington Inn**	▽▽	$99-$139 (SAVE)	323
72 p. 274	Quality Inn & Suites	▽▽	$85-$150	324

CONSHOHOCKEN

Map Page	Hotel	Diamond Rated	Rate Range	Page
75 p. 274	Residence Inn by Marriott Philadelphia/Conshohocken	▽▽▽	$174-$286	87

Map Page	Restaurants	Diamond Rated	Cuisine	Price Range	Page
97 p. 274	Spring Mill Cafe	▽▽▽	French	$10-$37	88
98 p. 274	Coyote Crossing	▽▽▽	Mexican	$8-$28	88
99 p. 274	Blackfish	▽▽▽	Continental	$10-$34	87

WEST CONSHOHOCKEN

Map Page	Hotel	Diamond Rated	Rate Range	Page
78 p. 274	**Philadelphia Marriott West**	▽▽▽	$188-$309 (SAVE)	418

Map Page	Restaurant	Diamond Rated	Cuisine	Price Range	Page
102 p. 274	**Savona**	▽▽▽▽	Northern Italian	$20-$55	419

CINNAMINSON, NJ

Map Page	Hotel	Diamond Rated	Rate Range	Page
81 p. 274	**Sleep Inn**	▽▽	$80-$150 (SAVE)	317

Map Page	Restaurant	Diamond Rated	Cuisine	Price Range	Page
105 p. 274	The Jug Handle Inn	▽▽	American	$7-$20	318

MOUNT LAUREL, NJ

Map Page	Hotels	Diamond Rated	Rate Range	Page
84 p. 274	Residence Inn by Marriott Mount Laurel at Bishop's Gate	▽▽▽	$118-$194	321
85 p. 274	Philadelphia/Mount Laurel Homewood Suites by Hilton	▽▽▽	$109-$199	321
86 p. 274	**DoubleTree Suites by Hilton Hotel Mt. Laurel**	▽▽▽	$109-$309 (SAVE)	320
87 p. 274	**Hotel ML**	▽▽▽	$99-$299 (SAVE)	320
88 p. 274	**The Westin Mount Laurel**	▽▽▽	$99-$399 (SAVE)	321
89 p. 274	Super 8	▽▽	$69-$109	321
90 p. 274	**Aloft Mount Laurel**	▽▽▽	Rates not provided (SAVE)	320
91 p. 274	**Red Roof Inn #7066**	▽▽	Rates not provided (SAVE)	321
92 p. 274	**Courtyard by Marriott Mt. Laurel**	▽▽▽	$132-$252 (SAVE)	320
93 p. 274	**Wyndham Philadelphia-Mount Laurel**	▽▽▽	$109-$189 (SAVE)	321
94 p. 274	Fairfield Inn & Suites by Marriott Mt. Laurel	▽▽▽	$132-$217	320
95 p. 274	**La Quinta Mt. Laurel-Philadelphia**	▽▽▽	$79-$249 (SAVE)	321
96 p. 274	**Staybridge Suites**	▽▽▽	$149-$359 (SAVE)	321
97 p. 274	Hilton Garden Inn-Mt. Laurel	▽▽▽	$109-$179	320
98 p. 274	Extended Stay America Pacilli Place Philadelphia/Mt. Laurel	▽▽	Rates not provided	320
99 p. 274	Hampton Inn Philadelphia/Mt. Laurel	▽▽▽	$89-$149	320
100 p. 274	**Hyatt Place Mt. Laurel**	▽▽▽	$99-$199 (SAVE)	321

MOUNT LAUREL, NJ (cont'd)

Map Page	Hotels (cont'd)	Diamond Rated	Rate Range	Page
101 p. 274	**Hyatt house Mt. Laurel**	▽▽▽	$99-$189 SAVE	320
102 p. 274	Comfort Inn & Suites	▽▽▽	$89-$129	320
103 p. 274	Candlewood Suites Mt. Laurel	▽▽	Rates not provided	320

Map Page	Restaurants	Diamond Rated	Cuisine	Price Range	Page
117 p. 274	Miller's NJ Ale House	▽▽	American	$8-$20	322
118 p. 274	Stefano's Ristorante	▽▽	Italian	$12-$27	322
119 p. 274	Sage Diner	▽▽	American	$5-$27	322
120 p. 274	CHUlicious	▽▽	Chinese	$8-$20	321
121 p. 274	Singapore Restaurant and Sushi Bar	▽▽	Japanese	$5-$20	322

CHERRY HILL, NJ

Map Page	Hotels	Diamond Rated	Rate Range	Page
106 p. 274	**Days Inn & Suites**	▽▽	$80-$155 SAVE	317
107 p. 274	Crowne Plaza Philadelphia/Cherry Hill	▽▽▽	Rates not provided	316
108 p. 274	**Holiday Inn Philadelphia-Cherry Hill**	▽▽▽	Rates not provided SAVE	317
109 p. 274	Extended Stay America-Philadelphia/Cherry Hill	▽▽	Rates not provided	317

Map Page	Restaurants	Diamond Rated	Cuisine	Price Range	Page
133 p. 274	Seasons 52 Fresh Grill	▽▽▽	New American	$10-$30	317
134 p. 274	Brio Tuscan Grille	▽▽▽	Italian	$10-$29	317
135 p. 274	Siri's Thai French Cuisine	▽▽	Thai	$9-$29	317
136 p. 274	Caffe' Aldo Lamberti	▽▽▽	Italian	$10-$38	317
137 p. 274	Norma's	▽▽	Eastern Mediterranean	$6-$27	317
138 p. 274	Oh Yoko! Sushi	▽▽	Japanese	$9-$20	317
139 p. 274	Il Villaggio	▽▽▽	Italian	$9-$32	317

SPRINGFIELD (DELAWARE COUNTY)

Map Page	Hotels	Diamond Rated	Rate Range	Page
112 p. 274	Courtyard by Marriott Philadelphia Springfield	▽▽▽	$139-$229	393
113 p. 274	Days Inn Springfield/Philadelphia Int'l Airport	▽▽	$90-$199	393

Map Page	Restaurant	Diamond Rated	Cuisine	Price Range	Page
146 p. 274	Tavola Restaurant and Bar	▽▽	American	$9-$26	393

GLOUCESTER CITY, NJ

Map Page	Hotel	Diamond Rated	Rate Range	Page
116 p. 274	Quality Inn	▽▽	$75-$126	318

VOORHEES, NJ

Map Page	Hotels	Diamond Rated	Rate Range	Page
119 p. 274	Hampton Inn Philadelphia/Voorhees	▽▽▽	$109-$149	323
120 p. 274	Hampton Inn-Cherry Hill/Voorhees	▽▽▽	$89-$189	323

Map Page	Restaurants	Diamond Rated	Cuisine	Price Range	Page
149 p. 274	Ritz Seafood	▽▽	Seafood	$9-$25	323
150 p. 274	Passariello's Pizzeria & Italian Eatery	▽	Italian	$7-$16	323
151 p. 274	A Little Cafe	▽▽	American	$22-$32	323

RUNNEMEDE, NJ

Map Page	Hotel	Diamond Rated	Rate Range	Page
123 p. 274	**La Quinta Inn & Suites Runnemede**	▽▽▽	$89-$239 [SAVE]	322

RIDLEY PARK

Map Page	Hotel	Diamond Rated	Rate Range	Page
126 p. 274	SpringHill Suites by Marriott Philadelphia Airport/ Ridley Park	▽▽▽	$118-$206	380

DEPTFORD, NJ

Map Page	Hotels	Diamond Rated	Rate Range	Page
129 p. 274	Residence Inn by Marriott Deptford	▽▽▽	$125-$229	318
130 p. 274	Fairfield Inn by Marriott Philadelphia/Deptford	▽▽	$97-$160	318

ESSINGTON

Map Page	Hotels	Diamond Rated	Rate Range	Page
133 p. 274	**Red Roof Inn Philadelphia Airport**	▽▽	Rates not provided [SAVE]	109
134 p. 274	**Wyndham Garden Hotel Philadelphia Airport**	▽▽▽	$89-$239 [SAVE]	109
135 p. 274	The Clarion Hotel Conference Center	▽▽▽	$109-$229	109
136 p. 274	Holiday Inn Express Philadelphia Airport	▽▽▽	$129-$159	109

THOROFARE, NJ

Map Page	Hotel	Diamond Rated	Rate Range	Page
139 p. 274	**BEST WESTERN West Deptford Inn**	▽▽	$110 [SAVE]	323

CHESTER

Map Page	Hotel	Diamond Rated	Rate Range	Page
142 p. 274	**BEST WESTERN PLUS Philadelphia Airport South at Widener University**	▽▽▽	$120-$150 [SAVE]	83

HADDONFIELD, NJ

Map Page	Hotel	Diamond Rated	Rate Range	Page
145 p. 274	Haddonfield Inn	▽▽▽	Rates not provided	319

LANGHORNE

Map Page	Restaurants	Diamond Rated	Cuisine	Price Range	Page
58 p. 274	J. B. Dawson's	▽▽	American	$9-$28	182
59 p. 274	Piccolo Trattoria	▽▽	Italian	$6-$23	182

AMBLER

Map Page	Restaurants	Diamond Rated	Cuisine	Price Range	Page
65 p. 274	Bridget's Steakhouse	▽▽▽	Steak	$11-$39	56
66 p. 274	Trax Restaurant and Cafe	▽▽▽	American	$24-$29	56

ABINGTON

Map Page	Restaurants	Diamond Rated	Cuisine	Price Range	Page
78 p. 274	Lee's Hoagie House of Abington	▽	Sandwiches	$5-$17	44
79 p. 274	Alexander's Kitchen Bar	▽▽	American	$9-$20	44

BLUE BELL

Map Page	Restaurant	Diamond Rated	Cuisine	Price Range	Page
82 p. 274	Blue Bell Inn	▽▽▽	Steak Seafood	$11-$40	69

HUNTINGDON VALLEY

Map Page	Restaurant	Diamond Rated	Cuisine	Price Range	Page
85 p. 274	White Elephant Restaurant	▽▽	Thai	$9-$25	160

MOUNT HOLLY, NJ

Map Page	Restaurant	Diamond Rated	Cuisine	Price Range	Page
⑧⑧ p. 274	Robin's Nest	▼▼	American	$9-$29	319

FLOURTOWN

Map Page	Restaurant	Diamond Rated	Cuisine	Price Range	Page
⑨① p. 274	Scoogi's	▼▼	Italian	$10-$30	111

ARDMORE

Map Page	Restaurant	Diamond Rated	Cuisine	Price Range	Page
⑩⑧ p. 274	Mikado Thai Pepper	▼▼	Asian	$8-$20	56

BALA-CYNWYD

Map Page	Restaurant	Diamond Rated	Cuisine	Price Range	Page
⑪① p. 274	Al Dar Bistro	▼▼	Mediterranean	$7-$24	57

BRYN MAWR

Map Page	Restaurant	Diamond Rated	Cuisine	Price Range	Page
⑪④ p. 274	Tango	▼▼▼	American	$7-$29	74

MAPLE SHADE, NJ

Map Page	Restaurant	Diamond Rated	Cuisine	Price Range	Page
⑫④ p. 274	P.J. Whelihan's Pub & Restaurant	▼▼	American	$6-$19	319

HAVERTOWN

Map Page	Restaurant	Diamond Rated	Cuisine	Price Range	Page
⑫⑦ p. 274	Nais Cuisine	▼▼	French	$15-$27	146

COLLINGSWOOD, NJ

Map Page	Restaurant	Diamond Rated	Cuisine	Price Range	Page
⑬⓪ p. 274	The Pop Shop	▼▼	Comfort Food	$5-$11	318

MARLTON, NJ

Map Page	Restaurants	Diamond Rated	Cuisine	Price Range	Page
⑭② p. 274	Mexican Food Factory	▼▼	Mexican	$6-$17	319
⑭③ p. 274	Joe's Peking Duck House	▼▼	Chinese	$8-$29	319

BELLMAWR, NJ

Map Page	Restaurant	Diamond Rated	Cuisine	Price Range	Page
⑮④ p. 274	Club Diner	▼▼	American	$6-$13	313

GIBBSBORO, NJ

Map Page	Restaurant	Diamond Rated	Cuisine	Price Range	Page
⑮⑦ p. 274	The ChopHouse	▼▼▼	Steak	$13-$50	318

DOWNTOWN PHILADELPHIA
- Restaurants p. 291
- Hotels & Restaurants map & index p. 266

ALEXANDER INN   (215)923-3535   37

Historic Hotel
$119-$159

Address: 301 S 12th St 19107 **Location:** Jct Spruce and 12th sts. ⓜ 12th-13th & Locust, 141. **Facility:** A fireplace is featured in the lobby at this seven-story brick building, which was constructed in 1900. An intimate combination parlor/breakfast room boasts comfortable seating. 48 units. 7 stories, interior corridors. **Parking:** no self-parking. **Terms:** cancellation fee imposed. **Amenities:** safes. **Activities:** exercise room. **Featured Amenity: continental breakfast.** *(See ad this page.)*

SAVE 🍴▶ BIZ 🛜 ✕
/SOME UNITS 🗄 🖨

Located in the heart of the City near the Historic District, theatres, restaurants and shopping.

BEST WESTERN PLUS INDEPENDENCE PARK HOTEL
(215)922-4443   18

Historic Hotel
$99-$320

AAA Benefit:
Members save up to 20%!

Address: 235 Chestnut St 19106 **Location:** Between 2nd and 3rd sts. Located in Old City Historic District. ⓜ 2nd, 63. **Facility:** Built in 1856, this small property boasts a boutique-style appeal. No matter what your daily activities entail, make sure you join fellow guests for the afternoon cookies and tea served in the lobby. 36 units. 5 stories, interior corridors. **Parking:** street only. **Terms:** resort fee. **Guest Services:** valet laundry. **Featured Amenity: full hot breakfast.**

SAVE 🍴▶ CALL 📶 BIZ 🛜 ✕ 📺
/SOME UNITS HS 🗄 🖨 🚃

COURTYARD BY MARRIOTT PHILADELPHIA DOWNTOWN
(215)496-3200   13

Hotel $167-$275 **Address:** 21 N Juniper St 19107 **Location:** Just n of Market St. Adjacent to. City Hall. ⓜ 13th, 67. **Facility:** 499 units. 17 stories, interior corridors. **Parking:** on-site (fee) and valet. **Pool(s):** heated indoor. **Activities:** hot tub, exercise room. **Guest Services:** valet and coin laundry.

AAA Benefit:
Members save 5% or more!

🍴 🍸 CALL 📶 🏊 BIZ 🛜 ✕ 🗄 📺
/SOME UNITS 🖨 🚃

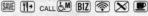

Get AAA/CAA travel information in the

digital and printed formats you prefer

(See map & index p. 266.)

DOUBLETREE BY HILTON PHILADELPHIA CENTER CITY
(215)893-1600

 Hotel $89-$309

 AAA Benefit: Members save 5% or more!

 **Address:** 237 S Broad St 19107 **Location:** Jct Broad and Locust sts. Located on Avenue of the Arts. Walnut-Locust, 117. **Facility:** 481 units. 26 stories, interior corridors. **Parking:** valet and street only. **Terms:** 1-7 night minimum stay, cancellation fee imposed. **Amenities:** video games, safes. **Dining:** 2 restaurants. **Pool(s):** heated indoor. **Activities:** sauna. **Guest Services:** valet laundry.

EMBASSY SUITES HOTEL PHILADELPHIA - CENTER CITY
(215)561-1776 **6**

Hotel $159-$579 **Address:** 1776 Benjamin Franklin Pkwy 19103 **Location:** On 18th St; between Cherry and Race sts. Suburban, 221. **Facility:** 288 units. 28 stories, interior corridors. **Parking:** on-site (fee) and valet. **Terms:** 1-7 night minimum stay, cancellation fee imposed. **Amenities:** video games. **Activities:** exercise room. **Guest Services:** valet and coin laundry.

AAA Benefit: Members save 5% or more!

FOUR POINTS BY SHERATON - PHILADELPHIA CITY CENTER
(215)496-2700 **3**

 Hotel $109-$459

 AAA Benefit: Members save up to 15%, plus Starwood Preferred Guest® benefits!

 Address: 1201 Race St 19107 **Location:** Jct 12th St; just n to entrance. Race-Vine, 119. **Facility:** 92 units. 10 stories, interior corridors. **Parking:** on-site (fee). **Terms:** 3 day cancellation notice-fee imposed. **Amenities:** video games, safes. **Activities:** exercise room. **Guest Services:** valet laundry.

FOUR SEASONS HOTEL PHILADELPHIA
215/963-1500 **5**

Hotel. Rates not provided. **Address:** 1 Logan Square 19103 **Location:** Corner of 18th St and Benjamin Franklin Pkwy. Suburban, 221. **Facility:** Guests are pampered by spectacular public areas featuring luxurious furnishings and beautiful flower arrangements. Spacious rooms are elegantly decorated and combine with service that goes above and beyond. 364 units, some two bedrooms. 8 stories, interior corridors. **Parking:** on-site (fee) and valet. **Amenities:** video games, safes. **Dining:** 2 restaurants, also, Fountain Restaurant, Swann Lounge & Cafe, see separate listings. **Pool(s):** heated indoor. **Activities:** sauna, hot tub, spa. **Guest Services:** valet laundry, area transportation.

▼ See AAA listing p. 287 ▼

Take your imagination to new destinations

with the online AAA/CAA Travel Guides

(See map & index p. 266.)

HAMPTON INN PHILADELPHIA CENTER CITY/ CONVENTION CENTER
(215)665-9100 **4**

Hotel
$139-$309

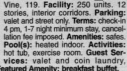
AAA Benefit: Members save 5% or more!

Address: 1301 Race St 19107 **Location:** At 13th and Race sts. Race-Vine, 119. **Facility:** 250 units. 12 stories, interior corridors. **Parking:** valet and street only. **Terms:** check-in 4 pm, 1-7 night minimum stay, cancellation fee imposed. **Pool(s):** heated indoor. **Activities:** hot tub, exercise room. **Guest Services:** valet and coin laundry, boarding pass kiosk. **Featured Amenity:** breakfast buffet. *(See ad p. 286.)*

SAVE ⁺† Y ⊇ BIZ 🛜 ✕ ▯ / SOME UNITS ▯ ▭ ▥

HILTON GARDEN INN PHILADELPHIA CENTER CITY
(215)923-0100 **10**

Hotel $139-$309 **Address:** 1100 Arch St 19107 **Location:** At Arch and 11th sts. Adjacent to convention center. Market East, 222. **Facility:** 279 units. 10 stories, interior corridors. **Parking:** on-site (fee). **Terms:** check-in 4 pm, 1-7 night minimum stay, cancellation fee imposed. **Pool(s):** heated indoor. **Activities:** hot tub, exercise room. **Guest Services:** valet and coin laundry.

AAA Benefit: Members save 5% or more!

†† Y CALL ♿M ⊇ BIZ HS 🛜 ✕ 📷 ▯ ▭ ▯ ▥

HILTON PHILADELPHIA AT PENN'S LANDING
(215)928-1234 **28**

Hotel
$99-$499

Hilton
HOTELS & RESORTS

AAA Benefit: Members save 5% or more!

Address: 201 S Columbus Blvd 19106 **Location:** Waterfront. Jct S Columbus Blvd and Dock St. Located at Penn's Landing-Delaware River. 2nd, 63. **Facility:** 348 units, some two bedrooms. 22 stories, interior corridors. **Parking:** valet and street only. **Terms:** cancellation fee imposed. **Amenities:** safes. **Dining:** Keating's River Grill, see separate listing. **Pool(s):** heated indoor. **Activities:** sauna, massage. **Guest Services:** valet laundry.

SAVE †† ⊹ Y CALL ♿M ⊇ ✚ BIZ $HS S🛜 ✕ 📷 ▯ ▯ / SOME UNITS 🔔 ▭ ▥

HOLIDAY INN EXPRESS MIDTOWN
(215)735-9300 **26**

Hotel
$169-$349

Address: 1305 Walnut St 19107 **Location:** Just e of Broad St. Walnut-Locust, 117. **Facility:** 168 units. 20 stories, interior corridors. **Parking:** on-site (fee). **Terms:** cancellation fee imposed. **Amenities:** video games. **Pool(s):** outdoor. **Guest Services:** valet laundry. **Featured Amenity:** breakfast buffet.

SAVE †† CALL ♿M ⊇ ✚ BIZ 🛜 ✕ ♣ ▯ / SOME UNITS 🔔 ▭ ▥

▼ See AAA listing p. 307 ▼

(See map & index p. 266.)

HOLIDAY INN EXPRESS PHILADELPHIA/PENN'S LANDING
215/627-7900 **1**

▼▼▼▼ **Hotel.** Rates not provided. **Address:** 100 N Columbus Blvd 19106 **Location:** Waterfront. I-95 exit 20 (Columbus Blvd/Washington St) to Columbus Blvd, then 1.2 mi n to jct Race St. Across from Penn's Landing-Delaware River. 🚇 2nd, 63. **Facility:** 184 units. 10 stories, interior corridors. **Parking:** on-site (fee). **Terms:** check-in 4 pm. **Amenities:** safes. **Activities:** exercise room. **Guest Services:** valet laundry, area transportation.

[icons]

HOME2 SUITES BY HILTON PHILADELPHIA CONVENTION CENTER
(215)627-1850 **9**

▼▼▼▼ **Extended Stay Hotel** $149-$399 **Address:** 1200 Arch St 19107 **Location:** Between Market and Arch sts. 🚇 Market East, 222. **Facility:** 248 units. 9 stories, interior corridors. *Bath:* shower only. **Parking:** street only. **Terms:** 1-7 night minimum stay, cancellation fee imposed. **Amenities:** safes. **Pool(s):** heated indoor. **Activities:** exercise room. **Guest Services:** valet and coin laundry.

AAA Benefit: Members save 5% or more!

[icons]

HOTEL MONACO PHILADELPHIA, A KIMPTON HOTEL
215/925-2111 **19**

▼▼▼▼
Historic Boutique Hotel
Rates not provided

Address: 433 Chestnut St 19106 **Location:** Jct 5th and Chestnut sts. 🚇 5th, 64. **Facility:** Enjoy the history of Philadelphia from this ultra-modern boutique hotel located across from Independence Hall. Originally built in 1907, this hotel now features plush fabrics, sleek designs and bold colors. 268 units. 9 stories, interior corridors. **Parking:** on-site (fee) and valet. **Amenities:** safes. **Dining:** Red Owl Tavern, see separate listing. **Activities:** bicycles, exercise room. **Guest Services:** valet laundry.

[icons]

HOTEL PALOMAR-PHILADELPHIA
215/563-5006 **25**

▼▼▼▼
Boutique Hotel
Rates not provided

[photo]

Address: 117 S 17th St 19103 **Location:** Corner of 17th and Samson sts. 🚇 15th-16th & Locust, 140. **Facility:** Located in downtown Center City, this lovely restored hotel is in the old Architects Building. The property successfully combines the building's historical Art Deco design with modern décor. 230 units. 25 stories, interior corridors. **Parking:** on-site (fee) and valet. **Amenities:** safes. **Activities:** exercise room. **Guest Services:** valet laundry.

[icons]

Upgrade to Plus or Premier membership for more of the benefits you need most

HYATT AT THE BELLEVUE
(215)893-1234 **30**

▼▼▼ ▼▼▼
Historic Hotel
$119-$449

HYATT
AAA Benefit: Members save 10%!

Address: 200 S Broad St 19102 **Location:** Between Walnut and Locust sts. 🚇 Walnut-Locust, 117. **Facility:** This elegantly appointed hotel is located in the historic Bellevue Building located downtown in the Avenue of the Arts district. All guests receive a complimentary pass to the 93,000-square-foot Sports Club. 172 units. 6 stories, interior corridors. **Parking:** valet and street only. **Terms:** 3 day cancellation notice-fee imposed. **Amenities:** safes. **Dining:** XIX (Nineteen) Restaurant, see separate listing. **Activities:** spa. **Guest Services:** valet laundry.

[icons]

THE INDEPENDENT HOTEL PHILADELPHIA
(215)772-1440 **34**

▼▼▼▼
Hotel
$129-$296

Address: 1234 Locust St 19107 **Location:** Just e of jct 13th St. 🚇 12th-13th & Locust, 141. **Facility:** 24 units. 5 stories, interior corridors. *Bath:* shower only. **Parking:** street only. **Terms:** cancellation fee imposed. **Guest Services:** valet laundry. **Featured Amenity:** continental breakfast.

[icons]

THE LATHAM HOTEL
(215)563-7474 **27**

▼▼▼▼
Historic Boutique Hotel
$129-$549

Address: 135 S 17th St 19103 **Location:** Jct 17th and Walnut sts. 🚇 15th-16th & Locust, 140. **Facility:** This smaller boutique hotel located in the heart of Center City blends a sleek, contemporary design with comfortable and plush furnishings. 139 units. 14 stories, interior corridors. **Parking:** on-site (fee) and valet. **Terms:** cancellation fee imposed. **Amenities:** safes. **Activities:** exercise room. **Guest Services:** valet laundry, area transportation.

[icons]

LE MERIDIEN PHILADELPHIA
(215)422-8200 **11**

▼▼▼▼
Historic Boutique Hotel
$139-$999

Le MERIDIEN **AAA Benefit:** Members save up to 15%, plus Starwood Preferred Guest® benefits!

Address: 1421 Arch St 19102 **Location:** Between Broad and 15th sts. 🚇 Suburban, 221. **Facility:** Serving as the former YMCA and district attorney's office, this hotel proves to be a contemporary, adaptive reuse of a historic building. City Hall and Love Park are nearby. 202 units. 10 stories, interior corridors. **Parking:** on-site (fee) and valet. **Terms:** cancellation fee imposed. **Amenities:** video games, safes. **Activities:** exercise room, massage. **Guest Services:** valet laundry.

[icons]

(See map & index p. 266.)

LOEWS PHILADELPHIA HOTEL (215)627-1200 [16]

Hotel
$149-$489

Address: 1200 Market St 19107 **Location:** Corner of 12th and Market sts. 13th, 67. **Facility:** This high-rise property features upscale contemporary furnishings and a gracious, accommodating staff. The lobby offers a lounge area off the front desk, perfect for watching your favorite sporting event. 581 units, some two bedrooms. 33 stories, interior corridors. **Parking:** valet only. **Terms:** check-in 4 pm, cancellation fee imposed. **Amenities:** safes. **Dining:** Bank and Bourbon, see separate listing. **Pool(s):** heated indoor. **Activities:** sauna, steamroom, spa. **Guest Services:** valet laundry.

MORRIS HOUSE HOTEL (215)922-2446 [31]

Historic Bed & Breakfast
$199-$499

Address: 225 S 8th St 19106 **Location:** Jct 8th and Locust sts; entrance on St. James Pl. 9th-10th & Locust, 142. **Facility:** The historic downtown B&B has just 15 rooms. Although limited in the public areas, they offer cozy historic and modern guest rooms. There is a beautiful courtyard area as well as a restaurant. 15 units, some efficiencies and kitchens. 3 stories, interior corridors. **Parking:** street only. **Terms:** 7 day cancellation notice-fee imposed, resort fee. **Guest Services:** coin laundry. **Featured Amenity: continental breakfast.**

OMNI HOTEL AT INDEPENDENCE PARK 215/925-0000 [20]

Hotel
Rates not provided

Address: 401 Chestnut St 19106 **Location:** Jct 4th St. 5th, 64. **Facility:** Located in Independence Park near multiple historic attractions, this European-style luxury hotel is equipped with elegant guest rooms and surely won't disappoint. 150 units. 13 stories, interior corridors. **Parking:** on-site (fee) and valet. **Amenities:** safes. **Dining:** video games. **Pool(s):** heated indoor. **Activities:** sauna, hot tub, exercise room, spa. **Guest Services:** valet and coin laundry.

PENN'S VIEW HOTEL (215)922-7600 [12]

Historic Hotel
$159-$349

Address: 14 N Front St 19106 **Location:** At Front and Market sts. Located in Old City Historic District. 2nd, 63. **Facility:** This charming 1828 structure, formerly a warehouse, offers elegant rooms with some upscale details; a few units have gas fireplaces. 51 units. 5 stories, interior corridors. **Parking:** on-site (fee). **Terms:** cancellation fee imposed. **Dining:** Ristorante Panorama, see separate listing. **Activities:** exercise room. **Guest Services:** valet laundry. **Featured Amenity: continental breakfast.**

PHILADELPHIA DOWNTOWN MARRIOTT HOTEL (215)625-2900 [14]

Hotel
$216-$355

MARRIOTT

AAA Benefit:
Members save 5% or more!

Address: 1201 Market St 19107 **Location:** Between 12th and 13th sts. Adjacent to convention center. 13th, 67. **Facility:** 1408 units. 23 stories, interior corridors. **Parking:** on-site (fee) and valet. **Terms:** check-in 4 pm. **Amenities:** safes. **Pool(s):** heated indoor. **Guest Services:** valet and coin laundry.

RADISSON BLU WARWICK HOTEL, PHILADELPHIA (215)735-6000 [35]

Hotel
$229-$599

Address: 220 S 17th St 19103 **Location:** Between Walnut and Locust sts; main entrance on 17th St. 15th-16th & Locust, 140. **Facility:** 301 units, some efficiencies. 21 stories, interior corridors. **Parking:** on-site (fee) and valet. **Terms:** 3 day cancellation notice-fee imposed. **Amenities:** safes. **Dining:** 2 restaurants, also, The Prime Rib, see separate listing. **Activities:** exercise room, massage. **Guest Services:** valet and coin laundry.

RESIDENCE INN BY MARRIOTT CENTER CITY PHILADELPHIA (215)557-0005 [15]

Extended Stay Hotel
$174-$286 **Address:** 1 E Penn Square 19107 **Location:** Jct Market and Juniper sts. 13th, 67. **Facility:** 290 units, some efficiencies. 27 stories, interior corridors. **Parking:** on-site (fee) and valet. **Terms:** check-in 4 pm. **Activities:** exercise room. **Guest Services:** valet and coin laundry.

AAA Benefit:
Members save 5% or more!

THE RITTENHOUSE 215/546-9000 [33]

Historic Hotel
Rates not provided

Address: 210 W Rittenhouse Square 19103 **Location:** Jct W Rittenhouse Square and Walnut St. 19th, 69. **Facility:** You will feel truly pampered at this exquisite historic property that features magnificent public spaces and a luxury spa for when you need a break from the bustling city. 116 units. 33 stories, interior corridors. **Parking:** on-site (fee) and valet. **Amenities:** video games, safes. **Dining:** 2 restaurants, also, Lacroix At The Rittenhouse, see separate listing. **Pool(s):** heated indoor. **Activities:** sauna, steamroom, spa. **Guest Services:** valet laundry, area transportation.

Visit AAA.com/searchfordiscounts
to save on dining, attractions,
hotels and more

(See map & index p. 266.)

THE RITZ-CARLTON PHILADELPHIA   215/523-8000 22

◤◤◤ ◤◤◤ **Classic Historic Hotel.**
Rates not provided. **Address:** Ten Avenue of the Arts 19102 **Location:** On Broad St; between Market and Chestnut sts. Near City Hall. City Hall, 118. **Facility:** The lobby, which is housed in a magnificent turn-of-the-20th-century domed building, is designed to wow. Staffers deftly anticipate guests' needs. 299 units. 32 stories, interior corridors. **Parking:** on-site (fee) and valet. **Amenities:** video games, safes. **Dining:** 10 Arts Bistro & Lounge by Eric Ripert, see separate listing. **Activities:** sauna, steamroom, exercise room, spa. **Guest Services:** valet laundry.

AAA Benefit:
Unequaled service at special member savings!

🍴 🛎 ☂ BIZ SHS 🛜 ✕ 📷 💻
/SOME UNITS 🛏 🖼 🚐

RODEWAY INN   (215)546-7000 29

◤◤ ◤◤ **Hotel** $79-$700 **Address:** 1208 Walnut St 19107 **Location:** Between 12th and 13th sts. 12th-13th & Locust, 141. **Facility:** 44 units. 7 stories, interior corridors. **Parking:** no self-parking. **Amenities:** safes.

🍴 🛜 ✕ 🖥 🖼 💻 🚐

SHERATON PHILADELPHIA DOWNTOWN   (215)448-2000 2

Hotel
$129-$499

AAA Benefit: Members save up to 15%, plus Starwood Preferred Guest® benefits!

Address: 201 N 17th St 19103 **Location:** Jct 17th and Race sts. Race-Vine, 119. **Facility:** 757 units. 29 stories, interior corridors. **Parking:** valet and street only. **Terms:** cancellation fee imposed. **Dining:** 2 restaurants. **Pool(s):** indoor. **Guest Services:** valet laundry.

SAVE 🍴 ☂ 🏊 🛗 BIZ SHS
🐾 ✕ 📷 💻
/SOME UNITS 🛏 🖥 🚐

SHERATON PHILADELPHIA SOCIETY HILL   (215)238-6000 32

◤◤◤ ◤◤◤
Hotel
$159

Sheraton

AAA Benefit: Members save up to 15%, plus Starwood Preferred Guest® benefits!

Address: One Dock St 19106 **Location:** Just s of jct 2nd and Walnut sts. 2nd, 63. **Facility:** 364 units. 4 stories, interior corridors. **Parking:** on-site (fee) and valet. **Terms:** cancellation fee imposed. **Amenities:** safes. **Pool(s):** heated indoor. **Activities:** exercise room. **Guest Services:** valet laundry, rental car service.

SAVE 🍴 🛎 ☂ 🏊 BIZ 🐾
✕ 📷 💻 /SOME UNITS 🛏 🖥 🚐

SOFITEL PHILADELPHIA   215/569-8300 24

◤◤◤ ◤◤◤
Contemporary Hotel
Rates not provided

Address: 120 S 17th St 19103 **Location:** Jct Sansom and 17th sts. 15th-16th & Locust, 140. **Facility:** This contemporary high-rise once housed the Philadelphia Stock Exchange. It features elegantly appointed guest rooms with feather-top beds and upscale modern furnishings. 306 units. 13 stories, interior corridors. **Parking:** on-site (fee) and valet. **Amenities:** video games, safes. **Dining:** 2 restaurants, also, Liberté, see separate listing, entertainment. **Activities:** exercise room, massage. **Guest Services:** valet laundry.

SAVE ECO 🍴 🛎 ☂ CALL 🛗
BIZ HS 🛜 ✕ 📷 💻
/SOME UNITS 🛏 🖥 🚐

SONESTA PHILADELPHIA   215/561-7500 17

◤◤◤ ◤◤◤
Hotel
Rates not provided

Address: 1800 Market St 19103 **Location:** Between 18th and 19th sts. 19th, 69. **Facility:** 439 units. 25 stories, interior corridors. **Parking:** on-site (fee) and valet. **Terms:** check-in 4 pm. **Amenities:** video games, safes. **Pool(s):** outdoor. **Activities:** exercise room. **Guest Services:** valet laundry.

SAVE ECO 🍴 🛎 ☂ 🏊 BIZ
🛜 ✕ 📷 🖥 💻 🚐

THE THOMAS BOND HOUSE B & B   215/923-8523 23

◤◤◤
Historic Bed & Breakfast
$125-$205

Address: 129 S 2nd St 19106 **Location:** Between Walnut and Chestnut sts; in Old City Historic District. 2nd, 63. **Facility:** The 1769 Georgian Revival home has a variety of rooms, from compact to comfortable, and a convenient location to Old City attractions. Rooms are furnished with antiques and reproductions. 12 units. 4 stories (no elevator), interior corridors. **Parking:** on-site (fee). **Terms:** 3 day cancellation notice-fee imposed.

SAVE 🍴 🛜 ✕ 🚐

THE WESTIN PHILADELPHIA   (215)563-1600 21

◤◤◤ ◤◤◤
Hotel
$109-$1999

WESTIN
HOTELS & RESORTS

AAA Benefit: Members save up to 15%, plus Starwood Preferred Guest® benefits!

Address: 99 S 17th St at Liberty Pl 19103 **Location:** Between Market and Chestnut sts. 15th, 68. **Facility:** A modern-style lounge, marble floors and elegant furnishings set the luxurious tone at this downtown hotel. An upscale shopping center is conveniently located within the building. 294 units. 15 stories, interior corridors. **Parking:** on-site (fee) and valet. **Terms:** cancellation fee imposed. **Amenities:** video games, safes. **Dining:** Winthorpe & Valentine Bar and Grill, see separate listing. **Activities:** sauna, exercise room, massage. **Guest Services:** valet laundry.

SAVE 🍴 🛎 ☂ BIZ 🐾 ✕ 📷 💻
/SOME UNITS 🛏 SHS 🖥 🚐

Recommend places you'd like us to inspect
at AAA.com/TourBookComments

(See map & index p. 266.)

THE WINDSOR SUITES
215/981-5678 **8**

Hotel
Rates not provided

Address: 1700 Benjamin Franklin Pkwy 19103 **Location:** At 17th St and Benjamin Franklin Pkwy. Suburban, 221. **Facility:** 125 efficiencies. 24 stories, interior corridors. **Parking:** on-site (fee) and valet. **Amenities:** safes. **Dining:** 2 restaurants. **Pool(s):** heated outdoor. **Activities:** exercise room. **Guest Services:** valet and coin laundry.

WYNDHAM PHILADELPHIA HISTORIC DISTRICT
(215)923-8660 **7**

Hotel
$129-$409

Address: 400 Arch St 19106 **Location:** Jct 4th and Arch sts. Located in Old City Historic District. 5th, 64. **Facility:** 364 units. 8 stories, interior corridors. **Parking:** on-site (fee). **Terms:** check-in 4 pm, cancellation fee imposed. **Pool(s):** outdoor. **Activities:** exercise room and coin laundry. **Guest Services:** valet and coin laundry.

WHERE TO EAT

10 ARTS BISTRO & LOUNGE BY ERIC RIPERT
215/523-8273 **65**

American. Fine Dining. $12-$35 **AAA Inspector Notes:** This restaurant is located against the rear wall in the open lobby, which features elegant marble columns and modern furnishings. Experience tried-and-true favorites such as macaroni and cheese, steak frites and pasta Bolognese. **Features:** full bar, happy hour. **Reservations:** suggested, for dinner. **Address:** Ten Avenue of the Arts 19102 **Location:** On Broad St; between Market and Chestnut sts; in The Ritz-Carlton Philadelphia. City Hall, 118. **Parking:** on-site (fee) and valet. B L D

AKI JAPANESE FUSION RESTAURANT & SAKE BAR
215/985-1838 **102**

Japanese. Casual Dining. $9-$26 **AAA Inspector Notes:** This restaurant offers a variety of sushi as well as cooked Japanese favorites, including salmon teriyaki and chicken katsu. This sleek downtown eatery also features a happy hour, which is popular for the delicious potables and half-priced appetizer menu. **Features:** full bar. **Reservations:** suggested, for dinner. **Address:** 1210 Walnut St 19107 **Location:** Just w of 12th St. 12th-13th & Locust, 141.
L D

A.KITCHEN
215/825-7030 **106**

American. Casual Dining. $8-$26 **AAA Inspector Notes:** This small restaurant just off Rittenhouse Square has an intimate atmosphere with dim lighting, cozy two-person tables and an open kitchen where guests can see the chefs preparing each meal. A variety of smaller dishes are offered ranging from Wagyu steak to hamachi crudo. The extensive wine and cocktail list allows for great pairings with any entrée choice. Make sure to call ahead, as there is limited seating. **Features:** full bar, patio dining, Sunday brunch. **Reservations:** suggested. **Address:** 135 S 18th St 19103 **Location:** Between Walnut and Sansom sts. 15th-16th & Locust, 140. **Parking:** street only. L D

Enjoy great member rates and benefits
at AAA/CAA Preferred Hotels

ALMA DE CUBA
215/988-1799 **107**

Cuban. Fine Dining. $5-$32 **AAA Inspector Notes:** Take a figurative journey to Old Cuba by stepping inside this intimate restaurant decorated with black-and-white photographs of Cuban scenes, ceiling fans and glass walls laminated with images of tobacco leaves. The menu continues in the same direction by lining up such favorites as vaca frita, a twice-cooked crispy skirt steak with onions, Cuban oregano, black beans and white rice. The delicious variety of classic cocktails provides perfect pairings. **Features:** full bar. **Reservations:** suggested. **Address:** 1623 Walnut St 19103 **Location:** Just e of jct Walnut and 17th sts. 15th-16th & Locust, 140. **Parking:** valet and street only. D

ALYAN'S
215/922-3553 **157**

Middle Eastern. Casual Dining. $5-$14 **AAA Inspector Notes:** This restaurant doesn't serve alcoholic beverages, but you're free to bring along your own. Since 1982, the modest, intimate spot has turned out great preparations of Middle Eastern cuisine such as kebabs, rib-eye steaks, Middle Eastern chicken cutlets and sandwiches, all of which can be eaten on site or boxed up for carry-out. **Features:** patio dining. **Location:** Jct South St. 9th-10th & Locust, 142. **Parking:** street only. L D

AMADA
215/625-2450 **51**

Spanish Small Plates. Fine Dining. $15-$45 **AAA Inspector Notes:** Find a wide variety of traditional tapas and entrées sharing menu space with Continental offerings at this sleek modern restaurant. Garlic shrimp, marinated olives, aged Manchego cheese and salchichon sausage bring a taste of Barcelona to Philly. The desserts and sangria don't fail; a meal here is not complete without at least one sampling of each. **Features:** full bar, Sunday brunch, happy hour. **Reservations:** suggested. **Address:** 217 Chestnut St 19106 **Location:** Between 2nd and 3rd sts. 2nd, 63. **Parking:** valet and street only. L D CALL

AMIS
215/732-2647 **150**

Italian. Casual Dining. $10-$26 **AAA Inspector Notes:** The city-casual restaurant offers a modern take on Roman fare. Highlights include fresh cheese, homemade pasta and salami, which are all paired with locally sourced veggies, seafood and Prime cuts of meat. The wine list offers a number of affordable gems. **Features:** full bar, Sunday brunch. **Reservations:** suggested. **Address:** 412 S 13th St 19147 **Location:** Between Pine and Lombard sts. Lombard-South, 116. **Parking:** street only. D CALL

ARIANA RESTAURANT
215/922-1535 **53**

Afghan. Casual Dining. $8-$16 **AAA Inspector Notes:** Not too spicy, this restaurant's menu reflects the delicate seasoning of the country's cuisine and draws influence from the traditional foods of many surrounding countries. As you settle down into this cozy spot, look around at the traditional Afghani clothing, photographs and rugs that decorate the dining room. A hookah lounge and appetizers are offered late at night. **Reservations:** suggested. **Address:** 134 Chestnut St 19106 **Location:** Between 2nd and Front sts. 2nd, 63. **Parking:** street only. D

AUDREY CLAIRE
215/731-1222 **143**

Mediterranean. Casual Dining. $17-$26 **AAA Inspector Notes:** This bring-your-own-bottle restaurant is a favorite of locals in the area. Delicious Mediterranean food is served in an active and loud atmosphere. When weather permits, outdoor seating is available in addition to their limited seating inside. A great spot for a group or couple, just make sure to have reservations ahead of time. **Reservations:** suggested. **Address:** 276 S 20th St 19103 **Location:** Jct 20th and Spruce sts. 15th-16th & Locust, 140. **Parking:** street only.
D

AZALEA
215/925-0000 **54**

American. Fine Dining. $11-$30 **AAA Inspector Notes:** Settle in to a large, tiger-skin-like upholstered armchair to admire the decorative mirrors and chandeliers adorning the dining room. Plush window treatments drape large windows overlooking Independence National Historic Park. Exceptionally personable service enhances the refined dining experience at this opulently furnished classic regional American restaurant. Once you decide on one of the well-prepared, attractively presented entrées, consult the extensive wine list for a proper complement. **Features:** full bar, Sunday brunch. **Reservations:** suggested. **Address:** 401 Chestnut St 19106 **Location:** Jct 4th St; in Omni Hotel at Independence Park. 5th, 64. **Parking:** valet only. B L D

(See map & index p. 266.)

BANK AND BOURBON   215/231-7300 (45)
▼▼▼ American. Casual Dining. $12-$34 **AAA Inspector Notes:** The inside of this open-kitchen concept restaurant blends a rustic tavern décor with elegant, contemporary furnishings. Light earth tones and modern lighting fill the dining room and surround the long wooden bar located in the center of the restaurant. The menu focuses on hearty fare such as roasted Lancaster chicken, a 24 day dry-aged burger and wild king salmon. As the name suggests, bourbon is a highlight here and an on-site expert can provide all the information you may need. **Reservations:** suggested, for dinner. **Address:** 1200 Market St 19107 **Location:** Corner of 12th and Market sts; in Loews Philadelphia Hotel. 🚇 13th, 67. **Parking:** on-site (fee) and valet.

[B] [L] [D] CALL ⚲M 🚇

BARBUZZO   215/546-9300 (77)
▼▼▼ Mediterranean. Fine Dining. $10-$17 **AAA Inspector Notes:** Tastefully done décor and exquisite, mouthwatering dishes are what you will find at this local favorite. A modern twist on traditional fare puts forth menu options such as pan-seared gnocchi with almond-milk pesto and braised short ribs with walnut-orange gremolata. Truly a must-go! **Features:** full bar. **Reservations:** suggested. **Address:** 110 S 13th St 19107 **Location:** Between Chestnut and Sansom sts. 🚇 Walnut-Locust, 117. **Parking:** street only. [L] [D] 🚇

BARCLAY PRIME   215/732-7560 (131)
▼▼▼▼ Steak. Fine Dining. $20-$100 **AAA Inspector Notes:** This luxury boutique steakhouse, hidden away in Rittenhouse Square, offers an elegant bar and lounge area with a white and black theme and dark wood accents. The dining room provides a dim and intimate atmosphere with decorative chandeliers and upscale furnishings. The menu consists of a variety of large portion, high-grade steaks served a la carte. **Features:** full bar. **Reservations:** suggested. **Address:** 237 S 18th St 19103 **Location:** Between Rittenhouse Square and Manning St. 🚇 15th-16th & Locust, 140. **Parking:** street only. [D] 🚇

BARRA RESTAURANT   215/238-6900 (52)
▼▼▼ Italian. Casual Dining. $9-$26 **AAA Inspector Notes:** This chic restaurant is located in the heart of the Old City Historic District and is the sister property of Birra in South Philly. Inside, guests will find modern décor with bright colors, a sleek bar and a large brick oven for their gourmet pizzas. The menu touches on a variety of foods, but we recommend sticking to their Italian specialties. **Features:** full bar, Sunday brunch, happy hour. **Address:** 239 Chestnut St 19106 **Location:** Jct 3rd and Chestnut sts, just e. 🚇 2nd, 63. **Parking:** street only. [L] [D] 🚇

BEAU MONDE   215/592-0656 (162)
▼▼ Northern French. Casual Dining. $10-$29 **AAA Inspector Notes:** A local favorite, this corner restaurant offers a cozy dining room as well as a wraparound outdoor patio when weather permits. The menu provides a variety of create-your-own savory and sweet crepes. Popular combinations include Beau Monde pizza, beef bourguignon with apples, and toasted almonds with caramel and vanilla ice cream. **Features:** full bar, patio dining, Sunday brunch. **Address:** 624 S 6th St 19147 **Location:** Corner of 6th and Bainbridge sts. 🚇 9th-10th & Locust, 142. **Parking:** street only.

[L] [D] CALL ⚲M 🚇

THE BELGIAN CAFE   215/235-3500 (3)
▼▼ Belgian. Casual Dining. $9-$20 **AAA Inspector Notes:** Don't be afraid to ask for guidance from your server on the detailed beer list, which includes a long lineup of Belgian beers. Warm and beautiful murals surround an eager crowd of young professionals and grad students at this art museum area spot. Give strong thought to trying the mussels, which are served in a variety of sauces—be sure to request bread for dipping. **Features:** full bar, Sunday brunch. **Address:** 601 N 21st St 19130 **Location:** Jct 21st and Green sts. 🚇 Spring Garden, 120. **Parking:** street only.

[L] [D] CALL ⚲M 🚇

BELLINI GRILL   215/545-1191 (119)
▼▼ Italian. Casual Dining. $12-$32 **AAA Inspector Notes:** Family-owned and -operated Bellini Grill welcomes you with a warm greeting from the owner. Be sure to make a reservation, as space in the dining room is limited. Bring your own wine to enjoy with the large portions of delicious food. **Features:** full bar. **Address:** 220 S 16th St 19102 **Location:** Between Locust and Walnut sts. 🚇 15th-16th & Locust, 140. **Parking:** street only. [L] [D] CALL ⚲M 🚇

BIBOU   215/965-8290 (179)
▼▼▼ French. Fine Dining. $26-$32 **AAA Inspector Notes:** Don't let the intimate dining room and close tables fool you. The menu changes often, but the restaurant's exquisite take on French cuisine is consistent. Staple items include duo de foie gras, which allows guests to experience foie gras seared as well as in a custard. Also, this restaurant allows guests to bring their favorite wine from home. **Reservations:** required. **Address:** 1009 S 8th St 19147 **Location:** Jct 8th and Kimball sts. 🚇 Ellsworth-Federal, 115. **Parking:** street only. [D] 🚇

BISTRO 7   215/931-1560 (33)
▼▼ French. Casual Dining. $24-$32 **AAA Inspector Notes:** *Classic.* This bring-your-own-bottle restaurant offers an intimate and active atmosphere with an open kitchen layout and limited seating available. The seasonally-changing menu incorporates a combination of French and American cuisine with fresh ingredients from local farmers. Check out the tasting menu when available to experience a variety of flavor and delicious combinations. Make sure to call ahead for reservations as this is a local favorite. **Reservations:** suggested. **Address:** 7 N 3rd St 19106 **Location:** Between Market and Church sts. 🚇 2nd, 63. **Parking:** street only. [D] 🚇

BISTRO LA BAIA   215/546-0496 (154)
▼▼ Italian. Casual Dining. $11-$16 **AAA Inspector Notes:** This intimate setting replicates the true Italian bistro: small, simple and quaint with food that's big on flavor, spice and taste. Only cash is accepted, and patrons should bring their own beer or wine. **Reservations:** suggested, for dinner. **Address:** 1700 Lombard St 19146 **Location:** SR 126 exit 12 (10th St) northbound, 0.5 mi w, then just s. 🚇 Lombard-South, 116. **Parking:** street only.

[L] [D] 🚇

BISTRO LA VIOLA   215/735-8630 (134)
▼▼ Italian. Casual Dining. $14-$18 **AAA Inspector Notes:** This dining room may be small, but the portions are anything but. Old-country flavors lend a distinctive touch to the homemade dishes. You can count on the friendly staff to welcome you warmly. Bring-your-own-bottle wine service is available at this cozy, cash-only eatery. **Reservations:** suggested. **Address:** 253 S 16th St 19102 **Location:** Between Locust and Spruce sts. 🚇 15th-16th & Locust, 140. **Parking:** street only. [L] [D] 🚇

BISTRO ST. TROPEZ   215/569-9269   55

▼▼▼ Regional French. Casual Dining. $8-$29 **AAA Inspector Notes:** Chef Rames draws tropical warmth from this downtown corner, where you'll sit down to daily changing dishes of Provençal French cuisine. Inside guests will be surrounded by panoramic views of the Schuylkill River and Historic 30th Street Train Station. Quality never wavers in Bistro St. Tropez's innovative preparations of fresh seafood, quality meats and fresh vegetables. **Features:** beer & wine, Sunday brunch, happy hour. **Reservations:** suggested, for dinner. **Address:** 2400 Market St 19103 **Location:** I-76 (Schuylkill Expwy) exit 344 (30th St Station), just w; across from PECO Building; in Market Design Center. ⊞ 22nd, 70. **Parking:** street only.

Ⓛ Ⓓ 🚲

THE BLACK SHEEP PUB & RESTAURANT
215/545-9473   130

▼▼ American. Casual Dining. $8-$23 **AAA Inspector Notes:** This charming Irish-inspired pub features a small dining room with dark wood furnishings, a cozy fireplace and windows that open up to 17th Street when weather permits. Additional bars and seating are open upstairs and downstairs during busy nights. Don't expect standard bar fare at this pub that puts forth options such as slow-braised short ribs. Servers are hard to come by as locals frequent this spot, so grab one when you can. **Features:** full bar, happy hour. **Address:** 247 S 17th St 19103 **Location:** Between Locust and Spruce sts. ⊞ 15th-16th & Locust, 140. **Parking:** on-site (fee).

Ⓛ Ⓓ 🚲

BLISS   215/731-1100   114

▼▼▼ New American. Fine Dining. $12-$36 **AAA Inspector Notes:** Find the chic, yet sophisticated, Bliss in the heart of the City Center. Boasting high ceilings, its interior is nicely appointed with mahogany wood accents and a tranquil blue wall decoration. Asian, French and Italian cuisines influence the chef's contemporary American dishes. The delightful menu may include a pan-seared sirloin with potato puree gratin and shallot-merlot glaze as well as sweet and sour crispy red snapper and stir-fried red chile prawns. Vegetarian offerings are plentiful. **Features:** full bar, Sunday brunch, happy hour. **Reservations:** suggested. **Address:** 220 S Broad St 19102 **Location:** Between Locust and Walnut sts. ⊞ Walnut-Locust, 117. **Parking:** on-site (fee). Ⓛ Ⓓ 🚲

BRIDGET FOY'S   215/922-1813   151

▼▼ American. Casual Dining. $11-$22 **AAA Inspector Notes:** This upbeat and dynamic restaurant tempts you with American, Mexican and Caribbean dishes that are as appealing to the eye as they are pleasing to the palate. The bustling South Street location exudes stylish contemporary flair with a gorgeous outdoor dining area perfect for people-watching. **Features:** full bar, patio dining, Sunday brunch, happy hour. **Address:** 200 South St 19147 **Location:** Jct 2nd St. ⊞ 2nd, 63. **Parking:** street only. Ⓛ Ⓓ 🚲

BUDDAKAN   215/574-9440   50

▼▼▼ Asian. Fine Dining. $15-$48 **AAA Inspector Notes:** With flowing white fabrics to either side, an imposing gilded statue of Buddha commands center stage at the elegant restaurant, which features a mezzanine dining area, open kitchen and a 20-person under-lit community table. The popular, ultra-chic dining room is a nice backdrop for dishes that fuse modern Asian cuisines. The signature dish is angry lobster, a wok-seared 3-pounder served in a nest of lobster mashed potatoes and served with wok-charred vegetables and coconut-curry sauce. **Features:** full bar. **Reservations:** suggested. **Address:** 325 Chestnut St 19106 **Location:** Between 3rd and 4th sts. ⊞ 5th, 64. **Parking:** valet and street only.

Ⓛ Ⓓ 🚲

THE CAMBRIDGE   267/455-0647   164

▼▼ American. Casual Dining. $10-$20 **AAA Inspector Notes:** This casual spot is decorated as an English pub with exposed-brick accents and windows that open up completely to South Street. The menu features upscale bar fare, including customizable burgers and savory appetizers. Sunday brunch is always a busy time with excellent breakfast foods and morning cocktails. **Features:** full bar, Sunday brunch, happy hour. **Reservations:** suggested, Sunday brunch. **Address:** 1508 South St 19146 **Location:** Between 15th and 16th sts. ⊞ Lombard-South, 116. **Parking:** street only.

Ⓓ 🚲

CAMPO'S DELI   215/923-1000   34

▼ Sandwiches. Quick Serve. $7-$10 **AAA Inspector Notes:** This small delicatessen has been around for a long time, thanks in part to its excellent cheesesteak. Families are welcomed here. **Features:** beer only. **Address:** 214 Market St 19106 **Location:** Jct Market and S Strawberry sts. ⊞ 2nd, 63. **Parking:** street only.

Ⓛ Ⓓ 🚲

THE CAPITAL GRILLE   215/545-9588   66

▼▼▼ Steak. Fine Dining. $13-$48 **AAA Inspector Notes:** Cherry wood and red leather assist in making this clubby dining room a beautiful spot to dine on excellent cuts of dry-aged beef. The staff is highly attentive and knowledgeable. **Features:** full bar, patio dining. **Address:** 1338 Chestnut St 19107 **Location:** Between Broad and 13th sts. ⊞ City Hall, 118. **Parking:** valet only.

Ⓛ Ⓓ 🚲

CARIBOU CAFÉ   215/625-9535   101

▼▼ French. Casual Dining. $10-$23 **AAA Inspector Notes:** The menu shows a clear French influence from the escargot hors d'oeuvres to the variety of gourmet crepes. The second-floor loft overlooks the first-floor bar. **Features:** full bar, Sunday brunch. **Reservations:** suggested, for dinner. **Address:** 1126 Walnut St 19107 **Location:** Corner of 12th and Walnut sts. ⊞ 12th-13th & Locust, 141. **Parking:** on-site (fee) and street. Ⓛ Ⓓ 🚲

CATAHOULA   215/271-9300   172

▼▼ Cajun. Casual Dining. $10-$19 **AAA Inspector Notes:** Don't be fooled by the small dining area and sleek high-top tables at Catahoula. Here you can sample big Louisiana flavors. Anything on the menu is a winner, but you must try the smoked Gouda grits. Just a short walk from the bustle of South Street, this cozy spot is a welcomed respite. **Features:** full bar, Sunday brunch. **Address:** 775 S Front St 19147 **Location:** Just s of jct Fitzwater St. ⊞ 2nd, 63. **Parking:** street only. Ⓓ LATE CALL 🅶Ⓜ 🚲

CHARLIE WAS A SINNER   267/758-5372   183

▼ Vegan Small Plates. Casual Dining. $7-$12 **AAA Inspector Notes:** This hip spot beautifully blends a fun cocktail bar atmosphere with an intimate dining room putting forth delicious small plates of vegan fare. These dishes are great for sharing and include such savory options as roasted Brussels sprouts with grain-mustard aioli and potato gnocchi with butternut squash barigoule. Be sure to save room for some incredible desserts or after-dinner liquors. **Features:** happy hour. **Reservations:** suggested. **Address:** 131 S 13th St 19107 **Location:** Between Sansom and Walnut sts. ⊞ 12th-13th & Locust, 141. **Parking:** street only. Ⓓ 🚲

CITY TAVERN   215/413-1443   80

▼▼▼
American Casual Dining $9-$27

AAA Inspector Notes: Many a founding father patronized the original City Tavern, which opened its doors on a prominent Independence Square spot in 1773. The tradition continues today in this re-creation, which aptly captures the Colonial spirit and style of its predecessor. A modern twist adds interest to dishes inspired by 18th-century recipes. Consider selections such as lobster pie served in a pewter pot, roast duckling, glazed duck, fried oysters or Sally Lunn bread. **Features:** full bar, patio dining. **Reservations:** suggested. **Address:** 138 S 2nd St 19106 **Location:** Corner of 2nd and Walnut sts. ⊞ 2nd, 63. **Parking:** valet and street only.

Menu on AAA.com Ⓛ Ⓓ 🐾 🚲

THE CONTINENTAL MIDTOWN   215/567-1800   68

▼▼ American. Casual Dining. $6-$32 **AAA Inspector Notes:** Raise a martini glass to this outstanding restaurant, which exudes retro style in everything, from its sleek blue vinyl booths to the hanging wicker chairs in the upstairs lounge and sunken living room below. You'll also want to send up a toast for the good food such as seared tuna with mushroom risotto, lush lobster macaroni and cheese, hefty burgers and triple-deckers, intriguing crab pad thai, and ingenious French onion soup dumplings. **Features:** full bar, Sunday brunch, happy hour. **Reservations:** suggested. **Address:** 1801 Chestnut St 19102 **Location:** At 18th St. ⊞ 19th, 69. **Parking:** street only. Ⓛ Ⓓ LATE 🚲

THE CONTINENTAL RESTAURANT & MARTINI BAR
215/923-6069 (38)

WWWW American. Casual Dining. $8-$32 **AAA Inspector Notes:** This restaurant nurtures the sultry atmosphere of the kind of place that Dean Martin and other Rat Packers would have frequented in their heyday. Order any of the many martinis from the bar, then nurse it along as you survey the setting, most notable for the overhead chandeliers crafted to resemble cocktail olives skewered with a toothpick. Drawing on the influences of many cultures, the menu spans from pad thai and hummus to miso soup and nicely presented Maryland crabcakes. **Features:** full bar, Sunday brunch, happy hour. **Reservations:** suggested. **Address:** 138 Market St 19106 **Location:** Jct 2nd St; in Old City Historic District. 2nd, 63. **Parking:** street only. L D LATE

CUBA LIBRE RESTAURANT & RUM BAR 215/627-0666 (40)

WWWW Cuban. Fine Dining. $8-$33 **AAA Inspector Notes:** A vibrant atmosphere replicating the streets of 1940s Havana is full of visual interest with lush vegetation, romantic balconies, stained glass, quaint murals and whirling fans. Energetic music still allows conversation, which may drift to eye-popping plates of spicy guava barbecue ribs, smoking ceviche platters and bronzed rum-, honey- and mango-coated salmon. Grilled spice-rubbed rib-eye with jalapeño chimichurri is a house specialty and ropa vieja also is recommended. **Features:** full bar, Sunday brunch, happy hour. **Reservations:** suggested. **Address:** 10 S 2nd St 19106 **Location:** Between Chestnut and Market sts. 2nd, 63. **Parking:** valet only. L D

CUCINA FORTE 215/238-0778 (173)

WW Italian. Casual Dining. $13-$32 **AAA Inspector Notes:** Cucina Forte's forte is classic Italian fare, which chef-owner Maria Forte prepares to raves. Relax in the tiny storefront while savoring ricotta gnocchi and chicken- and tomato-filled dream soup that indeed is a thing of dreams. Pleasant servers circulate through the homelike setting. **Reservations:** suggested. **Address:** 768 S 8th St 19147 **Location:** Between Catharine and Fitzwater sts. 9th-10th & Locust, 142. **Parking:** street only. D

THE DANDELION 215/558-2500 (91)

WWWW American. Gastropub. $13-$28 **AAA Inspector Notes:** This gastropub offers a limited menu, but each dish has a delicious array of ingredients. Equipped with multiple bars in an intimate setting, guests can find a huge variety of beer, wine and cocktails. A great spot for a drink and quick bite or for a full dining experience. **Features:** full bar, Sunday brunch, happy hour. **Reservations:** suggested. **Address:** 124 S 18th St 19103 **Location:** Corner of 18th and Samson sts. 19th, 69. **Parking:** street only.
L D LATE

D'ANGELO'S RISTORANTE ITALIANO 215/546-3935 (138)

WW Italian. Fine Dining. $10-$40 **AAA Inspector Notes:** Near Rittenhouse Square, this family-run restaurant prepares all the classics with Old World-style sauce. The extensive wine list makes for great entrée pairings. **Features:** full bar. **Reservations:** suggested, weekends. **Address:** 256 S 20th St 19103 **Location:** Between Locust and Spruce sts. 15th-16th & Locust, 140. **Parking:** street only. L D LATE

DANTE & LUIGI'S 215/922-9501 (174)

WW Italian. Casual Dining. $7-$30 **AAA Inspector Notes:** Traditional antipasti, secondi and primi are offered at the casual neighborhood restaurant. Your meal might span the menu from Caprese salad to calamari to lasagna Bolognese to luscious tiramisu. **Features:** full bar. **Reservations:** suggested. **Address:** 762 S 10th St 19147 **Location:** Corner of S 10th and Catharine sts. Lombard-South, 116. **Parking:** valet and street only. L D

DAVIO'S NORTHERN ITALIAN STEAKHOUSE
215/563-4810 (81)

WWWW Northern Italian. Fine Dining. $12-$55 **AAA Inspector Notes:** Situated in the historic Provident Bank Building in Center City, this dining room projects subdued elegance with high ceilings, attractive carved wood moldings, tall columns, arched windows and polished wood floors. An example from the menu is seared Provimi rib veal chop served with spinach, prosciutto ham, Reggiano cheese and polenta. **Features:** full bar. **Reservations:** suggested. **Address:** 111 S 17th St 19103 **Location:** Between Sansom and Chestnut sts. 15th-16th & Locust, 140. **Parking:** street only.
B L D CALL M

DAY BY DAY 215/564-5540 (98)

WWW American. Casual Dining. $7-$15 **AAA Inspector Notes:** The exciting and interesting menu at this popular brunch spot changes every few days. Eager, friendly servers are willing to make a couple of suggestions for those who cannot decide. This is a popular place among locals. **Features:** Sunday brunch. **Address:** 2101 Sansom St 19103 **Location:** Between 21st and 22nd sts. 22nd, 70. **Parking:** street only. B L

DEL FRISCO'S DOUBLE EAGLE STEAK HOUSE
215/246-0533 (69)

WWWW Steak. Fine Dining. $14-$59 **AAA Inspector Notes:** From the second you walk inside this restaurant you will be absolutely wowed by the dazzling and elaborately designed ceilings, massive marble columns and elegantly designed two-story wine vault placed at the center of the dining room. The lunch menu features some more casual items such as a prime cheeseburger or lobster shrimp club. However, the true specialties are the mouth-watering steaks, including prime rib-eye, filet mignon and veal porterhouse. **Features:** full bar. **Address:** 1426 Chestnut St 19102 **Location:** Jct 15th and Chestnut sts. City Hall, 118. **Parking:** street only.
L D CALL M

DEVIL'S ALLEY BAR AND GRILL 215/751-0707 (71)

WW American. Casual Dining. $10-$19 **AAA Inspector Notes:** Don't let the name scare you. This casual spot serves up excellent American fare, including smoked beef brisket, fried green tomatoes and pulled pork sliders. Inside, guests will find a bar/lounge area upstairs and a relaxed dining room with booth seating below. Be sure to make reservations for Sunday brunch as it tends to be very busy. **Features:** full bar, Sunday brunch, happy hour. **Address:** 1907 Chestnut St 19103 **Location:** Between 19th and 20th sts. 19th, 69. **Parking:** street only. L D

DEVON SEAFOOD GRILL 215/546-5940 (125)

WWW Seafood. Fine Dining. $13-$66 **AAA Inspector Notes:** Fin fans say there is nothing fishy about this grill, which serves large portions of fresh seafood from around the world, including mahi mahi from Costa Rica and 2-pound cold-water lobster from Maine. Its location directly off Rittenhouse Square provides great scenery for guests. **Features:** full bar, Sunday brunch, happy hour. **Reservations:** suggested. **Address:** 225 S 18th St 19103 **Location:** Between Walnut and Locust sts; at Rittenhouse Square. 15th-16th & Locust, 140. **Parking:** street only. L D LATE

DINARDO'S FAMOUS SEAFOOD 215/925-5115 (14)

WW Seafood. Casual Dining. $11-$48 **AAA Inspector Notes:** Located in the Old City Historic District, this restaurant has been serving up its famous Gulf Coast crabs since 1976. Large portions of crab steamed in a secret seasoning are a popular choice. Other great selections include New Orleans-style shrimp, filet mignon and a pescatore pasta dish with fresh shrimp, scallops, mussels and clams over linguine. The décor is a little dated, but the fresh seafood makes up for it. **Features:** full bar. **Reservations:** suggested. **Address:** 312 Race St 19106 **Location:** Between 3rd and 4th sts. 5th, 64. **Parking:** street only. L D

DI NIC'S ROAST BEEF & PORK 215/923-6175 (32)

W Sandwiches. Quick Serve. $5-$8 **AAA Inspector Notes:** Diners can grab a stool at the small counter in the center of the Reading Terminal Market to sample the sandwiches that have garnered high praise in this sandwich-crazed city. As the name suggests, roast beef and pork are the reigning crowd pleasers, but scalloppines also merit a slice of the raves. Favorite toppings include sharp provolone, greens and peppers. **Address:** 12th St & Filbert St 19107 **Location:** In Center City; in Reading Terminal Market. Market East, 222. **Parking:** street only. B L D

DMITRI'S 215/625-0556 (175)

WW Mediterranean. Casual Dining. $8-$20 **AAA Inspector Notes:** Your palate will note Mediterranean flavors in Dimitri's (mostly) Greek cuisine. In fact, you can watch as chefs prepare meals in the open kitchen, the focal point of this small but lively dining room. The restaurant lacks a liquor license but does provide BYOB service, so feel free to bring along a favorite wine to enjoy with your entrée. Striped bass served with steamed escarole and herbed rice is a favorite. **Features:** patio dining. **Address:** 795 S 3rd St 19147 **Location:** Jct 3rd and Catharine sts; in Queens Village area. 9th-10th & Locust, 142. **Parking:** street only. D

DOWN HOME DINER   215/627-1955   (44)
▼▼ American. Family Dining. $5-$13 **AAA Inspector Notes:**
Farm-fresh ingredients go into this busy diner's home-cooked dishes, which exemplify excellent taste. Scrumptious pancakes and Grandma's meatloaf are among choices priced to please the budget-conscious. **Address:** 1039 Reading Terminal Market 19107 **Location:** Jct 12th and Filbert sts. 11th, 66. **Parking:** street only.

[B] [L] [D] 🚇

EL FUEGO   215/592-1901   (90)
▼ Mexican. Quick Serve. $4-$10 **AAA Inspector Notes:** You can try several varieties of salsa and beer with the California-style burritos, tacos and quesadillas at El Fuego. Spice lovers should venture out and try the slow-cooked spicy beef. **Features:** beer only. **Address:** 723 Walnut St 19106 **Location:** Between 7th and 8th sts. 9th-10th & Locust, 142. **Parking:** street only.

[L] [D] 🚇

EL VEZ   215/928-9800   (76)
▼▼▼ Mexican. Casual Dining. $8-$28 **AAA Inspector Notes:**
The spirit of a Mexican fiesta and the cool style of Elvis Presley make strange but delicious bedfellows at this downtown establishment. Sample traditional Latin food created with a variety of Continental ingredients such as lump crabmeat, pineapple and Kobe steak. The overall dining experience at El Vez is joyful and different. Folks pack the place on the weekends, so be sure to make a reservation. **Features:** full bar, Sunday brunch. **Reservations:** suggested. **Address:** 121 S 13th St 19107 **Location:** Jct Sansom St. 12th-13th & Locust, 141. **Parking:** street only.

[L] [D] 🚇

FADO IRISH PUB   215/893-9700   (128)
▼▼ Irish. Casual Dining. $10-$17 **AAA Inspector Notes:** This casual spot is decorated with dark woods, a large wraparound bar and is busiest during large soccer or rugby sporting events. Traditional, hearty dishes can be found on the menu, like shepherd's pie, bleu cheese and lamb sliders and Harp-battered fish tacos. A nice selection of local and international beers make for great pairings. **Features:** full bar, Sunday brunch, happy hour. **Address:** 1500 Locust St 19103 **Location:** Jct Locust and 15th sts. 15th-16th & Locust, 140. **Parking:** street only.

[L] [D] 🚇

FAMOUS 4TH STREET DELICATESSEN   215/922-3274   (163)
▼▼ Deli. Casual Dining. $9-$27 **AAA Inspector Notes:**
Classic. For more than 85 years, locals have flocked here for delicatessen staples: overstuffed sandwiches of corned beef, salami, brisket, pastrami and turkey in addition to tasty smoked Nova, lox and salmon. If you'd prefer something in the entrée category, consider the breaded veal chop, stuffed cabbage or chicken in the pot. Breakfast choices and luscious desserts also merit a taste. Your check is brought to your table with a sweet treat: chocolate chip cookies. **Address:** 700 S 4th St 19147 **Location:** Jct Fitzwater and 4th sts. 9th-10th & Locust, 142. **Parking:** street only.

[B] [L] [D] 🚇

FARMICIA   215/627-6274   (42)
▼▼▼ Continental. Casual Dining. $8-$29 **AAA Inspector Notes:** With a changing menu full of fresh, local ingredients, this spot offers flavorful dishes and good value. The owners and staff are happy to guide patrons through the meal, offering wonderful wine and cocktail pairings for each course. Although there is a full bar available, feel free to bring your favorite wine as there is no corkage fee. **Features:** full bar, Sunday brunch, happy hour. **Address:** 15 S 3rd St 19106 **Location:** Between Chestnut and Market sts. 2nd, 63. **Parking:** street only.

[B] [L] [D] CALL 🚇

FERGIE'S PUB   215/928-8118   (82)
▼▼ Irish. Casual Dining. $6-$14 **AAA Inspector Notes:** Select from a vast array of imported draft beers to enjoy with Fergie's great standards, including fish and chips, Angus beef brisket, shepherd's pie, juicy burgers and freshly made soups. If you'd prefer other options, consider grilled salmon, crab cakes, vegetarian chili or spinach salad. **Features:** full bar, happy hour. **Address:** 1214 Sansom St 19107 **Location:** Just w of 12th St. 12th-13th & Locust, 141. **Parking:** street only. [L] [D] [LATE] 🚇

FEZ MOROCCAN CUISINE   215/925-5367   (158)
▼▼ Moroccan. Casual Dining. $13-$25 **AAA Inspector Notes:** Costumed waiters serve traditional dishes such as lamb tagine, shish kebab, couscous and baklava under a re-created Moroccan wedding tent. Diners can ask for help with the menu if they are having trouble choosing a few dishes to share as the staff are attuned to the needs of newcomers. Belly dancers and hookah (flavored tobacco filtered through water and smoked through a pipe) is offered on Friday and Saturday nights drawing in a raucous younger crowd. **Features:** full bar. **Reservations:** suggested. **Address:** 620 S 2nd St 19147 **Location:** Between South and Bainbridge sts. 2nd, 63. **Parking:** street only. [D] 🚇

FORK   215/625-9425   (36)
▼▼▼ American. Casual Dining. $16-$40 **AAA Inspector Notes:** Whether you sit at the large square bar or at one of the comfortable bench seats along the walls, you'll get a good look at the open kitchen that adjoins the dining area. Creative dishes are a feast for the palate, including grilled lobster over polenta and swordfish with black trumpet mushrooms. **Features:** full bar, Sunday brunch. **Reservations:** suggested, for dinner. **Address:** 306 Market St 19106 **Location:** Between 3rd and 4th sts. 2nd, 63. **Parking:** street only.

[L] [D] CALL 🚇

FOUNTAIN RESTAURANT   215/963-1500   (25)
▼▼▼▼ Continental. Fine Dining. $21-$44 **AAA Inspector Notes:** Overlooking Logan Square and the Swann Fountain, from which it gets its name, this restaurant excels on every level. Formally dressed staff members provide team service with grace and skill, meeting your every need as you navigate exquisite courses. An air of refined sophistication punctuates the dining room appointed in rich mahogany accents, gracious table appointments, original artwork, chandeliers and elegantly draped large windows. **Features:** full bar. **Reservations:** required. Semiformal attire. **Address:** 1 Logan Square 19103 **Location:** Corner of 18th St and Benjamin Franklin Pkwy; in Four Seasons Hotel Philadelphia. Suburban, 221. **Parking:** on-site (fee) and valet. [B] [L] [D] CALL 🚇

FOX AND HOUND   215/732-8610   (141)
▼▼ American. Casual Dining. $8-$16 **AAA Inspector Notes:** This is one of the best places in downtown Philadelphia to watch favorite sporting events in a lively atmosphere. This sports bar has all the essentials including ample seating, multiple TVs and a large variety of beer and cocktails. Expect huge crowds when any Philadelphia team is playing. **Features:** full bar, happy hour. **Address:** 1501 Spruce St 19102 **Location:** Jct 15th and Spruce sts. 15th-16th & Locust, 140. **Parking:** street only. [L] [D] 🚇

FRIDAY SATURDAY SUNDAY   215/546-4232   (140)
▼▼ American. Casual Dining. $21-$29 **AAA Inspector Notes:** Just off Rittenhouse Square, this bring-your-own-bottle restaurant is not much to look at from the outside, but has a charming homey setting once you enter. The dining area is small with decorative art pieces and cozy nooks for seating. The candles and dim lighting create a quiet and serene atmosphere. The menu provides a delicious variety of American cuisine using fresh, seasonal ingredients. **Features:** full bar. **Reservations:** suggested. **Address:** 261 S 21st St 19103 **Location:** Between Spruce and Locust sts. 22nd, 70. **Parking:** street only. [D] 🚇

GARCES TRADING COMPANY   215/574-1099   (120)
▼▼ Continental. Casual Dining. $8-$29 **AAA Inspector Notes:** This quaint restaurant resembles a European bistro with its cozy, small wood tables and long glass case at the entrance that sells an extensive variety of International meats and cheeses. While the GTC Burger is always a crowd favorite, those looking for a more refined meal may enjoy such entrées as sautéed Chatham cod or butternut squash cannelloni. Other additions include a variety of gourmet pizzas and cheeses from France, Italy and Spain. **Features:** full bar, Sunday brunch. **Address:** 1111 Locust St 19107 **Location:** Between 11th and 12th sts. 12th-13th & Locust, 141. **Parking:** street only.

[L] [D] 🚇

Keep your focus safely
on the road when driving

THE GARDEN RESTAURANT   215/278-7000   (8)

▼▼ ◆ American. Casual Dining. $14-$19 **AAA Inspector Notes:** After appreciating the spectacular Barnes Art Collection, guests can dine here. The seasonally changing menu focuses on fresh and local ingredients, with some foods coming from their own rooftop garden. When weather permits, feel free to enjoy the sun with a specialty cocktail in their outdoor courtyard. **Features:** full bar. **Address:** 2025 Benjamin Franklin Pkwy 19130 **Location:** Between 20th and 21st sts; in The Barnes Foundation. 🚇 19th, 69. **Parking:** on-site (fee). 🅛 CALL Ⓜ 🚇

GOOD DOG BAR & RESTAURANT   215/985-9600   (121)

▼▼▼ American. Casual Dining. $9-$21 **AAA Inspector Notes:** Luckily, you won't be expected to roll over or play dead to get the treats that are offered here. The restored 1920s tavern tempts you with upscale comfort food, including beet and goat cheese salad, truffled cheesesteak empanadas and the signature Good Dog burger, which is filled with Roquefort cheese and topped with caramelized onions. The staff, most of whom are tattooed and pierced, make a strong first impression, but they're sweet as pie. **Features:** full bar, happy hour. **Address:** 224 S 15th St 19102 **Location:** Just n of jct Locust St. 🚇 15th-16th & Locust, 140. **Parking:** street only.

🅛 🅓 [LATE] 🚇

GRACE'S TAVERN   215/893-9580   (168)

▼▼ American. Gastropub. $5-$14 **AAA Inspector Notes:** Although not much to look at from the outside, locals frequent this tavern for its extensive variety of beers and tasty dishes, including the can't-miss Kennett Square Burger. Inside guests will find dim lighting, a long wood bar and a handful of available tables. Friendly staff is always available to provide knowledge on the menu and make recommendations. **Features:** full bar, happy hour. **Address:** 2229 Grays Ferry Ave 19146 **Location:** Jct 23rd St and Grays Ferry Ave. 🚇 University City, 180. **Parking:** on-site (fee) and street.

🅛 🅓 [LATE] 🚇

HAN DYNASTY   215/922-1888   (48)

▼▼▼ Chinese. Casual Dining. $12-$23 **AAA Inspector Notes:** Spice lovers will rejoice at this truly authentic Szechuan restaurant set in an upscale converted-bank setting with grand décor complete with intricate vaulted ceilings and an elegantly appointed 20-foot bar. Entrées are all made to order and are able to be altered from mild to extremely spicy. During the winter months I recommend requesting a table away from the entrance. **Features:** full bar, happy hour. **Reservations:** suggested, weekends. **Address:** 123 Chestnut St 19106 **Location:** Between 2nd and Front sts. 🚇 2nd, 63. **Parking:** street only. 🅛 🅓 CALL Ⓜ 🚇

HARD ROCK CAFE   215/238-1000   (43)

▼▼ ▼ American. Casual Dining. $15-$23 **AAA Inspector Notes:** Rock 'n' roll memorabilia decorates the walls of the popular theme restaurant. Live music on the weekends contributes to the bustling atmosphere. On the menu is a wide variety of American cuisine—from burgers and sandwiches to seafood, steaks and pasta. **Features:** full bar. **Address:** 1113-31 Market St 19107 **Location:** Jct 12th St. 🚇 11th, 66. **Parking:** street only. [SAVE] 🅛 🅓 🚇

HARMONY VEGETARIAN RESTAURANT   215/627-4520   (24)

▼▼ Vegetarian. Casual Dining. $6-$13 **AAA Inspector Notes:** The all-vegetarian menu also is certified as kosher vegan. All of the delicious, healthful menu choices are prepared fresh to order, and you can ask for your meal to be hot and spicy if you prefer a little kick. **Address:** 135 N 9th St 19107 **Location:** Between Cherry and Race sts; in Chinatown. 🚇 8th and Market, 125. **Parking:** street only.

🅛 🅓 🚇

HOSTERIA DA ELIO   215/925-0930   (159)

▼▼ ▼ Italian. Casual Dining. $12-$27 **AAA Inspector Notes:** Tiny Hosteria Da Elio seats you in an inviting peach-hued dining room that overlooks the sidewalk or in a white and green one that leads to a small patio. Bring along a favorite bottle of wine to enjoy with host, owner and chef Elio's moderately priced specialties of traditional pasta and veal in addition to beef carpaccio and Gorgonzola or caprese salad. **Address:** 615 S 3rd St 19147 **Location:** Just s of jct South St. 🚇 9th-10th & Locust, 142. **Parking:** street only.

🅓 🚇

IMPERIAL INN   215/627-2299   (22)

▼▼ ▼ Chinese. Casual Dining. $6-$20 **AAA Inspector Notes:** The popular and reliable restaurant delivers an extensive variety of Szechuan, Mandarin and Cantonese dishes such as lychee duck with sweet fruity sauce to your table. For an authentic dim sum experience, time your visit for between 11 am and 3 pm. Service is prompt and efficient. **Features:** full bar. **Reservations:** suggested, weekends. **Address:** 142-46 N 10th St 19107 **Location:** Between Race and Arch sts; in Chinatown. 🚇 Chinatown, 124. **Parking:** street only. 🅛 🅓 🚇

IRISH PUB   215/925-3311   (95)

▼▼ Irish. Casual Dining. $4-$9 **AAA Inspector Notes:** A hand-carved walnut bar and walls lined with photographs and prints of sports and political figures decorate this bustling pub. In the midst of the theater district, the restaurant is a favorite place to savor hearty Irish-American cuisine. Stop in before or after a show. **Features:** full bar, patio dining, happy hour. **Address:** 1123 Walnut St 19107 **Location:** Between 11th and 12th sts. 🚇 12th-13th & Locust, 141. **Parking:** street only. 🅛 🅓 [LATE] 🚇

JANE G'S   215/563-8800   (75)

▼▼ ▼ Chinese. Casual Dining. $10-$29 **AAA Inspector Notes:** While the prices won't make you sweat, the mouth-numbing spice might! Traditional Szechuan dishes, whose spiciness can be adjusted from one to five, are offered. Those who don't enjoy a little heat in their entrées, however, should look elsewhere. Popular dishes include the dry pot, served in a large metal wok over an open flame, with bell peppers, chopped onions, chilies and other fresh vegetables mixed with your choice of protein. **Features:** full bar, happy hour. **Reservations:** suggested, for dinner. **Address:** 1930 Chestnut St 19103 **Location:** Between 19th and 20th sts. 🚇 19th, 69. **Parking:** street only. 🅛 🅓 CALL Ⓜ 🚇

JON'S BAR & GRILLE   215/592-1390   (155)

▼▼ ▼ American. Casual Dining. $7-$29 **AAA Inspector Notes:** Murals on the wall of the restaurant pay tribute to The Three Stooges, which is appropriate given that Larry was born in the building. You can sit indoors or out, and if you're part of a large party, this place can accommodate. **Features:** full bar, patio dining, Sunday brunch, happy hour. **Address:** 300 South St 19147 **Location:** Jct S 3rd and South sts. 🚇 9th-10th & Locust, 142. **Parking:** on-site (fee) and street. 🅛 🅓 [LATE] 🚇

JOY TSIN LAU CHINESE RESTAURANT   215/592-7227   (20)

▼▼ ▼ Chinese. Casual Dining. $7-$28 **AAA Inspector Notes:** Nibble a little of this and a little of that during an outstanding dim sum that features a sampling of more than 250 a la carte choices of appetizers and small entrées, including steak, chicken, seafood and duck prepared three ways. **Features:** full bar. **Address:** 1026 Race St 19107 **Location:** Between N 10th and N 11th sts; in Chinatown. 🚇 Chinatown, 124. **Parking:** street only. 🅛 🅓 [LATE] 🚇

JONES   215/223-5663   (60)

▼▼ Continental. Casual Dining. $10-$26 **AAA Inspector Notes:** Thanksgiving dinner, baked macaroni and cheese and Duncan Hines® chocolate layer cake with a glass of milk serve as textbook examples of the comfort food with a huge dose of style offered here. You also might "jones" for one of the more upscale dishes such as chicken and rock shrimp dumplings and hazelnut-crusted scallops. Prices are more than fair, given the restaurant's prime Old City location. **Features:** full bar, Sunday brunch. **Address:** 700 Chestnut St 19106 **Location:** Jct 7th St. 🚇 8th, 65. **Parking:** street only. 🅛 🅓 CALL Ⓜ 🚇

KABUL, CUISINE OF AFGHANISTAN   215/922-3676   (58)

▼▼ ▼ Afghan. Casual Dining. $15-$20 **AAA Inspector Notes:** Decorated with afghans and subtle lighting, this restaurant delivers a menu of traditional kebabs of marinated chicken, lamb or beef, as well as such dishes as lamb chops and scallion-filled dumplings with yogurt sauce. Servers are prompt. **Address:** 106 Chestnut St 19106 **Location:** Between 2nd and Front sts. 🚇 2nd, 63. **Parking:** street only. 🅓 🚇

KANELA   215/922-1773   133
ᗺᗺ ᗺᗺ Mediterranean. Casual Dining. $9-$32 **AAA Inspector Notes:** This popular BYOB attracts many locals with its incredible Mediterranean-focused menu and outdoor seating off Spruce Street. The warm salad of organic guinea fowl is highly recommended as a starter. Be sure to call ahead for reservations, as there are a limited amount of tables available. **Reservations:** suggested. **Address:** 1001 Spruce St 19107 **Location:** Jct 10th St. 9th-10th & Locust, 142. **Parking:** street only. [D] [🚇]

KARMA RESTAURANT & BAR   215/925-1444   57
ᗺᗺ ᗺᗺ Indian. Casual Dining. $11-$22 **AAA Inspector Notes:** Karma's lunch buffet lines up a variety of choices. If you come to this busy spot for dinner, you can choose from assorted rotian (Indian tandoori breads), tandoori khazana (traditional clay-oven dishes) and subzi mandi (vegetarian specialties). **Features:** full bar. **Address:** 114 Chestnut St 19106 **Location:** Between 2nd and Front sts; in Old City Historic District. 2nd, 63. [L] [D] [🚇]

KEATING'S RIVER GRILL   215/521-6509   108
ᗺᗺᗺ ᗺ American. Casual Dining. $12-$32 **AAA Inspector Notes:** The upscale, contemporary dining room has an open kitchen, elegant woodwork, a ceiling draped in flowing fabric and floor-to-ceiling windows that permit an excellent view of the Delaware River waterfront. A dining terrace opens from April to October. Included among offerings of American grill cuisine is a complimentary cheese fondue and bread starter. Crispy whole snapper with Asian slaw and ginger soy sauce is as appealing to the eye as to the palate. **Features:** full bar, happy hour. **Reservations:** suggested. **Address:** 201 S Columbus Blvd 19106 **Location:** Jct S Columbus Blvd and Dock St; in Hilton Philadelphia at Penn's Landing. 2nd, 63. **Parking:** on-site (fee) and valet. [B] [L] [D] [CALL] [♿M] [🚇]

KISSO SUSHI BAR   215/922-1770   13
ᗺᗺ ᗺᗺ Japanese. Casual Dining. $7-$23 **AAA Inspector Notes:** Diners sit at the sushi bar and watch impressive and skilled chefs create a meal before their eyes. Also offered is a large number of vegetarian dishes. Bring-your-own-bottle service is provided, so guests are encouraged to bring a favorite saki. For dessert, try cappuccino-flavored mochi. **Reservations:** suggested. **Address:** 205 N 4th St 19106 **Location:** Corner of Race and 4th sts. 5th, 64. **Parking:** street only. [L] [D] [🚇]

LACROIX AT THE RITTENHOUSE   215/790-2533   117
ᗺᗺ ᗺᗺ ᗺᗺ
American Fine Dining
$18-$75
AAA Inspector Notes: Large windows in the contemporary bi-level dining room give you a treetop view of Rittenhouse Square. Pleasant servers display a high standard of professionalism as they guide you around an innovative menu marked by such creations as chilled lemon grass consommé, stuffed pied de cochon and sautéed rabbit tenderloin en crepinette. **Features:** full bar, Sunday brunch, happy hour. **Reservations:** suggested. **Address:** 210 W Rittenhouse Square 19103 **Location:** Jct W Rittenhouse Square and Walnut St; in The Rittenhouse. 19th, 69. **Parking:** on-site (fee) and valet. *Menu on AAA.com*
[B] [L] [D] [🚇]

LA FAMIGLIA   215/922-2803   39
ᗺᗺᗺ ᗺ Italian. Fine Dining. $7-$43 **AAA Inspector Notes:** A Renaissance theme accents the narrow dining room, where you'll see marble tile, crimson wall coverings and gilded chandeliers, artwork and mirrors. The Old City favorite pleases its patrons with dishes made from homemade pasta, veal and rack of lamb. The outstanding wine cellar stores nearly 15,000 bottles of wine from Italy, France and California. **Features:** full bar. **Reservations:** suggested. Semiformal attire. **Address:** 8 S Front St 19106 **Location:** Between Chestnut and Market sts. 2nd, 63. **Parking:** street only.
[L] [D] [🚇]

LA LOCANDA DEL GHIOTTONE   215/829-1465   21
ᗺᗺ ᗺᗺ Italian. Casual Dining. $16-$31 **AAA Inspector Notes:** A lively atmosphere and some fresh, authentic Italian cuisine await in this cozy Old City staple. A variety of homemade dishes are featured, including spaghetti carbonara, pork osso buco and a gnocchi offering which changes daily. **Reservations:** suggested, weekends. **Address:** 130 N 3rd St 19106 **Location:** Jct 3rd and Cherry sts. 2nd, 63. **Parking:** street only. [D] [🚇]

LA VERANDA   215/351-1898   29
ᗺᗺᗺ ᗺ Italian. Family Dining. $10-$40 **AAA Inspector Notes:** Situated along Pier 3, this restaurant offers views of the Delaware River from its floor-to-ceiling windows. The décor resembles the interior of a cruise ship dining room, while the menu provides an array of seafood, steak and traditional favorites. **Features:** full bar. **Reservations:** suggested, weekends. **Address:** 5 N Columbus Blvd 19106 **Location:** At Pier 3, just n of Market St. 2nd, 63. **Parking:** valet only. [L] [D] [🚇]

LE CASTAGNE   215/751-9913   74
ᗺᗺᗺ ᗺ Northern Italian. Fine Dining. $16-$45 **AAA Inspector Notes:** Stylish and romantic décor can be found in this authentic restaurant. The smaller size, exposed brick walls and long white curtains provide an intimate atmosphere. The menu is filled with traditional favorites and homemade pasta dishes. The extensive wine list offers great parings for each entrée of choice. **Features:** full bar, happy hour. **Reservations:** suggested. **Address:** 1920 Chestnut St 19103 **Location:** Between 19th and 20th sts. 19th, 69. **Parking:** street only. [L] [D] [🚇]

LIBERTÉ   215/569-8300   85
ᗺᗺᗺ ᗺ French. Fine Dining. $14-$32 **AAA Inspector Notes:** The chic lounge looks onto the bustling Center City streets. An upscale cocktail and wine menu accompanies a menu of newly interpreted French fare, including salad niçoise, bouillabaisse and beef bourguignonne. **Features:** full bar, happy hour. **Reservations:** suggested, weekends. **Address:** 120 S 17th St 19103 **Location:** Jct Sansom and 17th sts; in Sofitel Philadelphia. 15th-16th & Locust, 140. **Parking:** on-site (fee) and valet. [L] [D] [LATE] [🚇]

LITTLE NONNA'S   215/546-2100   124
ᗺᗺ ᗺᗺ Italian. Casual Dining. $11-$26 **AAA Inspector Notes:** The chefs at nearby Barbuzzo opened this delightful little restaurant that offers a 40-seat intimate dining room and a small outdoor garden area when weather permits. In addition the open kitchen features a small counter area where guests can see their meals prepared right before them. The menu offers a delectable option of antipasti, fresh fish and pasta. I highly recommend sticking with their gourmet spaghetti and meatballs, the best I've have ever had. **Features:** beer & wine. **Reservations:** suggested, for dinner. **Address:** 1234 Locust St 19107 **Location:** Between 12th and 13th sts. 12th-13th & Locust, 141. **Parking:** street only. [L] [D] [🚇]

LOLITA   215/546-7100   73
ᗺᗺ ᗺᗺ Mexican. Casual Dining. $18-$24 **AAA Inspector Notes:** This local bring-your-own-bottle favorite offers the owner's delicious twist on traditional Mexican cuisine. Inside is an active and loud atmosphere with limited space and an open kitchen. When bringing your own beverages, feel free to bring a bottle of tequila and enjoy the variety of fresh fruit margarita mixers available. On the menu, diners cannot go wrong with the three chili-braised boneless short ribs. **Reservations:** suggested. **Address:** 106 S 13th St 19107 **Location:** Between Sansom and Chestnut sts. Walnut-Locust, 117. **Parking:** street only. [D] [🚇]

LOS CATRINES TEQUILA'S   215/546-0181   129
ᗺᗺ ᗺᗺ Mexican. Fine Dining. $10-$28 **AAA Inspector Notes:** Mexican culture and food come together in this sophisticated setting, which features white tablecloths, black-and-white photographs, a skeleton wedding mural and paintings of Mexican peasants. You can feel comfortable in the knowledge of the servers, who know as much about chicken mole and spicy tortilla soup as they do about the Mexican way of life. **Features:** full bar, happy hour. **Reservations:** suggested. **Address:** 1602 Locust St 19103 **Location:** Between 16th and 17th sts. 15th-16th & Locust, 140. **Parking:** street only. [L] [D] [🚇]

LOVASH INDIAN CUISINE

215/925-3881 (153)

WWW Northern Indian. Casual Dining. $9-$25 **AAA Inspector Notes:** Majoring in Northern Indian cuisine, Lovash also turns out some Southern Indian dishes. Create your own curry dishes in addition to vindaloo, saag, korma and jalfrezie. Bring along your favorite wine to enjoy with dinner. **Address:** 236 South St 19147 **Location:** Between 2nd and 3rd sts. 2nd, 63. **Parking:** street only.

(D) (🚷)

MAGGIANO'S LITTLE ITALY

215/567-2020 (31)

WWW Italian. Fine Dining. $10-$47 **AAA Inspector Notes:** Diners savor scrumptious, traditional favorites served in a bustling atmosphere reminiscent of Little Italy. The dining area projects an early-20th-century feel; loud conversations bouncing off high ceilings evoke a sense of the Roaring 20's. **Features:** full bar. **Reservations:** suggested. **Address:** 1201 Filbert St 19107 **Location:** At 12th and Filbert sts. 13th, 67. **Parking:** on-site (fee) and valet.

(L) (D) (🚷)

MAMA PALMA'S

215/735-7357 (144)

WWW Italian. Casual Dining. $8-$25 **AAA Inspector Notes:** Located just off Rittenhouse Square is this delightful cash-only pizzeria and Italian eatery. Guests are able to bring their own wine, but not beer as they have plenty on tap. They are most famous for their variety of brick-oven pizza served with the freshest ingredients. All dishes are able to be altered to guests' liking. This local favorite is only open for lunch on the weekends and open for dinner every day. **Features:** beer only. **Reservations:** suggested. **Address:** 2229 Spruce St 19103 **Location:** Corner of 23rd and Spruce sts; center. 22nd, 70. **Parking:** street only. (D) (🚷)

MAOZ VEGETARIAN

215/922-3409 (96)

W Vegetarian. Quick Serve. $5-$8 **AAA Inspector Notes:** This vegetarian-inspired quick-service restaurant offers scrumptious pitas and sandwiches. Falafel is a popular pick, but regardless of what guests order, they can pile up a variety of fresh produce toppings at the self-service bar. **Address:** 1115 Walnut St 19107 **Location:** Between 11th and 12th sts. 12th-13th & Locust, 141. **Parking:** on-site (fee) and street. (L) (D) CALL (🚷M) (🚷)

MARATHON GRILL

WWW American. Casual Dining. $10-$13 **AAA Inspector Notes:** If you're in a hurry, Marathon Grill ably gets you in and on your way. Numerous varieties of tasty salads and sandwiches are offered in addition to grill favorites. **Bar:** full bar.

(B) (L) (D) CALL (🚷M) (🚷)

For additional information, visit AAA.com

LOCATIONS:

Address: 121 S 16th St 19102 **Location:** Jct S 16th and Sansom sts. 15th-16th & Locust, 140. **Phone:** 215/569-3278

Address: 1818 Market St 19103 **Location:** Between 18th and 19th sts. 19th, 69. **Phone:** 215/561-1818

MARMONT STEAKHOUSE & BAR

215/923-1100 (35)

WWW American. Casual Dining. $8-$45 **AAA Inspector Notes:** One of the few budget-friendly options in Old City, this steakhouse satisfies patrons with well-seasoned steaks and chops as well as appetizers that are a meal on their own. The ample-size Philadelphia crabcake comes with a side of vegetables. Cocktail and dessert options are equally tempting. **Features:** full bar, patio dining. **Address:** 222 Market St 19106 **Location:** Between 2nd and 3rd sts. 2nd, 63. **Parking:** street only. (L) (D) (🚷)

MATYSON

215/564-2925 (64)

WWWW American. Fine Dining. $10-$27 **AAA Inspector Notes:** More upscale than the standard bring-your-own-bottle restaurant, this place offers fine dining and an intimate atmosphere. However, it is really the food that will impress you. With a seasonally changing menu and nothing but fresh and exotic ingredients, one cannot miss. **Reservations:** suggested. **Address:** 37 19th St 19103 **Location:** Between Market and Chestnut sts. 19th, 69. **Parking:** street only.

(L) (D) (🚷)

MCCORMICK & SCHMICK'S

215/568-6888 (56)

WWW Seafood. Fine Dining. $12-$46 **AAA Inspector Notes:** This place is all about seafood, which is imported from all over the world. Among good choices are Washington state oysters, Maine clams, delicate Hawaiian escolar and tuna from Ecuador. The club-like decor is cozy and the staff is attentive. **Features:** full bar, happy hour. **Reservations:** suggested. **Address:** One S Broad St 19107 **Location:** Between Market and S Broad sts. City Hall, 118. **Parking:** valet only. (L) (D) (🚷)

MCCROSSEN'S TAVERN

215/854-0923 (4)

WWW American. Casual Dining. $9-$19 **AAA Inspector Notes:** A 30-foot mahogany and black granite bar, white marble fireplace and stained-glass windows set in brick alcoves all lend to the striking visual appeal of this intimate dining room. A Mediterranean flair punctuates dishes of American and Italian cuisine. **Features:** full bar, Sunday brunch. **Reservations:** suggested. **Address:** 529 N 20th St 19130 **Location:** Between Hamilton and Spring Garden sts. Spring Garden, 120. **Parking:** street only.

(L) (D) (🚷)

MCGILLIN'S OLDE ALE HOUSE

215/735-5562 (72)

WW American. Gastropub. $6-$13 **AAA Inspector Notes:** *Historic.* Since 1860, this pub has been in continuous operation, making it the city's oldest tavern. Perhaps more popular for their drinks than food, they still offer a wide variety of sandwiches and salads, as well as chicken, steak and pasta dishes. There's also a lengthy list of bar munchies like pizza, wings, pot stickers and nachos. **Features:** full bar, Sunday brunch. **Address:** 1310 Drury St 19107 **Location:** Jct Market St, just s on Juniper St, just e. Walnut-Locust, 117. **Parking:** street only. (L) (D) (LATE) (🚷)

MISCONDUCT TAVERN

215/732-5797 (126)

WW American. Casual Dining. $8-$15 **AAA Inspector Notes:** This is a great spot for a quick bite with the menu providing a variety of upscale bar fare, including avocado fries, seared chicken sliders and house-made mac 'n cheese. Wash it all down with the extensive variety of beers from around the world. Expect large crowds during any big sporting event. **Features:** full bar, Sunday brunch, happy hour. **Address:** 1511 Locust St 19102 **Location:** Between 15th and 16th sts. 15th-16th & Locust, 140. **Parking:** street only.

(L) (D) (🚷)

MIXTO

215/592-0363 (147)

WW Latin American. Casual Dining. $8-$24 **AAA Inspector Notes:** Vibrant paintings surround you in Mixto's dining room, a welcoming bi-level spot marked by warm woods and exposed brick. Latin and Caribbean flavors infuse crabmeat, beef and cheese empanadas; crispy plantains; churrasco steak; and varied seafood and pork dishes. **Features:** full bar, Sunday brunch. **Address:** 1141 Pine St 19107 **Location:** Jct 12th St; in Center City. 12th-13th & Locust, 141. **Parking:** street only. (L) (D) (🚷)

MONK'S CAFE

215/545-7005 (136)

WW Belgian. Gastropub. $7-$24 **AAA Inspector Notes:** A dimly lit, joyous place, this café has the soul of Belgium in the heart of Philadelphia. A large selection of beer complements a menu of hearty fare that includes burgers, salads, sandwiches and upscale dinner entrées. Don't pass up their signature mussels. **Features:** full bar. **Address:** 264 S 16th St 19102 **Location:** Corner of 16th and Spruce sts. 15th-16th & Locust, 140. **Parking:** street only.

(L) (D) (LATE) (🚷)

MORIARTY'S RESTAURANT & IRISH PUB

215/627-7676 (105)

WW American. Casual Dining. $8-$24 **AAA Inspector Notes:** In a building that's been around since 1930, this restaurant seizes your attention at the entrance with a lengthy bar at which 27 draft beers and ales can be had. Continue on to the rest of the dining area, where you'll find inviting décor and many bar staples and Irish odds and ends. In addition to Irish favorites, you can order burgers, salads and Mexican fare. Flip over the menu to read about this place's history. **Features:** full bar, happy hour. **Address:** 1116 Walnut St 19107 **Location:** Between 12th and 11th sts; near S Quince St. 12th-13th & Locust, 141. **Parking:** street only.

(L) (D) (LATE) (🚷)

MORIMOTO   215/413-9070   59
▼▼▼ ▼▼▼ Japanese. Fine Dining. $26-$45 **AAA Inspector Notes:** Television's famed Iron Chef Masaharu Morimoto has brought his innovative Japanese cuisine to this sleek modern space near Independence National Historic Park. Choosing among specialties such as rare Kobe beef, black cod miso and sashimi can be daunting, so many let the chef choose by ordering the omakase, a multi-course tasting menu which highlights all the distinctive offerings. **Features:** full bar. **Reservations:** suggested. **Address:** 723 Chestnut St 19106 **Location:** Between 7th and 8th sts. 🚇 8th, 65. **Parking:** on-site (fee) and valet. L D 🚇

MORNING GLORY   215/413-3999   169
▼▼ ▼▼ American. Family Dining. $4-$15 **AAA Inspector Notes:** The many regulars who mill about at Morning Glory give you some indication that this place is worth investigating. The tasty breakfast dishes, sandwiches and other food compensate for the sometimes slow-paced service. If the weather is nice, head to a table outside. **Features:** Sunday brunch. **Address:** 735 S 10th St 19147 **Location:** At Fitzwater St. 🚇 Lombard-South, 116. **Parking:** street only.
B L 🅚 🚇

MOSHULU   215/923-2500   145
▼▼▼ ▼▼▼
International
Fine Dining
$15-$35
AAA Inspector Notes: The largest four-masted sailing ship in the world, the Moshulu has made many sea voyages since being launched in 1904. She now has been lovingly renovated into a premier restaurant/bar along the waterfront for diners' delight and pleasure. Cutting-edge cuisine is served impeccably in a setting elegantly decorated with natural wood accents, brass fittings and plush carpeting. **Features:** full bar, Sunday brunch. **Reservations:** suggested. **Address:** 401 S Columbus Blvd, Penn's Landing 19106 **Location:** Jct S Columbus Blvd and Dock St; on Penn's Landing-Delaware River Waterfront. 🚇 2nd, 63. **Parking:** on-site (fee) and valet. L D CALL 🅲🅼 🚇

MUSTARD GREENS   215/627-0833   160
▼▼ ▼▼ Chinese. Casual Dining. $7-$24 **AAA Inspector Notes:** Guests are treated to fresh and contemporary takes on Chinese cuisine, with plentiful vegetarian options. The friendly and capable staff is happy to guide guests toward dishes that best suit their taste buds and waistlines. This cozy eatery is extremely popular, so be prepared to spend your wait window-shopping on nearby South Street during the 6-7:30 pm dinner rush. **Features:** full bar. **Reservations:** suggested, weekends. **Address:** 622 S 2nd St 19147 **Location:** Between Bainbridge and South sts. 🚇 2nd, 63. **Parking:** street only.
D 🚇

MY THAI   215/985-1878   167
▼▼ ▼▼ Thai. Casual Dining. $10-$18 **AAA Inspector Notes:** With its candlelit, close-together tables, you might just make some new friends at this corner neighborhood restaurant that has been attracting locals since 1990. You'll know what you're ordering as the menu—dishes are marked as mild or spicy. If you don't see your favorite dish on the menu, be sure to inquire with the staff, who more often than not can fulfill your request. **Features:** full bar. **Address:** 2200 South St 19146 **Location:** Jct 22nd and South sts. 🚇 15th-16th & Locust, 140. **Parking:** on-site (fee) and street. D 🚇

NODDING HEAD BREWERY & RESTAURANT
215/569-9525   84
▼▼ ▼▼ American. Casual Dining. $5-$20 **AAA Inspector Notes:** After a trendy meal of baked Brie, quiche, jerk chicken or vegetarian fare, you'll nod your head in agreement that Nodding Head makes good food. You also can taste their own beer creations from the award-winning brewery. **Features:** full bar, Sunday brunch, happy hour. **Address:** 1516 Sansom St, 2nd Floor 19102 **Location:** Between 15th and Broad sts. 🚇 Walnut-Locust, 117. **Parking:** street only. L D 🚇

OCEAN HARBOR   215/574-1399   18
▼▼ ▼▼ Chinese. Casual Dining. $5-$15 **AAA Inspector Notes:** Be prepared for the frantic rush during the hours of dim sum, as this popular spot attracts many locals. Piping-hot and delicious items are available for sampling, or you can try a traditional favorite from Ocean Harbor's extended menu. **Features:** full bar. **Address:** 1023 Race St 19107 **Location:** Between 9th and 10th sts. 🚇 Chinatown, 124. **Parking:** street only. L D LATE 🚇

OCEAN PRIME   215/563-0163   94
▼▼▼ ▼▼▼ American. Fine Dining. $27-$49 **AAA Inspector Notes:** Though this restaurant sports a simple brick exterior, guests will be impressed when they walk into the elegantly appointed dining room featuring glass wine racks, modern leather furnishings and intimate lighting. The menu focuses on American cuisine and includes a selection of aged Prime steaks and savory seafood entrées. On select days, enjoy half-priced bottles of wine from the award-winning list. **Features:** full bar, happy hour. **Reservations:** suggested, weekends. **Address:** 124 S 15th St 19102 **Location:** Jct 15th and Samson sts. 🚇 Walnut-Locust, 117. **Parking:** street only. D CALL 🅲🅼 🚇

OYSTER HOUSE   215/567-7683   87
▼▼ ▼▼ Seafood. Casual Dining. $14-$28 **AAA Inspector Notes:** The constantly changing menu features well-seasoned seafood dishes, including Maine lobster, striped bass, sea scallops and a rotating selection of fresh oysters. Inside, chef's prepare food in the open, wraparound oyster bar located at the center of the restaurant. The buck-a-shuck happy hour from 5 to 7 pm draws a large and lively crowd. **Features:** full bar, happy hour. **Address:** 1516 Sansom St 19102 **Location:** Between 15th and 16th sts. 🚇 Walnut-Locust, 117. **Parking:** street only. L D LATE CALL 🅲🅼 🚇

PAESANO'S   215/440-0371   178
▼ Sandwiches. Quick Serve. $7-$9 **AAA Inspector Notes:** Most Philadelphians would consider this sandwich spot an absolute must-try while in town. The famous Paesano Beef Brisket Sandwich, which competed against Bobby Flay on the Food Network's show "Throwdown," will leave your taste buds craving more. The limited hours and parking make it tough to get to, but we highly recommend you make the trek. **Address:** 1017 S 9th St 19147 **Location:** Jct 9th and Kimball sts. 🚇 Ellsworth-Federal, 115. **Parking:** street only.
L 🚇

PAGODA NOODLE CAFE   215/928-2320   67
▼▼ ▼▼ Chinese. Casual Dining. $6-$28 **AAA Inspector Notes:** Recharge after exploring the nearby attractions and sites with any of at least eight budget-friendly noodle dishes in addition to rice platters, stir-fries and traditional selections. You'll get particular satisfaction from the Pagoda broth noodles. Swift servers navigate this café in the heart of the Old City. **Features:** full bar. **Address:** 125 Sansom Walk 19106 **Location:** Between Front and 2nd sts; just w of Penn's Landing; adjacent to Thomas Bond House Welcome Park. 🚇 2nd, 63. **Parking:** street only. L D 🚇

THE PALM RESTAURANT   215/546-7256   116
▼▼▼ ▼▼▼ American. Fine Dining. $31-$57 **AAA Inspector Notes:** This bustling restaurant is noted for Prime, dry-aged steaks and Nova Scotia lobsters. The huge portions are delivered by an attentive staff in an atmosphere that is fun and lively. At the end of the meal, servers present tempting pastries tableside. Caricature-lined walls lend to the feeling that patrons are dining in an art gallery. Even if you bring a big appetite you still may leave with a doggy bag. **Features:** full bar. **Reservations:** suggested. **Address:** 200 S Broad St 19102 **Location:** Corner of Walnut and Broad sts. 🚇 Walnut-Locust, 117. **Parking:** on-site (fee). L D 🚇

PASTRAMI & THINGS   215/567-6261   61
▼ Deli. Quick Serve. $4-$10 **AAA Inspector Notes:** Philly residents rave about this eatery's corned beef, but the menu also incorporates soups, salads and other sandwiches as well as tasty desserts. An upstairs dining area suits those not dropping in to pick up takeout fare. **Address:** 24 S 18th St 19103 **Location:** Jct 18th and Chestnut sts. 🚇 19th, 69. **Parking:** street only.
B L 🚇

PENANG   215/413-2531   26
▼▼ ▼▼ Asian. Casual Dining. $6-$20 **AAA Inspector Notes:** Malaysian and Thai dishes headline a menu of savory curries, smoky stir-fries and tasty noodle dishes. Don't neglect to try the specialty roti canai, a crispy pancake that's best eaten right off the grill. Accents of industrial steel add a modern touch to the spacious dining area. If you need menu guidance, don't be afraid to lean on the willing staff. **Features:** beer & wine. **Address:** 117 N 10th St 19107 **Location:** Between Cherry and Arch sts; in Chinatown. 🚇 8th and Market, 125. **Parking:** street only. L D 🚇

PERCH PUB
215/546-4090 123

WW WW American. Casual Dining. $8-$19 **AAA Inspector Notes:** "Perched" up on the second floor is this casual, relaxing eatery that provides exposed brick walls and floor-to-ceiling windows to view the attractive neon lights of Broad Street's Avenue of the Arts. The menu offers a variety of sandwiches, appetizers, snacks and salads. However, I recommend their gourmet burgers, which are customizable to each one's preference and include toppings such as applewood-smoked bacon jam, melted Gruyere cheese and garlic aioli. **Features:** full bar, Sunday brunch, happy hour. **Address:** 1345 Locust St 19107 **Location:** Jct Broad and Locust sts. Walnut-Locust, 117. **Parking:** street only. L D LATE

PHO & CAFE VIET HUONG
215/336-5030 181

WW Vietnamese. Casual Dining. $4-$14 **AAA Inspector Notes:** Authentic, fresh food is what keeps this restaurant afloat among a sea of competition. Do not let the disinterested servers or diner-like atmosphere stand in the way of some of the tastiest soups, bubble drinks and banh mi (Vietnamese hoagies) the city has to offer. Stop into the attached bakery for gooey sweets and fun Asian candies as well as sandwiches and traditional meats available to go. **Features:** beer & wine. **Address:** 1110 Washington Ave 19147 **Location:** Jct 11th St; in Wing Phat Plaza. Ellsworth-Federal, 115.

L D CALL

PHO XE LUA VIET THAI RESTAURANT
215/627-8883 16

WW Vietnamese. Casual Dining. $5-$12 **AAA Inspector Notes:** This most casual noodle house serves bowls of steaming pho topped with assorted grilled meats and seafood, fresh herb garnishes and rice. Vermicelli dishes come with much the same toppings. There also is a large selection of entrées that ring authentic such as salt-baked squid, snails with coconut and basil, stewed five-spice beef and a host of others. Some dishes require you to be a bit adventurous, while others are tamer. A loyal crowd keeps things busy at lunchtime. **Features:** full bar. **Address:** 907 Race St 19107 **Location:** Corner of 9th St. Chinatown, 124. **Parking:** no self-parking. L D

PIETRO'S COAL OVEN PIZZERIA
215/735-8090 110

WW WW Italian. Casual Dining. $9-$18 **AAA Inspector Notes:** After exploring Rittenhouse Square and JFK Plaza, hop on over to this Italian-style restaurant for a bite to eat. Pressed-tin ceilings, Georgian columns and a handmade cherry wood bar add to its historic appeal. Locals know Pietro's for its unique coal-oven pizzas that can be topped with an array of goodies like kalamata olives, sun-dried tomatoes and prosciutto. If you wish to forgo the pizza, large family-style salads and pasta dishes are other options. **Features:** full bar, Sunday brunch, happy hour. **Address:** 1714 Walnut St 19103 **Location:** Between 17th and 18th sts. 15th-16th & Locust, 140. **Parking:** street only. L D

PIZZERIA STELLA
215/320-8000 146

WW Pizza. Casual Dining. $9-$19 **AAA Inspector Notes:** Crispy thin-crust pizza with fresh, specialty toppings (smoked mozzarella, black truffle, fontina cheese, meatballs and baby spinach) share a starring role with the perfectly-seasoned salad, pasta and veggie dishes at this hip, modern spot. Guests will want to bring a group of friends and order several dishes to share. The homemade gelato in seasonal flavors is disturbingly good. **Features:** full bar. **Address:** 420 S 2nd St 19106 **Location:** Jct Lombard St. 2nd, 63. **Parking:** street only. L D CALL

PIZZERIA VETRI
215/600-2629 7

WW WW Pizza. Casual Dining. $8-$18 **AAA Inspector Notes:** See gourmet pizzas prepared right in front of your eyes at this cozy open-kitchen-concept restaurant located in the Art Museum neighborhood. Inside guests should expect a small dining room of about 30 chairs total and a small marble counter in front of the kitchen. In addition to their authentic Italian pizzas, guests can choose among scrumptious calzones, salads and desserts. **Features:** beer & wine. **Address:** 1939 Callowhill St 19130 **Location:** Between 19th and 20th sts. 19th, 69. **Parking:** street only. L D

Add AAA or CAA Associate Members to bring home the benefits of membership

PIZZICATO
215/629-5527 37

WW Italian. Casual Dining. $7-$26 **AAA Inspector Notes:** Although the name makes you immediately think of a pizzeria, this restaurant offers so much more. This trendy and contemporary spot features a variety of Italian options, some with an Asian influence oddly enough. You might try their ahi tuna, beef fillet, soup of the day (in my case, butternut squash) and scallops along with the pizza and pasta dishes. **Reservations:** suggested. **Address:** 248 Market St 19147 **Location:** Jct 3rd St. 2nd, 63. **Parking:** street only. L D CALL

THE PLOUGH AND THE STARS IRISH RESTAURANT & BAR
215/733-0300 47

WW WW Continental. Fine Dining. $8-$24 **AAA Inspector Notes:** Painted concrete columns with cornices and ceiling molding add to the ornate décor of this bustling dining room. A harp-shaped mezzanine overlooks the Irish pub. An emphasis on modern Irish cooking shows on a menu of contemporary European cuisine. **Features:** full bar, patio dining, happy hour. **Reservations:** suggested, weekends. **Address:** 123 Chestnut St 19106 **Location:** Just n of jct 2nd and Chestnut sts; entrance on 2nd St. 2nd, 63. **Parking:** street only. L D CALL

PORCINI RESTAURANT
215/751-1175 100

WW Italian. Casual Dining. $18-$26 **AAA Inspector Notes:** This cozy bring-your-own-bottle restaurant has a residential feel inside with its small dining room area, carpeted floors and enhanced fireplace. The modest restrictions in size can make it a little tight and a loud environment at times. The menu consists of homemade pasta dishes and sauces as well as traditional Italian favorites. Make sure to call ahead for reservations as this restaurant has restricted hours of operation. **Reservations:** suggested. **Address:** 2048 Sansom St 19103 **Location:** Between 20th and 21st sts. 22nd, 70. **Parking:** street only. D

POSITANO COAST BY ALDO LAMBERTI
215/238-0499 86

WW WW WW Southern Italian Small Plates. Casual Dining. $7-$30 **AAA Inspector Notes:** Seafood dishes dominate the menu at this eatery while other delicious Italian favorites, such as gnocchi in cheese sauce, capellini and a mixed antipasti plate also are worth a try. Perfect for a large, loud dinner party or an intimate meal for two in the lounge. **Features:** full bar, patio dining, happy hour. **Address:** 212 Walnut St 19106 **Location:** Jct 2nd St, just w. 2nd, 63. **Parking:** street only. L D CALL

THE PRIME RIB
215/772-1701 127

WW WW Steak. Fine Dining. $20-$50 **AAA Inspector Notes:** Located downtown, this dining room blends a sophisticated atmosphere with the comfort of booth and banquette seating. Black lacquer walls, leopard carpets and decorative lighting are employed to create a setting reminiscent of a 1940s dinner club. The formally-attired waitstaff offer gracious attentive service. **Features:** full bar, happy hour. **Reservations:** suggested. **Address:** 1701 Locust St 19103 **Location:** Between Walnut and Locust sts; main entrance on 17th St; in Radisson Blu Warwick Hotel, Philadelphia. 15th-16th & Locust, 140. **Parking:** valet and street only. D

PUB AND KITCHEN
215/545-0350 156

WW WW American. Gastropub. $9-$26 **AAA Inspector Notes:** Don't expect standard bar fare at this pub with a menu that frequently changes to provide the freshest ingredients in season. From the Barnegat scallop ceviche to the Hudson Canyon swordfish, you won't be disappointed. First-time guests should be sure to ask the knowledgeable staff about specials of the day and cocktail pairings. **Features:** full bar, patio dining, Sunday brunch, happy hour. **Address:** 1946 Lombard St 19146 **Location:** Corner of Lombard and 20th sts. 15th-16th & Locust, 140. **Parking:** street only. D LATE

PUMPKIN
215/545-4448 161

WW WW WW Mediterranean. Casual Dining. $30-$50 **AAA Inspector Notes:** This neighborhood restaurant packs a lot of flavor and creativity into a small, intimate space. The staff is welcoming and knowledgeable about the ever-changing menu, which focuses heavily on seafood and the freshest produce available. Only cash is accepted. This is a bring your own beer/wine restaurant. **Reservations:** suggested. **Address:** 1713 South St 19146 **Location:** Between 17th and 18th sts. Lombard-South, 116. **Parking:** street only. D

R2L
215/564-5337 **62**

▼▼▼▼ New American. Fine Dining. $26-$42 **AAA Inspector Notes:** With sweeping southern and western views of the city and sleek décor, guests will want to stop into this restaurant to bask in the cool vibe of its Center City clientele. While there, try one of the well-made dishes (the short ribs and lobster macaroni and cheese are divine) or seasonal cocktails. **Features:** full bar, happy hour. **Reservations:** suggested. **Address:** Between Market and Chestnut sts; 37th Floor of Two Liberty Place. 15th, 68. **Parking:** street only. D CALL ☊ 🚗

RACE STREET CAFE
215/627-6181 **12**

▼▼ American. Casual Dining. $8-$19 **AAA Inspector Notes:** Gather with friends or make new ones at this neighborhood restaurant and bar. Popular with the locals, this spot offers a variety of beers on draft that go well with the impressive menu selections such as the Moroccan-style lamb burger and horseradish-crusted tilapia. **Features:** full bar, Sunday brunch, happy hour. **Address:** 208 Race St 19106 **Location:** Between N Broad and N 2nd sts. 2nd, 63. **Parking:** street only. L D LATE 🚗

RALPH'S ITALIAN RESTAURANT
215/627-6011 **171**

▼▼ Southern Italian. Casual Dining. $9-$34 **AAA Inspector Notes:** In the Italian market area since the early 1900s, this family-run operation maintains a menu of tried-and-true, home-cooked cuisine, which is supplemented nightly with innovative specials. A tin ceiling and stucco walls lend to the Old World decor. **Features:** full bar. **Reservations:** suggested. **Address:** 760 S 9th St 19147 **Location:** Between Catharine and Fitzwater sts. 9th-10th & Locust, 142. **Parking:** street only. L D 🚗

RANGOON BURMESE RESTAURANT
215/829-8939 **27**

▼▼ Burmese. Casual Dining. $7-$17 **AAA Inspector Notes:** The kitchen's eclectic selections borrow ingredients and cooking methods from the traditions of India, Thailand and China. Sample yellow pea and onion soup or sweet and sour shrimp from a menu that designates entrées that are particularly spicy. **Features:** beer & wine. **Reservations:** suggested. **Address:** 112 N 9th St 19107 **Location:** Between Race and Arch sts; in Chinatown. 8th and Market, 125. **Parking:** street only. L D 🚗

RATCHADA THAI & LAOS CUISINE
215/467-1546 **180**

▼▼ Asian. Casual Dining. $9-$25 **AAA Inspector Notes:** You can look forward to a warm greeting from the husband-and-wife proprietors who do all they can to nurture a relaxing atmosphere. Taste the rich, savory flavors in Laotian and Thai dishes, including appetizers of soup and green papaya salads, healthy steamed entrées and piquant curries made with catfish, salmon, chicken and vegetarian ingredients. **Features:** full bar. **Address:** 1117 S 11th St 19147 **Location:** S of Washington Ave. Ellsworth-Federal, 115. **Parking:** street only. L D 🚗

RAW SUSHI & SAKE LOUNGE
215/238-1903 **78**

▼▼▼ Sushi. Casual Dining. $10-$29 **AAA Inspector Notes:** Fans will rejoice upon dining at this sexy eatery, with its oversized maki and fresh, colorful ingredients. A variety of cooked Japanese specialties are available for those with a less adventurous palate. Beverages include an array of sakes, wines and cocktails. Outdoor dining is available seasonally. **Features:** full bar, happy hour. **Reservations:** suggested, weekends. **Address:** 1225 Sansom St 19107 **Location:** Just e of 13th St. 12th-13th & Locust, 141. **Parking:** street only. L D 🚗

RAY'S CAFE
215/922-5122 **23**

▼▼ Regional Chinese. Casual Dining. $8-$19 **AAA Inspector Notes:** On the edge of Chinatown, this small café tempers the spices in its Taiwanese-style Chinese fare to suit your preference. You'll find an impressive selection of teas and coffees from all around the world. **Address:** 141 N 9th St 19107 **Location:** Just n of Market St; corner of Cherry St. Chinatown, 124. **Parking:** street only. B L D 🚗

RED OWL TAVERN
215/923-2267 **49**

▼▼ American. Casual Dining. $14-$26 **AAA Inspector Notes:** After touring Independence Hall, cross the street and visit this delightful restaurant and bar. Inside you will find a comforting atmosphere and décor featuring vaulted ceilings, exposed brick, beautiful wood furnishings and a long decorative bar at the center. If you're hungry, get ready to feast on hearty dishes such as beef short ribs on the bone, roasted herbed chicken pot pie or the house-made beef pastrami sandwich. Don't forget to also sample one of the specialty cocktails. **Features:** full bar, Sunday brunch, happy hour. **Address:** 433 Chestnut St 19106 **Location:** Jct 5th and Chestnut sts; in Hotel Monaco Philadelphia, A Kimpton Hotel. 5th, 64. **Parking:** on-site (fee) and valet. L D CALL ☊ 🚗

RISING TIDE
215/925-0266 **17**

▼▼ Chinese. Casual Dining. $6-$15 **AAA Inspector Notes:** Rising Tide gives you a taste of such authentic Chinese dishes as pork belly, bitter melon and cuttlefish, but you'll also be able to choose from a long list of shakes, smoothies and other healthy concoctions that blend ingredients like green barley, aloe vera and tapioca. If you're unfamiliar with the cuisine, ask the willing servers for translations and descriptions that will help you make sense of such dishes as preserved egg and pork congee casserole and teo chew-style squab. **Features:** full bar. **Address:** 937-939 Race St 19107 **Location:** Between 9th and 10th sts; in Chinatown. Chinatown, 124. **Parking:** street only. L D 🚗

RISTORANTE LA BUCA
215/928-0556 **113**

▼▼ Italian. Fine Dining. $11-$30 **AAA Inspector Notes:** If you don't find something appealing on this restaurant's table fish cart, which lines up fresh varieties including tuna, swordfish, Atlantic salmon and red snapper, you can turn to the tempting Italian fare such as penne alla arrabbiata, linguine and clams, and veal. The basement-level room feels slightly dated, but a large painted mural and exposed brick walls make it inviting nonetheless. **Features:** full bar. **Address:** 711 Locust St 19106 **Location:** Between 7th and 8th sts. 9th-10th & Locust, 142. **Parking:** street only. L D 🚗

RISTORANTE PANORAMA
215/922-7800 **30**

▼▼▼ Regional Italian. Fine Dining. $22-$30 **AAA Inspector Notes:** *Historic.* Veal, fish and homemade pasta are flavorful preparations on a menu of simple and fresh cuisine. Colorful, hand-painted wall murals add to the intimate trattoria atmosphere. The marvelous wine list features more than 100 by-the-glass selections, and varied wine flights have been selected for curious palates. The well-trained bar staff is capable. **Features:** full bar, happy hour. **Reservations:** suggested. **Address:** 14 N Front St 19106 **Location:** At Front and Market sts; in Penn's View Hotel. 2nd, 63. **Parking:** on-site (fee) and valet. D 🚗

ROSE TATTOO CAFE
215/569-8939 **5**

▼▼ Continental. Casual Dining. $11-$30 **AAA Inspector Notes:** In a 100-year-old Victorian building, Rose Tattoo Cafe makes you feel as though you're in the French Quarter in New Orleans. Most of what you'll find here are Cajun favorites such as jambalaya, but you also can have fresh seafood, ribs and chicken. The daily bread pudding is worth a splurge. **Features:** full bar. **Reservations:** suggested. **Address:** 1847 Callowhill St 19130 **Location:** Jct 19th and Callowhill sts. Spring Garden, 120. **Parking:** street only. L D 🚗

ROUGE
215/732-6622 **115**

▼▼▼ American. Casual Dining. $12-$28 **AAA Inspector Notes:** Specialties of French-Asian fare change often at Rouge, a sophisticated spot where you'll be treated with friendly ease. Sidewalk seating is prime real estate during the warmer months, with a comparable level of service. The restaurant's hamburger is often voted best in the city. **Features:** full bar, Sunday brunch. **Reservations:** suggested. **Address:** 205 S 18th St 19103 **Location:** Between Walnut and Chancellor sts; across from Rittenhouse Square. 15th-16th & Locust, 140. **Parking:** street only. L D 🚗

SABRINA'S CAFE 215/574-1599 176

♦♦ American. Casual Dining. $9-$23 **AAA Inspector Notes:** This cozy café is most famous for the scrumptious brunch offering signature favorites such as stuffed challah French toast with melted farmer's cream cheese. Expect long waits on the weekends. **Features:** Sunday brunch. **Address:** 910 Christian St 19147 **Location:** Between 9th and 10th sts; just n of Italian Market. 🚇 Ellsworth-Federal, 115. **Parking:** street only. [B] [L] [D] [🚇]

SABRINA'S CAFE & SPENCER'S TOO 215/636-9061 6

♦♦ American. Casual Dining. $6-$18 **AAA Inspector Notes:** Just like its two sister properties, this restaurant is most popular for its scrumptious brunch and hearty portions of buttermilk pancakes, cheese omelets and stuffed French toast just to name a few. However, if you're not in the mood to wait in line, the lunch and dinner menus will leave you anything but disappointed. Also remember that this restaurant allows you to bring your favorite beer or wine from home. **Features:** Sunday brunch. **Address:** 1804 Callowhill St 19130 **Location:** Jct 18th and Callowhill sts. 🚇 Race-Vine, 119. **Parking:** street only. [B] [L] [D] [🚇]

SALOON 215/627-1811 170

♦♦♦ Italian. Fine Dining. $10-$42 **AAA Inspector Notes:** An elegant saloon-style interior with elaborate wood moldings, antique art pieces and stained-glass lighting fixtures. The restaurant emits a small intimate dining atmosphere with private dining and a full bar/lounge area. The menu incorporates delicious traditional Italian cuisine with mouthwatering steaks. A local favorite, this place is highly recommended. **Reservations:** suggested. **Address:** 750 S 7th St 19147 **Location:** Between Catharine and Fitzwater sts. 🚇 9th-10th & Locust, 142. [L] [D] [🚇]

SAMPAN 215/732-3501 93

♦♦♦ Asian. Fine Dining. $10-$25 **AAA Inspector Notes:** Don't let the vibrant purple and green colors startle you; this restaurant is a can't-miss. Their modern take on Asian cuisine puts forth some of the best foods out there, including their scrumptious crispy Brussels sprouts and pork bao bun. Try to go during their happy hour, which offers great food and cocktail specials at an incredible value. **Features:** full bar, happy hour. **Reservations:** suggested. **Address:** 124 S 13th St 19107 **Location:** Between Sansom and Walnut sts. 🚇 Walnut-Locust, 117. **Parking:** on-site (fee) and street.
[D] [CALL] [🅜] [🚇]

SANG KEE PEKING DUCK HOUSE 215/925-7532 9

♦♦ Chinese. Family Dining. $7-$16 **AAA Inspector Notes:** If you're seeking a quick bite in Chinatown, this fantastic restaurant promises fast service. Sip the complimentary hot tea while you peruse the large menu, and if you have any questions the waitstaff will happily assist. As the name suggests, the roasted ducks you'll see hanging through the glass at the entrance are the specialty. **Features:** beer & wine. **Address:** 238 N 9th St 19107 **Location:** Just s of jct Vine St. 🚇 Chinatown, 124. **Parking:** street only.
[L] [D] [🚇]

SBRAGA 215/735-1913 149

♦♦♦♦ American. Fine Dining. $55-$95 **AAA Inspector Notes:** Classic. Kevin Sbraga's contemporary take on American cuisine is splendidly done at this incredible fine dining establishment. The prix-fixe seasonally changing four-course menu allows guests to choose from a small list of options and experience a truly divine meal from start to finish. Inside is a small dining room with modern touches, including a large open kitchen for guests to see top chefs preparing their meals right before them. **Features:** full bar. **Reservations:** suggested. **Address:** 440 S Broad St 19146 **Location:** Jct Broad and Pine sts. 🚇 Lombard-South, 116. **Parking:** street only.
[D] [CALL] [🅜] [🚇]

SEAFOOD UNLIMITED 215/732-3663 142

♦♦ Seafood. Casual Dining. $11-$18 **AAA Inspector Notes:** Pick up some raw seafood to cook at home or have it prepared here for savoring in the long, skinny dining room, which sports a modern feel. Marlin, catfish, tuna and rainbow trout are just some of the fish you can try. **Features:** full bar, Sunday brunch, happy hour. **Address:** 270 S 20th St 19103 **Location:** Jct S 20th and Spruce sts. 🚇 15th-16th & Locust, 140. **Parking:** on-site (fee) and street.
[D] [🚇]

SEIKO JAPANESE RESTAURANT 215/413-1606 1

♦♦ Japanese. Casual Dining. $7-$24 **AAA Inspector Notes:** Bright white floors and chairs, accented by neon orange walls, evoke the feeling of a hip Tokyo eatery at this Northern Liberties gem. A variety of fresh, flavorful maki rolls are offered, alongside cooked favorites such as edamame, vegetable tempura and chicken kat-su. Bring along your favorite wine or beer, as alcohol is not served. **Features:** beer & wine. **Address:** 604 N 2nd St 19123 **Location:** Between Green St and Fairmount Ave. 🚇 Spring Garden, 62. **Parking:** street only. [L] [D] [🚇]

SERAFINA RITTENHOUSE 215/977-7755 99

♦♦♦ Italian. Casual Dining. $9-$29 **AAA Inspector Notes:** This popular spot in downtown Philadelphia offers outdoor seating and a full bar for guests. This is a smaller restaurant that is able to open its floor-to-ceiling windows when the weather permits. The menu consists of a variety of Italian dishes, most famous for their wood oven-baked pizza. A local favorite great for a cocktail or dinner. **Features:** full bar, patio dining, Sunday brunch, happy hour. **Address:** 130 S 18th St 19103 **Location:** At 18th and Samson sts. 🚇 19th, 69. **Parking:** street only. [L] [D] [🛏] [🚇]

SERRANO 215/928-0770 41

♦♦ International. Casual Dining. $14-$25 **AAA Inspector Notes:** Serrano describes its cuisine as "international home cooking," but that doesn't really do it justice. Take a look at the menu and you'll find such fresh, made-to-order fare as stuffed grape leaves, chicken satay, balsamic bangers and mash, cowboy steak and three-mango salmon. Check out the intimate dining room's décor items from around the world. If you're in the mood for some after-dinner fun, head upstairs to Tin Angel, Serrano's music club. **Features:** full bar. **Address:** 20 S 2nd St 19106 **Location:** Between Market and Ranstead sts. 🚇 2nd, 63. **Parking:** street only. [D] [🚇]

SHIAO LAN KUNG 215/928-0282 19

♦♦ Chinese. Casual Dining. $8-$18 **AAA Inspector Notes:** Although choosing among the myriad restaurants in Chinatown can be overwhelming, it's hard to go wrong if you seek out the places where locals eat. Shiao Lan Kung is one of those places. Large portions, a casual setting and authentic spices make it a great choice. **Address:** 930 Race St 19107 **Location:** Between 9th and 10th sts; in Chinatown. 🚇 Chinatown, 124. **Parking:** street only.
[D] [LATE] [🚇]

SHIROI HANA JAPANESE RESTAURANT 215/735-4444 118

♦♦ Japanese. Casual Dining. $11-$35 **AAA Inspector Notes:** You'll face a wide array of choices ranging from sushi lunch box specials of tuna, whitefish, crab and salmon to donburi (steamed rice and toppings) of pork, chicken and beef to sushi and sashimi to nabe (hot pot) of beef, chicken or seafood. Count on prompt, pleasant service. **Features:** full bar. **Reservations:** suggested, dinner. **Address:** 222 S 15th St 19102 **Location:** Between Walnut and Locust sts; center. 🚇 15th-16th & Locust, 140. **Parking:** street only.
[L] [D] [🚇]

THE SIDECAR BAR AND GRILLE 215/732-3429 177

♦♦ American. Casual Dining. $10-$18 **AAA Inspector Notes:** Located a handful of blocks south of Rittenhouse Square, this hip spot is famous for its outstanding selection of upscale bar fare including cornmeal-crusted oysters, Carolina barbecue pulled pork and an herb-roasted turkey B.L.T. The atmosphere inside is warm and inviting, with large exposed brick walls and small wooden tables. With more than 10 seasonally changing beers on draft, a perfect pairing is available with any dish. **Features:** full bar, Sunday brunch, happy hour. **Address:** 2201 Christian St 19146 **Location:** Jct 22nd and Christian sts. 🚇 University City, 180. **Parking:** street only.
[D] [LATE] [🚇]

SILK CITY DINER, BAR & LOUNGE 215/592-8838 2

♦♦ American. Gastropub. $8-$18 **AAA Inspector Notes:** As famously seen on Food Network's Diners, Drive-ins and Dives, Silk City Diner's delicious gastropub menu features everything from spicy Buffalo wings by the pound to thyme-and-pepper-crusted tuna. If you didn't save room, we suggest you order a monstrous slice of Key lime pie to take with you. **Features:** full bar, Sunday brunch, happy hour. **Address:** 435 Spring Garden St 19123 **Location:** Jct 5th St; in Northern Liberties. 🚇 Spring Garden, 62. **Parking:** street only.
[D] [🚇]

SNOCKEY'S OYSTER AND CRAB HOUSE
215/339-9578 (182)

WWW Seafood. Casual Dining. $7-$51 **AAA Inspector Notes:** *Classic.* The classic neighborhood oyster house has been family-owned and -operated since 1912. The menu features a full raw bar, as well as fried and broiled seafood. Favorite choices are Mrs. Snockey's famous oyster stew, crab cakes and lobster specials. **Features:** full bar. **Address:** 1020 S 2nd St 19147 **Location:** Just n of jct S 2nd St and Washington Ave. **Parking:** street only. L D

SOUTH STREET SOUVLAKI
215/925-3026 (152)

WW Greek. Casual Dining. $5-$25 **AAA Inspector Notes:** Trendy, affordable traditional Greek cuisine is served here in large portions at affordable prices. For those on the go, curbside service also is available. The small dining area and bar create an active and loud atmosphere. The menu provides a variety of Mediterranean favorites, with the gyro being the most popular. **Features:** full bar. **Address:** 509 South St 19147 **Location:** Jct South and 5th sts. 9th-10th & Locust, 142. **Parking:** street only. L D

SOUTHWARK
215/238-1888 (166)

WWWW Continental. Fine Dining. $19-$26 **AAA Inspector Notes:** The menu at this cozy spot features a small selection of dishes, including house-made sausage, seared-scallops in warm spinach salad and the smoothest chicken liver mousse I have ever tasted. After the meal, diners can grab a seat at the bar for the best cocktails in Philadelphia. Drinks here are made the old fashioned way by knowledgeable, formally-attired bartenders using fresh squeezed juices and premium libations. **Features:** full bar. **Reservations:** suggested. **Address:** 701 S 4th St 19147 **Location:** Just s of jct Bainbridge St. 9th-10th & Locust, 142. **Parking:** street only. D

SPASSO ITALIAN GRILL
215/592-7661 (46)

WWWW Italian. Casual Dining. $11-$25 **AAA Inspector Notes:** Located in the Old City Historic District, the dining room features exposed original brick and stucco walls dating to the 1800s. An exhibition kitchen and crack-finished painted ceilings reinforce the ambience of a bustling trattoria and bar. Mock-marble tables and steel chairs are set on the sidewalk for seasonal al fresco dining. The menu offers a marriage of traditional Northern and Southern Italian dishes. Try the grilled bronzini served with peppers, zucchini and squash as a good sampler. **Features:** full bar, patio dining, happy hour. **Address:** 34 S Front St 19106 **Location:** Between Market and Chestnut sts. 2nd, 63. **Parking:** street only. L D

SPICE 28
215/928-8880 (70)

WWW Asian Fusion. Casual Dining. $8-$26 **AAA Inspector Notes:** Upon entering, guests are greeted by a neon-lit bar area and a contemporary dining room furnished with light woods and featuring intimate lighting. The menu's modern take on Asian fusion splendidly blends Szechuan and Thai cuisines to create a variety of savory and spicy options. **Features:** full bar, happy hour. **Reservations:** suggested, for dinner. **Address:** 1228 Chestnut St 19107 **Location:** Between 11th and 12th sts. 13th, 67. **Parking:** street only. L D

SQUARE 1682
215/563-5008 (88)

WWWW New American. Casual Dining. $11-$32 **AAA Inspector Notes:** The well-dressed, young Center City crew laughs over cocktails and appetizers in this sleek lounge on street level. Fortunately for vegetarians, the menu features a number of hearty options for them as well. The noise level and close proximity of the tables might not make it the best location for an intimate meal. **Features:** full bar, patio dining, Sunday brunch, happy hour. **Address:** 121 S 17th St 19103 **Location:** Jct Sansom St. 15th-16th & Locust, 140. **Parking:** street only. B L D LATE CALL M

STRANGELOVE'S
215/873-0404 (112)

WW American. Casual Dining. $10-$19 **AAA Inspector Notes:** This hip spot has become a local favorite with its outstanding selection of beverages and contemporary American fare. The intimate yet relaxed ambience provides the perfect atmosphere for a quick bite or for a full dining experience. The menu has both vegan and vegetarian options in addition to more meaty items such as their bacon barbecue sauce burger and seared chicken sandwich. The pimento cheese appetizer comes highly recommended to start your meal. **Features:** full bar, Sunday brunch, happy hour. **Address:** 216 S 11th St 19107 **Location:** Between Walnut and Locust sts. 12th-13th & Locust, 141. **Parking:** street only. L D LATE

TALULA'S GARDEN
215/592-7787 (111)

WWWW American. Fine Dining. $30-$50 **AAA Inspector Notes:** Just off Washington Square is where you'll find this Stephen Starr gem. The décor splendidly combines earthy tones and furnishings with an intimate fine-dining atmosphere. The "garden" aspect of the name rings true in their beautifully decorated outdoor patio. The cheese plates are a house specialty and a must-try, but all of the menu options provide fresh and succulent flavor. **Features:** full bar, patio dining, Sunday brunch, happy hour. **Reservations:** suggested. **Address:** 210 W Washington Square 19106 **Location:** Between Walnut and Locust sts. 9th-10th & Locust, 142. **Parking:** valet only. D

TEN STONE
215/735-9939 (165)

WW American. Casual Dining. $8-$12 **AAA Inspector Notes:** This pub and restaurant keeps the locals coming with their extensive draft beer list and the tasty dishes that accompany them, including a jerk chicken cheesesteak and cod fish tacos. Night owls can enjoy the 2 am nightly closing time. **Features:** full bar, Sunday brunch. **Address:** 2063 South St 19146 **Location:** Jct 21st and South sts. 15th-16th & Locust, 140. **Parking:** street only. L D LATE

TINTO
215/665-9150 (92)

WWW Spanish. Fine Dining. $10-$55 **AAA Inspector Notes:** If you've never tried pintxos, northern Spain's version of tapas, head to this intimate dining room for a taste. Expect a crowd, though, as it has quickly become one of the most popular restaurants in Center City. While waiting for a table, marvel at the display of corkscrews while sipping a glass of one of the handpicked wines. **Features:** full bar, happy hour. **Reservations:** suggested. **Address:** 114 S 20th St 19103 **Location:** Jct 20th and Sansom sts. 19th, 69. **Parking:** street only. D

TIRAMISU
215/587-7000 (104)

WWW Italian. Fine Dining. $12-$35 **AAA Inspector Notes:** You're likely to be surrounded by business-talking professionals and romance-seeking couples in the dining room of Tiramisu, which has an impressive wall of wines drawing from locales all over the world. The chef's delicious, daily changing specials complement a standing selection of beef, veal, poultry and pasta dishes. **Features:** full bar. **Reservations:** suggested. **Address:** 1519 Walnut St 19102 **Location:** Between 15th and 16th sts. 15th-16th & Locust, 140. **Parking:** street only. L D

TIR NA NOG, BAR & GRILL
267/514-1700 (28)

WW Irish. Casual Dining. $9-$27 **AAA Inspector Notes:** A beacon for the younger crowd, Tir na Nog whips up traditional Irish fare along the lines of fish and chips, potato-leek soup and the signature shepherd's pie. **Features:** full bar, Sunday brunch, happy hour. **Address:** 1600 Arch St 19103 **Location:** Between N 16th and N 17th sts; at The Phoenix. Suburban, 221. **Parking:** street only. L D LATE

TRIA
215/972-8742 (89)

WWW Continental. Casual Dining. $4-$10 **AAA Inspector Notes:** This tapas restaurant blends a variety of Continental items, creating a varied menu of salads, cheeses, sandwiches and desserts. The vast wine and beer menu is designed to complement any number of menu choices. Reservations are not accepted, so it's best to allow for a 30-minute wait during the weekends. **Features:** full bar, happy hour. **Address:** 123 S 18th St 19103 **Location:** Jct Sansom St. 19th, 69. **Parking:** street only. L D

TRIA
215/629-9200 (135)

WWW Continental. Casual Dining. $9-$11 **AAA Inspector Notes:** Continental flavor bursts from salads, cheese, sandwiches and desserts at Tria, which also presents a diverse wine and beer menu. You won't be able to make a reservation here, and a 15-minute wait is common on the weekends. This is the second, larger outpost of the popular eatery. **Features:** beer & wine, happy hour. **Address:** 1137 Spruce St 19107 **Location:** Jct 12th St. 12th-13th & Locust, 141. **Parking:** street only. D LATE

TWENTY MANNING GRILL 215/731-0900 (137)

▼▼▼ American. Casual Dining. $13-$27 **AAA Inspector Notes:** The white room accented by sunny yellow benches sets the ambient tone at this grill. The menu is quite a value considering that one can dine on raw oysters, homemade pizza and pasta, delicately smoked trout and roasted free-range chicken. The cocktail menu is equally charming, featuring herb-, fruit- and spice-infused syrups and liquors. **Features:** full bar, patio dining. **Address:** 261 S 20th St 19103 **Location:** Between Locust and Spruce sts. 15th-16th & Locust, 140. **Parking:** street only. [D] [🚐]

VARALLI RESTAURANT 215/546-6800 (122)

▼▼▼ Northern Italian. Fine Dining. $18-$24 **AAA Inspector Notes:** This stylish restaurant, located in the heart of the theater district, is a fun place to dine and people-watch through the large windows overlooking Broad Street. The kitchen uses only fresh ingredients in preparing wonderful Northern Italian fare and fresh seafood. **Features:** full bar, happy hour. **Reservations:** suggested. **Address:** 231 S Broad St 19107 **Location:** At S Broad and Locust sts. Walnut-Locust, 117. **Parking:** street only. [D] CALL [👥M] [🚐]

VARGA BAR 215/627-5200 (132)

▼▼ American. Casual Dining. $8-$21 **AAA Inspector Notes:** With 22 beers rotating on draft and food selections such as duck confit chicken wings and bourbon smoked baby back ribs, it's no wonder that locals frequent this neighborhood spot. The large selection of gourmet cheeses are great for those with a lighter appetite. Night owls will enjoy the daily 1 am closing time for the kitchen. **Features:** full bar, Sunday brunch, happy hour. **Address:** 941 Spruce St 19107 **Location:** Jct 10th and Spruce sts. 9th-10th & Locust, 142. **Parking:** street only. [D] [LATE] [🚐]

VETRI 215/732-3478 (139)

▼▼▼ ▼▼▼ Italian. Fine Dining. $155 **AAA Inspector Notes:** Dining at this restaurant is not just a meal, but a true culinary experience. The six-course, prix fixe chef's tasting menu for $155 takes a little more than two hours. The menu changes monthly to reflect the freshest ingredients and the chef prepares distinctive food concoctions that will leave the taste buds wanting more. Additional wine and beer pairings are available with each course. Make sure to call far in advance, as this small dining room is in high demand. **Features:** full bar. **Reservations:** required. **Address:** 1312 Spruce St 19107 **Location:** Between S 13th and Juniper sts. 12th-13th & Locust, 141. **Parking:** street only. [D] [🚐]

VIETNAM PALACE RESTAURANT 215/592-9596 (10)

▼▼ Vietnamese. Casual Dining. $8-$16 **AAA Inspector Notes:** Charbroiled beef short ribs leave you messy but satisfied at Vietnam Palace, where you also can contemplate aromatic pho (classic beef noodle soups) and well-prepared vermicelli and broken-rice dishes. **Features:** full bar, happy hour. **Address:** 222 N 11th St 19107 **Location:** Between Race and Vine sts; in Chinatown. Chinatown, 124. **Parking:** street only. [L] [D] [🚐]

VIETNAM RESTAURANT 215/592-1163 (11)

▼▼ Vietnamese. Casual Dining. $8-$15 **AAA Inspector Notes:** The décor is neat and casual with nothing to distract from the reason you're here, the food. Bowls of noodle soup come with various savory toppings and are garnished with fresh herbs and greens. Platters of vermicelli noodles and broken rice dishes have many of the same grilled, fried or lemongrass charbroiled toppings. **Features:** full bar. **Address:** 221 N 11th St 19107 **Location:** Between Race and Vine sts. Chinatown, 124. **Parking:** street only. [L] [D] CALL [👥M] [🚐]

VILLAGE WHISKEY 215/665-1088 (97)

▼▼▼ American. Casual Dining. $10-$26 **AAA Inspector Notes:** A polished wooden bar lined with more than 100 types of whiskey, Scotch and bourbon welcomes guests as they enter this intimate speakeasy. The menu features upscale pub fare, including raw oysters, french fries prepared in rendered duck fat and, most importantly, the best burgers in Philadelphia. Those looking to splurge can try the whiskey king topped with bleu cheese, bacon and foie gras. **Features:** full bar, Sunday brunch. **Address:** 118 S 20th St 19103 **Location:** Jct Sansom St. 19th, 69. **Parking:** street only. [L] [D] [LATE] [🚐]

VINTAGE WINE BAR & BISTRO 215/922-3095 (83)

▼▼ ▼▼ French. Casual Dining. $11-$22 **AAA Inspector Notes:** More than 60 by-the-glass wines complement this casual bistro's small menu of dishes, including mussels frites prepared from fresh ingredients that change weekly. If you need help putting together the perfect pairing, ask a capable staffer. **Features:** full bar, patio dining, happy hour. **Address:** 129 S 13th St 19107 **Location:** Just s of jct Sansom St. 12th-13th & Locust, 141. **Parking:** street only. [D] [LATE] CALL [👥M] [🚐]

WALNUT STREET SUPPER CLUB 215/923-8208 (103)

▼▼▼ Italian. Fine Dining. $17-$35 **AAA Inspector Notes:** Guests will feel that they've been transported back into the 1940s at this Italian fine-dining dinner club. Don't be surprised when your server takes center stage and performs outstanding renditions of famous singers like Frank Sinatra and Judy Garland. The menu tastefully blends traditional Italian favorites and a variety of Choice steaks. **Features:** full bar, happy hour. **Reservations:** suggested. **Address:** 1227 Walnut St 19107 **Location:** Between 12th and 13th sts. 12th-13th & Locust, 141. **Parking:** street only. [D] [🚐]

WINTHORPE & VALENTINE BAR AND GRILL
215/563-1600 . (63)

▼▼▼ American. Fine Dining. $10-$34 **AAA Inspector Notes:** Formal yet unpretentious describes nearly everything here, from the setting to the food to the service. You'll relax in the club-like dining room, which has original artwork and large, modern chandeliers, as you contemplate hearty regional chicken, lamb and seafood in addition to small plates and sandwiches from the grill. The aged natural Angus New York strip steak is highly recommended. **Features:** full bar, Sunday brunch. **Reservations:** suggested. **Address:** 99 S 17th St at Liberty Pl 19103 **Location:** Between Market and Chestnut sts; in The Westin Philadelphia. 15th, 68. **Parking:** on-site (fee) and valet. [B] [L] [D] [🚐]

XIX (NINETEEN) RESTAURANT   215/790-1919 (109)

▼▼▼ ▼▼▼
American
Fine Dining
$11-$40

AAA Inspector Notes: The elegant dining room, atop a luxurious historic hotel, has a domed ceiling, lovely wall murals with accompanying statues and fabulous views of the city. Delicately prepared seafood and chops are the focus and are complemented nicely by the extensive wine list. **Features:** full bar, Sunday brunch, happy hour. **Reservations:** suggested. **Address:** 200 S Broad St 19102 **Location:** Between Walnut and Locust sts; in Hyatt at The Bellevue. Walnut-Locust, 117. **Parking:** on-site (fee) and valet. [B] [L] [D] [🚐]

YAKITORI BOY 215/923-8088 (15)

▼▼ Japanese. Casual Dining. $5-$18 **AAA Inspector Notes:** This hip restaurant allows guests to try a variety of dishes from the "Japas" menu, which blends a tapas serving style and Japanese cuisine. With many dishes less than $5, diners are free to sample a little bit of everything, like bacon and quail egg, Karubi short rib and agedashi tofu. Sushi lovers aren't excluded, as there is a long list of standard and specialty rolls. Upstairs, find an always-popular karaoke bar open until 2 am daily. **Features:** full bar. **Address:** 211 N 11th St 19107 **Location:** Between Race and Spring sts. Chinatown, 124. **Parking:** street only. [D] [LATE] [🚐]

ZAVINO 215/732-2400 (79)

▼▼▼ Italian. Casual Dining. $13-$18 **AAA Inspector Notes:** When weather permits, the floor-to-ceiling glass walls open up for perfect people-watching on Sansom Street. Nosh on the homemade pastas, small plates and gourmet pizzas, but make sure to find a nice wine pairing on the restaurant's extensive wine list. **Features:** full bar, happy hour. **Address:** 112 S 13th St 19107 **Location:** Between Chestnut and Sansom sts. Walnut-Locust, 117. **Parking:** street only. [L] [D] [🚐]

CAPOGIRO GELATO CAFE 215/351-0900

[fyi] Not evaluated. Choose from 27 made-fresh-daily flavors of gelato at Capogiro Gelato Cafe. A seasonal array of flavors include hazelnut, Mexican chocolate, blood orange and avocado. The milk used to make the frozen treat is locally sourced from grass-fed, hormone-free cows, which makes it exquisitely creamy. Coffee, pre-made sandwiches and soups also are available. **Address:** 119 S 13th St 19107 **Location:** Jct Sansom St. 12th-13th & Locust, 141.

JIM'S STEAKS
215/928-1911

fyi Not evaluated. A word of warning when dining here: Order loudly and quickly upon reaching the front of the queue. You'll enjoy the cheesesteaks and hoagies served up at this late-night haunt. **Address:** 400 South St 19147 **Location:** Jct 4th St. 9th-10th & Locust, 142.

SONNY'S FAMOUS STEAKS
215/629-5760

fyi Not evaluated. This popular stop for late-night eats offers up a simple menu of steak sandwiches and burgers. **Address:** 228 Market St 19106 **Location:** Between 2nd and 3rd sts; in Old City Historic District. 2nd, 63.

SWANN LOUNGE & CAFE
215/963-1500

fyi Not evaluated. This small dining room is the epitome of subdued elegance. Diners can partake in casual offerings such as sandwiches, pizza or delicious, artistically presented entrées. An upscale buffet is a lunch option. Staff members provide formal, attentive service in an affable, casually upscale manner. The restaurant overlooks beautiful Logan Square and its famous Swann Fountain, from which it takes its name. **Address:** 1 Logan Square 19103 **Location:** Corner of 18th St and Benjamin Franklin Pkwy; in Four Seasons Hotel Philadelphia. Suburban, 221.

PHILADELPHIA (I-11) elev. 39'
• **Restaurants p. 308**
• **Hotels & Restaurants map & index p. 274**

ALOFT PHILADELPHIA
(267)298-1700

Hotel
$129

AAA Benefit: Members save up to 15%, plus Starwood Preferred Guest® benefits!

Address: 4301 Island Ave 19153 **Location:** Jct I-95 and SR 291 exit 13 northbound; exit 15 southbound. Eastwick, 161. **Facility:** 136 units. 5 stories, interior corridors. *Bath:* shower only. **Parking:** on-site (fee). **Terms:** cancellation fee imposed, resort fee. **Amenities:** safes. **Pool(s):** heated indoor. **Activities:** exercise room. **Guest Services:** valet and coin laundry.

CHESTNUT HILL HOTEL
215/242-5905   **2**

Historic Hotel. Rates not provided. **Address:** 8229 Germantown Ave 19118 **Location:** I-476 exit 19, 5.5 mi e. Located in a historic shopping district. Gravers, 261. **Facility:** Near shops and restaurants on Germantown Avenue, rooms at this Colonial-style hotel are individually decorated with antique reproductions. 36 units. 2-4 stories, interior corridors. **Amenities:** safes. **Dining:** Chestnut Grill and Sidewalk Cafe, see separate listing. **Activities:** exercise room.

COURTYARD BY MARRIOTT PHILADELPHIA AIRPORT
(215)365-2200   **19**

Hotel
$160-$263

COURTYARD Marriott

AAA Benefit: Members save 5% or more!

Address: 8900 Bartram Ave 19153 **Location:** I-95 exit 12B (airport), southbound; exit 10 northbound, follow SR 291 E 1 mi n. Located in a commercial area. Eastwick, 161. **Facility:** 152 units. 4 stories, interior corridors. **Parking:** on-site (fee). **Pool(s):** heated indoor. **Activities:** exercise room. **Guest Services:** valet and coin laundry, boarding pass kiosk, area transportation.

  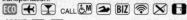

COURTYARD BY MARRIOTT PHILADELPHIA SOUTH AT THE NAVY YARD
(215)644-9200   **10**

Hotel
$181-$298

COURTYARD Marriott

AAA Benefit: Members save 5% or more!

Address: 1001 Intrepid Ave 19112 **Location:** I-95 exit 17, just s, then 0.3 mi w. AT&T, 111. **Facility:** 172 units. 5 stories, interior corridors. **Activities:** exercise room. **Guest Services:** valet and coin laundry, boarding pass kiosk.

CROWNE PLAZA - PHILADELPHIA WEST
(215)477-0200   **3**

Hotel $159-$499 **Address:** 4010 City Ave 19131 **Location:** I-76 (Schuylkill Expwy) exit 339, just s on US 1. Located in a commercial area near shopping and restaurants. Wissahickon, 230. **Facility:** 337 units. 8 stories, interior corridors. **Terms:** check-in 4 pm, cancellation fee imposed. **Pool(s):** heated indoor. **Activities:** hot tub, exercise room. **Guest Services:** valet and coin laundry, area transportation.

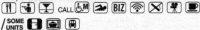

DOUBLETREE BY HILTON PHILADELPHIA AIRPORT
(215)365-4150   **14**

Hotel
$109-$329

DOUBLETREE BY HILTON

AAA Benefit: Members save 5% or more!

Address: 4509 Island Ave 19153 **Location:** I-95 exit 13 northbound; exit 15 southbound; 0.5 mi e, just e of SR 291. Eastwick, 161. **Facility:** 331 units. 9 stories, interior corridors. **Terms:** 1-7 night minimum stay, cancellation fee imposed. **Amenities:** safes. **Pool(s):** heated indoor. **Activities:** exercise room. **Guest Services:** valet laundry, boarding pass kiosk, area transportation.

EMBASSY SUITES-PHILADELPHIA AIRPORT
(215)365-4500   **20**

Hotel $139-$329 **Address:** 9000 Bartram Ave 19153 **Location:** I-95 exit 12B (airport) southbound, bear right on exit ramp to light, just n; exit 10 northbound, follow SR 291 E to Bartram Ave, then 1 mi n. Located in a commercial area. Eastwick, 161. **Facility:** 263 units. 5 stories, interior corridors. **Parking:** on-site (fee). **Terms:** 1-7 night minimum stay, cancellation fee imposed. **Pool(s):** heated indoor. **Activities:** hot tub, exercise room. **Guest Services:** valet and coin laundry, area transportation.

FAIRFIELD INN BY MARRIOTT - PHILADELPHIA AIRPORT
(215)365-2254   **18**

Hotel $118-$217 **Address:** 8800 Bartram Ave 19153 **Location:** I-95 exit 12B (airport), southbound; exit 10 northbound, follow SR 291 E to light, then 1.1 mi n. Located in a commercial area. Eastwick, 161. **Facility:** 109 units. 4 stories, interior corridors. **Amenities:** safes. **Pool(s):** heated indoor. **Activities:** exercise room. **Guest Services:** valet laundry.

(See map & index p. 274.)

FOUR POINTS BY SHERATON PHILADELPHIA AIRPORT
(215)492-0400 **11**

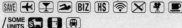

Hotel
$99

AAA Benefit: Members save up to 15%, plus Starwood Preferred Guest® benefits!

Address: 4101 Island Ave 19153 **Location:** Jct I-95 and SR 291 exit 13 northbound; exit 15 southbound. Located in a commercial area. Eastwick, 161. **Facility:** 177 units. 5 stories, interior corridors. **Parking:** on-site (fee). **Terms:** cancellation fee imposed. **Amenities:** Some: safes. **Pool(s):** outdoor. **Activities:** exercise room. **Guest Services:** valet laundry, rental car service.

FOUR POINTS BY SHERATON PHILADELPHIA NORTHEAST
(215)671-9600 **1**

Hotel
$125-$235

AAA Benefit: Members save up to 15%, plus Starwood Preferred Guest® benefits!

Address: 9461 E Roosevelt Blvd 19114 **Location:** I-276 (Pennsylvania Tpke) exit 351, 5 mi s on US 1. Located in a commercial area. **Facility:** 190 units. 6 stories, interior corridors. **Terms:** cancellation fee imposed. **Pool(s):** heated indoor. **Activities:** exercise room. **Guest Services:** valet and coin laundry, area transportation.

HAMPTON INN-PHILADELPHIA AIRPORT
(215)966-1300 **17**

Hotel
$129-$189

AAA Benefit: Members save 5% or more!

Address: 8600 Bartram Ave 19153 **Location:** I-95 exit 12B (airport), southbound; exit 10 northbound; just e of SR 291, then 1 mi n. Located in a commercial area. Eastwick, 161. **Facility:** 151 units. 6 stories, interior corridors. **Terms:** 1-7 night minimum stay, cancellation fee imposed. **Pool(s):** outdoor. **Activities:** exercise room. **Guest Services:** valet and coin laundry, area transportation. **Featured Amenity: breakfast buffet.**

HAWTHORN SUITES BY WYNDHAM PHILADELPHIA AIRPORT
(215)492-1611 **15**

Extended Stay Hotel
$111-$179

Address: 4630 Island Ave 19153 **Location:** I-95 exit 13 northbound; exit 15 southbound, 0.5 mi e; just e of SR 291. Eastwick, 161. **Facility:** 102 kitchen units. 2 stories (no elevator), exterior corridors. **Pool(s):** outdoor. **Activities:** exercise room. **Guest Services:** valet and coin laundry, area transportation.

Say YES to ERS text updates to stay posted when your tow truck is on the way

(See map & index p. 274.)

THE HILTON INN AT PENN   (215)222-0200 **7**

Hotel
$119–$359

AAA Benefit: Members save 5% or more!

Address: 3600 Sansom St 19104 **Location:** I-76 (Schuylkill Expwy) exit 345 eastbound; exit 346A (Sansom St) westbound; between 36th and 37th sts. 🚇 36th, 74. **Facility:** This elegantly appointed hotel is conveniently located in the University City neighborhood within walking distance of multiple shops, restaurants and University of Pennsylvania facilities. 243 units. 6 stories, interior corridors. **Parking:** on-site (fee) and valet. **Terms:** 1-7 night minimum stay, cancellation fee imposed. **Amenities:** safes. **Dining:** Penne Restaurant & Wine Bar, see separate listing, entertainment. **Activities:** exercise room. **Guest Services:** valet laundry. *(See ad p. 287.)*

SAVE 🍴 🧑‍🦽 🍸 CALL ㋔M BIZ HS 🛜 ✕ 🖥 🖨 /SOME UNITS 🖼 🚌

Hilton
HOTELS & RESORTS

Newly renovated on U Penn's campus. Easy walk to center city, restaurants and nightlife.

HILTON PHILADELPHIA CITY AVENUE   (215)879-4000 **5**

Hotel $139–$249 **Address:** 4200 City Ave 19131 **Location:** I-76 (Schuylkill Expwy) exit 339, 0.6 mi s on US 1. Located in a commercial area. 🚇 Bala, 218. **Facility:** 209 units. 12 stories, interior corridors. **Parking:** valet and street only. **Terms:** check-in 4 pm, 1-7 night minimum stay, cancellation fee imposed. **Amenities:** video games, safes. **Dining:** Delmonico's Steak House, see separate listing. **Pool(s):** heated indoor. **Activities:** exercise room. **Guest Services:** valet laundry.

AAA Benefit: Members save 5% or more!

🍴 🧑‍🦽 🍸 🏊 BIZ SHS 📶 ✕ 🖥 🖨 🖼 🚌

HOLIDAY INN PHILADELPHIA STADIUM   (215)755-9500 **9**

Hotel $129–$999 **Address:** 900 Packer Ave 19148 **Location:** I-95 exit 19 (Packer Ave), just s on Front St, then 0.7 mi w; jct Darien St. Located at Philadelphia Sports Complex. 🚇 AT&T, 111. **Facility:** 238 units. 11 stories, interior corridors. **Terms:** check-in 4 pm, cancellation fee imposed. **Pool(s):** outdoor. **Activities:** exercise room. **Guest Services:** valet and coin laundry.

🏋️ 🍴 🧑‍🦽 🍸 🏊 BIZ 📶 ✕ 🖥 🖨 🖼 🖥 /SOME UNITS HS 🚌

HOMEWOOD SUITES BY HILTON/PHILADELPHIA CITY AVENUE   (215)966-3000 **4**

Extended Stay Hotel
$139–$249 **Address:** 4200 City Ave 19131 **Location:** I-76 (Schuylkill Expwy) exit 339, 0.6 mi s on US 1. Located in a commercial area. 🚇 Bala, 218. **Facility:** 122 efficiencies, some two bedrooms. 12 stories, interior corridors. **Parking:** street only. **Terms:** 1-7 night minimum stay, cancellation fee imposed. **Amenities:** safes. **Pool(s):** heated indoor. **Activities:** exercise room. **Guest Services:** valet and coin laundry.

AAA Benefit: Members save 5% or more!

🍴 🏊 BIZ HS 🛜 🖥 🖨 🖼 🖥 🚌

HOMEWOOD SUITES UNIVERSITY CITY PHILADELPHIA   (215)382-1111 **8**

Extended Stay Hotel
$169–$399

HOMEWOOD SUITES BY HILTON

AAA Benefit: Members save 5% or more!

Address: 4109 Walnut St 19104 **Location:** I-76 (Schuylkill Expwy) exit 345 eastbound; exit 346A (Sansom St) westbound; jct 41st St. 🚇 40th, 77. **Facility:** 136 efficiencies. 11 stories, interior corridors. **Parking:** on-site (fee) and valet. **Terms:** 1-7 night minimum stay, cancellation fee imposed. **Pool(s):** heated indoor. **Activities:** hot tub, exercise room. **Guest Services:** valet and coin laundry, area transportation. **Featured Amenity:** breakfast buffet.

SAVE 🍴 CALL ㋔M 🏊 BIZ HS 🛜 ✕ 🖥 🖨 🖼 🖥 🚌

MICROTEL INN & SUITES BY WYNDHAM PHILADELPHIA AIRPORT   (215)492-0700 **16**

Hotel $70–$110 **Address:** 8840 Tinicum Blvd 19153 **Location:** I-95 exit 12B (airport) southbound, bear right on exit ramp to light, then just n; exit 10 northbound, follow SR 291 E signs to light, then 1 mi n. Located in a commercial area. 🚇 Eastwick, 161. **Facility:** 132 units. 3 stories, interior corridors. **Guest Services:** coin laundry, area transportation.

🛬 🍴 CALL ㋔M BIZ 🛜 🖥 /SOME UNITS 🖨 🖼 🖥 🚌

PHILADELPHIA AIRPORT MARRIOTT HOTEL   (215)492-9000 **21**

Hotel
$202–$332

MARRIOTT

AAA Benefit: Members save 5% or more!

Address: 1 Arrivals Rd 19153 **Location:** I-95 exit 10 northbound; exit 12A southbound. 🚇 Terminal B, 159. **Facility:** 419 units. 14 stories, interior corridors. **Parking:** on-site (fee). **Terms:** check-in 4 pm. **Amenities:** safes. **Activities:** exercise room. **Guest Services:** valet and coin laundry, boarding pass kiosk.

SAVE ECO 🛬 🍴 🧑‍🦽 🍸 CALL ㋔M BIZ SHS 📶 ✕ 🖥 /SOME UNITS 🖨 🖼

RENAISSANCE HOTEL PHILADELPHIA AIRPORT   (610)521-5900 **22**

Hotel
$140–$230

R
RENAISSANCE HOTELS

AAA Benefit: Members save 5% or more!

Address: 500 Stevens Dr 19113 **Location:** I-95 exit 9A (Essington/SR 420), just e on Wanamaker Ave, then 1.4 mi n on Industrial Way. Located in a commercial area. **Facility:** 351 units. 12 stories, interior corridors. **Amenities:** *Some:* safes. **Dining:** The Sanctuary, see separate listing. **Pool(s):** heated indoor. **Activities:** exercise room. **Guest Services:** valet laundry.

SAVE 🛬 🍴 🧑‍🦽 🍸 CALL ㋔M 🏊 BIZ SHS 📶 ✕ 🖥 /SOME UNITS 🖨 🖼

Find thousands of pet-friendly places to stay, play and dine with *The AAA PetBook*

(See map & index p. 274.)

SHERATON PHILADELPHIA UNIVERSITY CITY HOTEL
(215)387-8000 **6**

Hotel
$119-$399

AAA Benefit: Members save up to 15%, plus Starwood Preferred Guest® benefits!

Address: 3549 Chestnut St 19104 **Location:** I-76 (Schuylkill Expwy) exit 345, 0.5 mi w; jct 36th St; at University of Pennsylvania. 36th, 74. **Facility:** 332 units. 20 stories, interior corridors. **Parking:** on-site (fee). **Amenities:** safes. **Pool(s):** heated outdoor. **Activities:** exercise room. **Guest Services:** valet and coin laundry.

SHERATON SUITES PHILADELPHIA AIRPORT
(215)365-6600 **13**

Hotel
$129

AAA Benefit: Members save up to 15%, plus Starwood Preferred Guest® benefits!

Address: 4101 Island Ave 19153 **Location:** Jct I-95 and SR 291 exit 13 northbound; exit 15 southbound. Located in a commercial area. Eastwick, 161. **Facility:** 250 units. 8 stories, interior corridors. **Parking:** on-site (fee). **Terms:** cancellation fee imposed, resort fee. **Amenities:** safes. **Pool(s):** heated indoor. **Activities:** hot tub, exercise room. **Guest Services:** valet laundry.

WHERE TO EAT

THE ABBAYE
215/627-6711 **24**

American. Casual Dining. $5-$20 **AAA Inspector Notes:** Mingle with the regulars who drop in often to enjoy the upbeat and eccentric tavern atmosphere and great Sunday brunch, highlighted by homemade breads and muffins. An ever-changing variety of Belgian and local brews complements an eclectic menu that includes hearty sandwiches, salads and stews created to satisfy both vegetarians and carnivores. **Features:** full bar, Sunday brunch. **Address:** 637 N 3rd St 19123 **Location:** Jct Fairmount Ave; in Northern Liberties. Spring Garden, 62. **Parking:** street only. L D LATE

ABYSSINIA ETHIOPIAN RESTAURANT
215/387-2424 **41**

Ethiopian. Casual Dining. $6-$15 **AAA Inspector Notes:** The authentic Ethiopian cuisine at this restaurant is spicy-licious. Handwoven fabrics from Africa are indicative of the ethnic roots of this restaurant and its neighborhood. **Features:** full bar. **Reservations:** suggested, weekends. **Address:** 229 S 45th St 19104 **Location:** Jct Locust St. 46th, 78. **Parking:** street only.
B L D LATE

BAR FERDINAND
215/923-1313 **17**

Spanish. Casual Dining. $10-$30 **AAA Inspector Notes:** This incredible tapas-style restaurant in the Northern Liberties neighborhood has dark and incredibly detailed-oriented décor. Inside are original mosaic pieces and decorative carved stone and marble accents as well as elaborate lighting fixtures. The menu provides a huge variety of affordable cold and hot dishes that allow guests to try a variety of foods. I highly recommend being experimental and trying some of the exotic choices. **Features:** full bar, Sunday brunch, happy hour. **Reservations:** suggested. **Address:** 1030 N 2nd St 19116 **Location:** Just s of Girard Ave; in Liberties Walk Complex. Girard, 61. **Parking:** street only. D CALL

BITAR'S
215/755-1121 **43**

Eastern Mediterranean. Quick Serve. $4-$9 **AAA Inspector Notes:** Join the locals who have been coming to Bitar's, a family-run Lebanese lunch counter, for more than 30 years to enjoy its freshly made soups, salads and sandwiches, including vegetarian, chicken, lamb and beef varieties. Falafel, hummus and baba ghanoush satisfy a hunger, as do the many gyro preparations. **Address:** 947 Federal St 19147 **Location:** Jct S 10th St. Ellsworth-Federal, 115. **Parking:** street only. L D

BOBBY'S BURGER PALACE
215/387-0378 **40**

Burgers. Quick Serve. $6-$9 **AAA Inspector Notes:** This restaurant offers mouthwatering gourmet burgers inspired by famous chef Bobby Flay. While the menu also provides some sandwiches and salads, we recommend you focus on their specialty. On hot summer days, wash it all down with one of their 10 flavored milk shakes or malteds. **Features:** beer & wine. **Address:** 3925 Walnut St 19104 **Location:** I-76 (Schuylkill Expwy) exit 345 eastbound; exit 346A (Sansom St) westbound; between 39th and 40th sts. 40th, 77. **Parking:** street only. L D

BOMB BOMB BAR-BE-QUE GRILL
215/463-1311 **52**

Italian Barbecue. Casual Dining. $8-$26 **AAA Inspector Notes:** This local-favorite bar and restaurant has been in the same family for many years. History abounds, starting with the eatery's name. Browsing the great menu explains it all. **Features:** full bar. **Reservations:** suggested, weekends. **Address:** 1026 Wolf St 19148 **Location:** Corner of Wolf and S Broad sts. Snyder, 113. **Parking:** street only. L D

CHESTNUT GRILL AND SIDEWALK CAFE
215/247-7570 **6**

American. Casual Dining. $8-$20 **AAA Inspector Notes:** This restaurant is popular for its subterranean dining rooms and seasonal outdoor dining porches and patios. The all-day eclectic menu offers a range of light fare to full entrées. Choices include panko-coconut shrimp, three-nut-crusted Chilean sea bass and New Orleans catfish fingers. The 11 salads and 12 sandwich items will appeal to the more casual diner. **Features:** full bar, patio dining, early bird specials, Sunday brunch, happy hour. **Address:** 8229 Germantown Ave 19118 **Location:** I-476 exit 19, 5.5 mi e; in Chestnut Hill Hotel. Gravers, 261. L D

CHICKIE'S AND PETE'S CRAB HOUSE & SPORTS BAR

American. Casual Dining. $8-$20 **AAA Inspector Notes:** Head to this bustling bar and grill, a friendly, casual sports-themed restaurant. Don't miss a taste of Chickie's and Pete's famous patented crab fries. **Bar:** full bar. L D LATE

For additional information, visit AAA.com

LOCATIONS:
Address: 11000 Roosevelt Blvd 19116 **Location:** Jct US 1 and Halderman Ave; in Boulevard Plaza Center. **Phone:** 215/856-9890
Address: 1526 Packer Ave 19145 **Location:** Just w of jct Packer Ave and S Sydenham St. Oregon, 112. **Phone:** 215/218-0500
Address: 4010 Robbins Ave 19135 **Location:** I-95 exit 27 northbound, 1.3 mi w on Harbison Ave, just n on Frankford Ave, then just e; exit 30 southbound, 0.9 mi w on Cottman Ave, 1.2 mi s on Frankford Ave, then just e. Frankford Trans Ctr, 51.
Phone: 215/338-3060

CHUN HING
215/879-6270 **15**

Chinese. Casual Dining. $5-$15 **AAA Inspector Notes:** For more than a quarter century, family-owned Chun Hing has been around to accommodate your whim for Chinese food. Kitchen staff will gladly adjust each dish for your spiciness preferences. **Address:** 4160 Monument Rd 19131 **Location:** I-76 (Schuylkill Expwy) exit 339, just s on US 1, then sw; in Pathmark Super Center. Bala, 218. L D

CIRCLES
267/687-1778 **47**

Asian. Casual Dining. $8-$19 **AAA Inspector Notes:** This neighborhood restaurant provides a variety of Asian dishes but specializes in Thai cuisine with delicious curry dishes, rice noodle entrées and stir-fry dishes. The casual, homey decor inside provides a comforting atmosphere. Take-out orders are also available for those in a hurry. **Address:** 1514 Tasker St 19145 **Location:** Between 15th and 16th sts. Tasker-Morris, 114. **Parking:** street only.
D

(See map & index p. 274.)

CIRCLES CONTEMPORARY ASIAN 267/687-1309 19
▼▼ Asian Fusion. Casual Dining. $8-$19 **AAA Inspector Notes:** This cozy spot is decorated with fresh flowers and an abundance of candles to create an intimate and warm atmosphere. The menu touches on a variety of cuisines providing options ranging from cheese steak egg rolls to salmon pad thai. Spice levels are able to be altered to each individual's preference, and the Thai spring rolls as a great way to start any meal. Wash it all down with your favorite beer or wine from home at this BYOB establishment. **Address:** 812 N 2nd St 19123 **Location:** Between Poplar and Brown sts. Spring Garden, 62. **Parking:** street only. L D

COUNTRY CLUB RESTAURANT 215/722-0500 4
▼▼ American. Family Dining. $5-$14 **AAA Inspector Notes:** After pounding the pavement at what's argued to be the largest shopping mall in northeast Philadelphia, head to this busy, casual family eatery for some hearty comfort food. Your nose will tell you you're in the right spot once it sniffs the aromas wafting from the bakery, which prepares a multitude of luscious selections. Representative of the well-prepared dishes is the barbecue beef brisket, which is served with mashed potatoes and Brussels sprouts. Friendly staffers provide timely follow-up. **Address:** 1717 Cottman Ave 19111 **Location:** SR 73, 1 mi nw of jct US 1. B L D

DELMONICO'S STEAK HOUSE 215/879-4000 14
▼▼▼ Steak. Fine Dining. $15-$35 **AAA Inspector Notes:** This elegantly sophisticated yet comfortable restaurant offers live piano music nightly. The menu is renowned for its finest prime dry-aged steaks, finest ocean-caught fish, lamb and veal dishes, all presented in generous portions. Staff members offer attentive, personalized service under the alert eye of the maître d', who frequently visits diners at their tables. **Features:** full bar. **Reservations:** suggested, weekends. **Address:** 4200 City Ave 19131 **Location:** I-76 (Schuylkill Expwy) exit 339, 0.6 mi s on US 1; in Hilton Philadelphia City Avenue. Bala, 218. **Parking:** on-site (fee) and valet. D

DEREK'S 215/483-9400 10
▼▼▼ American. Fine Dining. $11-$34 **AAA Inspector Notes:** This restaurant offers a comfortable and cozy atmosphere with an elegant red and black theme with white accents. The menu consists of a variety of delicious American cuisine most famous for their wood-oven pizza and hearty signature burgers. A local favorite with two full bars make them a late-night hot spot. **Features:** full bar, Sunday brunch, happy hour. **Reservations:** suggested. **Address:** 4411 Main St 19127 **Location:** I-76 (Schuylkill Expwy) exit 338, 0.3 mi n on Green Ln, then 0.3 mi e; in Manayunk District. Manayunk, 231. **Parking:** street only. L D

DISTRITO 215/222-1657 29
▼▼▼ New Mexican. Casual Dining. $8-$32 **AAA Inspector Notes:** Fall through the rabbit hole into a whimsical world of nouveau Mexican cuisine. Bring a group to sample as many small-plate-style offerings as possible, especially the exquisite guacamole topped with shredded queso fresco. Kids and the young at heart will enjoy a seat at the restaurant's taxicab table. **Features:** full bar, Sunday brunch, happy hour. **Reservations:** suggested, weekends. **Address:** 3945 Chestnut St 19104 **Location:** Jct 40th St; in University City. 40th, 77. **Parking:** street only. L D

THE FAT HAM 215/735-1914 38
▼▼▼ American. Casual Dining. $6-$15 **AAA Inspector Notes:** From the chefs of Sbraga comes this modern take on American comfort foods served tapas-style. Inside, guests will find a cramped dining room that blends rustic elements with an elegant design. The beautifully appointed bar area is filled with an excellent selection of bourbons, whiskeys and other liquors. The menu provides unique adaptations of traditional Southern favorites, such as blackened catfish, crispy grits and green bean casserole. Note: The hot chicken is incredibly spicy! **Features:** full bar. **Address:** 3131 Walnut St 19104 **Location:** Between 31st and 32nd sts. 33rd, 72. **Parking:** street only. D

GREEN EGGS CAFE 215/226-3447 46
▼▼ American. Casual Dining. $9-$13 **AAA Inspector Notes:** If you've got a hankering for breakfast, you're in luck at the bright Green Eggs Cafe in South Philly, as they serve breakfast and lunch all day long. Fresh ingredients are used to create such classics as buttermilk pancakes, burgers, sweet potato fries and eggs Benedict. Delicious vegetarian options are available, too. **Features:** Sunday brunch. **Address:** 1306 Dickinson St 19147 **Location:** Just w of jct 13th St. Tasker-Morris, 114. **Parking:** street only. B L CALL M

GREEN EGGS CAFE 215/922-3447 22
▼▼ American. Casual Dining. $9-$13 **AAA Inspector Notes:** Hearty helpings of breakfast and lunch favorites, including buttermilk pancakes, breakfast burritos, burgers, eggs Benedict, sweet potato fries and grits fill the bellies of the local hipster set who love good food on the cheap. Delicious vegetarian options are available as well. **Features:** Sunday brunch. **Address:** 719 N 2nd St 19123 **Location:** Between Brown and Fairmount sts; in Northern Liberties. Spring Garden, 62. **Parking:** street only. B L

HONEY'S SIT 'N EAT 215/925-1150 20
▼▼ Comfort Food. Casual Dining. $6-$16 **AAA Inspector Notes:** Fresh, locally sourced ingredients enhance the flavors in a curious but wholly satisfactory mix of Jewish and Southern comfort foods. In addition to fried green tomatoes, Reubens, matzo ball soup and Frito chili pie, you can visit all day for breakfast favorites, including fluffy pancakes, tasty challah French toast, farm-fresh eggs scrambled with veggie sausage and heaping biscuits topped with blueberry preserves. On the weekend, be prepared for a long wait. **Address:** 800 N 4th St 19123 **Location:** Jct Brown St; in Northern Liberties. Spring Garden, 62. **Parking:** street only. B L

IL CANTUCCIO 215/627-6573 23
▼▼ Italian. Casual Dining. $8-$23 **AAA Inspector Notes:** You'll feel as if you're dining in someone's home when you sit down at one of the eight or nine tables in cozy Il Cantuccio. The bonus, of course, is that you don't have to cook or clean up. A half-wall separates guests from the kitchen, which occupies a corner of the dining room. It's a good idea to fill up on the well-prepared appetizers, salads and entrées since the desserts here are not a strong point. Be sure to bring cash, because it's the only method of payment accepted. **Reservations:** suggested, weekends. **Address:** 701 N 3rd St 19123 **Location:** At Fairmount Ave; in Northern Liberties. Spring Garden, 62. **Parking:** street only. L D

JACK'S FIREHOUSE RESTAURANT 215/232-9000 25
▼▼▼ American. Fine Dining. $8-$32 **AAA Inspector Notes:** In a converted firehouse, this moderately upscale dining room is decorated with rowing memorabilia. The seasonal sidewalk café is relaxed and comfortable. Sunday brunch is popular, as is the pork loin with sweet-onion marmalade. **Features:** full bar, patio dining, Sunday brunch, happy hour. **Reservations:** suggested. **Address:** 2130 Fairmount Ave 19130 **Location:** Just e of jct 22nd St and Fairmount Ave. Fairmount, 121. **Parking:** street only. L D

JAKE'S & COOPER'S WINE BAR 215/483-0444 11
▼▼▼ American. Fine Dining. $13-$32 **AAA Inspector Notes:** In the fashionable shopping district of Manayunk, this popular, often-crowded, bistro exudes an aura of warm elegance and casual chic. Creative food presentations such as the signature crab cakes and veal tournedos with lobster mashed potatoes reflect modern appeal. The ice cream is homemade. **Features:** full bar, Sunday brunch, happy hour. **Reservations:** suggested. **Address:** 4365 Main St 19127 **Location:** I-76 (Schuylkill Expwy) exit 338, 0.3 mi n on Green Ln, then just e; between Levering and Grape sts; in Manayunk District. Manayunk, 231. **Parking:** valet only. L D

JANNIE 215/722-6278 7
▼▼ Asian. Casual Dining. $5-$18 **AAA Inspector Notes:** After tromping through the stores in the shopping area, stop here to refuel on Chinese and Japanese food and consider the daily sushi and entrée specials. On display are tea sets that the owner has collected on international travels. **Features:** full bar. **Address:** 2117 Cottman Ave 19149 **Location:** 0.7 mi w of jct Roosevelt Blvd (US 1); in Cottman-Bustleton Shopping Center. L D CALL M

(See map & index p. 274.)

JG DOMESTIC   215/222-2363 [28]

WW WW American. Casual Dining. $12-$22 **AAA Inspector Notes:** Located just across the street from 30th Street train station, Jose Garces offers a fun, casual American restaurant focusing on local ingredients and hand-crafted specialty cocktails. The open concept, light wood furnishings, wraparound bar and abundance of plant life create a warm, inviting atmosphere. The JG domestic burger comes highly recommended, while others may be interested in day boat scallops with garbanzo bean salsa verde or Berkshire spareribs with bourbon molasses barbecue sauce. **Features:** full bar, happy hour. **Address:** 2929 Arch St 19104 **Location:** Jct N 30th and Arch sts; in Cira Centre. 30th, 220. **Parking:** on-site (fee).

L CALL ᎶM

JOHNNY MAÑANA'S   215/843-0499 [13]

WW WW Tex-Mex. Casual Dining. $7-$20 **AAA Inspector Notes:** Celebrate the Day of the Dead year-round at this kitschy Mexican eatery, where dinner platters are large and flavorful and a wide variety of tequilas await. Have a refreshing margarita or a glass of fiery tequila on the rocks. **Features:** full bar, happy hour. **Address:** 4201 Ridge Ave 19129 **Location:** US 1 exit Ridge Ave/Kelly Dr, just w. East Falls, 229. **Parking:** street only.

L D LATE

LAS CAZUELAS RESTAURANT   215/351-9144 [16]

WW WW Mexican. Casual Dining. $7-$19 **AAA Inspector Notes:** The small, intimate dining room is best described with adjectives such as cheerful, colorful and cozy. On the menu are dishes from the Puebla region of Mexico. Bring-your-own-bottle wine service is cheerfully provided, and the sounds of live guitar music fill the air on Friday, Saturday and Sunday evenings. Many specialties are prepared with mole poblano, a sauce made with five types of peppers, chocolate, plantains, croutons, raisins and sesame seeds. **Features:** patio dining, Sunday brunch. **Reservations:** suggested. **Address:** 426 W Girard Ave 19123 **Location:** Between 4th and 5th sts. Girard, 61. **Parking:** street only.

L D

LAS MARGARITAS   215/969-6600 [2]

WW WW Mexican. Casual Dining. $5-$17 **AAA Inspector Notes:** Sure you can get margaritas at this casual restaurant, but you'll also find tacos, burritos, enchiladas and traditional entrées. If you're watching your weight (or trying to lose it), ask about having your food prepared with lighter cheeses and creams. The dining room gets a burst of festivity from the gorgeous murals and vibrant colors. **Features:** full bar, happy hour. **Address:** 2538 Welsh Rd, Suite 40 19152 **Location:** Just e of jct Roosevelt Blvd (US 1); in Tremont Plaza Shopping Center. L D CALL ᎶM

LOS CABALLITOS CANTINA   215/755-3550 [50]

WW WW Mexican. Casual Dining. $7-$23 **AAA Inspector Notes:** Just ask any local for directions to The Cantina, as this place is known locally, and chances are your request will be easily met. When you're hit with a hankering for amazing margaritas and good, affordable food, this is the place to go. Local hipsters and their admirers often flock to this place for potent potables and dishes such as platanos machos (fried sweet plantains with cheese and lime sauce). The bar staff offers honest opinions about the lengthy tequila and mixed drink menu. **Features:** full bar, Sunday brunch, happy hour. **Address:** 1651 E Passyunk Ave 19148 **Location:** Between Tasker and Morris sts; in South Philadelphia. Tasker-Morris, 114.

L D LATE

MAD MEX   215/382-2221

WW WW Mexican. Casual Dining. $9-$17 **AAA Inspector Notes:** The upbeat and fast-paced restaurant displays nice Southwestern decor and serves good salsa. The sopaipillas are not to be missed. **Features:** full bar. **Address:** 3401 Walnut St 19104 **Location:** Between 34th and 35th sts. 36th, 74. **Parking:** street only.

L D LATE

MAKIMAN SUSHI   215/722-8800 [3]

WW WW Sushi. Casual Dining. $10-$27 **AAA Inspector Notes:** This spot offers innovative sushi and Japanese cuisine, with some Korean dish options available as well. The warm orange walls and modern Asian artwork enhance the intimacy of the experience. Bring your favorite wine or take advantage of the extensive take-out menu. **Reservations:** suggested, weekends. **Address:** 7324 Oxford Ave 19111 **Location:** Jct US 1, 1.9 mi w on Cottman Ave (SR 73), just nw. Ryers, 273. L D

MAMMA MARIA   215/463-6884 [48]

WW WW Italian. Casual Dining. $25-$55 **AAA Inspector Notes:** Whether you come for the $25 lunch or the $55 dinner, the only option at this casual Italian eatery is the prix fixe menu, which changes daily upon the chef's discretion. Guests won't be disappointed with the selection of homemade options including roasted eggplant, tortellini soup and pasta prepared three ways. Complimentary wine is offered during the meal, as well as an after-dinner limoncello drink. **Address:** 1637 Passyunk Ave 19148 **Location:** Between Morris and Tasker sts. Tasker-Morris, 114. **Parking:** street only.

L D

MARIGOLD KITCHEN   215/222-3699 [42]

WWWW American. Fine Dining. $24-$45 **AAA Inspector Notes:** Grab a favorite bottle of wine and bring it with you to this outstanding restaurant. Nothing is ordinary about the chef's innovative preparations such as escargots with honey mushrooms, Israeli couscous, pine nuts and parsley, toasted brioche with fried egg, fruitwood-smoked salmon, roasted beets and crispy shallots or a warm pignoli tart with figs and lavender ice cream. **Reservations:** suggested. **Address:** 501 S 45th St 19104 **Location:** Corner of Larchwood. 40th, 76. **Parking:** street only. D

MARRA'S CUCINA ITALIANA   215/463-9249 [51]

WW WW Italian. Family Dining. $8-$21 **AAA Inspector Notes:** Classic. A city institution since 1927, this restaurant is now into the fourth generation of family owners and operators. It hasn't changed much since its inception, probably not even in its décor, but why mess with what works? Grandmama's cooking prowess lives on in such dishes as irresistible fettuccine with pesto, hearty zuppa de pesce and crisp, bubbly pizza. **Features:** full bar. **Reservations:** suggested. **Address:** 1734 E Passyunk Ave 19148 **Location:** Jct S Iseminger St. Tasker-Morris, 114. **Parking:** street only.

L D

MAYFAIR DINER   215/624-8886 [8]

WW WW American. Family Dining. $7-$15 **AAA Inspector Notes:** Meatloaf, baked chicken and turkey give you a taste of the familiar here, which also merits kudos for the breakfast dishes such as the local favorite scrapple and eggs. Smartly uniformed staff members serve with efficient ease. Value prices and hearty portions contribute to this diner's popularity. **Address:** 7373 Frankford Dr 19136 **Location:** Between Tudor St and Bleigh Ave. Holmesburg Jct, 252.

B L D 24

MCNALLY'S TAVERN   215/247-9736 [5]

WW WW Sandwiches. Casual Dining. $4-$12 **AAA Inspector Notes:** If Philadelphia is famous for its sandwiches, this tavern should be required dining. A variety of spectacular homemade soups, desserts and sandwiches warm stomachs as the friendly (but saucy) staff warms the heart. The Schmitt, a cheesesteak featuring salami and McCall's special sauce, is so popular that it also is available at local sport venues and debuted nationally at Super Bowl XXXIX. **Features:** full bar. **Address:** 8634 Germantown Ave 19118 **Location:** I-476 exit 19, 4.9 mi e; in white and black building, across from the old trolley turn. Chestnut Hill West, 240. **Parking:** street only.

L D

MR. MARTINO'S TRATTORIA   215/755-0663 [49]

WW WW Italian. Casual Dining. $11-$20 **AAA Inspector Notes:** Take a step back in time and come to this charming family-owned and -operated restaurant that features a small rustic dining room with dark woods, exposed brick walls and dim lighting. The menu, like the days open, is very limited, but you won't be disappointed with the hearty cheese-filled pasta dishes or the always-popular balsamic chicken. Be sure to bring cash; credit cards are not accepted and there is no ATM inside. **Reservations:** suggested. **Address:** 1646 E Passyunk Ave 19148 **Location:** Between Morris and Tasker sts. Tasker-Morris, 114. **Parking:** street only. D

(See map & index p. 274.)

NEW DECK TAVERN   215/386-4600   33
▼▼ American. Casual Dining. $8-$17 **AAA Inspector Notes:**
Sit back and relax in this authentic Irish pub where the menu offers a
variety of American and Irish samplings. Try one of their draft beers
from around the world or enjoy something from the extensive collection of single-malt Scotches. **Features:** full bar. **Address:** 3408
Sansom St 19104 **Location:** I-76 (Schuylkill Expwy) exit 346A, just w
on South St, just n on 33rd St, just w on Walnut St, just n on 36th St,
then just w; in Sansom Commons. ▤ 36th, 74.
L D LATE ▥

NEW DELHI   215/386-1941   31
▼ Indian. Casual Dining. $10-$15 **AAA Inspector Notes:** This is
a traditional Indian restaurant decorated with art pieces, high ceilings
and an outdoor eating area. The buffet contains both meat and vegetable options as well as a full bar. I recommend trying the chicken
tikka masala. **Features:** full bar. **Address:** 4004 Chestnut St 19104
Location: Jct 40th St; in University City. ▤ 40th, 77. **Parking:** street
only. L D ▥

NIFTY FIFTY'S   215/676-1950
▼▼ American. Family Dining. $4-$13 **AAA Inspector Notes:**
Step back in time at this local chain, which features the self-
proclaimed world's largest soda fountain with more than 100 flavors
to choose from. Malts, shakes, burgers, sandwiches and fries are all
made with fresh ingredients on site. The kids will love the retro décor
and video game area. **Address:** 2491 Grant Ave 19114 **Location:**
Just e of jct US 1. B L D LATE

NORTH 3RD   215/413-3666   21
▼▼ American. Gastropub. $10-$19 **AAA Inspector Notes:**
One of the city's most popular date spots, this place plies you not
only with a delicious array of gastropub fare but also with an affordable price list (including reasonably priced wines by the bottle).
The dark, casually sexy interior displays a changing selection of
local art that just might have been created by your server. This
place is a big hit during its weekend brunch; if you're eager to try
it, get here early or be prepared to wait. **Features:** full bar, Sunday
brunch. **Address:** 801 N 3rd St 19123 **Location:** Jct Brown St; in
Northern Liberties. ▤ Spring Garden, 62. **Parking:** street only.
D LATE ▥

OREGON DINER   215/462-5566   54
▼▼ American. Casual Dining. $5-$18 **AAA Inspector Notes:**
Local favorites, such as cheesesteaks and cinnamon buns, share the
menu with typical diner fare that includes all-day breakfast. Families
and working families populate the diner during the day, while a college-
aged crowd takes over the night shift. **Features:** full bar. **Address:**
302 W Oregon Ave 19148 **Location:** I-95 exit 19, follow signs for
Packer Ave, just n on Front St, then just w.
B L D 24

OSTERIA   215/763-0920   26
▼▼▼ Italian. Fine Dining. $12-$30 **AAA Inspector Notes:**
Owners Marc Vetri and Jeff Benjamin aim to impress and rarely fail
to do so with their seasonal menu additions and thoughtfully chosen
wines and beers. You'll find great Tuscan cuisine, but if you love
pizza, give strong consideration to the legendary margherita or Lom-
barda. **Features:** full bar. **Reservations:** suggested. **Address:** 640 N
Broad St 19130 **Location:** Jct SR 611 and Wallace St. ▤ Spring
Garden, 120. **Parking:** street only. D ▥

PATTAYA THAI CUISINE   215/387-8533   32
▼▼ Thai. Casual Dining. $8-$17 **AAA Inspector Notes:** Expect modest décor and traditional menu items. While there are no
show-stoppers, the food is good and the variety pleasing from the red
curry salmon to the yellow curries. You'll also find a few exotic options, including spicy basil venison, ostrich with green curry and stir-
fried alligator with curry. **Features:** full bar, early bird specials.
Reservations: suggested, weekends. **Address:** 4006 Chestnut St
19104 **Location:** Between 40th and 41st sts. ▤ 40th, 77. **Parking:**
street only. L D ▥

PENNE RESTAURANT & WINE BAR   215/823-6222   36
▼▼▼ Italian. Casual Dining. $10-$28 **AAA Inspector Notes:**
The dining room enjoys a fun, stylish, casually upscale atmosphere
with an open kitchen. The modern restaurant emphasizes fresh handmade pasta and other regional specialties. An extensive wine program featuring 45 selections by the glass or flight complements the
outstanding bar menu. Pan-seared red snapper with mushroom risotto, Swiss chard and lobster sauce is a tasty dish. **Features:** full
bar, happy hour. **Reservations:** suggested. **Address:** 3600 Sansom
St 19104 **Location:** I-76 (Schuylkill Expwy) exit 345 eastbound; exit
346A (Sansom St) westbound; between 36th and 37th sts; in The
Hilton Inn at Penn. ▤ 36th, 74. **Parking:** valet and street only.
L D ▥

PHO PALACE   215/437-1898   1
▼ Vietnamese. Casual Dining. $7-$20 **AAA Inspector
Notes:** The delicious aromas of pho (a traditional beef- or chicken-
based soup) and smiles of the attentive staff will greet guests as soon
as they walk into this restaurant. Order a bowl for the table, then try
one of the tasty grilled meat dishes or vermicelli noodle bowls. **Address:** 15501 Bustleton Ave 19116 **Location:** I-276 (Pennsylvania
Tpke) exit 351, just s on US 1, 2.1 mi e on Street Rd, then 1.2 mi s.
▤ Somerton, 285. L D CALL ▣M ▥

POD   215/387-1803   34
▼▼▼ Japanese. Casual Dining. $9-$30 **AAA Inspector
Notes:** This restaurant boasts modern décor with a variety of colorful
lighting, enhanced furnishings and a full bar. The menu incorporates
the modern theme into traditional Asian cuisine such as dim sum pot
stickers with mustard aioli and braised-beef short ribs with udon
noodles. **Features:** full bar. **Reservations:** suggested. **Address:**
3636 Sansom St 19104 **Location:** I-76 (Schuylkill Expwy) exit 346A
(Sansom St), just w on South St. ▤ 36th, 74. **Parking:** street only.
L D ▥

THE RESTAURANT SCHOOL AT WALNUT HILL COLLEGE   215/222-4200   39
▼▼▼ Continental. Fine Dining. $13-$21 **AAA Inspector
Notes:** Dine at this large white Italianate mansion, which is part of the
culinary school. The student-operated restaurant offers an interesting,
eclectic mix in its offerings of American and European cuisine. The
re-created European courtyard is relaxed, and the dining room is
bathed in external light. **Features:** full bar, patio dining. **Reservations:** suggested. **Address:** 4207 Walnut St 19104 **Location:** Jct
Walnut and 42nd sts; in University City Plaza. ▤ 40th, 77.
D ▥

SABRINA'S CAFE @ POWELTON   215/222-1022   27
▼▼ American. Casual Dining. $7-$20 **AAA Inspector Notes:**
This casual eatery brings true comfort in a strikingly beautiful historic
building decorated with hardwood floors and original exposed stone
walls. However, it's the food that keeps people coming back. Stuffed
challah French toast and huevos rancheros are popular breakfast favorites (served all day), while hearty sandwiches like Mel's chicken
cutlet with marinated long hots and Angus beef burgers take over for
lunch. **Features:** Sunday brunch. **Address:** 227 N 34th St 19104 **Location:** Jct 34th St and Powelton Ave. ▤ 34th, 73. **Parking:** street
only. B L D ▥

THE SANCTUARY   610/521-5900   55
▼▼▼ American. Fine Dining. $6-$36 **AAA Inspector Notes:**
While coming or going, stop at this restaurant to grab a bite of contemporary regional American fare. With a contemporary, upscale and
casual style, the dining room is a nice spot to savor filet mignon,
which is topped with crumbled Gorgonzola cheese and served with
rosemary-roasted potatoes and a red wine demi-glace. **Features:** full
bar. **Reservations:** suggested. **Address:** 500 Stevens Dr 19113 **Location:** I-95 exit 9A (Essington/SR 420), just e on Wanamaker Ave,
then 1.4 mi n on Industrial Way; in Renaissance Hotel Philadelphia
Airport. B L D CALL ▣M

STANDARD TAP   215/238-0630   18
▼▼ American. Gastropub. $8-$26 **AAA Inspector Notes:** Ar-
guably the first of Philadelphia's gastropubs, the experience here provides exactly what one would expect and some things one would not.
Guests can view a flavorful and changing draft menu of local microbrews, a mouth-watering menu of burgers, pub snacks (diet-busting
gravy fries), grilled game and seafood and a small number of raw bar
offerings. While table service is available, small parties and singles
can cozy up to the bar. **Features:** full bar, Sunday brunch. **Address:**
901 N 2nd St 19123 **Location:** Jct Poplar St; in Northern Liberties.
▤ Spring Garden, 62. **Parking:** street only. D LATE ▥

(See map & index p. 274.)

TANDOOR INDIA
215/222-7122 (35)

♥♥ Indian. Casual Dining. $9-$16 **AAA Inspector Notes:** Looking for a budget-friendly option? Consider this Indian buffet-style restaurant with all the traditional favorites. Local students and faculty frequent this establishment for the quiet setting and exotic dishes. **Address:** 106 S 40th St 19104 **Location:** Between Sansom and Chestnut sts. 🚇 40th, 77. **Parking:** street only.

[L] [D] [🍴]

THAI SINGHA HOUSE
215/382-8001 (30)

♥♥ Thai. Casual Dining. $4-$18 **AAA Inspector Notes:** Sit and relax over a meal at this busy lunch stop in the University City district. Special three-course deals are available during certain times for under $11. **Features:** full bar, early bird specials. **Address:** 3900 Chestnut St 19104 **Location:** Jct 39th and Chestnut sts. 🚇 40th, 77. **Parking:** on-site (fee) and street. [L] [D] [🍴]

TONY LUKE'S BEEF AND BEER SPORTS BAR
215/465-1901 (53)

♥♥ Sandwiches. Casual Dining. $6-$9 **AAA Inspector Notes:** If you're looking for a hearty cheesesteak, go where Philadelphians go. This casual eatery offers friendly, speedy service and hearty dishes, including TL fries topped with Cheese Whiz and bacon, and the steak Italian with sharp provolone and sautéed spinach or broccoli rabe. You can check out drink specials when local sports events are on. **Features:** full bar. **Address:** 26 Oregon Ave 19148 **Location:** Just e of jct Front St. [L] [D] CALL [♿M]

THE VICTORCAFE
215/468-3040 (45)

♥♥♥ Italian. Casual Dining. $16-$36 **AAA Inspector Notes:** Historic. Established in 1919, this family-owned and -operated Italian restaurant has become a local favorite and a trademark of Philadelphia with its talented opera-singing staff. While feasting on a flavorful steak or hearty pasta dish, don't be alarmed when the bell rings and a server harmoniously sings his or her favorite musical or opera. **Features:** full bar. **Reservations:** suggested. **Address:** 1303 Dickinson St 19147 **Location:** Between 13th and Broad sts. 🚇 Tasker-Morris, 114. **Parking:** valet only. [D] [🍴]

WARMDADDY'S
215/462-2000 (44)

♥♥ American. Casual Dining. $8-$23 **AAA Inspector Notes:** Warmdaddy's features a flavorful menu of soul foods with a Creole twist. As you savor every bite of the shrimp and grits, gumbo ya-ya or fried chicken, your foot will be tapping to the live jazz and soul music played each night. The roof deck is a peaceful spot in the summertime. **Features:** full bar, Sunday brunch. **Reservations:** suggested, for dinner. **Address:** 1400 S Columbus Blvd 19147 **Location:** I-95 exit 20 (Columbus Blvd), just s. [L] [D]

WHITE DOG CAFE
215/386-9224 (37)

♥♥ American. Casual Dining. $12-$32 **AAA Inspector Notes:** Incredibly tasty dishes using local, organic and free-range ingredients can be had at this quaint café and pub located close to Drexel University and The University of Pennsylvania. Ask the friendly staff for great accompanying draft beers. **Features:** full bar, Sunday brunch, happy hour. **Address:** 3420 Sansom St 19104 **Location:** Between Walnut and Chestnut sts. 🚇 36th, 74. **Parking:** street only.

[L] [D] [🍴]

WINNIE'S LE BUS
215/487-2663 (12)

♥♥ American. Casual Dining. $6-$18 **AAA Inspector Notes:** Known for its weekend brunches, this homey restaurant delivers outstanding homemade bread and pastries, as well as delicious apple pie and fluffy banana walnut pancakes. Meatloaf is a menu staple. The lively atmosphere is welcoming to families. **Features:** full bar, Sunday brunch. **Reservations:** suggested, weekends. **Address:** 4266 Main St 19127 **Location:** I-76 (Schuylkill Expwy) exit 338, 0.3 mi n on Green Ln, then 0.5 mi e. 🚇 Manayunk, 231. **Parking:** street only. [B] [L] [D] [🍴]

ZESTY'S
215/483-6226 (9)

♥♥♥ Mediterranean. Casual Dining. $10-$50 **AAA Inspector Notes:** This local favorite is known for its cuisine served among stylish décor with granite tables, multiple fish tanks and a full wraparound bar. The menu is filled with all the traditional Greek favorites and offers delicious chicken lefkadas. The restaurant also serves as a great late-night stop and offers karaoke on selected nights. **Features:** full bar, Sunday brunch. **Reservations:** suggested. **Address:** 4382 Main St 19127 **Location:** I-76 (Schuylkill Expwy) exit 338, just n on Green Ln, then just e. 🚇 Manayunk, 231. **Parking:** street only. [L] [D] CALL [♿M] [🍴]

BROWN BETTY DESSERT BOUTIQUE
215/629-0999

[fyi] Not evaluated. Many of the recipes used at Brown Betty Dessert Boutique are from the lawyer-turned-baker owner's grandmother, who serves as the namesake of this popular and nationally recognized little eatery. The tempting menu offers cupcakes, cookies and other delicious sweets. **Address:** 1030 N 2nd St 19123 **Location:** Just s of jct Germantown Ave; in Liberties Walk Complex. 🚇 Girard, 61.

CACIA'S BAKERY
215/334-1330

[fyi] Not evaluated. Cacia's turns out delicious traditional Italian bread and focaccia, but you'll most likely visit the South Philly storefront for mouthwatering Sicilian-style pizza, which comes in varieties such as classic cheese and tomato, as well as spinach and broccoli and cheese. **Address:** 1526 Ritner St 19145 **Location:** Just w of Broad St. 🚇 Oregon, 112.

GENO'S STEAKS
215/389-0659

[fyi] Not evaluated. Try Cheez Whiz or provolone melted over classic Philly cheesesteaks at this famous outdoor eatery. **Address:** 1219 9th St 19147 **Location:** Jct E Passyunk Ave. 🚇 Ellsworth-Federal, 115.

JOHN'S ROAST PORK
215/463-1951

[fyi] Not evaluated. In addition to fabulous cheesesteak sandwiches, the restaurant whips up its namesake roast pork sandwiches, which many top with sharp provolone, greens and peppers. **Address:** 14 E Snyder Ave 19148 **Location:** I-95 exit 20 (Columbus Blvd), just e; at Weccacoe Ave; in South Philly.

MORE THAN JUST ICE CREAM
215/574-0586

[fyi] Not evaluated. Yes, you'll find more than just ice cream at this restaurant. In addition to extensive ice cream choices, the large menu also includes fresh salads, entrées and baked desserts. The cozy atmosphere is suitable for a relaxed lunch or dinner, or you can just grab a dessert on the run. **Address:** 1119 Locust St 19107 **Location:** Between 11th and 12th sts. 🚇 12th-13th & Locust, 141.

NBC SPORTS ARENA
267/443-6415

[fyi] Not evaluated. The NBC Sports Arena offers fans a one-of-a-kind sports viewing experience, featuring a 32-foot diagonal, LED HD television, high impact LED rings displaying the NBC sports ticker, and in-game promotions that will rival any live sports experience in the world, making for a true fourth stadium experience at the Philadelphia Sports Complex. With a full service menu, the NBC Sports Arena will be the best place to catch the game or host an unforgettable event. **Address:** 1100 Pattison Ave 19148 **Location:** At XFINITY Live! 🚇 AT&T, 111.

PAT'S KING OF STEAKS
215/468-1546

[fyi] Not evaluated. For more than 70 years, this place has served Philadelphia's famous cheesesteaks. **Address:** 1237 E Passyunk Ave 19147 **Location:** Jct 9th St and Passyunk Ave. 🚇 Ellsworth-Federal, 115.

STEVE'S PRINCE OF STEAKS
215/677-8020

[fyi] Not evaluated. Those who don't want to drive across town for an authentic cheesesteak should follow the locals to this spot. They will all be lined up to grab a sandwich or grinder (a hoagie served warm), many scarfing them down before they even make it back to the car. Read the ordering instructions on the wall, as not getting it right the first time sends diners to the back of the line to start over. **Address:** 2711 Comly Rd 19154 **Location:** Jct SR 63, 0.4 mi s on US 1/Roosevelt Blvd, just e.

(See map & index p. 274.)

TIFFIN STORE   215/922-1297

fyi Not evaluated. When the delivery service at this Indian restaurant became the talk of the town, the owners added a small dining room to accommodate the growing demand. Take advantage of the weekly lunch specials. **Address:** 710 W Girard Ave 19123 **Location:** Between 7th and 8th sts. Girard, 223.

TONY LUKE'S OLD PHILLY STYLE SANDWICHES
                                        215/551-5725

fyi Not evaluated. Flavorful cheesesteaks, chicken and roast pork sandwiches beckon to you from Tony Luke's sandwich stand. Sandwiches are served the "Italian" way, with broccoli rabe or spinach playing as big a role as the cheese. The savory indulgences make the occasional splurge worthwhile. **Address:** 39 E Oregon Ave 19148 **Location:** Between S Front and S Swanson sts.

Nearby New Jersey

BATSTO elev. 13'
• Part of Philadelphia area — see map p. 230

Established in 1766, Batsto became a prominent iron foundry and was of great military importance to the Patriots' cause during the Revolution. The village's prosperity grew after the war, a time when ironworks, glassworks, a brickyard, a gristmill and a sawmill provided livelihoods for nearly 1,000 people.

Fortunes dwindled when competition from cheap Pennsylvania coal forced the town's more expensive charcoal-fired furnaces to close in 1855. An 1874 fire burned half of Batsto to the ground, but 2 years later wealthy Philadelphia financier Joseph Wharton purchased the town site and the surrounding 100,000 acres.

INSIDER INFO:
The Pine Barrens

If most people don't know about New Jersey's Pine Barrens, it could be because the 450,000 year-round residents of this national reserve that overlies more than a million acres of the state's bottom half, prefer to keep a good thing to themselves.

Wedged between the roar of traffic along the New Jersey Turnpike and the Garden State Parkway, this quiet wilderness shows little evidence of the human settlement and enterprise that have occurred. Yet the Pines are far from barren.

The area's heart is a tapestry of impenetrable scrub and pitch pine, rivers, swamps and bogs where rebelling Colonials mined iron to make cannonballs. Villages, foundries and glassworks churned out the region's products until the late 1800s, after which the forest resumed full reign.

Local residents, affectionately called the "Pineys," learned to "work the woods" by selling its seasonal gifts and tending its cranberry and blueberry crops. Cranberries have been commercially raised in the Pine Barrens since about 1835, while the first commercial blueberry planting was made in 1916. The Pine Barrens account for approximately 25 percent of the state's agricultural income.

Many recreational opportunities exist in the Pine Barrens. Boating, canoeing, swimming, fishing and hunting are popular activities. Hikers can enjoy the Batona Trail, a marked wilderness trail that traverses the Pine Barrens, or explore old abandoned towns and the restored Batsto Village. More than 1,000 known sites in the vicinity show that man lived in this area as early as 10,000 B.C.

Left undisturbed are the woodland's wonders: a confusing tangle of sand roads cut during Colonial times, 12,000 acres of stunted pygmy pines in an area called the Plains, insectivorous plants, exotic orchids, ventriloquist tree frogs found almost nowhere else and a legendary winged creature known as the "Jersey Devil."

The muck soil in the Pine Barrens produces monobactum, a microorganism expected to revolutionize the antibiotics industry. An aquifer inside the Pine's deep sand beds holds 17 trillion gallons of water with the purity of glacial ice. The water in this shallow aquifer usually is at or near the surface, producing bogs, marshes and swamps. A maze of serpentine streams fed by the aquifer, stained the color of tea by cedar sap, rises within the low dome of land on which the Pines exist.

With development encroaching on all sides, the Pines' uniqueness becomes more apparent each year—except to local residents, who have always known it.

BATSTO HISTORIC VILLAGE is off CR 542 on Batsto Rd. This restored 19th-century village within Wharton State Forest *(see Recreation Areas Chart)* grew up around the Batsto Iron Works. Buildings include an iron master's mansion, a sawmill, a church, a gristmill, a general store, an icehouse, a post office and workers' houses. The visitor center houses a museum with permanent and changing historical exhibits. Visitors can take a cell phone audio tour.

Time: Allow 2 hours minimum. **Hours:** Grounds daily dawn-dusk. Visitor center open daily 9-4. Mansion tours are given when staff is available. Closed Jan. 1, Thanksgiving, Christmas and state holidays. Phone ahead to confirm schedule. **Cost:** Grounds and visitor center free. Mansion tour $3; $1 (ages 6-11). **Parking:** Sat.-Sun. and holidays $5, Memorial Day-Labor Day. **Phone:** (609) 561-3262 or (609) 561-0024.

BELLMAWR pop. 11,583
• Hotels & Restaurants map & index p. 274
• Part of Philadelphia area — see map p. 230

CLUB DINER   856/931-2880 (154)

American. Family Dining. $6-$13 **AAA Inspector Notes:** This eatery offers patrons simple home-style cooking in a casual, friendly atmosphere. Breakfast provides all the traditional favorites from omelets to French toast, while dinner provides a variety of pasta, hot sandwiches, seafood specialties and large steak entrées. **Address:** 20 N Black Horse Pike 08031 **Location:** I-295 exit 28, 0.8 mi s; New Jersey Tpke exit 3, just n. B L D 24

BLACKWOOD pop. 4,545
• Part of Philadelphia area — see map p. 230

HAMPTON INN-TURNERSVILLE   (856)228-4200

 Hotel $109-$182 **Address:**
5800 Black Horse Pike 08012 **Location:**
Just w of SR 42. **Facility:** 76 units. 5 stories, interior corridors. **Terms:** 1-7 night
minimum stay, cancellation fee imposed.
Pool(s): heated indoor. **Activities:** exercise room. **Guest Services:**
valet and coin laundry.

| **AAA Benefit:** |
| Members save 5% or more! |

BORDENTOWN pop. 3,924
• Part of Philadelphia area — see map p. 230

BEST WESTERN BORDENTOWN INN   (609)298-8000

Motel
$80-$120

| **AAA Benefit:** |
| Members save up to 20%! |

Address: 1068 US Hwy 206 S 08505
Location: New Jersey Tpke exit 7, 0.8
mi n. Next to a park. **Facility:** 100 units.
2 stories (no elevator), exterior corridors.
Pool(s): heated indoor. **Activities:**
sauna, hot tub, exercise room. **Guest
Services:** valet and coin laundry.

DAYS INN-BORDENTOWN   (609)298-6100

Motel
$70-$99

Address: 1073 US Hwy 206 N 08505
Location: New Jersey Tpke exit 7, 0.8
mi n. **Facility:** 129 units. 2 stories (no elevator), exterior corridors. **Amenities:**
safes. **Pool(s):** outdoor. **Activities:** exercise room. **Guest Services:** coin
laundry.

HAMPTON INN BORDENTOWN   (609)298-4000

 **Hotel** $99-$199 **Address:**
2004 US Hwy 206 S 08505 **Location:**
New Jersey Tpke exit 7, just s. **Facility:**
72 units. 4 stories, interior corridors.
Terms: 1-7 night minimum stay, cancellation fee imposed. **Pool(s):** heated indoor. **Activities:** exercise
room. **Guest Services:** valet and coin laundry.

| **AAA Benefit:** |
| Members save 5% or more! |

WHERE TO EAT

THE FARNSWORTH HOUSE RESTAURANT   609/291-9232

Italian. Casual Dining. $11-$43 **AAA Inspector Notes:**
Outside, a large likeness of an Early American fellow in a powdered
wig—presumably Thomas Farnsworth, who settled the area in
1682—welcomes diners. However, the menu is all Italian. Try the
chicken prepared several different ways, including chicken Francaise
and chicken Marsala. The tortellini and linguine are a hit, as well as
various versions of seafood, veal and steak. **Features:** full bar. **Reservations:** suggested. **Address:** 135 Farnsworth Ave 08505 **Location:** Center.

Pick up vibrant, top-quality travel guides
and atlases at AAA/CAA offices

MASTORIS DINER RESTAURANT   609/298-4650

American. Casual Dining. $6-$49 **AAA Inspector Notes:**
This casual family eatery with faux windows draped with curtains offers a simple dining room featuring meals with exceptional value. In
addition to Italian and Greek fare, the menu includes heaping servings of wholesome food such as burgers, wraps, seafood, steak and
sandwiches. The servers are fast and efficient. **Features:** full bar. **Address:** 144 Rt 130 08505 **Location:** N of jct US 206 and 130; I-295
exit 56 (US 130); New Jersey Tpke exit 7, 3 mi n.

BRIDGEPORT
• Part of Philadelphia area — see map p. 230

HAMPTON INN-BRIDGEPORT   (856)467-6200

Hotel $139-$159 **Address:**
2 Pureland Dr 08085 **Location:** I-295
exit 10, just se. **Facility:** 95 units. 4 stories, interior corridors. **Terms:** 1-7 night
minimum stay, cancellation fee imposed.
Pool(s): heated outdoor. **Activities:** exercise room. **Guest Services:**
coin laundry.

| **AAA Benefit:** |
| Members save 5% or more! |

BURLINGTON pop. 9,920, elev. 13'
• Part of Philadelphia area — see map p. 230

One of the first permanent settlements in the
western part of the colony, Burlington was established by members of the Society of Friends in 1677.
It became the capital of West Jersey and shared
that status with Perth Amboy after East and West
Jersey united. A strategic location on the Delaware
River between Trenton and Camden made the flourishing port so prosperous that its citizens—primarily
Quaker settlers and pacifists—were relatively uninvolved in the Revolution.

Venerable buildings that are open to the public by
appointment include the 1703 Old St. Mary's
Church, at Broad and Wood streets; the 1685 Revell
House, in the 200 block of Wood Street; the 1785
Friends Meeting House, on High Street near Broad
Street; the John Hoskins House, 202 High St.; the
1792 Friend's School, at York and Penn streets; and
the restored carriage house on Smith's Alley between High and Wood streets.

Burlington County Chamber of Commerce: 100
Technology Way, Suite 110, Mount Laurel, NJ
08054. **Phone:** (856) 439-2520.

**BURLINGTON COUNTY HISTORICAL SOCIETY
COMPLEX** is 2 blks. n. of US 130 at 451-459 High
St. The Corson Poley Center contains a library, museum, Children's History Center and three historic
houses: the Bard-How House, the Capt. James
Lawrence House and the James Fenimore Cooper
House. The museum displays a locally made
jinrikisha—an Asian hand-pulled carriage—as well
as a collection of tall case clocks and quilts. Another
exhibit, The American Revolution: A Global Conflict,
explores early American history. The Children's History Center offers interactive experiences for children ages 2 and up.

The library's genealogical records are available for research. **Hours:** Guided museum and 40-minute house tours are offered Tues.-Sat. 10-5. Children's History Center open Tues.-Sat. 10-5. Library open Wed.-Thurs. 1-5. Closed major holidays. **Cost:** Fee for house tour, Children's History Center or library and gallery $5. House tour, library and gallery $5. **Phone:** (609) 386-4773.

Bard-How House, 453 High St. in the Burlington County Historical Society Complex, was built around 1743 for merchant Bennett Bard and his wife, Sarah Pattison Bard. It was purchased in 1756 by butcher and tavern owner Samuel How. Period furnishings and other accessories decorate the restored house, including a tall case clock that dates from 1740.

Hours: Guided house tours are offered Tues.-Sat. 10-5. Closed major holidays. **Cost:** (includes Capt. James Lawrence House, James Fenimore Cooper House, and Burlington County Historical Society Complex library and gallery) $5. Tour only (includes Capt. James Lawrence House and James Fenimore Cooper House) $5. **Phone:** (609) 386-4773.

Capt. James Lawrence House, 459 High St. in the Burlington County Historical Society Complex, is the birthplace of the American naval hero of the War of 1812. The commander of the USS *Chesapeake* engaged in battle against the HMS *Shannon,* and the mortally wounded Lawrence issued his famous last command, remembered as "Don't give up the ship." The house is furnished in period and also contains a toy collection.

Hours: Guided house tours are offered Tues.-Sat. 10-5. Closed major holidays. **Cost:** (includes Bard-How House, James Fenimore Cooper House, and Burlington County Historical Society Complex library and gallery) $5. Tour only (includes Bard-How House and James Fenimore Cooper House) $5. **Phone:** (609) 386-4773.

James Fenimore Cooper House, 457 High St. in the Burlington County Historical Society Complex, is the birthplace of the author of the "Leatherstocking Tales," novels depicting the era of American frontiersmen and Native Americans. "The Last of the Mohicans" and "The Deerslayer" are among the best known titles in the series, written 1826-41. The 1780 Cooper House has five museum rooms.

Hours: Guided house tours are offered Tues.-Sat. 10-5. Closed major holidays. **Cost:** (includes Bard-How House, Capt. James Lawrence House, and Burlington County Historical Society Complex library and gallery) $5. Tour only (includes Bard-How House and Capt. James Lawrence House) $5. **Phone:** (609) 386-4773.

CAMDEN pop. 77,344, elev. 25'
• Part of Philadelphia area — see map p. 230

The site of William Cooper's ferryboat operation on the Delaware River in the 1680s grew into a city well-established in industry and transportation, especially after becoming the terminus for the Camden & Amboy Railroad in 1834. Yet echoes of the city's shipbuilding past remain ever-present.

The arrival of the **Tall Ships Philadelphia Camden 2015** offers those in the Delaware River region a glimpse into history—12 massive vessels, to be exact—at Penn's Landing and the Camden Waterfront from June 24-28.

Port facilities along the deep, broad Delaware River led to a boom in shipbuilding during World Wars I and II. The first nuclear-powered merchant ship, the *Savannah,* was built in Camden. On the cultural side, poet Walt Whitman—whose unfettered, subjective style revolutionized poetic expression in the mid-19th century—lived his last years in Camden. The tomb of the good gray poet is in Harleigh Cemetery on Haddon Avenue.

The Camden Riversharks play minor league baseball at Campbell's Field, 401 N. Delaware Ave., from late April through late September; for ticket and schedule information phone the box office at (866) 742-7579.

ADVENTURE AQUARIUM is on the banks of the Delaware River at 1 Riverside Dr. Sea life and wildlife can be seen and touched in a variety of exhibits, including the new KidZone, an interactive exhibit designed specifically for kids. Shark Realm, a 40-foot walk-through tunnel, houses more than 20 sharks and 850 other marine animals. The West African River Experience houses hippopotamuses and porcupines as well as a variety of African birds in an aviary. Films shown in a 4-D theater depict the wonders of underwater life. A Swim with the Sharks snorkeling program and special behind-the-scenes animal adventures also are offered.

Ferry/trolley service to the museum is available to and from the riverfront in Philadelphia May through September. **Time:** Allow 2 hours minimum. **Hours:** Daily 10-5. **Cost:** $25.95; $18.95 (ages 2-12). Adventure Combo with 4-D theater ticket $28.95; $21.95 (ages 2-12). **Parking:** $10. **Phone:** (856) 365-3300 or (800) 616-5297. City Hall, 144

BATTLESHIP *NEW JERSEY* is berthed at 62 Battleship Pl. on the Camden waterfront. This Iowa Class vessel, launched from the Philadelphia Navy Yard in 1942, is celebrated as the U.S. Navy's most decorated battleship. After serving in World War II, Korea, Vietnam and the Persian Gulf, the ship was decommissioned in 1990. Gun turrets, bridge communications, captain's and admiral's cabins, and enlisted men's bunks and mess area can be seen.

The 2-hour Fire Power Tour offers an in-depth look at the ship's weapons systems and the combat engagement center. The 90-minute Turret II Experience explores the battleship's legendary 16-inch gun turret.

Note: Video cameras, bags, backpacks and baby strollers are not permitted. Comfortable dress and shoes are recommended. A video version is available for those physically unable to take the tour. **Time:** Allow 2 hours minimum. **Hours:** Tours are offered every 15 minutes daily 9:30-5, May 1-Labor Day; daily 9:30-3, in Apr., day after Labor Day-Oct. 31 and Dec. 26-Dec. 31; Sat.-Sun. 9:30-3, Nov. 1-Dec. 31 and early Feb.-Mar. 31. Turret II Experience tours are offered Sat.-Sun. at 11 and 1. Closed Jan. 1, Thanksgiving and Christmas. **Cost:** Fire Power Tour $21.95; $17 (ages 6-11, 65+ and retired military with ID); free (ages 0-5 and active military with ID). Turret II Experience $29.95; $25.95 (ages 6-11, 65+ and retired military with ID); free (ages 0-5 and active military with ID). **Parking:** Fees vary by garage. **Phone:** (856) 966-1652 or (866) 877-6262. City Hall, 144

CAMDEN CHILDREN'S GARDEN is on the riverfront at 3 Riverside Dr., adjacent to Adventure Aquarium. It features a variety of themed gardens designed for children ages 12 and under, including a dinosaur garden, a fitness garden and a picnic garden. Storybook Gardens features the Giant's Garden, Three Little Pigs Garden and an English-style garden like the one depicted in the different versions of the movie "The Secret Garden." There also is a butterfly garden, a maze and a tree house. Indoor exhibits include the Philadelphia Eagles Butterfly House, Benjamin Franklin's Secret Workshop and the tropically landscaped Plaza de Aibonito.

Visitors also can ride the Garden Carousel, the Arrow River Train and the Spring Butterfly Ride, which raises riders 30 feet in the air to provide a butterfly's-eye view of the gardens. **Time:** Allow 2 hours minimum. **Hours:** Wed.-Sun. 10-4, July-Aug.; Thurs.-Sun. 10-4, Sept.-Dec.; phone for schedule, late Mar.-June 30. Closed Thanksgiving and Christmas. **Cost:** $6; $4 (visitors with a paid admission to Adventure Aquarium arriving through the Garden Gate); free (ages 0-2). **Phone:** (856) 365-8733. City Hall, 144

CAMDEN COUNTY HISTORICAL SOCIETY is .5 mi. n.w. on Haddon Ave. off US 130, .2 mi. n.e. on Vesper Blvd., then .2 mi. n.w. to 1900 Park Blvd. The society's museum contains fire-fighting equipment, Civil War artifacts, working Victrolas and a large collection of other vintage RCA items.

The brick, Georgian-style Pomona Hall, a Quaker mansion built in 1726 and extensively enlarged in 1788, is authentically restored and furnished in period. The society's library has maps, 18th- and 19th-century newspapers and an extensive collection of genealogical data. **Note:** The museum is currently closed and house tours have been temporarily suspended due to weather-related damage; phone for updates. **Hours:** House tours are given Thurs. and Sun. 12:30-3:30. Library open Wed. and Fri. 10-3, Thurs. 10-noon, Sun. noon-5. Closed major holidays. Phone ahead to confirm schedule. **Cost:** Museum or library $5; $4 (ages 65+ and students with ID). Pomona Hall tour $5. Museum and Pomona

Hall $8; $6 (students with ID). **Phone:** (856) 964-3333. Ferry Ave, 146

CARNEYS POINT pop. 7,382

• Part of Philadelphia area — see map p. 230

COMFORT INN & SUITES (856)299-8282

 Hotel $99-$150 **Address:** 634 Sodders Rd 08069 **Location:** I-295 exit 2B, just e on Pennsville-Auburn Rd, then 0.3 mi s. **Facility:** 63 units, some efficiencies. 3 stories, interior corridors. **Activities:** exercise room. **Guest Services:** coin laundry.

HOLIDAY INN EXPRESS HOTEL & SUITES (856)351-9222

Hotel $110-$140

Address: 506 S Pennsville-Auburn Rd 08069 **Location:** I-295 exit 2B, just e. **Facility:** 78 units. 3 stories, interior corridors. **Guest Services:** valet and coin laundry. **Featured Amenity:** breakfast buffet.

CHERRY HILL elev. 56'
• Hotels & Restaurants map & index p. 274
• Part of Philadelphia area — see map p. 230

GARDEN STATE DISCOVERY MUSEUM is at 2040 Springdale Rd., Suite 100. More than 20 interactive exhibit areas provide an entertaining and educational experience for children, especially for ages 1-10. The exhibits include re-creations of a diner, farmers market, newsroom, veterinary hospital, restaurant construction site, newspaper office and a miniature Philadelphia Flyers hockey rink. Other features include a rock wall, puppet shows, face painting and a variety of hands-on activities. There also is a collection of reptiles, insects and fish. The Little Discoveries area, which has a farmhouse and a barn, is suitable for toddlers under age 4.

Time: Allow 2 hours minimum. **Hours:** Mon.-Thurs. 9:30-8:30, Fri.-Sun. 9:30-5:30, July-Aug.; daily 9:30-5:30 (also Sat. 5:30-8:30, Oct.-Apr.), rest of year. Closed Thanksgiving and Christmas. **Cost:** $12.95; $11.95 (ages 55+ and grandparents); $5 (Mon.-Thurs. 5-8:30, July-Aug.); free (ages 0-1). Buy-one-get-one-free admission, active and retired military and their spouses and dependents with ID. **Phone:** (856) 424-1233.

CROWNE PLAZA PHILADELPHIA/CHERRY HILL
856/665-6666 **107**

 Hotel. Rates not provided. **Address:** 2349 W Marlton Pike (SR 70) 08002 **Location:** SR 70 at Cuthbert Blvd (SR 38 E); I-295 exit 34B southbound, 4 mi w. **Facility:** 408 units. 14 stories, interior corridors. **Terms:** check-in 4 pm. **Pool(s):** outdoor. **Activities:** exercise room. **Guest Services:** valet and coin laundry, boarding pass kiosk.

(See map & index p. 274.)

DAYS INN & SUITES   (856)663-0100 106

Motel
$80-$155

Address: 525 SR 38 E 08002 **Location:** I-295 exit 34B, 4 mi w on SR 70 to Cuthbert Blvd (SR 38 E), then just ne. **Facility:** 86 units. 2 stories (no elevator), exterior corridors. **Terms:** cancellation fee imposed. **Pool(s):** outdoor. **Activities:** exercise room. **Guest Services:** coin laundry. **Featured Amenity:** continental breakfast.

EXTENDED STAY AMERICA-PHILADELPHIA/CHERRY HILL
856/616-1200 109

Extended Stay Hotel. Rates not provided. **Address:** 1653 E SR 70 (Marlton Pike) 08034 **Location:** I-295 exit 34A, just e. **Facility:** 77 efficiencies. 3 stories, interior corridors. **Guest Services:** coin laundry.

HOLIDAY INN PHILADELPHIA-CHERRY HILL
856/663-5300 108

Hotel
Rates not provided

Address: 2175 W Marlton Pike 08002 **Location:** I-295 exit 34B, 2.5 mi w. **Facility:** 186 units. 6 stories, interior corridors. **Amenities:** safes. **Pool(s):** outdoor, heated indoor. **Activities:** exercise room. **Guest Services:** valet and coin laundry, rental car service.

WHERE TO EAT

BRIO TUSCAN GRILLE   856/910-8166 134

Italian. Fine Dining. $10-$29 **AAA Inspector Notes:** While the atmosphere is casual, upscale Tuscan villa-style décor lends a sophisticated touch to the dining experience. Both lunch and dinner offer all the attentiveness a diner expects. From the garlic, spinach and artichoke dip starter to beef, chicken, veal, seafood and homemade pasta entrées, there is a selection to satisfy all tastes. Among specialties are homemade mozzarella, crisp flatbreads and wood-fired oven-baked pizza, in addition to a selection of steak. **Features:** full bar, patio dining, Sunday brunch, happy hour. **Reservations:** suggested. **Address:** 901 Haddonfield Rd 08002 **Location:** I-295 exit 34B, 2.5 mi w.

CAFFE' ALDO LAMBERTI   856/663-1747 136

Italian. Fine Dining. $10-$38 **AAA Inspector Notes:** Contemporary describes both the décor and special dishes served at this café. The menu lists such traditional options as scampi, fra diavolo and many veal and pasta choices. Try the wild sea bass caramelized in a butter-lemon-wine sauce. Competent, crisply-dressed servers navigate the comfortable, modern dining room. **Features:** full bar, happy hour. **Reservations:** suggested. **Address:** 2011 Rt 70 W 08002 **Location:** I-295 exit 34B, 2.5 mi w; across from Garden State Park. **Parking:** valet and street only.

IL VILLAGGIO   856/795-1778 139

Italian. Fine Dining. $9-$32 **AAA Inspector Notes:** This bring-your-own-bottle establishment offers a warm, fine dining ambience with coordinating Italian artwork and an attractive brick fireplace. The menu does not disappoint with imported Italian meats and cheeses to provide all of the traditional favorites. Banquet facilities are available for any special occasion. **Features:** patio dining. **Reservations:** suggested, weekends. **Address:** 211 Haddonfield-Berlin Rd 08034 **Location:** I-295 exit 28, 1 mi n. Haddonfield, 149.

NORMA'S   856/795-1373 137

Eastern Mediterranean. Casual Dining. $6-$27 **AAA Inspector Notes:** This spot is two restaurants in one. Lunch offers a casual taste of Lebanon, with familiar salads and starters, shawarma, chicken kebabs, lamb shish and kafta kebabs, gyros and falafel. Dinner is Moroccan, with couscous specialties, kebabs, tagine and other favorites served in a bejeweled tented room of low tables with cushioned seating, traditional music and customs. Dinner could be an event. **Address:** 145 Barclay Farms Shopping Center (SR 70) 08002 **Location:** 0.4 mi w of jct SR 70 and I-295; 3.2 mi w of jct SR 70 and 73.

OH YOKO! SUSHI   856/857-9050 138

Japanese. Casual Dining. $9-$20 **AAA Inspector Notes:** Beatles music and posters, friendly staff and a large but pricey special maki menu can all be found here in this warm, cozy environment. Very fresh fish and ingredients are utilized in the dishes offered. Dressings, green tea ice cream and soy sauce are made in house. **Address:** 1428 Marlton Pike E 08034 **Location:** I-295 exit 34B, just w on SR 70; in Pine Tree Shopping Center.

SEASONS 52 FRESH GRILL   856/665-1052 133

New American. Fine Dining. $10-$30 **AAA Inspector Notes:** Embracing a distinctive concept, this restaurant focuses entirely on calorie-conscious dishes that reflect the current season. The menu changes 52 times a year. Modern and tasty choices include several types of flatbreads, salmon, chicken and an unusual offering of novelty dessert shots. Many by-the-glass options are among selections on the wine list. **Features:** full bar, patio dining, happy hour. **Address:** 2000 Rt 38, Suite 1145 08002 **Location:** I-295 exit 34B, 4 mi w on SR 70 to Cuthbert Blvd to SR 38 E, then 1.2 mi ne; in Cherry Hill Mall. **Parking:** on-site and valet.

SILVER DINER   856/910-1240

American. Family Dining. $7-$17 **AAA Inspector Notes:** The eatery with its chrome and glass plate exterior and the glow of neon, provides the traditional diner setting. Booths with juke boxes, counter service and friendly waitstaff add to the diner experience. The menu is extensive with salads, sandwiches and full meals. The desserts are made fresh and the fountain treats, shakes, floats and malts make for a great ending. Breakfast is available all day. **Address:** 2131 SR 38 E 08002 **Location:** I-295 exit 34B, 4 mi w on SR 70 to Cuthbert Blvd to SR 38 E, then 1.2 mi ne.

SIRI'S THAI FRENCH CUISINE   856/663-6781 135

Thai. Casual Dining. $9-$29 **AAA Inspector Notes:** Through the storefront window, passersby cannot help but notice the elegant dining room filled with patrons enjoying sophisticated Thai and French cuisine. Asian seasonings are evident in the seafood bouillabaisse spiked with lemongrass, as well as chicken with green curry. French influences can be found in the rack of lamb with Madeira rosemary au jus and the roast duck with berry glaze. Desserts are lovely and typically French. The restaurant implements a bring your own alcohol policy. **Reservations:** suggested. **Address:** 2117 Rt 70 W 08002 **Location:** I-295 exit 34B, 2.8 mi w on SR 70; at Track Town Shopping Center; opposite Garden State Park.

CINNAMINSON

- **Restaurants p. 318**
- **Hotels & Restaurants map & index p. 274**
- **Part of Philadelphia area — see map p. 230**

SLEEP INN   (856)829-0717 81

Hotel
$80-$150

Address: 208 Rt 130 N 08077 **Location:** 0.9 mi n of jct SR 73. **Facility:** 52 units. 2 stories, interior corridors. **Bath:** shower only. **Activities:** limited exercise equipment. **Featured Amenity:** full hot breakfast.

(See map & index p. 274.)

THE JUG HANDLE INN   856/665-9464   105
WW American. Casual Dining. $7-$20 **AAA Inspector Notes:**
Fill up on hearty portions of tasty food, such as fried Buffalo-style
wings, at this sports pub—a great place to catch a game with friends
over a few brews. **Features:** full bar, happy hour. **Address:** 10118 S
Fork Landing Rd 08077 **Location:** 0.9 mi s of jct US 130.

L   D   LATE

CLEMENTON pop. 5,000, elev. 96'
• Part of Philadelphia area — see map p. 230
CLEMENTON PARK & SPLASH WORLD, .7 mi. w.
of US 30 on White Horse Ave., is set on the shore
of a small lake. The amusement park has rides, car-
nival games and a children's section; the water park
has a variety of waterslides and a wave pool.

   Note: Bathing suits are required at the water
park; lockers and changing facilities are available.
Hours: Amusement park Mon.-Thurs. 11-8, Fri.-
Sun. 11-9, July-Aug. Water park Mon.-Thurs. 11-8,
Fri.-Sun. 11-7, July-Aug. Hours vary May-June and
in Sept.; phone ahead. **Cost:** (includes both parks)
$39.99; $29.99 (under 48 inches tall, ages 65+ and
physically impaired individuals); free (under 36
inches tall). Phone ahead to verify rates. **Parking:**
$10. **Phone:** (856) 783-0263. 🍴 🎢

COLLINGSWOOD pop. 13,926
• Hotels & Restaurants map & index p. 274
• Part of Philadelphia area — see map p. 230
THE POP SHOP   856/869-0111   130
WW Comfort Food. Casual Dining. $5-$11 **AAA Inspector
Notes:** Sample creative takes on classic grilled cheese at this retro-
style neighborhood soda shop which stakes a claim to fame in that
celebrity chef Bobby Flay once challenged the owners on his show.
Locals and tourists frequent this place for its warm service, upbeat
candy-colored dining area and family-friendly environment. Check the
website for fun weekly events such as team trivia. **Address:** 729
Haddon Ave 08108 **Location:** 1.2 mi e of jct US 30; on the main
street. 🚆 Collingswood, 147. **Parking:** street only.

B   L   D   🚆

DEPTFORD
• Hotels & Restaurants map & index p. 274
• Part of Philadelphia area — see map p. 230
FAIRFIELD INN BY MARRIOTT PHILADELPHIA/DEPTFORD
   (856)686-9050   130

WW Hotel $97-$160 **Address:**
1160 Hurffville Rd 08096 **Location:** SR
42 exit Deptford, Runnemede, Woodbury
to CR 544, just e to SR 41 S. **Facility:**
102 units. 4 stories, interior corridors.

AAA Benefit:
Members save 5%
or more!

Amenities: safes. **Pool(s):** heated indoor. **Activities:** exercise room.
Guest Services: valet laundry.
🍴 CALL 🅰M 🛎 BIZ 📶 ✕ 🔌 💲 /SOME UNITS 🖨

Check DrivingLaws.AAA.com
for local motor vehicle laws
when traveling

RESIDENCE INN BY MARRIOTT DEPTFORD
   (856)686-9188   129

WWW Extended Stay Hotel
$125-$229 **Address:** 1154 Hurffville Rd
08096 **Location:** SR 42 exit Deptford,
Runnemede, Woodbury to CR 544, just e
to SR 41 S. **Facility:** 102 efficiencies,
some two bedrooms. 3 stories, interior corridors. **Pool(s):** heated indoor. **Activities:** exercise room. **Guest Services:** valet and coin
laundry.

AAA Benefit:
Members save 5%
or more!

🍴 🛎 BIZ 📶 ✕ 🔌 💲 💻 /SOME UNITS 🖨

EASTAMPTON
• Part of Philadelphia area — see map p. 230
CHARLEY'S OTHER BROTHER   609/261-1555
WW American. Casual Dining. $9-$38 **AAA Inspector Notes:**
Families often drop in to this casual spot where there is something for
everyone. Nosh on such daily specials as stuffed flounder Oscar,
fried oysters, buffalo shrimp and stuffed or Milanese pork chops—
pork chop preparation and homemade soup choice changes every
day. Youngsters can order from the array of kid food on the children's
menu while adults narrow down their selection of steak, prime rib,
crab cakes or seafood of all kinds. **Features:** full bar, happy hour. **Address:** 1383 Monmouth Rd 08060 **Location:** Jct CR 537 and Jacksonville Rd. L   D   CALL 🅰M

GIBBSBORO pop. 2,274
• Hotels & Restaurants map & index p. 274
• Part of Philadelphia area — see map p. 230
THE CHOPHOUSE   856/566-7300   157
WWW Steak. Fine Dining. $13-$50 **AAA Inspector Notes:** As
you might expect, steaks rise to the top of the menu at this spot,
which has come to be known for its food, classic martinis and out-
standing service. Splurge on the delicious sides and sinful desserts.
Floor-to-ceiling windows add to the bright, airy feel of the dining area,
which is enhanced with wood accents and an inviting hearth. **Fea-
tures:** full bar, patio dining, happy hour. **Reservations:** suggested.
Address: 4 S Lakeview Dr 08026 **Location:** I-295 exit 32, 4 mi e on
Haddonfield-Berlin Rd (CR 561). **Parking:** valet and street only.

L   D

GLOUCESTER CITY pop. 11,456
• Hotels & Restaurants map & index p. 274
• Part of Philadelphia area — see map p. 230
QUALITY INN   (856)456-7400   116
WW Hotel $75-$126 **Address:** 1200 Crescent Blvd 08030 **Lo-
cation:** I-295 exit 23, 3 mi n on US 130. **Facility:** 63 units. 2 stories
(no elevator), interior/exterior corridors. **Activities:** exercise room.
Guest Services: valet and coin laundry.

BIZ 📶 🔌 💲 🖨

HADDONFIELD pop. 11,593, elev. 74'
• Hotels & Restaurants map & index p. 274
• Part of Philadelphia area — see map p. 230
   In 1701, Elizabeth Haddon was sent from England
by her father—who had no sons—to develop 550
acres southeast of Camden. In less than a year the in-
dustrious Quaker lass had built a house, begun the
colony and proposed marriage to Quaker missionary
John Estaugh (he accepted). Their romance is at the
center of "The Theologian's Tale" in Henry Wadsworth
Longfellow's "Tales of a Wayside Inn."

INDIAN KING TAVERN HOUSE MUSEUM, 1.5
blks. n. of Haddon Ave. at 233 Kings Hwy. E., was
built in 1750 and was for many years an important
social, political and military gathering place along
the historic Kings Highway. The three-and-a-half-
story structure is furnished in period and contains

(See map & index p. 274.)

historical displays. **Time:** Allow 30 minutes minimum. **Hours:** Thurs.-Sat. 10-noon and 1-4, Apr.-Sept. Hours vary rest of year. Closed Jan. 1, Thanksgiving and Christmas. Phone ahead to confirm schedule. **Cost:** Free. **Phone:** (856) 429-6792. ⊞ Haddonfield, 149

HADDONFIELD INN   856/428-2195 **145**
WWW **Bed & Breakfast.** Rates not provided. **Address:** 44 W End Ave 08033 **Location:** I-295 exit 28, 0.7 mi n on SR 168, 2.6 mi e on Kings Hwy, then just n. ⊞ Haddonfield, 149. **Facility:** You can walk around the shops of the historic district before retiring to your room, which features a fireplace and themed décor ranging from Tokyo to Cape Cod. 9 units. 3 stories, interior corridors. **Guest Services:** valet laundry.

MAPLE SHADE
• **Hotels & Restaurants map & index p. 274**
• **Part of Philadelphia area — see map p. 230**

CHARLIE BROWN'S STEAKHOUSE   856/779-8003
WW **Steak. Casual Dining. $9-$30 AAA Inspector Notes:** This budget-friendly steakhouse, famous for its prime rib, offers top quality fare without hurting your pocketbook. The young ones will not be disappointed with the kids' menu, and just might even try something green from the salad bar. Adults will love the quality steaks, chicken and rib dishes. The express lunches are great for those saddled with time constraints. **Features:** full bar, happy hour. **Address:** 114-116 E Main St 08052 **Location:** Corner of Main and Spruce (CR 537) sts.

P.J. WHELIHAN'S PUB & RESTAURANT   856/234-2345 **124**
WWW **American. Casual Dining. $6-$19 AAA Inspector Notes:** Sports lovers will rejoice at the sight of the island bar surrounded with flat-screen TVs. Hefty plates of wings, nachos, burgers and gooey desserts round out the menu. Food and drink specials are offered daily. **Features:** full bar. **Address:** 396 S Lenola Rd 08052 **Location:** I-295 exit 40, 3.4 mi w on SR 38.

MARLTON pop. 10,133
• **Hotels & Restaurants map & index p. 274**
• **Part of Philadelphia area — see map p. 230**

JOE'S PEKING DUCK HOUSE   856/985-1551 **143**
WW **Chinese. Casual Dining. $8-$29 AAA Inspector Notes:** Guests probably would not come to this small storefront restaurant for its looks, nor its service. However, the tasty noodle platters, soups and create-your-own entrées draw crowds. And we did not even mention the Peking duck—the memorable, standout signature dish. **Address:** 145 Rt 73 S 08053 **Location:** Jct SR 70, just s; in Marlton Crossing Shopping Center.

MEXICAN FOOD FACTORY   856/983-9222 **142**
WW **Mexican. Casual Dining. $6-$17 AAA Inspector Notes:** This restaurant is a great place to enjoy varied and creative dishes, many featuring fish as well as traditional favorites. Guacamole is homemade and good. Choices include grilled orange roughy with garlic and capers, grilled salmon or tuna with red onion and cilantro marmalade and jumbo shrimp over black pepper fettuccine with sweet chipotle cream sauce. Interesting art and great music give this place character. **Features:** full bar. **Address:** 601 W SR 70 08053 **Location:** Jct SR 73, 0.3 mi sw.

MOUNT HOLLY elev. 45'
• **Hotels & Restaurants map & index p. 274**
• **Part of Philadelphia area — see map p. 230**

Sharing the name of a nearby hill, Mount Holly was first settled by Quakers in 1676 and served as the capital of the state for 2 months in 1779. John Woolman, a Quaker abolitionist known for his 1774 journal, taught at the Old School House at 35 Brainerd St. Other historic buildings include the 18th- and 19th-century county buildings on High Street between Garden and Union streets.

Smithville Mansion, 2 miles east at 803 Smithville Rd. in nearby Eastampton, was the Victorian home of Hezekiah B. Smith, former owner of a local foundry and operator of the factory that produced the first "American Star" bicycles. Guided tours of the restored mansion are available May through October; phone (609) 265-5858. Also on the estate grounds is a building devoted to Smith's bicycles and an art gallery. Christmas and candlelight tours are offered in December.

HISTORIC BURLINGTON COUNTY PRISON MUSEUM is at 128 High St. The museum's interior still looks much the same as it did during its years as a prison. Exhibits includes a re-created warden's office and adjacent home, a maximum-security cell and a kitchen. One display details changes to American prison cells throughout history. Architect Robert Mills also designed several Washington, D.C.-area buildings as well as the Washington Monument.

Time: Allow 45 minutes minimum. **Hours:** Thurs.-Sat. 10-4, Sun. noon-4. Closed major holidays. **Cost:** $4; $2 (ages 55+ and students with ID); free (ages 0-4). **Phone:** (609) 265-5476 or (609) 518-7667.

CHARLIE BROWN'S STEAKHOUSE   609/265-1100
WW **Steak. Casual Dining. $9-$30 AAA Inspector Notes:** This budget-friendly steakhouse, famous for its prime rib, offers top quality fare without hurting your pocketbook. The young ones will not be disappointed with the kids' menu, and just might even try something green from the salad bar. Adults will love the quality steaks, chicken and rib dishes. The express lunches are great for those saddled with time constraints. **Features:** full bar, happy hour. **Address:** 949 Rt 541 08060 **Location:** To Burrs Rd jughandle and crossover.

ROBIN'S NEST   609/261-6149 **88**
WW **American. Casual Dining. $9-$29 AAA Inspector Notes:** Eclectic Victorian furnishings and prints of Mount Holly from the first half of the 20th century decorate the quaint dining rooms. In addition to fantastic homemade desserts (seriously, take some home for later), the menu offers quiche, sandwiches, salads and soups. Sunday brunch is popular. **Features:** full bar, patio dining, Sunday brunch, happy hour. **Reservations:** suggested. **Address:** 2 Washington St 08060 **Location:** Downtown.

MOUNT LAUREL
- **Hotels & Restaurants map & index p. 274**
- **Part of Philadelphia area — see map p. 230**

ALOFT MOUNT LAUREL   856/234-1880 90

Hotel
Rates not provided

AAA Benefit: Members save up to 15%, plus Starwood Preferred Guest® benefits!

Address: 558 Fellowship Rd 08054 **Location:** I-295 exit 36A, just se on SR 73 to Fellowship Rd, then just n. **Facility:** 154 units. 6 stories, interior corridors. *Bath:* shower only. **Amenities:** safes. **Pool(s):** heated indoor. **Activities:** exercise room. **Guest Services:** valet and coin laundry, area transportation.

CANDLEWOOD SUITES MT. LAUREL   856/642-7567 103

Extended Stay Hotel. Rates not provided. **Address:** 4000 Crawford Pl 08054 **Location:** New Jersey Tpke exit 4, 1 mi se on SR 73 S. **Facility:** 123 efficiencies. 3 stories, interior corridors. **Activities:** exercise room. **Guest Services:** valet and coin laundry.

COMFORT INN & SUITES   (856)727-0010 102

Hotel $89-$129 **Address:** 6000 Crawford Pl 08054 **Location:** New Jersey Tpke exit 4, 1 mi on SR 73 S. **Facility:** 90 units, some efficiencies. 3 stories, interior corridors. **Activities:** exercise room. **Guest Services:** valet and coin laundry.

COURTYARD BY MARRIOTT MT. LAUREL
                                     (856)273-4400 92

Hotel
$132-$252

COURTYARD Marriott

AAA Benefit: Members save 5% or more!

Address: 1000 Century Pkwy 08054 **Location:** New Jersey Tpke exit 4, just nw on SR 73 to Fellowship Rd, then just s; I-295 exit 36A, just se on SR 73 to Fellowship Rd, then just s. **Facility:** 151 units. 4 stories, interior corridors. **Pool(s):** heated indoor. **Activities:** hot tub, exercise room. **Guest Services:** valet and coin laundry, boarding pass kiosk.

DOUBLETREE SUITES BY HILTON HOTEL MT. LAUREL
                                     (856)778-8999 86

Hotel
$109-$309

DOUBLETREE BY HILTON

AAA Benefit: Members save 5% or more!

Address: 515 Fellowship Rd N 08054 **Location:** I-295 exit 36A, just se on SR 73 to Fellowship Rd, then just n. **Facility:** 204 units. 3 stories, interior corridors. **Terms:** 1-7 night minimum stay, cancellation fee imposed. **Amenities:** safes. **Pool(s):** heated indoor. **Activities:** hot tub, exercise room. **Guest Services:** valet and coin laundry.

EXTENDED STAY AMERICA PACILLI PLACE PHILADELPHIA/MT. LAUREL   856/608-9820 98

Extended Stay Hotel. Rates not provided. **Address:** 500 Diemer Dr 08054 **Location:** New Jersey Tpke exit 4, 1 mi se on SR 73, just n on Crawford Pl, then just e. Located in a corporate office park. **Facility:** 85 kitchen units. 3 stories, interior corridors. **Activities:** exercise room. **Guest Services:** coin laundry.

FAIRFIELD INN & SUITES BY MARRIOTT MT. LAUREL
                                     (856)642-0600 94

Hotel $132-$217 **Address:** 350 Century Pkwy 08054 **Location:** New Jersey Tpke exit 4 to SR 73 N, just s. **Facility:** 118 units. 4 stories, interior corridors. **Pool(s):** heated indoor. **Activities:** hot tub, exercise room. **Guest Services:** valet and coin laundry.

AAA Benefit: Members save 5% or more!

HAMPTON INN PHILADELPHIA/MT. LAUREL
                                     (856)778-5535 99

Hotel $89-$149 **Address:** 5000 Crawford Pl 08054 **Location:** New Jersey Tpke exit 4, 1 mi se on SR 73; I-295 exit 36A, 1.7 mi se on SR 73. Located behind Chili's. **Facility:** 125 units. 4 stories, interior corridors. **Terms:** 1-7 night minimum stay, cancellation fee imposed. **Pool(s):** outdoor. **Activities:** exercise room. **Guest Services:** valet and coin laundry.

AAA Benefit: Members save 5% or more!

HILTON GARDEN INN-MT. LAUREL   (856)234-4788 97

Hotel $109-$179 **Address:** 4000 Atrium Way 08054 **Location:** New Jersey Tpke exit 4, 1 mi se on SR 73, then just w. **Facility:** 140 units. 5 stories, interior corridors. **Terms:** 1-7 night minimum stay, cancellation fee imposed. **Pool(s):** heated indoor. **Activities:** hot tub, exercise room. **Guest Services:** valet and coin laundry, boarding pass kiosk.

AAA Benefit: Members save 5% or more!

HOTEL ML   (856)234-7300 87

Hotel
$99-$299

Address: 915 SR 73 N 08054 **Location:** New Jersey Tpke exit 4, northeast corner; I-295 exit 36A, just se. **Facility:** 280 units. 10 stories, interior corridors. **Terms:** check-in 4 pm. **Pool(s):** heated outdoor, heated indoor. **Activities:** hot tub, exercise room. **Guest Services:** valet and coin laundry, area transportation.

HYATT HOUSE MT. LAUREL   (856)222-1313 101

Extended Stay Hotel
$99-$189

HYATT house™

AAA Benefit: Members save 10%!

Address: 3000 Crawford Pl 08054 **Location:** I-295 exit 36A, 1.5 mi s on SR 73. **Facility:** 116 kitchen units, some two bedrooms. 3 stories (no elevator), exterior corridors. **Terms:** cancellation fee imposed. **Pool(s):** outdoor. **Activities:** exercise room. **Guest Services:** valet and coin laundry. **Featured Amenity:** breakfast buffet.

(See map & index p. 274.)

HYATT PLACE MT. LAUREL   (856)840-0770 100

Hotel
$99-$199

HYATT PLACE
AAA Benefit: Members save 10%!

Address: 8000 Crawford Pl 08054 **Location:** New Jersey Tpke exit 4, 1 mi se on SR 73; I-295 exit 36A, 1.7 mi se on SR 73. **Facility:** 124 units. 6 stories, interior corridors. **Terms:** cancellation fee imposed. **Pool(s):** outdoor. **Activities:** exercise room. **Guest Services:** valet laundry. **Featured Amenity:** breakfast buffet.

SAVE ⍾⧾ ⧾ CALL ⬥M ⬱ BIZ
⬤ ⬤ ⬤ ⬤ ⬤ / SOME UNITS ⬤ HS

LA QUINTA MT. LAUREL-PHILADELPHIA   (856)235-7500 95

Hotel
$79-$249

Address: 5000 Clover Rd 08054 **Location:** New Jersey Tpke exit 4, just se; I-295 exit 36A, 0.8 mi se. **Facility:** 63 units. 3 stories, interior corridors. **Amenities:** video games, safes. **Activities:** exercise room. **Guest Services:** valet and coin laundry. **Featured Amenity:** full hot breakfast.

SAVE ⍾⧾ CALL ⬥M BIZ HS ⬱
⬤ ⬤ ⬤ ⬤ ⬤ / SOME UNITS ⬤

PHILADELPHIA/MOUNT LAUREL HOMEWOOD SUITES BY HILTON   (856)222-9001 85

Extended Stay Hotel
$109-$199 **Address:** 1422 Nixon Dr 08054 **Location:** I-295 exit 36B, follow ramp to end, then just n. **Facility:** 118 efficiencies, some two bedrooms. 3 stories, interior corridors. **Terms:** 1-7 night minimum stay, cancellation fee imposed. **Pool(s):** heated indoor. **Activities:** hot tub, exercise room. **Guest Services:** valet and coin laundry.

AAA Benefit: Members save 5% or more!

⍾⧾ CALL ⬥M ⬱ BIZ ⬱ ⬤ ⬤ ⬤ ⬤
/ SOME UNITS ⬤

RED ROOF INN #7066   856/234-5589 91

Motel
Rates not provided

Address: 603 Fellowship Rd 08054 **Location:** I-295 exit 36A, just se on SR 73 to Fellowship Rd, then just s. **Facility:** 108 units. 2 stories (no elevator), exterior corridors. **Amenities:** video games, safes.

SAVE ⍾⧾ ⬱ ⬤
/ SOME UNITS ⬤ ⬤ ⬤ ⬤

RESIDENCE INN BY MARRIOTT MOUNT LAUREL AT BISHOP'S GATE   (856)234-1025 84

Extended Stay Hotel
$118-$194 **Address:** 1000 Bishops Gate Blvd 08054 **Location:** I-295 exit 40A, just e. **Facility:** 144 units, some two bedrooms, efficiencies and kitchens. 3 stories, interior corridors. **Pool(s):** heated indoor. **Activities:** hot tub, exercise room. **Guest Services:** valet and coin laundry, boarding pass kiosk.

AAA Benefit: Members save 5% or more!

⍾⧾ CALL ⬥M ⬱ BIZ HS ⬱ ⬤ ⬤ ⬤ ⬤
⬤ / SOME UNITS ⬤

STAYBRIDGE SUITES   (856)722-1900 96

Extended Stay Hotel
$149-$359

Address: 4115 Church Rd 08054 **Location:** New Jersey Tpke exit 4, 0.5 mi s on SR 73, then 0.5 mi w. **Facility:** 99 efficiencies, some two bedrooms. 3 stories, interior corridors. **Terms:** check-in 4 pm. **Pool(s):** heated indoor. **Guest Services:** valet and coin laundry. **Featured Amenity:** full hot breakfast.

SAVE ⍾⧾ ⬱ ⬤ BIZ HS ⬱
⬤ ⬤ ⬤ ⬤ / SOME UNITS ⬤

SUPER 8   (856)802-2800 89

Hotel $69-$109 **Address:** 560 Fellowship Rd 08054 **Location:** I-295 exit 36A, just s to Fellowship Rd. **Facility:** 80 units. 2 stories, interior corridors. **Bath:** shower only. **Guest Services:** coin laundry. ⍾⧾ ⬱ ⬤ ⬤ ⬤

THE WESTIN MOUNT LAUREL   (856)778-7300 88

Hotel
$99-$399

WESTIN HOTELS & RESORTS
AAA Benefit: Members save up to 15%, plus Starwood Preferred Guest® benefits!

Address: 555 Fellowship Rd 08054 **Location:** I-295 exit 36A, just se on SR 73 to Fellowship Rd, then just n. **Facility:** 173 units. 7 stories, interior corridors. **Parking:** on-site and valet. **Amenities:** safes. **Pool(s):** heated indoor. **Activities:** hot tub. **Guest Services:** valet laundry.

SAVE ⍾ ⬱ ⧾ CALL ⬥M ⬱
⬱ BIZ ⬱HS ⬱ ⬤ ⬤ ⬤
/ SOME UNITS ⬤ ⬤ ⬤

WYNDHAM PHILADELPHIA-MOUNT LAUREL   (856)234-7000 93

Hotel
$109-$189

Address: 1111 SR 73 08054 **Location:** New Jersey Tpke exit 4; I-295 exit 36A, 0.5 mi se. **Facility:** 243 units. 9 stories, interior corridors. **Amenities:** video games, safes. **Pool(s):** heated indoor. **Activities:** exercise room. **Guest Services:** valet laundry, rental car service, area transportation.

SAVE ECO ⍾ ⬱ ⧾ CALL ⬥M
⬱ BIZ ⬱ ⬤ ⬤ ⬤
/ SOME UNITS ⬤ ⬤ ⬤

WHERE TO EAT

CHULICIOUS   856/780-5240 120

Chinese. Casual Dining. $8-$20 **AAA Inspector Notes:** Painted a bright red color, this casual spot is popular for their authentic spices and flavors. The crystal wonton in chili oil is the signature appetizer and is highly recommended. An $8 lunch special is available Monday through Friday and includes a variety of poultry, tofu and seafood options. **Address:** 1200 S Church St 08054 **Location:** New Jersey Tpke exit 4, 2.1 mi e, then just n; in Village II.
L D

Remember, car seats, booster seats
and seat belts save lives

(See map & index p. 274.)

MILLER'S NJ ALE HOUSE　　　856/722-5690　117
▼▼ ▼▼ American. Casual Dining. $8-$20 **AAA Inspector Notes:**
This casual pub and restaurant provides an almost lodge-like feel
with their wood paneling and large wraparound bar at the center of
the restaurant. Flat-panel televisions flood the ceiling to provide
guests with ample viewing angles from any table. The large menu
touches on a bit of everything and includes pastas, burgers, steaks,
fajitas, and fresh seafood. **Features:** full bar, happy hour. **Address:**
554 Fellowship Rd 08054 **Location:** I-295 exit 36A, just se on SR 73
to Fellowship Rd, then just n. L D CALL M

SAGE DINER　　　856/727-0770　119
▼▼ ▼▼ American. Casual Dining. $5-$27 **AAA Inspector Notes:**
A favorite with the local crowd, this casual, unassuming diner serves
corned beef and cabbage, split pea soup, meatloaf, lasagna, chicken
cutlets, pasta and other home-style comfort foods. The menu features a page of breakfast choices and numerous sandwiches and
salads. Fluffy meringue towers above the lemon pie. Art Deco
touches decorate the dining room. **Address:** 1170 Rt 73 & Church
Rd 08054 **Location:** New Jersey Tpke exit 4, just se; I-295 exit 36A,
1 mi se. B L D LATE

SINGAPORE RESTAURANT AND SUSHI BAR
　　　856/802-2888　121
▼▼ ▼▼ Japanese. Casual Dining. $5-$20 **AAA Inspector Notes:**
If you're looking to get away from the local chain restaurants, you will
find this small, cozy restaurant a great value. The menu is filled with
an array of sushi rolls, bento boxes and traditional favorites. Great for
a quick bite and convenient to many nearby hotels. **Address:** 1215
SR 73 08054 **Location:** I-295 exit 36A, 2 mi se, off SR 73.
L D

STEFANO'S RISTORANTE　　　856/778-3663　118
▼▼ ▼▼ Italian. Casual Dining. $12-$27 **AAA Inspector Notes:** A
small, cozy Italian restaurant with friendly service and a warm atmosphere. You will often find the owner and chef, Paolo, cooking up
homemade favorites for her patrons. On the menu you will find Sicilian style pizza, an array of pasta dishes, homemade soups and
much more. Remember to bring your own wine and beer at this
BYOB establishment. **Reservations:** suggested, for dinner. **Address:** 3815 Church Rd 08054 **Location:** I-295 exit 36A, 0.4 mi s on
Beaver Ave, then just w. L D

NATIONAL PARK pop. 3,036, elev. 16'
• Part of Philadelphia area — see map p. 230

RED BANK BATTLEFIELD PARK (FORT MERCER)
is 2 mi. w. of I-295 at 100 Hessian Ave., on the riverfront. During the Revolutionary War Fort Mercer was
hastily built at this site to protect the Delaware River
and the port of Philadelphia from British forces. In October 1777, 400 Patriots under Gen. Christopher
Greene vanquished 1,200 Britons and Hessians led
by Count Van Donop. Also at the site is the restored
dwelling of Ann Whitall, who allegedly spun wool while
the battle raged around her home. **Hours:** Park open
daily dawn-dusk. House Thurs.-Sun. 1-4, Apr. 1 to
mid-Oct. Phone ahead to confirm schedule. **Cost:**
Free. **Phone:** (856) 853-5120.

PENNSVILLE pop. 11,888, elev. 19'
• Part of Philadelphia area — see map p. 230

FORT MOTT STATE PARK, 454 Fort Mott Rd., encompasses 104 acres on the Delaware River. Next
to the park is Finns Point National Cemetery, burial
ground for some 3,000 Confederate and Union soldiers. Visitors can walk along ramparts of the 1896
fort, which was built as a river defense during the
Spanish American War.

Seasonal ferry service connects Fort Mott and
Fort Delaware State Park on Pea Patch Island;
phone ahead for schedule. **Hours:** Daily 8-7:30, Memorial Day-Labor Day; 8-4, rest of year. **Cost:** Free.
Phone: (856) 935-3218.

HAMPTON INN　　　　　(856)351-1700
▼▼ ▼▼ ▼▼ Hotel $109-$209 **Address:**
429 N Broadway 08070 **Location:** I-295
exit 1, just se. **Facility:** 103 units. 4 stories, interior corridors. **Terms:** 1-7 night
minimum stay, cancellation fee imposed.
Pool(s): outdoor. **Activities:** exercise room. **Guest Services:** valet
and coin laundry.

> **AAA Benefit:**
> Members save 5%
> or more!

▥◄ ☂ CALL M ⇒ BIZ 🛜 🖥 🖨 🖵

SUPER 8 PENNSVILLE/WILMINGTON　　　(856)299-2992
▼▼ ▼▼ Hotel $79-$124 **Address:** 413 N Broadway 08070 **Loca-
tion:** I-295 exit 1, just se. **Facility:** 100 units. 4 stories, interior corridors. **Guest Services:** coin laundry. ▥◄ 🛜 🖥 🖵

RUNNEMEDE pop. 8,468
• Hotels & Restaurants map & index p. 274
• Part of Philadelphia area — see map p. 230

LA QUINTA INN & SUITES RUNNEMEDE
　　　　　(856)312-8521　123

▼▼ ▼▼ ▼▼
Hotel
$89-$239

Address: 109 E 9th Ave 08078 **Location:** New Jersey Tpke exit 3, 0.3 mi se,
then just e; I-295 exit 28, 1.2 mi se. **Facility:** 146 units. 7 stories, interior corridors. **Pool(s):** outdoor. **Activities:** game
room, exercise room. **Guest Services:**
coin laundry. **Featured Amenity: breakfast buffet.**

SAVE ▥ ☂ ⇒ BIZ 🛜 ☒
🖥 🖨 🖵 / SOME UNITS 🐾

SALEM pop. 5,146, elev. 14'
• Part of Philadelphia area — see map p. 230

Settled in 1675 by Quakers, Salem is one of the
oldest English settlements on the Delaware River.
Its early importance as a port made it a prize during
the Revolutionary War, when the city was occupied
by the British. After the war Camden surpassed
Salem as a shipping center, and attention turned to
agriculture.

The restored 1721 Alexander Grant House, 4
miles south of town at 79-83 Market St., displays objects from the Colonial and Federal periods. Hancock House State Historic Site was the scene of a
British-led massacre during the Revolutionary War.
In retaliation against the Quaker community for sup-
plying cattle to Gen. George Washington's starving
troops at Valley Forge, 300 men under Maj. John
Simcoe surprised and killed some 30 local mili-
tiamen asleep in the house; among the dead was
homeowner Judge William Hancock.

Built in 1734, the Hancock House is an excellent
example of the English Quaker style of dwelling
once prominent in the Lower Delaware Valley, which
incorporated a distinctive feature of zigzagging lines
of bricks at each end. The house is located at 3

Front St. in the nearby town of Hancocks Bridge, south of Salem via SR 49 to CR 658. It is open Wed.-Sat. 10-noon and 1-4, Sun. 1-4; phone (856) 935-4373.

One survivor of this bygone era is an oak tree estimated to be more than 5 centuries old. It stands at the entrance to the Friends Burial Ground, 112 W. Broadway. Beneath its branches early settler John Fenwick bargained with the Lenni Lenape Indians for the land on which Salem was established.

Salem County Chamber of Commerce 174 E. Broadway, P.O. Box 71, Salem, NJ 08079. **Phone:** (856) 351-2245.

SALEM COUNTY HISTORICAL SOCIETY is at 79-83 Market St. Founded in 1884, the site comprises four linked historic homes, one of which is the 1721 Alexander Grant Mansion House. Three rooms contain such exhibits as an early 18th-century cooking fireplace and kitchen utensils as well as local artwork and pottery. Other highlights include the reputed first law office in the U.S., a log cabin, a stone barn, and a genealogical and local history library. Changing exhibits also are presented.

Time: Allow 30 minutes minimum. **Hours:** Tues.-Sat. noon-4. Closed major holidays. **Cost:** Museum $5. Library research fee $5. **Phone:** (856) 935-5004. GT

THOROFARE
- Hotels & Restaurants map & index p. 274
- Part of Philadelphia area — see map p. 230

BEST WESTERN WEST DEPTFORD INN
(856)848-4111 139

Hotel
$110

AAA Benefit: Members save up to 20%!

Address: 98 Friars Blvd 08086 **Location:** I-295 exit 20, just e on Mid Atlantic Pkwy, then 0.4 mi n. **Facility:** 100 units. 2 stories, interior corridors. **Pool(s):** outdoor. **Activities:** limited exercise equipment. **Guest Services:** valet and coin laundry.

VOORHEES
- Hotels & Restaurants map & index p. 274
- Part of Philadelphia area — see map p. 230

HAMPTON INN-CHERRY HILL/VOORHEES
(856)346-4500 120

Hotel $89-$189 **Address:** 121 Laurel Oak Rd 08043 **Location:** I-295 exit 32, 2.3 mi e on Haddonfield-Berlin Rd, then s on White Horse Rd. Located in Voorhees Corporate Center.

AAA Benefit: Members save 5% or more!

Facility: 120 units. 4 stories, interior corridors. **Terms:** 1-7 night minimum stay, cancellation fee imposed. **Amenities:** video games. **Pool(s):** outdoor. **Activities:** exercise room. **Guest Services:** valet and coin laundry, area transportation.

HAMPTON INN PHILADELPHIA/VOORHEES
(856)751-1212 119

Hotel $109-$149 **Address:** 320 Rt 73 S 08043 **Location:** I-295 exit 32, 1.7 mi e on Haddonfield-Berlin Rd, 2.5 mi n on E Evesham Rd, 1.5 mi e on Kresson Rd, then just s. **Facility:** 118 units. 4 stories, interior corridors. **Terms:** 1-7 night minimum stay, cancellation fee imposed. **Pool(s):** heated indoor. **Activities:** exercise room. **Guest Services:** valet and coin laundry.

AAA Benefit: Members save 5% or more!

WHERE TO EAT

A LITTLE CAFE
856/784-3344 151

American. Casual Dining. $22-$32 **AAA Inspector Notes:** Bring your favorite wine from home and enjoy sophisticated Asian-influenced American dishes at this small, quaint spot, which rises above its humble location in a strip mall. The cozy dining room lacks size, but provides a warm, inviting atmosphere. **Reservations:** suggested. **Address:** 118 White Horse Rd E 08043 **Location:** I-295 exit 32, 3.8 mi e on CR 561 to White Horse Rd, then 1.1 mi s; in Plaza Shoppes. Lindenwold, 152.

PASSARIELLO'S PIZZERIA & ITALIAN EATERY
856/784-7272 150

Italian. Cafeteria. $7-$16 **AAA Inspector Notes:** Pick up a passport card upon entry, then prepare to enjoy a delicious meal of homemade Italian or American favorites. From baked gnocchi and calamari marinara to Buffalo wings and hoagies, this restaurant has a wide variety of affordable and satisfying dishes for the whole family. **Address:** 111 Laurel Oak Rd 08043 **Location:** I-295 exit 32, 2.3 mi e on Haddonfield-Berlin Rd, then just s on White Horse Rd.

RITZ SEAFOOD
856/566-6650 149

Seafood. Casual Dining. $9-$25 **AAA Inspector Notes:** Step inside this charming little storefront restaurant to find a casual, Asian-influenced dining room. Grab a seat to sample mainly seafood dishes with a similar Asian flair. Garlic and ginger-crusted salmon with Indonesian black beans, flash-fried devil fish with sweet chile scallion sauce and seafood stew with Asian noodles in Korean-style broth are a few such choices. However, there also are seafood shepherd's pie with lobster sauce and a few meat, rice and noodle dishes. **Reservations:** suggested, weekends. **Address:** 910 Rt 561 08043 **Location:** I-295 exit 32, 2.2 mi e; in Ritz Center.

WESTAMPTON
- Hotels & Restaurants map & index p. 274
- Part of Philadelphia area — see map p. 230

BEST WESTERN BURLINGTON INN
(609)261-3800 71

Hotel $99-$139

AAA Benefit: Members save up to 20%!

Address: 2020 Burlington Mt Holly Rd 08060 **Location:** New Jersey Tpke exit 5, just n. **Facility:** 88 units. 2 stories, interior corridors. **Pool(s):** heated indoor. **Activities:** exercise room. **Guest Services:** valet laundry.

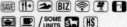

(See map & index p. 274.)

**COURTYARD BY MARRIOTT BURLINGTON MT. HOLLY/
WESTAMPTON** (609)261-6161 **67**

▼▼▼ **Hotel** $130-$213 **Address:**
30 Western Dr 08060 **Location:** New
Jersey Tpke exit 5, 0.3 mi n. **Facility:**
119 units. 4 stories, interior corridors.
Pool(s): heated indoor. **Activities:** exercise room. **Guest Services:** valet and coin laundry, area transportation.

> **AAA Benefit:**
> Members save 5%
> or more!

🍽 CALL 🖥M ➥ BIZ HS 🛜 ✕ 🛢 🖳
/ SOME UNITS 🍴

HILTON GARDEN INN MT. HOLLY/WESTAMPTON
609/702-1600 **70**

▼▼▼ **Hotel.** Rates not provided.
Address: 111 Hancock Ln 08060 **Location:** New Jersey Tpke exit 5. **Facility:**
113 units. 3 stories, interior corridors.
Terms: check-in 4 pm. **Pool(s):** heated indoor. **Activities:** exercise room. **Guest Services:** valet and coin laundry.

> **AAA Benefit:**
> Members save 5%
> or more!

🍴 🍽 CALL 🖥M ➥ BIZ HS 🛜 ✕ 🛢 🖳
🖳

HOLIDAY INN EXPRESS HOTEL & SUITES
(609)702-5800 **68**

▼▼▼ **Hotel** $99-$149 **Address:** 18 Western Dr 08060 **Location:** New Jersey Tpke exit 5, 0.3 mi n. **Facility:** 76 units. 3 stories, interior corridors. **Amenities:** safes. **Pool(s):** heated indoor. **Activities:** exercise room. **Guest Services:** valet and coin laundry.

🍴 CALL 🖥M ➥ BIZ 🛜 ✕ 🖳 / SOME UNITS 🛢 🍴

QUALITY INN & SUITES (609)845-9400 **72**

▼▼ **Hotel** $85-$150 **Address:** 2015 Burlington Mt Holly Rd 08060 **Location:** New Jersey Tpke exit 5, just n. **Facility:** 78 units. 2 stories (no elevator), interior corridors. **Activities:** exercise room. **Guest Services:** valet and coin laundry.

🍴 CALL 🖥M BIZ 🛜 ✕ 🛢 🍴 🖳

WILLIAMSTOWN pop. 15,567
• Part of Philadelphia area — see map p. 230

BEST WESTERN MONROE INN & SUITES
(856)340-7900

 Hotel
$99-$199

 AAA Benefit:
Members save up to 20%!

Address: 1151 N Black Horse Pike
08094 **Location:** New Jersey Tpke exit
3, 3.2 mi s on SR 168, then 9 mi s on SR
42; 2 mi s of jct CR 689. **Facility:** 44
units. 2 stories, interior corridors.
Pool(s): heated indoor. **Activities:** exercise room. **Guest Services:** valet and
coin laundry.

SAVE CALL 🖥M ➥ BIZ HS 🛜
🛢 🍴 🖳 / SOME UNITS 🐾

WOODBURY pop. 10,174, elev. 34'
• Part of Philadelphia area — see map p. 230

Woodbury was occupied by British troops in November 1777. Gen. Charles Cornwallis chose as his headquarters the home of John Cooper, a Continental Congress member denounced for his patriotism by his pacifist Quaker friends. A number of Revolutionary War-era buildings have been preserved.

"Light Horse" Harry Lee, father of Robert E. Lee, made Woodbury his headquarters during military campaigns in South Jersey in 1779. Other local notables include Commodore Stephen Decatur and Capt. James Lawrence, both of whom attended Woodbury Academy. The Hunter-Lawrence-Jessup House, 58 N. Broad St., was the boyhood home of Lawrence, known for his dying command "Don't give up the ship," uttered during the War of 1812. His former home now houses the Gloucester County Historical Society Museum. Exhibits include textiles, samplers, toys, dolls, military artifacts and a Colonial-era kitchen; phone (856) 848-8531.

Greater Woodbury Chamber of Commerce: P.O. Box 363, Woodbury, NJ 08096. **Phone:** (856) 845-4056.

CHARLIE BROWN'S STEAKHOUSE 856/853-8505

▼▼ Steak. Casual Dining. $9-$30 **AAA Inspector Notes:** This budget-friendly steakhouse, famous for its prime rib, offers top quality fare without hurting your pocketbook. The young ones will not be disappointed with the kids' menu, and just might even try something green from the salad bar. Adults will love the quality steaks, chicken and rib dishes. The express lunches are great for those saddled with time constraints. **Features:** full bar, happy hour. **Address:** 111 N Broad St 08096 **Location:** I-295 exit 24 (Gateway Blvd), s to N Broad St, then 1.2 mi s. L D

> This ends the Philadelphia section and
> resumes the alphabetical city listings
> for Pennsylvania.

PINE FORGE

GRACIE'S 21ST CENTURY CAFE AND CATERING
610/323-4004

▼▼▼ American. Fine Dining. $27-$44 **AAA Inspector Notes:** Caribbean influences distinguish the eclectic, innovative menu, which lists such specials as pan-seared shrimp, scallops and crab with basil-lemon creme. White chocolate mousse puff pastry with blueberry and mango chunks is simply delicious. **Features:** full bar. **Reservations:** suggested. **Address:** Manatawny Rd 19548 **Location:** Just se of jct Pine Forge Rd. D

PINE GROVE pop. 2,186

COMFORT INN (570)345-8031

▼▼ **Hotel** $70-$170 **Address:** 433 Suedberg Rd 17963 **Location:** I-81 exit 100, just e. **Facility:** 68 units. 3 stories, interior corridors. **Amenities:** safes. **Pool(s):** heated indoor. **Activities:** game room, exercise room.

🍴 CALL 🖥M ➥ BIZ 🛜 🛢 🍴 🖳 / SOME UNITS 🐾

HAMPTON INN PINE GROVE (570)345-4505

▼▼▼ **Hotel** $109-$159 **Address:**
481 Suedberg Rd 17963 **Location:** I-81
exit 100, just w. **Facility:** 81 units. 3 stories, interior corridors. **Terms:** 1-7 night
minimum stay, cancellation fee imposed.
Pool(s): heated indoor. **Activities:** exercise room. **Guest Services:** coin laundry.

> **AAA Benefit:**
> Members save 5%
> or more!

🍴 CALL 🖥M ➥ BIZ HS 🛜 🛢 🍴 🖳
/ SOME UNITS 🐾

Pittsburgh

Then & Now

It's a surprise, in fact, almost stunning. That would be the view of Pittsburgh's skyline as you emerge from the Fort Pitt Tunnel, where the Allegheny, Monongahela and Ohio rivers converge and modern monoliths soar majestically beyond. Shame on visitors expecting to see a gritty steel mill town engulfed in smoke, for Pittsburgh doesn't deserve the bad rap of its past—the city has cleaned itself up and undergone a renaissance. Steel mills have been replaced by high-tech and healthcare concerns, and more than 30 institutions of higher learning exist in what is locally known as "The College City."

Pittsburgh has received accolades for urban beauty, and a prime example is Point State Park, flanked by the three mighty rivers, a majestic fountain at one end and the skyscrapers of the downtown Golden Triangle at the other. The Three Rivers Heritage Trail guides hikers, joggers and cyclists along 21 miles of riverfront turf, while locals and tourists alike enjoy the equestrian paths and the occasional evening jazz concert at Riverview Park. An extensive trail system snakes through woodlands and steep valleys at Frick Park, while peaceful urban exploration via kayak or canoe is an option on the Allegheny River Trail.

For those seeking culture and entertainment, Pittsburgh delivers. Names like Heinz, Carnegie and Mellon grace buildings and other venues, reminders of the philanthropic families that figured prominently in the city's development. There's Heinz Hall, home of the Pittsburgh Symphony; Senator John Heinz History Center; and football arena Heinz Field. Mellon Bank Center carves out an impressive space in the skyline and Mellon Square is a modernist rooftop garden plaza. Carnegie Mellon University is one of the area's leading educational institutions, and the Carnegie Museums of Pittsburgh offer an unsurpassed learning experience to anyone captivated by art, science and natural history.

Carnegie Mellon University

What's nice about Pittsburgh is that it has big-city amenities, yet retains a small-town feel. The city's unique neighborhoods stand as proud symbols of ethnic diversity: Squirrel Hill, home of one of the region's largest Jewish populations; Bloomfield, known as "Little Italy"; the North Side, with traces of the old German community that immigrated in the early 19th century; and Polish Hill, where Polish immigrants settled in the late 1800s. In all, Pittsburgh has nearly 90 neighborhoods. AAA GEM attraction Cathedral of Learning pays homage to the area's ethnicity with its fascinating nationality classrooms.

All Pittsburghers come together to demonstrate spirit for their beloved sports teams: the Steelers (football), Penguins (hockey) and Pirates (baseball). At times, the city turns into a kaleidoscope of black and gold, as devoted

(Continued on p. 327.)

Destination Pittsburgh

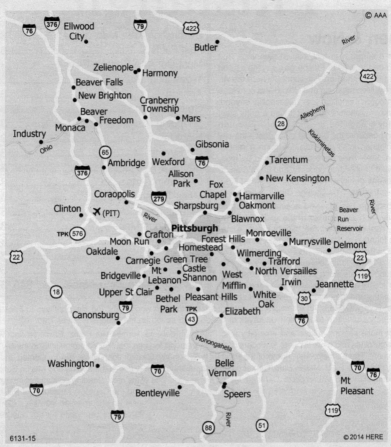

© AAA
6131-15
© 2014 HERE

This map shows cities in the Pittsburgh vicinity where you will find attractions, hotels and restaurants. Cities are listed alphabetically in this book on the following pages.

Fast Facts

ABOUT THE CITY

POP: 305,704 ▪ **ELEV:** 715 ft.

MONEY

SALES TAX: Pennsylvania's statewide sales tax is 6 percent. An additional 1 percent is collected by Allegheny County, as is a 7 percent lodging tax. The city levies a 5 percent amusements tax.

WHOM TO CALL

EMERGENCY: 911

POLICE (non-emergency): (412) 323-7800

TIME AND TEMPERATURE: (412) 391-9500

HOSPITALS: Allegheny General Hospital, (412) 359-3131 ▪ UPMC Mercy, (412) 232-8111 ▪ UPMC Passavant—McCandless, (412) 367-6700 ▪ UPMC Presbyterian, (412) 647-2345 ▪ UPMC St. Margaret, (412) 784-4000 ▪ Western Pennsylvania Hospital, (412) 578-5000.

WHERE TO LOOK AND LISTEN

NEWSPAPERS: The major daily newspaper is the morning *Post-Gazette,* found online at www.post-gazette.com. Smaller daily, weekly and special-interest papers also are published.

RADIO: Pittsburgh radio station KDKA (1020 AM) is a news/talk/weather station ▪ WDUQ (90.5 FM) is a member of National Public Radio.

VISITOR INFORMATION

Welcome Pittsburgh Information Center and Gift Shop: 120 Fifth Ave., Pittsburgh, PA 15222. **Phone:** (412) 281-7711 or (800) 359-0758.

Two other visitor centers also provide maps, brochures, event schedules and sightseeing companies.

They're at the Pittsburgh International Airport and at the Senator John Heinz History Center in the Strip District.

TRANSPORTATION

AIR TRAVEL: Pittsburgh International Airport (PIT), approximately 19 miles west via I-376 (Parkway West) and SR 60 is served by numerous major domestic and international carriers as well as commuter and cargo lines. For information on ground transportation, phone (412) 466-1275.

Allegheny County Airport (AGC), south of the city on Lebanon Church Road in West Mifflin, handles primarily corporate or private aircraft, although air taxis and charter services also are available.

RENTAL CARS: Hertz, at the Pittsburgh International Airport, offers discounts to AAA members; phone (412) 472-5955 or (800) 654-3080.

RAIL SERVICE: An Amtrak passenger service station is on the lower level of The Pennsylvanian, formerly Penn Central Station, at 1100 Liberty Ave. at Grant Street; phone (412) 471-6170, (800) 872-7245 or TTY (800) 523-6590.

BUSES: The Greyhound Lines Inc. terminal is at 55 11th St. near Liberty Avenue; phone (412) 392-6526 or (800) 231-2222.

TAXIS: The leading taxi company is Yellow Cab, (412) 321-8100. Cabs are metered, and standard fare is $4.60 per mile. A fuel surcharge of $1.10 may be charged.

PUBLIC TRANSPORTATION: Port Authority of Allegheny County Transit operates public transportation throughout the city and Allegheny County. The base fare is $2.50; exact change is required. Discounted fares are available through the purchase of weekly or monthly passes, which can be purchased at the transit's downtown service center at 534 Smithfield St. For route information, phone (412) 442-2000.

(Continued from p. 325.)
fans show off the colors adopted by all three teams—it's a brave soul who dons an opposing team's jersey. With the Steelers as the 2009 Super Bowl champs and the Penguins clinching the Stanley Cup title in June 2009, Pittsburgh has earned the right to call itself America's "City of Champions." These colossal events were enough to stop traffic, as blissful fans took to the streets to party or gather for pep rallies and parades.

Tradition also plays a part in the form of food icons and the friendly neighborhood grocer. Pittsburghers grew up with Isaly's Chipped Chopped Ham in the fridge, a household staple since the 1930s still satisfying cravings today. Many locals consider Sarris Candies to be one of the nation's best confectioners, and

numerous pubs and restaurants continue to serve pierogis, those soul-satisfying dumplings filled with such ingredients as potatoes, cheese, bacon and sauerkraut. Generations of Pittsburghers have sampled the namesake beer of Iron City Brewing Company, a fixture since 1861 and once delivered to homes via horse-drawn carriage. In the Strip District, named for a narrow plot of land between the river and the hillside, you'll find mom and pop businesses devoted entirely to popcorn, cheese, freshly baked bread, biscotti, coffee and other culinary delights. Stores like Pennsylvania Macaroni Company, with its remarkable selection of pastas, olive oil and all things Italian, and Wholey's Fish Market, where patrons still line up and take a number on busy Saturdays to snare a fresh catch, are like family to Strip District shoppers.

Must Do: AAA Editor's Picks

- Introduce yourself to Pittsburgh by visiting ♦ **Point State Park,** an urban green space with a dramatic view—this is where the Monongahela, Allegheny and Ohio rivers converge. Visit the ♦ **Fort Pitt Museum,** stroll along riverside walkways or take a seat by the fountain at the park's edge, where you'll spy such sites as PNC Park, Heinz Field and the ♦ **Carnegie Science Center** across the water.

- Spend time in the **Strip District** and explore its delightful mom-and-pop groceries, bakeries and restaurants touting everything from homemade lasagna to first-rate espresso. Do as the locals do and grab a hearty breakfast at **DeLuca's Restaurant,** shop for culinary specialties at the Pennsylvania Macaroni Company, and appreciate the circuslike atmosphere at **Wholey's,** a fish market.

- **See a game.** Whether you prefer hockey (Penguins), football (Steelers) or baseball (Pirates), this town comes to a standstill when its beloved sports teams are playing. And Pittsburgh has definitely earned bragging rights: the Steelers won the Super Bowl championship in February 2009, with the Penguins following suit by nabbing the Stanley Cup title in June 2009.

- Explore Pittsburgh's **Golden Triangle** area. This is the heart of downtown, and you'll experience trendy restaurants and varied nightlife opportunities. The cultural district presents an assortment of venues—the Benedum Center for the Performing Arts hosts ballet and Broadway performances, while the Cabaret at Theater Square offers year-round musical productions.

- Ride the **Duquesne Incline,** a funicular departing from the city's South Side neighborhood that scales Mount Washington. From your lofty perch, you'll have a birds-eye view of Pittsburgh that's especially dazzling at night.

- Tour the ♦ **Cathedral of Learning** at the University of Pittsburgh. As you approach the campus, you can't miss the massive Gothic Revival structure—the 42-story behemoth is said to be the world's second tallest educational building. Inside, you can explore some 27 nationality classrooms and learn about the culture and heritage of Pittsburgh's ethnic communities.

- Immerse yourself in Pittsburgh shopping and nightlife on **Carson Street** in "the Burgh's" South Side. Lined with funky shops, nightspots and eateries, Carson has a bit of a bohemian flair. The main drag is sandwiched between two large shopping complexes, Station Square (near the Smithfield Street Bridge) and Southside Works at the east end.

- All aboard! **Cruise Pittsburgh's three mighty rivers**—the Monongahela, Allegheny and Ohio. The riverboat captains of ♦ **Gateway Clipper Fleet** provide historical anecdotes as well as information concerning various landmarks during your sightseeing trip. **Just Ducky Tours** supplies amphibious vehicles that can explore city streets as well as slide into the water at any given moment.

- View thousands of stunning art and science objects at the ♦ **Carnegie Museums of Pittsburgh.** Discover the world of pop art at **The Andy Warhol Museum,** experience American and European works at the **Carnegie Museum of Art,** gaze at dinosaur fossils at the ♦ **Carnegie Museum of Natural History** and see a laser show, visit the planetarium or explore the **USS Requin** submarine at the ♦ **Carnegie Science Center.**

- Celebrate Pittsburgh's ethnic diversity by visiting some of its vibrant **neighborhoods.** Traces of Germany are reflected in the schnitzel, sausages and tasty brews of the North Side, while Bloomfield's "Little Italy" houses an assortment of Italian groceries. And while Squirrel Hill is the epicenter of the city's Jewish population, you'll also find Chinese, Middle Eastern and Greek culinary offerings.

Duquesne Incline

Pittsburgh 1-day Itinerary

AAA editors suggest these activities for a great short vacation experience.

Morning

- Start your day by visiting ᗡᗢ **Point State Park** to get your bearings while enjoying a scenic perspective of Pittsburgh's epicenter. The triangular-shaped park juts forth from downtown's edge, with a majestic fountain marking the point where the Allegheny, Monongahela and Ohio rivers meet. With a backdrop of soaring skyscrapers behind you, you'll have fun identifying landmarks across the water like Heinz Field and PNC Park on the North Shore. Visit the ᗡᗢ **Fort Pitt Museum** to learn how the fort's strategic position played an integral role in our nation's history.

- It's a quick hop over the Fort Duquesne Bridge to investigate a couple of the attractions you likely glimpsed from the park. On the North Shore, explore your choice of facilities affiliated with the ᗡᗢ **Carnegie Museums of Pittsburgh.** The ᗡᗢ **Carnegie Science Center** spans a variety of topics; whether you're intrigued by miniature railroads, sports challenges or aquarium life, you can tailor your experience to be as laid-back or interactive as you wish—and the Friday and Saturday night laser show dazzles viewers. Navigate your way through the **USS Requin,** a Tench-class submarine launched in 1945 now docked adjacent to the museum. If pop art captures your attention, swing by **The Andy Warhol Museum,** a shrine to the artist's various pursuits, including sculpture, painting, photography, film and video.

- If you're in an outdoors frame of mind, another option is to take one of the sightseeing cruises offered by the ᗡᗢ **Gateway Clipper Fleet,** departing from the city's South Shore across the Fort Pitt Bridge. In addition to appreciating prime city views, you'll learn about local history and the three rivers the vessel sails upon.

Afternoon

- For a real slice of Pittsburgh life, head to the Strip District, a narrow, mile-long pocket just northeast of downtown wedged between 11th and 33rd Streets. Most of the action takes place on the main drags of Smallman Street and Penn Avenue.

- Since the Strip is all about food, it's a phenomenal lunch stop, with plenty of options on Penn Avenue. Seafood aficionados on the run should stop by **Wholey's,** a market that also happens to serve up a mighty fine fish sandwich. If you're in the mood for a deli sandwich, burger or entrée salad, try **Deluca's Restaurant,** a local favorite that's also a popular breakfast haunt. To sample innovative Caribbean fare in an eclectic setting, head to **Kaya Restaurant,** around the corner on Smallman.

- After lunch, wander around the district and peruse the sidewalk vendors—a great place to grab that Steelers T-Shirt or whatever souvenir

Tour the USS *Requin* at the Carnegie Science Center

catches your eye. It's fun to browse the locally owned Italian groceries and sample such delectable goods as cheeses, olive oils, espresso, freshly baked breads, biscotti, chocolate and other confections. A sprinkling of unique shops offers fashion accessories and trinkets for the home and garden.

- You could also visit the University of Pittsburgh campus, about 3 miles east of the downtown area in the Oakland neighborhood. The must-see here is the ᗡᗢ **Cathedral of Learning,** the campuses' regal centerpiece and one of the world's tallest educational structures. A self-guiding tour will lead you through Nationality Rooms where you can learn about the cultures represented through taped narration.

Evening

- The South Side is a prime evening destination. Eateries and clubs are scattered along the stretch of Carson Street between the Station Square and Southside Works shopping and entertainment complexes. The **Hard Rock Cafe** at Station Square offers crowds, lively music and typical American fare. For more of a funky neighborhood feel, check out one of the spots along E. Carson Street: **Primanti Brothers Restaurant,** known for sliding French fries into their sandwiches, has been a hit with Pittsburghers since 1933, while **Ibiza Tapas & Wine Bar** offers innovative creations along with outdoor seating perfect for people-watching. **Dish Osteria and Bar,** a cozy bistro just off the main drag, serves classic Italian. After dinner, join the pub crawl among the street's cornucopia of nightspots.

Arriving
By Car

The primary highway from the north or the south is I-79, which passes through the western edge of the metropolitan area. Intersecting with east-west routes I-76 (Pennsylvania Turnpike) on the north and with I-70 on the south, I-79 funnels traffic into Pittsburgh via controlled-access I-279 (Parkway West) and the Fort Pitt Tunnel from Carnegie.

A second approach is I-279 (Parkway North) from Cranberry, and from the south via Banksville Road and I-279. US 19 Truck Route, using East Street from the north and West Liberty Avenue from the south, carries heavy commercial and industrial traffic into the city.

I-76 carries the bulk of east-west traffic through the area, interchanging en route with all major arteries; I-376 through the eastern suburbs provides the principal link to the heart of the city, arriving downtown via Grant Street exit 1C. Two other important east-west highways are US 22 and US 30, which combine upon nearing the city, then join expressways I-376 before entering the downtown area.

SR 28, first as the Allegheny Valley Expressway, then as E. Ohio Street, follows the north bank of the Allegheny River into the city's North Side, providing a route from northeast suburbs. **Note:** SR 28 is undergoing major construction. Similarly, SR 60 makes an easy connection from the northwestern suburbs along the south side of the Ohio River, picking up airport traffic before joining with US 22/30.

The primary highway into Pittsburgh is I-79

Getting Around
Street System

Pittsburgh's topography—a maze of hills and ravines sliced at an acute angle by two rivers converging to form a third—permits no consistent geometrical street layout. Instead, there is a patchwork of patterns dictated mainly by the lay of the land. A good street map is necessary for travel in this city.

From the Golden Triangle major thoroughfares fan out more or less parallel to the Allegheny and Monongahela rivers, with intervening streets perpendicular to the rivers near the Point but following the contours of the hills farther out. Fifth Avenue and Liberty Avenue are the primary arteries.

On the north side, at least the sections nearest the river, the picture is more regular, with avenues running parallel to the Allegheny River and streets perpendicular to it. All the major thoroughfares seem to converge on Allegheny Center, framed by N., E., S. and W. Commons. E. Ohio Street and Western Avenue feed in from the east and west, respectively; East Street, Federal Street, Brighton Avenue and Allegheny Avenue reach the center from the north.

The near edge of the hilly south side is the only part of the city that employs the designations East and West, using the Smithfield Street Bridge as the dividing line. Carson Street (SR 837), parallel to the river, is the main artery through this area.

Most of Pittsburgh's streets are named; there are relatively few areas of consecutively numbered thoroughfares. Two such locations are on the Point, where 1st through 7th avenues are numbered northward from the Monongahela River, and inland from the Allegheny River, where numbered streets increase as they proceed upstream.

A series of marked alternate routes known as the "Belt Routes" were developed to relieve congestion on the major highways and to aid travelers in and around the city. The five Belt Routes that loop Greater Pittsburgh and link various towns and highways are posted throughout the metropolitan area with color-coded signs (red, green, blue, yellow and orange).

The downtown speed limit, unless otherwise posted, is 25 mph, and on major thoroughfares, 35 mph. Unless a sign prohibits it, turning right at a red light after coming to a complete stop is legal. Similarly, so is turning left from one one-way street onto another. Pedestrians always have the right-of-way, particularly at marked crosswalks. Jaywalking, however, is illegal, and the law is strictly enforced. Driving during rush hours, about 6:30-9 a.m. and 4-6:30 p.m., should be avoided if possible.

Parking

As in any big city, parking downtown or near the major attractions is at a premium. On-street parking, when a space can be found, is governed by the meter system. However, commercial parking lots and garages are plentiful throughout. Rates range from $5 per hour to $25 per day.

Shopping

Pittsburgh's neighborhoods provide happy hunting grounds for those inclined to pop into trendy boutiques, bookstores and locally owned mom and pops offering unique home furnishings and all forms of bric-a-brac. You'll mostly find malls and their anchors in the suburbs, while themed complexes downtown and in its environs offer the shopper a little something extra—entertainment, cute bistros and other diversions amid popular chains and specialty retailers.

The downtown **Golden Triangle** is defined as the area roughly from Point State Park to Crosstown Boulevard, tucked between the Allegheny River on the north and the Monongahela River on the south. Department store aficionados on the prowl venture to the city's flagship **Macy's** (formerly Kaufmann's) at Fifth Avenue and Smithfield; the clock outside is a popular rendezvous point for Pittsburghers. If you're in the market for some classy baubles, make a beeline to the **Clark Building** at Liberty Avenue and Seventh Street. Considered the city's "diamond district," the art deco structure contains retail, wholesale and estate jewelers.

A couple of complexes ripe for retail exploration also are nestled within the Golden Triangle. The **Shops at One Oxford Center**, 301 Grant St., is a collection of specialty boutiques within a stunning glass atrium; standouts include Emphatics for chic yet pricey couture fashions and Kountz & Rider for fine menswear. **Fifth Avenue Place** reigns proudly at Fifth and Liberty, an impressive landmark crowned with a massive pyramid and steeple. It's a favorite haunt of downtown professionals who dash in during lunch to search for clothes and gifts; Betsy Ann Chocolates, purveyor of creamy truffles and other sinful treats, should not be ignored.

Forbes Avenue, near Carnegie Mellon University in the **Oakland** neighborhood is south of Fifth Avenue, and features shopping and dining near the school and medical centers.

East of downtown, there are several neighborhoods chock full of shopping delights. Closest to the Golden Triangle is the thriving **Strip District** (named for a narrow, mile-long stretch), where you'll find a delectable selection of culinary items—locals come here for pastas, exotic coffees, luscious pastries, gourmet finds and ethnic specialties. The Strip is in full swing on Saturday mornings, a colorful array of street performers, food and knick-knack vendors, and farmers displaying fresh produce. The **16:62 Design Zone**, extending from the district's 16th Street Bridge to the 62nd Street Bridge in Lawrenceville, hosts a plethora of businesses focusing on furniture and home décor. One of the city's oldest neighborhoods, **Lawrenceville** also contributes to the retail scene by way of eclectic boutiques and art studios—you'll find them dotted along Butler Street, Penn Avenue and Hatfield Street.

The **Shadyside** neighborhood is about 15 minutes east of downtown. Popular chains and specialty stores are sprinkled throughout upscale **Walnut**

Shop for gifts at Fifth Avenue Place

Street, with trendy cafés in-between perfect for refueling. **Ellsworth Avenue** presents a more local spin, punctuated with home accessory shops, antique dealers, art galleries and the occasional coffee place. You'll also stumble across some unique finds on the area's side streets.

The **South Craig Street** business district is the commercial hub of **Oakland**, another East End neighborhood. Refurbished row houses contain funky little bistros frequented by University of Pittsburgh and Carnegie Mellon University students, while businesses tout books, gifts and other knick-knacks. The shops of **Squirrel Hill**, east of Oakland, are mainly situated on Murray and Forbes. Kosher groceries, ethnic eateries and locally owned businesses selling novelty items from a variety of cultures give the area a real international flair, and it's fun hunting for resale clothing and souvenirs while indulging your sweet tooth at a bakery or coffeehouse.

The area south of downtown across the Monongahela River also holds allure for shoppers. Conveniently, there's a subway ("T") stop at the SAVE **Shops at Station Square**, situated on Carson Street at the Smithfield Street Bridge. Savor the view of Pittsburgh's skyline from this refurbished 19th-century railroad station with some 20 retailers, including SAVE **Hard Rock Cafe**. Station Square is also a popular dining, entertainment and nightlife venue. **Southside Works**, East Carson and 27th streets, is an outdoor complex complete with town square. High-end boutiques of both national and local stature are the draw here, and you'll also have your pick of the best-loved chains. Those just along for the ride can enjoy a movie or a meal, or browse the impressive selection at Joseph-Beth Booksellers. (Incidentally, the stretch of **East Carson Street** linking Station Square with Southside Works is inhabited by jewelry, antique and novelty stores as well as plenty of cafes, bars and coffeehouses.) Farther southeast across the Homestead Hi-Level Bridge and recognizable by its massive brick smokestacks, **Shopping At The Waterfront** provides open-air shopping and entertainment bordering the Monongahela River on the site of a former steel mill; the 260-acre retail behemoth's temptations are enhanced by the sweeping river view.

The suburban mall is alive and kicking in Pittsburgh, and if you arrived via plane you probably had your first taste of mall mania as you wandered past the vast assortment of shops and restaurants at **Pittsburgh Air Mall.** Near the airport off SR 60, **Robinson Town Centre** and **The Mall at Robinson** serve the western suburbs. The southern suburbs tout the 130-store **South Hills Village,** off US 19 between Upper St. Clair and Bethel Park. In Bethel Park at the intersection of US 19 and Fort Couch Road, **Village Square** specializes in such discounters as Burlington Coat Factory and Kohl's. In the South Hills off US 19 is the **Galleria of Mt. Lebanon,** which features Ann Taylor, Restoration Hardware, Williams-Sonoma and other chains. To the southeast in West Mifflin of SR 51 is **Century III Mall,** with 160 stores and restaurants.

Heading east on US 22 near the Pennsylvania Turnpike is **Monroeville Mall;** its 180 establishments are the commercial heart of this suburban region. Northeast of Pittsburgh off SR 28 exit 12A in

Taste exotic coffee in the Strip District

Tarentum is **Galleria at Pittsburgh Mills,** with JCPenney and Macy's. Farther out tucked into the North Hills are **McIntyre Square, North Hills Village, Northway Mall** and the upscale **Ross Park Mall**—all on McKnight Road. Branches of most large department stores can be found amid these four shopping complexes.

Nightlife

Pittsburghers like to mingle, and the city's thriving brew pubs and neighborhood bars provide the perfect setting for a game of pool, some friendly chat or nibbling on homemade pierogis and other flavorsome bites. Those musically inclined can opt for an evening at one of the live music venues or dance the night away to the pulsating beat of DJ-inspired tunes. Clubs providing entertainment may include cover charges and usually require drink minimums. To avoid surprises, phone ahead and confirm prices, opening hours, scheduled acts and dress codes.

If you appreciate well-crafted drafts, you've come to the right place. Ironically, copper tanks have replaced the altar at **Church Brew Works** (Lawrenceville/(412) 688-8200). Instead of sermons, this former cathedral now serves up piously named house brews and creative pub grub under its soaring ceilings—fans of dark lager should try the heavenly Pious Monk Dunkel. **Fat Heads Saloon** (South Side/(412) 431-7433) attracts all walks, from business types to partying sports fans. Knowledgeable bartenders in this bustling spot will provide tips on which of the tapped beers, bottles or artery-clogging headwiches (head-size sandwiches) are right for you.

German-style lagers are showcased at **Penn Brewery** (North Side/(412) 237-9400), where live polka tunes and an outdoor biergarten add to the merriment in a family style atmosphere—try their top-notch Penn Pilsner along with some authentic German fare. **Piper's Pub** (South Side/(412) 381-3977), offering a solid selection of English draughts and bottles, entertains a jolly assortment of British expats who gather to watch soccer and feast on across-the-pond favorites like bangers and mash. Belgian beer fans can indulge themselves with hard-to-find concoctions at **Sharp Edge Beer Emporium** (Friendship/(412) 661-3537), but whatever your preference, it's hard to go away unhappy with a menu touting some 300 international choices. The budget-minded should hit the weekday happy hour (4:30-6:30) for half-off Belgian drafts.

Pittsburgh's dance clubs appeal mostly to 20- and 30-somethings looking for a rousing party scene. The **Altar Bar** (Strip District/(412) 206-9719) "resurrects live music," a fitting description since it's housed within a former Catholic church. Coveted DJs spin tunes for postcollegiates out for a night of energetic dancing under colorful flashing lights in this sinfully upscale tri-level emporium, with bottle service and VIP areas available for those willing to throw down some coin. If you want some fog with your colored lights, check out **Diesel Club Lounge**

(South Side/(412) 651-4713), a big-city style multi-level club. Whether you're there for the stellar sound system, DJ-inspired gyrating or concerts appealing to varied age groups, you can check out the action from the catwalks looming above.

Pittsburgh offers a decent selection of live music venues showcasing diverse talent. Hipsters interested in listening to underground, alternative and indie bands frequent **Brillobox** (Lawrenceville/(412) 621-4900)—downstairs caters to diners, so venture upstairs to catch live acts. If you like the type of place where you're just a stone's throw away from the performers, **Club Café** (South Side/(412) 431-4950) hosts emerging and established artists presenting everything from jazz to blues to pop in a stylishly cozy spot catering to the sophisticated urbanite. **Moondog's** (Blawnox area/(412) 828-2040) is a little out of the way—you'll definitely need a set of wheels to get there—but the journey to this no-frills neighborhood pub is worth it for fans of quality rhythm and blues, country and rock.

The congregation at **Mr. Smalls** (Millvale/(412) 821-4447), in a former Catholic church, is now made up of reggae, punk, rock and hip-hop followers—the great acoustics also make this a popular concert stop for nationally known bands. The art deco inspired **Rex Theater** (South Side/(412) 381-6811), a Pittsburgh institution that has been around since the early 1900s, also delights with an array of local and national acts in a refurbished movie house. Purveyor of cutting-edge rock 'n' roll, the **31st Street Pub** (Strip District/(412) 391-8334) is a former biker bar with a crowd that depends on the type of band playing—punk, heavy metal, indie or whatever.

If you're into sipping an inventive cocktail, chatting with friends or just plain people watching, Pittsburgh has a healthy sampling of lounges to choose from. **Bossa Nova** (Downtown/(412) 232-3030) is a great place to order exotic drinks, sushi and Spanish tapas in an artsy setting; $5 martins are all the rage on Wednesday. Comfy couches and an outdoor deck will draw you into the casually funky **Firehouse Lounge** (Strip District/(412) 434-1230), where the day's worries are soothed away with imaginative libations—live jazz is presented on Thursday along with half-off wine bottles, while DJs spin on Friday and Saturday. Downtown professionals decompress at **Olive or Twist** (Downtown/(412) 255-0525), an upscale enclave known for its tantalizing menu of classic and contemporary martinis. Oenophiles usually land at the classy lounge within the **Sonoma Grille** (Downtown/(412) 697-1336), boasting some 100 wines by the glass with a collection largely influenced by West Coast vintners. For a tropical twist, head to **Tiki Lounge** (South Side/(412) 381-8454), where the South Pacific ambience will ease you into an island state of mind. Cocktails with names like Coconut Kiss, Head Hunter and Blue Shark help you unwind, and you get to keep the kitschy yet fun drink container as a souvenir.

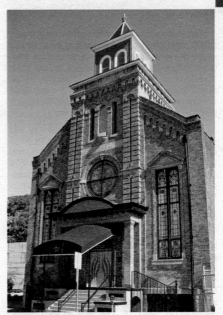
Check out The Altar Bar

Big Events

The **David L. Lawrence Convention Center** hosts many public events throughout the year. In mid-January there is the **Pittsburgh RV Show**, which features motor homes, travel trailers and fifth wheels as well as accessories. The **Pittsburgh International Auto Show**, held in February, gives car enthusiasts the opportunity to view new car, truck and motorcycle models. In early March, the **Pittsburgh Home and Garden Show** fills the center. Later that month is **Kid-a-palooza**, where children can meet some of their favorite characters at Cartoon Camp and have fun on indoor rides.

Over ten days in early June Pittsburgh celebrates the ⬙ **Three Rivers Arts Festival** at **Gateway Center** and **Point State Park** as well as throughout the **Cultural District**. There are programs and productions of just about everything cultural the city has to offer, including art, dance, music, theater and mime.

The ⬙ **Pittsburgh Three Rivers Regatta** occurs over Fourth of July weekend at Point State Park. In addition to the regatta, dozens of other events are held as well.

In late August, taste Mediterranean cuisine at the **Holy Trinity Greek Festival,** and experience **Shadyside Art Festival on Walnut Street,** which attracts artists, craftsmen, browsers and music aficionados. The **Pittsburgh Irish Festival** is held in early September at **The Riverplex at Sandcastle**. Mid-November begins the holiday season as downtown buildings show off their light displays at **Light-Up Night.**

Sports & Rec

That Pittsburghers are avid sports lovers is well known from the citywide celebrations that followed all the Steelers' Super Bowl victories and the Penguins' Stanley Cup victories. However, the city offers abundant and convenient opportunities for recreational pursuits as well; nearly every imaginable sport or recreational pastime is available. **Boating** is very popular on Pittsburgh's three rivers.

The focus for much recreation is the city and county parks. **Frick, Highland** and **Schenley** parks offer ball fields, **tennis** courts, **golf** courses and trails for **bicycling** and **hiking**. In winter, golf courses and hilly areas are popular for **cross-country skiing.** Information about facilities and current activities in the city parks can be obtained from the City Parks and Recreation Department; phone (412) 255-2539.

Allegheny County's **North Park** and **South Park** have plenty of the above activities as well as **swimming** pools, nearby bicycle rentals, **ice-skating** in winter and game preserves. In addition, North Park's lake offers **fishing,** boating and boat rentals. For more information about county park programs and activities contact Allegheny County Parks; phone (412) 350-7275. **The Rink at PPG Place,** (412) 394-3641, and **Schenley Park Rink,** (412) 422-6523, also offer ice-skating late November through early March.

Bicycling devotees have the advantage of a city bicycle route that links Highland, **Mellon,** Frick and Schenley parks. Near Highland Park is the **Washington Boulevard Cycling Track,** a half-mile

The David L. Lawrence Convention Center

slightly banked oval. The City Parks and Recreation Department can provide route information; phone (412) 255-2539. **Riverview Park** on the city's North Side features hiking trails and the Allegheny Observatory, an astronomy research center. Tours are offered April through October (by reservation only); phone (412) 321-2400.

Hiking is popular, as the number of hiking groups and programs attest. The Sierra Club and Venture Outdoors can furnish information about hiking, **canoeing** and **camping** in the area. In winter many of the city's hiking paths become **ski** trails. Besides the cross-country skiing provided by the city and county park areas, Allegheny County's **Boyce Park,** on Old Frankstown Road in nearby Plum, offers downhill skiing, cross-country skiing and **snow tubing.** Instruction and equipment rental are offered; phone (724) 733-4665. Equipment also can be rented at several ski shops, some of which also arrange ski trips and tours.

The **Three Rivers Heritage Trail** caters to bicyclists as well as walkers and joggers with its 22 miles of bicycle and pedestrian pathways; **in-line skating** is possible on some portions, too. The trail runs along the Allegheny, Monongahela and Ohio rivers. For route details and other information contact the Friends of the Riverfront Inc. at (412) 488-0212.

In addition to the courses in the parks, golf is available at a number of excellent public courses. Inquire at your hotel, for some might have a reciprocal golf club agreement for their guests with one of the local private or semiprivate courses.

Horseback riding is available at various stables and riding academies. Those who would rather watch equines than ride one can go to the **harness races** at **The Meadows Racetrack & Casino** *(see listing p. 411),* 25 miles south of Pittsburgh in Washington, where live harness racing is held year-round; for more information phone (724) 503-1200 or (877) 824-5050. There is **Thoroughbred racing** throughout the year at **Mountaineer Race Track and Gaming Resort** near Chester, W.Va., about an hour from Pittsburgh; phone (800) 804-0468.

Note: Policies concerning admittance of children to pari-mutuel betting facilities vary. Phone for information.

Among the swimming pools in Allegheny County, those in Boyce, **Settler's Cabin** and South Park provide waves for those who yearn for the surf. The fee is $5; $4 (ages 13–17); $3 (ages 6-12 and 60+); $1 (ages 0-5). Swimmers can choose a pool with or without waves.

Pittsburgh has 78 tennis courts in Schenley, Frick, Highland, **McKinley** and Mellon parks. Within Allegheny County you will find regional tennis courts at **West Park** and other public parks. Courts operate on a first-come, first-served basis. Because some require permits, it is a good idea to check with the city or county parks departments first; phone (412) 255-2539 or (412) 350-2455, respectively.

The National Football League's **Steelers** are popular among **football** fans; their home games are played at **Heinz Field.** Thanks to their sixth win in 2009, the Steelers have more Super Bowl victories than any other NFL franchise. Major League Baseball's **Pirates** are the stars during the **baseball** season; they play at **PNC Park.** The National Hockey League's **Penguins** play **hockey** at the **Consol Energy Center.** College sports also are big attractions, particularly the games played by the University of Pittsburgh's **Panthers.**

Performing Arts

The city's arts scene is growing, becoming more varied, more vital and more progressive. This is perhaps most apparent in Pittsburgh's theater offerings.

The **Pittsburgh Public Theatre** is a professional Equity company offering classical and modern dramas, including a new play each year. Its home is in the downtown **O'Reilly Theater,** designed by noted architect Michael Graves; phone (412) 316-1600 for ticket information. On the South Side, contemporary American plays are presented by the **City Theatre Company** during its October through May season. The always-interesting **Quantum Theatre** moves from one unique venue to another; phone (412) 362-1713. **Carnegie Mellon University's** theater is as active and excellent as ever; phone (412) 268-2082. **Point Park University's Pittsburgh Playhouse** in Oakland is the site of a wide range of classical and contemporary productions; phone (412) 624-7529 for ticket information. **University of Pittsburgh Repertory Theatre** (Pitt Rep) performs at the **Stephen Foster Memorial;** phone (412) 624-7529.

Dance of many kinds, from folk to modern, also is available. As they have for nearly 50 years, the **Duquesne University Tamburitzans** bring to vivid life the folk dances, songs and music of Old Eastern Europe; phone (412) 396-5185. The lavish **Benedum Center for the Performing Arts,** formerly the Stanley Theatre, is home to the acclaimed **Pittsburgh Ballet Theatre,** which performs October through April (412) 456-1390. The **Pittsburgh Dance Council** performs at the **Byham Theater.** Box office: (412) 456-6666.

The **August Wilson Center for African American Culture,** (412) 258-2700, named for the Pittsburgh native and playwright, is housed in a contemporary facility downtown on Liberty Avenue. Its offerings include dance, music and theater performances.

For orchestral music at its best, the **Pittsburgh Symphony** has few rivals. This orchestra packs the opulent 1926 **Heinz Hall,** 600 Penn Ave., September through June for its regular program series as well as for its Pops, Schooltime Concerts and Tiny Tots' series. Its excellent acoustics, elegant decor and dramatic architecture now form the backdrop for much of Pittsburgh's cultural activity. A courtyard with wrought-iron benches and water sculptures have been added to the hall. Phone (412) 392-4900 for ticket information.

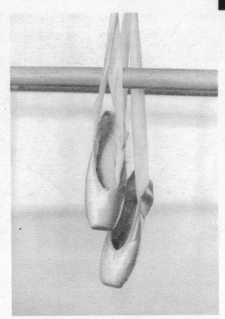

Check out the acclaimed Pittsburgh Ballet Theatre

The **Pittsburgh Opera** performs also at the Benedum Center for the Performing Arts. The **Pittsburgh Civic Light Opera** (CLO) also performs at the Benedum as well as at the Byham Theater.

The **CLO Cabaret** always entertains at the intimate **Cabaret at Theater Square.**

Contemporary American music is the specialty of the **Pittsburgh New Music Ensemble,** which performs at the **City Theatre.** Free chamber music concerts are held at The Frick Art Museum on Sundays, October through May. The Summer Concert in the Parks series provides a variety of free concerts, including bluegrass, folk and jazz in several of the city parks. Box office (412) 431-2489.

These are only a few of the possibilities; *Pittsburgh* magazine and the newspaper carry complete lists.

ATTRACTIONS

BEECHWOOD FARMS NATURE RESERVE is off SR 8 on Kittanning St. to 614 Dorseyville Rd. Headquarters for the Audubon Society of Western Pennsylvania, Beechwood Farms has more than 130 acres of fields, thickets, a pond and woodlands threaded by 5 miles of hiking trails. The environmental education center has a natural history library and bird observation room.

Education programs for children and adults are offered throughout the year. **Hours:** Trails daily dawn-dusk. Education center Tues.-Sat. 9-5 (also Tues. 5-7), Sun. 1-5. Closed major holidays. **Cost:** Free. **Phone:** (412) 963-6100.

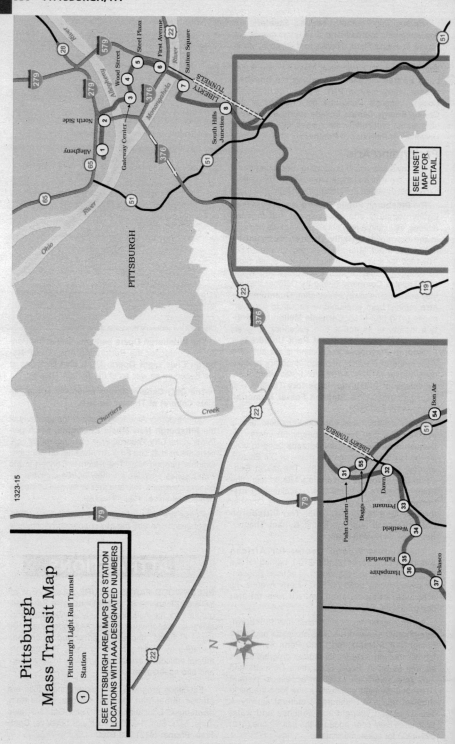

Pittsburgh
Mass Transit Map

Pittsburgh Light Rail Transit

① Station

SEE PITTSBURGH AREA MAPS FOR STATION
LOCATIONS WITH AAA DESIGNATED NUMBERS

1323-15

PITTSBURGH

Allegheny River

Monongahela River

Ohio River

Chartiers Creek

North Side

Allegheny

Gateway Center

Wood Street

Steel Plaza

First Avenue

Station Square

Steel Plaza

South Hills Junction

LIBERTY TUNNELS

SEE INSET MAP FOR DETAIL

Palm Garden

Boggs

Dawn

Pennant

Westfield

Fallowfield

Hampshire

Belasco

Bon Air

LIBERTY TUNNELS

① ② ③ ④ ⑤ ⑥ ⑦ ⑧
28 579 279 279 376 376 65 51 22 22 19 79 79
31 32 33 34 35 36 37 54 55

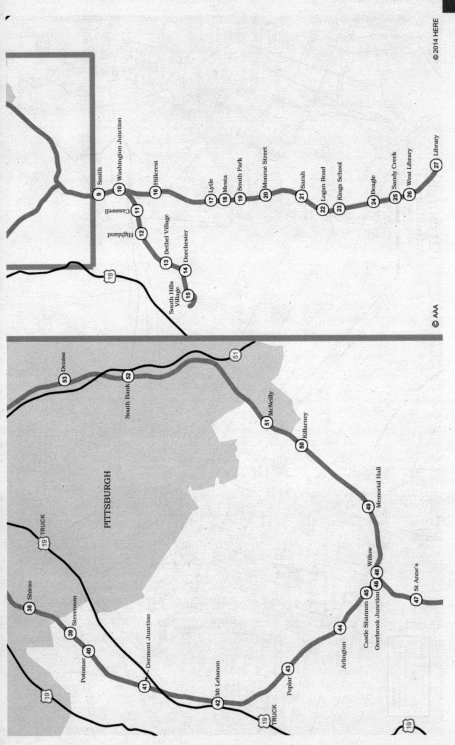

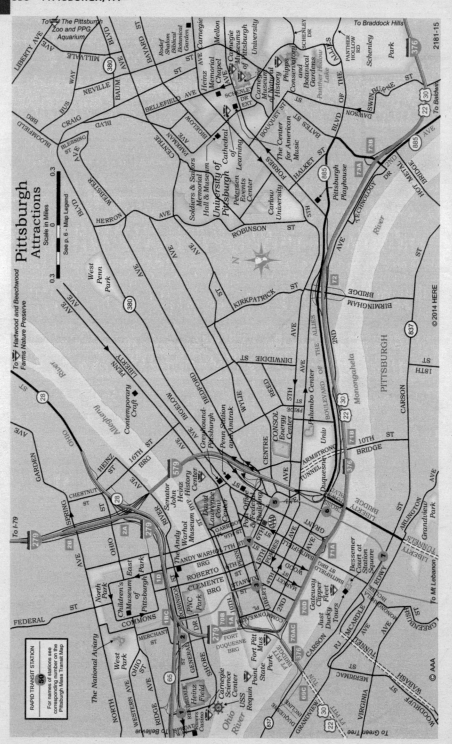

Pittsburgh Attractions

Scale in Miles

0.3 0 0.3

See p. 6 - Map Legend

To Hartwood and Beechwood Farms Nature Preserve

To The Pittsburgh Zoo and PPG Aquarium

To Braddock Hills

2181-15

© 2014 HERE

RAPID TRANSIT STATION 50

For names of stations see corresponding number on the Pittsburgh Mass Transit Map

BESSEMER COURT AT STATION SQUARE, s. end of the Smithfield Street Bridge, consists of a river walk lined with relics of the region's industrial heritage, including a 10-ton Bessemer converter built in 1930. A fountain show choreographed to music shoots water from hundreds of multicolored jets up to 40 feet in the air. **Time:** Allow 30 minutes minimum. **Hours:** Fountain show daily every 20 minutes from 9 a.m.-midnight, late Apr. to Fri. before Thanksgiving. Phone ahead to confirm schedule. **Cost:** Free. **Phone:** (412) 261-2811 or (800) 859-8959. Station Square, 7

CARNEGIE MUSEUMS OF PITTSBURGH, 4400 Forbes Ave. in Oakland, is based in the heart of the university area and is comprised of four cultural institutions. Adjoining contemporary and 19th-century buildings house Carnegie Museum of Art and Carnegie Museum of Natural History; the Andy Warhol Museum and Carnegie Science Center are located in the city's North Side district. Also included at 4400 Forbes Ave. are Carnegie Library and Carnegie Music Hall. **Hours:** Vary per museum. **Cost:** Varies per museum. **Phone:** (412) 622-3131.

The Andy Warhol Museum is at 117 Sandusky St. on the city's North Shore and is part of the Carnegie Museums of Pittsburgh. The facility is devoted to the life and work of one of the most influential artists of the second half of the 20th century. Installation art, extensive archival material and more than 500 canvases present the entire range of the Pittsburgh native's creative endeavors as a graphic artist, fine artist, filmmaker, music producer, stage designer, author and publisher.

Time: Allow 1 hour minimum. **Hours:** Tues.-Sun. 10-5 (also Fri. 5-10). Closed major holidays. Phone ahead to confirm schedule. **Cost:** $20; $10 (ages 3-18 and students with ID); half-price (Fri. 5-10). Phone ahead to confirm rates. **Phone:** (412) 237-8300. North Side, 2

Carnegie Library of Pittsburgh, 4400 Forbes Ave., was constructed in 1895 and is one of the nation's foremost public libraries. It contains more than 5.4 million items, including archives, audio recordings, books, electronic resources, magazines, newspapers and photographs. Cultural, educational and recreational programs also are offered throughout the year.

Guided tours are available by appointment. **Time:** Allow 1 hour minimum. **Hours:** Mon.-Thurs. 10-8, Fri.-Sat. 10-5:30, Sun. noon-5. **Cost:** Free. **Phone:** (412) 622-3114, or (412) 622-3121 for tour reservations.

Carnegie Museum of Art, 4400 Forbes Ave., part of the Carnegie Museums of Pittsburgh, displays American and European paintings, sculpture and decorative arts from the 16th century to the present. The Hall of Architecture's collection of monumental architectural casts is thought to be unique in the United States.

The Heinz Architectural Center surveys past and current architectural expression through the exhibition of drawings, models, photographs and related materials. Free gallery tours are given regularly. **Time:** Allow 3 hours minimum. **Hours:** Mon. and Wed.-Sat. 10-5 (also Thurs. 5-8), Sun. noon-5. Closed major holidays. **Cost:** (includes Carnegie Museum of Natural History) $17.95; $14.95 (ages 65+); $11.95 (ages 3-18 and students with ID). **Phone:** (412) 622-3131.

Carnegie Museum of Natural History, 4400 Forbes Ave., part of the Carnegie Museums of Pittsburgh, is known for its exhibits about earth sciences, life sciences and anthropology. Masterpiece specimens sparkle in Hillman Hall of Minerals and Gems where visitors can explore crystallography and mineral formations.

The Halls of African and North American Wildlife show animals in dioramas depicting realistic habitats. Mummies and other treasures from ancient Egypt are displayed in the Walton Hall of Ancient Egypt. The Alcoa Foundation Hall of American Indians includes exhibits about four societies: Tlingit of the Northwest Coast, Hopi of the Southwest, Lakota of the Plains and Iroquois of the Northeast. Polar World: Wyckoff Hall of Arctic Life traces the cultural history of Inuit peoples and their adaptation to the Arctic. Dinosaurs in Their Time presents fossils in scientifically-accurate poses, the result of current evidence.

Time: Allow 3 hours minimum. **Hours:** Mon. and Wed.-Sat. 10-5 (also Thurs. 5-8), Sun. noon-5. Guided tours are given Sat. at noon and 1, Sun. at 2 and 3. Closed major holidays. **Cost:** (includes Carnegie Museum of Art) $17.95; $14.95 (ages 65+); $11.95 (ages 3-18 and students with ID). **Phone:** (412) 622-3131.

Carnegie Science Center is at 1 Allegheny Ave. on the North Shore next to Heinz Field and is part of the Carnegie Museums of Pittsburgh. There are hundreds of hands-on exhibits covering the science of space flight, geology, physics, biology and energy; there are three live demonstration theaters, a laser show display, a four-story Omnimax theater and an authentic Cold War-era submarine.

The Buhl Planetarium offers high-definition, full-dome planetarium experiences. Model railroads and village scenes depicting turn-of-the-20th-century western Pennsylvania are displayed at the Miniature Railroad and Village.

Billed as the country's largest and most comprehensive robotics exhibition, roboworld features the Robot Hall of Fame as well as hands-on interactive exhibit stations showing how robots sense, think and act. Highmark SportsWorks invites visitors to run, bounce, climb and jump around more than two dozen experiences that explore the connection between science and sports.

Hours: Science Center Mon.-Fri. 10-5, Sat. 10-7. Omnimax movies every hour 6-10. Laser shows Fri.-Sat. at 5, 10, 11 and midnight (also Sat. at 7).

Closed Thanksgiving, Christmas and during Steelers home games with 1 and 4 p.m. kickoff times. **Cost:** (includes USS *Requin*) $18.95; $11.95 (ages 3-12). OMNIMAX $8.50; $6.50 (ages 3-12). **Parking:** $5. **Phone:** (412) 237-3400.

⬛ ⒯ 🅿 Allegheny, 1

USS *Requin* is at the Carnegie Science Center at 1 Allegheny Ave. and is part of the Carnegie Museums of Pittsburgh. The vessel features kiosks with touch screens offering visitors an opportunity to connect with submarine veterans and learn about the history of the *Requin* as well as submarines in general.

Note: Navigating the submarine requires full mobility. A virtual tour in the main lobby is offered for those unable to navigate the vessel. **Hours:** Hours vary; phone ahead. Closed Thanksgiving, Christmas and during Steelers home games with 1 and 4 p.m. kickoff times. Phone ahead to confirm schedule. **Cost:** USS Requin only, $5. Combination ticket with Carnegie Science Center $18.95; $11.95 (ages 3-12). **Phone:** (412) 237-1550. 🅿 Allegheny, 1

▼GEM CATHEDRAL OF LEARNING is on a 14-acre quadrangle at Bigelow Blvd., 5th Ave., Bellefield Ave. and Forbes Ave. The University of Pittsburgh's 42-story truncated Gothic stone tower was once known as the world's tallest schoolhouse.

Encircling the dramatic, Gothic-inspired Commons Room are 29 Nationality Classrooms, which reflect architectural and decorative styles ranging from classical, Byzantine and Romanesque to Renaissance, Tudor, Empire and folk. Based on cultural periods prior to 1787, each room was designed by artists and architects from nations that represent Pittsburgh's ethnic heritages and includes authentic period furnishings.

Visitors may lift the toggle switch as they enter each third floor room to activate a taped narration that describes the various room features. Third floor rooms explore such cultures as Austria, India, Africa, Israel and Japan. A sampling of heritages reflected in the first-floor classrooms, with audio descriptions and in-room written descriptions, includes Italy, Scotland, Greece, France, England and Germany. Additional classrooms are currently in the planning stages. Between mid-November and mid-January, the rooms are decorated in the traditional holiday manner of each nation represented.

Time: Allow 1 hour, 30 minutes minimum. **Hours:** Narrated audio tours of Nationality Rooms Mon.-Sat. 9-2:30, Sun. and holidays 11-2:30, May-Aug.; Sat. 9-2:30, Sun. and holidays 11-2:30, rest of year. Walk-in guided tours are offered 10:30-2:30 the day after Thanksgiving and Dec. 27-31. Closed Jan. 1, Thanksgiving, Christmas Eve, Christmas and day after Christmas. **Cost:** Free. Guided or audio tour $4; $2 (ages 6-18). **Phone:** (412) 624-6000.

THE CENTER FOR AMERICAN MUSIC, in the Stephen Foster Memorial on the University of Pittsburgh campus, is dedicated to American music and to Foster, a native of Pittsburgh and composer of

some of America's best-loved songs. The west wing houses a library and museum. Concerts and theater productions are presented regularly.

Hours: Museum Mon.-Fri. 9-4; closed university holidays. Library by appointment. **Cost:** Stephen Foster Memorial guided tour $5; $2.50 (senior citizens and students). Reservations are required 2 weeks in advance for guided tours. **Phone:** (412) 624-4100 for tour information.

CHILDREN'S MUSEUM OF PITTSBURGH is .5 mi. n. via the 6th St. Bridge at 10 Children's Way (Allegheny Center). Interactive exhibits for children of all ages encourage imaginative play and hands-on learning. Exhibit areas include a multimedia art studio, an attic, a garage, a creative workshop, a nursery, a theater and Waterplay. Traveling exhibits, classes, art displays and performers—including puppeteers and storytellers—also are offered.

Time: Allow 2 hours minimum. **Hours:** Daily 10-5. Closed major holidays. **Cost:** $14; $13 (ages 2-18 and 65+). Phone ahead to confirm rates. **Parking:** $6. **Phone:** (412) 322-5058. ⒯ 🅿 North Side, 2

CONTEMPORARY CRAFT is at 2100 Smallman St. at jct. 21st St. The society's gallery houses changing exhibits that showcase crafts made by local and international artists with contemporary themes. Lectures and studio classes also are offered. **Time:** Allow 1 hour minimum. **Hours:** Mon.-Sat. 10-5 (also Sun. 10-2, mid-Nov. to mid-Dec.). Closed major holidays. **Cost:** Donations. **Phone:** (412) 261-7003.

DUQUESNE INCLINE departs from the lower station at 1197 W. Carson St., .2 mi. w. of the s. end of Fort Pitt Bridge. The ride aboard the restored cable cars, which have been used by commuters since 1877, scales the wooded slopes of Mt. Washington. Visitors can get a panoramic view of Pittsburgh and see a pictorial history of the Steel City in the upper station. The viewing platform offers an opportunity to watch the hoisting equipment.

Hours: Trips depart Mon.-Sat. 5:30 a.m.-12:45 a.m., Sun. and holidays 7 a.m.-12:45 a.m. **Cost:** Round-trip $5; $2.50 (ages 6-11). Phone ahead to confirm rates. **Phone:** (412) 381-1665.

🅿 Allegheny, 1

FRICK ART & HISTORICAL CENTER, 7227 Reynolds St. in Point Breeze, is a 6-acre complex that includes Pittsburgh industrialist Henry Clay Frick's restored 19th-century home, Clayton; the Frick Art Museum; the reconstructed Alden and Harlow 1897 Greenhouse; and a welcome center. The Car and Carriage Museum features carriages and vintage automobiles. The Frick Art Museum contains Helen Clay Frick's art collection and hosts traveling exhibitions. **Note:** The Car and Carriage Museum is closed for a renovation and will not reopen until 2016. Phone ahead for updates. **Hours:** Tues.-Sun. 10-5. Closed Jan. 1, Easter, July 4, Thanksgiving, Christmas Eve and Christmas. **Cost:** Clayton $12;

$10 (senior citizens and students); $6 (ages 0-16). Other sites free. **Phone:** (412) 371-0600. 🍴

Car and Carriage Museum, 7227 Reynolds St. at Frick Art & Historical Center, displays classic automobiles, including Henry Clay Frick's 1914 Rolls Royce Silver Ghost Touring Car. Films detail the history of Pittsburgh's contribution to the automobile industry and aspects of the collection. **Note:** The Car and Carriage Museum will be closed for renovation in 2015 and is scheduled to reopen in early 2016. Phone ahead for updates. **Time:** Allow 1 hour minimum. **Hours:** Tues.-Sun. 10-5. Closed Jan. 1, Easter, July 4, Thanksgiving, Christmas Eve and Christmas. **Cost:** Free. **Phone:** (412) 371-0600.

Clayton, 7227 Reynolds St. at Frick Art & Historical Center, is the former estate of industrialist Henry Clay Frick and his family, who lived here 1883-1905. Visitors are introduced to the restored Victorian home, the only surviving home along Pittsburgh's once famous Millionaire's Row, on 75-minute guided tours. When the family moved into the Italianate-style house, there were 11 rooms; in 1891, architect Frederick J. Osterling built an additional 12 rooms. Most of the artifacts, furnishings and personal mementos of the Frick family are original to the house.

Hours: Guided tours are offered Tues.-Sun. 10-5. Closed Jan. 1, Easter, July 4, Thanksgiving, Christmas Eve and Christmas. **Cost:** $12; $10 (senior citizens and students with ID); $6 (ages 0-16). Reservations are recommended. **Phone:** (412) 371-0600.

The Frick Art Museum, 7227 Reynolds St. at Frick Art & Historical Center, presents Italian, Flemish and French paintings dating from the early Renaissance through the 18th century. Temporary exhibitions, concerts and lectures also are presented. **Time:** Allow 1 hour minimum. **Hours:** Tues.-Sun. 10-5. Closed Jan. 1, Easter, July 4, Thanksgiving, Christmas Eve and Christmas. **Cost:** Free. **Phone:** (412) 371-0600.

HARTWOOD, 200 Hartwood Acres, is a 629-acre estate designed in the style of a 16th-century English country manor. A 1-hour tour includes the Gothic Tudor mansion and its collection of antiques. Wooded trails are on the grounds. Concerts are given in summer.

Tours of the stable complex and hayrides are offered by appointment. **Time:** Allow 1 hour minimum. **Hours:** Guided tours are given Mon.-Sat. on the hour 10-3, Sun. noon-3. Old English Christmas and candlelight tours are sometimes offered late Nov.-Dec. 15; phone for hours. Closed major holidays. **Cost:** $6; $4 (ages 13-17 and 60+); $2 (ages 6-12); $1 (ages 0-5). Old English Christmas and candlelight tour $6. Cash only. Reservations are recommended for all tours. Reservations are required. **Phone:** (412) 767-9200.

HEINZ MEMORIAL CHAPEL is at the University of Pittsburgh, 5th and S. Bellefield aves. behind the Cathedral of Learning. The modern French Gothic interdenominational chapel boasts 73-foot-tall stained-glass windows, reputedly among the world's tallest. Other highlights include the organ, marble altar, carved woodwork, and interior and exterior stone carvings. Programs, concerts and recitals are offered. Thirty-minute guided tours are available by appointment. **Note:** The chapel will be closed Jan. 5-June 1, 2015 for renovation. **Time:** Allow 1 hour minimum. **Hours:** Mon.-Fri. 8:30-5, Sun. noon-5. **Cost:** Free. **Phone:** (412) 624-4157.

MONONGAHELA INCLINE departs from W. Carson St. across from Station Square. Offering a view of the city, the incline travels from the lower station on Carson Street to the terminus on Grandview Avenue, Mount Washington. The sidewalk along Grandview Avenue has circular overhangs providing views of the Golden Triangle. **Time:** Allow 30 minutes minimum. **Hours:** Mon.-Sat. 5:30 a.m.-12:45 a.m., Sun. and holidays 8:45 a.m.-midnight. **Cost:** One-way fare $2.50; $1.25 (ages 6-11); free (ages 0-5 and ages 65+). Phone ahead to confirm rates. **Phone:** (412) 442-2000. 🚇 Station Square, 7

THE NATIONAL AVIARY is at Allegheny Commons West at 700 Arch St. at jct. Ridge Ave. The bird zoo houses more than 500 birds from more than 150 species, many of them threatened or endangered. Visitors can participate in daily feedings, bird shows and interactive encounters. **Time:** Allow 1 hour minimum. **Hours:** Daily 10-5 (also 10-3 on Dec. 31). Closed Thanksgiving, Christmas Eve and

Heinz Memorial Chapel

Christmas. **Cost:** Aviary $14; $13 (ages 60+); $12 (ages 2-12). Aviary and bird show $19; $18 (ages 60+); $17 (ages 2-12). Aviary, bird show and bird feeding $20; $19 (ages 2-12); $18 (ages 2-12). **Phone:** (412) 323-7235. ⓣ 🏛 North Side, 2

**PHIPPS CONSERVATORY AND BO-
TANICAL GARDENS**—see Schenley Park p. 343.

PITTSBURGH CENTER FOR THE ARTS, 6300 5th Ave. in Mellon Park, features a fine arts and digital media school and galleries presenting the work of contemporary regional visual artists. Art exhibitions, classes, workshops, dance performances and lectures are offered for children and adults throughout the year. **Hours:** Tues.-Sat. 10-5 (also Thurs. 5-7), Sun. noon-5. Hours are extended mid-Nov. to late Dec.; phone ahead. Closed Jan. 1, Thanksgiving and Christmas. **Cost:** $5; $4 (ages 62+); $3 (students with ID); free (ages 0-12). **Phone:** (412) 361-0873.

THE PITTSBURGH ZOO & PPG AQUARIUM is off Butler St. w. of the Highland Park Bridge. The 77-acre site is home to 4,000 animals representing 400 species. Animals are featured in naturalistic exhibits such as a tropical forest, Asian forest and an African savanna. The Kids Kingdom offers sea lions and a petting zoo with deer and goats as well as a play area.

The PPG Aquarium features species from habitats such as the Amazon River, Antarctica, the tropics and Pennsylvania streams and rivers. The Water's Edge exhibit offers up close views of polar bears, sea otters and sand tiger sharks; two underwater tunnels afford views of the bears and sharks swimming overhead and around visitors.

A tram provides transportation within the park spring through fall. **Time:** Allow 2 hours minimum. **Hours:** Daily 9:30-6, Memorial Day weekend-Labor Day; 9-5, Apr. 1-Fri. before Memorial Day and day after Labor Day-Dec. 31; 9-4, rest of year. Gates close 1 hour, 30 minutes before closing time, Memorial Day weekend-Labor Day; gates close 1 hour before closing time, rest of year. Closed Jan. 1, Thanksgiving and Christmas. **Cost:** Apr.-Nov. $15; $14 (ages 60+); $13 (ages 2-13). Rest of year $11; $10 (ages 2-13 and 60+). **Phone:** (412) 665-3640. ⓣ

POINT STATE PARK is at the confluence of the Allegheny, Monongahela and Ohio rivers. The 36-acre park occupies land that was extremely valuable in the mid-18th century. In 1754 the French seized the area from the British, beginning events that led to the French and Indian War. The British regained supremacy in 1758 and one year later erected a new fort, which they named Fort Pitt for William Pitt, prime minister of England and friend of the Colonies. The fort served the frontier for the next three decades in the following struggles: Dunmore's War, Pontiac's Uprising, the Revolutionary War and the Indian wars of the late 18th century.

Fort Pitt Block House and Fort Pitt Museum *(see attraction listings)* as well as plaques, markers and other features interpret the history and significance of the area. One of the nation's largest fountains serves as the park's focal point and symbolizes the city's revitalized Golden Triangle. Set at the confluence of the three rivers, the fountain propels plumes of water to heights of 120 feet and is illuminated at night with white lights. It operates daily May through October.

Benches around the lawn areas and stone bleachers overlooking the Allegheny River and the North Side provide seating for the park's many outdoor events. Bicycle and footpaths connect to other recreation trails that traverse the city. **Hours:** Park daily 7 a.m.-11 p.m. **Cost:** Free. **Phone:** (412) 565-2850. 🏛 Gateway Center, 3

Fort Pitt Block House, 601 Commonwealth Pl. in Point State Park, was built in 1764 and is all that remains of Fort Pitt, the last vestige of British rule in western Pennsylvania. A significant amount of original architecture remains, and visitors can view 18th-century construction techniques. Exhibits, period artifacts and digital presentations are included, and educators are on site to assist with interpretation.

The Fort Pitt Society of the Daughters of the American Revolution have owned and preserved the site since 1894. **Hours:** Wed.-Sun. 10:30-4:30, Apr.-Oct.; Fri.-Sun. 10:30-4:30, rest of year. Phone ahead to confirm schedule. **Cost:** Free. **Phone:** (412) 471-1764. 🏛 Gateway Center, 3

Fort Pitt Museum, 101 Commonwealth Pl. in Point State Park, focuses on the early history of western Pennsylvania from the mid-1700s to the early 1800s. Exhibits illustrate the initial struggle between three groups, the French, English and Native Americans, who fought to lay claim to the region. Artifacts, dioramas, audiovisual presentations and computer simulations depict such events as the French and Indian War, Pontiac's Rebellion, the Revolutionary War, the early Native American wars in Ohio and Pittsburgh's early development as the "Gateway to the West." The museum is in a reproduction of one of the original bastions.

Time: Allow 1 hour minimum. **Hours:** Daily 10-5; closed major holidays except Memorial Day, July 4 and Labor Day. **Cost:** $6; $5 (ages 60+); $3 (ages 4-17 and students with ID). **Phone:** (412) 281-9284. 🏛 Gateway Center, 3

RODEF SHALOM BIBLICAL BOTANICAL GARDEN, near Carnegie Mellon University at 4905 5th Ave., displays more than 100 varieties of flora—each with a biblical name or reference. The one-third-acre setting is reminiscent of ancient Israel; a stream flowing through the garden represents the River Jordan. Parking is available behind the synagogue. **Time:** Allow 30 minutes minimum. **Hours:** Sun.-Thurs. 10-2, Sat. noon-1, June 1-Sept. 15

(also Wed. 7-9 p.m., June-Aug.). Guided tours depart on first Wed. of the month at 12:15, June-Sept. **Cost:** Free. **Phone:** (412) 621-6566.

SANDCASTLE, off I-376 exit 5, following signs to exit ramp off Homestead High Level Bridge, is a water park next to the Monongahela River with 15 waterslides, a lazy river, adult and children's pools, a wave pool and boardwalk.

Lockers may be rented for a fee. **Hours:** Open daily 11-6, June 7-Aug. 17; 11-5, Memorial Day and Labor Day weekends. **Cost:** $31.99; $21.99 (under 49 inches tall and ages 55+); free (ages 0-3). Prices may vary; phone ahead. **Parking:** $6. **Phone:** (412) 462-6666. 🍴

SCHENLEY PARK, on Schenley Dr., is one of the city's most popular green spaces. Among its amenities are a playground, swimming pool, 13 tennis courts, all-weather track, bridle trails and an 18-hole disc golf course. During the winter there are opportunities for ice-skating and cross-country skiing. **Hours:** Park daily dawn-dusk. Phone ahead to confirm schedule. **Phone:** (412) 682-7275 for park information. 🍴 🐾 🎡

Phipps Conservatory and Botanical Gardens, in Schenley Park at 1 Schenley Park, was donated to the city in 1893 by industrialist Henry Phipps. The grounds feature outdoor gardens and a 17-room Victorian glasshouse with exotic and native plants as well as several works of glass sculptures by artist Dale Chihuly, including a chandelier in the welcome center. Some of the conservatory's themed rooms are dedicated to ferns, orchids, palms and tropical forest plants. The Stove Room showcases plants found in the deep tropics, and it is transformed into a butterfly forest between spring and fall. A Japanese courtyard garden features bonsai. The Victoria Room recalls the Victorian era while the Broderie Room typifies gardens enjoyed by the French nobility during Louis XIV's reign.

Fountains, streams and waterfalls are incorporated throughout the themed areas, and many displays change seasonally. The Discovery Garden, geared toward children, has been designed with hands-on elements to allow youngsters to learn and play. In summer visitors get to enjoy the Aquatic Garden's water and floating plants in addition to the century-old statue of Neptune, the Roman sea god.

Guided tours are offered by appointment. **Time:** Allow 1 hour minimum. **Hours:** Daily 9:30-5 (also Fri. 5-10). Butterfly exhibit open May-Sept. Phone ahead for tour times. **Cost:** $15; $14 (ages 62+); $11 (ages 2-18). **Phone:** (412) 622-6914. 🍴 🎡

SENATOR JOHN HEINZ HISTORY CENTER, 1212 Smallman St., is an affiliate of the Smithsonian Institution and is the state's largest history museum. It features six floors of permanent and changing exhibits devoted to the history and heritage of western Pennsylvania; a library and

Phipps Conservatory and Botanical Gardens

archives; and the Western Pennsylvania Sports Museum, chronicling the region's professional and amateur sports figures.

The Pittsburgh: A Tradition of Innovation exhibition celebrates 250 years of Pittsburgh inventors and innovations that have changed the world, including the first liver transplant, the Polio vaccine, the nation's first radio station and the Ferris wheel. A large collection of glass along with interactive exhibits recall the days when Pittsburgh was known as America's Glass City. The Heinz 57 exhibit chronicles the history of Pittsburgh's H. J. Heinz Co. Interactive exhibits and games in Discovery Place help children understand how people in different times lived, worked and played.

Hours: Daily 10-5. Library and archives Wed.-Sat. 10-5. Closed Jan. 1, Easter, Thanksgiving and Christmas. **Cost:** $15; $13 (ages 62+); $6 (ages 6-17 and students with ID). **Phone:** (412) 454-6000. 🍴 🅿 Steel Plaza, 5

SOLDIERS & SAILORS MEMORIAL HALL & MUSEUM, 5th Ave. and Bigelow Blvd., honors the memory of veterans of all wars and conflicts. Exhibits feature military history, African-American regiments, Civil War memorabilia, Persian Gulf articles, uniforms, photographs and weapons. Guided tours are available by appointment. **Time:** Allow 1 hour minimum. **Hours:** Mon.-Sat. 10-4. Phone ahead for schedule updates. Closed major holidays. **Cost:** $10; $5 (ages 5-13 and 55+); free (veterans and military families). Reservations are required for films or special tours. **Phone:** (412) 621-4253, ext. 201.

THE WHEEL MILL is .2 miles e. off of Lincoln Hwy. (Fifth Ave.) to 6815 Hamilton Ave. The 80,000-square-foot indoor mountain biking and BMX bike park features ramps, half pipes, chutes and rooms full of paths that simulate trail conditions for riders. Classes, camps and special events are also offered. Both those who want to ride and spectators must sign a waiver before entering the park. Proof of insurance is also required for those 17 and under. **Hours:** M-F 2-10; Sat.-Sun 10-10. **Cost:** April 15-Oct. 14, M-F $12; $10 (8-12); $6 (0-7); Sat.-Sun. $20; $14 (8-12); $10 (0-7). Rest of year, M-F $19.99; $16.99 (8-12); $11.99 (0-7); Sat.-Sun. $25.99; $21.99 (8-12); $16.99 (0-7). Passes also available. **Phone:** (412) 362-3693. 🗙

GAMBLING ESTABLISHMENTS

• **Rivers Casino** is at 777 Casino Dr. **Hours:** Daily 24 hours. **Phone:** (412) 231-7777 or (877) 558-0777.

Sightseeing

Visitors who prefer sightseeing on their own should stop at VisitPittsburgh's Welcome Pittsburgh Information Center and Gift Shop at 120 Fifth Ave. Other branches are at the Pittsburgh International Airport and in Senator John Heinz History Center; phone (800) 359-0758. All centers provide brochures and maps of the Golden Triangle, Strip District, Design Zone (the city's interior design district) and Mount Washington. The Pittsburgh History and Landmarks Foundation, in Station Square, offers self-guiding tours as well as customized bus and walking tours for a range of historical sites in western Pennsylvania; phone (412) 471-5808.

Boat Tours

GATEWAY CLIPPER FLEET departs from 350 W. Station Square Dr. Narrated 1-hour sightseeing cruises on the city's three rivers are offered aboard the 1,000-passenger *Majestic*, the 600-passenger *Empress*, the 310-passenger *Duchess*, the 400-passenger *Princess*, and the 150-passenger *Countess*. Other cruises also are available, including Sunday ice cream socials, specialty entertainment cruises, and lunch and dinner cruises.

Hours: Sightseeing cruise departs Mon.-Fri. at 11, 12:15, 1:30, 2:45 and 4, May 26 to late Aug. (also Fri. Apr. 3-May 22). Passengers should arrive 10 minutes before departure to board. Phone ahead to confirm schedule. **Cost:** Sightseeing cruise $20; $10 (ages 3-12). **Phone:** (412) 355-7980. 🚃 Station Square, 7

JUST DUCKY TOURS departs from Station Square at 125 W. Station Square Dr. Fully narrated 1-hour city tours are offered aboard restored World War II amphibious vehicles, known as DUKWs (pronounced "ducks"), which traverse downtown streets then splash into the rivers. Landside highlights include PPG Tower, Grant Street and the theater district. After launching into one of three rivers near Heinz Field and PNC Park, the water cruise provides an offshore perspective of the Golden Triangle.

Time: Allow 1 hour minimum. **Hours:** Tours depart daily at 10:30, noon, 1:30, 3, 4 and 6 (also 4:30 on Sat.-Sun.), Apr.-Oct.; Sat.-Sun. at 10:30, noon, 1:30, 4:30 and 6 in Nov. **Cost:** $22; $15 (ages 3-12); $5 (ages 0-2). Reservations are recommended. **Phone:** (412) 402-3825. 🚃 Station Square, 7

Bus Tours

The Pittsburgh History and Landmarks Foundation, in Station Square, offers bus and walking tours for a range of historical sites in western Pennsylvania; phone (412) 471-5808.

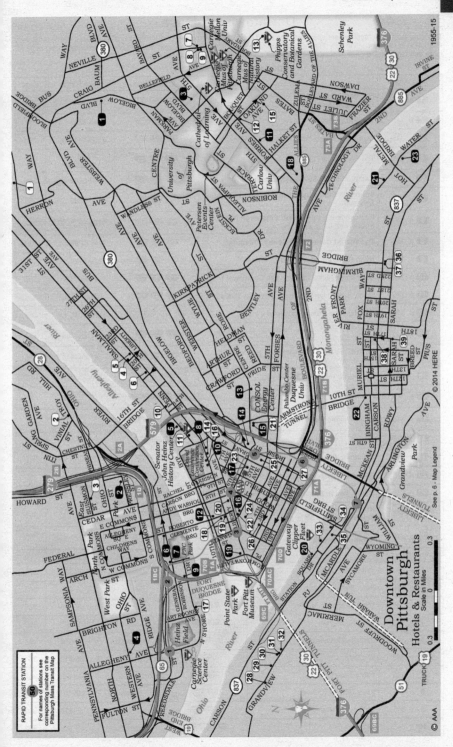

© 2014 HERE

1955-15

Downtown Pittsburgh
Hotels & Restaurants
Scale in Miles

See p. 6 - Map Legend

Downtown Pittsburgh

This index helps you "spot" where approved hotels and restaurants are located on the corresponding detailed maps. Hotel daily rate range is for comparison only. Restaurant price range is a combination of lunch and/or dinner. Turn to the listing page for more detailed rate and price information and consult display ads for special promotions.

DOWNTOWN PITTSBURGH

Map Page	Hotels	Diamond Rated	Rate Range	Page
1 p. 345	**Residence Inn by Marriott Pittsburgh University/Medical Center**	◊◊◊	$153-$263 [SAVE]	359
2 p. 345	**The Priory Hotel**	◊◊◊	$140-$275 [SAVE]	357
3 p. 345	**Wyndham Pittsburgh University Center**	◊◊◊	$159-$441 [SAVE]	360
4 p. 345	The Parador Inn	◊◊◊	Rates not provided	357
5 p. 345	**Hampton Inn & Suites Pittsburgh-Downtown**	◊◊◊	$134-$269 [SAVE]	356
6 p. 345	**SpringHill Suites by Marriott Pittsburgh North Shore** (See ad p. 360.)	◊◊◊	$153-$263 [SAVE]	359
7 p. 345	**Residence Inn by Marriott Pittsburgh North Shore** (See ad p. 358.)	◊◊◊	$160-$275 [SAVE]	358
8 p. 345	**The Westin Convention Center Pittsburgh**	◊◊◊	$149-$299 [SAVE]	360
9 p. 345	**Hyatt Place Pittsburgh-North Shore**	◊◊◊	$129-$499 [SAVE]	357
10 p. 345	Courtyard by Marriott Pittsburgh Downtown	◊◊◊	$188-$309	355
11 p. 345	Hilton Garden Inn Pittsburgh University Place	◊◊◊	$149-$179	356
12 p. 345	**Renaissance Pittsburgh Hotel**	◊◊◊◊	$195-$355 [SAVE]	358
13 p. 345	Cambria Hotel & Suites Pittsburgh at CONSOL Energy Center	◊◊◊	$169-$269	355
14 p. 345	DoubleTree by Hilton Hotel & Suites Pittsburgh Downtown	◊◊◊	$189-$309	355
15 p. 345	**Pittsburgh Marriott City Center**	◊◊◊	$188-$309 [SAVE]	357
16 p. 345	**Fairmont Pittsburgh**	◊◊◊◊	Rates not provided [SAVE]	355
17 p. 345	**Omni William Penn Hotel**	◊◊◊	Rates not provided [SAVE]	357
18 p. 345	Hampton Inn University Center/Pittsburgh	◊◊◊	$149-$179	356
19 p. 345	**Wyndham Grand Pittsburgh Downtown**	◊◊◊	$199-$369 [SAVE]	360
20 p. 345	**Sheraton Pittsburgh Station Square Hotel**	◊◊◊	$159-$425 [SAVE]	359
21 p. 345	**HYATT house Pittsburgh-South Side**	◊◊◊	$139-$279 [SAVE]	357
22 p. 345	**Holiday Inn Express Hotel & Suites Pittsburgh/ South Side** (See ad p. 356.)	◊◊◊	Rates not provided [SAVE]	357
23 p. 345	**SpringHill Suites by Marriott - Pittsburgh Southside Works** (See ad p. 359.)	◊◊◊	$132-$229 [SAVE]	359

Map Page	Restaurants	Diamond Rated	Cuisine	Price Range	Page
1 p. 345	The Church Brew Works	◊◊	American	$8-$30	361
2 p. 345	Penn Brewery Restaurant	◊◊	German	$9-$20	363
3 p. 345	Max's Allegheny Tavern	◊◊	German	$5-$16	362
4 p. 345	Kaya Restaurant	◊◊	Caribbean	$10-$29	362
5 p. 345	Deluca's Restaurant	◊	American	$6-$12	361
6 p. 345	Wholey's	◊	Seafood	$5-$12	364
7 p. 345	Lucca Ristorante	◊◊	Northern Italian	$18-$36	362
8 p. 345	Yuva India Restaurant	◊◊	Indian	$15-$26	364
9 p. 345	Ali Baba Restaurant	◊◊	Middle Eastern	$5-$16	360
10 p. 345	Lidia's	◊◊◊	Northern Italian	$9-$38	362

Map Page	Restaurants (cont'd)	Diamond Rated	Cuisine	Price Range	Page
⑪ p. 345	Eleven	◆◆◆	New American	$9-$45	361
⑫ p. 345	Joe Mama's Italian Deluxe	◆◆	Italian	$7-$15	362
⑬ p. 345	Café Phipps Conservatory and Botanical Gardens	◆	Natural/Organic	$7-$12	360
⑭ p. 345	The Original Fish Market	◆◆◆	Seafood	$10-$50	363
⑮ p. 345	India Garden	◆◆	Northern Indian	$6-$21	361
⑯ p. 345	Sonoma	◆◆◆	International	$9-$39	363
⑰ p. 345	Jerome Betti's Grille 36	◆◆	American	$7-$35	362
⑱ p. 345	Olive or Twist	◆◆	American	$12-$28	362
⑲ p. 345	Six Penn Kitchen	◆◆◆	New American	$9-$30	363
⑳ p. 345	Morton's The Steakhouse	◆◆◆	Steak	$27-$48	362
㉑ p. 345	**The Steelhead Brasserie & Wine Bar**	◆◆◆	American	$10-$32	363
㉒ p. 345	Caffe' Amante	◆◆	Continental	$6-$29	361
㉓ p. 345	The Terrace Room	◆◆◆	Continental	$10-$30	363
㉔ p. 345	NOLA On The Square	◆◆	New Creole	$9-$34	362
㉕ p. 345	The Carlton	◆◆◆	American	$10-$32	361
㉖ p. 345	Ruth's Chris Steak House	◆◆◆	Steak	$10-$60	363
㉗ p. 345	Chinatown Inn	◆◆	Chinese	$8-$20	361
㉘ p. 345	Monterey Bay Fish Grotto	◆◆◆	Seafood	$10-$39	362
㉙ p. 345	Isabela on Grandview	◆◆◆	New American	$12-$75	362
㉚ p. 345	Grandview Saloon	◆◆	American	$14-$49	361
㉛ p. 345	Tin Angel	◆◆◆	Continental	$39-$64	363
㉜ p. 345	Le Mont Restaurant	◆◆◆	Continental	$26-$48	362
㉝ p. 345	Hard Rock Cafe	◆◆	American	$13-$24 SAVE	361
㉞ p. 345	Grand Concourse Restaurant/Gandy Dancer	◆◆◆	American	$9-$42	361
㉟ p. 345	Kiku's of Japan	◆◆	Sushi	$14-$35	362
㊱ p. 345	Mallorca Restaurant	◆◆◆	Spanish	$8-$42	362
㊲ p. 345	Ibiza Tapas & Wine Bar	◆◆◆	Spanish	$5-$44	361
㊳ p. 345	Nakama Japanese Steakhouse and Sushi Bar	◆◆	Japanese	$9-$70	362
㊴ p. 345	Dish Osteria and Bar	◆◆	Italian	$15-$32	361

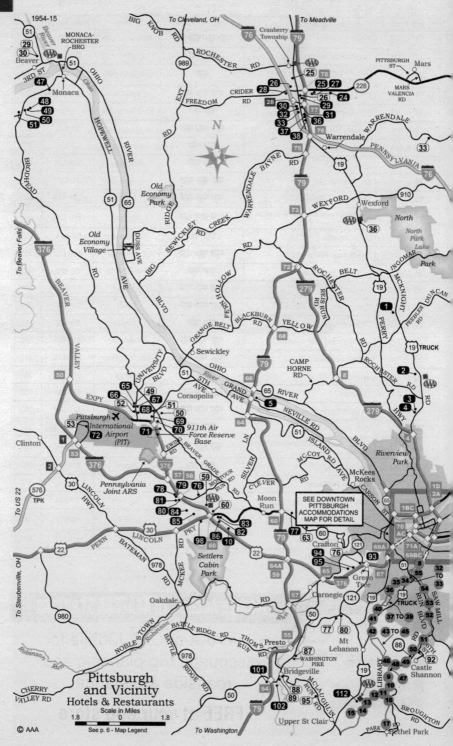

Pittsburgh
and Vicinity
Hotels & Restaurants

Scale in Miles

© AAA

See p. 6 - Map Legend

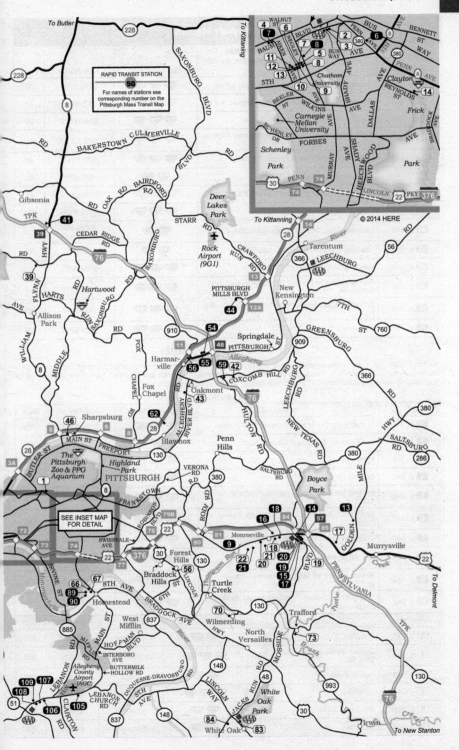

© 2014 HERE

✈ Airport Hotels

Map Page	PITTSBURGH INTERNATIONAL (Maximum driving distance from airport: 8.9 mi)	Diamond Rated	Rate Range	Page
70 p. 348	Courtyard by Marriott Pittsburgh Airport, 8.8 mi	▽▽▽	$146-$240	88
65 p. 348	DoubleTree by Hilton Pittsburgh Airport, 7.4 mi	▽▽▽	$159-$299 SAVE	88
66 p. 348	Hampton Inn Pittsburgh Airport, 7.4 mi	▽▽▽	$149-$179	88
72 p. 348	Hyatt Regency Pittsburgh International Airport, 0.7 mi	▽▽▽	$99-$359 SAVE	89
67 p. 348	La Quinta Inn Pittsburgh Airport, 7.3 mi	▽▽▽	$92-$194	89
68 p. 348	Pittsburgh Airport Super 8, 7.0 mi	▽▽	$60-$70	89
69 p. 348	Sheraton Pittsburgh Airport Hotel, 8.9 mi	▽▽▽	$99-$289 SAVE	89
79 p. 348	Comfort Suites, 7.3 mi	▽▽▽	$109-$199	204
84 p. 348	Extended Stay America Pittsburgh Airport, 8.5 mi	▽▽	Rates not provided	204
81 p. 348	MainStay Suites Pittsburgh Airport, 7.5 mi	▽▽	$90-$120	205
78 p. 348	Pittsburgh Airport Marriott, 7.3 mi	▽▽▽	$188-$309	205
80 p. 348	Residence Inn by Marriott Pittsburgh Airport Coraopolis, 7.7 mi	▽▽▽	$133-$219	205
85 p. 348	SpringHill Suites by Marriott-Pittsburgh Airport, 8.5 mi	▽▽▽	$132-$217	205
76 p. 348	Homewood Suites, 8.7 mi	▽▽▽	$129-$219	205

Pittsburgh and Vicinity

This index helps you "spot" where approved hotels and restaurants are located on the corresponding detailed maps. Hotel daily rate range is for comparison only. Restaurant price range is a combination of lunch and/or dinner. Turn to the listing page for more detailed rate and price information and consult display ads for special promotions.

PITTSBURGH

Map Page	Hotels	Diamond Rated	Rate Range	Page
1 p. 348	Home2 Suites by Hilton Pittsburgh/McCandless	▽▽▽	$129-$169	366
2 p. 348	La Quinta Inn & Suites Pittsburgh North	▽▽▽	$102-$215	366
3 p. 348	Hampton Inn	▽▽▽	$119-$184 SAVE	365
4 p. 348	Comfort Inn	▽▽▽	$103-$125	364
5 p. 348	Fairfield Inn & Suites by Marriott Pittsburgh Neville Island	▽▽▽	$104-$171	365
6 p. 348	SpringHill Suites by Marriott Pittsburgh Bakery Square	▽▽▽	$139-$229	368
7 p. 348	Courtyard by Marriott Pittsburgh/Shadyside	▽▽▽	$153-$252	365
8 p. 348	The Inn on Negley	▽▽▽	Rates not provided	366
9 p. 348	Residence Inn by Marriott-Wilkins (See ad p. 367.)	▽▽▽	$104-$171 SAVE	366
10 p. 348	Courtyard by Marriott Pittsburgh Airport Settlers Ridge	▽▽▽	$139-$229	365

Map Page	Restaurants	Diamond Rated	Cuisine	Price Range	Page
1 p. 348	Tessaro's	▽▽	American	$10-$26	369
2 p. 348	Casbah Mediterranean Kitchen & Wine Bar	▽▽▽	Mediterranean	$8-$30	368
3 p. 348	Buffalo Blues	▽▽	Wings	$7-$21	368
4 p. 348	Cafe Sam	▽▽▽	International	$6-$25	368
5 p. 348	The Elbow Room	▽▽	American	$5-$20	368
6 p. 348	La Feria	▽▽	Peruvian	$4-$14	369

Map Page	Restaurants (cont'd)	Diamond Rated	Cuisine	Price Range	Page
⑦ p. 348	Pamela's	◆	American	$5-$8	369
⑧ p. 348	Thai Place	◆◆	Thai	$9-$22	369
⑨ p. 348	Shady Grove	◆◆	American	$10-$18	369
⑩ p. 348	China Palace	◆◆	Chinese	$6-$22	368
⑪ p. 348	Girasole	◆◆◆	Northern Italian	$10-$22	369
⑫ p. 348	Cappy's Cafe	◆	American	$6-$10	368
⑬ p. 348	Sushi Too	◆◆	Japanese	$7-$24	369
⑭ p. 348	The Cafe at The Frick Art & Historical Center	◆◆	New American	$8-$15	368

MONROEVILLE

Map Page	Hotels	Diamond Rated	Rate Range	Page
⑬ p. 348	Super 8 Pittsburgh/Monroeville	◆◆	$80-$175	203
⑭ p. 348	Hampton Inn Monroeville/Pittsburgh	◆◆◆	$109-$159	202
⑮ p. 348	**Holiday Inn Pittsburgh-Monroeville**	◆◆◆	$95-$159 SAVE	202
⑯ p. 348	Extended Stay America-Pittsburgh-Monroeville	◆◆	Rates not provided	202
⑰ p. 348	**SpringHill Suites by Marriott Pittsburgh Monroeville** *(See ad p. 203.)*	◆◆◆	$97-$160 SAVE	203
⑱ p. 348	**Courtyard by Marriott Pittsburgh Monroeville** *(See ad p. 202.)*	◆◆◆	$104-$171 SAVE	202
⑲ p. 348	Comfort Suites Monroeville	◆◆◆	$100-$144	202
⑳ p. 348	**Red Roof Inn Pittsburgh East - Monroeville**	◆◆	Rates not provided SAVE	203
㉑ p. 348	**DoubleTree by Hilton Hotel Pittsburgh - Monroeville Convention Center**	◆◆◆	$99-$169 SAVE	202

Map Page	Restaurants	Diamond Rated	Cuisine	Price Range	Page
⑰ p. 348	Luccia Shea's	◆◆	American	$7-$36	203
⑱ p. 348	Rudy's Submarines	◆	American	$4-$10	204
⑲ p. 348	Gateway Grill	◆◆	American	$5-$20	203
⑳ p. 348	Taipei-Tokyo	◆◆	Chinese	$5-$22	204
㉑ p. 348	Shogun	◆◆	Japanese	$8-$40	204
㉒ p. 348	Monterey Bay Fish Grotto	◆◆◆	Seafood	$8-$39	204

CRANBERRY TOWNSHIP

Map Page	Hotels	Diamond Rated	Rate Range	Page
㉔ p. 348	Hilton Garden Inn Pittsburgh/ Cranberry	◆◆◆	$149-$199	91
㉕ p. 348	Pittsburgh Marriott North	◆◆◆	$154-$253	92
㉖ p. 348	Hampton Inn Cranberry	◆◆◆	$99-$189	91
㉗ p. 348	Courtyard by Marriott Pittsburgh North/Cranberry Woods	◆◆◆	$146-$240	91
㉘ p. 348	Residence Inn by Marriott Pittsburgh Cranberry Township	◆◆◆	$167-$275	92
㉙ p. 348	**Fairfield Inn by Marriott Pittsburgh Cranberry Township**	◆◆◆	$118-$194 SAVE	91
㉚ p. 348	**Hyatt Place Pittsburgh/Cranberry** *(See ad p. 91.)*	◆◆◆	$84-$199 SAVE	91
㉛ p. 348	Candlewood Suites	◆◆◆	$149-$189	90
㉜ p. 348	**Red Roof Inn Pittsburgh North Cranberry Township**	◆◆	Rates not provided SAVE	92
㉝ p. 348	Holiday Inn Express Cranberry Township	◆◆◆	Rates not provided	91

Map Page	Restaurants	Diamond Rated	Cuisine	Price Range	Page
㉕ p. 348	Monte Cello's Cranberry	◆◆	American	$5-$18	92
㉖ p. 348	Flavor of India	◆◆	Indian	$11-$15	92

MARS

Map Page	Hotels	Diamond Rated	Rate Range	Page
㊱ p. 348	Super 8-Cranberry	◆◆	$90-$175	194
㊲ p. 348	Comfort Inn Cranberry Township	◆◆	$99-$159	193
㊳ p. 348	**DoubleTree by Hilton Pittsburgh Cranberry**	◆◆◆	Rates not provided [SAVE]	194

GIBSONIA

Map Page	Hotel	Diamond Rated	Rate Range	Page
㊶ p. 348	Quality Inn & Suites Pittsburgh-Gibsonia	◆◆	$90-$200	129

Map Page	Restaurant	Diamond Rated	Cuisine	Price Range	Page
㉝ p. 348	The Pines Tavern	◆◆◆	Traditional American	$10-$36	129

TARENTUM

Map Page	Hotel	Diamond Rated	Rate Range	Page
㊸ p. 348	**SpringHill Suites by Marriott Pittsburgh Mills** (See ad p. 368.)	◆◆◆	$111-$194 [SAVE]	403

MONACA

Map Page	Hotels	Diamond Rated	Rate Range	Page
㊼ p. 348	Fairfield Inn & Suites by Marriott	◆◆◆	$132-$169	201
㊽ p. 348	Comfort Suites	◆◆◆	$109-$155	201
㊾ p. 348	The Inn	◆◆	Rates not provided	201
㊿ p. 348	Holiday Inn Express Hotel & Suites-Center Township	◆◆◆	Rates not provided	201
51 p. 348	Hampton Inn Beaver Valley/Pittsburgh	◆◆◆	$134-$164	201

HARMARVILLE

Map Page	Hotels	Diamond Rated	Rate Range	Page
54 p. 348	**Holiday Inn Express** (See ad p. 367.)	◆◆	Rates not provided [SAVE]	134
55 p. 348	Super 8	◆◆	$70-$110	134
56 p. 348	Valley Motel	◆	Rates not provided	134

OAKMONT

Map Page	Hotel	Diamond Rated	Rate Range	Page
59 p. 348	Doone's Inn at Oakmont	◆◆◆	Rates not provided	216

Map Page	Restaurants	Diamond Rated	Cuisine	Price Range	Page
㊷ p. 348	Somma Pizza & Sports Bar	◆	American	$5-$18	216
㊸ p. 348	Chelsea Grille	◆◆	American	$7-$30	216

BLAWNOX

Map Page	Hotel	Diamond Rated	Rate Range	Page
62 p. 348	**Comfort Inn & Suites** (See ad p. 365.)	◆◆◆	$99-$249 [SAVE]	68

CORAOPOLIS

Map Page	Hotels	Diamond Rated	Rate Range	Page
65 p. 348	**DoubleTree by Hilton Pittsburgh Airport**	◆◆◆	$159-$299 [SAVE]	88
66 p. 348	Hampton Inn Pittsburgh Airport	◆◆◆	$149-$179	88
67 p. 348	La Quinta Inn Pittsburgh Airport	◆◆◆	$92-$194	89

CORAOPOLIS (cont'd)

Map Page	Hotels (cont'd)	Diamond Rated	Rate Range	Page
68 p. 348	Pittsburgh Airport Super 8	♦♦	$60-$70	89
69 p. 348	**Sheraton Pittsburgh Airport Hotel** (See ad p. 89.)	♦♦♦	$99-$289 [SAVE]	89
70 p. 348	Courtyard by Marriott Pittsburgh Airport	♦♦♦	$146-$240	88
71 p. 348	**Embassy Suites-Pittsburgh International Airport**	♦♦♦	$139-$279 [SAVE]	88
72 p. 348	**Hyatt Regency Pittsburgh International Airport**	♦♦♦	$99-$359 [SAVE]	89

Map Page	Restaurants	Diamond Rated	Cuisine	Price Range	Page
49 p. 348	Jacksons Restaurant-Rotisserie-Bar	♦♦♦	American	$10-$40	90
50 p. 348	Hyeholde Restaurant	♦♦♦	Continental	$25-$42	89
51 p. 348	Armstrong's Restaurant	♦♦	American	$6-$20	89
52 p. 348	Wings, Suds & Spuds	♦	American	$5-$12	90
53 p. 348	Olive Press	♦♦♦	Mediterranean	$8-$35	90

MOON RUN

Map Page	Hotels	Diamond Rated	Rate Range	Page
76 p. 348	Homewood Suites	♦♦♦	$129-$219	205
77 p. 348	Pittsburgh Comfort Inn	♦♦	$109-$299	205
78 p. 348	Pittsburgh Airport Marriott	♦♦♦	$188-$309	205
79 p. 348	Comfort Suites	♦♦♦	$109-$199	204
80 p. 348	Residence Inn by Marriott Pittsburgh Airport Coraopolis	♦♦♦	$133-$219	205
81 p. 348	MainStay Suites Pittsburgh Airport	♦♦	$90-$120	205
82 p. 348	**Red Roof Inn Plus Pittsburgh South - Airport**	♦♦	Rates not provided [SAVE]	205
83 p. 348	**Hyatt Place Pittsburgh Airport** (See ad p. 364.)	♦♦♦	$89-$209 [SAVE]	205
84 p. 348	Extended Stay America Pittsburgh Airport	♦♦	Rates not provided	204
85 p. 348	SpringHill Suites by Marriott-Pittsburgh Airport	♦♦♦	$132-$217	205
86 p. 348	**Holiday Inn Express & Suites Pittsburgh Airport**	♦♦♦	$109-$229 [SAVE]	204

Map Page	Restaurants	Diamond Rated	Cuisine	Price Range	Page
59 p. 348	Ya Fei	♦♦	Chinese	$7-$19	206
60 p. 348	Ditka's Restaurant	♦♦♦	Steak	$10-$60	205

HOMESTEAD

Map Page	Hotels	Diamond Rated	Rate Range	Page
89 p. 348	**Hampton Inn & Suites Pittsburgh Waterfront**	♦♦♦	$149-$219 [SAVE]	157
90 p. 348	Courtyard by Marriott Pittsburgh-Waterfront	♦♦♦	$146-$240	157

Map Page	Restaurants	Diamond Rated	Cuisine	Price Range	Page
66 p. 348	Mitchell's Fish Market	♦♦♦	Seafood	$17-$30	157
67 p. 348	P.F. Chang's China Bistro	♦♦♦	Chinese	$10-$25	157

GREEN TREE

Map Page	Hotels	Diamond Rated	Rate Range	Page
93 p. 348	Holiday Inn Express Hotel & Suites Pittsburgh West-Greentree	♦♦♦	$109-$399	131
94 p. 348	Hampton Inn Pittsburgh Green Tree	♦♦♦	$109-$199	131
95 p. 348	**DoubleTree by Hilton Pittsburgh-Green Tree**	♦♦♦	$189-$289 [SAVE]	131

Map Page	Restaurants	Diamond Rated	Cuisine	Price Range	Page
(76) p. 348	Vincent's of Green Tree	▽▽	Italian	$7-$19	132
(77) p. 348	Tamarind Savoring India	▽▽	Indian	$7-$15	132

OAKDALE

Map Page	Hotel	Diamond Rated	Rate Range	Page
(98) p. 348	Quality Inn Pittsburgh Airport	▽▽	$95-$199	216

BRIDGEVILLE

Map Page	Hotels	Diamond Rated	Rate Range	Page
(101) p. 348	Hampton Inn	▽▽▽	$139-$189	72
(102) p. 348	**Holiday Inn Express** (See ad p. 366.)	▽▽▽	Rates not provided (SAVE)	72

Map Page	Restaurants	Diamond Rated	Cuisine	Price Range	Page
(87) p. 348	Peters Place	▽▽	American	$8-$42	72
(88) p. 348	Tambellini Bridgeville Restaurant	▽▽	Italian	$6-$25	72
(89) p. 348	LaBella Bean Coffee House & Eatery	▽	American	$3-$10	72

WEST MIFFLIN

Map Page	Hotels	Diamond Rated	Rate Range	Page
(105) p. 348	Holiday Inn Express Hotel & Suites	▽▽▽	Rates not provided	420
(106) p. 348	**SpringHill Suites by Marriott-West Mifflin** (See ad p. 420.)	▽▽▽	$104-$171 (SAVE)	420
(107) p. 348	Hampton Inn -West Mifflin	▽▽▽	$109-$179	420
(108) p. 348	Comfort Inn-West Mifflin	▽▽	$94-$159	420
(109) p. 348	Extended Stay America-Pittsburgh-West Mifflin	▽▽	Rates not provided	420

BETHEL PARK

Map Page	Hotel	Diamond Rated	Rate Range	Page
(112) p. 348	Crowne Plaza Pittsburgh South	▽▽▽	$119-$219	62

BEAVER

Map Page	Restaurants	Diamond Rated	Cuisine	Price Range	Page
(29) p. 348	Bert's Wooden Indian	▽▽	American	$4-$15	57
(30) p. 348	The Wooden Angel	▽▽	American	$12-$40	57

WEXFORD

Map Page	Restaurant	Diamond Rated	Cuisine	Price Range	Page
(36) p. 348	Miyako Japanese Steak & Seafood	▽▽	Japanese	$8-$33	421

ALLISON PARK

Map Page	Restaurant	Diamond Rated	Cuisine	Price Range	Page
(39) p. 348	The Tuscan Inn	▽▽	Northern Italian	$14-$29	53

SHARPSBURG

Map Page	Restaurant	Diamond Rated	Cuisine	Price Range	Page
(46) p. 348	Gran Canal Caffe	▽▽	Italian	$14-$25	388

FOREST HILLS

Map Page	Restaurant	Diamond Rated	Cuisine	Price Range	Page
(56) p. 348	Drews Family Restaurant	▽▽	American	$4-$16	112

CRAFTON

Map Page	Restaurant	Diamond Rated	Cuisine	Price Range	Page
(63) p. 348	Sapporo Japanese Steakhouse	▽▽	Japanese	$7-$38	90

WILMERDING

Map Page	Restaurant	Diamond Rated	Cuisine	Price Range	Page
70 p. 348	The Station Brake Cafe	◈◈	American	$13-$26	427

TRAFFORD

Map Page	Restaurant	Diamond Rated	Cuisine	Price Range	Page
73 p. 348	Parente's Ristorante	◈◈	Italian	$7-$24	404

MOUNT LEBANON

Map Page	Restaurant	Diamond Rated	Cuisine	Price Range	Page
80 p. 348	DeBlasio's	◈◈	Italian	$6-$30	207

WHITE OAK

Map Page	Restaurants	Diamond Rated	Cuisine	Price Range	Page
83 p. 348	China House	◈◈	Chinese	$3-$15	422
84 p. 348	Luciano's Italian Brick Oven	◈◈	Italian	$7-$17	422

CASTLE SHANNON

Map Page	Restaurant	Diamond Rated	Cuisine	Price Range	Page
92 p. 348	Calabria's	◈◈	Italian	$7-$27	79

UPPER ST. CLAIR

Map Page	Restaurant	Diamond Rated	Cuisine	Price Range	Page
95 p. 348	Piccolina's	◈◈◈	Northern Italian	$7-$33	408

DOWNTOWN PITTSBURGH

- Restaurants p. 360
- Hotels & Restaurants map & index p. 345

CAMBRIA HOTEL & SUITES PITTSBURGH AT CONSOL ENERGY CENTER (412)381-6687 **13**

◈◈◈ Hotel $169-$269 **Address:** 1320 Centre Ave 15219 **Location:** I-579 exit 7th Ave, s on Bigelow Ave, then just se. Next to CONSOL Hockey Stadium. 🅟 Steel Plaza, 5. **Facility:** 142 units. 7 stories, interior corridors. **Parking:** on-site (fee). **Pool(s):** heated indoor. **Activities:** hot tub, exercise room. **Guest Services:** valet and coin laundry, area transportation.

COURTYARD BY MARRIOTT PITTSBURGH DOWNTOWN (412)434-5551 **10**

◈◈◈ Hotel $188-$309 **Address:** 945 Penn Ave 15222 **Location:** I-279 exit 70B (Fort Dusquesne Blvd), 0.5 mi ne; center. 🅟 Wood Street, 4. **Facility:** 182 units. 9 stories, interior corridors. **Parking:** on-site (fee) and valet. **Activities:** exercise room. **Guest Services:** valet and coin laundry, area transportation.

AAA Benefit:
Members save 5% or more!

DOUBLETREE BY HILTON HOTEL & SUITES PITTSBURGH DOWNTOWN (412)281-5800 **14**

◈◈◈ Hotel $189-$309 **Address:** One Bigelow Square 15219 **Location:** Jct Bigelow Square and 6th St; just n of Grant St. 🅟 Steel Plaza, 5. **Facility:** 337 units, some two and three bedrooms. 20 stories, interior corridors. **Parking:** on-site (fee) and valet. **Terms:** off-site registration, 1-7 night minimum stay, cancellation fee imposed. **Amenities:** video games. *Some:* safes. **Pool(s):** heated indoor. **Activities:** exercise room. **Guest Services:** valet laundry.

AAA Benefit:
Members save 5% or more!

FAIRMONT PITTSBURGH 412/773-8800 **16**

◈◈◈◈ Contemporary Hotel
Rates not provided

Address: 510 Market St 15222 **Location:** Between Market St and 5th Ave; in cultural district. 🅟 Gateway Center, 3. **Facility:** This eco-friendly property adds a new realm of high-end hospitality. Upscale amenities include a water filter station and a 24/7 fitness center. 185 units. 12 stories, interior corridors. **Parking:** on-site (fee) and valet. **Amenities:** safes. **Dining:** entertainment. **Activities:** sauna, steamroom, spa. **Guest Services:** valet laundry.

(See map & index p. 345.)

HAMPTON INN & SUITES PITTSBURGH-DOWNTOWN
(412)288-4350

Hotel
$134-$269

AAA Benefit: Members save 5% or more!

Address: 1247 Smallman St 15222 **Location:** Jct 11th and Smallman sts, just e. Steel Plaza, 5. **Facility:** 143 units. 8 stories, interior corridors. **Terms:** check-in 4 pm, 1-7 night minimum stay, cancellation fee imposed. **Pool(s):** heated indoor. **Activities:** hot tub, exercise room. **Guest Services:** valet and coin laundry. **Featured Amenity:** breakfast buffet.

HAMPTON INN UNIVERSITY CENTER/PITTSBURGH
(412)681-1000

Hotel $149-$179 **Address:** 3315 Hamlet St 15213 **Location:** I-376 exit 72A, 0.6 mi e, then e. **Facility:** 132 units. 8 stories, interior corridors. **Parking:** on-site (fee), winter plug-ins.

AAA Benefit: Members save 5% or more!

Terms: 1-7 night minimum stay, cancellation fee imposed. **Activities:** limited exercise equipment. **Guest Services:** complimentary laundry, area transportation.

HILTON GARDEN INN PITTSBURGH UNIVERSITY PLACE
(412)683-2040

Hotel $149-$179 **Address:** 3454 Forbes Ave 15213 **Location:** Jct Forbes Ave and McKee Pl. **Facility:** 202 units. 9 stories, interior corridors. **Parking:** on-site (fee) and valet. **Terms:** 1-7 night minimum stay, cancellation fee imposed. **Activities:** exercise room. **Guest Services:** valet and coin laundry, area transportation.

Take Your **Imagination** to New Destinations

Use AAA Travel Guides online to explore the possibilities.

Go to AAA.com/travelguide today.

▼ See AAA listing p. 357 ▼

(See map & index p. 345.)

HOLIDAY INN EXPRESS HOTEL & SUITES PITTSBURGH/SOUTH SIDE 412/488-1130 22

▼▼▼
Hotel
Rates not provided

Address: 20 S 10th St 15203 **Location:** At 10th St Bridge; south side. 🅿 First Avenue, 6. **Facility:** 125 units. 6 stories, interior corridors. **Parking:** on-site (fee). **Terms:** check-in 4 pm. **Pool(s):** heated indoor. **Activities:** exercise room. **Guest Services:** valet and coin laundry, area transportation. **Featured Amenity: breakfast buffet.** *(See ad p. 356.)*

HYATT HOUSE PITTSBURGH-SOUTH SIDE
(412)390-2477 21

▼▼▼
Hotel
$139-$279

H HYATT house™
AAA Benefit: Members save 10%!

Address: 2795 S Water St 15203 **Location:** I-376 exit 72A, right on 2nd Ave, then just s. **Facility:** 136 units, some two bedrooms. 6 stories, interior corridors. *Bath:* shower only. **Pool(s):** heated indoor. **Activities:** exercise room. **Guest Services:** valet and coin laundry, area transportation. **Featured Amenity: breakfast buffet.**

HYATT PLACE PITTSBURGH-NORTH SHORE
(412)321-3000 9

▼▼▼
Hotel
$129-$499

⊞ HYATT PLACE™
AAA Benefit: Members save 10%!

Address: 260 N Shore Dr 15212 **Location:** I-279/376 exit 70B (Fort Duquesne Blvd), exit 6C, stay right, n on 6th St/Roberto Clemente Bridge (which becomes Federal St), w on W General Robinson St, s on Mazeroski Way, then just w. Across from PNC Park. 🅿 North Side, 2. **Facility:** 178 units. 7 stories, interior corridors. **Parking:** on-site (fee). **Terms:** cancellation fee imposed. **Pool(s):** heated indoor. **Activities:** exercise room. **Guest Services:** valet laundry, area transportation. **Featured Amenity: breakfast buffet.**

OMNI WILLIAM PENN HOTEL 412/281-7100 17

▼▼▼ ▼▼▼
Classic Historic Hotel
Rates not provided

Address: 530 William Penn Pl 15219 **Location:** Jct 6th St and William Penn Pl. 🅿 Steel Plaza, 5. **Facility:** This service-oriented hotel in the heart of bustling Pittsburgh has an ambiance of understated elegance. The hotel employs a discreetly attentive staff and offers elegantly appointed rooms. 596 units. 17 stories, interior corridors. **Parking:** on-site (fee) and valet. **Amenities:** video games, safes. **Dining:** 3 restaurants, also, The Terrace Room, see separate listing. **Activities:** exercise room, massage. **Guest Services:** valet laundry.

THE PARADOR INN 412/231-4800 4

▼▼▼ **Bed & Breakfast. Rates not provided. Address:** 939 Western Ave 15233 **Location:** At North Shore. 🅿 Allegheny, 1. **Facility:** This Caribbean-theme B&B on Pittsburgh's Northern Shore has gorgeous antique furnishings that are reminiscent of the islands; service is friendly. 9 units. 3 stories (no elevator), interior corridors. **Guest Services:** complimentary laundry.

PITTSBURGH MARRIOTT CITY CENTER
(412)471-4000 15

▼▼▼
Hotel
$188-$309

Ⅿ MARRIOTT
AAA Benefit: Members save 5% or more!

Address: 112 Washington Pl 15219 **Location:** Center Ave; just e of Crosstown Blvd. Opposite the Civic Arena. 🅿 Steel Plaza, 5. **Facility:** 402 units. 12 stories, interior corridors. **Parking:** on-site (fee) and valet. **Dining:** The Steelhead Brasserie & Wine Bar, see separate listing. **Pool(s):** heated indoor. **Activities:** sauna, exercise room. **Guest Services:** valet and coin laundry, area transportation.

THE PRIORY HOTEL (412)231-3338 2

▼▼▼
Historic Country Inn
$140-$275

Address: 614 Pressley St 15212 **Location:** I-376 exit 70B, 3 blks w on E Ohio St to Cedar Ave, then 3 blks s. 🅿 North Side, 2. **Facility:** This historic inn, which was built in 1888 to house Benedictine priests traveling through Pittsburgh, has been restored to 19th-century elegance and is gracefully appointed. 42 units. 4 stories, interior corridors. **Terms:** cancellation fee imposed. **Amenities:** safes. **Guest Services:** valet laundry, area transportation. **Featured Amenity: continental breakfast.**

(See map & index p. 345.)

RENAISSANCE PITTSBURGH HOTEL

(412)562-1200

Historic Hotel
$195-$355

RENAISSANCE HOTELS

AAA Benefit: Members save 5% or more!

Address: 107 6th St 15222 **Location:** I-376 E exit 70B (Liberty Ave), just e, then just n. Gateway Center, 3. **Facility:** This historic hotel is located in the heart of the theater district. The lobby—with a unique 1906 rotunda, white marble walls and a mosaic ceiling—is magnificent. 300 units. 14 stories, interior corridors. **Parking:** on-site (fee) and valet. **Terms:** check-in 4 pm. **Amenities:** safes. **Activities:** exercise room. **Guest Services:** valet laundry.

RESIDENCE INN BY MARRIOTT PITTSBURGH NORTH SHORE

(412)321-2099

Extended Stay Hotel
$160-$275

Residence Inn Marriott

AAA Benefit: Members save 5% or more!

Address: 574 W General Robinson St 15212 **Location:** I-279 exit 70B (Fort Duquesne Blvd), left on 6th St, corner of Federal and General Robinson sts; across from PNC Park. North Side, 2. **Facility:** 180 kitchen units, some two bedrooms. 10 stories, interior corridors. **Parking:** on-site (fee). **Pool(s):** heated indoor. **Activities:** game room, exercise room. **Guest Services:** area transportation. **Featured Amenity:** breakfast buffet. (See ad this page.)

▼ See AAA listing this page ▼

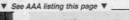

Residence Inn North Shore

- Conveniently located across the street from PNC Park and a few blocks from Heinz Field
- 180 urban designed suites with a full kitchen and areas for sleeping, working, eating and relaxing
- Complimentary breakfast buffet
- Indoor stationary lap pool & fitness room
- Complimentary Area Shuttle
- Entertainment Area
- Exterior Patio and fire pit
- Pet friendly

Residence Inn® **Marriott**

Residence Inn Pittsburgh North Shore
574 West General Robinson Street
Pittsburgh, PA 15212
412-321-2099 • www.marriott.com
DISCOUNTS »»REWARDS

(See map & index p. 345.)

RESIDENCE INN BY MARRIOTT PITTSBURGH UNIVERSITY/MEDICAL CENTER   (412)621-2200 ❶

Extended Stay Hotel
$153-$263

Residence Inn Marriott

AAA Benefit: Members save 5% or more!

Address: 3896 Bigelow Blvd 15213 **Location:** On SR 380. **Facility:** 174 kitchen units, some two bedrooms. 9 stories, interior corridors. **Parking:** on-site (fee). **Amenities:** safes. **Pool(s):** heated indoor. **Activities:** hot tub, exercise room. **Guest Services:** valet and coin laundry, area transportation. **Featured Amenity:** breakfast buffet.

SPRINGHILL SUITES BY MARRIOTT PITTSBURGH NORTH SHORE   (412)323-9005 ❻

Hotel
$153-$263

SPRINGHILL SUITES Marriott

AAA Benefit: Members save 5% or more!

Address: 223 Federal St 15212 **Location:** Corner of Federal and General Robinson sts. North Side, 2. **Facility:** 198 units. 10 stories, interior corridors. **Parking:** on-site (fee). **Pool(s):** heated indoor. **Activities:** exercise room. **Guest Services:** valet and coin laundry, area transportation. **Featured Amenity:** breakfast buffet. (See ad p. 360.)

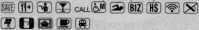

SHERATON PITTSBURGH STATION SQUARE HOTEL   (412)261-2000 ❷⓪

Hotel
$159-$425

Sheraton HOTELS & RESORTS

AAA Benefit: Members save up to 15%, plus Starwood Preferred Guest® benefits!

Address: 300 W Station Square Dr 15219 **Location:** Waterfront. I-376 exit Grant St, south end of Smithfield St Bridge. Located on Monongahela River. Station Square, 7. **Facility:** 399 units, some two bedrooms. 15 stories, interior corridors. **Parking:** on-site (fee). **Terms:** cancellation fee imposed. **Amenities:** safes. **Pool(s):** heated indoor. **Activities:** sauna, hot tub, steamroom, exercise room, massage. **Guest Services:** valet laundry, area transportation.

SPRINGHILL SUITES BY MARRIOTT - PITTSBURGH SOUTHSIDE WORKS   (412)488-8003 ❷❸

Hotel
$132-$229

SPRINGHILL SUITES Marriott

AAA Benefit: Members save 5% or more!

Address: 2950 S Water St 15203 **Location:** US 22/30 exit 2A (Forbes Ave), right to McDevitt Pl, left to CR 885, right to Hot Metal St, then left. **Facility:** 115 units. 6 stories, interior corridors. **Parking:** on-site (fee). **Pool(s):** heated indoor. **Activities:** hot tub, exercise room. **Guest Services:** valet and coin laundry, area transportation. **Featured Amenity:** breakfast buffet. (See ad this page.)

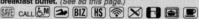

▼ See AAA listing this page ▼

SpringHill Suites Pittsburgh Southside Works

Style and space. Beautifully priced.

Spacious suites and vibrant lobbies offer flexible spaces perfect for working, meeting or relaxing.

- FREE Wi-Fi
- Relaxing indoor pool & fitness center
- Market is open 24/7 for snacks & necessities
- Complimentary new breakfast

SPRINGHILL SUITES® Marriott

2950 South Water Street
Pittsburgh, PA 15203
412-488-8003 • marriott.com

DISCOUNTS ››› REWARDS

Get AAA/CAA travel information in the digital and printed formats you prefer

▼ See AAA listing p. 359 ▼

THE WESTIN CONVENTION CENTER PITTSBURGH
(412)281-3700 [8]

Hotel
$149-$299

WESTIN HOTELS & RESORTS **AAA Benefit:** Members save up to 15%, plus Starwood Preferred Guest® benefits!

Address: 1000 Penn Ave 15222 **Location:** Jct 10th St; at Liberty Center. Adjacent to convention center. Wood Street, 4. **Facility:** 616 units. 26 stories, interior corridors. **Parking:** on-site (fee) and valet. **Terms:** cancellation fee imposed. **Amenities:** safes. **Dining:** 2 restaurants, also, The Original Fish Market, see separate listing. **Pool(s):** heated indoor. **Activities:** sauna, steamroom, exercise room, massage. **Guest Services:** valet laundry, area transportation.

[SAVE] [CALL] [BIZ] / SOME UNITS

WYNDHAM GRAND PITTSBURGH DOWNTOWN
(412)391-4600 [19]

Hotel
$199-$369

Address: 600 Commonwealth Pl 15222 **Location:** Jct I-279/376/SR 885; in Gateway Center. Opposite Point State Park. Gateway Center, 3. **Facility:** 712 units, some two bedrooms, three bedrooms and kitchens. 24 stories, interior corridors. **Parking:** on-site (fee) and valet. **Terms:** cancellation fee imposed. **Pool(s):** heated indoor. **Activities:** exercise room. **Guest Services:** valet laundry, area transportation.

[SAVE] [CALL] [BIZ] [HS] / SOME UNITS

WYNDHAM PITTSBURGH UNIVERSITY CENTER
(412)682-6200 [3]

Hotel
$159-$441

Address: 100 Lytton Ave 15213 **Location:** Just nw of 5th Ave; City Center. **Facility:** 251 units. 9 stories, interior corridors. **Parking:** on-site (fee). **Terms:** check-in 4 pm, 3 day cancellation notice. **Amenities:** video games. **Pool(s):** heated indoor. **Activities:** exercise room. **Guest Services:** valet and coin laundry, area transportation.

[SAVE] [CALL] [BIZ] [HS] / SOME UNITS

WHERE TO EAT

ALI BABA RESTAURANT   412/682-2829 [9]

Middle Eastern. Casual Dining. $5-$16 **AAA Inspector Notes:** In business since 1972, the Oakland eatery is popular with both the university crowd and museumgoers. It is one of the few traditional Middle Eastern restaurants left in the city. **Features:** beer only. **Address:** 404 S Craig St 15213 **Location:** Just nw of Forbes Ave. **Parking:** street only. [L] [D]

CAFÉ PHIPPS CONSERVATORY AND BOTANICAL GARDENS
412/622-6914 [13]

Natural/Organic. Casual Dining. $7-$12 **AAA Inspector Notes:** Inside a beautiful GEM attraction, the cafe prepares healthful fare along the lines of wraps, salads, daily soups and sandwiches, including the Grecian chicken sandwich. In addition to many unique beverage options, this place serves limited alcohol. Modern décor revolves around a "green" theme. **Address:** 700 Frank Curto Dr 15213 **Location:** I-376 exit 72A, 1 mi ne; in Phipps Conservatory and Botanical Gardens. **Parking:** street only. [ECO] [L]

(See map & index p. 345.)

CAFFE' AMANTE
412/391-1226 (22)

Continental. Casual Dining. $6-$29 **AAA Inspector Notes:** Within walking distance of the Theater District and many other downtown sites, this restaurant is known for its Italian flair and specializes in roast rack of lamb, stuffed veal, and several seafood dishes. **Features:** full bar. **Reservations:** suggested. **Address:** 120 5th Ave, Suite 200 15222 **Location:** Jct Market St; center; in Fifth Avenue Place, 2nd Floor. Gateway Center, 3. **Parking:** on-site (fee). L D

THE CARLTON
412/391-4099 (25)

American. Fine Dining. $10-$32 **AAA Inspector Notes:** The daily changing menu might include innovative choices such as seafood Wellington, veal chops and fresh fish, particularly well-prepared salmon. A soft atmosphere punctuates the dining room. The wine list features many reasonably priced selections. **Features:** full bar. **Address:** 500 Grant St, BNY Mellon Bldg, Lobby Level 15219 **Location:** 3 blks n of Liberty Ave. Steel Plaza, 5. L D

CHINATOWN INN
412/261-1292 (27)

Chinese. Casual Dining. $8-$20 **AAA Inspector Notes:** The only remaining business from the city's historic Chinatown, this restaurant offers many styles of Chinese cuisine and is a hot spot for lunch and dinner. It's a very affordable option in the downtown business district. Service is very pleasant but fast and furious due to the volume of business that the restaurant experiences. **Features:** full bar. **Address:** 520 3rd Ave 15219 **Location:** Corner of 3rd Ave and Ross St; adjacent to PNC Corp Offices. First Avenue, 6. **Parking:** street only. L D CALL M

THE CHURCH BREW WORKS
412/688-8200 (1)

American. Gastropub. $8-$30 **AAA Inspector Notes:** Formerly a Catholic church, this building now houses a distinctive brewing house. Wooden pews offer booth seating, the altar now serves as the microbrewery, and the confessional boxes are restrooms. Brewery creations include several homemade beers and handcrafted birch beer and ginger ale. **Features:** full bar. **Address:** 3525 Liberty Ave 15201 **Location:** Corner of 36th and Liberty Ave; in Lawrenceville area. **Parking:** on-site (fee) and street. L D

DELUCA'S RESTAURANT
412/566-2195 (5)

American. Family Dining. $6-$12 **AAA Inspector Notes:** In the Historic Strip District, the popular diner is a Pittsburgh tradition. Patrons seat themselves at the counter, a table or booth before noshing on a hearty breakfast or tasty lunch. **Address:** 2015 Penn Ave 15222 **Location:** Between 20th and 21st sts. Steel Plaza, 5. **Parking:** street only. B L

DISH OSTERIA AND BAR
412/390-2012 (39)

Italian. Family Dining. $15-$32 **AAA Inspector Notes:** Neo-European-style dining is offered in intimate rooms bathed in a soft candlelight glow. The food is authentic, with no meatballs to be found. The seasonally changing menu accommodates fresh fish and regional market availability. Reservations for six or more people aren't available Friday and Saturday nights. **Features:** full bar, happy hour. **Reservations:** suggested. **Address:** 128 S 17th St 15203 **Location:** Corner of Sarah St; on south side. First Avenue, 6. **Parking:** street only. D LATE

ELEVEN
412/201-5656 (11)

New American. Fine Dining. $9-$45 **AAA Inspector Notes:** Modern and upscale dining is what you will get when you dine at Eleven. The service is superb along with the menu. For an appetizer, try the calamari, which is lightly fried with shrimp and zucchini. For dinner, the smoked pork chop with potatoes parsnip puree and spinach is excellent. But save room for the desserts, all of which are made with a special flair by the pastry chef. **Features:** full bar. **Reservations:** suggested. **Address:** 1150 Smallman St 15222 **Location:** Jct Smallman and 12th sts; in Historic Strip District. Wood Street, 4. **Parking:** on-site (fee) and valet. L D

GRAND CONCOURSE RESTAURANT/GANDY DANCER
412/261-1717 (34)

American. Casual Dining. $9-$42 **AAA Inspector Notes:** *Historic.* This splendidly restored railroad station boasts a stained-glass ceiling and grand marble staircase that sweep diners back to the Victorian era. On the menu are fresh seafood and meat entrees. Lush flavor characterizes the signature chocolate truffle cake. **Features:** full bar, patio dining, early bird specials, Sunday brunch, happy hour. **Reservations:** suggested. **Address:** 100 W Station Square Dr 15219 **Location:** I-376 exit 72A on south end of Smithfield St Bridge; in Pittsburgh and Lake Erie Railroad Terminal Building. Station Square, 7. **Parking:** on-site (fee). L D

GRANDVIEW SALOON
412/431-1400 (30)

American. Casual Dining. $14-$49 **AAA Inspector Notes:** Atop Mount Washington, this restaurant features floor-to-ceiling windows and two seasonal cliffside decks that afford outstanding views of the city skyline and the Three Rivers area. The dining room nurtures a casual, light and airy atmosphere. Examples of Mediterranean-influenced American cuisine include great steaks and Greek appetizers. Portions are large. **Features:** full bar. **Address:** 1212 Grandview Ave 15211 **Location:** Atop Mt. Washington; just e of Duquesne Incline. Allegheny, 1. L D

HARD ROCK CAFE
412/481-7625 (33)

American. Casual Dining. $13-$24 **AAA Inspector Notes:** Rock 'n' roll memorabilia decorates the walls of the popular theme restaurant. Live music on the weekends contributes to the bustling atmosphere. On the menu is a wide variety of American cuisine—from burgers and sandwiches to seafood, steaks and pasta. **Features:** full bar. **Address:** 230 W Station Square Dr 15219 **Location:** Jct Carson and Smithfield sts; in Station Square. Station Square, 7. **Parking:** on-site (fee). SAVE L D CALL M

IBIZA TAPAS & WINE BAR
412/325-2227 (37)

Spanish. Fine Dining. $5-$44 **AAA Inspector Notes:** Patrons visit the contemporary eatery for classic Spanish dishes, including tapas small-plate portions and full entrees. Near bars and shopping on the city's exciting strip, this place also offers great outdoor seating. **Features:** full bar, patio dining, happy hour. **Address:** 2224 E Carson St 15203 **Location:** In South Side District. **Parking:** on-site and valet. D

INDIA GARDEN
412/682-3000 (15)

Northern Indian. Casual Dining. $6-$21 **AAA Inspector Notes:** This restaurant offers a variety of freshly prepared, additive-free seafood, poultry, lamb and vegetarian dishes. Tandoori preparations are the specialty. All entrées can be seasoned to guests' tastes. **Features:** beer only. **Reservations:** suggested. **Address:** 328 Atwood St 15213 **Location:** I-376 E exit Forbes Ave; jct Bates St. **Parking:** street only. L D

(See map & index p. 345.)

ISABELA ON GRANDVIEW
412/431-5882 ㉙
▼▼▼▼ New American. Fine Dining. $12-$75 AAA Inspector Notes: This upscale restaurant, which seats 60 people, has a minimalist décor package so as not to compete with dazzling 210 degree window views of the city skyscape and Three Rivers area. A daily changing menu of contemporary American cuisine is offered as a seven-course, prix fixe dinner and is the only offering on Saturday. Optional wine pairings are available from the highly-selective list of domestic and imported wines. Features: full bar. Reservations: suggested. Address: 1318 Grandview Ave 15211 Location: Atop Mt. Washington; just w of Duquesne Incline. 🅰 Allegheny, 1. Parking: on-site (fee) and valet. [D] [🚉]

JEROME BETTI'S GRILLE 36
412/224-6287 ⑰
▼▼ American. Casual Dining. $7-$35 AAA Inspector Notes: Voted Pittsburgh's best sports restaurant every year since it opened. Sample flatbread sandwiches served deep fried, blackened, grilled or stuffed. The place is frequented by locals and celebrities. Other attractions include generously portioned appetizers, numerous flat-panel HDTVs, a full bar and never-ending views of the riverfront or stadium skyline from the patio. Features: full bar. Address: 393 N Shore Dr 15212 Location: Corner of W General Robinson St and Mazeroski Way sts; near Heinz Field. 🅰 North Side, 2. [L] [D] [🚉]

JOE MAMA'S ITALIAN DELUXE
412/621-7282 ⑫
▼▼ Italian. Casual Dining. $7-$15 AAA Inspector Notes: Folks who want to go back in time to a 1960s-era diner need look no further. The retro-style dining area is casual, and staffers provide friendly service. The large menu features salads, sandwiches, omelets and pasta dishes to satisfy any palate. Features: full bar, Sunday brunch. Address: 3716 Forbes Ave 15213 Location: Corner of Forbes and Oakland aves; in Oakland area. Parking: on-site (fee). [L] [D]

KAYA RESTAURANT
412/261-6565 ④
▼▼ Caribbean. Casual Dining. $10-$29 AAA Inspector Notes: This trendy restaurant specializes in Caribbean and Jamaican cuisines. The bar is busy serving up specialty martinis and other flavorful tropical drinks. Features: full bar, Sunday brunch. Address: 2000 Smallman St 15222 Location: Jct 20th St. 🅰 Steel Plaza, 5. Parking: street only. [L] [D] [🚉]

KIKU'S OF JAPAN
412/765-3200 ㉟
▼▼ Sushi. Casual Dining. $14-$35 AAA Inspector Notes: In the popular Station Square area, this restaurant offers an extensive selection of sushi, as well as teriyaki and tempura dishes served in the traditional style. The dining room has a classic Japanese decor, and servers don Japanese costumes. Features: full bar. Reservations: suggested. Address: 225 W Station Square Dr 15219 Location: Jct Carson and Smithfield sts. 🅰 Station Square, 7. Parking: on-site (fee). [L] [D] [🚉]

LE MONT RESTAURANT
412/431-3100 ㉜
▼▼▼▼ Continental. Fine Dining. $26-$48 AAA Inspector Notes: The restaurant affords breathtaking views of Three Rivers, the Golden Triangle and the entire city. Attractive presentation marks such dishes as crispy duck with cherry sauce. Professional servers are prompt and attentive. Features: full bar. Reservations: suggested. Address: 1114 Grandview Ave 15211 Location: Atop Mt. Washington; adjacent to Duquesne Incline. 🅰 Allegheny, 1. Parking: on-site (fee) and valet. [D] [🚉]

LIDIA'S
412/552-0150 ⑩
▼▼▼ Northern Italian. Fine Dining. $9-$38 AAA Inspector Notes: The restaurant offers a cozy but relaxing atmosphere for a special occasion or just a night out on the town. Upscale taste is evident throughout the restored warehouse. The staff is helpful in making suggestions from among appetizers, salads, entrées and wines. The full bar area is equipped with a variety of beers. Features: full bar, Sunday brunch. Reservations: suggested. Address: 1400 Smallman St 15222 Location: In Historic Strip District. 🅰 Steel Plaza, 5. Parking: on-site (fee). [L] [D] [🚉]

LUCCA RISTORANTE
412/682-3310 ⑦
▼▼ ▼▼ Northern Italian. Casual Dining. $18-$36 AAA Inspector Notes: Within walking distance of the University of Pittsburgh and Carnegie-Mellon University, the restaurant is in the middle of the South Craig Street shopping area. Outdoor seating is an option when the weather permits. Features: full bar. Reservations: suggested. Address: 317 S Craig St 15213 Location: Jct Forbes Ave. [L] [D]

MALLORCA RESTAURANT
412/488-1818 ㊱
▼▼▼ Spanish. Fine Dining. $8-$42 AAA Inspector Notes: Spanish and Portuguese cuisine makes up the menu. The tuxedoed staff provides friendly and attentive service that evokes an Old World feel. Features: full bar, patio dining. Address: 2228 E Carson St 15203 Location: Just s of Birmingham Bridge. Parking: street only. [L] [D]

MAX'S ALLEGHENY TAVERN
412/231-1899 ③
▼▼ German. Casual Dining. $5-$16 AAA Inspector Notes: A Bavarian theme prevails in this tavern which has accents of dark wood and subtle German music piped in the background. The menu includes such traditional Old World favorites as schnitzel and homemade apple strudel. Families are welcome. Features: full bar, senior menu. Address: 537 Suismon St 15212 Location: Corner of Middle and Suismon sts; in North Shore area. 🅰 North Side, 2. [L] [D] [🚉]

MONTEREY BAY FISH GROTTO
412/481-4414 ㉘
▼▼▼▼ Seafood. Fine Dining. $10-$39 AAA Inspector Notes: Beautiful views of the city are available from this seafood restaurant. Features: full bar. Reservations: suggested. Address: 1411 Grandview Ave 15211 Location: Atop of Mt. Washington. 🅰 Allegheny, 1. Parking: on-site and valet. [L] [D] [🚉]

MORTON'S THE STEAKHOUSE
412/261-7141 ⑳
▼▼▼ Steak. Fine Dining. $27-$48 AAA Inspector Notes: Patrons should make sure to reserve ahead for the popular, well-known steakhouse. Large portions, including huge cuts of fine beef and plentiful seafood, are the norm. Even the vegetables are over-sized, with baked potatoes big enough for sharing. Features: full bar. Address: 625 Liberty Ave 15222 Location: Between 6th and 7th sts. 🅰 Wood Street, 4. Parking: valet and street only. [D] CALL [♿M] [🚉]

NAKAMA JAPANESE STEAKHOUSE AND SUSHI BAR
412/381-6000 ㊳
▼▼▼ Japanese. Casual Dining. $9-$70 AAA Inspector Notes: This trendy restaurant grills scallops, shrimp, chicken and steak on a smoke-free hibachi. Fresh, traditional sushi bar choices, such as avocado and California rolls, soft-shell crab and many others, delight sushi fans. Features: full bar. Reservations: suggested. Address: 1611 E Carson St 15203 Location: Corner of 17th St; on south side. 🅰 First Avenue, 6. Parking: on-site (fee) and valet. [L] [D] [🚉]

NOLA ON THE SQUARE
412/471-9100 ㉔
▼▼ New Creole. Casual Dining. $9-$34 AAA Inspector Notes: If you are nostalgic for the Big Easy, this high-energy brasserie capably gets you in the mood. Jazz plays while guests contemplate a bowl of gumbo or crayfish soup. Delicious Creole and Cajun cuisine has a contemporary twist and includes wood-fired flatbread, muffaletta, po'boys, alligator and frogs legs. Of course, for dessert, the beignets are recommended to add a sweet nostalgic touch. Decorated in New Orleans-style with original artwork, restored tin ceilings and familiar artifacts. Features: full bar. Reservations: suggested. Address: 24 Market Square 15222 Location: On Market Square. 🅰 Gateway Center, 3. Parking: valet and street only. [L] [D] [🚉]

OLIVE OR TWIST
412/255-0525 ⑱
▼▼ American. Casual Dining. $12-$28 AAA Inspector Notes: Conveniently located in the Cultural District of downtown and within walking distance of both PNC Park and Heinz Field, the restaurant is home of the original Black and Gold Martini. Features: full bar. Address: 140 6th St 15222 Location: Jct Penn Ave, just n; center. 🅰 Gateway Center, 3. Parking: street only. [L] [D] [🚉]

(See map & index p. 345.)

THE ORIGINAL FISH MARKET   412/227-3657 (14)
▼▼▼ Seafood. Casual Dining. $10-$50 **AAA Inspector**
Notes: A fish market feel prevails in the noisy, busy atmosphere.
In addition to a full sushi bar, the restaurant offers varied seafood
selections, which are flown in daily and prepared in many styles.
Steaks and pork chops also share menu space. The friendly staff
provides attentive, timely service. **Features:** full bar. **Reserva-
tions:** suggested. **Address:** 1001 Liberty Ave 15222 **Location:**
Jct 10th St; at Liberty Center; in The Westin Convention Center
Pittsburgh. 🚇 Wood Street, 4. **Parking:** on-site (fee) and valet.
L D CALL &M 🚇

PENN BREWERY RESTAURANT   412/237-9400 (2)
▼▼ German. Casual Dining. $9-$20 **AAA Inspector Notes:**
German beers and cuisine dominate this intimate restaurant's menu.
An outdoor biergarten has brick and stone while heavy wooden fur-
nishings and brewing memorabilia decorate the main dining room.
Service is friendly and prompt. The décor includes different countries'
flags hanging from the rafters, wood tables and benches, and memo-
rabilia items dating back to the early 19th century. **Features:** full bar.
Address: 800 Vinial St 15212 **Location:** Just ne of 16th St Bridge.
L D CALL &M

PRIMANTI BROTHERS RESTAURANT
▼ American. Casual Dining. $6-$18 **AAA Inspector Notes:**
Looking for a sandwich that offers piled-high fries and coleslaw on top
of each sandwich, then this is the place to be. The bar restaurant
theme is every Pittsburgher's dream with memorabilia for each sports
fan. **Bar:** full bar. L D LATE CALL &M
For additional information, visit AAA.com
LOCATIONS:
Address: 3803 Forbes Ave 15230 **Location:** I-376 exit Bates St, jct
Atwood St and Forbes Ave. **Phone:** 412/621-4444
Address: 2 S Market Pl 15230 **Location:** In Market Place area.
🚇 Gateway Center, 3. **Phone:** 412/261-1599
Address: 1832 E Carson St 15203 **Location:** Corner of 19th and
Carson sts; in South Side District. **Phone:** 412/381-2583
Address: 46 18th St 15230 **Location:** Just nw of jct 18th St and
Mulberry Hwy; in Historic Strip District. 🚇 Steel Plaza, 5.
Phone: 412/263-2142

RUTH'S CHRIS STEAK HOUSE   412/391-4800 (26)
▼▼▼ Steak. Fine Dining. $10-$60 **AAA Inspector Notes:**
The main fare is steak, which is prepared from several cuts of
prime beef and cooked to perfection, but the menu also lists lamb,
chicken and seafood dishes. Guests should come hungry because
the side dishes, which are among the a la carte offerings, could
make a meal in themselves. **Features:** full bar. **Reservations:**
suggested. **Address:** 6 PPG Pl 15222 **Location:** In PPG 6th
Building. 🚇 Gateway Center, 3. **Parking:** on-site (fee).
L D CALL &M 🚇

SIX PENN KITCHEN   412/566-7366 (19)
▼▼▼ New American. Casual Dining. $9-$30 **AAA Inspector**
Notes: A great spot for a business lunch or relaxed pre-theater
dinner, this restaurant satisfies guests with creative meals that reflect
the seasonal availability of ingredients, which are locally grown or
raised. **Features:** full bar, Sunday brunch. **Reservations:** suggested.
Address: 146 6th St 15222 **Location:** Center. 🚇 Gateway Center,
3. **Parking:** on-site (fee). L D 🚇

SONOMA   412/697-1336 (16)
▼▼▼ International. Fine Dining. $9-$39 **AAA Inspector**
Notes: This unique farm-to-table restaurant is set in the heart of
downtown. It is home to the creations of chef-owner Yves Carreau,
who makes regular changes to the menu based on the availability of
the freshest ingredients, many of which are from local farms. To further enhance your experience, you can select from an award-winning
wine list designed to complement the meal. A vegetarian menu also
is available. Sunday brunch with live jazz is served from 11 am to 2
pm each week. **Features:** full bar, Sunday brunch. **Reservations:**
suggested. **Address:** 947 Penn Ave 15222 **Location:** I-279 exit 70B
(Fort Duquesne Blvd), 0.5 mi ne; center. 🚇 Wood Street, 4.
Parking: on-site (fee). L D CALL &M 🚇

THE STEELHEAD BRASSERIE & WINE BAR
                                        412/394-3474 (21)
▼▼▼   **AAA Inspector Notes:** This restaurant
                      offers guests a casual dining experience
American   with all the enjoyment of fine dining. The
Casual Dining   menu mostly features fish selections
$10-$32   which are flown in daily. Also available
                      are roasted Amish chicken, New York
strip steak and lamb. Attentive, efficient
staff can only enhance your overall dining experience. A full bar
offers frozen drinks and an extensive beer and wine list. **Features:** full bar. **Reservations:** suggested. **Address:** 112 Washington Pl 15219 **Location:** Center Ave; just e of Crosstown Blvd;
in Pittsburgh Marriott City Center. 🚇 Steel Plaza, 5. **Parking:** on-
site (fee). *Menu on AAA.com* B L D CALL &M 🚇

THE TERRACE ROOM   412/553-5235 (23)
▼▼▼ Continental. Fine Dining. $10-$30 **AAA Inspector**
Notes: *Classic.* Restored to its 1916 splendor, this elegant dining
room boasts ornate ceilings, a wall-length mural and center palm
trees. The menu delivers creative Mediterranean cuisine, such as
turkey Devonshire with white cheese sauce over toasted bread.
Live music is offered Thursday and Friday. **Features:** full bar,
Sunday brunch. **Reservations:** suggested, weekends. **Address:**
530 William Penn Pl 15219 **Location:** Jct 6th St and William Penn
Pl; in Omni William Penn Hotel. 🚇 Steel Plaza, 5. **Parking:** on-
site (fee) and valet. B L D CALL &M 🚇

TIN ANGEL   412/381-1919 (31)
▼▼▼ Continental. Fine Dining. $39-$64 **AAA Inspector**
Notes: This restaurant offers a splendid nighttime view of downtown
Pittsburgh and its rivers. The four-course dinner includes a large veg-
etable boat with clam dip. **Features:** full bar. **Reservations:** sug-
gested. **Address:** 1200 Grandview Ave 15211 **Location:** Atop Mt.
Washington; just w of Duquesne Incline. 🚇 Allegheny, 1. **Parking:**
on-site (fee). D 🚇

(See map & index p. 345.)

WHOLEY'S   412/391-3737   6
◆ Seafood. Quick Serve. $5-$12 **AAA Inspector Notes:** The popular retail fish market prepares Pittsburgh-style fish sandwiches. Seating is limited. **Address:** 1711 Penn Ave 15222 **Location:** Just n; in Historic Strip District. ⊞ Steel Plaza, 5. **Parking:** street only.

L D 🚊

YUVA INDIA RESTAURANT   412/681-5700   8
◆◆ Indian. Casual Dining. $15-$26 **AAA Inspector Notes:** In Oakland close to Carnegie Mellon and Pitt, the restaurant is particularly popular for its all-you-can-eat lunch buffet. **Features:** full bar, Sunday brunch. **Address:** 412 S Craig St 15213 **Location:** Just nw of Forbes Ave. **Parking:** street only. L D

PITTSBURGH (G-2) elev. 764'
• Restaurants p. 368
• Hotels & Restaurants map & index p. 348

COMFORT INN   (412)415-3867   4
◆◆◆ **Hotel** $103-$125 **Address:** 4607 McKnight Rd 15237 **Location:** I-279 exit 4, 4 mi n on US 19. **Facility:** 50 units. 3 stories, interior corridors. **Activities:** limited exercise equipment.
CALL 🛎M BIZ 🛜 ⊠ 🖵 / SOME UNITS 🐾 🗄 🖾

Visit the AAA and CAA senior driving

websites for valuable resources

▼ See AAA listing p. 205 ▼

▼ *See AAA listing p. 68* ▼

(See map & index p. 348.)

COURTYARD BY MARRIOTT PITTSBURGH AIRPORT SETTLERS RIDGE (412)788-4404 **10**

▼▼▼ **Hotel** $139-$229 **Address:** 5100 Campbells Run Rd 15205 **Location:** I-376 exit 60B (Crafton/SR 60 S), just n. **Facility:** 124 units. 5 stories, interior corridors. **Pool(s):** heated indoor. **Guest Services:** valet and coin laundry, area transportation.

AAA Benefit: Members save 5% or more!

COURTYARD BY MARRIOTT PITTSBURGH/SHADYSIDE (412)683-3113 **7**

▼▼▼ **Hotel** $153-$252 **Address:** 5308 Liberty Ave 15224 **Location:** Jct Baum Blvd and Liberty Ave. **Facility:** 132 units. 6 stories, interior corridors. **Parking:** on-site (fee) and valet. **Pool(s):** heated indoor. **Activities:** exercise room. **Guest Services:** valet and coin laundry, area transportation.

AAA Benefit: Members save 5% or more!

FAIRFIELD INN & SUITES BY MARRIOTT PITTSBURGH NEVILLE ISLAND (412)264-4722 **5**

▼▼▼ **Hotel** $104-$171 **Address:** 5850 Grand Ave 15225 **Location:** I-79 exit 65, 0.5 mi ne towards Neville Island. **Facility:** 110 units. 4 stories, interior corridors. **Pool(s):** heated indoor. **Activities:** hot tub, exercise room. **Guest Services:** valet and coin laundry, area transportation.

AAA Benefit: Members save 5% or more!

HAMPTON INN (412)939-3200 **3**

▼▼▼ Hotel $119-$184

AAA Benefit: Members save 5% or more!

Address: 4575 McKnight Rd 15237 **Location:** I-279 exit 4, 4 mi n on US 19. **Facility:** 107 units. 4 stories, interior corridors. **Terms:** 1-7 night minimum stay, cancellation fee imposed. **Pool(s):** heated indoor. **Activities:** hot tub, exercise room. **Guest Services:** valet and coin laundry. **Featured Amenity:** full hot breakfast.

▼ See AAA listing p. 72 ▼

HOME2 SUITES BY HILTON PITTSBURGH/MCCANDLESS
(412)630-8400   **1**

Hotel $129-$169 **Address:** 8630 Duncan Ave 15237 **Location:** I-279 exit 4, 7 mi n on US 19 Truck Babcock, then left to Duncan Ave. **Facility:** 119 units. 4 stories, interior corridors. **Terms:** 1-7 night minimum stay, cancellation fee imposed. **Amenities:** *Some:* video games. **Pool(s):** heated indoor. **Activities:** exercise room. **Guest Services:** complimentary and valet laundry.

AAA Benefit: Members save 5% or more!

THE INN ON NEGLEY   412/661-0631   **8**

Bed & Breakfast. Rates not provided. **Address:** 703 S Negley Ave 15232 **Location:** 0.3 mi n of 5th Ave. Located in a historic district. **Facility:** The guest rooms make this beautiful inn a must-stay while in the city. All rooms have flat-screen TVs, custom furniture and deep soaking tubs. 8 units. 3 stories (no elevator), interior corridors. **Terms:** age restrictions may apply.

LA QUINTA INN & SUITES PITTSBURGH NORTH
(412)366-5200   **2**

Hotel $102-$215 **Address:** 4859 McKnight Rd 15237 **Location:** I-279 exit 4, 7 mi n on US 19. Adjacent to North Hills Village Mall. **Facility:** 146 units. 7 stories, interior corridors. **Terms:** check-in 4 pm. **Activities:** exercise room. **Guest Services:** valet and coin laundry.

RESIDENCE INN BY MARRIOTT-WILKINS
(412)816-1300   **9**

Extended Stay Hotel $104-$171

Residence Inn Marriott

AAA Benefit: Members save 5% or more!

Address: 3455 William Penn Hwy 15235 **Location:** I-76 (Pennsylvania Tpke) exit 57, 3.5 mi n. **Facility:** 124 units, some two bedrooms, efficiencies and kitchens. 4 stories, interior corridors. **Terms:** check-in 4 pm. **Amenities:** safes. **Pool(s):** heated indoor. **Activities:** exercise room. **Guest Services:** valet and coin laundry. **Featured Amenity:** breakfast buffet. *(See ad p. 357.)*

(See map & index p. 348.)

SPRINGHILL SUITES BY MARRIOTT PITTSBURGH BAKERY SQUARE   (412)362-8600   **6**

▼▼▼▼ **Hotel** $139-$229 **Address:** 134 Bakery Square Blvd 15206 **Location:** SR 28 exit Highland Park Bridge, right to Washington Blvd to Penn Ave, then just e. Located in Bakery Square with high end restaurants and shopping. **Facility:** 110 units. 6 stories, interior corridors. **Pool(s):** heated indoor. **Activities:** massage. **Guest Services:** valet and coin laundry, area transportation.

> **AAA Benefit:** Members save 5% or more!

▼ See AAA listing p. 403 ▼

Style and space. Beautifully priced.

ALADDIN'S EATERY   412/421-5100

▼▼ Lebanese. Casual Dining. $5-$14 **AAA Inspector Notes:** Middle Eastern traditions and flavorings inspire the menu, which lines up chicken, beef and lamb dishes along the lines of chicken mishwi, stuffed kibbeh shells, shish kebab, assorted pita "pizzas" and a Mediterranean marinated and char-grilled lamb plate. Vegetarians also aren't neglected and can assemble a meal that might start with an appetizer combination with hummus, tabbouleh, baba, falafel and dawali. **Features:** beer & wine. **Address:** 5878 Forbes Ave 15217 **Location:** In shopping district of Squirrel Hill. **Parking:** on-site (fee) and street.

BUFFALO BLUES   412/362-5837   **3**

▼▼ Wings. Casual Dining. $7-$21 **AAA Inspector Notes:** The high-energy spot serves a good variety of foods. The wings have repeatedly won accolades. **Features:** full bar. **Address:** 216 S Highland Ave 15206 **Location:** Jct Alder St and Highland Ave. **Parking:** street only.

THE CAFE AT THE FRICK ART & HISTORICAL CENTER   412/371-0600   **14**

▼▼ New American. Casual Dining. $8-$15 **AAA Inspector Notes:** This restaurant, set among the beautiful grounds of an estate, prides itself in working with a palette of fresh, seasonal ingredients. Fresh flowers are used as garnishes is some dishes. For casual, peaceful dining, diners can relax on the outdoor patio or in the sunny bistro. Homemade pastries are delicious. **Reservations:** required. **Address:** 7227 Reynolds St 15208 **Location:** I-376 exit 77 to Braddock Ave, 1.3 mi nw to Penn Ave, 0.3 mi w to S Homewood Ave, then just s to circle.

CAFE SAM   412/621-2000   **4**

▼▼▼ International. Casual Dining. $6-$25 **AAA Inspector Notes:** Near Shadyside Hospital, this cafe is an unexpected treat. In a converted home, it nurtures a romantic atmosphere in the evenings. Southwest, Northern Italian, Californian and Asian influences factor into menu offerings. The patio opens seasonally. **Features:** full bar. **Address:** 5242 Baum Blvd 15224 **Location:** Jct Liberty St; in Shadyside area.

CAPPY'S CAFE   412/621-1188   **12**

▼ American. Casual Dining. $6-$10 **AAA Inspector Notes:** Featuring a friendly staff and casual, pub-like dining in a cozy setting, this eatery serves up traditional fare of sandwiches, burgers, and salads. **Features:** full bar. **Address:** 5431 Walnut St 15232 **Location:** Between S Aikens and Bellefonte sts. **Parking:** street only.

CASBAH MEDITERRANEAN KITCHEN & WINE BAR   412/661-5656   **2**

▼▼▼ Mediterranean. Fine Dining. $8-$30 **AAA Inspector Notes:** This trendy, upscale restaurant has an extensive wine list and a creative and artistic menu. The grilled Hawaiian prawns and caramelized Nantucket bay scallop appetizers are two local favorites. The foods are presented as works of art with a multitude of colors and textures utilized within each dish. You won't know whether to eat your food or take a picture of it! **Features:** full bar. **Address:** 229 S Highland Ave 15206 **Location:** Jct Alder St and S Highland Ave; in Shadyside area. **Parking:** on-site and street.

CHINA PALACE   412/687-7423   **10**

▼▼ Chinese. Casual Dining. $6-$22 **AAA Inspector Notes:** The staff is highly attentive, dishes are very well prepared and the restaurant's lively setting is fun. Some tables are tightly spaced. **Features:** full bar. **Address:** 5440 Walnut St 15232 **Location:** Between Copeland and Bellefonte sts; in Shadyside area. **Parking:** on-site (fee) and street.

THE ELBOW ROOM   412/441-5222   **5**

▼▼ American. Casual Dining. $5-$20 **AAA Inspector Notes:** A Shadyside neighborhood favorite, the popular family-friendly restaurant/pub has a relaxed atmosphere. On the menu are burgers, specialty sandwiches, pasta, fresh salads and such appetizers as buffalo wings. This place is known for its designer cocktails. **Features:** full bar, Sunday brunch. **Address:** 5533 Walnut St 15232 **Location:** Between Bellefonte and Ivy sts; across from Banana Republic; in Shadyside area. **Parking:** on-site (fee).

(See map & index p. 348.)

GIRASOLE   412/682-2130 11
WWWW Northern Italian. Casual Dining. $10-$22 **AAA Inspector Notes:** Girasole, which means sunflower in Italian, presents a menu of contemporary Northern Italian cuisine in its small Shadyside eatery. On the seasonally changing menu are pasta, fish and meat specials at dinner and sandwiches at lunch. **Features:** full bar. **Address:** 733 Copeland St 15232 **Location:** Between Walnut and Elmer sts; in Shadyside area. **Parking:** street only. L D

LA FERIA   412/682-4501 6
WW WW Peruvian. Casual Dining. $4-$14 **AAA Inspector Notes:** This combination restaurant/gallery is a Shadyside attraction. Daily changing entrees include vegetarian, chicken and meat selections. Salads, sandwiches, soups and delicious desserts also are available. All spices are imported from Peru, but many of the other ingredients that the country introduced to the world are locally grown. Guests can bring their own wine. **Address:** 5527 Walnut St 15232 **Location:** Between Filbert St and Urn Way; in Shadyside area. **Parking:** street only. L D

MAD MEX   412/366-5656
WWW WW Mexican. Casual Dining. $7-$16 **AAA Inspector Notes:** The colorful décor and lively music will make for a fun experience. The kitchen dishes creative steak, seafood and chicken dishes using authentic Mexican ingredients, as well as tacos, enchiladas, quesadillas, sizzling fajitas and "Mad Mex" burritos. At the restaurant's large bar area, guests can order from a wide range of beers in bottles or on draft, as well as specialty drinks. **Features:** full bar. **Address:** 7905 McKnight Rd 15237 **Location:** 8 mi n on US 19. L D

PAMELA'S   412/683-1003 7
WW American. Family Dining. $5-$8 **AAA Inspector Notes:** This popular breakfast spot has been serving diners since 1980. The bountiful breakfast menu features quiche, French toast, croissants, omelets, bacon and eggs offered all day long. It's best known for its plentiful hotcakes and crêpes with your choice of fruit toppings. A great place for Sunday brunch; anticipate a 30- to 45-minute wait time on the weekend. **Features:** Sunday brunch. **Address:** 5527 Walnut St 15232 **Location:** Between Bellefonte and Ivy sts; in Shadyside area. **Parking:** street only. B L

SHADY GROVE   412/697-0909 9
WW WW American. Casual Dining. $10-$18 **AAA Inspector Notes:** Nestled in the busy shopping district of Shadyside, this trendy restaurant/bar is a great place to grab a bite to eat and relax after shopping. Seasonal outdoor seating is available. **Features:** full bar. **Address:** 5500 Walnut St 15232 **Location:** Corner of Walnut and Bellefonte sts; in Shadyside area. **Parking:** on-site (fee). L D LATE

THE SPAGHETTI WAREHOUSE   412/261-6511
WW WW Italian. Casual Dining. $4-$17 **AAA Inspector Notes:** The Italian-style restaurant chain sustains a festive family atmosphere. All entrees include bottomless tossed salad or soup. Patrons enjoy plentiful portions of such classic dishes as ravioli, lasagna, baked penne or the richly flavored cannelloni Florentine. Splurging on one of the many desserts, such as tiramisu, espresso mousse cake or carrot cake, is worthwhile. **Features:** full bar. **Address:** 2601 Smallman St 15222 **Location:** At 26th St. L D

SUSHI TOO   412/687-8744 13
WWW Japanese. Casual Dining. $7-$24 **AAA Inspector Notes:** The Shadyside restaurant sustains a traditional Japanese atmosphere and has a tatami room on the second floor. The menu includes tempura, teriyaki, bento boxes, noodles, nabemono and donburi. A sushi bar is in the main dining room. **Features:** full bar. **Address:** 5432 Walnut St 15232 **Location:** Between Copeland and Bellefonte sts. **Parking:** street only. L D

TESSARO'S   412/682-6809 1
WWW WWW American. Casual Dining. $10-$26 **AAA Inspector Notes:** The menu at this eatery focuses on burgers, sandwiches, beef, poultry, pork and seafood selections prepared simply over an open-flame hardwood grill. The entree portions are well-known for their enormous size. Guests can expect a friendly dining experience in the casual neighborhood restaurant. **Features:** full bar. **Address:** 4601 Liberty Ave 15224 **Location:** Jct Taylor St. **Parking:** street only. L D

THAI PLACE   412/687-8586 8
WW WW Thai. Casual Dining. $9-$22 **AAA Inspector Notes:** In the busy section of Shadyside, this restaurant offers a huge menu of dishes served in large portions. Even though meals leave bellies full, it is a good idea to leave a little room for homemade coconut ice cream or seasonal mangoes with sweet sticky rice. **Features:** full bar. **Address:** 5528 Walnut St 15232 **Location:** Center; in Walnut Street Shopping District. **Parking:** on-site (fee). L D CALL 🐾M

PITTSTON pop. 7,739

COMFORT INN PITTSTON   (570)655-1234
WW WW Hotel $39-$179 **Address:** 400 Hwy 315 18640 **Location:** I-81 exit 175 northbound, 1 mi n; exit 175B southbound, just w; in Pittston Crossings Plaza. **Facility:** 90 units. 5 stories, interior corridors. **Activities:** exercise room. **Guest Services:** valet and coin laundry.
🛬 🍴 📶 ✖ 🛏 📠 💻 / SOME UNITS 🐾

WHERE TO EAT

COOPER'S ON THE WATERFRONT   570/654-6883
WW WW Seafood. Casual Dining. $9-$40 **AAA Inspector Notes:** Facing the Susquehanna River, the waterfront dining room affords great views. Toy trains on an elevated track, as well as plenty of nautical touches, serve as decoration. Seafood—such as the combination platter—is at the heart of the menu. **Features:** full bar. **Address:** 304 Kennedy Blvd 18640 **Location:** Center. D

PLEASANT HILLS pop. 8,268
• **Part of Pittsburgh area — see map p. 326**

PRIMANTI BROTHERS RESTAURANT   412/653-6779
WW American. Casual Dining. $6-$18 **AAA Inspector Notes:** Looking for a sandwich that offers piled-high fries and coleslaw on top of each sandwich, then this is the place to be. The bar restaurant theme is every Pittsburgher's dream with memorabilia for each sports fan. **Features:** full bar. **Address:** 830 Clairton Blvd (Rt 51) 15236 **Location:** Just s from Century Three Mall. L D LATE CALL 🐾M

PLEASANTVILLE (D-3) pop. 892, elev. 1,635'

PITHOLE CITY, s. on SR 227, then 2.5 mi. e./n.e. to 14118 Pithole Rd., was a flourishing settlement during the oil boom of the mid-1860s, but it only lasted a little more than a year. In September 1865 the population was 15,000, and the town had 57 hotels, a post office and a daily newspaper; by December the following year, the population had dwindled to less than 2,000. Today there are very few remains of the vanished town except for cellar holes in a hillside meadow.

Use travel time to share driving tips
and rules of the road with your teens

Visitors can walk the grassy paths that were once streets; interpretive signs are available. **Time:** Allow 1 hour minimum. **Hours:** Grounds dawn-dusk. Visitor Center hours vary; phone for schedule. **Cost:** Free. $3; $2 (ages 3-16); free (ages 0-2). **Phone:** (814) 827-2797.

PLYMOUTH MEETING pop. 6,177

- Hotels & Restaurants map & index p. 274
- Part of Philadelphia area — see map p. 230

COURTYARD BY MARRIOTT-PHILADELPHIA PLYMOUTH MEETING   (610)238-0695 61

Hotel
$146-$240

COURTYARD Marriott

AAA Benefit: Members save 5% or more!

Address: 651 Fountain Rd 19462 **Location:** I-476 exit 20; I-276 (Pennsylvania Tpke) exit 333, just w on Plymouth Rd (Norristown), just e on Germantown Pike, then just e on Hickory Rd. Located in a commercial area. **Facility:** 157 units. 4 stories, interior corridors. **Pool(s):** heated indoor. **Activities:** hot tub, exercise room. **Guest Services:** valet and coin laundry.

  CALL 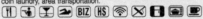   / SOME UNITS

DOUBLETREE SUITES BY HILTON PHILADELPHIA WEST
(610)834-8300 62

Hotel $109-$209 **Address:** 640 Fountain Rd 19462 **Location:** I-476 exit 20; I-276 (Pennsylvania Tpke) exit 333, just w on Plymouth Rd (Norristown), just e on Germantown Pike, then just e on Hickory Rd. Located in a commercial area. **Facility:** 253 units. 7 stories, interior corridors. **Terms:** check-in 4 pm, 1-7 night minimum stay, cancellation fee imposed. **Amenities:** safes. **Pool(s):** heated indoor. **Activities:** hot tub, exercise room. **Guest Services:** valet and coin laundry, area transportation.

AAA Benefit: Members save 5% or more!

HAMPTON INN PLYMOUTH MEETING   (610)567-0900 64

Hotel $129-$179 **Address:** 2055 Chemical Rd 19462 **Location:** I-476 exit 18B (Norristown/Chemical Rd) northbound, 0.3 mi w; exit southbound, use ramp to I-276 (Pennsylvania Tpke) and exit immediately at exit 333, Germantown Pike E ramp, just e to Chemical Rd, then 1 mi s. Located in a commercial area. **Facility:** 136 units. 5 stories, interior corridors. **Terms:** 1-7 night minimum stay, cancellation fee imposed. **Pool(s):** outdoor. **Activities:** exercise room. **Guest Services:** valet and coin laundry, area transportation.

AAA Benefit: Members save 5% or more!

SPRINGHILL SUITES BY MARRIOTT PHILADELPHIA/ PLYMOUTH MEETING   (610)940-0400 63

Hotel
$146-$240

SPRINGHILL SUITES Marriott

AAA Benefit: Members save 5% or more!

Address: 430 Plymouth Rd 19462 **Location:** I-276 (Pennsylvania Tpke) exit 333, follow signs for Plymouth Rd (Norristown), then just w. Located in a commercial area. **Facility:** 199 units. 8 stories, interior corridors. **Pool(s):** heated indoor. **Activities:** exercise room. **Guest Services:** valet and coin laundry. **Featured Amenity:** breakfast buffet.

WHERE TO EAT

REDSTONE AMERICAN GRILL   610/941-4400 94

American. Casual Dining. $13-$39 **AAA Inspector Notes:** Smoked rotisserie chicken in the open kitchen fills the air at this casual-upscale American restaurant. Attractive exposed-stone accents and dark wood furnishings decorate the beautiful dining room. The buffalo jumbo shrimp with blue cheese is a great beginning to any meal. **Features:** full bar, patio dining, happy hour. **Reservations:** suggested, weekends. **Address:** 512 W Germantown Pike 19462 **Location:** I-276 (Pennsylvania Tpke) exit 333, 0.5 mi n.

POCONO MOUNTAINS AREA

The name Poconos comes from a Native American word meaning "a stream runs between two mountains." In this case the stream is the Delaware River, which separates Pennsylvania from New Jersey, cutting through a ridge of the Appalachian Mountains and, in the process, forming Mount Minsi in Pennsylvania and Mount Tammany in New Jersey.

The area's 2,400 square miles, spread out among northeast Pennsylvania's Carbon, Monroe, Pike and Wayne counties, encompass rolling hills and some of the loveliest waterfalls in the East.

Folks have been coming to these mountains for rest and recreation since the mid-19th-century. Just 2 hours from both New York City and Philadelphia, the area was (and is today) a ready-made respite for big-city residents eager for a nearby escape.

Summer resorts and boardinghouses near the Delaware River opened to handle the vacationers who came by railroad to relax in the fresh, crisp mountain air and enjoy Mother Nature's bounties. Travelers still come to savor the great outdoors, but they now come year-round and more than likely arrive by car-all the better to explore this vacationland's vast mix of activities.

This map shows cities in the Pocono Mountains Area where you will find attractions, hotels and restaurants. Cities are listed alphabetically in this book on the following pages.

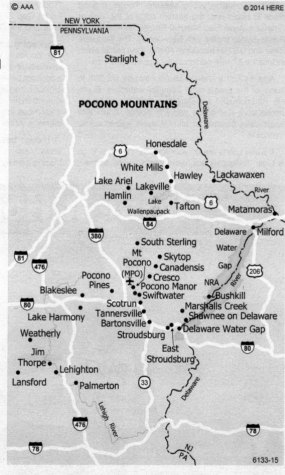

And the choice of accommodations has expanded as well. Today's visitors can select from plush lodges (many with their own golf courses and spas), historic country inns, quaint bed and breakfasts, simple mom and pop motels, an assortment of chain hotels-and, of course, the romantic couples-only resorts with their heart-shaped tubs and 7-foot-tall champagne glass whirlpool towers that have lured honeymooners to the area since the early 1960s.

You won't find any large cities here (all the better for relaxation). Stroudsburg and East Stroudsburg are about as big as it gets, but there are plenty of small, friendly towns to explore, brimming with Victorian architecture, galleries, historic homes, museums and shops.

If it's recreation you're seeking, though, a good place to begin is at the eastern edge of the area at Delaware Water Gap National Recreation Area, which Pennsylvania shares with New Jersey. The Delaware River and US 209 bisect this 40-mile-long parcel which includes a 27-mile portion of the Appalachian Trail.

And it's just a short drive (or hike) off US 209 to some of the area's most beautiful waterfalls. Bushkill, Raymondskill and Dingmans falls can all be admired from numerous vantage points. Trails and boardwalks suitable for all skill levels lead to scenic overlooks.

If water sports are on your agenda, the place to go is Lake Wallenpaupack, near Hawley in the northern part of the Poconos. One of the state's largest man-made lakes, it was created in 1926 to provide hydro-electric power. With 52 miles of shoreline and a depth of 60 feet, it's a huge watery playground.

Winter brings skiing to the Pocono Mountains. While the Pennsylvania slopes will never rival those in the Rockies (the tallest mountains here are just over 2,000 feet and artificial snow is often used), Pocono ski resorts are known for their family-friendly atmosphere. An assortment of state parks, state forests, rivers, streams, and lakes provide a rich backdrop for white-water rafting, canoeing, horseback riding, hiking, golfing and biking.

Or, if you prefer spectator sports and you're a NASCAR fan, Pocono Raceway (known as the "Tricky Triangle") near Long Pond is the site of two Sprint Cup Series races, the Pocono 400 held in June and the GoBowling.com 400 in August.

Shopping and being pampered in a spa are also high on many vacationers' lists. Outlets, malls and specialty shops cater to all tastes and budgets, and a popular pastime is combing the boutiques and the antiques and arts and crafts stores along the area's historic main streets. And spending an afternoon in a luxurious spa is a relaxing way to rejuvenate after taking in all the activities the Poconos have to offer.

Though beautiful all year, the Poconos are particularly scenic in the fall when the leaves change to blazing crimson, gold and orange.

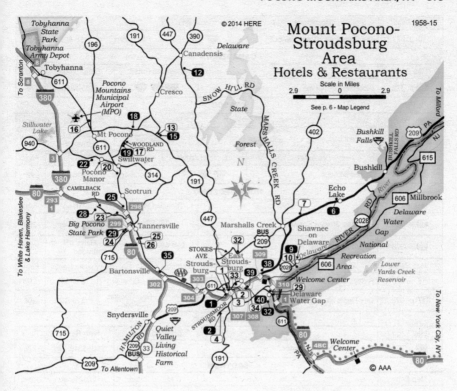

1958-15

Mount Pocono-
Stroudsburg
Area
Hotels & Restaurants

Scale in Miles

2.9   0   2.9

See p. 6 - Map Legend

© 2014 HERE

© AAA

Mount Pocono-Stroudsburg Area

This index helps you "spot" where approved hotels and restaurants are located on the corresponding detailed maps. Hotel daily rate range is for comparison only. Restaurant price range is a combination of lunch and/or dinner. Turn to the listing page for more detailed rate and price information and consult display ads for special promotions.

STROUDSBURG

Map Page	Hotels	Diamond Rated	Rate Range	Page
1 this page	Hampton Inn - Stroudsburg/Poconos	◈◈◈	$119-$199	400
2 this page	Stroudsmoor Country Inn	◈◈◈	$89-$330	400

Map Page	Restaurants	Diamond Rated	Cuisine	Price Range	Page
① this page	Sarah Street Grill	◈◈	American	$9-$26	400
② this page	Newberry's Yard of Ale	◈◈	American	$10-$22	400
③ this page	Siamsa Irish Pub	◈◈	Irish	$9-$29	400
④ this page	Stroudsmoor Country Inn	◈◈◈	Traditional American	$11-$30	401

MARSHALLS CREEK

Map Page	Hotel	Diamond Rated	Rate Range	Page
6 this page	**Pocono Palace Resort**	◈◈	Rates not provided (SAVE)	194

Map Page	Restaurant	Diamond Rated	Cuisine	Price Range	Page
⑦ this page	Big "A" Grillehouse	◈◈	American	$8-$32	194

SHAWNEE ON DELAWARE

Map Page	Hotel	Diamond Rated	Rate Range	Page
9 this page	The Shawnee Inn and Golf Resort	◈◈◈	Rates not provided	389

Map Page	Restaurant	Diamond Rated	Cuisine	Price Range	Page
⑩ p. 373	The Gem & Keystone Brewpub	▽▽	American	$8-$26	389

CANADENSIS

Map Page	Hotel	Diamond Rated	Rate Range	Page
⑫ p. 373	Brookview Manor Inn	▽▽▽	$155-$250	76

CRESCO

Map Page	Hotel	Diamond Rated	Rate Range	Page
⑮ p. 373	Crescent Lodge	▽▽▽	Rates not provided	92

Map Page	Restaurant	Diamond Rated	Cuisine	Price Range	Page
⑬ p. 373	Crescent Lodge	▽▽▽	Continental	$16-$29	92

MOUNT POCONO

Map Page	Hotels	Diamond Rated	Rate Range	Page
⑱ p. 373	**Paradise Stream Resort**	▽▽	Rates not provided (SAVE)	208
⑲ p. 373	**Mount Airy Casino Resort**	▽▽▽▽	Rates not provided (SAVE)	208

Map Page	Restaurants	Diamond Rated	Cuisine	Price Range	Page
⑯ p. 373	Baileys Grille & Steakhouse	▽▽	Steak	$16-$36	208
⑰ p. 373	Guy Fieri's Mt. Pocono Kitchen	▽▽	New Comfort Food	$13-$28	208

POCONO MANOR

Map Page	Hotel	Diamond Rated	Rate Range	Page
㉒ p. 373	**The Inn at Pocono Manor**	▽▽▽	$119-$249 (SAVE)	375

SCOTRUN

Map Page	Hotel	Diamond Rated	Rate Range	Page
㉕ p. 373	Great Wolf Lodge	▽▽▽	Rates not provided	384

TANNERSVILLE

Map Page	Hotels	Diamond Rated	Rate Range	Page
㉘ p. 373	**The Chateau Resort & Conference Center** *(See ad p. 402.)*	▽▽	$89-$324 (SAVE)	402
㉙ p. 373	**Days Inn-Tannersville**	▽▽	$66-$130 (SAVE)	402

Map Page	Restaurants	Diamond Rated	Cuisine	Price Range	Page
㉓ p. 373	**Barley Creek Brewing Company**	▽▽	American	$11-$24	402
㉔ p. 373	**Tandoor Palace Restaurant & Bar**	▽▽	Indian	$12-$21	403
㉕ p. 373	Legendary Tannersville Inn	▽▽	American	$9-$33	403
㉖ p. 373	**Smuggler's Cove**	▽▽	Seafood	$7-$35	403

DELAWARE WATER GAP

Map Page	Hotel	Diamond Rated	Rate Range	Page
㉜ p. 373	Water Gap Country Club	▽▽	Rates not provided	93

Map Page	Restaurant	Diamond Rated	Cuisine	Price Range	Page
㉙ p. 373	Sycamore Grille	▽▽▽	American	$8-$30	93

BARTONSVILLE

Map Page	Hotel	Diamond Rated	Rate Range	Page
㉟ p. 373	**Baymont Inn & Suites**	▽▽	$90-$150 (SAVE)	57

EAST STROUDSBURG

Map Page	Hotels	Diamond Rated	Rate Range	Page
㉞ p. 373	**Days Inn East Stroudsburg**	▽▽	$60-$120 (SAVE)	101

EAST STROUDSBURG (cont'd)

Map Page	Hotels (cont'd)	Diamond Rated	Rate Range	Page
㊴ p. 373	Super 8 East Stroudsburg	▽▽	$55-$149	101
㊵ p. 373	**Budget Inn & Suites**	▽▽▽	$70-$116 SAVE	101

Map Page	Restaurants	Diamond Rated	Cuisine	Price Range	Page
㉜ p. 373	**Peppe's Bistro**	▽▽▽	Northern Italian	$9-$33	102
㉝ p. 373	Holy Guacamole	▽	Mexican	$3-$7	101
㉞ p. 373	**The Roasted Tomato**	▽▽	American	$9-$22	102

SWIFTWATER

Map Page	Restaurant	Diamond Rated	Cuisine	Price Range	Page
⑳ p. 373	Desaki	▽▽▽	Japanese	$15-$50	401

POCONO MANOR

- Hotels & Restaurants map & index p. 373
- Part of Pocono Mountains Area — see map p. 371

THE INN AT POCONO MANOR (570)839-7111 ㉒

▽▽▽▽
Historic
Resort Hotel
$119-$249

Address: 1 Manor Dr 18349 **Location:** I-380 exit 3, just e on SR 314, follow signs for 1.3 mi. **Facility:** Originally opened in 1902, this resort offers a relaxed charm and sweeping views of the region. Extensive recreational facilities will keep the whole family occupied. 181 units, some two bedrooms. 7 stories, interior corridors. **Terms:** check-in 4 pm, 3 day cancellation notice. **Dining:** 3 restaurants. **Pool(s):** outdoor, heated indoor. **Activities:** fishing, regulation golf, cross country skiing, ice skating, recreation programs in summer, bicycles, playground, game room, trails, exercise room, spa. **Guest Services:** area transportation.

POCONO PINES pop. 1,409

- Part of Pocono Mountains Area — see map p. 371

VAN GILDER'S JUBILEE RESTAURANT & PUB 570/646-2377

▽▽ Comfort Food. Casual Dining. $7-$23 **AAA Inspector Notes:** Heaping portions of comfort food hit the spot from breakfast through dinner. If you're coming for the famed wings, you should know that since they're such a popular menu item they're only offered on Sunday and Thursday nights. An outdoor deck is open during the warmer months, while the connected lounge serves as a year-round sports bar. **Features:** full bar. **Address:** Rt 940 18350 **Location:** I-380 exit 3, 4 mi w. [B] [L] [D]

POINT MARION (I-2) pop. 1,159, elev. 817'

Point Marion is part of the Laurel Highlands *(see place listing p. 183).*

FRIENDSHIP HILL NATIONAL HISTORIC SITE is 3 mi. n. on SR 166; self-guiding tours begin at the visitor center. The scenic 661-acre site features the Gallatin House, home of Albert Gallatin 1789-1832. Gallatin served as the federal treasury secretary for Presidents Jefferson and Madison. Gallatin also was an ardent abolitionist. Ten miles of nature and hiking trails wind through the site.

Time: Allow 1 hour minimum. **Hours:** Grounds daily dawn-dusk. Gallatin House daily 9-5, May-Sept.; Sat.-Sun., Nov.-Mar.; Fri.-Mon. in April and Oct. Closed Jan. 1, Memorial Day, Labor Day, Thanksgiving and Christmas. Phone ahead to confirm schedule. **Cost:** Free. **Phone:** (724) 725-9190.

POINT PLEASANT (G-12) elev. 92'

- Part of Philadelphia area — see map p. 230

Before its settlement in the mid-1700s Point Pleasant was the site of Native American quarries for argillite, which was used in making arrowheads and knife blades. The Delaware River, another natural resource, provides many recreational opportunities for area visitors and residents.

RECREATIONAL ACTIVITIES

Tubing

- **Bucks County River Country** is at 2 Walters Ln. Other activities are offered. **Hours:** Daily 9-7, mid-May to early Sept.; last departure is at 4:30. Thurs.-Mon. 9-5, early Sept.-late Oct.; last departure is at 3. **Phone:** (215) 297-5000.

POTTSTOWN (A-8) pop. 22,377, elev. 144'

- Hotels p. 376 • Restaurants p. 376
- Part of Philadelphia area — see map p. 230

As early as 1714 an iron forge was established north of the present site of Pottstown, and iron making quickly became the area's principal industry. When Colonial ironmaster John Potts founded the city in 1752, he named it Pottsgrove. In 1815 it was incorporated as Pottstown. The city remains a busy industrial and trade center.

TriCounty Area Chamber of Commerce: 152 High St., Suite 360, Pottstown, PA 19464. **Phone:** (610) 326-2900.

Shopping areas: Coventry Mall, SR 100 and SR 724, is the major shopping center. It includes Boscov's and Kohl's.

POTTSGROVE MANOR is .7 mi. n. of jct. SRs 100 and 422 at 100 W. King St. The restored 1752 home of John Potts, Colonial ironmaster and town founder, provides a look at the lifestyle of his family, servants and slaves. Guided tours are given of the house, which contains 18th-century Pennsylvania furnishings, slave quarters and original woodwork. Changing exhibits also are featured.

Time: Allow 1 hour minimum. **Hours:** Tues.-Sat. 10-4, Sun. 1-4. Tours begin on the hour. Last tour begins 1 hour before closing. Closed major holidays. Phone ahead to confirm schedule. **Cost:** Free. $2. **Phone:** (610) 326-4014.

WELKINWEIR is off I-76 exit 312, 8.3 mi. n. on SR 100 then .7 mi. w. at 1368 Prizer Rd. This is the former estate of Everett and Grace Rodebaugh; both were dedicated to environmental issues and helped found the Green Valleys Association, which protects the five watersheds of northern Chester County. The arboretum features formal gardens, a wildlife sanctuary and hiking trails. The site is connected to the Horse-Shoe Trail, where horseback riding is permitted; from there visitors can continue on to French Creek State Park *(see Recreation Areas Chart)*.

Educational programs for children, adults and families are offered throughout the year. **Time:** Allow 3 hours minimum. **Hours:** Mon.-Fri. 9-4:30, early May-late Sept.; 9-4, rest of year (weather permitting). Closed major holidays. **Cost:** Donations. **Phone:** (610) 469-4990. 🏕

COMFORT INN & SUITES   (610)326-5000
🛇🛇🛇 Hotel $99-$179 **Address:** 99 Robinson St 19464 **Location:** SR 100, 1 mi n of jct US 422. Located in a commercial area. **Facility:** 119 units. 4 stories, interior corridors. **Pool(s):** heated outdoor. **Activities:** exercise room. **Guest Services:** valet and coin laundry.
🛇 CALL 🅜 🖧 BIZ 🛜 ✕ 🖪 🖾 🖳
/SOME UNITS 🛇

WHERE TO EAT

COVENTRY PUB   610/323-5790
🛇🛇 American. Casual Dining. $7-$20 **AAA Inspector Notes:** This older pub doesn't try to be fancy but it has kept locals coming in for years with its neighborly service and relaxed atmosphere. While the menu provides an option of sandwiches and snacks, most people come for their signature item, a hand-carved piled-high roast beef sandwich. An excellent selection of beers and cocktails are available to wash it all down. **Features:** full bar. **Address:** 1440 S Hanover St 19465 **Location:** 2.4 mi s of jct US 422 and SR 100.
Ⓛ Ⓓ

POTTSVILLE (G-9) pop. 14,324, elev. 636'

Pottsville was named for John Pott, a pioneer ironworker who built a small iron furnace in 1806. The founding of the city coincided with the beginning of the vital iron and steel industry, which prospered for more than a century.

Pottsville also was part of northeastern Pennsylvania's anthracite coal mining region. Pottsville sports the 90-foot-high Henry Clay Monument, a memorial to the presidential candidate who supported legislation favorable to the area's coal industry. The monument,

built in 1855, is said to be the nation's oldest cast-iron statue.

Schuylkill County Visitors Bureau: 300 S. Centre St., Pottsville, PA 17901. **Phone:** (570) 622-7700 or (800) 765-7282.

Shopping areas: Schuylkill Mall, 6 miles north on SR 61, has about 100 stores, including The Bon-Ton and Sears.

JERRY'S CLASSIC CARS AND COLLECTIBLES MUSEUM, downtown at 394 S. Centre St. (US 209), houses an impressive collection of more than 20,000 antiques and memorabilia on two floors. The majority of items relates to 1950s and '60s pop culture. The museum features hand-painted murals and themed sections, including a bandstand, kitchen and soda fountain. There are usually about 15 classic cars on display; the models chosen from the collection are changed regularly.

Time: Allow 1 hour minimum. **Hours:** Fri.-Sun. noon-5, May-Oct. **Cost:** $10; $8 (ages 6-12 and senior citizens); free (ages 0-5). **Phone:** (570) 628-2266. 🔲GT

YUENGLING BREWERY, Fifth and Mahantongo sts., offers tours of America's oldest brewery; it was established in 1829. Visitors observe various facets of the production process and sample the finished product at the tour's end.

The plant is not in operation on Saturdays. **Note:** Full mobility is required; there are many steps. Closed shoes are required; openings around the foot are not permitted. **Time:** Allow 1 hour, 15 minutes minimum. **Hours:** Tours depart Mon.-Fri. at 10 and 1:30 (also Sat. 11-1, Apr.-Dec.); tours depart in groups of 50 guests. Closed major holidays. **Cost:** Free. **Phone:** (570) 628-4890.

GREYSTONE RESTAURANT   570/628-4220
🛇🛇🛇
Continental Fine Dining $18-$30 — **AAA Inspector Notes:** *Historic.* In a circa 1894 former brick hotel downtown, the dining room offers an element of charm supported by exposed stone and wood walls and copper-topped tables. Another seating option is the dining terrace. An extensive list of wines, imported and domestic beers and 30 martinis complements a seasonally changing menu. Wild game is frequently featured. Broiled mahi mahi served atop asparagus spears and mashed potatoes is worth trying. **Features:** full bar, patio dining. **Reservations:** suggested. **Address:** 315 N Centre St 17901 **Location:** Jct Laurel Blvd and Centre St; downtown. Ⓓ

PUNXSUTAWNEY (F-4) pop. 5,962, elev. 1,236'

Each Feb. 2, the nation awaits the prognostication of one of the town's most respected citizens: Punxsutawney Phil—the official groundhog of 🐾 Groundhog Day. As they have each year since 1887, believers trek at dawn to Gobbler's Knob and rout the rodent from his den to determine whether there will be an early spring or 6 more weeks of winter, a legend based on the European tradition of-Candlemas Day (Feb. 2), where a burrowing animal is used to predict the length of winter.

This annual occurrence was immortalized in the 1993 movie "Groundhog Day," in which a television weatherman (played by comedian Bill Murray) reluctantly comes to Punxsutawney to cover the event, only to awake the next morning and find himself reliving every facet of the preceding day over, again and again.

On the other 364 days of the year, Phil and his family reside at the "groundhog zoo" at the Punxsutawney Memorial Library, just off the town's historic Barclay Square at 301 E. Mahoning St. A glass window lets visitors see the animals and their habitat from either inside or outside the building.

A series of 32 colorful, larger-than-life fiberglass statues honoring Punxsutawney's most famous resident can be seen in public spaces around town. The chamber of commerce has maps that show the placement of each of the Phils, as they are called.

Area residents enjoy the outdoors year-round on the Mahoning Shadow Trail, a 15-mile rails-to-trails conversion that runs between Punxsutawney and Fordham, beckoning walkers, runners, bicyclists and cross-country skiers. The trail, which mostly follows Mahoning Creek, crosses a railroad bridge and passes coke ovens and a waterfall. Trail maps are available at the chamber of commerce office.

Punxsutawney Area Chamber of Commerce: 102 W. Mahoning St., Punxsutawney, PA 15767. **Phone:** (814) 938-7700 or (800) 752-7445.

PUNXSUTAWNEY WEATHER DISCOVERY CENTER, 201 N. Findley St., features interactive exhibits relating to weather forecasting—both the scientific kind and folklore (where Punxsutawney Phil comes in). Visitors can watch weather videos in the theater, experience the power of a tornado, create a thunderstorm and try their hand at giving a TV weather forecast. **Time:** Allow 1 hour minimum. **Hours:** Mon. and Thurs.-Sat. 10-4, Jan.-March; Mon.-Tues. and Thurs.-Sat. 10-4, Sept.-Dec. and Apr.-May; Mon.-Sat. June-Aug. **Cost:** $5; free (ages 0-1). **Phone:** (814) 938-1000.

QUAKERTOWN pop. 8,979
• Part of Philadelphia area — see map p. 230

BEST WESTERN MOTOR INN   (215)536-2500

Hotel
$95-$109

AAA Benefit:
Members save up to 20%!

Address: 1446 W Broad St 18951 **Location:** E of jct SR 313 and 309. Located in a commercial area. **Facility:** 40 units. 2 stories (no elevator), interior corridors. **Activities:** exercise room. **Guest Services:** coin laundry.

HAMPTON INN-QUAKERTOWN   (215)536-7779

Hotel $119-$149 **Address:** 1915 John Fries Hwy (SR 663) 18951 **Location:** I-476 (Pennsylvania Tpke) exit 44, just e. **Facility:** 79 units. 3 stories, interior corridors. **Terms:** check-in 4 pm, 1-7 night minimum stay, cancellation fee imposed. **Pool(s):** heated indoor. **Activities:** hot tub, exercise room. **Guest Services:** valet and coin laundry.

AAA Benefit:
Members save 5% or more!

HOLIDAY INN EXPRESS HOTEL & SUITES QUAKERTOWN
215/529-7979

Hotel. Rates not provided. **Address:** 1918 John Fries Hwy (SR 663) 18951 **Location:** I-476 (Pennsylvania Tpke) exit 44, just e. **Facility:** 78 units. 3 stories, interior corridors. **Pool(s):** heated indoor. **Activities:** exercise room. **Guest Services:** valet laundry.

QUALITY INN & SUITES   (215)538-3000

Hotel $79-$159 **Address:** 1905 John Fries Hwy (SR 663) 18951 **Location:** I-476 (Pennsylvania Tpke) exit 44, just e. **Facility:** 60 units. 2 stories (no elevator), exterior corridors. **Amenities:** safes. **Activities:** exercise room. **Guest Services:** valet and coin laundry.

SPRINGHILL SUITES BY MARRIOTT   (215)529-6800

Hotel $101-$166 **Address:** 1930 John Fries Hwy (SR 663) 18951 **Location:** I-476 (Pennsylvania Tpke) exit 44, just e. **Facility:** 89 units. 3 stories, interior corridors. **Bath:** shower only. **Pool(s):** heated indoor. **Activities:** hot tub, exercise room. **Guest Services:** valet and coin laundry.

AAA Benefit:
Members save 5% or more!

WHERE TO EAT

THE SPINNERSTOWN HOTEL RESTAURANT & TAP ROOM
215/536-7242

American. Casual Dining. $9-$30 **AAA Inspector Notes:** Serving locals and travelers for the past 250 years, this restaurant mixes American and Continental dishes on its menu. A comfortable country-inn atmosphere prevails at the establishment, which, despite its name, has no lodging facilities. **Features:** full bar. **Reservations:** suggested, weekends. **Address:** 2195 Spinnerstown Rd 18951 **Location:** I-476 (Pennsylvania Tpke) exit 44, just w on SR 663, then 0.5 mi n.

QUARRYVILLE (I-10) pop. 2,576, elev. 488'
• Part of Pennsylvania Dutch Country area — see map p. 220

About 7 miles south on US 222 is the Robert Fulton Birthplace, the restored stone house where the artist, inventor and engineer was born in 1765. His drawings, miniature portraits and invention models, including the steamship *Clermont*, are exhibited on weekends during the summer; phone (717) 548-2679.

Keep a current AAA/CAA

Road Atlas in every vehicle

RADNOR

• Part of Philadelphia area — see map p. 230

RADNOR HOTEL   610/688-5800
WWWW Hotel. Rates not provided. **Address:** 591 E Lancaster Ave 19087 **Location:** I-476 (Pennsylvania Tpke) exit 13, 0.3 mi w on US 30. Located in a commercial area. (🏃) Radnor, 107. **Facility:** 171 units. 4 stories, interior corridors. **Amenities:** *Some:* safes. **Dining:** 2 restaurants, also, Glenmorgan Bar & Grill, see separate listing. **Activities:** exercise room, spa. **Guest Services:** valet laundry, area transportation.

🍴 🛗 🍽 BIZ 📶 ✕ 🛖 💻
/SOME UNITS 🎱 🖥 🚐

WHERE TO EAT

GLENMORGAN BAR & GRILL   610/341-3188
WW W American. Casual Dining. $9-$38 **AAA Inspector Notes:** The restaurant honors the region's Welsh immigrant heritage by naming itself for County Glamorgan, the largest county in Wales. The dining room's casually upscale décor employs natural mahogany, polished chrome, steel and nickel. The centerpiece is a 28-seat oval bar. On the menu are such tasty delicacies as honey-tamari salmon, grilled Jail Island salmon and pub steak au poivre. **Features:** full bar, Sunday brunch, happy hour. **Reservations:** suggested. **Address:** 593 E Lancaster Ave 19087 **Location:** I-476 (Pennsylvania Tpke) exit 13, 0.3 mi w on US 30; in Radnor Hotel. (🏃) Radnor, 107.

🄻 🄳 LATE 🚐

READING (H-10) pop. 88,082, elev. 237'

Thomas and Richard Penn, sons of William Penn, founded Reading in 1748 and named it for their ancestral home in England. The settlement was a supply base for forts along the Blue Mountains during the French and Indian War. In Reading originated the first Civil War regiment, volunteer band, flag and women's aid society. Modern Reading has become a major industrial center, with many clothing manufacturers maintaining retail outlet stores.

Reading contains a wealth of 18th- and 19th-century buildings, many noted for their elaborate use of decorative glass and wrought iron, in its five historic districts: Callowhill, which centers on the city's commercial area; Prince, which contains preserved 19th-century workers' homes, factories and commercial structures; Centre Park, which displays some of the city's finest Victorian structures; Penn's Common; and Queen Anne.

On the east side of Reading on the summit of Mount Penn is the Pagoda, a seven-story 1908 Japanese building that affords panoramas of the city and the Schuylkill Valley. About 8 miles northwest via SR 183 is the Blue Marsh Lake Recreation Area *(see Recreation Areas Chart).*

The GoggleWorks Center for the Arts, (610) 374-4600, is an art gallery where you can watch artists at work; there also is a theater that shows foreign and independent films. The site comprises several buildings at the intersection of Washington and 2nd streets and includes the former Thomas A. Wilson & Co. factory, a company that produced optical glass in the late 19th century. The company quickly expanded its horizons to become an innovator in occupational safety products, the first of which was a protective lens to protect the vision of those working in metal processing. The front desk offers maps of the galleries.

Greater Reading Visitor Center Kiosk: 201 Washington St., Reading, PA 19601. The kiosk inside the GoggleWorks Center for the Arts is staffed on weekends; brochures available daily. **Phone:** (610) 375-4085 or (800) 443-6610.

Shopping areas: Carter's, Reading China & Glass and Lee and Wrangler are among the stores that fill the more than 450,000 square feet of retail space at **VF Outlet Center,** 801 Hill Ave. Boscov's, Burlington Coat Factory, Baby Depot and Luxury Linens anchor **Fairgrounds Square Mall,** 3050 N. Fifth Street Hwy.

BERKS COUNTY HERITAGE CENTER is .4 mi. s. off SR 183 at 1102 Red Bridge Rd. This interpretive complex focuses on the history of the rural wagon industry and canal transportation. The complex includes Wertz's Covered Bridge (also known as Red Bridge), the longest single-span covered bridge in the state, and the 5-mile Union Canal Bicycle and Walking Trail, which traces a former canal towpath. The C. Howard Hiester Canal Center, Melcher's Grist Mill, Deppen Cemetery, Gruber Wagon Works, the Bicentennial Eagle Memorial and Veteran's Memorial also are featured.

A stone farmhouse serves as the information center. **Hours:** Grounds open 8-dusk. Guided tours of Gruber Wagon Works and Hiester Canal Center are given Tues.-Sat. 10-4, Sun. noon-5, May 1-last Sun. in Oct. Last tour begins 1 hour before closing. **Cost:** Grounds free. C. Howard Hiester Canal Center or Gruber Wagon Works $5; $4 (ages 61+); $3 (ages 7-18). Combination ticket $8; $6 (ages 61+); $4 (ages 7-18). **Phone:** (610) 374-8839.

C. Howard Hiester Canal Center, next to Berks County Heritage Center's information center at 1102 Red Bridge Rd., has a collection of artifacts representing 19th-century travel on the Union and Schuylkill canals. Videotapes offer historic information. Among the large exhibits are a tugboat pilothouse, a tollbooth and a coal scow that was converted to a houseboat for the Hiester family, who operated a boatyard.

Time: Allow 1 hour minimum. **Hours:** Guided tours are given Tues.-Sat. 10-4, Sun. noon-5, May 1-last Sun. in Oct. Last tour begins 1 hour before closing. **Cost:** $5; $4 (ages 61+); $3 (ages 7-18). Combination ticket with Gruber Wagon Works $8; $6 (ages 61+); $4 (ages 7-18). **Phone:** (610) 374-8839.
GT 🍴

Gruber Wagon Works, 1 Red Bridge Rd. at the Berks County Heritage Center, started in 1882 as a one-man trade shop and grew to a mass-production wagon manufacturing company. The building was moved from its original site in Mount Pleasant and meticulously restored, complete with tools and machinery used by Gruber craftsmen.

Time: Allow 1 hour minimum. **Hours:** Guided tours are given Tues.-Sat. 10-4, Sun. noon-5, May 1-last Sun. in Oct. Last tour begins 1 hour before closing. **Cost:** $5; $4 (ages 61+); $3 (ages 7-18).

Combination ticket with C. Howard Hiester Canal Center $8; $6 (ages 61+); $4 (ages 7-18). **Phone:** (610) 374-8839. GT

BERKS HISTORY CENTER, 940 Centre Ave., contains displays that depict local history, including fine arts, industry, transportation and Pennsylvania German arts and crafts. A museum displays changing art exhibits and an antique transportation collection including a Conestoga wagon, a 1902 Duryea automobile and a horse-drawn streetcar. Across the street, Henry Janssen Library collection includes 30,000 photographs, almost 600 maps, newspapers dating to 1796 and other items relating to Berks County history and genealogy.

Time: Allow 1 hour minimum. **Hours:** Tues.-Sat. 9-4. Closed major holidays, day before Thanksgiving and holiday weekends. Phone ahead to confirm schedule. **Cost:** Museum $7; $5 (ages 65+); $4 (ages 4-17). Library $7; ages 0-11 are not permitted. **Phone:** (610) 375-4375.

SAVE **MID-ATLANTIC AIR MUSEUM,** SR 183 to the Reading Regional Airport at 11 Museum Dr., following signs, displays both military and civilian aircraft dating from 1917 to 2006. Among the more than 65 airplanes displayed are two classic commercial airliners, a 1952 Martin 4-0-4 and a Vickers Viscount; the first night fighter ever built; a 1944 Douglas DC-3; a 1943 North American B-25 Mitchell; and a 1944 P-61 Black Widow, the first "night fighter" ever built.

Note: When using GPS for directions, use 1054 Arnold Road, Reading PA, 19605. **Time:** Allow 1 hour minimum. **Hours:** Daily 9:30-4. Last tour begins 1 hour before closing. Closed major holidays. **Cost:** $8; $6 (ages 65+); $3 (ages 6-12). **Phone:** (610) 372-7333.

READING PUBLIC MUSEUM, 500 Museum Rd., presents art, science and civilization displays. A 25-acre arboretum, a planetarium and changing exhibits also are featured. **Hours:** Museum daily 11-5. Planetarium star shows Mon.-Fri. at 4 and Sun. at 1, 2, 3 and 4; phone for laser light show schedule. Closed Presidents' Day, July 4, Labor Day, Thanksgiving, Christmas and New Year's Day.

Cost: Museum $10; $6 (ages 4-17, ages 65+ and students with ID). Planetarium star or music show $8; $5 (ages 4-17, ages 65+ and students with ID). Fees may be charged for special events and exhibitions. **Phone:** (610) 371-5850.

THE ABRAHAM LINCOLN HOTEL (610)372-3700
▼▼ **Historic Hotel** $88-$184 **Address:** 100 N 5th St 19601 **Location:** At 5th and Washington sts; downtown. **Facility:** Clad in brick with touches of wrought iron, this National Historic Hotel offers an elegantly appointed lobby. 104 units. 18 stories, interior corridors. **Parking:** on-site (fee). **Terms:** cancellation fee imposed. **Dining:** The Abe Saloon and Victorian Lounge, see separate listing, entertainment. **Activities:** exercise room. **Guest Services:** valet laundry.

COMFORT INN (610)371-0500

Hotel
$80-S165
Address: 2200 Stacey Dr (5th Street Hwy) 19605 **Location:** US 222 business route, just s of Warren St Bypass (SR 12 E). Located in a commercial area. **Facility:** 60 units. 2 stories (no elevator), interior corridors. **Amenities:** safes. **Activities:** exercise room. **Guest Services:** valet laundry. **Featured Amenity:** breakfast buffet.

HOLIDAY INN EXPRESS HOTEL & SUITES 610/372-0700
▼▼ **Hotel.** Rates not provided. **Address:** 2389 Bernville Rd (Rt 183) 19605 **Location:** US 222 exit SR 183, 1 mi s. Located at entrance to Reading Regional Airport. **Facility:** 70 units, some efficiencies. 3 stories, interior corridors. **Activities:** exercise room. **Guest Services:** valet and coin laundry.

 WHERE TO EAT

THE ABE SALOON AND VICTORIAN LOUNGE 610/372-7777
▼▼ American. Casual Dining. $7-$19 **AAA Inspector Notes:** As the name suggests, this restaurant is split in two rooms: a classic American pub with dark-wood furnishings and a beautiful Victorian dining room (only open at certain times). The menu provides a variety of casual fare, including beer-battered haddock fish and chips, a grilled Reuben and the popular "Honest Abe's Pub Burger." **Features:** full bar, happy hour. **Address:** 100 N 5th St 19601 **Location:** At 5th and Washington sts; downtown; in The Abraham Lincoln Hotel. **Parking:** on-site (fee).

ALEBRIJE MEXICAN RESTAURANT
▼▼ Mexican. Casual Dining. $9-$17 **AAA Inspector Notes:** Top dogs on Alebrije's Mexican and Tex-Mex menu include pollo patio (shrimp and chicken served with Mexican rice) and chicken ranchero (chicken marinated with ranchero sauce and served with rice and beans). A desert mural provides a nice backdrop in the casual dining room, which features Tex-Mex décor appointments. **Bar:** full bar.
For additional information, visit AAA.com
LOCATIONS:
Address: 3805 Perkiomen Ave 19606 **Location:** US 422 business route, 0.8 mi w of jct US 422. **Phone:** 610/370-0900
Address: 3225 N 5th Street Hwy 19605 **Location:** Jct US 222B (5th Street Hwy) and SR 12 (Warren Street Bypass), 0.8 mi e on US 222B; in Plaza 222 Shopping Center. **Phone:** 610/939-9288

CHEF ALANS AMERICAN BISTRO 610/685-4000
▼▼ American. Casual Dining. $4-$20 **AAA Inspector Notes:** With a tropical-Mediterranean décor theme, this restaurant employs mosaic tiles, Tuscan walls, eclectic lighting and artwork, and an abundance of plants and palm trees to provide a fun, contemporary, casual dining experience. The menu features tropical salads, brick-oven pizza, gourmet burgers, steaks, fresh seafood, pasta dishes, prime rib, rotisserie chicken and creative specials. Try the delicious butterflied filet mignon, charbroiled and topped with crabmeat imperial. **Features:** full bar, happy hour. **Address:** 3050 N 5th Street Hwy 19605 **Location:** Jct US 222B (N 5th Street Hwy) and SR 12 (Warren Street Bypass), 0.6 mi e on US 222B; in Fairgrounds Square Mall.

JUDY'S ON CHERRY 610/374-8511
▼▼ Mediterranean Small Plates. Fine Dining. $8-$32 **AAA Inspector Notes:** *Historic.* In a late-19th-century former market building, this restaurant merges brick walls, polished wood floors, an open kitchen and an arched wood ceiling whose center portion forms a cupola-like effect. Dishes are hearth-fired in a 3-ton stone oven. Try one of the gourmet pizzas such as crab pizza Dijonnaise, the rack of lamb with balsamic black-pepper vinaigrette or the clay-roasted snapper a la Portuguese. **Features:** full bar. **Reservations:** suggested. **Address:** 332 Cherry St 19602 **Location:** Between 3rd and 4th sts; downtown. **Parking:** street only.

STOKESAY CASTLE LORD'S DINING ROOM
610/375-6100

American Fine Dining
$30-$54

AAA Inspector Notes: As guests walk into the elegant dining room, they will be captivated by the wood-beam cathedral ceiling, upscale furnishings, beautiful stone fireplace and wrought iron chandeliers. The contemporary American-focused menu provides an abundance of flavorful dishes including coffee-dusted sea scallops and roasted rack of wild boar. Those looking for a more casual dining experience may be interested in the Knight's Pub, located right next door. **Features:** full bar. **Reservations:** suggested. **Address:** 141 Stokesay Castle Ln 19606 **Location:** US 422 business route, 3.4 mi w of jct US 422. [D] CALL 🔔M

THAI CUISINE RESTAURANT
610/929-6993

🛡️🛡️ Thai. Casual Dining. $6-$19 **AAA Inspector Notes:** This dining room has a cozy, casual atmosphere and is decorated with Thai tapestries and ceramics. On the menu are seafood specials and vegetarian dishes prepared with fresh, natural ingredients. Seafood curry is prepared with salmon, scallops, tuna, mussels, clams, crabmeat, six varieties of vegetables and a creamy coconut red curry sauce. Bring-your-own-bottle wine service is provided. **Reservations:** suggested, weekends. **Address:** 502 Eisenbrown St 19605 **Location:** Jct US 222B (N 5th Street Hwy) and SR 12 (Warren Street Bypass), 0.3 mi ne on US 222 business route, just n on George St, then just e. [L] [D]

TROOPER THORN'S
610/685-4944

🛡️🛡️ Irish. Casual Dining. $3-$22 **AAA Inspector Notes:** The eatery is a great spot to sit back, relax and enjoy a pint and a meat pie. The menu offers selections from Ireland, Scotland and England. Live, authentic Irish music is offered weekly. **Features:** full bar. **Address:** 451 Morgantown Rd 19611 **Location:** US 222 and SR 10, 1 mi s. [L] [D]

UGLY OYSTER DRAFTHAUS
610/373-6791

American Gastropub
$5-$20

AAA Inspector Notes: The establishment offers the true taste of an old Irish pub. Created in the style of a Guinness pub, the Ugly Oyster was constructed in York, England, taken apart, imported and reassembled by the same master craftsmen on the site of the city's oldest tavern. House specialties include oysters, fish and chips, Prime steaks and a large selection of imported English and Irish beers. **Features:** full bar. **Address:** 21 S 5th St 19602 **Location:** Corner of Cherry and 5th sts; downtown. *Menu on AAA.com* [L] [D]

RIDLEY PARK pop. 7,002
• **Hotels & Restaurants map & index p. 274**
• **Part of Philadelphia area — see map p. 230**

SPRINGHILL SUITES BY MARRIOTT PHILADELPHIA AIRPORT/RIDLEY PARK   (610)915-6600 **126**

🛡️🛡️🛡️ Hotel $118-$206 **Address:** 598 W Sellers Ave 19078 **Location:** I-95 exit 8 (Ridley Park), just nw on Stewart Ave, just n on US 13, then 0.6 mi e. Near Philadelphia International Airport. 📶 Crum Lynne, 170. **Facility:** 130 units. 5 stories, interior corridors. **Pool(s):** heated indoor. **Activities:** exercise room. **Guest Services:** valet and coin laundry, area transportation.

AAA Benefit:
Members save 5% or more!

✈️ 🍴 CALL 🔔M 🏊 🛗 BIZ HS 📶 ✕ 🖨 📷
💻 ⛽

ROARING SPRING (H-5) pop. 2,585,
elev. 1,200'

BARE MEMORIAL FOUNTAIN is at 740 Spang St. In 1850 the community took its name from the sound of the spring hitting the rocks. Today the rocks are gone but varicolored sprays of water rise to a height of 25 feet above the basin of the original spring site. **Hours:** The fountain operates daily noon-11, mid-Apr. until freezing weather. Hours may vary in cooler weather; phone ahead to confirm. **Phone:** (814) 224-5141.

ROBESONIA pop. 2,061

HEIDELBERG FAMILY RESTAURANT   610/693-5060

🛡️ American. Family Dining. $4-$18 **AAA Inspector Notes:** Bring the family for a tasty introduction to Pennsylvania Dutch cuisine. Homemade chicken potpie, flavorful soups, strawberry angel food cake and coconut cream pie are wholesome, filling examples of what you'll find on the menu. The restaurant caters to families with its friendly atmosphere and unpretentious setting. **Address:** 910 W Penn Ave 19551 **Location:** 1.5 mi w on US 422.
[B] [L] [D]

OZGOOD'S NEIGHBORHOOD GRILL & BAR   610/693-6685

🛡️🛡️ American. Casual Dining. $6-$22 **AAA Inspector Notes:** Before chains made neighborhood bar and grills all look the same, this casual spot was making signature salads, soft-pretzel sandwiches, fantastic seafood offerings and friendly service an everyday thing. Also on the menu are classic comfort foods, including smothered meatloaf, bourbon ham steak and freshly made cheesecake. **Features:** full bar, patio dining. **Address:** 319 E Penn Ave 19551 **Location:** Center. [L] [D]

ROCKHILL (H-6) pop. 371
• **Part of Pennsylvania Dutch Country area — see map p. 220**

Rockhill Trolley Museum, jct. SR 994 and US 522 at 430 Meadow St., across from the East Broad Top Railroad, chronicles the history of the trolley through photographs and various displays. Excursions on trolleys dating from the 1890s are offered. Special fall and winter theme excursions also are offered.

Hours: Museum and trolley excursions Sat.-Sun. 11-4:20, Memorial Day weekend-Oct. 31. Trolley departures at 11:15, 12:30, 1:45, 3 and 4:20. Phone ahead for special seasonal excursion schedules. Phone ahead to confirm schedule. **Cost:** $8; $4 (ages 3-12). **Phone:** (814) 447-9576 Sat.-Sun. during season.

RONKS (H-10) pop. 362, elev. 380'
• **Restaurants p. 382**
• **Attractions map p. 221**
• **Hotels & Restaurants map & index p. 225**
• **Part of Pennsylvania Dutch Country area — see map p. 220**

A restored 1738 water-driven gristmill and the largest covered bridge in Lancaster County is located .25 mi. s of US 30 at jct. S. Ronks and S. Soudersburg rds. A film about the Pennsylvania Dutch also is shown at Mill Bridge Camp Resort. Phone ahead to verify schedule; (717) 687-8181 or 800-645-2744.

THE AMISH VILLAGE, 199 Hartman Bridge Rd., offers 25-minute tours of an 1840 farmhouse furnished in the Old Order Amish style. The tour includes the great room (used for community meetings), kitchen, bedrooms and basement, and the guide offers insight into Amish history, clothing, furniture and their way of life. Other buildings include a

(See map & index p. 225.)

barn, schoolhouse, blacksmith shop, store and springhouse. Visitors are permitted to feed the farm animals.

The 90-minute Backroads Bus Tour is a narrated tour in a 14-passenger bus along country roads where buggies and farmers are often seen. The tour includes at least one stop; options include an Amish home, a quilt shop, a pretzel bakery or a bake shop. Picnicking is permitted after tours. **Time:** Allow 1 hour, 30 minutes minimum. **Hours:** Village Mon.-Sat. 9-5, Sun. 10-5, Mar.-Dec.; Sat.-Sun. 10-4, rest of year. Farmhouse only (weather permitting) daily 10-4, in Dec.; Sat.-Sun. 10-4, Jan.-Feb. Backroads Bus Tour depart daily on the hour 10-4, Mar.-Dec. **Cost:** Amish Village $9; $5.50 (ages 5-12); free (0-4). Backroads Bus Tour $20; $13 (ages 0-12). Village and bus tour $26; $$16 (ages 5-12); $13 (ages 0-4). Reservations are recommended for bus tour. **Phone:** (717) 687-8511. 🚗

CHERRY CREST ADVENTURE FARM, 150 Cherry Hill Rd., has a 5-acre maze with 2.5 miles of paths cut into a cornfield. Amenities include wagon rides, a petting zoo, logic mazes, a straw bale racing course, pedal carts, a hay tunnel and children's activities. Festivals and events also are presented.

Time: Allow 1 hour, 30 minutes minimum. **Hours:** Maze and farm activities open Tues.-Fri. 10-5, Sat. 10-dusk, July 3-Sept. 3; Thurs. 10-5, Fri.-Sat. 10-10, Oct. 4-Nov. 3; Fri. (also Labor Day) 10-5, Sat. 10-dusk, Sept. 7-15. Last maze admission 90 minutes before closing. Farm activities (no maze) Sat. (also Memorial Day) noon-5, May 28-June 25. Open weather permitting. Phone ahead to confirm schedule. **Cost:** Farm activities $10. Farm activities and maze $15. **Phone:** (717) 687-6843 or (866) 546-1799. 🍴 🚗

STRASBURG RAIL ROAD CO. is 1 mi. e. on SR 741E. Forty-five-minute excursions through the heart of Pennsylvania Dutch Country are offered on one of America's oldest short-line railroads. Restored steam locomotives pull vintage passenger and dining cars. Guided behind-the-scenes tours of the restoration shop are available. Special excursions include a Day Out With Thomas, the Easter Bunny Train, the Wine & Cheese Train, the Great Train Robbery, Steampunk unLimited, the Night Before Christmas Train, the Christmas Train and Santa's Paradise Express. Themed dinner trains also are available.

Time: Allow 1 hour minimum. **Hours:** Trains depart daily, mid-Mar. to early Nov.; Sat.-Sun., early Nov.-late Dec. Phone ahead for departure times and to confirm schedule. **Cost:** Coach fares $14; $8 (ages 3-11). Upgrades are available for open-air, dining and first-class cars for an extra fee. Behind-the-scenes tour $18; advance reservations recommended. Special excursion rates vary. Other combination ticket packages and day passes also

are available. Phone ahead to confirm rates. **Phone:** (717) 687-7522 or (866) 725-9666. 🍴 🚗

CANDLELIGHT INN BED & BREAKFAST   717/299-6005   **65**

🛏🛏🛏 **Classic Bed & Breakfast.** Rates not provided. **Address:** 2574 Lincoln Hwy E 17572 **Location:** Jct US 30 (Lincoln Hwy) and SR 896, 0.3 mi e. Located in a rural area. **Facility:** Victorian décor is found throughout this B&B, which is in a restored 1920s home at the edge of town. Some guest rooms feature a fireplace, casting a warm glow throughout the room on cool nights. 7 units. 3 stories (no elevator), interior corridors. **Terms:** age restrictions may apply. 📶 ✕ 🅦 ☎

DAYS INN LANCASTER PA DUTCH COUNTRY   (717)390-1800   **62**

◆◆ ◆◆
Hotel
$59-$169

Address: 34 Eastbrook Rd 17572 **Location:** Jct US 30 (Lincoln Hwy), just n on SR 896. Located in a commercial tourist area. **Facility:** 51 units, some efficiencies. 2 stories (no elevator), interior corridors. **Amenities:** safes. **Activities:** limited exercise equipment. **Guest Services:** coin laundry. **Featured Amenity:** continental breakfast.

SAVE BIZ 📶 ✕ 🛏 🖼 💻

EASTBROOK INN   (717)393-2550   **64**

◆◆ ◆◆
Motel
$65-$109

Address: 21 Eastbrook Rd 17572 **Location:** Jct US 30 (Lincoln Hwy), just n on SR 896. Located in a commercial tourist area. **Facility:** 54 units. 3 stories (no elevator), interior corridors. **Featured Amenity:** continental breakfast.

SAVE 📶 🛏 🖼 💻

HERSHEY FARM INN   (717)687-8635   **67**

◆◆ ◆◆
Hotel
$50-$170

Address: 240 Hartman Bridge Rd 17572 **Location:** Jct US 30 (Lincoln Hwy), 1.5 mi s on SR 896. **Facility:** 60 units, some two bedrooms. 1-2 stories (no elevator), interior/exterior corridors. **Dining:** Hershey Farm Restaurant, see separate listing. **Pool(s):** outdoor. **Activities:** fishing, playground. **Guest Services:** coin laundry.

SAVE 🍴 🏊 BIZ 📶 ✕ 💻
/ SOME UNITS 🛏 🖼

LA QUINTA INN & SUITES   (717)392-8100   **63**

◆◆ ◆◆
Hotel
$82-$189

Address: 25 Eastbrook Rd 17572 **Location:** Jct US 30 (Lincoln Hwy), just n on SR 896. **Facility:** 77 units. 3 stories, interior corridors. **Pool(s):** heated indoor. **Activities:** hot tub, exercise room. **Guest Services:** coin laundry. **Featured Amenity:** continental breakfast.

SAVE CALL &M 🏊 BIZ 📶 ✕
🛏 🖼 💻 / SOME UNITS 🐾

(See map & index p. 225.)

QUIET HAVEN MOTEL   717/397-6231   **61**

 Motel $52-$96 **Address:** 2556 Siegrist Rd 17572 **Location:** Jct SR 340, 0.5 mi s on SR 896, 0.3 mi e. Located in a quiet rural area. **Facility:** 15 units. 1 story, exterior corridors. **Terms:** 3 day cancellation notice.

SLEEP INN & SUITES   (717)687-5226   **66**

Motel
$110-$185

Address: 2869 Lincoln Hwy E 17572 **Location:** On US 30 (Lincoln Hwy), just e. **Facility:** 51 units. 2 stories, interior corridors. **Pool(s):** heated indoor. **Activities:** exercise room. **Guest Services:** coin laundry.

WHERE TO EAT

DIENNER'S COUNTRY RESTAURANT   717/687-9571   **35**

American. Casual Dining. $3-$12 **AAA Inspector Notes:** The staff is dressed in Amish attire at this cute, cozy restaurant that is most famous for their buffet option featuring home-cooked favorites like mac and cheese, rotisserie chicken and mashed potatoes. The salad and dessert bar also allow guests to pick and choose exactly what they want. Be sure to call ahead and check wait times as it can get busy on certain days. **Address:** 2855 Lincoln Hwy E 17572 **Location:** On US 30 (Lincoln Hwy), just e. B L CALL

HERSHEY FARM RESTAURANT   717/687-8635   **37**

Regional American Family Dining $6-$26

AAA Inspector Notes: This restaurant in the heart of Pennsylvania Dutch Country lays out a smorgasbord of home-cooked fare, including soups, salad and such hot dishes as sliced roast beef, fried chicken and potpie. A country theme is prevalent in the warm, cozy dining room. Scenic trails with vegetable and flower gardens and a rustic waterfall wind out back. **Address:** 240 Hartman Bridge Rd 17572 **Location:** Jct US 30 (Lincoln Hwy), 1.5 mi s on SR 896; in Hershey Farm Inn. *Menu on AAA.com* B L D

JENNIE'S DINER   717/397-2507   **33**

American. Casual Dining. $6-$17 **AAA Inspector Notes:** You can expect a wait on weekend mornings at this place, which is popular with truckers traveling on US 30, as well as with locals. Expect affordable, comfort fast food here, with such highlights as scrapple, chicken-fried steak and dumplings. Focus on breakfast or the hand-written menu of daily specials for the best value. A diner in the truest sense, service is quick and the décor is simple. **Address:** 2575 Lincoln Hwy E 17572 **Location:** Jct US 30 (Lincoln Hwy) and SR 896, 0.3 mi e. B L D 24

KATIE'S KITCHEN   717/687-5333   **36**

American. Casual Dining. $7-$13 **AAA Inspector Notes:** For those looking to avoid the long lines at the buffet down the road, pick this casual kitchen serving traditional Amish food. Outside is a large grassy yard with a play set so the kids can burn some energy while you stretch. Lunch items include wraps, fresh or grilled sandwiches, burgers and dogs. Dinner is classic farm cooking where the roast beef, chicken breast platter, ham steak and haddock fillet always are winners. If dining on a Tuesday, the roaust Amish wedding meal is a must try. **Address:** 200 Hartman Bridge Rd 17572 **Location:** Jct US 30 (Lincoln Hwy), 1 mi s on SR 896. B L D

MILLER'S SMORGASBORD & BAKERY   717/687-6621   **34**

Regional American Family Dining $8-$24

AAA Inspector Notes: The focus of the menu at this eatery is on traditional Lancaster County favorites such as carved beef, turkey, ham, fried chicken, creamy cheesecake and gourmet apple pie. The inviting building features traditional turn-of-the-20th-century architecture. **Address:** 2811 Lincoln Hwy E 17572 **Location:** US 30 (Lincoln Hwy), 1.8 mi e of jct SR 896. B L D

ROYERSFORD pop. 4,752

• Part of Philadelphia area — see map p. 230

STAYBRIDGE SUITES ROYERSFORD/VALLEY FORGE   610/792-9300

Extended Stay Hotel. Rates not provided. **Address:** 88 Anchor Pkwy 19468 **Location:** I-422 exit Royersford, just n. **Facility:** 105 efficiencies, some two bedrooms. 4 stories, interior corridors. **Pool(s):** heated indoor. **Activities:** exercise room. **Guest Services:** valet and coin laundry, area transportation.

/ SOME UNITS

ST. BONIFACE (G-4) elev. 2,054'

SELDOM SEEN COAL MINE, off SR 36, following sign, presents electric train rides that carry visitors into an underground coal mine. Tours depict the past, present and future of coal mining. A visitor center and museum also are offered. **Time:** Allow 2 hours minimum. **Hours:** Visitor center 11-5. Tours Thurs.-Sun. noon-5, July-Aug.; Sat.-Sun. noon-5, in June. **Cost:** Donations. $10; $6 (ages 4-12). Phone ahead to confirm rates. **Phone:** (814) 247-6305, or (814) 674-8939 on days mine is closed or during off-season.

ST. MARYS (E-5) pop. 13,070, elev. 1,702'

St. Marys was founded on December 8, 1842, by German immigrants escaping religious persecution; it was named in honor of the Blessed Virgin Mary. Today it is the industrial and retail hub of Elk County and in close proximity to the largest free-roaming elk herd east of the Mississippi.

St. Marys Area Chamber of Commerce: 53 S. St. Marys St., St. Marys, PA 15857. **Phone:** (814) 781-3804.

STRAUB BREWERY INC., 303 Sorg St., was founded in 1872 and is still owned and operated by the Straub family. One of the smallest breweries in the country, Straub distributes in Mid-Atlantic states. **Note:** Open-toe shoes are not permitted on tours. **Time:** Allow 30 minutes minimum. **Hours:** Tours are Tues.-Wed. at 10:30 and Thurs.-Fri. at 10:30 and 12:30. Closed major holidays. Phone ahead to confirm schedule. **Cost:** Free. Ages 0-11 are not permitted on tours. **Phone:** (814) 834-2875.

BEST WESTERN PLUS EXECUTIVE INN   (814)834-0000

Hotel
$99-$149

AAA Benefit:
Members save up to 20%!

Address: 1002 Earth Rd 15857 **Location:** SR 255, south end of town. Located in a commercial area. **Facility:** 57 units. 3 stories, interior corridors. **Pool(s):** heated outdoor. **Activities:** exercise room. **Guest Services:** valet laundry.

ST. MICHAEL (H-4) pop. 408, elev. 1,598'

JOHNSTOWN FLOOD NATIONAL MEMORIAL is at 733 Lake Rd. The memorial is on the site of the former South Fork Dam. When the dam broke and sent a 40-foot wall of water crashing through the Conemaugh Valley in 1889, Johnstown was devastated and more than 2,200 people died. The visitor center presents a 35-minute film titled "Black Friday" and contains a model of the dam as well as exhibits about local geography and events leading up to the flood.

Rangers conduct programs in summer. **Time:** Allow 1 hour minimum. **Hours:** Daily 9-5. Film is shown every hour 9:15-4:15. Closed Jan. 1, Martin Luther King Jr. Day, Presidents Day, Veterans Day, Thanksgiving and Christmas. **Cost:** (valid for 7 days) $4; free (ages 0-15). **Phone:** (814) 495-4643.

SANATOGA pop. 8,378
• Part of Philadelphia area — see map p. 230

CUTILLO'S RESTAURANT   610/327-2910

American. Casual Dining. $8-$32 **AAA Inspector Notes:** *Historic.* Housed in a late-1700s building that functioned historically as a hotel and tavern, this restaurant overlooks a creek and has two levels of dining rooms with large windows and hanging plants. Dine-in and takeout menus feature American and Italian fare, including classic seafood fettuccine, crabcake Française, godmother filet mignon and prime rib. **Features:** full bar. **Reservations:** suggested, weekends. **Address:** 2688 E High St 19464 **Location:** US 422 exit Sanatoga, just n to E High St, 0.6 mi w. L D

SARVER

KING'S FAMILY RESTAURANT   724/295-2220

American. Family Dining. $6-$15 **AAA Inspector Notes:** Fast and friendly service is offered here. The menu is large in size with descriptive menu items and pictures. The restaurant is also known for its ice cream and dessert menu. **Address:** 400 Buffalo Plaza 16055 **Location:** SR 28 exit 17, 1 mi ne on SR 356. B L D

SAYRE pop. 5,587

BEST WESTERN GRAND VICTORIAN INN
(570)888-7711

Hotel
$139-$199

AAA Benefit:
Members save up to 20%!

Address: 255 Spring St 18840 **Location:** SR 17 exit 61, just s. **Facility:** 100 units. 4 stories, interior corridors. **Pool(s):** heated indoor. **Activities:** sauna, hot tub. **Guest Services:** valet laundry.

HAMPTON INN SAYRE   (570)882-1166

Hotel $99-$209 **Address:** 3080 N Elmira St 18840 **Location:** US 220 exit Sayre/S Waverly, just n. **Facility:** 70 units. 4 stories, interior corridors. **Terms:** 1-7 night minimum stay, cancellation fee imposed. **Pool(s):** heated indoor. **Activities:** exercise room. **Guest Services:** valet and coin laundry.

AAA Benefit:
Members save 5%
or more!

MICROTEL INN & SUITES BY WYNDHAM   (570)888-0001

Hotel $79-$179 **Address:** 1775 Elmira St 18840 **Location:** US 220 exit Athens, 0.8 mi. **Facility:** 77 units. 4 stories, interior corridors. **Guest Services:** valet and coin laundry.

WHERE TO EAT

THE BRI MARIE INN AND RESTAURANT   570/888-8800

New American. Fine Dining. $8-$28 **AAA Inspector Notes:** A water fountain in the lobby of this renovated Queen Victorian house sets the mood for elegant, creative dining. Prepared-to-order steaks, pan-roasted duck breast with mango chutney, Kobe burgers, crab au gratin, Yuengling clams and roasted beet salad with goat cheese are just a sampling of the great selections offered. An English-style pub offers a relaxing spot to unwind before dinner. **Features:** full bar, patio dining. **Reservations:** suggested. **Address:** 119 S Elmer Ave 18840 **Location:** Downtown; in historic district. **Parking:** on-site (fee) and street. L D

ORIGINAL ITALIAN GRILLE   570/888-3100

Italian. Casual Dining. $6-$15 **AAA Inspector Notes:** The fine authentic food begins with the freshest ingredients, real Italian cheeses and house-made sauces. Favorites include chicken parmigiana, homemade Sicilian hand-tossed dough, fettuccine Alfredo, shrimp scampi, clam linguine and more, all complemented with imported and domestic wines and beer. It's uniquely located in a totally renovated historic railroad station. **Features:** full bar, patio dining. **Address:** 718 N Lehigh Ave 18840 **Location:** SR 17 exit 61, 0.6 mi s on SR 199 S. L D

SCENERY HILL

CENTURY INN DINING ROOM   724/945-6600
▼▼▼ American. Casual Dining. $7-$32 **AAA Inspector
Notes:** *Historic.* This dining room is restored to period in the historic
1794 inn. Signature dinners include roast turkey, stuffed pork chop
and Thomas Jefferson's peanut soup. Shepherd's pie is a top lunch
choice. Tasty breads, soups and desserts are homemade. **Features:**
full bar. **Reservations:** suggested. **Address:** 2175 E National Pike
(US 40) 15360 **Location:** Center. ⓛ ⒟

SCHNECKSVILLE (G-11) pop. 2,935,
elev. 669'

LEHIGH VALLEY ZOO is at 5150 Game Preserve
Rd. The 29-acre zoo features almost 300 animals
representing 88 species, from African penguins to
zebras. The zoo collection also includes 26 species
classified as endangered, threatened or of concern.
Events, activities and educational programs are
regularly scheduled. Pets are not permitted. **Time:**
Allow 1 hour, 30 minutes minimum. **Hours:** Daily
10-4, Apr.-Oct.; 10-3, rest of year. Closed Jan. 1,
Thanksgiving and Christmas. **Cost:** Apr.-Oct. $13;
$12 (ages 65+); $11 (ages 2-12). Mar. and Nov. $10.
Rest of year $8. **Phone:** (610) 799-4171. ⓘ

SCHWENKSVILLE (A-9) pop. 1,385,
elev. 148'
• **Part of Philadelphia area — see map p. 230**

PENNYPACKER MILLS, 5 Halderman Rd., is the
former home of Samuel Pennypacker, Pennsylvania's 25th governor. The house was built in the early
18th century and after Pennypacker bought the
house in 1900 he had an architect transform it into a
Georgian-style Colonial Revival mansion. Historical
documents and original family furnishings and artifacts can be seen. Special events and exhibits are
offered throughout the year.

Time: Allow 30 minutes minimum. **Hours:** Tues.-
Sat. 10-4, Sun. 1-4. Closed major holidays. **Cost:**
Donations. **Phone:** (610) 287-9349. Ⓖⓣ 🅰

SCOTRUN
• **Hotels & Restaurants map & index p. 373**
• **Part of Pocono Mountains Area — see map
p. 371**

GREAT WOLF LODGE   570/688-9899 ㉕
▼▼▼ Hotel. Rates not provided. **Address:** 1 Great Wolf Dr
18355 **Location:** I-80 exit 298, just n on SR 611. **Facility:** 401 units,
some two bedrooms. 4 stories, interior corridors. **Terms:** check-in 4
pm. **Amenities:** safes. **Dining:** 2 restaurants. **Pool(s):** heated outdoor, heated indoor. **Activities:** hot tub, miniature golf, recreation programs, game room, exercise room, spa. **Guest Services:** coin
laundry.
ECO 🍴 ⏍ 🛏 📶 ✉ 🔋 🖥 ▣

SCOTTDALE (H-2) pop. 4,384, elev. 1,050'

Scottdale is part of the Laurel Highlands *(see
place listing p. 183).*

WEST OVERTON MUSEUMS are 1 mi. n. on SR
819 at 109 W. Overton Rd. The complex includes
the Distillery Museum, converted from the 1859 Old
Farm distillery and gristmill, the 1838 Abraham

Overholt Homestead, and Springhouse—the birthplace of industrialist Henry Clay Frick. The museums' displays reflect life in a 19th-century rural-
industrial village.

Time: Allow 1 hour, 30 minutes minimum. **Hours:**
Daily noon-5, first weekend in May to late Oct.
Phone for winter special event schedule. **Cost:** $8;
$7 (ages 65+ and active military); $5 (ages 7-11).
Phone: (724) 887-7910. ⒼⓉ

SCRANTON (E-10) pop. 76,089, elev. 753'
• **Hotels p. 386 • Restaurants p. 386**

Scranton and Lackawanna County played an important part in the Industrial Revolution—four anthracite blast furnaces built in the 1840s and 1850s
by the Scranton brothers helped supply more than
80 percent of the anthracite coal that fueled the
growth of American industry. Miles of track, industrial sites and mine tunnels remain.

At 700 Lackawanna Ave. (I-81 exit 185) is the
1908 Lackawanna Station, a former railroad depot
that has been restored and converted into the
Radisson Lackawanna Station Hotel Scranton. The
lobby of the neo-Classical structure displays a mosaic floor, a barrel-vaulted Tiffany stained-glass
ceiling and Siena marble and faience tile murals;
phone (570) 342-8300.

The Suraci Gallery, Mahady Gallery and The
Maslow Study Gallery for Contemporary Art at Marywood University, the Linder Gallery at Keystone College and The Hope Horn Gallery at the University of
Scranton feature paintings, sculpture, prints and
photographs. Theater, concert and musical presentations are offered at the schools throughout the
year. Phone (570) 348-6278 for Marywood University; (570) 945-5141 for Keystone College and (800)
229-3526 for Scranton University information.

(800) 229-3526. Outdoor concerts are presented
May through September at The Toyota Pavilion at
Montage Mountain, (570) 961-9000. Additional theater,
concert and musical presentations are offered at The
Theater at Lackawanna College, (570) 955-1455; and
Scranton Cultural Center, (570) 346-7369.

Pop culture has brought Scranton, which serves
as the fictional setting of the NBC comedy "The Office," a lot of attention in recent years. Though not
filmed here, the show's characters often discuss
local restaurants, attractions and the mining history.
The sitcom's opening credits show some of the
city's landmarks, including the "Scranton Welcomes
You" sign. A highlight for fans is visiting The Mall at
Steamtown to have their picture taken in front of it;
now that it no longer resides near the expressway,
photo ops have greatly improved.

Lots of recreational opportunities can be found at
Lackawanna State Park *(see Recreation Areas
Chart),* McDade Park and Merli-Sarnoski Park. The
PNC Field, off I-81 exit 182 at the base of Montage
Mountain, plays host to the New York Yankees'

class AAA-affiliate, the Scranton/Wilkes-Barre Rail-Riders, in spring and summer; phone (570) 969-2255.

Lackawanna County Convention and Visitors Bureau: 99 Glenmaura National Blvd., Scranton, PA 18507. **Phone:** (570) 496-1701 or (800) 229-3526.

Shopping areas: One of Scranton's major shopping centers is The Mall at Steamtown, on Lackawanna Avenue, with more than 70 specialty stores anchored by Boscov's and The Bon-Ton. Viewmont Mall, on US 6 Bus. Rte. off I-81 exit 191A, features JCPenney, Macy's and Sears.

ANTHRACITE HERITAGE MUSEUM is at 22 Bald Mountain Rd. in McDade Park. The museum is dedicated to collecting, interpreting and preserving the history and culture of Pennsylvania's hard-coal region. Exhibits also highlight various immigrant groups who settled in the region and depict their influence on local history and industry. A brief film showcasing the industry's history also can be seen.

Guided tours are available by appointment. **Time:** Allow 1 hour minimum. **Hours:** Mon.-Sat. 9-5, Sun. noon-5, Apr.-Nov.; Tues.-Sat. 9-5, Sun. noon-5, rest of year. Closed major holidays. **Cost:** $7; $6 (ages 65+); $5 (ages 3-11); free (active military with ID). Guided tour additional $2. Phone ahead to confirm rates. **Phone:** (570) 963-4804.

EVERHART MUSEUM OF NATURAL HISTORY, SCIENCE & ART, in Nay Aug Park at 1901 Mulberry St., features a diverse collection of exhibits, including galleries dedicated to American fine and folk art; Dorflinger glass; African art; ethnographic and ancient world collections; fossils, rocks and minerals; and bird and mammal specimens. The museum also presents changing exhibits that focus on American history, art and culture. Educational programs are offered throughout the year.

Hours: Mon. and Thurs.-Fri. noon-4, Sat. 10-5, Sun. noon-5, Feb.-Dec. Closed Jan. 1, Easter, July 4, Thanksgiving and Christmas. **Cost:** $7; $5 (ages 65+ and students with ID); $3 (ages 6-12). **Phone:** (570) 346-7186.

HOUDINI TOUR & MAGIC SHOW, off I-81 exit 190, then w. 2 mi. to 1433 N. Main Ave., is dedicated to the memory of famed escape artist and magician Harry Houdini. Guided tours showcase Houdini memorabilia, including photographs, props and posters. Rare Houdini films and a live magic show also are included. Haunted: Mind Mysteries & The Beyond is a 3-hour show, and 90-minute ghost walk tours of Scranton also are offered.

Hours: Daily 1-6, July 1-Labor Day weekend; Sat.-Sun. and holiday weekends 1-4 by appointment, rest of year. Haunted show offered Sat. evenings; times vary. Ghost walk tours offered nightly; times vary. Phone ahead to confirm schedule. **Cost:** $17.95; $14.95 (ages 0-11). Haunted show $35. Ghost walk tour $20; $15 (ages 2-11). Phone to verify rates. Reservations are required for Haunted

show and ghost walk. **Phone:** (570) 342-5555, or (570) 383-1831 for Haunted show reservations.

LACKAWANNA COAL MINE TOUR at 1 Bald Mountain Rd. in McDade Park. Visitors are taken via railcar 300 feet underground to the floor of the coal mine, then on a guided walking tour through the mine's three veins. Underground temperatures remain at a constant 53 degrees Fahrenheit; jackets are available on loan. Above ground, an interpretive center houses wall mural exhibits. A theater shows an orientation film.

Time: Allow 1 hour minimum. **Hours:** Ticket office daily 10-3, Apr.-Nov. First tour begins at 11; last tour begins at 3. Visitors must arrive 15 minutes prior to tour departure. Closed Easter and Thanksgiving. Phone ahead to confirm schedule. **Cost:** $10; $9.50 (ages 62+); $9 (active military with ID); $7.50 (ages 3-12). **Phone:** (570) 963-6463.

SCRANTON IRON FURNACES is off I-81 exit 185 at 159 Cedar Ave. These four stone stacks are remnants of the Lackawanna Iron & Coal Co. blast furnaces, which were built 1848-57. The furnaces, catalysts for the development of Scranton, were the second largest producers of iron in the nation. Visitors can take self-guiding tours of the grounds, which offer educational exhibits. **Time:** Allow 15 minutes minimum. **Hours:** Sat.-Sun. and Mon. holidays 9-5, Memorial Day weekend-Labor Day; by appointment rest of year. **Cost:** Free. **Phone:** (570) 963-4804.

STEAMTOWN NATIONAL HISTORIC SITE is off I-81 exit 185 at jct. Cliff and Lackawanna aves. The National Historic Site is on the railroad yard of the Delaware, Lackawanna and Western Railroad and covers more than 40 acres. It features one of the country's largest collections of period locomotives, freight and passenger cars and railway maintenance vehicles. A visitor center, turntable and roundhouse also can be seen.

History and technology museums detail many aspects of railroading, including advances in railroad development and the types of jobs that the industry required. "Steel and Steam," an 18-minute film chronicling the evolution of railroads in the early 1900s, is regularly shown in a 250-seat theater, but occasionally a different film related to railroading is shown instead. Half-hour steam and diesel train excursions offer views of the grounds and traverse a portion of the former main line. Park rangers and volunteers lead several themed walking tours as well.

Ages 16 and under must be accompanied by an adult. **Time:** Allow 2 hours, 30 minutes minimum. **Hours:** Daily 9-5, Apr.-Dec.; 9-4, rest of year (weather permitting). "Steel and Steam" is presented every 30 minutes 9:30-4. Train excursions are offered Wed.-Sun., mid-Apr. to early Dec. (also Mon.-Tues., July-Aug.); phone for departure times. Walking tour schedules vary; phone ahead. Closed Jan. 1, Thanksgiving and Christmas.

Cost: $7; free (ages 0-16). Train excursion fare $5; free (ages 0-5). Additional fees for some excursions.

Phone: (570) 340-5200, or (570) 340-5204 for train reservations. 🚉

Electric City Trolley Station and Museum is off I-81 exit 185 to Lackawanna Ave., following signs to 300 Cliff St., on the grounds of Steamtown National Historic Site. The facility displays trolleys, photographs and a model trolley that children can control. A 10-minute film details the history of trolleys. Approximately 10-mile 1-hour trolley excursion rides also are offered.

Although the museum is on the grounds of a national park, the site is operated by Lackawanna County; therefore, National Parks passes are not valid. **Time:** Allow 30 minutes minimum. **Hours:** Museum daily 9-5, May.-Dec.; Wed.-Sun. 10-4, rest of year. Trolley rides depart Thurs.-Sun. at 10:30, noon, 1:30 and 3, May-Oct. Tickets must be purchased 15 minutes before scheduled departures. Closed Jan. 1, Easter, Thanksgiving and Christmas. Phone ahead to confirm schedule. **Cost:** Museum $6; $5 (ages 62+); $4 (ages 4-17). Trolley ride $8; $7 (ages 62+); $6 (ages 4-17). Combination ticket $10; $9 (ages 62+); $8 (ages 4-17). **Phone:** (570) 963-6590.

COMFORT SUITES   (570)347-1551

Hotel
$110-$180

Address: 44 Montage Mountain Rd 18507 **Location:** I-81 exit 182 northbound; exit 182A southbound. **Facility:** 100 units, some two bedrooms and efficiencies. 4 stories, interior corridors. **Pool(s):** heated indoor. **Activities:** hot tub, game room, exercise room. **Guest Services:** valet and coin laundry, area transportation. **Featured Amenity:** full hot breakfast.

COURTYARD BY MARRIOTT SCRANTON WILKES-BARRE   (570)969-2100

Hotel
$111-$183

COURTYARD Marriott
AAA Benefit: Members save 5% or more!

Address: 16 Glenmaura National Blvd 18507 **Location:** I-81 exit 182, 0.5 mi se on Montage Mountain Rd. **Facility:** 120 units. 3 stories, interior corridors. **Pool(s):** heated indoor. **Activities:** hot tub, exercise room. **Guest Services:** valet and coin laundry, boarding pass kiosk, area transportation.

HAMPTON INN-SCRANTON AT MONTAGE MOUNTAIN
                                      (570)342-7002
Hotel $129-$219 **Address:** 22 Montage Mountain Rd 18507 **Location:** I-81 exit 182 northbound; exit 182A southbound. **Facility:** 129 units. 4 stories, interior corridors. **Terms:** 1-7 night minimum stay, cancellation fee imposed. **Pool(s):** heated indoor. **Activities:** hot tub, game room, exercise room. **Guest Services:** valet and coin laundry, area transportation.

AAA Benefit: Members save 5% or more!

HILTON SCRANTON & CONFERENCE CENTER 570/343-3000
Hotel. Rates not provided. **Address:** 100 Adams Ave 18503 **Location:** I-81 exit 185, just w of jct Lackawanna Ave, Jefferson Ave and Spruce St; downtown. **Facility:** 175 units. 7 stories, interior corridors. **Parking:** on-site (fee). **Amenities:** safes. **Dining:** 2 restaurants. **Pool(s):** heated indoor. **Activities:** hot tub, exercise room. **Guest Services:** valet and coin laundry, rental car service, area transportation.

AAA Benefit: Members save 5% or more!

RADISSON LACKAWANNA STATION HOTEL SCRANTON
                                      (570)342-8300
Classic Historic Hotel $119-$239 **Address:** 700 Lackawanna Ave 18503 **Location:** I-81 exit 185, jct Lackawanna Ave, Jefferson Ave and Spruce St; downtown. **Facility:** This historic hotel in the center of town is in a converted train station and features elegant common areas. Of special note is the large stained-glass skylight above the lobby. 146 units. 6 stories, interior corridors. **Parking:** on-site (fee). **Amenities:** Some: safes. **Dining:** Carmen's 2.0 Restaurant, see separate listing, entertainment. **Activities:** sauna, exercise room. **Guest Services:** valet laundry.

SPRINGHILL SUITES BY MARRIOTT SCRANTON WILKES-BARRE   (570)207-1212
Hotel $111-$183 **Address:** 19 Radcliffe Dr 18507 **Location:** I-81 exit 182 northbound; exit 182A southbound, just e to Montage Mountain Rd, just se to Glenmaura Blvd, just e on National Blvd, then just n. **Facility:** 102 units. 4 stories, interior corridors. **Pool(s):** heated indoor. **Activities:** hot tub, exercise room. **Guest Services:** valet and coin laundry, area transportation.

AAA Benefit: Members save 5% or more!

TOWNEPLACE SUITES BY MARRIOTT SCRANTON WILKES-BARRE   (570)207-8500
Extended Stay Hotel $97-$160 **Address:** 26 Radcliffe Dr 18507 **Location:** I-81 exit 182 northbound; exit 182A southbound, 0.5 mi se on Montage Mountain Rd, then just se to Glenmaura Blvd. **Facility:** 110 units, some two bedrooms, efficiencies and kitchens. 4 stories, interior corridors. **Terms:** check-in 4 pm. **Pool(s):** heated indoor. **Activities:** hot tub, exercise room. **Guest Services:** valet and coin laundry, area transportation.

AAA Benefit: Members save 5% or more!

WHERE TO EAT

BLU WASABI   570/307-3282
Japanese. Casual Dining. $8-$39 **AAA Inspector Notes:** The bistro-style place vibrates with energy from background music and a lively crowd. Makimono, hand rolls and raw bar choices are offered, as are entrées of lobster, filet mignon, strip and rib-eye steaks prepared in Japanese style. Soups and entrée salads such as the Blu salad with grilled marinated salmon, pine nuts and tangerine on mixed greens with spicy lemon dressing are examples of the dilemma of so many choices. Many vegetarian choices round out the healthy menu. **Features:** full bar. **Address:** 1008 Scranton Carbondale Hwy 18508 **Location:** I-81 exit 191A, just e on US 6.

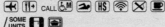
Find thousands of pet-friendly places to stay, play and dine with *The AAA PetBook*

CARMEN'S 2.0 RESTAURANT
570/558-3929

▼▼▼ New Italian. Fine Dining. $13-$38 **AAA Inspector Notes:** Italian marble and a vaulted Tiffany-glass ceiling are among upscale appointments in the formal dining room. Tempting creations include salmon, steak, veal and other specialty entrées. Top off the meal with a sinfully sweet dessert from the stocked cart. **Features:** full bar, Sunday brunch. **Address:** 700 Lackawanna Ave 18503 **Location:** I-81 exit 185, jct Lackawanna Ave, Jefferson Ave and Spruce St; downtown; in Radisson Lackawanna Station Hotel Scranton.

B L D

CASA BELLA RISTORANTE
570/969-9006

▼▼ Italian. Casual Dining. $14-$19 **AAA Inspector Notes:** Innovative Italian dining offers traditional and classic with some specialties in seafood such as the delectable sole Francaise—so delicate and delicious. Casual servers attend to all needs with finesse. A limited wine list with good paired choices is offered. **Features:** full bar. **Address:** 330 W Market St N 18508 **Location:** I-80 exit 190, 1.6 mi w on N Main Ave, then just n. D

COOPER'S SEAFOOD HOUSE & SHIP'S PUB
570/346-6883

Seafood
Casual Dining
$8-$34

AAA Inspector Notes: It's hard to imagine that any more kitsch could be stuffed into this fun casual restaurant and tavern. The menu offers a fairly common selection of seafood dishes broiled and fried. The walls are packed with a truly unique mix of nautical and pirate artifacts, old photos of Scranton, movie-star memorabilia and even dioramas of popular TV shows. The men's restroom is a shrine to the Beatles. **Features:** full bar. **Address:** 701 N Washington Ave 18509 **Location:** At Washington Ave and Pine St; center. *Menu on AAA.com* L D LATE

KILDARE'S IRISH PUB
570/344-4030

▼▼ Irish Comfort Food. Casual Dining. $8-$15 **AAA Inspector Notes:** The atmosphere here is the first thing to grab you—the artifacts, authentic furnishings and whole architectural elements from Irish pubs that have been packed up and shipped here to make for a distinct look and feel. The menu offers a solid selection of freshly prepared food, including Celtic classics such as shepherd's pie and Guinness stew, as well as familiar pub fare with burgers, salads, flatbreads and fish and chips. **Features:** full bar, patio dining, Sunday brunch, happy hour. **Address:** 199 Jefferson Ave 18503 **Location:** I-81 exit 185, jct Lackawanna Ave, Jefferson Ave and Spruce St; downtown. **Parking:** on-site and street. L D CALL &M

LA TOLTECA
570/969-0966

▼▼ Mexican. Casual Dining. $6-$25 **AAA Inspector Notes:** A festive dining room with carved and brightly painted tables and chairs sets the mood for casual dining. Friendly servers help with selecting traditional Mexican cuisine from a vast menu. Margaritas in every flavor make a great accompaniment for one of the combination dinners. **Features:** full bar. **Address:** 46 Viewmont Dr 18508 **Location:** I-81 exit 191 (US 6 E), just s; across from Viewmont Mall. L D CALL &M

NEW AMBER INDIAN RESTAURANT
570/344-7100

▼▼ Indian. Casual Dining. $10-$23 **AAA Inspector Notes:** The choice at this restaurant is extensive—from spicy hot vindaloo to delicious kebabs cooked in a traditional tandoor oven. The dining experience here is pleasant with friendly servers ready to help with selections. A wide variety of choices are offered at the lunch buffet. **Features:** full bar. **Address:** 3505 Birney Ave 18507 **Location:** I-81 exit 182 northbound; exit 182B southbound, 0.7 mi w, then 0.8 mi s on US 11. L D

SELINSGROVE pop. 5,654

COMFORT INN
570/374-8880

▼▼ ▼▼ Hotel. Rates not provided. **Address:** 613 N Susquehanna Tr 17870 **Location:** US 11 and 15, just n of US 522. Located in a commercial area. **Facility:** 62 units. 2 stories (no elevator), interior corridors. **Pool(s):** outdoor. **Activities:** exercise room. **Guest Services:** valet and coin laundry.

🍴 🍸 🏊 BIZ 📶 🛗 💻 /SOME UNITS 🔌 📷

HOLIDAY INN EXPRESS & SUITES SELINSGROVE
(570)743-9275

▼▼ ▼▼ Hotel $104-$359 **Address:** 651 N Susquehanna Tr 17870 **Location:** US 11 and 15, just n of US 522. Located in a commercial area. **Facility:** 74 units. 3 stories, interior corridors. **Terms:** cancellation fee imposed. **Activities:** exercise room. **Guest Services:** valet and coin laundry.

CALL &M HS 📶 ✖ 🛗 📷 💻

SELLERSVILLE pop. 4,249
• Part of Philadelphia area — see map p. 230

THE WASHINGTON HOUSE
215/257-3000

▼▼▼

American
Casual Dining
$5-$28

AAA Inspector Notes: Originally a farmhouse in the 1700s, this converted restaurant provides an intimate and homey atmosphere. Inside guests will find beautiful wood moldings, a decorative glass wine cellar and elaborate art pieces. The menu provides a variety of American cuisine with some European influences including Wiener schnitzel and Prussian peasant pork and noodles. **Features:** full bar, patio dining, Sunday brunch, happy hour. **Reservations:** suggested. **Address:** 136 N Main St 18960 **Location:** Just off SR 309 on Bethlehem Pike; midway between Quakertown and Montgomeryville. **Parking:** on-site and street. *Menu on AAA.com* L D

SEVEN SPRINGS (H-3) pop. 26, elev. 2,520'

Seven Springs is part of the Laurel Highlands *(see place listing p. 183).*

RECREATIONAL ACTIVITIES
Skiing and Snowboarding

• **Seven Springs Mountain Resort** is at 777 Waterwheel Dr. Snow tubing and summer activities also are offered. **Hours:** Daily, Dec.-Apr. (weather permitting); phone for schedule. **Phone:** (814) 352-7777 or (800) 452-2223.

SHAMOKIN DAM pop. 1,686
• Restaurants p. 388

ECONO LODGE INN & SUITES
(570)743-1111

▼▼ ▼▼ Hotel $79-$139 **Address:** 3249 N Susquehanna Tr 17876 **Location:** US 11 and 15, just n of jct SR 61. **Facility:** 118 units. 2 stories (no elevator), exterior corridors. **Pool(s):** outdoor. **Activities:** limited exercise equipment. **Guest Services:** valet and coin laundry.

🍴 🍸 🏊 📶 💻 /SOME UNITS 🔌 🛗 📷

HAMPTON INN SELINSGROVE/SHAMOKIN DAM
(570)743-2223

Hotel
$108-$161

AAA Benefit: Members save 5% or more!

Address: 3 Stettler Ave 17876 **Location:** US 11 and 15, 1 mi s of jct SR 61. Located in a commercial area. **Facility:** 75 units. 3 stories, interior corridors. **Terms:** 1-7 night minimum stay, cancellation fee imposed. **Pool(s):** heated indoor. **Activities:** hot tub, exercise room. **Guest Services:** valet and coin laundry. **Featured Amenity: full hot breakfast.**

PHILLIPS MOTEL   570/743-3100

Motel. Rates not provided. **Address:** 2943 N Susquehanna Tr 17876 **Location:** 3 mi n of Selinsgrove. Located in a commercial area. **Facility:** 47 units. 1 story, exterior corridors.

WHERE TO EAT

SKEETER'S PIT BBQ   570/743-2727

Barbecue. Quick Serve. $7-$20 **AAA Inspector Notes:** This is a great family-friendly stop for traditional barbecue like tender ribs, pulled pork and roasted chicken. The best part is the setting, high on a bluff with great views of the river from the dining room and the large outdoor patio. **Features:** beer only, patio dining. **Address:** 106 Victor Ln 17876 **Location:** Off US 15, just n of jct US 11.

[L] [D] CALL [&M]

TEDD'S LANDING   570/743-1591

American. Casual Dining. $10-$33 **AAA Inspector Notes:** At family-friendly Tedd's Landing you can enjoy lovely views of the river from the dining room as you feast on the specialty of the house: fresh seafood. Clam chowder, bacon-wrapped scallops and delicate orange roughy are among the offerings. Heavy wood accents and stone walls contribute to the restaurant's rustic ambience. **Features:** full bar. **Reservations:** suggested, weekends. **Address:** 45 Rt 11 17876 **Location:** 0.5 mi n. [D]

SHANKSVILLE (H-4) pop. 237, elev. 2,230'

Shanksville is part of the Laurel Highlands *(see place listing p. 183)*.

On Sept. 11, 2001, United Airlines Flight 93 crashed in a field in this rural farming and mining community. One of four commercial airliners hijacked that morning, Flight 93 was the only one that did not crash into a prominent American building. The plane left from Newark, N.J., bound for San Francisco, Calif., but its course was changed to Washington, D.C. by four terrorists. Passengers and crew members learned of the day's earlier attacks on the twin towers of the World Trade Center and the Pentagon when they telephoned authorities and family members. With extreme courage, they fought the four hijackers, thwarting their plan to fly the plane into a Washington, D.C. landmark. The crash site is now home to a temporary memorial to these 33 passengers and seven crew members. The first phase of a National Park Service permanent memorial was dedicated Sept. 10, 2011.

FLIGHT 93 NATIONAL MEMORIAL is on Lambertsville Rd., about 3 mi. s. of US 30 (Lincoln Hwy.). A memorial overlooks the crash site of Flight 93 and honors the 40 heroes aboard who sacrificed their lives in order to thwart a terrorist attack on the U.S. Capitol on Sept. 11, 2001. National Park Service volunteers and staff inform visitors of that day's events. A self-guided audio cell phone tour is available.

Next to the Memorial Plaza, visitors can walk alongside the marble Wall of Names and view outdoor exhibit panels. The first phase of the memorial construction was dedicated Sept. 10, 2011. Future phases will include a Visitor Center Complex, Flight Path walkway and learning center that will include exhibits with multimedia displays. Projected opening is late 2015.

Note: Different areas of the site will be under construction through 2015, but the memorial will remain accessible to visitors. **Hours:** 9-7, April to mid-Oct.; 9-5, rest of year. Last entry 30 min. before closing. Closed President's Day, Christmas, New Year's Day. **Cost:** Free. **Phone:** (814) 893-6322.

SHARON (E-1) pop. 14,038, elev. 854'

Evolving from a mill built on the Shenango River in 1802, Sharon is an industrial city that was founded on steel products. Frank H. Buhl, known as the father of industrial Shenango Valley, built a Romanesque castle in 1890 as a wedding present to his wife. One hundred years later the home was purchased and restored by Jim and Donna Winner. Buhl Mansion now operates as a luxury bed and breakfast and spa. Tours of the mansion, which showcases quality reproductions of works by some of the art world's greats, are available by appointment; phone (724) 346-3046.

VisitMercerCountyPA: 50 N. Water Ave., Sharon, PA 16146. **Phone:** (724) 346-3771 or (800) 637-2370.

Shopping areas: Reyers, in Sharon City Center at 40 S. Water Ave., stocks more than 175,000 pairs of shoes and carries 300 name brands. The Winner Outlet, in a four-story building at 32 W. State St., sells discount bridal, sport and cruise wear along with collectibles and giftware.

SHARPSBURG pop. 3,446
• Hotels & Restaurants map & index p. 348
• Part of Pittsburgh area — see map p. 326

GRAN CANAL CAFFE   412/781-2546   46

Italian. Casual Dining. $14-$25 **AAA Inspector Notes:** This gem is located in the center of town. The menu offers a variety of Italian cuisine while the bar is small in size but large in its wine selection. **Features:** full bar. **Reservations:** suggested, weekends. **Address:** 1021 N Canal St 15215 **Location:** Center. [D]

SHARTLESVILLE (G-10) pop. 455, elev. 568'

ROADSIDE AMERICA, off I-78/US 22 exit 23 at 109 Roadside Dr., is an extensive exhibit of miniature villages and towns depicting the growth and development of rural America. The 8,000-square-foot exhibit includes model trains that represent more than a half-century's work on the part of the builder. **Time:** Allow 1 hour minimum. **Hours:** Mon.-Fri. 9-6:30, Sat.-Sun. 9-7, July 1-Labor Day; Mon.-Fri. 10-5, Sat.-Sun. 10-6, rest of year. Closed Christmas. **Cost:** $9.75; $6.75 (ages 6-11). **Phone:** (610) 488-6241.

SHAWNEE ON DELAWARE (F-12) elev. 338'

- **Hotels & Restaurants map & index p. 373**
- **Part of Pocono Mountains Area — see map p. 371**

In this quaint town nestled in the foothills of the Poconos, visitors can secure outfitters for trips on the Delaware River as well as rent canoes, kayaks and other gear. River Road, which travels through Shawnee on Delaware, is a good route for navigating the adjacent Delaware Water Gap National Recreation Area.

The Shawnee Playhouse presents live theater performances, ballet, children's shows and other entertainment in a charming structure dating from 1904; for information phone (570) 421-5093.

RECREATIONAL ACTIVITIES

Skiing and Snowboarding

- **Shawnee Mountain** is off I-80 exit 309 to US 209N. Snow tubing also is offered. **Hours:** Mon.-Thurs. 1-5:30, Fri. 1-7:30, Sat.-Sun. 9-7:30, mid-Dec. to mid-Mar. (weather permitting). **Phone:** (570) 421-7231 or (800) 233-4218.

THE SHAWNEE INN AND GOLF RESORT   570/424-4000   9

Historic Resort Hotel. Rates not provided. **Address:** 124 Shawnee Inn Dr 18356 **Location:** Waterfront. I-80 exit 309, 1 mi n on SR 209, 0.7 mi e on Buttermilk Falls Rd, then just n. **Facility:** Built in 1911, this small family resort is big on character with classic-style rooms and ample recreation, including the golf course spread out over an island in the middle of the Delaware River. 99 units, some efficiencies and cottages. 4 stories, interior corridors. **Terms:** check-in 4 pm. **Dining:** The Gem & Keystone Brewpub, see separate listing. **Pool(s):** heated indoor. **Activities:** hot tub, fishing, regulation golf, par 3 golf, tennis, recreation programs, bicycles, playground, game room, trails, exercise room, spa. **Guest Services:** valet and coin laundry.

 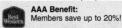

WHERE TO EAT

THE GEM & KEYSTONE BREWPUB   570/424-0990   10

American. Casual Dining. $8-$26 **AAA Inspector Notes:** This casual restaurant is rightfully proud to serve the well-crafted beers brewed on the resort premises, but the menu also holds great appeal for diners. Fresh fish, steak, burgers and chicken from the wood grill have great flavors and the dishes show a bit of creativity and even sophistication not usually seen at a brewpub. Dining options include the clubby upstairs room, the lower-level tavern and the outdoor patio. **Features:** full bar, patio dining. **Reservations:** suggested. **Address:** 1 River Rd 18356 **Location:** I-80 exit 309, 1 mi n on SR 209, 0.7 mi e on Buttermilk Falls Rd, then just n; at The Shawnee Inn and Golf Resort. L D CALL M

SHILLINGTON pop. 5,273

BEST WESTERN PLUS READING INN & SUITES
(610)777-7888

Hotel
$129-$329

AAA Benefit: Members save up to 20%!

Address: 2299 Lancaster Pike 19607 **Location:** I-76 (Pennsylvania Tpke) exit 286, 9 mi n on US 222. Located in a commercial area. **Facility:** 142 units. 4 stories, interior corridors. **Amenities:** safes. **Pool(s):** outdoor. **Activities:** exercise room. **Guest Services:** valet and coin laundry. **Featured Amenity: full hot breakfast.**

SHIPPENSBURG pop. 5,492

- **Restaurants p. 390**

BEST WESTERN SHIPPENSBURG HOTEL
(717)532-5200

Hotel
$70-$150

AAA Benefit: Members save up to 20%!

Address: 125 Walnut Bottom Rd 17257 **Location:** I-81 exit 29, 0.5 mi w on SR 174. **Facility:** 59 units. 2 stories (no elevator), interior corridors. **Amenities:** safes. **Pool(s):** heated indoor. **Activities:** sauna, hot tub, exercise room. **Guest Services:** coin laundry.

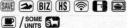

DYKEMAN HOUSE BED & BREAKFAST   717/530-1919

Historic Bed & Breakfast. Rates not provided. **Address:** 6 W Dykeman Rd 17257 **Location:** I-81 exit 24, 2.1 mi n on SR 696, then just e. **Facility:** A winding driveway leads guests past a spring-fed pond that serves as a trout hatchery and straight to the inviting 1850s Georgian-Italianate home. 3 units. 2 stories (no elevator), interior corridors. **Bath:** shower only. **Terms:** check-in 4 pm, age restrictions may apply.

MCLEAN HOUSE   717/530-1390

Historic Bed & Breakfast $70 **Address:** 80 W King St 17257 **Location:** I-81 exit 29, 1.5 mi w on SR 174, then 1 mi s on US 11. **Facility:** Built in 1798, the manor house is accented with antiques and a colorful collection of family memorabilia, all of which radiates a welcoming, homey ambiance. 4 units. 2 stories (no elevator), interior corridors. **Bath:** some shared. **Terms:** check-in 4 pm.

SHIPPEN PLACE HOTEL   717/532-4141

Hotel. Rates not provided. **Address:** 32 E King St 17257 **Location:** I-81 exit 29, 1.5 mi w on SR 174, then 0.8 mi s on US 11; just n of jct SR 696; downtown. **Facility:** 57 units. 4 stories, interior corridors. **Guest Services:** valet laundry.

WHERE TO EAT

CJ'S AMERICAN PUB & GRILL   717/532-5612
♥♥ American. Casual Dining. $9-$29 **AAA Inspector Notes:** At CJ's the atmosphere is suitable for any occasion, whether a family night out or a place to watch a sporting event. Seating is available in the dining room and lounge. The menu lists a nice selection of sandwiches and entrées with a variety of beef, ribs, pasta, chicken and fish dishes. One of the signature dishes is Chicken Chesapeake. Desserts are homemade. **Features:** full bar, happy hour. **Address:** 487 E King St 17257 **Location:** I-81 exit 29, 1.5 mi w on SR 174. L D

MEILIN'S HOUSE   717/532-9411
♥♥ Japanese. Casual Dining. $8-$25 **AAA Inspector Notes:** If the language barrier of an all-Chinese staff is not much of an issue for you, then it's more than worth your while to visit this place for its wonderful food. Try edamame, Jimmy's roll, other tasty sushi and varied à la carte items. In a strip mall, this place has a small sushi bar, two hibachi tables and some separate dining tables if you prefer privacy. **Address:** 825 W King St 17257 **Location:** I-81 exit 24, just w on SR 533/US 11. L D

SHIPPENVILLE pop. 480

SWEET BASIL FAMILY DINING AND JACK'S SALOTTO
                                                814/226-7013
♥♥ Italian. Casual Dining. $7-$15 **AAA Inspector Notes:** This great family dining place serves several homemade dishes of traditional pasta with sausage and meatballs, hand-tossed pizza and penne Siciliano. Freshly prepared cannoli and tiramisu are worth the splurge for dessert. **Features:** full bar, Sunday brunch. **Address:** 21108 Paint Blvd (SR 66) 16254 **Location:** Just s of jct US 322 and SR 66. L D CALL ℰM

SHREWSBURY pop. 3,823

HAMPTON INN   (717)235-9898
♥♥♥ Hotel $101-$149 **Address:**
1000 Far Hills Dr 17349 **Location:** I-83   **AAA Benefit:**
exit 4, just e. **Facility:** 84 units. 3 stories,   Members save 5%
interior corridors. **Terms:** 1-7 night   or more!
minimum stay, cancellation fee imposed.
Pool(s): heated indoor. **Activities:** hot tub, exercise room. **Guest Services:** valet and coin laundry.
⊞✚ CALL ℰM 🛍 BIZ HS 🛜 ✦ 🖥 📺 💻

SIGEL

FARMER'S INN   814/752-2942
♥ American. Family Dining. $4-$16 **AAA Inspector Notes:** At the beginning of the farm, the amazing restaurant and ice cream parlor makes most food items from scratch. Guests can sit in the many high-back rocking chairs on the porch while their little ones feed the farm animals. A wildlife zoo features more exotic animals such as bears and mountain lions. **Address:** 759 Schaffer Rd 15860 **Location:** 2 mi n on SR 949; 3 mi n of SR 36.
B L D CALL ℰM

SKYTOP

• Part of Pocono Mountains Area — see map p. 371

SKYTOP LODGE   570/595-7401
[fyi] Not evaluated. **Address:** One Skytop 18357 **Location:** On SR 390. Facilities, services, and décor characterize a mid-scale property. Situated on a private mountaintop, this historic resort stands like a stone fortress overlooking the activities taking place on the acreage surrounding the property.

SLIPPERY ROCK (F-2) pop. 3,625, elev. 1,299'

Four miles south of Slippery Rock near the junction of SRs 173 and 528, visitors will find the Old Stone House, built in 1822 by John K. Brown as a stagecoach stop on the Pittsburgh-Franklin Pike. The restored tavern and stagecoach stop is furnished in period. The Slippery Rock University History Department offers tours of the house weekends May through October, and during special events; phone (724) 738-2409.

JENNINGS ENVIRONMENTAL EDUCATION CENTER, 4 mi. s. at SRs 8, 173 and 528, protects remnants of a prairie ecological system that dates back 6,000 years, when a major prairie extended out of the Midwest into Pennsylvania. A stand of blazing star, a rare, wild prairie flower, blooms in late July. Maple sugaring demonstrations begin in mid-March. Environmentally based programs occur throughout the year. Five miles of hiking trails also are available.

Time: Allow 30 minutes minimum. **Hours:** Grounds daily dawn-dusk. Educational center Mon.-Fri. 8-4. Phone ahead to confirm schedule. **Cost:** Free. **Phone:** (724) 794-6011. ⛩

APPLEBUTTER INN   724/794-1844
♥♥♥ Classic Bed & Breakfast. Rates not provided. **Address:** 666 Centreville Pike 16057 **Location:** Jct SR 108 and 173, 1 mi s on SR 173. **Facility:** Built in 1844 on land granted to encourage westward settlement, this eleven-room farmhouse features bricks formed and fired on the premises. 11 units. 2 stories (no elevator), interior corridors. *Bath:* shower only. **Activities:** hot tub, massage.
⊞✚ BIZ 🛜 ✕

SMETHPORT (D-5) pop. 1,655, elev. 1,560'

Smethport, first settled in 1811, quickly grew and became a thriving borough in 1853. Main Street is the Mansion District and is lined with Victorian mansions of former local barons. Many of the estates were built as wedding gifts. Hamlin Lake Park offers boating, fishing, in-line skating, swimming and tennis.

Just southwest of Smethport in Mount Jewett is Kinzua Bridge State Park, which covers 329 acres. Within the park is the Kinzua Sky Walk, a pedestrian walkway built on the towers of the old Kinzua Viaduct, which upon completion in 1882 received worldwide acclaim for being the world's highest and longest railroad bridge. The Kinzua Sky Walk extends 600 feet and features an octagon-shaped overlook at the end. A section of the overlook's floor is made of glass so visitors can look down into the Kinzua Gorge. A visitors center is under construction and is scheduled to open in fall 2015. For more information phone (814) 965-2646.

Smethport Visitor Center 119 W. Main St., Smethport, PA 16749. **Phone:** (814) 887-5630.

Self-guiding tours: Maps detailing a walking tour of the Mansion District are available at the Hamlin Memorial Library, McKean County Courthouse and Smethport Visitor Center.

SMOKETOWN pop. 357
• Hotels & Restaurants map & index p. 225
• Part of Pennsylvania Dutch Country area — see map p. 220

MILL STREAM COUNTRY INN   717/299-0931
 Hotel. Rates not provided. **Address:** 170 Eastbrook Rd 17576 **Location:** Jct SR 340, 0.3 mi s on SR 896. **Facility:** 52 units. 2-3 stories (no elevator), exterior corridors. **Pool(s):** outdoor.

SMOKETOWN INN (OF LANCASTER COUNTY)
717/397-6944

Hotel
$59-$89
Address: 190 Eastbrook Rd 17576 **Location:** Jct SR 340, just s on SR 896. **Facility:** 22 units, some two bedrooms, efficiencies and kitchens. 2 stories (no elevator), interior corridors. **Terms:** 2 night minimum stay - seasonal and/or weekends, 3 day cancellation notice.

WHERE TO EAT

GOOD 'N PLENTY RESTAURANT   717/394-7111
Regional
American
Family Dining
$8-$21
AAA Inspector Notes: Crafts and quilts are on display in the country-cozy dining room where you'll sit for family-style meals presented on large platters. Meat, relishes, homemade bread and starches are wholesome and filling, while the desserts are varied and tempting. **Address:** 150 Eastbrook Rd 17576 **Location:** US 30 (Lincoln Hwy), 1 mi n on SR 896; 0.5 mi s of SR 340.

SOMERSET (H-4) pop. 6,277, elev. 2,250'
• Restaurants p. 392

Somerset is part of the Laurel Highlands (see place listing p. 183).

SOMERSET HISTORICAL CENTER is 4 mi. n. of Somerset on SR 985. The museum examines southwestern Pennsylvania's rural life 1750-1950. Two re-created farmsteads, a covered bridge, a sugar camp, a cider press and a genealogical library are included. A visitor center contains exhibits and farm machinery from western Pennsylvania. Tours begin in the visitor center with a 12-minute video about the history and impact of rural life on the mountain barrier area.

Time: Allow 1 hour minimum. **Hours:** Tues.-Sat. 9-5, Sun. noon-5, Apr.-Oct.; Tues.-Fri. 9-5, rest of year. Tour times vary; last tour begins at 3:30. Closed holidays. **Cost:** $6; $5.50 (ages 65+); $3 (ages 3-11). **Phone:** (814) 445-6077.

WINERIES
• **Glades Pike Winery** is on SR 31 at 2208 Glades Pike. **Hours:** Tours and tastings Mon.-Fri. 11-6. Tours are available by appointment. Closed Jan. 1, Easter and Christmas. **Phone:** (814) 445-3753.

A-1 ECONOMY INN   814/445-4144

Motel
Rates not provided
Address: 1138 N Center Ave 15501 **Location:** Just e via Water Works Rd, just n on SR 601. **Facility:** 19 units. 1 story, interior corridors. **Guest Services:** coin laundry, area transportation. **Featured Amenity:** continental breakfast.

BUDGET HOST INN   (814)445-7988
 Motel $45-$95 **Address:** 799 N Center Ave 15501 **Location:** I-70/76 (Pennsylvania Tpke) exit 110, 0.3 mi s. Located in a busy commercial area. **Facility:** 27 units. 2 stories (no elevator), exterior corridors. **Terms:** 3 day cancellation notice-fee imposed.

COMFORT INN   (814)445-9611
Hotel
$105-$150
Address: 202 Harmon St 15501 **Location:** I-70/76 (Pennsylvania Tpke) exit 110, just s. **Facility:** 102 units. 2-3 stories, interior corridors. **Pool(s):** outdoor. **Activities:** exercise room. **Guest Services:** valet laundry. **Featured Amenity:** continental breakfast.

DOLLAR INN   814/445-2977
 Motel. Rates not provided. **Address:** 1146 N Center Ave 15501 **Location:** I-70/76 (Pennsylvania Tpke) exit 110, 0.3 mi s, then just n on SR 601/N Central Ave; at top of hill. Located in a quiet area. **Facility:** 16 units. 1 story, exterior corridors.

THE GEORGIAN INN OF SOMERSET   814/443-1043
Historic Country Inn $135-$215 **Address:** 800 Georgian Inn Dr 15501 **Location:** I-70/76 (Pennsylvania Tpke) exit 110, 0.5 mi e, then 0.3 mi n on SR 601. Located at Horizon Outlet Center. **Facility:** This 1915 Georgian mansion sits on a picturesque hill and has been restored to its original elegance. The inn features 12-foot-high ceilings, oak floors and is decorated uniquely in American antiques. 16 units. 3 stories (no elevator), interior corridors. **Terms:** 7 day cancellation notice-fee imposed.

GLADES PIKE INN   814/443-4978
Historic Bed & Breakfast. Rates not provided. **Address:** 2684 Glades Pike Rd 15501 **Location:** I-70/76 (Pennsylvania Tpke) exit 110, 6 mi w on SR 31; exit 91, 13 mi e on SR 31. **Facility:** Surrounding this historic 1842 B&B are many bike and hiking trails; road and mountain bikes are available along with maps. 5 units. 2 stories (no elevator), interior corridors. **Activities:** downhill & cross country skiing, bicycles.

HAMPTON INN (814)445-9161

▼▼▼▼ **Hotel** $119-$169 **Address:** 324 Laurel Crest Rd 15501 **Location:** I-70/76 (Pennsylvania Tpke) exit 110, just sw. **Facility:** 110 units. 5 stories, interior corridors. **Terms:** 1-7 night minimum stay, cancellation fee imposed. **Pool(s):** heated outdoor. **Activities:** exercise room. **Guest Services:** coin laundry.

AAA Benefit: Members save 5% or more!

[🍴] CALL [🅼] [🏊] [BIZ] [🛜] [✕] [🛗] [▯] / SOME UNITS [🖥]

QUILL HAVEN COUNTRY INN 814/443-4514

▼▼▼▼ **Historic Bed & Breakfast** $105-$150 **Address:** 1519 N Center Ave 15501 **Location:** I-70/76 (Pennsylvania Tpke) exit 110, just e via Water Works Rd, then 1.1 mi n on SR 601. **Facility:** This B&B, built in 1918, reflects the Arts and Crafts style. The owners have opened their home to guests who enjoy good hospitality. The Bridal Suite has a large hot tub. 4 units. 2 stories (no elevator), interior corridors. **Terms:** check-in 4 pm, 7 day cancellation notice. **Activities:** hot tub. **Guest Services:** valet laundry.

[🍴] [🛜] [✕] [☎]

WHERE TO EAT

HOSS'S FAMILY STEAK & SEA 814/445-3788

▼ Steak. Casual Dining. $8-$29 **AAA Inspector Notes:** Folks can bring the whole family to enjoy this restaurant's 100-item salad bar, homemade soups and bread, steaks, fresh seafood and chicken entrées. **Address:** 1222 N Center Ave 15501 **Location:** I-70/76 (Pennsylvania Tpke) exit 110, just e via Water Works Rd, then just n on SR 601. [L] [D]

KING'S FAMILY RESTAURANT 814/445-5311

▼▼▼ American. Family Dining. $6-$13 **AAA Inspector Notes:** Fast and friendly service is offered here. The menu is large in size with descriptive menu items and pictures. The restaurant is also known for its ice cream and dessert menu. **Address:** 1180 N Center Ave 15501 **Location:** I-70/76 (Pennsylvania Tpke) exit 110, just e via Water Works Rd, then 0.5 mi n on SR 601. [B] [L] [D] CALL [🅼]

OAKHURST TEA ROOM 814/443-2897

▼▼▼
American
Casual Dining
$7-$32

AAA Inspector Notes: Established in 1933, the casual restaurant is a local favorite for home-style, Pennsylvania Dutch fare. Everything is homemade-from roast beef, ham and turkey to bread, soup and dessert. The lunch buffet is loaded with tempting selections. **Features:** full bar, Sunday brunch. **Reservations:** suggested. **Address:** 2409 Glades Pike 15501 **Location:** 5.4 mi w on SR 31. *Menu on AAA.com* [L] [D] CALL [🅼]

PINE GRILL RESTAURANT 814/445-2102

▼▼▼ American. Casual Dining. $7-$20 **AAA Inspector Notes:** This family-run business has been serving since 1941 and offers well-prepared entrées. The main menu features grilled rainbow trout and grilled albacore white tuna salad topped with tomato-corn chutney and balsamic vinaigrette. Original pine walls and tile floors lend to the rustic décor of the dining room. **Features:** full bar. **Address:** 800 N Center Ave 15501 **Location:** I-70/76 (Pennsylvania Tpke) exit 110, 0.3 mi s. [L] [D] CALL [🅼]

SOUDERTON (H-11) pop. 6,618, elev. 428'
• Part of Philadelphia area — see map p. 230

ASHER'S CHOCOLATES is at 80 Wambold Rd. Visitors can watch a video presentation and take a self-guiding tour through a glass corridor for an inside look at the chocolate-making process. **Hours:** Tours are offered Mon.-Fri. 10-3:30. Closed major holidays. **Cost:** Free. **Phone:** (215) 721-3276 or (800) 438-8882.

SOUTH STERLING
• Part of Pocono Mountains Area — see map p. 371

THE FRENCH MANOR INN AND SPA 570/676-3244

▼▼▼ ▼▼▼
Country Inn
Rates not provided

Address: 50 Huntingdon Dr 18445 **Location:** SR 191, 0.4 mi w. **Facility:** The beautiful inn is fashioned after a stone château in the south of France. Rooms in the main house have a quaint and distinct charm; other buildings have more space and balconies with stunning views. 19 units. 2 stories (no elevator), interior/exterior corridors. **Terms:** age restrictions may apply. **Dining:** The French Manor Restaurant, see separate listing. **Pool(s):** heated indoor. **Activities:** hot tub, sledding, trails, exercise room, spa. **Guest Services:** valet laundry, area transportation. **Featured Amenity:** full hot breakfast.

[SAVE] [🔑] [🍴] [🧍] [🍽] [🏊] [🛜] [✕] / SOME UNITS [▯] [🖥]

WHERE TO EAT

THE FRENCH MANOR RESTAURANT 570/676-3244

▼▼▼▼
French
Fine Dining
$35-$50

AAA Inspector Notes: In a beautiful manor modeled after a château in the south of France, the dining room offers a stately atmosphere for elegant dining. It features a 30-foot vaulted ceiling with massive wood beams, dual fireplaces and pecky cypress wall paneling. The menu centers on gourmet French cuisine and features such specialty items as filet mignon a la homard, filled with broiled lobster and napped in mushroom cognac cream. Service is skilled and diligent. **Features:** full bar, patio dining. **Reservations:** suggested. Semiformal attire. **Address:** 50 Huntingdon Dr 18445 **Location:** SR 191, 0.4 mi w; in The French Manor Inn and Spa. *Menu on AAA.com* [B] [D]

SOUTH WILLIAMSPORT (E-8) pop. 6,379, elev. 522'

The city hosts the Little League World Series each summer.

WORLD OF LITTLE LEAGUE MUSEUM is at 525 US 15, next to the Little League World Series stadium. Displays interpret the history and growth of Little League Baseball and Softball since the organization was founded in 1939. The museum includes uniforms, Major League Baseball players' Little League items, a 1934 Babe Ruth uniform and high-tech interactive experiences.

Time: Allow 1 hour minimum. **Hours:** Daily 9-5. Closed Jan. 1, Easter, Thanksgiving and Dec. 24-25 and 31. Phone ahead to confirm schedule. **Cost:** $5; $3 (ages 62+); $2 (ages 5-12). Audio guide rental $3; free (AAA members). **Phone:** (570) 326-3607.

SPEERS pop. 1,154

• Part of Pittsburgh area — see map p. 326

THE BACK PORCH RESTAURANT   724/483-4500

▼▼ American. Casual Dining. $11-$34 **AAA Inspector Notes:** *Historic.* Brick fireplaces and farmhouse antiques decorate this restored 1806 home. Succulent spare ribs, marinated in soy sauce and brown sugar, have been on the menu since the mid-1970s. The white-chocolate cheesecake is delightfully decadent. **Features:** full bar. **Reservations:** suggested, for dinner. **Address:** 114 Speers St 15012 **Location:** I-70 exit 40; under exit bridge on river by marina.

[L] [D]

SPRINGFIELD (DELAWARE COUNTY)

• Hotels & Restaurants map & index p. 274
• Part of Philadelphia area — see map p. 230

COURTYARD BY MARRIOTT PHILADELPHIA SPRINGFIELD
(610)543-1080 [112]

▼▼▼ **Hotel** $139-$229 **Address:** 400 W Sproul Rd 19064 **Location:** I-476 exit 3, 0.7 mi e on Baltimore Pike, then 1 mi n. 🅟 Thomson Avenue, 13. **Facility:** 92 units. 3 stories, interior corridors.

AAA Benefit: Members save 5% or more!

Pool(s): heated indoor. **Activities:** hot tub, exercise room. **Guest Services:** valet and coin laundry, boarding pass kiosk, area transportation.

[Y] CALL [&M] [🚐] [BIZ] [HS] [🛜] [✖] [🛗] [💻] / SOME UNITS [🖨] [🚍]

DAYS INN SPRINGFIELD/PHILADELPHIA INT'L AIRPORT
(610)544-4700 [113]

▼▼ **Hotel** $90-$199 **Address:** 650 Baltimore Pike 19064 **Location:** I-476 exit 3, 2 mi e. 🅟 Leamy Ave, 15. **Facility:** 131 units. 2 stories (no elevator), exterior corridors. **Amenities:** safes. **Activities:** limited exercise equipment. **Guest Services:** coin laundry, area transportation.

[✈] [🍴] [Y] CALL [&M] [🛜] [💻] / SOME UNITS [🛗] [🚍]

WHERE TO EAT

TAVOLA RESTAURANT AND BAR   610/543-1200 [146]

▼▼ American. Casual Dining. $9-$26 **AAA Inspector Notes:** Come to this casual spot and enjoy delicious brick-oven pizzas and hearty sandwiches inside the cozy dining room or on the beautiful outdoor patio that overlooks a professionally manicured golf course. Every Sunday there is a brunch buffet featuring a custom omelet bar. **Features:** full bar, patio dining, Sunday brunch. **Address:** 400 W Sproul Rd 19064 **Location:** I-476 exit 3, 0.7 mi e on Baltimore Pike, then 1 mi n. 🅟 Thomson Avenue, 13. [L] [D] [🚍]

SPRINGS (I-3) elev. 2,474'

Springs is part of the Laurel Highlands *(see place listing p. 183).*

SPRINGS MUSEUM, off SR 669 at 134 River Rd., depicts the lives of Casselman Valley settlers in the mid-18th century. Two buildings house domestic, farm and shop relics. Displays include an early schoolroom, post office, country store and barn. A farmers market is held every Saturday, Memorial Day weekend to mid-September. The Folk Festival is held the first Friday and Saturday in October; it includes craft and farm equipment demonstrations, musical entertainment and a hay ride.

Time: Allow 1 hour minimum. **Hours:** Wed.-Fri. 1-5, Sat. 9-2, Memorial Day weekend-early Oct.; by appointment rest of year. **Cost:** Free. Folk Festival $5; $2 (ages 6-18). **Phone:** (814) 662-2625.

SPRUCE CREEK (G-6) pop. 240, elev. 777'

INDIAN CAVERNS INC., 4 mi. n.e. on SR 45, contains limestone formations and Native American artifacts, including a tablet of petroglyphs. The caverns are electrically lighted and the constant temperature is 56 F. Visitors can also pan for gems and feed fish on the property.

Time: Allow 1 hour minimum. **Hours:** Guided tours daily 10-5, Memorial Day-Labor Day; Sat.-Sun. 10-5, Apr. 1-day before Memorial Day and day after Labor Day-Oct. 31. Last tour begins 1 hour before closing. **Cost:** $13; $12 (ages 65+ and students and military with ID); $11 (ages 4-12). **Phone:** (814) 632-7578 or (570) 322-0350.

STARLIGHT

• Part of Pocono Mountains Area — see map p. 371

THE INN AT STARLIGHT LAKE   570/798-2519

▼▼ **Historic Country Inn.** Rates not provided. **Address:** 289 Starlight Lake Rd 18461 **Location:** Waterfront. Off SR 370, 1 mi n, follow signs. Next to Starlight Lake. **Facility:** Situated in the Endless Mountains, this 1909 inn offers a tranquil setting far from city noise and traffic. Guest rooms and baths are very modest. 21 units. 1-3 stories (no elevator), interior/exterior corridors. **Activities:** boat dock, fishing, tennis, bicycles, playground, game room, limited exercise equipment.

[🍴] [Y] [🛜] [✖] [🦆] [W] [☎] / SOME UNITS [🔔]

STATE COLLEGE (F-6) pop. 42,034, elev. 1,174'

• Hotels p. 394 • Restaurants p. 397

The Pennsylvania State University *(see attraction listing),* founded as an agricultural college in 1855, is located in the fertile Nittany Valley of central Pennsylvania. The school, established to teach methods of soil conservation, became Pennsylvania State College in 1874. A community slowly grew up around the school, and it was incorporated as the Borough of State College in 1896. Today Penn State University offers undergraduate degrees in 190 programs and some 160 graduate degree programs. The commonwealth's largest university, Penn State has more than 98,000 students at 27 locations statewide, including nearly 46,200 at the University Park campus in State College.

State College features mountain bike trails and opportunities for fly-fishing.

Central Pennsylvania Convention & Visitors Bureau: 800 E. Park Ave., State College, PA 16803. **Phone:** (814) 231-1400 or (800) 358-5466.

THE PENNSYLVANIA STATE UNIVERSITY, at University Park, is the commonwealth's largest university and is noted for its beautiful campus. Campus parking is provided for a fee daily until 9 p.m. (central campus) and until 5 p.m. (other areas). **Phone:** (814) 865-4700.

The Arboretum at Penn State lies on the n.w. section of campus between Shortlidge and Bigler rds. Due to the great size of the project, portions of the

370-acre site are opening in phases. The 35-acre H.O. Smith Botanic Gardens is open, and it features more than 700 species and 17,000 plants, an overlook pavilion, fountain, boardwalk, rose and fragrance garden, lotus pond, esplanade, sub-tropical-themed terrace and pollinators' gardens. The Childrens Gate Garden is designed for visitors from ages 3 to 12, and includes information about the region's biodiversity. The main biking and hiking trail is the Bellefonte Central Rail Trail, a 1.3-mile crushed-limestone path following the old railroad bed.

Future additions will include additional themed gardens, an education center and a conservatory. Docent-led tours are sometimes available with 2 weeks' advance notice. **Time:** Allow 1 hour minimum. **Hours:** Daily dawn-dusk (weather permitting). **Cost:** Donations. Fees may be charged for tours. **Phone:** (814) 865-9118 or (814) 867-2591.

The Berkey Creamery, Department of Food Science, College of Agricultural Sciences is at jct. Bigler and Curtin rds. on Penn State's University Park campus. Visitors can view the processing procedures at the creamery from the observation room. The creamery produces cheese, ice cream, milk, yogurt and other products. **Hours:** Observation room open Mon.-Fri. 8-5; phone ahead to see if production will be in progress. **Cost:** Free. **Phone:** (814) 865-7535.

Earth and Mineral Sciences Museum and Art Gallery, on the ground floor at 16 Deike Building on Burrowes Rd. on Penn State's University Park campus, contains gemstones, minerals and fossils representing more than 22,000 specimens. Also on display are mineral industries-related art and mining and scientific equipment. Interactive earthquake, tornado and GeoWall exhibits are offered.

Time: Allow 30 minutes minimum. **Hours:** Mon.-Fri. 9:30-5. Closed university holidays, Jan. 1, Christmas, day after Christmas and Dec. 27-31. **Cost:** Free. **Phone:** (814) 865-6336.

Frost Entomological Museum, on Curtin Rd. on Penn State's University Park campus, houses more than 2 million insects in its collection, including mounted, live, land and aquatic specimens. There are numerous exhibits, photographs and models. **Note:** The museum is undergoing renovation and is scheduled to reopen in summer of 2015. Phone ahead for updates. **Time:** Allow 30 minutes minimum. **Hours:** Mon.-Fri. 9:30-4:30. Closed major holidays and university breaks. **Cost:** Free. **Phone:** (814) 865-1895.

Old Main is on Pollock Rd. on Penn State's University Park campus. It is the Central Administration building and was built 1856-63; it was rebuilt 1929-30. It contains the Land Grant Frescoes by American muralist Henry Varnum Poor. **Hours:** Mon.-Fri. 8-5. Closed major holidays. **Cost:** Free. **Phone:** (814) 865-7517.

Palmer Museum of Art, Penn State, on Curtin Rd. at Penn State's University Park campus, offers American and international exhibitions of paintings, sculpture, prints, drawings, photographs and ceramics. Special exhibitions feature works of art from other museums and public and private collections. Educational programs, films and musical performances also are presented. Guided tours are available by appointment. **Time:** Allow 30 minutes minimum. **Hours:** Tues.-Sat. 10-4:30, Sun. noon-4. Closed some holidays. **Cost:** Free. **Phone:** (814) 865-7672.

Penn State All-Sports Museum, in Beaver Stadium on the University Park campus, contains memorabilia of the Penn State Nittany Lions sports teams, the Heisman trophy, photographs of former players and displays of 19 current and former varsity sports.

Time: Allow 30 minutes minimum. **Hours:** Tues.-Sat. 10-4, Sun. noon-4, mid-Mar. to mid-Dec.; Fri.-Sat. 10-4, Sun. noon-4, rest of year. Home football game weekend schedule varies; phone ahead. Closed major holidays except July 4. **Cost:** $5; $3 (children, senior citizens and students with ID). **Phone:** (814) 865-0044.

Penn State University Archives is in the Paterno Library at jct. Curtin Rd. and Allen St. on the University Park campus; parking is available at the Nittany Lion Inn parking deck. The archives include more than 1200 collections documenting the history of Penn State and the State College area.

. **Time:** Allow 30 minutes minimum. **Hours:** Mon.-Thurs. 8-6, Fri. 8-5, during spring and fall semesters; Mon.-Fri. 8-5, during summer semester. Closed major holidays. **Cost:** Free. **Phone:** (814) 865-1793.

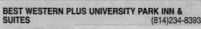

CARNEGIE INN & SPA, AN ASCEND HOTEL COLLECTION MEMBER   (814)234-2424

Contemporary
Country Inn
$129-$199

Address: 100 Cricklewood Dr 16803 **Location:** I-99/US 322 exit 71 (Toftrees/Woodycrest). **Facility:** Located next to a golf course, the contemporary property has the ambiance and theme of a Scottish country house. Offered is individually decorated, traditional-style guest rooms and a new full-service spa. 20 units. 3 stories, interior corridors. **Parking:** on-site and valet. **Terms:** 3 day cancellation notice. **Activities:** spa. **Guest Services:** valet laundry, area transportation. **Featured Amenity:** full hot breakfast.

SAVE 🅿️ 🍽️ 👨‍🦽 🍷 🛜 ❌ / SOME UNITS 🔌 🖨️ 💻

COMFORT SUITES   (814)235-1900

▽▽▽ Hotel $89-$149 **Address:** 132 Village Dr 16803 **Location:** SR 26, 1.1 mi on US 322 W (Atherton St), just ne; center. **Facility:** 77 units. 3 stories, interior corridors. **Amenities:** safes. **Pool(s):** heated indoor. **Activities:** hot tub, exercise room. **Guest Services:** valet and coin laundry.

🍽️ 🏊 HS 🛜 ❌ 🔌 🖨️ 💻 / SOME UNITS 🔌

COUNTRY INN & SUITES BY CARLSON   (814)234-6000

▽▽▽ Hotel $79-$159 **Address:** 1357 E College Ave 16801 **Location:** 0.6 mi off US 322 Bypass on SR 26 S. **Facility:** 113 units. 5 stories, interior corridors. **Terms:** cancellation fee imposed. **Amenities:** safes. **Pool(s):** heated indoor. **Activities:** hot tub, exercise room. **Guest Services:** valet and coin laundry, area transportation.

🅿️ 🍽️ CALL 👨‍🦽 🏊 BIZ HS 🛜 ❌ 🔌 🖨️ 💻

COURTYARD BY MARRIOTT   (814)238-1881

▽▽▽ Hotel $118-$194 **Address:** 1730 University Dr 16801 **Location:** US 322, 1.5 mi e of jct SR 26. **Facility:** 78 units. 3 stories, interior corridors. **Pool(s):** heated indoor. **Activities:** hot tub, exercise room. **Guest Services:** valet and coin laundry.

AAA Benefit: Members save 5% or more!

🅿️ 🍽️ 👨‍🦽 🍷 BIZ HS 🛜 ❌ 🔌 💻 / SOME UNITS 🖨️

DAYS INN PENN STATE   (814)238-8454

▽▽ 💎 Hotel $104-$250 **Address:** 240 S Pugh St 16801 **Location:** Just e of SR 26 northbound; 0.4 mi n of jct US 322 business route; downtown. **Facility:** 186 units. 5-6 stories, interior corridors. **Amenities:** video games. **Dining:** Mad Mex, see separate listing. **Pool(s):** heated indoor. **Activities:** exercise room. **Guest Services:** valet laundry, area transportation.

🅿️ 🍽️ 🍷 BIZ HS 🛜 🎮 🔌 💻 / SOME UNITS 🔌 🖨️

FAIRFIELD INN & SUITES BY MARRIOTT STATE COLLEGE   (814)238-3871

▽▽▽ Hotel $62-$160

FAIRFIELD INN & SUITES Marriott

AAA Benefit: Members save 5% or more!

Address: 2215 N Atherton St 16803 **Location:** US 322 exit N Atherton St, 0.8 mi e. **Facility:** 83 units. 3 stories, interior corridors. **Pool(s):** heated indoor. **Activities:** hot tub, exercise room. **Guest Services:** valet and coin laundry. **Featured Amenity:** breakfast buffet.

SAVE 🅿️ 🍽️ CALL 👨‍🦽 🏊 BIZ HS 🛜 ❌ 💻 / SOME UNITS 🔌 🖨️

▼ See AAA listing p. 394 ▼

HAMPTON INN & SUITES AT WILLIAMSBURG SQUARE
(814)231-1899

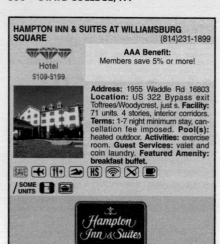

Hotel
$109-$199

AAA Benefit: Members save 5% or more!

Address: 1955 Waddle Rd 16803 **Location:** US 322 Bypass exit Toftrees/Woodycrest, just s. **Facility:** 71 units. 4 stories, interior corridors. **Terms:** 1-7 night minimum stay, cancellation fee imposed. **Pool(s):** heated outdoor. **Activities:** exercise room. **Guest Services:** valet and coin laundry. **Featured Amenity:** breakfast buffet.

Only 4 miles from Penn State campus & downtown State College. Free hot breakfast & WiFi.

Plan complete trip routings with the online and mobile TripTik® Travel Planner

---

HAMPTON INN STATE COLLEGE
(814)231-1590

Hotel $89-$179 **Address:** 1101 E College Ave 16801 **Location:** SR 26, 0.7 mi s of jct US 322. **Facility:** 119 units. 3 stories, interior corridors. **Terms:** 1-7 night minimum stay, cancellation fee imposed. **Pool(s):** heated outdoor. **Activities:** exercise room. **Guest Services:** valet laundry.

AAA Benefit: Members save 5% or more!

HILTON GARDEN INN
(814)272-1221

Hotel $99-$159 **Address:** 1221 E College Ave 16801 **Location:** 0.5 mi off US 322 Bypass on SR 26 S. **Facility:** 103 units. 4 stories, interior corridors. **Terms:** 1-7 night minimum stay, cancellation fee imposed. **Pool(s):** heated indoor. **Activities:** hot tub, exercise room. **Guest Services:** valet and coin laundry.

AAA Benefit: Members save 5% or more!

HOLIDAY INN EXPRESS AT WILLIAMSBURG SQUARE
(814)867-1800

Hotel $99-$599

Address: 1925 Waddle Rd 16803 **Location:** US 322 Bypass exit Toftrees/Woodycrest, just s. **Facility:** 106 units. 4 stories, interior corridors. **Terms:** 30 day cancellation notice-fee imposed. **Activities:** exercise room. **Guest Services:** valet and coin laundry. **Featured Amenity:** breakfast buffet.

NITTANY BUDGET MOTEL
(814)238-0015

Motel
$49-$225

Address: 2070 Cato Ave 16801 **Location:** SR 26, 2.6 mi s of jct US 322 business route. **Facility:** 23 units. 1 story, exterior corridors. **Featured Amenity:** continental breakfast.

THE NITTANY LION INN OF THE PENNSYLVANIA STATE UNIVERSITY
(814)865-8500

Historic Hotel
$129-$409

Address: 200 W Park Ave 16803 **Location:** US 322, 0.5 mi w of jct SR 26. **Facility:** Located on the campus of Penn State University, this 1931 Colonial-style inn offers traditional-style rooms decorated in PSU colors. 223 units. 3 stories, interior corridors. **Parking:** on-site and valet. **Terms:** cancellation fee imposed. **Amenities:** video games. **Activities:** hot tub, regulation golf, exercise room. **Guest Services:** valet laundry, area transportation. *(See ad p. 396.)*

THE PENNSYLVANIA STATE UNIVERSITY-THE PENN STATER CONFERENCE CENTER HOTEL
(814)863-5000

Hotel
$99-$389

Address: 215 Innovation Blvd 16803 **Location:** US 322 E/220 N exit Penn State University/Innovation Park exit "A", 0.5 mi e. **Facility:** 300 units. 5 stories, interior corridors. **Parking:** on-site and valet. **Terms:** closed 12/24-1/2, cancellation fee imposed. **Dining:** 2 restaurants. **Pool(s):** heated indoor. **Activities:** hot tub, exercise room. **Guest Services:** valet laundry, area transportation. *(See ad p. 396.)*

QUALITY INN PENN STATE
(814)234-1600

Motel $59-$329 **Address:** 1274 N Atherton St 16803 **Location:** US 322 business route, 1 mi w of jct SR 26. **Facility:** 97 units. 3 stories, interior corridors. **Activities:** exercise room. **Guest Services:** valet and coin laundry.

RAMADA CONFERENCE CENTER & GOLF HOTEL
(814)238-3001

Hotel $79-$389 **Address:** 1450 S Atherton St 16801 **Location:** US 322 business route, 1.4 mi e of jct SR 26. **Facility:** 284 units. 2 stories, interior/exterior corridors. **Terms:** check-in 4 pm, cancellation fee imposed. **Pool(s):** outdoor, heated indoor. **Activities:** hot tub, game room, exercise room. **Guest Services:** valet and coin laundry.

RESIDENCE INN BY MARRIOTT STATE COLLEGE
(814)235-6960

Extended Stay Hotel
$132-$217 **Address:** 1555 University Dr 16801 **Location:** US 322 business route, 1.5 mi e of jct SR 26. **Facility:** 81 units, some two bedrooms, efficiencies and kitchens. 3 stories, interior corridors. **Amenities:** video games. **Pool(s):** heated indoor. **Activities:** hot tub, exercise room. **Guest Services:** valet and coin laundry.

AAA Benefit:
Members save 5% or more!

SLEEP INN
(814)235-1020

Hotel $69-$139 **Address:** 111 Village Dr 16803 **Location:** US 322 business route, 1 mi w of jct SR 26. **Facility:** 100 units. 3 stories, interior corridors. **Activities:** exercise room. **Guest Services:** valet and coin laundry.

SPRINGHILL SUITES BY MARRIOTT STATE COLLEGE
(814)867-1807

Hotel
$90-$263

SPRINGHILL SUITES Marriott

AAA Benefit:
Members save 5% or more!

Address: 1935 Waddle Rd 16803 **Location:** US 322 Bypass exit Toftrees/Woodycrest, just s; in Williamsburg Square. **Facility:** 72 units. 4 stories, interior corridors. **Pool(s):** heated indoor. **Activities:** hot tub, exercise room. **Guest Services:** valet and coin laundry. **Featured Amenity:** breakfast buffet.

TOFTREES GOLF RESORT & CONFERENCE CENTER
(814)234-8000

Resort Hotel
$79-$499

Address: One Country Club Ln 16803 **Location:** I-99/US 322 exit 71 (Toftrees/Woodycrest). **Facility:** This golf resort offers spacious public areas and grounds. Penn State University is nearby. 102 units. 2-3 stories (no elevator), interior corridors. **Terms:** check-in 4 pm, cancellation fee imposed. **Dining:** Down Under Steak House, see separate listing. **Pool(s):** heated outdoor. **Activities:** regulation golf, tennis, exercise room, massage. **Guest Services:** valet and coin laundry.

WHERE TO EAT

THE ALLEN STREET GRILL
814/231-4745

American. Casual Dining. $8-$32 **AAA Inspector Notes:** This not-to-be-missed restaurant is on the second floor of a historic downtown hotel, across from Penn State. The second floor patio affords the best location for people watching with a favorite beer or wine from their award-winning, extensive list. Popular menu items include crab and mango spring rolls, Maryland crab bisque and Jacks' roadhouse steak charbroiled with spice sweet vinaigrette. Their desserts are homemade and not to be missed. **Features:** full bar. **Address:** 100 W College Ave 16801 **Location:** Center of downtown; in Hotel State College. **Parking:** on-site (fee) and street. L D

Choose real ratings you can trust from
professional inspectors who've been there

AMERICAN ALE HOUSE & GRILL
814/237-9701

▼▼▼▼
**American
Casual Dining
$9-$32**

AAA Inspector Notes: The restaurant serves creative cuisine in a casual, bustling environment. Entrées include daily prime rib, seafood and pasta dishes, sandwiches and salads. Breakfast is served only on Sundays from 11 am to 2 pm. Dining on the seasonal patio is a nice diversion. **Features:** full bar. **Reservations:** suggested. **Address:** 821 Cricklewood Dr 16803 **Location:** US 322 business route exit Toftrees/Woodycrest, just n to Toftrees, e to Cricklewood Dr, 0.5 mi n, then e. L D

THE DINER
814/238-5590

▼ Comfort Food. Cafeteria. $6-$16 **AAA Inspector Notes:** *Classic.* The beginnings of this part fast-food part diner-style restaurant began in 1926 when it became home of the grilled sticky (cinnamon roll). As the location and ownership evolved, the basic philosophy remained the same--provide great comfort food fast. This downtown diner has carved a niche over time with their classic macaroni and cheese dish. A 1950s style pervades the dining areas with retro mirrors and lights for a truly nostalgic experience. **Address:** 126 W College Ave 16801 **Location:** Center of downtown; across from Penn State University. **Parking:** on-site and street.

B L D CALL &M

DOWN UNDER STEAK HOUSE
814/234-8000

▼▼ American. Casual Dining. $9-$32 **AAA Inspector Notes:** The casual restaurant, overlooking the golf course, specializes in steaks and seafood. A pub-like bar also is featured. **Features:** full bar. **Address:** 1 Country Club Ln 16803 **Location:** I-99/US 322 exit 71 (Toftrees/Woodycrest); in Toftrees Golf Resort & Conference Center.

B L D CALL &M

FACCIA LUNA PIZZERIA
814/234-9000

▼▼ Italian. Casual Dining. $7-$15 **AAA Inspector Notes:** Opened in 1991 by two Penn State fraternity brothers, this neighborhood trattoria specializes in wood-oven pizza, stromboli, such fresh pasta dishes as the spinach ricotta ravioli, appetizers, sandwiches and great entrée salads from ingredients never comprising quality and freshness. Draped in Tuscan tones, with walls lined in framed black-and-white photographs and a patio dining area, this spot offers a casual dining experience. Plan ahead as this is a busy restaurant. **Features:** full bar. **Address:** 1229 S Atherton St 16801 **Location:** 1.3 mi e on US 322 business route. L D

HERWIGS AUSTRIAN BISTRO
814/272-0738

▼▼
**Austrian
Casual Dining
$9-$22**

AAA Inspector Notes: Austrian food prevails in this small but busy place, where the friendly owners cook and serve each meal themselves. Gluten-free selections now available. Reservations are highly recommended and the place is BYOB. Sunday brunch is offered on home-game weekends. **Reservations:** suggested. **Address:** 132 W College Ave 16801 **Location:** Just e of SR 26 northbound; downtown. **Parking:** on-site (fee). L D

MAD MEX
814/272-5656

▼▼ Mexican. Casual Dining. $7-$15 **AAA Inspector Notes:** This happening Mexican restaurant is convenient to the Penn State campus. Happy hour offers great deals on beer and special margaritas. Namesake burritos include vegetarian choices, wild-with-flavor salsa, dips, shared appetizers, enchiladas and fajitas. Check for age restriction hours. **Features:** full bar. **Address:** 240 S Pugh St 16801 **Location:** Just e of SR 26 northbound; 0.4 mi n of jct US 322 business route; downtown; in Days Inn Penn State. **Parking:** on-site (fee). L D

MARIO'S ITALIAN RESTAURANT
814/234-4273

▼▼▼ Italian. Casual Dining. $12-$27 **AAA Inspector Notes:** Only a mile from Penn State's main campus, this restaurant offers great Italian cooking including wood-fired pizza, rotisserie chicken, veal, chicken, lamb and pork slow roasted to tenderness. The original vodka sauce is delicious as is their own rum cake and tiramisu. **Features:** full bar. **Address:** 1272 N Atherton St 16803 **Location:** US 322 business route, 1 mi w of jct SR 26. L D

OLDE NEW YORK
814/237-1582

▼▼ International. Casual Dining. $8-$25 **AAA Inspector Notes:** This casual restaurant lives up to its name with a diverse ethnic representation of all cuisine types from the old neighborhoods of New York City. Pierogies, egg rolls, galumpkis (cabbage rolls), agnolotti (pasta with goat cheese and red peppers), jaw-breaking deli sandwiches made your way, entree salads, kase wurst, nachos, potato pancakes, wings, burgers and lots more. Choose from 12 draught beers on tap with micros, imports and domestics as well. **Features:** full bar. **Address:** 2298 E College Ave 16801 **Location:** SR 26, 2 mi n of jct US 322. L D CALL &M

OTTO'S PUB AND BREWERY
814/867-6886

▼▼ American. Gastropub. $10-$25 **AAA Inspector Notes:** This brewpub offers trendy and ever-popular items such as beer-battered fish, pulled pork sandwich, braised short ribs, crab cakes, bacon-wrapped meatloaf and wild salmon. Try one of the wood-fired oven pizzas made from their own beer-infused pizza dough. All menu items go well with one of their hand-crafted beers. **Features:** full bar. **Address:** 2235 N Atherton St 16803 **Location:** US 322 business route, 2.9 mi w of jct SR 26. L D

PENANG
814/861-6088

▼▼ Asian. Casual Dining. $7-$23 **AAA Inspector Notes:** This small restaurant lined with stone tiles and accented with modern hanging lights specializes in Malaysian and Thai cuisines. Their extensive menu includes maki, temaki and hand rolls that can be enjoyed at the intimate sushi bar with noodles fried or in soup. Poultry, pork, beef and seafood are accented with green or red curries, garlic, ginger, exotic herbs and spices. Many vegetarian choices are offered and they now offer a classic Chinese menu. **Address:** 1221 N Atherton St 16803 **Location:** US 322 business route, 1 mi w of jct SR 26. L D CALL &M

THE TAVERN RESTAURANT
814/238-6116

▼ Traditional American. Casual Dining. $8-$30 **AAA Inspector Notes:** Serving the area since 1948, this restaurant is decorated in the Colonial style and features a museum-like collection of lithographs, Penn State memorabilia and Civil War pictures. Menu favorites are succulent prime rib and crab cakes. Service is attentive. **Features:** full bar, Sunday brunch. **Address:** 220 E College Ave 16801 **Location:** SR 26 southbound, 5 blks n of US 322 business route. **Parking:** street only. L D

THE WAFFLE SHOP-NORTH
814/238-7460

▼ American. Family Dining. $6-$14 **AAA Inspector Notes:** A favorite among the locals, this great waffle shop offers a menu that ranges from very tasty waffles, with or without fresh fruit toppings, to light-and-fluffy pancakes, omelets and sausages, to name a few items for breakfast. Lunch offers large portions of entrée salads and freshly made sandwiches. Cash only. **Address:** 1229 N Atherton St 16803 **Location:** US 322 business route, 1 mi w of jct SR 26.

B L

THE WAFFLE SHOP-WEST
814/235-1816

▼ American. Family Dining. $6-$12 **AAA Inspector Notes:** This place is great for made-to-order waffles and omelets, fluffy pancakes, thick bacon, fresh-squeezed orange juice and other delicious breakfast items. Don't overlook lunches, as they are delicious, too, with freshly made entrée salads, sandwiches and other sides. Cash only. **Address:** 1610 W College Ave 16801 **Location:** SR 26, 1.6 mi s of jct US 322 business route. B L

ZOLA NEW WORLD BISTRO
814/237-8474

▼▼▼ New Mediterranean. Casual Dining. $10-$34 **AAA Inspector Notes:** This contemporary bistro atmosphere provides a distinctive dining experience. Try the crispy whole red snapper, crab cakes, Prince Edward Island mussels, lobster macaroni and cheese made with black truffles and Guyere cheese or perhaps one of six-cheese fondues for two. An award-winning wine list enhances and complements all courses. Chocolate fondant, orange panna cotta or crème brûlée are delicious for dessert. **Features:** full bar. **Reservations:** suggested, for dinner. **Address:** 324 W College Ave 16801 **Location:** On SR 26, just s of Atherton St. **Parking:** on-site and street. L D CALL &M

STEWARTSTOWN (I-9) pop. 2,089, elev. 870'

WINERIES
- **Naylor Vineyards and Wine Cellar** is 2 mi. n. on SR 24 at 4069 Vineyard Rd. **Hours:** Tours and tastings Mon.-Sat. 10-6, Sun. noon-5. Closed major holidays. **Phone:** (717) 993-2431 or (800) 292-3370. **GT**

STRASBURG (I-10) pop. 2,809, elev. 469'
- **Attractions map p. 221**
- **Part of Pennsylvania Dutch Country area — see map p. 220**

Though first settled by French Huguenots, Strasburg evolved into a community of German immigrants in the Pennsylvania Dutch Country. The town is noted for its quaint atmosphere; the availability of Amish food and arts and crafts; and its many railroad exhibits, both model and real. The Lancaster County Art Association, 149 Precision Ave. next to Strasburg Public Library, presents rotating exhibits of local artists' works. Classes, events and workshops are presented throughout the year. The gallery is open Wed.-Sat. 11-4 and Sun. 1-4 except for major holidays and between Christmas and New Year's Day; phone (717) 687-7061.

CHOO CHOO BARN, TRAINTOWN, U.S.A., e. on SR 741 at 226 Gap Rd., is a 1,700-square-foot model train display of Lancaster County. The exhibit has 22 operating model trains and more than 150 animated figures and vehicles. **Time:** Allow 1 hour minimum. **Hours:** Daily 10-5, early Mar.-Dec. 31. Last admission is 30 minutes before closing. Closed Easter, Thanksgiving and Christmas. **Cost:** $7.50; $4.50 (ages 3-11). **Phone:** (717) 687-7911.

THE NATIONAL TOY TRAIN MUSEUM, 1.5 mi. e. on SR 741 and .2 mi. n. on Paradise Ln., displays antique and contemporary toy trains. Five operating layouts can be viewed. A video about toy trains also is presented. **Time:** Allow 1 hour minimum. **Hours:** Daily 10-5, June-Aug.; Fri.-Mon. 10-5, May and Sept.-Oct.; Sat.-Sun. 10-5, Apr. and Nov.-Dec. Phone ahead for extended hours. Last admission 30 minutes before closing. Closed Christmas. **Cost:** $7; $6 (ages 65+); $4 (ages 6-12); $22 (family, two adults and three children). **Phone:** (717) 687-8976.

RAILROAD MUSEUM OF PENNSYLVANIA, 1 mi. e. on SR 741E at 300 Gap Rd., traces the history of railroads in Pennsylvania through restored locomotives, railcars and artifacts. The museum takes visitors from the colorful era of 19th-century wood-burning engines to modern streamliners. An orientation video played in an early 20th-century passenger depot sets the tone.

The museum's collection of more than 100 vintage locomotives and railcars, which includes steam, diesel and electric locomotives, and passenger and freight cars, were all either made or operated in Pennsylvania. The beautifully restored rolling stock is displayed on five tracks inside the massive main hall. Additional pieces can be seen in the outdoor train yard with a working 1928 turntable.

Some of the cars are open for inspection—including the cab of a steam locomotive, a caboose and a passenger car—and can be walked through. Others can be seen up-close courtesy of stairways and platforms that allow for viewing the inside of the equipment. An observation bridge provides excellent views of the rolling stock from above. A self-guided mobile device tour is available.

Visitors can pretend to be an engineer and operate a train, including the throttle, brakes and horn, in the museum's cab simulator built from a Norfolk Southern diesel locomotive. In addition, the museum's education center in a late Victorian-era freight station has hands-on activities and an extensive model train layout. Railroad memorabilia such as lanterns, tools, china and clocks also can be seen. Special events are held throughout the year.

Note: The outdoor train yard is not always accessible due to weather or safety reasons. **Time:** Allow 1 hour, 30 minutes minimum. **Hours:** Mon.-Sat. 9-5, Sun. noon-5, Apr.-Oct.; Tues.-Sat. 9-5, Sun. noon-5, rest of year. Closed Jan. 1, Thanksgiving and Christmas. **Cost:** $10; $9 (ages 65+); $8 (ages 3-11). **Phone:** (717) 687-8628.

SIGHT & SOUND THEATRES, LANCASTER COUNTY, on SR 896, presents live theatrical performances based on Bible stories in a 2,000-seat theater featuring a 300-foot wraparound stage and special effects. Live animals are part of the cast. A 1-hour behind-the-scenes guided tour also is available.

Hours: "Moses," Jan. 2-Apr. 18. "Joseph," May 22-Oct. 17. "Miracle of Christmas," Nov. 7-Jan. 2. Performances Tues.-Sat.; phone for curtain times. **Cost:** $52-$67; $29-$52 (ages 13-18); $19-$21 (ages 2-12). Reservations are recommended. **Phone:** (800) 377-1277.

ISAAC'S FAMOUS GRILLED SANDWICHES   717/687-7699

Deli Sandwiches. Quick Serve. $8-$12 **AAA Inspector Notes:** The modern, New York-style delicatessen specializes in overstuffed grilled sandwiches named after birds, plants and flowers. Salads and homemade soups also are popular. A tropical feel is prevalent in the colorful, casual dining room. **Address:** Rt 741 E (226 Gap Rd) 17579 **Location:** On SR 741, 0.5 mi e; in Shops of Traintown. **L D**

STROUDSBURG (F-11) pop. 5,567, elev. 420'
- **Hotels p. 400 • Restaurants p. 400**
- **Hotels & Restaurants map & index p. 373**
- **Part of Pocono Mountains Area — see map p. 371**

Col. Jacob Stroud, who served in the French and Indian War, settled in what is now Stroudsburg in 1769. Because of the strategic location 3 miles west of the Delaware Water Gap, Fort Penn was built around his home in 1776. Two years later the post sheltered refugees from the Wyoming Massacre

(See map & index p. 373.)

(see Wyoming p. 428). The town was formally established in 1799 when Stroud and his son sold lots in their spaciously platted site.

The 1795 Stroud Mansion, built by the colonel for his son, still stands at 900 Main Street; it serves as headquarters for the Monroe County Historical Association. Artifacts are on display and a research library is on site. A 1-hour guided tour is offered at Tuesday-Friday (also first and third Saturdays of the month) at 11 and 2. Phone (570) 421-7703.

The Sherman Theater, 524 Main St., opened in 1929. Among the evening's entertainment was a performance by comedians Stan Laurel and Oliver Hardy. Vaudeville shows were given in the theater's early days and then in later years the building became a movie house. These days live entertainment has returned, and performances are offered throughout the year. Phone (570) 420-2808.

Pocono Mountains Visitors Bureau: 1004 Main St., Stroudsburg, PA 18360. **Phone:** (570) 421-5791 or (800) 762-6667.

Self-guiding tours: Brochures about the area, including the historic downtown and hiking and biking in northeast Pennsylvania, are available at the visitors bureau.

Shopping areas: Downtown Stroudsburg's restored historic buildings are home to an array of antique, arts and crafts, apparel and specialty stores.

QUIET VALLEY LIVING HISTORICAL FARM is 3.5 mi. s.w. on US 209 Bus. Rte., then 1.5 mi. s.e. to 347 Quiet Valley Rd. This 115-acre living-history museum is a restored late 18th- through 19th-century Pennsylvania German farm. Guides in period clothing conduct tours of historic buildings, which include a house, barn, cabin, smoke house, springhouse, icehouse, dry house, maple sugar house and tool sheds. A bake oven can be seen, and crafts are demonstrated daily. Corn, flax, potatoes, rye and wheat are grown, and farm animals include chickens, goats, horses, pigs, rabbits, sheep, turkeys, a cow and a mule.

Special themed events are held select weekends throughout the year. During Farm Animal Frolic in May visitors can pet baby farm animals, enjoy pony or wagon rides, and watch sheep shearing. In October, Harvest Festival features folk entertainment, children's activities, and traditional craft demonstrations such as spinning, weaving and basket making. The Old Time Christmas celebration includes a living nativity scene and a visit from Pennsylvania German folk figure Belschnikel.

Pets are not permitted. **Time:** Allow 2 hours, 30 minutes minimum. **Hours:** Tours of historic farm museum Tues.-Sat. (also Labor Day) 10-5, Sun. noon-5, third Sat. in June-Labor Day. Farm Animal Frolic Sat. 10-4, Sun. noon-4, Memorial Day weekend and the previous weekend. Harvest Festival Sat.-Sun. 10-5, Columbus Day weekend. Old

Time Christmas tours are offered every 15 minutes Sat.-Sun. 3-7, the first and second full weekends in Dec. **Cost:** $10; $5 (ages 3-12). Phone ahead to verify special event admission. **Phone:** (570) 992-6161. 🎫

HAMPTON INN & SUITES STROUDSBURG/BARTONSVILLE
570/369-1400

[fyi] Hotel $139-$209 Too new to rate, opening scheduled for May 2015. **Address:** 700 Commerce Blvd 18360 **Location:** I-80 exit 302. **Amenities:** 109 units, coffeemakers, microwaves, refrigerators, pool, exercise facility. **Terms:** 1-7 night minimum stay, cancellation fee imposed.

AAA Benefit: Members save 5% or more!

HAMPTON INN - STROUDSBURG/POCONOS
(570)424-0400 **1**

Hotel $119-$199 **Address:** 114 S 8th St 18360 **Location:** I-80 exit 307 (SR 191 N), just w on Ann St, then just e; downtown. Located in a commercial area. **Facility:** 100 units. 4 stories, interior corridors. **Terms:** 1-7 night minimum stay, cancellation fee imposed. **Pool(s):** heated indoor. **Activities:** exercise room. **Guest Services:** valet and coin laundry.

AAA Benefit: Members save 5% or more!

STROUDSMOOR COUNTRY INN   (570)421-6431 **2**

Country Inn $89-$330 **Address:** 231 Stroudsmoor Rd 18360 **Location:** I-80 exit 307, 1 mi s on SR 191 to Stroudsmoor Rd, then 0.7 mi w. Located in a semi-rural area. **Facility:** Made up of multiple buildings, the property is scattered across a lushly landscaped hillside. The lobby offers true country elegance with dark woods, leather furnishings, a stone fireplace and wood floors. 62 units. 1-2 stories (no elevator), interior/exterior corridors. **Terms:** 7 day cancellation notice-fee imposed. **Dining:** restaurant, see separate listing. **Pool(s):** heated indoor. **Activities:** hot tub, bicycles, exercise room, spa.

WHERE TO EAT

NEWBERRY'S YARD OF ALE   570/517-0130 **2**

American. Casual Dining. $10-$22 **AAA Inspector Notes:** Not just another downtown ale house, this inviting restaurant has an interesting menu with sandwiches, specialty pizzas and entrées like citrus scallops, Parmesan-crusted snapper and cider glazed pork chops. Of course there is a great selection of craft and imported beers and a welcoming, family-friendly ambiance. **Features:** full bar. **Address:** 622 Main St 18360 **Location:** Between 6th and 7th aves; downtown. **Parking:** street only.

SARAH STREET GRILL   570/424-9120 **1**

American. Casual Dining. $9-$26 **AAA Inspector Notes:** Sporting a casual tavern atmosphere, the dining room is decorated with works by local artists. The lounge welcomes musicians and features singer/songwriter music six nights a week. Seating is offered on the seasonal dining deck and beer garden. The 18-ounce Delmonico steak is a favorite on a menu of burgers, specialty pizzas and varied pasta dishes served with homemade sauces. Sushi is available Tuesday through Sunday evenings. **Features:** full bar, Sunday brunch. **Address:** 550 Quaker Alley 18360 **Location:** Between 5th and 6th sts; on Sarah St; just nw of SR 191; center.

SIAMSA IRISH PUB   570/421-8434 **3**

Irish. Casual Dining. $9-$29 **AAA Inspector Notes:** You're not likely to encounter leprechauns at Siamsa Irish Pub, but the Irish spirit is nonetheless alive and well. Celtic comfort foods pair with American favorites and such creative salads as Brie and pear with apple chutney. **Features:** full bar, Sunday brunch. **Address:** 636 Main St 18360 **Location:** Jct 7th and Main sts. **Parking:** street only.

(See map & index p. 373.)

STROUDSMOOR COUNTRY INN   570/421-6431 ④

WWW Traditional American. Casual Dining. $11-$30 **AAA Inspector Notes:** The dining room features a subdued, charmingly elegant country inn atmosphere, with a popular upscale soup and salad bar. Continental influences flavor offerings of American cuisine such as broiled New Zealand rack of lamb marinated with virgin olive oil, herbs and spices. Lavish buffets—seafood, filet mignon and champagne brunch—are presented on the weekends. This place is known for its homemade rice pudding and roasted turkey. They also bake an excellent apple pie. **Features:** full bar, Sunday brunch. **Reservations:** suggested. **Address:** 231 Stroudsmoor Rd 18360 **Location:** I-80 exit 307, 1 mi s on SR 191 to Stroudsmoor Rd, then 0.7 mi w.

Ⓑ Ⓛ Ⓓ

SUGARLOAF

TOM'S KITCHEN FAMILY RESTAURANT   570/788-3808

WWW American. Family Dining. $6-$14 **AAA Inspector Notes:** Quaint, comfortable, pleasant and decorated with country crafts and folk art, the family restaurant serves wholesome food made from scratch in the immaculate kitchen. Among local favorites are meatloaf, chicken croquettes, roast turkey with stuffing and lasagna with meatballs. Soups and daily specials also are offered. This place is known for its homemade pies and apple dumplings, which are made from fresh, in-season fruits. **Features:** Sunday brunch. **Address:** 656 State Rt 93 18249 **Location:** I-80 exit 256, 2 mi s; I-81 exit 145, 2 mi n. Ⓑ Ⓛ Ⓓ

SUNBURY (F-8) pop. 9,905, elev. 446'

Sunbury, on Shamokin Creek and the Susquehanna River, was the site of Pennsylvania's largest frontier fort, Fort Augusta. The powder magazine from the 1756 fort still stands. The Hunter House, 1150 N. Front St., contains a research library and a permanent exhibit of artifacts recovered from archaeological digs made on the site of the fort; phone (570) 286-4083.

Sunbury had one of the world's first central station incandescent electric lighting plants. It was built by Thomas Edison in 1883. The plant was treated with much suspicion by the townspeople, most of whom were afraid to cross the threshold to look inside.

At S. Second Street are the Keithan Bluebird Gardens, featuring a variety of trees, azaleas and rhododendrons. The gardens reach peak bloom March through May. On SR 147 is the Shikellamy Marina & Fabridam, where a 3,000-acre lake is formed by what is said to be the world's largest inflatable dam.

Shopping areas: Susquehanna Valley Mall, on US 11/15, is the town's main shopping center. Its major stores are The Bon-Ton, Boscov's, JCPenney and Sears.

SWIFTWATER

- **Hotels & Restaurants map & index p. 373**
- **Part of Pocono Mountains Area — see map p. 371**

DESAKI   570/839-2500 ⑳

WWW Japanese. Fine Dining. $15-$50 **AAA Inspector Notes:** After a long day of skiing or hiking in the Poconos area, families and couples can come here and enjoy an entertaining hibachi grill show or dine on a variety of delicious sushi rolls. Those looking to avoid driving should call ahead and ask about the complimentary shuttle service available for certain hotels and resorts. An 18 percent gratuity is included in all meals. **Features:** full bar. **Address:** 2054 Rt 611 18370 **Location:** I-80 exit 298, 2.4 mi n. Ⓓ CALL Ⓛ Ⓜ

TAFTON (E-11) elev. 1,532'

- **Part of Pocono Mountains Area — see map p. 371**

Tafton is near Lake Wallenpaupack *(see Hawley p. 146 and Recreation Areas Chart)*, the state's third largest man-made lake. Preseason stocking makes this a good location for fishing.

TAMAQUA (F-10) pop. 7,107, elev. 810'

STONEHEDGE GARDENS is at 51 Dairy Rd., just e. of jct. SRs 309 and 443. Herb, hosta, water, perennial and nature gardens comprise Stonehedge Gardens' 7 acres. Ponds, a creek and 2 miles of hiking trails also are part of the complex. A visitor center includes a library resource room and an art gallery featuring works by local artists. Educational programs and special events are offered throughout the year.

Guided tours are available by appointment. **Time:** Allow 30 minutes minimum. **Hours:** Grounds daily noon-dusk. Visitor center Fri.-Sun. noon-6. **Cost:** Donations. **Phone:** (570) 386-4276.

TANNERSVILLE (F-11) elev. 1,276'

- **Hotels p. 402 • Restaurants p. 402**
- **Hotels & Restaurants map & index p. 373**
- **Part of Pocono Mountains Area — see map p. 371**

Shopping areas: The Crossings Premium Outlets, I-80 exit 299, following signs, is a rambling, two-story shopping experience featuring approximately 100 high-end outlet stores. Shopping choices offering selections from head to toe include Ann Taylor, Brooks Brothers, Cole Haan, Chico's, Guess, Michael Kors, Polo Ralph Lauren, Rockport and Tommy Hilfiger. Young fashionistas can shop at Carter's, Gymboree and OshKosh B'gosh, while those in search of accessory, housewares and gift bargains can peruse the shelves at Coach, Corningware Corelle & More and Yankee Candle.

CAMELBEACH WATERPARK is about 3 mi. w. of I-80 exit 299, following signs. The park's more than 30 acres feature FlowRider, a surf ride; a lazy river; more than 35 slides; a wave pool; a scenic chairlift ride; two family slides; miniature golf and two children's areas. Pharaoh's Phortress houses eight waterslides, a water obstacle course, a four-story tipping bucket, wading lagoons, fountains, sprinklers and water guns.

Picnicking is permitted for a fee; tents, tables and food are available. Pets are not permitted. **Time:** Allow 3 hours minimum. **Hours:** Daily 11-6, late May-Labor Day (some extended hours late June to Late Aug.). Phone ahead to confirm schedule. **Cost:** $39.99; $29.99 (0-47 inches, ages 65+ and military with ID); $19.99 (from 3-6). Phone ahead to verify admission prices. **Phone:** (570) 629-1661. 🍴 🎿

RECREATIONAL ACTIVITIES

Skiing

- **Camelback Mountain Resort** is about 3 mi. w. of I-80 exit 299, following signs. Snow tubing also is available. **Hours:** Ski area Mon.-Thurs. 9-9, Fri. 9

(See map & index p. 373.)

a.m.-10 p.m., Sat. 8:30 a.m.-10 p.m., Sun. 8:30 a.m.-9 p.m., early Dec. to mid-Apr. Snow tubing park Mon.-Fri. 3-9, Sat.-Sun. and holidays 9-9, early Dec.-late Mar. **Phone:** (570) 629-1661 for conditions report and to verify schedule.

THE CHATEAU RESORT & CONFERENCE CENTER
(570)629-5900 **28**

Resort Hotel
$89-$324

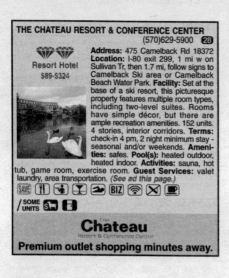

Address: 475 Camelback Rd 18372 **Location:** I-80 exit 299, 1 mi w on Sullivan Tr, then 1.7 mi, follow signs to Camelback Ski area or Camelback Beach Water Park. **Facility:** Set at the base of a ski resort, this picturesque property features multiple room types, including two-level suites. Rooms have simple décor, but there are ample recreation amenities. 152 units. 4 stories, interior corridors. **Terms:** check-in 4 pm, 2 night minimum stay - seasonal and/or weekends. **Amenities:** safes. **Pool(s):** heated outdoor, heated indoor. **Activities:** sauna, hot tub, game room, exercise room. **Guest Services:** valet laundry, area transportation. *(See ad this page.)*

Chateau
Resort & Conference Center

Premium outlet shopping minutes away.

DAYS INN-TANNERSVILLE (570)629-1667 **29**

Hotel
$66-$130

Address: 126 Hill Motor Lodge Rd 18372 **Location:** I-80 exit 299, just s on SR 715. **Facility:** 72 units. 1-2 stories (no elevator), exterior corridors. **Terms:** cancellation fee imposed. **Amenities:** safes. **Dining:** Tandoor Palace Restaurant & Bar, see separate listing. **Pool(s):** outdoor. **Guest Services:** coin laundry. **Featured Amenity:** continental breakfast.

WHERE TO EAT

BARLEY CREEK BREWING COMPANY
570/629-9399 **23**

American
Gastropub
$11-$24

AAA Inspector Notes: This bustling place set in the shadows of Camelback Mountain is housed in an unusual post-and-beam timber-frame building. An area favorite for American and English pub food, highlights include barbecue rock Cornish hen served on a bed of fire-roasted corn salsa. A seasonal outdoor park is available when weather permits. Horseshoe pits, bocce ball courts and a large covered deck are featured. **Features:** full bar, happy hour. **Address:** 1774 Sullivan Tr 18372 **Location:** I-80 exit 299, just n on SR 715, then 1.1 mi w on Sullivan Tr to jct Camelback Rd. *Menu on AAA.com* L D CALL M

▼ *See AAA listing this page* ▼

AAA Vacations® packages ...

unforgettable experiences and unrivaled value

(See map & index p. 373.)

LEGENDARY TANNERSVILLE INN   570/629-3131
 American. Casual Dining. $9-$33 **AAA Inspector Notes:** If the season is right, grab a seat on the veranda or the solarium at the Legendary Tannersville Inn. Opened in 1847 as a hotel, you'll find typical American fare such as crab cakes, barbecue ribs, steak and fried chicken served here. A murder mystery night is hosted every Friday. **Features:** full bar. **Address:** 2977 Rt 611 18372 **Location:** I-80 exit 299, just n on SR 715, then 1 mi s. L D LATE

SMUGGLER'S COVE   570/629-2277 26

Seafood
Casual Dining
$7-$35

AAA Inspector Notes: Posters and a variety of bric-a-brac dot the relaxed dining room. The menu features a good selection of fresh seafood and a few steaks. Specialties include prime rib, live lobsters, a salad bar and crab cakes. **Features:** full bar, early bird specials. **Reservations:** suggested. **Address:** 2972 Rt 611 18372 **Location:** I-80 exit 299, just n on SR 715, then 1 mi s. L D

TANDOOR PALACE RESTAURANT & BAR
570/619-0068 24

Indian
Casual Dining
$12-$21

AAA Inspector Notes: Serving traditional Indian cuisine, the restaurant has two dining rooms: one in a 170-year-old railroad dining car and another decorated with Indian paintings. The menu lists tandoor preparations in addition to other chicken, lamb, goat, seafood and many vegetarian dishes. Good choices are tandoori chicken (chicken marinated overnight in yogurt and spices and roasted in a clay oven) and methi malai mutter (a rare blend of creamed, chopped fenugreek leaves, spinach and green peas). **Features:** full bar. **Address:** 126 Motor Hill Lodge Rd 18372 **Location:** I-80 exit 299, just s on SR 715; in Days Inn-Tannersville. L D

GABEL'S ICE CREAM & FAST FOOD   570/629-0370
fyi Not evaluated. Step back into a time gone by at this popular ice cream stand which has been in operation since the 1950s. A variety of sandwiches, including burgers, gyros, cheesesteaks and wraps, are available. The hot dog featuring shredded cheddar, onions and homemade chili is a favorite. There are no restrooms on-site. **Address:** SR 611 & Alger Ave 18372 **Location:** Jct SR 715, just s.

TARENTUM (G-2) pop. 4,530, elev. 777'
• Hotels & Restaurants map & index p. 348
• Part of Pittsburgh area — see map p. 326

TOUR-ED MINE & MUSEUM, off SR 28 exit 14 then .1 mi. n. on Bull Creek Rd., offers guided tours of a deep coal mine. The mantrip carries visitors one-half-mile down into the mine where the tour begins. Displays feature actual equipment in working condition and illustrate the coal-mining process. A museum exhibits a company store, a miner's log cabin and coal jewelry. Haunted mine tours are offered in October.

The underground temperature is a constant 54 F. **Note:** A jacket and comfortable walking shoes are recommended. **Time:** Allow 1 hour minimum. **Hours:** Wed.-Mon. 10-4, Memorial Day weekend-Labor Day; by appointment, May 1-day before Memorial Day. Haunted Mine Thurs. 7-10 and Fri.-Sat 7-11, in Oct. Last tour begins 1 hour before closing. **Cost:** $10; $9 (ages 3-12 and senior citizens). Haunted mine tour Thurs. $10; Fri.-Sat. $12. Ages 0-9 are not recommended on haunted mine tour. **Phone:** (724) 224-4720.

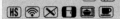
SPRINGHILL SUITES BY MARRIOTT PITTSBURGH MILLS   (724)274-1064 44
Hotel
$111-$194

AAA Benefit: Members save 5% or more!

Address: 3015 Pittsburgh Mills Blvd 15084 **Location:** SR 28 exit Pittsburgh Mills Blvd; in Pittsburgh Mills shopping area. **Facility:** 115 units. 5 stories, interior corridors. **Pool(s):** heated indoor. **Activities:** exercise room. **Guest Services:** valet and coin laundry. **Featured Amenity:** breakfast buffet. (See ad p. 368.)

TIPTON (G-5) pop. 1,083, elev. 994'

DELGROSSO'S AMUSEMENT PARK, 4352 E. Pleasant Valley Blvd., features more than 30 rides and a water park including 5 large water slides and activity pool. **Hours:** Open daily at 11, June 2-Aug. 23; Sat.-Sun. and holidays in May and Sept. Closing times vary. Phone ahead to confirm schedule.

Cost: All-day ride pass June-Aug. $19.95; May and Sept. $16.95. Individual ride tickets 50c (all rides require more than one ticket) Phone ahead to confirm rates. **Phone:** (814) 684-3538 or (866) 684-3538.

TITUSVILLE (D-2) pop. 5,601, elev. 1,174'

Native Americans used the slick film on Oil Creek to mix their war paints, and enterprising settlers bottled and sold it as a medicinal concoction called Seneca Oil. Not until 1859 when Col. Edwin Drake drilled a well, did oil begin to revolutionize industry and spur progress around the world. Titusville's status as birthplace of the oil industry earned Oil Creek Valley its title of "the valley that changed the world," and the city became a wealthy boom town. Pennsylvania was the nation's number one oil producer until 1901, when production peaked and the oil industry began striking richer fields in the West.

Today evidence of the town's wealth can be found downtown on Main and Perry streets, which are lined with mansions showcasing varying architectural designs, including Queen Anne and Victorian.

Titusville Chamber of Commerce: 202 W. Central Ave., Titusville, PA 16354. **Phone:** (814) 827-2941.

Self-guiding tours: Visitors can stroll past fine examples of architecture while touring the tree-lined streets of Titusville. A brochure is available at the chamber of commerce.

DRAKE WELL MUSEUM is .5 mi. s. on SR 8, then 1.2 mi. e. on E. Bloss St. The museum marks the spot where Edwin Drake drilled the world's first commercially successful oil well in 1859. Photographs and outdoor working oil field equipment trace the evolution of the modern petroleum industry. The exhibit "There's a Drop of Oil and Gas in

Your Life Every Day" features a multisensory orientation theater. A replica of Drake's well, an operating oil lease with pump jacks and a steel drilling rig and pumping jacks are also on display.

A 10-mile paved bicycle trail and 52 miles of hiking trails connect Drake Well and Oil Creek State Park *(see Recreation Areas Chart)*. **Hours:** Tues.-Sat. 9-5, Sun. noon-5, Apr.-Dec.; Wed.-Sat. 9-5, Sun. noon-5, rest of year. Closed winter holidays. Phone ahead to confirm schedule. **Cost:** $10; $8 (ages 65+); $5 (ages 3-11); free (active military and their family with ID). **Phone:** (814) 827-2797.

OIL CREEK AND TITUSVILLE RAILROAD, 409 S. Perry St., offers 3-hour train trips in restored 1930s passenger cars. Narrated excursions, departing from a renovated 1896 freight station, recount the area's 19th-century oil boom. The train contains the only operating railway post office car in the United States. Trips also depart from the Drake Well Museum *(see attraction listing)*, south of Titusville, and Rynd Farm, north of Oil City. Murder mystery dinner trains and holiday-themed train trips also are available.

Hours: Train departs from the Perry Street station Wed.-Sun. at 11 (also Sat.-Sun. at 3), Oct. 1-19; Wed.-Thurs. and Sat.-Sun. at 1, July-Aug.; Sat.-Sun. at 1, in June and Sept. Phone ahead to confirm schedule. **Cost:** $19; $17 (ages 60+); $13 (ages 3-12); $50 (family, two adults with two children). Reservations are recommended. **Phone:** (814) 676-1733.

TOWANDA (D-9) pop. 2,919, elev. 771'

Towanda was the boyhood home of composer Stephen Collins Foster and the home of staunch Abraham Lincoln supporter David Wilmot, who founded the Republican Party.

FRENCH AZILUM, 4.3 mi. s. on SR 187, then 3.8 mi. e. on SR 2014 (French Asylum Rd.), following signs, was founded in 1793 as a refuge for French Royalists fleeing the Revolution. About 50 log buildings were erected, none of which still stand. After Napoleon's pardon, many immigrants left the area. Highlights include outbuildings with early Americana, the 1836 LaPorte House containing period furnishings, a 14-minute video about the site's history, three display cabins and scenic grounds.

Hours: Fri.-Mon. 11-5, mid-May to Labor Day weekend; Sat.-Sun. weekend after Labor Day to mid-Oct. Last tour begins 1 hour before closing. Phone ahead to confirm schedule. **Cost:** $5; $3 (students with ID); free (ages 0-12). **Phone:** (570) 265-3376.

BEST WESTERN PLUS TOWANDA INN   (570)268-7000

Hotel
$135-$150

AAA Benefit: Members save up to 20%!

Address: 44 Peace Ln 18848 **Location:** On US 6 E. **Facility:** 65 units. 3 stories, interior corridors. **Terms:** 3 day cancellation notice-fee imposed. **Pool(s):** heated indoor. **Activities:** exercise room. **Guest Services:** valet and coin laundry. **Featured Amenity:** continental breakfast.

FAIRFIELD INN & SUITES BY MARRIOTT TOWANDA WYSOX   (570)265-5553

Hotel
$146-$240

AAA Benefit: Members save 5% or more!

Address: 1248 Golden Mile Rd 18848 **Location:** On US 6 E. **Facility:** 88 units. 3 stories, interior corridors. **Pool(s):** heated indoor. **Activities:** exercise room. **Guest Services:** valet and coin laundry. **Featured Amenity:** breakfast buffet.

FAIRFIELD INN & SUITES® Marriott

In the Endless Mountain Region on Historic Rt. 6 there's a new hotel to discover, experience & enjoy.

WHERE TO EAT

VILLA SENA   570/265-9986
Italian. Casual Dining. $4-$18 **AAA Inspector Notes:** The casual restaurant's dining room has large windows overlooking the Bradford County Airport and the nearby mountains. A full bar complements a menu of Italian-American cuisine, including steaks, veal, seafood, chicken and a variety of pasta dishes. **Features:** full bar, patio dining. **Address:** RR 2, Box 76A 18848 **Location:** 1.2 mi s on Old US 220 (Towanda-Monroeton Rd). L D

TRAFFORD pop. 3,174

- **Hotels & Restaurants map & index p. 348**
- **Part of Pittsburgh area — see map p. 326**

PARENTE'S RISTORANTE   412/373-0566 73
Italian. Casual Dining. $7-$24 **AAA Inspector Notes:** Family-owned and -operated for more than 10 years, the kitchen prepares good Italian fare. On the menu is a selection of pasta dishes as well as meats and fish. Guests can expect to eat a lot because most amply portioned entrées come with soup and salad. The local theater contributes to dinner and theater events. **Features:** full bar. **Reservations:** suggested, weekends. **Address:** 427 Cavitt Ave 15085 **Location:** Center. **Parking:** on-site and street. L D

TREVOSE pop. 3,550
• Hotels & Restaurants map & index p. 274
• Part of Philadelphia area — see map p. 230

COMFORT INN TREVOSE   (215)638-4554
▼▼▼ Hotel $85-$105 Address: 2779 Lincoln Hwy N 19053 Location: I-276 (Pennsylvania Tpke) exit 351, 0.5 mi s. Located in a commercial area. Facility: 87 units. 3 stories, interior corridors. Pool(s): outdoor. Activities: exercise room. Guest Services: valet laundry.

CROWNE PLAZA PHILADELPHIA-BUCKS COUNTY
HOTEL   215/364-2000

Hotel
Rates not provided

Address: 4700 Street Rd 19053 Location: I-276 (Pennsylvania Tpke) exit 351, just s on US 1, then 0.3 mi w on SR 132. Located in a commercial area. Trevose, 286. Facility: 214 units. 6 stories, interior corridors. Terms: check-in 4 pm. Pool(s): heated indoor. Activities: sauna, hot tub, exercise room. Guest Services: valet and coin laundry, rental car service, area transportation.

RADISSON HOTEL PHILADELPHIA NORTHEAST
                                    (215)638-8300
▼▼▼ Hotel $119-$199 Address: 2400 Old Lincoln Hwy 19053 Location: I-276 (Pennsylvania Tpke) exit 351, 1 mi s on US 1; jct Roosevelt Blvd and Old Lincoln Hwy. Located in a commercial area. Facility: 274 units, some efficiencies. 6 stories, interior corridors. Terms: cancellation fee imposed. Amenities: Some: safes. Pool(s): outdoor, heated indoor. Activities: exercise room. Guest Services: valet and coin laundry.

RED ROOF INN PHILADELPHIA TREVOSE
                                    215/244-9422
Motel
Rates not provided

Address: 3100 Lincoln Hwy 19053 Location: I-276 (Pennsylvania Tpke) exit 351, 0.5 mi s on US 1 at US 132. Located in a commercial area. Trevose, 286. Facility: 162 units. 2 stories (no elevator), exterior corridors. Amenities: video games, safes. Guest Services: coin laundry.

TROUT RUN

FRY BROTHERS TURKEY RANCH   570/998-9400
▼ American. Family Dining. $6-$11 AAA Inspector Notes: Family owned for four generations, this mountaintop restaurant has been serving hungry travelers for more than 65 years. Relax in the cozy and inviting country pine decor and enjoy their specialty turkey dinners along with a full menu of tasty comfort foods. Address: 27 SR 184 17771 Location: US 15 exit Steam Valley (SR 184).

B L D

TROY (D-8) pop. 1,354, elev. 1,136'

FARM MUSEUM & HISTORIC VILLAGE (BRADFORD COUNTY HERITAGE ASSOCIATION) is on SR 14 in Alparon Park, .5 mi. n. of jct. US 6. Exhibits, which include re-creations of a general store,

icehouse, blacksmith shop and woodworking shop, allow visitors to imagine what rural life was like in America's past. Examples of agricultural equipment and farming implements are displayed. Also on the grounds are an 1822 house; an herb garden; a carriage house with a carriage, wagon and sleigh collection; a maple sugar house; a one-room schoolhouse; a barbershop; and a children's church. The Pennsylvania Heritage Festival is held the third weekend in September.

Hours: Thurs.-Sat. 9-4, Sun. 1-4, late Apr.-late Oct.; by appointment rest of year. Phone ahead to confirm schedule. Cost: $7; $5 (ages 60+); $3 (students grades K-12); free (ages 0-5). Phone: (570) 297-3410.

TUNKHANNOCK (WYOMING COUNTY)

COMFORT INN & SUITES TUNKHANNOCK   (570)836-4100
▼▼▼ Hotel $149-$179 Address: 5 N Eaton Rd 18657 Location: 0.4 mi s; just across bridge. Facility: 77 units, some efficiencies. 3 stories, interior corridors. Amenities: safes. Pool(s): heated indoor. Activities: picnic facilities, exercise room. Guest Services: coin laundry.

HAMPTON INN TUNKHANNOCK   (570)996-5866
▼▼▼
Hotel
$139-$179

AAA Benefit:
Members save 5% or more!

Address: 209 E Tioga St 18657 Location: Jct SR 92 and US 6, just n; on US Business Rt 6. Facility: 67 units. 4 stories, interior corridors. Terms: 1-7 night minimum stay, cancellation fee imposed. Pool(s): heated indoor. Activities: hot tub, exercise room. Guest Services: valet and coin laundry. Featured Amenity: full hot breakfast.

WHERE TO EAT

TWIGS RESTAURANT & CAFE   570/836-0433
▼▼ American. Casual Dining. $6-$25 AAA Inspector Notes: This cute corner brick restaurant with distinctive copper and glass hanging lights, stained-glass windows, antique ceiling tiles and modern art makes for an eclectic, cozy dining spot. Locals frequent this place for delicious, trendy foods that burst with homemade flavor such as their wraps, panini and entree salads. Features: full bar, patio dining. Address: 1 E Tioga St 18657 Location: On US 6; center. Parking: street only. L D

TYRONE (G-5) pop. 5,477, elev. 909'

GARDNERS CANDY MUSEUM, 30 W. 10th St., is in an 1890s candy store. A re-created candy kitchen, candy-making utensils, Easter bunny molds, candy boxes and other memorabilia are displayed. A 45-minute video depicts a tour of the candy factory. Hours: Mon.-Sat. 9:30-9, Sun. 1-9. Closed major holidays. Cost: Free. Phone: (814) 684-0857 for the museum.

UNION DALE (D-11) pop. 267, elev. 1,697'

RECREATIONAL ACTIVITIES
Skiing and Snowboarding
- **Elk Mountain Ski Resort** is off I-81 exit 206 at 344 Elk Mountain Rd. **Hours:** Daily 8:30 a.m.-10 p.m., day after Christmas-late Mar.; 8:30-4:30, Dec.1-late Dec. Phone ahead to confirm schedule. **Phone:** (570) 679-4400, or (800) 233-4131 for ski conditions.

UNIONTOWN (I-2) pop. 10,372, elev. 1,022'

Uniontown is in the Laurel Highlands *(see place listing p. 183)* of southwestern Pennsylvania, an area filled with historic sites and outdoor recreation outlets. Spelunking, bicycling and white-water rafting are popular.

Founded in 1776, the town is on Route 40, the historic National Road, which was built 1811-18. It is the birthplace of Gen. George C. Marshall, who laid out the plan in which America would provide economic aid to Europe after World War II—the Marshall Plan. Southeast of town is the grave of Gen. Edward Braddock *(see Fort Necessity National Battlefield p. 112).* About 5 miles west on the National Road/US 40 is Searights Toll House, one of two remaining such structures; there were originally six in the state.

Fayette Chamber of Commerce: 65 W. Main St., Uniontown, PA 15401. **Phone:** (724) 437-4571.

COAL AND COKE HERITAGE CENTER on US 119 on the grounds of Penn State Fayette, The Eberly Campus, in the lower level of the library. This museum chronicles the local coal and coke industries, which fueled the Pittsburgh steel industry, through an extensive collection of items donated by families of former industry employees. The technical aspect of the industry is presented along with the human element of the workers—the problems and opportunities they encountered, the communities ("patches") they formed, and the ethnic and cultural backgrounds of the immigrants as well as the African Americans who arrived from the South. The collection includes artifacts, clothing and photographs.

Among the items in the research archives are documents, maps, newspapers and oral histories. **Time:** Allow 30 minutes minimum. **Hours:** Mon.-Fri. 10-3 when school is in session and other times by appointment, mid-Jan. to mid-Dec. **Cost:** Donations. **Phone:** (724) 430-4158.

LAUREL CAVERNS is about 3 mi. e. on US 40, then 5 mi. s. on Skyline Dr. to 200 Caverns Park Rd. A maze cave with more than 3 miles of passages, the caverns have been explored since the late 1700s. Guided tours include the Grand Canyon and other limestone formations. A view from Chestnut Ridge covers two states and 4,000 square miles. An indoor miniature golf course also is available. Cavern temperatures remain at a constant 52 degrees Fahrenheit.

Warm clothing is recommended. **Time:** Allow 1 hour minimum. **Hours:** Daily 9-5, May 1-late Oct. **Cost:** $12; $11 (ages 65+); $10 (grades 6-12); $9 (grades K-5). **Phone:** (724) 438-3003 or (800) 515-4150.

FAIRFIELD INN BY MARRIOTT UNIONTOWN   (724)434-1800

 **Hotel** $97-$183 **Address:** 283 McClellandtown Rd 15401 **Location:** Jct US 40/119, just e. **Facility:** 69 units. 3 stories, interior corridors. **Pool(s):** heated indoor. **Guest Services:** valet laundry.

AAA Benefit: Members save 5% or more!

HAMPTON INN   (724)430-1000

Hotel $110-$159 **Address:** 698 W Main St (US 40) 15401 **Location:** 1.8 mi w on US 40. **Facility:** 86 efficiencies. 3 stories, interior corridors. **Terms:** 1-7 night minimum stay, cancellation fee imposed. **Pool(s):** heated indoor. **Activities:** sauna, hot tub, steamroom, exercise room.

AAA Benefit: Members save 5% or more!

HERITAGE INN OF UNIONTOWN   724/437-7829

Motel $59-$109 **Address:** 222 W Main St 15401 **Location:** 0.6 mi w on US 40. **Facility:** 19 units. 1 story, exterior corridors. **Terms:** cancellation fee imposed. **Guest Services:** valet laundry.

INNE AT WATSON'S CHOICE AND HARVEST HOUSE BED & BREAKFAST   724/437-4999

 Historic Bed & Breakfast $105-$215 **Address:** 234 Balsinger Rd 15401 **Location:** Jct US 40/119, 3 mi w on SR 21, 0.3 mi nw, follow signs. **Facility:** Picnic-basket lunches are a specialty at this 1820 country farmhouse featuring German architecture. The B&B offers traditional rooms, as well as large one-bedroom units and newly constructed private cabins. 12 units, some cabins. 1-2 stories (no elevator), interior corridors. **Terms:** closed 1/1-2/28, 2 night minimum stay - seasonal and/or weekends, 8 day cancellation notice-fee imposed.

MG MOTEL   724/437-0506

Motel
$54-$64

Address: 7909 National Pike (US 40) 15401 **Location:** US 40 W, 2.2 mi w. **Facility:** 10 units. 1 story, exterior corridors.

SUPER 8   (724)425-0261

Hotel $84-$156 **Address:** 701 W Main St 15401 **Location:** 1.8 mi w on US 40. **Facility:** 61 units. 3 stories, interior corridors. **Guest Services:** valet and coin laundry.

UNIONTOWN HOLIDAY INN   (724)437-2816

Hotel $119-$179 **Address:** 700 W Main St 15401 **Location:** 1.8 mi w on US 40. **Facility:** 178 units. 2 stories (no elevator), interior corridors. **Pool(s):** heated indoor. **Activities:** hot tub, playground, game room, limited exercise equipment. **Guest Services:** valet and coin laundry.

WHERE TO EAT

ALL STAR ASIAN BUFFET   724/430-8185
◆ Asian. Casual Dining. $6-$18 **AAA Inspector Notes:** Located in a shopping center, this Asian buffet restaurant has a variety of menu options. The buffet price includes Mongolian grill and sushi stations. Crab legs are the special on Fridays. The service and atmosphere are casual. **Address:** 203 Walmart Dr 15401 **Location:** SR 43 exit 15, 1.9 mi w; in Fayette Crossing Shopping Center.
Ⓛ Ⓓ

ANGELINA'S PICCOLO   724/437-2782
◆ Italian. Casual Dining. $7-$16 **AAA Inspector Notes:** In Oliver Square just outside of historic downtown, the casual restaurant prepares Italian food, including daily made breads and soups. This place closes earlier than typical restaurants, so it's a good idea to get here early. **Address:** 104 Oliver Plaza 15401 **Location:** On SR 51; in Oliver Plaza. Ⓛ Ⓓ

DI MARCO'S BISTRO & CANTINA   724/438-1611
◆◆ American. Casual Dining. $8-$25 **AAA Inspector Notes:** Built in a remodeled Victorian home, half of the downtown restaurant is dining room, half is lounge. The large bar features 50 draft beers and has a good wine list. The extensive menu is mostly American with a Southwestern flair. The chicken chili is great, but the daily specials also should be considered. Children are welcome. **Features:** full bar. **Reservations:** suggested. **Address:** 26 Morgantown St 15401 **Location:** Between W South and W Church sts; center.
Ⓛ Ⓓ

EAT'N PARK   724/439-0440
◆ American. Casual Dining. $5-$11 **AAA Inspector Notes:** Casual, family restaurant with friendly but sometimes inattentive service. There's a salad bar buffet, and Sunday brunch is a good value. The menu has many choices of American cuisine and homemade desserts. The strawberry pie is incredible. Free cookies are given to the kids at the end of the meal. A special dietary menu, offered at all locations, includes gluten-free, reduced sodium, small portions and vegetarian options. **Features:** Sunday brunch. **Address:** 519 W Main St 15401 **Location:** 0.8 mi w on US 40.
Ⓑ Ⓛ Ⓓ CALL Ⓜ

GENERATIONS, A RESTAURANT   724/437-3204
◆◆ Italian. Casual Dining. $17-$25 **AAA Inspector Notes:** In a beautiful renovated Victorian home from the 1800s, the casually upscale Italian restaurant in historic downtown nurtures a warm atmosphere, and many regulars are happy to make conversation with diners, even if they've never met. A private dining room is available. Chicken Romano is fabulous, and the homemade desserts are not to be forgotten. **Features:** full bar. **Reservations:** suggested, weekends. **Address:** 181 W Main St 15401 **Location:** Between N Mount Vernon Ave and Kensington St; in historic downtown. Ⓓ

MELONI'S   724/437-2061
◆
Italian
Casual Dining
$7-$20
AAA Inspector Notes: This restaurant is located in an old-fashioned neighborhood, where the service and atmosphere are casual and the food is tasty and filling. Lasagna, spaghetti and Italian sausage sandwiches are specialties. The menu also lists a handful of American choices. There is a good selection of beer and wines to choose from at the bar. **Features:** full bar. **Address:** 105 W Main St 15401 **Location:** Center. *Menu on AAA.com*
Ⓛ Ⓓ

MING HING CHINESE RESTAURANT   724/438-8883
◆ Chinese. Casual Dining. $6-$15 **AAA Inspector Notes:** In a shopping center, the small dine-in or carry-out Chinese restaurant is known for good food, and while table service isn't offered, there are still tables at which guests can dine. A kind and gracious husband-and-wife pair operates this place. Those who want to eat on the premises must arrive at least 30 minutes before closing; otherwise, carry-out is the only option. **Address:** 629 Pittsburgh Rd 15401 **Location:** SR 43 exit 15, just e, 0.8 mi n, then just e. Ⓛ Ⓓ

TITLOW TAVERN & GRILLE   724/437-6749
◆◆ American. Casual Dining. $7-$25 **AAA Inspector Notes:** The tavern offers a casual atmosphere and a large menu with a variety of seafood, steaks and vegetarian dishes. **Features:** full bar. **Reservations:** suggested, weekends. **Address:** 92 W Main St 15401 **Location:** Center; in Highland House Hotel. **Parking:** on-site (fee) and valet. Ⓛ Ⓓ

UPPER BLACK EDDY
• Part of Philadelphia area — see map p. 230

THE BRIDGETON HOUSE ON THE DELAWARE   610/982-5856
◆◆◆ Bed & Breakfast. Rates not provided. **Address:** 1525 River Rd 18972 **Location:** Waterfront. On SR 32; center. **Facility:** Enjoy elegant views of the Delaware River from this beautiful B&B, which offers an outdoor area consisting of a fountain, garden, covered tea room and a dock. Luxury suites and a penthouse are available. 11 units. 3 stories (no elevator), interior corridors. **Terms:** age restrictions may apply.

UPPER DELAWARE SCENIC AND RECREATIONAL RIVER (D-11)

The Upper Delaware Scenic and Recreational River comprises 73 miles of the Upper Delaware River from just north of Port Jervis, N.Y., to Hancock, N.Y. Along this stretch the river changes from long, placid eddies to swift water and challenging rapids. It is paralleled on the New York side by SR 97 (Upper Delaware Scenic Byway), which has several scenic overlooks. The best road from which to see the river on the Pennsylvania side is the northern section of SR 191, which at times is only a few feet above the water.

Almost all land along the river is privately owned; public river access areas are located on both the Pennsylvania and New York shores. Private campgrounds and canoe liveries are available near the river.

The Upper Delaware was an important transportation route for Native Americans and early settlers. In 1828 the Delaware and Hudson Canal opened, bringing coal-laden boats from the Pennsylvania interior to the port of New York. However, problems soon developed at the point where the canal crossed the river: Slow-moving boats being towed across the river were constantly colliding with the huge log and timber rafts that were coursing down the river to sawmills and shipyards in Trenton, N.J., and Philadelphia, Pa.

To solve the problem and improve the canal's efficiency, the company approved a plan to build the canal above the water. John Roebling, who later designed the Brooklyn Bridge, built the Delaware Aqueduct, known today as Roebling Bridge, to cross the river and carry canal traffic from Lackawaxen, Pa., to Minisink Ford, N.Y. The aqueduct is considered to be the oldest wire suspension bridge in America. The adjacent tollhouse contains exhibits interpreting the history of the Delaware and Hudson Canal, John Roebling and the Delaware Aqueduct.

Beavers, foxes, white-tailed deer, minks, muskrats, otters, rabbits and squirrels populate the area. Birds include bald eagles, great blue herons,

Canada geese and several varieties of hawks and ducks.

On the banks of the Upper Delaware Scenic and Recreational River lies the Zane Grey Museum, in Lackawaxen, Pa. The renowned Western author began his writing career and lived at the site with his wife, Dolly, 1905-18.

Recreational opportunities include boating, canoeing, fishing and rafting. In summer the National Park Service offers a variety of programs and recreational activities, including cultural and natural history walks and guided hikes.

Information stations are located at some public boating access sites, including on Scenic Dr. in Lackawaxen, Pa., and in Skinners Falls, N.Y. Phone (570) 729-7134 (headquarters) or (845) 252-7100 (river conditions).

UPPER ST. CLAIR pop. 19,229
- Hotels & Restaurants map & index p. 348
- Part of Pittsburgh area — see map p. 326

KING'S FAMILY RESTAURANT   412/833-9095

▼▼ American. Family Dining. $6-$15 **AAA Inspector Notes:** Fast and friendly service is offered here. The menu is large in size with descriptive menu items and pictures. The restaurant is also known for its ice cream and dessert menu. **Address:** 155 McMurray Rd 15241 **Location:** Just sw of jct Washington Rd.

B   L   D

PICCOLINA'S   412/257-1880 95

▼▼▼ Northern Italian. Fine Dining. $7-$33 **AAA Inspector Notes:** The Pinebridge Commons spot focuses on traditional Italian dishes and such delicious specials as lemon chicken with sliced Sicilian olives, capers and fresh lemon juice. **Features:** full bar. **Reservations:** suggested. **Address:** 1580 McLaughlin Run Rd 15241 **Location:** SR 50 (Bridgeville), 2.5 mi e, follow Orange Belt; in Pinebridge Commons.   L   D

VALLEY FORGE (A-9) elev. 98'
- Part of Philadelphia area — see map p. 230

Valley Forge began as an iron forge on Valley Creek in the 1740s. A sawmill and gristmill were added by the time of the Revolutionary War, making Valley Forge an important supply center for the Colonists. However, it did not escape the attention of the British, who destroyed the forge and mills in 1777. Only ruins marked the site when George Washington chose Valley Forge for his winter of 1777-78 encampment (see Valley Forge National Historical Park this page).

Valley Forge Convention & Visitors Bureau: 1000 First Ave., Suite 101, King of Prussia, PA 19406. **Phone:** (610) 834-1550.

FREEDOMS FOUNDATION AT VALLEY FORGE, 1601 Valley Forge Rd. (SR 23), was founded in 1949 as an educational institution to promote responsible citizenship. The 85-acre campus features the Independence Garden, the Medal of Honor Grove, the Faith of Our Fathers Chapel, the Bill of Responsibilities and the American Credo monuments. The Medal of Honor Grove and the campus are open to the public. **Time:** Allow 30 minutes

minimum. **Hours:** Mon.-Fri. 8-4. **Cost:** Donations. **Phone:** (610) 933-8825.

▼ VALLEY FORGE NATIONAL HISTORICAL PARK (A-8) elev. 154'
- Part of Philadelphia area — see map p. 230

Extending east from the village of Valley Forge along SR 23, the 3,500-acre Valley Forge National Historical Park was the site of the 6-month winter/spring encampment by the Continental Army. From Dec. 19, 1777, to June 19, 1778, Gen. George Washington and 12,000 soldiers survived against terrible odds and kept the British Army contained in Philadelphia.

During that harsh winter some 2,000 troops died from disease brought on by supply shortages, exposure and poor sanitation. Still, during those 6 months the army was reorganized, Baron von Steuben developed a uniform system of drill and the Continental Army left Valley Forge better trained and more efficient.

The visitor center, at the junction of SR 23 and N. Gulph Road, has exhibits and presents a short film. Maps outlining a self-guiding driving tour, which includes the National Memorial Arch, Washington's Headquarters, Washington Memorial Chapel (see attraction listings), the reconstructed huts of Muhlenberg's Brigade and the original entrenchment lines and fortifications are available here. One-hour audio driving tours on CD can also be purchased. Seasonal trolley tours begin from this location.

A stop at any of the Storytelling Benches located throughout the park will offer insight into the Valley Forge army encampment and its impact on the Revolutionary War. The Once Upon A Nation benches are staffed seasonally and can be found at the visitor center and Washington's Headquarters. Vault tours offer a behind-the-scenes look at a collection of historic documents. Audio cell phone, bicycle, trolley, ranger-led and gallery tours also are available.

Allow 2 hours minimum. Park open daily 7 a.m.-dusk. Visitor center and Washington's Headquarters open daily 9-6, mid-June through Sept. 30; 9-5, rest of year; closed Jan. 1, Thanksgiving and Christmas. Varnum's Quarters Sat.-Sun. noon-4, Memorial Day-Labor Day. Varnum's picnic area daily 7 a.m.-dusk, Apr.-Oct. Narrated 90-minute trolley tours depart daily, mid-June through Labor Day; Sat.-Sun., Apr. 1 to mid-June and day after Labor Day-Nov. 30 (weather permitting). Holiday tours offered in late Nov. and late Dec. Vault tours are given by appointment. Phone for schedule of other tours.

Park free. Trolley tour $16.50; $13.50 (senior citizens and students and active military with ID); $8.50 (ages 0-11). Audio CD $14.95. Phone (610) 783-1099 for the visitor center, (610) 783-1074 for trolley tours, (610) 783-1020 for vault tours, (484) 396-1034 for cell phone tour (English) or (484) 396-1015 for cell phone tour (Spanish).

NATIONAL MEMORIAL ARCH, off SR 23 in Valley Forge National Historical Park, commemorates the patriotism and suffering of George Washington and the men who were under his command; it was dedicated in 1917. The final design was inspired by the Arch of Titus in Rome. The inner walls of this 60-foot high granite memorial contain bronze plaques listing the names of the general officers at Valley Forge. **Hours:** Daily dawn-dusk. **Cost:** Free. **Phone:** (610) 783-1099 for the park visitor center.

WASHINGTON MEMORIAL CHAPEL is at 1600 Valley Forge Park Rd. (SR 23) within Valley Forge National Historical Park. The Episcopal chapel was built in 1903 as a memorial to Gen. George Washington and contains artifacts, relics, woodcarvings and windows depicting national history. The National Patriot's Bell Tower houses 58 bells and the Veteran's Wall of Honor. **Time:** Allow 30 minutes minimum. **Hours:** Daily 10-5. **Cost:** Donations. **Phone:** (610) 783-0120.

WASHINGTON'S HEADQUARTERS is 3 mi. w. of the visitor center on SR 23W in Valley Forge National Historical Park. The house, which contains Revolutionary War-era furnishings, was rented by Gen. George Washington during the Continental Army's encampment Dec. 19, 1777, to June 19, 1778, and served as his command post for coordinating the daily operations of the entire army.

The structure is also known as the Potts House. Park rangers are available to answer questions. Displays that chronicle Washington as a leader can be seen in the 1917 Valley Forge Train Station building next door. **Time:** Allow 30 minutes minimum. **Hours:** Visitor center daily 9-5 (also 5-6, mid-June to mid-Aug.). Headquarters 9-5, Mar.-Dec.; Sat.-Sun. 10-4 (also Presidents Day), Jan.-Feb. Train station 9-5, Mar.-Dec. Closed Jan. 1, Thanksgiving and Christmas. Phone ahead to confirm schedule. **Cost:** Free. **Phone:** (610) 783-1099 for the park visitor center.

VOLANT (F-1) pop. 168, elev. 1,033'

If you're traveling along I-79 or I-80 and have an itch to go shopping for something special that can't be found in every mall or chain store, take the nearest Volant exit to visit this quaint town with nearly two dozen specialty shops lining Main Street (SR 208). The focal point of the old-fashioned small town is Volant Mill, which dates back to 1812. Volant had a flourishing business district in the late 19th- and early 20th centuries thanks to the mill and the railroad, but with the Great Depression came less growth; the mill eventually closed in the 1960s and the trains ceased in the mid-1970s and Volant settled into its new role as a typical small rural town. However, in 1984 an antique and country gift store opened up in the Volant Mill building. More shops gradually opened along Main Street, creating a specialty shopping district which is a popular destination still.

Amish families reside on nearby farms, so horses and buggies are common sights in the area. Neshannock Creek, excellent for trout fishing, runs through Volant and fly fishing is quite popular. Also popular is the annual trout stocking day in March, which is just one of many planned festivities in a busy calendar of events schedule where almost every month offers at least one way to celebrate a holiday or the arrival of a new season.

Shopping areas: The Volant Village Shops include nearly two dozen specialty shops along Main Street (SR 208) with a wide assortment of merchandise, including furniture, leather goods, rugs, kitchen supplies, soaps and lotions, garden flags, scrapbook materials, collectibles, home furnishings, jewelry, handmade Amish goods and artwork by regional artists. There are also coffees, teas, spices, jams, relishes and nostalgic candies. During autumn, which is a particularly lovely time to visit the area, many of the shops' inventories are enhanced with Halloween, Thanksgiving and Christmas decorations.

WARMINSTER
• Part of Philadelphia area — see map p. 230

HOLIDAY INN EXPRESS & SUITES WARMINSTER - DOYLESTOWN   215/443-4300
▼▼▼▼ **Hotel.** Rates not provided. **Address:** 240 Veterans Way 18974 **Location:** I-276 exit 343, 1 mi n on Blair Mill Rd, 0.9 mi w on W Moreland Ave, 2 mi n on Jacksonville Rd, then just w. 🖼 Warminster, 298. **Facility:** 92 units, some efficiencies. 3 stories, interior corridors. **Amenities:** safes. **Pool(s):** heated indoor. **Activities:** hot tub, exercise room. **Guest Services:** valet and coin laundry.
CALL 🈁 🅜 🚗 BIZ HS 🛜 🎫 🍽 💻 🚇

WARREN (D-3) pop. 9,710, elev. 1,174'
• Restaurants p. 410

Kinzua Dam, 6 miles east on SR 59, offers scenic views of the dam and Allegheny Reservoir, and a wide variety of summer and winter recreational activities are available. A visitor center in the Big Bend Access Area is open based on the availability of volunteers; phone (814) 726-0661, or (814) 726-0164 for lake conditions. *See Allegheny National Forest p. 46 and Recreation Areas Chart.*

Warren County Visitors Bureau: 22045 US 6, Warren, PA 16365. **Phone:** (814) 726-1222 or (800) 624-7802.

WARREN COUNTY HISTORICAL SOCIETY, 210 Fourth Ave., is housed in an Italian Renaissance house built in 1873. Period rooms include a formal parlor, a Victorian room and a general store. A research library contains archives, genealogy records and a photograph collection. **Time:** Allow 30 minutes minimum. **Hours:** Mon.-Fri. 8:30-4:30. Closed major holidays. **Cost:** Donations. **Phone:** (814) 723-1795.

ALLEGHENY INN & SUITES   (814)723-8881
▼▼ ▼▼ **Hotel** $74-$106 **Address:** 204 Struthers St 16365 **Location:** 1.5 mi w on US 6 exit Ludlow St, w on Allegheny, then s. **Facility:** 56 units. 3 stories, interior/exterior corridors.
🍽 🛜 ✕ 🎫 🍽 💻 /SOME UNITS 🅢

HAMPTON INN & SUITES OF WARREN (814)723-2722

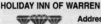 **Hotel** $130-$144 **Address:** 3291 Market St 16365 **Location:** I-86 exit 37, 10 mi s on US 62. **Facility:** 69 units. 4 stories, interior corridors. **Terms:** 1-7 night minimum stay, cancellation fee imposed. **Pool(s):** heated indoor. **Activities:** exercise room. **Guest Services:** valet and coin laundry.

AAA Benefit: Members save 5% or more!

CALL

HOLIDAY INN OF WARREN (814)726-3000

Hotel $119-$129

Address: 210 Ludlow St 16365 **Location:** Jct US 6, just n on US 62 N (Ludlow St). **Facility:** 110 units. 4 stories, interior corridors. **Dining:** Tootsie's Restaurant, see separate listing. **Pool(s):** heated indoor. **Activities:** sauna, exercise room. **Guest Services:** valet laundry.

WHERE TO EAT

CHIODO'S FERRO CUCINA 814/723-5773

 Italian. Casual Dining. $7-$25 **AAA Inspector Notes:** Since 2001, good authentic Italian fare has been prepared and served here in generous portions. A large selection of antipasti, pasta, chicken, veal, steaks and seafood prepared in all ways imaginable is offered. Prime rib is featured on Friday, Saturday and Sunday only. **Features:** full bar. **Address:** 1413 Pennsylvania Ave 16365 **Location:** On US 6 and 62.

TOOTSIE'S RESTAURANT 814/726-3000

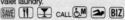 American. Casual Dining. $7-$27 **AAA Inspector Notes:** Patrons will find a casual atmosphere in the restaurant as well as friendly service. The steakhouse menu reflects an all-American cuisine. **Features:** full bar. **Address:** 210 Ludlow St 16365 **Location:** Jct US 6, just n on US 62 N (Ludlow St); in Holiday Inn of Warren.

WARRINGTON
• Part of Philadelphia area — see map p. 230

HAMPTON INN - WARRINGTON/DOYLESTOWN
(215)343-8400

 Hotel $149-$209 **Address:** 1570 Easton Rd 18976 **Location:** 2.4 mi s of jct US 202 and SR 611. **Facility:** 78 units. 5 stories, interior corridors. **Terms:** 1-7 night minimum stay, cancellation fee imposed. **Amenities:** safes. **Pool(s):** heated indoor. **Activities:** exercise room. **Guest Services:** valet and coin laundry.

AAA Benefit: Members save 5% or more!

HOMEWOOD SUITES WARRINGTON (215)343-1300

 Extended Stay Hotel $149-$259

 HOMEWOOD SUITES BY HILTON

AAA Benefit: Members save 5% or more!

Address: 2650 Kelly Rd 18976 **Location:** 2.4 mi s of jct US 202 and SR 611. **Facility:** 96 efficiencies, some two bedrooms. 5 stories, interior corridors. **Terms:** 1-7 night minimum stay, cancellation fee imposed. **Pool(s):** heated indoor. **Activities:** game room, exercise room. **Guest Services:** valet and coin laundry. **Featured Amenity:** full hot breakfast.

WHERE TO EAT

JANNIE RESTAURANT 215/343-3889

 Asian. Casual Dining. $9-$30 **AAA Inspector Notes:** Located in a storefront of a small shopping center, this restaurant features a beautiful large dining room with polished stone floors, a mirror-finish brass ceiling, decorative lighting suspended with large rectangular carved-plaster bases, Oriental murals and sculptures, and impressive displays of Oriental vases and teapots. A combination of Chinese and Japanese cuisines is available, including sushi bar items, sashimi and tempura. **Features:** full bar. **Reservations:** suggested. **Address:** 118 Easton Rd 18976 **Location:** Jct County Line and Easton (SR 611) rds, just w; in Warrington Crossing Plaza.

WASHINGTON (H-1) pop. 13,663, elev. 1,039'
• Restaurants p. 412
• Part of Pittsburgh area — see map p. 326

The Washington and Jefferson College Memorial Library was founded by a gift from Benjamin Franklin; phone (724) 223-6070. The school, which started in 1781, is said to be the oldest college west of the Allegheny Mountains.

The Duncan Miller Glass Museum, 525 Jefferson Ave., exhibits fine pressed and hand-blown glass made 1893-1955. It is open for guided tours Thurs.-Sun. 11-4 (except holidays), early Apr.-late Dec. and by appointment year-round. A $4 fee is charged for adults, $1 for ages 13-18, and ages 0-12 can take the tour free of charge. Phone (724) 225-9950.

Self-guiding tours: Washington County is home to 22 of the state's 210 covered bridges. A brochure highlighting their history is available at various information stands in the area, including Courthouse Square.

Shopping areas: Tanger Outlet Center, .5 mi. e. off I-79 exit 41 (Racetrack Rd.) at 2200 Tanger Blvd., features nearly 75 stores, including Ann Taylor Factory Store, Calvin Klein, Carter's, Izod, Old Navy and Nike Factory Store.

DAVID BRADFORD HOUSE is at 175 S. Main St. David Bradford was a leader in the 1791-94 Whiskey Rebellion, a protest against high excise taxes that hurt the grain producers of western Pennsylvania. The house is furnished in 18th-century style. **Hours:** Thurs.-Fri. (also first Sat. of each month) 11-4, May-Dec. By appointment rest of year.

Last tour begins at 3. Candlelight tours are given Dec. 2-4. **Cost:** $5; $4 (students and senior citizens). **Phone:** (724) 222-3604.

LEMOYNE HOUSE, 49 E. Maiden St., was the home of abolitionist and doctor Francis Julius LeMoyne. Built in 1812, the early Greek Revival stone mansion served as LeMoyne's office and apothecary shop and was a station for the Underground Railroad. The site, furnished in period antiques, now houses the Washington County Historical Society headquarters and the LeMoyne Historic Garden. **Hours:** Tues.-Fri. 11-4. Last tour begins 1 hour before closing. Closed major holidays. **Cost:** $5; $4 (students). **Phone:** (724) 225-6740.

PENNSYLVANIA TROLLEY MUSEUM is at 1 Museum Rd., off I-79 exit 41 (Racetrack Rd.) or from I-79N exit 40 (Meadow Lands), following signs. The museum offers trolley rides, exhibits and a film. A 1-hour guided tour includes a 4-mile scenic trolley ride and the original car barn showcasing nine streetcars. An additional 1-hour guided tour of 30 trolleys also is offered.

Hours: Museum, Mon.-Fri. 10-4, Sat.-Sun. 10-5, Memorial Day-Labor Day; Fri. 10-4, Sat.-Sun 10-5, Mar. 17-May 24 and Sept. 11-Dec. 13. Guided tours depart on the hour; last tour begins one hour before closing. Tour of 30 trolleys departs at 1 (except during special events), Apr.-Nov. Closed Easter. **Cost:** $9; $8 (ages 62+); $6 (ages 3-15). Trolley Display Building Tour additional $4; $2 (ages 3-15). Phone ahead to confirm rates. Fees may be charged for special events. **Phone:** (724) 228-9256.

GAMBLING ESTABLISHMENTS

- **The Meadows Racetrack & Casino** is at 210 Racetrack Rd. **Hours:** Daily 24 hours. **Phone:** (724) 503-1200 or (877) 824-5050.

CAMBRIA SUITES WASHINGTON   (724)223-5555
Contemporary Hotel $129-$199 **Address:** 451 Racetrack Rd 15301 **Location:** I-79 exit 41, just e. Near outlet shopping and casino. **Facility:** 105 units, some two bedrooms and efficiencies. 4 stories, interior corridors. **Amenities:** video games. **Pool(s):** heated indoor. **Activities:** exercise room, massage. **Guest Services:** valet and coin laundry, area transportation.

CANDLEWOOD SUITES   (724)873-7300
Extended Stay Hotel $120 **Address:** 255 Meadowland Blvd 15301 **Location:** I-79 exit 41, just e. **Facility:** 84 efficiencies. 4 stories, interior corridors. **Activities:** limited exercise equipment. **Guest Services:** complimentary and valet laundry.

COMFORT INN MEADOWLANDS   (724)746-9700
Hotel $125-$200
Address: 237 Meadowlands Blvd 15301 **Location:** I-79 exit 41, just e. **Facility:** 70 units. 3 stories, interior corridors. **Pool(s):** heated indoor. **Activities:** limited exercise equipment. **Guest Services:** valet laundry. **Featured Amenity: breakfast buffet.** *(See ad this page.)*

COMFORT SUITES WASHINGTON   (724)884-0299
Hotel $119-$174 **Address:** 2110 N Franklin Dr 15301 **Location:** I-70 exit 15, just w on US 40, then right. **Facility:** 67 units. 3 stories, interior corridors. **Activities:** limited exercise equipment. **Guest Services:** coin laundry.

Gear up with head-to-toe savings
at AAA.com/searchfordiscounts

▼ *See AAA listing this page* ▼

COUNTRY INN & SUITES BY CARLSON   (724)884-1450

 Hotel $140-$214 **Address:** 245 Meadowlands Blvd 15301 **Location:** I-79 exit 41, just e, then left. **Facility:** 81 units. 4 stories, interior corridors. **Terms:** cancellation fee imposed. **Pool(s):** heated indoor. **Activities:** exercise room. **Guest Services:** coin laundry.

COURTYARD BY MARRIOTT PITTSBURGH/WASHINGTON MEADOW LANDS   (724)222-5620

 Contemporary Hotel $125-$229 **Address:** 1800 Tanger Blvd 15301 **Location:** I-79 exit 41, just e, then just s. **Facility:** 124 units, some efficiencies. 5 stories, interior corridors. **Pool(s):** heated indoor. **Activities:** hot tub, exercise room. **Guest Services:** valet and coin laundry, area transportation.

> **AAA Benefit:**
> Members save 5% or more!

DOUBLETREE BY HILTON HOTEL PITTSBURGH-MEADOW LANDS   (724)222-6200

 Hotel $129-$219 **Address:** 340 Racetrack Rd 15301 **Location:** I-79 exit 41, 0.5 mi e. **Facility:** 138 units, some two bedrooms. 7 stories, interior corridors. **Terms:** check-in 4 pm, 1-7 night minimum stay, cancellation fee imposed. **Amenities:** *Some:* safes. **Pool(s):** outdoor. **Activities:** exercise room. **Guest Services:** valet and coin laundry, area transportation.

> **AAA Benefit:**
> Members save 5% or more!

HAMPTON INN & SUITES   (724)222-4014

 Hotel $109-$189 **Address:** 475 Johnson Rd 15301 **Location:** I-79 exit 41, 0.5 mi e. **Facility:** 103 units. 5 stories, interior corridors. **Terms:** 1-7 night minimum stay, cancellation fee imposed. **Pool(s):** heated indoor. **Activities:** hot tub, exercise room. **Guest Services:** valet and coin laundry, area transportation.

> **AAA Benefit:**
> Members save 5% or more!

HAMPTON INN WASHINGTON   (724)228-4100

 Hotel $124-$250 **Address:** 119 Murtland Rd 15301 **Location:** I-70 exit 19A, just e on US 19. **Facility:** 111 units. 5 stories, interior corridors. **Parking:** winter plug-ins. **Terms:** 1-7 night minimum stay, cancellation fee imposed. **Pool(s):** heated indoor. **Activities:** exercise room. **Guest Services:** complimentary laundry.

> **AAA Benefit:**
> Members save 5% or more!

HYATT PLACE PITTSBURGH SOUTH/MEADOWS RACETRACK & CASINO   (724)222-7777

[fyi] Hotel $129-$349 Too new to rate, opening scheduled for March 2015. **Address:** 212 Racetrack Rd 15301 **Location:** I-79 exit Racetrack Rd. **Amenities:** 155 units.

> **AAA Benefit:**
> Members save 10%!

MICROTEL INN & SUITES BY WYNDHAM   (724)705-7676

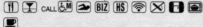 Hotel $95-$130 **Address:** 501 Racetrack Rd 15301 **Location:** I-79 exit 41, just e. **Facility:** 80 units. 3 stories, interior corridors. **Amenities:** safes. **Activities:** exercise room. **Guest Services:** coin laundry.

RAMADA   (724)225-9750

Hotel
$82-$130

Address: 1170 W Chestnut St 15301 **Location:** I-70 exit 15, 0.5 mi e on US 40. **Facility:** 92 units. 2 stories (no elevator), interior/exterior corridors. **Pool(s):** outdoor. **Guest Services:** valet laundry.

RED ROOF INN WASHINGTON, PA   724/228-5750

Motel
Rates not provided

Address: 1399 W Chestnut St 15301 **Location:** I-70 exit 15, just e on US 40. **Facility:** 110 units. 2 stories, interior/exterior corridors. **Amenities:** safes.

SPRINGHILL SUITES BY MARRIOTT   (724)223-7800

 Hotel $118-$194 **Address:** 16 Trinity Point Dr 15301 **Location:** I-70 exit 20, just w; in Trinity Point Plaza. **Facility:** 86 units. 4 stories, interior corridors. **Pool(s):** heated indoor. **Activities:** hot tub, exercise room. **Guest Services:** valet and coin laundry.

> **AAA Benefit:**
> Members save 5% or more!

WHERE TO EAT

HOG FATHER'S OLD FASHIONED BBQ   724/229-1227

 Barbecue. Casual Dining. $7-$20 **AAA Inspector Notes:** All-American barbecue food is flavored with great Carolina-style sauce that's remarkably close to the real thing. Barbecue shrimp, coleslaw and the pulled pork sandwich are all winners. Service is casual. During the winter, diners seated near the door may get a little too close to the weather for comfort. **Features:** beer only. **Address:** 1301 Jefferson Ave 15301 **Location:** I-70 exit Jefferson Ave, just off exit.

UNION GRILL   724/222-2860

 American. Casual Dining. $9-$28 **AAA Inspector Notes:** Tucked downstairs, below ground level is this rustic spot accented in brick and wood. Fresh ingredients enhance the flavor of such dishes as eggplant parmigiana and lobster ravioli. **Features:** full bar. **Address:** 13 1/2 E Wheeling St 15301 **Location:** Center. **Parking:** street only.

Get AAA/CAA travel

information in the digital and

printed formats you prefer

WASHINGTON CROSSING HISTORIC PARK (H-12) elev. 52'

• Part of Philadelphia area — see map p. 230

Washington Crossing Historic Park is divided into two areas: the Thompson's Mill section is 1.5 miles southeast of New Hope via SR 32, and the McConkey's Ferry section is 5 miles farther south on SR 32. A bridge crosses the Delaware River and allows visitors to enter New Jersey's Washington Crossing State Park. The 500-acre park is dedicated to the memory of George Washington and the 2,400 soldiers who crossed the Delaware on Christmas night in 1776 to attack and capture Trenton, N.J., then garrisoned by Hessian mercenaries. A re-enactment of the crossing of the Delaware is held at 1 p.m. on Christmas. Other events are presented throughout the year. Picnicking is permitted.

The park and recreation areas are open daily dawn-dusk (weather permitting). The visitor center is open Tues.-Sun. 10-5; closed some holidays. Historic building schedules vary. Phone ahead to confirm schedules.

Grounds free. Historic building admission (which includes Bowman's Hill Tower, Durham Boat House, McConkey's Ferry Inn, Thompson-Neely Farmstead and Visitor Center) $11; $6 (ages 4-11); free (active military with ID). Durham Boat House, McConkey's Ferry Inn and Visitor Center only $6. Additional fees may be charged for special events. Phone (215) 493-4076.

McCONKEY'S FERRY SECTION, 5 mi. s. of New Hope on SR 32 at 1112 River Rd. within Washington Crossing Historic Park, focuses on the site where Gen. George Washington and his troops embarked on their historic crossing. The Mahlon K. Taylor House, the restored 1817 home of an influential businessman of the period, can be viewed from the outside (it is only open to large tour groups). Also depicted is the 19th-century village of Taylorsville, which grew as the Delaware Canal prospered.

Hours: Tours Mon.-Sun. 10-4. Closed some holidays. Phone ahead to confirm schedule. **Cost:** (includes all McConkey's Ferry section sites as well as Bowman's Hill Tower and Thompson-Neely Farmstead in the Thompson's Mill Section) $11; $6 (ages 4-11); free (active military with ID). McConkey's Ferry Section only $6. Additional fees may be charged for special events. **Phone:** (215) 493-4076.

Durham Boat House, within McConkey's Ferry Section of Washington Crossing Historic Park at 1112 River Rd., stores replicas of iron ore boats such as those used by Washington during the Christmas crossing of the Delaware River.

Hours: Mon.-Sun. 10-4. Closed some holidays. Phone ahead to confirm schedule. **Cost:** (includes Bowman's Hill Tower, McConkey's Ferry Inn, Thompson-Neely Farmstead and Visitor Center) $11; $6 (ages 4-11); free (active military with ID). Durham Boat House, McConkey's Ferry Inn and Visitor Center only $6. Additional fees may be charged for special events. **Phone:** (215) 493-4076.

Hibbs House, within McConkey's Ferry Section of Washington Crossing Historic Park at 1112 River Rd., is a restored tenant house built in the late 1830s. Open-hearth cooking demonstrations in the furnished home are given periodically throughout the year. **Note:** The Hibbs House is currently closed; phone for updates. **Phone:** (215) 493-4076.

McConkey's Ferry Inn, within McConkey's Ferry Section of Washington Crossing Historic Park at 1112 River Rd., is a restored stone building, the earliest parts of which date from the 1750s. George Washington is believed to have dined at the inn before crossing the Delaware.

Hours: Mon.-Sun. 10-4. Closed some holidays. Phone ahead to confirm schedule. **Cost:** (includes Bowman's Hill Tower, Durham Boat House, Thompson-Neely Farmstead and Visitor Center) $11; $6 (ages 4-11); free (active military with ID). Durham Boat House, McConkey's Ferry Inn and Visitor Center only $6. Additional fees may be charged for special events. **Phone:** (215) 493-4076.

Visitor Center, within McConkey's Ferry Section of Washington Crossing Historic Park at 1112 River Rd., features visitor facilities, an exhibits gallery and a film that depicts the sites' significance. **Hours:** Mon.-Sun. 10-5. Closed some holidays. Phone ahead to confirm schedule. **Cost:** (includes Bowman's Hill Tower, Durham Boat House, McConkey's Ferry Inn, Thompson-Neely Farmstead and Visitor Center) $11; $6 (ages 4-11); free (active military with ID). Durham Boat House, McConkey's Ferry Inn and Visitor Center only $6. **Phone:** (215) 493-4076.

THOMPSON'S MILL SECTION, 1.5 mi. s.e. of New Hope on SR 32 within Washington Crossing Historic Park, preserves 18th-century buildings, Bowman's Hill Tower and soldiers' gravesites. These locations are available for exterior grounds visitation only. **Hours:** Schedule varies per site. **Cost:** Varies per site. **Phone:** (215) 493-4076.

Bowman's Hill Tower, within Thompson's Mill Section of Washington Crossing Historic Park at River Rd. & Lurgan Rd., was completed in 1931 and presents a commanding 14-mile view of the Delaware River Valley. Washington Crossing can be seen to the south. An elevator takes visitors to an observation point within the 125-foot tower; the top is then reached by 23 stone stairs.

Hours: Mon.-Sun. 10-4, Apr.-Dec. (weather permitting). Closed some holidays. Phone ahead to confirm schedule. **Cost:** (includes Durham Boat House, McConkey's Ferry Inn, Thompson-Neely Farmstead and Visitor Center) $11; $6 (ages 4-11); free (active military with ID). Tower only $6. Additional fees may be charged for special events. **Phone:** (215) 862-3166.

Bowman's Hill Wildflower Preserve is within Thompson's Mill Section of Washington Crossing Historic Park at 1635 River Rd., across from Thompson-Neely Farmstead. It includes a 134-acre wildflower area with a visitor center, native plant exhibits, about a dozen hiking trails and indoor exhibits. Picnicking is permitted in the front, outside the deer fence. **Hours:** Preserve daily 8:30-dusk.

Visitor center Tues.-Sun. 9-5 (also Memorial Day and Labor Day holidays). Guided tours depart Tues.-Sun. at 2, Apr.-Oct. Closed Thanksgiving and Christmas Eve-New Year's Day. **Cost:** $5; $3 (ages 62+ and students with ID); $2 (ages 4-14). **Phone:** (215) 862-2924. ⊞

Soldiers' Graves, within Thompson's Mill Section of Washington Crossing Historic Park, mark the burial place of Continental soldiers who died during the encampment. **Hours:** Daily dawn-dusk. Phone for Memorial Day access. Closed some holidays. **Cost:** Free. **Phone:** (215) 493-4076.

Thompson-Neely Farmstead, within Thompson's Mill Section of Washington Crossing Historic Park at 1638 River Rd., built in the 1700s, was the scene of a military hospital during the Bucks County encampment. A barn, a reconstructed 19th-century gristmill and other restored farm outbuildings are nearby.

Hours: Thurs.-Sun. 10-4, Apr.-Dec. Closed some holidays. Phone ahead to confirm schedule. **Cost:** (includes Bowman's Hill Tower, Durham Boat House, McConkey's Ferry Inn and Visitor Center) $11; $6 (ages 4-11); free (active military with ID). Farmstead only $6. Additional fees may be charged for special events. **Phone:** (215) 493-4076.

WATERFORD (C-2) pop. 1,517, elev. 1,192'

In 1753 the French built Fort LeBoeuf, which eventually fell to the British. A 21-year-old George Washington, then a major in the British Virginia Militia, delivered a message from Gov. Robert Dinwiddie asking the French to withdraw from the area. The French refused, and eventually tensions erupted into the French and Indian War. A statue of Washington stands near the site.

Also of interest on S. High Street is the Amos Judson House, a restored two-story Federal Greek Revival home built in 1820. The museum contains circa 1840 furnishings and a model of the fort as well as a library with genealogical information. Next door is the Fort LeBoeuf Museum at 123 S. High St.; it sits on the original site of the French fort. Inside are exhibits related to Native Americans who lived in the area as well as the French and British fur trade. Across the street is the restored 1826 Eagle Hotel, a stone structure built in the Federal and Georgian styles. This once was an important stagecoach stop and now houses a restaurant.

Brotherton's Bridge, on Niemeyer Road, is a covered bridge over LeBoeuf Creek. Swimming, boating, fishing and camping are available at nearby Lake LeBoeuf *(see Recreation Areas Chart).*

WAYNE (B-9) elev. 400'
• Part of Philadelphia area — see map p. 230

In the mid-1800s banker J. Henry Askin developed a community he named Louella, in honor of his two daughters, Louisa and Ella. With railroad connections to Philadelphia, the rural Victorian village was populated by the families of commuting businessmen. Askin's financial difficulties forced him to sell the property, but Louella continued to grow and attract urbanites. The town was later renamed for Revolutionary War general Anthony Wayne.

Wayne is home to Valley Forge Military Academy and College, site of a monument commemorating the World War II Battle of the Bulge. The Radnor Historical Society, 113 W. Beech Tree Ln., is housed in a 1789 farmhouse and provides information about area history Tuesday-Saturday; phone (610) 688–2668.

CHANTICLEER GARDEN, 786 Church Rd., is a 35-acre garden situated on the former estate of pharmaceutical magnate Adolph Rosengarten Sr. Featured are landscaped courtyards; flowering trees and shrubs; vegetable and herb gardens; tropical plants; perennials and annuals; and woodlands and ponds. The Minder Ruin Garden displays plantings among the foundation of a razed stone house. The Rosengarten house contains family furniture, decorative arts and fresh flower arrangements from the garden; participants may tour the garden on their own following the house tour.

Time: Allow 1 hour minimum. **Hours:** Garden open Wed.-Sun. 10-5, early Apr.-early Nov. (also Fri. 5-8, May-Aug.). House tours depart Fri.-Sat. at 11, Apr. 3-Oct. 3. **Cost:** Garden $10; free (ages 0-12). House tour $15 (reservations required). **Phone:** (610) 687-4163. ⊞

COURTYARD BY MARRIOTT PHILADELPHIA DEVON
(610)687-6633

▼▼▼▼
Hotel
$167-$275

COURTYARD
Marriott

AAA Benefit: Members save 5% or more!

Address: 762 W Lancaster Ave 19087 **Location:** US 30, 0.8 mi e of jct Waterloo Rd. Located in Devon Square Business Center. 🅟 Strafford, 204. **Facility:** 149 units. 3 stories, interior corridors. **Pool(s):** heated indoor. **Activities:** exercise room. **Guest Services:** valet and coin laundry, boarding pass kiosk.

SAVE ECO ⓉⓉ CALL 🅖Ⓜ 🔁 BIZ
📶 ⊠ 🐾 🔒 💻
/SOME UNITS 📶 🅟

COURTYARD BY MARRIOTT PHILADELPHIA VALLEY FORGE/KING OF PRUSSIA
(610)687-6700

▼▼▼▼
Hotel
$146-$240

COURTYARD
Marriott

AAA Benefit: Members save 5% or more!

Address: 1100 Drummers Ln 19087 **Location:** US 202 exit Swedesford Rd, 0.3 mi s. Located in a commercial area. **Facility:** 150 units. 3 stories, interior corridors. **Pool(s):** heated indoor. **Activities:** exercise room. **Guest Services:** valet and coin laundry, boarding pass kiosk.

SAVE ECO ⓉⓉ CALL 🅖Ⓜ 🔁 BIZ
📶 ⊠ 🐾 🔒 💻
/SOME UNITS 📶

EMBASSY SUITES PHILADELPHIA-VALLEY FORGE
(610)647-6700

Hotel
$109-$289

AAA Benefit:
Members save 5%
or more!

Address: 888 Chesterbrook Blvd 19087
Location: US 202 exit Chesterbrook
Blvd. Located in Chesterbrook Complex.
Facility: 229 units, some two bedrooms.
5 stories, interior corridors. **Terms:** 1-7
night minimum stay, cancellation fee imposed. **Pool(s):** heated indoor. **Activities:** hot tub, exercise room. **Guest
Services:** valet and coin laundry, area
transportation. **Featured Amenity:**
breakfast buffet.

WHERE TO EAT

BLACK POWDER TAVERN   610/293-9333
American. Casual Dining. $10-$22 **AAA Inspector Notes:**
This restaurant's varied menu touches upon multiple cuisines and
provides a delicious option of small plates, sandwiches, salads and
dinner entrées. An all-beef banh-mi-style hot dog and cedar plank
salmon are among its signature items. An extensive variety of craft
beers and homemade desserts pair well with any entrée. **Features:**
full bar, patio dining, Sunday brunch, happy hour. **Address:** 1164
Valley Forge Rd 19087 **Location:** SR 252, just n of jct US 202.
[L] [D]

RISTORANTE PRIMAVERA   610/254-0200
Italian. Casual Dining. $11-$22 **AAA Inspector Notes:**
Large pictures of flowers decorate the walls of this slightly upscale
dining room, which is softly illuminated by a large skylight. An extensive selection of wine complements dishes of homemade pasta, veal
and fish, as well as pizza cooked in wood-fired ovens. **Features:** full
bar. **Reservations:** suggested, weekends. **Address:** 384 W Lancaster Ave 19087 **Location:** 0.8 mi w on US 30. ⓑ Strafford, 204.
Parking: valet only. [L] [D] 🚲

WAYNESBORO (I-7) pop. 10,568, elev. 713'

Tucked into rolling hills and surrounded by peach
and apple orchards, Waynesboro dates back to
1749. Like many other towns in the vicinity, it lays
claim to a historical footnote; abolitionist John Brown
taught Sunday school nearby while preparing for his
ill-fated Harper's Ferry, W.Va., raid. Later, Waynesboro became an early 20th-century retreat for Washington, D.C., residents seeking escape from
summer heat and humidity.

Greater Waynesboro Chamber of Commerce: 5
Roadside Ave., Waynesboro, PA 17268. **Phone:**
(717) 762-7123.

RENFREW MUSEUM AND PARK, 1010 E. Main St.,
houses the Nicodemus Collection of Decorative Arts
within a 200-year-old restored German farmstead. The
collection features ceramics, painted furniture, metalware and objets d'art from the 19th century displayed
in a homelike setting. A visitor center offers a DVD presentation, a 200-piece Shenandoah pottery collection
and a display of antique tools. The park has nature
and hiking trails, and a 150-seat pavilion. Fly-fishing is
offered on Antietam Creek. Guided tours of the museum house are available.

Time: Allow 1 hour minimum. **Hours:** Park daily
dawn-dusk. Visitor center and museum Tues.-Fri.
noon-4, Sat.-Sun. 1-4, mid-Apr. to mid-Oct. Phone
ahead to confirm schedule. **Cost:** Visitor center free.
Museum $6; $5 (ages 65+); $4 (ages 7-12). **Phone:**
(717) 762-4723. 🏛

WAYNESBURG (I-1) pop. 4,176, elev. 938'

Waynesburg was named for Revolutionary War
hero Gen. "Mad" Anthony Wayne. The town is the seat
of Greene County, named for another Revolutionary
War hero, Gen. Nathanael Greene. A statue of Greene
is atop the 1850 county courthouse, a fine example of
Greek Revival architecture. The old log courthouse,
144 E. Greene Street, now houses the Cornerstone
Genealogical Society; phone (724) 627-5653. Also in
town is Waynesburg University, one of the first colleges in the United States to grant degrees to women.

Greene County Tourist Promotion Agency: 19 S.
Washington St., Waynesburg, PA 15370. **Phone:**
(724) 627-8687 or (877) 280-8687.

GREENE COUNTY HISTORICAL SOCIETY is off
I-79 exit 14, about 1 mi. e. on SR 21, then .6 mi. s.
on A Kern Rd. and just e. to 918 Rolling Meadows
Rd. The museum is housed in an 1860s building
that served as the Greene County Poor Farm
through 1964.

The 52-room structure offers local history exhibits, including Monongahela cultural items, saltglaze pottery, quilts, Depression-era glassware, a
sports history exhibit and a country store. Glassware
and equipment from the former 1908-77 James
Bryan Dairy also are on display. **Time:** Allow 1 hour
minimum. **Hours:** Tues.-Sat. 10-3. **Cost:** $5; $3
(ages 6-12 and 65+). **Phone:** (724) 627-3204. 🏛

COMFORT INN   (724)627-3700
Hotel $95-$130 **Address:** 100 Comfort Ln 15370 **Location:** I-79 exit 14, just e. **Facility:** 72 units. 3 stories, interior corridors.
Amenities: safes. **Guest Services:** coin laundry.

ECONO LODGE   (724)627-5544
Hotel $90 **Address:** 126 Miller Ln 15370 **Location:** I-79
exit 14, just w. **Facility:** 57 units. 2 stories (no elevator), exterior
corridors.

HAMPTON INN & SUITES   (724)802-1010
Hotel $139-$199 **Address:**
227 Greene Plaza 15370 **Location:** I-79
exit 14, just w. **Facility:** 92 units. 5 stories, interior corridors. **Terms:** 1-7 night
minimum stay, cancellation fee imposed.
Pool(s): heated indoor. **Activities:** hot tub, exercise room. **Guest
Services:** valet and coin laundry.

AAA Benefit:
Members save 5%
or more!

SUPER 8-WAYNESBURG   (724)627-8880
Motel $56-$110 **Address:** 100 Stanley Dr 15370 **Location:** I-79 exit 14, just w. **Facility:** 56 units. 3 stories (no elevator), interior corridors. **Terms:** cancellation fee imposed.

WEATHERLY (F-10) pop. 2,525, elev. 1,086'

• Part of Pocono Mountains Area — see map p. 371

RECREATIONAL ACTIVITIES

White-water Rafting

• [SAVE] **Whitewater Challengers Raft Tours** is at 288 N. Stagecoach Rd.; visitors are then bused to the rafting location. Other activities also are available. **Hours:** White-water rafting daily 9-5, Apr.-June and Sept.-Oct. Summer rafting in calmer waters daily 9-5, July-Aug. **Phone:** (570) 443-9532 or (800) 443-8554.

WELLSBORO (D-7) pop. 3,263, elev. 1,315'

If Wellsboro's lantern-lit streets, town green and Victorian mansions seem vaguely reminiscent of Massachusetts or Vermont, it is because the town was founded by New England colonists in 1806. In the mountainous region of north-central Pennsylvania, Wellsboro is an all-year recreation center.

Tioga County Visitors Bureau: 2053 SR 660, P.O. Box 139, Wellsboro, PA 16901. **Phone:** (570) 724-0635 or (888) 846-4228.

Self-guiding tours: Walking and driving tour information is available from the visitors bureau.

[SAVE] **ANIMALAND ZOOLOGICAL PARK,** 4181 SR 660, features a paved path through a very nicely landscaped park where visitors can observe a variety of animals, including deer, sheep, fowl, a Siberian tiger, black bears, buffalo, alpaca, miniature horses, monkeys, peacocks and pheasants. A 2-mile self-guiding walking tour is available.

Food is available June-Aug. **Hours:** Park daily 10-5, May-Oct. **Cost:** $8; $7 (students and senior citizens); $5 (ages 3-12). Phone ahead for current prices. **Phone:** (570) 724-4546. [icons]

GRAND CANYON OF PENNSYLVANIA, 10 mi. w. on SR 660, was formed by the Pine Creek River. Forty-seven miles long and up to 1,450 feet deep, it is the highlight of the Pennsylvania Wilds, a 2 million-acre area in north central Pennsylvania set aside for recreational opportunities. The area offers spectacular panoramas.

Leonard Harrison and Colton Point state parks *(see Recreation Areas Chart)* encompass the east and west rims, respectively. **Hours:** 8 a.m. to dusk. **Cost:** Free. **Phone:** (570) 724-3061 for Leonard Harrison and Colton State parks.

SHERWOOD MOTEL 570/724-3424

Motel
$75-$125

Address: 2 Main St 16901 **Location:** Just n on US 6 and SR 287; downtown. **Facility:** 42 units, some two bedrooms. 2 stories (no elevator), interior/exterior corridors. **Pool(s):** heated outdoor. **Activities:** playground.

[SAVE] [icons]

WHERE TO EAT

PENN WELLS DINING ROOM 570/724-2111

American
Casual Dining
$7-$27

AAA Inspector Notes: The European dining room is traditional, with linen tablecloths and crystal. Homemade Italian specialties are the primary focus of the menu. Visit on Friday to enjoy the fish fry. Tempting desserts include Reese's cup chocolate pie and rice pudding. Reservations suggested in summer and weekends. **Features:** full bar, Sunday brunch. **Address:** 62 Main St 16901 **Location:** Just n on US 6 and SR 287; downtown. [B] [L] [D]

THE STEAK HOUSE 570/724-9092

Steak. Casual Dining. $9-$30 **AAA Inspector Notes:** Homemade soups and dinners of fresh roasted turkey, fresh seafood and steaks are popular offerings at this casual family restaurant. Generously portioned dishes are simply presented but wholesome and filling. The country-style décor is inviting. Service is attentive but unrushed. **Features:** full bar. **Address:** 29 Main St 16901 **Location:** Center. [D]

TIMELESS DESTINATION 570/724-8499

Italian. Casual Dining. $8-$34 **AAA Inspector Notes:** The fine cuisine is diversified and trendy to satisfy every appetite. Menu options range from gourmet pizzas, pasta, chicken, seafood and specialty pork and veal dishes to calzones, stromboli, sandwiches and wraps, burgers and salads. Special seating is available for up to 50 people. **Features:** full bar, happy hour. **Address:** 77 Main St 16901 **Location:** Center. [L] [D]

WEST CHESTER (B-8) pop. 18,461, elev. 424'

• Restaurants p. 418
• Part of Philadelphia area — see map p. 230

Graced by many handsome Greek Revival and Victorian houses, West Chester is surrounded by the rich farmland of Chester County. During the Revolutionary War several major skirmishes occurred nearby, including the battles of Brandywine and Paoli. In 1842 West Chester became the home of the *Jeffersonian,* one of the few newspapers in the North to support the South. A rioting mob soon wrecked the paper's offices, and eventually the postmaster general prohibited its distribution by mail.

A building of note is the Chester County Courthouse, built in 1724.

AMERICAN HELICOPTER MUSEUM & EDUCATION CENTER, 1220 American Blvd., demonstrates the past and future of rotor-wing aircraft. More than 30 civilian and military aircraft are displayed, including a rare V-22 Osprey with tilted rotors.

Hands-on exhibits demonstrate helicopter design and operation. **Time:** Allow 1 hour minimum. **Hours:** Wed.-Sat. 10-5, Sun. noon-5. Last admission 1 hour before closing. Closed Thanksgiving and Christmas. **Cost:** $10; $8 (senior citizens and students with ID). **Phone:** (610) 436-9600.

CHESTER COUNTY HISTORICAL SOCIETY, 225 N. High St., has six galleries of permanent and changing exhibits featuring early American furniture and decorative arts. Included are clocks, ceramics, crystal and silver, clothing, textiles, letters, diaries, photographs and dolls. A research library specializes in genealogy and area history. **Time:** Allow 1 hour minimum. **Hours:** Wed.-Sat. 9:30-4:30. Closed federal holidays. Closed major holidays. **Cost:** $6; $5 (ages 65+); $3.50 (ages 6-17 and students with ID); free (active military with ID). **Parking:** $2-$5. **Phone:** (610) 692-4800.

QVC STUDIO TOUR, 1200 Wilson Dr., provides a behind-the-scenes look inside the cable shopping channel's works. **Time:** Allow 1 hour minimum. **Hours:** Tours depart daily at 10:30, noon, 1, 2:30 and 4. Closed Jan. 1, Easter, Thanksgiving and Christmas. **Cost:** $7.50; $5 (ages 6-12). Not recommended for ages 0-5. **Phone:** (800) 600-9900.

DAYS HOTEL AND CONFERENCE CENTER WEST CHESTER BRANDYWINE VALLEY (610)692-1900

Hotel $79-$129 **Address:** 943 S High St 19382 **Location:** 1.5 mi s on US 202 and 322; jct US 322 business route. Located in a commercial area. **Facility:** 141 units. 3 stories, interior corridors. **Terms:** 3 day cancellation notice-fee imposed. **Amenities:** *Some:* safes. **Pool(s):** outdoor. **Activities:** exercise room. **Guest Services:** valet and coin laundry.

HOLIDAY INN EXPRESS & SUITES WEST CHESTER 610/399-4600

Hotel. Rates not provided. **Address:** 1310 Wilmington Pike 19382 **Location:** 3 mi s on US 202 and 322. Located in a commercial area. **Facility:** 75 units. 3 stories, interior corridors. **Amenities:** safes. **Pool(s):** heated indoor. **Activities:** exercise room. **Guest Services:** valet and coin laundry.

HOTEL WARNER (610)692-6920

Hotel
$119-$299

Address: 120 N High St 19382 **Location:** Between Chestnut St and Prescott Alley; downtown. **Facility:** 80 units. 5 stories, interior corridors. **Terms:** resort fee. **Amenities:** safes. **Pool(s):** heated indoor. **Activities:** limited exercise equipment. **Guest Services:** valet and coin laundry. **Featured Amenity:** continental breakfast.

MICROTEL INN & SUITES BY WYNDHAM WEST CHESTER   (610)738-9111

Hotel
$79-$149

Address: 500 Willowbrook Ln 19382 **Location:** US 202 exit Matlack St, just se. Located in Willowbrook Industrial Park. **Facility:** 100 units. 3 stories, interior corridors. **Activities:** exercise room. **Guest Services:** coin laundry. **Featured Amenity: continental breakfast.**

SAVE CALL 🄼 BIZ 🛜 ✕ 🎥 / SOME UNITS 🍴 🖥 🖵

WHERE TO EAT

AVALON   610/436-4100

Italian. Fine Dining. $18-$25 **AAA Inspector Notes:** This charming restaurant provides an intimate and warm dining atmosphere with its beautiful wood-burning fireplace, polished stone floors and professional staff. The sophisticated menu blends the rustic cuisine with upscale dining to provide outstanding flavors. A four-course prix-fixe menu also is available. Guests are able to bring their favorite wine from home Sunday through Tuesday. **Features:** full bar, happy hour. **Reservations:** suggested, weekends. **Address:** 116 E Gay St 19382 **Location:** Between N Matlack and N Walnut sts. **Parking:** street only. D CALL 🄼

CARMINE'S PIZZA AND EATERY   610/436-6009

Italian. Casual Dining. $6-$20 **AAA Inspector Notes:** Convenient to shopping, you will find this Italian eatery great for a quick bite. The open kitchen and booth seating provide a very casual setting. The menu provides all the traditional favorites and a large variety of pizzas, pastas and sandwiches. **Features:** beer only. **Address:** 947 Paoli Pike 19380 **Location:** Just w of US 202; in West Goshen Shopping Center. L D

DILWORTHTOWN INN   610/399-1390

American. Fine Dining. $23-$56 **AAA Inspector Notes:** This Colonial inn offers an intimate fine dining experience with dim lighting, multiple fireplaces and a candle-lit atmosphere. The use of multiple dining rooms create a homey feel for guests. The service is top notch with friendly and conversant staff members. The menu provides a variety of American cuisine that changes weekly to deliver the freshest ingredients. A truly great experience from start to finish. **Features:** full bar, patio dining. **Reservations:** suggested. **Address:** 1390 Old Wilmington Pike 19382 **Location:** 4 mi s on US 202 and 322, 0.3 mi w; in Historic Dilworthtown Village. D

DOC MAGROGAN'S   610/429-4046

Seafood. Casual Dining. $8-$30 **AAA Inspector Notes:** This casual seafood spot specializes in oysters, but you can't go wrong with any of the hearty dishes they provide, including their classic lobster roll and Thai chile-glazed salmon. The atmosphere is friendly and upbeat, and guests can expect a variety of events during the week, including all-you-can-eat crab legs and happy hour. **Features:** full bar, happy hour. **Address:** 117 E Gay St 19380 **Location:** Between Matlack and Walnut sts; downtown. **Parking:** street only. L D

HIGH STREET CAFFE   610/696-7435

Cajun. Casual Dining. $8-$28 **AAA Inspector Notes:** In a small downtown storefront, the High Street Caffe sports contemporary French appointments. Although a full bar is available, guests are able to bring their own wine Sunday, Monday and Tuesday. Cajun and Creole influences are apparent on the menu, but it also features exotic ingredients such as kangaroo and ostrich. The chicken-and-andouille gumbo and molasses-marinated pork tenderloin with caramelized onions are delicious. **Features:** full bar. **Reservations:** suggested. **Address:** 322 S High St 19382 **Location:** On SR 100 (High St); downtown. **Parking:** on-site and street. L D

IRON HILL BREWERY   610/738-9600

American. Casual Dining. $10-$29 **AAA Inspector Notes:** This casual eatery offers a variety of tasty American dishes to go alongside their handcrafted beer selection. The signature egg rolls make a great start to any meal. When weather permits, enjoy the outdoor seating area situated on the sidewalk of always busy Gay Street. **Features:** full bar, Sunday brunch, happy hour. **Address:** 3 W Gay St 19380 **Location:** Between Church and High sts; downtown. **Parking:** street only. L D

LIMONCELLO   610/436-6230

Italian. Fine Dining. $8-$30 **AAA Inspector Notes:** Downtown is where you'll find this delightful restaurant. Its limited size and open kitchen provide a lively atmosphere. The delectable and diverse menu offers homemade pasta dishes, specialty veal entrées, gourmet pizzas, and seafood and poultry favorites. **Features:** full bar, patio dining, happy hour. **Reservations:** suggested. **Address:** 9 N Walnut St 19380 **Location:** Between E Market and E Gay sts; downtown. **Parking:** street only. L D 🐄

PIETRO'S PRIME   484/760-6100

Steak Seafood. Fine Dining. $10-$48 **AAA Inspector Notes:** Downtown West Chester makes up for its limited amount of upscale steakhouses with this "prime" restaurant offering a variety of flavorful cuts of meat and scrumptious seafood selections. Try to go during lunch to get the most value for your dollar. **Features:** full bar, patio dining, early bird specials, happy hour. **Reservations:** suggested. **Address:** 125 W Market St 19382 **Location:** Between Church and Darlington sts; downtown. **Parking:** on-site (fee) and street. L D CALL 🄼 🐄

TECA   610/738-8244

Italian. Casual Dining. $7-$35 **AAA Inspector Notes:** This popular spot is one of the few wine bars in downtown. Pair a glass with outrageously tasty dishes, including more than 10 types of bruschetta, savory Italian cured meats and cheeses, gourmet pizzas and hearty pasta dishes. You'll also enjoy comfort whether you're dining in their upbeat and colorful dining room or outside on their often-crowded sidewalk patio. **Features:** full bar, patio dining, happy hour. **Address:** 38 E Gay St 19380 **Location:** Between Walnut and High sts; downtown. **Parking:** street only. L D

WEST CONSHOHOCKEN pop. 1,320

- **Hotels & Restaurants map & index p. 274**
- **Part of Philadelphia area — see map p. 230**

PHILADELPHIA MARRIOTT WEST   (610)941-5600 **78**

Hotel
$188-$309

MARRIOTT

AAA Benefit: Members save 5% or more!

Address: 111 Crawford Ave 19428 **Location:** I-76 (Schuylkill Expwy) exit 331B eastbound; exit 332 westbound, 0.5 mi e on SR 23. Located in a commercial area. 🅟 Conshohocken, 235. **Facility:** 288 units. 17 stories, interior corridors. **Parking:** on-site and valet. **Pool(s):** heated indoor. **Activities:** hot tub, exercise room. **Guest Services:** valet laundry.

SAVE 🍴 🛎 Y 🛏 BIZ SHS 🛜 ✕ 🎥 🛗 🖵 / SOME UNITS 🖥 🖵

(See map & index p. 274.)

WHERE TO EAT

SAVONA
610/520-1200 (102)

▼▼▼▼

Northern Italian Fine Dining $20-$55

AAA Inspector Notes: Sleek, contemporary ambience prevails at this restaurant. Among excellently prepared cuisine inspired by the French and Italian Riviera are sophisticated seafood preparations such as sautéed Dover sole with lemon-pine nut butter sauce and Mediterranean sea bass with zucchini carpaccio. Filet mignon with caramelized onion tart and roasted baby lamb rack also are local favorites. An extensive wine list features more than 1,000 international and domestic varieties. **Features:** full bar. **Reservations:** suggested. **Address:** 100 Old Gulph Rd 19428 **Location:** I-76 (Schuylkill Expwy) exit 330, 0.3 mi s on SR 320 to jct Old Gulph Rd; in Village of Gulph Mills. Matsonford, 100. **Parking:** valet only. [L] [D]

WEST HAZLETON pop. 4,594

CANDLEWOOD SUITES
(570)459-1600

▼▼▼▼ **Extended Stay Hotel** $78-$95 **Address:** 9 Bowman's Mill Rd 18202 **Location:** I-81 exit 145 southbound; exit SR 93 S northbound to Tom Hicken Rd. **Facility:** 124 efficiencies. 5 stories, interior corridors. **Activities:** exercise room. **Guest Services:** valet and coin laundry.

CALL BIZ HS 📶   / SOME UNITS

FAIRFIELD INN & SUITES BY MARRIOTT - HAZLETON
(570)453-0300

▼▼▼ **Hotel** $76-$125 **Address:** 118 SR 93 18201 **Location:** I-81 exit 145, just s; I-80 exit 256, 3.2 mi se. Located in a commercial area. **Facility:** 100 units. 3 stories, interior corridors.

> **AAA Benefit:** Members save 5% or more!

Pool(s): heated indoor. **Activities:** sauna, hot tub, exercise room. **Guest Services:** valet and coin laundry.

🍴 CALL 📶 BIZ HS 📶 ✕ 💻 / SOME UNITS 🔌 📺

HAMPTON INN HAZLETON
(570)454-3449

▼▼▼ **Hotel** $99-$159 **Address:** 1 Top of the 80s Rd 18202 **Location:** I-81 exit 145, just w on SR 93; I-80 exit 256, 3.5 mi se on SR 93. Overlooking Conyngham Valley. **Facility:** 122 units. 3 stories, interior corridors. **Terms:** 1-7 night minimum stay, cancellation fee imposed. **Dining:** Top of the 80's Restaurant, see separate listing. **Pool(s):** outdoor. **Activities:** exercise room. **Guest Services:** valet laundry.

> **AAA Benefit:** Members save 5% or more!

🍴 CALL 📶 BIZ 📶 💻 / SOME UNITS 🔌 📺

WHERE TO EAT

TOP OF THE 80'S RESTAURANT
570/454-8795

▼▼▼ American. Casual Dining. $10-$48 **AAA Inspector Notes:** Perched high on top of a mountain just off I-81 and overlooking the Conyngham Valley, this quaint restaurant offers patrons scenic views from every seat in the house. The evening hours are a real treat as the sun sets behind the mountains and casts a beautiful ray of light in the valley and through the restaurant's windows. The menu features something for everyone with familiar salads and sandwiches at lunch and steaks, seafood, chicken dishes and pastas filling out the dinner menu. **Features:** full bar. **Reservations:** suggested, for dinner. **Address:** 3 Top of the 80s Rd 18202 **Location:** I-81 exit 145, just w on SR 93; I-80 exit 256, 3.5 mi se on SR 93; in Hampton Inn Hazleton. [L] [D] CALL 📶

WEST LAWN pop. 1,715

AUSTIN'S RESTAURANT & BAR
610/678-5500

▼▼▼ American. Casual Dining. $7-$28 **AAA Inspector Notes:** With brick walls and pillars and a beamed wood ceiling, Austin's contemporary dining room bustles and has an open kitchen as its focal point. The menu lists steak, seafood, ribs, chicken, pasta and bountiful salads. Delicious desserts such as cheesecake are made on the premises. **Features:** full bar, happy hour. **Address:** 1101 Snyder Rd 19609 **Location:** US 222 exit Spring Ridge Dr, 2 mi s on Van Reed Rd. [L] [D]

WEST MIDDLESEX pop. 863

HOLIDAY INN EXPRESS HOTEL & SUITES
724/982-4600

▼▼▼ Hotel. Rates not provided. **Address:** 3060 Spangler Rd 16159 **Location:** I-80 exit 4B (SR 60), just w to SR 18, then just n to Spangler Rd. **Facility:** 78 units, some kitchens. 3 stories, interior corridors. **Pool(s):** heated indoor. **Activities:** hot tub. **Guest Services:** valet and coin laundry.

CALL 📶 🏊 🏋 BIZ HS 📶 ✕ 🔌 💻 / SOME UNITS 📺

PARK INN BY RADISSON SHARON
(724)528-2501

▼▼▼ Hotel $99-$175 **Address:** 3377 New Castle Rd 16159 **Location:** I-80 exit 4B (SR 60), just w to SR 18, then just s. **Facility:** 153 units, some two bedrooms. 3 stories, interior corridors. **Terms:** 3 day cancellation notice-fee imposed. **Dining:** 2 restaurants. **Pool(s):** heated indoor. **Activities:** sauna, hot tub, game room, exercise room. **Guest Services:** valet and coin laundry.

🍴 🍷 CALL 📶 🏊 BIZ 📶 💻 / SOME UNITS 🔌 📺

SUPER 8-WEST MIDDLESEX
(724)528-3888

▼▼ Hotel $65-$155 **Address:** 3369 New Castle Rd 16159 **Location:** I-80 exit 4B (SR 60), just w to SR 18, then just s. **Facility:** 52 units. 3 stories, interior corridors.

🍴 CALL 📶 BIZ 📶 🔌 💻 / SOME UNITS 📺

WEST MIFFLIN (G-2) pop. 20,313

- Hotels & Restaurants map & index p. 348
- Part of Pittsburgh area — see map p. 326

KENNYWOOD PARK is at 4800 Kennywood Blvd. A traditional family amusement park, Kennywood has 14 children's rides and 34 adult rides, including six roller coasters and three water rides. Game arcades, landscaped gardens and daily stage shows are offered. Kennywood features buildings dating from 1898.

Time: Allow 3 hours minimum. Hours: Open daily at 10:30, mid-May to late Aug.; closing times vary. Rides and attractions begin opening at 11. Park

▼ See AAA listing this page ▼

Add a refreshing perspective to your travel experience.

Start your day with our new complimentary breakfast buffet and shop the nearby Waterfront, a restaurant and retail complex.

- FREE high speed Internet
- Spacious indoor pool & fitness center
- Complimentary hot breakfast buffet

SPRINGHILL SUITES®
Marriott

schedule varies early May to mid-May and late Aug.-late Oct. Phone ahead to confirm schedule. Cost: $40.99; $27.99 (under 46 inches tall); $20.99 (ages 55+); free (ages 0-2). Admission after 5 p.m. $25.99; $13.99 (ages 55+). Prices are subject to change in 2015. Phone: (412) 461-0500. [⑪]

COMFORT INN-WEST MIFFLIN   (412)653-6600   108
▼▼▼ Hotel $94-$159 Address: 1340 Lebanon Church Rd 15236 Location: 0.6 mi e of jct SR 51. Facility: 73 units. 4 stories, interior corridors. Terms: check-in 4 pm. Activities: exercise room. Guest Services: valet laundry.

EXTENDED STAY AMERICA-PITTSBURGH-WEST MIFFLIN
412/650-9096   109
▼▼ Extended Stay Hotel. Rates not provided. Address: 1303 Lebanon Church Rd 15122 Location: 0.5 mi e of jct SR 51. Facility: 101 kitchen units. 4 stories, interior corridors. Guest Services: coin laundry.

HAMPTON INN -WEST MIFFLIN   (412)650-1000   107
▼▼▼ Hotel $109-$179 Address: 1550 Lebanon Church Rd 15236 Location: 0.7 mi e of jct SR 51. Facility: 69 units. 3 stories, interior corridors. Terms: 1-7 night minimum stay, cancellation fee imposed. Pool(s): heated outdoor. Activities: exercise room. Guest Services: valet laundry, area transportation.

AAA Benefit:
Members save 5% or more!

HOLIDAY INN EXPRESS HOTEL & SUITES
412/469-1900   105
▼▼▼ Hotel. Rates not provided. Address: 3122 Lebanon Church Rd 15122 Location: 1.5 mi e of jct SR 51. Facility: 91 units. 4 stories, interior corridors. Activities: exercise room. Guest Services: valet and coin laundry, area transportation.

SPRINGHILL SUITES BY MARRIOTT-WEST MIFFLIN
(412)653-9800   106

▼▼▼ Hotel $104-$171

SPRINGHILL SUITES Marriott

AAA Benefit: Members save 5% or more!

Address: 1000 Regis Ave 15236 Location: 0.8 mi e of jct SR 51 and Lebanon Church Rd. Facility: 94 units. 4 stories, interior corridors. Pool(s): heated indoor. Activities: exercise room. Guest Services: valet and coin laundry, area transportation. Featured Amenity: breakfast buffet. (See ad this page.)

WEST READING pop. 4,212

CANDLEWOOD SUITES   610/898-1910
▼▼▼ Extended Stay Hotel. Rates not provided. Address: 55 S 3rd Ave 19611 Location: Jct Penn Ave. Facility: 74 kitchen units. 3 stories, interior corridors. Activities: exercise room. Guest Services: valet and coin laundry.

WHERE TO EAT

CHEF ALANS AMERICAN BISTRO   610/375-4012

▼▼ ▼▼ American. Casual Dining. $6-$20 **AAA Inspector Notes:** This upscale and contemporary yet casual dining experience includes a tropical-Mediterranean décor theme that incorporates mosaic tiles, Tuscan walls, eclectic lighting and artwork, and an abundance of plants and palm trees. Your menu choices include tropical salads, brick-oven pizzas, gourmet burgers, steaks, fresh seafood, pasta dishes, prime rib, rotisserie chicken and creative specials. **Features:** full bar, happy hour. **Address:** 555 Penn Ave 19611 **Location:** Jct 6th and Penn aves; in West Reading Shopping Center. ⬜L⬜ ⬜D⬜ CALL ⬜M⬜

GNA RISTORANTE & PIZZERIA   610/376-1155

▼▼ ▼▼ Italian. Casual Dining. $5-$25 **AAA Inspector Notes:** Whether you're seeking a quick takeout meal, a casual drink at the bar or a classic evening of dining, this restaurant will meet your needs. Friendly staffers happily guide you through a lengthy menu of favorites. **Features:** full bar. **Address:** 421 Penn Ave 19611 **Location:** Between 4th and 5th sts. ⬜L⬜ ⬜D⬜

THIRD & SPRUCE CAFE   610/376-5254

▼▼ ▼▼ American. Casual Dining. $6-$20 **AAA Inspector Notes:** Neon fusion and Art Deco merge at this popular café where hipsters of all ages meet. The interesting décor and sweeping two-story bar area make for a fun atmosphere. More than 35 draft beers pair with simple dishes from a lengthy menu. Plenty of TVs show sporting events. **Reservations:** suggested, for dinner. **Address:** 238 S 3rd Ave 19611 **Location:** Jct Penn and S 3rd aves, just e. ⬜L⬜ ⬜D⬜ ⬜LATE⬜

WEST READING TAVERN   610/376-9232

▼▼ ▼▼ American. Casual Dining. $5-$23 **AAA Inspector Notes:** Perhaps the county's best-kept secret, the tavern has long been a favorite among locals, and with good reason. Seafood specialties such as Chesapeake Bay fisherman's soup are especially good as are Baltimore pasta and Dun Wurkyn, this place's microbrewed lager. Fireplaces and dark wood tones lend to a cozy atmosphere. **Features:** full bar, happy hour. **Address:** 606 Penn Ave 19611 **Location:** Between 6th and 7th sts. **Parking:** street only. ⬜L⬜ ⬜D⬜

WEXFORD

- Hotels & Restaurants map & index p. 348
- Part of Pittsburgh area — see map p. 326

ATRIA'S RESTAURANT & TAVERN   724/934-3660

▼▼ ▼▼ American. Casual Dining. $10-$28 **AAA Inspector Notes:** Guests feel right at home in the dining room of this eatery, which is decorated in bright shades of yellow, green and red, and has rich wood tables and chairs. Tasty and well-seasoned entrees fill the large menu. This place is great for a fast sit-down lunch or relaxed dinner. **Features:** full bar. **Address:** 12980 Perry Hwy 15090 **Location:** I-76 (Pennsylvania Tpke) exit 28 (Cranberry), 3.2 mi s on US 19. ⬜L⬜ ⬜D⬜

KING'S FAMILY RESTAURANT   724/935-0320

▼▼ ▼▼ American. Family Dining. $6-$15 **AAA Inspector Notes:** Fast and friendly service is offered here. The menu is large in size with descriptive menu items and pictures. The restaurant is also known for its ice cream and dessert menu. **Address:** 105 VIP Dr, Rt 910 15090 **Location:** I-79 exit 73, just n of jct SR 910/Wexford Bayne Rd and VIP Dr. ⬜B⬜ ⬜L⬜ ⬜D⬜

MIYAKO JAPANESE STEAK & SEAFOOD   724/933-7253 ㊱

▼▼ ▼▼ Japanese. Casual Dining. $8-$33 **AAA Inspector Notes:** Chefs prepare fresh vegetables, steak, seafood and chicken dishes right in front of patrons on a hibachi grill at this eatery. The chef puts on some crafty and skilled knife demonstrations while preparing the food. **Features:** full bar. **Address:** 10636 Perry Hwy 15090 **Location:** On US 19; in Wexford Shopping Center. ⬜L⬜ ⬜D⬜ CALL ⬜M⬜

WHITE HAVEN (F-10) pop. 1,097, elev. 1,120'

White Haven is a year-round outdoor recreation destination. White-water rafting is popular on the Lehigh River spring through fall, and nearby Hickory Run State Park *(see Recreation Areas Chart)* offers ice fishing, snowmobiling and cross-country skiing in winter.

COMFORT INN-POCONO MOUNTAIN   (570)443-8461

▼▼ ▼▼ Hotel $69-$259 **Address:** Rt 940 at I-80 & 476 18661 **Location:** I-476 exit 95, just e; I-80 exit 277 (Lake Harmony). **Facility:** 100 units. 5 stories, interior corridors. **Amenities:** safes. **Pool(s):** heated indoor. **Activities:** hot tub, game room, exercise room. **Guest Services:** coin laundry.
🛁 BIZ 🛜 ⬜ ⬜ ⬜ / SOME UNITS ⬜

HOLIDAY INN EXPRESS & SUITES-WHITE HAVEN/LAKE HARMONY   570/443-2100

▼▼▼ Hotel. Rates not provided. **Address:** Rt 940 at I-80 & 476 18661 **Location:** I-476 exit 95, just e; I-80 exit 277 (Lake Harmony). **Facility:** 75 units. 3 stories, interior corridors. **Pool(s):** heated indoor. **Activities:** hot tub, limited exercise equipment.
CALL ⬜M⬜ 🛁 BIZ HS 🛜 ✕ ⬜ / SOME UNITS ⬜ ⬜

WHERE TO EAT

POWERHOUSE EATERY   570/443-4480

▼▼ ▼▼ American. Casual Dining. $7-$53 **AAA Inspector Notes:** Perched high atop a side of mountain and overlooking the interstate, this eatery was converted from a power plant. Original valves, gaskets, boilers and brick walls now make up the decor of the dining room. High ceilings, light-wood tones and dressed tables add to the ambience. The menu features American cuisine with some Italian influences thrown in for flavor. Seafood, chicken parmigiana, rack of lamb, veal and a New York strip steak often highlight the menu features. Lunch is more casual. **Features:** full bar. **Reservations:** suggested, weekends. **Address:** 60 Powerhouse Rd 18661 **Location:** I-80 exit 273, 0.3 mi w. ⬜L⬜ ⬜D⬜

WHITE MILLS (E-11) pop. 659, elev. 922'
• Part of Pocono Mountains Area — see map p. 371

DORFLINGER GLASS MUSEUM, .5 mi. e. of US 6 on Long Ridge Rd., features more than 900 pieces of cut, engraved, etched, gilded and enameled crystal. The restored house of a glass worker is open for tours on select dates. **Time:** Allow 30 minutes minimum. **Hours:** Wed.-Sat. 10-4, Sun. 1-4, May-Oct.; Sat. 10-4, Sun. 1-4, in Nov. **Cost:** $5; $4 (ages 55+); $2 (ages 6-18). **Phone:** (570) 253-1185.

The Dorflinger-Suydam Wildlife Sanctuary, jct. Elizabeth St. and Long Ridge Rd. at the Dorflinger Glass Museum, offers nature trails for observing indigenous wildlife and waterfowl within its 600 acres. Pets are not permitted. The Wildflower Music Festival is held on Saturdays in July and August. **Time:** Allow 30 minutes minimum. **Hours:** Daily dawn-dusk. **Cost:** Free. **Phone:** (570) 253-1185.

Recommend places
you'd like us to inspect at
AAA.com/TourBookComments

WHITE OAK   pop. 7,862

- Hotels & Restaurants map & index p. 348
- Part of Pittsburgh area — see map p. 326

CHINA HOUSE   412/678-8800   83

♥♥ Chinese. Casual Dining. $3-$15 **AAA Inspector Notes:** This restaurant offers a full buffet in addition to an extensive menu. Fast, friendly service is the norm. Most folks leave with a doggie bag in hand. **Features:** full bar. **Address:** 2001 Lincoln Way 15131 **Location:** Jct SR 48 and Lincoln Hwy; in Oak Park Mall.

L D CALL &M

LUCIANO'S ITALIAN BRICK OVEN   412/672-7428   84

♥♥ Italian. Casual Dining. $7-$17 **AAA Inspector Notes:** Diners hungry for pizza frequent this place, which offers traditional, deep-dish, pan, Chicago and white varieties. The menu also lists other great entrees, including eggplant parmigiana and veal piccata. Delivery and takeout are available. **Features:** full bar. **Address:** 1212 Long Run Rd 15131 **Location:** Jct SR 48 and Lincoln Hwy, just s on SR 48. L D CALL &M

WILKES-BARRE   (E-10) pop. 41,498, elev. 593'

- Restaurants p. 424

In the Wyoming Valley on the Susquehanna River, Wilkes-Barre was named for John Wilkes and Isaac Barre, members of the British Parliament and Colonial sympathizers. They also are honored by a monument in Public Square.

The Wyoming Valley was the scene of the Yankee-Pennamite Wars, a land struggle between Pennsylvania and Connecticut from 1769-85. Many skirmishes were fought on Wilkes-Barre's River Common, a 35-acre park on River Street between North and South streets. Within the park, which dates from 1770, are the Luzerne County Court House and numerous historic markers. Eventually Congress ruled in favor of Pennsylvania, though Connecticut did not relinquish its claims to the disputed area until 1800.

The F.M. Kirby Center for the Performing Arts is housed in a restored 1930s Art Deco movie palace. The center is home to the Northeastern Pennsylvania Philharmonic Orchestra and Ballet Theatre Pennsylvania. It offers a full program of drama, comedy, opera and musicals; phone (570) 826-1100.

The Luzerne County Historical Society operates a museum at 69 S. Franklin St. with exhibits about the coal mining industry as well as Native American artifacts, rocks, minerals and fossils of local origin; phone (570) 822-1727.

Frances Slocum State Park offers a variety of recreational facilities. *See Recreation Areas Chart.*

Luzerne County Convention and Visitors Bureau: 56 Public Sq., Wilkes-Barre, PA 18701. **Phone:** (570) 819-1877 or (888) 905-2872.

Shopping areas: The Wyoming Valley Mall on SR 309 Bus. Rte. offers more than 90 stores, including The Bon-Ton, JCPenney, Macy's and Sears.

SORDONI ART GALLERY, 150 S. River St., is on the campus of Wilkes University. The gallery displays paintings, sculpture, watercolors, photographs and other media of Modern and contemporary American artists. Changing exhibits also are on display. **Hours:** Tues.-Sun., noon-4:30. Closed university breaks; phone ahead for schedule updates. **Cost:** Free. **Phone:** (570) 408-4325.

GAMBLING ESTABLISHMENTS

- **Mohegan Sun at Pocono Downs** is at 1280 SR 315. **Hours:** Daily 24 hours. **Phone:** (570) 831-2100 or (888) 946-4672.

BEST WESTERN GENETTI HOTEL & CONFERENCE CENTER   (570)823-6152

Hotel
$99-$169

 **AAA Benefit:** Members save up to 20%!

Address: 77 E Market St 18701 **Location:** Jct Washington St; downtown. **Facility:** 72 units. 5 stories, interior corridors. **Pool(s):** heated outdoor. **Activities:** bicycles, exercise room. **Guest Services:** valet and coin laundry.

SAVE ✈ ⓘ Ⓨ CALL &M ⊃
BIZ 📶 ✕ 🛏 🖵 💻
/ SOME UNITS S HS

COMFORT INN & SUITES   (570)823-0500

Hotel
$89-$149

Address: 1067 Wilkes-Barre Township Blvd (Rt 309) 18702 **Location:** I-81 exit 165 southbound; exit 165B northbound on SR 309 business route. **Facility:** 65 units. 4 stories, interior corridors. **Pool(s):** heated indoor. **Activities:** exercise room. **Guest Services:** valet and coin laundry. **Featured Amenity:** breakfast buffet.

SAVE Ⓨ CALL &M ⊃ 📶 ✕
🛏 🖵 💻

DAYS INN   (570)826-0111

Hotel
$65-$250

Address: 760 Kidder St 18702 **Location:** I-81 exit 170B to exit 1 (SR 309 S business route), just w; I-76 (Pennsylvania Tpke) exit 105 to exit 1 (SR 115 N). Across from Wyoming Valley Mall. **Facility:** 75 units. 4 stories, interior corridors. **Amenities:** safes. **Guest Services:** coin laundry. **Featured Amenity:** continental breakfast.

SAVE 🛏↻ 📶 🛏 🖵 💻
/ SOME UNITS S 🖵

ECONO LODGE ARENA   (570)823-0600

Hotel
$69-$99

Address: 1075 Wilkes-Barre Township Blvd 18702 **Location:** I-81 exit 165 southbound; exit 165B northbound, on SR 309 business route. **Facility:** 103 units. 3 stories, interior corridors. **Guest Services:** valet and coin laundry. **Featured Amenity:** full hot breakfast.

SAVE 🛏↻ 📶 🛏 🖵 💻
/ SOME UNITS S

EXTENDED STAY AMERICA WILKES-BARRE HWY 315
570/970-2500

 Extended Stay Hotel. Rates not provided. **Address:** 1067 Hwy 315 18702 **Location:** I-81 exit 170B to exit 1 (SR 309 S business route), 0.3 mi n. **Facility:** 72 efficiencies, some two bedrooms. 4 stories, interior corridors. **Activities:** exercise room. **Guest Services:** valet and coin laundry.

FAIRFIELD INN & SUITES BY MARRIOTT WILKES-BARRE SCRANTON
(570)208-4455

Hotel
$111-$194

FAIRFIELD INN & SUITES **Marriott**

AAA Benefit: Members save 5% or more!

Address: 884 Kidder St 18702 **Location:** I-81 exit 170B to exit 1 (SR 309 S business route), then 0.5 mi w. **Facility:** 110 units. 4 stories, interior corridors. **Pool(s):** heated indoor. **Activities:** hot tub, exercise room. **Guest Services:** valet and coin laundry, area transportation. **Featured Amenity: full hot breakfast.**

HAMPTON INN & SUITES-WILKES-BARRE
(570)824-1005

Hotel
$99-$229

Hampton

AAA Benefit: Members save 5% or more!

Address: 876 Schechter Dr 18702 **Location:** I-81 exit 168 (Highland Park Blvd), just w. Across from Wyoming County Mall. **Facility:** 113 units. 5 stories, interior corridors. **Terms:** 1-7 night minimum stay, cancellation fee imposed. **Pool(s):** heated indoor. **Activities:** hot tub, exercise room. **Guest Services:** valet and coin laundry, area transportation.

HILTON GARDEN INN-WILKES-BARRE
(570)820-8595

Hotel $109-$199 **Address:** 242 Highland Park Blvd 18702 **Location:** I-81 exit 168, just s. **Facility:** 123 units. 4 stories, interior corridors. **Terms:** 1-7 night minimum stay, cancellation fee imposed.

AAA Benefit: Members save 5% or more!

Pool(s): heated indoor. **Activities:** hot tub, exercise room. **Guest Services:** valet and coin laundry, area transportation.

HOLIDAY INN EXPRESS EAST
570/825-3838

Hotel. Rates not provided. **Address:** 1063 Hwy 315 18702 **Location:** I-81 exit 170B to exit 1 (SR 309 S business route) to SR 315, just s. **Facility:** 117 units. 5 stories, interior corridors. **Pool(s):** heated indoor. **Activities:** hot tub, exercise room. **Guest Services:** valet laundry, area transportation.

HOLIDAY INN WILKES BARRE - EAST MOUNTAIN
(570)822-1011

Hotel
$130-$170

Address: 600 Wildflower Dr 18702 **Location:** I-81 exit 170A, 0.5 mi se on SR 115; I-476 exit 105, w on SR 115. **Facility:** 152 units. 7 stories, interior corridors. **Terms:** 2 night minimum stay - seasonal. **Pool(s):** heated indoor. **Activities:** sauna, hot tub, tennis, playground, exercise room. **Guest Services:** valet and coin laundry, area transportation.

HOST INN ALL SUITES
(570)270-4678

Extended Stay Hotel
$109-$199

Address: 860 Kidder St 18702 **Location:** I-81 exit 170B to exit 1 (SR 309 S business route), 0.5 mi w. **Facility:** 66 kitchen units. 3 stories, interior corridors. **Amenities:** safes. **Pool(s):** heated indoor. **Activities:** hot tub, exercise room. **Guest Services:** valet and coin laundry, area transportation. **Featured Amenity: continental breakfast.**

MICROTEL INN & SUITES BY WYNDHAM WILKES-BARRE
(570)970-3760

Hotel $72-$103 **Address:** 1185 Rt 315 18702 **Location:** 1.5 mi n of jct SR 115 and 309. **Facility:** 101 units. 4 stories, interior corridors. **Pool(s):** heated indoor. **Activities:** hot tub, limited exercise equipment. **Guest Services:** coin laundry, area transportation.

MOHEGAN SUN AT POCONO DOWNS
888/946-4672

Contemporary Hotel. Rates not provided. **Address:** 1280 Hwy 315 18702 **Location:** I-81 exit 170B (SR 309 S business route) to exit 1, 1 mi n. **Facility:** This nice slice of Vegas in northeastern Pennsylvania has a thoroughly modern casino and a stylish hotel to match. Rooms have a sleek but unpretentious style and the full staff is eager to serve. 238 units. 7 stories, interior corridors. **Bath:** shower only. **Parking:** on-site and valet. **Terms:** check-in 4 pm. **Amenities:** safes. **Dining:** 7 restaurants, also, Ruth's Chris Steak House, see separate listing, nightclub, entertainment. **Activities:** exercise room, spa. **Guest Services:** valet laundry.

QUALITY INN & SUITES CONFERENCE CENTER
(570)824-8901

Hotel
$79-$129

Address: 880 Kidder St 18702 **Location:** I-81 exit 170B to exit 1 (SR 309 S business route) off expressway, 0.5 mi w. Located in a commercial area. **Facility:** 118 units. 2 stories (no elevator), exterior corridors. **Amenities:** Some: safes. **Guest Services:** valet and coin laundry, area transportation. **Featured Amenity: full hot breakfast.**

RED ROOF INN WILKES-BARRE ARENA 570/829-6422

Motel
Rates not provided

Address: 1035 Hwy 315 18702 **Location:** I-81 exit 170B to exit 1 (SR 309 S business route) to SR 315, just n. **Facility:** 115 units. 3 stories, exterior corridors. **Amenities:** safes.

THE WOODLANDS INN, AN ASCEND HOTEL COLLECTION MEMBER (570)824-9831

Hotel $99-$219 **Address:** 1073 Hwy 315 18702 **Location:** I-81 exit 170B to exit 1 (SR 309 S business route), 0.3 mi n. Near Mohegan Sun at Pocono Downs. **Facility:** 150 units, some efficiencies and kitchens. 2-9 stories, interior corridors. **Terms:** check-in 4 pm. **Dining:** 2 restaurants. **Pool(s):** outdoor, heated indoor. **Activities:** hot tub, tennis, exercise room, spa. **Guest Services:** valet and coin laundry.

WHERE TO EAT

HAYSTACKS 570/822-4474

American. Cafeteria. $6-$15 AAA Inspector Notes: Friendly servers and a varied menu with such items as salads, sandwiches, roast turkey, steak, chicken, fish and baked meatloaf bring local folks back. Most of the tempting desserts are prepared in house, the blue cheese salad dressing is special, and the cornbread is considered a signature item. **Features:** beer & wine. **Address:** 116 Wilkes-Barre Township Blvd 18706 **Location:** Jct Highland Park Blvd, 0.5 mi n. [B] [L] [D]

KATANA 570/825-9080

Japanese. Casual Dining. $10-$31 AAA Inspector Notes: The sushi and hibachi chefs prepare delicious ahi, eel, tuna and salmon sashimi, steak, chicken and seafood hibachi while diners watch. The trendy place is popular with the locals. **Features:** full bar. **Address:** 41 S Main St 18701 **Location:** Just off Public Square; in Mid Town Village Shopping Plaza. **Parking:** on-site (fee). [L] [D]

MIRAKUYA JAPANESE RESTAURANT 570/820-0901

Japanese. Casual Dining. $8-$32 AAA Inspector Notes: Fine sushi and sashimi presentations are served along with creatively prepared Japanese steak dishes. Diners can sit at the sushi bar and observe the lovely creations being made or watch the entertainment at the hibachi grill. **Features:** full bar. **Address:** 695 Kidder St 18702 **Location:** I-81 exit 170B to exit 1 (SR 309 S business route), 0.6 mi w. [L] [D]

RUTH'S CHRIS STEAK HOUSE 570/208-2266

Steak. Fine Dining. $34-$49 AAA Inspector Notes: The main fare is steak, which is prepared from several cuts of Prime beef and cooked to perfection, but the menu also lists lamb, chicken and seafood dishes. Guests should come hungry because the side dishes, which are among the a la carte offerings, could make a meal in themselves. **Features:** full bar. **Reservations:** suggested. **Address:** 1280 Hwy 315 18702 **Location:** I-81 exit 170B (SR 309 S business route) to exit 1, 1 mi n; in Mohegan Sun at Pocono Downs. **Parking:** on-site and valet. [L] [D] [LATE] CALL [&M]

THAI THAI 570/824-9599

Thai. Casual Dining. $9-$22 AAA Inspector Notes: Authentic Thai cuisine is presented in eye-pleasing, colorful portions made from fresh ingredients that are local when possible. The elegant, bold-colored dining room is offset by delicate curtains allowing light from two street-side walls of windows. Friendly servers are available to recommend any menu items if needed. You might opt for the pad phed nor mai, which has sauteed bamboo shoots, string beans, bell pepper, Kaffir lime and basil leaf, red curry paste and coconut milk. **Address:** 41 S Main St 18701 **Location:** In Mid Town Village Shopping Plaza; just off public square. **Parking:** street only. [L] [D]

WILLIAMSPORT (E-8) pop. 29,381, elev. 528'

• Restaurants p. 426

Once known as the lumber capital of the world, modern Williamsport's strong manufacturing base complements its rich history. Among its highlights is Millionaires' Row, a street lined with Victorian-era mansions built by lumber barons. The city also is the birthplace of Little League Baseball. On West Fourth Street south of Max M. Brown Memorial Park is Carl E. Stotz Field, the original Little League field named after the league's founder.

Lycoming County Visitor Information Center: 210 William St., Williamsport, PA 17701. **Phone:** (570) 327-7700 or (800) 358-9900.

Shopping areas: Lycoming Mall, I-80 Lycoming Mall exit, features The Bon-Ton, JCPenney, Macy's and Sears. A shopping area along W. Fourth Street features stores and boutiques within a historic district.

HIAWATHA RIVERBOAT TOURS, 2205 Hiawatha Blvd. in Susquehanna State Park, offers 1-hour paddle-wheeler cruises along the Susquehanna River. A pre-recorded tape narrates the history of the river. Theme cruises also are available.

Hours: Sightseeing cruises depart Tues.-Sat. at 11:30, 1, 2:30 and 4, Sun. at 1, 2:30 and 4, June-Aug.; Sat.-Sun. at 1, 2:30 and 4 in May and Sept.-Oct. Tickets are sold 1 hour before departure. **Cost:** $8.50; $8 (ages 61+); $4.50 (ages 3-12). **Phone:** (570) 326-2500 or (800) 248-9287.

THOMAS T. TABER MUSEUM OF THE LYCOMING COUNTY HISTORICAL SOCIETY, SR 180 Maynard St. exit to 858 W. Fourth St., exhibits artifacts from 10,000 B.C. to the present. Exhibits include an art gallery, blacksmith shop, carpenter shop, Victorian parlor and gristmill. Displays about the lumber industry, Native Americans and The Shempp Toy Train Collection also are featured.

Time: Allow 1 hour minimum. **Hours:** Tues.-Fri. 9:30-4, Sat. 11-4 (also Sun. 1-4, May-Oct.). Closed major holidays. **Cost:** $7.50; $6 (ages 65+); $5 (ages 3-12); $20 (family, two adults and children). **Phone:** (570) 326-3326.

WILLIAMSPORT TROLLEY TOUR departs from the Victorian gazebo next to the Peter Herdic Transportation Museum at 810 Nichols Pl., from Susquehanna State Park and from the Third Street parking garage. The 75-minute tour visits Williamsport's Millionaires' Row, the impressive mansions built by the town's lumber barons. The tour also includes stops at the original birthplace of Little League Baseball and the *Hiawatha* paddlewheel riverboat. The tour is accompanied by audio narration. The museum chronicles the history of transportation in the area.

Tickets are sold at the Peter Herdic Transportation Museum and at the Hiawatha House in Susquehanna State Park. **Hours:** Museum Tues.-Sat. 10-3, June-Aug.; Fri.-Sat. 10-3, rest of year. Tours depart Nichols Place Tues.-Fri. at 10:45, 12:15 and 1:45, Sat. at 10:45 and 12:15, June-Aug. Tours depart Susquehanna State Park Tues.-Fri. at 11, 12:30 and 2, Sat. at 11 and 12:30, June-Aug. Tours depart Third Street parking garage Tues.-Fri. at 11:20, 12:50 and 2:20, Sat. at 11:20 and 12:50, June-Aug. **Cost:** (includes the museum) $5; $4 (ages 60+); $3 (ages 0-11). **Phone:** (570) 326-2500 or (800) 248-9287.

WORLD OF LITTLE LEAGUE MUSEUM—see South Williamsport p. 392.

BEST WESTERN WILLIAMSPORT INN (570)326-1981
Hotel $80-$190
AAA Benefit: Members save up to 20%!
Address: 1840 E 3rd St 17701 **Location:** I-180 exit 25 (Faxon St), 0.5 mi e. **Facility:** 132 units. 2 stories (no elevator), exterior corridors. **Pool(s):** outdoor. **Activities:** exercise room. **Guest Services:** valet and coin laundry, area transportation.

CANDLEWOOD SUITES 570/601-9100
Extended Stay Hotel. Rates not provided. **Address:** 1836 E 3rd St 17701 **Location:** I-180 exit 25 (Faxon St), 0.5 mi e. **Facility:** 122 efficiencies. 3 stories, interior corridors. **Pool(s):** heated indoor. **Activities:** picnic facilities, exercise room. **Guest Services:** complimentary and valet laundry, area transportation.

COMFORT INN (570)601-9300
Hotel $110-$140
Address: 1959 E 3rd St 17701 **Location:** I-180 exit 23A westbound; exit 23 eastbound, just w. **Facility:** 78 units. 3 stories, interior corridors. **Pool(s):** heated indoor. **Activities:** exercise room. **Guest Services:** valet and coin laundry. **Featured Amenity:** continental breakfast.

FAIRFIELD INN & SUITES BY MARRIOTT WILLIAMSPORT (570)601-9200
Hotel $76-$125 **Address:** 104 Maynard St 17701 **Location:** I-180 exit 28 (Maynard St), just n. Across from Pennsylvania College of Technology. **Facility:** 83 units. 3 stories, interior corridors. **Pool(s):** heated indoor. **Activities:** exercise room. **Guest Services:** valet and coin laundry, area transportation.
AAA Benefit: Members save 5% or more!

GENETTI HOTEL & SUITES (570)326-6600
Historic Hotel $129-$229
Address: 200 W 4th St 17701 **Location:** Jct William St; downtown. Next to Community Arts Center. **Facility:** The tall profile of this 1922 parlor-style hotel dominates the small town's skyline. Rooms here vary greatly in layout and décor style. 208 units, some two bedrooms, efficiencies and kitchens. 10 stories, interior/exterior corridors. **Terms:** cancellation fee imposed. **Pool(s):** outdoor. **Activities:** game room, exercise room. **Guest Services:** valet and coin laundry, area transportation. **Featured Amenity:** full hot breakfast.

HAMPTON INN & SUITES WILLIAMSPORT - FAXON EXIT (570)601-5800
Hotel $115-$259 **Address:** 66 Liberty Ln 17701 **Location:** I-180 exit 25, just n. **Facility:** 113 units. 5 stories, interior corridors. **Terms:** 1-7 night minimum stay, cancellation fee imposed. **Pool(s):** heated outdoor. **Activities:** hot tub, exercise room. **Guest Services:** valet and coin laundry.
AAA Benefit: Members save 5% or more!

HAMPTON INN WILLIAMSPORT DOWNTOWN (570)323-6190
Hotel $119-$175 **Address:** 140 Via Bella 17701 **Location:** I-180 exit 27B eastbound; exit 26 westbound, jct US 220 and SR 15 S. **Facility:** 110 units. 5 stories, interior corridors. **Terms:** 1-7 night minimum stay, cancellation fee imposed. **Pool(s):** heated indoor. **Activities:** hot tub, exercise room. **Guest Services:** valet and coin laundry.
AAA Benefit: Members save 5% or more!

HOLIDAY INN DOWNTOWN WILLIAMSPORT 570/327-8231
Hotel. Rates not provided. **Address:** 100 Pine St 17701 **Location:** I-180 exit 27B eastbound; exit 26 westbound; jct US 220 and SR 15 S; downtown. **Facility:** 102 units. 5 stories, interior corridors. **Pool(s):** heated indoor. **Activities:** exercise room. **Guest Services:** valet and coin laundry, area transportation.

HOLIDAY INN EXPRESS & SUITES DOWNTOWN WILLIAMSPORT 570/327-5292
Hotel. Rates not provided. **Address:** 90 Pine St 17701 **Location:** I-180 exit 27B eastbound; exit 26 westbound; jct US 220 and SR 15 S; downtown. **Facility:** 96 units, some efficiencies. 5 stories, interior corridors. **Pool(s):** heated indoor. **Activities:** exercise room. **Guest Services:** valet and coin laundry, area transportation.

RESIDENCE INN BY MARRIOTT WILLIAMSPORT
(570)505-3140

WWWW **Extended Stay Hotel** $108-$177 **Address:** 150 W Church St 17701 **Location:** I-180 exit 27B eastbound; exit 26 westbound; just w of Market St; downtown. **Facility:** 97 units, some two bedrooms, efficiencies and kitchens. 4 stories, interior corridors. **Terms:** check-in 4 pm. **Pool(s):** heated indoor. **Activities:** hot tub, exercise room. **Guest Services:** valet and coin laundry, boarding pass kiosk.

AAA Benefit: Members save 5% or more!

TOWNEPLACE SUITES BY MARRIOTT WILLIAMSPORT
(570)567-7467

WWW **Extended Stay Hotel** $97-$160 **Address:** 10 W Church St 17701 **Location:** I-180 exit 27B eastbound; exit 26 westbound; at Market St; downtown. **Facility:** 81 units, some two bedrooms, efficiencies and kitchens. 4 stories, interior corridors. **Pool(s):** heated indoor. **Activities:** hot tub, exercise room. **Guest Services:** valet and coin laundry.

AAA Benefit: Members save 5% or more!

WILLIAMSPORT SUPER 8
(570)368-8111

WWW **Hotel** $90-$160 **Address:** 2815 Old Montoursville Rd 17701 **Location:** I-180 exit 23B eastbound; exit 23 westbound. Near the airport. **Facility:** 43 units. 3 stories (no elevator), interior corridors. **Terms:** 2 night minimum stay - seasonal and/or weekends, cancellation fee imposed. **Activities:** recreation programs.

WHERE TO EAT

33 EAST
570/322-1900

WWWW American. Fine Dining. $17-$32 **AAA Inspector Notes:** Located in a restored Art Deco building, the dining room and bar have a metropolitan air. The menu includes preparations such as grilled spicy shrimp, crab cakes and fresh salads with walnuts, pears or strawberries and goat cheese. Entrées include their penne with lobster, tomato and Asiago cream and Parmesan-crusted grouper with potato-bacon hash. Desserts such as the rich banana cheesecake tortilla are made in house. **Features:** full bar. **Address:** 33 E 3rd St 17701 **Location:** Just e of Market St. **Parking:** street only. D

BARREL 135
570/322-7131

WW New American. Casual Dining. $8-$30 **AAA Inspector Notes:** This place serves a good mix of creative, well-prepared cuisine in a cozy relaxed setting. A good wine and cocktail list and an outdoor patio add to the appeal. **Features:** full bar, patio dining, Sunday brunch. **Reservations:** suggested. **Address:** 135 W 3rd St 17701 **Location:** Between Williams and Pine sts; downtown. **Parking:** street only. L D

BULLFROG BREWERY & RESTAURANT
570/326-4700

WW American. Casual Dining. $7-$20 **AAA Inspector Notes:** This downtown microbrewery produces a great selection of beers and also offers an interesting menu of sandwiches, steaks, salads and some creative twists on mac 'n' cheese and burgers. Products from local farms and producers add to the local flavor. There is live music on some nights. **Features:** full bar, Sunday brunch. **Address:** 229 W 4th St 17701 **Location:** Jct 4th St and Government Pl. **Parking:** street only. L D LATE

Keep your focus safely

on the road when driving

DI SALVO'S
570/327-1200

WWWWW
Italian
Casual Dining
$10-$40

AAA Inspector Notes: On the edge of town in a residential neighborhood, this restaurant got its roots as a homemade pasta shop. It has evolved into a family passion for great food prepared using family recipes with an imaginative flair. Most of their pastas are made in house. The seafood is the freshest available. A regional wine list offers the best wines of Italy for exceptional pairing. **Features:** full bar. **Address:** 341 E 4th St 17701 **Location:** Between Penn and Basin sts; downtown. L D

LE JEUNE CHEF
570/320-2433

WWWW
Continental
Fine Dining
$6-$30

AAA Inspector Notes: This restaurant is a training facility of the Pennsylvania College of Technology, which allows student chefs to hone their skills. Well-prepared and artistically presented classical cuisine is fittingly complemented by an extensive selection of wines. The menu is prix fixe during the academic year. **Features:** full bar. **Reservations:** suggested. **Address:** One College Ave 17701 **Location:** Jct I-180 and US 220 and 15 exit Maynard St, n to college entrance, follow signs; on Pennsylvania College of Technology campus. *Menu on AAA.com*
L D

THE PETER HERDIC HOUSE
570/322-0165

WWW Continental. Fine Dining. $22-$35 **AAA Inspector Notes:** *Historic.* In a restored 1854 Victorian mansion built by Peter Herdic, a 19th-century Pennsylvania lumber baron, the fine-dining establishment is an architectural, as well as historical and culinary treat. The menu offers seasonal local and organic ingredients when available. A local favorite, roasted hen with lemon is from a local farm. The rack of lamb, crab cakes, wild Alaskan salmon, macadamia-crusted halibut, and pear, walnut and Gorgonzola salad all are excellent choices. **Features:** full bar, patio dining. **Address:** 407 W 4th St 17701 **Location:** W of Market St; between Elmira and Center sts; downtown. D

VINCENZO'S ITALIAN CUISINE
570/327-1551

WW Italian. Casual Dining. $5-$18 **AAA Inspector Notes:** Hand-painted murals make a backdrop depicting a scene in Italy that sets the mood for great authentic Italian cuisine. Rich traditional sauces and delicate seafood sauces accompany freshly made pastas. Antipasti, entrée salads, signature carne, pesce and pollo dishes as well as some vegetarian choices make for delicious choices. The cannoli, cheesecake, tiramisu or spumoni should not be missed. You can bring your own wine here. **Features:** beer only. **Address:** 99 Maynard St 17701 **Location:** I-180 exit 28, just n.
L D CALL M

WILLOW GROVE pop. 15,726

- Hotels & Restaurants map & index p. 274
- Part of Philadelphia area — see map p. 230

COURTYARD BY MARRIOTT PHILADELPHIA WILLOW GROVE
(215)830-0550 **49**

WWWW
Hotel
$160-$263

COURTYARD Marriott

AAA Benefit: Members save 5% or more!

Address: 2350 Easton Rd (Rt 611) 19090 **Location:** I-276 (Pennsylvania Tpke) exit 343, just n. Located in commercial area. **Facility:** 149 units. 3 stories, interior corridors. **Terms:** check-in 4 pm. **Pool(s):** heated indoor. **Activities:** hot tub, exercise room. **Guest Services:** valet and coin laundry, boarding pass kiosk.

(See map & index p. 274.)

HAMPTON INN-WILLOW GROVE   (215)659-3535 **51**

WWW Hotel $99-$199 **Address:** 1500 Easton Rd 19090 **Location:** I-276 (Pennsylvania Tpke) exit 343, 0.3 mi s on SR 611. **Facility:** 150 units. 5 stories, interior corridors. **Terms:** 1-7 night minimum stay, cancellation fee imposed. **Guest Services:** valet laundry.

AAA Benefit: Members save 5% or more!

SPRINGHILL SUITES BY MARRIOTT PHILADELPHIA WILLOW GROVE   (215)657-7800 **50**

WWW Hotel $132-$217

AAA Benefit: Members save 5% or more!

Address: 2480 Maryland Rd 19090 **Location:** I-276 (Pennsylvania Tpke) exit 343, 0.3 mi s on SR 611, then 0.3 mi w. Located in a commercial area. **Facility:** 155 units. 4 stories, interior corridors. **Pool(s):** heated indoor. **Activities:** exercise room. **Guest Services:** valet and coin laundry. **Featured Amenity:** breakfast buffet.

WHERE TO EAT

OOKA JAPANESE SUSHI & HIBACHI STEAK HOUSE   215/659-7688 **75**

WW Japanese. Casual Dining. $13-$29 **AAA Inspector Notes:** Expect efficient service from the kimono-clad waitresses in this casual dining room. Peruse the extensive menu, which offers sushi, sashimi, tempura, tonkatsu, teriyaki and bento box preparations as well as non-raw-fish sushi. You might decide on the seafood teriyaki: lobster tail, shrimp and sea scallops served with sautéed broccoli, carrots, red onions and a side order of white rice. **Address:** 1109 Easton Rd 19090 **Location:** I-276 (Pennsylvania Tpke) exit 343, 0.4 mi s on SR 611. Willow Grove, 296.

WILLOW STREET (I-9) pop. 7,578, elev. 482'
• Part of Pennsylvania Dutch Country area — see map p. 220

HANS HERR HOUSE is 4 mi. s. on US 222, then .7 mi. s. to 1849 Hans Herr Dr. Built in 1719, this is believed to be the oldest building in Lancaster County and the oldest Mennonite meetinghouse in America. The medieval-style Germanic stone house has been depicted in several paintings by Andrew Wyeth, a descendant of Hans Herr. The site includes the restored house, a Mennonite farm exhibit, a blacksmith shop, a native American longhouse and a visitor center.

Time: Allow 1 hour minimum. **Hours:** Mon.-Sat. 9-4, Apr.-Nov. Herr House tours are given at 9, 11, 1 and 3. Last tour begins one hour before closing. Longhouse tours at 10, noon and 2. Closed Easter weekend and Thanksgiving. Phone ahead to confirm schedule. **Cost:** Herr House or Longhouse tour $8; $4 (ages 7-12). Combination ticket $15; $7 (ages 7-12). **Phone:** (717) 464-4438.

WILMERDING pop. 2,190
• Hotels & Restaurants map & index p. 348
• Part of Pittsburgh area — see map p. 326

THE STATION BRAKE CAFE   412/823-1600 **70**

WW American. Casual Dining. $13-$26 **AAA Inspector Notes:** This classy cafe offers a menu of delicious customer-appreciation specials, health-conscious choices, seafood, steaks and pasta-bilities, among other things. Live entertainment is offered on certain nights. **Features:** full bar. **Reservations:** suggested. **Address:** 500 Station St 15148 **Location:** Center. **Parking:** street only.

WINDBER pop. 4,138

RIZZO'S RESTAURANT   814/467-7908

WW Italian. Casual Dining. $7-$22 **AAA Inspector Notes:** Two dining rooms are traditional and two are contemporary at this warm, cozy restaurant. Chicken captiva, a boneless breast sautéed and topped with mustard sauce, cheese, fresh crab and bacon bits, is a house specialty. The chocolate cheesecake is delicious. **Features:** full bar. **Reservations:** suggested, weekends. **Address:** 2200 Graham Ave 15963 **Location:** Just n of jct SR 56 and 160, just e.

WIND GAP (F-11) pop. 2,720

The 1,168-acre Jacobsburg Environmental Education Center, 835 Jacobsburg Rd., encompasses the remains of the 18th-century village of Jacobsburg and the site of the second Henry Gun Factory; phone (610) 746-2801.

RED CARPET INN   (610)863-7782

WW Motel $70-$125 **Address:** 1395 Jacobsburg Rd 18091 **Location:** SR 33 exit Wind Gap/Bath (SR 512 S), just s, follow signs. **Facility:** 28 units. 2 stories (no elevator), interior/exterior corridors. **Terms:** cancellation fee imposed.

WHERE TO EAT

J & R'S SMOKEHOUSE   610/863-6162

WW American. Casual Dining. $8-$22 **AAA Inspector Notes:** With a relaxed atmosphere derived from a Southern motif that includes neon cacti, this spot features steaks, seafood, pasta and chicken. However, the specialty is barbecued ribs. This restaurant prides itself in providing meats that are 100 percent free of growth hormones and antibiotics. The casual dining room is accented calmly with light wood tones, low ceilings and Native American-themed artwork. The staff provides Southern hospitality. A breakfast buffet is set up Sunday 9 am to 12:30 pm. **Features:** full bar. **Address:** 1420 Jacobsburg Rd 18091 **Location:** SR 33 exit SR 512, just w.

WOMELSDORF (H-9) pop. 2,810, elev. 434'
• Restaurants p. 428

CONRAD WEISER HOMESTEAD is .5 mi. e. on US 422. The frontier stone home was built by Conrad Weiser, Colonial interpreter and peacemaker during the French and Indian War. The parklike 26-acre estate was designed by the sons of renowned landscape architect Frederick L. Olmsted. Two monuments and the family cemetery are on the grounds.

Time: Allow 1 hour minimum. **Hours:** Grounds open daily dawn-dusk. House Sat.-Sun. noon-4, June 1-Labor Day; first Sun. of the month noon-4,

Mar. 10-May 30 and Oct.-Dec. Phone ahead to confirm schedule. **Cost:** Grounds and house, free $5. **Phone:** (610) 589-2934. 🏚

THE STOUCH TAVERN 1785   610/589-4577
▼▼▼▼ American. Fine Dining. $7-$27 **AAA Inspector Notes:** *Historic.* Built in 1785, this tavern has five dining rooms decorated in the early-American style, complete with lanterns, antiques and paintings. A large stone fireplace and exposed wood ceiling beams reinforce the Colonial ambience. George Washington visited this place in 1793 when he was president. **Features:** full bar. **Reservations:** suggested. **Address:** 138 W High St 19567 **Location:** Center. **Parking:** on-site and street. [L] [D]

WOODWARD (F-7) pop. 110, elev. 1,145'

WOODWARD CAVE, 2 mi. w. off SR 45 on Woodward Cave Dr., is one of the state's largest caverns. A 50-minute, half-mile guided tour through five rooms is offered. The cave maintains a constant temperature of 48 F.

Warm clothing and proper footwear are recommended. **Hours:** Daily 9:30-5 (also Fri.-Sat. 5-6), in July; Sun.-Fri. 10-4, Sat. 9:30-5, late May-June 30 and early to late Aug.; Sat.-Sun. 10-4, mid-Apr. to late May and late Aug. to mid-Oct. Closed Easter. Phone ahead to confirm schedule. **Cost:** $11; $5.50 (ages 4-12). Phone ahead to confirm rates. **Phone:** (814) 349-9800. 🏚

WORCESTER (A-10) elev. 233'
• Part of Philadelphia area — see map p. 230

PETER WENTZ FARMSTEAD, 2100 Schultz Rd. with entrance on Shearer Rd., is an 18th-century Pennsylvania German working farm of more than 90 acres with a Georgian mansion furnished in period. The house twice was used by George Washington as headquarters during the Revolutionary War. Period crafts and farming demonstrations are given during special events offered throughout the year.

Time: Allow 1 hour minimum. **Hours:** Tues.-Sat. 10-4, Sun. 1-4. Last tour begins 30 minutes before closing. Closed major holidays. **Cost:** Donations. **Phone:** (610) 584-5104.

WRIGHTSVILLE pop. 2,310

ACCOMAC INN   717/252-1521
▼▼ Continental. Casual Dining. $15-$40 **AAA Inspector Notes:** *Historic.* On the Susquehanna River, this converted 18th-century inn and ferry crossing is renowned for its expertly prepared and artfully presented food. Beef tenderloin medallions with mushroom-Madeira sauce and brandy is prepared tableside and the decadent desserts are made in house. **Features:** full bar, Sunday brunch. **Reservations:** suggested. **Address:** 6330 S River Dr 17368 **Location:** US 30 exit Wrightsville, 1.5 mi n, follow signs. [L] [D]

WYOMING (E-10) pop. 3,073, elev. 557'

With the outbreak of the Revolution, the Wyoming Valley's importance as a granary led to a number of attacks by Tory and Native American forces. On July 3, 1778, 1,200 Native Americans and renegade whites defeated 300 frontiersmen 4 miles north of Kingston near Forty Fort, leaving the settlements of the Wyoming Valley unprotected. The next day the Native Americans passed up and down the valley in a series of raids that became known as the Wyoming Massacre. In reprisal, Gen. John Sullivan led an expedition up the Susquehanna River, devastating the area and breaking the Native Americans' grip on the region.

A monument at Fourth Street and Wyoming Avenue marks the site of a grave for victims of the Wyoming Massacre.

The Swetland Homestead at 885 Wyoming Ave. is the 1803 Swetland family home; additions were made as the family acquired additional members and wealth. The period rooms span 70 years and can be toured by appointment; phone (570) 823-6244, Ext. 3.

WYOMISSING pop. 10,461

COUNTRY INN & SUITES BY CARLSON   610/373-4444
▼▼ ▼▼ Hotel. Rates not provided. **Address:** 405 N Park Rd 19610 **Location:** US 422 exit N Wyomissing Blvd, just n to Park Rd, then just w. Located in a commercial area. **Facility:** 102 units. 3 stories, interior corridors. **Pool(s):** heated indoor. **Activities:** hot tub, exercise room. **Guest Services:** valet and coin laundry.
📶⁺ CALL 🅖Ⓜ 🔌 BIZ 🛜 🛏 🗄 🖥

COURTYARD BY MARRIOTT READING WYOMISSUNG
                                         (610)378-1137
▼▼▼▼ Hotel $146-$240 **Address:** 150 N Park Rd 19610 **Location:** US 422 exit N Wyomissing Blvd, just n to Park Rd, then 0.7 mi w. Located in a commercial area. **Facility:** 135 units. 6 stories, interior corridors. **Pool(s):** heated indoor. **Activities:** hot tub, exercise room. **Guest Services:** valet and coin laundry, boarding pass kiosk.
Ⓨ CALL 🅖Ⓜ 🔌 BIZ HS 🛜 ✕ 🛏 🖥 / SOME UNITS 🗄

AAA Benefit:
Members save 5% or more!

CROWNE PLAZA READING HOTEL   (610)376-3811
▼▼▼▼ Hotel $149-$249 **Address:** 1741 W Papermill Rd 19610 **Location:** US 422 exit Papermill Rd. **Facility:** 255 units. 2-4 stories, interior corridors. **Terms:** 3 day cancellation notice-fee imposed. **Pool(s):** heated indoor. **Activities:** exercise room. **Guest Services:** valet laundry, area transportation.
🍴 🥤 Ⓨ CALL 🅖Ⓜ 🔌 BIZ HS 🛜 ✕ 📹 🖥 / SOME UNITS 🅂🄻 🛏 🗄

DAYS INN READING/WYOMISSING   (610)374-1500
▼▼ Hotel $79-$130 **Address:** 910 Woodland Rd 19610 **Location:** US 422 exit Papermill Rd, just e. **Facility:** 101 units. 4 stories, interior corridors. **Activities:** exercise room. **Guest Services:** valet and coin laundry.
📶⁺ CALL 🅖Ⓜ BIZ 🛜 ✕ 🛏 🗄 🖥

HAMPTON INN   (610)374-8100
▼▼▼▼ Hotel $119-$189 **Address:** 1800 Papermill Rd 19610 **Location:** US 422 exit Papermill Rd. Opposite Berkshire Mall. **Facility:** 142 units. 5 stories, interior corridors. **Terms:** 1-7 night minimum stay, cancellation fee imposed. **Pool(s):** heated indoor. **Activities:** exercise room. **Guest Services:** valet laundry.
📶⁺ CALL 🅖Ⓜ 🔌 BIZ 🛜 🛏 🗄 🖥

AAA Benefit:
Members save 5% or more!

HOMEWOOD SUITES-READING/WYOMISSING (610)736-3100

▼▼▼▼ **Extended Stay Hotel** $129-$214 **Address:** 2801 Papermill Rd 19610 **Location:** US 422 exit Papermill Rd, 1.8 mi nw; US 222 exit Spring Ridge Rd. Located in a commercial area. **Facility:** 119 efficiencies, some two bedrooms. 4 stories, interior corridors. **Terms:** 1-7 night minimum stay, cancellation fee imposed. **Pool(s):** heated outdoor. **Activities:** exercise room. **Guest Services:** valet and coin laundry, area transportation.

AAA Benefit: Members save 5% or more!

[🍴] CALL [📶M] [🏊] [BIZ] [HS] [📶] [✕] [🔒] [🖥] [💻] / SOME UNITS [🐾]

THE INN AT READING HOTEL & CONFERENCE CENTER
(610)372-7811

▼▼▼▼ **Hotel** $89-$199 **Address:** 1040 N Park Rd 19610 **Location:** US 222 exit N Wyomissing Blvd, just n, then 0.3 mi e. **Facility:** 171 units. 1-2 stories, interior corridors. **Terms:** cancellation fee imposed. **Pool(s):** heated outdoor. **Activities:** exercise room. **Guest Services:** valet laundry.

[🍴] [🍽] [🍸] CALL [📶M] [🏊] [BIZ] [📶] [✕] [💻] / SOME UNITS [🐾] [🔒] [🖥]

VIVA BISTRO & TAPAS LOUNGE 610/685-5299

▼▼ ▼▼ Mediterranean. Casual Dining. $12-$28 **AAA Inspector Notes:** The restaurant's ownership presented itself a mission: to bring an uplifting experience to casual diners in a friendly, warm and cozy European-Mediterranean atmosphere. Mission accomplished! Healthy fresh seafood, pasta, steaks, veal and chicken are served with quality wines, spirits and signature drinks. Lending to the ambience are nightly live entertainment and Sunday jazz lunches. **Features:** full bar, patio dining, happy hour. **Address:** 901 Hill Ave 19610 **Location:** US 422 exit N Wyomissing Blvd, just n to Park Rd, then 1 mi w. [L] [D] [LATE] CALL [📶M]

THE WORKS 610/375-2700

▼▼▼ American Family Dining $9-$20

AAA Inspector Notes: In a renovated historic factory building, this restaurant is a fun, friendly place to bring the family. The kitchen prepares a nice selection of sandwiches, pizza, entrées and children's meals, with most items made from scratch. The back section of the building houses more than 150 entertaining arcade games. **Features:** full bar. **Address:** 1109 Bern Rd 19610 **Location:** Off Penn Ave (SR 423 business route); just e of jct State Hill Rd.

[L] [D] CALL [📶M]

WYSOX

COMFORT INN (570)265-5691

▼▼ ▼▼ Hotel $150-$170 **Address:** 898 Golden Mile Rd 18854 **Location:** On US 6 E. **Facility:** 51 units. 3 stories, interior corridors. **Pool(s):** heated indoor. **Activities:** sauna, exercise room. **Guest Services:** coin laundry.

[🍴] [🏊] [BIZ] [📶] [✕] [🔒] [🖥] [💻] / SOME UNITS [🐾]

STONE MOUNTAIN INN ON KEENE SUMMIT B&B
570/265-8846

[fyi] Not evaluated. **Address:** 1995 Keene Summit Rd 18854 **Location:** SR 6, 2 mi n, follow signs. Facilities, services, and décor characterize a mid-scale property. Located on 70 country acres, this B&B offers an outdoor patio for relaxation and a campfire for evening enjoyment. Walls are lined with local artwork for sale.

THE RIVER STONE INN 570/265-8882

▼▼ ▼▼ American. Casual Dining. $9-$25 **AAA Inspector Notes:** Situated in the Endless Mountains, this restaurant offers dinner-special nights. Tuesday is T-bone night, Friday is beer-battered haddock night and Saturday is prime rib night. Their house favorite is the 14-ounce rib-eye steak. A few Greek dishes along with some pasta dishes round out a varied menu. Try a cocktail or cold beer in their Wildfire Grille. **Features:** full bar. **Address:** 47 Leisure Dr 18848 **Location:** On US 6 E; in The River Stone Inn. [L] [D] CALL [📶M]

YARDLEY pop. 2,434
• Part of Philadelphia area — see map p. 230

HAMPTON INN & SUITES NEWTOWN (215)860-1700

▼▼▼ Hotel $119-$229

AAA Benefit: Members save 5% or more!

Address: 1000 Stony Hill Rd 19067 **Location:** I-95 exit 49, just sw. Located in a commercial area. **Facility:** 137 units, some efficiencies. 3 stories, interior corridors. **Terms:** 1-7 night minimum stay, cancellation fee imposed. **Pool(s):** outdoor. **Activities:** exercise room. **Guest Services:** valet and coin laundry. **Featured Amenity:** full hot breakfast.

[SAVE] [🍴] CALL [📶M] [🏊] [BIZ] [📶] [🔒] [🖥] [💻] / SOME UNITS [HS]

YORK (I-8) pop. 43,718, elev. 375'
• Hotels p. 431 • Restaurants p. 432

York served as the national capital Sept. 30, 1777, to June 27, 1778, while the British occupied Philadelphia. It was in York that Congress received the news of Gen. John Burgoyne's surrender, adopted the Articles of Confederation, issued the first National Thanksgiving Proclamation and learned that France was to send aid to the Colonies.

Capitalizing on the region's legacy as an industrial and manufacturing center, today's York County bills itself as the Factory Tour Capital of the World. More than a dozen factories, producing everything from pretzels to motorcycles, welcome visitors. A booklet detailing all of the city's tours is available at the Visitors Information Center.

Strand-Capitol Performing Arts Center, jct. George and Philadelphia streets, features the historic 1906 Capitol Theatre and the 1925 Strand Theatre. Performances run throughout the year; phone (717) 846-1111.

Heritage Rail Trail County Park is a 21-mile biking, hiking and horseback riding trail that runs from the Colonial Courthouse to the Mason Dixon Line, where it connects to Maryland's 20-mile Northern Central Railroad Trail. In winter, cross-country skiing and snowshoeing are permitted. The trail runs along an operational railroad line, so never get too close to the tracks. The park is open daily 8 a.m.-dusk; phone (717) 840-7440.

York County Convention and Visitors Bureau: York County Visitors Information Center at Harley-Davidson, 1425 Eden Rd., York, PA 17402. Or visit the Downtown York Visitors Information Center at Central Market, 34 W. Philadelphia St.; phone (717) 852-9675 or (888) 858-9675. **Phone:** (717) 852-6006.

Self-guiding tours: Literature about self-guiding walking tours is available from the York County Heritage Trust, (717) 848-1587, at 250 E. Market St. The York County Convention and Visitors Bureau also usually stocks them at their two locations.

Shopping areas: The York Galleria, 2 miles east of I-83 on US 30, is the area's largest mall; anchor stores are The Bon-Ton, Boscov's, JCPenney and Sears. West Manchester Mall, 1 mile west of I-83 on US 30, features Kohl's and Wal-Mart.

Two miles east of I-83 on US 30 across from York Galleria, Christmas Tree Hill offers holiday-themed gifts and home decor in a post-Revolutionary War mansion.

Many farmers markets specialize in Pennsylvania Dutch and German cuisine and include Central Market House, 34 W. Philadelphia St., held Tues., Thurs. and Sat. 6-2; Market & Penn Farmers Market, 380 W. Market St., held Tues. and Fri.-Sat. 6-3; and New Eastern Market, 201 Memory Ln., held Fri. 7-6.

RICHARD M. NIXON ENVIRONMENTAL EDUCATION CENTER, on Nixon Dr. in Richard M. Nixon County Park, has 181 acres of undisturbed environment. Its goal is to conserve and preserve the area's flora and fauna and teach about the importance of our environment. A natural history museum features dioramas, interactive displays, geological specimens from the area and more than 180 mounted specimens representing 15 countries. A large collection of York County taxidermy mounts also are on display.

Dioramas represent views of the African savannah, Arctic Circle and Northern Rocky Mountains. A bird observation window, a working indoor honeybee hive, live snakes and a touch room are included. A reference library and more than six miles of hiking trails also are on site. **Time:** Allow 1 hour minimum. **Hours:** Park grounds 8-dusk. Center Tues.-Sat. 8:30-4:30, Sun. noon-4:30. Closed major holidays. **Cost:** Free. **Phone:** (717) 428-1961.

VAUGHN L. BEALS TOUR CENTER AT HARLEY-DAVIDSON VEHICLE OPERATIONS is .7 mi. e. of jct. I-83 and US 30, at 1425 Eden Rd. The tour center highlights Harley-Davidson manufacturing and assembly operations. A children's area and a theater featuring a short video also are offered. During 1-hour guided factory tours, visitors view manufacturing and assembly of Touring, Softail, CVO and Trike motorcycles. The 2-hour Steel Toe Tour is an enhanced tour experience.

Note: Fully enclosed, low-heeled shoes are required. Cameras are only allowed in the tour center. Tours fill quickly and are offered on a first-come, first-served basis. **Hours:** Tour center Mon.-Fri. 8-4. Factory tours are offered 9-2. Steel Toe tour departs Mon.-Fri. at 9:30 and noon, late Aug. to mid-June. There typically is no production on Fridays. Closed major holidays. Phone ahead to confirm schedule. **Cost:** One-hour factory tour free. Steel Toe Tour $35. Ages 0-11 are not permitted on plant tour. **Phone:** (877) 883-1450.

WOLFGANG CANDY, 50 E. 4th Ave., is a factory where chocolate-covered pretzels, truffle cookies and peanut butter bears are made. The visitor center has a small collection of antique candy items like sugar molds and glass candy jars. A tour includes a video of the candy-making process and a demonstration of how chocolate is tempered and hollowed for fillings.

Hours: Tours depart Mon.-Thurs. at 1. The presentation is not offered the weeks before and during Easter and Christmas. **Cost:** Free. Reservations are recommended for tours. **Phone:** (717) 843-5536, 112 for tour information or (800) 248-4273.

YORK BARBELL MUSEUM AND USA WEIGHTLIFTING HALL OF FAME is off I-83N exit 24 at 3300 Board Rd. Exhibits detail the history of Olympic lifting, power lifting, bodybuilding and strongman competitions as well as the life accomplishments of Bob Hoffman, an industry pioneer and founder of York Barbell. Also on display are numerous late 19th- to early 20th-century trophies, sculptures, barbells, books and plaques. Special events are held throughout the year. **Hours:** Daily 9:30-4:30 (also Fri. 4:30-6). Phone ahead to confirm schedule. **Cost:** Free. **Phone:** (717) 767-6481 or (800) 358-9675.

YORK COUNTY HERITAGE TRUST includes several properties on E. Market, W. Market and W. Princess sts. Exhibits at the Historical Society Museum depict life in York County up to the 20th century. A reproduction of the original York village square with a one-room cabin, print shop, apothecary and toy store can be viewed. Decorative arts, folk art and exhibits about York's role in the Revolutionary and Civil wars are displayed. The Library & Archives houses an extensive collection on a variety of topics, including genealogy, local history and military history.

The Agricultural & Industrial Museum highlights the Golden Age of industrial development from south central Pennsylvania's early years to the present. Exhibits showcase industrial equipment and the history of transportation and include a working three-story gristmill and a 72-ton giant A-frame ammonia compressor.

The Victorian-era Bonham House, occupied by the Bonham family 1875-1965, displays artwork by patriarch Horace Bonham as well as furnishing styles from the 1850s-1930s. The Fire Museum in the 1903 station showcases more than 200 years of local firefighting with photographs, uniforms, vintage vehicles and the original fire-horse stalls. The Colonial Complex *(see attraction listing)* focuses on the Revolutionary period.

Tickets may be purchased at any of the sites except Bonham House. **Hours:** All museums open early Tues.-Sat., Apr. to late Nov.; times vary by museum. Agricultural & Industrial Museum, 10-4. Historical Society Museum, 9-4:30. Library & Archives, 9-5. Fire Museum, 10-4. Bonham House Sat. by appointment, early Apr.-late Nov.; tours depart from the Historical Society Museum. Phone ahead to confirm tour schedule. Closed major holidays.

Cost: One-day ticket (includes Colonial Complex and all open sites and museums) $15; $13.50 (ages 65+); $7 (students ages 8-18 with ID). **Phone:** (717) 848-1587.

Colonial Complex, 157 W. Market St., is part of York County Heritage Trust and consists of restored 18th- and 19th-century buildings and a replica of York's colonial courthouse that are seen by a guided tour. The 1741 half-timbered Golden Plough Tavern housed travelers passing through rural Pennsylvania. The stone circa 1751 General Horatio Gates House is the supposed site where the Marquis de Lafayette gave a toast, which prevented the overthrow of Gen. George Washington as head of the Continental Army. Gen. Gates was the hero of the Battle of Saratoga.

The Colonial Court House is a reproduction of the one in which the Second Continental Congress voted to adopt the Articles of Confederation in 1777 during the Congress' 9-month term in York.

Hours: Tues.-Sat. 10-4, early Apr.-late Nov. Tours are given on the hour 10-3 (except noon). Phone ahead to confirm tour schedule. Closed major holidays. **Cost:** One-day ticket (includes all open York County Heritage Trust sites and museums) $15; $13.50 (ages 65+); $7 (students ages 8-18 with ID). **Phone:** (717) 848-1587.

BEST WESTERN WESTGATE INN (717)767-6931

Hotel
$80-$140

AAA Benefit: Members save up to 20%!

Address: 1415 Kenneth Rd 17408 **Location:** I-83 exit 21B northbound, 2 mi w on US 30, then just n; exit 22 southbound, 0.5 mi s on SR 181, 1.7 mi w on US 30, then just n. Located in a commercial area. **Facility:** 104 units. 3 stories, interior corridors. **Activities:** exercise room. **Guest Services:** coin laundry. **Featured Amenity:** continental breakfast.

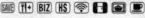

COMFORT INN & SUITES (717)699-1919

Hotel $95-$169 **Address:** 2250 N George St 17402 **Location:** I-83 exit 22, just n. Located in a commercial/residential area. **Facility:** 129 units. 4 stories, interior corridors. **Activities:** exercise room. **Guest Services:** valet and coin laundry.

COUNTRY INN & SUITES BY CARLSON YORK (717)747-5833

Hotel
$129-$189

Address: 245 St. Charles Way 17402 **Location:** I-83 exit 16A, 0.3 mi se. Located in a quiet area. **Facility:** 67 units. 3 stories, interior corridors. **Terms:** cancellation fee imposed. **Pool(s):** heated indoor. **Activities:** hot tub, exercise room. **Guest Services:** valet and coin laundry. **Featured Amenity:** full hot breakfast.

COURTYARD BY MARRIOTT YORK   (717)840-7840

WWW **Hotel** $111-$183 **Address:** 2799 Concord Rd 17402 **Location:** I-83 exit 21A northbound; exit 21 southbound, 3.5 mi e on US 30, then just s on SR 24. Located behind a shopping mall. **Facility:** 103 units. 4 stories, interior corridors. **Pool(s):** heated indoor. **Activities:** hot tub, exercise room. **Guest Services:** valet and coin laundry, area transportation.

AAA Benefit: Members save 5% or more!

FOUR POINTS BY SHERATON YORK   (717)846-4940

WWW **Hotel** $115-$300

FOUR POINTS BY SHERATON

AAA Benefit: Members save up to 15%, plus Starwood Preferred Guest® benefits!

Address: 1650 Toronita St 17402 **Location:** I-83 exit 21A northbound; exit 21 southbound, just ne. Located in a commercial area. **Facility:** 146 units. 5 stories, interior corridors. **Pool(s):** heated indoor. **Activities:** hot tub, exercise room. **Guest Services:** valet and coin laundry.

HAMPTON INN   (717)840-1500

WWW **Hotel** $109-$189 **Address:** 1550 Mt. Zion Rd 17402 **Location:** I-83 exit 21A northbound; exit 21 southbound, 3.5 mi e on US 30, then just n on SR 24. Next to a shopping mall. **Facility:** 144 units. 5 stories, interior corridors. **Terms:** 1-7 night minimum stay, cancellation fee imposed. **Pool(s):** heated outdoor. **Activities:** exercise room. **Guest Services:** valet and coin laundry.

AAA Benefit: Members save 5% or more!

HAMPTON INN & SUITES YORK SOUTH   (717)741-0900

WWW **Hotel** $109-$189 **Address:** 2159 S Queen St 17403 **Location:** I-83 exit 16B, just s. **Facility:** 100 units. 4 stories, interior corridors. **Terms:** 1-7 night minimum stay, cancellation fee imposed. **Pool(s):** heated indoor. **Activities:** exercise room. **Guest Services:** valet and coin laundry.

AAA Benefit: Members save 5% or more!

HERITAGE HILLS GOLF RESORT AND CONFERENCE CENTER   717/755-0123

WWW **Resort Hotel** Rates not provided

Address: 2700 Mount Rose Ave 17402 **Location:** I-83 exit 18, 1 mi e on SR 124. Located in a quiet area. **Facility:** After enjoying 36-holes of golf, grab some food and take in the sun on the large outdoor brick patio at Knickers Pub, or stay cool in the elegant lobby area furnished with marble floors and spacious seating. 104 units. 5 stories, interior corridors. **Dining:** 2 restaurants, also, Ironwoods Restaurant, see separate listing. **Activities:** regulation golf, miniature golf, exercise room, spa. **Guest Services:** valet laundry.

HOLIDAY INN EXPRESS & SUITES   717/741-1000

WWW **Hotel.** Rates not provided. **Address:** 140 Leader Heights Rd 17403 **Location:** I-83 exit 14, just w on SR 182. Located in a quiet area. **Facility:** 135 units. 5 stories, interior corridors. **Pool(s):** heated outdoor. **Activities:** exercise room. **Guest Services:** valet and coin laundry.

HOMEWOOD SUITES BY HILTON   (717)434-1800

WWW **Extended Stay Hotel** $159-$189 **Address:** 200 Masonic Dr 17406 **Location:** I-83 exit 22, just e, then right. **Facility:** 91 efficiencies, some two bedrooms. 4 stories, interior corridors. **Terms:** 1-7 night minimum stay, cancellation fee imposed. **Pool(s):** heated indoor. **Activities:** exercise room. **Guest Services:** valet and coin laundry.

AAA Benefit: Members save 5% or more!

WINGATE BY WYNDHAM YORK   (717)848-2100

WWW **Hotel** $88-$199 **Address:** 105 State St 17404 **Location:** I-83 exit 21B northbound; exit 21 southbound, 0.3 mi w on US 30, then just n. **Facility:** 70 units. 3 stories, interior corridors. **Terms:** cancellation fee imposed. **Amenities:** safes. **Pool(s):** heated indoor. **Activities:** hot tub, exercise room. **Guest Services:** valet laundry.

WYNDHAM GARDEN YORK   (717)846-9500

WW **Hotel** $109-$169 **Address:** 2000 Loucks Rd 17408 **Location:** I-83 exit 21B, 2.5 mi w on US 30, then just n; exit 22 southbound, 0.5 mi s on SR 181, 2.2 mi w on US 30, then just n. Adjacent to a shopping mall. **Facility:** 180 units. 2 stories, interior corridors. **Terms:** check-in 4 pm, 7 day cancellation notice. **Amenities:** video games. **Pool(s):** outdoor, heated indoor. **Activities:** exercise room. **Guest Services:** valet and coin laundry.

THE YORKTOWNE HOTEL   717/848-1111

WWW **Historic Hotel** Rates not provided

Address: 48 E Market St 17401 **Location:** SR 462 eastbound and I-83 business route, just e of square, follow signs. Located in downtown business district. **Facility:** Built in 1925, the lobby of this city center hotel is splendidly appointed with patterned carpet, potted ferns, a grand piano and nice chandeliers. 120 units, some two bedrooms and efficiencies. 11 stories, interior corridors. **Parking:** street only. **Dining:** Off Center Grill, see separate listing. **Activities:** spa. **Guest Services:** valet and coin laundry, area transportation.

WHERE TO EAT

CRIMSON AMERICAN GRILL   717/793-3605

WW **American. Casual Dining.** $8-$23 **AAA Inspector Notes:** The attractive dining rooms present an upscale, yet comfortable, setting in which to enjoy well-prepared entrees of veal, steak, seafood and chicken. Crab imperial is a signature dish. Servers in crisp attire are professional and attentive. **Features:** full bar, patio dining, happy hour. **Address:** 1839 S Queen St 17403 **Location:** I-83 exit 16B, 1 mi w. [L] [D] CALL

CRIMSON AMERICAN GRILL   717/793-3605

▼▼ ▼▼ American. Casual Dining. $8-$23 **AAA Inspector Notes:** This casual eatery is perfect for every occasion, including cocktails with friends or a romantic dinner for two. The outdoor patio is available to be enjoyed year-round; it's covered and heated during winter months. The menu offers a modern take on American fare and includes steaks, salads, burgers, fresh seafood and poultry. **Features:** full bar, patio dining, happy hour. **Address:** 1839 S Queen St 17403 **Location:** I-83 exit 16B, 1 mi w. [L] [D] CALL [&][M]

EL SERRANO   717/757-4963

▼▼ Mexican Small Plates. Casual Dining. $6-$20 **AAA Inspector Notes:** Authentic dishes are served at this casual eatery. Portions are large, so a big appetite is helpful. **Features:** full bar. **Address:** 3410 E Market St 17402 **Location:** I-83 exit 19A southbound; exit 19 northbound, 2.3 mi e on SR 462. [L] [D]

FUJIHANA JAPANESE STEAKHOUSE AND SUSHI
717/845-8988

▼▼ ▼▼ Japanese. Casual Dining. $13-$33 **AAA Inspector Notes:** Sit at the great sushi bar to sample the raw offerings, at a hibachi grill table for entertainment with your authentic Japanese meal or in private seats in the sushi area if you prefer not to sit with strangers. Servers in Japanese garb wander through the casually upscale dining area. **Features:** full bar. **Address:** 935 Loucks Rd 17404 **Location:** I-83 exit 22, just w. [L] [D] CALL [&][M]

IRONWOODS RESTAURANT   717/755-0123

▼▼ ▼▼ Continental. Casual Dining. $8-$33 **AAA Inspector Notes:** Grilled filet mignon and cream of crab soup are specialties at this intimate restaurant, which has vaulted ceilings and classic décor. The stylish location and expansive windows provide incredible views of the golf course's rolling green hills. Varied influences are evident in the excellent fresh fare. **Features:** full bar, happy hour. **Reservations:** suggested. **Address:** 2700 Mount Rose Ave 17402 **Location:** I-83 exit 18, 1 mi e on SR 124; in Heritage Hills Golf Resort and Conference Center. [D]

ISAAC'S FAMOUS GRILLED SANDWICHES   717/751-0515

▼ Deli Sandwiches. Quick Serve. $8-$12 **AAA Inspector Notes:** The modern, New York-style delicatessen specializes in overstuffed grilled sandwiches named after birds, plants and flowers. Salads and homemade soups also are popular. A tropical feel is prevalent in the colorful, casual dining room. **Address:** 2960 Whiteford Rd 17402 **Location:** I-83 exit 21A northbound, 3 mi e on US 30, then just n on SR 24; exit 21 southbound; in Village at Meadowbrook Shopping Center. [L] [D]

JR'S FRESH CUT FRENCH FRIES   717/741-2379

▼ American. Casual Dining. $1-$8 **AAA Inspector Notes:** When you're in the downtown area, search out this historic Central Market house for great barbecue, hamburgers, sandwiches and hand-cut french fries. Seating is limited. **Address:** 34 W Philadelphia St 17402 **Location:** City Center; in Historic Central Market House. **Parking:** street only. [L]

KELLY'S INN   717/755-3896

▼▼ ▼▼ American. Casual Dining. $6-$23 **AAA Inspector Notes:** Start with clams or oysters casino at this inn, have a hearty turtle or Maryland crab soup and follow that with an entrée of broiled or fried flounder; those are just a few of the extensive seafood items available at this inn. Great burgers and salads also are featured for a smaller appetite, as are broasted chicken and panini-style sandwiches. The lounge is open for lunch and allows smoking. **Features:** full bar. **Address:** 1906 N Sherman St 17406 **Location:** Just n of jct US 30 (Arsenal Rd) and Sherman St. [D] [✎]

THE LEFT BANK RESTAURANT & BAR   717/843-8010

▼▼ ▼▼ American. Casual Dining. $19-$36 **AAA Inspector Notes:** This chic bistro exudes a cosmopolitan atmosphere. Mediterranean preparations of seafood, steak and lamb are stylishly presented and appropriately seasoned. Aromatic bread is baked on the premises. Creative desserts appeal to both the eye and palate. **Features:** full bar, happy hour. **Reservations:** suggested. **Address:** 120 N George St 17401 **Location:** I-83 business route, just n of SR 462/74. **Parking:** street only. [L] [D]

MARKET ST. VIET THAI CAFE   717/846-9302

▼▼ ▼▼ Thai. Casual Dining. $6-$17 **AAA Inspector Notes:** Don't let the outward appearance of this restaurant mislead you. This place offers great Viet-Thai cuisine and over-the-top-friendly service. It is a real gem. Menu items include Chinese, Vietnamese and Thai dishes such as pad thai, kung pao chicken and yellow, green and red curries in addition to a host of authentic homemade desserts. If you enjoy this type of cuisine, you're in for a real treat that's affordable to boot. **Address:** 917 E Market St 17403 **Location:** Between Tremont and Albemarle sts. [L] [D]

OFF CENTER GRILL   717/848-1111

▼▼ ▼▼ Continental. Casual Dining. $8-$25 **AAA Inspector Notes:** Situated on one of the busiest streets in historic downtown, the restaurant's large windows offer great views of the action. Come hungry because both the lunch and dinner portions are large. You'd be wise to save room for the specialty mandarin orange napoleon with passion fruit sorbet dessert. **Features:** full bar, Sunday brunch. **Address:** 48 E Market St 17401 **Location:** SR 462 eastbound and I-83 business route, just e of square, follow signs; in The Yorktowne Hotel. **Parking:** valet only. [B] [L] [D] [LATE]

ROUND THE CLOCK DINER & COFFEE SHOP   717/848-5344

▼ American. Family Dining. $6-$24 **AAA Inspector Notes:** This appropriately named diner is open round the clock for road-weary travelers from I-83 and US 30. Menu choices quiet your hungry appetite. **Address:** 222 Arsenal Rd (US 30) 17402 **Location:** I-83 exit 21A northbound; exit 21 southbound, just ne. [B] [L] [D] [24]

WHITE ROSE BAR AND GRILL   717/848-5369

▼▼ ▼▼ American. Casual Dining. $7-$29 **AAA Inspector Notes:** Located on a busy corner in downtown York, this restaurant gets a lot of business thanks to an extensive menu and happy hour specials. The crab-pretzel appetizer and their locally ground-fresh burgers are among the most popular items. The outdoor seating areas provides a great spot for people-watching. **Features:** full bar, patio dining, Sunday brunch, happy hour. **Reservations:** suggested, for dinner. **Address:** 48 N Beaver St 17401 **Location:** Jct Philadelphia and Beaver sts; downtown. **Parking:** street only. [L] [D]

ZELIENOPLE (F-1) pop. 3,812, elev. 911'
• Part of Pittsburgh area — see map p. 326

Zelienople was founded in 1802 by Baron Dettmar Basse and named for his daughter Zélie. The 10-room Federal period Passavant House was Basse's gift to Zélie in 1808. The 1805 three-story Buhl House was built by another founding father, Christian Buhl. Both are open for guided tours Mon.-Fri.; phone (724) 452-9457 for tour information.

Zelienople-Harmony Area Chamber of Commerce: 111 W. New Castle St., P.O. Box 464, Zelienople, PA 16063. **Phone:** (724) 452-5232.

434

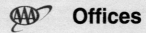 **Offices**

Main office listings are shown in **BOLD TYPE** and toll-free member service numbers appear in *ITALIC TYPE*.
All are closed Saturdays, Sundays and holidays unless otherwise indicated.
The addresses, phone numbers and hours for any AAA/CAA office are subject to change.
The type of service provided is designated below the name of the city where the office is located:

✤ Auto travel services, including books and maps, and on-demand TripTik ® routings.
● Auto travel services, including selected books and maps, and on-demand TripTik ® routings.
■ Books/maps only, no marked maps or on-demand TripTik ® routings.
▲ Travel Agency Services, cruise, tour, air, car and rail reservations; domestic and international hotel reservations; passport photo services; international and domestic travel guides and maps; travel money products; and International Driving Permits. In addition, assistance with travel related insurance products including trip cancellation, travel accident, lost luggage, trip delay and assistance products.
❂ Insurance services provided. If only this icon appears, only insurance services are provided at that office.
€ Car Care Plus Facility provides car care services.
▨ Electric vehicle charging station on premises.

AAA NATIONAL OFFICE: 1000 AAA DRIVE, HEATHROW, FLORIDA 32746-5063, (407) 444-7000

PENNSYLVANIA

ALLENTOWN—AAA EAST CENTRAL, 2072 DOWNYFLAKE LN, 18103. WEEKDAYS (M-F) 9:00-5:00, THU 9:00-8:00, SAT 10:00-2:00. (610) 434-5141 ✤ ▲ ❂

ALTOONA—AAA EAST CENTRAL, 1634 VALLEY VIEW BLVD, 16602. WEEKDAYS (M-F) 9:00-5:00, SAT 9:00-12:00. (814) 946-1277 ✤ ▲

ARDMORE—AAA MID-ATLANTIC, 30 GREENFIELD AVE, 19003. WEEKDAYS (M-F) 9:00-5:30, THU 9:00-7:00, SAT 9:00-1:00. (610) 649-9000 ✤ ▲ ❂

BEDFORD—AAA SOUTHERN PENNSYLVANIA, 9613 LINCOLN HWY STE 103, 15522. WEEKDAYS (M-F) 9:00-5:00, FRI 9:00-7:00, SAT 9:00-12:00. (814) 623-5196, *(800) 222-1469.* ✤ ▲ ❂

BETHLEHEM—AAA EAST CENTRAL, 1520 STEFKO BLVD, 18017. WEEKDAYS (M-F) 9:00-5:00, THU 9:00-8:00, SAT 10:00-2:00. (610) 867-7502 ✤ ▲ ❂

BLOOMSBURG—AAA MID-ATLANTIC, 1040 SCOTT TOWN CENTER, 17815. WEEKDAYS (M-F) 9:00-5:30, SAT 9:00-3:00. (570) 784-3380 ✤ ▲ ❂

BRADFORD—AAA EAST CENTRAL, 587 SOUTH AVE, 16701. WEEKDAYS (M-F) 9:00-5:00. (814) 368-3113 ✤

BUTLER—AAA EAST CENTRAL, 138 CLEARVIEW CIR, 16001. WEEKDAYS (M-F) 9:00-5:30, SAT 9:00-12:30. (724) 287-2713 ✤ ▲ ❂

CAMP HILL—AAA CENTRAL PENN, 4680 E TRINDLE RD, 17011. WEEKDAYS (M-F) 9:00-5:00, WED 9:00-6:00, SAT 9:00-12:00. (717) 761-6811 ✤ ▲ ❂

CARBONDALE—AAA NORTH PENN, 18 S MAIN ST, 18407. WEEKDAYS (M-F) 9:00-5:00, SAT 9:00-12:00. (570) 282-1390 ✤ ▲ ❂

CARLISLE—AAA CENTRAL PENN, 1911 W TRINDLE RD, 17013. WEEKDAYS (M-F) 9:00-5:00, WED 9:00-6:00, SAT 9:00-12:00. (717) 243-1844 ✤ ▲ ❂

CHAMBERSBURG—AAA SOUTHERN PENNSYLVANIA, 1666 LINCOLN WAY E, 17202. MON/WED/FRI 9:00-9:00, TUE/THU 9:00-6:00, SAT 9:00-6:00. (717) 264-4191, *(800) 222-1469.* ✤ ▲ ❂

CLIFTON HEIGHTS—AAA MID-ATLANTIC, 5233 W BALTIMORE AVE, 19018. WEEKDAYS (M-F) 7:00-7:00, SAT 8:00-5:00, SUN 10:00-4:00. (610) 605-2114 ✤ ▲ ❂ € ▨

CRANBERRY TOWNSHIP—AAA EAST CENTRAL, 20510 RT 19 #103-104, 16066. WEEKDAYS (M-F) 9:00-7:00, SAT 9:00-3:00. (724) 772-1122 ✤ ▲ ❂

DOWNINGTOWN—AAA MID-ATLANTIC, 105 QUARRY RD, 19335. WEEKDAYS (M-F) 7:00-7:00, SAT 8:00-4:00, SUN 10:00-4:00. (484) 237-2230 ✤ ▲ ❂ €

EASTON—AAA NORTHAMPTON COUNTY, 3914 HECKTOWN RD, 18045. MON/WED/FRI 9:00-5:00, TUE/THU 9:00-8:00, SAT 9:00-1:00. (610) 258-2371 ✤ ▲

ERIE—AAA EAST CENTRAL, 4430 BUFFALO RD, 16510. WEEKDAYS (M-F) 9:00-5:00. (814) 897-9508 ✤ ▲

ERIE—AAA EAST CENTRAL, 6660 PEACH ST UNIT #2, 16509. WEEKDAYS (M-F) 9:00-5:00, SAT 9:00-1:00. (814) 866-0246 ✤ ▲ ❂

FAIRLESS HILLS—AAA MID-ATLANTIC, 110 LINCOLN HWY, 19030. WEEKDAYS (M-F) 9:00-5:30, SAT 9:00-3:00. (215) 269-2034 ✤ ▲ ❂

FRANKLIN—AAA EAST CENTRAL, 491 ALLEGHENY BLVD #200, 16323. WEEKDAYS (M-F) 8:30-5:00. (814) 432-3960 ✤

GETTYSBURG—AAA CENTRAL PENN, 1275 YORK RD #10, 17325. WEEKDAYS (M-F) 9:00-5:00, WED 9:00-6:00, SAT 9:00-12:00. (717) 334-1155 ✤ ▲

GLEN MILLS—AAA MID-ATLANTIC, 1810 WILMINGTON PIKE, 19342. WEEKDAYS (M-F) 9:00-5:30, SAT 9:00-3:00. (610) 808-9000 ✤ ▲ ❂

GREENSBURG—AAA EAST CENTRAL, 5142 RT 30 #135, 15601. WEEKDAYS (M-F) 9:00-5:00, SAT 10:00-2:00. (724) 834-8300 ✤ ▲ ❂

GROVE CITY—AAA EAST CENTRAL, 24 PINE GROVE VILLAGE DR, 16127. WEEKDAYS (M-F) 8:30-5:00. (724) 458-8930 ✤

HANOVER—AAA SOUTHERN PENNSYLVANIA, 1000 CARLISLE ST, 17331. MON/WED/FRI 9:00-9:00, TUE/THU 9:00-6:00, SAT 9:00-6:00. (717) 637-2400, *(800) 222-1469.* ✤ ▲ ❂

HARRISBURG—AAA CENTRAL PENN, 2301 PAXTON CHURCH RD, 17110. WEEKDAYS (M-F) 9:00-5:00, WED 9:00-6:00, SAT 9:00-12:00. (717) 657-2244, *(800) 498-4222.* ✤ ▲

HARRISBURG—AAA CENTRAL PENN, 2301 PAXTON CHURCH RD, 17110. WEEKDAYS (M-F) 9:00-5:00, WED 9:00-6:00, SAT 9:00-12:00. (717) 657-2244 ✤ ▲

HERMITAGE—AAA EAST CENTRAL, 1749 E STATE ST, 16148. WEEKDAYS (M-F) 8:30-5:00, SAT 8:30-12:00. (724) 981-9141 ✤ ❂

HONESDALE—AAA NORTH PENN, 1126 MAIN ST, 18431. WEEKDAYS (M-F) 9:00-5:00, SAT 9:00-12:00. (570) 253-0160 ✤ ▲ ❂

HUMMELSTOWN—AAA CENTRAL PENN, 1142 MAE ST, 17036. WEEKDAYS (M-F) 9:00-5:00, WED 9:00-6:00, SAT 9:00-12:00. (717) 533-3381 ✤ ▲ ❂

HUNTINGDON—AAA CENTRAL PENN, 608 WASHINGTON ST, 16652. WEEKDAYS (M-F) 9:00-5:00, WED 9:00-6:00, SAT 9:00-12:00. (814) 643-1030 ✤ ▲

INDIANA—AAA EAST CENTRAL, 1169 WAYNE AVE, 15701. WEEKDAYS (M-F) 8:30-5:00, THU 8:30-7:00, SAT 9:30-1:30. (724) 349-4193 ✚ ▲

JOHNSTOWN—AAA SOUTHERN PENNSYLVANIA, 500 GALLERIA DR #112, 15904. MON/WED/FRI 10:00-9:00, TUE/THU 10:00-6:00, SAT 10:00-6:00. (814) 269-3641, *(800) 222-1469.* ✚ ▲ ○

KING OF PRUSSIA—AAA MID-ATLANTIC, 139 E DEKALB PIKE, 19406. WEEKDAYS (M-F) 9:00-5:30, SAT 9:00-3:00. (610) 337-6800 ✚ ▲ ○

KITTANNING—AAA EAST CENTRAL, 11 FRANKLIN VILLAGE MALL, 16201. WEEKDAYS (M-F) 8:30-5:00, SAT 8:30-12:00. (724) 543-1924 ✚ ▲

LANCASTER—AAA CENTRAL PENN, 101 W JAMES ST, 17603. WEEKDAYS (M-F) 9:00-5:00, WED 9:00-6:00, SAT 9:00-12:00. (717) 397-4444 ✚ ○

LANCASTER—AAA CENTRAL PENN, 804 ESTELLE DR, 17601. WEEKDAYS (M-F) 9:00-5:00, WED 9:00-6:00, SAT 9:00-12:00. (717) 898-6900 ✚ ▲ ○

LANSDALE—AAA EAST CENTRAL, 1250 N BROAD ST, 19446. WEEKDAYS (M-F) 9:00-5:00, THU 9:00-8:00, SAT 10:00-2:00. (215) 855-8600 ✚ ▲ ○

LEBANON—AAA CENTRAL PENN, 984 ISABEL DR, 17042. WEEKDAYS (M-F) 9:00-5:00, WED 9:00-6:00, SAT 9:00-12:00. (717) 273-8533 ✚ ▲

LEWISBURG—AAA EAST CENTRAL, 530 1/2 N DERR DR, 17837. WEEKDAYS (M-F) 8:30-5:00. (570) 524-7455 ●

LEWISTOWN—AAA CENTRAL PENN, 33 N BROWN ST, 17044. WEEKDAYS (M-F) 9:00-5:00, WED 9:00-6:00, SAT 9:00-12:00. (717) 242-2221 ✚

LITITZ—AAA CENTRAL PENN, 727 S BROAD ST, 17543. WEEKDAYS (M-F) 9:00-5:00, WED 9:00-6:00, SAT 9:00-12:00. (717) 626-3040 ✚ ▲ ○

LOCK HAVEN—AAA SOUTHERN PENNSYLVANIA, 12 ORIOLE RD, 17745. WEEKDAYS (M-F) 9:00-5:00. (570) 748-2405, *(800) 222-1469.* ✚ ▲ ○

LOWER BURRELL—AAA EAST CENTRAL, 2501 LEECHBURG RD STE E, 15068. WEEKDAYS (M-F) 9:00-5:00, SAT 9:00-2:00. (724) 339-4440 ✚ ▲

MEADVILLE—AAA EAST CENTRAL, 18939 PARK AVE PLZ #7, 16335. WEEKDAYS (M-F) 8:30-5:00, SAT 8:30-12:00. (814) 724-2247 ✚ ▲ ○

MONROEVILLE—AAA EAST CENTRAL, 2725 MOSSIDE BLVD, 15146. WEEKDAYS (M-F) 9:00-7:00, SAT 9:00-3:00. (412) 858-4640 ✚ ▲ ○

NEW CASTLE—AAA EAST CENTRAL, 40 EAST ST, 16101. WEEKDAYS (M-F) 9:00-5:00, SAT 10:00-2:00. (724) 658-8551 ✚ ▲ ○

PHILADELPHIA—AAA MID-ATLANTIC, 1801 MARKET ST, 19103. WEEKDAYS (M-F) 9:00-5:00. (215) 399-1180 ✚ ▲ ○

PHILADELPHIA—AAA MID-ATLANTIC, 2260 OREGON AVE STE H5, 19145. WEEKDAYS (M-F) 9:00-5:30, SAT 9:00-3:00. (215) 399-1000 ✚ ▲ ○

PHILADELPHIA—AAA MID-ATLANTIC, 9475 ROOSEVELT BLVD, 19114. WEEKDAYS (M-F) 9:00-5:30, SAT 9:00-3:00. (215) 671-1700 ✚ ▲ ○

PITTSBURGH—AAA EAST CENTRAL, 160 FT COUCH RD, 15241. WEEKDAYS (M-F) 9:00-7:00, SAT 9:00-3:00. (412) 833-5203 ✚ ▲ ○

PITTSBURGH—AAA EAST CENTRAL, 1760 PARK MANOR BLVD, 15205. WEEKDAYS (M-F) 9:00-7:00, SAT 9:00-3:00. (412) 809-2800 ✚ ▲ ○

PITTSBURGH—AAA EAST CENTRAL, 4790 MCKNIGHT RD, 15237. WEEKDAYS (M-F) 9:00-7:00, SAT 9:00-3:00. (412) 367-7600 ✚ ▲ ○

PITTSBURGH—AAA EAST CENTRAL, 538 SMITHFIELD ST, 15222. WEEKDAYS (M-F) 8:30-5:00. (412) 338-4300 ✚ ▲ ○

PITTSBURGH—AAA EAST CENTRAL, 5900 BAUM BLVD, 15206. WEEKDAYS (M-F) 8:30-5:00. (412) 363-5100, *(800) 441-5008.* ✚ ○

PITTSBURGH—AAA EAST CENTRAL, 5900 BAUM BLVD, 15206. WEEKDAYS (M-F) 8:30-5:00, SAT 10:00-3:00. (412) 363-5100 ✚ ▲ ○

PITTSBURGH—AAA EAST CENTRAL, 9 CLARITON BLVD, 15236. WEEKDAYS (M-F) 9:00-7:00, SAT 9:00-3:00. (412) 655-6100 ✚ ▲ ○

POTTSVILLE—AAA SCHUYLKILL COUNTY, 340 S CENTRE ST, 17901. WEEKDAYS (M-F) 8:30-5:00, SAT 9:00-12:00. (570) 622-4991 ✚ ▲ ○

POTTSVILLE—AAA SCHUYLKILL COUNTY, 340 S CENTRE ST, 17901. WEEKDAYS (M-F) 8:30-5:00, SAT 9:00-12:00. (570) 622-4991 ✚ ▲ ○

READING—AAA READING-BERKS, 920 VAN REED RD, 19610. WEEKDAYS (M-F) 9:00-5:00, WED 9:00-7:00, SAT 9:00-12:00. (610) 374-4531, *(800) 373-4339.* ✚ ▲ ○

READING—AAA READING-BERKS, 920 VAN REED RD, 19610. WEEKDAYS (M-F) 9:00-5:00, WED 9:00-7:00, SAT 9:00-12:00. (610) 374-4531 ✚ ▲ ○

ROCHESTER—AAA EAST CENTRAL, 300 ADAMS ST, 15074. WEEKDAYS (M-F) 9:00-5:00, SAT 10:00-2:00. (724) 775-8000 ✚ ▲ ○

ROYERSFORD—AAA EAST CENTRAL, 70 BUCKWALTER RD, 19468. WEEKDAYS (M-F) 10:00-6:00, THU 10:00-8:00, SAT 10:00-2:00. (610) 323-6300 ✚ ▲ ○

SCRANTON—AAA NORTH PENN, 1035 N WASHINGTON AVE, 18509. WEEKDAYS (M-F) 9:00-5:00, THU 9:00-7:00, SAT 9:00-1:00. (570) 348-2511, *(800) 982-4306.* ✚ ▲ ○

SCRANTON—AAA NORTH PENN, 1035 N WASHINGTON AVE, 18509. WEEKDAYS (M-F) 9:00-5:00, THU 9:00-7:00, SAT 9:00-1:00. (570) 348-2511 ✚ ▲ ○

SHREWSBURY—AAA SOUTHERN PENNSYLVANIA, 14625 MT AIRY RD STE #104, 17361. MON/WED/FRI 9:00-9:00, TUE/THU 9:00-6:00, SAT 9:00-6:00. (717) 235-7883, *(800) 222-1469.* ✚ ▲ ○

SOMERSET—AAA EAST CENTRAL, 110 N CENTER AVE, 15501. WEEKDAYS (M-F) 8:30-5:00, FRI 8:30-7:00. (814) 443-6526 ✚

SOUTH WILLIAMSPORT—AAA NORTH PENN, 1 E 6TH AVE, 17702. WEEKDAYS (M-F) 8:30-5:00, MON 8:30-8:00. (570) 323-8431 ✚ ▲ ○

ST. MARYS—AAA EAST CENTRAL, 1375 BUCKTAIL RD, 15857. WEEKDAYS (M-F) 8:30-5:00. (814) 834-7838 ✚ ▲

STATE COLLEGE—AAA SOUTHERN PENNSYLVANIA, 200 SHILOH RD, 16801. MON/WED/FRI 9:00-9:00, TUE/THU 9:00-6:00, SAT 9:00-6:00. (814) 237-0305, *(800) 222-1469.* ✚ ▲ ○

STROUDSBURG—AAA NORTH PENN, 1527 N 9TH ST, 18360. WEEKDAYS (M-F) 9:00-5:00, SAT 9:00-12:00. (570) 421-2500 ✚ ▲ ○

SUNBURY—AAA EAST CENTRAL, 1001 MARKET ST, 17801. WEEKDAYS (M-F) 8:30-5:30. (570) 286-4507 ✚ ▲

TAMAQUA—AAA SCHUYLKILL COUNTY, 202 E BROAD ST, 18252. WEEKDAYS (M-F) 8:30-5:00, SAT 9:00-12:00. (570) 668-1003 ■ ▲ ○

TOWANDA—AAA NORTH PENN, 306 ENNIS LN, 18848. WEEKDAYS (M-F) 9:00-5:00, SAT 9:00-12:00. (570) 265-6122 ✚ ▲ ○

TUNKHANNOCK—AAA NORTH PENN, 208 W TIOGA ST, 18657. WEEKDAYS (M-F) 9:00-5:00. (570) 836-5104 ✚ ▲ ○

UNIONTOWN—AAA EAST CENTRAL, 111 W MAIN ST, 15401. WEEKDAYS (M-F) 8:30-5:00, FRI 8:30-7:00. (724) 438-8575 ✚ ▲

436

WARREN—AAA EAST CENTRAL, 2285 MARKET ST, 16365. WEEKDAYS (M-F) 9:00-5:00. (814) 723-6660

WARRINGTON—AAA MID-ATLANTIC, 865 EASTON RD STE 100, 18976. WEEKDAYS (M-F) 9:00-5:30, SAT 9:00-3:00. (215) 343-2660

WASHINGTON—AAA EAST CENTRAL, 196 MURTLAND AVE, 15301. WEEKDAYS (M-F) 8:30-5:00, SAT 8:30-12:00. (724) 222-3800

WAYNE—AAA MID-ATLANTIC, 849 W LANCASTER AVE, 19087. WEEKDAYS (M-F) 7:00-7:00, SAT 8:00-5:00, SUN 10:00-4:00. (610) 263-8150

WAYNESBURG—AAA EAST CENTRAL, 184 GREENE PLZ, 15370. WEEKDAYS (M-F) 9:30-5:30. (724) 627-3434

WELLSBORO—AAA NORTH PENN, 9 CHARLESTON ST, 16901. WEEKDAYS (M-F) 8:30-5:00. (570) 724-4134

WEST CHESTER—AAA MID-ATLANTIC, 707 E GAY ST, 19380. WEEKDAYS (M-F) 7:00-7:00, SAT 8:00-5:00, SUN 10:00-4:00. (610) 696-8100

WEXFORD—AAA EAST CENTRAL, 10548 PERRY HWY, 15090. WEEKDAYS (M-F) 9:00-7:00, SAT 9:00-3:00. (724) 933-3000

WHITE OAK—AAA EAST CENTRAL, 2001 LINCOLN WAY #8, 15131. WEEKDAYS (M-F) 10:00-6:00, SAT 10:00-2:00. (412) 675-3400

WILKES-BARRE—AAA MID-ATLANTIC, 679-E KIDDER ST, 18702. WEEKDAYS (M-F) 9:00-5:30, SAT 9:00-3:00. (570) 819-1920

WILLOW GROVE—AAA MID-ATLANTIC, 2506 W MORELAND RD, 19090. WEEKDAYS (M-F) 7:00-7:00, SAT 8:00-5:00, SUN 10:00-4:00. (215) 392-9620

YORK—AAA SOUTHERN PENNSYLVANIA, 2840 EASTERN BLVD, 17402. WEEKDAYS (M-F) 8:00-5:00. (717) 600-8900, *(800) 222-1469.*

YORK—AAA SOUTHERN PENNSYLVANIA, 2840 EASTERN BLVD, 17402. MON/WED/FRI 9:00-9:00, TUE/THU 9:00-6:00, SAT 9:00-6:00. (717) 600-8700, *(800) 222-1469.*

Metric Equivalents Chart

TEMPERATURE

To convert Fahrenheit to Celsius, subtract 32 from the Fahrenheit temperature, multiply by 5 and divide by 9. To convert Celsius to Fahrenheit, multiply by 9, divide by 5 and add 32.

ACRES

1 acre = 0.4 hectare (ha)   1 hectare = 2.47 acres

MILES AND KILOMETERS

Note: A kilometer is approximately 5/8 or 0.6 of a mile. To convert kilometers to miles multiply by 0.6.

Miles/Kilometers		Kilometers/Miles	
15	24.1	30	18.6
20	32.2	35	21.7
25	40.2	40	24.8
30	48.3	45	27.9
35	56.3	50	31.0
40	64.4	55	34.1
45	72.4	60	37.2
50	80.5	65	40.3
55	88.5	70	43.4
60	96.6	75	46.6
65	104.6	80	49.7
70	112.7	85	52.8
75	120.7	90	55.9
80	128.7	95	59.0
85	136.8	100	62.1
90	144.8	105	65.2
95	152.9	110	68.3
100	160.9	115	71.4

Celsius ° / Fahrenheit °

Celsius °		Fahrenheit °
100	BOILING	212
37		100
35		95
32		90
29		85
27		80
24		75
21		70
18		65
16		60
13		55
10		50
7		45
4		40
2		35
0	FREEZING	32
-4		25
-7		20
-9		15
-12		10
-15		5
-18		0
-21		-5
-24		-10
-27		-15

LINEAR MEASURE

Customary	Metric
1 inch = 2.54 centimeters	1 centimeter = 0.4 inches
1 foot = 30 centimeters	1 meter = 3.3 feet
1 yard = 0.91 meters	1 meter = 1.09 yards
1 mile = 1.6 kilometers	1 kilometer = .62 miles

LIQUID MEASURE

Customary	Metric
1 fluid ounce = 30 milliliters	1 milliliter = .03 fluid ounces
1 cup = .24 liters	1 liter = 2.1 pints
1 pint = .47 liters	1 liter = 1.06 quarts
1 quart = .95 liters	1 liter = .26 gallons
1 gallon = 3.8 liters	

WEIGHT

If You Know:	Multiply By:	To Find:
Ounces	28	Grams
Pounds	0.45	Kilograms
Grams	0.035	Ounces
Kilograms	2.2	Pounds

PRESSURE

Air pressure in automobile tires is expressed in kilopascals. Multiply pound-force per square inch (psi) by 6.89 to find kilopascals (kPa).

24 psi = 165 kPa	28 psi = 193 kPa
26 psi = 179 kPa	30 psi = 207 kPa

GALLONS AND LITERS

Gallons/Liters				Liters/Gallons			
5	19.0	12	45.6	10	2.6	40	10.4
6	22.8	14	53.2	15	3.9	50	13.0
7	26.6	16	60.8	20	5.2	60	15.6
8	30.4	18	68.4	25	6.5	70	18.2
9	34.2	20	76.0	30	7.8	80	20.8
10	38.0	25	95.0	35	9.1	90	23.4

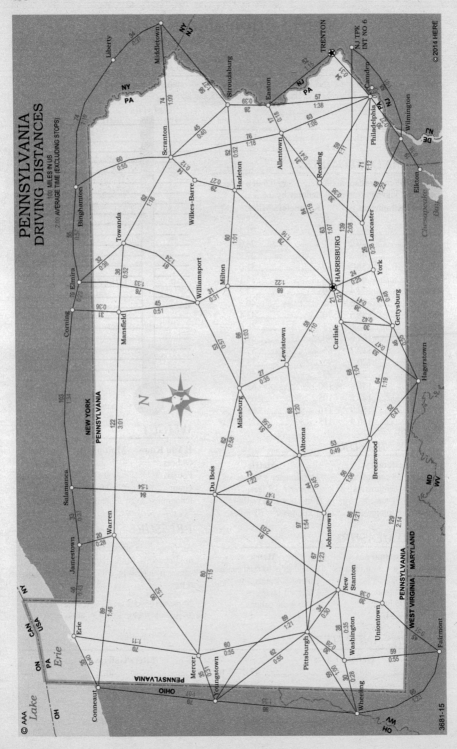

PENNSYLVANIA
DRIVING DISTANCES

100 MILES IN US
2:00 AVERAGE TIME (EXCLUDING STOPS)

Points of Interest Index

 Attractions appear at the top of each category
and offer a Great Experience for Members®.

Index Legend

NB..	national battlefield		NR..	national river
NBP..	national battlefield park		NS..	national seashore
NC..	national cemetery		NWR....................................	national wildlife refuge
NF..	national forest		PHP................................	provincial historic(al) park
NHM..............................	national historic(al) monument		PHS................................	provincial historic(al) site
NHP..............................	national historic(al) park		PP....................................	provincial park
NHS..............................	national historic(al) site		SF..	state forest
NL..	national lakeshore		SHM..........................	state historic(al) monument
NME..................................	national memorial		SHP..........................	state historic(al) park
NMO................................	national monument		SHS..........................	state historic(al) site
NMP..............................	national military park		SME................................	state memorial
NP..	national park		SP....................................	state park
NRA..............................	national recreation area		SRA..........................	state recreation area

CHILDREN'S ACTIVITIES

EVENTS & FESTIVALS

HISTORIC SITES & EXHIBITS

OUTDOORS & SCIENCE

SHOPPING & NIGHTLIFE

SPORTS & RECREATION

TOURS & SIGHTSEEING

Photo Credits

Page numbers are in bold type. Picture credit abbreviations are as follows:
- (i) numeric sequence from top to bottom, left to right ■ (AAA) AAA Travel library.

- (Cover) Marsden Hartley, Flower Abstraction (detail), 1914, Oil on canvas; 42 3/8 x 34 7/8 in., Pennsylvania Academy of the Fine Arts, Philadelphia, PA, 2003.1.4 / Courtesy of Pennsylvania Academy of the Fine Arts
- **2** (i) © Jim, the Photographer / flickr
- **2** (ii) © kyle.tucker95 / flickr
- **2** (iii) © AppalachianViews / Shutterstock.com
- **2** (iv) © Nagel Photography / Shutterstock.com
- **12** (i) Courtesy of Berry Manor Inn
- **12** (ii) © Chris Dew / Killarney Lodge
- **12** (iii) Courtesy of Hyatt Hotels
- **12** (iv) Courtesy of Montpelier Plantation and Beach
- **12** (v) © Elisa Rolle / Wikimedia Commons
- **12** (vi) Courtesy of The Shores Resort & Spa
- **12** (vii) Courtesy of Alexander Holiday Homes
- **12** (viii) Courtesy of Bryce View Lodge
- **12** (ix) Courtesy of Vista Verde Guest Ranch
- **13** Courtesy of Divi Resorts
- **18** (i) © iStockphoto.com / Ron_Thomas
- **18** (ii) © iStockphoto.com / ThomasTakacs
- **19** © C Borland/PhotoLink / Getty Images
- **20** (i) Courtesy of Wikimedia Commons
- **20** (ii) Courtesy of Wikimedia Commons
- **23** (i) © L. Albee / Longwood Gardens
- **23** (ii) © Jon Bilous / Shutterstock.com
- **23** (iii) © K. Jensen / Shutterstock.com
- **23** (iv) © Nagel Photography / Shutterstock.com
- **23** (v) © Michael G. Mill / Shutterstock.com
- **24** (i) © Jim, the Photographer / flickr
- **24** (ii) © iStockphoto.com / gkuchera
- **24** (iii) © iStockphoto.com / aimintang
- **24** (iv) © kyle.tucker95 / flickr
- **229** © iStockphoto.com / trekandshoot
- **233** © Nikreates / Alamy
- **234** © Purestock / Alamy
- **235** Courtesy of Philadelphia Zoo
- **236** © Dan Leeth / Alamy
- **237** © R. Kennedy / GPTMC
- **238** © iStockphoto.com / travelif
- **239** © Randy Duchaine / Alamy
- **240** © iStockphoto.com / TonnyWong
- **241** © Nikreates / Alamy
- **248** © Zoonar/G Whitton / age fotostock
- **250** Courtesy of Please Touch Museum
- **252** © Tetra Images /age fotostock
- **254** © Jason O. Watson / Alamy
- **256** Courtesy of National Constitution Center
- **258** © CORBIS / age fotostock
- **260** Courtesy of Wikimedia Commons
- **263** © brillianthues / flickr
- **325** Courtesy of Carnegie Mellon University
- **328** © iStockphoto.com / PhilAugustavo
- **329** © Photojunkie / Wikimedia Commons
- **330** © iStockphoto.com / cosmonaut
- **331** © Images-USA / Alamy
- **332** © iStockphoto.com / YelenaYemchuk
- **333** © ereyesleblanc / flickr
- **334** © Jim West / Alamy
- **335** © Karramba Production / Shutterstock.com
- **341** © iStockphoto.com / aimintang
- **343** © Philip Scalia / Alamy